MONUMENTA MUSICA EUROPEA

GENERAL EDITOR
FULVIA MORABITO

SECTION II
RENAISSANCE
VOL. 1

CENTRO STUDI OPERA OMNIA LUIGI BOCCHERINI – ONLUS
MMX

FLORENCE, BNC, PANCIATICHI 27

TEXT AND CONTEXT

EDITED BY
GIOIA FILOCAMO

TRANSLATED BY BONNIE J. BLACKBURN

✤

BREPOLS

TURNHOUT

MMX

D/2010/0095/142

ISBN 978-2-503-51518-2

MONUMENTA MUSICA
EUROPEA

GENERAL EDITOR
FULVIA MORABITO

SECTION II
RENAISSANCE
VOL. 1

CONTENTS

PREFACE

THE EARLY SIXTEENTH-CENTURY MANUSCRIPT Panciatichi 27 of the Biblioteca Nazionale Centrale in Florence has been well known to musicologists and Italianists for some time both for the presence among its pages of vocal and instrumental pieces that are among the most famous musical and literary texts of the Renaissance, and for its many *unica*. Although some pieces have already appeared a modern edition, there has been no systematic study of the entire manuscript or a complete publication, both of which are necessary for a better understanding of its structure and its historical context, finally allowing a comprehensive view.

Realizing the edition of a musical manuscript is not the same as making an edition of each of the pieces contained in it. Throughout the course of my work I have sought to adhere to this simple and lapidary assumption, fully aware that the pieces that flowed into MS Panciatichi 27 arrived from various directions and often derived from independent traditions. This perception has long been firmly established in studies of the written transmission of medieval and Renaissance music, and is confirmed each time one encounters a miscellaneous collection such as the one edited here. Although nearly all compositions (two excepted) are in the hand of one copyist, the musical pieces in Panciatichi 27 do not derive from the same source, nor have they followed similar paths of transmission: in some there are unequivocal signs of an older origin, whereas others might in fact be the result of compositional experimentation in the course of compiling the manuscript. Some pieces were transcribed from musical prints barely off the press, and others were 'modernized' through the personal intervention (mostly mediocre) of the principal scribe of the manuscript. On the other hand, manuscript collections copied in the age of print — such as Panciatichi 27 — are always rather heterogeneous in their contents: for the most part we deal with miscellanies devised according to the taste of a single person or a group, in which various genres are mixed according to subjective criteria. The transmission process that differentiates one piece from another thus furnishes valuable information if one wishes to investigate the history and evolution of an individual piece, but if the object of the study is first of all the product that contains it — as in this case — the stemma of an individual piece serves only to understand at which point in its trajectory it has been 'photographed' in the manuscript. A certain amount of research for each individual piece is thus necessary in order to draw judicious conclusions that will apply to the whole manuscript, but in this edition the reader will not find the apparatus laden with detailed lists of the variants among the musical and poetic readings of each piece that have come down to us (even if sometimes it has been necessary to fill in lacunae and correct errors); nevertheless, each musical concordance has been examined and compared with the reading in Panciatichi 27, but the results of such an analysis have been stated only insofar as they cast light on the process of the manuscript's tradition. The investigation thus focuses on the understanding of the manner in which the anthology in Panciatichi 27 was created, the provenance of the material contained in the manuscript, and the underlying rationale for its compilation.

That this rationale is far from linear is evident. Even verifying such a basic fact as the complete number of pieces contained in the manuscript has posed various problems in the course of the work. Over many years of study I have been constrained to modify this aspect several times: in the past, in fact, the multipart pieces were catalogued as separate pieces (as, for example, the series of Lamentations now listed as no. 178 or the music written on fols. 211*v*-212*r*: the latter was always interpreted as individual pieces, but is in fact the continuation of the *Dies ire* no. 185, which begins on the preceding opening). A more problematic case has been the *Amen* of fols. 210*v*–211*r* (no. 183): although based on the chant of the classic sequence *Dies irae*, it has not been possible to determine with certainty either the polyphonic order or whether it belongs — as an *Amen* — to the neighbouring pieces. Unnoticed before now, moreover, were two texts notated without any music in the manuscript (nos. 112bis and 147). On the whole, therefore, the pieces in the manuscript are 185 + 2 without music (no. 112bis is classified in this edition as 'bis' because it has no autonomous use, whereas I believe no. 147 was included in the manuscript with the intent of using it in some manner, even if it was later set aside or totally forgotten).

'Musical concordance' is a complex concept. I realized 'on the spot' how difficult it was to seek to give a single definition, and in the recension stage I myself changed my ideas several times on what to include under the category of 'concordance'. The difficulty arises from the fact that many pieces have in common with others only three, two, or even one voice; and sometimes we are dealing with decorated versions of single parts. In these circumstances one must make a judgement based on merit: is it a question of an independent reworking of a given theme, or rather of the same piece that circulated in a different arrangement? Evaluations such as these are easy prey to personal opinions, and that which one scholar classifies as a concordance may be catalogued instead by another as simply a 'related' piece. This divergent evaluation may therefore explain situations in which the listing of concordances of a specific piece produces a different result from an analogous list published elsewhere. The edition, nevertheless, registers some musical and poetic concordances that, as far as I know, have never been mentioned before in specific studies.

In my opinion, the strong accent placed on poetic concordances is necessary. In addition to the more than two hundred musical sources (manuscript and print) listed here, the four hundred literary sources represent a sort of 'anomaly' in the usual panorama of musical editions, generally uninterested in a full recension of literary concordances. And, while one can be reasonably confident of having listed nearly all the musical concordances known today — thanks to the help of overlapping repertories — one cannot say the same of poetic concordances: there are in fact no systematic inventories of literary sources of the fifteenth and sixteenth centuries usable as repertories, not even ones that are partially exhaustive. One has to deal instead with myriad specific studies, often traceable only though bibliographical cross-references. If it is difficult therefore to track down the current location of incunables or sixteenth-century prints (the lists of libraries signalled here from time to time should certainly be considered only partial), the situation with poetic manuscripts is of course still more critical, since the detailed inventories indispensable for tracing the texts they contain are often lacking. It is realistic to accept, therefore, that the poetic concordances listed in the edition represent only a fraction of those that have survived.

In connection with the texts contained in Panciatichi 27 there is always the problem represented by the sometimes garbled textual incipits, which for us users represent a sort of title of the piece. Sometimes they appear in the form of a heading above the music, but at other times they are under the first notes of one or more voices. Some of the pieces presented in this form are clearly instrumental, but for others the question is legitimate whether they once carried texts that have not yet been identified. The scrutiny of so many poetic sources has enabled the identification of some of these so far unknown: it has been possible, for example, to determine for the first time the continuation of incipits such as *Ogi è 'l tempo, peccatore* (no. 42), *Guarda le vestimente* (no. 80), and *Son su passo de la morte* (no. 112bis). To be sure, the mathematical certainty that we are in fact dealing with the texts understood by Scribe A in Panciatichi 27 can only come once musical concordances emerge that are furnished with the same texts (complete or partial), but tracking down the possible continuations of a garbled incipit yields information at least on the presumed genre (devotional or secular) of the piece set. It is not to be excluded that in the future we may succeed in finding new or more complete texts through a systematic search of poetic sources of the fifteenth and sixteenth centuries. For obvious reasons I have undertaken this in only a limited form, often guided by the red threads singled out in the vast bibliography consulted, and by chance (which at times 'helps the bold'!).

Just as all the authors of the poetic texts traced here have been identified thanks to literary concordances, many composers too have been identified thanks to musical concordances. On the other hand, some attributions have been hypothesized on the basis of different, 'unofficial' considerations (Brumel for no. 121, Cara for no. 125, Isaac for nos. 169 and 170). Through the intersection of the concordances it has been possible to attribute almost thirty pieces beyond those named in the manuscript, and in three other cases the concordances have yielded alternative names to those indicated in Panciatichi 27. Many of these attributions have already been indicated in specialist studies, but for at least one piece I am sure that an identification has been made here for the first time. And it is not insignificant, since it regards the paternity of the only piece in five voices in the manuscript, a piece that had a fairly wide circulation and is anonymous also in Petrucci: *Hor oires una canzon* (no. 57) is attributed to Johannes de Stokem in the manuscript fragments conserved at Iserlohn.

Finally, the dating of the manuscript. If for some time Panciatichi 27 was generically placed in the first decade of the sixteenth century, systematic editing of the source has permitted a more circumscribed dating: certainly after the publication of the fourth book of Frottole by Petrucci (between 7 February and 22 December 1505), and perhaps after 29 May 1506, the date of printing of the second book of Lamentations by Petrucci. This concerns the main corpus of the manuscript copied by Scribe A, whereas the two pieces added by Scribe B are datable after 9 October 1510, the publication date of *Canzoni nove* by Antico.

I close this preface by emphasizing that for all the problems a critical edition solves, many others are raised. Regarding Panciatichi 27, whoever will make use of the present investigation to continue the study of this important manuscript — which in my opinion owes much of its cultural importance to its position at the crossroads between manuscript and print traditions — can reflect on the unanswered questions. It is a manuscript that in some way serves as a spokesman for a rather free mentality, which has established the content according to personal taste, assembling the pieces with a particular rationale, but one that is not entirely obvious and still bears investigation. I believe that the typical environment for this rather free mentality, mixing pieces with various purposes (sacred, devotional, secular) is that of a Mantuan confraternity, even if I cannot pinpoint it exactly. I base this opinion above all on the high number of laude and *contrafacta*, but above all the unusual presence of sections of the Requiem. This is my conclusion, based more on a general impression than on concrete facts. *Au fond* a critical edition is a point of departure for further discussion: it furnishes information to be interpreted, and in the best of cases proposes a point of view. Fortunately, no critical edition can be labelled 'definitive', and I truly hope that this one, in particular, is not, but instead will serve to increase debate, the foundation of knowledge.

ACKNOWLEDGEMENTS

M Y INTEREST IN THE MUSICAL MANUSCRIPT Panciatichi 27 dates back some fourteen years. Fresh with the enthusiasm of finishing a demanding philological study of the production of the first Italian polyphonist of whom we have notice (Giovanni da Cascia) for the *tesi di laurea* at the University of Bologna, I immediately sought another field of investigation that might fittingly compete with the preceding one on the level of 'masochism'. My indecision was short-lived, and guided by Giuseppina La Face Bianconi, I prepared myself zealously to begin the research that sees the light of day with this publication. I hadn't the slightest idea of what type of work awaited me, of the time frame (which revealed itself as somewhat short of geological), of the amount of scholarly literature to be read, and of the questions of various natures that would arise. New problems were always turning up, and I solved them slowly: I was on the brink of abandoning the project many times, feeling discouraged and inadequate, too small for such a large work. All this made it very clear to me why there had never yet been a modern edition of 'my manuscript' — in general I allow myself such familiarity with the paper object only verbally, born after so many years of companionship — and why so many scholars had not yet undertaken the enterprise.

After having digested the initial idea, work was begun in earnest during the three years of study for the *Dottorato di ricerca in Filologia musicale* at Cremona (University of Pavia). Still, I owe the greater part of this experience to my studies abroad. After having spent three months at Oxford as a Visiting Junior Research Fellow, thanks to the invaluable support of Reinhard Strohm, I won an Erasmus-Socrates scholarship, which allowed me to transfer to Oxford University for the entire year 1999. I was associated with the University college Lady Margaret Hall, which became my home, and I was able to enjoy with genuine amazement the splendid libraries situated almost at every angle of the city. The lively and stimulating scholarly atmosphere greatly increased my knowledge. I have indelible memories of that time, thanks to which I developed a new love for what I was doing. Apart from new acquaintances, many of whom have left a strong personal imprint on my life, my first enthusiasm for what I was studying grew also thanks to the teaching I had the good fortune to receive in that prestigious university: I will never forget Reinhard Strohm's wonderful lectures on early polyphony, at which I marvelled each time not only for their enormous richness, but above all for the critical acumen and methodology that I absorbed. From those lectures I learned that nothing must be taken for granted, that the 'common places' need to be verified every time, and that what one can 'see' can also be explained in a different way than it seems at first acquaintance. And then I recall with particular pleasure the singing sessions organized by the indefatigable Margaret Bent: meetings 'out of hours', after dinner, in the seminar room of All Souls College. From her too I learned much: with a small group (sometimes only three or four) we spent a couple of hours singing polyphonic music directly from facsimiles of the old manuscripts. This was an experience I had never had before, which I found of inestimable value for one who, like me, had to confront difficult editorial problems: musical palaeography learned on the fly, which I treasured immensely. To my Oxford stay also dates the most important encounter of my scholarly career, that with Bonnie Blackburn, who became at that time the supervisor of my dissertation at the Faculty of Music of the University. To her I owe above all her injections of energy and confidence, of which I had great need at the time. From her I had much more than I would ever have expected from an academic contact: the innumerable 'straightenings' of my path, at times uncertain, facilitated — but more correctly I should say alone permitted — the completion of my doctoral thesis. I learned as much from her confirmations as from her polite objections (firm, and sometimes deliciously ironic): her enthusiasm and generosity have been for me almost the only comfort in difficult moments related to the drafting of the work.

The conclusion of the *Dottorato di ricerca* saw a dissertation entitled *Il repertorio profano con testo italiano del codice Panciatichi 27*: about a third of the repertory was studied, and much remained to be done. Shortly thereafter I won two-year post-doctoral fellowship at the University of Bologna. Under the supervision of Giuseppina La Face — who had already put at my disposal her collection of microfilms of fifteenth- and sixteenth-century literary and musical sources for the doctoral thesis — the project took shape to complete the musical edition of the manuscript. Albert Dunning proposed that I publish the work, which would have inaugurated the new series *Monumenta Musica Europea* that he had founded for the publisher Brepols. Enthused by this generous proposal, I continued to work on completing the edition thanks to two other stays abroad in important places. I benefited from an Audrey Lumsden-Kouvel Fellowship for three months at the Newberry Library in Chicago, followed by a two-month fellowship at the Herzog August Bibliothek in Wolfenbüttel. Both experiences permitted me to work with ease in very well provisioned libraries, to meet colleagues from other disciplines coming from all parts of the world, and above all to spend a period of complete concentration on the project. During my stay in the States I also spent some time at the Musicological Archives for Renaissance Manuscript Studies at the School of Music of the University of Illinois at Urbana-Champaign, directed by Herbert Kellman. Never was a host more cordial or hospitable, and only thanks to my visits to Urbana was I able to answer many questions regarding the imposing number of musical sources that it was necessary to examine. Not only was I able to see all the microfilms I requested, but much of the work already accomplished and in progress was put at my disposal at the prestigious American institution: a spirit of scholarly generosity that I cannot let pass unmentioned, which I admire profoundly, and which I experienced in analogous form only during my stay in Oxford.

In these years I also worked frequently in other libraries, in which I always had a warm reception and specific help. I cite only those I visited most often: at Florence the manuscript room of the Biblioteca Nazionale Centrale and the Morrill Music Library at the Villa I Tatti (Harvard University); at Bologna the Biblioteca del Dipartimento di Musica e Spettacolo of the University, the Museo Internazionale e Biblioteca della Musica (*ex* Civico Museo Bibliografico Musicale), the Biblioteca Universitaria, the Biblioteca Comunale dell'Archiginnasio, the Biblioteca del Dipartimento di Italianistica, and the Biblioteca di Casa Carducci; at Oxford the Bodleian Library, the Taylorian Institution, and the library of the Faculty of Music; at Chicago the Regenstein Library of the University of Chicago; at Urbana-Champaign the library of the School of Music; at London the British Library; at Rome the Biblioteca Casanatense, the Biblioteca Nazionale Centrale, the Biblioteca dell'Accademia Nazionale dei Lincei e Corsiniana, the Biblioteca Apostolica Vaticana; at Milan the Biblioteca dell'Archivio Storico Civico e Biblioteca Trivulziana; at Venice the Biblioteca Nazionale Marciana; at Cremona the library of the Facoltà di Musicologia. My special thanks go to the Biblioteca Nazionale Centrale in Florence for allowing the reproduction of images from Panciatichi 27. Over the years I have in fact visited many other libraries, archives, and institutions, and have exchanged letters, e-mail, and telephone calls with many Italian and foreign librarians and archivists. To all of them I owe thanks for having contributed to the enrichment of the information contained in my work, but to mention them individually is absolutely impossible; as representative I name only one: Gianluigi Perino of the Biblioteca Comunale of Treviso, who, in an epoch in which the use of pen and ink seems necessary only for the shopping list, sent me by post (five pages in A4 format) a detailed list of MS 181 that he had copied out in person. The gesture struck me to the point that, although never having met this diligent librarian, I decided that he deserved to be named as the formal representative of the category.

Antonio Rossi placed at my complete disposition his substantial experience as an Italianist: a precise and generous scholar, he has never been stingy with advice and opinions, and has been very close to me, tolerating in good spirits my frequent questions, my second thoughts, and my visits to his house in Switzerland that always went on for too many hours.

I have had recourse to other scholars over the years for help on more marginal matters, though always precious: Jeffrey Dean, Giuliano Di Bacco, David Fallows, William Prizer, Cesarino Ruini, Claudio Vela, Blake Wilson. I have profited from the learned advice of Leofranc Holford-Strevens at different times, especially in times of sheer emergency: my gratitude to him is huge. In the last stages I also benefited much from the authoritative experience as a liturgist and musicologist of Giulio Cattin, who gave me advice and support with the true affection of a father.

To Adam Gilbert I owe the realization of a dream: to hear the performance of many of the pieces of Panciatichi 27, some for the first time after nearly five hundred years. The dream became a reality in the course of three concerts (organized by the Associazione culturale *L'Orfeo* of Spoleto) performed in Umbria at the end of 2003 by the Ensemble Ciaramella, directed by Adam himself, and his suggestions have been extremely precious for the musical edition of the pieces. The experience was then repeated at a concert during the prestigious meeting of the American Musicological Society in Seattle, Washington during November 2004, which hosted the group and presented music taken from the manuscript.

In the last years of work on the manuscript I had the help of another musicologist, normally devoted to studies of nineteenth-century Italian opera: Marco Beghelli. His collaboration, begun more as a game, subsequently proved indispensable. Endowed with a sense of scholarly curiosity certainly 'above average', Marco became the companion of many hours dedicated to the discovery and use of repertories, online and not, which contributed greatly to the outcome of this publication. The many musicological discussions I had with him have been of immense use, paradoxically perhaps just because they were exchanged with a scholar expert in other planets who looked at the problems from a different angle. And his passionate assistance during the phase of the study of the liturgical and paraliturgical pieces contained in Panciatichi 27 will remain memorable.

Finally, I thank the person who probably knows as much about this work as I, if not more. With incredible tenacity Bonnie Blackburn has followed this extremely long editorial adventure, with constant attention and an unlimited dosage of human sensibility. It is not possible to enumerate the incalculable quantity of information, advice, and encouragement that I have had the good fortune to receive from her; without slighting the contribution of other scholars, she is the indispensable reference point for those who approach these Renaissance musical questions. Her constant assistance on this publication took an incredible number of hours from her life: no thanks are adequate to express my eternal gratitude, and I hope that my words will at least succeed in transmitting a part of it. As if this were not enough, Bonnie then took on herself the burden of preparing the English translation of the Italian text, but only those who do not know this extraordinary scholar can think that her work resulted in a simple translation: she has continually corrected oversights and serious errors, has improved and 'polished' my prose, has suggested directions for the work and very useful clarifications. All with her usual discretion, with a delicate capacity to generate each time the same simple comment: 'Bonnie is right!'

My husband Fabrizio Ammetto has been a constant support along the way, from the time of the doctoral thesis to the publication of the edition. To him I owe thanks for his technical expertise, very sensible musical advice, lucid editorial suggestions, and an unending dose of patience. Together with Bonnie Blackburn, Fabrizio is certainly the world expert on the manuscript: 'my' Panciatichi 27 has become also 'his' Panciatichi 27, and between us it has been a constant subject of discussion over many years, even from our first romantic encounters. My husband's passion for contrapuntal problems has been providential in many cases (how many incorrect passages he has fixed!), as, on the other hand, has his computer literacy: he was the excellent transcriber of the music on the computer (including the Renaissance music fonts created expressly by Antonio Gessi), as well as the designer of the layout of all the pages. I am not ashamed to say that, without Fabrizio, this work would never have the aspect that it has. To my husband I dedicate, with affection, esteem, and gratitude (and with a touch of melancholy), the edition of 'our' manuscript: a sort of child that we adopted together at birth, which has then grown up, and is now finally ready to walk. The paradoxical repercussion is that both of us can hardly bear to separate from him.

At this point, it remains to thank the excellent editors of the book: Roberto Illiano, Fulvia Morabito, and Massimiliano Sala. Three special persons, three dear friends. Together with them, I am grateful to the publisher, Brepols, which has tolerated very generously not only my delays but also my frequent uncertainties on the massive whole of the work.

The years spent working on the edition of Panciatichi 27 have been much longer than Albert Dunning would have hoped. This volume comes out with a single regret: that Albert did not live to see it. His premature death on 2 June 2005 is one of the great sorrows that has accompanied the preparation of this work. To his memory I dedicate my grateful thought: that if Albert had not believed in me, and had not patronized the publication of the study, perhaps the edition of Panciatichi 27 would never have come to light. Of Albert's spiritual presence a visible testimony is the famous painting on the jacket of this book: Titian's *Amor sacro e amor profano*. After much investigation of what would be the best image to represent the edition, I found that this painting combines the two fundamental souls of the repertory of Panciatichi 27: precisely the sacred and the profane. Titian painted this masterwork at the age of about 25, in the very epoch of the compilation of Panciatichi 27; it was commissioned by the learned humanist and Venetian official Nicolò Aurelio for his wedding in 1514 with Laura Bagarotto. For Albert the visual aspect of the cover was very important, and I was delighted when he approved my proposal, with its 'allegorical' character, for the edition. The problem remained, however, how to use the beautiful painting graphically, in view of its inconvenient oblong format. The last time I saw Albert (Easter 2005) — then very ill, but still very lucid, ironic, and an exemplary host in his gorgeous Dutch house in Loenen aan de Vecht, where his splendid wife Jeanine was doing her utmost to cheer up the last weeks of his life — I succeeded in extracting from him permission to use just a part of the painting in a rather unorthodox manner by splitting it. Normally adverse to operations of this type, that day Albert responded: «Fine, but remember that to cut a painting by Titian is a very great responsibility!»: it was his last reference to my work. It remains with me, and I often recall the liberating laughter that followed his joke while he was driving rapidly on the motorway.

Spoleto – Bologna, Summer 2009   *Gioia Filocamo*

SOURCES

PRELIMINARY NOTE

MUSICAL AND TEXTUAL MANUSCRIPTS

The musical manuscripts listed here were copied between about 1430-40 and 1570-90, with a single exception datable to 1613 (BolM 34).[1] An asterisk (★) after the number of the piece indicates a musical concordance, but with a different text, although different texts are not specified for variants such as: *Defecerunt vedo ormai / Defecerunt donna ormai* (no. 37), or *Arda el ciel e 'l mundo tuto / Crida el ciello e 'l mondo tuto* (no. 43). A different symbol (§) after the number of the piece indicates a musical concordance, but without text. The literary sources, however, comprise a period from the mid-fourteenth to the second half of the sixteenth century, with the exception of *Ver.Civ. 1212* (see the relative entry).

MUSICAL AND TEXTUAL PRINTS

The sources that have been taken into consideration for concordances are musical prints from 1501 to 1568 and printed literary sources published between 1470 and ca. 1580. An asterisk (★) after the number of the piece indicates a musical concordance, but with a different text. A different symbol (§) after the number of the piece indicates a musical concordance, but without the text.

After the siglum (in bold) follow the title page of the print (normalized as regards the resolution of abbreviations, words joined or separated, use of capital and lower-case letters, accents, and punctuation) and the location or locations of exemplars. An asterisk (★) after the library indicates the copy consulted, together with its shelfmark. The phrases 'a petizione di' / 'ad instanza di' are rendered as 'at the request of' / 'at the instance of'. Abbreviations are to be resolved in the following manner: 'no d.' = no date; 'no pl.' = no place; 'no pr.' = no printer; 'no typ. info.' = no typographical information.

---

[1]. See the entry for no. 168, n. 2.

I. MUSICAL MANUSCRIPTS

AugsS 25 = AUGSBURG, Staats- und Stadtbibliothek, 4° Mus. 25
No. **56**★

AugsS 142a = AUGSBURG, Staats- und Stadtbibliothek, 2° 142a (*olim* Cim. 43)
Nos. **36**★, **160**§

BarcC 454 = BARCELONA, Biblioteca de Catalunya (*ex* Biblioteca Central), 454
Nos. **89**, **126**, **131**

BasU 5-9 = BASEL, Öffentliche Bibliothek der Universität, F.X.5-9
(5 partbooks)
No. **177**

BasU 10 = BASEL, Öffentliche Bibliothek der Universität, F.X.10
(Bassus partbook only)
No. **36**★

BasU 17-20 = BASEL, Öffentliche Bibliothek der Universität, F.X.17-20
(4 partbooks)
No. **66**

BasU 22 = BASEL, Öffentliche Bibliothek der Universität, F.IX.22
'Bonifazius Amerbachs Orgelbuch' (keyboard tablature)
Nos. **21**, **54**, **89**, **139**

BasU 22-4 = BASEL, Öffentliche Bibliothek der Universität, F.X.22-24
(only Superius, Altus, Bassus partbooks: the Tenor partbook is lost; the leaves of the Altus partbook after piece no. 40
are missing)
No. **66**

BasU 26c = BASEL, Öffentliche Bibliothek der Universität, F.VI.26c
(organ treatise, in tablature)
No. **139**§

BerlS 30 = BERLIN, Staatsbibliothek, Preußischer Kulturbesitz, N. Mus. ant. theor. 30
(theory treatise with musical pieces on the initial pages)
No. **69**

BerlS 22048 = BERLIN, Staatsbibliothek, Preußischer Kulturbesitz, Mus. 22048
(one folio only)
No. **93**

BerlS 40021 = BERLIN, Staatsbibliothek, Preußischer Kulturbesitz, Mus. 40021 (*olim* Z 21)
Nos. **21**, **58**★, **75**★, **138**★

BerlS 40026 = BERLIN, Staatsbibliothek, Preußischer Kulturbesitz, Mus. 40026
'Orgeltabulatur des Leonhard Kleber' (keyboard tablature)
Nos. **36**★ (twice), **127**, **139**

BerlS 40196 = BERLIN, Staatsbibliothek, Preußischer Kulturbesitz, Mus. 40196
No. **66**

BerlS 40632 = BERLIN, Staatsbibliothek, Preußischer Kulturbesitz, Mus. 40632
(German lute tablature)
No. **21**

BolA 179 = Bologna, Biblioteca Comunale dell'Archiginnasio, A 179 (*olim* 16.b.III.20)
Nos. **31**, **45**

BolM 13 = Bologna, Museo Internazionale e Biblioteca della Musica (*ex* Civico Museo Bibliografico Musicale), Q.13 (*olim* 138)[2]
No. **45**

BolM 15 = Bologna, Museo Internazionale e Biblioteca della Musica (*ex* Civico Museo Bibliografico Musicale), Q.15 (*olim* 37)
No. **48**★

BolM 16 = Bologna, Museo Internazionale e Biblioteca della Musica (*ex* Civico Museo Bibliografico Musicale), Q.16 (*olim* 109)
Nos. **16**★, **36**★, **40**, **56**, **64**★, **75**, **83**★, **89**

BolM 17 = Bologna, Museo Internazionale e Biblioteca della Musica (*ex* Civico Museo Bibliografico Musicale), Q.17 (*olim* 148)
Nos. **89**, **111**, **127**

BolM 18 = Bologna, Museo Internazionale e Biblioteca della Musica (*ex* Civico Museo Bibliografico Musicale), Q.18 (*olim* 143)
Nos. **21**§, **52**, **54**, **56**, **59**, **66**§, **75**, **89**, **93**, **131**, **138**★

BolM 19 = Bologna, Museo Internazionale e Biblioteca della Musica (*ex* Civico Museo Bibliografico Musicale), Q.19 'Codice Rusconi'
No. **120**

BolM 34[3] = Bologna, Museo Internazionale e Biblioteca della Musica (*ex* Civico Museo Bibliografico Musicale), Q.34 (in score format)
No. **168**§

BolU 2216 = Bologna, Biblioteca Universitaria, 2216
No. **48**★

BratM 33 = Bratislava, Miestne Pracovisko Matice Slovenskej, Inc. 33 (formerly at Košice, Knižnica Dominikánov, III A 13)
(binding fragments; missing since the last restoration in 1968, but partially known through a photocopy now at Budapest, Országos Széchényi Könyvtár, MS 495)
No. **56**★

BruxR 90 / TournaiV 94 = Brussel/Bruxelles, Koninklijke Bibliotheek van België / Bibliothèque Royale de Belgique, IV.90 (Superius partbook); Tournai, Bibliothèque de la Ville, 94 (Tenor partbook)[4]
No. **127**

BruxR 11239 = Brussel/Bruxelles, Koninklijke Bibliotheek van België / Bibliothèque Royale de Belgique, 11239
Nos. **89**, **127**

BurHu = Burgos, Monasterio de las Huelgas, s.s.
'Las Huelgas Codex'
No. **20**

CambM 18 = Cambrai, Médiathèque Municipale, 18 (*olim* 20)
No. **81**★

CambM 125-8 = Cambrai, Médiathèque Municipale, 125-128 (*olim* 124)
(4 partbooks)
No. **126**

---

[2]. The manuscript has monophonic music, but it also has as its unique polyphonic piece no. 45.
[3]. See the entry for no. 168, n. 2.
[4]. These two partbooks have recently been joined by the newly discovered Altus (Brussel/Bruxelles, Koninklijke Bibliotheek van België / Bibliothèque Royale de Belgique, IV.1274). The only concordance with Panc.27, however, is not expanded since it does not include the Altus part.

ChN 25 = Chicago, Newberry Library, Case MS minus VM 140.C25
'Vincenzo Capirola's Lute Book' (Italian lute tablature)
Nos. **89, 127**

CoimU 48 = Coimbra, Biblioteca Geral da Universidade, M.48
(in score format)
No. **177**

CTL G12 = Cape Town, National Library of South Africa (*ex* South African Public Library), Grey 3.b.12
Nos. **9, 15, 16, 26, 36, 40★, 45, 47★, 51, 58, 60, 74, 75★,**[5] **76, 79, 81, 83, 91, 93★, 114, 116**

CV F84 = Città del Vaticano, Biblioteca Apostolica Vaticana, Ferraioli 84
(although the manuscript contains 63 texts altogether, only 16 of them have music)
No. **69** (text only)

CV G27 = Città del Vaticano, Biblioteca Apostolica Vaticana, Cappella Giulia XIII.27
'Codice Medici'
Nos. **16★, 21, 36★, 40, 54★, 56, 75, 89, 96, 127, 168**

CV S15 = Città del Vaticano, Biblioteca Apostolica Vaticana, Cappella Sistina 15
No. **126**

CV S35 = Città del Vaticano, Biblioteca Apostolica Vaticana, Cappella Sistina 35
No. **21**

CV S41 = Città del Vaticano, Biblioteca Apostolica Vaticana, Cappella Sistina 41
No. **115**

CV S42 = Città del Vaticano, Biblioteca Apostolica Vaticana, Cappella Sistina 42
No. **94**

DijM 517 = Dijon, Bibliothèque Municipale, 517 (*olim* 295)
Nos. **40, 56, 59, 64★**

DresL 505 = Dresden, Sächsische Landesbibliothek - Staats- und Universitätsbibliothek, Mus. 1/D/505 (formerly at Annaberg, Bibliothek der St. Annenkirche, 1248)
'Annaberg Chorbuch'
No. **138★**

ErlU 473/4 = Erlangen, Universitätsbibliothek, 473/4 (*olim* 793)
No. **66★**

EsM 24 = El Escorial, Real Monasterio de San Lorenzo, Biblioteca y Archivo de Música, IV.a.24
No. **64★**

FirC B2441 = Firenze, Biblioteca del Conservatorio Luigi Cherubini, Basevi 2441
Nos. **12, 37, 43, 66, 145**

FirD 21 = Firenze, Duomo, Archivio Musicale dell'Opera di S. Maria del Fiore, 21
(the earliest layer is a Superius partbook, to which additions have been made in choirbook format)
No. **45**

FirN BR62 = Firenze, Biblioteca Nazionale Centrale, Banco Rari 62
(two fragments only)
No. **69★**

FirN BR229 = Firenze, Biblioteca Nazionale Centrale, Banco Rari 229 (*olim* Magliabechiano XIX.59)
Nos. **16★, 21§, 40, 54§, 56, 73, 75, 89, 96§, 105§, 127, 138§, 168**

---

[5]. But through its alternative text the Panc.27 piece refers to the text present only in CTL G12.

FirN BR230 = FIRENZE, Biblioteca Nazionale Centrale, Banco Rari 230 (*olim* Magliabechiano XIX.141)
 Nos. **87**, **92**, **93**

FirN BR337 = FIRENZE, Biblioteca Nazionale Centrale, Banco Rari 337 (*olim* Palatino 1178)
 (Bassus partbook only)
 Nos. **11**, **43**, **66**§, **68**, **84**, **151**

FirN M107bis = FIRENZE, Biblioteca Nazionale Centrale, Magliabechiano XIX.107 bis
 Nos. **21**, **54**, **89** or **92** (index only; see the relevant entries), **96**§, **127**★

FirN M117 = FIRENZE, Biblioteca Nazionale Centrale, Magliabechiano XIX.117
 No. **127**

FirN M121 = FIRENZE, Biblioteca Nazionale Centrale, Magliabechiano XIX.121
 'Libro di Marietta Pugi'
 Nos. **13**★, **36**★, **40**, **75**§, **149**

FirN M178 = FIRENZE, Biblioteca Nazionale Centrale, Magliabechiano XIX.178
 Nos. **16**★, **40**, **54**, **75**, **89**, **96**, **105**★, **127**

FirR 2356 = FIRENZE, Biblioteca Riccardiana, 2356
 Nos. **40**, **83**, **89**, **127**

FirR 2794 = FIRENZE, Biblioteca Riccardiana, 2794
 Nos. **40**, **89**, **127**

FMU 20 = FRANKFURT AM MAIN, Universitätsbibliothek Johann Christian Senckenberg, Fragm. Lat. VII 20
 No. **36**★

GreifU 640-1 = GREIFSWALD, Universitätsbibliothek, BW 640-641 (*olim* E^b 133)
 (Superius and Bassus partbooks only, copied from the print RhauSym [RISM 1538/8] with additions)
 Nos. **66**, **89**, **177**

HeilbS 2 = HEILBRONN, Stadtarchiv, Musiksammlung X/2
 (Bassus partbook only)
 Nos. **21**, **54**, **55**, **168**

HerdF 9822 = HERDRINGEN, Schloss Fürstenberg, Bibliothek, Fü 9822 (*olim* 9822-9823) (formerly at PADERBORN, Erzbischöfliche Akademische Bibliothek)
 (Superius and Bassus partbooks only)
 No. **66**★

HKK 7 = HRADEC KRÁLOVÉ, Krajské Muzeum, Literární Archiv, II.A.7
 'Speciálník'
 No. **83**★

HKK 20 = HRADEC KRÁLOVÉ, Krajské Muzeum, Literární Archiv, II.A.20
 (Bassus partbook only)
 Nos. **59**, **168**§

IserV 124 = ISERLOHN, Evangelische Kirkengemeinde, Varnhagen Bibliothek, IV.36.F124
 (fragments recovered from the binding of an incunabulum)
 No. **57**§

JenaU 31 = JENA, Thüringer Universitäts- und Landesbibliothek, 31
 No. **21**

KasL 53/2 = KASSEL, Landesbibliothek und Murhardsche Bibliothek der Stadt Kassel, 8° Mus. 53/2
 (Superius partbook only)
 No. **40**

KøbK 291 = København, Det Kongelige Bibliotek, Thott 291, 8°
    No. **40**

KøbK 1848 = København, Det Kongelige Bibliotek, Ny Kongelige Samling 1848, 2°
    Nos. **54**, **89**, **127**

KönU 150 = Königsberg (Kaliningrad), former Staats- und Universitätsbibliothek, Gen. 2. 150
    (German lute tablature; missing since World War II)
    No. **66**

KrakJ 40098 = Kraków, Biblioteka Jagiellońska, Mus. 40098 (formerly at Berlin, Preussische Staatsbibliothek, Mus. 40098 (*olim* Z 98 and Z 8037)
    'Glogauer Liederbuch' (3 partbooks)
    Nos. **56**★, **73**§

LeipU 49-50 = Leipzig, Universitätsbibliothek, Bibliotheca Albertina, Thomaskirche 49/50 & 50
    (5 partbooks)
    No. **127**★

LeipU 51 = Leipzig, Universitätsbibliothek, Bibliotheca Albertina, Thomaskirche 51 (1-2)
    (Tenor and Bassus partbooks only)
    No. **66**★

LeipU 1494 = Leipzig, Universitätsbibliothek, Bibliotheca Albertina, 1494
    'Mensuralkodex des Nikolaus Apel'
    Nos. **11**★, **36**★ (twice), **54**§, **54**★, **68**

LinzL 529 = Linz, Oberösterreichische Landesbibliothek (*ex* Bundesstaatliche Studienbibliothek), 529
    No. **64**★

LonB A31922 = London, British Library, Additional 31922
    'Henry VIII Manuscript'
    Nos. **21**, **36**★, **40**, **64**★, **127**

LonB A35087 = London, British Library, Additional 35087
    No. **36**★

LonB E3051 = London, British Library, Egerton 3051
    (the same MS as WashC M6: LonB E3051 has the first 61 folios; WashC M6 has fols. 80-99; the remaining folios are lost)
    Nos. **66**, **93**, **145**

LonB RXVI = London, British Library, Royal 20 A. XVI
    No. **127**

MaaR = Maastricht, Rijksarchief van Limburg, s.s.
    (fragments)
    No. **40**

MadP 1335 = Madrid, Biblioteca del Palacio Real, 1335 (*olim* 2-I-5)
    'Cancionero de Palacio'
    Nos. **65**, **66**

MilA 5 = Milano, Biblioteca Ambrosiana, S.P.II.5
    'Codice Borromeo' (the MS contains poems and a musical lauda (*Hora mai sono in età*); among the texts there are poems and writings by Girolamo Savonarola)
    No. **159** (text only)

MilB 49 = Milano, Biblioteca Nazionale Braidense, AD.XIV.49
    No. **48**★

MilD 1 = MILANO, Archivio della Veneranda Fabbrica del Duomo, Sezione Musicale, Librone 1 (*olim* 2269)
Nos. **60**, **99**, **129**

MilD 2 = MILANO, Archivio della Veneranda Fabbrica del Duomo, Sezione Musicale, Librone 2 (*olim* 2268)
Nos. **21**, **81**★

MilT 55 = MILANO, Biblioteca dell'Archivio Storico Civico e Biblioteca Trivulziana, Triv. 55
Nos. **33**, **93**

ModD IV = MODENA, Duomo, Biblioteca e Archivio Capitolare, Mus. IV
Nos. **3**, **115**

ModE 8 = MODENA, Biblioteca Estense Universitaria, γ.L.11.8
(Bassus partbook only)
No. **168**

ModE 9 = MODENA, Biblioteca Estense Universitaria, α.F.9.9 (It. 1221)
Nos. **78**, **87**

MontA 871 = CASSINO, Biblioteca Statale del Monumento Nazionale di Montecassino, 871
Nos. **40**§, **45**, **158** (index only)

MünS 272 = MÜNCHEN, Bayerische Staatsbibliothek, Musiksammlung, Mus. 272
(German lute tablature)
Nos. **21**, **54**

MünS 352b = MÜNCHEN, Bayerische Staatsbibliothek, Cim. 352b (*olim* Mus. 3725)
'Buxheimer Orgelbuch' (keyboard tablature)
Nos. **64**§, **83**★

MünS L5023 = MÜNCHEN, Bayerische Staatsbibliothek, Latino Monacensis 5023
Nos. **64**★, **83**

MünU 322-5 = MÜNCHEN, Universitätsbibliothek der Ludwig-Maximilians-Universität, 8° 322-325 (*olim* Cim. 44a)
(4 partbooks)
No. **131**

MünU 326 = MÜNCHEN, Universitätsbibliothek der Ludwig-Maximilians-Universität, 8° 326 (*olim* Cim. 44b)
(Altus partbook only)
Nos. **66**★, **177**

MünU 718 = MÜNCHEN, Universitätsbibliothek der Ludwig-Maximilians-Universität, 4° Cod. 718
(German lute and viola da gamba tablature)
Nos. **21** (twice), **36**★

NHY 91 = NEW HAVEN, Yale University, Beinecke Rare Book and Manuscript Library, 91
'Mellon Chansonnier'
No. **40**

PadCap 17 = PADOVA, Biblioteca Capitolare, A.17
No. **60**

ParisN F1597 = PARIS, Bibliothèque Nationale de France, Fonds Fr. 1597
'Chansonnier Lorraine'
Nos. **51**, **89**, **95**, **127**

ParisN F2245 = PARIS, Bibliothèque Nationale de France, Fonds Fr. 2245
No. **127**

ParisN F12744 = Paris, Bibliothèque Nationale de France, Fonds Fr. 12744
    No. **96**

ParisN F15123 = Paris, Bibliothèque Nationale de France, Fonds Fr. 15123 (*olim* Suppl. Fr. 2637)
    'Chansonnier Pixérécourt'
    Nos. **40, 56, 64★, 83, 158**

ParisN NAF4379 = Paris, Bibliothèque Nationale de France, Nouvelles Acquisitions Françaises 4379
    (the codex consists of four MSS bound together, the first of which has 42 pages from SevC 43)
    Nos. **36★, 64★**

ParisN NAL401 = Paris, Bibliothèque Nationale de France, Nouvelles Acquisitions Latines 401
    No. **31**

ParisN Rés27 = Paris, Bibliothèque Nationale de France, Département de la Musique, Rés. Vmd. 27
    (Italian lute tablature)
    Nos. **9** (twice), **12, 21** (twice), **37, 43, 52, 54, 116, 124, 151**

ParisN Rés57 = Paris, Bibliothèque Nationale de France, Département de la Musique, Rés. Vmc. 57
    'Chansonnier Nivelle de la Chaussée'
    No. **64★**

ParisN Rés676 = Paris, Bibliothèque Nationale de France, Département de la Musique, Rés. Vm.^{7} 676
    Nos. **12, 13★, 21§, 33, 36★, 40, 43, 54, 56, 62, 63, 65, 66, 68, 78, 83, 87, 89, 113, 116, 138★, 145, 149, 151**

ParisN Ro2973 = Paris, Bibliothèque Nationale de France, Rothschild 2973 (I.5.13)
    'Chansonnier de Jean de Montchenu'
    Nos. **40, 64★**

ParmaP Par3597 = Parma, Biblioteca Palatina, Parmense 3597
    No. **20**

PavU A361 = Pavia, Biblioteca Universitaria, Aldini 361
    No. **45**

PavU A362 = Pavia, Biblioteca Universitaria, Aldini 362
    No. **40**

PerA 431 = Perugia, Biblioteca Comunale Augusta, 431 (*olim* G.20)
    Nos. **13★, 20, 36★** (twice), **40, 56, 62, 64★, 75, 83**

PesO 1144 = Pesaro, Biblioteca Oliveriana, 1144 (*olim* 1193)
    (lute tablature, partly French and partly Italian)
    Nos. **33, 64★**

PozR 1361 = Poznań, Miejska Biblioteka Publiczna im. Edwarda Raczyńskiego, Dział Zbiorów Specjalnych 1361
    No. **45**

PrahaS 47 = Praha, Strahovský Klášter – Knihovna, D.G.IV.47
    'Strahov Codex'
    No. **83**

RegB 220-2 = Regensburg, Bischöfliche Zentralbibliothek, B. 220-222
    (4 partbooks)
    No. **177**

RegB 940-1 = Regensburg, Bischöfliche Zentralbibliothek, A.R. 940-941
    (5 partbooks)
    Nos. **21, 59★, 66★, 177**

RMN = Rocca di Mezzo, Chiesa di S. Maria della Neve, Museo d'Arte Sacra Cardinale Agnifili, s.s.
No. **115**

RomaCa 2856 = Roma, Biblioteca Casanatense, 2856 (*olim* O.V.208)
Nos. **16★, 40, 56★, 75, 83, 89, 127**

SegC = Segovia, Archivo Capitular de la Catedral, s.s.
Nos. **21, 36★** (twice), **54★, 55★, 56, 64★, 73★, 89, 105, 127, 131, 138★, 168**

SevC 20 = Sevilla, Biblioteca Capitular y Colombina, 5.5.20 (*olim* Z Tab. 137, N° 25)
No. **131**

SevC 43 = Sevilla, Biblioteca Capitular y Colombina, 5.1.43 (*olim* Z Tab. 135, N° 33)
(138 folios of an original 188; eight pages are lost, while 42 pages are in ParisN N4379)
Nos. **40, 56, 68, 73, 83**

SGS 461 = St. Gallen, Stiftsbibliothek, 461
'Fridolin Sicher Liederbuch'
Nos. **57, 97, 128**

SGS 462 = St. Gallen, Stiftsbibliothek, 462
'Johannes Heer Liederbuch'
Nos. **21★, 36★, 54★, 89**

SGS 463 = St. Gallen, Stiftsbibliothek, 463
'Aegidius Tschudi Liederbuch' (Superius and Altus partbooks only)
Nos. **36★, 54, 66★, 89, 96, 103, 105** (index only), **115, 177**

SGS 530 = St. Gallen, Stiftsbibliothek, 530
'Orgeltabulatur des Fridolin Sicher' (keyboard tablature)
Nos. **11★, 54, 89, 94, 98, 103, 105, 126, 168**

SienaC 2 = Siena, Biblioteca Comunale degli Intronati, K.I.2
No. **98**

SionC 87-4 = Sion (Sitten), Archives du Chapitre de la Cathédrale, 87-4
(Bassus partbook only)
Nos. **66★** (twice), **177**

StuttL 39 = Stuttgart, Württembergische Landesbibliothek, Musica folio I 39
No. **138★**

TorN 27 = Torino, Biblioteca Nazionale Universitaria, Riserva musicale I.27 (*olim* q^m III.59)
Nos. **21, 127, 166**

TournaiV 94 = Tournai, Bibliothèque de la Ville, 94
(Tenor partbook): see **BruxR 90 / TournaiV 94**

TrenC 1947/4 = Trento, Biblioteca Comunale, 1947/4
No. **64§**

TrenF 133 = Trento, Biblioteca Musicale Laurence Feininger, FC 133
No. **48**

TrenM 89 = Trento, Museo Castello del Buonconsiglio, Monumenti e Collezioni Provinciali (*ex* Museo Provinciale d'Arte), 1376 (*olim* 89)
No. **56§**

TrenM 91 = Trento, Museo Castello del Buonconsiglio, Monumenti e Collezioni Provinciali (*ex* Museo Provinciale d'Arte), 1378 (*olim* 91)
No. **83**

UlmS 236 = Ulm, Von Schermar'sche Familienstiftung, Bibliothek, 236a-d
(4 partbooks)
No. **66★**

UlmS 237 = Ulm, Von Schermar'sche Familienstiftung, Bibliothek, 237a-d
(4 partbooks)
Nos. **11§, 21, 40**

UppsU 76a = Uppsala, Universitetsbiblioteket, Vokalmusik i Handskrift 76a
Nos. **40, 56, 127**

UppsU 76e = Uppsala, Universitetsbiblioteket, Vokalmusik i Handskrift 76e
(Superius partbook only; MS copy of two printed volumes: PeIsaac [RISM I 88] and *Misse Gaspar* [...], Venice, Ottaviano Petrucci, 7 January 1506 (1507 modern style) [RISM G 450])
Nos. **21, 81★**

UppsU 478-80 = Uppsala, Universitetsbiblioteket, Utl. vok. mus. tr. 478-480
(Altus, Tenor, and Bassus partbooks only; MS addition to a copy of Johann Walther, *Wittembergisch* [...] *Gesangbüchlein*, Wittenberg, Georg Rhaus Erben, 1551 [RISM W 173]: each volume adds four pages bound to the beginning and 16 pages bound to the ending)
No. **66★**

VenM I145 = Venezia, Biblioteca Nazionale Marciana, It. IX.145 (= 7554) (formerly at Biblioteca dei Padri Somaschi della Salute, 22)
(consisting of two originally separate and quite distinct manuscripts)
Nos. **20** (twice), **48**

VerCap 690 = Verona, Biblioteca Capitolare, DCXC (DCC, 350)
No. **45**

VerCap 757 = Verona, Biblioteca Capitolare, DCCLVII (DCCLXVII, 438)
Nos. **21§, 54§, 56§, 57§, 83§, 89§, 127§, 168§**

VerCap 758 = Verona, Biblioteca Capitolare, DCCLVIII (DCCLXVIII)
Nos. **60, 94**

VerCap 760 = Verona, Biblioteca Capitolare, DCCLX (DCCLXX)
No. **177**

WarN P364 = Warszawa, Biblioteka Narodowa, Poliński 364[6] (formerly at Kraków, Klasztor Św. Ducha [St. Spiritus Spiritus Convent], s.s.)
(keyboard tablature; destroyed, but available in microfilm)[7]
No. **21**

WarU 5892 = Warszawa, Biblioteka Uniwersytecka, Oddział Zbiorów Muzycznych, RM 5892 (formerly at Breslau, Musikalisches Institut bei der Universität, Mf. 2016)
Nos. **11★, 16§, 21, 138★**

WashC J6 = Washington, DC, Library of Congress, M2.171.J6 Case
(a collection of theoretical treatises, with some polyphony)
Nos. **45, 76**

WashC L25 = Washington, DC, Library of Congress, M2.1.L25 Case
'Laborde Chansonnier'
Nos. **40, 56★, 64★, 127**

---

[6]. In Brzezińska 1987, p. 148, the number is cited as 564.

[7]. «Willi Apel obtained a microfilm copy of the Cracow Tablature for the Isham Memorial Library of Harvard University shortly before the German invasion of Poland of 1939. The manuscript was presumed destroyed. After the war Professor Apel had a microfilm returned to Poland» (see Insko 1992, p. iv).

WashC M6 = Washington, DC, Library of Congress, M2.1.M6 Case
(the same MS as LonB E3051: LonB E3051 has the first 61 folios; WashC M6 has fols. 80-99; the remaining folios are missing)
'Wolffheim Fragment'
Nos. **21**, **115**★

WienN 11883 = Wien, Österreichische Nationalbibliothek, Handschriftensammlung, 11883
No. **21**

WienN 18688 = Wien, Österreichische Nationalbibliothek, Musiksammlung, Mus. 18688
'Lauten-Tablatur des Stephan Craus aus Ebenfurt' (lute tablature added to Hans Judenkünig, *Ain schöne kunstliche Underweisung* [...], Wien, Hans Singriener, 1523 [RISM J 687])
No. **21**

WML 6 = London, Private Collection of Nessa Glen (formerly at Wertheim am Main, Fürstlich Löwenstein'sche Bibliothek, Musikalien n° 6)
(German lute tablature)
No. **54**§

WolfA 78 = Wolfenbüttel, Herzog August Bibliothek, 78 Quodlibetica 4°
No. **36**§

WolfA G287 = Wolfenbüttel, Herzog August Bibliothek, Guelferbytanus 287 Extravagantium
Nos. **40**, **56**, **64**★

WrocK 352 = Wrocław (Breslau), Biblioteka Kapitulna, 352
(lute tablature, partly Italian and partly German)
No. **66**

WrocU 428 = Wrocław (Breslau), Biblioteka Uniwersytecka, Oddział Rękopisów, I. F. 428
'Viadrina Codex'; 'Grüner Codex'
No. **126**

ZwR 78/2 = Zwickau, Ratsschulbibliothek, LXXVIII, 2 (= VollBM 1)
(4 partbooks)
No. **36**§

ZwR 78/3 = Zwickau, Ratsschulbibliothek, LXXVIII, 3 (= VollBM 12)
(3 partbooks)
Nos. **21**§, **54**§, **55**§, **59**§, **73**§, **127**§, **168**§

ZwR 86/2 = Zwickau, Ratsschulbibliothek, LXXXVI, 2 (= VollBM 6)
(Altus and Bassus partbooks only)
No. **21**

II. Musical Prints

AntCanzoni = *Canzoni nove con alcune scelte de varii libri di canto*, Rome, Andrea Antico, 9 October 1510
    Basel⋆, Öffentliche Bibliothek der Universität, kk.II.32
    Nos. 21,[8] **179**, **180**

AttMotetz = *Motetz nouvellement composez*, Paris, Pierre Attaingnant, no d.[9]
    (4 partbooks)
    Eichstätt, Universitätsbibliothek Eichstätt-Ingolstadt (*ex* Staatliche Bibliothek Eichstätt) [A, imperfect]; Paris⋆, Bibliothèque Nationale de France, Département de la Musique, Rés. Vm.[7] 182; Versailles, Bibliothèque Municipale [S]
    No. **94**

AttTrezeMotetz = *Treze motetz musicaulx avec ung prelude, le tout reduict en la tabulature des orgues espinettes et manicordions et telz semblables intrumentz*, Paris, Pierre Attaingnant, 1 April 1531
    (keyboard tablature)
    München⋆, Bayerische Staatsbibliothek, Mus.pr. 234 [lost, but a photocopy is preserved]
    No. **36**⋆

Baena = [Gonzalo de Baena], *Arte novamente inventada pera aprender a tanger*, Lisbon, Germão Galharde, 5 January 1540
    (keyboard tablature)
    Madrid⋆, Biblioteca del Palacio Real, VIII/1816
    Nos. **56**, **89**, **131**

EgenLieder = *[Lieder zu 3 & 4 Stimmen]*, [Frankfurt am Main, Christian Egenolff, ca. 1535]
    (Superius partbook only, in 3 books)
    Paris⋆, Bibliothèque Nationale de France, Département de la Musique, Rés. Vm.[7] 504 [S]
    Nos. **21**, **40**, **54**, **55**, **59**, **127**, **128**, **139**, **168**

FormGerle = *Tabulatur auff die Laudten etlicher Preambel, Teutscher, Welscher und Francösischer Stück, von Liedlein, Muteten, und schönen Psalmen, mit drey und vier Stymmen, durch Hanns Gerle Luttinisten ordentlich gesetz [...]*, Nuremberg, Hieronymus Formschneider, 1533
    (German lute tablature)
    Berlin, Staatsbibliothek, Preußischer Kulturbesitz; London⋆, British Library [2 copies, both imperfect], Hirsch IV.1604
    No. **127**

FormTrium = *Trium vocum carmina a diversis musicis composita*, Nuremberg, Hieronymus Formschneider, 1538
    (3 partbooks)
    Berlin, Freie Universität Berlin, Universitätsbibliothek; Berlin-Charlottenburg, Bibliothek der Hochschule für Musik und Darstellende Kunst; Jena⋆, Thüringer Universitäts- und Landesbibliothek, 4 Mus. 6.c (2)
    Nos. **21**§, **54**§, **55**§, **75**§, **89**§, **127**§, **128**§, **131**§, **168**§

GardFesta1543 = *Il vero libro di madrigali a tre voci di Constantio Festa novamente racolti et con una nova gionta stampatti et corretti a tre voci*, Venice, Antonio Gardano, 1543
    (3 partbooks)
    Kraków⋆, Biblioteka Jagiellońska, Mus.ant.pract. F 270
    No. **59**⋆

GardFesta1556 = *Di Constantio Festa il primo libro di madrigali a tre voci novamente da Antonio Gardano ristampati et corretti*, Venice, Antonio Gardano, 1556
    (3 partbooks)

---

[8]. Manuscript fragment: beginning of Tenor only.
[9]. In RISM B I, p. 102, the date is hypothesized as 1528; the online catalogue of the Bibliothèque Municipale of Versailles gives the date 1529; the online catalogue of the Bibliothèque Nationale de France has ca. 1530.

BOLOGNA, Museo Internazionale e Biblioteca della Musica (*ex* Civico Museo Bibliografico Musicale) [B]; MÜNCHEN⋆, Bayerische Staatsbibliothek, 4° Mus.pr. 117/1; VERONA, Biblioteca dell'Accademia Filarmonica [B]; WIEN, Österreichische Nationalbibliothek
No. **59**⋆

GardFesta1564 = *Di Constantio Festa il primo libro di madrigali a tre voci, novamente per Antonio Gardano ristampati et corretti,* Venice, Antonio Gardano, 1564
(3 partbooks)
PADOVA, Biblioteca Universitaria [B]; REGENSBURG⋆, Fürst Thurn und Taxis Hofbibliothek und Zentralarchiv, F.K.Musik No. 53
No. **59**⋆

GiuCant1523 = *Cantus monastici formula noviter impressa* [...] [Colophon:] *Cantorinus et processionarius* [...] *secundum ritum congregationis cassinensis alias sancte Iustine* [...], Venice, Luca Antonio Giunta, 30 April 1523
BOLOGNA⋆, Museo Internazionale e Biblioteca della Musica (*ex* Civico Museo Bibliografico Musicale), Lit. 21 [imperfect]; BOSTON, Public Library, Music Department; CITTÀ DEL VATICANO, Biblioteca Apostolica Vaticana; RAVENNA, Istituzione Biblioteca Classense
(the printed and online versions of EDIT 16 indicate another copy at the Biblioteca Ambrosiana in Milan; aided by the librarians, I have carefully looked for this copy on the spot, but without success)
No. **45**

GiuCant1536 = *Cantus monastici formula noviter impressa* [...] [Colophon:] *Cantorinus et processionarius* [...] *secundum ritum congregationis cassinensis alias sancte Iustine* [...], Venice, Luca Antonio Giunta, February 1535 (1536 modern style)
BOLOGNA, Biblioteca Comunale dell'Archiginnasio; BOLOGNA⋆, Museo Internazionale e Biblioteca della Musica (*ex* Civico Museo Bibliografico Musicale), Lit. 22; BOSTON, Public Library, Music Department; CESENA, Biblioteca dell'Abbazia di S. Maria del Monte; CHICAGO, Newberry Library; CREMONA, Biblioteca Statale (*ex* Governativa); GENOVA, Biblioteca della Badia dei Benedettini di S. Andrea della Castagna; MINNEAPOLIS (MN), Minneapolis Public Library; MONREALE, Biblioteca Popolare Pax - S. Martino delle Scale; PADOVA, Biblioteca Universitaria; PALERMO, Biblioteca Centrale della Regione Siciliana Alberto Bombace; RAVENNA, Istituzione Biblioteca Classense; REGGELLO, Biblioteca dell'Abbazia di Vallombrosa; ROCHESTER (NY), Sibley Music Library, Eastman School of Music, University of Rochester; ROMA, Biblioteca della Basilica di S. Paolo; ROMA, Biblioteca Nazionale Centrale Vittorio Emanuele II; ST. MEINRAD (IN), Archabbey Library of St. Meinrad; SIENA, Biblioteca Comunale degli Intronati; TEOLO, Biblioteca del Monumento Nazionale di Praglia
(the printed and online versions of EDIT 16 indicate another copy at the Biblioteca Ambrosiana in Milan; aided by the librarians, I have carefully looked for this copy on the spot, but without success)
No. **45**

GiuJosqII = *Libri secundi missarum Josquin* [...], Rome, Jacopo Giunta, Giovanni Giacomo Pasoti, Valerio Dorico, June 1526
(4 partbooks)
BARCELONA, Biblioteca de Catalunya (*ex* Biblioteca Central) [AT]; LONDON, British Library [SB]; PARIS, Bibliothèque Nationale de France, Département de la Musique; REGENSBURG, Bischöfliche Zentralbibliothek [AT]; WIEN⋆, Österreichische Nationalbibliothek, SA.77.C.30. 1-4 Mus 18
No. **115**

GünNew = *Das erst Buch. Ein newes Lautenbüchlein mit vil feiner lieblichen Liedern für die jungen Schuler* [...] *durch mich Hansen Newsidler Lutennisten und Burger zu Nürnberg offentlich aussgangen,* Nuremberg, Hans Günther, 1544
(German lute tablature)
KARLSRUHE⋆, Badische Landesbibliothek, Mus. A 674
No. **66**

GutNew = *Das erst Buch. Ein newes Lautenbüchlein mit vil feiner lieblichen Liedern für die jungen Schuler* [...] *durch mich Hansen Newsidler Lutennisten unnd* [*sic*] *Burger zu Nürnberg offentlich aussgangen,* Nuremberg, Christoff Gutknecht, 1547
(German lute tablature)
NÜRNBERG⋆, Bibliothek des Germanische Nationalmuseum, quer-8° M.261 (Postinc.)
No. **66**

HanZanger = *Practicae musicae praecepta, pueritiae instituendae gratia, ad certam methodum revocata, per Joannem Zangerum oenipontanum,* Leipzig, Georg Hantzsch, 1554
(theory treatise with musical examples)
AUGSBURG, Staats- und Stadtbibliothek; BERLIN, Staatsbibliothek, Preußischer Kulturbesitz; DARMSTADT, Universitäts- und Landesbibliothek (*ex* Hessische Landes- und Hochschulbibliothek) [imperfect]; GOTHA, Forschungs- und

Landesbibliothek; GÖTTINGEN, Niedersächsische Staats- und Universitätsbibliothek; HEILBRONN, Stadtarchiv; ITHACA (NY), Cornell University Library, Kroch Library Rare & Manuscripts; JENA, Thüringer Universitäts- und Landesbibliothek; MÜNCHEN, Bayerische Staatsbibliothek; ÖREBRO, Karolinska Läroverkets Bibliotek; PARIS, Bibliothèque Nationale de France, Département de la Musique; PARIS, Bibliothèque Sainte-Geneviève [imperfect]; STUTTGART, Württembergische Landesbibliothek; WASHINGTON★, DC, Library of Congress, ML 171.Z26 (case); WOLFENBÜTTEL, Herzog August Bibliothek [2 copies]

Nos. **124**§, **128**§

LiberSac1523 = *Liber sacerdotalis nuperrime ex libris sanctae Romanae ecclesiae et quarundam aliarum ecclesiarum* [...], Venice, Melchiorre Sessa and Pietro Ravani, 20 July 1523

BOLOGNA, Museo Internazionale e Biblioteca della Musica (*ex* Civico Museo Bibliografico Musicale); BRONI, Biblioteca della Collegiata di S. Pietro Apostolo; CITTÀ DEL VATICANO★, Biblioteca Apostolica Vaticana, Racc.Gen. Liturgia IV.398; FIRENZE, Biblioteca Nazionale Centrale; LUCCA, Biblioteca Statale (*ex* Governativa); MESSINA, Biblioteca Provinciale dei Frati Minori Cappuccini Madonna di Pompei; MILANO, Biblioteca e Archivio del Capitolo Metropolitano; MILANO, Biblioteca Nazionale Braidense; NOVARA, Biblioteca Comunale Carlo Negroni; PARMA, Biblioteca Palatina, Sezione Musicale; ROMA, Biblioteca Angelica; ROMA, Biblioteca Casanatense; TRENTO, Biblioteca Musicale Laurence Feininger; TRENTO, Fondazione Biblioteca S. Bernardino; TREVISO, Biblioteca Comunale; VENEZIA, Biblioteca Nazionale Marciana

No. **45**

LiberSac1537 = *Liber sacerdotalis nuperrime ex libris sanctae Romanae ecclesiae et quarundam aliarum ecclesiarum* [...], Venice, Vittore Ravani & C., May 1537

AMELIA, Biblioteca del Seminario Vescovile; BERGAMO, Civica Biblioteca - Archivi Storici Angelo Mai; BOLOGNA, Biblioteca Provinciale dei Frati minori dell'Emilia. Sezione Biblioteca dell'Osservanza; CAVA DE' TIRRENI, Biblioteca Comunale Canonico Aniello Avallone; CITTÀ DEL VATICANO, Biblioteca Apostolica Vaticana; MESSINA, Biblioteca Provinciale dei Frati Minori Cappuccini Madonna di Pompei; MESSINA, Biblioteca Regionale Universitaria; MILANO★, Biblioteca Ambrosiana, G-H.V.24 [imperfect]; MILANO, Biblioteca e Archivio del Capitolo Metropolitano; MILANO, Biblioteca Nazionale Braidense; MODENA, Biblioteca Estense Universitaria; MODENA, Duomo, Biblioteca e Archivio Capitolare; PADOVA, Biblioteca del Monumento Nazionale di S. Giustina; PERUGIA, Biblioteca S. Basilio del Seminario Arcivescovile; PIACENZA, Biblioteca del Seminario Vescovile; ROMA, Biblioteca Casanatense; TRENTO, Biblioteca Provinciale dei Padri Cappuccini

No. **45**

MeruloFesta = *Di Constantio Festa il primo libro de' madrigali a tre voci nuovamente ristampati et corretti per Claudio Merulo da Coreggio*, Venice, Claudio Merulo da Correggio, 1568

(3 partbooks)

BRESSANONE, Biblioteca del Seminario Vescovile Vinzentinum; KRAKÓW★, Biblioteka Jagiellońska, Mus.ant.pract. F 275

No. **59**★

Motetti1520 = *Motetti e canzone. Libro primo*, [Rome], no pr., [1520?][10]

(4 partbooks)

NEW YORK★, Pierpont Morgan Library, 001476-79 [imperfect]

No. **175**

MüllerHeckel = *Lautten Büch, von mancherley schönen und lieblichen Stucken, mit zweyen Lautten zusamen zuschlagen, und auch sonst das mehrer Theyl allein für sich selbst.* [...] *durch Wolffen Heckel von München, Burger zu Strassburg in ein verstendige Tabulatur* [...] *gebracht*, Strasburg, Christian Müller, 1562

(German lute tablature)

BASEL, Öffentliche Bibliothek der Universität [T]; BERLIN, Staatsbibliothek, Preußischer Kulturbesitz [T, imperfect]; BRUSSEL/BRUXELLES, Koninklijke Bibliotheek van België / Bibliothèque Royale de Belgique [T]; DRESDEN, Sächsische Landesbibliothek – Staats- und Universitätsbibliothek; KRAKÓW, Biblioteka Jagiellońska [T]; LONDON, British Library [S, imperfect]; LONDON, Royal College of Music [S, imperfect]; MÜNCHEN, Bayerische Staatsbibliothek [S]; PARIS, Bibliothèque Nationale de France, Département de la Musique (formerly at PARIS, Bibliothèque Geneviève Thibault), [S]; TRIER, Stadtbibliothek [S]; WIEN★, Österreichische Nationalbibliothek, S.A.76.C.27

No. **21**

---

[10]. RISM B I, p. 101, gives «Roma, A. Antico, 1521». Based also on the study of Catherine W. Chapman (CHAPMAN 1964), Martin Picker concludes that this print cannot have been produced by Antico, and dates from 1520; see PICKER 1977, p. 214.

PeBossI1509 = *Tenori e contrabassi intabulati col sopran in canto figurato per cantar e sonar col lauto. Libro primo. Francisci Bossinensis opus*,Venice, Ottaviano Petrucci, 27 March 1509
(Italian lute tablature)
Paris, Bibliothèque Nationale de France, Département de la Musique [according to Stanley Boorman, this copy contains parts of the second edition, which he dates 1515; see Boorman 2006, p. 716]; Sevilla, Biblioteca Capitular y Colombina; Wien★, Österreichische Nationalbibliothek, S.A.77.C.25; Private Collection[11]
Nos. **12, 52, 61★, 66**

PeBossI1515 = *Tenori e contrabassi intabulati col sopran in canto figurato per cantar e sonar col lauto. Libro primo. Francisci Bossinensis opus*,Venice, Ottaviano Petrucci, 27 March 1509[12]
(Italian lute tablature)
Chicago★, Newberry Library, Case VM.1490.B.74 [imperfect]
Nos. **12, 52, 61★, 66**

PeCantiC = *Canti C. N°. Cento cinquanta*,Venice, Ottaviano Petrucci, 10 February 1503 (1504 modern style)
Paris, Bibliothèque Nationale de France, Département de la Musique; Treviso, Biblioteca Capitolare della Cattedrale; Wien★, Österreichische Nationalbibliothek, 47.355-4°
Nos. **36★, 40**

PeDalza = *Intabulatura de lauto libro quarto. Padoane diverse. Calate a la spagnola. Calate a la taliana. Tastar de corde con li soi recercar drietro. Frottole. Joanambrosio [Dalza]*, Venice, Ottaviano Petrucci, 31 December 1508
(Italian lute tablature)
Brussel/Bruxelles, Koninklijke Bibliotheek van België / Bibliothèque Royale de Belgique; Chicago, Newberry Library [imperfect];Wien★, Österreichische Nationalbibliothek, S.A.77.C.26
No. **116**

PeFroI = *Frottole, libro primo*, Venice, Ottaviano Petrucci, 28 November 1504
Madrid, Private Collection; München★, Bayerische Staatsbibliothek, Rar. 878/1; Wien, Österreichische Nationalbibliothek; Private Collection[13]
Nos. **12, 17, 37, 52, 61★, 66, 93**

PeFroIII1505 = *Frottole, libro tertio*,Venice, Ottaviano Petrucci, 6 February 1504 (1505 modern style)
Madrid, Private Collection; München★, Bayerische Staatsbibliothek, Rar. 878/3; Private Collection[14]
Nos. **43, 65, 84, 85, 145, 148, 150**

PeFroIII1507 = *Frottole, libro tertio*,Venice, Ottaviano Petrucci, 26 November 1507
Regensburg, Bischöfliche Zentralbibliothek;Wien★, Österreichische Nationalbibliothek, S.A.77.C.2 (3)
Nos. **43, 65, 84, 85, 145, 148, 150**

PeFroIV1505 = *Strambotti, ode, frottole, sonetti, et modo de cantar versi latini e capituli. Libro quarto*,Venice, Ottaviano Petrucci, [between 7 February and 22 December 1505, the publication dates of the third and fifth books of Frottole][15]
München★, Bayerische Staatsbibliothek, Rar. 878/4 [imperfect]; Private Collection[16]
Nos. **38, 53, 63**

PeFroIV1507 = *Strambotti, ode, frottole, sonetti, et modo de cantar versi latini e capituli. Libro quarto*,Venice, Ottaviano Petrucci, 31 July 1507
Wien★, Österreichische Nationalbibliothek, S.A.77.C.2 (4) (this may be the copy formerly in the Fugger collection; see Boorman 2006, p. 600)
Nos. **38, 53, 63**

---

[11]. A further copy was advertised for sale by Sotheby's of London on 5 December 2003 (Lot 145), with an estimated price of € 86,000-120,000: see Boorman 2006, p. 716 and NJE 28/II, p. 243.

[12]. According to Stanley Boorman, the correct date of this print would be the beginning of 1515, perhaps February; see Boorman 2006, pp. 780-785.

[13]. David Fallows notes that at a Sotheby auction on 23 May 2007 a private individual purchased a copy of this volume, together with four other Petrucci prints (see Fallows 2007, p. 421, n. 7).

[14]. David Fallows notes that at a Sotheby auction on 23 May 2007 a private individual purchased a copy of this volume, together with four other Petrucci prints (see Fallows 2007, p. 421, n. 7). It is not clear whether this is the edition of 1505 or 1507.

[15]. Stanley Boorman hypothesizes August 1505; see the discussion on the paper used in Boorman 2006, pp. 600-601.

[16]. David Fallows notes that at a Sotheby auction on 23 May 2007 a private individual purchased a copy of this volume, together with four other Petrucci prints (see Fallows 2007, p. 421, n. 7). It is not clear whether this is the edition of 1505 or 1507.

PeFroV = *Frottole, libro quinto*, Venice, Ottaviano Petrucci, 23 December 1505
> MÜNCHEN★, Bayerische Staatsbibliothek, Rar. 878/5; PARIS, Bibliothèque Sainte-Geneviève [imperfect]; WIEN, Österreichische Nationalbibliothek
> No. **151**

PeIsaac = *Misse Henrici Izac: Charge de deul. Misericordias Domini. Quant yay au cor. La Spagna. Comme feme*, Venice, Ottaviano Petrucci, 20 October 1506
> (4 partbooks)
> BERLIN, Staatsbibliothek, Preußischer Kulturbesitz; BOLOGNA★, Museo Internazionale e Biblioteca della Musica (*ex* Civico Museo Bibliografico Musicale), Q.68; GÜSSING, Franziskaner-Kloster, Bibliothek [T, imperfect]; LONDON, British Library; MILANO, Biblioteca del Conservatorio Giuseppe Verdi [S]; WIEN, Österreichische Nationalbibliothek [SAT]
> Nos. **21**, **81**★

PeJosqII1505 = *Missarum Josquin liber secundus*, Venice, Ottaviano Petrucci, 30 June 1505
> (4 partbooks)
> BOLOGNA★, Museo Internazionale e Biblioteca della Musica (*ex* Civico Museo Bibliografico Musicale) [SAB], Q.63; FIRENZE, Biblioteca Marucelliana [B]; MILANO, Biblioteca del Conservatorio Giuseppe Verdi [STB]; ROCHESTER (NY), Sibley Music Library, Eastman School of Music, University of Rochester [S, imperfect]; WOLFENBÜTTEL, Herzog August Bibliothek
> No. **115**

PeJosqII1515Gothic = *Missarum Josquin liber secundus*, Fossombrone, Ottaviano Petrucci, 11 April 1515
> (4 partbooks)
> ASSISI, Biblioteca Comunale; BARCELONA, Biblioteca de Catalunya (*ex* Biblioteca Central) [A]; BERLIN, Staatsbibliothek, Preußischer Kulturbesitz; BOLOGNA★, Museo Internazionale e Biblioteca della Musica (*ex* Civico Museo Bibliografico Musicale), Q.72; GÜSSING, Franziskaner-Kloster, Bibliothek, [T]; LONDON, British Library [imperfect]; ROCHESTER (NY), Sibley Music Library, Eastman School of Music, University of Rochester [SB]; WIEN, Österreichische Nationalbibliothek [SAT]
> No. **115**

PeJosqII1515Roman = *Missarum Josquin liber secundus*, Fossombrone, Ottaviano Petrucci, 11 April 1515[17]
> (4 partbooks)
> BERGAMO, Civica Biblioteca - Archivi Storici Angelo Mai [S]; BRUSSEL/BRUXELLES, Koninklijke Bibliotheek van België / Bibliothèque Royale de Belgique [B]; CITTÀ DEL VATICANO★, Biblioteca Apostolica Vaticana, Cappella Sist. 235-238 (2); LONDON, British Library [imperfect]; SZOMBATHELY, Püspöki Könyvtár [B]; WIEN, Österreichische Nationalbibliothek [STB]
> No. **115**

PeLamI = *Lamentationum Jeremie prophete liber primus*, Venice, Ottaviano Petrucci, 8 April 1506
> BOLOGNA, Museo Internazionale e Biblioteca della Musica (*ex* Civico Museo Bibliografico Musicale); LONDON★, British Library, K.1.d.6★ (1) [imperfect]; PADOVA, Biblioteca Antoniana; PARIS, Bibliothèque Nationale de France, Département de la Musique [imperfect]
> No. **45**

PeLamII = *Lamentationum liber secundus. Auctores Tronboncinus. Gaspar. Erasmus*, Venice, Ottaviano Petrucci, 29 May 1506
> BOLOGNA, Museo Internazionale e Biblioteca della Musica (*ex* Civico Museo Bibliografico Musicale) [imperfect]; LONDON★, British Library, K.1.d.6★ (2) [imperfect]; PARIS, Bibliothèque Nationale de France, Département de la Musique [imperfect]
> No. **174**

PeLaudeII = *Laude libro secondo*, Venice, Ottaviano Petrucci, 11 January 1507 (1508 modern style)
> SEVILLA★, Biblioteca Capitular y Colombina, 12.1.3
> Nos. **4** (twice), **9**, **45**, **47**★, **115**★, **175**

PeMotA1502 = *Motetti A. Numero trentatre*, Venice, Ottaviano Petrucci, 9 May 1502
> BOLOGNA★, Museo Internazionale e Biblioteca della Musica (*ex* Civico Museo Bibliografico Musicale), Q.53
> Nos. **51**, **60**, **90**, **91**, **94**, **95**, **98**, **99**, **102**, **103**, **124**, **126**, **129**, **130**

---

[17]. Ca. 1519 or later, according to NOBLE 1978, pp. 442-443.

PeMotA1505 = *Motetti A. Numero trentatre,*Venice, Ottaviano Petrucci, 13 February 1504 (1505 modern style)
BUDAPEST★, Országos Széchényi Könyvtár, ZR 523
Nos. **51, 60, 91, 94, 95, 98, 99, 102, 103, 124, 126, 129, 130**

PeMotB = *Motetti de passione, de cruce, de sacramento, de Beata Virgine et huiusmodi. B,* Venice, Ottaviano Petrucci, 10 May 1503
BOLOGNA★, Museo Internazionale e Biblioteca della Musica (*ex* Civico Museo Bibliografico Musicale), Q.56 [imperfect]; BUDAPEST, Országos Széchényi Könyvtár [imperfect]; LONDON, British Library; PARIS, Bibliothèque Nationale de France, Département de la Musique [imperfect]
No. **115**

PeOdh1501 = *Harmonice musices Odhecaton A,* Venice, Ottaviano Petrucci, dedication dated «decimo octavo cal. Iunias. Salutis anno. MDI» (= 15 May or 14 June 1501?)[18]
BOLOGNA★, Museo Internazionale e Biblioteca della Musica (*ex* Civico Museo Bibliografico Musicale), Q.51 [imperfect]
Nos. **21, 55, 56, 57, 59, 73, 89, 96, 97, 111, 127, 128, 131, 139**

PeOdh1503 = *Harmonice musices Odhecaton A,* Venice, Ottaviano Petrucci, 14 January 1502 (1503 modern style)
SEVILLA★, Biblioteca Capitular y Colombina, 12.1.29 [imperfect]; PRIVATE COLLECTION[19]
Nos. **21, 54, 55, 56, 57, 59, 73, 89, 96, 97, 105, 111, 127, 128, 131, 139, 168**

PeOdh1504 = *Harmonice musices Odhecaton A,* Venice, Ottaviano Petrucci, 25 May 1504
MADRID, Private Collection, *olim* MADRID, Biblioteca de la Casa Ducal de Medinaceli; NEW YORK, Pierpont Morgan Library; PARIS, Bibliothèque Nationale de France, Département de la Musique; TREVISO★, Biblioteca Capitolare della Cattedrale, Stampa Mus. 5 [imperfect]; WASHINGTON, DC, Library of Congress
Nos. **21, 54, 55, 56, 57, 59, 73, 89, 96, 97, 105, 111, 127, 128, 131, 139, 168**

PeSpinI = [FRANCESCO SPINACINO], *Intabulatura de lauto. Libro primo,* Venice, Ottaviano Petrucci, *post* 27 February 1507
(Italian lute tablature)
KRAKÓW★, Biblioteka Jagiellońska, Mus.ant.pract. P 680
Nos. **21, 54, 64★, 139**

PeSpinII = [FRANCESCO SPINACINO], *Intabulatura de lauto. Libro secondo,* Venice, Ottaviano Petrucci, 31 March 1507
(Italian lute tablature)
KRAKÓW★, Biblioteka Jagiellońska, Mus.ant.pract. P 680 (2)
Nos. **36★, 55, 64★, 89, 131**

PetreiusNewI = *Ein newgeordent künstlich Lautenbuch, in zwen Theyl getheylt [...] dergleichen vormals nie im Truck, aber yetzo durch mich Hansen Newsidler Lutinisten und Bürger zu Nürnberg, offenlich außgangen [...],* Nuremberg, Johann Petreius, 1536
(German lute tablature)
BERLIN, Staatsbibliothek, Preußischer Kulturbesitz; BERN, Stadt- und Universitätsbibliothek; HALLE AN DER SAALE, Martin-Luther-Universität, Universitäts- und Landesbibliothek Sachsen-Anhalt; KØBENHAVN, Det Kongelige Bibliotek; LEIPZIG, Städtische Bibliotheken, Muzikbibliothek [2 copies]; MÜNCHEN, Bayerische Staatsbibliothek [imperfect]; STRASBOURG, Bibliothèque du Séminaire Protestant [imperfect]; WASHINGTON, DC, Library of Congress; WOLFENBÜTTEL★, Herzog August Bibliothek, 2.14 Mus; ZOFINGEN, Stadtbibliothek
Nos. **21, 54** (twice)

PetreiusNewII = *Der ander Theil des Lautenbuchs [...] dergleichen vormals nie im Truck, aber yetzo durch mich Hansen Newsidler Lutinisten und Bürger zu Nürnberg, offenlich außgangen [...],* Nuremberg, Johann Petreius, 1536
(German lute tablature)
BERLIN, Staatsbibliothek, Preußischer Kulturbesitz; BRUSSEL/BRUXELLES, Koninklijke Bibliotheek van België / Bibliothèque Royale de Belgique [imperfect]; HALLE AN DER SAALE, Martin-Luther-Universität, Universitäts- und Landesbibliothek Sachsen-Anhalt; NÜRNBERG, Bibliothek des Germanische Nationalmuseum; WOLFENBÜTTEL★, Herzog August Bibliothek, 2.14 Mus
Nos. **55, 59, 89, 128, 131**

---

[18]. Interpreting «iunias» as a printing error for 'iulias', since there is no 18th before the kalends of June in the Roman calendar, Leofranc Holford-Strevens has brought about a new reading of the Latin dedication of the *Odhecaton,* proposing to interpret the day mentioned as 14 June (see BLACKBURN 1996, p. 34 and n. 24).

[19]. David Fallows notes that at a Sotheby auction on 23 May 2007 a private individual purchased a copy of this volume, together with four other Petrucci prints (see FALLOWS 2007, p. 421, n. 7).

PhalChansons = *Des chansons reduictz en tabulature de lut à deux, trois, et quatre parties* [...] *Livre premier*, Louvain, Jacques Bathen and Reynier Velpen (Pierre Phalèse), 1545
(French lute tablature)
BESANÇON★, Bibliothèque Municipale, 247975
No. **54**★

Razzi = *Libro primo delle laudi spirituali da diversi autori eccell. e divoti autori, antichi e moderni composte* [...] *raccolte da fra S. Razzi* [...] *Nuovamente stampate*, Venice, Francesco Rampazetto at the instance of Giunti di Firenze, 1563
Assisi, Biblioteca della Porziuncola (Basilica di S. Maria degli Angeli); BOLOGNA★, Museo Internazionale e Biblioteca della Musica (*ex* Civico Museo Bibliografico Musicale), R.211; BRUSSEL/BRUXELLES, Koninklijke Bibliotheek van België / Bibliothèque Royale de Belgique; FIRENZE, Biblioteca del Conservatorio Luigi Cherubini [2 copies]; FIRENZE, Biblioteca Nazionale Centrale; FRATTA POLESINE, Private Collection of Giorgio Fanan; KRAKÓW, Biblioteka Jagiellońska; LONDON, British Library, [2 copies]; LUCCA, Biblioteca Statale (*ex* Governativa); MILANO, Biblioteca dell'Archivio Storico Civico e Biblioteca Trivulziana; OXFORD, Bodleian Library (formerly at TENBURY WELLS, St. Michael's College); ROMA, Biblioteca dell'Accademia Nazionale dei Lincei e Corsiniana; ROMA, Biblioteca Musicale Governativa del Conservatorio S. Cecilia [2 copies]; ST. PETERBURG, Rossijskaja Nacional'naja Biblioteka; STRASBOURG, Bibliothèque Nationale et Universitaire; VENEZIA, Biblioteca Nazionale Marciana
(although RISM indicates a copy also in PARIS, Bibliothèque Nationale de France, Département de la Musique, there is no trace of the print either in the card catalogue of the library or in that of the Fonds du Conservatoire, nor in the two bibliographical catalogues in current use: CATALOGUE PARIS and MUSIQUES ANCIENNES)
Nos. **45, 69, 76, 149**★

RhauSym = *Symponiae iucundae atque adeo breves quatuor vocum* [...], Wittenberg, Georg Rhau, 1538
(4 partbooks)
DRESDEN, Sächsische Landesbibliothek - Staats- und Universitätsbibliothek; HEILBRONN, Stadtarchiv; JENA, Thüringer Universitäts- und Landesbibliothek; MÜNCHEN★, Bayerische Staatsbibliothek, Mus.pr. 12/6; ROSTOCK, Universitätsbibliothek; ZWICKAU, Ratsschulbibliothek [S]
Nos. **66**★, **177**

ScottoFesta1547 = *Il vero libro di madrigali a tre voci di Constantio Festa novamente raccolti et con una nova gionta di madrigali di Iacomo Fogliano, & de altri autori nuovamente stampati, & corretti*, Venice, Ottaviano Scotto, 1547
(3 partbooks)
BARCELONA★, Biblioteca de la Institució Milà i Fontanals, Consejo Superior de Investigaciones Científicas (*ex* Biblioteca del Instituto Español de Musicología) [B], Fondo Reserva, 65 (*olim* B-3); TRENTO, Biblioteca Comunale [STB imperfect]
No. **59**★

ScottoFesta1551 = *Di Constantio Festa il primo libro di madrigali a tre voci novamente ristampato, et da molti errori occorsi nelle prime stampe emendato. Aggiontovi anchora alcuni madrigali a tre voci di Iacomo Fogliano*, Venice, Girolamo Scotto, 1551
(3 partbooks)
BOLOGNA★, Museo Internazionale e Biblioteca della Musica (*ex* Civico Museo Bibliografico Musicale) [T], S.133
No. **59**★

ScottoFesta1559 = *Di Constantio Festa il primo libro di madrigali a tre voci: novamente ristampato, et da molti errori occorsi nelle prime stampe emendato, aggiontovi ancora alcuni madrigali a tre voci di Iacomo Fogliano*, Venice, Girolamo Scotto, 1559
(3 partbooks)
PARIS★, Bibliothèque Nationale de France, Département de la Musique, Rés. Vm.⁷ 589
No. **59**★

WyssHeckel = *Lautten Buoch, von mancherley schönen und lieblichen Stucken, mit zweyen Lautten zusamen zeschlagen, und auch sonst das mehrer Theyl für sich selbst alleyn.* [...] *durch Wolffen Heckel von München, Burger zu Strassburg* [...] *in ein verstendliche Tabulatur* [...] *gebracht*, Strasburg, Urban Wyss (Weiss), 1556
(German lute tablature)
HAMBURG, Staats- und Universitätsbibliothek Carl von Ossietzky, Musikabteilung [T, lost]; KRAKÓW★, Biblioteka Jagiellońska [T], Mus.ant.pract. H 690
(although RISM indicates a copy also in PARIS, Bibliothèque Nationale de France, Département de la Musique, there is no trace of the print either in the card catalogue of the library or in that of the Fonds du Conservatoire, nor in the two bibliographical catalogues in current use: CATALOGUE PARIS and MUSIQUES ANCIENNES)
No. **21**

III. Textual Manuscripts

Berg.C. 1 = Bergamo, Civica Biblioteca – Archivi Storici Angelo Mai, Cassaforte 1.1 (*olim* Δ.VII.15)
    Nos. **29/114**, **64**, **76**

Berl.M. 17 = Berlin, Staatliche Museen der Stiftung Preußischer Kulturbesitz, Kupferstichkabinett, 78.B.17 (*olim* Hamilton 674)
    Nos. **40**, **56**

Berl.S. H.348 = Berlin, Staatsbibliothek, Preußischer Kulturbesitz, Hamilton 348 (*ex* Biblioteca di S. Francesco della Vigna in Venezia)
    Nos. **13**, **27**, **29/114**, **64**, **76**, **147**

Bol.Arciv. 4880 = Bologna, Biblioteca Arcivescovile, 4880 (*olim* Aula 2ª C.VI.4)
    No. **13**

Bol.Car. 34 = Bologna, Biblioteca di Casa Carducci, non Carducciano 34
    No. **64**

Bol.FM. 10 = Bologna, Archivio Storico della Provincia di Cristo Re dei Frati Minori dell'Emilia Romagna, Sez. VII, Piana 10
    Nos. **19**, **63**

Bol.U. 12 = Bologna, Biblioteca Universitaria, 12, II.4
    No. **13**

Bol.U. 157 = Bologna, Biblioteca Universitaria, 157
    No. **13**

Bol.U. 1242 = Bologna, Biblioteca Universitaria, 1242
    No. **19**

Bol.U. 1737 = Bologna, Biblioteca Universitaria, 1737
    No. **76**

Bol.U. 2618 = Bologna, Biblioteca Universitaria, 2618
    No. **13**

Bol.U. 2672 = Bologna, Biblioteca Universitaria, 2672
    No. **76**

Bol.U. 2690 = Bologna, Biblioteca Universitaria, 2690
    No. **19**

Bol.U. 2845 = Bologna, Biblioteca Universitaria, 2845
    Nos. **13**, **64**, **76**, **147**

Bol.U. 2932 = Bologna, Biblioteca Universitaria, 2932
    No. **76**

Bol.U. 3795 = Bologna, Biblioteca Universitaria, 3795
    No. **19**

Bol.U. 4019 = Bologna, Biblioteca Universitaria, 4019
    Nos. **13**, **27**, **29/114**, **69**, **76**

Borg.P. M.76725 = Borgomanero, Biblioteca Pubblica e Casa della Cultura - Fondazione Achille Marazza, Molli 76725
Nos. **13**, **29/114**, **64**

Brambilla = An incomplete manuscript signalled by Ettore Brambilla (see Brambilla 1903, with table), but whose current location is unknown. It appears to date from the end of the fifteenth century, in southern Italian (perhaps it comes from L'Aquila), and copied throughout by a single hand, probably of a friar. It is in Gothic letters, and contains 35 quinterns, the last of which are damaged by a spot that progressively increases
Nos. **13**, **64**

Br.Q. 16 = Brescia, Biblioteca Civica Queriniana, A.VI.16
No. **19**

Br.Q. 23 = Brescia, Biblioteca Civica Queriniana, A.VI.23
Nos. **19**, **78**

Como.C. = Como, Archivio Storico della Diocesi, Fondo Curia Vescovile, s.s.
No. **13**

CV. BL.3679 = Città del Vaticano, Biblioteca Apostolica Vaticana, Barberiniano Latino 3679 (*olim* XLIV.40)
Nos. **30**, **76**

CV. BL.3695 = Città del Vaticano, Biblioteca Apostolica Vaticana, Barberiniano Latino 3695 (*olim* XLIV.56)
No. **13**

CV. BL.3711 = Città del Vaticano, Biblioteca Apostolica Vaticana, Barberiniano Latino 3711 (*olim* XLIV.72)
Nos. **30**, **69**, **76**

CV. BL.4047 = Città del Vaticano, Biblioteca Apostolica Vaticana, Barberiniano Latino 4047 (*olim* XLV.141)
Nos. **29/114**, **30**, **147**

CV. Ca.193 = Città del Vaticano, Biblioteca Apostolica Vaticana, Capponi 193
Nos. **19**, **53**, **116**, **149**

CV. Ch.120 = Città del Vaticano, Biblioteca Apostolica Vaticana, Chigi L.IV.120
Nos. **29/114**, **64**

CV. Ch.176 = Città del Vaticano, Biblioteca Apostolica Vaticana, Chigi L.V.176
No. **180**

CV. Ch.266 = Città del Vaticano, Biblioteca Apostolica Vaticana, Chigi L.VII.266
Nos. **29/114**, **30** (twice), **47**, **64**, **76**, **147**

CV. OL.251 = Città del Vaticano, Biblioteca Apostolica Vaticana, Ottoboniano Latino 251
No. **76**

CV. OL.3322 = Città del Vaticano, Biblioteca Apostolica Vaticana, Ottoboniano Latino 3322
No. **13**

CV. P.113 = Città del Vaticano, Biblioteca Apostolica Vaticana, Patetta 113
No. **29/114**

CV. P.341 = Città del Vaticano, Biblioteca Apostolica Vaticana, Patetta 341
No. **64**

CV. P.1513 = Città del Vaticano, Biblioteca Apostolica Vaticana, Patetta 1513
No. **13**

CV. ReL.478 = Città del Vaticano, Biblioteca Apostolica Vaticana, Reginense Latino 478
No. **13**

CV. Ro.229 = Città del Vaticano, Biblioteca Apostolica Vaticana, Rossi 229 (*olim* VIII.168)
No. **13**

CV. Ro.424 = Città del Vaticano, Biblioteca Apostolica Vaticana, Rossi 424 (*olim* IX.114)
    Nos. **30**, **36**, **67**, **69**, **76**, **159**

CV. Ro.651 = Città del Vaticano, Biblioteca Apostolica Vaticana, Rossi 651 (*olim* X.32)
    No. **29/114**

CV. Ro.1002 = Città del Vaticano, Biblioteca Apostolica Vaticana, Rossi 1002 (*olim* XI.152)
    No. **30**

CV. VL.3195 = Città del Vaticano, Biblioteca Apostolica Vaticana, Vaticano Latino 3195
    No. **180**

CV. VL.3213 = Città del Vaticano, Biblioteca Apostolica Vaticana, Vaticano Latino 3213
    No. **13**

CV. VL.5133 = Città del Vaticano, Biblioteca Apostolica Vaticana, Vaticano Latino 5133
    No. **76**

CV. VL.5159 = Città del Vaticano, Biblioteca Apostolica Vaticana, Vaticano Latino 5159
    Nos. **19**, **33**, **35**, **49**, **53**

CV. VL.5170 = Città del Vaticano, Biblioteca Apostolica Vaticana, Vaticano Latino 5170
    Nos. **1**, **19**, **33**

CV. VL.7714 = Città del Vaticano, Biblioteca Apostolica Vaticana, Vaticano Latino 7714
    Nos. **13**, **30**, **76**

CV. VL.8191 = Città del Vaticano, Biblioteca Apostolica Vaticana, Vaticano Latino 8191
    No. **19**

CV. VL.13026 = Città del Vaticano, Biblioteca Apostolica Vaticana, Vaticano Latino 13026
    Nos. **29/114**, **64**, **76**, **147**, **159**

CV. VL.13704 = Città del Vaticano, Biblioteca Apostolica Vaticana, Vaticano Latino 13704
    No. **53**

Fer.C. 211 = Ferrara, Biblioteca Comunale Ariostea, II.211
    Nos. **29/114**, **76**, **147**

Fer.C. 408 = Ferrara, Biblioteca Comunale Ariostea, I.408
    No. **49**

Fir.L. Ant.158 = Firenze, Biblioteca Medicea Laurenziana, Antinori 158
    Nos. **145**, **149**

Fir.L. Ash.480 = Firenze, Biblioteca Medicea Laurenziana, Ashburnham 480
    Nos. **29/114**, **30**, **76**, **147**, **159**

Fir.L. Ash.539 = Firenze, Biblioteca Medicea Laurenziana, Ashburnham 539
    No. **30**

Fir.L. Ash.567 = Firenze, Biblioteca Medicea Laurenziana, Ashburnham 567
    No. **30**

Fir.L. Ash.598 = Firenze, Biblioteca Medicea Laurenziana, Ashburnham 598
    No. **13**

Fir.L. Ash.852 = Firenze, Biblioteca Medicea Laurenziana, Ashburnham 852
    Nos. **13**, **147**

Fir.L.Ash.1177 = Firenze, Biblioteca Medicea Laurenziana, Ashburnham 1177
    No. **13**

Fir.L.Ash.1402 = Firenze, Biblioteca Medicea Laurenziana, Ashburnham 1402
  Nos. **13**, **29/114**, **64** (twice), **76**, **147**

Fir.L. R.121 = Firenze, Biblioteca Medicea Laurenziana, Redi 121
  No. **30**

Fir.L. S.17 = Firenze, Biblioteca Medicea Laurenziana, Segni 17
  No. **30**

Fir.M. 262 = Firenze, Biblioteca Marucelliana, C.262
  Nos. **30**, **69**, **76**, **147**, **159**

Fir.N. 4 = Firenze, Biblioteca Nazionale Centrale, II.VII.4 (*olim* Magliabechiano VII.1008)
  Nos. **30**, **76**

Fir.N. 12 = Firenze, Biblioteca Nazionale Centrale, II.XI.12
  Nos. **29/114**, **30**

Fir.N. 35 = Firenze, Biblioteca Nazionale Centrale, II.XI.35
  Nos. **30**, **76**, **159**

Fir.N. 42 = Firenze, Biblioteca Nazionale Centrale, II.IX.42
  No. **68**

Fir.N. 54 = Firenze, Biblioteca Nazionale Centrale, II.X.54
  No. **19**

Fir.N. 58 = Firenze, Biblioteca Nazionale Centrale, II.IX.58
  Nos. **29/114**, **147**

Fir.N. 75 = Firenze, Biblioteca Nazionale Centrale, II.II.75
  No. **53**

Fir.N. 140 = Firenze, Biblioteca Nazionale Centrale, II.IX.140
  Nos. **29/114**, **30**, **64**, **76**, **147**

Fir.N. 291 = Firenze, Biblioteca Nazionale Centrale, II.III.291
  No. **13**

Fir.N. 700 = Firenze, Biblioteca Nazionale Centrale, II.IV.700
  Nos. **29/114**, **76**

Fir.N. II.IV.3 = Firenze, Biblioteca Nazionale Centrale, II.IV.3
  No. **13**

Fir.N. II.VIII.3 = Firenze, Biblioteca Nazionale Centrale, II.VIII.3 (*olim* Magliabechiano XIII.47)
  No. **76**

Fir.N. B.228 = Firenze, Biblioteca Nazionale Centrale, Baldovinetti 228 (*olim* Palatino 428)
  Nos. **33**, **35**, **63**, **87**

Fir.N. CS.488 = Firenze, Biblioteca Nazionale Centrale, Conventi Soppressi F.3.488
  No. **30**

Fir.N. LF.13 = Firenze, Biblioteca Nazionale Centrale, Landau Finaly 13
  No. **76**

Fir.N. LF.236 = Firenze, Biblioteca Nazionale Centrale, Landau Finaly 236
  Nos. **30**, **69**

Fir.N. LF.249 = Firenze, Biblioteca Nazionale Centrale, Landau Finaly 249
  Nos. **30**, **147**

Fir. N. LF.302 = FIRENZE, Biblioteca Nazionale Centrale, Landau Finaly 302
    Nos. **29/114, 76**

Fir. N. M.27 = FIRENZE, Biblioteca Nazionale Centrale, Magliabechiano VII.27
    Nos. **29/114, 30, 64, 76, 147**

Fir. N. M.30 = FIRENZE, Biblioteca Nazionale Centrale, Magliabechiano VII.30
    Nos. **29/114, 76, 147**

Fir. N. M.85 = FIRENZE, Biblioteca Nazionale Centrale, Magliabechiano XI.85
    No. **30**

Fir. N. M.285 = FIRENZE, Biblioteca Nazionale Centrale, Magliabechiano VII.285
    No. **147**

Fir. N. M.367 = FIRENZE, Biblioteca Nazionale Centrale, Magliabechiano VII.367
    Nos. **30, 159**

Fir. N. M.376 = FIRENZE, Biblioteca Nazionale Centrale, Magliabechiano VII.376
    No. **19**

Fir. N. M.686 = FIRENZE, Biblioteca Nazionale Centrale, Magliabechiano VII.686
    Nos. **69, 76, 147**

Fir. N. M.690 = FIRENZE, Biblioteca Nazionale Centrale, Magliabechiano VII.690
    Nos. **30** (twice), **67, 159**

Fir. N. M.735 = FIRENZE, Biblioteca Nazionale Centrale, Magliabechiano VII.735
    No. **149**

Fir. N. M.738 = FIRENZE, Biblioteca Nazionale Centrale, Magliabechiano VII.738
    No. **13**

Fir. N. M.744 = FIRENZE, Biblioteca Nazionale Centrale, Magliabechiano VII.744
    No. **30**

Fir. N. M.1083 = FIRENZE, Biblioteca Nazionale Centrale, Magliabechiano VII.1083
    Nos. **64, 69, 76, 159**

Fir. N. M.1114 = FIRENZE, Biblioteca Nazionale Centrale, Magliabechiano VII.1114
    No. **30**

Fir. N. M.1163 = FIRENZE, Biblioteca Nazionale Centrale, Magliabechiano VII.1163
    No. **30**

Fir. N. M.VII.117 = FIRENZE, Biblioteca Nazionale Centrale, Magliabechiano VII.117
    Nos. **19, 63**

Fir. N. NA.701 = FIRENZE, Biblioteca Nazionale Centrale, Nuovi Acquisti 701
    Nos. **19, 63, 87, 116**

Fir. N. P.13 = FIRENZE, Biblioteca Nazionale Centrale, Palatino 13
    No. **29/114**

Fir. N. P.169 = FIRENZE, Biblioteca Nazionale Centrale, Palatino 169
    No. **69**

Fir. N. P.172 = FIRENZE, Biblioteca Nazionale Centrale, Palatino 172
    No. **30**

Fir. N. P.173 = FIRENZE, Biblioteca Nazionale Centrale, Palatino 173
    Nos. **15, 69, 76**

Fir.N. P.219 = FIRENZE, Biblioteca Nazionale Centrale, Palatino 219
  No. **30**

Fir.N. P.445 = FIRENZE, Biblioteca Nazionale Centrale, Palatino 445
  No. **30**

Fir.N. T.227 = FIRENZE, Biblioteca Nazionale Centrale, Tordi 227
  Nos. **19, 145**

Fir.R. 1094 = FIRENZE, Biblioteca Riccardiana, 1094
  No. **30**

Fir.R. 1106 = FIRENZE, Biblioteca Riccardiana, 1106
  No. **13**

Fir.R. 1119 = FIRENZE, Biblioteca Riccardiana, 1119
  Nos. **29/114, 76**

Fir.R. 1258 = FIRENZE, Biblioteca Riccardiana, 1258
  No. **116**

Fir.R. 1294/2760 = FIRENZE, Biblioteca Riccardiana, 1294 and 2760
  No. **13**

Fir.R. 1413 = FIRENZE, Biblioteca Riccardiana, 1413
  Nos. **29/114, 69, 76, 159**

Fir.R. 1473 = FIRENZE, Biblioteca Riccardiana, 1473
  Nos. **30, 69, 76, 147**

Fir.R. 1501 = FIRENZE, Biblioteca Riccardiana, 1501
  No. **30**

Fir.R. 1502 = FIRENZE, Biblioteca Riccardiana, 1502
  Nos. **29/114, 30, 64, 76, 147**

Fir.R. 1661 = FIRENZE, Biblioteca Riccardiana, 1661
  No. **13**

Fir.R. 1666 = FIRENZE, Biblioteca Riccardiana, 1666
  Nos. **29/114, 147**

Fir.R. 1720 = FIRENZE, Biblioteca Riccardiana, 1720
  No. **30**

Fir.R. 1721 = FIRENZE, Biblioteca Riccardiana, 1721
  No. **30**

Fir.R. 1763 = FIRENZE, Biblioteca Riccardiana, 1763
  No. **13**

Fir.R. 2723 = FIRENZE, Biblioteca Riccardiana, 2723
  Nos. **33, 63**

Fir.R. 2816 = FIRENZE, Biblioteca Riccardiana, 2816
  No. **30**

Fir.R. 2893 = FIRENZE, Biblioteca Riccardiana, 2893
  No. **30**

Fir.R. 2894 = FIRENZE, Biblioteca Riccardiana, 2894
  No. **30**

Fir.R. 2895 = FIRENZE, Biblioteca Riccardiana, 2895
Nos. **29/114, 69, 76, 147**

Fir.R. 2896 = FIRENZE, Biblioteca Riccardiana, 2896
No. **30**

Fir.R. 2929 = FIRENZE, Biblioteca Riccardiana, 2929
Nos. **29/114, 30, 76, 147**

Fir.R. 2971 = FIRENZE, Biblioteca Riccardiana, 2971
No. **30**

Fir.R. 3112 = FIRENZE, Biblioteca Riccardiana, 3112
Nos. **29/114, 30, 69, 76, 159** (index only)

FrattaPol.Fanan = FRATTA POLESINE, Private Collection of Giorgio Fanan (former Private Collection of Remo Giazotto)
No. **76**

Gub.Maz = A parchment manuscript that belonged to Giuseppe Mazzatinti, with anonymous laude in musical and dialogue
form of the Disciplinati of Gubbio. The current location is unknown. It is mentioned in MAZZATINTI 1880 (with a
complete table on p. 87), MAZZATINTI 1886, and MAZZATINTI 1889
No. **64**

Lon.B.A.16439 = LONDON, British Library, Additional 16439
No. **33**

Lon.B.A.27549 = LONDON, British Library, Additional 27549
No. **13**

Luc.S. 1302 = LUCCA, Biblioteca Statale (*ex* Governativa), 1302
No. **13**

Man.C. 4 = MANTOVA, Biblioteca Comunale, 4 (*olim* A.I.4)
Nos. **93, 179**

Mil.A. 3 = MILANO, Biblioteca Ambrosiana, Y 3 sup.
Nos. **29/114, 64, 147**

Mil.A. 25 = MILANO, Biblioteca Ambrosiana, D 25 sup.
No. **159**

Mil.A. 35 = MILANO, Biblioteca Ambrosiana, C 35 sup.
Nos. **30, 76**

Mil.A. 80 = MILANO, Biblioteca Ambrosiana, ✠ 80 sup.
No. **13**

Mil.A. 94 = MILANO, Biblioteca Ambrosiana, D 94 suss.
No. **13**

Mil.A.T.502 = MILANO, Biblioteca Ambrosiana, Trotti 502
No. **64**

Mil.B. 27 = MILANO, Biblioteca Nazionale Braidense, AC.IX.27
Nos. **64, 76**

Mil.B. 28 = MILANO, Biblioteca Nazionale Braidense, AC.IX.28
No. **13**

Mil.T. 92 = MILANO, Biblioteca dell'Archivio Storico Civico e Biblioteca Trivulziana, Triv. 92
Nos. **13, 29/114, 64, 76**

Mil. T. 383 = MILANO, Biblioteca dell'Archivio Storico Civico e Biblioteca Trivulziana, Triv. 383
No. **64**

Mil. T. 545 = MILANO, Biblioteca dell'Archivio Storico Civico e Biblioteca Trivulziana, Triv. 545
No. **13**

Mil. T. 913 = MILANO, Biblioteca dell'Archivio Storico Civico e Biblioteca Trivulziana, Triv. 913
Nos. **29/114**, **64**, **76**

Mod. E. 81 = MODENA, Biblioteca Estense Universitaria, γ.D.6.29 (Campori 81)
Nos. **12**, **19**

Mod. E. 381 = MODENA, Biblioteca Estense Universitaria, α.G.5.11 (It. 381)
No. **13**

Mod. E. 809 = MODENA, Biblioteca Estense Universitaria, α.M.7.15 (It. 809)
Nos. **19** (twice), **63**, **93**

Mod. E. 1168 = MODENA, Biblioteca Estense Universitaria, α.M.7.32 (It. 1168)
Nos. **62**, **80**

Mod. E. 1277 = MODENA, Biblioteca Estense Universitaria, γ.X.2.9 (Campori App. 1277)
No. **30**

Mün. S. I240 = MÜNCHEN, Bayerische Staatsbibliothek, It. 240
Nos. **15**, **36**, **76**

Mün. S. I265 = MÜNCHEN, Bayerische Staatsbibliothek, It. 265
No. **19**

Nap. N. 1 = NAPOLI, Biblioteca Nazionale Vittorio Emanuele III, XVII.1
Nos. **62**, **80**

Nap. N. 14 = NAPOLI, Biblioteca Nazionale Vittorio Emanuele III, VII.F.14
No. **13**

Nap. N. 31 = NAPOLI, Biblioteca Nazionale Vittorio Emanuele III, S.Q.IX.B.31
(variants and manuscript texts in the print: *Opere de M. Antonio Thebaldeo* […], Modena, Domenico Rococciola, 13 October 1498)
No. **19**

Nap. N. 38 = NAPOLI, Biblioteca Nazionale Vittorio Emanuele III, XIV.C.38
Nos. **29/114**, **64**, **76**

NY. C. 195 = NEW YORK, Columbia University, Plimpton 195
No. **13**

Ox. B. CI.99 = OXFORD, Bodleian Library, Canonici It. 99
Nos. **1**, **53**, **155**

Ox. B. CI.180 = OXFORD, Bodleian Library, Canonici It. 180
No. **13**

Ox. B. CI.193 = OXFORD, Bodleian Library, Canonici It. 193
No. **76**

Ox. B. CI.208 = OXFORD, Bodleian Library, Canonici It. 208
No. **13**

Ox. B. CI.240 = OXFORD, Bodleian Library, Canonici It. 240
No. **13**

Ox.B. CI.263 = OXFORD, Bodleian Library, Canonici It. 263
Nos. **13**, **76**

Ox.B. CI.301 = OXFORD, Bodleian Library, Canonici It. 301
No. **13**

Ox.B. CL.317 = OXFORD, Bodleian Library, Canonici Liturg. 317
No. **13**

Ox.B. CL.363 = OXFORD, Bodleian Library, Canonici Liturg. 363
No. **13**

Pad.Civ. 4 = PADOVA, Biblioteca Civica, A 4 (*olim* Fondo De Visiani, 4.II)
No. **29/114**

Pad.U. 1151 = PADOVA, Biblioteca Universitaria, 1151
No. **13**

Pad.U. 1357 = PADOVA, Biblioteca Universitaria, 1357
No. **13**

Pal.C. 8 = PALERMO, Biblioteca Comunale, 4 Qq A 8
No. **13**

Paris.JA. 2075 = PARIS, Musée Jacquemart-André (Bibliothèque de l'Institut), I 2075
No. **19**

Paris.N. F.1719 = PARIS, Bibliothèque Nationale de France, Fonds Fr. 1719
No. **127** (twice)

Paris.N. I.559 = PARIS, Bibliothèque Nationale de France, Fonds It. 559
Nos. **29/114**, **64**

Paris.N. I.560 = PARIS, Bibliothèque Nationale de France, Fonds It. 560
No. **19**

Paris.N. I.607 = PARIS, Bibliothèque Nationale de France, Fonds It. 607
No. **64**

Paris.N. I.618 = PARIS, Bibliothèque Nationale de France, Fonds It. 618
No. **76**

Paris.N. I.1020 = PARIS, Bibliothèque Nationale de France, Fonds It. 1020
No. **87**

Paris.N. I.1543 = PARIS, Bibliothèque Nationale de France, Fonds It. 1543
No. **53**

Parma.P. Pal.37 = PARMA, Biblioteca Palatina, Palatino 37
Nos. **13**, **147**

Parma.P. Par.201 = PARMA, Biblioteca Palatina, Parmense 201 (*olim* HH.IX.70.201)
No. **19**

Parma.P. Par.3072 = PARMA, Biblioteca Palatina, Parmense 3072
No. **19**

Pav.U.A.355 = PAVIA, Biblioteca Universitaria, Aldini 355
No. **13**

Pav.U.A.378 = PAVIA, Biblioteca Universitaria, Aldini 378
No. **13**

Pav.U.A.474 = PAVIA, Biblioteca Universitaria, Aldini 474
No. **29/114**

Pes.O. 54 = PESARO, Biblioteca Oliveriana, 54
Nos. **1**, **33**, **63** (twice), **87**, **149**

Piac.C. L.15 = PIACENZA, Biblioteca Comunale Passerini-Landi, Landi 15
(stolen in 1985, but a microfilm is preserved)
Nos. **29/114**, **64**, **76**, **147**

Piac.C. P.245 = PIACENZA, Biblioteca Comunale Passerini-Landi, Pallastrelli 245
No. **64**

Prato.R. 186 = PRATO, Biblioteca Roncioniana, Fondo Cesare Guasti 186
(MS missing from the library at least since 1981, the date of the publication of the inventory of the Fondo Cesare Guasti, edited by Francesco De Feo (DE FEO 1981); the description of MS 186 (on p. 135), given that it is physically lacking, was taken from the *Inventario dei Manoscritti della Raccolta Guasti di Prato* (NICASTRO 1924))
No. **76**

Rav.C. 63 = RAVENNA, Istituzione Biblioteca Classense, 63
Nos. **13**, **69**

Rav.C. 177 = RAVENNA, Istituzione Biblioteca Classense, 177
No. **29/114**

Rav.C. 464 = RAVENNA, Istituzione Biblioteca Classense, 464
Nos. **13**, **30**

Rim.C. 38 = RIMINI, Biblioteca Civica Alessandro Gambalunga, SC–MS 38 (*olim* D IV 206)
Nos. **15**, **30**, **36**, **67**, **69**, **76**, **159**

Roma.Al. 224 = ROMA, Biblioteca Universitaria Alessandrina, 224
No. **76**

Roma.Al. 301 = ROMA, Biblioteca Universitaria Alessandrina, 301
No. **13**

Roma.Ang. 1482 = ROMA, Biblioteca Angelica, 1482
Nos. **27**, **76**

Roma.Ang. 2274 = ROMA, Biblioteca Angelica, 2274
Nos. **30**, **64**, **67**, **76**, **159**

Roma.Ang. 2275 = ROMA, Biblioteca Angelica, 2275
Nos. **30** (twice), **64**, **76**

Roma.Ca. 817 = ROMA, Biblioteca Casanatense, 817 (*olim* d.VI.36)
No. **13**

Roma.Ca. 1432 = ROMA, Biblioteca Casanatense, 1432 (*olim* d.VI.1)
No. **69**

Roma.Ca. 3828 = ROMA, Biblioteca Casanatense, 3828
No. **64**

Roma.Co. 3 = ROMA, Biblioteca dell'Accademia Nazionale dei Lincei e Corsiniana, Corsini 43.D.3 (*olim* Rossi 185)
Nos. **30**, **67**, **159**

Roma.Co. 27 = ROMA, Biblioteca dell'Accademia Nazionale dei Lincei e Corsiniana, Corsini 44.G.27 (*olim* Rossi 27)
No. **29/114**

Roma.Co. 33 = ROMA, Biblioteca dell'Accademia Nazionale dei Lincei e Corsiniana, Corsini 43.C.33 (*olim* Rossi 146)
Nos. **30, 76**

Roma.N. S.413 = ROMA, Biblioteca Nazionale Centrale Vittorio Emanuele II, Sessoriano 413 (*olim* 241)
No. **19**

Roma.N. V.24 = ROMA, Biblioteca Nazionale Centrale Vittorio Emanuele II, Varia 24
Nos. **29/114, 147**

Roma.N. VE.483 = ROMA, Biblioteca Nazionale Centrale Vittorio Emanuele II, Vittorio Emanuele 483
No. **30**

Roma.S. 2 = ROMA, Biblioteca del Senato della Repubblica, Canneto sull'Oglio II,2
No. **13**

Sev.C. 31 = SEVILLA, Biblioteca Capitular y Colombina, 7.2.31
Nos. **19, 63**

Sev.C. 52 = SEVILLA, Biblioteca Capitular y Colombina, 7.1.52
No. **13**

Siena.C. 13 = SIENA, Biblioteca Comunale degli Intronati, I.VIII.13
Nos. **29/114, 147**

Siena.C. 14 = SIENA, Biblioteca Comunale degli Intronati, I.VIII.14
Nos. **69, 147**

Siena.C. 15 = SIENA, Biblioteca Comunale degli Intronati, I.VIII.15
Nos. **69, 147**

Siena.C. 16 = SIENA, Biblioteca Comunale degli Intronati, I.VIII.16
No. **159**

Siena.C. 17 = SIENA, Biblioteca Comunale degli Intronati, I.VIII.17
Nos. **30** (twice), **69, 147**

Siena.C. 41 = SIENA, Biblioteca Comunale degli Intronati, G.X.41
Nos. **30, 69, 147**

Siena.C. II.37 = SIENA, Biblioteca Comunale degli Intronati, I.II.37 (*olim* A.7.1)
No. **13**

Siena.C. VIII.37 = SIENA, Biblioteca Comunale degli Intronati, I.VIII.37
No. **30**

Spithöver = Laudario of Jacopone da Todi, preceded by his life derived from the 'Franceschina',[20] current location unknown
No. **29/114**

Stock.K. 5 = STOCKHOLM, Kungliga Biblioteket, V. u. 5 (*olim* Theol. in 4° no. 27)
No. **13**

---

[20]. 'Franceschina', or *Specchio dell'Ordine Minore*, of fra Jacopo Oddi, from Perugia (d. 1483), in two manuscripts: one parchment from the town of Norcia, having come from the Monastero di S. Chiara, contains the oldest redaction and is decorated with illuminated representations; the other, parchment and paper, from the Biblioteca Comunale in Perugia, with a more extended redaction and illustrated with realistic representations in colour, was formerly in the Biblioteca Comunale in Assisi, and then passed to the bookdealer Spithöver. A notice is found in TOBLER 1878, and TENNERONI 1909. Further notices on the manuscripts of the 'Franceschina' can be found in ROSSI 1882.

Tessier = *olim* Venezia, Collection of the Cav. Andrea Tessier [cod. ★], current location unknown[21]
      Nos. **29/114**, **64**, **76**

Trev.C. 22 = Treviso, Biblioteca Comunale, 22
      No. **13**

Trev.C. 188 = Treviso, Biblioteca Comunale, 188
      No. **13**

Trev.C. 220 = Treviso, Biblioteca Comunale, 220
      No. **76**

Ven.C. C.128 = Venezia, Biblioteca d'Arte del Museo Civico Correr, Cicogna 128 (*olim* Cicogna 1932)
      Nos. **29/114**, **64**

Ven.GR. 120 = Venezia, Biblioteca Giustinian-Recanati, II.CXX (*ex* Biblioteca dei Padri Somaschi della Salute, 40)
      Nos. **13**, **27**, **29/114**, **64**, **76**, **88**

Ven.GR. 121 = Venezia, Biblioteca Giustinian-Recanati, II.CXXI
      Nos. **27**, **76**

Ven.M. I.3 = Venezia, Biblioteca Nazionale Marciana, It. I.3 (= 4889)
      No. **13**

Ven.M. I.9 = Venezia, Biblioteca Nazionale Marciana, It. XI.9 (= 7401)
      No. **13**

Ven.M. I.28 = Venezia, Biblioteca Nazionale Marciana, It. V.28 (= 5644)
      No. **13**

Ven.M. I.30 = Venezia, Biblioteca Nazionale Marciana, It. I.30 (= 5023)
      No. **13**

Ven.M. I.38 = Venezia, Biblioteca Nazionale Marciana, It. I.38 (= 5028)
      No. **13**

Ven.M. I.61 = Venezia, Biblioteca Nazionale Marciana, It. I.61 (= 4973)
      No. **29/114**

Ven.M. I.66 = Venezia, Biblioteca Nazionale Marciana, It. XI.66 (= 6730)
      No. **49**

Ven.M. I.75 = Venezia, Biblioteca Nazionale Marciana, It. I.75 (= 5184)
      No. **13**

Ven.M. I.77 = Venezia, Biblioteca Nazionale Marciana, It. IX.77 (= 6634)
      Nos. **29/114**, **30**, **64**, **76**, **147**

Ven.M. I.78 = Venezia, Biblioteca Nazionale Marciana, It. IX.78 (= 6453)
      Nos. **15**, **30**, **36**, **67**, **69**, **76**, **159**

Ven.M. I.79 = Venezia, Biblioteca Nazionale Marciana, It. IX.79 (= 7551)
      Nos. **29/114**, **30**, **69**

Ven.M. I.80 = Venezia, Biblioteca Nazionale Marciana, It. IX.80 (= 6357)
      Nos. **29/114**, **64** (twice), **76**

---

[21]. The last mention of this manuscript that can be traced is perhaps the following by Carlo Frati: «All the manuscripts [of Tessier], 130 in total, but of limited value» were sold «to the Rosenthal firm in Munich» after the death of Andrea Tessier on 10 January 1896 (see Frati 1909, pp. 52-53).

Ven.M. I.153 = Venezia, Biblioteca Nazionale Marciana, It. IX.153 (= 7058)
Nos. **29/114**, **64**

Ven.M. I.182 = Venezia, Biblioteca Nazionale Marciana, It. IX.182 (= 6284) (*ex* Biblioteca di S. Mattia di Murano, 40)
Nos. **13**, **27** (twice), **29/114**, **64**, **76** (twice), **147**

Ven.M. I.230 = Venezia, Biblioteca Nazionale Marciana, It. IX.230 (= 7068)
Nos. **64**, **76**, **147**

Ven.M. I.257 = Venezia, Biblioteca Nazionale Marciana, It. IX.257 (= 6365)
No. **76**

Ven.M. I.269 = Venezia, Biblioteca Nazionale Marciana, It. IX.269 (= 5443)
No. **13**

Ven.M. I.313 = Venezia, Biblioteca Nazionale Marciana, It. IX.313 (= 7565)
Nos. **29/114**, **64**, **76**, **147**

Ven.M. I.324 = Venezia, Biblioteca Nazionale Marciana, It. IX.324 (= 6654)
Nos. **29/114** (twice), **147**

Ven.M. I.486 = Venezia, Biblioteca Nazionale Marciana, It. IX.486 (= 6767)
No. **76**

Ven.M. IZ.60 = Venezia, Biblioteca Nazionale Marciana, It. Zan.60 (= 4752)
No. **19**

Ver.Cap. 737 = Verona, Biblioteca Capitolare, DCCXXXVII (DCCXLVII)
Nos. **29/114**, **30**, **76**

Ver.Cap. 811 = Verona, Biblioteca Capitolare, DCCCXI (DCCCXV)
No. **13**

Ver.Civ. 1212 = Verona, Biblioteca Civica, 1212
'Canzoniere di fra Jacopone da Todi' (the codex is an authoritative transcription of the fifteenth century of an old laudario on parchment preserved at the Biblioteca di S. Maria delle Grazie in Bergamo; edited between 1760 and 1772 by fra Giovanni Domenico da Bergamo of the Reformed Minorites, the laudario contains 139 laude traditionally attributed to Jacopone da Todi; see Biadego 1892, p. 36)
Nos. **29/114**, **64**

Vic.A. 32bis = Vicenza, Archivio di Stato, Ospedale di San Marcello busta 32 bis, 'libro B'
No. **13**

Vic.C. 65 = Vicenza, Biblioteca Civica Bertoliana, 65 (G.2.7.17)
No. **13**

Vic.C. 111 = Vicenza, Biblioteca Civica Bertoliana, 111 (G.2.8.17)
No. **29/114**

IV. Textual Prints

Altissimo1525 = *Opere nuove dello Altissimo poeta fiorentino dove si lauda una donna dal capo alli piedi. Et altri strambocti bellissimi composti da più varii auctorii*, Florence, A[ntonio] T[ubini], at the request of Bartolomeo di Matteo Castelli, 15 March 1524 (1525 modern style)
Firenze★, Biblioteca Nazionale Centrale, Palatino E.6.6.154 I/5
(the catalogue Edit 16, both online and printed, lists another copy at Vatican City, Biblioteca Apostolica Vaticana; with the help of the librarians, I carefully searched for this exemplar at the library, but without success)
No. **62**

Aq1502Bes = *Opere del facundissimo Seraphino Aquilano collecte per Francesco Flavio*, Rome, Giovanni Besicken, 29 November 1502
Madrid, Biblioteca Nacional de España; München, Bayerische Staatsbibliothek; New Haven, Yale University, Beinecke Rare Book and Manuscript Library; Roma★, Biblioteca Nazionale Centrale Vittorio Emanuele II, 69.1.F.9; Ventimiglia, Biblioteca Civica Aprosiana
No. **49**

Aq1502Bon = *Opere del facundissimo Seraphino Aquilano collette per Francesco Flavio […]*, Venice, Manfredo Bonelli, 24 December 1502
Bologna★, Biblioteca di Casa Carducci, 1.a.368 [imperfect]; Bologna, Biblioteca Universitaria [imperfect]; Cambridge (MA), Harvard University, Houghton Library; Firenze, Biblioteca Nazionale Centrale; London, British Library; Napoli, Biblioteca Oratoriana del Monumento Nazionale dei Girolamini; New York, New York Public Library, Humanities–Rare Books Division; Oxford, Bodleian Library; Paris, Bibliothèque Nationale de France; Parma, Biblioteca Palatina; Venezia, Biblioteche della Fondazione Giorgio Cini; Venezia, Biblioteca Nazionale Marciana
No. **49**

Aq1503Baz = *Opere del facundissimo Seraphino Aquilano collette per Francesco Flavio. E per Caligula Bazalero aggiunto quanto è la terza parte de le altre impressioni […]*, Bologna, Caligola Bazalieri, 30 May 1503
Bologna★, Biblioteca Universitaria, Raro A.16; Città del Vaticano, Biblioteca Apostolica Vaticana; Firenze, Biblioteca Nazionale Centrale
Nos. **49**, **53**

Aq1503Bes = *Opere dello elegante poeta Seraphino Aquilano finite et emendate con la loro apologia et vita d'esso poeta*, Rome, Giovanni Besicken, 5 October 1503
Firenze, Biblioteca Riccardiana [imperfect]; University Park★ (PA), Pennsylvania State University Libraries, Rare Books, Italian Collection, PQ4619.C5.1503
No. **49**

Aq1503Bon = *Opere del facundissimo Seraphino Aquilano con la zonta collecte per Francesco Flavio […]*, Venice, Manfredo Bonelli, 30 August 1503
Città del Vaticano★, Biblioteca Apostolica Vaticana, Capponi IV. 719 (3) [imperfect]; Washington, DC, Folger Shakespeare Library
No. **49**

Aq1503Man = [Serafino Aquilano], *[Opere]*, Milan, Pietro Martire Mantegazza, at the instance of Giovanni Giacomo da Legnano and brothers, 24 April 1503
Durham★ (NC), Duke University, Perkins Library, EC537S [imperfect]
No. **49**

Aq1503Pac = *Strambotti, sonecti, ballatecte, egloghe, epistole et capitoli del facundissimo Seraphino Aquilano. Et ancora molti altri belli strambotti et sonecti composti da più diverse persone agiunti di poi del primo originale*, [Florence], no pr., at the request of ser Piero Pacini da Pescia, [ca. 1503?]
Firenze★, Biblioteca Nazionale Centrale, Landau Finaly 176 [imperfect]
No. **49**

Aq1503Rug = *Opere del facundissimo Serafino Aquilano collecte per Francesco Flavio* […], Bologna, Girolamo Ruggeri, 10 February 1503
FRANKFURT AM MAIN★, Universitätsbibliothek Johann Christian Senckenberg, IL 1930/476
No. **49**

Aq1504Bon = *Opere del facundissimo Seraphino Aquilano con la zonta collecte per Francesco Flavio et da più persone* […], Venice, Manfredo Bonelli, 15 July 1504
TREVISO★, Biblioteca Comunale, III.91.G.13381
Nos. **49**, **53**

Aq1504Man = *Opere del facundissimo Seraphino Aquilano coletto per Francesco Flavio. Agiunte et regiunte* […], Milan, Pietro Martire and brothers Mantegazza, at the instance of Gottardo da Ponte, 27 September 1504
FIRENZE, Private Collection (Antonio Rossi mentions this exemplar, pointed out to him by Neil Harris; see ROSSI 2005, p. 472, n. 4); ROMA★, Biblioteca Casanatense, Rari 215
Nos. **49**, **53**

Aq1505Bon(A) = *Opere del facondissimo Seraphino Aquilano. Collecte per Francisco Flavio con la zonta et più azonta novamente da excellentissime persone corectissime* […], Venice, Manfredo Bonelli, at the request of Niccolò Zoppino, 30 April 1505
ROMA★, Biblioteca Nazionale Centrale Vittorio Emanuele II, 69.1.F.6
Nos. **49**, **53**

Aq1505Bon(B) = *Opere dello elegante poeta Seraphino Aquilano finite et emendate con la gionta, zoè apologia et vita d'esso poeta* […], Venice, Manfredo Bonelli, 31 November 1505
LONDON, British Library; ROMA★, Biblioteca Casanatense, Vol.Misc. 2082/1 [imperfect]; VENEZIA, Biblioteca Nazionale Marciana
No. **53**

Aq1505Son = *Poema di Seraphino novamente cum diligentia da Hieronymo Soncino impresso cum molte cose adiuncte* […], Fano, Girolamo Soncino, 11 March 1505
AREZZO, Istituzione Biblioteca Città di Arezzo; CITTÀ DEL VATICANO★, Biblioteca Apostolica Vaticana, Capponi V. 772; FANO, Biblioteca Comunale Federiciana; LONDON, British Library; NEW YORK, Jewish Theological Seminary of America Library; OXFORD, Bodleian Library; REGGIO NELL'EMILIA, Biblioteca Municipale Antonio Panizzi; ROMA, Biblioteca Angelica [imperfect]
Nos. **49**, **53**

Aq1506Bon = *Opere dello elegante poeta Seraphino Aquilano* […], Venice, Manfredo Bonelli, 26 November 1506
TREVISO★, Biblioteca Comunale, Misc. 606 (3)
No. **53**

Aq1507Bon = *Opere dello elegante poeta Seraphino Aquilano* […], Venice, Manfredo Bonelli, 20 September 1507
ROVERETO★, Biblioteca Civica Girolamo Tartarotti, Ar.IV.1.10C (c) [imperfect]; VALÈNCIA, Universitat de València, Biblioteca General e Històrica
No. **53**

Aq1507Son = *Poema di Seraphino novamente cum diligentia da Hieronymo Soncino impresso* […], Pesaro, Girolamo Soncino, *post* 5 February 1507
FIRENZE★, Biblioteca Marucelliana, 1.GG.X.51 [imperfect]
Nos. **49**, **53**

Aq1508Bon = *Opere dello elegante poeta Seraphino Aquilano* […], Venice, Manfredo Bonelli, 20 March 1508
LONDON, British Library; MODENA★, Biblioteca Estense Universitaria, α.X.10.18
No. **53**

Aq1509Son = *Poema di Seraphino* […], Pesaro, Girolamo Soncino, 22 June 1509
FANO, Biblioteca Comunale Federiciana; FIRENZE, Biblioteca Nazionale Centrale; NEW HAVEN, Yale University, Beinecke Rare Book and Manuscript Library; ROMA★, Biblioteca Nazionale Centrale Vittorio Emanuele II, 69.6.I.12; STUTTGART, Württembergische Landesbibliothek
Nos. **49**, **53**

Aq1510Rus = *Opere dello elegante poeta Seraphino Aquillano [...]*,Venice, Giorgio Rusconi, 23 December 1510
    GENÈVE, Fondation Barbier-Müller (Université, Faculté des Lettres); ROMA★, Biblioteca Universitaria Alessandrina,
    Misc.XIII.a.19.2
    No. **53**

Aq1510Tub = *Strambotti, sonetti, canzone, egloghe, pistole et capitoli del Seraphino Aquilano. Et altri strambotti et sonetti [...]*,
    [Florence?, Antonio Tubini?, ca. 1510?]
    SEVILLA★, Biblioteca Capitular y Colombina, 4.1.34 (2)
    No. **49**

Aq1511Leg = *Opere del facundissimo Seraphino Aquilano ultimamente impresse per compassione de le incorrectione degli altri [...]*,
    Milan, [Giovanni Giacomo da Legnano], 20 September 1511
    AOSTA★, Biblioteca del Seminario Maggiore, C.679
    Nos. **49, 53**

Aq1512Bin = *Opere de lo elegante poeta Seraphino Aquillano [...]*,Venice, Alessandro Bindoni, 1512
    NAPOLI★, Biblioteca Nazionale Vittorio Emanuele III, S.Q.XXVI.L.31
    No. **53**

Aq1513Lov = *Poema vulgare de Seraphino Aquilano [...]*,Venice, Simone da Lovere, 24 January 1513
    GENOVA★, Biblioteca Universitaria, Rari M.VIII.24
    No. **53**

Aq1513Ses = [SERAFINO AQUILANO], *[Opere]*,Venice, Melchiorre Sessa, 23 September 1513
    MADRID★, Biblioteca Nacional de España, R.2705/1 [imperfect]
    No. **53**

Aq1515Leg = *Opere del facundissimo Seraphino Aquilano ultimamente impresse per compassione de le incorrectione degli altri [...]*,
    Milan, [Giovanni Giacomo da Legnano], 20 September 1515 (title page), 20 August 1515 (colophon)
    BERGAMO, Civica Biblioteca - Archivi Storici Angelo Mai; CITTÀ DEL VATICANO★, Biblioteca Apostolica Vaticana,
    Capponi VI. 138 (2) [imperfect]; FIRENZE, Biblioteca Nazionale Centrale; LONDON, British Library; PADOVA,
    Biblioteca Universitaria
    Nos. **49, 53**

Aq1516Bin = *Opere dello elegante poeta Seraphino Aquillano [...]*,Venice, Alessandro Bindoni, 30 November 1516
    FANO, Biblioteca Comunale Federiciana; LONDON, British Library; TORINO★, Biblioteca Nazionale Universitaria,
    Ris. 29/7 (1); WIEN, Österreichische Nationalbibliothek
    No. **53**

Aq1516Cas(A) = *Opere del facundissimo Seraphino Aquilano ultimamente impresse per compassione de le incorrectione degli altri [...]*,
    Milan, Bernardino da Castello, at the instance of Nicolò Gorgonzola, 13 March 1516 (but on the title page: 20 April
    1516)
    CITTÀ DEL VATICANO★, Biblioteca Apostolica Vaticana, R.G. Lett.It. V.217; PHILADELPHIA, University of
    Pennsylvania Library, J. Robert van Pelt Library
    Nos. **49, 53**

Aq1516Cas(B) = *Opere del facundissimo Seraphino Aquilano ultimamente impresse per compassione de le incorrectione degli altri [...]*,
    Milan, Bernardino da Castello, at the instance of Giovanni Giacomo da Legnano and brothers, 20 April 1516 (title
    page), 22 August 1516 (colophon)
    LONDON, British Library; MILANO★, Biblioteca dell'Archivio Storico Civico e Biblioteca Trivulziana, Rari Triv. L
    75; PHILADELPHIA, University of Pennsylvania Library, J. Robert van Pelt Library
    Nos. **49, 53**

Aq1516Giu = *Opere dello elegantissimo poeta Seraphino Aquilano novamente con diligentia impresse con molte cose aggiunte [...]*,
    Florence, Filippo Giunta, December 1516
    BARCELONA, Biblioteca de la Universitat; BOLOGNA★, Biblioteca Comunale dell'Archiginnasio, 8.X.IV.69; CITTÀ
    DEL VATICANO, Biblioteca Apostolica Vaticana [imperfect]; FIRENZE, Biblioteca Nazionale Centrale; LONDON, British
    Library; MADRID, Biblioteca Nacional de España; MILANO, Biblioteca Ambrosiana; MILANO, Biblioteca Nazionale
    Braidense; MODENA, Biblioteca Estense Universitaria; MONTPELLIER, Bibliothèque Municipale; PARIS, Bibliothèque
    Mazarine; PRINCETON, University Library; RAVENNA, Istituzione Biblioteca Classense; ROMA, Biblioteca Casanatense;
    ROMA, Biblioteca Nazionale Centrale Vittorio Emanuele II; TORINO, Biblioteca Nazionale Universitaria;VALÈNCIA,

Universitat de València, Biblioteca General e Història; WIEN, Österreichische Nationalbibliothek
Nos. **33**, **49**, **53**

Aq1516Son = *Opere volgari di Seraphino Aquilano* […] *di novo con somma diligentia et emendatione* […] *impresse in Fano*, Fano, Girolamo Soncino, 20 March 1516
CAMBRIDGE (MA), Harvard University, Houghton Library; FANO★, Biblioteca Comunale Federiciana, C-Sonc. 22; LOS ANGELES, University of California Library; MÜNCHEN, Bayerische Staatsbibliothek; VENEZIA, Biblioteca d'Arte del Museo Civico Correr; VICENZA, Biblioteca Civica Bertoliana [imperfect]
Nos. **49**, **53**

Aq1518Mon = *Opere de lo elegante poeta Seraphino Aquillano* […], [Venice, Guglielmo da Monferrato, 1518-19?]
FIRENZE★, Biblioteca Nazionale Centrale, Palatino 2.4.1.9
No. **53**

Aq1519Ses = *Opere dello elegante poeta Seraphino Aquillano* […], Venice, Melchiorre Sessa and Pietro Ravani, 15 October 1519
PHILADELPHIA, University of Pennsylvania Library, J. Robert van Pelt Library; TREVISO, Biblioteca Comunale; VENEZIA★, Biblioteca Nazionale Marciana, 83.C.215,1
No. **53**

Aq1520Pen = *Stramboti novi sopra ogni preposito, composti per lo excellentissimo e famoso poeta Seraphino da L'Aquila*, [Venice?, Giacomo Penzio?, 1520?]
CHANTILLY★, Bibliothèque du Musée Condé, XI.G.62
No. **33**

Aq1522Rus = *Opere de lo elegante poeta Seraphino Aquillano* […], Venice, Giorgio Rusconi, 12 March 1522
CAMBRIDGE★ (MA), Harvard University, Houghton Library, Coll. Ital. 7323.5.10★; NAPOLI, Biblioteca Nazionale Vittorio Emanuele III
No. **53**

Aq1523Vim = *Opere del facundissimo Seraphino Aquilano ultimamente impresse per compassione de le incorrectione degli altri* […], Milan, Agostino da Vimercate, at the instance of Giovanni Giacomo da Legnano and brothers, 12 June 1523
MILANO, Biblioteca Ambrosiana [imperfect]; MILANO★, Biblioteca dell'Archivio Storico Civico e Biblioteca Trivulziana, Rari Triv. M 1621
Nos. **49**, **53**

Aq1529Mor = *Strambotti novi sopra ogni preposito composti per lo famosissimo poeta Seraphino da L'Aquila*, Brescia, Giovanni Antonio da Gandino, 1529
NEW YORK★, New York Public Library, Spencer Collection, Ital. 1529 Ciminelli
No. **33**

Aq1530Zop = *Del Seraphino Aquilano poeta elegantissimo l'opere d'amore con ogni diligentia corrette et alla sua integrità ridotte nuovamente* […], Venice, Niccolò Zoppino, 1530
L'AQUILA, Biblioteca Provinciale Salvatore Tommasi; CAMBRIDGE, University Library; CITTÀ DEL VATICANO★, Biblioteca Apostolica Vaticana, Ferraioli V. 4368; PARIS, Bibliothèque Mazarine; ROMA, Biblioteca Nazionale Centrale Vittorio Emanuele II; UDINE, Biblioteca Civica Vincenzo Joppi; VENEZIA, Biblioteca Nazionale Marciana
Nos. **33**, **49**, **53**

Aq1548Basc = *Di Seraphino Aquilano poeta elegantissimo opere, nuovamente ricorrette, et con diligentia impresse* […], Venice, Niccolò Bascarini, 1548
BERLIN, Staatsbibliothek, Preußischer Kulturbesitz; BOLOGNA★, Biblioteca di Casa Carducci, 3.l.201; CHIAVARI, Biblioteca della Società Economica; EDINBURGH, National Library of Scotland; MODENA, Biblioteca Estense Universitaria; NAPOLI, Biblioteca dell'Accademia Pontaniana; NAPOLI, Biblioteca Nazionale Vittorio Emanuele III; NAPOLI, Biblioteca Oratoriana del Monumento Nazionale dei Girolamini; NAPOLI, Biblioteca Universitaria; OXFORD, Bodleian Library; PARIS, Bibliothèque Nationale de France, Fonds de l'Arsenal; PESCARA, Biblioteca Comunale Vittoria Colonna; VENEZIA, Biblioteca Nazionale Marciana; VENTIMIGLIA, Biblioteca Civica Aprosiana; VERCELLI, Biblioteca Civica; WASHINGTON, DC, Library of Congress; WOLFENBÜTTEL, Herzog August Bibliothek
Nos. **33**, **49**, **53**

AqMis = *Soneti del Seraphin*, Brescia, Bernardino Misinta, [*post* 1500]
PARIS★, Bibliothèque Nationale de France, Rés. Yd. 1249
No. **35**

AqStramb(A) = *Stramboti novi sopra ogni preposito, composti per lo excellentissimo e famoso poeta Seraphino da L'Aquila*, no typ. info.
London⋆, British Library, C.20.c.22/24
No. **33**

AqStramb(B) = *Strambotti novi sopra ogni proposito composti per lo famosissimo poeta Seraphino da Lagla* [*sic*], no typ. info.
München⋆, Bayerische Staatsbibliothek, P.o.it. 331/15; Zwickau, Rathsschulbibliothek
No. **33**

AqVav = *Strambotti novi sopra ogni proposito. Composti per lo eccellentissimo et famoso poeta Seraphino da L'Aquila. Con una epistola agionta novamente*, no pl., Giovanni Andrea Vavassori, no d.
London⋆, British Library, G.10729
No. **33**

BelcLBart = *Laude di Feo Belcari*, [Florence, Bartolomeo de' Libri, ca. 1480]
Bryn Mawr (PA), Bryn Mawr College, Marjorie Walter Goodhart Medieval Library; Firenze⋆, Biblioteca Nazionale Centrale, A.5.31
No. **30**

BelcLBen = *Laude di Feo Belcari*, no pl., [printer of Benignus' *Dialectica*?, ca. 1480]
Firenze⋆, Biblioteca Nazionale Centrale, Banco Rari 374 [imperfect] (formerly in Firenze, Private Collection of Tammaro De Marinis)
No. **30**

BelcR1485 = [Feo Belcari], *Qui comincia la rapresentatione da Habram quando Iddio gli comandò che gli facessi sacrificio in sul monte d'Isaac suo flgluolo* [*sic*], [Florence, Bartolomeo de' Libri], 24 October 1485
Firenze⋆, Biblioteca Nazionale Centrale, Palatino E.6.4.115
No. **30**

Busti1488 = [Bernardino de' Busti], *Corona de la beatissima Vergene Maria*, [Milan, Giovanni Antonio de Honate, ca. 1488]
current location unknown; formerly in Milano, Private Collection of Gaetano Melzi, then Firenze, Private Collection of Tammaro De Marinis; see photograph of the first page in Galli 1947, Tav. V
Nos. **13, 64**

Busti1489 = [Bernardino de' Busti], *Corona de la beatissima Vergene Maria*, [Milan, Giovanni Antonio de Honate, ca. 1488-89]
Milano⋆, Biblioteca Ambrosiana, Inc. 447
Nos. **13, 64**

Busti1490 = [Bernardino de' Busti], *Corona de la beatissima Vergine Maria*, Milan, Leonhard Pachel, 29 May 1490
Milano⋆, Biblioteca Nazionale Braidense, AN.IX.6
Nos. **13, 64**

Busti1492S = [Bernardino de' Busti], *Thesauro spirituale*, Milan, Ulrich Scinzenzeler, 16 March 1492
Città del Vaticano, Biblioteca Apostolica Vaticana [3 copies]; Liège, Bibliothèque de l'Université de Liège; Milano⋆, Biblioteca Ambrosiana, Inc. 485; Milano, Biblioteca dell'Archivio Storico Civico e Biblioteca Trivulziana; Paris, Bibliothèque Mazarine
Nos. **13, 64**

Busti1492Z = [Bernardino de' Busti], *Thesauro spirituale*, Milan, Antonio Zaroto, 1 June 1492
Milano⋆, Biblioteca Ambrosiana, Inc. 502
Nos. **13, 64**

Busti1494 = [Bernardino de' Busti], *Thesauro spirituale integro*, Milan, Ulrich Scinzenzeler, 3 December 1494
Bologna⋆, Biblioteca Universitaria, A.V.B.IX.61 [imperfect]; München, Bayerische Staatsbibliothek
Nos. **13, 64**

Busti1517 = [Bernardino de' Busti], *Thesauro spirituale*, Milan, Rocco da Valle and brothers, at the instance of Nicolò Gorgonzola, 3 August 1517
London⋆, British Library, 1606/986; Sevilla, Biblioteca Capitular y Colombina
Nos. **13, 64**

BustiPon = [BERNARDINO DE' BUSTI], *Corona de la beatissima Vergene Maria*, [Milan], Gottardo da Ponte, [*ante* March 1531]
SEVILLA★, Biblioteca Capitular y Colombina, 14.2.3 (4)
Nos. **13, 64**

Chasse = *La chasse et le depart d'amours faict et compose par reverend père en dieu messire Octovien de Sainct Gelaiz evesque d'Angoulesme et par noble homme Blaise d'Auriol bachelier en chascun droit demourant a Thoulouze*, Paris, Antoine Vérard, 9 April 1509
LONDON★, British Library, C.34.m.2; PARIS, Bibliothèque de l'Institut National d'Histoire de l'Art, Collections Jacques Doucet
No. **40**

Collectanio1514Lov = *Collectanio de cose spirituale, zoè sonetti, laude, capituli, stanze et cantico del dispresio del mundo con la sententia de Pilato, de diversi et preclari auctori*, Venice, Simone da Lovere, 1514
MODENA★, Biblioteca Estense Universitaria, α.C.7.11/1
Nos. **42, 69**

Collectanio1514Rus = *Collectanio de cose nove spirituale, zoè sonetti, laude, capituli et stantie, con la sententia de Pilato composte da diversi et preclarissimi poeti hystoriato. Recollecto per mi Nicolò dicto Zopino*, Venice, Giorgio Rusconi, 10 February 1514
MILANO★, Biblioteca dell'Archivio Storico Civico e Biblioteca Trivulziana, Rari Triv. L 366
Nos. **42, 69**

Colletanio = *Colletanio di cose nove spirituali nel quale contiensi sonetti, laude, capitoli, & stantie, composte da diversi & preclarissimi poeti, novamente ristampato, & con ogni diligentia revisto & historiato*, no typ. info.
RIMINI★, Biblioteca Civica Alessandro Gambalunga, BQ 390 [imperfect]
No. **42**

Colletanio1509 = *Colletanio de cose nove spirituale, zoè sonetti, laude, capituli et stantie, con la sententia di Pilato composte da diversi et preclarissimi poeti hystoriato*, Venice, Niccolò Zoppino, 31 January 1509
MILANO, Biblioteca dell'Archivio Storico Civico e Biblioteca Trivulziana [imperfect]; SEVILLA★, Biblioteca Capitular y Colombina, 14.1.10 (1)
Nos. **42, 69**

Colletanio1510 = *Colletanio de cose nove spirituale, zoè sonetti, laude, capituli et stantie, con la sententia di Pilato composte da diversi et preclarissimi poeti hystoriato*, Venice, Giorgio Rusconi, 9 December 1510
NAPOLI, Biblioteca Nazionale Vittorio Emanuele III; TREVISO, Biblioteca Comunale; VENEZIA★, Biblioteca Nazionale Marciana, Misc. 2229.2 [imperfect]
Nos. **42, 69**

Colletanio1513 = *Colletanio de cose nove spirituale, zoè sonetti, laude, capituli et stantie, con la sententia de Pilato composte da diversi et preclarissimi poeti hystoriato. Recollecto per mi Nicolò dicto Zopino*, Venice, Giorgio Rusconi, 5 May 1513
VENEZIA★, Biblioteche della Fondazione Giorgio Cini, Fo.an.tes. 169
Nos. **42, 69**

Colletanio1521 = *Colletanio de cose nove spirituale, zoè sonetti, laude, capituli et stantie, composte da diversi et preclarissimi poeti historiato con altre cose agiunte*, Venice, Niccolò Zoppino and Vincenzo Di Paolo, 15 July 1521
MILANO★, Biblioteca dell'Archivio Storico Civico e Biblioteca Trivulziana, Rari Triv. L 2480; MODENA, Biblioteca Estense Universitaria
Nos. **42, 69**

Colletanio1524 = *Colletanio de cose nove spirituale, zoè sonetti, laude, capituli et stantie, composte da diversi et preclarissimi poeti historiato con altre cose agiunte*, Venice, Niccolò Zoppino and Vincenzo Di Paolo, 20 October 1524
FIRENZE, Biblioteca Nazionale Centrale; MILANO★, Biblioteca dell'Archivio Storico Civico e Biblioteca Trivulziana, Triv. L 652; RAVENNA, Istituzione Biblioteca Classense
Nos. **42, 69**

Colletanio1537 = *Colletanio di cose nove spirituale nel quale contiensi sonetti, laude, capitoli, et stantie, composte da diversi et preclarissimi poeti, novamente ristampato, et con ogni diligentia revisto et historiato*, Venice, Niccolò Zoppino, 1537
CITTÀ DEL VATICANO★, Biblioteca Apostolica Vaticana, Capponi V. 757 (3)
Nos. **42, 69**

Compendio = *Compendio de cose nove spirituale, zoè sonetti, laude, capituli et stantie composte da diversi et praeclarissimi poeti historiato,* [Venice?], no pr., [15…]
    Roma★, Biblioteca Casanatense, Vol. Inc. 2035/7 (*olim* Inc. 2358/7)
    Nos. **42, 69**

Compendio1483 = *Compendio devotissimo de varie cose sancte et spirituale. Hic inde per lo catolico et divoto homo Ubertino da Busti: con summa carità recollecte et insudate* […], [Milan, Giovanni Antonio de Honate, ca. 1483]
    Milano★, Biblioteca dell'Archivio Storico Civico e Biblioteca Trivulziana, Triv. Inc. E 31
    Nos. **29/114, 64, 76**

Contrasto = *Il contrasto del Denaro et del Homo,* [Florence], no pr., [*ante* December 1515]
    Sevilla★, Biblioteca Capitular y Colombina, 6.3.29 (25)
    No. **11**

Fior1505 = *Fioreti de laudi da diversi doctori compilati, ad consolation et refrigerio de ogni persona spirituale,* Brescia, Giacomo Britannico, [ca. 1505]
    Città del Vaticano★, Biblioteca Apostolica Vaticana, Inc. Ferr. VI.1102; London, British Library; Milano, Biblioteca dell'Archivio Storico Civico e Biblioteca Trivulziana [imperfect]; Venezia, Biblioteca d'Arte del Museo Civico Correr
    Nos. **13, 27, 29/114, 30, 64, 76, 112, 112bis, 147, 159**

Fior1509 = *Fioretto de cose nove nobilissime et degne de diversi auctori noviter stampate* […], Venice, Niccolò Zoppino, 31 January 1508 (1509 modern style)
    Roma★, Biblioteca Angelica, RR.3.17
    No. **43**

Fior1510 = *Fioretto de cose nove nobilissime et degne de diversi auctori noviter stampate* […], Venice, Giorgio Rusconi, 26 November 1510
    Modena★, Biblioteca Estense Universitaria, α.Z.7.29/1; Venezia, Biblioteca Nazionale Marciana [imperfect]; Washington, DC, Folger Shakespeare Library
    No. **43**

Fior1518 = *Fioretto de cose nove nobilissime et de diversi auctori noviter stampate* […], Venice, Giorgio Rusconi, 28 September 1518
    Milano, Biblioteca dell'Archivio Storico Civico e Biblioteca Trivulziana; Roma★, Biblioteca dell'Accademia Nazionale dei Lincei e Corsiniana, 130.C.3
    No. **43**

Fior1521 = *Fioretto de cose nove nobilissime et degne de diversi auttori noviter stampate e uno capitulo azonto novamente contra de quello melasaratumo* […], Venice, Niccolò Zoppino and Vincenzo Di Paolo, 12 February 1521
    Napoli★, Biblioteca Nazionale Vittorio Emanuele III, S.Q.XXV.G.22
    No. **43**

Fior1522 = *Fioretto de cose nove nobilissime et de diversi auctori noviter stampate* […], Venice, Giovanni Francesco and Giovanni Antonio Rusconi, 14 August 1522
    Milano★, Biblioteca dell'Archivio Storico Civico e Biblioteca Trivulziana, Triv. M 1233; Venezia, Biblioteche della Fondazione Giorgio Cini
    No. **43**

Giust1474 = *Incomenciano le devotissime et sanctissime laude le quale compose el nobele et magnifico messere Leonardo Iustiniano,* Venice, [Bartolomeo da Cremona and/or Bartolomeo di Carlo Vercellese], [*ante* 1 December] 1474
    Bergamo, Civica Biblioteca – Archivi Storici Angelo Mai; London, British Library; Milano, Biblioteca Ambrosiana; Milano, Biblioteca dell'Archivio Storico Civico e Biblioteca Trivulziana; Napoli, Biblioteca Nazionale Vittorio Emanuele III [2 copies]; Oxford, Bodleian Library; Ravenna, Istituzione Biblioteca Classense; Roma★, Biblioteca dell'Accademia Nazionale dei Lincei e Corsiniana, 51.C.36; Venezia, Biblioteca d'Arte del Museo Civico Correr [imperfect]; Venezia, Biblioteche della Fondazione Giorgio Cini
    Nos. **27, 29/114, 76**

Giust1475 = *Laude del excellentissimo misier Lunardo Iustiniano patricio venetian e de altri sapientissimi homini,* Vicenza, Leonhard Achates, 1475
    Firenze★, Biblioteca Nazionale Centrale [2 copies], E.6.4.122; London, Society of Antiquaries; Manchester, John Rylands Library; Milano, Biblioteca Ambrosiana; Milano, Biblioteca dell'Archivio Storico Civico e Biblioteca

Trivulziana; New York, Pierpont Morgan Library; Paris, Bibliothèque Nationale de France [2 copies, one of them imperfect]; Parma, Biblioteca Palatina [imperfect]; Vicenza, Biblioteca Comunale Bertoliana
Nos. **27, 29/114, 76**

Giust1483 = *Laude del excellentissimo misier Lunardo Iustiniano patricio venetian e d'altri sapientissimi homini*, Venice, Bernardino Celerio, August 1483
Ancona⋆, Biblioteca Comunale Luciano Benincasa, Inc. 45; London, British Library; Los Angeles, University of California Library; Roma, Biblioteca Casanatense; St. Peterburg, Rossijskaja Nacional'naja Biblioteka; Sevilla, Biblioteca Capitular y Colombina; Venezia, Biblioteca Nazionale Marciana
Nos. **27, 29/114, 76**

Giust1490 = *Incominciano le devotissime et sanctissime laude composte per el nobile et magnifico misser Leonardo Iustiniano*, Venice, Dionisio Bertocco, 22 June 1490
Firenze, Biblioteca della Cassa di Risparmio, Fondo Roberto Ridolfi; London, British Library; Lugano, Biblioteca Cantonale; Padova, Biblioteca Antoniana; Paris, Bibliothèque Mazarine; Parma⋆, Biblioteca Palatina, Inc.Parm. 243; Washington, DC, Library of Congress, Rare Book Division
Nos. **27, 29/114, 76**

Giust1495 = *Incomincia le devotissime et sanctissime laude composte per el nobile et magnifico misser Lonardo Iustiniano*, Brescia, Bernardino Misinta, 17 March 1495
Brescia, Biblioteca Civica Queriniana; Città del Vaticano⋆, Biblioteca Apostolica Vaticana, Inc.Ferr. IV.8136 (3); Milano, Biblioteca dell'Archivio Storico Civico e Biblioteca Trivulziana; Milano, Biblioteca Nazionale Braidense
Nos. **27, 29/114, 76**

Giust1506 = *Laude devotissime et sanctissime, composte per el nobile et magnifico misser Leonardo Iustiniano di Venetia*, Venice, Bernardino Vitali, 25 May 1506
Milano, Biblioteca dell'Archivio Storico Civico e Biblioteca Trivulziana [imperfect]; Napoli, Biblioteca Nazionale Vittorio Emanuele III; Venezia⋆, Biblioteca della Fondazione Querini Stampalia, Piano IV H.3
Nos. **27, 29/114, 76**

Giust1517 = *Laude devotissime et sanctissime composte per el nobile et magnifico misier Leonardo Iustiniano di Venetia*, Venice, Bernardino Vitali, 16 September 1517
Cambridge⋆, University Library, F151.e.2.15; Parma, Biblioteca Palatina [imperfect]
Nos. **27, 29/114, 76**

Historia = *Questa si è la historia della mal maritada, con certe altre canzone*, no pl., no pr., [ca. 1530]
Firenze⋆, Biblioteca Riccardiana, Ed. rare 689
No. **116**

Inamormento = *Incomenza lo inamormento di Floro. Opera nova composta per lo excellentissimo poeta Piero de Noceto da Lucca* […], Venice, Alessandro Bindoni, 8 June 1510
Modena⋆, Biblioteca Estense Universitaria, α.Z.7.29/5
Nos. **66, 93**

Infantia1513 = *Libro chiamato Infantia Salvatoris, in lo quale se contiene la vita e li miracoli et passione de Iesu Christo e la creatione de Adamo, et molte altre cose, le quale lezendo si poterano intendere*, Venice, Giovanni Tacuino, 27 June 1513
current location unknown (according to Essling, II/1, no. 1774, who found it in a library catalogue)
No. **13**

Infantia1515 = *Libro chiamato Infantia Salvatoris, in lo quale si contiene la vita e li miraculi et la passione de Jesu Christo, e la creatione de Adamo, et molte altre cose, le quale lezendo si poteranno intendere*, [Venice], no pr., [ante December 1515]
Sevilla⋆, Biblioteca Capitular y Colombina, 6.3.26 (4)
No. **13**

Infanzia1541 = [*Infanzia del Salvatore, sua vita, miracoli e passione etc., con un lamento di Maria Vergine*], Rome, Valerio and Luigi Dorico, 1541
current location unknown (indicated by Capponi 1747, p. 25)
No. **13**

JacopBen = *Laude de lo contemplativo et extatico B. F. Jacopone de lo ordine de lo Seraphico S. Francesco* […], Venice, Bernardino Benali, 5 December 1514
Bergamo, Civica Biblioteca - Archivi Storici Angelo Mai; Città del Vaticano⋆, Biblioteca Apostolica Vaticana,

Rossiana 6436; F𝚒𝚛𝚎𝚗𝚣𝚎, Biblioteca Marucelliana; F𝚒𝚛𝚎𝚗𝚣𝚎, Biblioteca Nazionale Centrale; G𝚎𝚗𝚘𝚟𝚊, Biblioteca Universitaria; G𝚛𝚘𝚝𝚝𝚊𝚏𝚎𝚛𝚛𝚊𝚝𝚊, Biblioteca Statale del Monumento Nazionale (Biblioteca della Badia Greca); L𝚒𝚟𝚘𝚛𝚗𝚘, Biblioteca Comunale Labronica Francesco Domenico Guerrazzi; L𝚞𝚌𝚌𝚊, Biblioteca Statale (*ex* Governativa); L𝚞𝚐𝚘 𝚍𝚒 R𝚘𝚖𝚊𝚐𝚗𝚊, Biblioteca Comunale Fabrizio Trisi; M𝚒𝚕𝚊𝚗𝚘, Biblioteca Nazionale Braidense; P𝚊𝚛𝚖𝚊, Biblioteca Palatina [lost]; P𝚒𝚜𝚊, Biblioteca Universitaria; R𝚘𝚖𝚊, Biblioteca Casanatense; R𝚘𝚖𝚊, Biblioteca Nazionale Centrale Vittorio Emanuele II; S𝚙𝚘𝚕𝚎𝚝𝚘, Biblioteca Comunale Giosuè Carducci [lost]; V𝚎𝚗𝚎𝚣𝚒𝚊, Biblioteca della Fondazione Querini Stampalia [imperfect];V𝚎𝚗𝚎𝚣𝚒𝚊, Biblioteche della Fondazione Giorgio Cini

Nos. **29/114, 64**

JacopMis = *Incipiunt laudes quas fecit sanctus frater Iacobonus de Tuderto ordinis fratrum minorum, ad utilitatem et consolationem* […], Brescia, Bernardino Misinta, at the instance of Angelo Britannico, 10 July 1495

B𝚛𝚎𝚜𝚌𝚒𝚊, Biblioteca Civica Queriniana; C𝚒𝚝𝚝à 𝚍𝚎𝚕 V𝚊𝚝𝚒𝚌𝚊𝚗𝚘★, Biblioteca Apostolica Vaticana [2 copies, one of them imperfect; the other was consulted], Inc.Ferr. IV.8136 (2); D𝚎𝚗 H𝚊𝚊𝚐, Koninklijke Bibliotheek; L𝚘𝚗𝚍𝚘𝚗, British Library; M𝚒𝚕𝚊𝚗𝚘, Biblioteca dell'Archivio Storico Civico e Biblioteca Trivulziana; M𝚒𝚕𝚊𝚗𝚘, Biblioteca Nazionale Braidense; N𝚎𝚠 H𝚊𝚟𝚎𝚗, Yale University, Beinecke Rare Book and Manuscript Library; S𝚊𝚗 M𝚊𝚛𝚒𝚗𝚘 (CA), Henry E. Huntington Library

No. **64**

JacopSper = *Laude del contemplativo B. F. Iacopone, de l'ordine del Seraphico S. Francesco* […], Venice, al segno della Speranza, 1556

A𝚜𝚜𝚒𝚜𝚒, Biblioteca del Centro di Documentazione Francescana del Sacro Convento di S. Francesco; C𝚒𝚝𝚝à 𝚍𝚎𝚕 V𝚊𝚝𝚒𝚌𝚊𝚗𝚘, Biblioteca Apostolica Vaticana; F𝚒𝚎𝚜𝚘𝚕𝚎, Biblioteca Bandiniana; F𝚒𝚛𝚎𝚗𝚣𝚎, Biblioteca Nazionale Centrale; M𝚎𝚜𝚜𝚒𝚗𝚊, Biblioteca Regionale Universitaria; M𝚒𝚕𝚊𝚗𝚘, Biblioteca dell'Archivio Storico Civico e Biblioteca Trivulziana; M𝚘𝚍𝚎𝚗𝚊★, Biblioteca Estense Universitaria, A.LVIII.L.20; P𝚊𝚍𝚘𝚟𝚊, Biblioteca del Convento dei Frati Cappuccini; P𝚊𝚍𝚘𝚟𝚊, Biblioteca del Seminario Vescovile; P𝚒𝚜𝚊, Biblioteca Universitaria; R𝚘𝚖𝚊, Biblioteca dell'Accademia Nazionale dei Lincei e Corsiniana; R𝚘𝚖𝚊, Biblioteca Nazionale Centrale Vittorio Emanuele II; R𝚘𝚖𝚊, Biblioteca del Pontificio Ateneo Antonianum; V𝚎𝚗𝚎𝚣𝚒𝚊, Biblioteca d'Arte del Museo Civico Correr

No. **64**

Lamento = *Lamento de una giovaneta la quale fu volunterosa de esser presto maridata. Et una frottola del gallo. Et uno exordio sponsalitio*, no pl., no pr., [*ante* 1526 according to E𝚍𝚒𝚝 16 on line]

F𝚒𝚛𝚎𝚗𝚣𝚎★, Biblioteca Nazionale Centrale, Palatino E.6.5.3 II/21

No. **68**

Lamento1524 = *Lamento de una giovinetta la quale fu voluntarosa d'esser presto maridata. Et una frottola del gallo. Et uno exordio sponsalitio*, [Venice], Francesco Bindoni, October 1524

C𝚑𝚊𝚗𝚝𝚒𝚕𝚕𝚢★, Bibliothèque du Musée Condé, XI.G.62

No. **68**

Lamento1526 = *Lamento de una giovenetta la quale fu voluntarosa d'esser presto maridata. Et una frottola del gallo. Et uno exordio sponsalitio*, Venice, Francesco Bindoni, March 1526

L𝚘𝚗𝚍𝚘𝚗★, British Library, C.20.c.22/7

No. **68**

LaudeBonac = *Laude facte e composte da più persone spirituali* […] *Et tutte le infrascripte laude ha raccolto et insieme ridotto Iacopo di maestro Luigi de' Morsi cittadino fiorentino*, Florence, Francesco Bonaccorsi, at the request of Iacopo de' Morsi, 1 March 1485 (1486 modern style)

A𝚝𝚕𝚊𝚗𝚝𝚊 (GA), Emory University Library; Á𝚟𝚒𝚕𝚊, Biblioteca Pública; B𝚎𝚛𝚕𝚒𝚗, Staatsbibliothek, Preußischer Kulturbesitz; C𝚊𝚖𝚋𝚛𝚒𝚍𝚐𝚎 (MA), Harvard University, Houghton Library [imperfect]; C𝚒𝚝𝚝à 𝚍𝚎𝚕 V𝚊𝚝𝚒𝚌𝚊𝚗𝚘, Biblioteca Apostolica Vaticana [3 copies]; C𝚕𝚊𝚛𝚎𝚖𝚘𝚗𝚝 (CA), Honnold Library (Bodman Collection), Associated Colleges [2 copies, one of them imperfect]; F𝚒𝚛𝚎𝚗𝚣𝚎, Biblioteca della Cassa di Risparmio, Fondo Roberto Ridolfi; F𝚒𝚛𝚎𝚗𝚣𝚎, Biblioteca Nazionale Centrale [imperfect]; F𝚒𝚛𝚎𝚗𝚣𝚎, Biblioteca Riccardiana; F𝚘𝚕𝚒𝚐𝚗𝚘, Biblioteca Ludovico Jacobilli; L𝚘𝚗𝚍𝚘𝚗, British Library; M𝚒𝚕𝚊𝚗𝚘, Biblioteca e Archivio del Capitolo Metropolitano [imperfect]; M𝚒𝚕𝚊𝚗𝚘, Biblioteca dell'Archivio Storico Civico e Biblioteca Trivulziana; M𝚒𝚕𝚊𝚗𝚘, Biblioteca Nazionale Braidense [imperfect]; N𝚊𝚙𝚘𝚕𝚒, Biblioteca Nazionale Vittorio Emanuele III; N𝚊𝚙𝚘𝚕𝚒, Biblioteca Universitaria [imperfect]; O𝚡𝚏𝚘𝚛𝚍, Bodleian Library; P𝚊𝚛𝚖𝚊, Biblioteca Palatina [imperfect]; R𝚒𝚎𝚝𝚒, Biblioteca Comunale Paroniana [imperfect]; R𝚘𝚖𝚊, Biblioteca dell'Accademia Nazionale dei Lincei e Corsiniana [imperfect]; V𝚎𝚗𝚎𝚣𝚒𝚊★, Biblioteca Nazionale Marciana [2 copies], Inc. 1155

Nos. **15, 30, 36, 67, 69, 76, 159**

LaudeBonar = *Laude spirituali di Giesù Christo, della Madonna, et di diversi santi, et sante del Paradiso [...] di nuovo ristampate*, Bologna, Pellegrino Bonardo, [ca. 1560][22]
Bologna★, Biblioteca Universitaria, Raro C.17; Firenze, Biblioteca Nazionale Centrale; Roma, Biblioteca Nazionale Centrale Vittorio Emanuele II; Siena, Biblioteca Comunale degli Intronati
Nos. **29/114, 30, 64, 69, 147, 159**

LaudeFort = *Laude devote per la natività del nostro Signore Giesù Christo. Ristampate con aggiunta di due laude bellissime*, Florence - Pistoia, Pier Antonio Fortunati, no d.
Firenze★, Biblioteca Nazionale Centrale, Palatino E.6.7.55 II/35
No. **69**

LaudeGiacc = *A laude e gloria del onnipotente Iddio e della gloriosa Virgine Maria incomincia il libro delle laude di Iesu Christo e della Madonna e di diversi santi et sante composto da diversi personi spirituali [...] Nuovamente restampato [...]*, Bologna, Anselmo Giaccarelli, 12 March 1551
Siena★, Biblioteca Comunale degli Intronati, Misc. Fil. e Pol. XVII.10
Nos. **29/114, 64, 159**

LaudeMisc = *Laude facte et composte da più persone spirituali [...] E oltre a quelle che già per lo tempo passato furon impresse s'è fatta ora in questa nova impressione una aggiunta di più d'altrettante*, [Florence, Antonio Miscomini and Bartolomeo de' Libri, ca. 1495]
Bryn Mawr (PA), Bryn Mawr College, Marjorie Walter Goodhart Medieval Library; Cambridge, University Library [one page only]; Corvallis (OR), Oregon State University Library; Firenze, Accademia della Crusca; Firenze, Biblioteca Nazionale Centrale [2 copies]; London, British Library; Lucca, Biblioteca Statale (*ex* Governativa); Milano, Biblioteca dell'Archivio Storico Civico e Biblioteca Trivulziana; Milano, Biblioteca Nazionale Braidense [imperfect]; Paris, Bibliothèque Mazarine [imperfect]; Venezia★, Biblioteca Nazionale Marciana, Inc. 720
Nos. **15, 29/114, 30, 36, 64, 67, 69, 76, 147, 159**

LaudeNat = *Laude devote per la natività del nostro Signore Giesù Christo. Con una aggiunta di dua laude bellissime*, no pl., no pr., [ca. 1580]
Firenze★, Biblioteca Nazionale Centrale, Palatino E.6.5.2/30; Milano, Biblioteca dell'Archivio Storico Civico e Biblioteca Trivulziana
No. **69**

LaudeSper = *Laude devote composte da diverse persone spirituali [...]*, Venice, al segno della Speranza, 1556
Bologna★, Biblioteca di Casa Carducci, 4.b.346; Chiavari, Biblioteca della Società Economica; Fiesole, Biblioteca Bandiniana; Firenze, Biblioteca Nazionale Centrale; Genova, Biblioteca Universitaria; Messina, Biblioteca Regionale Universitaria; Milano, Biblioteca dell'Archivio Storico Civico e Biblioteca Trivulziana; Padova, Biblioteca del Seminario Vescovile; Pisa, Biblioteca Universitaria; Roma, Biblioteca dell'Accademia Nazionale dei Lincei e Corsiniana; Roma, Biblioteca del Pontificio Ateneo Antonianum
Nos. **15, 30, 36, 67, 69, 159**

LaudeVecchie = *Libro di laude. Laude facte et composte da più persone spirituali [...] Et oltre a quelle che già per lo tempo passato furono impresse s'è facta ora in questa nuova impressione un'aggiunta di più d'altrettante*, [Florence, Gianstefano di Carlo], at the request of ser Piero Pacini da Pescia, [1502-07][23]
Firenze, Accademia della Crusca [imperfect]; Firenze, Biblioteca della Cassa di Risparmio, Fondo Roberto Ridolfi;

---

[22]. The copy in the Biblioteca Nazionale, Rome, has on the title page, under the ornament, «Prero De Venetia: 1579»; see Mischiati 2001, p. 749.

[23]. The dating is that of Giovanni Ponte (Ponte 1969, p. 26, n. 69), who explains it as follows: it would certainly be later than 1502 (because it includes, on fol. 77*r*, a lauda «in honore della tavola di Sancta Maria impruneta per intercedere gratia per uno Gonfaloniere a vita»), and before 1507-08, since it does not include *Dolor pianto e penitenzia* (= 'Carro della morte'), a text that had «a rapid and wide diffusion». This text is found on fol. 87*v* of Florence, Biblioteca Riccardiana, MS 1251, *Epistole e Vangeli volgarizzati* (edited in Ponte 1969, pp. 36-37), preceded by the rubric «La chanzona. del trionfo della morte andato. una .sera. di charnovale torno. 1507, conposto da m. Chastelano Castelanj». William Prizer has now discovered a document that fixes the date of *LaudeVecchie* as 1507 (modern style), the year in which the 'Carro della morte' was devised (see Prizer 2004b, p. 202). Adolfo Tura (Tura 2001, p. 97, no. 58) posits that the printer was Gianstefano di Carlo: Bartolomeo de' Libri — traditionally considered to be the printer of the book — printed his last book on 25 April 1500 (Augustinus Papiensis, *Scrutinium*), and then his son-in-law Gianstefano di Carlo would have taken over the business. Tura does not explain, however, his reason for assigning the date to ca. 1514. My thanks to Bonnie Blackburn for having called Prizer's article to my attention, and Blake Wilson for having referred me to the books by Ponte and Tura.

FIRENZE, Biblioteca Nazionale Centrale [imperfect]; FIRENZE★, Biblioteca Riccardiana, Ed. rare 196.2 [imperfect]; MILANO, Biblioteca dell'Archivio Storico Civico e Biblioteca Trivulziana; PARMA, Biblioteca Palatina; ROMA, Biblioteca Casanatense; VENEZIA, Biblioteche della Fondazione Giorgio Cini; VENEZIA, Biblioteca Nazionale Marciana [imperfect]

Nos. **15** (twice), **29/114**, **30**, **36**, **64**, **67**, **69**, **76**, **147**, **159**

LaudiBad = *Laudi devote per la natività del nostro Sig. Giesù Christo. Con una aggiunta di due laudi bellissime*, Florence, alle Scale di Badia, [ca. 1550]

FIRENZE★, Biblioteca Nazionale Centrale, Banco Rari 183/5 (*olim* Miscellanee 979.5)

No. **69**

LaudiGiunti = *Scelta di laudi spirituali di diversi eccellentiss. e devoti autori antichi e moderni; nuovamente ricorrette, e messe insieme*, Florence, Giunti, 1578

FIRENZE, Biblioteca Nazionale Centrale; MILANO, Biblioteca dell'Archivio Storico Civico e Biblioteca Trivulziana; ROMA, Biblioteca dell'Accademia Nazionale dei Lincei e Corsiniana; VENEZIA★, Biblioteca Nazionale Marciana, 227.D.136,1

Nos. **67**, **69**, **76**, **159**

LaudiRiccardiana = *[Laudi]*, no typ. info.

FIRENZE★, Biblioteca Riccardiana, Ed. rare 196.3 [imperfect]

Nos. **30**, **36**, **67**, **69**, **76**, **159**

Non1500a = *Non aspectò giamai con tal disio. Con certe altre zentilece […]*, [Florence?], no pr., [ca. 1500?]

ZWICKAU★, Ratsschulbibliothek, 5.5.52/16

No. **19**

Non1500b = *Non expectò già mai con tal desio. Con la risposta […]*, no pl., no pr., [ca. 1500]

ZWICKAU★, Ratsschulbibliothek, 5.4.52/20

No. **19**

Non1520 = *Non expectò giamai con la risposta*, [Venice, Francesco? Bindoni, ca. 1520]

LONDON★, British Library, C.20.c.22/26

No. **19**

Non1524 = *No expettò giamai, con molte altre canzone […]*, Venice, Francesco Bindoni, April 1524

CHANTILLY★, Bibliothèque du Musée Condé, XI.G.62

No. **19**

Non1527 = *Non expettò già mai, con molte altre canzone*, Venice, Francesco Bindoni, January 1527 (1528 modern style)

LONDON★, British Library, C.57.l.7/l3

No. **19**

Non1540M = *Non espettò giamai. Con la risposta. Et altre belle canzonette*, Milan, Giovanni Antonio Borgo, [ca. 1540]

LONDON★, British Library, 11426.c.65

No. **19**

Non1540R = *Non aspettò giamai con tal desio con la resposta, con altri capitoli, e strambotti, e a ciascaduno proposito*, [Rome?], no pr., [ca. 1540]

NEW YORK★, New York Public Library, Spencer Collection, Ital. 154-

No. **19**

Non1568 = *Non aspettò già mai con tal disio*, Florence, no pr., 1568

WOLFENBÜTTEL★, Herzog August Bibliothek, LK Sammelbd. 64

No. **19**

NonF = *Non aspettò già mai con tal desio*, [Florence], no pr., no d.

FIRENZE★, Biblioteca Nazionale Centrale, Palatino E.6.5.3 II/28; LUCCA, Biblioteca Statale (*ex* Governativa)

No. **19**

NonM = *Non aspettò già mai con tal desio*, no typ. info.

MILANO★, Biblioteca dell'Archivio Storico Civico e Biblioteca Trivulziana, Triv. M 715/1

No. **19**

NonVav1 = *Non espettò giamai con tal disio*, Venice, Giovanni Andrea Vavassori, [*post* 1530]
    MILANO★, Biblioteca dell'Archivio Storico Civico e Biblioteca Trivulziana, Rari Triv. H 290
    No. **19**

NonVav2 = *Non expettò giamai con tal desio*, [Venice], Giovanni Andrea Vavassori, [*post* 1530]
    ROMA★, Biblioteca Paolo Baffi della Banca d'Italia, Salottino del Governatore 55
    No. **19**

Opera1515 = *Opera de cose nove spirituale*, […] *con la sententia de Pilato, et molte altre belle cose, composte da diversi et preclarissimi doctori*, [Venice, Bernardino Benali?, ca. 1515]
    BOLOGNA★, Biblioteca Universitaria, A.V.B.IX.60
    Nos. **13, 42, 69**

OperaFregoso = *Opera nova del magnifico cavaliero miser Antonio Phileremo Fregoso la quale tracta de doi philosophi* […], Venice, Giorgio Rusconi, 1 September 1513
    CITTÀ DEL VATICANO★, Biblioteca Apostolica Vaticana, Stamp.Ferr. V.8015 (3); LUCCA, Biblioteca Statale (*ex* Governativa)
    No. **13**

OperaNova = *Opera nova de laude facte et composte da più persone spirituali* […], Venice, Giorgio Rusconi, at the instance of Niccolò Zoppino, 4 March 1512
    FIRENZE, Biblioteca Nazionale Centrale [imperfect]; MILANO, Biblioteca dell'Archivio Storico Civico e Biblioteca Trivulziana; MILANO, Biblioteca del Museo Poldi Pezzoli; ROMA, Biblioteca dell'Accademia Nazionale dei Lincei e Corsiniana; SEVILLA, Biblioteca Capitular y Colombina; VENEZIA★, Biblioteca Nazionale Marciana, Rari V.459 [imperfect]
    Nos. **15** (twice), **29/114, 30, 36, 64, 67, 69, 76, 147, 159**

Operetta1512 = *Questa si è una operetta piacevole et dilectevole da intendere, composta per uno che finge aver cercato tutto el mondo et di varie et diverse cose intenderite da legere o recetare dove se fa qualche convito*, Rome, at the instance of Giovanni Battista Carminate, 1512
    SEVILLA★, Biblioteca Capitular y Colombina, 6.3.29 (4)
    No. **68**

Operetta1515 = *Questa si è una operetta piacevole et dilectevole da intendere, composta per uno chi se finge aver cercato tutto el mondo et assai altre cose che per gentileza se potranno recetare in qualche convito*, [Rome], no pr., [ca. 1515]
    MÜNCHEN★, Bayerische Staatsbibliothek, Res. 4° P.o.it. 331/4
    No. **68**

Operetta1521 = *Operetta de uno che finge avere cercato tutto il mondo, con molte altre gentilezze aggiunte, cosa da recitare a qualche convito et da legere piacevolissima*, Rome, at the instance of Domenico detto il Venezianello, 10 May 1521
    MÜNCHEN★, Bayerische Staatsbibliothek, Rar. 1091 (*olim* Res. 4° P.o.it. 2509/1)
    No. **68**

Patientia = *Patientia ognun me dice*, no pl., no pr., [ca. 1500]
    VENEZIA★, Biblioteca Nazionale Marciana, Misc. 1945.3
    No. **116**

Petr1470 = [FRANCESCO PETRARCA], [*Canzoniere e Trionfi*], Venice, Vindelino da Spira, 1470
    BRESCIA, Biblioteca Civica Queriniana [imperfect]; BRUSSEL/BRUXELLES, Koninklijke Bibliotheek van België / Bibliothèque Royale de Belgique; CAMBRIDGE, King's College Library [2 copies, one of them imperfect]; CAMBRIDGE (MA), Harvard University, Houghton Library; CHANTILLY, Bibliothèque du Musée Condé; CHICAGO, Newberry Library; CITTÀ DEL VATICANO★, Biblioteca Apostolica Vaticana, [2 copies, both imperfect], Inc.Barber. AAA.I.4; COLOGNY, Fondation Martin Bodmer, Bibliotheca Bodmeriana; COMO, Biblioteca dei Musei Civici [imperfect]; DUBLIN, Trinity College Library; FIRENZE, Biblioteca Medicea Laurenziana; FIRENZE, Biblioteca Nazionale Centrale [imperfect]; GENOVA, Biblioteca Durazzo [imperfect]; ITHACA (NY), Cornell University Library, Kroch Library Rare & Manuscripts; LEUVEN, Katholieke Universiteit, Universiteitsbibliotheek; LIVERPOOL, Public Libraries, Central Library; LONDON, British Library [2 copies]; MANCHESTER, John Rylands Library; MILANO, Biblioteca dell'Archivio Storico Civico e Biblioteca Trivulziana; MILANO, Biblioteca Nazionale Braidense [imperfect]; NAPOLI, Biblioteca Nazionale Vittorio Emanuele III [imperfect]; NEW YORK, Pierpont Morgan Library; OXFORD, Bodleian Library; PARIS, Bibliothèque Nationale de France; PHILADELPHIA, Rosenbach Museum and Library; ROMA, Biblioteca dell'Accademia Nazionale dei Lincei e Corsiniana; ROMA, Biblioteca Nazionale Centrale Vittorio Emanuele II; STOCKHOLM,

Kungliga Bibliteket; Tʀɪᴇsᴛᴇ, Biblioteca Civica Attilio Hortis; Vᴇɴᴇᴢɪᴀ, Biblioteca Nazionale Marciana [2 copies]; Wᴀsʜɪɴɢᴛᴏɴ, DC, Library of Congress; Wɪᴇɴ, Österreichische Nationalbibliothek

No. **180**

Pianto1477 = [Eɴsᴇʟᴍɪɴᴏ ᴅᴀ Mᴏɴᴛᴇʙᴇʟʟᴜɴᴀ], *El pianto de la Verzene Maria*, [Vicenza, Hermann Liechtenstein, ca. 1477]

Mᴏᴅᴇɴᴀ★, Biblioteca Estense Universitaria, α.C.6.13/1

No. **13**

Pianto1478 = *Pianti devotissimi de la Madona*, [Milan], Filippo da Lavagna, [ca. 1478]

Pʀᴏᴠɪᴅᴇɴᴄᴇ★ (RI), Annmary Brown Memorial Library, Brown University, 298

No. **13**

Pianto1481H = Eɴsᴇʟᴍɪɴᴏ ᴅᴀ Mᴏɴᴛᴇʙᴇʟʟᴜɴᴀ, *Il devotissimo pianto de la gloriosa Vergine Maria* […], [Rome, Georg Herolt, ca. 1481]

Rᴏᴍᴀ★, Biblioteca dell'Accademia Nazionale dei Lincei e Corsiniana, 51.E.24

No. **13**

Pianto1481L = Eɴsᴇʟᴍɪɴᴏ ᴅᴀ Tʀᴇᴠɪsᴏ [= ᴅᴀ Mᴏɴᴛᴇʙᴇʟʟᴜɴᴀ], *Devotissimo pianto de la gloriosa Virgine Maria*, Venice, Luca di Domenico, 17 March 1481

Bᴏʟᴏɢɴᴀ★, Biblioteca Universitaria, A.V.B.X.29; Cɪᴛᴛà ᴅᴇʟ Vᴀᴛɪᴄᴀɴᴏ, Biblioteca Apostolica Vaticana; Lᴏɴᴅᴏɴ, British Library; Mɪʟᴀɴᴏ, Biblioteca dell'Archivio Storico Civico e Biblioteca Trivulziana; Vɪᴄᴇɴᴢᴀ, Biblioteca Civica Bertoliana

No. **13**

Pianto1483 = *Incomincia il pianto della gloriosa Vergine Maria composto per messere Antonio Cornazzano*, [Milan], Christoph Valdarfer, [ca. 1483]

Pᴀʀɪs★, Bibliothèque Nationale de France, Rés. Yd. 1465

No. **13**

Pianto1490 = *Incomenza lo pianto de la nostra advocata Verzine Maria composto per miser Antonio Cornazano*, [Brescia, Bernardino Misinta, ca. 1490]

Vᴇʀᴏɴᴀ★, Biblioteca Civica [imperfect: only two folios remain, one bound at the beginning and the other at the end of the first fascicle of eight folios of *De fide et vita Cristi* by Antonio Cornazano, Venice, Tommaso di Piasi, 15 November 1492], Inc. 327

No. **13**

Pianto1493 = [Eɴsᴇʟᴍɪɴᴏ ᴅᴀ Mᴏɴᴛᴇʙᴇʟʟᴜɴᴀ], *Incomincia il gran lamento de la Virgine Maria madre del nostro Signore Iesu Christo*, [Venice, Bernardino Benali, ca. 1493]

Mɪʟᴀɴᴏ, Biblioteca Nazionale Braidense [imperfect]; Vᴇɴᴇᴢɪᴀ★, Biblioteca d'Arte del Museo Civico Correr, Inc. H.133

No. **13**

Pianto1495 = *Il pianto della gloriosa Vergine Maria composto per messere Antonio Cornazzano*, [Milan, Filippo Mantegazza, ca. 1495]

Oxʏғᴏʀᴅ★, Private Collection of David Rogers [imperfect]

No. **13**

Pianto1505 = *Pianto devotissimo de la Madona hystoriado. Composto per el magnifico misser Leonardo Iustiniano in terza rima, nel qual tracta la passione del nostro Signor Iesu Christo cosa nuova*, Venice, Bartolomeo Zani, 27 June 1505

Pᴀʀᴍᴀ★, Biblioteca Palatina, GG.III.274

No. **13**

Pianto1537 = *Incomincia il pianto della gloriosa Vergine Maria composto per messer Antonio Cornazzano poeta clarissimo*, Milan, Giovanni Antonio Borgo, 8 August 1537

Pᴀʀɪs★, Bibliothèque Nationale de France, Rés. Yd. 1466

No. **13**

PiantoOratione = *Incomenza la oratione in la quale si prega la Beata Vergine, che narri il suo lamento e pianto per la morte del suo dilecto figliolo, facta e composta vulgare da fra Guglielmo da Trevisio de l'ordine di frati heremitani di sancto Augustio*, no typ. info.

Pᴇsᴀʀᴏ★, Biblioteca Oliveriana, ms. 1547/VI (formerly at Pᴇsᴀʀᴏ, Private Collection of Giuliano Vanzolini) [imperfect:

this is an «imperfect incunable whose last leaves have been added in handwriting» (see CREMA 2002, pp. 613-614, n. 16)]
No. **13**

Rado = *Stramboti de misser Rado e de madonna Margarita. Cosa nova*, no typ. info.
CHANTILLY★, Bibliothèque du Musée Condé, XI.G.62
No. **116**

Ricco1511 = *Opere de Antonio Ricco neapolitano intitulata Fior de Delia. Stampata novamente* […], Venice, Melchiorre Sessa, 1
October 1511
FIRENZE, Biblioteca Nazionale Centrale; LONDON★, British Library, 11426.aa.36
No. **33**

Ricco1520 = *Opere de Antonio Ricco neapolitano intitulata Fior de Delia stampata novamente* […], Venice, Melchiorre Sessa and
Pietro Ravani, 30 March 1520
LONDON★, British Library, C.107.aa.23/3; PISA, Biblioteca Universitaria
No. **33**

RispSon = *Rispecti, sonetti et canzone nuovamente stampati*, no typ. info.
FIRENZE★, Biblioteca Nazionale Centrale, Palatino D.4.7.16
No. **63**

SepteDolori = *E septe dolori che dà l'amore* […], [Florence, Bartolomeo de' Libri, ca. 1500]
ROMA★, Biblioteca Casanatense, Vol.Inc. 1661 (*olim* Inc. 1703)
No. **19**

SetteDolori = *Li sette dolori de lo amore* […], [Florence, alla Badia?], no d.
MÜNCHEN, Bayerische Staatsbibliothek; PARIS★, Bibliothèque Nationale de France, Rés. Yd. 624; SEVILLA, Biblioteca
Capitular y Colombina
No. **19**

SolaVirtus = *Sola virtus. Fior de cose nobilissime et degne de diversi auctori* […], Venice, Simone da Lovere, 14 October 1514
VENEZIA★, Biblioteca Nazionale Marciana, Misc. 2429.2
No. **43**

TebEp1500Bes = *Epistola del Tibaldeo de Ferrara che finge che l'abia facta una donna e mandata a lui. E capitolo medesimamente
d'amore a sdruzolo bellissimo. E canzona di patientia. E più canzonette morale* […], [Rome, Giovanni Besicken, *post* 1500]
ROMA★, Biblioteca Casanatense, Vol.Inc. 1686 (*olim* Inc. 1729)
No. **19**

TebEp1500Sil = *Epistola del Tibaldeo de Ferrara che finge che l'abbia facta una donna e mandata a lui. E capitolo medesimamente
d'amore asdruzolo bellissimo. E canzona di patienza. E più canzonette morale* […], [Rome, Eucharius Silber, ca. 1500]
ROMA★, Biblioteca Casanatense, Vol.Inc. 1505 (*olim* Inc. 1545)
No. **19**

TebEp1506 = *Epistola del Tibaldeo de Ferrara che finge che l'abbia facta una dona e mandata a lui* […], [Rome, Eucharius Silber,
post 1506]
MÜNCHEN★, Bayerische Staatsbibliothek, P.o.it. 4° 331/12
No. **19**

TebEp1509 = *Epistola del Tibaldeo de Ferrara che finge che l'abia facta una donna e mandata a lui* […], [Rome, Eucharius Silber,
ca. 1509]
MILANO★, Biblioteca Nazionale Braidense, AM.X.51; SEVILLA, Biblioteca Capitular y Colombina
No. **19**

TebEp1545 = *Epistola del Tibaldeo, cioè Non aspettò già mai con tal desio* […], Bologna, at the instance of Giovanni di Francesco
Benvenuto Cartolaio, 1545
MILANO★, Biblioteca dell'Archivio Storico Civico e Biblioteca Trivulziana, Rari Triv. H 715/2
No. **19**

TebEp1557 = *Epistola del Tibaldeo, cioè Non aspettò già mai con tal disio* […], Florence, presso il Vescovado, 1557
OXFORD★, Bodleian Library, Mason L.295
No. **19**

TebOp1498 = *Opere de M. Antonio Tebaldeo da Ferrara*, Modena, Domenico and Francesco Rococciola, 13 October 1498
Bologna, Biblioteca di Casa Carducci [imperfect]; Cassino, Biblioteca Statale del Monumento Nazionale di Montecassino; Fermo, Biblioteca Comunale; Ferrara, Biblioteca Comunale Ariostea [imperfect]; København, Det Kongelige Bibliotek; Lucca, Biblioteca Statale (*ex* Governativa); Modena★, Biblioteca Estense Universitaria, α.X.6.9; Napoli, Biblioteca Nazionale Vittorio Emanuele III; Paris, Bibliothèque Nationale de France; Verona, Biblioteca Capitolare [imperfect]
No. **19**

TebOp1500 = *Opere del Thebaldeo de Ferrara* […],Venice, Giovanni Battista Sessa, 7 July 1500
Modena★, Biblioteca Estense Universitaria, α.J.7.3/1
No. **19**

TebSon1499 = *Soneti capituli et egloge del prestantissimo M. Antonio Thebaldeo*, Milan, Ulrich Scinzenzeler, at the instance of Giovanni da Legnano, 4 June 1499
Baltimore, Walters Art Gallery; Firenze, Biblioteca Nazionale Centrale; London, British Library; Milano, Biblioteca dell'Archivio Storico Civico e Biblioteca Trivulziana; Milano, Biblioteca Nazionale Braidense; Napoli, Biblioteca Oratoriana del Monumento Nazionale dei Girolamini; Paris, Bibliothèque Nationale de France; Parma★, Biblioteca Palatina, Inc.Parm. 671
No. **19**

VitaSB = *La vita di san Bernardino*, [Florence, Lorenzo Morgiani and Johann Petri, *post* 28 August 1496]
Milano★, Biblioteca dell'Archivio Storico Civico e Biblioteca Trivulziana, Triv. Inc. E 16
No. **30**

PART I

THE MANUSCRIPT PANCIATICHI 27

1. Physical Description

THE MUSICAL MANUSCRIPT PANCIATICHI 27 of the Biblioteca Nazionale Centrale in Florence (hereafter 'Panc.27') is a manuscript in oblong octavo format; it measures 15.3 × 21 cm, retains the eighteenth-century binding in boards and leather, and is currently in a good state of preservation. It comprises 216 folios bound in 27 quaternions of eight leaves each, to which have been added two vellum flyleaves (one precedes the initial quaternion, the other follows the last fascicle), originally belonging to a twelfth-century breviary,[1] which function as protection for the entirely paper contents of the book. Three supplementary blank leaves of new paper — surely added during the restoration of the book — have been inserted before the first flyleaf and after the last parchment folio.[2] After the last fascicle of the manuscript there are in fact nine original blank pages followed by a folio from the breviary in parchment and by the three blank pages newly added. A paper attached to the inside back cover contains the following annotation: «Cc. 216 di cui bianche le cc. 121-129, 157-206, 214-215: più n. 14 cc. di guardia in principio, di cui membranacea la c. 4 e scritta la c. 5, e n. 13 cc. di guardia in fine, di cui membr. la carta n. 10. | 29.XI.1935.XIV | [at the right] I.R.».[3]

The proper title page of the volume follows the first parchment page. It carries an inscription — certainly added by a late hand — stating the miscellaneous contents of the manuscript: «Cantilene | sacre e profane». Above the 'title' is a name that has been cancelled and is only partly legible today: «fratris Honofrij [... + ...]» (see FIG. 1). The handwriting appears to be of the sixteenth century, but is nevertheless different from those in the rest of the manuscript: it may belong to a former owner (the first owner? the person who commissioned the manuscript?) of the book, who thus inscribed his property. Somewhat lower, the *ex libris* of the Panciatichi library[4] carries the number of the old shelfmark of the volume: «III.2.8».[5]

After the title page, ten blank folios of original paper precede the first fascicle of the music. The first of these contains two groups of arabic numerals annotated by the same hand that wrote the numbers in the manuscript itself: (a) '4.97 - 7 - 2 - 1.06';[6] (b) '2 - 48 - 10 - 96'.[7]

---

[1]. See MORPURGO *ET AL.* 1887-1962, p. 54.

[2]. The manuscript was restored perhaps in 1960. On the library card for Panc.27 labelled 'Elenco dei Lettori che hanno studiato il Manoscritto' the following annotation is found: «Restaurato. V. registro restauri 1960 n. 61».

[3]. In the date, the roman numeral 'XIV' refers to the fourteenth year of the fascist era. The siglum «I.R.» can no longer be understood today.

[4]. The *ex libris* contains the inscription in Greek «ΕΚ ΤΗΣ ΒΙΒΛΙΟΘΗΚΗΣ ΤΩΝ ΠΑΝΤΖΙΑΤΙΚΩΝ» = «From the library of the Panciatichi family». The circular inscription surrounds the image of a bird (a pelican?) holding in its beak a banderole with the words «Pius esto». The *ex libris* was added by Antonmaria Biscioni, who was the curator of the Panciatichi library from 1720 to 1755, the same period in which the manuscript was rebound in the current binding. The Panciatichi family came originally from Pistoia, but transferred to Florence in the sixteenth century, on the express invitation of the Medici. The first appears to have been Niccolò di Gualtieri (1513-84), great grandfather of Lorenzo and Bandino. Parallel with his Cardinal cousin Bandino, the canon Lorenzo Panciatichi (1635-1676) was the initiator of the famous collection. We have, however, no inventory of it; thus we do not know whether Lorenzo owned the current Panc.27. The family retained possession of the library until 1859, when Marchese Ferdinando Panciatichi sold 153 volumes (the oldest and most precious ones) to the Biblioteca Palatina in Florence for 2,000 scudi. But one of the volumes from that sale was never found; the then librarian of the Palatina, Francesco Palermo, informed Marchese Panciatichi, who decided to remedy the loss by donating a further 218 manuscripts. Today in fact there are 370 manuscripts in the fondo Panciatichi – above all literary and juridical material – kept in the Biblioteca Nazionale Centrale, where the patrimony of the Biblioteca Palatina was transferred (see the preface of Berta Maracchi Biagiarelli in MORPURGO *ET AL.* 1887-1962, pp. vii-xxiii).

[5]. The erroneous shelfmark 1-III.28 is reported in BASILE - MARCHAND 1989-92, I, p. 53. In the Panciatichi library the numbers referred to the topographical arrangement in cupboards, in which the volumes were placed in numerical order. The overall subdivision was organized in 13 classes of materials (see INNOCENTI 1984, p. 424).

[6]. The '7' and the '2' are listed in column format under the 7 of '4.97', and therefore the final number '1.06', is of course the product of the sum of $97 + 7 + 2$.

[7]. The first three numbers are aligned horizontally, but the '96' is placed under the '48', separated by the '2' and the '48', in the typical layout that helps in manual calculation: 96 is in fact the product of 2×48.

FIG. 1: Title page of MS Panc.27. Photo Mario Setter – GAP.

The pages prepared for music in Panc.27 have six staves each, and the writing surface covers a space that measures ca. 12 × 18 cm. Not all the folios with staves contain music: some lack notes completely (89r, 104r, 120v, 129r–130r, 145v–146r, 156v–207r, 213v–216r), whereas others (121r–128v) lack even staves. Folio 216v contains a few rhythmic rules, probably intended for performance or instruction; absent, however, from the note values and the mensuration signs listed there is an illustration of the triplet contained in pieces nos. 2 (second and fifth staves of folios 1v and 2r) and 103 (fol. 71r, fourth stave), and two time signatures: the archaic sign of *prolatio minor* (a circle containing two vertical dots), used only in piece no. 45 (fol. 28v), and the more common *tempus perfectum cum prolatione minori diminutum* (an empty circle with a vertical or oblique stroke).

The 27 quaternions of the manuscript have the same type of paper. (For their internal arrangement, see the section I.4.a on the repertory.) The watermark of the paper used in Panc.27 is very similar to Briquet no. 1007 (see FIG. 2b),[8] which is a further refinement of the more archaic appearance of watermark no. 1006 (see FIG. 2a).

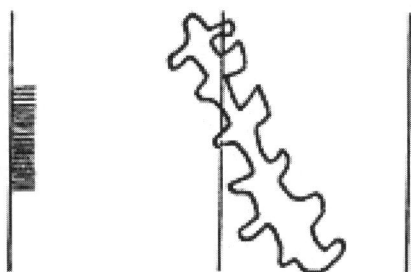

FIG. 2a: Briquet watermark no. 1006.

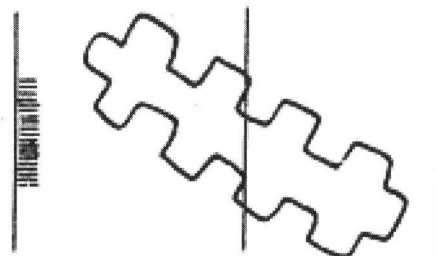

FIG. 2b: Briquet watermark no. 1007.

---

[8]. «Bande écotée» (see BRIQUET I, p. 77).

The tracings reproduced in Briquet represent a range of variants of the same type of watermark characterizing a type of paper produced in Emilia Romagna, used above all in Ferrara, Reggio Emilia, and Parma between the last decade of the fifteenth century and the second decade of the sixteenth. The watermark of Panc.27 (see Fig. 3) has five lateral projections of a similar shape to those in watermark no. 1007, except that this has only four projections. No other paper music manuscript listed in CC has this type of watermark, which never appears complete on any page of the manuscript.

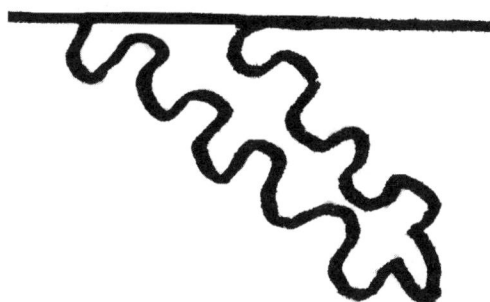

Fig. 3: The watermark of MS Panc.27. The horizontal line represents the upper margin of the paper.

The manuscript has two numberings, both in arabic numerals placed at the top right of the recto of every folio: one in an older hand up to 120r, and a modern one — in red ink — from 121r on. This characteristic has made some think that the present Panc.27 was composed of two different manuscripts joined together (the first up to fol. 120v and the second from fol. 121r to the end),[9] but Jeppesen subsequently changed his mind on this hypothesis because of the largely regular disposition of the gatherings.[10] Moreover, the same copyist worked in both parts of the manuscript, and this serves to support the idea that the whole manuscript was conceived as a unit from the very beginning.

At least two scribes were involved in entering the music and the words:[11] the first (A) — an older hand (perhaps that of a professional?) — has filled the larger part of the manuscript in a fairly orderly fashion in a somewhat restricted amount of time.[12] It is very likely he was responsible both for the numbering up to fol. 120r and for placing the individual arabic numerals amply distributed after

[9]. See Morpurgo et al. 1887-1962, p. 54, Jeppesen 1935, p. lxiii, and CC I, p. 232.

[10]. See Jeppesen 1969, p. 38.

[11]. A change relevant to the copying of the poetic and musical text appears to have happened between 1375 and 1475: from the last quarter of the fifteenth century, the scribe of the poetic text and the musical notator were fused in a single professional (see the discussion in Bent 1969, Earp 1983, Bent 1984, and King 1999). Earp states further that shortly before 1450 «copyists on the continent finally gave up even the pretence of trying to show the correlation of word and music, and began to copy manuscripts music first, a much easier working method. The music symbols are placed equidistantly, and the text later underlaid below» (Earp 1991, p. 197). In Panc.27, however, some situations make one think of the newer method of working, whereas others are closer to the older practice. On fol. 53v, for example, the *residuum* of the poetic text is written with darker ink, whereas that of the text under the notes is the same as that used for the music: this demonstrates that, effectively, words and notes above them were written at the same time. The same situation seems true also on fols. 77v-78r. But it is also true that, at least in two cases (133v-134r and 135v-136r), the differences in the consistency of the ink show that the copying of the poetic text happened later than that of the musical notation. Probably, therefore, both methodologies of working were used in parallel, at least by Scribe A.

[12]. Only the analysis of the inks helps clarify this important palaeographical aspect. From what I have personally been able to observe in the manuscript, however, it appears that the more faded and the bolder colours cannot be considered useful in postulating periods of scribal inactivity between one stage and another. The lightest inks and the darkest inks are found together from the beginning to the end of Panc.27; thus I believe that the preparation of the volume happened in a concentrated period of time.

the barlines (final or sectional) of 60 compositions up to fol. 143*r*.[13] the hand seems to be the same, as demonstrated both by the colour of the inks in the various annotations and a comparison with the form of the numeral '3' placed next to the mensuration sign of several pieces (see FIG. 4).[14]

FIG. 4: Fol. 1*v* (detail). Example of the *ductus* of Scribe A: the forms of the notes are all rather angular and the general disposition of the text and music is fairly regular. The illustration shows an interesting detail: in addition to appearing at the end of the voices, the numeral '3' indicates the triplets in the middle of the second and the fifth staves, thus confirming the responsibility of the same hand for both annotations. Photo Mario Setter – GAP.

---

[13]. Jeppesen called attention to the presence of these numbers in the manuscript: they indicate the sum of the values of the *semibreves* in each piece to which they refer, with the exception of the final *longae*, and have been inserted at the end in order to exercise some 'control' over the rhythmic values copied from the model in question (JEPPESEN 1969, p. 38). Personally, I find this perplexing, principally because the numbers in question occur only after a limited number of pieces, whereas the scribe remains the same, even for the other pieces with similar characteristics and provided with concordant sources. In my opinion, the numbers have a different function: perhaps to prepare *contrafacta* or intabulations on the basis of the pieces in the codex. The ink, moreover, clearly shows that all these numbers were added later with respect to the musical notation of each piece in question: there is too great a difference in the intensity of the colour between the end of the piece and the number added immediately after it. On this argument see FILOCAMO 2004, whose content has been brought up to date and condensed in this book in section I.4.b.

[14]. My thanks to Bonnie Blackburn, both for having aroused my curiosity and spurred me to look further into this truly interesting aspect of the manuscript, and for having suggested this second and efficacious analytical method.

Scribe B is uniquely responsible for the section 207v–209r (pieces nos. 179 and 180). He was certainly was not a professional copyist: his *ductus* is mercantile and more recent in contrast to A's. The music and the poetic text are presented in a confused and disordered manner in these four pages, with a noticeably less pleasing visual appearance, more difficult to decipher with respect to the rest of the manuscript (see FIG. 5).

FIG. 5: Fol. 207v (detail). Example of the *ductus* of Scribe B. Photo Mario Setter – GAP.

Moreover, the particular position of the pages chosen, in the final section of the manuscript and after several fascicles with blank staves, is telling: Scribe B has copied two compositions present in the first musical print published by Andrea Antico.[15] In addition, the second piece sets a Petrarchan canzone, the only poetic text of the Florentine crown set to music in Panc.27. Many scholars have pointed to the fact that the change in repertory from the fixed poetic forms to the canzone was a function of the new desire for musical variety and a greater significance of the poetic text[16] united with the desire to hear music with more elevated verse of greater artistic value,[17] but all agree in considering the new manner a novelty of the beginning of the Cinquecento.[18] Together, many factors, therefore, suggest that the intervention of Scribe B is later in time than the work of A.

On the possibility that there was a third scribe (A') I am not at all convinced.[19] The principal element that distinguishes him from A would consist in the presence of more rounded forms of the lozenges and in a more careless writing of the text, but after a careful analysis of the whole manuscript I lean more towards the opinion that the copyist was the same. I cannot prove this conclusively, of course, but the fact that often the more rounded traits appear for a few notes at the beginning, at the end, or in the middle of a piece is not sufficient to convince me of the presence of a third person at work with pen and ink. I think it is more realistic to posit that the same Scribe A sometimes interrupted his work, returning to it in a different mood, with more or less haste, or with greater or lesser tiredness: sometimes is it really difficult, in fact, to determine with precision whether a specific trait of writing belongs to Scribe A or rather to the presumed A', given that the passage from one to another *ductus* is rather gradual (see FIG. 6).[20] (For example, slightly after the middle of the fourth stave there is an angular *b semibrevis*. This is preceded and followed by round note shapes: it is impossible to think that

---

[15]. *Canzoni nove con alcune scelte de varii libri di canto*, Rome, 9 October 1510 (AntCanzoni).

[16]. PIRROTTA 1994, pp. 246-247.

[17]. EINSTEIN 1951, p. 334.

[18]. PRIZER 1991, p. 15. Bartolomeo Tromboncino inaugurated the new trend, setting to music Petrarch's *Sì è debile il filo a cui s'attene*, contained in the seventh book of Frottole published by Petrucci (Venice, 6 June 1507).

[19]. Jeppesen hypothesizes that a colleague contemporaneous with Scribe A contributed to the compilation of Panc.27 (JEPPESEN 1969, p. 38).

[20]. Further examples of the mixture of writing traits can be found on fol. 24v (sixth stave) as well as fol. 89v (fourth stave).

there would be a change of scribe for a single note. Cf. also the *e* four notes later. None of these notes appears to have been corrected.)

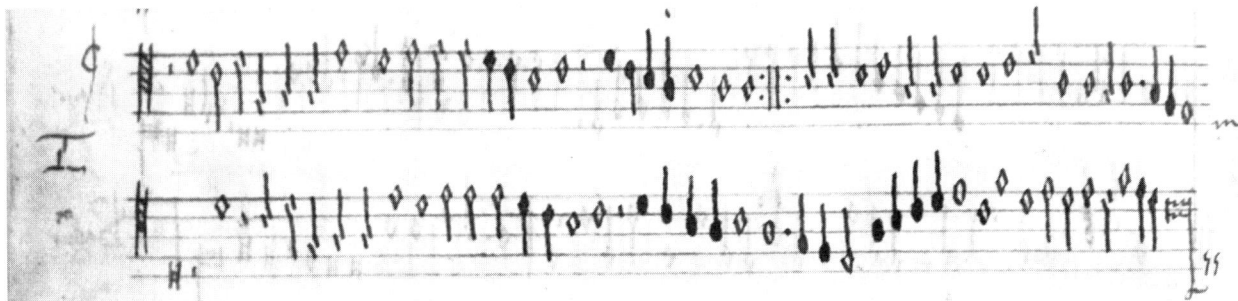

FIG. 6: Fol. 112*v* (detail). The figure illustrates how in the third and fourth staves there are present at the same time two types of *ductus*, differentiated especially in the forms of the heads of the *semiminimae*. Photo Mario Setter - GAP.

The poetic text underneath the notes likewise often reveals traits that associate the two presumed Scribes A and A' if, as seems plausible, the musical and the textual scribe can be conjoined in a single professional.[21]

Occasionally the inscriptions *Vidi* and *Iustus* appear in the manuscript, written with fine penstrokes in the outer margin — lower or side — of some folios of the manuscript.[22] Although these rubrics were certainly added by the scribe who wrote the texts of the codex, the criterion for their appeareance is not clear, nor what significance should be attributed to them.

In the Panc.27 codex the disposition of the music is in choirbook format, and the voices are placed principally according to the rule that the Superius and Tenor appear on the verso of the preceding folio, Altus and Bassus on the recto of the following: in this manner one can see the whole composition on each opening of the volume without the necessity to turn pages. Sometimes this regular disposition is not respected: these are cases in which the piece has evidently been added later, and therefore occupies the residual space, sometimes only one side of the folio.

The music of Panc.27 is written in white mensural notation and shares the writing characteristics of other manuscripts and prints originating between the second half of the fifteenth century and the end of the sixteenth. Occasionally, black notation is used, but only to distinguish notes in plainchant sung before the polyphony or to indicate alternative readings.

The manuscript contains various graphic details that permit one to hypothesize its use in performance: there are often corrections in pitches by means of cancellations,[23] erasures,[24] additions,[25] alternative musical readings (as in FIG. 7),[26] and curved lines that join the syllables to specific notes, clarifying the text underlay (see FIG. 8).[27] Other indications relative to performance can be seen on fol. 210*v*: the compound ligature has, above or below every *brevis*, the numeral '2' referring to the length of the note; on fol. 15*v* a cancellation moves forward «-nisti?» (the final part of «venisti?»); on fol. 68*r* there is an alternative repositioning of words in the Bassus.

---

[21]. One example among many: the calligraphic comparison between the writing *Meskim* on fol. 72*v* — presumed to be that of Scribe A' — and the writing of the following fol. 73*r* — clearly copied by Scribe A — shows an indubitable commonality of traits relative to the text.

[22]. The inscription *Vidi* appears on fols. 10*v*–11*r* and 11*v*-12*r*; fol. 14*r* has the more specific wording *Vidi totum*. The indication *Iustus* is present on fols. 7*v*-8*r*, 19*r*, 20*r*, 22*r*, 28*r*, 51*v*, and 110*r*.

[23]. For example, on fols. 86*v* and 208*r*.

[24]. As on fols. 46*v*, 63*r*, 75*v*, 85*v*, and 134*r*.

[25]. Fol. 26*r* includes a conspicuous paste-over on the fifth stave that covers a portion of the musical text.

[26]. Other examples on fols. 15*r*, 17*v*-18*r*, 18*v*, 40*v*, 46*v*, and 73*v*-74*r*.

[27]. Further examples on fols. 82*v* (second and third staves), 103*v* (sixth stave), 191*v* (second stave), 192*v* (second and third staves).

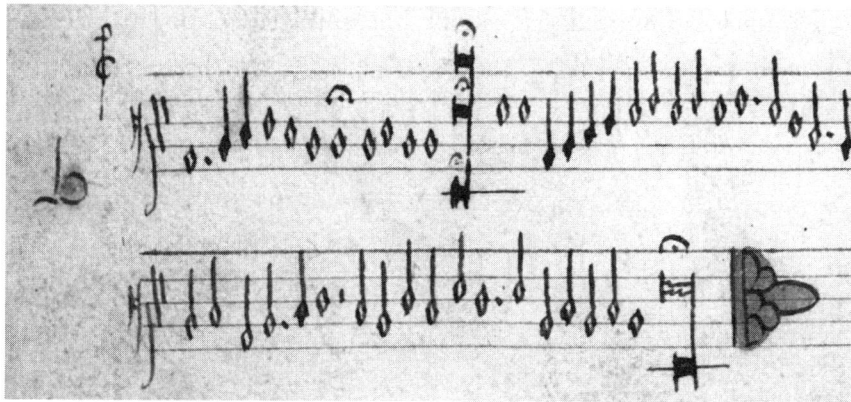

FIG. 7: Fol. 51*v*, fifth and sixth staves (detail). Photo Mario Setter - GAP.

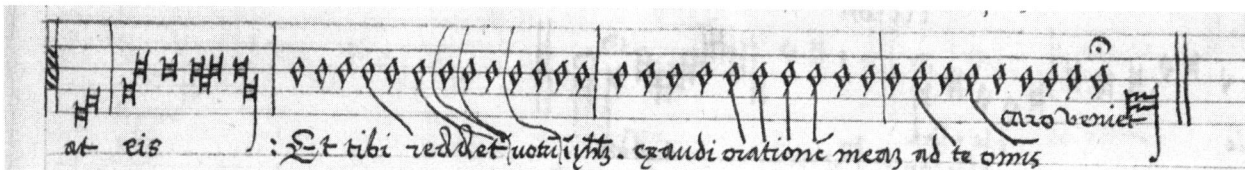

FIG. 8: Fol. 210*r*, second stave. The curved lines clarify the placement of the syllables under the notes. Photo Mario Setter - GAP.

Sometimes words have been cancelled outright from a certain point and repositioned a little ahead (see FIG. 9).[28]

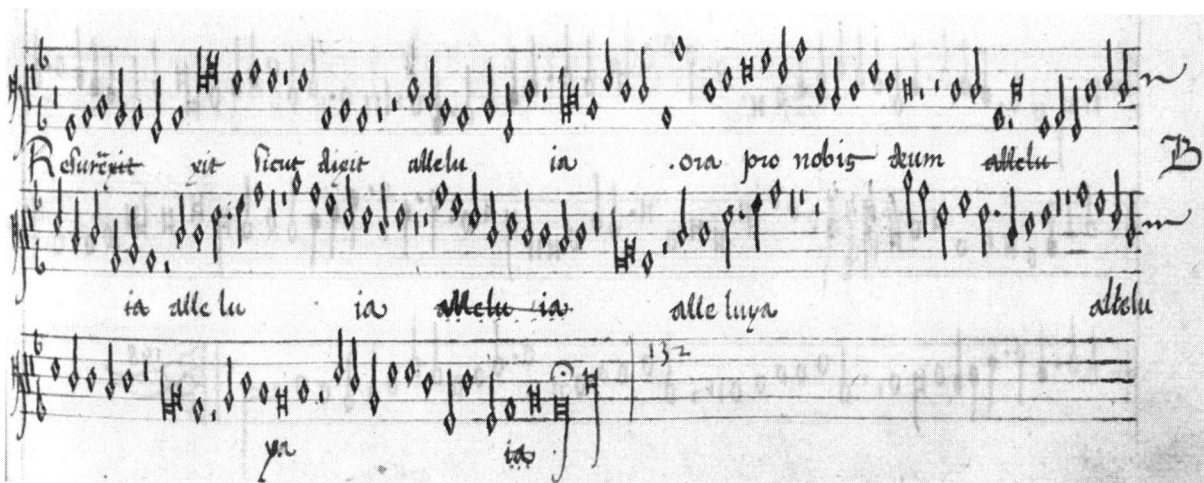

FIG. 9: Fol. 63*r*, last three staves. The invocation *Alleluia* has been cancelled and repositioned directly afterwards twice. Photo Mario Setter - GAP.

The appearance of the rhythmic rules on the last folio of the manuscript (see FIG. 15) should not be undervalued. Dietrich Kämper's hypothesis also fits well with the presence of the characteristics just mentioned: «Some manuscripts around 1500, in which instrumental music plays an important part, reveal their function of teaching manuals and musical exercise in the frequent appendices containing 'regulae de cantu figurato'».[29]

---

[28]. Other examples on fols. 67*v*, 137*r*, 148*v*, and 155*v*.

[29]. KÄMPER 1976, p. 38.

57

Panc.27 is not a richly illuminated manuscript. The only decorations present are a few touches of red, green, and yellow: they consist mostly of modest ornaments placed at the end of closing barlines in the musical voices that appositely mark the conclusions of the compositions.

2. GATHERING STRUCTURE

GATHERING I

fols.

1. *Disperso per lo mundo peregrino* CTB
                                                                                                    1
2. *Ave Maria, gratia plena* ST

    2. *Ave Maria, gratia plena* AB
                                                                                                    2
    3. *Ave Maria, gratia plena* ST

        3. *Ave Maria, gratia plena* AB
                                                                                                    3
        4. *Ave Maria, gratia plena* ST + 5. *Qui seminant in lacrimis* ST

            4. *Ave Maria, gratia plena* AB + 5. *Qui seminant in lacrimis* AB
                                                                                                    4
            6. (= 132) *Ave Maria, gratia plena* ST + 7. *Vidimus enim stellam eius in Oriente* CT

            6. (= 132) *Ave Maria, gratia plena* AB + 7. *Vidimus enim stellam eius in Oriente* AB
                                                                                                    5
            8. *Ave Maria, [gratia plena]* (Prima pars) ST

        8. *Ave Maria, [gratia plena]* (Prima pars) AB

        8. *Ave Maria, [gratia plena]* (Secunda pars) ST
                                                                                                    6
    8. *Ave Maria, [gratia plena]* (Secunda pars) [AB]
                                                                                                    7
    9. *Ave Maria, gratia plena* ST

9. *Ave Maria, gratia plena* AB
                                                                                                    8
10. *O admirabile comertium!* CT

GATHERING II

fols.

10. *O admirabile comertium!* AB
                                                                                                    9
11. *A la bataglia* (Prima pars) ST

    11. *A la bataglia* (Prima pars) AB
                                                                                                    10
    11. *A la bataglia* (Secunda pars) ST

        11. *A la bataglia* (Secunda pars) A[B]
                                                                                                    11
        11. *A la bataglia* (Tertia pars) ST

            11. *A la bataglia* (Tertia pars) A[B]
                                                                                                    12
            12. *Aimè el cor, aimè la testa* ST

            12. *Aimè el cor, aimè la testa* AB
                                                                                                    13
            13. *Ave Regina, Virgo gloriosa / Sofrire son disposto [ogni tormento]* STAB

        14. *Ave victorioso* CTAB
                                                                                                    14
        15. *A Maria, fonte d'amore / Vive lieto [e non temere]* ST

    15. *A Maria, fonte d'amore / Vive lieto [e non temere]* AB
                                                                                                    15
    16. *Amice, ad quid venisti? attende tibi* ST

16. *Amice, ad quid venisti? attende tibi* B
                                                                                                    16
17. *Alma, svegliate oramai* CTA[B] + 18. *Cucù, cucù, ognon canti cucù* B

Gathering III

fols.

19. *Non expectò giamai con tal desio* CTAB + 20. *Qui nos fecit ex nihilo* [T₁T₂] — 17

21. *Benedictus* ST

21. *Benedictus* [A]B — 18

22. *Benedicamus Domino* CTAB + 23. *Benedicamus Domino* CTCt + 24. *Benedicamus Domino* CTAB

25. *Benedicamus Domino* CTB + 26. *Benedicamus Domino* CTB — 19

27. *Poi che sei dal mondo tolta* STAB + 28. *Ave Maria, gratia [plena]* CT

29. *Cum desiderio vo cercando* CTAB — 20

30. *Chi serve a Dio cum purità di cor[e]* CTCt + 31. *Lauda Sion Salvatorem* CTCt

32. *Cantons cantons laisons melenconie* CTCt — 21

33. *Contento in foco sto como fenice* STAB + 34. *Detro mia gioia* [T]

35. *Fortuna, che te giova de straciarme* CTAB — 22

36. *Poi che t'ebi nel core / Fortuna desperata* ST

36. *Poi che t'ebi nel core / Fortuna desperata* AB — 23

37. *Defecerunt vedo ormai* ST + 38. *O mia infelice sorte* CT

37. *Defecerunt vedo ormai* AB + 38. *O mia infelice sorte* AB — 24

39. *Dies ire, dies illa* CTAB

Gathering IV

fols.

40. *De tous biens playne [est ma maistresse]* CTCt — 25

41. *Altera autem die* [Prima pars] CT

41. *Altera autem die* [Prima pars] AB — 26

41. *Altera autem die* (Secunda pars) CTAB

42. *Ogi è 'l tempo, peccatore* CTCt — 27

43. *Arda el ciel e 'l mundo tuto* ST + 44. *Utile consilium* CT

43. *Arda el ciel e 'l mundo tuto* AB + 44. *Utile consilium* AB — 28

45. *Cum autem venissem ad locum* CTCt

46. *Christi corpus ave, de sancta Virgine natum* CT[B] — 29

47. *Dolce Regina* ST + 48. *Gaude Virgo, mater Christi* CT

47. *Dolce Regina* AB + 48. *Gaude Virgo, mater Christi* AB — 30

49. *Deh, fusse qui [chi mi to' el somno! Somno]* CTAB

50. *Deh, non più tante parole* CTAB — 31

51. *Da pacem, Domine* ST

51. *Da pacem, Domine* AB — 32

52. *Deh sì, deh no, deh sì* CTAB

60

GATHERING V

GATHERING VI

GATHERING VII

GATHERING VIII

62

Gathering IX

Gathering X

Gathering XIII

fols.

126. *Propter gravamen [et tormentum] (Secunda pars)* AB
97

127. *Ales regres, [vuidez de ma presence]* ST

   127. *Ales regres, [vuidez de ma presence]* Ct
98

   128. *La alfonsina* ST

     128. *La alfonsina* Ct
99

     129. *Ave stella matutina* S[T]

       129. *Ave stella matutina* AB
100

       130. *Ibo mihi ad montem mirrhe* ST

       130. *Ibo mihi ad montem mirrhe* AB
101

       131. *Mater patris [et filia]* ST

     131. *Mater patris [et filia]* Ct
102

      132. (= 6) *Ave Maria, gratia plena* ST + 133. Letanie. *Sancta Maria, ora pro nobis* CATB

   132. (= 6) *Ave Maria, gratia plena* AB + 134. *Sancta Maria, ora pro nobis* CTB
103

   135. (Libera me, Domine) Duo. *Dies illa, dies ire - Tremens factus sum - Requiem eternam* [B₁B₂]

RULED STAVES WITHOUT MUSIC

136. *Verbum caro factum est* STCt
104

Gathering XIV

fols.

137. *Alleluia* STB
105

138. *Alleluia* ST

  138. *Alleluia* AB
106

  139. *Fortuna d'um gran tempo* ST

    139. *Fortuna d'um gran tempo* Ct
107

    140. *Tenebre facte sunt* CT

      140. *Tenebre facte sunt* AB
108

      141. *Ave sanctissima Maria* CT

      141. *Ave sanctissima Maria* AB
109

      142. (= 86) *Verbum caro factum est* CTCt

    143. *Se per te mia fin serà* CTAB + 144. *Verbum caro factum est* CT

    145. *Se non dormi, donna, ascolta* ST + 146. *Siamo, done, trei romeri* CT
110

    + 147. *Alzando li oghii vidi Maria bella* (text only)

  145. *Se non dormi, donna, ascolta* AB + 146. *Siamo, done, trei romeri* Ct
111

  148. *Signora, anci, mea dea* CTAB + 149. *La virtù se vol seguire* S

150. *Signora, anci, mia dea* [C]TAB + 149. *La virtù se vol seguire* TCt
112

151. *Poca pace e molta guerra* ST + 152. *Se l'ortolana vene a la cità* ST

65

Gathering XV

fols.

151. *Poca pace e molta guerra* AB + 152. *Se l'ortolana vene a la cità* AB

— 113

153. *[…]* ST + 154. *[F]ammi ciò che vòi, crudel signora* CT

153. *[…]* AB + 154. *[F]ammi ciò che vòi, crudel signora* AB

155. *In foco ardente moro como fenice* ST + 156. *Seràno li […] mei tanto cocenti* ST

— 114

+ 157. *Non naque al mondo mai el più scontento* S

155. *In foco ardente moro como fenice* AB + 156. *Seràno li […] mei tanto cocenti* Ct

+ 157. *Non naque al mondo mai el più scontento* TCt

— 115

158. *Poiché vivo sopra la terra* ST

158. *Poiché vivo sopra la terra* Ct + 159. *Giù per la mala via* CTAB

— 116

160. *Caminata* CT

160. *Caminata* AB

— 117

161. (Magnificat) *Et exultavit* CT

161. (Magnificat) *Et exultavit* AB

— 118

162. *Kyrie [eleison]* ST

162. *Kyrie [eleison]* AB

— 119

163. (Magnificat) *Et exultavit* ST

163. (Magnificat) *Et exultavit* AB

— 120

Ruled staves without music

Gathering XVI

fols.

Blank

— 121

Blank

Blank

— 122

Blank

Blank

— 123

Blank

Blank

— 124

Blank

Blank

— 125

Blank

Blank

— 126

Blank

Blank

— 127

Blank

— 128

Blank

66

Gathering XVII

fols.

Ruled staves without music

Ruled staves without music
— 129

Ruled staves without music

164. *Felix namque* (Prima pars) ST
— 130

164. *Felix namque* (Prima pars) AB

164. *Felix namque* (Secunda pars) ST
— 131

164. *Felix namque* (Secunda pars) AB + B «alio modo notatum»

165. *Lucis Creator optime* ST
— 132

165. *Lucis Creator optime* B

166. *Magni[fic]at anima mea Dominum* [ST]
— 133

166. *Magni[fic]at anima mea Dominum* [B]

166. *Magni[fic]at anima mea Dominum* ST
— 134

166. *Magni[fic]at anima mea Dominum* [B]

167. (Magnificat) *Anima mea Dominum* STB
— 135

167. (Magnificat) *Anima mea Dominum* AB

167. (Magnificat) *Anima mea Dominum* ST
— 136

Gathering XVIII

fols.

167. (Magnificat) *Anima mea Dominum* A[B]

167. (Magnificat) *Anima mea Dominum* ST
— 137

167. (Magnificat) *Anima mea Dominum* AB

168. *Helas, [que devera mon cueur]* CT
— 138

168. *Helas, [que devera mon cueur]* [Ct]

169. *Non desina* CT
— 139

169. *Non desina* AB

170. *Turis* CT
— 140

170. *Turis* B

171. *Bianca più che neve sei chiamata* ST
— 141

171. *Bianca più che neve sei chiamata* B

172. *Sine fraude* CT
— 142

172. *Sine fraude* B

173. *Ave Maria, gratia plena* [ST]
— 143

173. *Ave Maria, gratia plena* [AB]

174. *Incipit lamentatio Ieremie prophete* CT
— 144

67

Gathering XIX

174. *Incipit lamentatio Ieremie prophete* AB
145
RULED STAVES WITHOUT MUSIC
   RULED STAVES WITHOUT MUSIC
146
   175. *Ave Maria, gratia plena* [ST]
      175. *Ave Maria, gratia plena* AB
147
     176. *Incipit oratio Ieremie prophete* CT
       176. *Incipit oratio Ieremie prophete* AB
148
        176. *Incipit oratio Ieremie prophete* [CT]

        176. *Incipit oratio Ieremie prophete* [AB]
149
      177. *Rex autem David* CT
    177. *Rex autem David* AB
150
     178. *Incipit lamentatio Ieremie prophete* [ST]
   178. *Incipit lamentatio Ieremie prophete* [AB]
151
   178. *Incipit lamentatio Ieremie prophete* ST
178. *Incipit lamentatio Ieremie prophete* AB
152
178. *Incipit lamentatio Ieremie prophete* ST

Gathering XX

178. *Incipit lamentatio Ieremie prophete* AB
153
178. *Incipit lamentatio Ieremie prophete* [ST]
   178. *Incipit lamentatio Ieremie prophete* [AB]
154
   178. *Incipit lamentatio Ieremie prophete* ST
     178. *Incipit lamentatio Ieremie prophete* AB
155
    178. *Incipit lamentatio Ieremie prophete* [ST]
      178. *Incipit lamentatio Ieremie prophete* [AB]
156
       RULED STAVES WITHOUT MUSIC

       RULED STAVES WITHOUT MUSIC
157
      RULED STAVES WITHOUT MUSIC
    RULED STAVES WITHOUT MUSIC
158
     RULED STAVES WITHOUT MUSIC
   RULED STAVES WITHOUT MUSIC
159
   RULED STAVES WITHOUT MUSIC
RULED STAVES WITHOUT MUSIC
160
RULED STAVES WITHOUT MUSIC

68

Gathering XXI

Ruled staves without music

Ruled staves without music

    Ruled staves without music

    Ruled staves without music

        Ruled staves without music

        Ruled staves without music

            Ruled staves without music

            Ruled staves without music

            Ruled staves without music

            Ruled staves without music

        Ruled staves without music

        Ruled staves without music

    Ruled staves without music

    Ruled staves without music

Ruled staves without music

Ruled staves without music

161
162
163
164
165
166
167
168

Gathering XXII

Ruled staves without music

Ruled staves without music

    Ruled staves without music

    Ruled staves without music

        Ruled staves without music

        Ruled staves without music

            Ruled staves without music

            Ruled staves without music

            Ruled staves without music

            Ruled staves without music

        Ruled staves without music

        Ruled staves without music

    Ruled staves without music

    Ruled staves without music

Ruled staves without music

Ruled staves without music

169
170
171
172
173
174
175
176

69

Gathering XXIII

Ruled staves without music

Ruled staves without music
— 177

Ruled staves without music

Ruled staves without music
— 178

Ruled staves without music

Ruled staves without music
— 179

Ruled staves without music

Ruled staves without music
— 180

Ruled staves without music

Ruled staves without music
— 181

Ruled staves without music

Ruled staves without music
— 182

Ruled staves without music

Ruled staves without music
— 183

Ruled staves without music

Ruled staves without music
— 184

Gathering XXIV

Ruled staves without music

Ruled staves without music
— 185

Ruled staves without music

Ruled staves without music
— 186

Ruled staves without music

Ruled staves without music
— 187

Ruled staves without music

Ruled staves without music
— 188

Ruled staves without music

Ruled staves without music
— 189

Ruled staves without music

Ruled staves without music
— 190

Ruled staves without music

Ruled staves without music
— 191

Ruled staves without music

Ruled staves without music
— 192

Gathering XXV

Ruled staves without music

Ruled staves without music — 193

Ruled staves without music

Ruled staves without music — 194

Ruled staves without music

Ruled staves without music — 195

Ruled staves without music

Ruled staves without music — 196

Ruled staves without music

Ruled staves without music — 197

Ruled staves without music

Ruled staves without music — 198

Ruled staves without music

Ruled staves without music — 199

Ruled staves without music

Ruled staves without music — 200

Ruled staves without music

Gathering XXVI

fols.

Ruled staves without music

Ruled staves without music — 201

Ruled staves without music

Ruled staves without music — 202

Ruled staves without music

Ruled staves without music — 203

Ruled staves without music

Ruled staves without music — 204

Ruled staves without music

Ruled staves without music — 205

Ruled staves without music

Ruled staves without music — 206

Ruled staves without music

Ruled staves without music — 207

179. *Tuto el mundo è fantasia* ST

179. *Tuto el mundo è fantasia* A[B] — 208

180. *Di pensier in pensier, di monte in monte* ST

fols.

180. *Di pensier in pensier, di monte in monte* AB

181. *Requiem eternam dona eis, Domine* CT

209

    181. *Requiem eternam dona eis, Domine* AB

182. *Kyrie eleison* CT + 183. *Amen* [?] + 184. (Libera me, Domine) *Tremens factus sum ego - Dies illa, dies ire* 210
- *Requiem eternam* [B₁] + 185. *Dies ire, dies illa* [B₁]

    182. *Kyrie eleison* AB + 183. *Amen* TAB + 184. (Libera me, Domine) *Tremens factus sum ego –
Dies illa, dies ire – Requiem eternam* [B₂] + 185. *Dies ire, dies illa* [B₂]

211

185. *Dies ire, dies illa - [Tuba mirum]* [B₁]

    185. *Dies ire, dies illa - [Tuba mirum]* [B₂]

212

186. *Dies ire, dies illa* CT

186. *Dies ire, dies illa* AB

213

Ruled staves without music

214

Ruled staves without music

Ruled staves without music

215

Ruled staves without music

Ruled staves without music

Ruled staves without music

216

[Rules of mensural notation]

72

3. LIST OF COMPOSITIONS

	Incipit	Fols.	vv.	Author of the text	Composer	Presence of numbers
1.	*Disperso per lo mundo peregrino*	1r	3			
2.	*Ave Maria, gratia plena*	1v–2r	4		Lorenzo Bergomozzi	×
3.	*Ave Maria, gratia plena*	2v–3r	4		Giacomo Fogliano	×
4.	*Ave Maria, gratia plena*	3v–4r	4		Marchetto Cara / [Bartolomeo Tromboncino]	×
5.	*Qui seminant in lacrimis*	3v–4r	4			×
6.	*Ave Maria, gratia plena* (= 132)	4v–5r	4			
7.	*Vidimus enim stellam eius in Oriente*	4v–5r	4			×
8.	*Ave Maria, [gratia plena]*	5v–7r	4		Musipula	×
9.	*Ave Maria, gratia plena*	7v–8r	4		Bartolomeo Tromboncino	
10.	*O admirabile comertium!*	8v–9r	4			×
11.	*A la bataglia*	9v–12r	4	[Gentile Aretino (Becchi?)]	Henricus Isaac	×
12.	*Aimè el cor, aimè la testa*	12v–13r	4		[Marchetto Cara]	
13.	*Ave Regina, Virgo gloriosa / Sofrire son disposto [ogni tormento]*	13v	4	[Enselmino da Montebelluna]		
14.	*Ave victorioso*	14r	4			
15.	*A Maria, fonte d'amore / Vive lieto [e non temere]*	14v–15r	4	[Francesco degli Albizzi]		
16.	*Amice, ad quid venisti? attende tibi*	15v–16r	3		Alexander Agricola	×
17.	*Alma, svegliate oramai*	16v	4		[Giovanni Brocco]	
18.	*Cucù, cucù, ognon canti cucù*	16v	[3]		Pamphilus	
19.	*Non expectò giamai con tal desio*	17r	4	[Antonio Tebaldi]		
20.	*Qui nos fecit ex nihilo*	17r	2			
21.	*Benedictus*	17v–18r	4		Henricus Isaac	×
22.	*Benedicamus Domino*	18v	4			
23.	*Benedicamus Domino*	18v	3			
24.	*Benedicamus Domino*	18v	4			
25.	*Benedicamus Domino*	19r	3			
26.	*Benedicamus Domino*	19r	3			
27.	*Poi che sei dal mondo tolta*	19v	4	[Leonardo Giustinian]	Ben	
28.	*Ave Maria, gratia [plena]*	19v	2			
29.	*Cum desiderio vo cercando*	20r	4	[Bianco da Siena]		
30.	*Chi serve a Dio cum purità di cor[e]*	20v	3	[Feo Belcari]		
31.	*Lauda Sion Salvatorem*	20v	3			
32.	*Cantons cantons laisons melenconie*	21r	3		Jo[hannes?] Vilet	
33.	*Contento in foco sto como fenice*	21v	4	[Angelo Poliziano]		
34.	*Detro mia gioia*	21v	[3]			
35.	*Fortuna, che te giova de straciarme*	22r	4			
36.	*Poi che t'ebi nel core / Fortuna desperata*	22v–23r	4	[Francesco degli Albizzi]		×
37.	*Defecerunt vedo ormai*	23v–24r	4		[Marchetto Cara]	
38.	*O mia infelice sorte*	23v–24r	4			
39.	*Dies ire, dies illa*	24v	4			
40.	*De tous biens playne [est ma maistresse]*	25r	3			×
41.	*Altera autem die*	25v–26v	4			
42.	*Ogi è 'l tempo, peccatore*	27r	3			
43.	*Arda el ciel e 'l mundo tuto*	27v–28r	4			
44.	*Utile consilium*	27v–28r	4			
45.	*Cum autem venissem ad locum*	28v	3		[Johannes de Quadris]	
46.	*Christi corpus ave, de sancta Virgine natum*	29r	3	[St. Anselm of Aosta?]		
47.	*Dolce Regina*	29v–30r	4			
48.	*Gaude Virgo, mater Christi*	29v–30r	4			
49.	*Deh, fusse qui [chi mi to' el somno! Somno]*	30v	4	[Serafino Aquilano]		

	Incipit	Fols.	vv.	Author of the text	Composer	Presence of numbers
50.	*Deh, non più tante parole*	31r	4			
51.	*Da pacem, Domine*	31v–32r	4			
52.	*Deh sì, deh no, deh sì*	32v	4		[Marchetto Cara / Bartolomeo Tromboncino]	×
53.	*La nocte aquieta ogni fiero animale*	33r	4			
54.	*La mora*	33v–34r	3		[Henricus Isaac]	×
55.	*La stangetta*	34v–35r	3		[Henricus Isaac / Jacob Obrecht / Gaspar van Weerbeke]	×
56.	*Helas, [que poura devenir]*	35v–36r	4		Firminus Caron	×
57.	*Hor oires una canzon*	36v–37r	5		[Johannes de Stokem]	
58.	*[…]*	37v–38r	3			×
59.	*Ne doibt [on prendre quant on donne]*	38v–39r	3	[Jean II, duc de Bourbon]	Loyset Compère	
60.	*Mater digna Dei*	39v–40r	4		[Gaspar van Weerbeke]	×
61.	*Io son de gabbia, non de bosco ocello / Iste confesor Domini*	40v	4		[Michele Pesenti]	
62.	*L'ucelo me chiama [che perdo giornata]*	40v–41r	3	[Francesco Galeota]		
63.	*Io son l'ucello che sopra i rami d'oro*	41r	4		[Marchetto Cara]	
64.	*Canti zoiosi e dolce melodia / Jo hay pris amor [à ma devise]*	41v	3			×
65.	*Io mi voglio lamentare*	42r	4		[Giovanni Brocco]	
66.	*In te, domine, speravi*	42v–43r	4		Josquin des Prez	×
67.	*Egli è il tuo bon Iesù*	42v–43r	4	[Feo Belcari]	Frater Dionisius Placentinus	
68.	*A la caza / Iamo a la caza*	43v–45r	4			
69.	*Iesù, Iesù, Iesù*	45v–46r	4	[Feo Belcari]		
70.	*Alto Iesù, figl[i]olo de Maria*	45v–46r	3			
71.	*Ave maris stella*	46v	3			
72.	*Aures ad nostras [deitatis preces]*	47r	3			
73.	*Helas, [le bon temps que j'avoie]*	47v–48r	3		Johannes Tinctoris / [Loyset Compère]	
74.	*Miserere [mei, Deus]*	48v–49r	4			
75.	*Les bien amore / Omnis labor habet finem*	49v–50r	3	[Jean d'Auton]	Henricus Isaac	×
76.	*O Iesù dolce, o infinito amore*	50v	3	[Leonardo Giustinian]		
77.	*O misero stato*	51r	4			
78.	*Oimè, che moro [per ti, dona crudele]*	51v	4		Marchetto Cara	
79.	*O gloriosa Domina*	52r	3			
80.	*Guarda le vestimente*	52r	3			
81.	*Omnis laus in fine canitur*	52v–53r	4		[Henricus Isaac]	×
82.	*O madre di Iesù, o dea eterna*	52v–53r	4			
83.	*O gloriosa Regina mundi*	53v–54r	3		[Johannes Touront]	×
84.	*La speranza me tien vivo*	54v–55r	4			×
85.	*Se conviene a un cor vilano*	55v–56r	4		[Eneas]	
86.	*Verbum caro factum est (= 142)*	56v	3			
87.	*Mille prove [ho già facto per levarmi]*	56v	3			
88.	*Memento mei*	57r	3			
89.	*Si dedero [somnum oculis meis]*	57v–58r	3		Alexander Agricola	×
90.	*Surge, propera, amica mea*	58v–59r	4		Johannes de Pinarol	×
91.	*O pulcherrima mulierum*	59v–60r	4		Gaspar van Weerbeke	×
92.	*Si dedero [el mio core al dio d'amore]*	60v–61r	4		[Giacomo Fogliano]	
93.	*Se ben or [non] scopri el fuoco*	60v–61r	4		[Bartolomeo Tromboncino]	
94.	*Regina celi letare*	61v–63r	4		Antoine Brumel	×
95.	*O quam glorifica [luce coruscas]*	63v–64r	3		Alexander Agricola	×
96.	*Helas, que il est à mon gré*	64v–65r	4		Johannes Japart	
97.	*Helas, [ce n'est pas sans rayson]*	65v–66r	4		Johannes de Stokem	
98.	*Virgo Maria, non est tibi similis nata*	66v–67r	4		Gaspar van Weerbeke	×
99.	*Christi mater, ave*	67v–68r	4		Gaspar van Weerbeke	×
100.	*Trista è la sorte di chi serve al vento*	68v–69r	4			

	Incipit	Fols.	vv.	Author of the text	Composer	Presence of numbers
101.	*Piange Pisa*	68v–69r	4		Bar[tholomeus?] Pisanus	
102.	*Stella celi extirpavit*	69v–70r	4			×
103.	*Adonai, [sanctissime Domine]*	70v–71r	4		Gaspar van Weerbeke	×
104.	*Tristitia vestra convertetur in gaudium*	71v–72r	4		Renaldo	×
105.	*Meskim [es u cutkin ru?]*	72v	3		[Jacob Obrecht]	×
106.	*Quemadmodum desiderat cervus*	73r	3			×
107.	*Veni Creator Spiri[tus]*	73v–74r	3			
108.	*Kyrie eleison*	74v–75r	3			
109.	*Lucis Creator optime*	75v–76r	3			×
110.	*[…]*	76v	4			
111.	*Regina celi [letare]*	77r	3		Loyset Compère	×
112.	*Miserere al mio perire*	77v–78r	4			
112bis.	*Son su passo de la morte* (text only)	78r	–			
113.	*Sconsolata phylomena*	78v	4			
114.	*Cum desiderio vo cercando*	79r	3	[Bianco da Siena]		
115.	*Tu solus qui facis mirabilia*	79v–80r	4		Josquin des Prez	
116.	*'Patientia' [ognun me dice]*	80v–81r	4			×
117.	*Verbum caro, panem verum*	81v–82r	4			
118.	*Incipit oratio Ieremie prophete*	82v–84r	3			
119.	*(Credo) Patrem omnipotentem*	84v–86r	2			
120.	*O Domine Iesu Christe*	86v–87r	4		[Antoine Brumel]	
121.	*O Domine Iesu Christe*	87v–88r	4	[Pope Gregory I 'the Great'?]	[Antoine Brumel?]	×
122.	3i toni. *Nunc dimittis servum tuum*	88v	3			
123.	*Magnificat anima mea Dominum*	89v–91r	4			
124.	*La Spagna*	91v–94r	4		Johannes Ghiselin	×
125.	*Regina celi [letare]*	94v–95r	3		Antonio Peragulfo	×
126.	*Propter gravamen [et tormentum]*	95v–97r	4		Loyset Compère	×
127.	*Ales regres, [vuidez de ma presence]*	97v–98r	3	[Jean II, duc de Bourbon]	Hayne van Ghizeghem	×
128.	*La alfonsina*	98v–99r	3		Johannes Ghiselin	×
129.	*Ave stella matutina*	99v–100r	4		Gaspar van Weerbeke	×
130.	*Ibo mihi ad montem mirrhe*	100v–101r	4		[Gaspar van Weerbeke]	×
131.	*Mater patris [et filia]*	101v–102r	3		Antoine Brumel	×
132.	*Ave Maria, gratia plena* (= 6)	102v–103r	4			
133.	Letanie. *Sancta Maria, ora pro nobis*	102v	4			
134.	*Sancta Maria, ora pro nobis*	103r	3			
135.	*(Libera me, Domine)* Duo. *Dies illa, dies ire – Tremens factus sum ego – Requiem eternam*	103v	2			
136.	*Verbum caro factum est*	104v	3			
137.	*Alleluia*	105r	3		Dominicus	×
138.	*Alleluia*	105v–106r	4		[Henricus Isaac]	×
139.	*Fortuna d'um gran tempo*	106v–107r	3		[Josquin des Prez]	×
140.	*Tenebre facte sunt*	107v–108r	4			
141.	*Ave sanctissima Maria*	108v–109r	4	[Pope Sixtus IV?]		
142.	*Verbum caro factum est* (= 86)	109v	3			
143.	*Se per te mia fin serà*	110r	4			
144.	*Verbum caro factum est*	110r	2			
145.	*Se non dormi, donna, ascolta*	110v–111r	4		[? C. (= Marchetto Cara? / Loyset Compére?)]	
146.	*Siamo, done, trei romeri*	110v–111r	3			
147.	*Alzando li oghii vidi Maria bella* (text only)	110v	–			
148.	*Signora, anci, mea dea*	111v	4		Bartolomeo Tromboncino	
149.	*La virtù se vol seguire*	111v–112r	3			
150.	*Signora, anci, mia dea*	112r	4		[Bartolomeo Tromboncino]	
151.	*Poca pace e molta guerra*	112v–113r	4		[Bartolomeo Tromboncino]	×

	Incipit	Fols.	vv.	Author of the text	Composer	Presence of numbers
152.	*Se l'ortolana vene a la città*	*112v–113r*	4			×
153.	*[…]*	*113v–114r*	4			
154.	*[F]ammi ciò che vòi, crudel signora*	*113v–114r*	4			
155.	*In foco ardente moro como fenice*	*114v–115r*	4			
156.	*Seràno li […] mei tanto cocenti*	*114v–115r*	3			
157.	*Non naque al mondo mai el più scontento*	*114v–115r*	3			
158.	*Poiché vivo sopra la terra*	*115v–116r*	3			×
159.	*Giù per la mala via*	*116r*	4	[Feo Belcari]		
160.	*Caminata*	*116v–117r*	4			
161.	(Magnificat) *Et exultavit*	*117v–118r*	4			
162.	*Kyrie [eleison]*	*118v–119r*	4			
163.	(Magnificat) *Et exultavit*	*119v–120r*	4			
164.	*Felix namque*	*130v–132r*	4			×
165.	*Lucis Creator optime*	*132v–133r*	3			×
166.	*Magni[fic]at anima mea Dominum*	*133v–135r*	3			×
167.	(Magnificat) *Anima mea Dominum*	*135v–138r*	4			×
168.	*Helas, [que devera mon cueur]*	*138v–139r*	3		Henricus Isaac	×
169.	*Non desina*	*139v–140r*	4			
170.	*Turis*	*140v–141r*	3			
171.	*Bianca più che neve sei chiamata*	*141v–142r*	3			
172.	*Sine fraude*	*142v–143r*	3			×
173.	*Ave Maria, gratia plena*	*143v–144r*	4			
174.	*Incipit lamentatio Ieremie prophete*	*144v–145r*	4		[Erasmus (Lapicida?)]	
175.	*Ave Maria, gratia plena*	*146v–147r*	4		[Bartolomeo Tromboncino]	
176.	*Incipit oratio Ieremie prophete*	*147v–149r*	4			
177.	*Rex autem David*	*149v–150r*	4		[Adrian Willaert?]	
178.	*Incipit lamentatio Ieremie prophete*	*150v–156r*	4			
179.	*Tuto el mundo è fantasia*	*207v–208r*	4		[Jo(hannes?) Hesdimois]	
180.	*Di pensier in pensier, di monte in monte*	*208v–209r*	4	[Francesco Petrarca]		
181.	*Requiem eternam dona eis, Domine*	*209v–210r*	4			
182.	*Kyrie eleison*	*210v–211r*	4			
183.	*Amen*	*210v–211r*	2?			
184.	(Libera me, Domine) *Tremens factus sum ego - Dies illa, dies ire - Requiem eternam*	*210v–211r*	2			
185.	*Dies ire, dies illa*	*210v–211r*	2			
186.	*Dies ire, dies illa*	*212v–213r*	4			

4. The Contents

(A) The Repertory

PANC.27 IS A MISCELLANEOUS MANUSCRIPT comprising 185 polyphonic pieces[30] plus two without music: *Alzando gli oghii vidi Maria bella*[31] and *Son su passo de la morte*.[32] Two compositions are present twice in the manuscript (although with slight differences),[33] and the three parts of the *Libera me* of the Requiem Mass placed on fol. 103*v* (no. 135) are found again in the regular sequence on fols. 201*v*-211*r* (no. 184), but with the voices inverted[34] (which in fact produces no different effect, since the parts are written in the same clef, and thus the piece can tranquilly be considered a duplicate).

The musical repertory in the manuscript dates approximately from the end of the fifteenth to the beginning of the sixteenth century, and includes various types of liturgical, devotional, and secular compositions for two voices (7 pieces), three voices (63 pieces), four voices (113 pieces), and five voices (one piece only, no. 57); for one piece (no. 183) the arrangement remains uncertain.[35] The poetic texts of the polyphonic compositions are in Italian, Latin, French, and in one case Flemish; some exhibit bilingualism (Italian/French, Italian/Latin). In only three cases (nos. 58, 110, and 153) does the manuscript have music without text or any kind of heading, although inferences have been drawn about their genres.[36]

The following listing, divided into groups organized in decreasing numerical order, summarizes schematically the types of repertory in Panc.27 and offers a better overview of the contents than a commentary (the abbreviations in parentheses are to be resolved as follows: U = textual and musical *unicum*; MU = musical *unicum*; TU = textual *unicum*):

- LITURGICAL AND PARALITURGICAL LATIN COMPOSITIONS:
  - mass sections: nos. 5 (MU, anon.), 20?, 21, 22? (MU, anon.), 23? (MU, anon.), 24? (MU, anon.), 25? (MU, anon.), 26?, 108 (MU, anon.), 119 (MU, anon.), 135/184 (MU, anon.), 137? (MU, Dominicus), 138, 162 (MU, anon.), 181 (MU, anon.), 182 (MU, anon.);
  - *Ave Maria*: nos. 2 (MU, Laurentius Bergomotius Mutinensis), 3, 4, 6/132 (MU, anon.), 8 (MU, Musipula), 9, 28 (MU, anon.), 173, 175;
  - antiphons: nos. 10 (MU, anon.), 51, 98, 102, 130?, 131, 164? (MU, anon.);
  - hymns: nos. 71 (MU, anon.), 72 (MU, anon.), 79, 107 (MU, anon.), 109 (MU, anon.), 117 (MU, anon.), 165 (MU, anon.);
  - *Magnificat*: nos. 123 (MU, anon.), 161 (MU, anon.), 163 (MU, anon.), 166, 167 (MU, anon.);
  - Lamentations: nos. 118 (MU, anon.), 174, 176 (MU, anon.), 178 (MU, anon.);
  - sequences: nos. 39 (MU, anon.), 183 (*Amen*, MU, anon.), 185 (MU, anon.), 186 (MU, anon.);
  - *Regina celi*: nos. 94, 111, 125 (MU, Antonius Peragulfus Lucensis);

---

[30]. BECHERINI 1959a, pp. 118-122, gives 179; JEPPESEN 1969, p. 38, says 187, as does CC I, p. 232; RISM B IV/5, pp. 140-150, counts 189 pieces.

[31]. *Alzando gli oghii vidi Maria bella*, fol. 110*v* (no. 147), cannot be a *contrafactum* of the preceding composition; graphically it appears to suggest instead the *residuum*. I thank Claudio Vela for having suggested the possibility, subsequently confirmed, that this text has no relationship with the preceding one. It is in fact a text frequently found in manuscript literary sources, and is well known also in relation to the copious literature on *contrafacta*.

[32]. In this case too I thank an Italianist who located the incipit of no. 112bis: Antonio Rossi (see the relevant entry).

[33]. *Ave Maria gratia plena* on fols. 4*v*-5*r* (no. 6) corresponds to the version on fols. 102*v*-103*r* (no. 132), and *Verbum caro factum est* on fol. 56*v* (no. 86) is equivalent to the music and poetry of the piece on fol. 109*v* (no. 142). This fact supports the hypothesis that Panc.27 has — at least in part — been copied from several sources.

[34]. See the entries for nos. 135 and 184.

[35]. See the relative entry.

[36]. See the relevant entries.

- litanies: nos. 133 (MU, anon.), 134 (MU, anon.);
- canticle: no. 122 (MU, anon.);
- *Plantus Mariae*: no. 45;
- other prayers based on the Old and New Testaments: nos. 7 (MU, anon.), 16, 41 (MU, anon.), 74, 86/142 (MU, anon.), 89, 90, 91, 103, 104 (MU, Renaldo), 106 (MU, anon.), 115, 136 (MU, anon.), 140 (MU, anon.), 144 (MU, anon.), 177;
- other prayers: nos. 46, 48, 60, 83, 99, 120, 121 (MU, anon., but perhaps attributable to Brumel),[37] 126, 129, 141 (MU, anon.).

- • COMPOSITIONS WITH ITALIAN SECULAR TEXTS:
  - strambotti: nos. 1 (MU, anon.), 33 (MU in this form, anon.), 35 (MU, anon.), 49? (MU, anon.), 53, 62, 63, 78, 80? (MU, anon.), 87, 92, 100 (MU, anon.), 154 (U, anon.), 155 (MU, anon.), 156 (U, anon.), 157 (U, anon.);
  - barzellette:[38] nos. 12, 37? (or lauda?), 43, 50? (U, anon.), 65? (or oda?), 66, 84, 85, 93, 113, 116, 145, 149, 151, 158?, 179;
  - instrumental pieces with an Italian title: nos. 54, 55, 124, 128, 139, 160;
  - unidentified forms: nos. 68, 101 (U, Bar[tholomeus?] Pisanus), 143 (U, anon.), 152 (U, anon.), 171 (U, anon.);
  - ode: nos. 38, 65? (or barzelletta?), 148 (MU in this form: Bartolomeo Tromboncino is the author of the Superius, whereas the rest is reworked or composed *ex novo*), 150;
  - ballate antiche: nos. 17, 52;
  - canons: nos. 18 (U, anon.), 34 (U, anon.);
  - canzone: no. 180;
  - canti carnascialeschi: nos. 11, 146 (U, anon.);
  - capitolo ternario: no. 19 (MU, anon.);
  - sapphic ode: no. 61 (TU).

- • LAUDE:
  - *contrafacta*: nos. 13, 15, 36 (MU in this form, anon.), 37? (or barzelletta?), 64, 69;
  - other laude: nos. 14? (MU, anon.), 27 (MU, Ben), 29 (MU, anon.), 30 (MU, anon.), 31?, 42 (MU, anon.), 47, 67 (MU, Frater Dionisius Placentinus), 70 (U, anon.), 76, 77? (U, anon.), 82 (U, anon.), 88? (MU, anon.), 112 (MU, anon.), 112bis (text only), 114, 147 (text only), 159 (MU, anon.).

- • SECULAR COMPOSITIONS WITH FRENCH TEXT:
  - chansons: nos. 32? (U, Jo[hannes?] Vilet), 40 (MU in this form, anon.), 56, 59, 73, 75, 96, 97, 127, 168;
  - instrumental piece with a French heading: no. 57?

---

[37]. See the relevant entry.

[38]. On the differentiation between the designations 'frottola' and 'barzelletta' for musical compositions, see PIRROTTA 1994. Paolo Trovato, on the other hand, strenuously insists on the complete inaccuracy of the designation 'frottola', despite Petrucci's use: «As to the specific meaning of *frottola* in the musical sense ('barzelletta', that is ballata with eight-syllable lines), the equivalence between *frottola* and *barzelletta* (or *bargeleta*) is already attested at the end of the Quattrocento [...]. If one takes into account that, of the 653 compositions transmitted by the ten surviving books of Frottole published by Petrucci, 382 are counted as barzellette or, as some prefer to say, frottole, the correctness of the term chosen by Petrucci appears undeniable (it is a question of *frottole* by synecdoche: the most frequent or conspicuous part for the whole, that is for the different poetic forms as a whole). The fact is that the term frottola becomes — because of the known (and completely different) precedent in the fourteenth-century homonymous poetic form and the ambiguity between the specific musical sense ('barzelletta') and the generic one (of the kind included in the Petrucci corpus of 'poesia per musica', or 'vocal polyphonic compositions on secular texts', etc.) — an equivocal term and of little use for us historians» (see TROVATO 2005, p. 259). In this book I accept Trovato's plea, and thus adopt the term 'barzelletta' instead of the usual 'frottola' or the compromise 'frottola/barzelletta'.

- SECULAR COMPOSITIONS WITH LATIN TEXT:
  - instrumental pieces with a Latin heading: nos. 169? (U, anon.), 170? (U, anon.), 172? (U, anon.);
  - proverbs: nos. 44? (U, anon.), 81.

- TEXTLESS: nos. 58, 110 (MU, anon., perhaps instrumental), 153? (MU, anon., perhaps a canto carnascialesco).

- FLEMISH SONG: no. 105.

Even if it is not easy to make a precise count (in view of the many question marks next to some of the pieces), one thing, however, is certain: the pieces that can be labelled as secular, including the textless ones, comprise less than half of the total pieces: 75 (+ one?, that is no. 37, which is perhaps a lauda)[39] out of 187 (here I include in the total count also the two texts without music). Some of these, moreover, have been absorbed as lauda *contrafacta* and have thus changed their 'social' aspect: from secular to devotional.

One can gain a precise idea of the general layout of the contents of Panc.27 by looking at the scheme given in this book (pp. 59-72), which reproduces the gathering structure of the manuscript, folio by folio, also taking into account the following: the appearance of the sixteenth gathering, completely blank, without even ruled staves, is suggestive of the hypothesis that a second manuscript began here, subsequently joined to the first.[40] Some pieces form a bridge between various paper fascicles,[41] but gathering XVI begins in fact without any kind of link with the previous gathering. (I have already said, however, that the idea that Panc.27 resulted from the assembly of two different manuscripts has already been discounted by scholars.) The overall organization of the contents of the book, however, is rather confused: although the initial part clearly demonstrates the intention to organize the musical material alphabetically — at least in the upper area of the openings (the remaining space was in fact utilized to write compositions outside the alphabetical order) — this intention later gave way to a spotty alphabetical ordering, or even a completely casual one.

More specifically: in gatherings I and II the intention to order the pieces alphabetically is clear, but from gathering III onwards the alphabetical disruptions are in fact frequent, though it is still possible to recognize the general idea to keep together some pieces whose incipit is linked by the same letter. To give only some examples (and omitting the alphabetical disjunctions present, which at times clearly are due to filling the remaining space left free after copying the pieces considered in some sense 'principal'), the pieces that begin with 'L' on fols. 33r-35r precede those with 'H' on fols. 35v-37r, and those that begin systematically with 'S' on fols. 55v-61r precede those ordered by 'R' on fols. 61v-63r. In gathering IX, on the other hand, an alphabetical order is not even broadly recognizable, whereas on fols. 74v-78r of the tenth gathering pieces beginning with 'K' are followed by those with 'L' and then with 'M' (although interspersed with a textless piece and a *Regina celi*). After this, sections unified from an alphabetical point of view can be found here and there, such as on fols. 86v-88r (with two pieces having the same incipit: *O Domine Iesu Christe*), on fols. 97v-100r (with various pieces beginning with 'A'), on fols. 105r-106v (with two *Alleluia*), and on fols. 109v-113r (dedicated almost exclusively to the letter 'S',

---

[39]. I include in the total the secular pieces with Italian text, the pieces with French text, the secular pieces with Latin text, the textless pieces, and the Flemish song.

[40]. On fol. 121r in fact begins the foliation in red ink, described in the paragraph on the physical appearance of the manuscript.

[41]. Between gatherings I and II we find *O admirabile comertium!* (no. 10); between V and VI *L'ucelo me chiama [che perdo giornata]* (no. 62); between VI and VII *Miserere [mei, Deus]* (no. 74); between VIII and IX *Helas, que il est a mon gré* (no. 96); between X and XI *'Patientia' [ognun me dice]* (no. 116); between XII and XIII *Propter gravamen [et tormentum]* (no. 126); between XIV and XV *Poca pace e molta guerra* (no. 151) and *Se l'ortolana vene a la città* (no. 152); between XVII and XVIII *[Magnificat] Anima mea Dominum* (no. 167); between XVIII and XIX *Incipit lamentatio Ieremie prophete* (no. 174); between XIX and XX *Incipit lamentatio Ieremie prophete* (no. 178); between XXVI and XXVII *Di pensier in pensier, di monte in monte* (no. 180).

with few exceptions). Following this the alphabetical disorder in the sequence of pieces increases, even if in gathering XV itself there are a few sections that seem to reflect a particular ordering. Gathering XVI orders 'L' and 'M' up to the beginning of gathering XVIII, and from fol. 144v a section dedicated to 'I' begins, but interspersed with pieces with a different incipit. The last fascicle does not observe any alphabetical sequence at all.

From a point of view of repertory, the physical placement of the pieces does not follow any strict logic. If there was a clear intention to begin the manuscript with a sequence of six *Ave Maria*, there then follow secular pieces that all begin with 'A'. Similar situations, which bring together in an offhand manner sacred and secular pieces, and devotional and instrumental works, are absolutely normal in this manuscript. The unique exceptions, comprising at least seven folios, are: fols. 1v–9r (all liturgical), 32v–39r (secular), 81v–91r (liturgical), 99v–106r (liturgical), 117v–138r (liturgical, but with a completely blank fascicle in the middle), 143v–156r (liturgical). There are not lacking, however, other less extensive sections where it seems possible to trace some kind of intention to order the repertory more precisely. For example, the six pieces of the Requiem on fols. 209v–213r (nos. 181-186), the five *Benedicamus Domino* on fols. 18v–19r (nos. 22-26), the four strambotti on fols. 113v–115r (nos. 154-157), the three pieces in the 'bird cycle' on fols. 40v–41r (nos. 61-63), the two instrumental pieces on fols. 33v–35r (nos. 54 and 55), the two hymns on fols. 46v–47r (nos. 71 and 72), the two chansons on fols. 64v–66r (nos. 96 and 97), the two pieces with the same incipit *O Domine Iesu Christe* on fols. 86v–88r (nos. 120 and 121), the two *Alleluia* on fols. 105r–106r (nos. 137 and 138), the two *Magnificat* on fols. 133v–138r (nos. 166 and 167), the two pieces copied from AntCanzoni on fols. 207v–209r (nos. 179 and 180). Other examples could be added, though the continuous sequence is disturbed by intervening pieces (as for the six *Ave Maria* at the beginning, nos. 2, 3, 4, 6, 8, 9, or the three Lamentations nos. 174, 176, and 178, or also the two *Magnificat* nos. 161 and 163).

The overall contents clearly privilege the liturgical destination of the pieces, and this can also be noticed when analysing the space occupied. Homogeneous zones conspicuous from this point of view are, for example, fols. 1v–9r, 73r–76r, 81v–91r, 99v–106r, 117v–138r (which, however, includes the completely blank gathering XVI), 143v–156r, 209v–213r. It is clear that precisely this repertory stands at the centre of the interests of the compiler of the manuscript, a repertory with which it opens[42] and closes. Although of lesser importance quantitatively, we do find analogous homogeneous spaces occupied uninterruptedly by secular repertory: fols. 9v–13r, 32v–39r (with the uncertainty of no. 58 on fols. 37v–38r), 110v–117r (but including laude nos. 147 and 159), 138v–143r.

The compositions with liturgical and paraliturgical Latin texts reflect three principal themes:[43]
1. Marian (38 instances + one duplicated): nos. 2 (MU), 3, 4, 6/132 (MU), 8 (MU), 9, 28 (MU), 45, 48, 60, 71 (MU), 79, 83, 90, 91, 94, 95, 98, 99, 102, 111, 123 (MU), 125 (MU), 126, 129, 130, 131, 133 (MU), 134 (MU), 141 (MU), 161 (MU), 162 (MU), 163 (MU), 164 (MU), 166, 167 (MU), 173, 175;
2. Christological (11 instances + one duplicated): nos. 7 (MU), 10 (MU), 46, 72 (MU), 86/142 (MU), 115, 117 (MU), 120, 121 (MU), 136 (MU), 144 (MU);
3. Liturgy of the Dead (9 instances + one duplicated): nos. 39 (MU), 74, 106 (MU), 135/184 (MU), 181 (MU), 182 (MU), 183 (*Amen*, MU), 185 (MU), 186 (MU).

The subjects treated in the lauda texts can also be subdivided into three principal themes:
1. Marian (7 instances + one uncertain): nos. 13, 15, 47, 64, 82 (U), 88? (MU), 112, 147 (text only);

---

[42]. Although the manuscript begins with a strambotto, this seems an expedient not to waste an unused page. The true intention of the scribe was more probably to begin with the *Ave Maria* of Lorenzo Bergomozzi.

[43]. The identification of the chants that form the basis of many of the liturgical or paraliturgical pieces has often permitted the confirmation of the subject. Chants have been identified in the 32 following cases: nos. 3, 21, 23, 24, 25, 26, 39, 51, 71, 72 (from STÄBLEIN 1956), 79, 94, 95, 107, 111, 117, 119, 122, 123, 125, 138, 161, 162, 163, 165, 166, 167, 181, 182, 183, 185, 186.

2. Christological (9 instances + one doubtful): nos. 14? (MU), 27 (MU), 29 (MU), 31, 36, 67 (MU), 69, 70 (U), 76, 114;
3. Fear of Death (5 instances): nos. 30 (MU), 42 (MU), 112 (U), 112bis (text only), 159 (MU).

From this brief analysis it is clear that 46/47 pieces in Panc.27 refer to the cult of the Virgin, and 21/22 devote their attention to Christ. Fifteen pieces are directed to death instead, in the sense that they serve to honour and celebrate it, or else sing of its threat. On the whole, therefore, the attention dedicated to these three themes covers slightly less then half the pieces in the manuscript. On the significance I personally attribute to such a preponderance, see the section on the provenance of the manuscript.

The truly imposing number of *unica* in Panc.27, divided here into three categories (U, MU, TU) to aid qualification, is the most interesting section of the repertory, since we are dealing with pieces that circulated contemporaneously; it is precisely in this context that the peculiarities connected with the specific environment that produced the manuscript that hosts them are manifested.

The *unica*, both musical and textual (U) are 20 altogether: 11 pieces with secular Italian text, to which 4 laude should be added, one piece with French text, and 4 secular pieces with Latin text. The musical *unica* (MU) are 70: 49 liturgical and paraliturgical Latin pieces (the three duplicated pieces are counted only once), to which are to be added 9 pieces with secular Italian text, 9 laude, one piece with French text, and 2 textless pieces. Lastly, the only textual *unicum* (TU) is a piece with a secular Italian text. Counting instead the group of musical and textual *unica* with those that are musical *unica*, we obtain the impressive number of 89. This means that almost half the compositions present in Panc.27 are found only in this source, organized as follows: 49 liturgical and paraliturgical Latin piece, 20 pieces with secular Italian text, 12 laude, 4 secular pieces with Latin text, 2 pieces with French text, and 2 textless pieces.

This picture lends itself to some practical considerations. Musically speaking, none of the 89 *unica* is by a named author, while attributions have been found for only the following pieces, here listed in the order of their appearance: no. 2 (Laurentius Bergomotius Mutinensis), no. 8 (Musipula), no. 27 (Ben), no. 32 (Jo[hannes?] Vilet), no. 67 (Frater Dionisius Placentinus), no. 101 (Bar[tholomeus?] Pisanus), no. 104 (Renaldo), no. 125 (Antonius Peragulfus Lucensis), no. 137 (Dominicus), no. 148 (Bartolomeo Tromboncino, Superius only).[44] With the exception of Tromboncino, some of these names are practically unknown or documentable with too many uncertainties.[45] For the rest, we are dealing with persons who are either linked to a local place so securely that they have no further need of identification — I refer to Dominicus, Musipula, Renaldo — or are clearly known in a wider territorial region, but still have not left an indelible mark on the musical history of their time. These last can be better identified thanks to the use of a probable last name (Vilet) or a toponym (*Lucensis* = from Lucca, *Mutinensis* = from Modena, *Pisanus* = from Pisa, *Placentinus* = from Piacenza). And while Antonius Peragulfus Lucensis and Laurentius Bergomotius Mutinensis are in fact known musicians, for Bar[tholomeus?] Pisanus and Frater Dionisius there is no certain identity. I think that the necessity to specify the place name was necessary because Panc.27 was not compiled in any of the cities indicated in the toponyms: a logical deduction, which serves to reinforce the hypothesis that the manuscript comes from a centre where products and new ideas arrived easily.

Many composers have been traced through concordances. The phenomenon of the lack of attributions for the vast majority of the pieces in the manuscript is obviously due to several considerations: the fan of hypotheses ranges from the disinterest of the copyist in what seems of primary importance to modern scholars, to a complete lack of information, perhaps passing through the consideration that to write the name of a composer well known to everyone would seem otiose. In addition to this, there is the phenomenon of the reworking of well-known pieces, which happened in various circumstances and for various reasons (adaptations for performance, compositional experiments, and so forth). In the

---

[44]. See the Remarks on no. 150, which also includes those on no. 148.
[45]. See the section on biographical notices on the musicians.

following I list only the attributions taken from concordances[46] worth mentioning because they are considered plausible:[47] Bartolomeo Tromboncino alternating with Cara for nos. 4 (assigned to Cara in Panc.27), 52 (also assigned to Cara), 93, 150, 151, 175; Marchetto Cara for nos. 12, 37, 52 (alternating with Tromboncino), 63, perhaps 145;[48] Henricus Isaac for nos. 54, 55 (alternating with Weerbeke and Obrecht, less probable), 81, 138; Giovanni Brocco for nos. 17, 65; Antoine Brumel (nos. 120 and perhaps 121); Gaspar van Weerbeke (nos. 60, 130); Eneas (no. 85); Giacomo Fogliano (no. 92); Johannes Hesdimois (no. 179); Erasmus (Lapicida?) for no. 174; Johannes de Quadris (no. 45); Josquin des Prez (no. 139); Jacob Obrecht (no. 105); Michele Pesenti (no. 61); Johannes Prioris (no. 111, alternating with Compère, to whom it is assigned in Panc.27); Johannes de Stokem (no. 57); Johannes Touront (no. 83); Adrian Willaert (no. 177?).[49]

Following these acquisitions, therefore, it is possible to weigh the balance of the known composers in the manuscript. Considering only the plausible attributions and adding those indicated in the manuscript to those gained from concordances, this is the classification of the composers represented in Panc.27, excluding those to whom a single piece has been attributed: in our current state of knowledge, the music most represented in the manuscript is by Isaac (8 appearances), followed by Weerbeke (7 pieces). Tromboncino's contribution is noteworthy (5 certain appearances, plus 2 attributed also to Cara, and a Superius securely by him), as is Cara's (with 3 certain pieces, plus 2 attributed also to Tromboncino, and another possible one, but without proof). Following, at some distance, are Brumel (3 appearances, with a fourth hypothesized), Agricola, and Josquin (3 each), and then Compère (2 certain appearances and one attributed also to Prioris), Brocco, Fogliano, Ghiselin, and Stokem (2 pieces each).

How trustworthy is this classification? Certainly one can deduce from it a norm for the taste circulating at the beginning of the Cinquecento. The musicians most represented are in fact the most famous ones in Italy, and those whose pieces are widely diffused in musical manuscripts and contemporary prints. Therefore we are dealing with very up-to-the-date composers, and in fact some of the pieces included in Panc.27 were veritable successes in the 'hit parade' of that time.[50] But from this data, unfortunately, no certain information allows us to pinpoint the precise area in which the manuscript was compiled. We know for certain that the music travelled separately from its composers (above all when famous),[51] and therefore to infer that the presence of one composer or another can tell us something very significant is not prudent. Moreover, in the case of Panc.27 we are not even faced with musicians whose presence prevails to a significant extent: the number of attributions is relatively small, and the distance between the attributions to one composer or to another is truly derisory. It would be much wiser, therefore, to trust in the composers of the *unica* if the goal is to individuate the circumscribed geographical zone in which the manuscript was compiled.

The same might be said for the authors of the poetic texts set in Panc.27, none of which is mentioned in the manuscript. Some names have been traced thanks to the help of concordances, but much more marginally compared with the musical attributions. The reason for this discrepancy is simple: generally the musical sources do not include any indication of the authors of the text. The search therefore has to be conducted on the basis of literary sources, often not very rewarding. As in music, in fact, in literature too we experience the phenomenon of 'culpable' overattribution when we deal with famous writers: it is therefore indispensable to winnow what is found and submit it to effective skimming by linguistic experts who know how to evaluate the plausibility of an attribution.[52]

---

[46]. No. 121 is an exception: Brumel is not noted in any concordance, but the name rests on a hypothetical attribution. See the relevant entry.

[47]. In the individual entries, however, various discussions of the dubious attributions will be found.

[48]. See the relevant entry.

[49]. See the relevant entry.

[50]. The pulse of the diffusion of the pieces can be taken via the list of concordances for each entry.

[51]. On this phenomenon see, for example, LOCKWOOD 1979: through the activities of copyists and informers in contact with France, the music of Jean Mouton reached Ferrara even before he himself arrived at the end of 1515.

[52]. To note only a single example, see the enormous winnowing Antonio Rossi accomplished after so many years of work on the lyric verse attributed to Serafino Aquilano.

Feo Belcari is the name most frequently found (with 4 appearances), followed by Francesco degli Albizzi, Leonardo Giustinian, and Jean II, duc de Bourbon, with 2 appearances each. As in the case of musicians, therefore, I do not believe it is prudent to make deductions based on the presence of some poets instead of others to evaluate Panc.27. Indeed, in the case of poets, it seems to me that the terrain is even more of a minefield. There are in fact far more poetic manuscripts and prints of the fifteenth and sixteenth centuries than surviving coeval musical sources, and this surely indicates that also at that time the literary book had more diffusion than the musical book. Therefore, we can reasonably hypothesize that the names of poets circulated even more easily than those of musicians, and this fact renders the attempt to delineate a specific area of provenance for the manuscript via the poets even more complicated.

The *contrafacta* and secular 'travestimenti' are an important part of the repertory of Panc.27. In some cases the contrafaction is 'declared', in the sense that it is explicit in the heading or under the music of the piece in question, as in nos. 13, 15, 36, 61, 64, 75. In other cases the *contrafacta* have been unmasked in the course of work, or have been hypothesized here: nos. 37 (a dubious case), 58?, 69, 109, 138, 173. In total, we have to do with 10 pieces that are almost securely contrafacted and 2 uncertain cases. Of the 10 certain pieces, only 6 (nos. 13, 15, 36, 64, 69, 109) are true and proper *contrafacta*, revealed in the sense that they superimpose a devotional text over the original secular one. The other 3 cases propose substitutions (always indicated) of a different type: no. 138 from sacred to sacred, no. 75 from secular to secular, and no. 61 a double contrafaction, from an original Horatian ode to a Latin hymn, and then from this last to an Italian secular text.

The number of pieces contrafacted is significant in the general economy of the book, and this fact lends itself at least to an evaluation. The frequent signposting of the famous musical model of these pieces in Panc.27 makes one think that the compiler of the manuscript felt it important: certainly he knew much secular music, and at the same time he knew where to go to find a substitute text and reuse it in the music. My opinion is that this compiler could draw on a reservoir of Italian poetry with ease, and often attempted to compose music *ex novo* on texts drawn from the many poetic collections in circulation. It is logical to imagine that all this could happen easily only in a culturally up-to-date centre, where the exchanges of ideas were frequent.

That the principal scribe of Panc.27 (Scribe A) frequently and willingly intervened personally in the musical repertory in the manuscript is demonstrated by various 'editorial' alterations, some of them rather awkward contrapuntally. The Remarks in the entries for individual pieces clarify the nature of these changes (sometimes simply compositional 'experiments' with respect to the traditional versions), but perhaps it is worthwhile here to discuss some notable examples to assess the quality of the alterations. The most striking case is surely that of Isaac's *Benedictus* (no. 21), where no fewer than three alternative ornamented bass lines absent from any other concordant source have been added, and therefore are certainly attributable to the experimental fancy of the scribe. No. 164 too has important alternative readings, always in the Bassus: in the *Prima pars* of the piece the copyist wrote a melody to substitute for the ten bars of rest, whereas in the *Secunda pars* the new Bassus replaces the preceding one completely in the sense that it fills almost completely the bars of rest. Alternative readings of lesser scope are found also in nos. 19 and 33: in both cases the scribe invents a whole section substituting for the 'official' one (the ending of the Cantus in no. 19, and the final section of the Bassus of no. 33), but in truth in neither of the two cases are we really certain which the 'official' version is. Thus, while no. 19 is a musical *unicum*, for no. 33 the version in Panc.27 represents a branch of the tradition independent of that attested in concordant sources, since its Altus is present only in Panc.27 and the Bassus is different from that of the two concordances. The same could be said of nos. 36 and 40 (*Poi che t'ebi nel core / Fortuna desperata* and *De tous biens playne [est ma maistresse]*), pieces that are very well known and which circulated in various versions throughout Europe: the Altus of no. 36 in Panc.27 does not in fact appear in any of the known concordances, and the same is true of the Contra in no. 40. Also the extremely problematic counterpoint expressed in the joining of two mediocre lower voices to the higher one in no. 70 (the lauda *Alto Iesù, figl[i]olo de Maria*) makes one think that it is a scribal experiment, just as the uncertain polyphonic situation of the *Amen* no. 183, where one doesn't know how to align the four voices convincingly. Finally, the situation of no. 148 is special: this version of *Signora, anci, mia dea* is surely a re-elaboration of the same piece in Panc.27 (no. 150): the same Cantus, the Tenor and Bassus varied, and a completely different Altus.

From these few examples one could argue that Scribe A was not simply a passive copyist from his models. Interested in varying what he copied at time, he can be considered a second-rate composer who exercised his ability with the aim perhaps of performing what he copied or composed (as witnessed by various unmistakable 'performance' signs in the manuscript, discussed in the section on its physical appearance). Here we should again recall the opinion of Dietrich Kämper, who singles out some manuscripts of the beginning of the Cinquecento for their clear function as teaching manuals and musical exercises, demonstrated by the presence in appendices of illustrations of rhythmic rules for the music.[53] In the specific case of Panc.27, moreover, Scribe A has added to about a third of the pieces little arabic numbers at the end of voices or sections that, expressing the sums (not always correct!) of *semibreves* contained in every voice, were probably used to rework the pieces themselves in other forms (*contrafacta* or intabulations).[54] And I believe that the copyist of Panc.27 intended to fill the entire manuscript with music; otherwise, of what use would it be to place the rhythmic rules on the last page of the book?

The principal scribe of Panc.27 was not very interested in the tradition of the poetic texts carried by the pieces, whether sacred or secular. Fifty-two pieces in fact are provided with only a textual incipit (generally under the first notes in one or more voices); these are nos. 8, 11, 12, 16, 28, 31, 34, 35, 39, 40, 44, 54, 56, 59, 62, 68, 71, 73, 74, 75, 80, 82, 87, 88, 92, 93, 95, 96, 97, 101, 103, 105, 107, 109, 111, 113, 116, 124, 125, 126, 127, 131, 158, 159, 160, 162, 163, 164, 168, 169, 171, 172. Another 19 include instead only a general inscription, positioned as a sort of heading (nos. 14, 21, 32, 42, 47, 49, 50, 55, 57, 72, 77, 78, 81, 89, 128, 139, 143, 151, 170). This graphic presentation might be related to the type of performance suggested or used: this is what has been hypothesized by some scholars who have investigated this problem, coming to different conclusions.[55] That there does not seem to have been a consistent interest on the part of the scribe with respect to the texts set to music, appears to me a further indication strengthening the hypothesis that this person was a dilettante composer who cared more about the music than the text, music he collected in part because of its author, in part because it constituted a repertory uniquely linked to his territory, and in part because it was the fruit of his creativity.

---

[53]. See KÄMPER 1976, p. 38.

[54]. On this specific subject see the paragraph that follows below.

[55]. While Louise Litterick strongly maintains that, in Italian sources, the absence of text is a clear indication of instrumental performance (LITTERICK 1980, p. 480 and LITTERICK 1981, p. 117), Warwick Edwards and Jon Banks incline towards a less clear-cut opinion. Edwards does not think it useful to qualify everything without text as implicitly destined for instruments, and prefers the ambiguous definition of 'songs without words' to designate the neutral field of such late fifteenth-century compositions (EDWARDS 1981, p. 91); studying the SegC repertory, Banks appeals instead to the possibility that in the presence of only the textual incipit of a piece, the motivations could be threefold: (a) the text was so well known that it was pointless to add it; (b) it suggested a performance of vocalization without words; (c) the destination was truly instrumental (BANKS 1999, p. 295). The possibility of vocalization as performance practice in pieces without text had earlier been suggested also by Litterick, although with scant conviction relative to Italian sources (LITTERICK 1980, notes 7 and 11).

(B) The Function of the Arabic Numbers: 'Servants' or 'Masters'?[56]

About a third of the repertory of Panc.27 exhibits an interesting detail: small arabic numerals —
written in the hand of Scribe A (who was responsible for the foliation of the manuscript up to fol. 120r,
most of the musical notation, and the poetic texts of the piece) — without any indication whatever that
would clarify their function. These numerals appear sometimes at the end of every voice, occasionally
only at the end of some of them or specific sections within them, and other times alone or together
with others, even past fol. 120r.[57] Upon closer inspection, it appears that the copyist has recorded the
sum of the values of the *semibreves* contained in each vocal or instrumental part, always excluding the
final *longa* and often some long internal notes that serve to demarcate the sections.

This curious phenomenon has already been discussed by Knud Jeppesen, who solved the problem
rather rapidly: the numbers represent a means of control by which the scribe could assure himself that
he had the correct count in his version and had not overlooked anything in copying from his model in
other sources.[58] But the explanation of the illustrious scholar leaves some questions unanswered: if the
purpose of the numbers was only editorial, what sense would it make to limit them to only a third of
the compositions in the manuscript, without indicating them also in other pieces that were certainly
copied from contemporaneous sources by the same scribe? Examination of the inks shows, furthermore,
that the insertion of the numbers was not made at the same time as the musical and poetic texts were
entered. The numbers could have been added later, after the notation of the music in each part. Various
elements, therefore, reinforce my scepticism on the presumed function of the numbers as representing
some kind of editorial control in the process of copying from other sources.

To attempt to shed light on the problem, it is necessary to delve deeper into the complicated
question. No fewer than 66 cases, distributed among 60 compositions,[59] have various arabic numbers at
the end of every voice. Most frequently there is only one number, whereas in other cases the numbers
are more than one per voice, positioned graphically one next to the other or one over the other (see
Figs. 4, 12, 13, and 14). On the whole, these pieces do not show any predilection either for a specific
poetic-musical form or for a particular mensuration.[60]

The complete list of the pieces and their sections is as follows: nos. 2, 3, 4, 5, 7, 8a, 8b, 10, 11a, 16,
21, 36, 40, 52, 54, 55, 56, 58, 60, 64, 66, 75, 81, 83, 84, 89, 90, 91, 94a, 94b, 95, 98, 99, 102, 103, 104, 105,
106, 109, 111, 116, 121, 124a, 124c, 125, 126a, 127, 128, 129, 130, 131, 137, 138, 139, 151, 152, 158,
164b, 165, 166a, 166b, 167a, 167b, 167c, 168, 172.

Within the cases considered the following groups can be distinguished:
I. compositions in which there is agreement between the number(s) and the sum of the values of the
   semibreves present, excluding the *longa/brevis* at the end of the piece or the end of a section (43
   cases altogether);

---

[56]. This section is a condensation of what I published in my article FILOCAMO 2004, brought up to date in the light
of new ideas in the last years.

[57]. The fact that the numbers are present in both sections of the manuscript, marked with different types of numbering,
validates the hypothesis that the 'architectonic' conception of the whole manuscript was unitary from the beginning.

[58]. «Nach den meisten Kompositionen (oder Stimmen) folgen einige rätselhafte Zahlen; bei näherer Betrachtung
werden sie jedoch verständlich als die Anzahl der Semibreven der einzelnen Stimmen vermerkend (wobei doch die mit
Fermaten versehenen 'finales' nicht mitgezählt wurden). Offenbar stellen sie Kontrollzeichen dar, wodurch der Schreiber
beim Nachzählen sich vergewisserte, bei der Kopie seiner Vorlagen aus anderen Quellen nichts übersprungen zu haben»
(JEPPESEN 1970, p. 38).

[59]. Although the pieces are technically 60, there are sometimes sections of compositions that I have analysed as
separate pieces because they have arabic numbers that relate exclusively to those sections. When necessary (nos. 8, 94, 124,
166, 167), alphabetical letters have been placed next to the ordinal number to designate the portion of the piece considered
(a, b, c: see TABLE 2 below): if we add these single sections to the pieces that do not contain internal sections, we arrive at a
total of 66 cases.

[60]. The compositions that begin in *tempus imperfectum diminutum* are, however, in the clear majority within this group
of pieces (56 out of 66 cases), but this is a tendency shared with other pieces in the rest of the manuscript.

II. pieces in which the number agrees with the sum of the values of the *semibreves*, including the final note (only 2 cases);[61]

III. compositions in which, without taking into account hypothetical errors or oversights on the part of the scribe, there is no agreement between the number(s) and the sum of the values of the *semibreves* present, excluding the final *longa* and/or the *longa/brevis* at the end of a section (12 cases);[62]

IV. pieces in which, owing to a probable counting error by the scribe, there is no agreement between the number(s) and the sum of the values of the *semibreves*, including or excluding the value of the final *longa* and/or the *longa/semibrevis* at the end of a section (9 cases).

Within the four groups there are further internal divisions: TABLE 1 includes all 66 cases in Panc.27, while TABLE 2 gives details and comments on every single case.

The characteristics of the first and second groups of pieces might support Jeppesen's opinion on the placement of the numbers, and thus indicate control over the counting of the rhythmic values from the models,[63] but there are, on the other hand, situations that do not at all confirm the general validity of this idea (see TABLE 2). The examples that follow illustrate some of the cases in which it is not possible to explain the presence of the numbers in relation to copying from a model:[64]

– in two cases in Group I (nos. 84 and 151) at the end of the Superius a greater number of *semibreves* is indicated than actually present. The only plausible explanation for this numbering is that the scribe wished to make clear his intention to hold out the final *longa* until the completion of the number placed in the other voices, to make the highest voice conclude simultaneously with the other three parts. In this case there does not seem to be any possible relation between the number added in the Superius and control of copying, and all the more so because in various analogous examples the copyist noted the number exactly (lower or higher) of the *semibreves* relative to the single voices (see FIG. 10);

– the rubric «alio mo(do) notat(um)» of no. 164b (Group I) might perhaps be interpreted as a warning connected with the process of 'entrance/exit' of the piece 'in/from' the manuscript (see FIG. 11);

– in no. 167a (Group I) the presence of the crossed-out number in the Tenor — relating, moreover, to a musical section that is silent in that voice — would confirm that the placement of the arabic numbers has nothing to do with the process of copying the piece. This case confirms that the number was certainly not placed to control the transcription of music from a model (see FIG. 12);

– how is it that in no. 60 (Group III) some musical sections were not counted? It might have been a deliberate decision on the part of the copyist: perhaps it was not useful to determine the quantity because it didn't serve to 'export' those sections elsewhere (see FIG. 13);

– why, in no. 116 (Group IV), were the initial rests clearly excluded from the explicit counting of the numbers? Perhaps the scribe decided that there was no point in including their value in the

---

[61]. In reality, the difference in numbering between the two compositions in question and the pieces of the previous group is not substantial. In all the other pieces the final *longa* is outside the count of musical values; for these two pieces, the value of the last note is included, but it is necessary to consider that in both pieces the final note is not the effective conclusion of the piece: the first ends the notation of the notes anticipating a ripresa, and the second refers to its continuation, that is the third part of the piece, which is structurally and/or graphically separated from that which precedes it. The presence of this second grouping of pieces, therefore, is purely theoretical. In reality the two pieces discussed here could easily have been included in Group I.

[62]. These pieces have small internal sections (initial, intermediate, or concluding) or single notes not counted that, if eliminated, would sometimes restore the agreement between the number(s) and the sum of the *semibreves* indicated.

[63]. Something similar has been noticed by Richard Sherr: in connection with the possible significance of certain *signa congruentiae* in some Petrucci prints, Sherr offers an interpretation of several numbers present in the motet *Sancti Dei omnes*, attributed to Mouton and found in MS CV S42 (fols. 11*v*-15*r*). It is a question of counts relative to the sum of *semibreves* (as happens in Panc.27): slash marks over the music, with arabic numbers placed in the margin indicating the number of *semibreves* up to that point. Such signs correspond exactly, in each voice, to the page turns in a late sixteenth-century copy of the same piece in MS Vatican City, Biblioteca Apostolica Vaticana, Cappella Sistina, 76 (fols. 158*v*-164*r*). Sherr comes to the following conclusion: «So here we can prove that markings of this sort were intended to aid the copying process into choirbook format» (SHERR 1990, p. 267). Examining the concordances of Panc.27, however, none of these shows numbers usable as a control in connection with the copying process.

[64]. Other cases that contradict the copying hypothesis can be deduced from an attentive reading of TABLE 2.

calculation because the initial rests in all the voices are musical silences: since it was a simultaneous rest, in fact, it was perfectly legitimate to ignore it if the rhythmic count was designed for reusing the section instead of acting as a simple control (see FIG. 14).

FIG. 10: *La speranza me tien vivo*, fol. 54*v*, Superius and Tenor, and fol. 55*r*, Altus and Bassus. Photo Mario Setter – GAP.

FIG. 11: *Felix namque*, *Secunda pars*, fol. 131*v*, Superius and Tenor; fol. 132*r*, Altus and Bassus. Photo Mario Setter – GAP.

FIG. 12: (Magnificat) *Anima mea*, fol. 135v, Superius, Tenor, and Bassus; fol. 136r, Altus and Bassus [cont.]. Photo Mario Setter – GAP.

Fig. 13: [Gaspar van Weerbeke], *Mater digna Dei*, fol. 39*v*, Superius and Tenor; fol. 40*r*, Altus and Bassus. Photo Mario Setter – GAP.

FIG. 14: *'Patientia' [ognun me dice]*, fol. 80*v*, Superius and Tenor; fol. 81*r*, Altus and Bassus. Photo Mario Setter - GAP.

The conclusions that emerge from the repertory analysed suggest that for the majority of the pieces (of Groups I and II) accompanied by the presence of numbers in Panc.27 Jeppesen's hypothesis is valid. I would expand it as follows: the scribe might have added the numbers to assure himself of having copied correctly from his model or directly from the original *tabula compositoria* on which the pieces were perhaps initially composed,[65] with the sole aim of being sure he had copied the rhythmic values exactly ('editorial' purpose). But Jeppesen's hypothesis does not fit the compositions of Groups III and IV at all. And if from one piece to another the scribe is the same, why should he change his editorial attitude as 'copyist' in the decision to note or not the sum of the *semibreves*? Why are only certain pieces, and not others, characterized by the presence of these numbers? And why are only sections of pieces or even single voices involved? I do not intend to weaken Jeppesen's hypothesis as a whole — that the addition of the numbers is a direct consequence of the act of copying — but I would like to include other interpretative possibilities for the compositions that do not fit his hypothesis. I believe that the numbers might have served in a different way expressly for musicians to verify during the performance that the polyphony and the rhythm were both correct ('performative' purpose); or, more likely, they might have been useful to plan rhythmic-mensural frameworks for future *contrafacta* or instrumental intabulations ('reworking' purpose).

I do not think that Panc.27 was destined to function solely as a 'souvenir cabinet' for its users. Rather, I believe that it was a 'living' manuscript, prepared for practical ends, even to project new compositions on the basis of those already existing. The probability that the added numbers served to reveal at a glance the precise length of a section or a whole piece in order to create other versions on that basis is perhaps more plausible than the hypothesis that they were added only to control the rhythmic precision of vocal or instrumental performers. Besides, Panc.27 has various *contrafacta* and secular 'travestimenti'; at least 31 compositions have at the minimum one concordance with another text,[66] and only 12 of these lack numbers at the end of their voices.[67] I believe that, rather than having extrapolated the numbers from a control exercised over his models, the Panciatichi scribe himself could have decided to put them in with a view to future compositional projects originating in the reuse of models that were already at hand.[68] And in fact, beyond the numerous *contrafacta* and secular

---

[65]. In an epoch-making article (LOWINSKY 1948, republished, with small changes, in LOWINSKY 1989, II, no. 34, pp. 797-800), Edward Lowinsky discerned in the *Compendium musices* of Auctor Lampadius — first printed in 1537 and then in 1554, both in Bern — the first distinction between the old and new methods of composition: the old one consisted of the use of various *tabulae* of wood or slate, one for each voice of the composition, which permitted cancellation and rewriting; the new method prefigured the use of a true score where one could write the musical parts on paper simultaneously. Lampadius attributes the introduction of the new system to Josquin des Prez, but Isaac too is mentioned among the innovators (pp. 19-20). Although it was preceded by two contributions (KINKELDEY 1910 and SCHWARTZ 1920), Lowinsky's article set in motion a series of chain reactions, summarized by Jessie Ann Owens (see OWENS 1997, pp. 4-5). Owens, however, invites us to rethink Lowinsky's interpretation of the question, because she maintains that the passage from 'successive' to 'simultaneous' composition in reality reflects the musical style, not the compositional process (p. 33). One of the conclusions emerging from her study is: «Composers of complex vocal polyphony during the period from roughly 1450 to 1600 neither needed nor used scores for composing. Scores were used for studying music, particularly after the middle of the sixteenth century, and they were used in composition by composers of keyboard music accustomed to using them in performance. Instead of scores, composers worked on short segments in quasi-score format and on longer segments in separate parts (for example, choirbook format)» (p. 313). In his review («Il Saggiatore musicale», VII, 2000, pp. 179-189) Stefano La Via criticized Owens's clear convictions that categorically exclude the use of the score from the panorama of Renaissance composition: the *quasi-score* (or *pseudo-score*) format, he thinks, was assimilated too easily by Owens with writing in separate parts (pp. 185 and 187), whereas it would be more useful to retain a more flexible attitude in the face of a variety of compositional methods used by Renaissance musicians (p. 189).

[66]. Nos. 11, 13, 15, 16, 21, 33, 36, 40, 47, 48, 54, 55, 56, 58, 59, 61, 64, 66, 69, 73, 75, 81, 83, 93, 105, 111, 115, 127, 138, 149, 168.

[67]. Nos. 13, 15, 33, 47, 48, 59, 61, 69, 73, 93, 115, 149.

[68]. As far as we know, the following pieces were not exploited as sacred or secular 'travestimenti' (subdivided into sections where Scribe A has counted sections independently from the rest of the composition): nos. 2, 3, 4, 5, 7, 8a, 8b, 10, 52, 60, 84, 89, 90, 91, 94a, 94b, 95, 98, 99, 102, 103, 104, 106, 109, 116, 121, 124a, 124c, 125, 126a, 128, 129, 130, 131, 137, 139, 151, 152, 158, 164b, 165, 166a, 166b, 167a, 167b, 167c, 172. The total is 41 pieces, but 47 cases in all.

'travestimenti' identified, there are various intabulations concordant with a variety of pieces in the manuscript.

On the other hand, further elements reinforce the hypothesis that Panc.27 was prepared for performance purposes,[69] beginning with its physical makeup: paper rather than parchment, the small oblong format, its light weight and consequently easy manageability, the absence of precious miniatures or finely decorated capital letters, the easy legibility of the textual and musical script. The ingenious placement of small arabic numbers could have served the *magister* or the most unsophisticated performers to control rhythm and polyphony, or could have suggested the basis for new adaptations of the piece: the numbers define the precise length of rhythmic sections, ready to migrate easily elsewhere, to be adapted perhaps also to new poetic texts that were metrically compatible with the original ones. The fact that many pieces lack the numbers in some voices (or sections) might indicate that the intention was to 'export' only limited portions of music. If Scribe A of Panc.27 was an active intermediary between users (performers or not) and the authoritative (and less authoritative) versions of the pieces he copied, perhaps we can consider his activity as 'prospective', and not merely a mechanical copying. Despite the musical errors present, the hypothesis that an active circle of users sounding, singing, and exporting music revolved around Panc.27 seems to me more than plausible. And the numbers on the whole should perhaps be read as the key to distinguishing vital movements of musical polyphony from the interior to the exterior of this manuscript.[70] But Scribe A also noted down sums of arabic numbers on one of the blank pages at the beginning of the manuscript. Moreover, Renaissance culture was amply impregnated with the new modes of perception linked to the mercantile growth of the fourteenth century: constant arithmetical activity is among the most outstanding developments and invades discourse (including musical discourse) penetrating into thinking that became much more empirical, inductive, and quantitative.[71] Might the calculation of the *semibreves* even have served to plan lauda *contrafacta* also to gain indulgences to atone for one's own sins?

---

[69]. This is not the same as saying that correct performances took place on the basis of the readings in Panc.27, which often have gaps or downright mistakes.

[70]. Apart from the two Vatican manuscripts cited earlier — in which the placement of the numbers had a different function with respect to what happens in Panc.27 — I am aware of the presence of arabic numbers not explainable as simple indications of rhythmic duration in only two other musical sources. One case is mentioned in GIALDRONI – ZIINO 1995 (I thank John Nádas for drawing this article to my attention). Unfortunately, in this case, and like the authors of the contribution (*ibidem*, p. 189), I have not been able to ascertain a plausible meaning for such added numbers. The second example was mentioned to me by Warwick Edwards, who has written about it in EDWARDS 1974. In the essay he cites four English manuscript partbooks (Walsingham Consort Books) from the end of the sixteenth century, and a separate page that lists the compositions. Next to the titles of the pieces and their ordinal number appear, at the left, arabic numbers equivalent to the sum of the values of the *semibreves* of the pieces in the Bassus partbook. Repetitions are not counted, whereas the calculation continues in the case of the note values included in the first and second endings (p. 212). The noting of the count, reminiscent of Panc.27, is lacking for only a very few of the listed pieces. Renaissance theorists as well willingly investigated numbers: both Ugolino of Orvieto and Giovanni Spataro held that it was good practice to conclude every piece with its 'complete number' relative to the mensuration in question (see BLACKBURN ET AL. 1991, pp. 1030-1031); it does not seem to me, however, that this usage has anything to do with the problem under discussion.

[71]. See WILSON 1992, p. 12.

TABLE 1

Categories of the numerical references in some compositions of Panc.27 (indicated here with arabic numerals)

Abbreviations: br = *brevis/es*, lg = *longa/ae*, sb = *semibrevis/es*

TYPE	GROUPS				
	I	**II**	**III**		**IV**
	number(s) corresponding to the sum of sb values, excluding the final lg and/or the lg/br at the end of a section	number(s) corresponding to the sum of sb values, including the final note	number(s) not corresponding (at least in one voice) to the sum of sb values (passages or notes deliberately overlooked), excluding the final lg and/or the lg/br at the end of a section		number(s) not corresponding (at least in one voice) to the sum of sb values, including the final lg and/or the lg/br at the end of a section
			number(s) corresponding, disregarding passages or notes deliberately overlooked	number(s) not corresponding, disregarding passages or notes deliberately overlooked	
a¹: the same number (referring to the whole composition) present in all the voices	16, 40, 54, 58, 75, 81, 84, 89, 95, 105, 106, 109, 128, 137, 139, 151, 168	52	10, 83, 90, 103, 125		
a²: the same number (referring to only one section of the composition) present in all the voices	8a, 164b		94b	8b	130
a³: the same numbers (referring to the whole composition) present in all the voices					
a⁴: the same numbers (each referring to one section) present in all the voices	91, 99, 127, 131, 167a, 167b		3		167c
b¹: a number (referring to the whole composition) disagreeing in the various voices	5, 7, 55, 56, 98, 111, 138, 172		102		36
b²: a number (referring to only one section of the composition) disagreeing in the various voices	11a, 94a				124c
b³: numbers (each referring to one section) disagreeing in the various voices	4, 64			2, 60	66, 116
c¹: the same number (referring to the whole composition) present only in some voices	152				21
c²: the same number (referring to only one section of the composition) present only in some voices		124a			
c³: the same numbers (each referring to one section) present only in some voices	121, 126a				
d: a number (referring to only one section of the composition) present only in some voices	129				
e¹: a number (referring to the whole composition) present only in one voice	165				
e²: numbers (referring to several sections of the composition) present only in one voice			166a		104
e³: a number (referring to only one section of the composition) present only in one voice	166b				158

TABLE 2

Comprehensive list of the arabic numbers present in the individual voices (S/C, A, T, B/Ct) of the relevant compositions, subdivided into groups
(for the meaning of the groups and types see TABLE 1)

Note: in the column referring to the individual voices, '–' indicates that the voice in question has no number(s); if there is no entry, the voice is not present

GROUP I

Type	No.	Incipit	Fols.	vv.	S/C	A	T	B/Ct	Remarks
a^1	16	*Amice, ad quid venisti? attende tibi*	15v–16r	3	80		80	80	80 = no. of sb in bb. 1-40
	40	*De tous biens playne [est ma maistresse]*	25r	3	118		118	118	118 = no. of sb in bb. 1-59
	54	*La mora*	33v–34r	3	129		129	129	129 = no. of sb in bb. 1-64
	58	*[...]*	37v–38r	3	130		130	130	130 = no. of sb in bb. 1-65
	75	*Les bien amore / Omnis labor habet finem*	49v–50r	3	104		104	104	104 = no. of sb in bb. 1-52
	81	*Omnis laus in fine canitur*	52v–53r	4	64	64	64	64	64 = no. of sb in bb. 1-32
	84	*La speranza me tien vivo*	54v–55r	4	72	72	72	72	72 = no. of sb in bb. 1-36 The S has 60 sb, but the number 72 at the end of the voice surely indicates that the last note (in b. 31) is extended to the conclusion of the other voices
	89	*Si dedero [somnum oculis meis]*	57v–58r	3	150		150	150	150 = no. of sb in bb. 1-75
	95	*O quam glorifica [luce coruscas]*	63v–64r	3	158		158	158	158 = no. of sb in bb. 1-79
	105	*Meskim [es u cutkin ru?]*	72v	3	58		58	58	58 = no. of sb in bb. 1-29
	106	*Quemadmodum desiderat cervus*	73r	3	55		55	55	55 = no. of sb in bb. 1-27
	109	*Lucis Creator optime*	75v–76r	3	94		94	94	94 = no. of sb in bb. 1-47
	128	*La alfonsina*	98v–99r	3	124		124	124	124 = no. of sb in bb. 1-62
	137	*Alleluia*	105r	3	68		68	68	68 = no. of sb in bb. 1-34
	139	*Fortuna d'um gran tempo*	106v–107r	3	92		92	92	92 = no. of sb in bb. 1-46

95

Type	No.	Incipit	Fols.	vv.	S/C	A	T	B/Ct	Remarks
	151	*Poca pace e molta guerra*	112v–113r	4	55	55	55	55	55 = no. of sb in bb. 1-26 The S has 43 sb, but the number 55 at the end of the voice surely indicates that the last note (in b. 21) is extended to the conclusion of the other voices
	168	*Helas, [que devera mon cueur]*	138v–139r	3	117		117	117	117 = no. of sb in bb. 1-58
a²	8a	*Ave Maria, [gratia plena] (Prima pars)*	5v–6r	4	66	66	66	66	66 = no. of sb in bb. 6-38 (the count excludes the initial part of the section, bb. 1-5, comprising the intonation *Ave Maria*, concluding with a fermata)
	164b	*Felix namque (Secunda pars)*	131v–132r	4	74	74	74	74	74 = no. of sb in bb. 51-87 The alternative B with the rubric «alio mo(do) notat(um)» also has the no. 74 at the end
a⁴	91	*O pulcherrima mulierum*	59v–60r	4	46 62	46 62	46 62	46 62	46 = no. of sb in bb. 1-23 62 = no. of sb in bb. 25-55
	99	*Christi mater, ave*	67v–68r	4	14 18 68	14 18 68	14 18 68	14 18 68	14 = no. of sb in bb. 1-7 18 = no. of sb in bb. 9-17 68 = no. of sb in bb. 19-52
	127	*Ales regres, [vuidez de ma presence]*	97v–98r	3	64 40		64 40	64 40	64 = no. of sb in bb. 1-32 40 = no. of sb in bb. 34-53
	131	*Mater patris [et filia]*	101v–102r	3	114 42		114 42	114 42	114 = no. of sb in bb. 1-57 42 = no. of sb in bb. 59-72
	167a	*(Magnificat) Anima mea Dominum* (bb. 1-82)	135v–136r	4	42 132	42 132	42	42 132	42 = no. of sb in bb. 1-14 132 = no. of sb in bb. 16-81 Under the number 42 the T also gives the number 132, but crossed out, since the T is silent in the section *Qui respexit* to which it must refer
	167b	*(Magnificat) Anima mea Dominum* (bb. 83-127)	136v–137r	4	52 51	52	52 51	52 51	52 = no. of sb in bb. 83-108 51 = no. of sb in bb. 110-126
b¹	5	*Qui seminant in lacrimis*	3v–4r	4	54	54	50	54	54 = no. of sb in bb. 1-27 50 = no. of sb in bb. 1-25
	7	*Vidimus enim stellam eius in Oriente*	4v–5r	4	51	54	51	54	51 = no. of sb in bb. 1-26/I 54 = no. of sb in bb. 1-27

Type	No.	Incipit	Fols.	vv.	S/C	A	T	B/Ct	Remarks
	55	*La stangetta*	34v–35r	3	115		119	119	115 = no. of sb in bb. 1-57 119 = no. of sb in bb. 1-59
	56	*Helas [que poura devenir]*	35v–36r	4	124	127	124	124	124 = no. of sb in bb. 1-62 127 = no. of sb in bb. 1-63
	98	*Virgo Maria, non est tibi similis nata*	66v–67r	4	96	104	96	104	96 = no. of sb in bb. 1-47 104 = no. of sb in bb. 1-51
	111	*Regina celi [letare]*	77r	3	86		88	88	86 = no. of sb in bb. 1-44 (the count would be correct, taking into account the oversight of bb. 12/II-13/I) 88 = no. of sb in bb. 1-44
	138	*Alleluia*	105v–106r	4	82	83	83	83	82 = no. of sb in bb. 1-41 (the count would be correct, taking into account the oversight of b. 23/I) 83 = no. of sb in bb. 1-41
	172	*Sine fraude*	142v–143r	3	117		117	112	117 = no. of sb in bb. 1-58 112 = no. of sb in bb. 1-58 (the count would be correct, taking into account the oversight of bb. 7/II and 47/II-49/I)
b²	11a	*A la bataglia (Prima pars)*	9v–10r	4	58	59	58	58	58 = no. of sb in bb. 1-29 59 = the count in the A, corresponding to the no. of sb present, even if there is one too many in b. 13/I
	94a	*Regina celi letare ([Prima pars])*	61v–62r	4	124	125	124	124	124 = no. of sb in bb. 1-62 125 = no. of sb in bb. 1-63/I
b³	4	*Ave Maria, gratia plena*	3v–4r	4	8 27 23 14	8 27 23 16	8 27 23 16	8 27 23 16	8 = no. of sb in bb. 1-4 27 = no. of sb in bb. 6-18 23 = no. of sb in bb. 21-31 14 = no. of sb in bb. 33-39 16 = no. of sb in bb. 33-40
	64	*Canti zoiosi e dolce melodia / Jo hay pris amor [à ma devise]*	41v	3	60 46		62 46	60 46	60 = no. of sb in bb. 1-30 62 = no. of sb in bb. 1-31 46 = no. of sb in bb. 34-56
c¹	152	*Se l'ortolana vene a la cità*	112v–113r	4	33	–	33	33	33 = no. of sb in bb. 1-11

Type	No.	Incipit	Fols.	vv.	S/C	A	T	B/Ct	Remarks
c³	121	*O Domine Iesu Christe*	87v-88r	4	108 13	108 13	– –	108 13	108 = no. of sb in bb. 1-54 13 = no. of sb in bb. 56-61
	126a	*Propter gravamen [et tormentum] (Prima pars)*	95v-96r	4	– – – –	– – – –	– – – 194	124 6 64 194	124 = no. of sb in bb. 1-62 6 = no. of sb in bb. 64-66 64 = no. of sb in bb. 68-99 194 = total of the preceding numbers (124+6+64)
d	129	*Ave stella matutina*	99v-100r	4	–	50	–	50	50 = no. of sb in bb. 1-25
e¹	165	*Lucis Creator optime*	132v-133r	3	–		–	84	84 = no. of sb in bb. 1-28
e³	166b	*Magni[fi]c[at] anima mea Dominum (bb. 104-124)*	134v-135r	3	40		–	–	40 = no. of sb in bb. 104-123

GROUP II

Type	No.	Incipit	Fols.	vv.	S/C	A	T	B/Ct	Remarks
a¹	52	*Deh sì, deh no, deh sì*	32v	4	62	62	62	62	62 = no. of sb in bb. 1-31 (although in the C the count does not include the superfluous value of the note in b. 16)
c²	124a	*La Spagna (Prima pars)*	91v-92r	4	90	90	–	–	90 = no. of sb in bb. 1-30 The number 90 is written midway between the end of the S and the end of the T: it is not clear whether it refers to one or the other voice

98

GROUP III/1

Type	No.	Incipit	Fols.	vv.	S/C	A	T	B/Ct	Remarks
a^1	10	O admirabile comertium!	8v–9r	4	90	90	90	90	90 = no. of sb in bb. 1–45
	83	O gloriosa Regina mundi	53v–54r	3	200		200	200	200 = no. of sb in bb. 1–100
	90	Surge, propera, amica mea	58v–59r	4	190	190	190	190	190 = no. of sb in bb. 1–95
	103	Adonai, [sanctissime Domine]	70v–71r	4	126	126	126	126	126 = no. of sb in bb. 1–63
	125	Regina celi [letare]	94v–95r	3	248		248	248	248 = no. of sb in bb. 1–124
a^2	94b	Regina celi letare ([Secunda pars])	62v–63r	4	132	132	132	132	132 = no. of sb in bb. 64–129
a^4	3	Ave Maria, gratia plena	2v–3r	4	38 / 42	38 / 42	38 / 42	38 / 42	38 = no. of sb in bb. 1–19 / 42 = no. of sb in bb. 21–41
b^1	102	Stella celi extirpavit	69v–70r	4	144	147	144	144	144 = no. of sb in bb. 1–72 (in the S the count does not include the initial section) / 147 = no. of sb in bb. 1–74/I
e^2	166a	Magnif[fic]at anima mea Dominum (bb. 1–61)	133v–134r	3	– / – / –		– / – / –	16 / 58 / 43	16 = no. of sb in bb. 1–8 / 58 = no. of sb in bb. 10–38 / 43 = no. of sb in bb. 40–60 / In the S the count does not include the initial intonation / Magnificat in black notes

99

GROUP III/2

Type	No.	Incipit	Fols.	vv.	S/C	A	T	B/Ct	Remarks
a^2	8b	*Ave Maria, gratia plena (Prima pars)*	*6v–7r*	4	58	58	58	58	58 = no. of sb in bb. 40-68 The count in the S does not include the lacuna of b. 67/I
b^3	2	*Ave Maria, gratia plena*	*1v–2r*	4	34 14 25	34 14 15	34 1 25	34 14 –	34 = no. of sb in bb. 1-17 14 (1 is an error for 14) = no. of sb in bb. 19-25 25 (15 is an error for 25) = no. of sb in bb. 26-38/I The absence of the number 25 in the B is perhaps due to the fact that the sb in the third section in effect are 24 (this sum takes into account the oversight of b. 32/I)
	60	*Mater digna Dei*	*39v–40r*	4	50 48	50 40	50 40	50 40	50 = no. of sb in bb. 7-31 48 (40 is an error for 48) = no. of sb in bb. 39-62

GROUP IV

Type	No.	Incipit	Fols.	vv.	S/C	A	T	B/Ct	Remarks
a³	130	*Ibo mihi ad montem mirrhe*	100v-101r	4	100 99	100 99	100 99	100 99	S, A, T, B: 101 sb. The piece is not divided into sections, so the double numbering is inexplicable
a⁴	167c	(Magnificat) *Anima mea Dominum* (bb. 128–229)	137v-138r	4	116 85	116	85	116 85	116 = no. of sb in bb. 128-185 / 85 is an error for 84 = no. of sb of bb. 187-228 / In the B, moreover, the 'correct' count would be 82, taking into account the oversight of b. 218
b¹	36	*Poi che t'ebi nel core / Fortuna desperata*	22v-23r	4	111	112	112	112	112 (111 is an error for 112) = no. of sb in bb. 1-56
b²	124c	*La Spagna (Tertia pars)*	93v-94r	4	84	90	83	90	84 (83 is an error for 84) = no. of sb in bb. 61-88 / 90 = no. of sb in bb. 61-90
b³	66	*In te, domine, speravi*	42v-43r	4	23 40	23 42	23 42	23 42	23 is an error for 22 (excluding the br of b. 12) or 24 (including the br of b. 12) = no. of sb in bb. 1-12 / 40 = no. of sb in bb. 13-32 / 42 = no. of sb in bb. 13-33
	116	*'Patientia' [ognun me dice]*	80v-81r	4	55 15 56	55 15 54	55 15 53	55 15 56	55 = no. of sb in bb. 1-29 (without counting the initial rest and those supplied in bb. 17/I and 26/I) / 15 = no. of sb in bb. 31/II-38 / 56 = no. of sb in bb. 39-67 (without counting the supplied rests in bb. 39/I and 51/I); 53 and 54 are errors for 56, even if in the A the 'correct' count would be 52, taking into account the oversight of bb. 62 and 67, and in the T would be 55, considering the oversight of the dot in b. 64/I
c¹	21	*Benedictus*	17v-18r	4	110	–	110	110	110 is an error for 114 (= the total of sb in bb. 1-57), unless the count does not take into account the length of the composition in the version for three voices (without the added A), which then begins with b. 3
e²	104	*Tristitia vestra convertetur in gaudium*	71v-72r	4	75 52	– –	– –	– –	75 is an error for 74 = no. of sb in bb. 1-37 / 52 = no. of sb in bb. 38-63
e³	158	*Poiché vivo sopra la terra*	115v-116r	3	103		–	–	103 is an error for 104 = no. of sb in bb. 1-52

Out of a total of 185 musical pieces, 71 are plausibly attributable to composers, some of which are known only through their presence in Panc.27: (a) 42 pieces are attributed in the manuscript; (b) another 29 may be attributed thanks to the aid of concordances; (c) 4 transmit a plausible multiple attribution (this group includes pieces already included in the second grouping).

The group of composers present in Panc.27 includes important names and scarcely known ones, all normalized here in spelling and listed in alphabetical order together with the pieces attributed to them in Panc.27 or in the respective concordances. The biographical notices of known composers are easily found in articles in the most recent musical dictionaries, indicated here (if present); the additional information concerns specific controversial aspects (of identity or otherwise) and updated references. Greater attention, however, is given to the minor composers and those rarely attested; their presence in Panc.27 may cast light not only on their origin and the provenance of the manuscript, but also on the tradition of the repertory included in it.

Alexander Agricola (Ghent, ca. 1446 – Valladolid, 15 August 1506)

16: *Amice, ad quid venisti? attende tibi*

89: *Si dedero [somnum oculis meis]*

95: *O quam glorifica [luce coruscas]*

Just, Martin - Calella, Michele. 'Agricola, (Ackerman), Alexander', in: MGG I, cols. 211-215.

Wegman, Rob C. - Fitch, Fabrice - Lerner, Edward R. 'Agricola [Ackerman], Alexander', in: NG I, pp. 225-229.

Bar[tholomeus?] Pisanus

101: *Piange Pisa*

Scholars have not agreed on the resolution of the abbreviation of the name. Knud Jeppesen reads «Bar[nardo?] Pisan[o]»,[72] but Johannes Wolf transcribed it as «Bartholomeus Pisanus».[73] William Prizer refers to a «Messer Bartolomeo Pisani»: the name figures in a list of the employees at the Ferrarese court compiled in 1470,[74] but Giulio Cattin has commented that 1470 is too early for the production of barzellette, even though the poetic form of *Piange Pisa* is not known.[75] Adriano Franceschini mentions a book «Quadragesimale Magistri Bartholomei de Pisis» in the Archivio del Capitolo dei canonici at Ferrara Cathedral. This is fra Bartolomeo Albisi (Albizi) of Pisa,[76] a well-known person but very old and with no known musical interests: he entered the order of the Friars Minor, and in 1342 was guardian of the convent in Pisa until his death, which happened perhaps after 1360.[77]

No musical dictionaries have an entry for Bartolomeo Pisano; there is, however, an entry for Bernardo Pisano (Pagoli), but without reference to *Piange Pisa*. Bernardo is a Florentine composer born in 1490 who died in 1548, important also for the partbooks of his music published by Petrucci in 1520. Apart from the consideration of his age — this musician would have been very young in the years when Panc.27 was compiled — the identification of Bernardo with the author of *Piange Pisa* does not make much sense, even for stylistic reasons, since he is an author known for madrigalistic compositions. The *opera omnia* dedicated to Bernardo Pisano edited by Frank D'Accone[78] do not include the piece in Panc.27. Among the many musicians called «Bartolomeo» attested in Florence and listed by D'Accone, none is qualified as 'Pisano'.[79] The same is true for the musicians listed by Lockwood only in the English version of his book on the Ferrarese court (p. 345).

---

[72]. Jeppesen 1969, p. 268.

[73]. DTÖ 32, p. 238.

[74]. Prizer 1985, pp. 28-29, n. 103.

[75]. Cattin 1990, p. 252, n. 109.

[76]. Franceschini 1982, p. 85.

[77]. DBI II, pp. 16-17.

[78]. CMM 32/I.

[79]. D'Accone 1997, pp. 731-732, 754-755, 761, 781.

Ben

27: *Poi che sei dal mondo tolta*

No repertory known to me mentions a musician called «Ben»; it is possibly an abbreviation for another name (Benedictus/Benedetto?), perhaps only known locally.

Laurentius Bergomotius Mutinensis (*fl.* sec. XVI *in.*)

2: *Ave Maria, gratia plena*

This person is mentioned by Giovanni Spataro, who calls him «Laurentio Burgomozo da Mutina».[80] Lorenzo was born in Modena in 1480 and was a singer in the cathedral there from 1506 to 1513, when he transferred to the private chapel of Leo X. He remained there at least until 1521, and then returned to Modena, where he died in 1549. The name 'Bergomozzi' is well documented in Modena;[81] in the Archivio di Stato in Modena (fondo Cancelleria ducale, Particolari, busta 150) there is a Latin document dated 20 December 1505 that mentions a certain Cesare Bergomozzi, which confirms the existence of this surname already in the early years of the sixteenth century.

In the fondo Cancelleria ducale, Particolari, busta 134, two sixteenth-century documents have been preserved relating to a Lorenzo Bergami (but catalogued under «Bergomi»); on the back of the older one is written: «Lorenzo Bergami sacerdote Reggiano», and both letters begin with «Lorenzo Bergami da Reggio». According to an archivist at Modena, both letters were written by the same hand, but at different times, which may be confirmed by the fact that both treat the same matter (credits to be extracted from a certain Pelegrino Sanguineti). There is no way of verifying if this priest Lorenzo has anything to do with (or in fact is identical to) the singer Lorenzo in the Duomo of Modena, but the qualification «Mutinensis» (= 'from Modena') in Panc.27 would not rule out that elsewhere he could have been called 'da Reggio': the place name 'Mutinensis' might indeed include the province of Reggio Emilia, since the duchy of Modena and Reggio at that time were a single entity.[82] The «Lorenzo da Modena» documented at Ferrara in the years 1476-77[83] is evidently a different person.

Giovanni Brocco (*fl.* early 16th century)

17: *Alma, svegliate oramai*

65: *Io mi voglio lamentare*

Luisi, Francesco. 'Brocco, Giovanni Antonio', in: MGG III, cols. 954-955.

Boorman, Stanley. 'Brocco, Giovanni', in: NG IV, pp. 412-413.

In the manuscript ModE 9 — in which there are only three names of musicians over only seven pieces — the name of Giovanni Brocco appears in two different versions: «Io. broc[us]» and «Io. Ant[onius] broc[us]». For Jeppesen the two forms referred to one person, that is «Ioannes Brocchus *Vero[nensis]*», mentioned with his toponym in PeFroI (*Aymè che doglia è questa*, fol. 16r), and without it in the same Book I (*Alma svegliate hormai*, fol. 2r), as well as in seven instances in the third book of Frottole.[84] The identification of the frottolist, who almost certainly was a member of the scuola degli Accoliti of Verona,[85] with the Veronese archpriest of Arbizzano Giovanni Broco — a humanist to whom attention has been drawn by Messedaglia[86] — has also been hypothesized by all the scholars

---

[80]. See Blackburn *et al.* 1991, p. 983, referring to the autograph letter of Spataro to Pietro Aaron of 23 May 1524 (pp. 300-306: 305).

[81]. The family stemma is described in Di Crollalanza III, *Appendice*, p. 169: «Arms: silver, with five snaking flames, three red and two black, in alternation, moving from the chief towards the tip of the pale; with the chief attached in silver, with five iron arrows, arising out of the partition, and placed in the pale».

[82]. Amorth 1998, pp. 7-8.

[83]. Lockwood 1987, *Appendice V*, p. 396.

[84]. Boorman 2006, p. 1261.

[85]. Paganuzzi 1976, p. 95.

[86]. Messedaglia 1944, pp. 84, 100-101. On 11 March 1500 Broco (or Brocchi?) carved the following inscription on a Roman sepulchral pillar: «Prodidit luci lapidem Ioannes Brochus et plebis Dominus Sacerdos quem diu in terris tenuit

who have dealt with the problem,[87] but it is also possible that the two partially agreeing names refer to different people: it is striking, in fact, that in the first mention in ModE 9 the second name Antonius is lacking; it appears only in the second mention, and then is 'withdrawn' from the third.[88] The same composer also turns up in a manuscript containing music from the church, MS DCCLIX (DCCLXIX) of the Biblioteca Capitolare in Verona,[89] and Giuseppina La Face hypothesizes that he might be identifiable with the Magister Iohannes whose name appears over the sonnet on fol. 7★r of MS ModE 9.[90]

ANTOINE BRUMEL (Diocese of Laon?, ca. 1460 - Mantua?, after 11 May 1512)

94: *Regina celi letare*
120: *O Domine Iesu Christe*
121?: *O Domine Iesu Christe*
131: *Mater patris [et filia]*

PIETSCHMANN, Klaus. 'Brumel (Brumet, Brummel, Brommel, Brunel, Brunello), Antoine' in: MGG III, cols. 1120-1126.
HUDSON, Barton. 'Brumel [Brummel, Brommel, Brunel, Brunello], Antoine', in: NG IV, pp. 494-498.

? C.

145: *Se non dormi, donna, ascolta*
    See the catalogue, no. 145, n. 1.

MARCHETTO CARA (Verona, ca. 1465 - Mantua, late October 1525)

4?: *Ave Maria, gratia plena* (attributed elsewhere also to Tromboncino)
12: *Aimè el cor, aimè la testa* (attributed elsewhere also to Tromboncino)
37: *Defecerunt vedo ormai*
52?: *Deh sì, deh no, deh sì* (attributed elsewhere also to Tromboncino)
63: *Io son l'ucello che sopra i rami d'oro*
78: *Oimè, che moro [per ti, dona crudele]*
145?: *Se non dormi, donna, ascolta* (or Loyset Compère?)

SCHMIDT, Lothar. 'Cara (de Cara, Carra) Marchetto, (Marco, Marcetus, Marcus)', in: MGG IV, cols. 160-168.
PRIZER, William F. 'Cara [Carra], Marchetto [Marco, Marcus, Marchettus]', in: NG V, pp. 108-111.

FIRMINUS CARON (fl. ca. 1460-75)

56: *Helas que pourra devenir*

GALLAGHER, Sean. 'Caron, Firminus', in: MGG IV, cols. 243-247.
FALLOWS, David. 'Caron, Firminus', in: NG V, pp. 176-177.

    An author well attested in many fifteenth- and sixteenth-century sources (the CC lists no fewer than 39 manuscripts), he is always identified with the single name 'Caron'. The only exception

---

vetustas lumine cassum MD XI Martii» (see PAGANUZZI 1976, pp. 110 and 152, n. 12). Paganuzzi continues: «The cippus, used as an architectonic element, supports two arches through which one enters into the courtyard of the canonry, and on a capital Brocco's arms are sculpted: a fess crossing over two shoots, or sprouts ('brocchi'), one rose at the top, the other at the base (according to Messedaglia). On the fess are carved the letters D.I.A.B., the last damaged at the bottom, which, on the basis of the inscription mentioned earlier, taking into account the meaning of *brocco* portrayed in the coat of arms, might be interpreted as *Dominus Ioannes Arbisani Brochus* [see the illustration in PAGANUZZI 1976, p. 111, fig. 58]. A similar coat of arms without letters is also found on the campanile, placed there after the earlier tower, demolished in 1936, was reconstructed (1939). Messedaglia called attention to the Virgilian allusion in *lumine cassum* (*Aen*. 11. 85): if we recall that the MS DCCLIX of the Biblioteca Capitolare of Verona contains a *Salve Regina* of Giovanni Brocco, who is certainly the frottolist, it is difficult not to think that the humanist archpriest and the musician are the same person» (see PAGANUZZI 1976, p. 110).

[87]. JEPPESEN 1969, pp. 279-280, PAGANUZZI 1976, p. 110; LUISI 1985, LA FACE BIANCONI 1990, p. 14.

[88]. *Mai più serà lo core mio contento*, fols. 66v-67r and the textless piece on fols. 94v-95r are assigned to «Io. Broc[us]»; *Se me abandoni fa che tu me rendi*, fols. 95v-96r is attributed to «Io. Ant[onius] broc[us]».

[89]. «Io. Broc[us]» appears over the *Salve Regina* on fols. 50v-51v reproduced in PAGANUZZI 1976, p. 111. On the manuscript see SPAGNOLO 1996, pp. 558-559.

[90]. LA FACE BIANCONI, p. 14.

is «F. caron» in the *Missa L'homme armé* in MS San Pietro B 80 in the Biblioteca Apostolica Vaticana, fols. 99*r*-113*r*. Thanks to Tinctoris we are able to resolve the initial as his baptismal name «Firminus»: the theorist in fact cites his name in full in the nineteenth chapter (*De nono decimo effectu*) in the *Complexus effectuum musices* (1472-75).[91] He names him again twice in full in the Prologue of his *Liber de arte contrapuncti* (1477)[92] and in the eighth chapter of Book 3,[93] as well as three other times with only his surname: twice in his *Proportionale musices* (before 1476)[94] and once more in his *Liber de arte contrapuncti*, Book 2, chapter 33;[95] the contexts clarify that Tinctoris was referring to a contemporary musician. From a document preserved in the Bibliothèque Municipale in Amiens[96] we have a notice of a Firminus Caron who lived in Amiens in 1422, possibly an ancestor of our Caron. Other conjectures as to his first name are 'Jean' (less probable) or the 'Philippe' Caron cited by Jules Houdoy[97] as *enfant d'autel* in Cambrai Cathedral, son of Jean. Many scholars have insisted in the identification of the composer with Philippe;[98] documents conserved at Brussels, however, demonstrate that the composer cannot be Philippe.[99]

LOYSET COMPÈRE (Hainaut, ca. 1445 – Saint-Quentin, 16 August 1518)

59: *Ne doibt [on prendre quant on donne]*

73?: *Helas, [le bon temps que j'avoie]* (attributed elsewhere also to Tinctoris)

111?: *Regina celi* (attributed elsewhere also to Prioris in a version that differs only in the opening notes)

126: *Propter gravamen [et tormentum]*

145?: *Se non dormi, donna, ascolta* (or Marchetto Cara?)

FINSCHER, Ludwig. 'Compère, Loyset (Aluyseto)', in: MGG IV, cols. 1446-1545.

RIFKIN, Joshua - DEAN, Jeffrey - FALLOWS, David - HUDSON, Barton. 'Compère, Loyset', in: NG VI, pp. 180-184.

FRATER DIONISIUS PLACENTINUS

67: *Egli è il tuo bon Iesù*

As attested also in the CC,[100] the name of «Dionisius Placentinus» (= 'of Piacenza') appears only in Panc.27. Therefore it is unlikely that he can be identified with the Dionisio da Piacenza contained in the *Dizionario biografico piacentino* of Luigi Mensi:[101] a Lateran Canon Regular with no clear connection with musical activity, abbot of the abbey of Fiesole who wrote the life of the reverend mother Battista da Genova (secular name Tommasina Vernazza, 1497-1587), Lateran Canonness, published in the fourth volume of her spiritual works edited in 1602.[102]

Pietro Canal mentions a certain «fra Dionisio Memmo who from September 1506 was an organist in the ducal chapel of Venice, and in 1516 went to London, where, on account of his valour, he acquired the favour of the king».[103] And Antonio Bertolotti relates that «the Marchese [Francesco Gonzaga], having finally gathered the best musicians that could be found, on 12 January 1511 ordered the testing of the new chapel, for which a friar of the Crutched Friars, a Venetian

---

[91]. SEAY 1975, p. 176.

[92]. *Ibidem*, p. 12.

[93]. *Ibidem*, p. 156.

[94]. SEAY 1978, pp. 10 and 49.

[95]. SEAY 1975, p. 143.

[96]. The document is reproduced in THOMSON 1959, I, after p. 14, and discussed on pp. 13-15.

[97]. HOUDOY 1880, p. 83.

[98]. From THOMSON 1959 to ROTH 1991, pp. 290-293; see other studies at n. 5, p. 296 of HAGGH 1991.

[99]. HAGGH 1991, pp. 296, 299-315.

[100]. CC V, p. 145.

[101]. MENSI 1899, p. 164.

[102]. *Delle opere spirituali della reverenda et divotiss. vergine di Christo, donna Battista da Genova* [...] *T. IV. Con la vita della medesima descritta dal m.r.p.d. Dionisio da Piacenza* [...] *Hor prima dato in luce. Con tre tavole molto copiose, et utili*, Verona, Angelo Tamo, 1602. There is a copy in Florence, Biblioteca Nazionale Centrale, Palatino 14.X.1.6.4[II].

[103]. CANAL (1879) 1881, p. 23 (677).

gentleman and excellent clavicembalist, was called from Venice. Canal believes that this friar might be fra Dionisio Memmo, who from September 1507 was organist of the ducal chapel in Venice».[104] But neither one nor the other reference shows any link between this Dionisio and Piacenza.

Another interesting suggestion arises from a book that is no longer extant: the lost tenth book of Frottole published by Petrucci in Fossombrone in 1512. We know that it listed a certain «Dionis[ius] dit Papin da Mantua», of whom Canal found no notice in the Archivio Gonzaga, «which perhaps is an indication and result of not being in the service of the court: but there were some frottole by Papino in the tenth book of Petrucci».[105] The provenance 'da Mantua' most likely refers to the place in which the musician was in service at the time, and not to his city of origin. On Petrucci's tenth book of Frottole Claudio Sartori comes to our aid: «This tenth book of Petrucci's Frottole was also cited in the catalogue of publications by Petrucci prepared by Bottrigari and reproduced by Gaspari on the manuscript leaf he added to the book by Schmid in the Biblioteca del Conservatorio di Bologna, and by Augusto Vernarecci (op. cit. [that is VERNARECCI 1882], p. 126)». The book was certainly in the collection of Ferdinand Columbus,[106] and a copy belonged to the famous owner of Petrucci prints Ercole Bottrigari, who listed the names of the composers present: «Philippus Mantuan. Organ., Io: Hesdimitis, Io: Scrivano, Franciscus F., G. B. Ferro, Dionis. dit. Papin da Mantua, Pietro da Lodi».[107]

DOMINICUS

137: *Alleluia*

LUISI, Francesco. 'Dominicus', in: DEUMM II, p. 517.

On the identity of this «Dominicus», attested in this graphic form only in Panc.27, various hypotheses can be suggested. For example, Canal mentioned a «messer Domenichino» who in 1515 was *Maestro de' canti* at the court of Mantua.[108] The name «dominicus de feraria» appears only in MS Canon. Misc. 213 of the Bodleian Library in Oxford (*O dolçe conpagno se tu voy cantare*, fol. 135r), compiled between 1428 and 1436 but with a repertory that partly goes back to the 1380s:[109] possibly this reference is to the choreographer and dancing-master Domenico da Piacenza, but this identification would be unlikely for a Dominicus in the Panciatichi manuscript who was the author of an *Alleluia*. Enrico Peverada mentions a «Domenico da Ferrara di Giacomo», a singer and choir director in Ferrara Cathedral from 1460 to 1472.[110] The duties of this don Domenico, however, were not continuous: on 26 September 1460 we find Roberto de Anglia as the singer charged «ad

---

[104]. BERTOLOTTI 1890, p. 30. On Memo see the relevant entries by John M. Ward in NG (XVI, p. 379) and by Dietrich Helms in MGG (XI, cols. 1522-1523).

[105]. CANAL (1879) 1881, p. 21 (675).

[106]. CHAPMAN 1968, no. 40.

[107]. See CANAL (1879) 1881, p. 21 (675), n. 1 and BOORMAN 2006, p. 724.

[108]. CANAL (1879) 1881, p. 23 (677).

[109]. FALLOWS 1995, pp. 19-20.

[110]. «On the eleventh of February 1460 appeared the new 'magister ad docendum clericos in cantu' and also the rector of the chapel of S. Giovanni Battista *sub organo*, the *cantor* don Domenico, son of mastro Giacomo [...], of whom it is said that he is from Argenta, at one time a carpenter, now a 'canipario' (administrator) of the Marchese, son of the late Giovanni *Chiarieli*, living in Ferrara in the district of the Rotta. The change of profession and — above all — of rank of mastro Giacomo might indicate that the singer Domenico also had some fortune at court and therefore in the wake of his son the father too achieved a not negligible advance in Este service; but we cannot state this with certainty. At any rate, at the date mentioned above, the singer don Domenico and his father mastro Giacomo — the latter present and consenting — promise to pay to the 'massaro' (administrator) of the fabric of the cathedral ser Vincenzo Lardi '22 lire di marchesini' for bed linen consigned by the administrator. Don Domenico, characterized as 'cantore conducto ad docendum clericos Ferrarie in cantu', reappears on 22 August 1463: the act now calls him 'Ferrarese priest'» (see PEVERADA 1991, pp. 129-130 and n. 80, with references to the relevant archival documents). «On the 11th of the following month, on the *cantor* don Domenico the vicar general Raffaele Primadicci confers the chapel of St. Sebastian in the cathedral» (see PEVERADA 1991, p. 130, n. 81, with references to the relevant archival documents). The presence of the same singer don Domenico is again attested at two meetings of the chaplains of the cathedral held on 17 February 1467 and 13 January 1468, as well as at two pastoral visits of the chapel on 10 May 1470 and 4 June 1472 (see PEVERADA 1991, p. 130, nn. 84, 85, and 86, with references to the relevant archival documents).

docendum clericos Ferrarie».[111] According to what Adriano Franceschini reports, a «Dominicus» owned a book of Virgilian works that had previously belonged to Francesco de Lignamine, bishop of Ferrara from 1446 to 1460;[112] though there is no proof, it is possible that he might be the same Domenico investigated by Peverada, considering that before leaving for Rome, the bishop De Lignamine gave his library to the chapter of the canons at Ferrara Cathedral.[113]

More prudent, perhaps, is the identification proposed by Knud Jeppesen[114] with the musician Domenico who in 1517 was in the service of the Marchese of Mantua, perhaps the same person also called «cantore Domenichino» who together with the heir Federico Gonzaga left for Rome in 1510 to become a hostage of Pope Julius II.[115] Possibly his too are the frottola *Se per seguire el gregie*, present together with the indication «Domi» in the anthology *Canzone, Sonetti, Strambotti et Frottole. Libro primo* printed in Siena by Pietro Sambonetto on 30 August 1515 (RISM 1515/2), and the motet *Virgo prudentissima* published in the *Motetti del Fiore. Libro primo* printed in Lyons in 1532 by Jacques Moderne (RISM 1532/10), attributed to «Domin.».

Other musicians to consider are perhaps the «Domenico del Reame trombeta» at the court of Ferrara from 1484 to 1486,[116] the «Domenico organista» at Ferrara from 1492 to 1505,[117] and the older «Don Domenico controbasso», who worked there from 1472 to 1478.[118] Other homonyms are attested in Ferrara more sporadically: «Domenego trombeta» (1457),[119] «Domenico da Piacenza» (1471), and «Domenico da Vizenza trombeta» (1478).[120]

The contrapuntist «Giovanni Dominico» who lived in the middle of the sixteenth century mentioned in GERBER (1812) 1966, I, col. 916, who in 1566 published in Venice the collection *Cantiones sacrae 5 vocum*, appears to be too late to be taken into consideration here.[121]

ENEAS

85: *Se conviene a un cor vilano*

LUISI, Francesco. 'Eneas', in: DEUMM II, p. 656.

The name appears uniquely over the piece *Se conviene a un cor villano* printed in PeFroIII, and there are no biographical notices in any repertory, to my knowledge. Probably deriving from the second edition (the first edition of 1837-44 does not include the entry) of the *Biographie universelle des musiciens et bibliographie générale de la musique* of François-Joseph Fétis[122] is a misunderstanding that remained attached to the name of this musician. Fétis classifies the composer as 'Dupré (Eneas)', linking it to Petrucci's seventh and ninth books of Frottole. Similarly Robert Eitner, who continues to call him 'Dupre, Eneas'.[123] The CC also contains the entry 'Dupre, Eneas', which refers uniquely to Panc.27.[124] Knud Jeppesen, instead, distinguishes 'Eneas' from 'Elias Dupre',[125] while the list of composers in RISM B IV/5 contains uniquely 'Dupré, Eneas (Elias)' (p. 674), and next to the incipit *Se conviene a un cor vilano* reports 'Dupré (E)' (p. 657), referring only to the piece in Panc.27, where

---

[111]. PEVERADA 1991, pp. 130-131.

[112]. An unidentified hand has added the rubric «habet Dominicus»; see FRANCESCHINI 1977, p. 86, n. 1.

[113]. *Ibidem*, p. 52.

[114]. JEPPESEN 1968, p. 153.

[115]. BERTOLOTTI 1890, pp. 31 and 29.

[116]. LOCKWOOD 1987, *Appendice V*, pp. 398-399.

[117]. *Ibidem*, pp. 401-405.

[118]. *Ibidem*, pp. 394-397.

[119]. This notice comes from William Prizer's review of the English edition of LOCKWOOD 1987 (in: *Journal of the American Musicological Society*, XL, 1987, pp. 95-105: 101).

[120]. LOCKWOOD 1987, *Appendice V*, pp. 393, 394, 397.

[121]. See also FÉTIS III, p. 36 and EITNER III, p. 226. This musician is possibly Giovanni Domenico del Giovane da Nola, born between 1510 and 1520 (I owe this suggestion to Bonnie Blackburn, with thanks).

[122]. FÉTIS III, p. 84.

[123]. EITNER III, p. 281.

[124]. CC V, p. 147.

[125]. JEPPESEN 1969, p. 275.

instead the attribution is «[Eneas]» (p. 146). In point of fact, nothing authorizes us to think that 'Elias Dupré' and 'Eneas' are the same person, and both DEUMM (vol. II) and the NG (vol. VII) dedicate separate entries to the two people. Stanley Boorman does the same in his recent catalogue of Petrucci sources, distinguishing 'Dupre, Helias' from 'Eneas':[126] with the first name are associated no fewer than 7 compositions, attested in the seventh book of Frottole (3 pieces), the ninth book (3 pieces), and the second book of Frottole intabulated for voice and lute by Bossinensis (one piece).

ERASMUS (LAPICIDA?) (ca. 1440/45 - Vienna, 19 November 1547)

174: *Incipit lamentatio Ieremie prophete*

CALELLA, Michele. 'Lapicida, (Lapicide), Erasmus (Rasmo)', in: MGG X, cols. 1202-1204.

WEISS, Susan Forscher. 'Lapicida, [Steinschneider], Erasmus [Rasmo]', in: NG XIV, p. 267.

Generally, one tends of think that the «Erasmus» of the Lamentation in Panc.27 (perhaps copied from PeLamII) is the long-lived 'Lapicida'[127] known from various pieces attested in German and Italian sources. Curiously, in Stanley Boorman's catalogue both the Lamentation and the frottola *Pietà cara signore | La pietà ha chiuso le porte* (assigned in Petrucci only to «Rasmo») are indexed under 'Erasmus, Desiderius'.[128] Already August Wilhelm Ambros was not convinced that the Rasmo of Petrucci was the same as Lapicida.[129]

GIACOMO FOGLIANO (Modena, 1467/68 - Modena, 10 April 1548)

3: *Ave Maria, gratia plena*

92: *Si dedero [el mio core al dio d'amore]*

SCHMIDT, Lothar. 'Fogliano (Fogliani, Foglianus, Foianus, Folianus), Giacomo (Jacopo, Jacobus)', in: MGG VI, cols. 1394-1398.

SLIM, H. Colin. 'Fogliano [da Modena], Giacomo [Fogliani, Jacopo]', in: NG IX, pp. 56-57.

See also PRIZER 2004, pp. 405-406 and p. 405, n. 15.

JOHANNES GHISELIN (VERBONNET) (Picardy, before 1460? - after 1507)

124: *La Spagna*

128: *La alfonsina*

PIETSCHMANN, Klaus. 'Ghiselin (alias Verbonnet), Johannes', in: MGG VII, cols. 871-875.

GOTTWALD, Clytus. 'Ghiselin [Verbonnet], Johannes', in: NG IX, pp. 813-814.

See also RIFKIN 2003, p. 321, n. 175.

HAYNE VAN GHIZEGHEM (ca. 1445 - before 1497)

127: *Ales regres, [vuidez de ma presence]*

BORGHETTI, Vincenzo. 'Hayne van Ghizeghem', in: MGG VIII, cols. 1123-1129.

LITTERICK, Louise. 'Hayne [Ayne, Haine, Heyne, Scoen Hayne] van Ghizeghem [Ghiseghem]', in: NG XI, pp. 288-289.

JO[HANNES?] HESDIMOIS

179: *Tuto el mundo è fantasia*

Another mysterious name absent from modern music dictionaries, «Hesdimois» might refer to the provenance of the musician from the French city of Hesdin, now in Pas-de-Calais, even if in this case the correct heading should have been 'Hesdinois'.[130] The best-known musician coming from this city is Nicolle des Celliers de Hesdin, known simply as 'Hesdin',[131] whose full name is documented only on the epitaph of his tomb in Beauvais Cathedral, where he was master of the choirboys at least from 1536 till his death in 1538. We also have a notice of a Pierre Hesdin, documented first at the

---

[126]. BOORMAN 2006, p. 1265.

[127]. The adjective is explained by Armando Petrucci: it refers to a stonecutter of epitaphs (see PETRUCCI 1992, p. 41).

[128]. BOORMAN 2006, p. 1265.

[129]. AMBROS III, p. 190.

[130]. As confirmation, see the entry 'Hesdin' in GRAND ROBERT DES NOMS PROPRES II, p. 1440.

[131]. See the relevant entry by Joshua Rifkin in NG XI, pp. 457-458.

court of Henry II of France, and then as singer in the Papal Chapel from 1547 to 1559.[132]

Perhaps because it took for granted his French provenance, the CC turned the name of the composer into the French 'Jean Hesdimois', although his name appears in AntCanzoni only in the form «Jo. Hesdimois».[133]

A certain «Io. Hesdimitis» (the same person?) appears among the authors in the tenth book of Petrucci's Frottole, now lost.[134] Already Robert Eitner, in the *Quellen-Lexicon*, hypothesized the substantial identity between Hesdimitis and Hesdimois;[135] so does Stanley Boorman in his Petrucci catalogue raisonné, referring to the note by Bottrigari transcribed by Gaspari on the composers of the tenth book of Frottole, in the description of the same book, now lost, and in the index of names.[136]

HENRICUS ISAAC (Flanders or Brabant, ca. 1450/55 - Florence, 26 March 1517)

11: *A la bataglia*

21: *Benedictus (Missa Quant j'ay au cueur)*

54: *La mora*

55?: *La stangetta* (attributed elsewhere also to Obrecht and to Weerbeke; see the catalogue, no. 55, n. 2)

75: *Les bien amore / Omnis labor habet finem*

81: *Omnis laus in fine canitur*

138: *Alleluia*

168: *Helas, [que devera mon cueur]*

STAEHELIN, Martin. 'Isaac (Isaak, Ysac, Ysach, Yzac etc.), Heinrich (Henrich, Henricus, Arrigo di Fiandra/de Alemania, Arrigo d'Ugo/Ugonis, Arrigo Tedesco)', in: MGG IX, cols. 672-691.

STROHM, Reinhard - KEMPSON, Emma. 'Isaac [Ysaak, Ysac, Yzac], Henricus [Heinrich, Arrigo d'Ugo, Arrigo Tedesco]', in: NG XII, pp. 576-590.

JOHANNES JAPART (ca. 1450 - after 1500?)

96: *Helas, que il est à mon gré*

ATLAS, Allan W. 'Japart, Jean (Johannes)', in: MGG IX, cols. 935-936.

ATLAS, Allan W., rev. ALDEN, Jane. 'Japart [Japarte, Jappart, Zaparth, ?Gaspart], Jean [Janni, Johannes]', in: NG XII, pp. 890-891.

See also ATLAS 2005 — who retains the possibility of the identification of Japart with the singer Frater Johannes de Francia and that Japart was in contact with Petrus Castellanus, Petrucci's editor — and the forthcoming *Jean Japart: The Collected Works*, edited by Allan W. Atlas, New York, Broude Trust (Masters and Monuments of the Renaissance).

JOHANNES DE QUADRIS (before 1410 - after 1456, but certainly dead by 1457)

45: *Cum autem venissem ad locum*

BORGHETTI, Vincenzo. 'Johannes de Quadris, (Quatris)', in: MGG IX, cols. 1107-1110.

CATTIN, Giulio. 'Johannes de Quadris [Quatris]', in: NG XIII, pp. 143-144.

JOSQUIN DES PREZ (? near Saint-Quentin, ca. 1450/55 - Condé-sur-l'Escaut, 27 August 1521)

66: *In te, domine, speravi*

115: *Tu solus qui facis mirabilia*

139: *Fortuna d'um gran tempo*

FINSCHER, Ludwig. 'Josquin des Prez', in: MGG IX, cols. 1210-1282.

MACEY, Patrick - NOBLE, Jeremy - DEAN, Jeffrey - REESE, Gustave. 'Josquin (Lebloitte dit) des Prez [Josse, Gosse, Joskin, Jossequin, Josquinus, Jodocus, Judocus, Juschino; Desprez, des Près, des Prés, de Prés, a Prato, de Prato, Pratensis]', in: NG XIII, pp. 220-266.

See also FALLOWS 2009.

---

[132]. ABERT 1927, p. 200.

[133]. CC V, p. 170.

[134]. On the book and the musicians listed in it see the final part of the entry on Frater Dionisius Placentinus.

[135]. See EITNER V, p. 131: 'Hesdimois, Jean (Joannes Hesdimitis)'.

[136]. BOORMAN 2006, pp. 46, 303, 724, 1268.

Musipula

8: *Ave Maria*

As far as is known, only the CC mentions the name «Musipula», with the unique reference to Panc.27.[137]

Jacob Obrecht (Ghent, ca. 1458 – Ferrara, 1505)

55?: *La stangetta* (attributed elsewhere also to Isaac and to Weerbeke; see the catalogue, no. 55, n. 2)

105: *Meskim [es u cutkin ru?]*

Finscher, Ludwig. 'Obrecht, (Hobrecht, Hoebrecht, Obreth, Obret, Hobertus), Jacob (Jacop, Copkin)', in: MGG XII, cols. 1258-1272.

Wegman, Rob C. 'Obrecht, [Hobrecht], Jacob', in: NG XVIII, p. 267.

Pamphilus

18: *Cucù, cucù, ognon canti cucù*

The name «Pamphilus» is reported only in Jeppesen 1969 (p. 288) and in CC, with the unique reference to the attestation of Panc.27.[138] I have not found any new information on this mysterious person, except the suggestion that links him to the name of the poet Panfilo Sasso, itself a pseudonym of Sasso de' Sassi (Modena, ca. 1455 – Lonzano, Ravenna, 1527): however, I think it highly unlikely that the reference in Panc.27 is to the poet, since it would be the unique case in the whole manuscript in which a poet is mentioned. Too late is the possible identification with the maestro di cappella Joseph Panfilus who lived in France at the end of the 1560s,[139] as well as that with the trombonist «Pamfilo di Ansano Maria, detto Tromboncino» who lived in the 1540s.[140]

Antonius Peragulfus Lucensis (fl. sec. XVI in.)

125: *Regina celi*

The CC gives Panc.27 as the unique reference to this author.[141] It is unlikely that he can be identified with the theorist Antonio da Lucca, the Servite friar who lived in the fifteenth century who was occupied with various problems of mensural notation, but appears to have left no compositions. He is instead the musician and singer in office in Lucca Cathedral mentioned by Luigi Nerici,[142] who instructed the choirboys and held the title of 'praecentor'.[143] A greatly appreciated musician, he surely maintained his post at Lucca at least from 15 March 1507 to 23 April 1509.[144] In that year the cathedral canons gave preference to the priest Vincenzo Bianchi, and Peragulfo left. That Antonio was not a priest seems attested by the fact that in the meetings of the chaplains of the cathedral he is never called 'presbiter' (a term attached to all the other names). Peragulfo, however, was permitted to enjoy the distributions as 'concappellano', and in the meetings is indicated as «Dominus Peragulfus».[145]

The English theorist John Hothby mentions a «Pelagulfus» together with other musicians in his *Dialogus in arte musica*, a treatise perhaps conceived at Lucca Cathedral and written down by one of Hothby's own students.[146] According to Reinhard Strohm the musicians mentioned here would have been well known to students, and would in part have been represented in MS Lucca,

---

[137]. CC V, p. 203.

[138]. *Ibidem*, p. 209.

[139]. Vander Straeten VI, p. 447.

[140]. D'Accone 1997, pp. 792 and 849.

[141]. CC V, p. 212.

[142]. Nerici 1880, pp. 44-45, 80, 269.

[143]. Eitner VII, p. 360.

[144]. The document of his nomination is transcribed in full in Nerici 1880, p. 80, n. 40. At n. 41 is the documentary reference to Peragulfo's dismissal.

[145]. Nerici 1880, pp. 44-45, 269.

[146]. Strohm 1993, p. 596. See also Seay 1955, who gives the complete text of the *Dialogus*. The passage in question — which cites 14 other musicians — is on fol. 82r, transcribed by Seay on p. 95.

Archivio di Stato, 238.[147] Strohm hypothesizes that some of the composers cited by Hothby were his personal acquaintances; among these «Pelagulfus» is probably Antonio Peragulfo.[148] We also owe to Reinhard Strohm, who was the first to study the Lucca MS,[149] the recent acquisitions of more pages of the same codex: at the moment we know 76 pages containing 27 pieces, the last of which is the hymn *Qui pace Christi* by «A. Peragulfus» (Hand D, fol. 60*v*): this, therefore, is the second composition attributable to this musician, hitherto known only thanks to the *Regina celi* in Panc.27.[150]

MICHELE PESENTI (Verona, ca. 1470 – May 1528)

61: *Io son de gabbia, non de bosco ocello / Iste confesor Domini*
LUISI, Francesco. 'Pesenti, (Pesentus) [Veronese], Michele (Michael)', in: MGG XIII, cols. 374-376.
PRIZER, William F. 'Pesenti [Vicentino], Michele', in: NG XIX, pp. 484-485.

JOHANNES DE PINAROL (ca. 1467 – Brescia, ca. 1536)

90: *Surge propera amica mea*
SHERR, Richard. 'Pinarol, Johannes de', in: NG XIX, p. 749.
LUISI, Francesco. 'Pinarol, Giovanni (Ioannes)', in: DEUMM VI, p. 20.

Robert Eitner thought that Pinarol was Dutch,[151] but Francesco Luisi hypothesizes instead that the composer was Brescian by birth.[152] Panc.27 is the unique musical manuscript to attribute a piece to Pinarol. It is not clear why François-Joseph Fétis considered the musician to be Belgian[153] in view of the fact that the name is linked to only two attestations (*Fortuna desperata* in PeCantiC, fols. 68*v*-69*r*, and *Surge propera amica mea* in Panc.27 and in PeMotA; see catalogue no. 90), which carry the ascription «Jo./Io. Pinarol/de Pinarol».

Some documentary notices on this musician have fortunately come down to us in the studies of Paolo Guerrini. A contract, registered partly on 13 October and partly on 26 November 1507, found in an administrative book in the archive of the monastery of S. Eufemia in Brescia, attests the restoration and enlargement of the local organ on the part of «Zohan da li organi» (identified with 'Giovanni di Pinerolo'), organ builder and organist in the service of the Duomo of Brescia.[154] Other documents show Pinarol working as organ builder and organist at Brescia from June 1514: one of these is dated 4 November 1514, and five other notices are documentable from 6 Feburary to 23 July 1515.[155] In 1517 Pinarol was organist of the Duomo of Brescia and was fifty years old: he

---

[147]. Also belonging to this corpus are MSS Lucca, Archivio Arcivescovile, 97 and Pisa, Archivio Arcivescovile, Biblioteca Maffi, Cartella 11/III; all the three sources are reproduced and studied in a facsimile (STROHM 2008). See also the entry by Bonnie Blackburn for 'Hothby, John' in: NG XI, pp. 749-751: 750.

[148]. STROHM 1993, p. 591.

[149]. STROHM 1968.

[150]. I thank Reinhard Strohm, who kindly communicated the news of this discovery before reporting it in his presentation at the *Medieval and Renaissance Music Conference 2007* (Institut für Musikwissenschaft, Universität Wien, 7-11 August), and Bonnie Blackburn, who gave me a résumé of his paper *Entdeckung mit Fortsetzungen: der neueste Forschungsstand zum 'Chorbuch Lucca'*.

[151]. EITNER VII, p. 450.

[152]. See the relevant entry in DEUMM VI, p. 20.

[153]. FÉTIS VII, p. 59. CC does the same, accepting uncritically that Pinarol's baptismal name was 'Jean' (see CC V, p. 214).

[154]. The information comes from GUERRINI 1942, pp. 137-138.

[155]. The document of 1514 is found on fol. 23*r* of the *Liber boletarum fabrice ecclesie maioris [Brixie]*, MS F.VII.24 of the Biblioteca Civica Queriniana, formerly belonging to the Archivio Storico Civico, but transferred there from the Archivio Capitolare: «Mag.r Ioannes de pinarolo Organista conductus ad hoc sub die X Iunii prox. pret. ad reformandum organa S. Marie eccles. cathedralis et facta pulsare cum salario duc. XX in anno et ad rationem anni, quod salarium incipiat et currere die primo augusti prox. pret., ut latius in instr. rogato per d. Leonardum malvetium alium Canc. comunis brixie [*in margine* et registratum in libro diversarum locationum f. 73], habuit bull. pro eius salario trium mensium de libris XV cum dimidia planet […]». The notice comes from GUERRINI 1939, pp. 212-213.

affirms this in a memorandum presented to the civic tax authority in this very year.[156] In 1536 he was substituted (perhaps owing to his death) by Vincenzo Parabosco of Piacenza as organist of the cathedral: Parabosco's employment contract is dated 11 August 1536.[157]

JOHANNES PRIORIS (fl. ca. 1485 - 1512)

111?: *Regina celi* (attributed elsewhere also to Compère in a version that differs only in the opening notes)

PLANCHART, Alejandro Enrique. 'Prioris, Johannes', in: MGG XIII, cols. 944-946.

LITTERICK, Louise. 'Prioris, Johannes', in: NG XX, pp. 382-384.

Notices on this musician can be found in dictionary entries. Here I shall mention only some suggestions on his identification. Edmond Vander Straeten hypothesized a Flemish origin, considering the name «Prioris» as the translation of the words 'de Veurste' or 'de Vorste' (= 'the first'), a Latinization of the name of a musician who was a native of the Low Countries.[158] The first certain document that concerns him dates from 1503, when he is mentioned as the master of the French Royal Chapel.[159] David Fallows suggests other identifications: a «Johannes Prepositi» appears in documents of the choir of the French Royal Court at the beginning of the 1460s, a «Johannes Praepositus» is known in Ferrara in 1449-50, and a «Jo. Praepositi» is in the papal chapel in 1450-51.[160]

RENALDO (= RAYNALDUS FRANCIGENA?)

104: *Tristitia vestra convertetur in gaudium*

The identity of this person is not ascertainable with certainty. In addition to Panc.27, only the 'Rusconi manuscript' (BolM 19) contains compositions attributed to «Renaldo»: 11 in total (7 motets, 2 masses, and 2 Magnificats).[161] The name «Raynaldino» appears in the registers of the Milanese ducal chapel in 1474[162] and might refer to the same musician as in BolM 19, and even to the «Raynaldus francigena» who was *Magister cantus* at Padua in 1489-90, qualified as 'presbiter'. The attribution «Franci» in the index of PeMotB, referring to *Parce Domine* (fols. 36v-37r), might also refer to the same person.[163] But the name «Raynaldino» might also refer to the Raynaldus Odenoch from Flanders who was a singer in Treviso Cathedral from 1477 to 1479.[164] A «Raynaldus de Odena» or «de Honderic» (the same as the one at Treviso?) sang in the papal chapel from 1491 to 1493 («de Odena» in Italian documents might mean 'from Audenarde' [= a Flemish city]).[165] Another possible

---

[156]. See GUERRINI 1926, p. 247 and n. 1, who reports the text of the memorandum preserved in the Biblioteca Civica Queriniana of Brescia: «[1517] — *Quarta Ioannis: n. 72, Poliza de Iohan da gli organi de pinerol organista in dom de brexa; / Mi Zohan ssto de età de anni 50 / Et ho una caseta per mio uso apreso sancto francescho. Iuravit — Petrus Stella, V. Girellus, Franc. de hippolitis* [...]».

[157]. MOLMENTI 1895, p. 130.

[158]. VANDER STRAETEN I, p. 126.

[159]. This is a letter of 8 June 1503 from the Ferrarese ambassador to Duke Ercole I in which he says that he will send a mass by Prioris, master of the chapel of Louis XII. See NG XX, p. 382.

[160]. FALLOWS 1999, p. 715.

[161]. *Paradisi portas aperuit nobis*, fols. 7v-8r; *Illuminavit cum Dominum splendoris*, fols. 23v-25r; *Hec dies quam fecit Dominum*, fols. 25v-26r; *Regina celi letare*, fols. 30v-32r; *O Jhesu Christe miserere mei*, fols. 36v-37r; *O Domine Yhesu Christe*, fols. 45v-46r; *Ave sanctissima Maria*, fols. 50v-52r; [*Missa*], fols. 131v-141r; [*Missa Benedictus Dominus Deus*], fols. 176v-185r; [Magnificat] Octavi toni. *Et exultavit*, fols. 190v-193r; [Magnificat] Quarti toni. *Et exultavit*, fols. 193v-196r.

[162]. See SARTORI 1956, pp. 64 and 66, and REESE 1990, p. 232.

[163]. See BOORMAN 2006, p. 933, DRAKE 2002, p. 5, and REESE 1990, p. 232.

[164]. On Raynaldus Odenoch's stay in Treviso, Christopher Reynolds corrects a persistent error in dating (see REYNOLDS 1995, p. 117, n. 11): the singer remained there until 1479, and not till 1488, as appears in all bibliographical references from the 1920s on (see CASIMIRI 1941, p. 12 and p. 13, n. 1: «In all likelihood, *Raynaldus* came to Padua from Treviso, where he was a singer at the cathedral from 1477 to 1488» [but D'ALESSI 1925, p. 14 writes «from 1487»]. In the documents from Treviso he is called «presbiter Raynaldus Odenoch de Flandria cantor stipendiatus in ecclesia cathedrali tarvisiana». See also D'ALESSI 1925, p. 14; D'ALESSI 1938, p. 157; REESE 1990, p. 232).

[165]. See HABERL 1888, pp. 56, 58, 123; LOCKWOOD 1979, p. 237; REESE 1990, p. 232.

identification might lead to the Raynaldus who was nominated as *maestro di cappella* of Rieti Cathedral in 1471-72.[166] For Jeppesen too «Renaldo» and «Raynaldo» could be the same person: a Frenchman active as singer in the church of the Madonna della Steccata of Parma (the chapel choir was instituted in 1528)[167] — the city in which he probably died in October 1529[168] —, whose compositions are unknown.[169] And whereas for Reese all these hypothetical identifications might relate to the same person,[170] Knud Jeppesen is convinced that the priest «Don Rinaldo» traceable at the end of the fifteenth century in various cities of the Veneto (Treviso and Padua)[171] is certainly not identifiable with Raynaldo of Parma, who was not a priest, but rather a married layperson (in the chapel choir of Parma he was in fact succeeded by his son Ernoul Caussin, called «de rainaldino», on 18 October 1529).[172] Robert Eitner has the entry 'Renaldo (Renaldino) Benedictus',[173] which is exactly what is written in RISM.[174] The misunderstanding probably derives from the annotation in vol. III (*Musica vocale profana*) of Gaetano Gaspari's *Catalogo della Biblioteca musicale "G. B. Martini" di Bologna*:[175] «Renaldo (elsewhere in the manuscript called Renaldino), and on fol. 177 with the addition Benedictus». In fact the composer is never called «Renaldino» in the manuscript in question (BolM 19), and fol. 177 contains neither the rubric «Benedictus» nor any allusion to our man.[176] This ambiguous and incorrect annotation in Gaspari's catalogue has thus led its readers to the eccentric notion that «Benedictus» was part of Renaldo's name, and upon close inspection, the only rubrics of BolM 19 that might have caused this misunderstanding could be those on fols. 152*v* («Benedictus dormit») and 153*r* («Benedictus mortuus est»), inscriptions that in fact refer to the Benedictus of the *Missa Parva* of Antoine de Févin (fols. 141*v*-155*r*), in which two of the four voices are silent.[177] Four (other?) persons with the same name are attested in Ferrara at different times: a «Raynoldo trombeta» in 1470,[178] a «Rainaldo del Chitarrino» from 1471 to 1499,[179] a «Rainaldetto Cambrai» from 1474 to 1476[180] and a «Rinaldo da Forli [*sic*]» in 1481.[181] Frank D'Accone also notes a piffaro player «Renaldo di Michele da Cesena» in the first half of the fifteenth century and documented in that profession in Florence,[182] and also a «Don Rinaldo Francioso, maestro di canto e cantore» in the paylists of the SS. Annunziata in Florence from 22 November 1482 to 21 March 1483.[183]

---

[166]. See SACCHETTI-SASSETTI 1940, p. 123 and REESE 1990, p. 232. Christopher Reynolds hypothesizes that this same Renaldo may have transferred immediately afterwards to Rome, where he may be identified with «Rainaldus de Meis» (see REYNOLDS 1995, p. 117, n. 11).

[167]. PELICELLI 1916, p. 4.

[168]. *Ibidem*, p. 5, PELICELLI 1931, p. 197, and REESE 1990, p. 232.

[169]. JEPPESEN 1968, p. 162.

[170]. CC as well associates Renaldo with the two diminutives «Reynaldino» and «Renaldino» (see CC V, p. 221).

[171]. Jeppesen adds Concordia to the cities as well, but Reynolds corrects the information, since this Raynaldus taught there in 1552. He would therefore be a later person (see REYNOLDS 1995, p. 117, n. 11).

[172]. See PELICELLI 1931, pp. 141-142, JEPPESEN 1968, p. 162, n. 2, and REESE 1990, p. 232.

[173]. EITNER VIII, p. 189.

[174]. RISM B IV/5, p. 679.

[175]. GASPARI, III, p. 4.

[176]. Fol. 177 instead has the Kyrie of the *Missa Dictes moy toutes* of Antoine de Févin.

[177]. REESE 1990, p. 232, n. 203, is also confusing, for, in the original English version of the book as well (p. 220, n. 188), he erroneously gives fol. 177 and refers to vol. IV of the catalogue rather than the third.

[178]. LOCKWOOD 1987, *Appendice V*, p. 394.

[179]. *Ibidem*, pp. 394-403.

[180]. *Ibidem*, pp. 395-396. Reynolds thinks that Rainaldetto de Cambrai may be identical with Rainaldus de Meis, who reached Rome in the autumn of 1472, and remained in service at the Cappella of S. Pietro until 1472 (see REYNOLDS 1995, p. 117).

[181]. LOCKWOOD 1987, *Appendice V*, p. 398.

[182]. D'ACCONE 1997, p. 793.

[183]. D'ACCONE 1961, p. 334 and n. 97.

JOHANNES DE STOKEM (? Stockem, near Liège, ca. 1445 - 2/3 October 1487 or after 1501)[184]

57: *Hor oires una canzon*

97: *Helas, [ce n'est pas sans rayson]*

VENDRIX, Philippe. 'Stokem (Prato, Pratis, Stockem, Stokhem, Stoken, Stoccken, Stoecken, Sthoken), Johannes de', in: MGG XV, cols. 1528-1529.

STARR, Pamela F. 'Stokem [Prato, Pratis, Stockem, Stokhem, Stoken, Stoccken, Stoecken, Sthoken], Johannes de', in: NG XXIV, p. 423.

JOHANNES TINCTORIS (Braine-l'Alleud, near Nivelles, prov. Barbant, ca. 1435 - Nivelles or Italy, before 12 October 1511)

73?: *Helas, [le bon temps que j'avoie]* (attributed elsewhere also to Compère)

CALELLA, Michele. 'Tinctoris, Johannes, in reality Jehan le Taintenier', in: MGG XVI, cols. 838-842.

WOODLEY, Ronald. 'Tinctoris, Johannes [Le Taintenier, Jehan]', in: NG XXV, pp. 497-501.

JOHANNES TOURONT (*fl.* ca. 1450-75/80)

83: *O gloriosa Regina mundi*

PLANCHART, Alejandro Enrique. 'Touront (Thauranth, Toront, Thourot, Tonrroutt), Iohannes', in: MGG XVI, cols. 974-976.

KIRNBAUER, Martin. 'Touront [Thauranth, Toront, Thourot, Tonrroutt], Johannes', in: NG XXV, pp. 660-661.

See also the entry for no. 83, n. 1.

BARTOLOMEO TROMBONCINO (in or near Verona, ca. 1470 - in or near Venice, after 1534 or after 1535)

4?: *Ave Maria, gratia plena* (attributed elsewhere also to Cara)

9: *Ave Maria, gratia plena*

52?: *Deh sì, deh no, deh sì* (attributed elsewhere also to Cara)

93: *Se ben or [non] scopri el fuoco*

148: *Signora, anci mea dea*

150: *Signora, anci, mia dea*

151: *Poca pace e molta guerra*

175: *Ave Maria, gratia plena*

LUISI, Francesco. 'Tromboncino (Trombonzino, Trombonsin, Tromboncin, Tromboncinus, Trombonus), Bartolomeo (Bortolo, Bortholamio, Bortolameo)', in: MGG XVI, cols. 1069-1077.

PRIZER, William F. 'Tromboncino [Trombonzin, Trombecin etc.], Bartolomeo', in: NG XXV, pp. 758-762.

JO[HANNES?] VILET

32: *Cantons cantons laisons melenconie*

The identity of this person is mysterious. David Fallows proposes two possibilities, attested in two manuscripts, which he believes might coincide with the Vilet of Panc.27, or else be different persons: «villete» documented in *Quessa cy dea suis* (Trent, Archivio Diocesano Tridentino, 93★, fol. 372*v*), and «Jacobus viletti» in *Ein buer gein holtze* (MünS 352b, fol. 62*r-v*).[185] This Jacobus might

---

[184]. Although Adalbert Roth discovered a document (a supplication) that confirms that Stokem died in the first days of October of 1487, Fallows is rather dubious and writes: «The supplication, dated 4 October 1487, is for a benefice at the cathedral of Erlau, Hungary, vacant through the death of 'Johannes de Prato, alias Stokem'. Very often such supplications were made on the basis of erroneous information; from the moment in which Stokem was paid as a member of the papal chapel towards the end of September 1487, someone must have put himself forward very speedily to assure the benefice so unexpectedly left vacant. If, as I am convinced, Stokem was still alive after 1487, it would be easier to propose him as the composer of the Mass *Allez regretz*, attributed in Jena MS 21 to 'Jo. de pratis' (printed in *Werken van Josquin des Prés: Missen*, no. 20). In his commentary in the NJE 7, 1997, Thomas Noblitt sets out a lengthy reasoning to demonstrate why the work cannot be by Josquin des Prez». Fallows is completely convinced that Stokem should be considered a «composer active in the years following 1490» (see FALLOWS 2005, p. 675 and n. 35).

[185]. See FALLOWS 1999, p. 723 and EITNER X, p. 87, who in the entry 'Viletti, Jacob' says that he is known only for a piece for three voices present in MünS 352b.

also be «Jacobus Villette, presbyter Cameracensis [...] in iure baccalaureus», a singer and chaplain of Ferdinand, King of Sicily, to whom papal documents concede benefices on 13 May 1473, and who in October 1480 was paid as a singer in the chapel in Naples.[186] Also, «le petit Villette», son of the singer 'Jehan Villette', is called 'enfant de chapelle' in 1446, and then singer at the court of Savoy from 1449 to 1466.[187]

The CC turns his name into 'Joan Vilet', although the entry refers only to the name attested in Panc.27. Another entry, on the other hand, is dedicated to 'Jacobus Viletti (= Vilette)' with the single reference to the MS in Trent.[188]

GASPAR VAN WEERBEKE (Oudenaarde, ca. 1445 – after 1516 or after 1517)

55?: *La stangetta* (attributed elsewhere also to Isaac and to Weerbeke; see the catalogue, no. 55, n. 2)
60: *Mater digna Dei*
91: *O pulcherrima mulierum*
98: *Virgo Maria, non est tibi similis nata*
99: *Christi mater, ave*
103: *Adonai, [sanctissime Domine]*
129: *Ave stella matutina*
130: *Ibo mihi ad montem mirrhe*

WINKLER, Heinz-Jürgen. 'Gaspar van Weerbeke', in: MGG VII, cols. 569-574.

CROLL, Gerhard - LINDMAYR-BRANDL, Andrea. 'Weerbeke [Werbeke, Werbeck], Gaspar [Jaspar, Gaspart]', in: NG XXVII, pp. 207-210.

ADRIAN WILLAERT (Bruges or Roulaers, ca. 1490 – Venice, 7 December 1562)

177?: *Rex autem David* (see also the catalogue of the piece, n. 1)

HORN, Wolfgang. 'Willaert (Vuillaert, Wigliaert, etc.), Adrian (often only Adrien, M. Adriano, etc.)', in: MGG XVII, cols. 943-965.

LOCKWOOD, Lewis - ONGARO, Giulio - FROMSON, Michele - OWENS, Jessie Ann. 'Willaert [Vuigliart etc.], Adrian [Adriano]', in: NG XXVII, pp. 389-400.

---

[186]. FALLOWS 1999, p. 723. See also EITNER X, p. 87, who refers to VANDER STRAETEN IV, p. 29.

[187]. FALLOWS 1999, p. 723. The two Villette, father and son, had already been mentioned by Marie-Thérèse Bouquet: Jacob was nominated as Bishop of Nice in 1463 (see BOUQUET 1968, pp. 250-254, 295).

[188]. CC V, p. 247.

Although there are 185 pieces in Panc.27, the texts that have been traced are in fact two more: in addition to the musical pieces must be added *Son su passo de la morte* (no. 112bis) and *Alzando li oghii vidi Maria bella* (no. 147). In the manuscript itself none of the texts is attributed, and the names of the authors found so far have been identified through poetic concordances. Apart from the texts traditionally attributed to the evangelists, only 22 others have a secure or attributable paternity (nos. 11, 13, 15, 19, 27, 29/114, 30, 33, 36, 46?, 49, 59, 62, 67, 69, 75, 76, 121?, 127, 141?, 159, 180). In some cases, noted in the individual entries, there are conflicting attributions.

The situation with poets is analogous to that with composers: we find famous names, but run up against more problematic names, rarely attested. As in the section on the biographies of musicians, we refer to dictionaries and specific studies, if possible. No entries are given for the authors of texts who, though mentioned in the concordances, have been considered improbable (the most notable case is that of Jacopone da Todi).

Francesco degli Albizzi

15: *A Maria, fonte d'amore*
36: *Poi che t'ebi nel core*

Completely missing from the traditional biographical dictionaries and encyclopedias, Francesco degli Albizzi, as David Fallows has suggested, was perhaps the brother of Piero di Luca degli Albizzi, who was the author of the canzone morale *A qualunque animal che vive in terra* and among the 'approbatores' of the Commune of Pontedera in August 1412.[189] In confirmation of this hypothesis, in the entry in DBI 'Albizzi, Luca' (Florence, 19 March 1382 - [Florence], 5 August 1458) it says that Luca, by «Lisabetta di Niccolò de' Bardi (d. 1425) and Aurelia di Niccolò de' Medici (d. 1475), bore the children Piero, Lisabetta, Maso, Antonio, Francesco, Giovambattista, Lorenzo, Girolamo; Masetto was a natural son».[190] The MS *CV. BL. 3711* mentions the relationship explicitly at least twice: on p. 79 «franchesco dalbizo di luca» refers to the lauda *Molti son da Giesù nel ciel chiamati* (pp. 79-80), and on p. 87 we find the rubric «La sopra scricta lauda fece franchesco dalbizo di Luca» in reference to *O infinita charità di Dio* (pp. 85-87).

Lodovico Frati mentions a «Francesco d'Albizo de Prato di Fiesole»,[191] to whom the text *De vogliate contemplare* on fols. 148v-149r of the MS *Rim. C. 38* is attributed,[192] but Galletti suggests that he may be identified with Franceschino degli Albizi, referring to Ammirato's *Famiglie fiorentine*.[193]

---

[189]. See Fallows 1999, p. 736, who emphasizes that Francesco contributed more poems than any other author (except Belcari) to the print *LaudeBonac*.

[190]. See DBI II, p. 26.

[191]. To be exact, «Franciesco Dalbizo pe [*sic*] Prati di Fiesole», on fol. 148v of the MS.

[192]. See Frati 1918, p. 195.

[193]. I have consulted a copy of *Delle famiglie nobili fiorentine di Scipione Ammirato* (Florence, Gio. Donato, e Bernardino Giunti & Compagni, 1615) in the Herzog August Bibliothek in Wolfenbüttel, A:4.1 Geogr. 2°(3): on p. 27 is mentioned «Franceschino poeta», friend of Petrarch and author of poetry still appearing in print in Ammirato's day: he would be the son of Taddeo, who «fu Commessario di quel grand'esercito, il quale fù sconfitto da Castruccio à Fucecchio l'anno 1328 […]. Hebbe Taddeo tra gli altri figliuoli Franceschino non solo amico del Petrarca, ma il quale scrisse anchor egli poesie, & trouansi hoggidì stampate delle sue compositioni. Morì intorno l'anno 1350. Onde il Pet. come di persona morta disse ne' Trionfi *Sennuccio & Franceschin, che fur sì humani.* & nel Sonetto, oue della morte di Sennuccio fa mentione, prega il detto Sennuccio, che fra gli altri, giunto che sarà in cielo, saluti Franceschino. *Ma ben ti priego, ch'alla terza sfera | Guitton saluti & messer Cino e Dante, | Franceschin nostro, & tutta quella schiera.* // Ricciardo figliuolo di Franceschino (quel che è stato infino à quest'hora à tutta la famiglia celato) fù poeta anchor egli, si come in vn libro di rime appresso Riccardo Riccardi è ritrouato. […] Scrisse anchor versi, come nell'allegato libro si legge, Franceschino figliuolo di Ricciardo, il quale, non si hauendo prima di lui hauuta mentione, non è posto nell'albero. Appariscono di costui non più che due ballate, l'vna che incomincia. *Ben so che pare il mio lieue coraggio* & l'altra *S'io mi pur taccio, & non dimostro come.* Che si vede, che hanno in se spirito poetico, & quasi riceuuto per heredità di mano in mano dal padre, & dall'auolo, come ne' tempi più freschi si vidde ne due Strozzi

ST. ANSELM OF AOSTA (Aosta 1033 - Canterbury 1109)

46?: *Christi corpus ave, de sancta Virgine natum*

ZINI, Zino. 'Anselmo, santo, d'Aosta', in: GDE I, pp. 893-894.

FEO BELCARI (Florence, 4 February 1410 - Florence,16 August 1484)

30: *Chi serve a Dio cum purità di cor[e]*

67: *Egli è il tuo bon Iesù*

69: *Iesù, Iesù, Iesù*

159?: *Giù per la mala via*[194]

MARTI, Mario. 'Belcari, Feo', in: DBI VII, pp. 548-551.

BÀRBERI-SQUAROTTI, Giorgio. 'Belcari, Feo', in: GDE III, pp. 132-133.

BIANCO DA SIENA (Florence?, ca. 1350 - Venice, 1434?)[195]

29/114: *Cum desiderio vo cercando*

BRAMBILLA AGENO, Franca. 'Bianco da Siena', in: DBI X, pp. 220-223.

ENSELMINO DA MONTEBELLUNA (or 'DA TREVISO') (*fl.* between the end of the thirteenth century and the first half of the fourteenth. 1362 is the *terminus ante quem*)[196]

13: *Ave Regina, Virgo gloriosa*

MOSCHELLA, Maurizio. 'Enselmino (Anselmo, Guglielmo) da Montebelluna (da Treviso)', in: DBI XLII, pp. 804-806.

BÀRBERI-SQUAROTTI, Giorgio. 'Enselmino da Montebelluna', in: GDE VI, p. 441.

FRANCESCO GALEOTA (Naples, ca. 1446 - ?, 1497)

62: *L'ucelo me chiama [che perdo giornata]*

COLLETTI, Marco. 'Galeota, Francesco', in: DBI LI, pp. 416-420.

BÀRBERI-SQUAROTTI, Giorgio. 'Galeota, Francesco', in: GDE IX, pp. 23-24.

GENTILE ARETINO (GENTILE BECCHI?)[197] (Urbino, ca. third decade of the fifteenth century - Arezzo, 1497)

11: *A la bataglia*

GRAYSON, Cecil. 'Becchi, Gentile', in: DBI VII, pp. 491-493.

LEONARDO GIUSTINIAN (Venice, between 1381 and 1386, ca. 1383 - Venice, 10 November 1446)

76: *O Iesù dolce, o infinito amore*

27: *Poi che sei dal mondo tolta*

PIGNATTI, Franco. 'Giustinian, Leonardo', in: DBI LVII, pp. 249-255.

GALETTI, Paola. 'Giustiniani (o Giustiniàn, Zustiniàn)' family, in: GDE IX, pp. 653-654.

BORGHETTI, Vincenzo. 'Giustinian (Giustiniani, Giustiniano), Leonardo', in: MGG VII, cols. 1029-1031.

FALLOWS, David. 'Giustiniani [Giustinian], Leonardo', in: NG IX, p. 916.

POPE GREGORY I 'THE GREAT' (Rome, slightly earlier than the mid-sixth century, ca. 540 - Rome, 12 March 604)

121?: *O Domine Iesu Christe*

---

padre & figliuolo, & molto prima ma in materia d'historia ne tre Villani, Giovanni, Matteo, & Filippo, questi figliuol di Matteo, & essi lor due fratelli. [...]».

[194]. On the contested authorship of the text, see n. 1 of this entry.

[195]. David Fallows hypothesizes 1412 as the date of his death, without, however, clarifying the reason: see FALLOWS 1999, p. 737.

[196]. As attested by a manuscript copied in the same year, «Sermones quadragesimales Voraginis, cum corio rubeo, quondam fratris Henselmini» (see GARGAN 1978, pp. 122 and 249, n. 14, where reference is made to other documents in the Archivio di Stato in Treviso that show his presence in the Augustinian monastery of S. Margherita (Treviso) from 1333 to 1348).

[197]. See the entry for no. 11, n. 1.

Boesch Gajano, Sofia. 'Gregorio I, santo', in: Enciclopedia dei papi I, pp. 546-574.

Dyer, Joseph. 'Gregor I (Gregor der Große)', in: MGG VII, cols. 1562-1564.

McKinnon, James W. 'Gregory the Great [Gregory I]', in: NG X, pp. 376-377.

Jean d'Auton (ca. 1466-1527)

75: *Les bien amore*

Sozzi, Lionello. 'Jean d'Auton', in: GDE XI, p. 430.

Jean II, duc de Bourbon (1427-1488)

59: *Ne doibt on prendre quant on donne*

127: *Ales regres, [vuidez de ma presence]*

Fallows 1999, p. 728.

Francesco Petrarca (Arezzo, 20 July 1304 - Arquà, Padua, 18/19 July 1374)

180: *Di pensier in pensier, di monte in monte*

Orlando, Sandro. 'Petrarca, Francesco', in: GDE XV, pp. 830-838.

Steinheuer, Joachim. 'Petrarca, Francesco', in: MGG XIII, cols. 397-403.

Haar, James. 'Petrarch [Petrarca, Francesco]', in: NG XIX, pp. 498-499.

Angelo Poliziano (Montepulciano, Siena, 14 July 1454 - Florence, 29 September 1494)

33: *Contento in foco sto como fenice*

Bigi, Emilio. 'Poliziano, Angelo', in: GDE XVI, pp. 269-274.

Glowotz, Daniel. 'Poliziano (Politian, Politiano, Politianus, Politien, Polizian), Angelo (Agnolo, Agnolus, Ange, Angelus), eigentl. Agniolo Ambrogini', in: MGG XIII, col. 730.

Haar, James. 'Poliziano [Ambrogini Poliziano], Angelo', in: NG XX, pp. 33-34.

Serafino Aquilano (Serafino Ciminelli) (L'Aquila, 6 January 1466[198] - Rome, 10 August 1500)

49: *Deh, fusse qui [chi mi to' el somno! Somno]*

Vigilante, Magda. 'Ciminelli, Serafino (Serafino Aquilano)', in: DBI XXV, pp. 562-566.

Pozzi, Mario. 'Serafino Aquilano', in: GDE XVIII, p. 595.

Fenlon, Iain. 'Serafino de' Ciminelli dall'Aquila (Serafino Aquilano)', in: MGG XV, cols. 597-598.

Haar, James. 'Serafino de' Ciminelli dall'Aquila [Serafino Aquilano]', in: NG XXIII, p. 109.

Rossi 2002, *Nota bio-bibliografica*, pp. liii-lxv.

Rossi 2005, *Nota bio-bibliografica aggiornata*, pp. 29-37.

Pope Sixtus IV (Celle Ligure, Savona, 21 July 1414 - Rome, 13 August 1484)

141?: *Ave sanctissima Maria*

Lombardi, Giuseppe. 'Sisto IV', in: Enciclopedia dei papi II, pp. 701-717.

Planchart, Alejandro Enrique. 'Sixtus IV, eigentl. Francesco della Rovere, Francesco da Savona', in: MGG XV, cols. 868-869.

Antonio Tebaldi, called 'il Tebaldeo' (Ferrara, 1463 - Rome, 1537)

19: *Non expectò giamai con tal desio*

De Vendittis, Luigi. 'Tebaldeo, il (Antonio Tebaldi)', in: GDE XIX, p. 807.

---

[198]. Antonio Rossi says that «Moscardi fixes the date of his birth as 6 January, but without indicating the source of his information»: see Moscardi 1899, p. 260 and Rossi 2005, p. 29.

5. PROVENANCE, FUNCTION, AND DATE

(A) THE GEOGRAPHICAL PROVENANCE

GIVEN PANC.27'S WIDESPREAD REPERTORIAL CONNECTIONS with other musical sources of various kinds, many well-known scholars have been concerned with the provenance of the manuscript. A diversity of opinions have been expressed, summarized as follows.

Bianca Becherini and Knud Jeppesen traced the origin of the manuscript to Florence or Tuscany, an opinion that Giulio Cattin once shared;[199] he subsequently changed his mind and declared himself strongly in favour of northern Italy.[200] Whereas Becherini centred her hypothesis above all on the Savonarolan nature of the repertory,[201] Jeppesen gave more weight to the textual references to Tuscany found in compositions such as *A la bataglia* or *Piange Pisa*.[202]

For Allan Atlas the manuscript was compiled in northern Italy, probably at Mantua. He based his conclusion both on the nature of the readings — always distant from those found in Florentine sources, but similar to those of northern sources such as the *Odhecaton* and VerCap 757, and the very strong repertorial connections with the manuscript ParisN Rés676 (Mantuan or Ferrarese)[203] as well as the probably Paduan ModE 9[204] — and on the physical structure of the manuscript: the gatherings in quaternions would confirm its origin in northern *scriptoria*, whereas the Tuscans preferred quinternions.[205] But while it is undeniable that many readings in Panc.27 are connected with those of the *Odhecaton*, it is equally true that none of the eight concordances with VerCap 757 shows any closeness to the readings in Panc.27. The considerable number of concordances with ParisN Rés676 is in itself at least an indication of a shared environment: if it is not possible to speak of a direct filiation between the readings of Panc.27 and those of ParisN Rés676, the impression immediately arises that the two anthologies, which are also very similar in the types of repertory they include, were conceived in the same geographical area and in a similar if not identical cultural environment. But I do not believe that it is advisable to speak of strong ties with ModE 9, which shares with Panc.27 only two pieces with very distant readings,[206] plus one piece that has only the Superius in common with the similarly texted piece in Panc.27.[207] Besides, Bonnie Blackburn has demonstrated that Florentine manuscripts were not always made up of quinternions; thus the physical makeup of the object cannot constitute incontrovertible proof of its provenance.[208]

---

[199]. CATTIN 1973a, p. 183.

[200]. CATTIN 1972a, p. 485, n. 81. Even though this study would appear to precede CATTIN 1973a chronologically, it is certain that it contains his reflections developed subsequently, confirming his final opinion of northern Italy as the provenance of the manuscript also in CATTIN 1983a, p. 41, n. 47.

[201]. A new method of very homorhythmic 'psalmodizing' distinguishes the repertory close to Savonarola. Panc.27 might be a manuscript expressly compiled to remember the preacher (BECHERINI 1954, pp. 113-116).

[202]. See JEPPESEN 1969, p. 39. But while the text of *A la bataglia* (missing in Panc.27, but recoverable from the concordant sources) recounts a precise event, the battle of Sarzanello in 1487 fought by Florentine troops against the Genovese (see entry no. 11), *Piange Pisa* cannot be connected plausibly with any historical event, since in the manuscript there is only an incipit and I have not found any concordance with a poetic text of the time that has the same beginning. In confirmation that the reference to Tuscany is nevertheless plausible, is the Pisan citizenship of the composer (see the entry 'Bar[tholomeus?] Pisanus' in the biographies of composers).

[203]. Prizer assigns the provenance to Mantua with some assurance, on the basis of precise references contained in some texts in the manuscript (see PRIZER 1990). The MS ParisN Rés676, probably compiled from 4 to 26 October 1502, is available in facsimile (LESURE 1979).

[204]. The Estense manuscript is dated «Padua, 4 October 1496». It is published in facsimile (RMF 13), and there is a modern edition of the strambotti (LA FACE BIANCONI 1990).

[205]. ATLAS 1975-76, I, p. 252 and ATLAS 1993, p. 25, n. 28. In neither of the two studies is it clarified, however, why a Mantuan origin is to be preferred.

[206]. Nos. 78 and 87.

[207]. No. 62.

[208]. BLACKBURN 1981b, p. 121, n. 2. Howard Mayer Brown reinforces the objection, pointing out that in Florentine shops one could buy single quinternions and quaternions already ruled for music, ready to be used by the scribe (BROWN 1983, I, p. 6).

The opinion of the north Italian provenance of Panc.27 is shared by William Prizer,[209] who in the past had assigned the preparation of the manuscript to Ferrara or Mantua, based on the presence of three strambotti of the 'bird cycle'. In the manuscript, in fact, the three compositions are transcribed one following the other,[210] and they belong to the group of 'responses' between Mantua and Ferrara that also include *Io son l'ocel che con le debil ali* by Pesenti and *Io son l'ocello che non pò volare* by Tromboncino:[211] humorous musical cannon shots between two courts that from the last decade of the Quattrocento on strongly integrated their political and cultural affairs. In 1492, in fact, the elder daughter of the Ferrarese Duke Ercole d'Este married the Mantuan Marchese Francesco II Gonzaga: with Isabella all the proverbial cultural refinement in which the children of the powerful Duke Ercole and his wife Eleonora d'Aragona were brought up was transferred to the provincial marquisate.[212] A famous patron as well as a virtuoso musician, Isabella promoted a dense network of cultural relations between her new home and her native duchy. Exchanges of artists, books, music, instrumentalists, and much else have been amply documented in the Este correspondence: this extensive collection of letters testifies to the cultural liveliness and competent interest in the arts that nearly all the children of Ercole cultivated throughout their lives, but it also reveals a marked tendency to mutual rivalry, never appeased, and that in fact drew its most vital sap from the patronage of the arts.

Recently, Prizer himself reconsidered the provenance of Panc.27: without clarifying the reasons, he suggested it came «from Ferrara, or less likely, from Milan».[213] In his subsequent studies, however, Milan is no longer mentioned, and Ferrara remains the most cogent hypothesis.[214]

Giulio Cattin based his most recent opinion on both repertorial and linguistic considerations. He inventoried and studied in depth the MS CTL G12, assigning its provenance to northern Italy specifically in the light of the manifest similarity of its contents with Panc.27:[215] the second section of CTL G12 is surprisingly close to the contents of Panc.27, since the two manuscripts share no fewer than 21 compositions (with no other source does CTL G12 have such a large part of its repertory in common),[216] and in five cases they share exclusive concordances. According to Cattin, the repertory of CTL G12 is also strongly connected with that of ParisN Rés676,[217] a source that shares no fewer than 24 pieces with Panc.27. The manuscripts CTL G12 and Panc.27 would therefore derive from a similar but not the same north Italian environment,[218] since in both one finds the circulation of liturgical, devotional, and secular pieces.

To the observations collected so far on the question of the provenance of Panc.27 other aspects can be added. For example, the hypothesis that Panc.27 was compiled in Tuscany is no longer sustainable.[219] Even if the presence of musical pieces such as *A la bataglia* or *Piange Pisa* might indicate Florence, it is not wise to extrapolate conclusions on the origin of a manuscript based solely on the presence of texts containing geographical or political references. The pieces circulated, and textual adaptations to new situations were surely made, thus rendering the particularized function irrelevant.[220] In this specific case, both compositions mentioned are without their poetic text, having only the incipit. Likewise

---

[209]. Prizer 1985, p. 29.

[210]. In the spelling of Panc.27: *Io son de gabbia, non de bosco ocello* by Pesenti (no. 61), the anonymous *L'ucelo me chiama [che perdo giornata]* (no. 62), and *Io son l'ucello, che sopra i rami d'oro* by Cara (no. 63).

[211]. Prizer 1985, p. 28. The complete cycle, consisting of five pieces, is edited in Filocamo 2003.

[212]. The ducal pair had six children, all with strong musical interests: Isabella (1474-1539), Beatrice (1475-1497), Alfonso (1476-1534), Ferrante (1477-1540), Ippolito (1479-1520), and Sigismondo (1480-1524).

[213]. Prizer 2001, p. 24, n. 60.

[214]. Prizer 2005, p. 240, n. 73, defines Panc.27 «as North-Italian and probably Mantuan. I believe it is more likely, however, that the manuscript stems from Ferrara».

[215]. Regarding the origin of CTL G12, Cattin in fact said Florence (Cattin 1972a); he then changed his mind and pointed in the direction of northern Italy in Cattin 1983a, p. 41, n. 47.

[216]. Cattin 1972a, p. 485.

[217]. Cattin 1973a, p. 183.

[218]. The diverging musical readings of the exclusive concordance *A Maria, fonte d'amore*, for example, for Cattin would separate the two witnesses, excluding a direct reciprocal relationship (*ibidem*, pp. 205-206).

[219]. As stated in CC I, p. 232.

[220]. The concept is well evaluated in Strohm 1981, p. 320.

the presence of canti carnascialeschi[221] might support the manuscript's connection with Florence, the cradle of this genre, but the linguistic inflections of the texts in Panc.27 are clearly northern. The two phenomena, however, are not incompatible: Prizer has noted the presence of canti carnascialeschi in the north Italian repertory,[222] which also appear in southern sources.[223] To these elements it should be added that the survival of the tropes of the Benedicamus attested in *Qui nos fecit ex nihilo* seems to be typically northern.[224]

Among the most recent contributions to a more precise identification of the zone in which Panc.27 originated, that of Keith Polk merits mention: referring on several occasions to the musical MS AugsS 142a,[225] he shows the strong connections of a specific section with the Mantuan environment.[226] Although compiled in Augsburg, the manuscript contains a small homogeneous section of courtly Italian dances for three voices,[227] and shares with Panc.27 a unique concordance that has, in the current state of research, the characteristic of being exclusive: the dance *Caminata*. In the German manuscript, *Caminata* is filled out with 'polyphonic variations' that no one had noticed so far: fols. 20v–21r do not, in fact, contain generic monodic trumpet calls, as was thought in the past, but rather perfectly functional polyphony.[228] This polyphonic reconstruction varies the base version of *Caminata* and spices it up with 'adventurous' diminutions completely absent in Panc.27. Polk reinterprets a contemporary inscription placed on fol. 24r in AugsS 142, already noted by other scholars,[229] and connects the rubric[230] directly to the presence of the Italian repertory in the preceding folios, hypothesizing the presence of a middleman as 'hinge' between the German environment and the Italian one: Ulrich Schubinger 'the Younger', a German trombonist hired by Francesco Gonzaga in 1502 who lived in Mantua almost without interruption until the end of the second decade of the Cinquecento.[231] Polk hypothesizes that Ulrich sent his colleague Jacob Hurlacher in Augsburg various pieces performed at the Mantuan court, and these could have passed in this way into the German manuscript:[232] Ulrich was Jacob's direct predecessor as a trombonist in the civic band of Augsburg, and the two persons could have been warm friends.[233] Personally, I am not entirely convinced that the hypothetical connection between the two German instrumentalists is the answer: the presence of such a debated inscription hardly seems to me proof of their relationship, also because it is placed outside the portion containing the Italian repertory and thus perhaps does not in fact refer to it. It is certain, however, that the section in question unquestionably

---

[221]. As *Siamo, done, trei romeri* (no. 146) and probably no. 153, without text.

[222]. Prizer 1980, p. 98 and Prizer 1996a.

[223]. As, for example, in PerA 431.

[224]. Piece no. 20. See Robertson, Anne W. 'Benedicamus Domino', in: NG III, pp. 237-239: 238.

[225]. There is a facsimile of the manuscript (Augsburger Liederbuch 1997) and a modern edition (Jonas 1983).

[226]. Polk 1992, p. 141 and Polk 1996, p. 332.

[227]. The section is the work of a single scribe, who does not appear before or after this point; it goes from fol. 18v to fol. 21v, spanning the third and fourth fascicles of the manuscript. The compositions appear in the following order: *Mantüaner danz* [= *La gambetta*], fols. 18v-19r; [*Mir ist ein schöns brauns Meidelein*], fol. 19v; [*Passamezzo moderno*], fol. 20r; [*La monina*], fol. 20v; [*Caminata*], fols. 20v-21r; [...], fol. 21v. The titles in square brackets have been taken from concordances, some of which are found in the musical MS Royal Appendix 59-62 of the British Library in London (in four partbooks, ca. 1550-60, and copied in northern Italy: see CC IV, pp. 433-434). The six pieces are edited and discussed in Filocamo 2009b.

[228]. I owe this discovery to the perspicacity of Fabrizio Ammetto, whom I thank.

[229]. The rubric was read as «Dem Ersam vnd weisen Jacob stat pfeyfer sol mir | Fraintlichen grus [...] main fraintlichen grus [...]» in Bente 1968, p. 232; similarly in Gottwald 1974, p. 7 and Jonas 1983, II, p. 39.

[230]. Corrected to: «Dem Eersam und Weisen Jacob stat pfeyfer sol mir daf[ür] Vernommen», translated as 'The honourable and wise city musician Jacob [Hurlacher] is the source of this' (Polk 1992, p. 141). Then follows «Fraintlichen grus Mein fraintlichen grus».

[231]. As proved by two letters (one of 16 June 1502 and the other of 6 October 1519) written by Francesco Gonzaga to his treasurer (Prizer 1981, p. 160 and n. 31).

[232]. Brown and Polk have noticed in German musical sources the tendency «to reflect a practice of ensemble performance, whether vocal, instrumental, or mixed, which characterized German civic, intellectual, and monastic communities keen to appropriate an international repertory» (see Brown - Polk 2001, p. 127).

[233]. Polk 1992, p. 141.

connects the piece *Caminata* with the «Mantuan dance» at the beginning.[234] I therefore think that it would not be hazardous to hypothesize the provenance of *Caminata* from the Gonzaga court, just as one can legitimately speak of a relation (even if indirect) between the version of the piece in Panc.27 and that in AugsS 142a.[235]

Another indication of the connection between Panc. 27 and the Mantuan environment might be the impressive number of concordances that the manuscript shares with the musical MS ParisN Rés676, certainly a product of the Po valley. As mentioned earlier, Prizer assigns it to Mantua with assurance.[236] The exclusive concordance *Sconsolata phylomena*,[237] whose musical reading shows a certain closeness between the two versions,[238] reinforces the hypothesis that the two manuscripts share the same geographical origin.

Another assessment by Prizer, this time related to the contents of PeLaudeII, draws Panc.27 close to Mantua: he holds that much of the repertory contained in the Petrucci print can reasonably be connected with the Gonzaga court,[239] and, while no reading can be considered a direct model, Panc.27 shares no fewer than six concordances with PeLaudeII.

(B) The Function of the Manuscript

The discussion of the heterogeneous repertory of Panc.27 has shown, next to so many secular pieces, the unusual presence of musical pieces clearly connected with the Liturgy of the Dead, as well as a high number of laude and *contrafacta*. No collections of musical laude have come down to us from this period in history: all the polyphonic laude that we know from the manuscripts are mixed in with other types of compositions, but Panc.27, CTL G12, and ParisN Rés676 are undeniably among the richest witnesses of the devotional repertory. And not just this. Even some of the *contrafacta* present in Panc.27 are found in the other two manuscripts with similar content. I believe, therefore, that Giulio Cattin's idea is completely creditable: that both CTL G12 and Panc.27 were compiled in an environment in which a common repertory circulated, sacred and secular, and perhaps one could hypothesize that the principal compiler of Panc.27 was an amateur musician, a member of a confraternity that actively engaged in singing laude.[240] Such a compiler might well concide with Scribe A: a dilettante composer who brought together in a manuscript book pieces by known authors and personal experiments, up-to-date pieces, and original variants to known pieces. This person might have crafted the collection according to his own taste, with the deliberate goal of performing its contents (as is proved by the many indications that are clearly performance oriented, and the table of rhythmic values on the last folio of the manuscript).

Although the vast interest in polyphony cultivated in the Italian Church since the fourteenth century has long been known, at first 'unofficial' and extemporized,[241] polyphonic practice seems to

---

[234]. *Mantüaner danz* [= *La gambetta*]. A reference to *La gambetta* can also be detected in the colourful lexicon of the Mantuan poet Teofilo Folengo (see CATTIN 1975, pp. 204-205).

[235]. On this see the Remarks to no. 160, as well as FILOCAMO 2009b.

[236]. See n. 203 above. The simple style of the laude in ParisN Rés676 would point to their use in one of the numerous confraternities of the lower middle classes (see PRIZER, *Popular Piety*, n. 276 below).

[237]. Piece no. 113.

[238]. Among the pieces in common, most of the variants are graphic. The single substantial variant present is certain the result of an error in ParisN Rés676.

[239]. PRIZER 1993b, pp. 180-181. Already in his *Courtly Pastimes* Prizer advanced the same hypothesis, justified by the fact that as well as containing pieces by Tromboncino and Cara, the «Don Philippo» of PeLaudeII might be the Filippo Lappacino of Francesco II's chapel. For Prizer this music could have been performed in the chapel of S. Maria dei Voti, in the Mantuan cathedral of S. Pietro: in support of this opinion would be the observation that of the 56 laude, no fewer than 21 are on a Marian subject (PRIZER 1980, pp. 27-28). Boorman accepts these conclusions somewhat cautiously, although he considers it improbable that Petrucci acquired music from Mantua (BOORMAN 2006, p. 678).

[240]. Singing laude is an activity that is amply documented in many different social groups in Renaissance cities, especially in the richest and most vital ones.

[241]. It is enough to recall the performance in *cantus planus binatim* (see GALLO 1966 and GALLO 1985).

have gained ground little by little and then been imposed in an official and legitimate manner even in the most secluded religious communities. This was due to the particular climate that contemporaneously saw polyphony resounding not only in lay environments, but also where 'civic liturgy' was practised: the court chapels and cathedrals. The stimulus for innovation also fermented within the Benedictine communities that were renewed through the Santa Giustina reform promoted in 1409 by Ludovico Barbo: the compilation of some musical manuscripts clearly emanating from this environment and containing polyphonic liturgical pieces goes back to the second half of the Quattrocento. In 1504 the *Congregatio Casinensis, alias S. Justine de Padua* received official approval, and in 1506 the first Cantorino was printed in Venice. From the second edition (1523) onwards some of the pieces appear with a polyphonic *imprimatur*, thus sanctioning the entrance of music for several voices alongside monodic practice.[242] But despite this reformist stimulus within the Church, it is nevertheless more probable that the creative environment for Panc.27 was that of the urban confraternities.

The hypothesis of a link between the manuscript and a confraternity setting becomes even more plausible if one recalls the typical social context in which Renaissance confraternities operated up to about the third decade of the sixteenth century. It has to do with composite realities born on the wave of the extraordinary urban development that characterized Italy since the thirteenth century, in spontaneous response to the weakness of the parochial structure of the secular Church:[243] the affiliated members belonged to various social categories, and heterogeneity characterized the activity as much as the organizational arrangement of the devotional institution. The rich, the bourgeois, merchants, artisans: all participated together in the variegated human aspect of the confraternity, where every member accomplished precise tasks and worked actively with the principal goal of meriting a 'good death'. The senses of guilt and widespread insecurity provoked by life in the city — a difficult existence often mingled with personal uprootings, violence, and injuries — were placated through charitable and penitential practices. 'Social inversion' was one of the prevailing methods in organizational activities: the rich exceptionally performed activities that were 'humbling' for them — such as distributing alms to the poor — while the less well off offered their prayers for the salvation of the souls of the more fortunate; on occasion some members even took on the role of inquisitors to support the regular processes of the ecclesiastical tribunal; others nearly supplanted the clergy in the organization of prayers within the confraternity.[244] In sum, a variegated world, vitalized precisely by the frequent inversion of roles. Renaissance confraternities experienced a great amount of permeability between the different cultures that encountered each other there, and clothing was exchanged in an almost cathartic way: a fluid microcosm that in reality reflected the dynamic image of the city itself, with its various inhabitants of differing social levels, the contradictions, and the thousand serious and gay faces. This phenomenon is often described as 'laicization of religion', destined to placate the spiritual unease of the urban laity.[245] This state of things lasted as long as the parishes did not actively assume control of the confraternities: that happened after the 1530s, and changed for ever both their internal organization and social and cultural attitudes to them. Under clerical patronage, the earlier institutions became 'monochromatic' from the human point of view, limiting themselves to reproducing rigorously the ruling social hierarchies: no longer the closeness between the various members coming from different levels of the social scale, who humiliated or raised themselves in imitation of the example of Christ, no longer the exchange of roles, no longer occasions to make merry together in the ritual and traditional banquets. The institution of the confraternity will thus completely change its face and social configuration, and will become the unambiguous expression

---

[242]. For the topic see the extensive study CATTIN 1970.

[243]. See GOLDTHWAITE (1995) 1999, pp. 102-103.

[244]. On this see the analysis in WEISSMAN 1991, pp. 201-220, to which the following discussion on the musical aspects owes much inspiration.

[245]. See GOLDTHWAITE (1995) 1999, pp. 111 and 114.

of members belonging to the same environment, specialized to all effects:[246] even its expressions, therefore, flattened to a single plane devoid of variants.

Returning to the beginning of the Cinquecento, it seems to me possible to reason in terms parallel to the discussion so far with reference to one of the cultural products of the society of the time: the musical manuscript. Understandably the idea that the same object should contain motets and secular pieces, laude and dances, fragments of the Requiem and canti carnascialeschi, as happens in Panc.27, disconcerts whomever has the task to study such variety in an attempt to seek out any internal coherence. But on the basis of what has just been outlined in relation to the social environments in which the confraternities of the fifteenth and early sixteenth centuries modelled their own structure, I believe that it is possible to consider Panc.27 as the child of a cultural conception that benefited from the fluidity of the confines of its own pragmatic basis. Certainly the manuscript was a product of the first decade of the Cinquecento, an epoch in which such permeable cultural hetereogenity was still thoroughly the rule in the active life of the confraternities. The presence of *contrafacta*, sometimes made piquant by an explicit reference to the secular musical model, seems to me to indicate how much the lay culture expressed in Panc.27 was strongly entwined with the devotional as well as the liturgical culture: three tightly knit cultural environments (liturgical/devotional/secular) in a manner which to our eyes might seem rather irreverent.[247] The notion of the exchange of institutional roles, which happened explicitly in the Renaissance confraternity, is found primarily in the pieces that masquerade as *contrafacta* and secular 'travestimenti'. Nothing surprising, then. Panc.27, like other sources with analogous contents — but perhaps considerably more so than these because it is more varied in the types of compositions it hosts — might therefore be the logical fruit of an environment of composite cultural forces, a mirror of the social and human variety of the users it presupposes. For this is what we are dealing with: not a memorial repository, but a book that was used in some manner. The phenomenon of the *contrafactum* can be explained as the expression of a culture of inversion, especially when its original musical form is openly signalled where it would be superfluous to do so, since the music is completely notated. In a culture that does not trace lines of demarcation too precisely between what is sacred and what is secular, 'cantasi come' and *contrafacta* probably help to mitigate social diversity within the same environment, and I believe that in Panc.27 these pieces should be read through this lens: if the manuscript was connected with the activity of a Renaissance confraternity, which seems probable to me, its varied contents, at once secular/devotional/liturgical, would constitute an indirect proof. The cultural fluidity manifested by the uninhibited juxtaposition of pieces with different character would essentially mirror the analogous culture of inversion of the social roles of those affiliated with it.

The members of confraternities were assigned well-defined roles that were often attended to with extreme zeal. Different duties with specific obligations subdivided the responsibilities of the institution down to the last detail. The festive occasions formed an integral part of the prescribed programmes as well, with the declared scope of recomposing disputes arising from time to time and renewing peace and good harmony among the members. It appears that feasts of this type often lost any connotation of piousness, and broke out into true and proper carnival excesses: banquets, tourneys, fights between animals, and similar amenities, made alluring by further inversions of the usual social roles.[248] Therefore, the confraternities too certainly needed secular music — instrumental

---

246. On the subject, see also WEISSMAN 1991, pp. 212-216, in which it is also underlined how, once the festive component and the characteristic social inversion that was so prevalent earlier faded, the Baroque confraternities irremediably lost a good part of the attracting force that had been exercised by the Renaissance ones precisely because of their internal dynamism.

247. On the phenomenon of contrafaction based on chanson models see CATTIN 1984.

248. See WEISSMAN 1991, pp. 210-211, who considers the rehabilitation of the festive component on the part of the confraternities as «perhaps one of the most striking contributions of contemporary Early Modern European social history» (p. 210).

music for entertainment, dances, various frottolistic forms, canons,[249] chansons[250] — for the exigencies 'necessitated' by the festive occasions in which all the members participated with lively enthusiasm: how much would the performance of courtly music on these occasions have aided the inversion of social roles? I believe that such performances in these contexts would have contributed much to reinforcing the sense of belonging to the community of all those affiliated with a particular confraternity: to hear the same music enjoyed by the nobles at court, 'disguised' or in its original clothing, must surely have served to arouse in artisans, merchants, and bourgeois, apart from the momentary emotive closeness to the nobles, also the illusion of sharing their leisure and pleasures:[251] the world thus appeared more equal for a day, the differences between the confraternity brothers were levelled for a moment, and the less well off perhaps felt less envy towards those who had more than they did. If such feelings really circulated during these feasts, it must have created an intensification of civic character that would be interesting to investigate in detail: a not indifferent contribution to the social concord between various classes that lived together in the city. How much weight can we attribute to the music in this sense? Is it reasonable to think that the music served also as social glue during this type of occasion, contributing thus in part even to the characteristic prosperity of the Renaissance city, itself the child of a deliberately weighed social equilibrium? If it is legitimate to consider the Renaissance city as an autonomous microcosm, preoccupied in equal measure as much with its well-being as with its spiritual salvation, the confraternities thus assumed a role of primary importance and reflected the dynamics intimately: spiritual life became the interface of the material one, the obverse of the same medal. And the singing of laude became a glue for all the social categories: they were sung in fact in the courtly chapels as well as in public civic processions. It is probable that the different compositional styles of the laude, more or less complex, can be referred to the different contexts of their origin: the highest-status users surely enjoyed more elaborate structures, while the simpler laude can perhaps be attributed to those contexts in which they constituted alternative prayers for those who did not know how to read.[252] Even the flagellants used them on various occasions. Singing laude surely brought together rich and poor during public processions on the most important religious feasts.

It is a singularly curious fact that a miscellaneous source such as Panc.27 should contain fragments of the Requiem Mass — something rather rare in contemporary sources — and that prompts us to enquire into the reason for their presence in Panc.27. Following further in the same interpretative direction discussed just before this, one could probably add 'more wood to the fire' by considering the pieces from the Requiem to be among those pieces useful for the activities of any confraternity. The historians of the phenomenon have amply explained that one of the most urgent inducements to affiliate oneself with lay groups was the widespread need to procure oneself a 'good death', decent in form and directed as far as possible towards the hope of Paradise. The shelter of the confraternity offered a remedy for the living and the dead in equal measure: those still alive remembered the dead, praying regularly for them, with the aim of shortening the time their souls would have to pass in Purgatory, but at the same time they prayed for themselves, for the same end in the prospect of inevitable death.[253] The cult of Purgatory in fact gained increasing momentum at the end of the fifteenth century, and this is clearly noticeable also in the function underlying much musical production of the time.[254] Through

[249]. Both perpetual canons in Panc.27 (nos. 18 and 34) are furnished with resolutions. In Petrucci's earliest prints, the presence of such rubrics is connected with the market aimed at amateurs (see BLACKBURN 2001b, p. 53).

[250]. The primary audience for chansons seems to have been the aristocracy and the upper middle classes (see PRIZER 1991, pp. 3-6).

[251]. Even when they distributed alms to the most needy on behalf of the confraternity, the bourgeois and artisans played at being nobles: certainly they could have felt themselves generous and magnanimous with sufficient adaptation to the role required by the task (see WEISSMAN 1991, p. 204).

[252]. On the question of various compositional styles in the lauda see GLIXON 1990, p. 30 and PRIZER 1993b, pp. 175-180.

[253]. See BLACK 1989, pp. 30, 105, 106. On the Panc.27 Requiem sections see FILOCAMO 2009c.

[254]. See BROWN 1990, pp. 744-773: 765. Bonnie Blackburn offers an eloquent example of how diffuse and flexible the practice of praying to obtain indulgences was, also in a musical environment (see BLACKBURN 1999): the prayer examined there, *Ave sanctissima Maria*, has a polyphonic musical setting in Panc.27 (no. 141).

indulgences the civic mercantile culture trafficked in prayers that were useful in the ascent towards Paradise, and those who could not pay depended on the support of the confraternity. To pray for the dead was considered one of the imperative duties of its members, and Requiem Masses were an integral part of the customary rites that often took place at secondary altars of churches.[255] We also know how much the dominant bourgeois mentality in the overall organizational structure of the confraternities inevitably ended up by contaminating even their most devotional aspect,[256] and thus we can reasonably assume that every prayer for the benefit of the living or dead had the goal of assuring oneself a well-quantified encounter. The advantage in question could be of various natures: it was useful for one's own sinful soul, and, moreover, by praying in return for compensation, one gained 'discounts for third parties' in Purgatory or money for oneself in this life. In the end, even those who prayed for the dead who were not related to them, and who did it freely, on their own death could hope to receive in exchange the same favour from relatives and friends of the defunct. It was a mercantile *do ut des* that produced of course a form of partial 'life insurance' (and on death) *ante litteram*, in a period in which all forms of guaranteed social assistance for citizens were totally lacking. It seems indeed that for many people the affiliation with one confraternity or another was strongly conditioned in the first place precisely by the attention devoted to the cult of the dead, and therefore «Laudesi companies tended to be more attractive to older married couples […]. Flagellant groups, practicing a cathartic flagellation ritual, on the other hand, attracted unmarried males from their late adolescence through their early thirties».[257] (And in Panc.27 five pieces with Italian text allude to the fear of death.) Even what has been said in relation to the cult of deceased ancestors seems to me strongly relatable to the discourse of the inversion of roles played out in Renaissance confraternities: in what other circumstances would people of the middle classes be able to ensure such attention that unrelated people could be persuaded to pray for their own dear departed? This was normally an exclusive privilege of nobles, prodigal with splendid displays even in funeral ceremonies, and who could easily enlist persons who prayed or sang in honour of the deceased of their own family.[258] Praying for the dead with the help of polyphonic song in the context of the confraternity was a luxury for those who could not afford to hire a group of singers privately: if need be, the institution took on the task, to the relief and comfort of friends and relatives of the deceased, who could thus benefit from funerals and prayers in some sense comparable to the rites of the nobles or to their proud cult of the ancestors. Adding up the elements, therefore, one can hypothesize with a certain measure of credibility that the presence of Requiem pieces in Panc.27 refers to their use within a confraternity fully active in singing as well.

Yet another piece of the mosaic, it seems to me, can usefully be inserted in the same picture: the presence of some fifty pieces specifically dedicated to or connected with the cult of the Virgin. From about the last third of the Quattrocento, the Marian cult assumes an importance it had not had up to that point, above all thanks to the institution of the feast of the Immaculate Conception[259] and the later official recognition of the cult of the Rosary.[260] All this had interesting repercussions on Marian iconography as well, which began to take on stronger overtones of the image of the Apocalypse.[261] Certainly, the contemporary affirmation of the cult of Purgatory contributed to bringing the figure of

---

[255]. See Goldthwaite (1995) 1999, pp. 116-117.

[256]. Blake Wilson has efficiently clarified the social implications in the Florentine context (Wilson 1992).

[257]. See Weissman 1991, p. 212.

[258]. In such cases, however, the singers too drew spiritual utility for themselves, praying at the same time for themselves and for the listeners (see Blackburn 1997).

[259]. The doctrine of the Immaculate Conception was encouraged as much by the Franciscans as it was opposed by the Dominicans (see Black 1989, p. 28). The Franciscan Pope Sixtus IV began the road towards official recognition of the doctrine in February 1477, through the document *Cum praecelsa*. But it was only four centuries later that what up till then was only a simple popular belief acquired the status of dogma, which happened with the promulgation of the bull *Ineffabilis Deus* of 8 December 1854 signed by Pius IX (see Blackburn 1999, p. 178).

[260]. The devotion to the Rosary was sanctioned by Pius V after 1571: the Pope associated the naval victory of the Holy League against the Turks in the Battle of Lepanto with the intercession of the Virgin, encouraged by prayers and meditations on the Rosary (cfr. Black 1989, p. 30).

[261]. On this see Blackburn 1999, p. 185.

the Virgin closer to the devotion of the faithful: as a woman and the mother of God, Mary could be approached in a 'more confidential' manner, thanks to her role as mediatrix between the human world and the divine world, also for prayers destined to shorten the time spent in Purgatory. As an obvious consequence, the cult of the Virgin encouraged female devotion as well as the institution of Marian confraternities.[262] Such a change of horizon had notable consequences also for music, and the end of the Quattrocento saw a great flourishing of motets on Marian topics.[263] An analogous discourse could be made for the image of Christ, which in like manner becomes more humanized and accessible, also in iconography. The believer thus establishes a new relation, emotively closer and more deeply felt, and in music as well there are various Latin pieces and laude with Christological subjects.[264]

(C) The Dating

The discussion of the dating of Panc.27 has always found scholars to be more or less in agreement on the first years of the sixteenth century, without further specification. Some of the texts set to music go back to precise periods or moments, though they do not furnish much help in identifying the date of the manuscript. For example, the poetic text *Chi serve a Dio con purità di cor[e]* was in existence at least since 1449, the year in which the first known performance of the *Rappresentazione di Abramo e Isacco* took place in Florence.[265] For the piece *Fortuna d'un gran tempo*, Edward Lowinsky considered various connections with the contemporary cultural context,[266] then proposed the date of 1499, under the immediate impression of the fall of the house of Sforza.[267] The text *Aimè el cor, aimè la testa*[268] was explicitly mentioned in a letter that Maria Savorgnan sent to her lover Pietro Bembo on 19 August 1500.[269] Moreover, *Vivi lieto e non temere*, the stated basis of the *contrafactum A Maria, fonte d'amore*,[270] is mentioned, together with *L'ocelo da le rame d'oro*, in a letter dated 2 August 1494 that the Mantuan student Don Acteon Mauri wrote to Francesco II Gonzaga.[271] The presence of the composition *A la bataglia* — positioned, in addition, in the initial part of the manuscript — securely establishes carnival of 1488 as the earliest *terminus post quem* for the compilation of Panc.27.[272]

But the most interesting indications that are useful in fixing a date for the preparation of Panc.27 surely come from the musical sources that share concordances with the manuscript. The relation with printed sources, however, changes from piece to piece, in the sense that, if one ascertains that a certain piece has been copied from a print, that does not mean that all the other pieces also present in the same print will have perforce been the models for their concordances in Panc.27. The stemmata therefore have been drawn up piece by piece, not source by source: the entire content of a manuscript (or a

---

[262]. See BLACK 1989, pp. 30 and 103.

[263]. See BROWN 1990.

[264]. There are some twenty cases also in Panc.27.

[265]. See no. 30, n. 2.

[266]. See LOWINSKY 1943.

[267]. Piece no. 139. See LOWINSKY 1976, pp. 71-72.

[268]. Piece no. 12.

[269]. DIONISOTTI 1950, p. 21, letter no. 37: «Io poso chantare la chancion che dice *Haimè il cor, aimè la testa*, el primo per amore di voi, ché ogni strada mi è chiusa di vedervi, la testa per gli afanni sustenuti: in modo che certo sto male, e se non fose per far alegro el mio nimicho, ogi di leto non serei levata. […]». Dionisotti comments on p. xxii: «Scrive lei (37): "Io poso chantare la chancion che dice *Haimè il cor, aimè la testa*", e intende dell'affanno amoroso che le urge in cuore e degli affanni invece familiari e privati che le martellano la testa con femminee emicranie. In realtà questo amore investe cuore e testa alla pari, forse anzi più l'una che l'altro; non tanto è un'esplorazione primaverile, quanto è una misura e affermazione meridiana con occidui presentimenti, della vita. Perciò anche è così denso di sottintesi letterari, è nella sua sostanza stessa una avventura letteraria».

[270]. Piece no. 15.

[271]. See entry no. 15, n. 1.

[272]. See entry no. 11.

print) is therefore simply the sum of the particular cases.[273] The detailed results for this purpose can be verified in the single entries for the pieces, but as far as the dating of Panc.27 is concerned, it is useful here to summarize the most important evidence: more than twenty musical pieces of the main body of Panc.27 have been copied from the following Petrucci prints: *Odhecaton*, *Motetti A*, Frottole books I, III, and IV, and perhaps the second book of Lamentations. Moreover, two texts were taken from the literary print *Fior1505*. The main body of Panc.27 was most likely prepared in a restricted period of time, as can be deduced from the inks; thus one can hypothesize that Scribe A finished copying after the date of publication of PeFroIV1505 (between 7 February and 22 December 1505). The *terminus post quem* would slip to after 29 May 1506 — the printing date of the only known exemplar of PeLamII — if one could be absolutely sure that the version of the Lamentations on fols. 144*v*-145*r* was copied from Petrucci. The manuscript was then taken over by Scribe B, who copied into it two pieces (nos. 180 and 181) taken directly from AntCanzoni, a print published on 9 October 1510.[274]

By intersecting the data that I have found in the Archivio di Stato in Mantua[275] with that extrapolated from specific studies and with unpublished material collected by William Prizer[276] I have been able to draw up a list of lay confraternities active in Mantua in the first decade of the Cinquecento:[277] (a) Confraternita di S. Pietro martire, a Dominican confraternity founded in 1444/1445[278] (in the Archivio di Stato in Mantua I found references relative to the year 1490);[279] (b) Confraternita del Preziosissimo Sangue, at the basilica of S. Andrea, construction of which began in 1472; it houses the most important relic in Mantua, a phial said to contain the blood of Christ;[280] (c) Confraternita del Santissimo Sacramento,[281] established at the church of S. Maria della Carità in 1494[282] (in the Archivio di Stato in Mantua I found references relative to the year 1529).[283] To these well-documented confraternities, which were certainly active during the period of the compilation of Panc.27, can perhaps be added the Compagnia di S. Maria della Passione mentioned by Roberto Brunelli, but without specifying the years

---

[273]. As Margaret Bent has shown, sharing the same repertory alone cannot constitute an efficient point of departure if one wishes to distinguish a true relation between musical sources (see BENT 1981).

[274]. See the part on the evaluation of the concordant witnesses.

[275]. I have examined various collections of documents: Trascrittori di libri [Davari, busta 7]; Maestri di musica, cantori e suonatori [Davari, busta 16]; Teatro e musica [Davari, busta 24].

[276]. My warmest thanks go to William Prizer for his generosity in placing at my disposition the still unpublished results of his research on the topic. The provisional title of his study is *Popular Piety in Renaissance Mantua: The Lauda and Flagellant Confraternities*. Here I shall limit myself to a brief mention of the documents cited by Prizer in more extended form, citing only those that are indispensable. His study should nevertheless appear soon, and will facilitate the verification of the information summarized here.

[277]. To the list cited here should be added the ca. twenty confraternities attested in the Mantuan territory (see PRIZER, *Popular Piety* cit.).

[278]. See MEERSSEMAN 1977, pp. 812-813, BRUNELLI 1986, p. 82, and MURPHY 1999, p. 46. Prizer mentions a fifteenth-century chronicle that claims 1445 as the year of foundation (the document is MS 718 of the Biblioteca Comunale in Mantua), which came about because of the interest of the Dominican friar Pietro Equo. The same manuscript specifies that all the members of the confraternity should be poor, and no one should be accepted who is famous or guilty of immoral conduct. Prizer also indicates that what Meersseman reports on the Mantuan confraternity is inaccurate and based on the report in DONESMONDI 1612, I, p. 380 (who gives 1444 as the date of foundation). Also, MS 491 (*olim* E.I.13) of the same library contains the Rules, which mention singing of the «devozioni», probably laude, and the practice of flagellation (see PRIZER, *Popular Piety*).

[279]. Archivio Gonzaga, busta 3362.

[280]. See BRUNELLI 1986, p. 82 and MURPHY 1999, p. 46. Prizer indicates 1459 as the year of foundation, «established by Pius II in Mantua at the Diet of Mantua» (see PRIZER, *Popular Piety*).

[281]. Or del Corpo Santissimo. The confraternities devoted to the Holy Sacrament originated in the twelfth century and concentrated on frequent communion and eucharistic devotions: they were normally connected with a parish and under clerical control. Their number increased significantly in the end of the fifteenth and the first half of the sixteenth century (see MURPHY 1999, p. 51. At n. 23 there is a useful bibliography on confraternities. See also BENDISCIOLI 1960, p. 82).

[282]. See BRUNELLI 1986, p. 82 and MURPHY 1999, p. 51. Prizer does not mention this one in his study on Mantuan confraternities.

[283]. Archivio Gonzaga, busta 3362.

in which it was active.[284] Prizer calls it the Compagnia della Scopa Segreta,[285] a flagellant confraternity founded between 1446 and 1454; before this last date it met in the church of S. Maria in Gradaro.[286] To these can be added the Scopa di S. Maria della Misericordia, a Dominican confraternity founded at the beginning of the fourteenth century,[287] as well as the Compagnia di S. Maria del Carmine, a Carmelite confraternity attested certainly from 1399 to 1601.[288]

Prizer's researches list other more or less contemporaneous associations that were operating in Mantua: the Scopa Bianca del Crocifisso, documented from the end of the thirteenth century probably up to 1432; the Scopa Negra di S. Maria Gentile (Confraternita della Morte), documented with certainty from the beginning of the fourteenth century; the Scopa Bianca di S. Giovanni Battista in Tempio, founded at the end of the fourteenth century and still attested during a pastoral visit at the end of 1584; the Compagnia de la Gloriosa Vergine, founded in the mid-fifteenth century;[289] the Scopa di S. Gotardo, founded in 1466 and attested in documents at least till July 1470;[290] the Compagnia di S. Nicola da Tolentino, in existence at least from December 1473 to November 1499.

There is also the Confraternita del Cristo Flagellato, which I have found mention of in 1537 in the Archivio di Stato in Mantua, but I do not know whether it was already active in the first decade of the sixteenth century.[291] From the late 1530s, in fact, the Mantuan confraternities came under increasing pressure to adapt to the models of religious comportment imposed by the clergy and the Gonzaga: the religious independence of the laity was condemned as subversive and dangerous, as much from a religious as from a political point of view. The Gonzaga therefore began to control the office of bishop, which was held by preference by a member of the family. A process was initiated whereby the confraternities were progressively subordinated to the clergy, as can be verified throughout Italy. But in a certain sense the Mantuan experience was unique, because the religious interests were strongly intertwined with the dynastic ones.[292] A direct consequence of the changed state of affairs was a consistent reduction in the religious autonomy of the laity, and after 1538 the Mantuan confraternities were reorganized according to the wishes of the ecclesiastical hierarchy, which assumed direct control over them.

For the moment, it is not possible to establish more precisely which context generated Panc.27. But I do not at all exclude (rather, I welcome it!) that other scholars will succeed in the future in defining more precisely the cultural background that gave rise to the manuscript. What is certain, however, is that the source was clearly prepared in a place where it was not difficult to find recent manuscripts and printed books: a city with a court that was very interested in culture is surely a very fitting place and better still if provided with other libraries.[293] The principal scribe of the manuscript was in contact not only with musical books but also with anthologies of poetry: this is demonstrated

---

284. See BRUNELLI 1986, p. 82.

285. All the companies called 'Scopa' refer to the use of flagellation: the 'scopa' (or 'scova') was in fact the flagellum adopted to whip the body. Singing of laude was an integral part of the rite of flagellation, above all during the celebration of Maundy Thursday, with the special rite of the Mandatum (see PRIZER, *Popular Piety*).

286. *Ibidem.*

287. Prizer speaks about this at length in his unpublished study, documenting the recitation of prayers in Italian, the singing of laude, and the practice of flagellation.

288. Prizer devotes considerable space to this confraternity too, clarifying that at least part of the members consisted of flagellants. Among the most important tasks of the confraternity was attending to the death rites of the members, which gave ample opportunity for singing laude in processions and during the rites.

289. As attested in the Chronicle of S. Pietro Martire (MS 718 in the Biblioteca Comunale of Mantua).

290. As attested in the Registro notarile cittadino of 1466 preserved in the Archivio di Stato in Mantua, fol. 442*v*.

291. Prizer's study on Mantuan confraternities does not refer to this one.

292. Cardinal Ercole Gonzaga (1505-63), son of Isabella d'Este and Francesco II Gonzaga, lived in Mantua from 1537 to 1561 and promoted a series of reforms that reduced the autonomy of the laity, above all in the confraternities. The same Ercole later held the reins of the duchy for 17 years, thus bringing about the combination of temporal and spiritual power. This turned out to be convenient both from the point of view of the incipient reform movement in the Church, and for the political needs of the dominant family. See MURPHY 1999, pp. 46-47 and 53.

293. It is known that Mantua was a pulsating cultural centre, where there was no lack of books or libraries and the various civic circles interacted between them. On the exchange between courts and monasteries, for example, see LECCISOTTI 1939 and CATTIN 1970, pp. 281-282, n. 76.

by the various texts circulating in poetic collections of the time that receive musical settings only in Panc.27. These are *unica*, but only from a strictly musical point of view: the examination of over four hundred literary sources listed in this edition underlines in fact the enormous circulation of the literary repertory at the beginning of the sixteenth century. Scribe A was fully acquainted with it, to the point where he dipped with both hands into this enormous reservoir containing not only secular but also devotional poetry in the Italian language.

6. EVALUATION OF THE CONCORDANT SOURCES

M ANY MUSICAL MANUSCRIPTS SHARE CONCORDANCES with Panc.27. That fact, however, is not always significant for the purpose of constructing a network of informative repertorial relationships with the manuscript. A high number of pieces in common, of course, might establish what type of repertory was most popular in a certain period in a particular geographic area, but it cannot in itself be considered the only useful element in defining the contacts between one source and another. As already mentioned above, even if we can trace the model of a piece with certainty, it is by no means given that other Panc.27 pieces also present in the source containing that model come from it as well. The circulation of pieces in the Renaissance happened in a rather scattered fashion, and thus the only certain method of establishing filiations among sources is to reconstruct their specific traditions piece by piece. I do think it is useful, however, to list here the sources that share concordances with Panc.27 — including reprints —, starting with a minimum number of five (arbitrarily considered the minimum significant), and to comment briefly on the relationship with their versions of the pieces in Panc.27. The survey that follows includes the time period and presumed provenance of the sources, in order to facilitate the determination of possible further contextual relations among the concordances. In addition, I have listed those pieces for which the model has been traced.

(A) RELATIONSHIPS WITH MUSICAL SOURCES

MANUSCRIPTS WITH AT LEAST 5 CONCORDANCES: **LeipU 1494** (plus one duplicated concordance): perhaps from the University of Leipzig, ca. 1490-1504; **FirC B2441**: from Milan (PRIZER 1996b, p. 26) or Tuscany (JEPPESEN 1969, p. 50), shortly after 1510, but most likely 1512-13; **FirN M107bis**: from Florence, after 1503, but probably around 1510; **FirN M121**: from Florence, end of the first decade of the 16th c.; **LonB A31922**: from the English court, ca. 1513-20; **ParisN F15123**: of Florentine provenance, mid-1480s, perhaps not later than 1484; **SevC 43**: Neapolitan provenance, or Florentine (BOORMAN 1981), early 1480s.

PRINTS WITH 5 CONCORDANCES: **PeSpinII** (Italian lute tablature): printed in Venice, 31 March 1507; **PetreiusNewII** (German lute tablature): printed in Nuremberg, 1536.

None of the versions of the concordances contained in these sources was the model for the pieces in Panc.27. Except for LonB A31922, these are manuscripts earlier or contemporaneous with Panc.27. ParisN F15123 also has an exclusive concordance: no. **153**.

MANUSCRIPT WITH 6 CONCORDANCES: **FirN BR337** (Bassus partbook only): probably from Florence, ca. 1520.

A manuscript later than the preparation of Panc.27, the versions of the Bassus parts are not close to those of the pieces in Panc.27.

MANUSCRIPTS WITH AT LEAST 7 CONCORDANCES: **PerA 431** (plus one duplicated concordance): from a Franciscan convent in the Neapolitan area for the sacred repertory, perhaps Ortona (CATTIN 1983a, pp. 35-39), ca. 1490; **RomaCa 2856**: from Ferrara? (RIFKIN 2003 contests this traditional opinion), ca. 1479-81, or 1485-90 (THOMAS 2001, p. 367), or early 1490 (RIFKIN 2003, pp. 313-323); **ZwR 78/3** (three partbooks): from Zwickau, after 1520.

PRINTS WITH AT LEAST 7 CONCORDANCES: **PeLaudeII** (plus one duplicated concordance): printed in Venice, 11 January 1507, but 1508 modern style; **PeFroI**: printed in Venice, 28 November 1504; **PeFroIII1505**: printed in Venice, 6 February 1504, but 1505 modern style; **PeFroIII1507**: printed in Venice, 26 November 1507.

At least two pieces (nos. **52** and **66**) were certainly copied from PeFroI (whereas two others are uncertain: nos. **12** and **17**). No. **17**, however, has an exclusive concordance with PeFroI. The model of no. **85** was the version in PeFroIII1505, and perhaps no. **150** as well was copied from one of the two printings of Petrucci's third book of Frottole. For no. **84** the provenance from the same book remains uncertain. There are two exclusive concordances with this last print: nos. **85** and **150**.

Manuscripts with 8 concordances: **BolM 16**: probably from the Neapolitan area, or from Rome (Fuller 1969, p. 86 and Thomas 2001, p. 367), 1487-1490s; **FirN M178**: probably from Florence, early 1490s; **VerCap 757**: from Verona, ca. 1490-1500.
None of the concordant versions contained in these sources was the model for the pieces in Panc.27, even if all three manuscripts were compiled before Panc.27.

Manuscripts with at least 9 concordances: **SGS 463** (Superius and Altus partbooks only; 8 concordances plus one indicated only in the index): from Glarus, Switzerland, or its environs, shortly after 1540; **SGS 530** (keyboard tablature): from Sankt Gallen, ca. 1512-21, with additions in 1531.
Prints with 9 concordances: **EgenLieder** (Superius only, in three books): printed in Frankfurt am Main, ca. 1535; **FormTrium** (three partbooks): printed in Nuremberg, 1538.
The date and format of all these manuscript and printed sources excludes the hypothesis that any of one of them was the source for the pieces in Panc.27, confirmed also by the analysis of the versions themselves.

Manuscript with at least 10 concordances: **ParisN Rés27** (Italian lute tablature, with two repeated concordances): probably from Venice, ca. 1505-10, after 1507 to ca. 1510 (Fabris 2001 and Fabris 2005, p. 483).
This is a source without Superius, perhaps of a professional who had no need of one because he knew it by memory. It is therefore impossible to think that it was the model for any of the pieces in Panc.27.

Manuscripts with 11 concordances: **BolM 18**: from Bologna, ca. 1502-05; **CV G27**: from Florence, or from Rome (Thomas 2001, p. 367), 1492-94/5.
None of the versions of the concordances contained in these sources was the model for the pieces in Panc.27, even though both manuscripts were prepared before Panc.27.

Manuscripts with at least 13 concordances: **SegC** (plus one duplicate concordance): Spanish provenance, perhaps from the royal court at Segovia, or from Toledo (Thomas 2001, p. 367), late 1490s, or 1502 (Thomas 2001, p. 367); **FirN BR229**: from Florence, ca. 1492-95.
Print with 13 concordances: **PeMotA1505**: printed in Venice, 13 February 1504, but 1505 modern style.
The two manuscripts were not the model for any version contained in Panc.27. For PeMotA1505, see the comments below to PeMotA1502.

Prints with 14 concordances: **PeOdh1501**: printed in Venice, dedication dated «decimo octavo cal. Iunias. Salutis anno. MDI» [= 15 May or 14 June 1501?]; **PeMotA1502**: printed in Venice, 9 May 1502.
At least six pieces (nos. **60**, **95**, **98**, **103**, **126**, **129**) were certainly copied from Petrucci's *Motetti A* (from 1502 or from 1505), and two others with a certain probability (no. **99** — despite the transposition — and no. **130**). The provenance of nos. **91** and **102** remains uncertain: in this last the Panciatichi scribe has even corrected an error present in the model. With *Motetti A* Panc.27 shares no fewer than four exclusive concordances: nos. **51** in the version for four voices (with added A), **90**, **102**, **130**. For PeOdh1501 see the comments below to PeOdh1503 and PeOdh1504.

Prints with 17 concordances: **PeOdh1503**: printed in Venice, 14 January 1502, but 1503 modern style; **PeOdh1504**: printed in Venice, 25 May 1504.

132

Nine Panc.27 pieces (nos. **54, 56, 59, 73, 89, 96, 97, 128, 139**) had the *Odhecaton* as model. It is not possible to determine which of the known printings served as source, but certainly no. **128** was not taken from the copy of PeOdh1504 now in Treviso, and for no. **139** it could not have been PeOdh1501. Two other pieces probably come from the *Odhecaton* (nos. **127** and **131**), and the other two remain uncertain (nos. **55** and **57**).

Manuscript with 21 concordances: **CTL G12**: from a monastery of the Congregazione di Santa Giustina in northern Italy (the Po Plain area) for the sacred repertory, and linked with the courts of Mantua and Ferrara for the frottolistic texts, ca. 1500 for the first part and 1510/15 for the second.

Despite the high number of musical concordances and the substantial contemporaneity between Panc.27 and CTL G12, it is not possible to speak of a direct filiation for any of the Panc.27 pieces. The two manuscripts, however, share no fewer than five exclusive concordances (nos. **15, 26, 74, 79, 114**), and in four cases (nos. **16, 36,**[294] **75** and **81**) include with the music a text that is absent in the other concordances. (Moreover, only Panc.27 and CTL G12 set to music, though with different settings, the text of no. **41**.) Furthermore, the common geographical provenance of the two manuscripts is attested by the version of no. **83** — where both include the final «Amen» and the same conjunctive error —, and of nos. **36** and **116**.

Manuscript with 24 concordances: **ParisN Rés676**: from Mantua or Ferrara (for Prizer 1990 it comes from Mantua), from 4 to 26 October 1502.

The musical versions of ParisN Rés676 are always rather distant from the Panciatichi concordances. As in the case of MS CTL G12, however, the common environment with Panc.27 is certain, as is also confirmed by the exclusive concordance no. **113**.

Two other printed sources have been singled out as models for the pieces in Panc.27, even if they do not share a large number of concordances with the manuscript: **AntCanzoni** (printed in Rome, 9 October 1510) was certainly the model for nos. **179** and **180**, and **PeLamII** (printed in Venice, 29 May 1506) might be the model for no. **174**. This fact further confirms that the sharing of a large number of concordances is not a fundamental element in the evaluation of the repertorial relationships between sources, and it does not necessarily establish direct contacts between them even if it can undoubtedly indicate a common geographical area for the repertory and can aid in determining the provenance of one source from a specific region.

The presence of exclusive musical concordances is also useful in pointing to interesting connections between sources, although it is not in itself an obvious element to trace possible models for pieces in Panc.27. Here is the list, which does not include those sources mentioned earlier:
- **AugsS 142a** (from Augsburg; ca. 1505-13): no. **160**;
- **BolM 19** (from northern Italy, perhaps from Cento or Bologna; ca. 1518): no. **120**;
- **ModIV** (probably from Modena, copied for the use of the cathedral choir; ca. 1520-30): no. **3**;
- **TorN 27** (from Piedmont; early 16th c.): no. **166**;
- **PeFroIV1505** (printed in Venice; between 7 February and 22 December 1505): nos. **38** and **53**;
- **PeFroIV1507** (printed in Venice; 31 July 1507): nos. **38** and **53**;
- **PeLaudeII** (printed in Venice; 11 January 1507, but 1508 modern style): no. **4** (two versions: the one on fols. 47*v*-48*r* is much closer to the Panciatichi version).

Further significant relationships, of various kinds, can also be mentioned:
- • no. **31** shares with the MSS **BolA 179** (perhaps from a Dominican convent in Brescia; dated 28 July 1467) and **ParisN NAL401** (from the Benedictine monastery in Polirone, today S. Benedetto

---

[294]. With a different Altus.

Po, in the province of Mantua; dated 1475 and 1477)[295] a probable geographical and cultural relationship: both manuscripts reproduce, however, a version of the piece with only two voices in common;

• no. **45** is found also in **BolM 13** (from the same Benedictine monastery of Polirone; dated 1482), a manuscript that apart from this polyphonic piece contains only monophony;

• the version of no. **92** is very close to that in **FirN BR230** (from Florence; ca. 1525), but this is a very late source.

I believe that it would be useful to compile a 'hit parade' of the pieces in Panc.27 that takes into account their diffusion in other sources. Although we can never be entirely sure whether the sources listed constitute the whole of the sources produced — rather, it is highly probable that only a fraction of these has survived, not quantifiable in percentual terms with respect to the presumed total — an inventory of what has come down to us invites reflection on the more or less comprehensive data in our possession. With regard to the fifteenth- and sixteenth-century musical sources, in fact, the existence of various repertories and specific studies permits a fairly complete picture of what remained. And even if what has survived is surely only a part of what once existed, at least we can 'photograph' pratically everything. The following, therefore, is the situation with the pieces in Panc.27 that circulated most widely, the listing of which stops at those with at least five concordances, and also includes the reprints: no. **21** (41 concordances), no. **127** (31 concordances), no. **40** (30 concordances), no. **89** (29 concordances), nos. **54** and **66** (27 concordances), nos. **36** and **56** (23 concordances), no. **64** (19 concordances), no. **59** (17 concordances), no. **45** (16 concordances), nos. **83** and **168** (14 concordances), no. **131** (12 concordances), nos. **75** and **115** (11 concordances), nos. **55** and **177** (10 concordances), no. **96** (9 concordances), nos. **73, 128, 138** (8 concordances), nos. **16, 93, 105, 126, 139** (7 concordances), nos. **12, 43, 57, 60, 94** (6 concordances), nos. **11, 52, 81, 145** (5 concordances).

(B) Relationships with Literary Sources

For only two pieces are we in a position to posit with a certain degree of likelihood the provenance of their poetic text from a literary source: nos. **112** and **112bis** were almost certainly copied from **Fior1505**.

A very detailed discussion of the presence of texts set to music in Panc.27 in literary sources cannot arrive at precise conclusions. In fact, while we can be reasonably sure of knowing almost all the contemporary musical sources that have come down to us — thanks also to the help of inventories, specialized studies, and critical editions — thus making it possible to draw prudent conclusions by comparing the data in our possession with that already acquired, we cannot, on the other hand, believe that the same procedure can be carried out with the literary sources. Unfortunately, there do not yet exist systematic repertories for these types of sources, just as there are few critical editions based on specific sources. As a consequence, therefore, the investigation of literary sources carried out for this edition was undertaken in a rather disordered and haphazard manner: beginning with single bibliographical references contained in specific studies. If we can therefore speak of results, it needs to be kept in mind that it is a question of very partial ones, with no pretence of exhaustiveness, because I have absolutely no idea what portion of the existing manuscripts and prints I have been able to see.

Having made this necessary statement, I turn to the quantitive data that I can supply in relation to the textual repertory set to music in Panc.27. There will be no qualitative discussions of the texts, since with the exception of the cases cited of the texts of nos. **112** and **112bis**, it is almost impossible to succeed in positing the copying from a literary source with any degree of plausibility. Also in this case, sources with fewer than five texts in common with Panc.27 are not cited.[296]

---

[295]. I thank Stefania Roncroffi for the information on the provenance of both manuscripts.
[296]. As with the list of the musical sources, also for the literary ones I count as concordances those found in reprints.

MANUSCRIPTS WITH 5 CONCORDANCES: **Bol.U. 4019** (probably belonged to a Compagnia dei Bianchi; second half of the 15th c.), **CV.VL.5159** (from the Romagna and the Marche; early 16th c.), **CV.VL.13026**, **Fir.L. Ash.480** (15th c.), **Fir.L. Ash.1402**, **Fir.M. 262** (15th c.), **Fir.N. 140** (15th c.), **Fir.N. M.27** (probably for monastic use; second half of 15th c.), **Fir.R. 1502** (15th c.), **Fir.R 3112**, **Pes.O. 54** (from the Marche; early 16th c., perhaps 1504), **Roma.Ang. 2274** (early 16th c.), **Ven.M. I.77** (belonged to the Compagnia dei Battuti di S. Zenobi in Florence; 15th c.).

MANUSCRIPTS WITH 6 CONCORDANCES: **Berl.S. H.348** (from the Venetian Franciscan convent of S. Francesco ad vineas; after 1474, ca. 1490; it depends directly on the *editio princeps Giust1474*),[297] **CV. Ch.266** (copied by the Florentine Filippo di Lorenzo Benci; ca. 1448-56, with additions up to 1464; it contains laude in the Umbrian-Tuscan tradition), **CV. Ro.424** (from an Umbrian-Tuscan laudistic cultural environment; ca. 1480-90), **Ven.GR. 120** (perhaps commissioned in a monastic environment; ca. 1450-60), **Ven.M. I.182** (from a monastic environment; 1475-77. The Giustinian repertory was copied from the *editio princeps Giust1474*).

PRINTS WITH 6 CONCORDANCES: **LaudeBonar** (printed in Bologna; ca. 1560), **LaudeSper** (printed in Venice; 1556), **LaudiRiccardiana** (no typ. info.).

MANUSCRIPTS WITH 7 CONCORDANCES: **Rim.C. 38**,[298] **Ven.M. I.78** (16th-c., an exact copy of the print *LaudeBonac*).

PRINT WITH 7 CONCORDANCES: **LaudeBonac** (printed in Florence; 1 March 1485, but 1486 modern style).

PRINTS WITH 10 CONCORDANCES: **Fior1505** (printed in Brescia; ca. 1505), **LaudeMisc** (printed in Florence; ca. 1495), **LaudeVecchie** (printed in Florence; ca. 1502-07/08), **OperaNova** (printed in Venice; 4 March 1512).

From these few partial data, however, something interesting emerges: the frequent dependence of manuscripts on printed sources, often incunables. The texts most frequently found in the literary sources examined are laude, and, as can be verified by consulting the relevant entries in the edition, 12 laudistic texts have a musical setting uniquely in Panc.27: nos. **14, 27, 29/114, 30, 42, 67, 70, 77, 82, 88, 112, 159**.[299] In the present state of our knowledge, the text among these last that circulated the most widely seems to be no. **30** (71 concordances), followed by nos. **29/114** (70 concordances), **159** (25 concordances), **27** (14 concordances), **67** (13 concordances), **42** (11 concordances), **88** and **112** (one concordance each). For nos. **14, 70, 77**, and **82** I have not found any literary concordance.

It can be said that some texts set to music seem exceedingly popular. Citing only the numbers that exceed the twenty concordances so far singled out, we have nos. **13** (98 concordances), **76** (84 concordances), **30** (71 concordances), **29/114** (70 concordances), **64** (58 concordances), **19** (49 concordances), **69** (43 concordances), **53** (34 concordances), **49** (27 concordances), and **159** (25 concordances), apart from the very widely circulated Petrarchan no. **180**.[300]

Often some texts travelled together with others. Always taking into account the limited nature of my research, it is nevertheless a fact that when in one source I traced the presence of text no. **29/114**, I found there also the texts of nos. **30, 64, 67, 69, 76, 147**, and **159**.[301] Further tendencies to 'voyage' together link nos. **49** and **53, 42** and **69, 13** and **69**.

---

[297]. Only five laude from the *editio princeps* of 1474 are not present in MS *Berl.S. H.348*.

[298]. In LUISI 1983, I, p. 126, it is said that the MS was copied from *LaudeVecchie* or its reprint *OperaNova*.

[299]. To this list should be added no. **36**, whose musical setting in Panc.27 is a *unicum* in this specific form. Moreover, the text *Ave Regina, Virgo gloriosa* of no. **13** is set to music only in Panc.27, but elsewhere the piece circulated with the text *Sofrire son disposto [ogni tormento]*.

[300]. To this list should also be added no. **147** (41 concordances), without music in Panc.27.

[301]. Nos. **15** and **36** too are mostly present in the sources that have the preceding texts.

PART II

CRITICAL COMMENTARY
AND TRANSCRIPTIONS

Explanatory Notes

Texts

In the catalogue, each text taken into consideration has been supplied — where possible — with an edition, critical apparatus, and specific bibliography. The following remarks are intended to set out in detail both the criteria adopted and the arrangement of the information on the texts of the compositions.

General Criteria
- Titles of all the poetic texts according to the reading of the heading or the whole initial line in Panc.27. In case this is incomplete, what is present is reported; the remainder, placed in square brackets, is taken from the source from which the complete text is drawn.
- Double title in cases where Panc.27 expressly indicates that it is a *contrafactum* or a *cantasi come* (nos. 13, 15, 36, 61, 64, 75). Number 68 also has a double title, though it is not a *cantasi come*.
- Indication of the name of the poet at the upper left; since it is always taken from concordances (except in the case of Jean II, duc de Bourbon), it is placed in square brackets. At the right the name of the composer is indicated if given in Panc.27; if taken from a concordant source, the name appears in square brackets. Square brackets also enclose any amplification of the names themselves.
- Disposition of the text and the *residuum* according to the metric and poetic form; the indication of the refrain follows the presentation in the source used.
- Indication of the nature of each piece that has been sufficiently identified. For the texts of the Mass and Office it is common that the same text can be used on different feasts, but the old and modern liturgical books often indicate only the incipit, cross-referring to the page on which the text appears complete. In such cases these references are not indicated in the entries relative to the pieces in this edition, which are limited to the main uses present in modern liturgical books (in general those with musical notation in AM, AR, GR, LR, LU, PM, and those with the complete text in BR and MR). It should be borne in mind that the modern use may not always coincide with that of the epoch and of the place in which Panc.27 was compiled. Since that time, in fact, some feasts of the liturgical calendar have been added, moved, or suppressed, and many texts have been eliminated or have changed their function, also in regard to individual local traditions. For the oldest usages and details, the repertories inventoried in AMS, CAO, CS, and IGC should be consulted.
- A list of all the other sources that share the same text and music. Next to each witness are the foliation and the indication of other information present in the source in question (name of the poet, name of the composer, useful rubrics, other annotations). Implicit attributions are normalized and placed in parentheses. The incipits of the concordant pieces have been normalized as regards the resolution of abbreviations and the separation or joining of words. If the incipit is not noted, it is to be understood that it largely agrees with that given in Panc.27, unless further graphic variants are indicated.
- Listing of the modern editions of the poetic text. For the liturgical texts the most common liturgical books have been used; whenever these give a beginning similar to that in the piece in Panc.27, the reference is noted together with the liturgical use indicated there. For texts deriving from the Bible reference is also made to the Clementine Vulgate. For the pieces from the Ordinary of the Mass liturgical books are indicated only if they include chants connected with the music in Panc.27.

- Presentation of the *Commentary on the text*. The editorial remarks indicate differences in the text among the various voices in Panc.27 and errors or metric irregularities in the reading of the manuscript, with proposed conjectural emendations suggested by the concordances. Among other observations, the explanation of obscure words is included.
- Reproduction of the texts from concordances that include parts of the text absent in Panc.27. Among the poetic concordances, the one with the most extensive text has been published. These texts have been edited with the same editorial criteria used for the texts of Panc.27, but irregularities in metre or form and instances of different words, or of strophes placed differently among the various sources, are not indicated. The extensive concordances of Latin liturgical or paraliturgical texts have not been listed.
- Omission of the cancellations or corrections made immediately by the scribes, except in a few cases where such interventions have editorial relevance.
- A list of the specific bibliographical contributions relative to each text or composition.

THE TEXT
- Regularization of the punctuation according to modern criteria.
- Preference accorded to the poetic reading of the *Superius/Cantus*. The text given is that of the highest voice except where a different reading is worthy of greater consideration: such cases, however, are noted.
- Regularization of the formal poetic structure.
- Indication of the reprise in strophic forms by means of an indented repetition of the *incipit*; this incipit is placed as it is indicated from time to time in the source used.
- Indication of deletions in angle brackets.
- Indication of additions in square brackets.
- Correction of evident errors, signalling the editorial intervention in the apparatus.
- The use of ellipses in the case of short gaps, and of the *crux desperationis* for more extensive readings that cannot be deciphered because of damage to the witness (erasures, cancellations, tears, trimmed margins, etc.) or because the writing is illegible.

SPELLING
- Regularization of the joining or separating of words.
- Resolution of the abbreviations and symbols.
- Resolution of the Tironian *et* as *e* or *et*, and preservation of the Latin conjunction *et*.
- Normalization of the interjections *ai* and *de* to *ahi* and *deh*.
- Normalization of the inflections of the verbs *avere* and *essere* by adding or removing etymological or pseudo-etymological *h* (e.g. *a, ano, he, habia, havesti*).
- Joining of *poi* and *che* where the conjunction has a causal meaning; where the meaning is temporal *poi* and *che* are kept separate.
- Joining of *al fin* in cases where the adverb has temporal value; where it has final value *al* and *fin* are kept separate.
- Distinction between *che 'l* and *ch'el*, on the basis of the function of the article and the pronoun *il* or *el*.
- Indication, by means of an apostrophe, of aphaeresis, elision, and truncation.
- Addition of accents according to modern usage.
- Normalization of the use of capital and lower-case letters.
- Transcription of *j* as *i*, except in terms and names in French (e.g. *Japart, Jo*).
- Transcription of *y* as *i*, with the exception of the terms *cygno, Kyrie, phylomena, transtyberina*, French terms (e.g. *playne, rayson, royne, vuydez*), and Latin terms derived from Greek.
- Preservation of phonosyntactic doublings, indicated by means of a superscript point preceding them (e.g. ˙*llei*).

- Use of the single form *s*, which is found in two graphic forms, long *s* and short *s*.
- Transcription of consonantal *u* as *v*.
- Preservation of *x* (e.g. *caxon, expectò*).
- Preservation of the Latinizing spelling *ph* (e.g. *Pamphilus, phenice, phylomena, prophetia, seraphini*).
- Preservation of the Latin group *ti* + vowel (e.g. *patientia, abitatio', reverentia, licentia, partiale*).

PHONETICS

- Elimination of the *i* without diacritic function in words with affricate *c* and palatal *g* (e.g. *legie, regie, piangie, incierto, ogniun/ogniuno*).
- Preservation of the oscillation of consonants, now single, now double, in order to maintain the linguistic patina. Such preservation is maintained even in rhyme position (e.g. *tera:guera:erra*, but also *tuto:fructo, laccio:stratio, pace:brazze*).
- Elimination of superfluous *h*, etymological or pseudo-etymological, including those indicating a velar sound of the *c* and guttural of the *g* (e.g. *hormai, anchora, humana, chui, tho, hor, ognhora, habitatio', bochon, humil, homo, honore, focho, cha, scholpito, hora, biancha, challe, chontrario, chome*). Such *h*, on the other hand, are preserved in Italian names (e.g. *Chriaco, Hercole, Honorato, Zacchagnino*).
- Preservation of *m* for *n* at the end of a word (e.g. *sum, um, bem, ciascum, im*).
- Preservation of the simple Latin preposition *cum*.
- Preservation of the group *ct* in Latinizing spellings (e.g. *fructo, nocte, conducto, pecto*).
- Normalization of the spelling *ngn* to *gn* (e.g. *ongnun, ongni, sengnato*).
- Normalization of the spelling *lgl* and *gl* + vowel to *gli* + vowel (e.g. *volglio, figla*).
- With notice, intervention has been made in rhymes where correction is necessary; imperfect rhymes, however, are preserved.

ABBREVIATIONS

- In the critical apparatus of each piece the following abbreviations are used:

    A = *Altus / Alto*
    B = *Bassus*
    B_1 = *Bassus I*
    B_2 = *Bassus II*
    C = *Cantus*
    Ct = *Contra*
    S = *Superius / Soprano*
    T = *Tenor / Tinore*
    T_1 = *Tenor I*
    T_2 = *Tenor II*

CRITICAL APPARATUS TO THE MUSIC

- The variants indicated are reported as follows: running number(s) of the modern edition (arabic number), followed by the section(s) relative to the remark (roman number); abbreviation of the relevant voice(s). In the listing of variants, if the note names do not appear next to the indication of the original rhythmic value, it is to be understood that they have the same pitches corresponding to those of the reading in question.

MUSICAL TRANSCRIPTIONS

GENERAL INFORMATION

- Numbering and titles of the compositions according to the same criteria used for the presentation of the texts.
- Indication of the name of the poet and of the composer according to the same criteria used for the version in the catalogue of compositions.

– Indication of the presence of text — complete or incomplete — in each voice. The text underlay follows Panc.27 except for the *residuum*; italics distinguish the textual repetitions present in the source.

– The text underlaid is that edited in the catalogue of compositions, and preserves any supplements; the cancelled parts of the text are not, however, given under the music.

– Although in some pieces a textual incipit appears under the music, the texts have not been underlaid syllabically because the text is question is unknown, and therefore it is impossible to reconstruct its metric and poetic form (nos. 44, 80, 88, 101). But also some textual incipits identifiable with known texts are not syllabified under the music because it cannot be proved that they were intended as vocal in Panc.27 (nos. 11, 39, 40, 56, 59, 68, 71, 73, 74, 92, 95, 96, 97, 103, 105, 107, 109, 111, 116, 125, 126, 127, 131, 137, 138, 159, 162, 163, 164, 168).

– Only the heading is retained, even if otherwise unknown, of those pieces that have no text underlaid (nos. 32, 42, 50, 77, 143); in the particular case of no. 57 the heading transmitted in Panc.27 is retained even though it is probably not a textual incipit (see the relevant entry).

– Also in the cases where the incipit of a known text (nos. 21, 49, 72, 78, 87, 89, 151) or a hypothetical one (nos. 14, 47, 75) appears only as a heading, it is not underlaid in the music.

– Instrumental pieces, or those presumed so, have only the heading present in Panc.27 (nos. 55, 128, 139, 170); the text is also underlaid, unsyllabified, if present in one or more voices.

– The few original inscriptions *Iustus* (nos. 9, 25, 29, 35, 43, 78, 143), *Vidi* (no. 11), and *Vidi totum* (no. 14) placed at the end of some pieces or of sections are retained.

Music

– In the transcription into modern scores, the voices are arranged retaining their original labels (expanded within square brackets, if necessary):
   Superius / Cantus / Soprano;
   Altus / Contratenor Altus / Alto;
   Tenor / Tinore;
   Bassus / Contra / Contratenor Bassus.

– When the names of the voices are missing, they are deduced from their function/clef/range/disposition in the MS (nos. 17, 20, 21, 34, 46, 90, 92, 95, 97, 102, 115, 118, 119, 123, 129, 135, 166, 168, 173, 175, 178, 179, 184, 185).

– In those cases in which two voices have the same role, they are distinguished as *Tenor I - Tenor II* (nos. 20, 57, 119), and as *Bassus I - Bassus II* (nos. 135, 184, 185).

– The monodic intonations present in nos. 102, 123, 166, and 181 are preserved.

– Only piece no. 183 should not be considered as presented in score format (see the relevant entry).

– The modern transcriptions are preceded by the following original information for each voice: name of the voice, clef, key signature (preserving the position and occasional doubling at the distance of an octave), mensuration sign (only if present), range. In pieces nos. 71 and 107 the notes added in parentheses to the range refer to the increase in tessitura due to the presence of alternative readings.

– The circular canons for three voices (nos. 18 and 34) have been resolved following the indications of their relative inscriptions. The single voice present in the MS is repeated till the end of the exposition of the third entry: the repeated part is indicated within square brackets. In the second entry the sign ' introduces the re-entry of the *dux*.

– Modern clefs are used: treble, transposing treble, and bass.

– The original mensuration signs are transcribed in the following manner:
   ¢ , ᴄ , ᴄ2 , ⊙ → ¢

   ⏀ , ⦸ , ᴏ , ᴏ3 , ¢3 → 3/2

   ᴄ → 6/4

142

In the cases where the original sign is missing, or is different from one voice to another, the appropriate sign is added within square brackets.

- Changes of mensuration within a piece, besides being indicated by a modern time signature, are also shown by the original mensuration sign above the top stave (nos. 11, 68, 97, 122, 123, 129, 131, 167); in this case it means that all voices have the same sign (an exception is signs within square brackets). If different among each other, then all the original mensuration signs are placed above the corresponding staves (nos. 126, 146, 167).
- Rhythmic values have been halved.
- Excessive rhythmic values present in cadential situations have been absorbed by silently lengthening the relative measures.
- Final *longae* (or at the end of a section), generally transcribed as modern breves, have instead been adapted to the length of the other voices. More generally, their value has been adjusted to the measure chosen in the modern edition appropriate to the indication of the mensuration sign.
- Ligatures are indicated with the sign ⌐.
- Coloration is indicated between small opening and closing half-brackets ⌐ ¬. In cases of long sections in coloration the tempo has been changed momentarily, specifying the equivalence of the unit of the modern measure. At the end of the section the initial mensuration returns.
- The local accidentals present in the MS are regularly transcribed before the note to which they refer, and their effect lasts through the bar. The accidentals above the stave are taken from concordant readings when considered correct, and/or suggested by the editor; their effect is limited to the single note to which they refer. In only two cases (nos. 5 and 117) such accidentals are placed under the note to which they refer.
- The transcription of single vertical bars in the original (thin or solid), double or repetition signs, are given in the following manner:
  - the transition from *Prima Pars* to *Secunda/Tertia Pars* is always rendered with ‖ (even if the MS has nothing or has only a single bar);
  - ‖ (which indicates the end of a section) is rendered with ‖;
  - the change of mensuration is rendered with │, unless the MS has ▮;
  - │ is rendered with │, or with a modern opening/closing repetition sign;
  - ‖ is rendered with a modern opening/closing repetition sign;
  - : ‖ : is rendered with a modern opening/closing repetition sign;
  - a *custos* and │ are rendered with a modern opening/closing repetition sign;
  - │ at the end of a section with various lines of text placed under the music is rendered with a modern closing repetition sign.
- Some *signa congruentiae, custodes,* and inscriptions «ut supra» are interpreted and resolved. In doubtful cases they are given in the transcription or in the apparatus.
- The final fermata is added in square brackets in cases where its absence is clearly due to the copyist's inadvertence. If instead the fermata is present in only one voice out of 3 or 4 it is not indicated.
- Editorial additions of missing music are enclosed in square brackets.
- Some repeated notes have been joined editorially with dotted ties.
- Alternative notes are retained and transcribed with black notes.
- Alternative readings annexed to pieces nos. 19, 21, 33, 164 have been transcribed in full.
- The arabic numbers present at the end of some of the pieces or sections have been preserved and indicated.

1.

Disperso per lo mundo peregrino

fol. 1r (3 vv.)

Disperso per lo mundo peregrino
vo suspirando sempre in vesta bruna.
Il ciel m'è contra, e 'l mio crudel destino,
le stelle, li pianeti e la fortuna.
5   Io son el più scontento e 'l più meschino
che mai nascese soto [de] la luna.
Invidia, male lingue e zilosia
son caxon del bando e doglia mia.

Italian secular piece (strambotto toscano).

Commentary on the text:

3	the *residuum* begins here
6	hypometric; corrected according to the three literary sources
8	the line ends with a question mark, which has been deleted

Readings emended in the edition:

Bar	Voice	Original
37/II–38/I	T	dotted *minima* and *semiminima*
40	C	*longa* with fermata

Textual concordances (mss): • *CV. VL.5170* (36*v*), «Ser[aphino]» • *Ox.B. CI.99* (104*r*) • *Pes.O. 54* (104*r*)

Modern editions of the text: Filocamo 2000, pp. 94-95 (after Panc.27); Saviotti 1892, p. 343 (after *Pes.O. 54*); Spongano 1971, p. 82 (after *Ox.B. CI.99*).

Remarks: The question mark at the end of the last line deleted here — not found in any of the three concordant literary sources — suggests the hypothesis that the text of this strambotto was copied from another literary source, so far unknown. It is likely that the initial conception of the MS Panc.27 did not foresee *Disperso per lo mundo peregrino* as the opening piece: it occupies only the first recto, and the ink is noticeably darker than in the following pieces, which are copied in choirbook format (Superius and Tenor on the verso, Altus and Bassus on the recto). It is the only secular piece in the fascicle, and the initial letter of the incipit ('D') also contrasts strikingly with the layout of the first gathering of the codex: it is followed by no fewer than six *Ave Maria* settings, as well as two devotional texts that begin with different letters ('Q' [*Qui seminant in lacrimis*] and 'V' [*Vidimus enim stellam eius in Oriente*]), probably added later to fill in the empty staves on folios 3*v*-5*r*. The literary text is in strambotto form; the music must be repeated for each of the following three couplets, included here in the form of a *residuum*.

1.

DISPERSO PER LO MUNDO PEREGRINO

fol. 1*r*

2.

Ave Maria, gratia plena

fols. 1*v*-2*r* (4 vv.)

Laurentius Bergomotius Mutinensis

Ave Maria, gratia plena, Dominus tecum;
benedicta tu in mul[i]eribus,
et benedictus fructus ventris tui, Iesus.
Sancta Maria, mater Dei,
5   ora pro nobis peccatoribus,
nunc et in hora mortis.
Amen.

Prayer to the Blessed Virgin Mary (LU, p. 1861) based on Luke 1:28 («et ingressus angelus ad eam dixit | ave gratia plena Dominus tecum | benedicta tu in mulieribus», Vulgata, p. 1606) and 1:42 («et [Elisabeth] exclamavit voce magna et dixit | benedicta tu inter mulieres et benedictus fructus ventris tui», Vulgata, p. 1607). It is recited, silently, at the beginning of all the Hours and at the end of Compline (BR, pp. 1, 110). See also AMS, p. 244; CAO III, pp. 5, 64; CAO IV, pp. 40, 42, 476; CS, pp. 424-425, 428-429; IGC, p. 55.

Commentary on the text:

6   «nostre» lacking after «mortis»

Readings emended in the edition:

Bar	Voice	Original
38/II	A	*brevis* with fermata

Modern editions of the music: Banks 1993, II, pp. 16-17 (after Panc.27); Jeppesen 1935, pp. 161-162 (after Panc.27).

Remarks: This *Ave Maria* surely was intended as the opening piece of Panc.27. No other pieces attributed to Laurentius Bergomotius are known, either in manuscript or print; does such an honorific place suggests that this Lorenzo «Mutinensis» (= 'of Modena') might be the copyist of the whole manuscript?

Bibliography: AMS, p. 244; Banks 1993, I, p. 264; CAO III, pp. 5, 64; CAO IV, pp. 40, 42, 476; CS, pp. 424-425, 428-429; Filocamo 2004; IGC, p. 55.

2.
AVE MARIA, GRATIA PLENA
fols. 1*v*–2*r*

Laurentius Bergomotius Mutinensis

San - cta Ma - ri - a, ma - ter De - i, o - ra pro no -

- - bis pec - - - ca - to - ri - bus, nunc et in ho - ra

mor - . - tis. A - - - - men.

3.

AVE MARIA, GRATIA PLENA

fols. *2v–3r* (4 vv.)

IACOBUS FOGLIANUS MUTINENSIS

Ave Maria, gratia plena, Dominus tecum;
benedicta tu in mulieribus,
et benedictus fructus ventris, Iesus.
Sancta Maria, mater Dei,
5   ora pro nobis peccatoribus,
nunc et in hora mortis.
Amen.

For the text see no. 2.

COMMENTARY ON THE TEXT:

3   «tui» lacking after «ventris»
6   «nostre» lacking after «mortis»

READINGS EMENDED IN THE EDITION:

BAR	VOICE	ORIGINAL
incipit	T	flat also on the top line, perhaps intended to refer to the *e´* in bar 6
42	S, B	*longa* with fermata

MUSICAL CONCORDANCES (MSS): • ModD IV (44*v*–45*r*), modern hand: «Fogliani Jacobus»

MODERN EDITIONS OF THE MUSIC: BANKS 1993, II, pp. 17–18 (after Panc.27); JEPPESEN 1935, pp. 163–164 (after Panc.27).

REMARKS: The only other concordance for this piece is quite distant from the Panc.27 version; it is better to consider it a 'concordance with variants'. The incipit of the most widely used Gregorian melody of *Ave Maria* (for example LU, p. 1861) is quoted at the beginning of the Bassus and Superius.

BIBLIOGRAPHY: BANKS 1993, I, p. 264; CAO III, pp. 5, 64; CAO IV, pp. 40, 42, 476; CS, pp. 424–425, 428–429; FILOCAMO 2004; IGC, p. 55.

3.

AVE MARIA, GRATIA PLENA

fols. *2v-3r*

Iacobus Foglianus Mutinensis

Sanc - ta Ma - ri - a, ma - ter De - i, o - ra pro no - bis

pec - ca - to - - - ri - bus, nunc et in ho - ra mor - tis,

nunc et in ho - ra mor - tis. A - - - - men.

4.

Ave Maria, gratia plena

fols. 3*v*-4*r* (4 vv.)

Marcetus [Cara] / [Bartolomeo Tromboncino]

Ave Maria, gratia plena, Dominus tecum;
benedicta tu in mulieribus,
et benedictus fructus ventris tui, Iesus.
Sancta Maria, mater Dei,
5   ora pro nobis peccatoribus,
nunc et in hora mortis nostre.
Amen.

For the text see no. 2.

Readings emended in the edition:

Bar	Voice	Original
32	T, B	*longa* with fermata

Musical concordances (prints): • PeLaudeII (17*v*-18*r*), «M. C.» • PeLaudeII (47*v*-48*r*), «B. T.»

Modern editions of the music: Banks 1993, II, pp. 19-20 (after Panc.27); Jeppesen 1935, pp. 82-83 (after PeLaudeII, 47*v*-48*r*).

Remarks: Petrucci's two versions are not identical: some rests are placed differently, and some notes lack stems. The version of Panc.27 is closer to that of fols. 47*v*-48*r*, despite some graphic differences. Two significant variants separate the piece in Panc.27 from the other Petrucci version.

Bibliography: Banks 1993, I, p. 264; Boorman 2006, pp. 677, 890; CAO III, pp. 5, 64; CAO IV, pp. 40, 42, 476; CS, pp. 424-425, 428-429; Filocamo 2004; Freeman 1991, p. 202; Glixon 1990, pp. 36-38; IGC, p. 55.

4.

AVE MARIA, GRATIA PLENA

fols. 3v–4r

Marcetus [Cara] / [Bartolomeo Tromboncino]

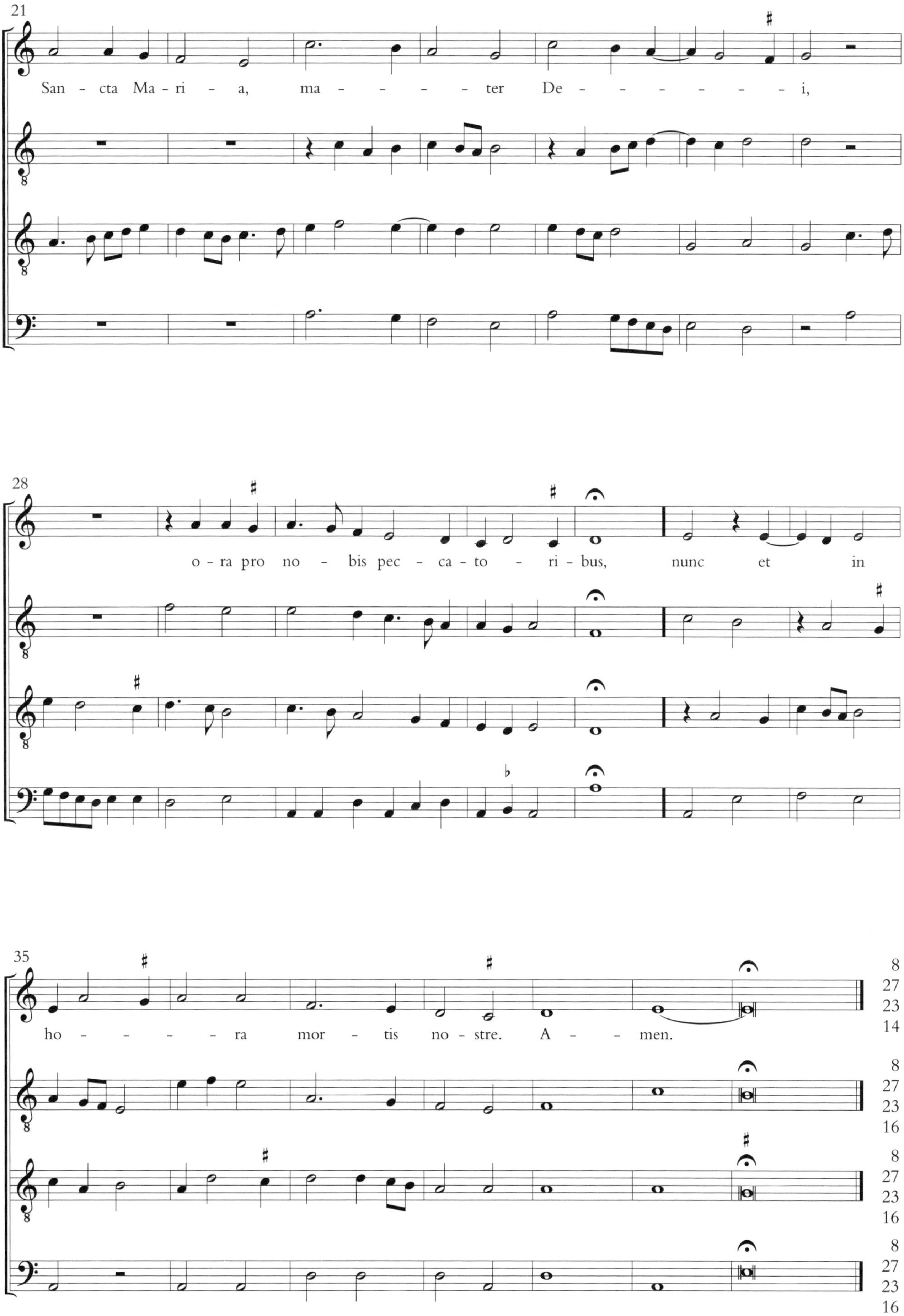
21
San - cta Ma - ri - a, ma - - - - ter De - - - - - - - i,
28
o - ra pro no - bis pec - ca - to - ri - bus, nunc et in
35
ho - - - - ra mor - tis no - stre. A - - men.
8
27
23
14
8
27
23
16
8
27
23
16
8
27
23
16

5.

Qui seminant in lacrimis

fols. 3*v*-4*r* (4 vv.)

Qui seminant in lacrimis,
in exultatione metent.

The beginning of the Tract for the Mass of the Common of two or more Martyrs, out of Paschal Time (GR, pp. [24]-[25]; LU, pp. 1164-1165; MR [*Commune Sanctorum*], fol. 7*r*). See also AMS, p. 244.

COMMENTARY ON THE TEXT:

2   MR has «gaudio» instead of 'exultatione'

READINGS EMENDED IN THE EDITION:

BAR	VOICE	ORIGINAL
11/II	A	*a g*

TEXT FROM MR [*Commune Sanctorum*], fol. 7*r* (*In communi plurimorum martyrum extra Tempus Paschale. Post septuagesimam. Tractus*):

Qui seminant in lachrymis,
in gaudio metent.

V. Euntes ibant, et flebant,
mittentes semina sua.

V. Venientes autem venient cum exultatione,
portantes manipulos suos.

MODERN EDITIONS OF THE TEXT: AMS, pp. 30, 41.

MODERN EDITIONS OF THE MUSIC: BANKS 1993, II, p. 159 (after Panc.27).

REMARKS: The piece is written in darker ink than the *Ave Maria* on the same opening. It seems clear that *Qui seminant in lacrimis* was added later to fill the empty space at the bottom of the opening.

BIBLIOGRAPHY: AMS, p. 244; BANKS 1993, I, pp. 286-287; FILOCAMO 2004; IGC, p. 349.

5.
QUI SEMINANT IN LACRIMIS
fols. 3*v*–4*r*

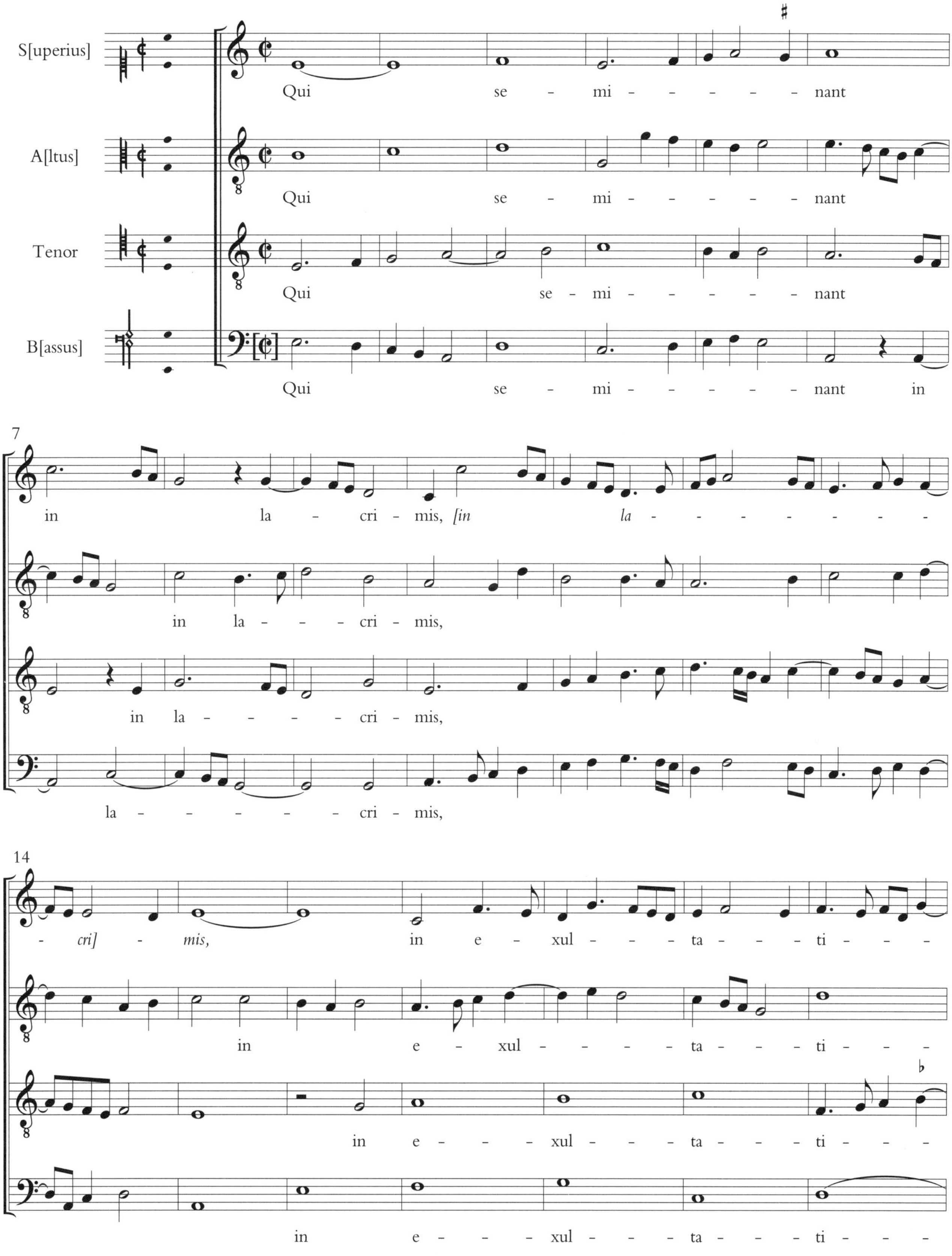

- o - ne ... me - tent.

- o - ne ... me - tent.

- o - ne ... me - tent.

- o - ne ... me - tent.

6.

Ave Maria, gratia plena

fols. 4*v*-5*r* (4 vv.)

      Ave Maria, gratia plena, Dominus tecum;
      benedicta tu in mulieribus,
      et benedictus fructus ventris tui, Iesus.
      Sancta Maria, mater Dei,
5   ora pro nobis peccatoribus,
      nunc et in hora mortis nostre.
      Amen.

For the text see no. 2.

MUSICAL CONCORDANCES (MSS): • Panc.27 (102*v*-103*r*)

MODERN EDITIONS OF THE MUSIC: BANKS 1993, II, pp. 21-22 (after Panc.27).

REMARKS: Bars 9-11 of the Superius are written at the end of the voice, preceded and followed by an insertion sign; that arrangement probably indicates the copying process from another source. The piece appears twice in Panc.27 (nos. 6 and 132), with small melodic and rhythmic variants.

BIBLIOGRAPHY: BANKS 1993, I, pp. 264-265; CAO III, pp. 5, 64; CAO IV, pp. 40, 42, 476; CS, pp. 424-425, 428-429; FREEMAN 1991, p. 202; IGC, p. 55.

6.
AVE MARIA, GRATIA PLENA
fols. 4v–5r

tu – – i, Ie – – sus. San – cta Ma – ri – a, ma – – – – ter

De – i, o – ra pro no – bis pec – ca – to – ri – – – – – – bus,

nunc et in ho – ra mor – tis no – stre. A – men.

7.

Vidimus enim stellam eius in Oriente

fols. 4*v*–5*r* (4 vv.)

Vidimus enim stellam eius in Oriente,
et venimus cum muneribus adorare eum.

Based on Matthew 2:2 («[Magi] dicentes | ubi est qui natus est rex Iudaeorum | vidimus enim stellam eius in oriente | et venimus adorare eum», Vulgata, p. 1528). It has been used, for example, as: antiphon to the Benedictus, fourth day within the Octave of Epiphany (AR, p. 332; AM, p. 299; BR, p. 243); responsory versicle for the second Nocturns of Epiphany (LR, pp. 76-77); Alleluia verse (GR, p. 52*r*; LU, p. 460; MR, p. 43), and Communion (GR, p. 52*v*; LU, p. 462; MR, p. 44) of the Mass for Epiphany. See also AMS, pp. 243, 251, CAO III, p. 537, and IGC, p. 440.

Commentary on the text:

1	MR lacks «enim»
2	MR gives «dominum» instead of 'eum'

Readings emended in the edition:

Bar	Voice	Original
17/II-18/I	T	*c′* instead of *b*

Modern editions of the text: AMS, p. 25; CAO III, p. 537.

Modern editions of the music: Banks 1993, II, pp. 202-203 (after Panc.27).

Remarks: The piece is written in darker ink than the *Ave Maria* on the same opening. It seems clear that *Vidimus enim stellam eius in Oriente* was added later to fill the empty space at the bottom of the opening.

Bibliography: AMS, pp. 243, 251; Banks 1993, I, p. 293; CAO III, p. 537; CS, p. 379; Filocamo 2004; IGC, p. 440.

7.
Vidimus enim stellam eius in Oriente
fols. 4*v*-5*r*

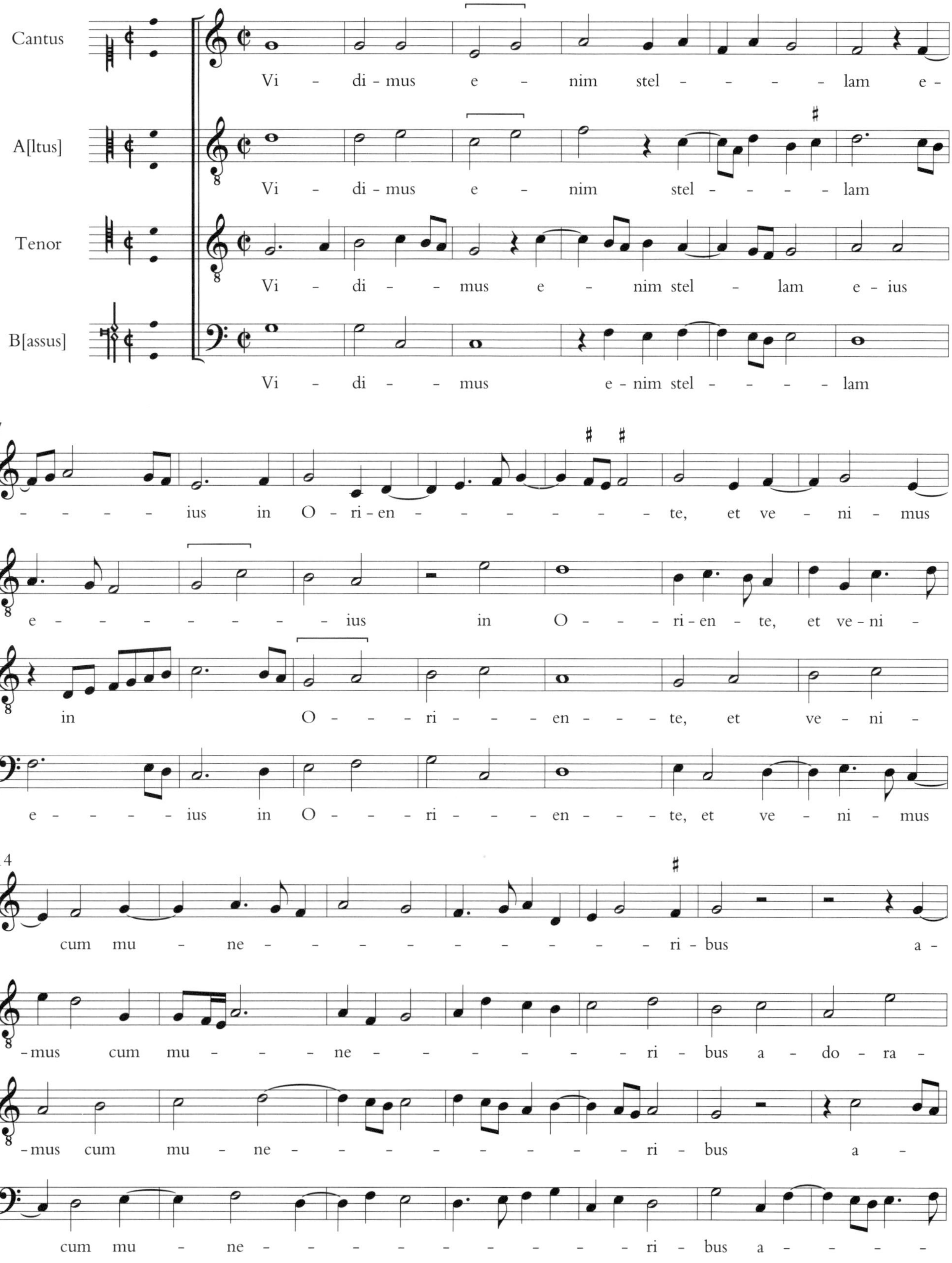

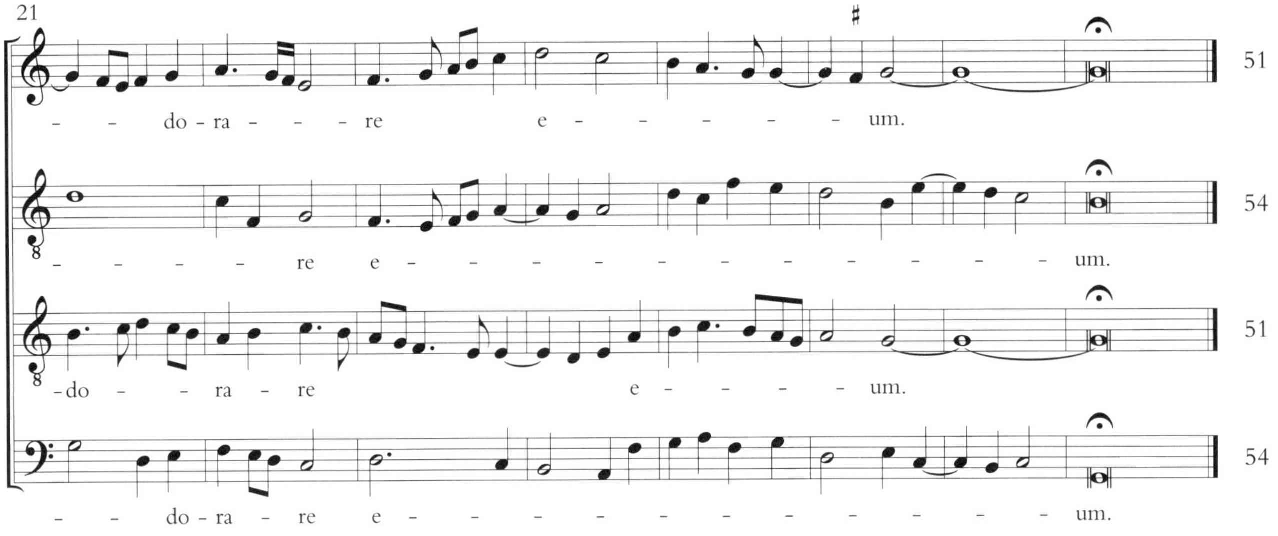
21
- - do - ra - - - re e - - - - - - um.
51
- - - - - re e - - - - - - - - - - - - um.
54
-do - - ra - re e - - - - um.
51
- - do - ra - re e - - - - - - - - - - - - um.
54

8.

Ave Maria, [gratia plena]

fols. 5v-7r (4 vv.)

MUSIPULA

Ave Maria

Sancta Maria

For the text see no. 2.

READINGS EMENDED IN THE EDITION:

BAR	VOICE	ORIGINAL
6/I	A	*a′* instead of *g′*
32/II	A	*minima* rest
58/II-59/I	A	*b c′ d′*
66/I	S	flat before *f″*
67/II	S	extra *d″* between *e″* and *c″*
74/II	B	superfluous *breve c* after *g*
75	B	*longa* with fermata

MODERN EDITIONS OF THE MUSIC: BANKS 1993, II, pp. 22-25 (after Panc.27); JEPPESEN 1935, pp. 165-167 (after Panc.27).

REMARKS: The types of errors suggest that the scribe copied from a source no longer extant.

BIBLIOGRAPHY: BANKS 1993, I, p. 265; CAO III, pp. 5, 64; CAO IV, pp. 40, 42, 476; CS, pp. 424-425, 428-429; FILOCAMO 2004; FREEMAN 1991, pp. 202 and 205; IGC, p. 55.

8.
AVE MARIA, [GRATIA PLENA]
fols. 5*v*–7*r*

Musipula

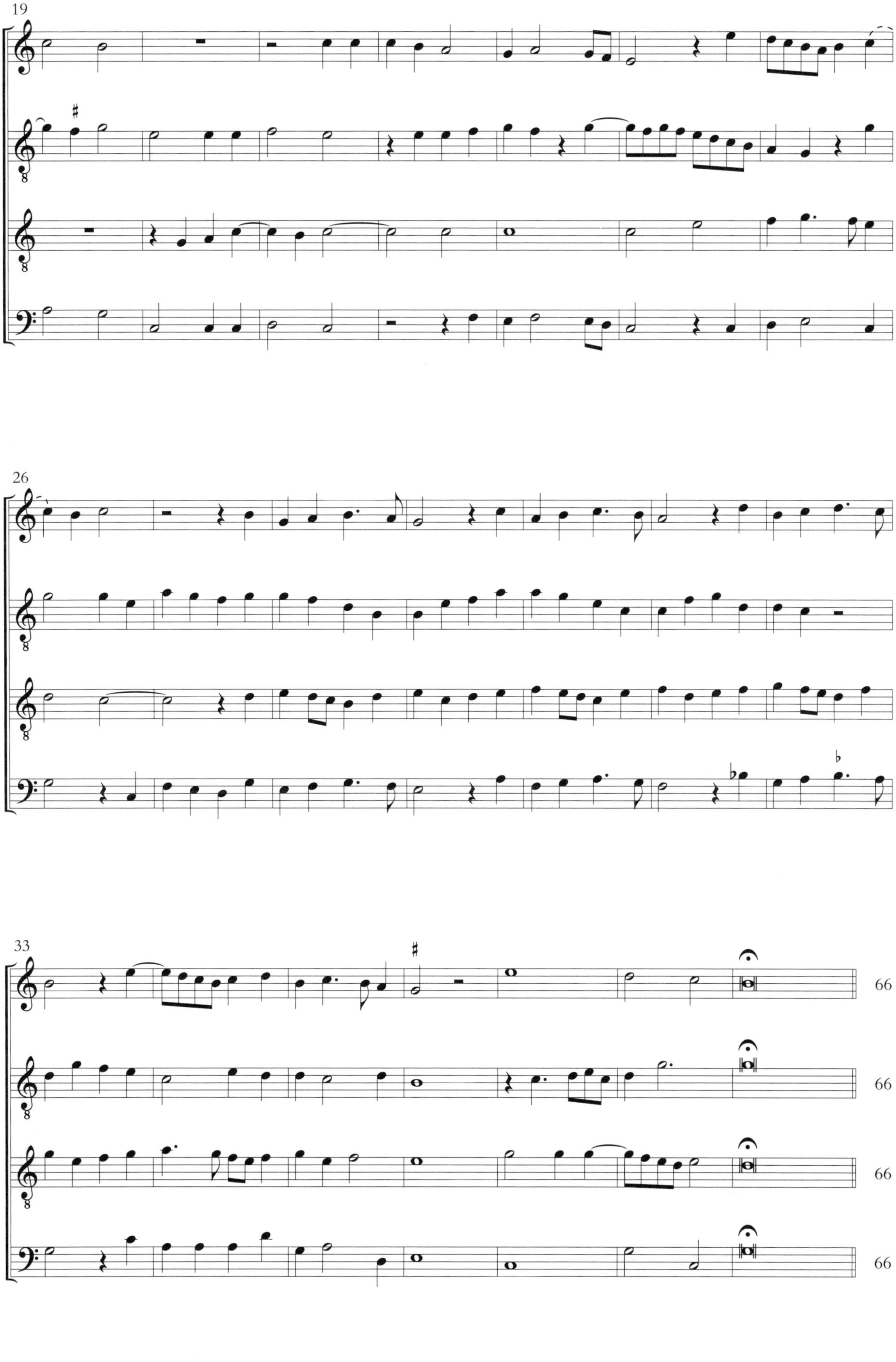
19
26
33
66
66
66
66

Secunda pars

San – cta   Ma – ri –   – a

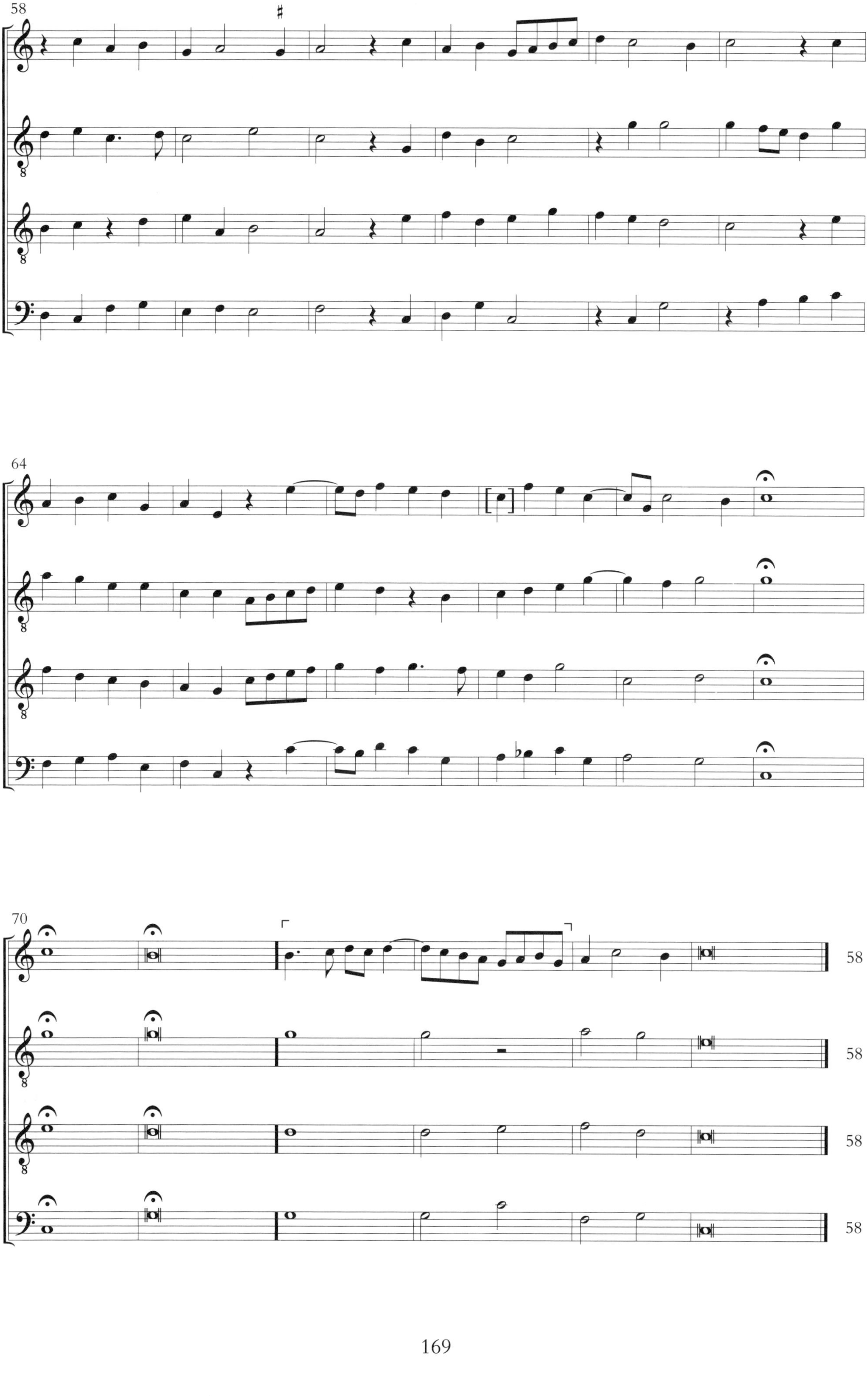
58
64
70
58
58
58
58

9.

AVE MARIA, GRATIA PLENA

fols. 7*v*-8*r* (4 vv.)

B[ARTOLOMEO] T[ROMBONCINO]

Ave Maria, gratia plena, Dominus tecum;
benedicta tu in mulieribus,
et benedictus fructus ventris tui, Iesus.
Sancta Maria, mater Dei,
5   ora pro nobis peccatoribus,
nunc et in hora mortis nostre.
Amen.

For the text see no. 2.

READINGS EMENDED IN THE EDITION:

BAR	VOICE	ORIGINAL
51-52	A	*longa* with fermata
51-53	S	*brevis* with fermata
53	A	*longa* with fermata
between 53 and 54	T	superfluous *c″ longa* with fermata

MUSICAL CONCORDANCES (MSS): • CTL G12 (88*v*-89*r*, *olim* 88*v*-89*r*) • ParisN Rés27 (52*r*) • ParisN Rés27 (55*v*)

MUSICAL CONCORDANCES (PRINTS): • PeLaudeII (39*v*-40*r*), «B. T.»

MODERN EDITIONS OF THE MUSIC: BANKS 1993, II, pp. 25-27 (after Panc.27); GREENBERG – MAYNARD 1975, pp. 137-139 (after PeLaudeII); JEPPESEN 1935, pp. 64-65 (after PeLaudeII).

REMARKS: At the end of each voice part the word «Iustus» appears for the first time. A comparison of the inks suggests that the inscription is probably contemporary with the copying of the piece. There are substantial musical variants from the version published by Petrucci. A number of graphic differences and two substantial variants distance the piece from CTL G12 as well, even though Cattin holds that the CTL G12 version is closer to Panc.27 than to that of PeLaudeII (CATTIN 1973a, p. 209).

BIBLIOGRAPHY: BANKS 1993, I, pp. 265-266; BOORMAN 2006, p. 892; CAO III, pp. 5, 64; CAO IV, pp. 40, 42, 476; CATTIN 1973a, p. 209; CS, pp. 424-425, 428-429; GREENBERG – MAYNARD 1975, pp. 135-136; IGC, p. 55.

9.
AVE MARIA, GRATIA PLENA
fols. 7v–8r

B[artolomeo] T[romboncino]

S[uperius]

A-ve Ma-ri-a,

A[ltus]

A-ve Ma-ri-a,

T[enor]

A-ve Ma-ri-a,

B[assus]

A-ve Ma-ri-a,

gra-ti-a ple-na, Do-mi-nus te-cum; be-ne-

gra-ti-a ple-na, Do-mi-nus te-cum; be-ne-

gra-ti-a ple-na, Do-mi-nus te-cum; be-ne-

gra-ti-a ple-na, Do-mi-nus te-cum

-di-cta tu in mu-li-e-ri-bus, et be-

-di-cta tu in mu-li-e-ri-bus, et be-

-di-cta tu in mu-li-e-ri-bus, et be-

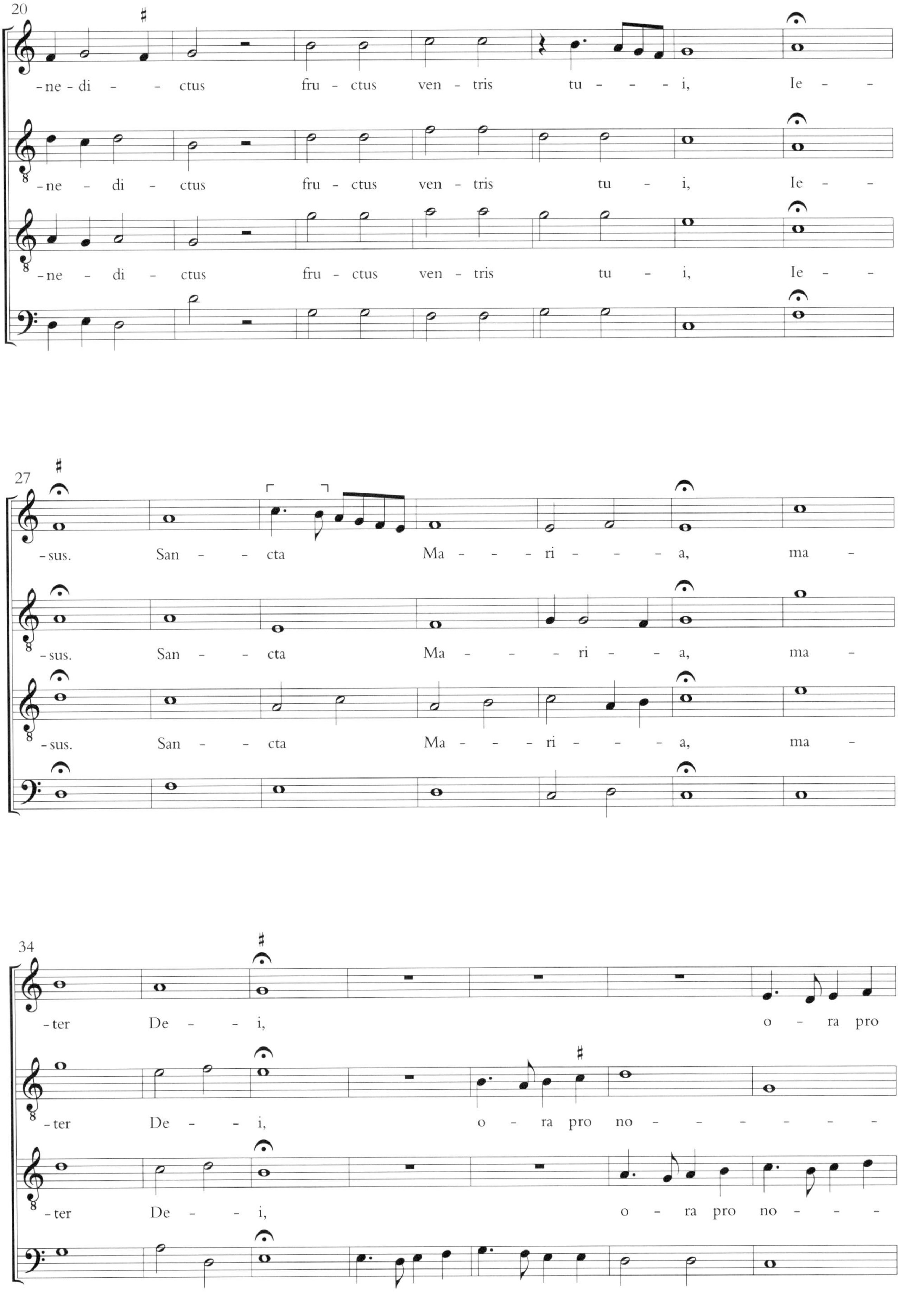
20
-ne - di - - ctus fru - ctus ven - tris tu - - - i, Ie - -
-ne - di - ctus fru - ctus ven - tris tu - i, Ie - -
-ne - di - ctus fru - ctus ven - tris tu - i, Ie - -
27
-sus. San - - cta Ma - - ri - - - a, ma -
-sus. San - - cta Ma - - - ri - - a, ma -
-sus. San - - cta Ma - - - ri - - - - a, ma -
34
-ter De - - i, o - ra pro
-ter De - - i, o - ra pro no - - - - - - -
-ter De - - i, o - ra pro no - - -

41
no - - - - bis pec - ca - to - ri - bus, nunc et in
- - - - - bis pec - ca - - - - to - ri - bus, nunc et in
- - - - - bis pec - ca - - - - to - ri - bus, nunc et in
47
ho - ra mor - - - - tis no - - - stre.
ho - ra mor - - - - tis no - stre.
ho - ra mor - - - - tis no - stre.
54
A - - - - - - - - - men.
Iustus
A - - - - - - - - - - - - - - men.
Iustus
A - - - - - - - - - - - - - - men.
Iustus
Iustus

10.

O ADMIRABILE COMERTIUM!

fols. 8*v*-9*r* (4 vv.)

O admirabile comertium!
Creator generis humani,
animatum corpus sumens,
de Virgine nasci dignatus est;
5   et procedens homo sine semine,
largitus est nobis suam deitatem.

Antiphon for the post-Christmas season used for the feast of the Circumcision (*Ad Laudes et per Horas*: AM, p. 271; AR, p. 294; BR, p. 220. *In II. Vesperis*: LU, pp. 442-443) and in various hours of the Office of the Blessed Virgin Mary after Christmas (BR [*Commune Sanctorum*], p. 81). See also CAO III, p. 362; IGC, p. 301.[1]

COMMENTARY ON THE TEXT:

1   comertium] commertium A, B

READINGS EMENDED IN THE EDITION:

BAR	VOICE	ORIGINAL
19/II	A	the flat before *e'* probably refers to the *e'* in the following bar
32/I	B	*c* instead of *B flat*

MODERN EDITIONS OF THE TEXT: CAO III, p. 362.

MODERN EDITIONS OF THE MUSIC: BANKS 1993, II, pp. 137-138 (after Panc.27).

REMARKS: The ink is darker, but for the first time it is used to write a composition that is not added in an empty portion of the page. Perhaps the piece was copied later; it interrupts, in fact, the alphabetical sequence dedicated to the letter 'A'.

BIBLIOGRAPHY: BANKS 1993, I, pp. 282-283; CAO III, p. 362; FILOCAMO 2004; IGC, p. 301.

---

[1]. Sherr shows that the antiphon was also used in the Saturday Office of the Virgin (SHERR 1997, p. 196). My thanks to Bonnie Blackburn for pointing this out.

10.
O ADMIRABILE COMERTIUM!

fols. *8v–9r*

Cantus: O ad-mi-ra-bi-le co-mer-ti-um! Cre-a-tor ge-ne-ris hu-ma-ni, a-ni-ma-tum cor-pus su-mens, de Vir-gi-ne na-sci di-gna-tus est;

A[ltus]: O ad-mi-ra-bi-le co-mer-ti-um! Cre-a-tor ge-ne-ris hu-ma-ni, a-ni-ma-tum cor-pus su-mens, de Vir-gi-ne na-sci di-gna-tus est;

Tenor: O ad-mi-ra-bi-le co-mer-ti-um! Cre-a-tor ge-ne-ris hu-ma-ni, a-ni-ma-tum cor-pus su-mens, de Vir-gi-ne na-sci di-gna-tus est;

Bassus: O ad-mi-ra-bi-le co-mer-ti-um! Cre-a-tor ge-ne-ris hu-ma-ni, a-ni-ma-tum cor-pus su-mens, de Vir-gi-ne na-sci di-gna-tus est;

et pro-ce-dens ho-mo si – ne se-mi-ne,

et pro-ce-dens ho-mo si – ne se-mi-ne,

et pro-ce-

et pro-ce-

lar-gi-tus est no-bis su-am de-i-ta – tem.

lar-gi-tus est no-bis su-am de-i-ta-tem.

-dens ho-mo si – ne se – mi – ne, lar-gi-tus est no-bis su-am de-i-ta – tem.

-dens ho-mo si – ne se-mi-ne, lar-gi-tus est no-bis su-am de-i-ta – tem.

176

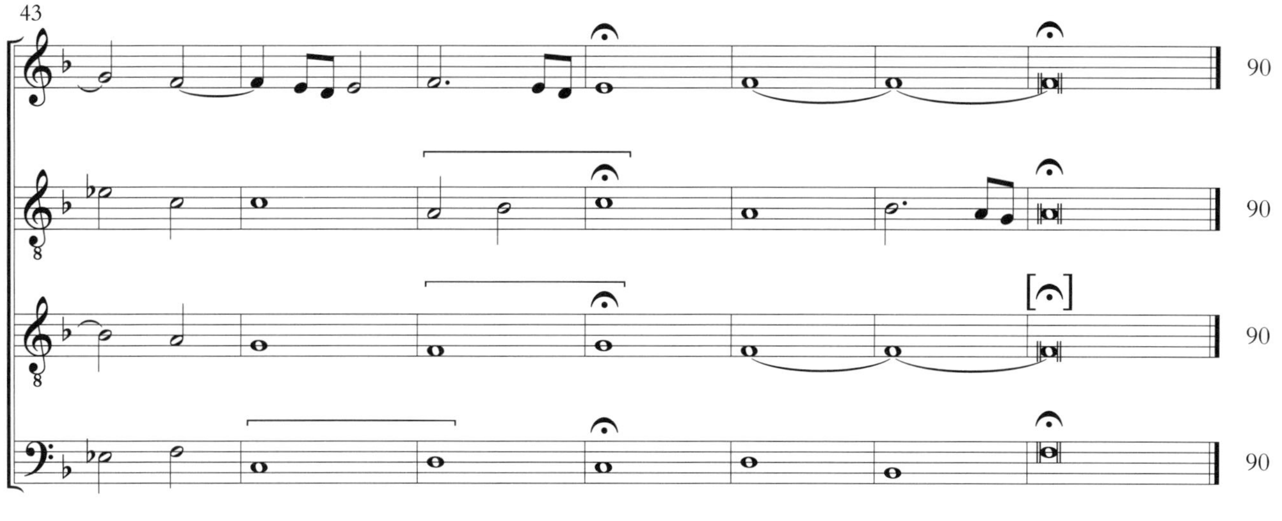
43
90
90
90
90

11.

A LA BATAGLIA

fols. 9v-12r (4 vv.)

[Gentile Aretino (Becchi?)[1]]   [Henricus] Isaac

A la bataglia

Italian secular piece (canto carnascialesco). Although *A la bataglia* had been considered in the past to be an instrumental piece by some scholars (WOLF 1908, pp. 221-224; TORREFRANCA 1939, pp. 51-52; OSTHOFF 1969, p. 89), in reality — on the basis of McGee's reconstruction — the music fits the poetic text expressly created for a precise event: the public investiture of Niccolò Orsini, count of Pitigliano, as Captain General of the Florentine army on 17 July 1485 (MCGEE 1983b, p. 5).[2] Recently, however, the reconstruction of the occasion that gave birth to the composition has been enriched with a new angle: F. William Kent published a passage from a letter of 29 December 1487, sent (from Florence) by a certain Ambrogio Angeni to Antonio di Alessandro da Filicaia (merchant in Nantes), in which it is said that Isaac is preparing a composition that demonstrates «gran fantaxia» for carnival of 1488, and in a third letter of 5 February 1488 Angeni says that Isaac has composed *La Guera di Serezana*, which he promises to send but instead does not. These discoveries therefore permit a secure dating after the end of 1487: in this way Isaac would easily have had the time to make himself at home in Florence, and the piece therefore was composed as a commemoration of the battle, not for the investiture of Niccolò Orsini. From a letter of April 1488 we even know that the piece did not please: a failure perhaps due to the performance or, more likely, its compositional style, which is unlike that of other carnival songs (see KENT 2004 and WILSON 2006).[3]

---

[1]. This Gentile Aretino is perhaps identifiable with Gentile Becchi, Bishop of Arezzo (1473-97) and teacher of Lorenzo il Magnifico (see NOVATI 1907, p. 322, n. 2). Although probable, there is no definite proof of this (see MCGEE 1983a, p. 289).

[2]. Both contributions by McGee (MCGEE 1983a and MCGEE 1983b) reconstruct the historical events concerning the quarrel between Florence and Genoa. By means of the identification of some names contained in the text Timothy McGee was able to pinpoint the precise occasion that saw the two cities striving for the control of a useful outlet on the western sea coast, but direct conflict was postponed on many occasions. The definitive solution to the dispute was to be the battle of Sarzanello — a castle in the Val di Magra near the city of Sarzana — on 22 June 1487 (BECHERINI 1953, p. 5 gives the erroneous date of 15 April 1487). The Florentines won, but seven years later the fortress surrendered to King Charles VIII of France. Niccolò Orsini was named commander of the Florentine army on 24 June 1485 at 6.30 a.m., but his public investiture, with related celebrations throughout the city, was planned for 17 July. In a short time, therefore, it was necessary to organize the solemn ceremony, which foresaw a sumptuous display and the contribution of the city musicians. The chronicle of the Florentine herald Francesco Filarete describes in detail what happened during the festivities (FRANCESCO FILARETE, *Ceremonie notate in tempi*, Florence, Archivio di Stato, Carte di correde, 61), and from other similar reports it is clear that after the speeches on the part of the city officials it was customary to declaim a poem created on purpose for the occasion (MCGEE 1983b, p. 7). For McGee, the poem *A la bataglia* was probably the poem destined for Orsini's investiture ceremony, and the music of Isaac — present in Florence for only a few months (D'ACCONE 1963, pp. 465-466, indicates that the musician arrived there during the late autumn of 1484 at the instigation of Lorenzo il Magnifico himself) — would therefore have been written in a very short time after the poem for which it was intended, which was surely commissioned after the June nomination (Jessie Owens too notes that quickness in composition was characteristic of the Flemish composer: OWENS 1997, pp. 272-274). According to this reconstruction it would be the oldest composition attributed to Isaac known so far. McGee hypothesizes that it was performed by the city musicians themselves, who, considering that the city registers of the time do not include salaried singers, would have given proof of their vocal abilities on the occasion. The proof of such performance would be the fragmentary presence of the text in MS FirN BR337, which leads to the hypothesis of an 'alternate' instrumental and vocal performance (MCGEE 1983a, p. 297).

[3]. I thank Adam Gilbert (who in turn informed me of the articles by Kent) and Blake Wilson: both kindly sent me the two precious articles, which bring up to date the state of our knowledge of the piece.

READINGS EMENDED IN THE EDITION:

BAR	VOICE	ORIGINAL
13/I	A	superfluous *c′ semibrevis*
55/I	T	*c′ minima*
110	A, B	*longa* with fermata
between 141 and 142	T	superfluous *semibrevis* rest
142/II	T	*minima*
148	A, B	*longa* with fermata

TEXTUAL CONCORDANCES (PRINTS): • *Contrasto* (2*v*), «Gentile Aretino», «Barzellecta morale che tracta delli adornamenti di bactaglie»

MUSICAL CONCORDANCES (MSS): • FirN BR337 (78*v*-80*r*), B only • LeipU 1494 (251*v*-252*r*), *O praeclarissima atque graciosa*[4] • SGS 530 (124*v*-126*r*), *O dulcedo virginalis* • UlmS 237 (S: 8*v*-9*r*, A: 7*v*-8*r*, T: 4*v*-5*v*; B: 5*v*-7*r*), textless • WarU 5892 (85*v*-86*r*), *Ave sanctissima civitas* (= *Prima pars - Secunda pars*); (86*v*-87*r*), *O virgo felix nondum edita* (= *Tertia pars*)

TEXT FROM FirN BR337:

     Alla battaglia, presto, alla battaglia
     armisi ognuno di suo corazza e maglia.

     Per parte dell'excelso capitano
     ognun sia presto armato e sia in camino.
5   Su, valenti signor, di mano in mano,
     signor Iulio e Organtino,
     o signor Paulo Orsino,
     schinier, falde e coraza, fiancaletto.
     Su, lancia in stocco e mazza,
10   afibbia questo braccialetto.
     Te' 'l caval, baio e 'l morelletto.
     Su, messer Hercole, Criaco e Cerbone,
     conte Rinuccio e 'l signor Honorato,
     sir di Piombino, Annibale e Guidone,
15   Giovan Savel, Malaspina e Currado!
     Ognun sia presto armato
     e a caval montato!
     Su, spade e sproni e alabarde.
     Alleardo, seguitiam lo stendardo!
20   Bolognesi et Galleschi,
     a lor che son prigioni et rotti,
     su, uom valenti e franchi stradiotti,
     su, buon soldati e docti,
     leviam di qui questa brutta canaglia.

TEXT FROM *Contrasto*:

     Alla battaglia, presto, alla battaglia
     armisi ognun di sua coraza et maglia.

     Per parte del excelso capitano
     ch'ognun sia presto armato et sia in camino.
5   Su, valenti signor, di mano in mano

---

[4]. See the complete text in HERCZOG 2005, p. 99.

Sarazenel si spaza.
Schinieri, falde et coraza,
arnesi, elmo et fiancalecto.
Su lance, stocchi et maza,
10   affibbia questo braccialecto.
To' il baio e 'l morellecto.
Su, messer Hercole, Criaco et Cerbone,
conte Rinuccio, signor Ornolfo,
sir di Piombino, Aniballe et Guidone,
15   Giovan Savel, Malespin e Curato!
Ognun sia presto armato
et a caval montato!
Su spade, sproni
le barde al leardo!
20   Vie' su, poltroni,
chi fia il più gagliardo?
Seguitiam lo stendardo.
Vie' su franchi Sforzeschi,
Bolognesi et Galleschi!
25   Su, buon valenti et franchi stradiocti!
Su, buon soldati et docti,
leviam di lì quella bructa canaglia!

Orsù buon conestabil, presto, avanti
col capitan marchese Gabriello,
30   siate in ordine et in punto tucti quanti.
Leviam color d'intorno a Serezanello
chi sono e Genovesi.
E non paiono rappresi
la gente maladecta.
35   Gli han trovati gli arnesi:
cavianglieli con l'accecta,
aspecta, aspecta, aspecta
o Scaramuccia. Su, Zacchagnin Corso,
Riccio Vecchiecti! Su, Borgo Rinaldi,
40   o Pierandrea et Francesco Arogorso,
Ferrando, Alfonso, e non è da star saldi.
Affrontiam que' ribaldi
or che siam freschi e caldi!
To' la celata,
45   ad me il gorzerino,
la mazza ferrata.
Vien via, Alexandrino,
la testiera al ronzino.
Su, Chriaco Borghese!
50   Su, Giovanni Albanese!
Lance, balestra, targoni e targecte,
partigiane, ronche, verrettoni e saecte.
Su, tamburi e trombecte!
Vie le vie lor, che son uomin di paglia!

55   All'arme, all'arme, orsù gente gagliarda!
Alfonso al ponte, alle mura, alle porte!
State parati. Ognun da lor si guarda,
benché sien presso loro scelte scorte.

```
        Vie' su, gagliardi et fieri,
60      innanzi e balestrieri,
        targoni, scudi et rotelle.
        Su lance, et scoppiectieri
        alle cinghie, alle selle!
        Sforacchiam lor la pelle.
65      Su archibusi, scoppiecti et spingarde.
        Lion tedesco, uso all'artiglierie
        far far 'tuffe taff', bronzine et bombarde
        a far buon colpi et non d'armeggerie.
        Sbarrate son le vie!
70      Assalta Corsecto,
        vie' su Zacchagnino,
        carca Schiavetto,
        diserra Alfonsino,
        tu non vali un quattrino.
75      Scampa, uccidi a morte,
        renditi ad me, sta forte!
        'San Giorgio!', 'Marzocco! Marzocco!',
        suona, percuoti, forbocta rintocco.
        'Palle palle!', 'Marzocco! Marzocco!',
        legagli strecti et pon lor buona taglia.
```

MODERN EDITIONS OF THE TEXT: BECHERINI 1953, p. 10 (after FirN BR337); HERCZOG 2005, pp. 93-94 (after FirN BR337); McGEE 1983a, pp. 299-302 (after *Contrasto* and FirN BR337); NOVATI 1907 (after *Contrasto*).

MODERN EDITIONS OF THE MUSIC: BECHERINI 1953, pp. 11-21 (after FirN BR337 and Panc.27); DTÖ 32, pp. 221-224 (after Panc.27); EDM 34, pp. 379-382 (after LeipU 1494); GREENBERG - MAYNARD 1975, pp. 286-298 (after Panc.27); KLÖCKNER 2004 (after UlmS 237); McGEE 1983a, pp. 299-302 (after FirN BR337); SM 8, pp. 292-295 (after SGS 530); THOMAS 1985.

REMARKS: There is no reason for the division into three parts. Although only the Bassus survives, the version of FirN BR337 (*Alla battaglia presto alla battaglia*) is quite close to Panc.27, though 25 lines of the text are provided (the printed version of the *Contrasto* has 80 lines, which do not exactly match those of FirN BR337 at the beginning). UlmS 237 is also close to Panc.27, but it is a late and peripheral source in partbooks and direct contact with Panc.27 is unlikely. The version in LeipU 1494 is more distant. It is interesting that there are so many contrafact texts for the piece, which has recently been identified as a work devised for the Florentine carnival of 1488 (KENT 2004 and WILSON 2006).

BIBLIOGRAPHY: BECHERINI 1953; CATTIN 1973a, p. 215; D'ACCONE 1963; FILOCAMO 2004; GHISI 1939a, p. 4; GREENBERG - MAYNARD 1975, pp. 284-285; HERCZOG 2005, pp. 85-105; KÄMPER 1976, p. 187; KENT 2004; McGEE 1983a; McGEE 1983b; OSTHOFF 1969, I, pp. 73-109; PICKER 1991, p. 106; SM 8, p. 361; TORREFRANCA 1939, pp. 51-52; TOSCANI 1993, p. 134; WILSON 2006.

11.
A LA BATAGLIA

fols. 9*v*–12*r*

[Gentile Aretino (Becchi?)]

[Henricus] Isaac

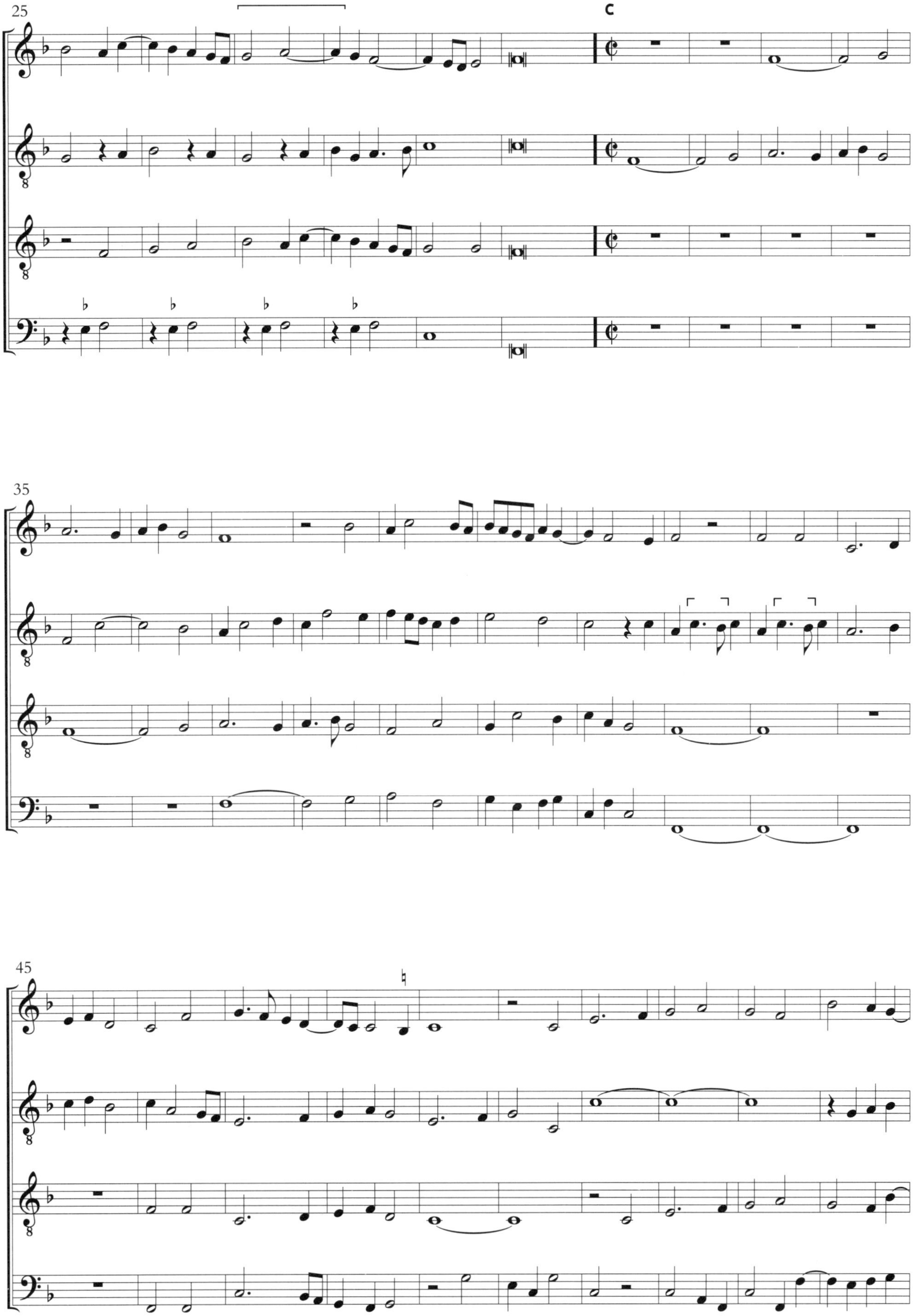
25
C
35
45

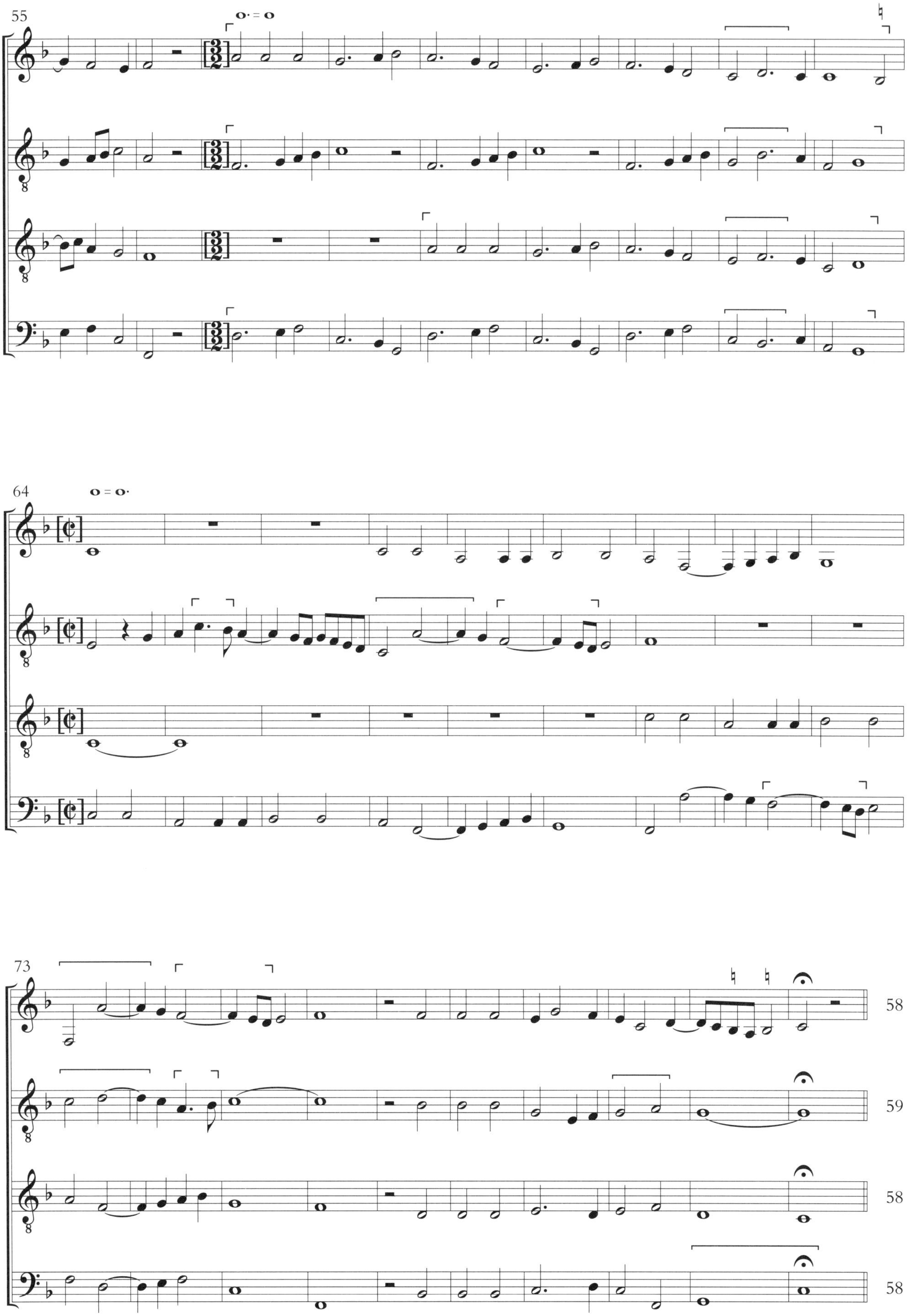
55
64
73
58
59
58
58

Secunda pars

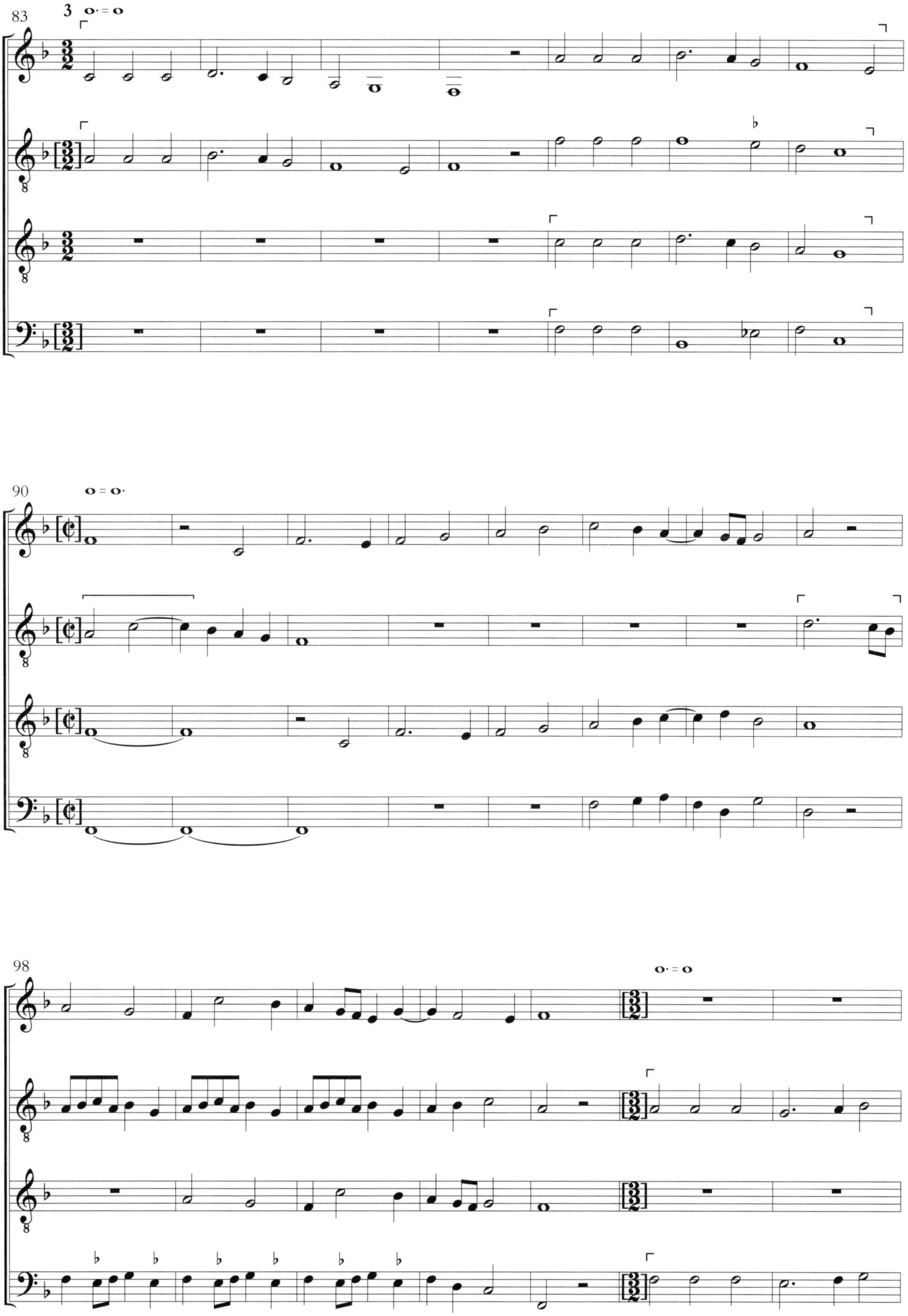

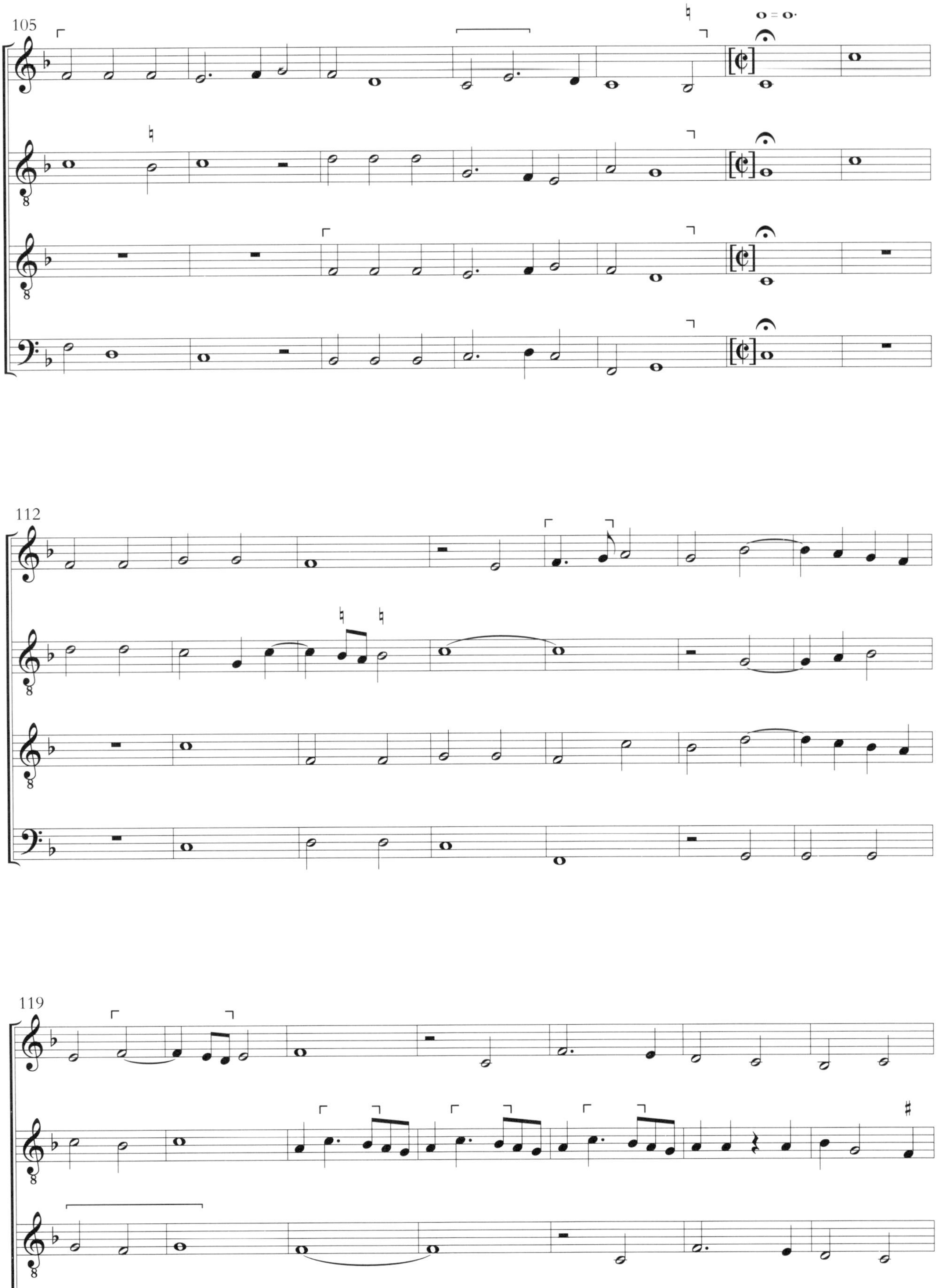
105
112
119

Vidi
Vidi
Vidi
Vidi

Tertia pars

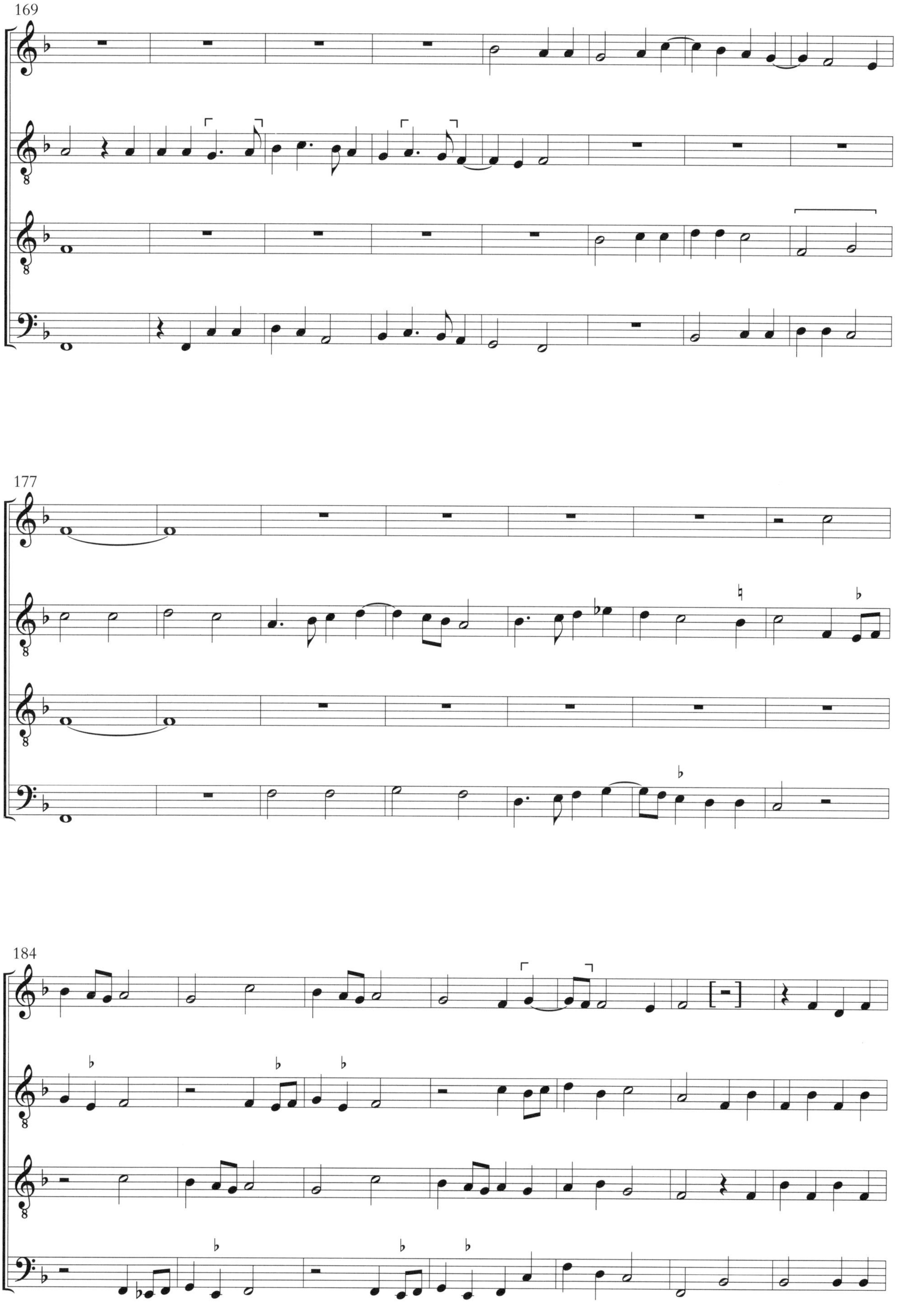
169
177
184

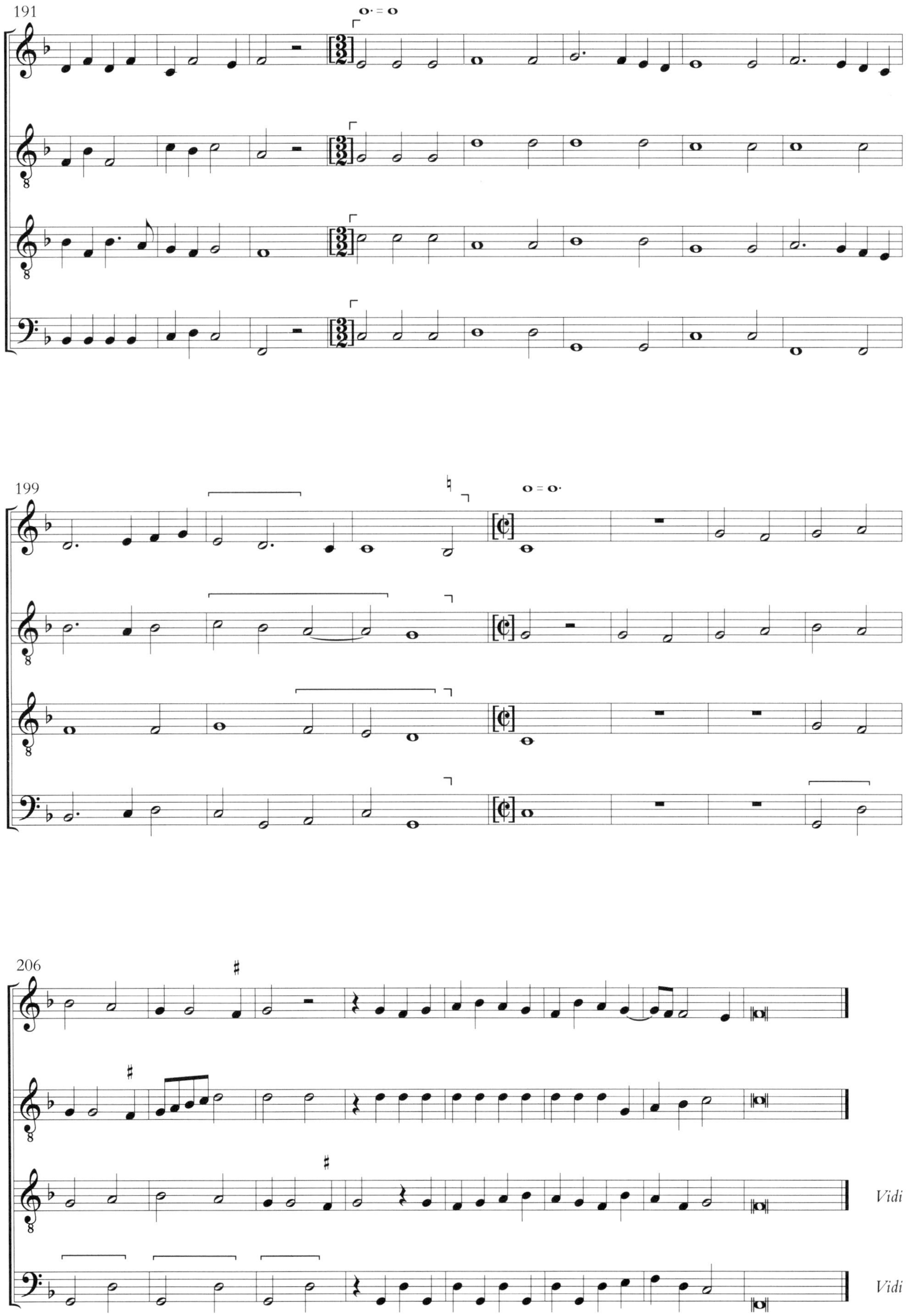
191
199
206
Vidi
Vidi

12.

AIMÈ EL COR, AIMÈ LA TESTA

fols. 12*v*-13*r* (4 vv.)

[MARCHETTO CARA]

Aimè el cor, aimè la testa

Italian secular piece (barzelletta).

READINGS EMENDED IN THE EDITION:

BAR	VOICE	ORIGINAL
5/I and 8/I	T	despite the *g♯′* in PeBossI1509 and its reprint, it is preferable to reserve the accidental for the following cadential *g′*
between 9 and 10	S, A, T, B	line
16-22	S, A, T, B	the repetition should probably be reserved for after the final repeat of the stanza of the frottola-barzelletta
17/I	T	despite the *g♯′* in PeBossI1509 and its reprint, it is preferable to reserve the accidental for the following cadential *g′*

TEXTUAL CONCORDANCES (MSS): • *Mod.E. 81* (70*v*-71*v*), *Oyme el cor oyme la testa*

MUSICAL CONCORDANCES (MSS): • FirC B2441 (7*v*-8*r*), *Oyme il cuor oyme la testa* • ParisN Rés27 (46*r*), *Oime lo capo oime la testa* • ParisN Rés676 (11*v*-12*r*), *Oime il core oime la testa*, «Marcheto»; index: «Cara»

MUSICAL CONCORDANCES (PRINTS): • PeBossI1509 (32*r*), *Oime il cor oime la testa*, «M. C.» • PeBossI1515 (32*r*), *Oime il cor oime la testa*, «M. C.» • PeFroI (2*v*-3*r*), *Oime el cor oime la testa*, «Marcvs Cara Vero.»

TEXT FROM ParisN Rés676:[1]

> Oimè il core, oimè la testa
> chi non ama non m'intenda,
> chi non fala non si emenda:
> dopo il falo el pentire resta.
> Oimè il core […]

5 | Oimè, Dio, ch'errore fece io
> ad amar un cor falace.
> Oimè, Dio, ch'el pentire mio
> non mi dà per questo pace.
> Oimè, il foco aspro e vivace
10 | mi consuma il tristo cor.
> Oimè, Dio, ch'el facto errore
> l'alma afflicta mi molesta.
> Oimè il core […]

---

[1]. PeBossI1509 (and its reprint) and PeFroI have the same amount of text as ParisN Rés676; in FirC B2441 the fourth stanza is lacking; in *Mod.E. 81* l. 36 is missing.

Oimè, che ben m'acorgea
da un cor falso esser tradito.
15 Oimè, ch'alora nol sapea
al mio error pigliar partito.
Oimè, il mio cieco appetito
m'ha conduto a questa sorte.
Oimè, io crido il mio mal forte,
20 ognor cresce e più m'infesta.
    Oimè il core […]

Doi dolzi ochi, un parlar dopio,
una troppo gran beltade,
fam che di dolore scopio
per la persa libertade.
25 Se per questa l'alma pate
ne fu causa il dolor cieco,
sì che ad effecto tal mi reco,
che 'l morire mi for festa.
    Oimè il core […]

Patientia, o core mio stolto!
30 Gode el mal si tu el cercasti,
se alora, quando fosti accolto,
ad Amore non reparasti.
Ti conven che pena atasti[2]
del previsto tuo falir,
35 che non giova il tuo pentire,
né cridare cum voce maesta.
    Oimè il core […]

MODERN EDITIONS OF THE TEXT: BORGHI 1995, pp. 154-156 (after FirC B2441); CESARI *ET AL.* 1954, p. 3★
(after PeFroI); DISERTORI 1964, p. 385 (after PeBossI1509); SCHWARTZ 1935, p. xxvii (after PeFroI).

MODERN EDITIONS OF THE MUSIC: BORGHI 1995, pp. 311-312 (after FirC B2441); CESARI *ET AL.* 1954,
p. 3 (after PeFroI); DISERTORI 1964, pp. 384-385 (after PeBossI1509); PIRROTTA 1984, pp. 183-184
(after PeBossI1509); REESE 1990, p. 172 (after PeFroI), 172-173 (after PeBossI1509); SCHWARTZ
1935, p. 1 (after PeFroI).

REMARKS: The versions of FirC B2441 and Paris N. Rés676 are distant from Panc.27, in addition to
including more text. The version of PeBossI1509 (and its reprint) is relatively close to Panc.27,
despite the missing Altus, and it too has more text. PeFroI is possibly the model for Panc.27: it has
much more text, and the music has graphic variants and a few passages that are slightly different.

BIBLIOGRAPHY: BOORMAN 2006, pp. 1001-1002; CATTIN 1986, p. 282, n. 13; DAHLHAUS (1968) 1988, pp.
249-257; LOWINSKY 1962, pp. 8-9; LUISI 1995, pp. 392-393, 397, 399; PRIZER 1980, pp. 117-118;
PRIZER 1991, p. 9; PRIZER 1996b, p. 38; SLIM 1988, p. 36, n. 17; TIBALDI 2005, pp. 542, 544.

---

2. The verb may derive from 'attastare', that is 'to feel' (see BATTAGLIA I, p. 807).

12.

AIMÈ EL COR, AIMÈ LA TESTA

fols. 12v–13r

[Marchetto Cara]

Ai-mè el cor, ai-mè la te - sta

13.

AVE REGINA, VIRGO GLORIOSA /
SOFRIRE SON DISPOSTO [OGNI TORMENTO]

fol. 13*v* (4 vv.)

[ENSELMINO DA MONTEBELLUNA][1]

Sofrire son disposto[2]

Ave Regina, Virgo gloriosa
che de Dio Padre te chiamasti ancilla,
del Figliol fosti madre, figlia e sposa.

Lauda (capitolo ternario). Contrafact on the music of the strambotto *Soffrire son disposto ogni tormento*.

---

[1]. In the poetic sources known, the text is often anonymous or carries different attributions: among the presumed names in succession have been Dante Alighieri (see GRAF 1884, p. 406), Francesco Petrarca (see BINI 1852, pp. ix-x; BEVILACQUA 1994, p. 159), Antonio del Beccaio *alias* Antonio da Ferrara (see BINI 1852, p. 157; BEVILACQUA 1994, p. 159), Biagio Saraceni (see MORSOLIN 1890, pp. 941-945, more likely the name of the copyist: SERENA 1891, p. 13; but in a letter of 3 October 2006 the dr. Maria Luigia De Gregorio, of the Archivio di Stato in Vicenza, notified me that Biagio di Giacomo Saraceno drew up the inventory of the movable goods of the Ospedale di San Marcello in Venice), Leonardo Giustinian (see BINI 1852, pp. vi-ix), Antonio Cornazano (ever since the *editio princeps*, by evident confusion with his *Vita di Nostra Donna*: ROGERS 1993, p. 7), Antonio Tebaldeo (see CREMA 2002, p. 616, n. 24), and Marco Bandarini (who instead paraphrased the text with occasional original additions: ZAMBRINI 1878, col. 719). The general tendency has been to consider the work of Tuscan origin, overlooking the linguistic factors pointing to the Veneto, or as a simple Italian version of the *Tractatus de planctu Beatae Virginis Mariae* attributed to St. Bernard (see GOFF (1964) 1973, p. 228): references to St. Bernard in MS *Bol. U. 12* and in MS *Ven.M. I.75*. Enselmino's paternity — today commonly accepted but discussed at length at the end of the nineteenth century, until the definitive clarification by Augusto Serena (SERENA 1893) — had nevertheless already been contemplated by Apostolo Zeno (ZENO 1752, I, p. 97, letter of 5 July 1704 to Antonfrancesco Marmi) and published by Girolamo Tiraboschi in the second edition of his *Storia della letteratura italiana* (TIRABOSCHI 1787-94, V, p. 595), on the basis of the explicit statement of a certain number of manuscripts and incunables (MORSOLIN 1891, pp. 543-544); however, the true paternity was not accepted in the first modern edition of the poem, where it was presented as anonymous (BINI 1852, pp. 3-21). Nevertheless, if one were to take a pedantically literal view of the various sources, Enselmino might instead appear as a mere 'compiler' of the *Pianto* (MORSOLIN 1891, pp. 544-545), of which he would have composed only the last capitolo giving thanks (*Gratiarum actio*) and, as a logical consequence, the initial one of the invocation to the Virgin (*Prohemio*), which begins *Ave regina virgo gloriosa*: this would appear to be confirmed by the incunable *Pianto 1481L*, which ends capitolo X with the words «Explicit Virginis beate lamentatio et intacte vulgariter compillata cum ritmis prolata ore fratris Enselmini de Trivisio ordinis fratrum heremitarum sancti Augustini» and then prefaces the last capitolo with the rubric «Incipit oratio sive gratiarum actio supradicti compillatoris». In favour of such a hypothesis would also be the circumstance that the first and last capitolo (XI) of the *Pianto* themselves have often been treated in the textual tradition as self-standing compositions: either because many witnesses omit the eleventh capitolo, but even more because the two compositions often have their own life, recopied in certain manuscripts in isolation and printed as independent laude in some anthologies (see ZENO 1752, I, pp. 96-97, BINI 1852, pp. v and 157; BIADENE 1887, p. 201; MORSOLIN 1891, p. 546; CREMA 2002, pp. 615-616 and n. 2). And in some of these cases of individual transmission, sometimes the first capitolo coincides only for about the first 20 lines. In particular, in the second half of the fifteenth century the two texts formed an integral part of the anthology *Corona de la beatissima Vergene Maria* compiled by Bernardino de' Busti. The first and the last capitolo are also the two unique sections of the *Pianto* which received a musical setting: the initial tercet is set in Panc.27; the first six tercets of the last capitolo, interspersed with a refrain composed of a concluding distich («Star con quella quam terra, pontus, ethera | colunt, adorant, predicant eternam»), were set to music by Filippo da Lurano (*Ne le tue braze o Vergene Maria* in PeLaudeII, fols. 51*v*-52*r*); see the modern edition in JEPPESEN 1935, p. 92 and LUISI 1983, II, pp. 79-80).

[2]. On the problem of the poetic and musical paternity of the strambotto *Soffrire son disposto ogni tormento* see LA FACE BIANCONI - ROSSI 1990.

This is the first tercet of the *Pianto della Vergine*, a sacred poem of 11 capitoli[3] in terza rima (but with a rhyming distich to end each capitolo), traditionally attributed to Enselmino (or Anselmo, or Guglielmo) da Montebelluna (or da Treviso), an Augustinian friar in the Convento of Santa Margherita at Treviso. The poem, known under various Latin and Italian titles (*Lamentum Virginis, Lamentatio beatae Virginis, Virginis sanctae lamentatio, Pianto devotissimo, Pietoso lamento, El pianto de la Verzene, Ploratus Virginis, Uno lamento di nostra donna*, etc.; see ANDREOSE 2001, p. 8 and n. 4), belongs to the rich medieval tradition of the *Planctus Mariae* (STICCA 1984; CREMA 2002, p. 613, n. 14) and enjoyed a particular success for over a century from its composition, and in a vast geographic area, among confraternities of various kinds (CREMA 2002, p. 616, n. 25), as proven by the great quantity of manuscripts and early printed sources that transmit it. On hypotheses concerning the dating of the *Pianto*, ascribable to the second quarter of the fourteenth century, see CREMA 2002, pp. 612-613, partially correcting that proposed by LINDER 1898 (and still confirmed in LONGO 1986, p. 206, n. 79: ca. 1325, more precisely between 1322 and 1327), indicating 1362 as *terminus ante quem* (by which time Enselmino was dead).[4] Without indicating the precise reasons, Alvise Andreose inclines towards the fifth decade of the Trecento (see ANDREOSE 2001, p. 7, n. 1).

READINGS EMENDED IN THE EDITION:

BAR	VOICE	ORIGINAL
16	A	*c′ d′* (the reading of PerA 431 has been adopted)
16	B	*d c* (the readings of the concordances have been adopted)
after 21	A	superfluous *c′ semibrevis*

TEXTUAL CONCORDANCES (MSS):[5] • *Berl.S. H.348* (125v-126v), only capitolo XI, (Leonardo Giustinian) • *Bol.Arciv. 4880* (37r-38v), only capitolo XI • *Bol.U. 12* (2r-24v: 2r-v), «sam Bernardo» • *Bol.U. 157* (174r-181v: 174r-v) • *Bol.U. 2618* (155r-157r), only capitolo XI • *Bol.U. 2845* (223-238: 223) • *Bol.U. 4019* (138r-151r: 138r) • *Borg.P.M.76725* (70v-94v: 70v-72r) • *Como.C* (50v-84r and 90v-92r: lauda no. 33, fols. 90v-92r)[6] • *CV. BL.3695* (23r-25r), only capitolo XI • *CV. OL.3322* (63r-81r), begins at l. 78[7] • *CV. P.1513* (186v-187r), only capitolo XI • *CV. ReL.478* (155r-183v: 156r-157r), «frate anselmo da treviso del ordene de li heremitani de sancto avgustino» • *CV. Ro.229*[8] (71r-113v: 71r-72v) • *CV.VL.3213* (391v-393v), only capitolo XI, «Maestro Antonio da Ferrara» • *CV.VL. 7714*

---

[3]. It exists in various versions, from a minimum of 9 to a maximum of 13 capitoli (uniquely in *Vic.A. 32bis*). The capitoli are effectively 9, to which have been added a proemium, sometimes divided into two parts (*Oratio sive obsecratio ad postulandam lamentationem beatae Virginis*), and a final prayer (*Oratio sive gratiarum actio*); see ANDREOSE 2001, p. 8 and n. 3.

[4]. The oldest of the datable manuscripts is *Fir.L. Ash.1177*, provided one reads 1354 (and not 1454) as the date of compilation, partially erased (AGNELLI 1902, p. xii); otherwise it would be the MS *Ven.M. I.3*, dated Venice, 28 November 1369 and compiled by Domenico de' Giuliani (MORPURGO 1883), or the MS *Fir.R. 1661*, dated 1371 and compiled by the Veronese notary Filippo de Humilitatibus (GRAF 1884, p. 401).

[5]. Among the manuscript poetic sources listed in ANDREOSE 2001 (p. 9, n. 6) the MS Vatican City, Biblioteca Apostolica Vaticana, Rossi 765 (*olim* X.145) is erroneously included, as is also MS Treviso, Biblioteca Comunale, 181. With regard to *Bol.U. 1737* (listed both in ANDREOSE 2001, p. 9, n. 6 and in CREMA 2002, p. 616, n. 24) it should be stated that it does not contain the first capitolo of the *Pianto*: in reality is it another lauda, with an identical incipit (fol. 6r: *Ave regina virgo gloriosa*). Quite another matter is the situation of the MS It. II.88 (= 4880) of the Biblioteca Nazionale Marciana of Venice: the parchment numbered as fol. 1, which in fact functions as the guardsheet, must originally have been intended for a copy of the *Pianto*, since the copyist wrote an 'I' at the beginning and the two initial lines of the first capitolo («Ave regina virgo gloriosa | che de dio padre te chiamasti ancilla»); aborting his work, the parchment leaf, turned upside down, was then used as the opening folio in the manuscript, otherwise of paper.

[6]. In this source, the nine capitoli that constitute the *Pianto* have been divided into separate laude, numbered from 18 to 27. The initial prayer (*Ave regina virgo gloriosa*) is found separately from the other five laude (nos. 28-32), as lauda no. 33 (see LARGHI 1998, pp. 61-63, who expands what has already been described in CASNATI - RE 1965).

[7]. The folio that should have contained *Ave Regina, Virgo gloriosa* has been torn out of the manuscript.

[8]. Despite the fact that Andreose — following BINI 1852 — lists, in addition to *CV. Ro.229*, a phantom 'cod. Rossi' among the concordances (see ANDREOSE 2001, p. 9, n. 6), I believe that they are the same manuscript, not two different ones.

(57r–59r), only capitolo XI • *Fir.L. Ash.598* (26r–48v: 26r–27r), «santo Bernardo» • *Fir.L. Ash.852* (1r–52v: 1r–3v), «secundum dominum franciscum petrarcam de florentia» • *Fir.L. Ash.1177* (57r–91r: 57r–58v) • *Fir.L. Ash.1402* (1r–41v: 1r–v, but fol. 2 is lacking, and therefore ll. 37-74 are missing) • *Fir.N. 291* (79r–85v: 79r) • *Fir.N. II.IV.3* (51r–73v), begins at l. 60, thus it lacks *Ave Regina, Virgo gloriosa* • *Fir.N. M.738* (53r–84v: 53r–54r) • *Fir.R. 1106* (49r–57r), begins at l. 152, thus it lacks *Ave Regina, Virgo gloriosa* • *Fir.R. 1294/2760* (62r–70r: 62r), «facto per Messer Franciescho Petracchi» • *Fir.R. 1661* (1r–12v: 1r) • *Fir.R. 1763* (61r–88v: 61r–64r), «santo Bernardo» • *Lon.B. A.27549* (105v–111v: 105v) • *Luc.S. 1302* (1r–32v: 1r–2r) • *Mil.A. 80* (125r–155r: 125r–v),[9] «fratrem enselminum ordinis santi augustini» • *Mil.A. 94* (41r–65r: 41r–42r) • *Mil.B. 28* (2r–27r: 2r–v) • *Mil.T. 92* ([242r]–[245r])[10] • *Mil.T. 545* (117v–138v, olim 127v–148v: 117v–118r, olim 127v–128r) • *Mod.E. 381* (117v–125r: 117v) • *Nap.N. 14* (203v–204v), only capitolo XI • *NY.C. 195* (172r–181v: 172r), «Io. bocacio florenteno» • *Ox.B. CI.180* (24r–26v), only capitolo XI • *Ox.B. CI.208* (75r–96v: 75r–v) • *Ox.B. CI.240* (71r–94v: 71r–72r) • *Ox.B. CI.263* (95r–115v: 95r–v),[11] «fato per man di miser Franzescho petrarcha» • *Ox.B. CI.301* (2r–34v: 2r–v), first leaf of text and any opening title lost; fol. 2r starts at l. 28 • *Ox.B. CL.317* (2ar–36v: 2ar–2br),[12] «[…] per sapientem et religiosum uirum fratrem Anselmum ordinis sancti Augustini» • *Ox.B. CL.363* (8v–47r: 8v–10r), «[…] compilatam vulgariter. A fratre enselmino de monte bellunam [sic] ordinis fratrum heremitarum sancti Augustini» • *Pad.U. 1151* (209r–237v: 209r–210r) • *Pad.U. 1357* (1r–26r: 1r–v), in the heading of the last prayer: «Le gratie de fradre Alselmino» • *Pal.C. 8* (113v–116r), only capitolo XI • *Parma.P. Pal.37* (111r–134v: 111r–v) • *Pav.U. A.355* (41r–42v), only capitolo XI • *Pav.U.A.378* (39r–79v: 39r–v), begins at l. 21, «lamentatio beate uirginis marie uulgariter compilata et in ritmis prolata ore Fratris Henselmi ordinis sancti Augustini» • *Rav.C. 63* (148v–152r), only capitolo XI • *Rav.C. 464* (34v–36r), only capitolo XI • *Roma.Al. 301* (184r–216v: 184r–185v) • *Roma.Ca. 817* (125r–167r: 125r–126r) • *Roma.S. 2* (28r–50r), begins at l. 68,[13] • *Sev.C. 52* (70v–97r: 71r–v) • *Siena.C. II.37* (1r–17v: 1r–2r), «La passione de Jesu Cristo» • *Stock.K. 5* (1r–51r: 1r–2v) • *Trev.C. 22* (1r–41r: 1r–2v), modern hand: «vulgariter a fratre Enselmino de Montebelluna Ordinis Fratrum heremitarum sancti Augustini» • *Trev.C. 188* (177r–179v), only capitolo XI • *Ven.GR. 120* (275v–286v), the first prayer is missing[14] • *Ven.M. I.3* (156r–187r: 156r–157r)[15] • *Ven.M. I.9* (182r–219v: 182r–183r) • *Ven.M. I.28* (78r–92r: 78r–v), «Incipit ploratus virginis Marie de morte filii suj in vulgare sermone quem composuit venerabilis frater Anselmus» • *Ven.M. I.30* (89r–111r: 89r–v) • *Ven.M. I.38* (1r–2r), only ll. 1419-1512[16] • *Ven.M. I.75* (118v–124v: 118v–119r), «hic rogitat pie diram bernardus noscere mortem ab ea sum plantum [sic] sui geniti que dei natum matrem» • *Ven.M. I.182* (275r–285r: 275r–v), «fatto per frate Henselmini da Trivisi dello ordine de romitani, molto divoto» • *Ven.M. I.269* (107r–141r: 107r–108r) • *Ver.Cap. 811* (69r–100r: 69r–70r) • *Vic.A. 32bis* (110r–113v), begins at l. 1309; on fol. 111v «Incipit liber XIII et ultimus» • *Vic.C. 65* (1r–43v: 1r–2v), «a fratre Henselmino ordinis fratrum heremitarum sancti Augustini»

---

[9]. In CREMA 2002, pp. 613-614, n. 16, it is erroneously reported that the last folio is 152r. The mistake is probably due to the fact that on that folio appears the rubric that attributes the *Pianto* to Enselmino.

[10]. According to Giuseppe Galli the text of the manuscript was copied directly from *Busti1490*, where it constitutes an integral part of the *Corona de la beatissima Vergene Maria* of Bernardino de' Busti (fols. 229r–254r): «Ave Regina virgo gloriosa | che de dio patre te ciamasti ancilla». Expl.: «ringratiando la tua cortesia | sarò ornato incorruptibile vesta» (see GALLI 1948, p. 116). The text is the same as that I have edited, up to the middle of l. 21. It then continues differently (see the complete text, given after *Busti1494*).

[11]. Fol. 95r–v contains *Ave rezina virgo gloriosa*, anonymous and without any heading; the same *Pianto* continues on fol. 96r, though it appears to be another poem introduced by the heading «Lamento de la nostra dona» and attributed to Petrarch.

[12]. Fol. 1 is a flyleaf, and the first two leaves of text are foliated 2a and 2b.

[13]. The title and the first lines of the *lamentatio* are missing owing to the removal of at least one folio between fols. 27 and 28 (see GRANDI 1989, p. 104, n. 27 and STATUTI SENATO, p. 44).

[14]. See LUISI 1983, I, p. 75.

[15]. The capitolo ends without the final distich.

[16]. See ANDREOSE 2001, p. 16.

Textual concordances (prints):[17] • *Busti 1488* (cap. LII)[18] • *Busti 1489* (c4*v*-c6*v*) • *Busti 1490* (b3*v*-b6*r*) • *Busti 1492S* (b1*r*-b2*v*), (Bernardino de' Busti) • *Busti 1492Z* (b1*r*-b3*r*), (Bernardino de' Busti) • *Busti 1494* (F4*v*-F7*v*), (Bernardino de' Busti) • *Busti 1517* (B2*r*-B4*r*), (Bernardino de' Busti) • *BustiPon* (cap. XVI) • *Fior 1505* (c2*r*-c3*r*) • *Infantia 1513* (lost)[19] • *Infantia 1515* (n3*r*-p4*r*: n3*r*-*v*), «compilato per Enselmino de triviso frate de S. Augustino» • *Infantia 1541* (lost), «Anselmini»[20] • *Opera 1515* (N1*r*-N3*v*), only capitolo XI • *OperaFregoso* (G2*r*-G4*r*), only capitolo XI, «Capitulo Del Gloria Vergine Maria Composta per Misser Antonio Thibaldeo» • *Pianto 1477*[21] (the whole print consists of the *Pianto*: a1*r*-a2*r*) • *Pianto 1478* (1*r*-41*r*: 1*r*) • *Pianto 1481H* (a1*r*-d7*v*: a1*r*-a2*r*), «intacte vulgariter compilata cum ritimis prolata ore fratris Enselmini de trivisio ordinis fratrum heremitarum sancti Augustini» • *Pianto 1481L* (a1*r*-f2*r*: a1*r*-*v*), «intacte vulgariter compillata cum ritmis prolata ore fratris Enselmini de Trivisio ordinis fratrum heremitarum sancti Augustini» • *Pianto 1483* (1*r*-32*v*: 1*r*-2*r*), «composto per Messere Antonio Cornazzano» • *Pianto 1490* ([1]*r*-[?]), begins at l. 126, thus *Ave Regina, Virgo gloriosa* is lacking,[22] «composto per Miser Antonio Cornazano» • *Pianto 1493* (2*r*-16*r*: 2*r*-*v*) • *Pianto 1495* (1*r*-30*r*: 1*r*),[23] «composto per Messere Antonio Cornazzano» • *Pianto 1505* (A2*r*-H2*r*: A2*r*-A3*v*), «composto per el magnifico misser Leonardo veneto» • *Pianto 1537* (a[1]*r*-[d8]*v*: a[1]*r*-a2*r*) • *PiantoOratione* (1*r*-[38*v*?]: 1*r*-2*r*),[24] «facta e composta vulgare da fra Guglielmo da Trevisio de l'ordine di frati heremitani di sancto Augustino»

Musical concordances (mss): • FirN M121 (18*v*-19*r*), *Sofferir son disposto ogni tormento* • ParisN Rés676 (83*v*-84*r*), *Soffrire io som disposto ogne tormento*, 3 vv. (without A) • PerA 431 (116*v*-117*r*, olim 126*v*-127*r*), *Sufferir so disposto omne tormento*

Text from *Pianto 1481L* ([Proemio]):

> Ave Regina, Virgo gloriosa,
> che de Dio Padre te chiamasti ancilla,
> del Figliol fosti madre, figlia e sposa.

---

[17]. Linder 1898 lists among the concordances also *Opera nuova spirituale non più posta in luce, composta per Marco Bandarini*, no pl., no pr., [ca. 1552] (Venice, Biblioteca Nazionale Marciana, Misc. 2397.4); the poem *La passione di Giesù, recitata da Maria Vergine* contained in it is only a free paraphrase of capitoli II-X of Enselmino's *Pianto*.

[18]. In this source and in *Busti 1489*, *Busti 1490*, *Busti 1492S*, *Busti 1492Z*, *Busti 1494*, *Busti 1517*, *BustiPon*, *Fior 1505* the comprehensive text is that indicated in note 10 (taken from the *Corona de la beatissima Vergene Maria* of Bernardino de' Busti) and given in complete form below.

[19]. According to Essling — who must have taken the notice from some book dealer's catalogue — the last ten folios included the *Pianto* (see Essling II/1, no. 1774).

[20]. Thus in Capponi 1747, p. 25.

[21]. This is the oldest edition of Enselmino's *Pianto* to have survived. The 1471 *editio princeps*, lost to this day, had erroneously attribuited the lines to «Messer Antonio Cornazzano, poeta clarissimo», from which a series of spurious reprints originated.

[22]. The two remaining folios of this print have been bound, one at the beginning and the other at the end, to a fascicle of eight folios containing the *De fide et vita Cristi* of Antonio Cornazano (Venice, Tommaso di Piasi, 1492). The recto of the first folio has the only title page, whereas the verso is blank; the second folio recto contains ll. 126-128 of the *Pianto*, and the verso has ll. 168-172 and 186-188.

[23]. The incunable is part of a private collection in Oxford. It was therefore not possible for me to verify on which folio *Ave Regina, Virgo gloriosa* ends.

[24]. After Vanzolini 1894: «[…] there are ten numbered capitoli, in addition to the *oratione*. // After fol. 30, the verso of which contains the first seven tercets of the ninth capitolo, two folios are lacking and thus twenty-eight tercets; moreover, through an error in pagination, the recto of fol. 33 (which would have that number, if the folios had been signed and my exemplar were complete) does not continue with the verso, but rather the recto of fol. 34, which in turn is followed by the verso of fol. 33, continuing with the verso of fol. 34. And after this two more folios are lacking, which should have contained a tercet and the closing couplet of capitolo IX, the indication of capitolo X, and the words «Questa è la rengratiatione facta a la Vergine Maria», and twenty-four tercets of capitolo X corresponding to the *Liber XIII* of the fragment published by Morsolin. At the end there is a single folio which would be fol. 37, after which the last is lacking, containing two tercets with the concluding couplet of the capitolo and, probably, the colophon».

Sì como te mostrasti a la Sibilla
5   nel cerchio d'oro col tuo figlio in brazo
atorno il sole quando più sentilla

per dar intender ad Octavian pazo
ch'al mondo era nato un mazor d'esso,
e de[25] ciascuno era pace e solazo;

10   e come l'angiolo Gabriel instesso
discese, quando fosti salutata
da lui che da Dio Padre ti fu messo;

e come fosti, o Verzene beata,
como la sancta scriptura favella,
15   da Isaia in figura dimostrata;

el naserà, ciò disse, una verzella
de la radice de Iesse, e un fiore
meraveioso ascenderà fuor d'ella;

e tu, verzella degna d'oni onore,
20   quel fior suave producesti in terra,
che tucto el mondo prese grande odore;

e come da Dio al mondo era gran guera
tu festi la pace, e come via
tu sei de ciascun fedele che erra;

25   cossì ti prego, o dolze Madre pia,
ched el ti piaqua di mostra[r]me alquanto
de la gran doglia tua, Vergen Maria,

e de la forte pena e 'l grave pianto,
che tu portasti quando il tuo figliolo
30   fo posto su la croce, e infin tanto

ched el fo passionato a sì gran dolo;
e poi fin ch'el fo zo del legno tolto,
e da Iosep revolto nel lenzuolo

e poscia fin ch'el fo da lui sepolto
35   dime, Raina, quanto, ch'io tin prego,
fo quel dolor ch'el cuor t'avea sì tolto;

a ciò ch'io possa sempre pianzer tiego
la passion del tuo figliol benigno
e ciascun fedel cristiano miego.

40   Io mi cognosco ben ch'io non son degno
de domandarte, Madre, questa gratia,
perch'io me sento pecator maligno.

Ancor mi sento, Madre, in contumatia

---

[25]. In the source «do» instead of 'de'.

del tuo fiolo e ti; ma tu se' quella
45   fontana di pietà che zascun satia.

Tu sei del mare la chiarita stella,
tu sei, Madonna, sì de gratia plena
che recogli zascun che a ti s'apella.

e di misericordia viva vena
50   tu sei regina, et ancor quella nave
ch'al porto de salute ciascun mena.

Però, Madona mia, non mi par grave
adomandarte questo, quando io sento
che tu se' tanto benigna e soave:

55   se tu mi conte, Madre, il tuo lamento
tu me farai d'onni voglia contento.

Text from *Busti1494* (F4*v*-F7*v*):

Ave Regina, Virgo gloriosa,
che de Dio Patre te chiamasti ancilla,
essendo sua intemerata sposa.

Sì como te monstrasti a la Sibilla
5   nel cerchio d'oro col to fiol in brazo
atorno il sole quando più sintilla

per far intendere a Octaviano pazo
ch'al mondo era nato un mazor d'esso,
che a ciascuno era pace e solazo;

10   e como l'angel Gabriel istesso
descese, quando fusti salutata
da lui che da Dio Patre a te fu messo.

Alora fusti, o Vergene beata,
sì como la sancta scriptura favella,
15   da Isaia in figura demonstrata;

el nascerà, dixe, una vergella
de la radice di Iese e un fiore
maraveglioso ascenderà for d'ella;

e tu, vergella digna d'ogni onore,
20   quel fior suave producesti in terra,
che a tut'il mondo porse grand'odore;

e como tra Dio e 'l mondo era gran guerra
tu fecisti la pace, e sei el ligno
che tuti li nostri inimici atterra.

25   Però benché cognosca che non son digno
de dimandarte, o Matre, alcuna gratia,
perché me sento peccator maligno,

benché ancor me veda in contumacia
30 del tuo fiol, perché tu sei quella
fontana de pietà che tuti sacia,

però me dai conforto e l'audacia
de supplicarte, o Vergineta bella;
me monstri del nemico la fallacia.

35 Tu sola sei del mar la ciara[26] stella,
tu sei regina sì de gratia plena,
che racolli ciascun ch'a te s'apella.

De misericordia sei viva vena,
40 tu sei la barca nostra e quella nave
che a porto de salute ognuno mena.

Però, Madonna mia, non me par grave
né anche de meritar alcuna pena
45 per invocar il tuo nome suave.

Amor me stringe e fa di te parlare,
o primicera di vergene prudente,
sì che de tropo ardir non m'imputare.

O saldo scudo de la felice gente
50 dal qual ogni sagitta indreto torna,
deh, non lassa ferir la mia mente.

O lume che questa vita e l'altra adorni,
che 'l cel de tua belleza inamorasti,
vene a salvarne ne li extremi giorni.

55 O sacro fonte de li penseri casti,
che 'l cogitato mal in bon ritorni
et in umilitade i grandi fasti,

umilia ormai la mente mia altera
che par che d'altra vita poco cura.
60 O Vergene sancta d'ogni parte intera,

pregote, poncella[27] immaculata e pura,
che sei di peccator speranza vera,
non lassi a me venir ria ventura.

Tu sei nostra nothera[28] e bona guida
65 in questo orribil e tempestoso mare
nel qual per gran paura ognuno crida.

Ma tu, Vergene pia, ne pòi salvare,
però l'anima mia in te si fida
ché la farai al porto applicare.

---

[26]. A Veneto-Lombarda linguistic form of 'chiara'.
[27]. I.e. 'pulzella'.
[28]. Probably a printing error of 't' for 'c' («nochera» = 'nocchiera').

70   Tu vedi che altro non ho se non affanno
     in questa fragil e sagurata vita,
     e forse venuto son a l'ultim'anno.

     Il tempo mio corre como sagita
     e il scampare longo cerco invano,
75   ché ogni cosa a morte sì m'invita.

     Sì, quasi son ne lo extremo passo
     e me ritrovo solo senza governo
     sì che ne vado a lo inferno basso.

     E benché sapia esser il foco eterno,
80   el vicio e l'error mio m'han facto un saxo,
     e quasi oblito[29] son dil ben superno.

     Succorre adonca presto al core lasso,
     perché se adimori[30] de adiutarme
     dal libro de la vita me vedo casso.

85   Non guardar me, ma chi dignò crearme
     a la imagin sua, e lui t'induca
     col tuo dolce risguardo recrearme.

     Benché sia de vil terra caduca,
     risguarda il cor contrito umiliato
90   e fa che al ben viver se reduca.

     O clarità del circolo stellato,
     non d'un splendore solo, ma diversi
     da cui è tut'il mondo illuminato,

     ascolta, prego, questi rimati versi
95   e volge il tuo volto irradiato
     a noi nel tempestoso mar submersi.

     E benché Italian, né Indi o Persi
     né altri possan a pien di te parlare
     né dir di toi merti como doversi,

100 non volia tu però abandonare
     colui il quale a te venire vole
     e soto il tuo filio militare.

     Gubernatrice de le superne scole,
     benché l'ingenio mio fia poco,
105 tacer le toi virtù molto mi dole.

     O lume sancto, o benedecto foco,
     senza il qual non se trova la via
     d'aver la pace del beato loco,

---

[29]. From 'oblire' = 'dimenticare'.
[30]. From 'addimorare' = 'indugiare'.

con fede torno a te, dolce Maria,
110   prima che povertà d'amor me spolia,
ché 'l tuo succorso benigno me dii.

Guarda con quanti spietati argolii[31]
questa fortuna pessima e ria
porta el mio legno in ruinosi scolii.

115   Smarito sono da la drita strada
e trasportato in Silla[32] contra volia,
se non m'adiuti mal conven che vada.

O dolce rifreno de la divina spada,
il tuo nato meco reconcilia,
120   sì che nel baratro infernal non cada.

Fa che adesso con la mente mesta
di mei peccati facia la vigilia
e poi vada a la eterna festa,

dove glorioso, con la corona in testa,
125   rigratiando la tua cortesia,
sarò ornato d'incorruptibil vesta.

MODERN EDITIONS OF THE TEXT: BEVILACQUA 1994, pp. 96-138 (after CIBOTTO 1960); BIADENE 1885, p. 275 (first seven and last five lines from *Sev.C. 52*); BINI 1852, pp. 3-21 (after *CV.Ro.229*); BRAMBILLA 1903, pp. 5-26 (does not give the text, but only the detailed apparatus of the variants with the respect to Linder's edition, from a mysterious Neapolitan manuscript, which is not any of those listed so far, and would also contain *Canti zoiosi e dolce melodia*); CALZAVARA 1950, pp. 7-66 (after LINDER 1898); CASNATI - RE 1965, pp. 17-18 (after *Como.C.*, lauda no. 26, which corresponds to capitolo VIII, from the initial line to l. 1084); CIBOTTO 1960 (after CALZAVARA 1950, but incorporating the suggestions in the article by Franco Riva, 'Su una nuova edizione de *El planto della verzene Maria* di Fra' Enselmino', in: *Studi storici veronesi*, III (1951-52), pp. 124-127); DI GIOVANNI 1874, pp. 433-437 (after *Pal.C. 8*); FINZI 1893, pp. 169-170 (only capitolo I after *Luc.S. 1302*); FINZI 1894, pp. 339-374 (after *Luc.S. 1302*); pp. 374-376 (after MS Lucca, Biblioteca Statale, 1491, that is MS 6 of Francesco Moücke, the eighteenth-century printer who transcribed it from MS *CV.VL.3213*); pp. 377-380 (after Moücke's copy, made from *OperaFregoso*); JEPPESEN 1935, pp. lxxix-lxxx (after PeLaudeII and *Berl.S. H.348*); LINDER 1898 (collation of 22 MSS, apart from *Trev.C. 22*); LUISI 1983, I, pp. 331-345 (after *Ven.GR. 120*); SERENA 1909, pp. 9-30.

MODERN EDITIONS OF THE MUSIC: ATLAS 1985, p. 223 (after PerA 431); HERNON 1972, pp. 456-458 (after PerA 431).

REMARKS: Although there are very many literary sources,[33] the text *Ave Regina, Virgo gloriosa* has a musical setting only in Panc.27. The concordant musical sources transmit instead the text of the strambotto *Soffrire son disposto ogni tormento*, and none of these seems to be related to Panc.27 because of the numerous graphic and substantive variants. From the types of musical errors (notes written a third

---

[31]. «Argolii» stands for 'orgogli' (= 'moti burrascosi del mare'. See BATTAGLIA I, p. 647).

[32]. «Silla» stands for 'Scilla' (symbolically, 'dangerous place for navigators').

[33]. I wish to thank Marco Beghelli for having helped me to organize the literary sources and their relevant bibliography. He also obtained the text from *Busti1494* for me. My thanks also to Antonio Rossi for having resolved several obscurities in the text.

too high or too low) it is logical to suppose that the scribe of Panc.27 copied the music from a model that is no longer extant.

BIBLIOGRAPHY: ANDREOSE 2001; ATLAS 1985, p. 273; BEVILACQUA 1994; BIADENE 1887, p. 201, n. 1; BOORMAN 2006, p. 992; BRAMBILLA 1903; BRIDGMAN 1953-56, pp. 234-235; CASNATI - RE 1965; CATTIN 1986, p. 309; CREMA 2002; CREMA 2005; DE ANGELIS 1818, p. 269; FINZI 1894; FRATI 1917, p. 464; GHISI 1939, pp. 71-72; HERNON 1972, pp. 291-293, 528; JEPPESEN 1935, p. xix; LA FACE BIANCONI - ROSSI 1990; LONGO 1986, pp. 202-206; LOWINSKY 1962, p. 9; LUISI 1983, I, p. 544; MORSOLIN 1890; MORSOLIN 1891; PERINI 1938, pp. 9-10; SCHUTTE 1980, pp. 11, 16-19; SERENA 1891; SERENA 1893; SERENA 1909.

13.
Ave Regina, Virgo gloriosa /
Sofrire son disposto [ogni tormento]
fol. 13*v*

[Enselmino da Montebelluna]

-ma - sti an – – – cil - la,   del   Fi - gliol   fo – – - sti   ma –

-dre,   fi - glia e   spo – – – – - sa.

14.

AVE VICTORIOSO

fol. 14*r* (4 vv.)

[Heading only]

Lauda? (strambotto toscano?).[1]

TEXT FROM PeLaudeII:

Ave victorioso e sancto legno,
per cui se aperse el ciel, chiuse l'inferno.
Salve tu, che salvasti el mondo degno
da brusar dentro al foco sempitreno [*sic*].
5 Como tu aiuti l'universo indegno,
e muti el mal perpetuo in ben eterno,
cossì noi te pregamo benché indegni,
ne aiuti in vita e al fin salvar ne degni.

REMARKS: This is the only time that the remark «Vidi totum» (centred at the bottom of the page, under two blank staves) is found, written in a paler ink than that used in the piece: perhaps as a note later added by the scribe himself to indicate the rechecking of his model.

BIBLIOGRAPHY: PRIZER 1993b, p. 194.

---

[1]. At fols. 16*v*-17*r* the musical print PeLaudeII contains a strambotto set by Marchetto Cara. BOORMAN 2006, p. 960 lists the version of PeLaudeII as concordant with that of Panc.27. In reality, the music does not agree with that of Panc.27, but the text could easily be adapted.

14.
AVE VICTORIOSO
fol. 14r

Vidi totum

15.

A MARIA, FONTE D'AMORE / VIVE LIETO [E NON TEMERE]

fols. 14*v*-15*r* (4 vv.)

[Francesco degli Albizzi]

A Maria, fonte d'amore,
vada og[n]i alma peccatrice;
mondaràla d'ogni errore
e farala venire alfin felice
5   perch'è madre del Signorre.
         A Maria, fonte d'amore

Chi vol gratia vada a quella,
che è del ciel porta serena,
e dil mondo chiara stella
che per recta via ci mena,
10   ciascun che 'i dona el core.
         A Maria, fonte d'amore

L'alma che è cum lei unita,
serà dal dracon diffessa,
et in ciel cum lei unita
e di gloria sempre acesa
15   dell'inmenso eterno ardore.
         A Maria [...]

Ogn'om lauda il nome sancto
di Maria, virgine bella,
piena de Spirito Sancto,
de' mortali secura stella,
20   e di gratia dispensatore.
         A Maria [...]

Lauda. Contrafact on the music of the barzelletta *Vivi lieto e non temere*.[1]

---

[1]. This barzelletta can be read in *Man. C. 4*, fols. 227*v*-228*r*, edited in Gallico 1961, pp. 105-106 (*Viva lieto e non timere*) and in Prizer 1986, p. 32 (*Vivi lieto e non temere*), but I have not found any setting. The incipit *Vivi lieto e non temere* is, however, mentioned, with *L'ocelo da le rame d'oro*, in a letter dated 2 August 1494 that the Mantuan student Don Acteon Mauri wrote to Francesco II Gonzaga, in which he says that the Ferrarese lutenist Pietrobono taught him these two pieces (see Prizer 1986, pp. 22-27 and Prizer 1991, p. 21; the letter is given in Prizer 1986, p. 24, n. 80 and in Lockwood 1987, p. 138). Lockwood suggests that *Vivi lieto e non temere* might be related to the barzelletta *Vivo lieto nel tormento*, present in the second book of Frottole published by Petrucci (see Lockwood 1987, p. 138).

COMMENTARY ON THE TEXT:

4	hypermetric
6	the *residuum* begins here
19	hypermetric
20	hypermetric

READINGS EMENDED IN THE EDITION:

BAR	VOICE	ORIGINAL
[1-3]	A	at the end of the *residuum*, which occupies three-quarters of the fifth stave of fol. 14*v*, there is a musical addition with the annotation «In loco expectationis contralti In p°» ['p°' = 'principio'?] (= 'at the beginning in place of the rests in the Altus'): an indication of an alternative reading for the rests of bars 1-3
43	A	*longa* with fermata

TEXTUAL CONCORDANCES (MSS): • *Fir.N. P.173* (169*v*), *Se a Maria fonte di amore*,[2] «Francesco di Albizo» • *Mün.S. I240* (25*r*) • *Rim.C. 38* (154*r*), «Di Francesco dalbizo» • *Ven.M. I.78* (87*r*), «Di Francesco Dalbizo»

TEXTUAL CONCORDANCES (PRINTS): • *LaudeBonac* (87*r*), «Di Francesco Dalbizo» • *LaudeMisc* (39*r*), «Francesco Dalbizo» • *LaudeSper* (42*r*), «Di Francesco Dalbizo» • *LaudeVecchie* (d5*r*), «Di Francesco Dalbizo» • *LaudeVecchie* (p2*v*-p3*r*), *Se a maria fonte d'amore*,[3] «Di francesco dalbizo» • *OperaNova* (29*r*), «Di Francesco Dalbizo» • *OperaNova* (114*v*), *Se a maria fonte d'amore*,[4] «Di francesco dalbizo»

MUSICAL CONCORDANCES (MSS): • CTL G12 (78*v*-79*r*, *olim* 77*v*-78*r*)

MODERN EDITIONS OF THE TEXT: GALLETTI 1863, pp. 83-84 (after *LaudeBonac*); PRIZER 1986, pp. 32-33 (after Panc.27).

MODERN EDITIONS OF THE MUSIC: CMM 76, pp. 36-37 (after CTL G12); PRIZER 1986, pp. 32-37 (after Panc.27).

REMARKS: Although it is the unique concordance, the version of CTL G12 is rather distant from that of Panc.27 because of numerous graphic variants (ligatures in place of separated notes and vice versa, repeated notes instead of long notes) and substantive variants (ornaments and a few different notes). In the poetic sources the indication «cantasi come *Accuelly m'a la belle*» is often found (see FALLOWS 1999, pp. 68-69 and WILSON 1998, p. 86): this chanson by Caron is not concordant with the piece in Panc.27, however.

BIBLIOGRAPHY: CATTIN 1973a, pp. 205-206; CATTIN 1986, pp. 303-304, n. 107; CMM 76, p. xxvii; FALLOWS 1999, p. 68; FEIST 1889, pp. 121, 175; PRIZER 1986, pp. 25-27; TENNERONI 1909, p. 53.

---

[2]. Despite the variant in the incipit, the whole first strophe is equivalent to that of Panc.27. See the modern edition in GALLETTI 1863, p. 268.

[3]. See n. 2.

[4]. See n. 2.

15.
A Maria, fonte d'amore /
Vive lieto [e non temere]
fols. 14v–15r

[Francesco degli Albizzi]

al - ma pec - ca - tri - - ce; mon - da - rà la

d'o - - - - gni er - ro - - - re e fa - ra -

-la ve - ni - - re al fin fe - li - - ce

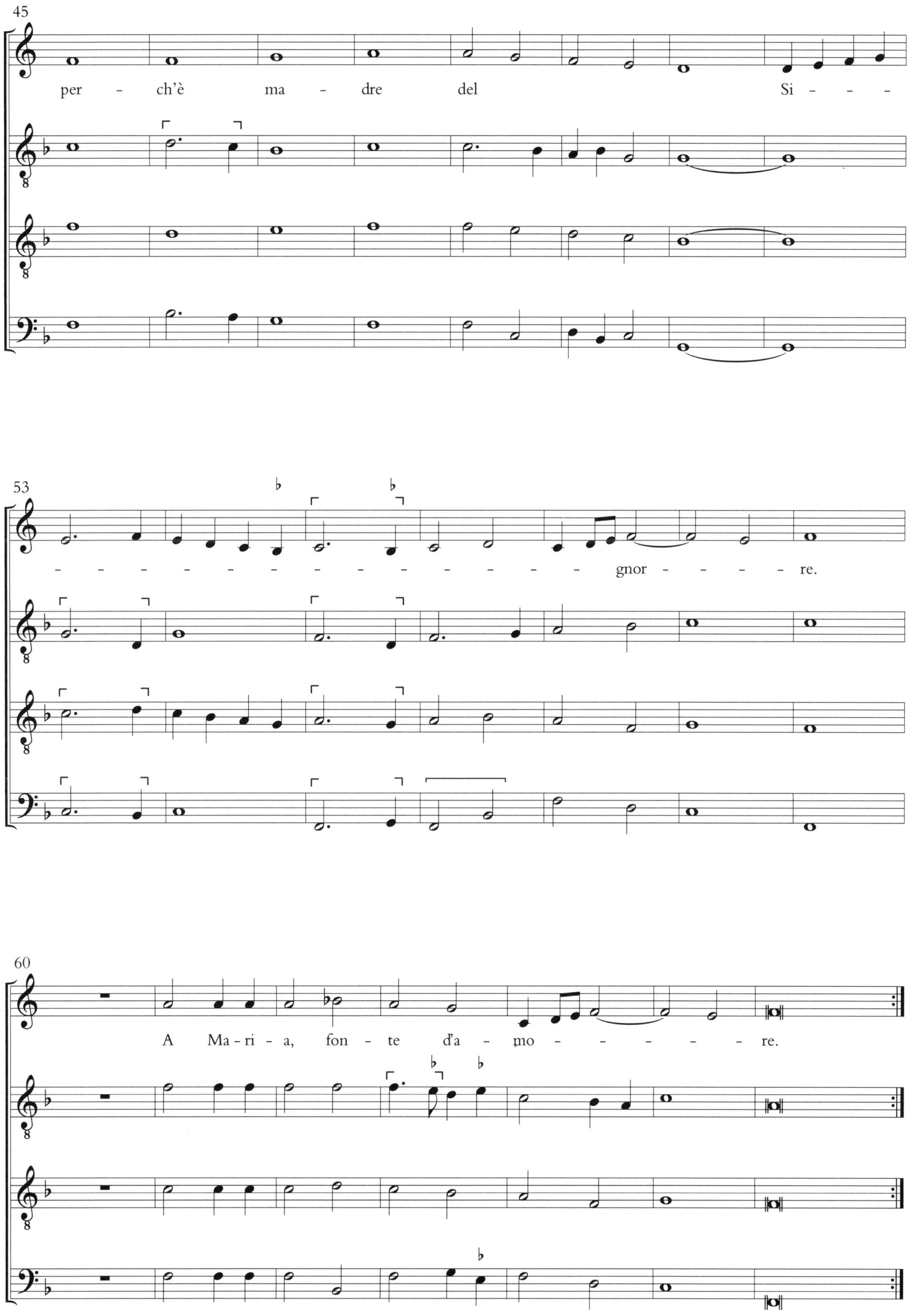
45
per - ch'è ma - dre del Si - - -
53
- - - - - - - - - - - - gnor - - - - re.
60
A Ma - ri - a, fon - te d'a - mo - - - - - - re.

16.

Amice, ad quid venisti? attende tibi

fols. 15*v*–16*r* (3 vv.)

Alexander Agricola

Amice, ad quid venisti? attende tibi

This is a combination of two biblical phrases: «amice ad quod/quid venisti» from Matthew 26:50 (Jesus' question to Judas, who has come to betray him, Vulgata, p. 1569) and the very common admonition «Attende tibi», present many times also in the Bible (for example Tobias 4:13, Ecclesiasticus 11:35 and 29:27, 1 Timothy 4:16). The continuation of the text found in CTL G12 is taken instead from the Gospel parable of the workers sent to the vineyard, in Matthew 20:13-14, Vulgata, p. 1556 («[13]at ille respondens uni eorum dixit | amice non facio tibi iniuriam | nonne ex denario convenisti mecum | [14]tolle quod tuum est et vade | volo autem et huic novissimo dare sicut et tibi»). No liturgical use is known of the text set in Panc.27 and in CTL G12; an antiphon with the text of Matthew 20:13-14 (up to «vade») occurs as the *Antifona ad Magnificat in Feria V. post Dom. Septuag.* (CAO III, p. 46; CS, p. 401).

Commentary on the text:

1   S: the syllables «-ni-sti» have been underlined with dots (i.e. cancelled) and then repositioned farther on

Musical concordances (mss):[1] • BolM 16 (24*v*-25*r*), *Dictes le moy* • CTL G12 (124*v*, *olim* 141*v*), 2 vv. (S and T only),[2] «Al agricola» • CV G27 (95*v*-96*r*, *olim* 102*v*-103*r*), *Dictes moy toutes* • FirN BR229 (116*v*-117*r*), *Dictes moy toutes*, «Alexander agricola» • FirN M178 (13*v*-14*r*), *Dictes moy toutes*, «Alexander» • RomaCa 2856 (69*v*-70*r*), *Dittes moy* • WarU 5892 (96*v*), textless

Text from CTL G12:

         Amice, ad quid venisti? attende tibi.
         Non facio tibi iniuriam. Tolle quod tuum est.

Modern editions of the music: Brown 1983, II, pp. 230-232 (after FirN BR229); CMM 22/IV, p. 64 (after Panc.27); CMM 22/V, pp. 24-25 (after FirN BR229); Wolff 1970, II, pp. 192-195 (after RomaCa 2856).[3]

Remarks: Apart from the textless version (WarU 5892), the piece has had two types of musical transmission: as a rondeau quatrain (*Dictes moy toutes voz pensées*) in five manuscripts, and with a Gospel text in two. The tradition, therefore, links the two MSS Panc.27 and CTL G12. Passing over the fact that the latter version does not transmit the Bassus, the comparison of the Superius and Tenor shows only a few graphic variants of slight significance: 11 ligatures *cum opposita proprietate*

---

[1]. The most frequent textual attestation appears to be that of the rondeau quatrain *Dictes moy toutes voz pensées*. A modern edition is found in Brown 1983, I, p. 255, from FirR 2794, fol. 8*v*, with corrections from KøbK 1848, p. 137.

[2]. The following page is lost.

[3]. With the Tenor from DijM 517 (191*v*-192*r*, *olim* 188*v*-189*r*, *Dictes moy toutes*, «Loyset compere»).

that are all separate notes in Panc.27. Certainly, therefore, the version of Panc.27 and that of CTL G12 derive from a common environment. From a musical point of view, the other concordances are more distant: there are many graphic variants in FirN M178 and in FirN BR229, and more substantial differences with BolM 16, RomaCa 2856, and WarU 5892.

BIBLIOGRAPHY: ATLAS 1975-76, I, p. 204; BROWN 1983, I, p. 255; CATTIN 1973a, p. 220; FALLOWS 1999, pp. 132-133; FILOCAMO 2004; POWERS 1994, pp. 427-428; WOLFF 1970, I, pp. 278-279.

16.
AMICE, AD QUID VENISTI? ATTENDE TIBI

fols. 15*v*-16*r*

Alexander Agricola

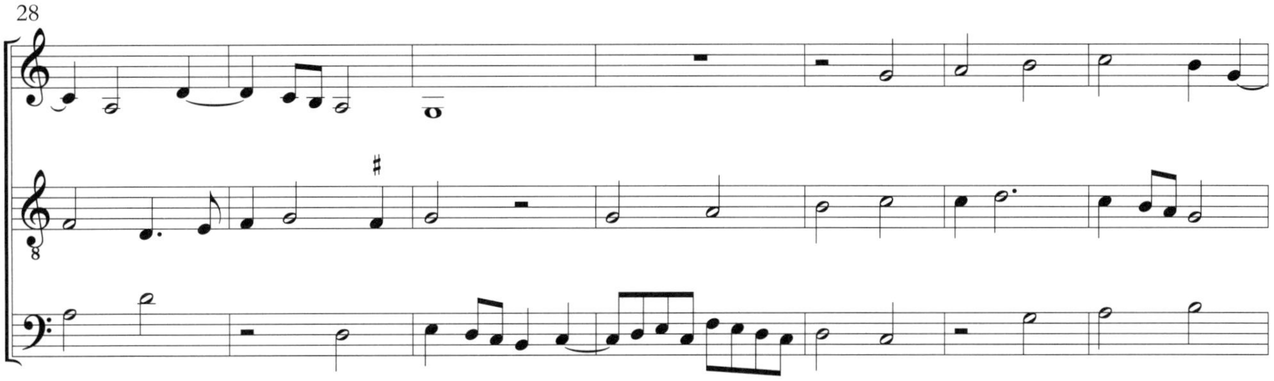
28

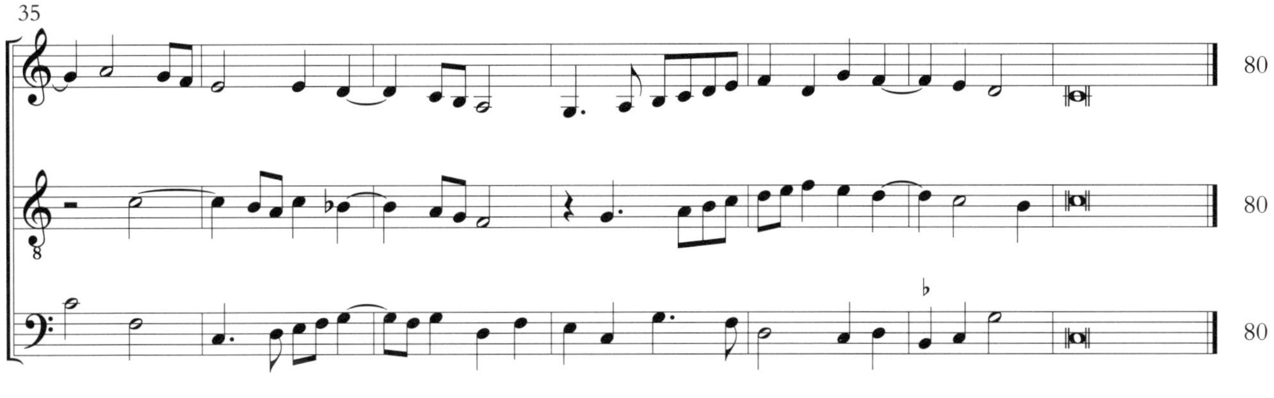
35
80
80
80

17.

Alma, svegliate oramai

fol. 16*v* (4 vv.)

[Giovanni Brocco]

Alma, svegliate oramai,
ancora cieca tu dormi.
    Alma, svegliate o[ramai]

Pon mente como in breve
sen va 'sto tempo leve;
5   dunque star non se deve
sopita como stai.
    Alma […]

O quanta è cosa dura
e non li poni cura,
che quel che li anni fura
10   non più ritorna mai.
    Alma […]

Conven che voglie mute
se brami tua salute,
e seguitar virtute,
che lieta alfin serai.
    Alma […]

15   'Sta fragiltade umana
segue sua voglia insana
e da ciel se aluntana.
Misera, tu che fai?
    Alma svegl[iate] […]

Italian secular piece (ballata antica).

Commentary on the text:

1   oramai] oranai C (repetition)
1-2   plausible as eight-syllable lines, the two lines have seven syllables in PeFroI: oramai] hormai;
           ancora] anchor
3   the *residuum* begins here

Musical concordances (prints): • PeFroI (2*r*), «Io. Broc.»

TEXT FROM PeFroI:

Alma, svegliate ormai,
ancor cieca tu dormi.
    Alma, svegliate ormai

Pon mente come in breve
sen va 'sto tempo leve;
5   donque star non si deve
sopita come stai.
    Alma […]

O quanto è cosa dura
e non li poni cura,
che quel che li anni fura
10   non più ritorna mai.
    Alma […]

Convien che voglie mute
se brami tua salute,
e seguitar virtute,
che lieta alfin serai.
    Alma […]

15   'Sta fragiltade umana
segue sua voglia insana
e dal ciel se aluntana.
Misera, tu che fai?
    Alma svegl[iate] […]

Ogni piacer che è in terra
20   alfin retorna in guerra.
Sol virtù mai non erra,
e tu neglecta stai.
    Alma […]

MODERN EDITIONS OF THE TEXT: CESARI *ET AL*. 1954, p. 3★ (after PeFroI); LUISI 2005, p. 203 (after PeFroI, only the first two strophes); PAGANUZZI 1976, p. 112 (after PeFroI); SCHWARTZ 1935, p. xxvii (after PeFroI).

MODERN EDITIONS OF THE MUSIC: CESARI *ET AL*. 1954, p. 3 (after PeFroI); SCHWARTZ 1935, p. 1 (after PeFroI).

REMARKS: Perhaps PeFroI is the model for the piece in Panc.27: if one discounts that the Bassus is written in the print in the baritone clef, the musical version is completely identical in the two sources. But the metric form of the textual refrain occasions some doubt: PeFroI standardizes all its lines in seven syllables, creating a more orthodox poetic version of the ballata; Panc.27, instead, opts for a clear metrical contrast between the refrain and the stanza, achieving a musically more efficient result in the refrain in relation to the text.

BIBLIOGRAPHY: BOORMAN 2006, p. 958; EINSTEIN 1949, I, pp. 68, 91-92.

17.
ALMA, SVEGLIATE ORAMAI
fol. 16*v*

[Giovanni Brocco]

18.

Cucù, cucù, ognon canti cucù

fol. 16*v* (3 vv.)

PAMPHILUS

Cucù, cucù, ognon canti cucù.

Perpetual canon.

MODERN EDITIONS OF THE MUSIC: JEPPESEN 1969, pp. 300-302 (after Panc.27).[1]

REMARKS: The inscription «In triplici post sextam et sextam circulo quoque» appears at the end of the single voice of this perpetual canon. It explains the resolution and means 'In each circle/circuit in triplicate after a sixth [*brevis*] and a sixth [*brevis*]'. Both this canon and the only other one present in the manuscript (no. 34) are relegated to a blank space at the bottom of the page, and in both cases the page on which they appear contains all four voices of a secular Italian song.

BIBLIOGRAPHY: GALLICO 1996, p. 63.

---

[1]. Jeppesen's transcription begins on the first beat. This solution does not seem to fit the character of the composition or the metrical accentuation of the words.

18.
CUCÙ, CUCÙ, OGNON CANTI CUCÙ
fol. 16v

Pamphilus

In triplici post sextam et sextam circulo quoque

B[assus]

Cu -

Cu - cù, cu - cù, o - gnon can - - - ti cu - cù, cu -

Cu - cù, cu - cù, o -

- cù, cu - cù, o - gnon can - - - ti cu - cù, cu - cù, cu-cù, cu-cù, cu -

- cù, cu-cù, cu-cù, cu - cù, cu - cù, cu - cù, cu - cù, cu-cù, cu-cù,

- gnon can - - - ti cu - cù, cu - cù, cu-cù, cu-cù, cu - cù, cu-cù, cu-

- cù, cu - cù, cu - cù, cu - cù, cu - cù, cu-cù, cu-cù, cu-cù, cu-

cu-cù, cu-cù, cu - cù, cu - cù. Cu - cù, cu - cù, o - gnon can - - -

- cù, cu - cù, cu - cù, cu-cù, cu-cù, cu-cù, cu-cù, cu - cù, cu - cù.

- cù, cu - cù. Cu - cù, cu - cù, o - gnon can - - - ti cu - cù,

- ti cu - cù, cu - cù, cu-cù, cu-cù, cu - cù, cu - cù, cu - cù,

222

19.

Non expectò giamai con tal desio

fol. 17r (4 vv.)

[Antonio Tebaldi, called 'il Tebaldeo']

> Non expectò giamai con tal desio
> servo la libertà né nave porto,
> cum quanto expecto tuo ritorno io

First tercet of a capitolo ternario, the so-called *Epistola del Tebaldeo*, which became part of the poet's *Opere* as the 'Epistola prima' (no. 274). It was very successful, even as a separate text.

Commentary on the text:

1		expectò] aspetto B
2		porto] a porto C (initial version)
3		io] lacking in the T

Readings emended in the edition:

Bar	Voice	Original
incipit	B	the mensuration sign is that of *tempus imperfectum cum prolatione imperfecta*, without a stroke
4/I	B	*semibrevis* with fermata
8	C	*longa* with fermata
8/1	A	*semibrevis* with fermata
10/II	C, A	fermata on the *semiminima* instead of on the *minima*

Textual concordances (MSS): • *Bol.FM. 10* (54v-55v), «Tib.» • *Bol.U. 1242* (51v-52v), «Quedam puella ad amantem», (Antonio Tebaldeo) • *Bol.U. 2690* (65v-67v), «Una certa puta ad il suo amante. Capitolo iij» • *Bol.U. 3795* (89v-92v), «Capitulo tercio» • *Br.Q. 16* (26r) • *Br.Q. 23* (1r-2v), «Capitulo» • *CV.Ca.193* (219r-220r), «Epistola di Tebaldeo» • *CV.VL.5159* (234r-235r), «Epistola Tibaldei» • *CV.VL.5170* (50v-52r), «Epistola amice ad amicum» • *CV.VL.8191* (11v)[1] • *Fir.N. 54* (71r-72r), «Tibaldeus ferrariensis» • *Fir.N. M.376* (39r-40r) • *Fir.N. M.VII.117* (48v-49r) • *Fir.N. NA.701* (55v-56r) • *Fir.N. T.227* (9r), «Pistola del Tibaldeo» • *Mod.E. 81* (47v-49r), «Epistola del Tibaldeo» • *Mod.E. 809* (149r-151r), «Tib.» • *Mod.E. 809* (195r-198r), «Non expecto cum La Risposta» • *Mün.S. I265* (11v-13r), «Tibaldeo» • *Nap.N. 31* (104r-105v), «6° capitolo. Epistola de una giovane al amante suo» • *Paris.JA. 2075* (61v-62r) • *Paris.N. I.560* (31r-32r) • *Parma.P. Par.201* (181r-182r), «Epistula Tibaldei» • *Parma.P. Par.3072* (22v-23r), (Antonio Tebaldeo), «Puella ad amantem» • *Roma.N. S.413* (204v-205r), «Quedam puella ad amantem» • *Sev.C. 31* (29v-30v), «Antonius Thebaldeus» • *Ven.M. IZ.60* (177v-178v), «Antoni Tibaldei»

---

[1]. Only ll. 1-4, found on the verso of the final guard sheet (parchment) of the manuscript.

Textual concordances (prints):[2] • *Non1500a* ([1]r-[2]r) • *Non1500b* ([1]r-v) • *Non1520* (A1r-v) • *Non1524* (A1r-v) • *Non1528* (A1r-v) • *Non1540M* (A1r-v) • *Non1540R* (A1r-A2r) • *Non1568* (A1v) • *NonF* (A1v) • *NonT* (A1v) • *NonV1* (A1r-v) • *NonV2* (A1r-v) • *SepteDolori* (a3r), «Epistola del Tibaldeo» • *SetteDolori* (a3r-v), «La Epistola del Tibaldeo» • *TebEp1500Bes* ([1]v), «Epistola del Tibaldeo de Ferrara che finge che l'habia facta una donna e mandata a lui» • *TebEp1500Sil* ([1]v), «Epistola del Tibaldeo de ferrara che finge che l'habbia facta una donna e mandata a lui» • *TebEp1506* ([1]v), «Epistola del Tibaldeo de ferrara che finge che l'habbia facta una dona e mandata a lui» • *TebEp1509* ([1]v), «Epistola del Tibaldeo de Ferrara che finge che l'habia facta una donna e mandata a lui» • *TebEp1545* (A1r-v), «Epistola del Tibaldeo» • *TebEp1557* (A1v), «Tibaldeo» • *TebOp1498* (O4r-O5v), (Antonio Tebaldeo) • *TebOp1500* (23r-23v) • *TebSon1499* (75v-76v), (Antonio Tebaldeo)

Text from *CV. VL.5159*:

> Non aspectò giamai con tal disio
> servo la libertà, né nave porto,
> con quanto el tuo ritorno ho spetato io,
>
> sperando a tanti mal trovar conforto.
5   Passato è el tempo, e non ti vegio ancora:
> dovresti pur venir, se non sei morto.
>
> Aimè, crudel, chi te sforciava alora,
> quando scrivisti a me: 'Suporta, aspecta!
> Aspecta, ch'io vivo senza dimora!'?
>
10   Tu inganni una che è sciocca e simplicetta,
> una che troppo t'ama e troppo crede,
> una percossa da mortal saetta;
>
> non aspectava già simil mercede,
> non sol di me, ma ancor di te mi dole:
15   qual infamia è magior che romper fede?
>
> O quante volte, risguardando el sole,
> umilmente el pregai che 'l s'afretasse,
> spronando i soi corsier più che non suole,
>
> acciò più presto el tempo s'apresasse!
20   Il tempo da te scripto, il tempo tanto
> già disiato da mie voglie lasse.
>
> Tu sei disposto pur de avere el vanto
> de mia misera morte: abilo adonca!
> Io non ho più suspir', non ho più pianto.
>
25   Già la terza sorella el stame tronca,
> sento el vechio Caron gionto a la riva
> per tòrme dentro in la sua cava conca;

---

[2]. The *editio princeps* of the *Opere de M. Antonio Thebaldeo da Ferrara* is *TebOp1498*, edited by a cousin of the poet, Iacopo Tebaldi; numerous subsequent editions are based on it (see Basile - Marchand 1989-92, I, pp. 90-109: 40 different printings till the mid-sixteenth century, of which more than ten are incunables), attested primarily through two branches derived from *TebSon1499* and *TebOp1500*. *TebOp1498* was explicitly designed to prevent the loss of Tebaldeo's verses and to remove the numerous textual corruptions; the huge success enjoyed by the *Epistola*, available on the market already three years before the *Opere*, still continued to occasion the appearance of pamphlets of a few folios (two or four fols.), often without indication of the publisher, in which the anonymous text was accompanied by a handful of other poems, also by other authors. In most of the cases, Tebaldeo's *Epistola* opens the collection, providing the title for the whole booklet, a further sign of its clear popularity. I thank Marco Beghelli for the summary of the situation of the poetic prints.

ma bench'io resti di mia vita priva
per te, non però bramo alcun tuo danno,
30   ma sol che la tua gloria al mondo viva;

et che felice sia ogne tuo anno,
felice ogne tua impresa, e la fortuna
ognor te exalti in più sublimo scanno;

e benigne le stelle, el sol, la luna,
35   l'aqua, la terra, a te sia morte e lenta,
e la vichieza senza noglia alcuna;

et si fiamma amorosa ti tormenta
per altra donna, si converta in pace
e faza la tua vita al fin contenta.

40   A te el mio male, a me el tuo gaudio piace;
e se forse te offendo per amarte,
perdonami: el gli è forza, el me dispiace.

Io te ho scripto più versi a parte a parte;
ora la debil man mia non si move,
45   sì che da mi non aspectar più carte.

El primo mesagier che con mie nove
viva a ti serà el mio spirto tristo,
prima venirà a ti che vada altrove;

et possa, signor mio, ch'el t'arà visto,
50   tornarà lieto a la superna corte,
se per amar se fa del celo aquisto.

Et perché infamia te serìa morte,
non vo' si legi o che se intenda mai
che fusti causa de mia dura sorte;

55   però te prego, poi che letto arai
questa epistola mia, la doni al foco:
se brami l'onor tuo, so che 'l farai.

Et se per caso alcun tu giongi al loco
ove sarò sepulta in tetra fossa,
60   non mi negare almen — questo fia poco —:

'Requiescite in pace, o infelice ossa'.

MODERN EDITIONS OF THE TEXT: BASILE - MARCHAND 1989-92, II/1, pp. 425-429, II/2, pp. 283-285.

REMARKS: An alternative reading appears in one section (bb. 9-12, Cantus), but adds very little of musical substance to the base text. The *ductus* of the script is more rounded with respect to the preceding piece and to the next piece on the same page.

BIBLIOGRAPHY: BASILE 1983, p. 173; CATTIN 1986, p. 297; CERUTI BURGIO 1972, p. 50; VECCHI GALLI 1986a, pp. 16-17, 28.

19.
NON EXPECTÒ GIAMAI CON TAL DESIO
fol. 17r

[Antonio Tebaldi, called 'il Tebaldeo']

Cantus: Non ex - pec - tò gia-mai con tal de - si - o

ser - vo la li - ber - tà né na - ve por - to,

cum quan - to ex - pec - to tu - o ri - tor - no i - o

cum quan - to ex - pec - to tuo ri - tor - no i - o

Bassus: Non ex - pec - tò gia - mai

20.

QUI NOS FECIT EX NIHILO

fol. 17*r* (2 vv.)

> Qui nos fecit ex nihilo,
> Deo Patri et Filio.

Benedicamus Domino trope.

MUSICAL CONCORDANCES (MSS): • BurHu (23*r-v*) • ParmaP Par3597 (10*v*-11*r*) • PerA 431 (161*r*), 3 vv. (with an additional B) •VenM I145 (8*r*) • VenM I145 (103*r-v*),[1] score format

TEXT FROM BurHu:

> Qui nos fecit ex nichilo,
> Patri eius cum Filio
> Sancto simul Paraclito
> Benedicamus Domino.
> 5   Alleluia, alleluia,
>   alleluia, alleluia.

TEXT FROM PerA 431 and VenM I145 (103*r-v*):

> Qui nos fecit ex nichilo:
> Patri eiusque Filio,
> Sancto simul Paraclito.
> Benedicamus Domino.
>
> 5   Adest nobis festivitas
>   et preclara solemnitas;
>   iam sol refulsit claritas.
>   Deo dicamus gratias.

MODERN EDITIONS OF THE MUSIC: ANGLÈS 1931, III, p. 42 (after BurHu); BANKS 1993, II, p. 158 (after Panc.27); CATTIN 1985, p. 54 (after CMM 79, I, pp. 70-71), p. 56 (after PerA 431); CMM 79, I, pp. 70-71 (after BurHu); DIEDERICHS 1986, pp. 390 (after VenM I145, fol. 8*r*, and fol. 103*r-v*), 392 (after Panc.27 and PerA 431).

REMARKS: This is a very old piece, which appears polyphonically for the first time in the early fourteenth-century MS BurHu in the form of Stimmtausch (voice exchange), which economizes the compositional process through the use of two melodic modules alternated between the two voices. Even the more recent version in Panc.27 retains this characteristic: bars 9-16 repeat, with voices inverted, the first eight bars.[2] The piece was copied later on the remainder of the page, as demonstrated by the darker ink and by the more spiky *ductus* of the musical notation. A comparison of the readings of the concordances excludes direct contacts among the various versions.

BIBLIOGRAPHY: BANKS 1993, I, p. 286; CATTIN 1983a, pp. 36-37; CATTIN 1985; GALLO 1985; STROHM 1985, pp. 90, 95.

---

[1]. Ornamented version.

[2]. I thank Giulio Cattin for these suggestions.

20.
Qui nos fecit ex nihilo
fol. 17*r*

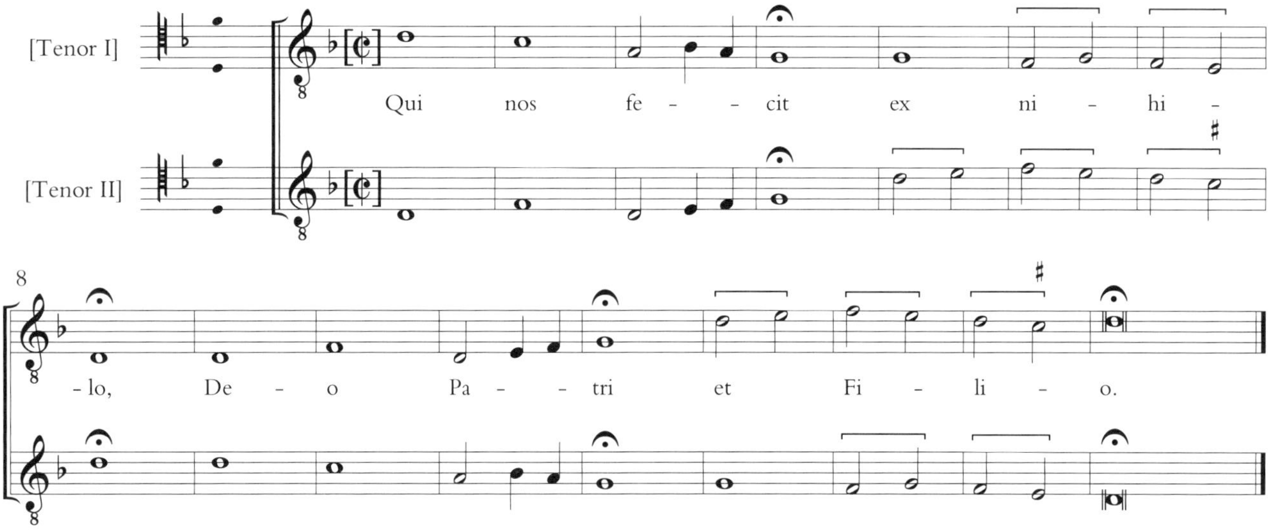

21.

Benedictus

fols. 17*v*-18*r* (4 vv.)

Isachina [= Henricus Isaac]

[Heading only]

Benedictus of the Ordinary of the Mass. Part of a parody mass (based on the rondeau cinquain *Quant j'ay au cueur* by Antoine Busnois), but also transmitted as a separate composition.

Readings emended in the edition:

Bar	Voice	Original
58	A	black notes

Musical concordances (mss):

(a) As a single movement section: • BasU 22 (30*v*-32*r*), 3 vv., «Isaac» • BerlS 40632 (19*v*-20*r*), 3 vv. • BolM 18 (63*v*-64*r*), «Absque verbis»[1] • CV G27 (50*v*-51*r*, *olim* 57*v*-58*r*), 3 vv., «Ysach» • FirN BR229 (9*v*-10*r*), textless, 3 vv., «Henricus yzac» • FirN M107bis (20*v*, *olim* 19*v*), 3 vv. • HeilbS 2 (no. 9), Ct only, «Isaac» • LonB A31922 (3*v*-4*r*), *B* (in a modern hand in the S: *Benedictus*), 3 vv. • MünS 272 (71*v*-72*r*) • MünU 718 (136*v*-137*r*), *Tenor Benedictus* • MünU 718 (150*v*), *Bassus Benedictus* • ParisN Rés27 (21*r*-22*r*) • ParisN Rés27 (55*r*-*v*), *Tenor e Contra de Benedictus* • ParisN Rés676 (77*v*-78*r*), 3 vv., «Isach», «Absque verbis»[2] • RegB 940-1 (no. 190), 3 vv., in the A partbook: «Cum tua quam cantare soles vox desyderetur, tempus id interea lepidus consume bibendo», and then «?» (associated with the rubric?) • SGS 462 (7*v*-8*r*), T: «Plytzgan», B: «Plitzgen» • TorN 27 (35*r*), 3 vv., «Isach» • UlmS 237 (S: 22*v*, T: 20*r*-*v*, B: 21*r*-*v*), 3 vv. • VerCap 757 (29*v*-30*r*), textless, modern hand: «Yzac Benedictus (a 3)» • WarN P364 (244-246), 3 vv. • WashC M6 (88*v*-89*r*), 3 vv. • WienN 18688 (86*v*-87*r*) • ZwR 78/3 (no. 9), textless, 3 vv., «Isaac» • ZwR 86/2 (no. 1)

(b) As part of a complete Mass: • BerlS 40021 (103*r*-112*r*: 110*v*-111*r*), 3 vv. • CV S35 (28*v*-37*v*: 34*v*-35*r*), 3 vv., «Ysach» • JenaU 31 (36*r*-50*r*: 47*v*-48*r*), 3 vv. • MilD 2 (144*v*-151*r*: 150*v*-151*r*), 3 vv., «Isac» • SegC (45*v*-54*r*: 52*v*-53*r*), «Ysaac» • UppsU 76e (22*r*-32*r*: 30*v*-31*r*), S only, «Henrici Izac» • WarU 5892 (49*r*-57*r*: 56*v*-57*r*), 3 vv., «Ysaac» • WienN 11883 (42*v*-51*r*: 50*v*-51*r*), lacking Agnus Dei, 3 vv.

Musical concordances (prints):

(a) As a single movement section: • AntCanzoni (43*r*), manuscript fragment: beginning of T only (bb. 1-9/I) • EgenLieder (III, no. 46), S only • FormTrium (no. 30), textless, but in the Jena copy only, added by hand: «H. Isac Benedictus qui venit», 3 vv. • MüllerHeckel (46-49) • PeOdh1501 (82*v*-83*r*), 3 vv., «Isac» • PeOdh1503 (82*v*-83*r*), 3 vv., «Izac» • PeOdh1504 (82*v*-83*r*), 3 vv.,[3] «Izac» • PeSpinI (4*r*-5*r*), *Benedictus de Isach*, (Francesco Spinacino) • PetreiusNewI (p3*r*-p4*v*) • WyssHeckel (46-49)

(b) As part of a complete Mass: • PeIsaac (no. 3), 3 vv., «Henricus Izac»

---

[1]. «Absque verbis» = 'without words'.

[2]. See n. 1.

[3]. The Washington copy of PeOdh1504 has a handwritten Altus voice underneath the Contra; it is not directly related to the version of Panc.27 because of numerous variants, including substantive ones. I thank Bonnie Blackburn for bringing this to my attention; a facsimile of the whole piece is included in the Appendix of Boorman - Beebe 2001.

MODERN EDITIONS OF THE MUSIC: BROWN 1983, II, pp. 18-20 (after FirN BR229); CMM 65/VII, pp. 43-83: 74-76 (after MilD 2); DISERTORI 1964, pp. 229-231 (after PeSpinI); DTÖ 28, p. 112 (after FirN BR229 and ZwR 78/3); EDM 77, pp. 56-84: 79-80 (after BerlS 40021); FANO 1962, pp. 38-73: 66-67 (after MilD 2); FERRARI 1994, pp. 2-3 (after ParisN Rés676); HEWITT 1942, pp. 379-380 (after PeOdh1504); MÖNKEMEYER 1985, I, p. 51 (after FormTrium); PLAMENAC 1928, pp. 44-45 (after SGS 462); SCHMIDT 1969, II, pp. 4-7 (after PeSpinI); SM 5, pp. 18-20 (after SGS 462); SM 6, pp. 28-29 (after BasU 22); STEVENS 1962, p. 1 (after LonB A31922).

REMARKS: Panc.27 is among the very few sources that transmit the composition for four voices (together with BolM 18, SegC, SGS 462, VerCap 757). One of the difficulties caused by the added Altus is, for example, the cadential passage at bars 19-20, where the presence of the f' prevents alteration of the f in the Tenor. From a strictly musical point of view, the version of Panc.27 cannot be linked with any of the concordances for four voices: in all four cases there are too many graphic and substantive variants. None of the concordances consulted has alternative passages in the Bassus: their presence in Panc.27 constitutes a unique attempt at ornamenting in three different ways a passage originally of four *longae* that descend by step (bb. 46-53). Thus, we are almost certainly faced with an experimental 'compositional' initiative of the scribe himself, who has profited from the space left on the staves to add these three variants at a later time.

BIBLIOGRAPHY: ATLAS 1975-76, I, pp. 126-127; BAKER 1978, I, pp. 293-294; BANKS 1993, I, p. 261; BOORMAN 2006, pp. 878-879; BOORMAN - BEEBE 2001, p. xiv; BROWN 1983, I, pp. 210-211; CHRISTOFFERSEN 1994, II, pp. 160-161; EDM 78, p. 331; HEWITT 1942, pp. 161-162; JUST 1975, II, pp. 95-96; LAMA DE LA CRUZ 1994, p. 178; PICKER 1991, pp. 27-28; PRIZER 1995, p. 184; STAEHLIN 1977, I, pp. 32-34, 20★-21★, III, pp. 76-81; WEISS 1998, pp. 27-28.

21.
BENEDICTUS
fols. 17v–18r

Isachina [= Henricus Isaac]

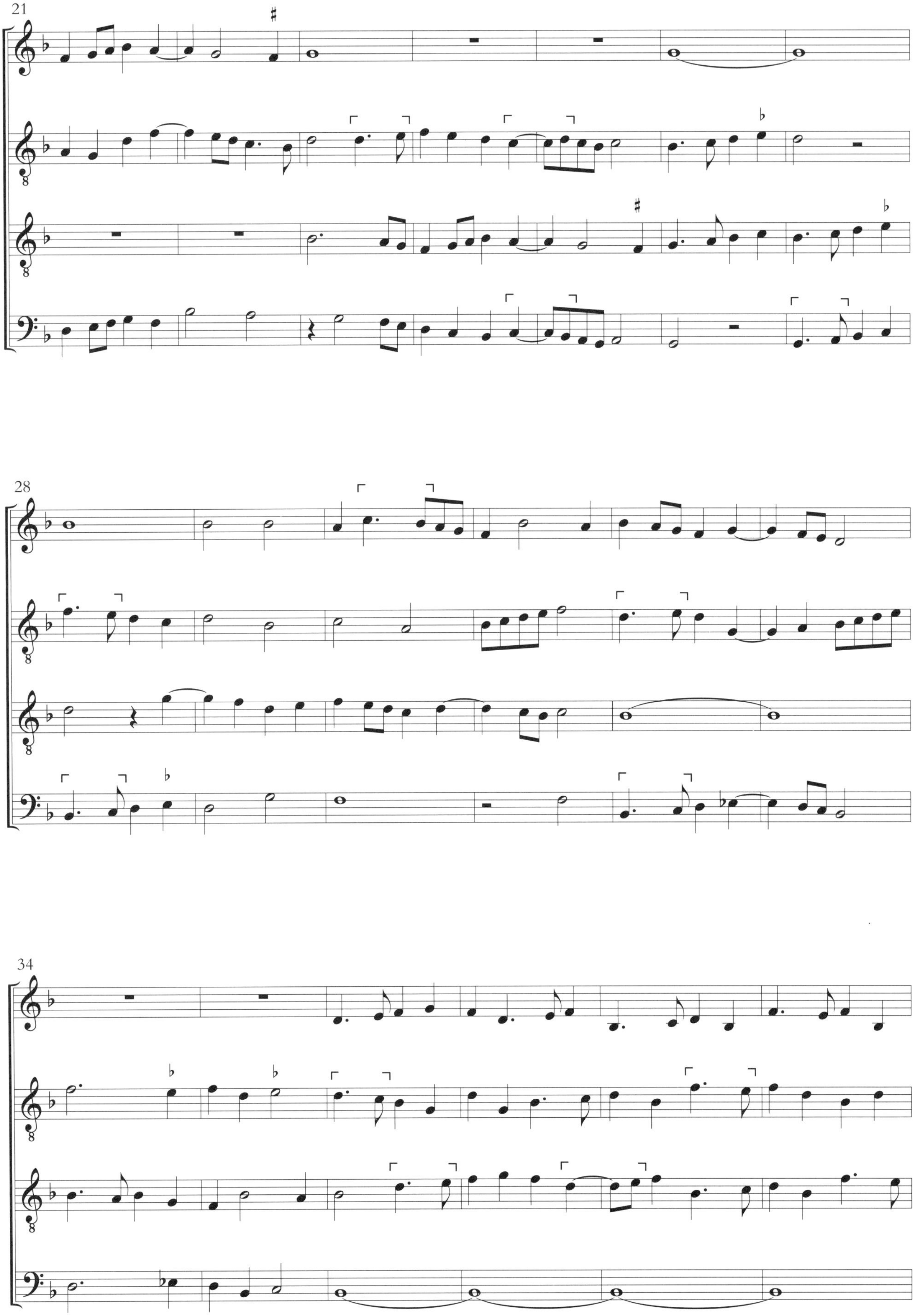
21
28
34

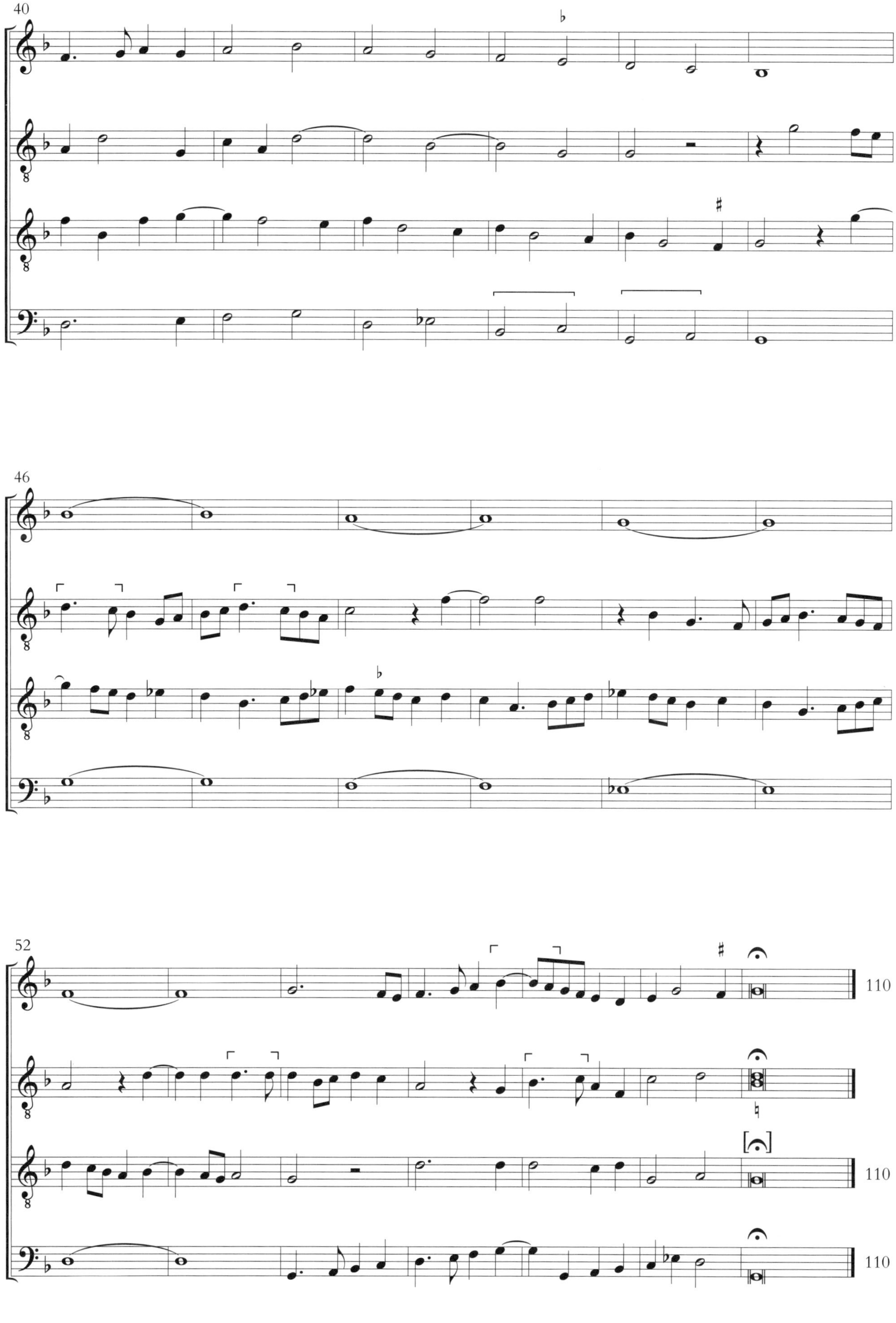
40
46
52
110
110
110

Three alternative readings of the Bassus (bb. 46–53)

22.

BENEDICAMUS DOMINO

fol. 18*v* (4 vv.)

Benedicamus Domino.

Concluding acclamation (to which the congregation responds «Deo gratias») used at the end of all the canonical hours (AM, pp. 1244-1249, 21 melodies; AR, pp. 447; AR, pp. 58★-62★, 15 melodies; BR, p. 109; LU, pp. 124-127, 12 melodies; LR, pp. 44-45, 2 melodies) and at the end of the Mass in place of the *Ita missa est* in Advent and Lent as well as for the Vigils, Ember Days, and Rogation Days (GR, pp. 11★, 18★, 31★, 35★, 41★, 47★, 55★, 57★, 59★; LU, pp. 22, 28, 40, 43, 48, 53, 60, 62, 63; MR, pp. 278, 279; PM, p. 83).

READINGS EMENDED IN THE EDITION:

BAR	VOICE	ORIGINAL
incipit	A	B flat signature

MODERN EDITIONS OF THE MUSIC: BANKS 1993, II, p. 46 (after Panc.27).

REMARKS: To accept the B flat in the Altus signature would mean that the whole piece is to be considered in the transposed Dorian mode. The Tenor, however, has no signature, and most of the Bs are in this part. Therefore it seems likely that the flat in the Altus is a mistake, and the piece is Mixolydian.

BIBLIOGRAPHY: BANKS 1993, I, p. 268; IGC, pp. 67-68; ROBERTSON 1988.

22.
BENEDICAMUS DOMINO
fol. 18*v*

23.

Benedicamus Domino

fol. 18*v* (3 vv.)

Benedicamus Domino.

For the text see no. 22.

Modern editions of the music: Banks 1993, II, p. 46 (after Panc.27).

Remarks: It seemed preferable to preserve the parallel fifths and octaves (Cantus-Contra, bb. 6/III-7; Cantus-Tenor, bb. 8/III-9), which were clearly intended by the composer. The chant in AM, p. 1248, AR, p. 61★, GR, p. 41★, LU, pp. 48 and 126 (*In Dominicis per annum*), and MR, p. 279 is paraphrased in the Tenor.

Bibliography: Banks 1993, I, p. 268; IGC, pp. 67-68; Robertson 1988.

23.
BENEDICAMUS DOMINO
fol. 18*v*

24.

Benedicamus Domino

fol. 18*v* (4 vv.)

Benedicamus Domino.

For the text see no. 22.

Readings emended in the edition:

Bar	Voice	Original
10/I	A	*g′ minima* and *f′ minima*

Modern editions of the music: Banks 1993, II, p. 48 (after Panc.27).

Remarks: It seemed preferable to preserve the various parallel fifths and octaves (Cantus-Bassus, bb. 4-5; Cantus-Bassus, bb. 6-7; Altus-Bassus, bb. 11-12; Cantus-Bassus, bb. 18-19; Tenor-Bassus, bb. 19-20). The melody of the Tenor in bars 14-10 (setting «Domino») corresponds to the third section of the chant in AR, p. 59★ (*Ad Laudes*) and LU, pp. 22 and 124 (*Ad Laudes*), and then to bars 14-20 of the Cantus of *Benedicamus Domino* no. 25. See also no. 25.

Bibliography: Banks 1993, I, p. 269; IGC, pp. 67-68; Robertson 1988.

24.
BENEDICAMUS DOMINO
fol. 18*v*

25.

Benedicamus Domino

fol. 19*r* (3 vv.)

Benedicamus Domino.

For the text see no. 22.

Modern editions of the music: Banks 1993, II, p. 47 (after Panc.27).

Remarks: It seemed preferable to preserve the parallel octaves (Cantus-Bassus, bb. 12-13), and the sometimes unorthodox counterpoint. The chant in AR, pp. 59★, GR, p. 11★, LR, p. 44, LU, p. 22 and of p. 124 (*Ad Laudes*) is taken over almost identically in the Cantus. The presence of the ritornello sign at the end of the Benedicamus section (b. 13) respects the 'tripartite' structure AAB of the chant, which repeats the first section. The melody of the Cantus in bars 14-20 (setting «Domino») corresponds exactly to bars 14-20 of the Tenor of *Benedicamus Domino* no. 24. The ink of the rubric «Iustus» is lighter than that of the piece.

Bibliography: Banks 1993, I, p. 268; IGC, pp. 67-68; Robertson 1988.

25.
BENEDICAMUS DOMINO
fol. 19*r*

Iustus

26.

BENEDICAMUS DOMINO

fol. 19r (3 vv.)

Benedicamus Domino.

For the text see no. 22.

MUSICAL CONCORDANCES (MSS): • CTL G12 (57r, *olim* 56r)

MODERN EDITIONS OF THE MUSIC: BANKS 1993, II, p. 47 (after Panc.27); CATTIN 1972a, p. 533 (after CTL G12).

REMARKS: The original reading of the Bassus in bar 9 has been preserved though it causes brief vertical clashes with the Cantus; each line has its own melodic logic. The counterpoint is acceptable if the piece is considered as two *bicinia*: Cantus-Tenor and Tenor-Bassus. The sole concordance is CTL G12; the two versions differ only in slight graphic variants, but the lower voice of CTL G12 ends with a different note (*d* with fermata instead of *a*). The beginning of the chant in GR, p. 18* and LU, p. 28 is paraphrased in the Cantus.

BIBLIOGRAPHY: BANKS 1993, I, p. 269; CATTIN 1972a, pp. 487-488; CATTIN 1973a, p. 197; IGC, pp. 67-68; ROBERTSON 1988.

26.
BENEDICAMUS DOMINO
fol. 19*r*

27.

POI CHE SEI DAL MONDO TOLTA

fol. 19v (4 vv.)

[LEONARDO GIUSTINIAN]   BEN

Poi che sei dal mondo tolta,
cerca Iesù Cristo, sposo
dolce, bello et amoroso
et in lui tuta ti volta.

5   Cerca Iesù tuo amatore:
nel presepio el vederai,
e tu 'n lui consolarai
l'alma tua e 'l tristo core.

Vederai el tuo Signore
10   quanto è mansueto e bello,
prenderai quel bel zoiello
nelle brace del bon core.

Vederai quel enfinito
et immenso e dolce amore;
15   vederai el candido fiore
la madre de Dio fiorito.

Trouveral acompagnato
cum Ioseph vechiarello,
vederai quel dolce agnello
20   che per noi fo passionato.

Però fa' che 'l to piacere,
alma, sia de lui pensare,
e da lui non te lasare,
mettiti cum lui a galdere.

25   Pensa che [in] 'sto mondo vano
ogni cosa è transitoria,
no tegnir ne la memoria
'sto terren amor mundano.

Pensa de Iesù ch'è summo,
30   dillectoso amor perfecto;
pensa te che 'l van dilecto
de 'sto mundo è tuto fumo.

[…]

Sapi che, chi vo' 'l seguire,
Iesù a tuti dà sua gloria;
75 pregam ‹che› tuti cum victoria
nui possiamo a lui salire.

Amen.

Lauda (oda).

COMMENTARY ON THE TEXT:

8	the original version «coro» is corrected to «core» to match the rhyme
17	the *residuum* begins here
18	hypometric
25	the logical addition is taken from the concordances
after 32	lines 33-72, present in concordances, are lacking
75	hypermetric

READINGS EMENDED IN THE EDITION:

BAR	VOICE	ORIGINAL
1/II	A	*f' e'*
5/I	B	flat before *F*

TEXTUAL CONCORDANCES (MSS): • *Berl.S. H.348* (136*v*-137*r*), (Leonardo Giustinian) • *Bol.U. 4019* (71*v*-72*r*) • *Roma.Ang. 1482* (117*r*-118*r*) • *Ven.GR. 120* (62*r*-63*v*), (Leonardo Giustinian) • *Ven. GR. 121* (76-78), (Leonardo Giustinian) • *Ven.M. I.182* (180*r*-*v*), «di messer lonardo» • *Ven.M. I.182* (264*r*-*v*), «di messer Lonardo»

TEXTUAL CONCORDANCES (PRINTS): • *Fior1505* (m4*r*-m5*v*) • *Giust1474* (D2*v*-D4*v*), (Leonardo Giustinian) • *Giust1475* (i5*v*-i7*r*), (Leonardo Giustinian) • *Giust1483* (g6*r*-*v*), (Leonardo Giustinian) • *Giust1490* (b8*v*-c1*v*), (Leonardo Giustinian) • *Giust1495* (a8*r*), (Leonardo Giustinian) • *Giust1506* (d7*v*-e1*r*), (Leonardo Giustinian) • *Giust1517* (d8*v*-e2*v*), (Leonardo Giustinian)

TEXT FROM *Giust1474*:

Poi che sei dal mondo tolta,
cerca Iesù Cristo, sposo
dolce, bello e amoroso
e in lui tuta te volta.

5 Cerca Iesù tuo amatore:
nel presepio el vederai,
e con lui consolarai
l'alma tua e 'l tristo core.

Vederai el tuo Signore
10 quanto è mansueto e bello,
prenderai quel bel zoiello
nelle braze del bon core.

Vederai quel infinito
et immenso e dolce amore;
15 vederai el candido fiore,
la madre de Dio fiorito.

Troverai 'l acompagnato
con Ioseph vechiarelo,
vederai quel dolce agnello
20 che per nui fo passionato.

Però fa' che 'l tuo piacere,
alma, sia de lui pensare,
e da lui non te lassare,
metite con lui a galdere.

25 Pensa ch'a 'sto mondo vano
ogni cossa è transitoria,
non tegnir ne la memoria
'sto teren amor mondano.

Pensa de Iesù ch'è sumo,
30 diletoso amor perfeto;
pensa te che 'l van dileto
de 'sto mondo è tuto fumo.

Guarda, alma, quanto è fello!
Questo mondo è tuto vano,
35 transitorio e pien d'afano,
e vitioso tuto quelo.

Deh, contempla un poco in Dio
e pensa de quella gloria
ne la qual, con gran victoria,
40 i anzoli canta cum dixio.

I anzoli canta tuti 'osanna';
alma, pensa che dolceza
è veder tanta beleza,
Iesù dolce, vera mana.

45 Donque, in 'sto mondo falace,
che se fa e che se sente?
Sol afani e grave stente
senza mai requie né pace.

Però, poi che tu sei tolta
50 de 'sto mondo e data a Dio,
fa che in lui sia el tuo dexio
e dal mondo tuta morta.

Non cognoscer più parenti,
siegui Iesù vero amore,
55 tuta piena de calore
vivi in lui senza spaventi.

Guarda quanto Iesù bello
è cortexe, tutto umile
verso ogni peccator vile,
60   mansueto come agnello.

Nella croce col suo sangue
el ne volse ricomprare,
per doverne liberare
e trarne tuti de l'angue.

65   Però ti vo confortare
ch'al ben far tu non si' stanca,
che in Iesù piatà non manca,
chi la vuol in lui trovare.

Donca poi che fuor del seculo
70   sei usita e data a Dio,
refudato el mondo rio,
stare tu pòi senza pericolo.

Sapi che, chi vuo' 'l seguire,
Iesù a tuti el dà suo gloria;
75   pregamo che con victoria
nui possiamo a lui salire.

MODERN EDITIONS OF THE TEXT: LUISI 1983, I, pp. 283-284 (after *Ven. GR. 120*).

MODERN EDITIONS OF THE MUSIC: LUISI 1983, II, p. 113 (after Panc.27).

REMARKS: A lauda text by an author widely diffused in poetic sources, but a musical *unicum* of respectable workmanship. The first four quatrains of the text are each underlaid in a single voice (Superius: ll. 1-4; Tenor: ll. 5-8; Altus: ll. 9-12; Bassus: ll. 13-16); the last quatrain written in the *residuum* (ll. 73-76) has been added in the margin of the folio, perhaps indicating a lengthy performance *ad libitum*, comprising the parts of the text not present in Panc.27.

BIBLIOGRAPHY: LUISI 1983, I, p. 550.

27.
POI CHE SEI DAL MONDO TOLTA
fol. 19v

[Leonardo Giustinian]   Ben

S[uperius]

Poi che sei dal mon - do tol - ta, cer - ca Ie - sù Cri - sto,
Cer - ca Ie - sù tuo a - ma - to - re: nel pre - se - pio el ve - de -
Ve - de - rai el tuo Si - gno - re quan - to è man - su - e - to e
Ve - de - rai quel en - fi - ni - to et im - men - so e dol - ce a-

A[ltus]

Poi che sei dal mon - do tol - ta, cer - ca Ie - sù Cri - sto,
Cer - ca Ie - sù tuo a - ma - to - re: nel pre - se - pio el ve - de -
Ve - de - rai el tuo Si - gno - re quan - to è man - su - e - to e
Ve - de - rai quel en - fi - ni - to et im - men - so e dol - ce a-

T[enor]

Poi che sei dal mon - do tol - ta, cer - ca Ie - sù Cri - sto,
Cer - ca Ie - sù tuo a - ma - to - re: nel pre - se - pio el ve - de -
Ve - de - rai el tuo Si - gno - re quan - to è man - su - e - to e
Ve - de - rai quel en - fi - ni - to et im - men - so e dol - ce a-

B[assus]

Poi che sei dal mon - do tol - ta, cer - ca Ie - sù Cri - sto,
Cer - ca Ie - sù tuo a - ma - to - re: nel pre - se - pio el ve - de -
Ve - de - rai el tuo Si - gno - re quan - to è man - su - e - to e
Ve - de - rai quel en - fi - ni - to et im - men - so e dol - ce a-

spo - so dol - ce, bel - lo et a - mo - ro - so et in lui tu - ta ti vol - ta.
-ra - i, e tu 'n lui con - so - la - ra - i l'al - ma tua e 'l tri - sto co - re.
bel - lo, pren - de - rai quel bel zo - iel - lo nel - le bra - ce del bon co - re.
-mo - re; ve - de - rai el can - di - do fio - re la ma - dre de Dio fio - ri - to.

spo - so dol - ce, bel - lo et a - mo - ro - so et in lui tu - ta ti vol - ta.
-ra - i, e tu 'n lui con - so - la - ra - i l'al - ma tua e 'l tri - sto co - re.
bel - lo, pren - de - rai quel bel zo - iel - lo nel - le bra - ce del bon co - re.
-mo - re; ve - de - rai el can - di - do fio - re la ma - dre de Dio fio - ri - to.

spo - so dol - ce, bel - lo et a - mo - ro - so et in lui tu - ta ti vol - ta.
-ra - i, e tu 'n lui con - so - la - ra - i l'al - ma tua e 'l tri - sto co - re.
bel - lo, pren - de - rai quel bel zo - iel - lo nel - le bra - ce del bon co - re.
-mo - re; ve - de - rai el can - di - do fio - re la ma - dre de Dio fio - ri - to.

spo - so dol - ce, bel - lo et a - mo - ro - so et in lui tu - ta ti vol - ta.
-ra - i, e tu 'n lui con - so - la - ra - i l'al - ma tua e 'l tri - sto co - re.
bel - lo, pren - de - rai quel bel zo - iel - lo nel - le bra - ce del bon co - re.
-mo - re; ve - de - rai el can - di - do fio - re la ma - dre de Dio fio - ri - to.

28.

Ave Maria, gratia [plena]

fol. 19*v* (2 vv.)

Ave Maria, gratia [plena]

For the text see no. 2.

Readings emended in the edition:

Bar	Voice	Original
16	T	there is a very faint *c* under the *c′* that has been erased, probably because it was considered a mistake

Modern editions of the music: Banks 1993, II, p. 28 (after Panc.27).

Remarks: The piece has been entered in darker ink on a blank portion of the page. The change of tactus after the line through the stave after bar 7 is hypothetical, but would seem plausible in relation to the cadential structure.

Bibliography: Banks 1993, I, p. 266; CAO III, pp. 5, 64; CAO IV, pp. 40, 42, 476; CS, pp. 424–425, 428–429; Freeman 1991, pp. 202 and 205; IGC, p. 55.

28.
AVE MARIA, GRATIA [PLENA]
fol. 19v

Cantus: A – ve Ma – ri – a

Tenor: A – ve Ma – ri – a, gra – ti – a

29.

Cum desiderio vo cercando

fol. 20r (4 vv.)

[Bianco da Siena]

Cum desiderio vo cercando
de trovar quello amoroso
Iesù Cristo dilectoso
per cui amor vo suspirando.

Lauda (ripresa only) (barzelletta). See also no. 114.

Commentary on the text:

1   hypermetric

Readings emended in the edition:

Bar	Voice	Original
29/II-III	T	*c′ b a* instead of *e′ d′ c′*

Textual concordances (mss): • *Berg.C. 1* (91v–92r), (Jacopone da Todi) • *Berl.S.H.348* (21r–v), (Jacopone da Todi) • *Bol.U. 4019* (124r–v) • *Borg.P. M.76725* (134v–135r) • *CV. BL.4047* (121v–122r) • *CV. Ch.120* (20v–21r, olim 170v–171r), «De Jacopone» • *CV. Ch.266* (34v–35r), «biancho iniesuato» • *CV.P.113* (118v–119r) • *CV.Ro.651* (160v–161r), (Bianco da Siena) • *CV.VL.13026* (6v–7r) • *Fer.C. 211* (119v–122v) • *Fir.L. Ash.480* (48r–49v) • *Fir.L. Ash.1402* (141v–142r) • *Fir.N. 12* (66r–68r) • *Fir.N. 58* (28r–v) • *Fir.N. 140* (29v–30v) • *Fir.N. 700* (26v–28r) • *Fir.N. LF.302* (18r–20r) • *Fir.N. M.27* (65r–67v), (Jacopone da Todi) • *Fir.N. M.30* (13v–15r) • *Fir.N. P.13* (247v–248v) • *Fir.R. 1119* (203r–204v) • *Fir.R. 1413* (253v–254v) • *Fir.R. 1502* (33r–34r) • *Fir.R. 1666* (14r–v) • *Fir.R. 2895* (49r–50v) • *Fir.R. 2929* (85v–87r, olim 84v–86r) • *Fir.R. 3112* (177v–179r, olim 171v–173r) • *Mil.A. 3* (111v–112r) • *Mil.T. 92* ([212]r–v) • *Mil.T. 913* (63r–64v) • *Nap.N. 38* (93r–94v) • *Pad. Civ. 4* (22v–23r) • *Paris.N. I.559* (104r–v), (Jacopone da Todi) • *Pav.U.A.474* (106v) • *Piac.C. L.15* (15v–17r, olim 10v–12r) • *Rav.C. 177* (77v–79r) • *Roma.Co. 27* (154r–v) • *Roma.N.V.24* (142v–143r) • *Siena.C. 13* (34v–35v), *Considerando io vo cercando*; at the end of the lauda the incipit of the ripresa is given in the correct form: *Con desiderio vo cercando* • *Spithöver* (no. 156), (Jacopone da Todi) • *Tessier* (84r) • *Ven.C. C.128* (61r–63r) • *Ven.GR. 120* (80v–82r), (Leonardo Giustinian) • *Ven.M. I.61* (82v–83r) • *Ven.M. I.77* (43v–44v) • *Ven.M. I.79* (9r–10r) • *Ven.M. I.80* (38v–40r) • *Ven.M. I.153* (112v–114r), in a later hand «Jacopone da Todi» • *Ven.M. I.182* (112v–113r), «di messer Lonardo», «pre beltrame» • *Ven.M. I.313* (25v–28r) • *Ven.M. I.324* (133v–134v) • *Ven.M. I.324* (140v–141r) • *Ver.Cap. 737* (40v–42r) • *Ver.Civ. 1212* (266–267), (Jacopone da Todi) • *Vic.C. 111* (98r–99r)

Textual concordances (prints): • *Compendio1483* (106r–107r) • *Fior1505* (c6v–c7v) • *Giust1474* (M2v–M3v), (Leonardo Giustinian) • *Giust1475* (b2r–b3r), (Leonardo Giustinian) • *Giust1483* (f2r–v), (Leonardo Giustinian) • *Giust1490* (g5v–g6v), (Leonardo Giustinian) • *Giust1495* (d2v–d3r), (Leonardo Giustinian) • *Giust1506* (p1r–p2v), (Leonardo Giustinian) • *Giust1517* (n8r–o1v), (Leonardo Giustinian) • *JacopBen* (✠[6v]), «De andare con disiderio cercando il divino amore Est Justiniani» • *LaudeBonar* (8r–v), *Con desio vo cercando*, «del Bianco Giesuatto» • *LaudeGiacc* (7v) • *LaudeMisc* (61v–62r) • *LaudeVecchie* (g5r–v) • *OperaNova* (53r–v)

252

TEXT FROM *Giust1474*:

Cum desiderio vo cercando
de trovare quello amoroso
Iesù Cristo dilectoso
per cui amore vo suspirando.

5   Suspirando per amore
vo circando il mio dilecto;
possa non trovare il mio core,
tanto è per amor constrecto.
Con desiderio puro aspecto
10   di trovare da lui mercede;
dato gli ho il core e la fede,
sempre a lui m'aricomando.

Ricomàndogli il cor mio,
poiché d'amore l'hai infiamato,
15   prego lui che il mio desio
no gli sia domenticato.
Quanto i' l'ho desiderato
non lo dico in questo canto,
ma più volte, con gran pianto,
20   per amore il vo chiamando.

Chiamo la speranza mia
senza la quale non trovo posa,
suspirando nocte e dia
d'amor sempre sto pensosa.
25   Non trovo nulla altra cosa
chi conforti la mia mente,
se l'amore non gli consente
d'avere quello ch'io adimando.

Adimando di vedere
30   la sua splendente facia,
e di poterlo tenere
solo un poco ne le bracia.
Tuto pare chi me disfacia
per desiderio amoroso.
35   Non posso tenere nascoso
quello che io sento desiando.

Quello che l'anima e il cor sente
non lo posso più cellare,
però lo dico a tuta zente
40   perché non posso altro fare.
L'amor mi fa lamentare
de inamorato lamento,
per zoglie e pena ch'io sento
canto e piango, sospirando.

45   Suspirando il core s'acende
a più ardente desio,
l'anima e l'affecto ascende
a la mente del cor mio.
Tanto amore mi struge

50 che più non sazo che me dire,
    se non che io penso morire
    si non ho quello ch'io domando.

    Se non ho quello che l'amore
    m'ha promesso per certanza;
55 altro non voria il mio core,
    se non morire in desianza,
    tanto son visso a speranza;
    altro nol sa che l'amore
    per lo quale a tute l'ore
60 me lamento consumando.

    Consumanto per amore
    chiamo che 'l venga la morte,
    zorno e nocte a tute l'ore
    prego che m'apra le porte,
65 poi ch'io son zonto a tal porto
    che non posso trovar loco:
    ardami d'amore il foco
    e sarà pagato el bando.

MODERN EDITIONS OF THE TEXT: BINI 1851, pp. 179-180 (after *CV. Ro.651*); GALLETTI 1863, p. 128 (after *LaudeMisc*); JEPPESEN 1935, p. XVI (after GALLETTI 1863); LONGO 1986, p. 398 (after *Borg.P. M.76725*); LUISI 1983, I, pp. 292-293 (after *Ven.GR. 120*); MAZZA 1960, p. 167 (after *Berg.C. 15*).

MODERN EDITIONS OF THE MUSIC: DIEDERICHS 1986, pp. 300-301 (after Panc.27); JEPPESEN 1969, pp. 41-42 (after Panc.27); LUISI 1983, II, pp. 30-31 (after Panc.27).

REMARKS: The piece has parallel octaves in two places between the Cantus and Bassus (bb. 9-10 and b. 25), clearly intended by the composer. The missing rest in the Cantus (b. 5/I) and the error in the Tenor passage (b. 29) are typical mistakes due to inattention in copying from a model that has not come down to us. The rubric «Iustus», written with the same type of ink as the piece, serves to reinforce the hypothesis that the scribe was referring to a model.

BIBLIOGRAPHY: D'ANCONA (1878) 1906, p. 479; FALLOWS 1999, p. 508; FEIST 1889, p. 131; FRATI 1917, pp. 476, 478; GHISI 1953a, pp. 52-56, 69; LONGO 1986, p. 221; LUISI 1983, I, p. 544; SCARDIN 1939, p. 90; TENNERONI 1909, p. 85; WILSON 1992, p. 172.

29.
CUM DESIDERIO VO CERCANDO
fol. 20*r*

[Bianco da Siena]

Cantus
Altus
Tenor
Bassus

Cum de - si - de - - - rio vo cer -

- can - - - - - - - do de tro - var quel - lo a -

- mo - - ro - - - so Ie - sù Cri - sto di - lec -

-to - - - - -so   per   cui a - mor   vo

su - - - -spi - ran - - - - -do.   *Iustus*

30.

Chi serve a Dio cum purità di cor[e]

fol. 20*v* (3 vv.)

[Feo Belcari]

Chi serve a Dio cum purità di cor[e]
vive contento e po' salvato more.

Cum quanti affani[1]

The lauda in the form of a barzelletta *Chi serve a Dio con purità di core*, commonly attributed to Feo Belcari, is attested both as a self-standing text, in anthologies of laude, and as an insertion in the *Rappresentazione di Abramo e Isacco*, also attributed to Belcari, as a song of praise sung by various people almost at the end of the play (see Newbigin 1981).[2]

Commentary on the text:

1   serve] servae C

Readings emended in the edition:

Bar	Voice	Original
7/II	T	*a semibrevis* instead of *g semibrevis*
8/I	C	*d' semibrevis* instead of *minima*

Textual concordances (mss):

(a) as an isolated lauda: • *CV. BL. 3679* (21*r*)[3] • *CV. BL. 3711* (38-39)[4] • *CV. Ch. 266* (50*r*) • *CV. Ro. 424* (136*r*) • *CV. VL. 7714* (116*r-v*) • *Fir. L. Ash. 480* (38*v*) • *Fir. M. 262* (29*v*-30*r*) • *Fir. N. 4* (3*r*) • *Fir. N. 35* (165*r-v*) • *Fir. N. 140* (33*v*) • *Fir. N. LF. 236* (2*v*) • *Fir. N. M. 27* (156*v*) • *Fir. N. M. 690* (75*v*-76*r*),

---

[1]. This section of text does not appear in any of the known concordances. It is possibly a comment by the scribe himself, who may have judged the extreme difficulty of the proposition illustrated in the text. In fact, «Cum quanti affani» is not written under the music, but instead occupies a clearly separate space that does not even suggest a normal *residuum*. Francesco Luisi, on the other hand, thinks that it is a reference to a secular text to be sung to the same melody, of which, however, no trace is to be found in the frottola repertory (see Luisi 1983, II, p. cxxvi).

[2]. This was one of the most successful *sacre rappresentazioni* in Tuscany, which explains the large number of attestations, both in manuscript and especially in print, resulting from the wide distribution of devotional works of limited typographical value. According to an annotation in the MSS *CV. Ro. 1002* (fol. 14*v*), *Fir. N. M. 367* (fol. 16*r*), and *Fir. N. CS. 488* (fol. 35*v*), the play was performed for the first time in 1449 in Florence in the church of Santa Maria Maddalena, in the place called «Cestelli», but its success continued for several decades and even outside the Tuscan orbit, as demonstrated, for example, by the report of a performance in the piazza of the Parma Duomo on Easter Day 1481 (see *Diario parmense ab anno* MCCCCLXVII *ad* MCCCCLXXXII *auctore anonimo nunc primum editum ex manuscripto codice Torelliano*, in *Rerum italicarum scriptores ab anno aere christianae quingentesimo ad millesimum quingentesimum ex insignium bibliothecarum codicibus*, edited by Ludovico Antonio Muratori, XXII, Milan, Tipografia della Società Palatina, 1733, cols. 243-398: 370).

[3]. The lauda is anonymous and lacks the beginning; only ll. 8-20 remain. The preceding poem carries the number 18, and breaks off at l. 23; the one that now follows is no. 21. In the poem no. 18 the loss of folios is noted, which obviously comprised the beginning of *Chi serve a Dio con purità di core*, which would be no. 20.

[4]. Rabboni 1991, p. 128 says «Lauda lacking the beginning; it begins with the line *da quella luce del sommo sprendore* [*sic*]», but instead the lauda is complete. With regard to the edition published here, however, the position of the second and third strophes is reversed.

(Feo Belcari) • *Fir.N. P.172* (5r–v) • *Fir.R. 1473* (75r–v) • *Fir.R. 1501* (27v–28r) • *Fir.R. 1502* (34r–v) • *Fir.R. 2894* (9r) • *Fir.R. 2896* (27v–28r) • *Fir.R. 2929* (206v–207r, olim 205v–206r) • *Fir.R. 3112* (84r, olim 76r) • *Rav.C. 464* (39v–40r), «Vestigium Cristi»[5] • *Rim.C. 38* (123r–v), «Di Feo Belcari» • *Roma.Ang. 2274* (40v–41r) • *Roma.Ang. 2275* (34v–35r, olim 41v–42r) • *Roma.Co. 33* (6r–v) • *Siena.C. 17* (2v–3r) • *Siena.C. 17* (49v–50r) • *Siena.C. 41* (19r–v) • *Ven.M. I.77* (67v) • *Ven.M. I.78* (12r–v), «Di Feo Belchari» • *Ven.M. I.79* (31v–32r) • *Ver.Cap. 737* (40r–v)

(b) as part of the *Rappresentazione di Abramo e Isacco*: • *CV.BL.4047* (108v–112v)[6] • *CV.Ch.266* (59r–62v: 62r–v),[7] «Feo Belchari» • *CV.Ro.1002* (4r–14v: 14r–v) • *Fir.L. Ash.539* (123r–127r: 127r), «per feo belchari cittadino fiorentino» • *Fir.L. Ash.567* (21r–24v, olim 23r–26v: 24r–v, olim 26r–v) • *Fir.L. R.121* (55r–68r: 67r–v), «Feo belcari» • *Fir.L. S.17* (2r–12v: 12r) • *Fir.N. 12* (46r–65v: 65v) • *Fir.N. CS.488* (25r–35v: 35r) • *Fir.N. LF.249* (1r–15v: 13v–14r) • *Fir.N. M.85* (165r–171v)[8] • *Fir.N. M.367* (1r–16r: 15r–v), «Feo Belchari» • *Fir.N. M.690* (105v–119r: 118v–119r), «Feo Belchari» • *Fir.N. M.744* (1v–16r: 15r–v) • *Fir.N. M.1114* (1r–13r: 12v–13r)[9] • *Fir.N. M.1163* (58v–71r: 70r–v), «feo belchari» • *Fir.N. P.219* (55r–66r: 65v–66r) • *Fir.N. P.445* (15r–26v: 26v) • *Fir.R. 1094* (150r–153v),[10] «Feo belchari» • *Fir.R. 1720* (49r–61v: 61v), «Feo belchari» • *Fir.R. 1721* (42r–57r: 56r–v) • *Fir.R. 2816* (178r–188v)[11] • *Fir.R. 2893* (14v–27v: 26r–27r) • *Fir.R. 2971* (14v–22v: 22r) • *Mil.A. 35* (187r–195v: 195r–v), «Feo Belchari» • *Mod.E. 1277* (15r–21v),[12] «Feo Belchari» • *Roma.Ang. 2275* (67r–80v, olim 74r–87v: 80r, olim 87r),[13] «feo belchari» • *Roma.Co. 3* (167–195: 193–194), «Feo Belchari» • *Roma.N. VE.483* (76v–85r: 85r) • *Siena.C.VIII.37* (150r–160v: 159v–160r)

Textual concordances (prints):

(a) as an isolated lauda: • *BelcLBart* (b2v–b3r), «Di Feo Belcari», «Come el servire a dio dilecta l'anima» • *BelcLBen* (b2v–b3r), «Di Feo Belcari», «Come el servire a dio dilecta l'anima» • *Fior1505* (d4r–v) • *LaudeBonac* (12r–v), «Di Feo Belcari» • *LaudeBonar* (9v), «Del Beato Giovanni Giesuato» • *LaudeMisc* (5r), «Di Feo Belcari» • *LaudeSper* (9r–v), «Di Feo Belcari» • *LaudeVecchie* (a4v), «Di Feo Belchari» • *LaudiRiccardiana* (e8v), «Feo Belchari» • *OperaNova* (4v), «Di Feo Belchari» • *VitaSB* (3v–4r), «Lauda di Feo Belchari»

(b) as part of the *Rappresentazione di Abramo e Isacco*:[14] • *BelcR1485* (10r–v), «composta per feo belchari»

---

[5]. There may remain a trace of an attribution in the sign «εr !» placed in the left margin of fol. 39v.

[6]. *Chi serve a Dio con purità di core* is lacking.

[7]. With additions (to the *Rappresentazione*) on fol. 109r.

[8]. The play breaks off at the line «che cel dicessi prima che a madonna»: the last folio has in fact got lost; it should have followed fol. 171v and contained *Chi serve a Dio con purità di core*.

[9]. Owing to a loss of folios, the play lacks the beginning: it starts with l. 89, «state su, servi miei fedeli e saggi» (14th octave). Although anonymous, it is nevertheless placed close to many other pieces by Belcari, and it cannot be excluded that the beginning mentioned the name of the poet.

[10]. The last two folios of the manuscript are lacking, which should have carried *Chi serve a Dio con purità di core*.

[11]. The manuscript is mutilated at the end, and thus of necessity lacks *Chi serve a Dio con purità di core*.

[12]. The text of the play occupies the last seven folios of the second (and last) fascicle of the manuscript, and ends with the line «seruendo sempre a dio com'i' t'o mostro». Then follows, partly cancelled, a further strophe that ends «fatica o spesa grande che ci auemmo». The lauda *Chi serve a dio con purità di core* is lacking.

[13]. On fol. 80r the lauda is mentioned only by its incipit: «[...] la famiglia di casa fa un ballo tondo e canta questa lauda Chi serve addio con purita di core».

[14]. The *editio princeps BelcR1485* was followed by a long series of editions, almost all issuing from Florentine printers (a few exemplars come from Siena), often without a printer's mark or at least with incomplete information, which after 1490 stabilized in a standard format (mostly fascicles in 4° of ca. 20 × 14 cm and only four leaves, provided with similar woodcuts: see Kristeller 1897, II, pl. 5 and Testaverde - Evangelista 1988, fig. 7), often preserved in a single copy (see Colomb de Batines 1852, pp. 6-8; D'Ancona 1872, I, pp. 42-43; Cioni 1961, pp. 64-73; Testaverde - Evangelista 1988). In many cases it appears that such fascicles formed part of whole collections of *sacre rappresentazioni* similar to Belcari's. This editorial production continued until the late seventeenth century; over forty different printings of the *Rappresentazione di Abramo e Isacco* are traceable today (a tenth of them incunables), all with similar titles but sometimes differing in the spelling of the Hebrew names and the length of the title or incipit. The poetic text itself is fairly stable, whereas there are significant variants in the stage directions. Only one of the distinguishable editorial traditions specifies in the *explicit*

Text from *LaudeSper.*:

> Chi serve a Dio con purità di core
> vive contento e poi salvato more.
>
> Se la virtù dispiace un poco al senso
> nel suo principio, quando è esercitata,
> 5   l'alma, che sente vero gaudio immenso,
> dentro dal core è tutta consolata:
> la mente sua si truova radiata
> da quella luce del sommo splendore.
>
> Quando ordinati son tutt'i costumi
> 10   dentro e di fuori el nostro etterno Dio,
> all'or si vegon quelli eccelsi lumi,
> che fanno viver l'uom lieto e giulìo:
> cantando va per un santo giulìo
> le gran dolcezze del perfetto amore.
>
> 15   Va giubilando e dice: «O gente stolta,
> cercando pace nei mondan diletti,
> se voi volete aver letitia molta,
> servite a Dio con tutti i vostri affetti:
> egli è quel fonte de' piacer perfetti
> 20   che fa giocondo ogni suo servidore».
>
> Amen.

MODERN EDITIONS OF THE TEXT:[15] ALLOCCO-CASTELLINO 1926, pp. 5-29: 28-29; BANFI (1963) 1974, pp. 37-62: 61-62 (basically after *BelcR1485* and previous modern editions); BONFANTINI 1942, pp. 126-147: 146; D'AMICO 1955, pp. 71-95: 94 (after D'ANCONA 1872); D'ANCONA 1872, I, pp. 44-59: 58 (basically after *BelcR1485*); DE BARTHOLOMAEIS 1943, II, pp. 237-255: 254-255 (after D'ANCONA 1872); FACCIOLI 1975, pp. 133-149: 149 (after DE BARTHOLOMAEIS 1943); GALLETTI 1833, pp. 1-23: 22-23 (after *Fir.N. M.690*); GALLETTI 1863, p. 7 (after *BelcLBart*); IMBRIANI 1883, pp. 2-15: 12 (basically after D'ANCONA 1872); PAPINI 1923, p. 97; PONTE 1974, pp. 29-46: 45-46 (mostly after D'ANCONA 1872 and BANFI 1963).

MODERN EDITIONS OF THE MUSIC: LUISI 1983, II, p. 186 (after Panc.27, with the text *O gloriosa verzene Maria*); OSTHOFF 1969, II, p. 33 (after Panc.27).

REMARKS: A widely diffused text,[16] also in the form of contrafacts, though a musical *unicum*, this simple piece might be due to the compositional initiative of the scribe of Panc.27, who would have written the music only for the ripresa (ll. 1-2). Therefore it is not clear whether he intended to end the composition at the close of the ripresa, or to repeat the same melody for each distich of the text, though that would go against the structural form of the barzelletta.

«festa di Habraam composta per Feo Belcari ciptadino fiorentino». The lauda *Chi serve a Dio con purità di core* occasionally appears on the last printed page.

[15]. In the strictly musical field, it should be mentioned that Belcari's text was also used as the libretto of a drama work by Ildebrando Pizzetti (*La sacra rappresentazione d'Abram e d'Isaac*, 1917, expanded version in 1926), with further editions of the relative texts: *Programma-Ricordo della Rappresentazione di Abramo ed Isac di Feo Belcari (4 febb. 1410 - 16 ag. 1484), eseguita al R. Politeama Fiorentino la sera del 9 giugno 1917 a benefizio delle Famiglie bisognose dei richiamati*, edited by Luigi Rasi, Florence, Tipografia Domenicana, 1917; *La rappresentazione di Abram e d'Isaac (secolo 15.) adattata nel testo a cura di Onorato Castellino, musiche di Ildebrando Pizzetti*, Milan, G. Ricordi, [1926].

[16]. I thank Marco Beghelli, who has disentangled the exceedingly complex relationships of the Belcari prints and has checked many modern editions.

BIBLIOGRAPHY: CARBONI - ZIINO 1973, pp. 282, 297-298; CATTIN 1978, p. 31, and n. 33; FRATI 1917, p. 472; GHISI 1953a, p. 69; LUISI 1983, I, p. 544; MARTELLI 1968, p. 65, n. 27; NEWBIGIN 1981; NEWBIGIN 1983, p. xiv; NOSOW 2000, pp. 234 and n. 43, 248; OSTHOFF 1969, I, pp. 30-31; PRIZER 1993b, p. 172 and n. 14; RABBONI 1991, pp. 73, 128-130; SMITH 1991, p. 20; TENNERONI 1909, p. 77.

30.

CHI SERVE A DIO CUM PURITÀ DI COR[E]

fol. 20*v*

[Feo Belcari]

Chi ser-ve a Di — o   cum pu-ri-tà   di co-r[e]

vi — ve con-ten — to   e po' sal-va — — to mo — re.

31.

Lauda Sion Salvatorem

fol. 20*v* (3 vv.)

Lauda Sion Salvatorem

Lauda-type composition (?)[1] based on the sequence text for the feast of Corpus Christi, traditionally attributed to St. Thomas Aquinas (GR, pp. 295-299; LU, pp. 945-949; MR, fol. XXIV*r-v*).

COMMENTARY ON THE TEXT:

1	Sion] Syon Ct

READINGS EMENDED IN THE EDITION:

BAR	VOICE	ORIGINAL
15	Ct	G

MUSICAL CONCORDANCES (MSS): • BolA 179 (183*v*-184*r*), 2 vv. (S and T only) • ParisN NAL401 (134*v*-135*r*), with a different Ct

TEXT FROM BolA 179[2] and ParisN NAL401:

> Lauda Sion Salvatorem,
> lauda ducem et pastorem,
> in hymnis et canticis.
>
> Ave corpus Domini.

TEXT FROM MR, fol. XXIV*r-v* (*In festo corporis Christi. Sequentia*):

> 1.   Lauda Sion Salvatorem,
> lauda ducem et pastorem,
> in hymnis, et canticis.

---

[1]. Both BolA 179 and ParisN NAL401, after the initial tercet, have a line that is foreign to the sequence *Lauda Sion Salvatorem* corresponding to the fermata passage. Reinforcing the possibility that the piece may be considered a lauda-type composition is its placement among other polyphonic laude in the final section of MS ParisN NAL401 (*[…] o Signore per tua bontate a quella sancta croce dove con alta voce ognor mi chiami* (110*v*), text only; *Peccatore moverai* (111*v*), text only; *Laudiamo l'amor divino* (113*r*), text only; *Benedeto ne sia lo giorno* (114*v*), text only; *Amor Iesu dilecto* (116*v*), text only; *Ave del ciel Maria* (128*v*), text only; *O verzeneta bella (133v)*, lined for music, but not notated; *Lauda Sion Salvatorem* (134*v*), text and music; *O Maria Magdalena* (147*v*), text and music; *O Maria diana stella* (153*r*), text and music). I thank Stefania Roncroffi for having alerted me to this concordance. Giulio Cattin (pers. com.) holds, on the other hand, that the piece is a motet constructed on the first lines of the sequence *Lauda Sion Salvatorem*. In favour of this hypothesis is the fact that the concluding fermata passage seems devised for the syllables of the final words of the sequence («Amen. Alleluia»), even if in the concordances one finds «Ave corpus Domini» instead. Bonnie Blackburn (pers. com.) favours the lauda hypothesis, not only because of the position of the piece among laude in ParisN NAL401, but also because the Latin text fits awkwardly in triple metre; moreover, the syllables «Ave corpus Domini» fit better than «Amen. Alleluia»; in the chant these words are clearly two phrases and not run together.

[2]. This version gives «ymnis» in place of «hymnis» as the unique difference.

2.   Quantum potes, tantum aude:
      quia maior omni laude,
      nec laudare sufficis.

3.   Laudis thema specialis,
      panis vivus et vitalis,
      hodie proponitur.

4.   Quem in sacre mensa cene,
      turbe fratrum duodene,
      datum non ambigitur.

5.   Sit laus plena, sit sonora,
      sit iucunda, sit decora
      mentis iubilatio.

6.   Dies enim sollemnis agitur,
      in qua mense prima[3] recolitur
      huius institutio.

7.   In hac mensa novi regis,
      novum pascha nove legis,
      phase vetus terminat.

8.   Vetustatem novitas,
      umbram[4] fugat veritas,
      noctem lux eliminat.

9.   Quod in cena Christus gessit,
      faciendum hoc expressit
      in sui memoriam.

10.   Docti sacris institutis,
      panem, vinum in salutis
      consecramus hostiam.

11.   Dogma datur christianis,
      quod in carnem transit panis,
      et vinum in sanguinem.

12.   Quod non capis, quod non vides,
      animosa firmat fides,
      preter rerum ordinem.

13.   Sub diversis speciebus,
      signis tantum, et non rebus,
      latent res eximie.

14.   Caro cibus, sanguis potus:
      manet Christus tamen totus
      sub utraque specie.

---

3. MR has «primo».
4. MR has «umbra».

15.   A sumente non concisus,
      non confractus, non divisus:
      integer accipitur.

16.   Sumit unus, sumunt mille:
      quantum isti, tantum ille:
      nec sumptus consumitur.

17.   Sumunt boni, sumunt mali:
      sorte tamen inequali,
      vite vel interitus.

18.   Mors est malis, vita bonis:
      vide paris sumptionis
      quam sit dispar exitus.

19.   Fracto demum sacramento,
      ne vacilles: sed memento,
      tantum esse sub fragmento,
      quantum toto tegitur.

20.   Nulla rei fit scissura:
      signi tantum fit fractura:
      qua nec status, nec statura
      signati minuitur.

21.   Ecce panis angelorum
      factus cibus viatorum:
      vere panis filiorum,
      non mittendus canibus.

22.   In figuris presignatur,
      cum Isaac immolatur:
      agnus pasche deputatur:
      datur manna patribus.

23.   Bone pastor, panis vere,
      Iesu nostri miserere:
      tu nos pasce, nos tuere:
      tu nos bona fac videre
      in terra viventium.

24.   Tu qui cuncta scis et vales:
      qui nos pascis hic mortales:
      tuos ibi commensales
      coheredes et sodales
      fac sanctorum[5] civium.

      Amen. Alleluia.

MODERN EDITIONS OF THE TEXT: AH 50, 584-585 (*In Festivitate Corporis Christi. Sequentia*).

MODERN EDITIONS OF THE MUSIC: BANKS 1993, II, p. 112 (after Panc.27).

---

[5]. MR has «sanctoru».

REMARKS: In addition to rhythmic and graphic variants, the BolA 179 version, older than that of Panc.27, lacks the Contra. Therefore a direct contact between the two sources can be excluded. Nor can there be any relationship with the version of ParisN NAL410, since the Contra is completely different. Curiously, both concordances have the line «Ave corpus Domini» at the fermata passage.

BIBLIOGRAPHY: BANKS 1993, I, p. 279; CHEVALIER II, no. 10222; DRAKE 2002, p. 50.

31.
LAUDA SION SALVATOREM
fol. 20*v*

Cantus

Lau-da Si - on Sal - va - to - rem

Tenor

Contra

Lau-da Si - on

32.

Cantons cantons laisons melenconie

fol. 21*r* (3 vv.)

Io[hannes?] Vilet[1]

[Heading only]

French chanson?

Readings emended in the edition:

Bar	Voice	Original
19	T	*longa* with fermata

Bibliography: Fallows 1999, p. 103.

---

[1]. This name, attested only here, has caused some perplexity in the past, so that in Morpurgo *et al.* 1887, p. 55, the adventurous completion 'Jo. vil[a]e[r]t' is suggested. On the possibility that it might in fact refer to Willaert, see the sceptical comment to the catalogue, no. 177, n. 1.

32.

CANTONS CANTONS LAISONS MELENCONIE

fol. 21*r*

Io[hannes?] Vilet

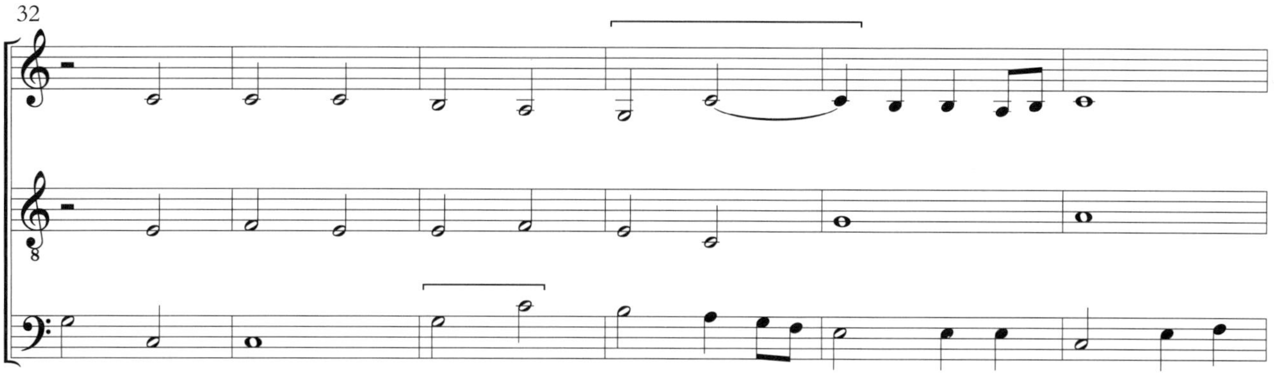
32

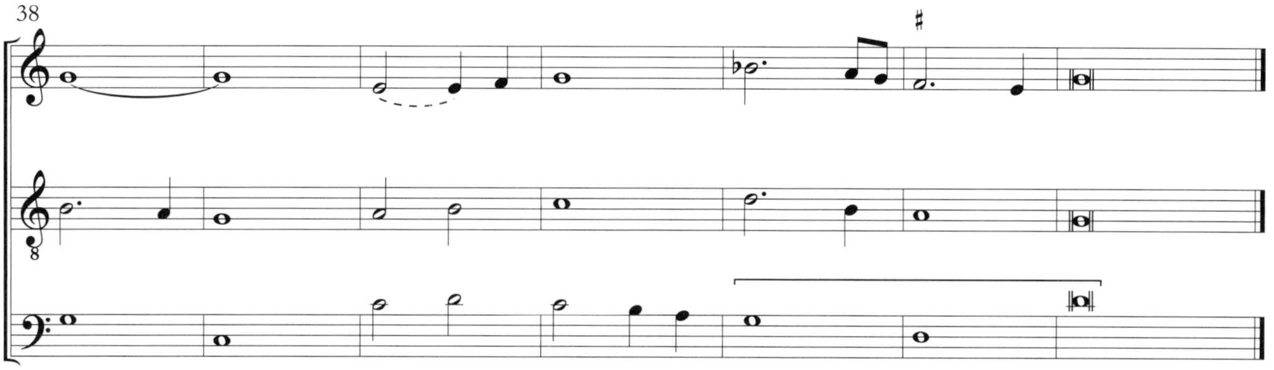
38

33.

Contento in foco sto como fenice

fol. 21*v* (4 vv.)

[Angelo Poliziano][1]   [...][2]

> Contento in foco sto como fenice,
> e como cigno canto nel morire,
> perché io spero doventar felice
> quando soferto arò pena e martìre.

Italian secular piece (strambotto toscano).

Textual concordances (mss): • *CV.VL.5159* (168*v*), (Serafino Aquilano) • *CV.VL.5170* (58*r*) • *Fir.N. B.228* (37*v*) • *Fir.R. 2723* (42*v*) • *Lon.B.A.16439* (34*r*) • *Pes.O. 54* (74*v*)

Textual concordances (prints): • *Aq1516Giu* (174*v*-175*r*), (Serafino Aquilano) • *Aq1520Pen* (A2*v*), (Serafino Aquilano) • *Aq1529Mor* ([2*v*]), (Serafino Aquilano) • *Aq1530Zop* (X6*v*), (Serafino Aquilano) • *Aq1548Basc* (174*v*-175*r*), (Serafino Aquilano) • *AqStramb(A)* (a2*v*), (Serafino Aquilano) • *AqStramb(B)* (2*r*), (Serafino Aquilano) • *AqVav* (a2*r*), (Serafino Aquilano) • *Ricco1511* (G3*r-v*),[3] (Antonio Ricco) • *Ricco1520* (G3*r-v*), (Antonio Ricco)

Musical concordances (mss): • MilT 55 (56*v*-57*r*), 3 vv. (without A, and different B) • ParisN Rés676 (31*v*-32*r*), after the text and music of *Contento in foco sto como fenice* there is the text of the contrafact *Ave di celli imperatrice santa* («Pro lauda Virginis Marie»), 3 vv. (without A, and different B) • PesO 1144 (70-71)

Text from *Lon.B.A.16439*:

> Contento in fuoco sto come phenice,
> et come cygno canto nel morire,

---

[1]. There is no autograph witness of Poliziano's *Rime*, nor is there a collection compiled under his direct supervision. The presence of *Contento in foco sto como fenice* both in *Fir.R. 2723* — a Medicean source copied while the poet was still alive and which constitutes the largest collection of his *Rime* — and in *Lon.B.A.16439*, also a Medicean manuscript and clearly intended as a systematic collection of Poliziano's oeuvre, convinces Daniela Delcorno Branca of the paternity of this text, which Carducci had already deemed authentic. The frequent and untrustworthy attribution to Serafino Aquilano follows upon the heels of his extraordinary success, but essentially appears in sources copied after his death (see Delcorno Branca 1979).

[2]. Remo Giazotto writes that the piece should be attributed to Lodovico Fogliano (Giazotto 1959, p. 13). He also says that the poetic text «is conserved in the State Library of Prague with the simple indication *Fogliano, 1504*. It appears that the copyist who was engaged to retranscribe it had recourse to the Trivulziana manuscript, which is certainly earlier than 1504» (Giazotto 1959, p. 95). Daniela Delcorno Branca does not appear to give much credence to Giazotto's statement: «With respect to the strambotto in question, Giazotto mentions its presence also in a manuscript of the State Library of Prague, without, however, giving the siglum» (Delcorno Branca 1971, p. 244).

[3]. The poem appears in this enlarged reprint of the works of Antonio Ricco (15th-16th century), whereas it was absent in the first edition, edited by the author himself (Antonio Ricco, *Fior de Delia*, Venice, Manfredo Bonelli, 15 March 1507, copy in the University of Pennsylvania Library, Philadelphia) as well as the second edition (Antonio Ricco, *Fior de Delia. Stampata Novamente [...]*, Venice, Manfredo Bonelli, 7 March 1508, held by the following libraries: Chicago, Newberry Library; Turin, Biblioteca Centrale della Facoltà di Lettere e Filosofia dell'Università; Udine, Biblioteca Civica Vincenzo Joppi; Washington, DC, Folger Shakespeare Library). It turns up later, for example, in the reprint of 1520 published in Venice by Melchiorre Sessa and Pietro Ravani, a copy of which is in the British Library.

però ch'i' spero diventar felice
quando soferto arò pena et martìre.
5   Amor, tu vederai quanto non lice
eser crudele al mio leal servire,
ché, conosciuta la mia pura fede,
spero che avrai di me qualche merzede.

MODERN EDITIONS OF THE TEXT: CARDUCCI 1863, p. 250 (after *Fir.R. 2723*); DELCORNO BRANCA 1983, p. 429 (ll. 1-4); DELCORNO BRANCA 1986, pp. 315-316; DELCORNO BRANCA 1987, p. 174; GIAZOTTO 1959, p. 95 (after MilT 55); JEPPESEN 1970, pp. 158-159 (after MilT 55).

MODERN EDITIONS OF THE MUSIC: GIAZOTTO 1959, p. 95 (after MilT 55); IVANOFF 1988, pp. 115-117 (after PesO 1144); JEPPESEN 1970, pp. 299-300 (after MilT 55); LUISI 1983, II, pp. 150 (after ParisN Rés676), 151 (after Panc.27).

REMARKS: Although with reciprocal graphic musical and textual differences, the MSS MilT 55 and ParisN Rés676 have the same version of the piece: this proves that there existed at least two different traditions of the composition, and the version of Panc.27 constitutes an independent branch. Here, the presence of an added Altus, a new Bassus, and an alternative version of the concluding section suggest that it was the copyist himself who is responsible for the changes. This goes together with the characteristic contrapuntal awkwardnesses often present in the *unica* of Panc.27, observable above all in the numerous parallel progressions (triads, bb. 6-7; fifths between the Tenor and Bassus, bb. 8-9; octaves between Superius and Altus, bb. 15-16).

BIBLIOGRAPHY: CATTIN 1983b, p. 385; DELCORNO BRANCA 1971, pp. 237, 239, 243-244, 246-249; DELCORNO BRANCA 1983, pp. 429-430; DELCORNO BRANCA 1987, pp. 157-158, 160, 174-176, 201, 203-204; PAGANI 1968, pp. 447-449, p. 456; SAVONA 1973, p. 364; ZAMBON 1983, pp. 411-425.

33.
CONTENTO IN FOCO STO COMO FENICE
fol. 21v

[Angelo Poliziano]

S[uperius]
A[ltus]
T[enor]
B[assus]

Con – ten - to in fo - co sto co - mo
per – – ché io spe – ro do – ven - tar

fe – – ni – – ce, e co - mo ci – gno
fe – – li – – ce quan - do so - fer - to a -

can - to nel mo – – ri – – – – – – re,
– rò pe - na e mar – – tì – – – – – re.

34.

DETRO MIA GIOIA

fol. 21*v* (3 vv.)

Detro mia gioia

Perpetual canon.

COMMENTARY ON THE TEXT:

1   «Detro» can be found in Boiardo with the meaning of 'dietro' (*Orlando innamorato*, lib. 2, can. 22.14.3, and lib. 2, can. 25.28.5; *Pastorale*, egloga 6.7 and egloga 8.83)[1]

REMARKS: The inscription «Circulo quoque o veniat alter post nonam ◊» appears at the end of the single voice of this perpetual canon. It explains the resolution and means 'In each circle/circuit of the canon let the other come after the ninth *semibrevis*'.[2] This canon was certainly performed: a short vertical line appears under two notes, each corresponding to the correct new entrance (bb. 5 and 9) after the *g*. But the ink of these signs is much lighter than that of the piece, suggesting that they were added after the canon was copied. It is not clear whether the text *Detro mia gioia* should be understood as a quinario or whether *Detro mia* is the beginning of a longer line ending with *gioia*; the placement of the text under the music leaves the question open, since «Detro mia» is found exactly under the first notes of the dux, whereas «gioia» is written under the last notes.

---

[1]. See LIZ II.

[2]. Even though «Circulo quoque post nonam ◊» would be sufficient as a resolution of the canon, «o veniat alter» might serve to reinforce the entrance of the succeeding voices, as if to say 'oh, let the other come!'. My thanks to Leofranc Holford-Strevens for this intriguing interpretation.

34.
DETRO MIA GIOIA
fol. 21v

Circulo quoque o veniat alter post nonam

[Tenor]

Detro mia gioia

35.

Fortuna, che te giova de straciarme

fol. 22r (4 vv.)

[…]¹

> Fortuna, che te giova de straciarme

Italian secular piece (strambotto toscano).

Readings emended in the edition:

Bar	Voice	Original
26/II	A	*minima* rest and *b minima*
28/II	A	*b* instead of *a*
32/I	A	*d' e'*

Textual concordances (mss): • *CV.VL.5159* (67*v*), (Serafino Aquilano) • *Fir.N. B.228* (12*r*)

Textual concordances (prints): • *AqMis* (c3*v*), (Serafino Aquilano)

Text from *Fir.N. B.228*:

> Fortuna, che ti giova di strazare
> el corpo mio che più non se defende?
> O Morte, at che ti iova non cavare
> l'alma di pene, poi che a 'tte s'arrende?
> 5   Oimè, che non mi iova di chiamare
> socorso, se 'l chiamar ognor m'offende.
> M'offende assai Fortuna che mi strugge,
> ma più m'offende Morte che mi fugge.

Remarks: Despite the fact that no other musical setting is known, the piece might be derived from a pre-existing model: this is suggested by the presence of the rubric «Iustus», surely written later, as shown by the lighter ink. Such a hypothetical copy might have been for three voices: the relationship between the Cantus, Tenor, and Bassus works well, but the Altus is rather awkward and needed editorial emendation. Perhaps it was the scribe himself who added the fourth voice, without however succeeding in avoiding contrapuntal problems.

---

¹. The attribution to Serafino Aquilano — implied in two of the three literary concordances — has not been accepted, either by Bauer Formiconi 1967 or by La Face Bianconi - Rossi 1999.

35.
FORTUNA, CHE TE GIOVA DE STRACIARME
fol. 22*r*

Iu[s]t[us]

36.

Poi che t'ebi nel core / Fortuna desperata

fols. 22*v*–23*r* (4 vv.)

[Francesco degli Albizzi]

Poi che t'ebi nel core,
Iesù clemente e pio,
crescì tanto el desio
ch'el arde a tute l'ore.

5   Ardime di splendore,
dolce e piatoso Idio,
ché ogni cosa in oblio
ho dato per tuo amore.

Lauda (oda) (a contrafact on the music of *Fortuna desperata | iniqua e maladecta*: a modern edition of this text is in Torrefranca 1939, p. 297, taken from ParisN Rés676, and in Lama de la Cruz 1994, p. 268, taken from SegC, fol. 174*r*. See also Meconi 2001a, p. xvi).

Commentary on the text:

5   the *residuum* begins here

Readings emended in the edition:

Bar	Voice	Original
54	A	*c′*

Textual concordances (mss): • *CV. Ro. 424* (124*v*), (Feo Belcari) • *Mün. S. I240* (68*r*) • *Rim. C. 38* (134*r*), «Franciesco Dalbizo» • *Ven. M. I. 78* (39*v*–42*r*, lacking fols. 40*r*–41*v*), «Francesco Dalbizo»

Textual concordances (prints): • *LaudeBonac* (39*v*), «Francesco Dalbizo» • *LaudeMisc* (15*r*–*v*), «Francesco Dalbizo» • *LaudeSper* (20*v*), «Di Francesco Dalbizo» • *LaudeVecchie* (b5*v*), «Francesco Dalbizo» • *LaudiRiccardiana* (g8*v*), «Francesco D'Albizo» • *OperaNova* (13*v*), «Di Francescho Dalbizo»

Musical concordances (mss): • AugsS 142a (46*v*–47*r*), *fortuna desperata*, 6 vv., «Allexannderr A[gricola]» • BasU 10 (8*r*), *Fortüna*, B only • BerlS 40026 (63*v*–64*v*), *Fortuna in ut*, «H[ans] B[uchner]» • BerlS 40026 (132*r*–133*v*), *Fortuna Quatuor in fa* • BolM 16 (132*v*–133*r*), *[F]ortuna disperata*, with a different A • CTL G12 (79*v*–80*r*, olim 78*v*–79*r*), with a different A • CV G27 (56*v*–57*r*, olim 63*v*–64*r*), *fortuna desperata*, with a different A, but also with an alternative B, «felice» • FirN M121 (25*v*–26*r*), *Fortuna disperata*, 3 vv. (without A) • FMU 20 (1*r*), 2 vv. (S and T only), *fortuna de[s]perata / O panis vite venerande* • LeipU 1494 (62*r*), *Fortuna / Virginis alme parens*, with a different A • LeipU 1494 (162*v*), *Ave stella fulgida*, 2 vv. (S and A only) • LonB A31922 (4*v*–5*r*), *Fortune esperee*, with a different A • LonB A35087 (11*v*–12*r*), *Fortuna desperata*, 3 vv. (without A) • MünU 718 (S: 119*r*; T: 129*v*–130*r*; B: 141*r*), *Forduna / Fortuna*, 3 vv. (without A) • ParisN NAF4379 (40*v*–41*r*), *fortuna desperata*, with a different A and added in a later hand • ParisN Rés676 (24*v*–25*r*), *Fortuna desperata iniqua e maladecta*, with a different A • PerA 431

(83v-84r, *olim* 93v-94r), *Fortuna desperata*, 3 vv. (without A) • PerA 431 (84v-85r, *olim* 94v-95r), *Fortuna desperata*, with a different A • SegC (174r), *fortuna disperata*, 3 vv. (without A), «Anthonius busnoys» • SegC (182v), *Fortuna disperata*, 3 vv., with a different B, «Josquin du pres» • SGS 462 (6v-7r), *fortuna desperata quae te dementia vertit*, with a different A • SGS 463 (no. 144), 2 vv. (S and A only), *Fortuna desperata quae te dementia cepit*, «Ionicus in Quintus»; index: «Fortuna desperata antiquum» • WolfA 78 (2v), textless, 3 vv. (without A) • ZwR 78/2 (no. 54), textless, with a different A

MUSICAL CONCORDANCES (PRINTS): • AttTrezeMotetz (83v-86r), *Fortuna* • PeCantiC (126v-127r), *Fortuna desperata*, with a different A • PeSpinII (38v-41r), *Fortuna desperata*

TEXT FROM *CV. Ro. 424*:

> Poi ch'i' t'ebbi nel core,
> Iesù clemente et pio,
> crescé tanto 'l disio
> che gli arde a tucte l'ore.

> 5 Non ti partir, Signore,
> da me, ché ti vogl'io,
> ché tutto il piacer mio
> è stare in questo ardore.

> Ardimi di splendore,
> 10 dolce et piatoso Idio,
> ch'ogni cosa in oblio
> ho dato per tuo amore.

> Ah quanto è grande errore
> amare il mondo rio,
> 15 ché 'l ben sancto et giulìo
> si cambia per dolore.

MODERN EDITIONS OF THE TEXT: GALLETTI 1863, p. 56 (after *LaudeBonac*); TARGIONI TOZZETTI 1901, p. 335 (after GALLETTI 1863).

MODERN EDITIONS OF THE MUSIC: ATLAS 1975-76, II, pp. 38-42 (after CV G27); BERNOULLI 1910, pp. 36-37 (after SGS 462); BROOKS 1951, III, pp. 201-203 (after SegC), 312-315 (after BolM 16), 317-320 (after PeCantiC), 322-325 (after LonB A31922); CMM 22/V, pp. 68-70 (after AugsS 142a); CMM 76, pp. 38-39 (after CTL G12), xxvii (A only after Panc.27); DTÖ 28, p. 190 (after ParisN NAF4379); EDM 32, p. 71 (after LeipU 1494, fol. 62r); EDM 34, p. 408 (after LeipU 1494, fol. 162v); EDM 91, pp. 98-100 (after BerlS 40026, fols. 63v-64v); EDM 92, pp. 61-63 (after BerlS 40026, fols. 132r-133v); GREENBERG - MAYNARD 1975, pp. 212-213 (after LonB A31922); HERNON 1972, pp. 356-358 (after PerA 431, fols. 83v-84r, *olim* 93v-94r), 359-364 (after PerA 431, fols. 84v-85r, *olim* 94v-95r); JONAS 1983, I, pp. 127-131 (after AugsS 142a); McMURTRY 1967, pp. 232-235 (after LonB A35087); MECONI 1999, pp. 471-472 (after ParisN NAF4379); MECONI 2001a; MOERK 1971, II, pp. 311-313 (after ParisN NAF4379); MOSER 1930, pp. 60-61 (after BerlS 40026, fols. 63v-64v); NJE 27, I, pp. 16-17 (after SegC, fol. 182v), with commentary in NJE 27c, pp. 77-78, throwing serious doubts on the ascription; NOE 4, pp. 30-32 (after SegC); RIFKIN 1999, pp. 556-557 (after ParisN NAF4379); ROKSETH 1930, p. 55 (after LonB A35087 and AttTrezeMotetz); SCHMIDT 1969, II, pp. 270-275 (after PeSpinII); SELF 1996, pp. 29-33 (various versions); SM 5, pp. 17-18 (after SGS 462); SMIJERS J/13, pp. 105 (after LonB A35087), 106 (after PeCantiC), 107 (after LonB A31922); SMIJERS J/53, pp. 25-27 (after LonB A35087), pp. 27-29 (after SegC, fol. 182v); STEVENS 1962, p. 2 (after LonB A31922); STROHM 1993, pp. 621-622 (after LonB A35087); WOLF O/1, pp. 136-137 (after ParisN NAF4379).

REMARKS: The piece had an enormous diffusion, in Italy and the rest of Europe. Drawing on 36 versions, Honey Meconi has reconstructed the tradition of *Fortuna desperata* over the course of a century, from the 1470s to the 1560s (see MECONI 2001a, pp. ix-xxxvii). She posits that the original musical structure was for three voices, originating as a Superius-Tenor *bicinium*, then enriched with a Contratenor (or Bassus). There exist various versions of the added Altus: in three cases (BolM 16, LonB A31922, Panc.27) the supplementary Altus is unique in each version; all the other instances transmit a common supplementary Altus. Only one manuscript (AugsS 142a, Agricola's version) increases the polyphonic structure yet further, giving it its own Altus and two more original voices. In addition, there are other musical versions of the piece that have in common with the preceding ones only the Superius–Tenor *bicinium*, only the Superius, or only the Tenor. The version in CTL G12 has the same music as the older ParisN NAF4379, but the lauda text in common only with Panc.27 (*Poi che t'ebi nel core*) and with various literary sources (in many of which the indication «cantasi come *Fortuna desperata*» appears). In view of the fact, therefore, that the musical version of Panc.27 does not derive from any source known to us, one may conclude that perhaps the copyist himself composed its Altus. It is interesting that the lauda text set to music is found in only two closely related manuscripts (CTL G12 and Panc.27): yet another testimony that the compilers of the two manuscripts surely drew on a common repertory, though not directly related to each other.

BIBLIOGRAPHY: ATLAS 1975-76, I, pp. 134-136; ATLAS 1981; BAKER 1978, I, pp. 458-459; BOORMAN 2006, pp. 977-978; CATTIN 1973a, p. 206; CATTIN 1978, p. 38; CMM 76, p. xxvii; EDM 92, p. 156; FALLOWS 1999, pp. 518-520; GALLICO 1996, pp. 147, 149-150, 183, 190-191; GREENBERG – MAYNARD 1975, pp. 210-211; HERNON 1972, pp. 522-523; JEPPESEN 1935, p. xix; LAMA DE LA CRUZ 1994, p. 268; LOACH 1969, I, pp. 316-317, 377-378; LUISI 1983, I, p. 193; MCMURTRY 1967, pp. 123-131; MECONI 2001a; ROSTIROLLA (1986) 2001, p. 178; WOLFF 1970, pp. 372-381.

36.
Poi che t'ebi nel core / Fortuna desperata
fols. 22v–23r

[Francesco degli Albizzi]

- te   e   pi – – – o,   cre – – – – – – scì

tan – to el   de – si – – – – – o

ch'el   ar – – de   a

tu – te l'o – – – – – – re,

a tu – te l'o – – – – re.

37.

Defecerunt vedo ormai

fols. 23v–24r (4 vv.)

[Marchetto Cara]

Defecerunt vedo ormai,
sicut fumus dies mei.
Tu, che summo bene sei,
audi vocem de' mei guai.
  Defecerunt vedo ormai,
  sicut fumus dies mei.

Italian secular piece (barzelletta) or lauda, partially based on Psalm 101:4 («quia defecerunt sicut fumus dies mei | et ossa mea sicut gremium aruerunt», Vulgata, p. 896).[1]

Commentary on the text:

1	«defecerunt» derives from the Latin verb *deficio, is, feci, fectum, ere* (= 'dissolve, pass away, fail')
1	vedo] ved B
1-2	«Defecerunt sicut fumus dies mei» (= 'For my days are vanished like smoke')

Readings emended in the edition:

Bar	Voice	Original
13	T	the first *g* in bar 13 coincides with the beginning of a new stave, on which the scribe has placed a flat that would seem to be a key signature. Probably, however, the copyist mechanically copied the B flat that applies only to the *b* in bar 12

Musical concordances (mss): • FirC B2441 (22v-23r), *Defecerunt donna hormai* • ParisN Rés27 (44r-v), *Deffecerunt donna hormai*

Musical concordances (prints): • PeFroI (4v-5r), *Defecerunt donna hormai*, «M. C.»

Text from FirC B2441:

Defecerunt donna ormai,
sicut fumus dies mei.
Se discesa dal ciel sei,
audi vocem de' miei guai.

5 T'ho servita già tanti anni
senza premio e senza fede.
Trame ormai di tanti affanni:
questo fia per mia mercede.
Se 'l martìr ogn'altro excede
10 certo son che 'l veder è asai.
  Defecerunt […]

---

[1]. Psalm 101 is the fifth Penitential Psalm. My thanks to Bonnie Blackburn for identifying the source of the text.

Non pigliar mio dir a gioco,
che se il duol più tempo dura,
tanto intenso e grave il foco
de mia pena acerba e dura,
15   e la mia aspra vita obscura
bon rimedio non fia mai.
        Defecerunt […]

Lasso me, che son conducto
or al fin de mie giornate,
e mi sento aver in tuto
20   perso il tempo de mie etade.
Deh, crudel, abi pietade,
che, inver, mai non errai.
        Defecerunt […]

Più parlar non posso: adio!
Vale, vale, ingrata, or vale.
25   Ben ti prego che 'l cor mio
me ritorni tal o quale,
ché servir chi me fa male
mai, crudel, io non sperai.
        Defecerunt […]

MODERN EDITIONS OF THE TEXT: BORGHI 1995, pp. 174-175 (after FirC B2441); CESARI *ET AL.* 1954, p. 4⋆ (after PeFroI); SCHWARTZ 1935, p. xxvii (after PeFroI).

MODERN EDITIONS OF THE MUSIC: BORGHI 1995, pp. 338-339 (after FirC B2441); CESARI *ET AL.* 1954, pp. 4-5 (after PeFroI); SCHWARTZ 1935, p. 3 (after PeFroI).

REMARKS: The version in Panc.27 does not seem to be derived from any of the known concordances. The textual variant in the first line («donna» instead of 'vedo') is present in all the other sources; the alternative third line, «Se discesa dal ciel sei», is found both in FirC B2441 and in PeFroI (the intabulation in ParisN Rés27 gives only the first line). The presence or absence of the B flat in the signature is one of the most interesting variants: only Panc.27 provides it in the Bassus; only FirC B2441 does not give it in the Altus; only Panc.27 has it erroneously at the beginning of the second stave in the Tenor. Apart from some graphic and rhythmic variants, FirC B2441 has two different notes (b. 10/I Altus: *e′* instead of *f′*; b. 11/II, Tenor: *c′* instead of *d′*); PeFroI differs in its large number of graphic and rhythmic variants (repeated notes instead of long notes and vice versa). The presence of a *signum congruentiae* on the final note of only the Tenor in Panc.27 is curious. *Defecerunt vedo ormai* begins the alphabetical section of Panc.27 devoted to the letter 'D': in the original plan devised by the scribe, this unique bilingual piece (Italian-Latin) in Panc.27 perhaps was intended to foreshadow the first piece in the manuscript dedicated to the Liturgy of the Dead (the sequence *Dies ire, dies illa*, no. 39). Perhaps this was the reason the scribe himself may have varied the text of the refrain of this barzelletta, transforming the sense of lament for unrequited love into a lauda-like invocation.

BIBLIOGRAPHY: BOORMAN 2006, p. 971; DE ROBERTIS 1966, pp. 357, 360; MIGLIORINI 1954; PRIZER 1980, pp. 116-117; PRIZER 1996b, p. 41.

37.

DEFECERUNT VEDO ORMAI

fols. 23*v*–24*r*

[Marchetto Cara]

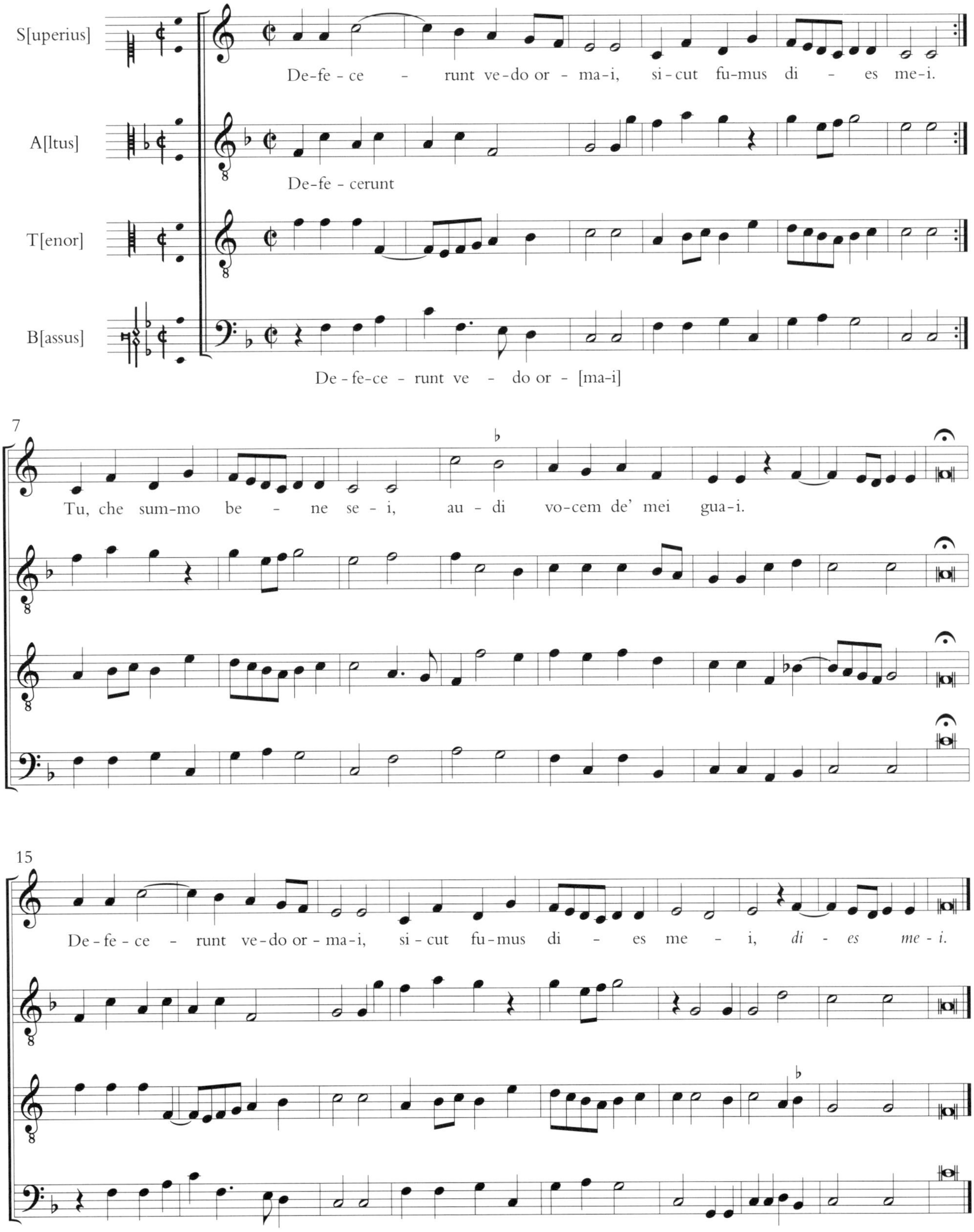

38.

O MIA INFELICE SORTE

fols. 23v-24r (4 vv.)

O mia infelice sorte,
a cui è dedicato
che ogn'or‹a› sia tormentato
d'una fera crudele.

Italian secular piece (oda).

COMMENTARY ON THE TEXT:

3   the hypermetre can be corrected on the basis of the reading in PeFroIV1505 (and its reprint)

MUSICAL CONCORDANCES (PRINTS): • PeFroIV1505 (49v); index: «Oda» • PeFroIV1507 (49v); index: «Oda»

TEXT FROM PeFroIV1505:

O mia infelice sorte,
a cui è dedicato
ch'ogn'or sia tormentato
da una fera crudele.

5   A che tanto fidele
ne fe' el celeste corso
che, con più me dà morso,
tanto più la desio?

      Il mio destin sì rio
10   Natura ha confirmato,
che quasi consumato
mi sento ogni vigore.

      Con più, dico, soccore
la vita che declina,
15   tanto più me ruina
con sua cruda licentia.

      Patirò con patientia
ogni martìr e stento,
perché forsi contento
20   serrò da poi la morte.

MODERN EDITIONS OF THE TEXT: SCHWARTZ 1935, p. xlv (after PeFroIV1505).

MODERN EDITIONS OF THE MUSIC: SCHWARTZ 1935, p. 93 (after PeFroIV1505).

REMARKS: The version in Panc.27 seems to derive from Petrucci: the only musical differences are merely graphic (PeFroIV1505 and its reprint end without fermatas on the *longae* of b. 12; it includes sharps referring to the *c′* in b. 1 of the Tenor and b. 11 of the Superius; it inverts the *minima-semibrevis* pattern in bb. 8/II-9/I of the Tenor). The composition surely does not end with the fermatas in bar 12: a refrain is implied, from the first bar to bar 9, where a barline is written. The piece was copied with darker ink than the previous piece on the same pages: certainly *O mia infelice sorte* was added later to fill up the last two staves, since it interrupts the alphabetical sequence of pieces dedicated to the letter 'D'.

BIBLIOGRAPHY: BOORMAN 2006, p. 998; PRIZER 1980a, p. 68; VELA 1984, p. 70.

38.
O MIA INFELICE SORTE
fols. *23v-24r*

O mia infelice sorte, a cui è dedicato che ogn'or sia tormentato d'una fera crudele, d'una fera crudele.

39.

Dies ire, dies illa

fol. 24v (4 vv.)

Dies ire, dies illa

Sequence of the Requiem Mass, traditionally attributed to Thomas of Celano (GR 97*-100*; LU, pp. 1810-1813; MR [*Commune Sanctorum*], fol. 41r-v).

Readings emended in the edition:

Bar	Voice	Original
9/II–10/I	B	flat in front of *b*
14/II–15	T	*c′ b a g f* instead of *e′ d′ c′ b a*
16/I	B	*semibrevis* rest
24	B	*longa* with fermata

Text from MR [*Commune Sanctorum*], fol. 41r-v (*Missa in commemoratione defunctorum. Sequentia*):

Dies ire, dies illa
solvet seclum in favilla:
teste David cum Sibylla.

Quantus tremor est futurus,
5   quando iudex est venturus,
cuncta stricte discussurus.

Tuba mirum spargens sonum,
per sepulchra regionum,
coget omnes ante thronum.

10   Mors stupebit et natura,
cum resurget creatura,
iudicanti responsura.

Liber scriptus proferetur,
in quo totum continetur,
15   unde mundus iudicetur.

Iudex ergo cum sedebit,
quidquid[1] latet apparebit:
nil inultum remanebit.

Quid sum miser tunc dicturus?
20   quem patronum rogaturus?
cum vix iustus sit securus.

---

[1]. MR has «quicquid».

Rex tremende maiestatis,
qui salvandos salvas gratis,
salva me, fons pietatis.

25   Recordare Iesu pie,
quod sum causa tue vie,
ne me perdas illa die.

Querens me, sedisti lassus:
redemisti, crucem passus:
30   tantus labor non sit cassus.

Iuste iudex ultionis,
donum fac remissionis
ante diem rationis.

Ingemisco, tamquam reus:
35   culpa rubet vultus meus:
supplicanti parce Deus.

Qui Mariam absolvisti,
et latronem exaudisti:
mihi quoque spem dedisti.

40   Preces mee non sunt digne:
sed tu bonus fac benigne:
ne perenni cremer igne.

Inter oves locum presta:
et ab hedis me sequestra,
45   statuens in parte dextra.

Confutatis maledictis,
flammis acribus addictis:
voca me cum benedictis.

Oro supplex et acclinis:
50   cor contritum quasi cinis:
gere curam mei finis.

Lachrymosa dies illa,
qua resurget ex favilla

iudicandus homo reus.
55   Huic ergo parce Deus.

Pie Iesu Domine,
dona eis requiem.

Amen.

MODERN EDITIONS OF THE TEXT: AH 54, pp. 269-270.

MODERN EDITIONS OF THE MUSIC: BANKS 1993, II, p. 74 (after Panc.27).

REMARKS: The scribal *ductus* of this piece is noticeably different from that of the preceding and following pages; the note shapes are much more rounded and the ink darker, but this does not seem sufficient to hypothesize the intervention of another music copyist. The beginning of the chant in GR 97★–100★ and LU, pp. 1810-1813 is quoted in the Cantus.

BIBLIOGRAPHY: BANKS 1993, I, p. 273; CHEVALIER I, no. 4626.

39.
Dies ire, dies illa
fol. 24v

Dies ire, dies illa

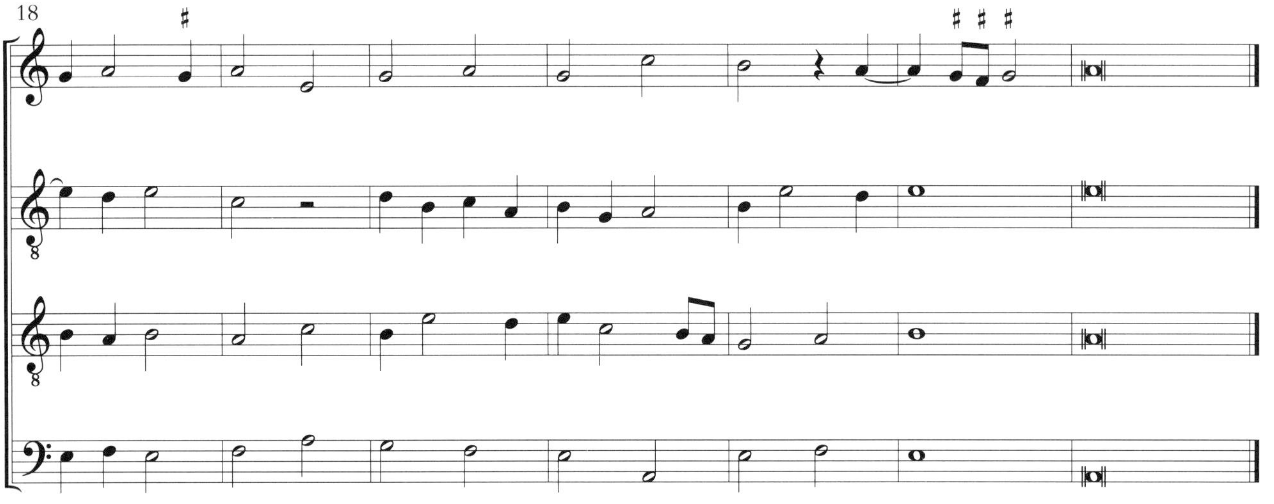
18

40.

De tous biens playne [est ma maistresse]

fol. 25r (3 vv.)

De tous biens playne

Chanson (rondeau quatrain).

COMMENTARY ON THE TEXT:

1   tous] tons C

READINGS EMENDED IN THE EDITION:

BAR	VOICE	ORIGINAL
60	C	*longa* with fermata

TEXTUAL CONCORDANCES (MSS): • *Berl.M. 17* (184r-v)[1]

TEXTUAL CONCORDANCES (PRINTS): • *Chasse* (O3v-Q3r)[2]

MUSICAL CONCORDANCES (MSS): • BolM 16 (133v-134r), with different Ct • CTL G12 (84v-85r, *olim* 83v-84r), *Cum defecerint ligna*,[3] with different Ct • CV G27 (57v-58r, *olim* 64v-65r), with different Ct; shares a Superius with a three-voice reworking found on the same opening[4] • DijM 517 (14v-15r), *De tous biens plaine est ma maistresse*, with different Ct, «Hayne», • FirN BR229 (187v-188r), *De tous biens plaine est ma maistresse*, with different Ct • FirN M121 (24v-25r), with different Ct • FirN M178 (34v-35r), with different Ct, «hayne» • FirR 2356 (32v-33r), with different Ct • FirR 2794 (18v-19r), *De tous biens plaine est ma maistraisse*, with different Ct • KasL 53/2 (no. 13), C only • KøbK 291 (5v-6r), *De tous biens plaine et [sic] ma maistresse*, with different Ct • LonB A31922 (40v-41r), with different Ct • MaaR (25r-v), C only • MontA 871 (344), textless, with different Ct • NHY 91 (42v-43r), *De tous biens plaine est ma maistresse*, with different Ct, «Heyne» • ParisN Rés676 (42v-43r), with different Ct • ParisN Ro2973 (25v-26r) *De tous biens plaine est ma mais[tres]se*, with different Ct • PavU A362 (34bisv-35r), with different Ct,[5] «Heyne» • ParisN F15123 (105v-106r), with different Ct • PerA 431 (70v-71r, *olim* 80v-81r), *De tous biens plaine est*, with different Ct • RomaCa 2856 (66v-67r), with different Ct, «Haine» • SevC 43 (39r; fol. 38 missing), 2 vv. (T and Ct; Cantus lost), only the T in common; MS index incomplete • UlmS 237 (C: 17r; T: 15r; Ct: 16r), with

---

[1]. BROWN 1983, I, p. 282 indicates that the version of the poem in *Berl.M. 17* is that of the *Chasse*. After the incipit in common, however, the continuation is different: the latter poem has been edited in LÖPELMANN 1923, no. 575.

[2]. Also the edition of PERKINS - GAREY 1979, II, pp. 324-325, affirms that: «The poem in *Chasse*, f. Piir, beginning *De tous biens pleine*, has nothing in common with the present poem except the initial line». By «present poem» is meant the poem that is given as the textual basis in Cynthia Cyrus (CYRUS 2000).

[3]. The text comes from Proverbs 26:20, 22 (VULGATA, p. 981): «²⁰Cum defecerint ligna extinguetur ignis et susurrone subtracto iurgia conquiescunt», «²²verba susurronis quasi simplicia et ipsa perveniunt ad intima ventris».

[4]. This is not a version for five voices, as is erroneously indicated in HEWITT 1942, p. 137 and in BROWN 1963, p. 205. The confusion arises from the deceptive disposition of the five voices (one Superius, two Tenores, and two Bassus) that appear on fols. 57v-58r (see ATLAS 1976, I, p. 137).

[5]. Probably a later addition to the manuscript since it is written in a hand different from that of the main scribe; the same is true several folios later on 50v-51r, where *Mon cuer de duel* also appears in a later hand.

different Ct • UppsU 76a (15*v*-16*r*), *De tous biens plaine est ma maistresse*, with different Ct, modern hand: «[Hayne de Ghizeghem]» • WashC L25 (62*v*-63*r*), *De tous biens plaine est ma maistresse*, with different Ct • WolfA G287 (52*v*-53*r*), *De tous biens plaine est ma maistresse*, with different Ct

MUSICAL CONCORDANCES (PRINTS): • EgenLieder (III, no. 16), C only • PeCantiC (143*v*-144*r*), with different Ct

TEXT FROM CYRUS 2000, p. xvii (after WashC L25):

> De tous biens plaine est ma maistresse,
> chacun lui doit tribut d'onneur.
> Car assouvye est en valeur
> autant que jamais fut deesse.
>
> 5   En la veant j'ay tel leesse
> que c'est paradis en mon cuer.
>   [De tous biens plaine…]
>
> Je n'ay cure d'autre richesse
> si non d'estre son serviteur,
> et pource qu'il n'est chois milleur
> 10   en mon mot porteray sans cesse:
>
>   [de tous biens plaine…]

MODERN EDITIONS OF THE TEXT: BROWN 1983, I, pp. 281-282 (after FirN BR229, and after JEPPESEN 1927, pp. 6-7); CMM 74, p. xxxviii; CYRUS 2000, p. xvii (after WashC L25); LÖPELMANN 1923, no. 575 (after *Berl.M. 17*: a different version of the poem than the one that normally circulated with music); PERKINS - GAREY 1979, II, pp. 323-325 (after NHY 91, with the variants from other sources); POPE - KANAZAWA 1978, p. 612 (after THIBAULT - DROZ (1927) 1976, pp. 20-21); RESTORI 1894, p. 391 (after PavU A362).

MODERN EDITIONS OF THE MUSIC: AMBROS II, *Musikbeilagen*, pp. 20-21 (after DijM 517); ATLAS 1975-76, II, pp. 43-45 (after CV G27); BARRET 1981, II, pp. 71-77 (after DijM 517); BROWN 2983, II, pp. 402-403 (after FirN BR229); CMM 74, pp. 14-15 (3 vv.), 16-17 (4 vv.); CYRUS 2000, pp. 3-5 (after WashC L25), 14-16 (after Panc.27), 20-22 (after PeCantiC), 31-33 (after CV G27); GUTIÉRREZ-DENHOFF 1988, pp. 77-78 (after WolfA G287); JEPPESEN 1927, pp. 7-8 (after KøbK 291); JONES 1971, II, pp. 194-196 (after FirR 2794); KOTTICK 1962, II, pp. 78-79 (after ParisN Ro2973); PEASE 1959, I, pp. 301-306 (after ParisN F15123); PERKINS - GAREY 1979, I, pp. 120-121 (after NHY 91); POPE - KANAZAWA 1978, pp. 320-323 (after MontA 871); MOERK 1971, II, pp. 117-118 (after SevC 43); SCHAVRAN 1978, II, pp. 76-79 (after PavU A362); STEVENS 1962, p. 30 (after LonB A31922); THIBAULT - DROZ (1927) 1976, pp. 20-21 (after DijM 517); THIBAULT - FALLOWS 1991, pp. 38-39 (after ParisN Ro2973); WOLFF 1970, II, pp. 186-188 (after RomaCa 2856)

REMARKS: Hayne van Ghizeghem's three-voice chanson *De tous biens plaine est ma maistresse* had a very wide diffusion in the fifteenth and sixteenth centuries: the piece circulated both in its original version and in various elaborated versions, anonymous as well as attributed (for three or four voices, with a different Contratenor, with only the Superius in common, with only the Tenor in common, etc.). Cynthia Cyrus has analysed as many as 28 reworkings of the piece (CYRUS 2000), and from her study it emerges that the original version of the piece is that contained in WashC L25. The reworking in Panc.27 is an *unicum* which shares the Cantus-Tenor duet with the original version, while the Contra was perhaps added by the scribe himself: in various places there are rather awkward contrapuntal passages (vertical clashes, parallel fifths and octaves, and empty fifths) which make this particular version somewhat deficient (see CYRUS 2000, p. 114). The musical concordances listed above include only the settings for three voices that share the Superius-Tenor duet with the version in Panc.27 (settings 1, 5, 6 of CYRUS 2000, with the exception of intabulations), apart from settings that use only the Superius.

BIBLIOGRAPHY: ATLAS 1975-76, I, pp. 136-139; BROWN 1963, pp. 204-206; BROWN 1983, I, pp. 281-282; CATTIN 1973a, p. 208; CATTIN 1975, p. 206; CMM 74, pp. xxxvii-xli; CYRUS 2000; FILOCAMO 2004; GUTIÉRREZ-DENHOFF 1985, pp. 35, 115, 125, 170-171, 186; GUTIÉRREZ-DENHOFF 1988, pp. 141-144; HERNON 1972, pp. 515-517; JEPPESEN 1927, pp. lxxxi-lxxxvii; JONES 1971, II, pp. 93-96; KÄMPER 1976, pp. 82-83; KOTTICK 1962, II, pp. 19-20; MARIX 1939, p. 237; MOERK 1971, I, pp. 135-136; PEASE 1959, I, pp. 44-46, 104; PERKINS - GAREY 1979, II, pp. 321-325; POPE - KANAZAWA 1978, pp. 611-612; POWERS 1994, pp. 475-479; SCHAVRAN 1978, I, pp. 135-143; THIBAULT - DROZ (1927) 1976, p. 117; THIBAULT - FALLOWS 1991, pp. xcvi-xcix; WOLFF 1970, I, pp. 263-276.

40.
DE TOUS BIENS PLAYNE [EST MA MAISTRESSE]
fol. 25*r*

De tous biens playne

299

41.

Altera autem die

fols. *25v–26v* (4 vv.)

Altera autem die,
que est post Parasceven,
convenerunt principes sacerdotum
et Pharisei ad Pilatum, dicentes:
5 «Domine, recordati sumus
quia seductor ille dixit adhuc vivens:
'Post tres dies resurgam'.
Iube ergo custodiri sepulchrum
usque in diem tertium,
10 ne forte veniant discipuli eius,
et furentur eum,
et dicant plebi:
'Surrexit a mortuis':
et erit novissimus error peior priore».
15 Ait illis Pilatus:
«Habetis custodiam:
ite, custodite sicut scitis».
Illi autem abeuntes
munierunt sepulchrum,
20 signantes lapidem, cum custodibus.

Gospel reading from Matthew 27:62-66 (Vulgata, p. 1573). This is the last section of the Gospel for Palm Sunday, which according to liturgical books is chanted *in tono Evangelii* (LU, p. 600; MR, pp. 149-150) and not simply recited.

Readings emended in the edition:

Bar	Voice	Original
87-88	C, A	*brevis–longa* ligature

Modern editions of the music: Banks 1993, II, pp. 8-12 (after Panc.27); Becherini 1954, p. 121 (after Panc.27, bb. 1-20).

Remarks: In bar 28 the double D-B flat chord is the only chord in first inversion in the whole piece. A long strip of paper covers bars 51-76 of the Bassus (fol. *26r*, fifth stave), under which there was surely other music, as demonstrated by the two stems that peep out above the strip, which correspond to bars 63-64, and also from the chestnut-coloured faded stain partly covered by the strip: probably the copyist first tried to cancel the passage, with an unsatisfactory result, in view of the ink stain that is still visible. He then decided on the slip, which certainly is a better solution to cover a passage that had become too dirty to be corrected. Regarding the text, it is interesting that only one other setting is known, but a different version (in the MS CTL G12): this confirms that Panc.27 and CTL G12 come from a common, though not exactly coinciding, environment.

Bibliography: Banks 1993, I, p. 263.

41.

Altera autem die

fols. 25*v*-26*v*

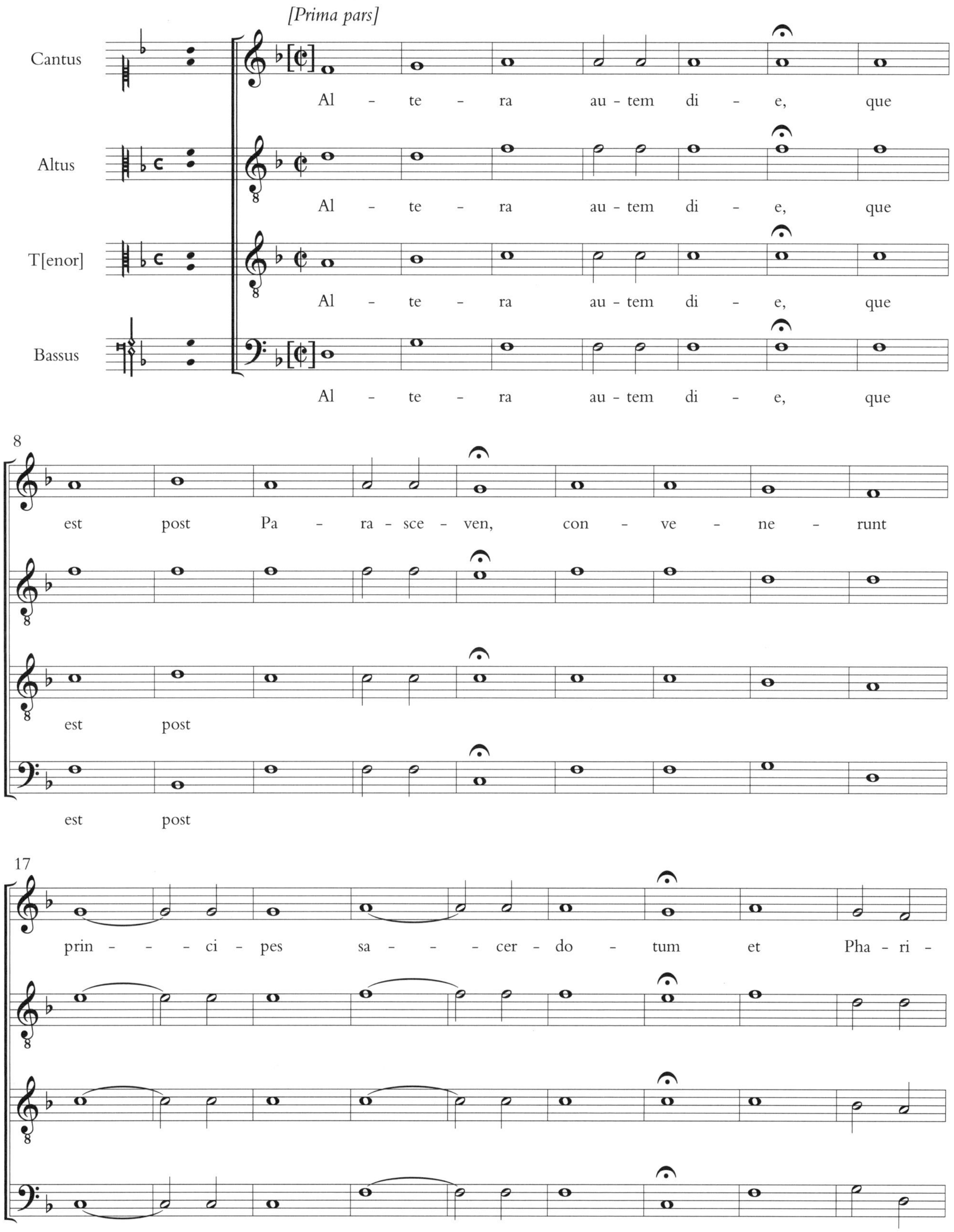

-se – i ad Pi – la – tum, di – cen – – – tes: «Do –

-mi – ne, re – cor – da – ti su – mus qui – a se – du – ctor il – le

di – xit ad – huc vi – vens: 'Post tres di –

303

e - ius, et fu - ren - tur e - um, et

di - cant ple - bi: 'Sur - re - - - xit a mor-tu - is': et

e - rit no - vis - - si - mus er - ror pe - ior pri - o - re».

Secunda pars

109

A - it il - - lis Pi - la - - tus: «Ha - be -

117

- tis cu - sto - di - am: i - te, cu - sto - di - te

126

sic - ut sci - tis». Il - li au - tem a - be - un - tes

305

mu – ni – e – – – runt se – pul – – chrum, si – – – gnan – tes

la – pi – dem, cum cu – sto – di – bus.

42.

OGI È 'L TEMPO, PECCATORE

fol. 27*r* (3 vv.)

[Heading only]

Lauda (barzelletta).

READINGS EMENDED IN THE EDITION:

BAR	VOICE	ORIGINAL
32	T	*brevis* with fermata
after 32	T	barline lacking
after 46	Ct	superfluous *G brevis*
52-53	Ct	*brevis*
after 62	Ct	superfluous *a semibrevis*
63/II	T	*b*
64	T	*b*

TEXTUAL CONCORDANCES (PRINTS): • *Colletanio* (D4*r*-D6*r*), «Pianto della Madonna in laude del Signore» • *Colletanio1509* (G3*v*-H1*v*), «Pianto de la Madonna in laude del signore» • *Colletanio1510* (G3*v*-H1*v*), «Pianto de la Madonna in laude del signore» • *Colletanio1513* (G3*v*-H1*v*), «Pianto de la Madona in laude del signore» • *Colletanio1514Lov* (G2*v*-G4*v*), «Pianto de la Madonna in laude del signore» • *Colletanio1514Rus* (G3*v*-H1*v*), «Pianto de la Madonna in laude del signore» • *Colletanio1521* (D3*v*-D5*v*), «Pianto de la Madonna in laude del signore» • *Colletanio1524* (D3*v*-D5*v*), «Pianto della Madonna in laude del signore» • *Colletanio1537* (D3*v*-D5*v*), «Pianto della Madonna in laude del Signore» • *Compendio* (B1*r*-B2*v*), «Laude del signore» • *Opera1515* (H1*r*-H3*r*), «Pianto della Madonna in la passion del nostro signore»

TEXT FROM *Colletanio1509*:

> Oggi è il tempo, o peccatore,
> lacrimar pel tuo peccato,
> poi che in croce t'ha lavato
> col suo sangue el Redemptore.

5   Di che vòi tu lacrimare
> se non piangi el tuo Signore?
> Ché oggi sol per te salvare
> pende in croce el Salvatore.
> Bene è impio et duro el core
10   che oggi non fa compagnia
> alla croce con Maria,
> che pel duol piangendo more.
>> Oggi è il tempo, o peccatore

> Ogni colpa oggi perdona
> el Signor, tucto clemente.

15   Una lacrima oggi dona
vita eterna a chi si pente.
Piange, ché benignamente
lui te aspecta a braccia aperte.
Piangi, ché ha per te soferte
20   tante pene el Creatore.
            Oggi è il tempo, o peccatore

Oggi puoi con amar pianto
conseguir quel bene eterno
dove è sempre riso et canto,
dove è gaudio sempiterno.
25   Che ti val poi, nell'inferno,
el perpetuo lacrimare?
Ché di lacrime un gran mare
non ti lava un solo errore.
            Oggi è il tempo, o peccatore

Peccator, se non ti dole
30   di Iesù l'aspro tormento,
oggi in cielo te accusa el sole
et nel mondo ogni elemento.
Peccator al pianger lento,
pensa che ogni creatura
35   et la pietra, ch'è sì dura,
fece segno di dolore.
            Oggi è il tempo, o peccatore

Se la croce oggi contempli,
specchio de l'umana vita,
tu vedrai con quanti exempli
40   che al ben far Iesù t'invita.
Sapientia, che è infinita,
carità, pace et clementia,
umilità con patientia
t'insegna oggi el Salvatore!
            Oggi è il tempo, o peccatore

45   Non per òr, non per argento
el Signor t'ha ricomprato,
ma con morte et gran tormento
ché sé stesso in pregio ha dato.
Facto agnello immaculato
50   per purgar l'error antico
che avea el servo col nimico
et ribello al suo factore.
            Oggi è il tempo, o peccatore

Peccator, se tu penserai
nel dolor che ebbe Maria,
55   certo so che piangerai
a la croce in compagnia.
«Voi che passate per via»
cridò lei, «fu mai tal duolo
qual sento io del mio figl[i]uolo,

60   morto sol per l'altrui errore!».
                Oggi è il tempo, o peccatore

      Quando in croce Iesù disse:
      «Ecco, donna, il tuo figl[i]uolo»,
      quella voce el cor trafisse
      che alla madre addoppiò el duolo.
65   O clementia, o exemplo suolo
      ch'era in croce et pur pregava!
      Per qualunque el tormentava,
      piglia exemplo, o malfatore.
                Oggi è il tempo, o peccatore

      Longin ceco, che pensasti
70   de ferire un pecto suolo,
      l'uno et l'altro cor passasti,
      della madre e del figl[i]uolo.
      Lei sentì tutto quel duolo,
      lei sentì le spine e i chiovi.
75   Or se a pianger non ti movi,
      ad chi serbi el tuo dolore?
                Oggi è il tempo, o peccatore

      Per te è facto ‹el› pellicano,
      col morir vince la morte.
      Lui ferito ti fa sano,
80   col suo sangue ti fa forte.
      Ne la extrema et dura sorte
      per te acquista oggi victoria.
      Piangi, dunque, per memoria
      di Iesù tuo redemptore.
                Oggi è il tempo, o peccatore

85   Chi creò la terra e 'l mare,
      chi creò el balsamo e 'l mele,
      chi per te volse mutare
      l'acqua in vin, ch'eri infidele,
      oggi ebbe aceto con fele.
90   Disse: «Sitio», et tu l'udisti,
      madre afflicta, che sentisti
      et gustasti quel sapore.
                Oggi è il tempo, o peccatore

REMARKS: The parallel twelfths in bars 23-25 between the Cantus and Contra have been retained. The counterpoint, for the rest, works well if each voice is read independently against the Tenor. The two superfluous notes after bars 46 and 62 and the missing rest (b. 58/I) in the Contra, together with the misplacement of the last two notes in the Tenor (a third lower) suggest typical mistakes owing to the scribe's oversight in copying from the model.

42.
OGI È 'L TEMPO, PECCATORE
fol. 27r

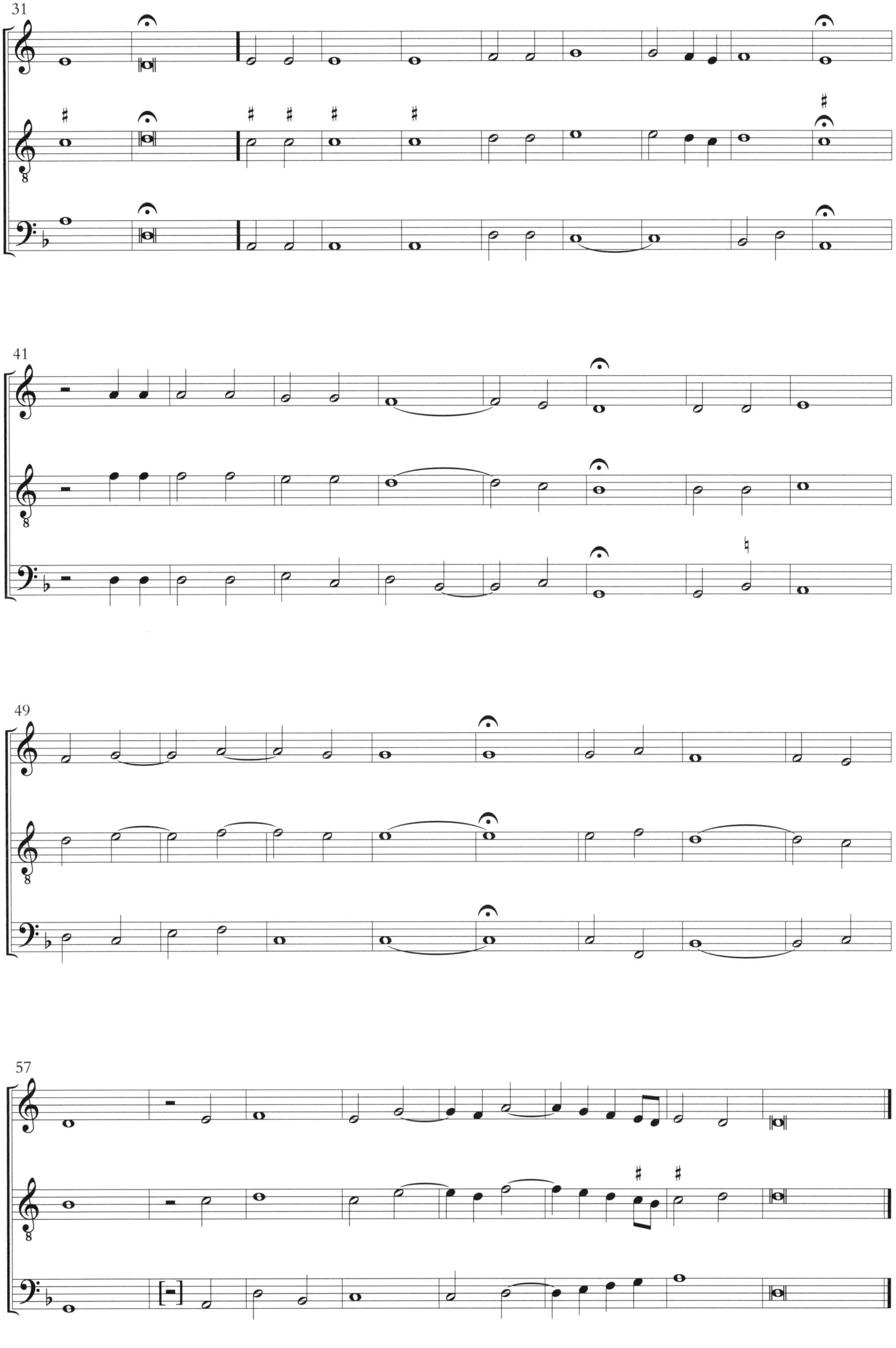
31
41
49
57

43.

ARDA EL CIEL E 'L MUNDO TUTO

fols. 27*v*–28*r* (4 vv.)

Arda el ciel e 'l mundo tuto,
poiché son in fiama e foco
condanato in questo loco
a servir senza alcun fructo.
   Arda el ciel e 'l mundo tuto,
   poiché son in fiama e foco

Italian secular piece (barzelletta).

COMMENTARY ON THE TEXT:

1   el ciel] e cielo S (repetition); e 'l mundo] e mundo S (first enunciation of the line)

READINGS EMENDED IN THE EDITION:

BAR	VOICE	ORIGINAL
after 6	B	superfluous *semibrevis A*
32	A	*longa* with fermata

TEXTUAL CONCORDANCES (PRINTS): • *Fior1509* (M1*v*-M2*r*) • *Fior1510* (M1*v*-M2*r*), «Barzelletta» • *Fior1518* (F5*v*-F6*r*) • *Fior1521* (M1*v*-M2*r*), «Barzelletta» • *Fior1522* ([g5*v*-g6*r*]), «Barzeletta» • *SolaVirtus* (M1*v*-M2*r*), «Barzelletta»

MUSICAL CONCORDANCES (MSS): • FirC B2441 (9*v*-10*r*) • FirN BR337 (32*v*), B only • ParisN Rés27 (43*r*-*v*), *Crida el ciello e 'l mondo tuto* • ParisN Rés676 (119*v*-120*r*)

MUSICAL CONCORDANCES (PRINTS): • PeFroIII1505 (46*v*-47*r*) • PeFroIII1507 (46*v*-47*r*)

TEXT FROM *Fior1509*:

  Arde il cielo e 'l mondo tutto,
  poich'io so 'n fiama e in fuoco
  destinato in ogni luoco
  a patire senza alcun fructo.

5 Infelice el nasimento
  che m'ha dato la mia sorte:
  ch'el mio mal sia nutrimento,
  de ch'io amo ognor più forte!
  Aimè ch'io bramo la morte,
10 in tal stato son conducto.
    Arde il cielo e 'l mondo tucto

Ahi[1] crudel, che te giova
d'un tuo servo farne stratio?
Tu hai di me pur facto prova,
né 'l tuo cor n'è ancor satio
15   de tenirme in tanto giatio,
in sospiri, in pianto, in lutto.
        Arde il cielo e 'l mondo tucto

Se 'l servir mio non t'è gratto
dame almanco libertade.
S'io son tuo preso e ligatto,
20   a che me usi crudeltade?
Se non hai di me pietade
serò presto arso, destructo.
        Arde il cielo e 'l mondo tucto

Pongo fine al mio tormento,
perch'io son all'ultim'ora.
25   Per te son arso in tormento,
e per te convien ch'io mora.
Per amarte, ingratta mora,
alla morte io son conducto.
        Arde il cielo e 'l mondo tucto

MODERN EDITIONS OF THE TEXT: BORGHI 1995, pp. 157-159 (after FirC B2441); CESARI *ET AL.* 1954, p. 46★ (after PeFroIII1505).

MODERN EDITIONS OF THE MUSIC: BORGHI 1995, pp. 315-316 (after FirC B2441); CESARI *ET AL.* 1954, pp. 127-128 (after PeFroIII1505).

REMARKS: While the versions of FirC B2441 and ParisN Rés676 are distinctly distant from Panc.27 (ParisN Rés676 even has different clefs in the Superius and Bassus), those of FirN BR337 and PeFroIII1505 (and its reprint) are unquestionably relatable to the manuscript. Leaving aside the partbook FirN BR337, the Superius and Tenor of the Petrucci print are almost identical (although the upper voice is written in the soprano clef). The Altus and Bassus, on the other hand, have enough rhythmic variants to discourage the hypothesis that Panc.27 was copied from that source. That the piece certainly had a model, however, can be confirmed by the rubric «Iustus» placed at the end of the Altus. The modal configuration of the piece is rather unusual: from the Dorian mode at the beginning it passes into Phrygian at the final cadence, corresponding to the long-held note in the Superius.

BIBLIOGRAPHY: BOORMAN 2006, p. 960; PRIZER 1996b, p. 38.

---

[1]. The source has «Hai».

43.
ARDA EL CIEL E 'L MUNDO TUTO
fols. 27v-28r

S[uperius]: Ar - da el ciel e 'l mun - do tu - to, poi - ché son in fia - ma e

A[ltus]

T[enor]

B[assus]: Ar - da el ciel

fo - co con - da - na - to in que - sto lo - co a ser - vir sen - za al - cun fruc - to.

Ar - da el ciel e 'l mun - do tu - to, poi - ché son in fia - ma e fo – – – co

Iustus

315

44.

Utile consilium

fols. *27v–28r* (4 vv.)

Utile consilium

If one leaves out of consideration the wide diffusion of the phrase, not found in known liturgical or paraliturgical texts, Italian or Latin, the incipit might be identified with the beginning of a proverb or some literary phrase, such as «Utile consilium modo, sed commune, dedisti» (Juvenal, Satire IX, l. 124), or «Utile consilium dominus ne despice servi; | nullius sensum, si prodest, tempseris umquam» (Cato, *Disticha*, III, ll. 10-11),[1] or «Utile consilium qui spernit, inutile sumit. | Qui nimis est tutus, retia jure subit» (Gualterus Anglicus, *Fabulae*, no. 20: *De hirundine et avibus*, ll. 13-14).[2] Alternatively, other possibilities are the proverbs: «Utile consilium dans est homo sepius altri (!), | qui per consilia sibimet nequit auxiliari»; «Utile consilium ne spernas, quod tibi trado, | in latebris mentis immo reconde tue!»; «Utile consilium qui spernit, inutile sumit»; «Utile consilium tibi do: sis semper honestus, | cum letis letus, cum mestis sis quoque mestus!».[3]

COMMENTARY ON THE TEXT:

1   consilium] conscilium C, A, T

MODERN EDITIONS OF THE MUSIC: BANKS 1993, II, p. 195 (after Panc.27).

REMARKS: Written in a different ink (or with a different pen), and with firmer strokes, compared with the composition directly above it. The piece was clearly copied in an empty space left on the opening; as in many other similar cases, the voice names are written out, and the highest voice is called «Cantus».

BIBLIOGRAPHY: BANKS 1993, I, p. 291.

---

[1]. In WALTHER 1967, p. 571, there is a slightly different version: «Utile consilium dominus ne despice servi! | Si prodest, sensum nullius tempseris umquam!».

[2]. In HERVIEUX 1884, II, p. 394. I thank Marco Beghelli for having suggested these hypotheses, and Leofranc Holford-Strevens, who clarified the reference to Gualterus Anglicus.

[3]. See the bibliographical references in WALTHER 1967, pp. 571-572.

44.
UTILE CONSILIUM
fols. 27*v*–28*r*

Cantus

Utile consilium

Altus

Utile consilium

Tenor

Utile consilium

Bassus

Utile consilium

45.

Cum autem venissem ad locum

fol. 28*v* (3 vv.)

[Johannes de Quadris]

Cum autem venissem ad locum,
ubi crucifigendus erat filius meus,
statuerunt eum
in medio omnis populi,
5   et vestibus expoliatis
nudum dimiserunt corpus sanctissimum.

Beginning of a *Planctus Mariae*, sung as a processional chant in the liturgy of Italian Benedictines on Maundy Thursday and Good Friday.

COMMENTARY ON THE TEXT:

6   dimiserunt] dimisserunt C, T

READINGS EMENDED IN THE EDITION:

BAR	VOICE	ORIGINAL
7	C	black *brevis*
10/II-III	C, T	black *brevis*
13	T	black *brevis*
14	T	black *brevis*
17	C, T	black *brevis*
30/II-31/I	C	black *brevis*

MUSICAL CONCORDANCES (MSS): • BolA 179 (183*v*-184*r*), 2 vv. (C and T only) • BolM 13 (38*v*-44*r*: 38*v*-39*r*), 2 vv. (C and T only) • CTL G12 (19*v*-25*r*, *olim* 18*v*-24*r*: 19*v*-20*r*, *olim* 18*v*-19*r*), with different Ct • FirD 21 (10*v*-11*r*), C only • MontB 871 (408-409), 4 vv. (only the C in common) • PavU A361 (8*v*-9*r*), 2 vv. (C and T only) • PozR 1361 (6*v*-7*r*), with different Ct • VerCap 690 (53*v*-58*r*: 53*v*-54*r*), 2 vv. (C and T only) • WashC J6 (122*v*-126*r*: 125*v*-126*r*), 2 vv. (C and T only)

MUSICAL CONCORDANCES (PRINTS):[1] • GiuCant1523 (73*v*-76*r*), 2 vv. (C and T only) • GiuCant1536 (58*v*-61*r*), 2 vv. (C and T only) • LiberSac1523 (267*v*-268*r*), «De processione ad sepulchrum […] In feria VI in parasceve», 2 vv. (C and T only) • LiberSac1537 (253*r*-*v*), «De processione», 2 vv. (C and T only) • PeLamI (47*v*-48*r*); index: «presbyter Johannes de Quadris», 2 vv. (C and T only) • PeLaudeII (5*v*-6*r*), 4 vv. (only the C in common) • Razzi (115*v*-116*r*), 2 vv. (C and T only)

---

[1]. I thank Peter Scott for kindly having given me some information from his doctoral dissertation on the two books of Lamentations printed by Petrucci (SCOTT 2004).

A   Cum autem venissem ad locum,
ubi crucifigendus erat filius meus,
statuerunt eum
in medio omnis populi,
5   et vestibus expoliatis
nudum dimiserunt corpus sanctissimum.

B   O dulcissime filie Sion,
o dulcissime, videte dolorem meum:
inspicite nudum
10   in medio omnis populi,
filium meum dulcissimum:
vulneratus est in medio eorum.

C   O vos, qui transitis per viam,
venite, et videte si est dolor sicut meus:
15   desolata sum nimis,
non est qui consoletur me;
salus mea infirmata est,
vita occiditur et a me tollitur.

D   O nimis triste spectaculum,
20   o crudele supplicium impensum filio!
O felix rex,
tam indecenti morte coronatur!
Pontifices iniquitatis,
tantumne in vestrum exardescitis Deum?

E   25   Attendite vos, o populi
et universe plebes, dolorem maximum:
morte turpissima
mactaverunt filium meum.
Vos, optime sorores,
30   flecte una mecum, de filio conqueramur.

F   Cum autem affixus fuisset,
levaverunt eum in altum
spinea corona coronatum;
stetit quidem vere despectus et illusus
35   et opbrobrijs repletus
et omni amaritudine saturatus.

G   O dulcissime fili mi,
inspice me desolatam,
et fac me mori tecum,
40   quia repleta est anima mea
angustijs et opbrobrijs,
et dolor circumdedit animam meam.

H   Cum autem completa sunt omnia,
caput suum inclinans ad me
45   loqutus est mihi:
mulier, ecce filius tuus.
Et conversus ad discipulum
dixit quoque ad eum: ecce mater tua.

H bis		*Cum vero deposuissent corpus*
		Jesu de cruce, statuerunt illud
	45	*in gremio matris sue,*
		in medio mulierum
		amarissime flentium,
		mestissima matre filium nimis deplorante.

I		Mortuum iam deposuerant,
	50	cum exanimis amplector corpus sanctissimum:
		nunc caput deosculabar,
		nunc pedes et vulnera,
		et amarissimis fletibus
		exanimata cecidi super terram.

L	55	Cum portaretur ad sepulchrum,
		illos sequebar amarissime plorando;
		et lamentabar
		post eos dicendo:
		sinite me osculari
	60	corpus sanctissimum dulcissimi filii.

M		Cum vero venissem ad locum
		ubi sepeliendus erat filius meus,
		statuerunt eum
		in medio mulierum,
	65	et sindone involventes
		sepultum dimiserunt corpus sanctissimum. Amen.

The following synoptic table illustrates the order of the single strophes of the text in the musical sources examined, set out according to decreasing degree of affinity:

	strophes							
PavU A361	A	B	C	D	E	I	L	M
PeLamI	A	B	C	D	E	I	L	M
CTL G12	A	B	C	D	E	M		
BolM 13	A	B	C	M	D	E		
VerCap 690	A	B	C	M	D	E		
LiberSac1523	A	B	M	C	D	E	*H bis*	
LiberSac1537	A	B	M	C	D	E	*H bis*	
WashC J6	A	B	C	D	E			
Razzi	A	B	M	C	D			
GiuCant1523	A	B	D	E	M			
GiuCant1536	A	B	D	E	M			
PozR 1361	A	B	C	F	G	H		
BolA 179	A							
MontB 871	A							
Panc.27	A							
PeLaudeII	A							
FirD 21	L	A	M	D				

MODERN EDITIONS OF THE TEXT: CATTIN 1972a, pp. 471-474 (after all sources); CATTIN 1977, pp. 250-254 (after FirD 21); MANCUSO 1984, II, p. 620 (after Razzi); PERZ - KOWALEWICZ 1976, pp. 157-158 (after PozR 1361); POPE - KANAZAWA 1978, p. 646 (after MontB 871), pp. 647-648 (after PavU A361); YOUNG 1933, I, p. 128 (after LiberSac1523).

MODERN EDITIONS OF THE MUSIC: BECHERINI 1954, p. 120 (after Panc.27, bb. 1-14); CATTIN 1968a, p. 14 (after PavU A361); CATTIN 1970, pp. 288-289 (after GiuCant1523 and GiuCant1536); CATTIN 1972a, pp. 512-513 (after CTL G12 and compared with the Ct of Panc.27); CATTIN 1972b, pp. 71-72 (after PeLamI); DIEDERICHS 1986, pp. 412-413 (after Panc.27), pp. 414-415 (after CTL G12), pp. 416-417 (after PozR 1361), pp. 418-420 (after MontB 871), pp. 421-422 (after PeLaudeII); MUZYKA STAROPOLSKA 1966, p. 30 (after PozR 1361); JEPPESEN 1935, pp. 8-9 (after PeLaudeII); MANCUSO 1984, II, pp. 622-624 (after Razzi); MORAWSKI 1972, I, p. 61 (after PozR 1361); PERZ - KOWALEWICZ 1976, pp. 467-468 (after PozR 1361); POPE - KANAZAWA 1978, pp. 479-482 (after MontB 871).

REMARKS: The piece in Panc.27 probably derives from a model that had an older version, as shown by the unusual mensuration sign (a circle containing two vertical dots that does not appear in the table of symbols drawn up by the copyist on fol. 216v), described as *prolatio minor* in BUSSE BERGER 1993, pp. 236-237; the overall rhythm in fact alternates between duple and triple metre. Even though the mensuration sign clearly indicates triple metre — attested also by the presence of various black *breves* in the Cantus and Tenor — the reworking of the piece in Panc.27 is more convincing in duple metre. The original musical version is certainly a *bicinium* Cantus-Tenor, a version that has travelled in various sources that have only this piece in common with Panc.27 (BolM 13, FirD 21, PavU A361, VerCap 690, GiuCant1523, GiuCant1536, LiberSac1523, LiberSac1537, PeLamI) and others that have more pieces in common (BolA 179, WashC J6, Razzi). The added Contra in Panc.27 is similar to that in CTL G12; the two sources, however, do not derive from a common model: CTL G12 has a 'modern' mensuration sign (circle alone) and does not have black *breves*. Perhaps it was the copyist himself who revised the lower voice in Panc.27: it is the only voice without black *breves* and produces rather clumsy contrapuntal progressions.

BIBLIOGRAPHY: BANKS 1993, I, p. 270; BOORMAN 2006, pp. 899-900; CATTIN 1968a, pp. 5-6; CATTIN 1968b, pp. 96-97, 99-100; CATTIN 1969; CATTIN 1970, pp. 289-292; CATTIN 1971b, pp. 35-42; CATTIN 1972a, pp. 468-476; CATTIN 1973a, pp. 192-193; CATTIN 1977; CORBIN 1960, pp. 114-120, 207-216; DAMILANO 1963, p. 79; GHISI 1937, pp. 107-108; GHISI 1953b; JEPPESEN 1935, p. lxxiv; SCOTT 2004, pp. 86-87; STICCA 1984, pp. 176-182.

45.

Cum autem venissem ad locum

fol. 28*v*

[Johannes de Quadris]

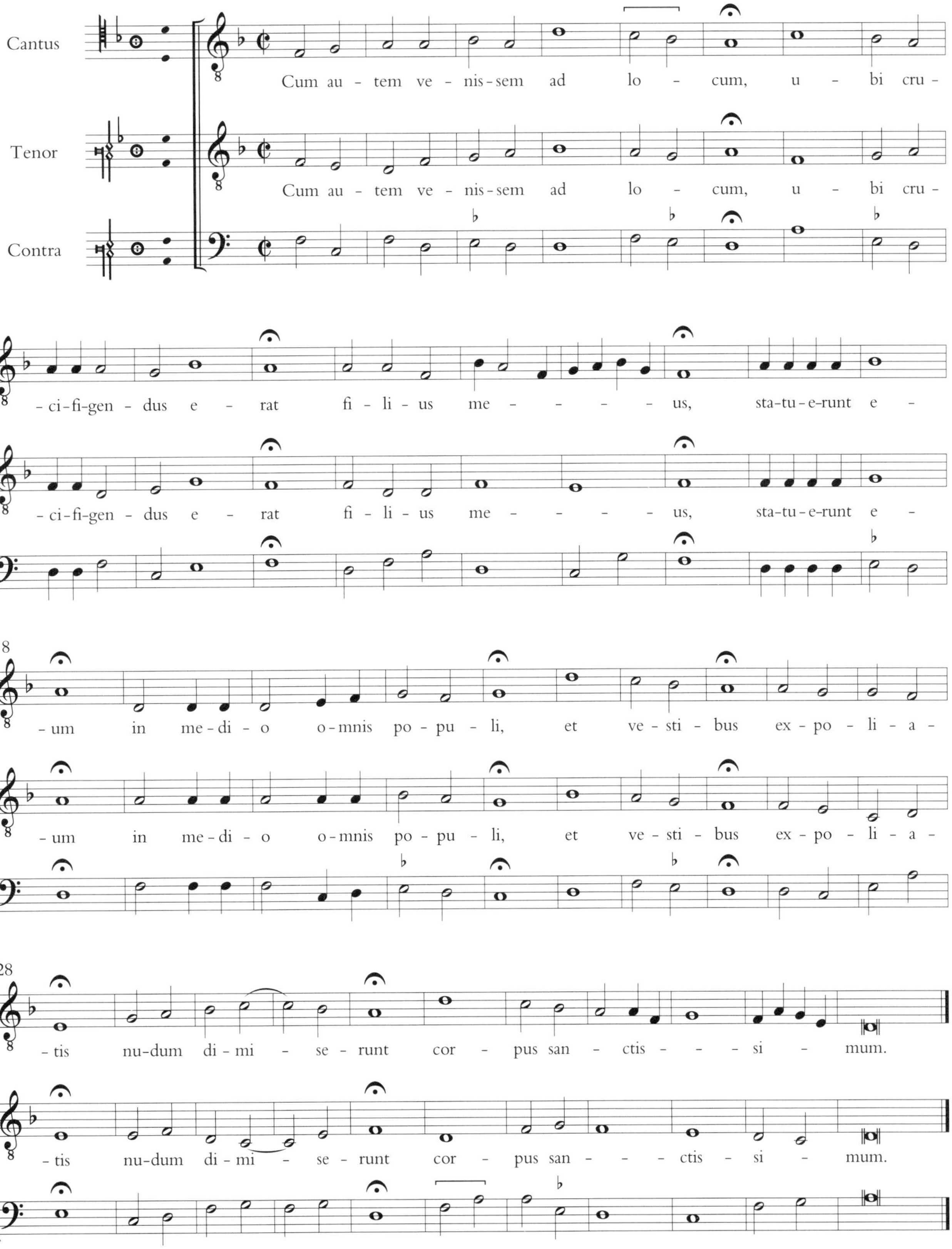

46.

CHRISTI CORPUS AVE, DE SANCTA VIRGINE NATUM

fol. 29r (3 vv.)

[ST. ANSELM OF AOSTA?]

> Christi corpus ave, de sancta Virgine natum,
> viva caro, deitas integra, verus homo.
> Salve vera salus, via, vita, redemptio mundi.
> Liberet a cunctis nos tua dextera malis.

First part of a prayer to the Eucharist attributed to St. Anselm. Widely diffused, it became an ejaculation suggested for the adoration of the Holy Sacrament during the two moments of the elevation, as witnessed, for example, in the *Vita scolastica* (ca. 1290-1300) of Bonvesin de la Riva, lines 401-404 and 407-410.

READINGS EMENDED IN THE EDITION:

BAR	VOICE	ORIGINAL
43	B	*brevis*
120	B	*brevis*

TEXT FROM BONVESIN DE LA RIVA, p. 67 (ll. 397-410):

> Presbyteri manibus tunc hostia quando levatur
> — hostia facta Deus integer est et homo —,
> tunc genibus flexis, capitis velamine dempto
> 400   carmina devote quattuor ista move:
> «Christi corpus, ave, sancta de Virgine natum,
> viva caro, deitas integra, verus homo.
> Salve, vera salus, via, vita, redempcio mundi,
> liberet a cunctis nos tua dextra malis».
> 405   Quando levat calicem manibus, cor surrige, iunctis
> ac infra totidem carmina scripta feras:
> «Christi sanguis, ave, celi sanctissime potus,
> unda salutaris crimina nostra lavans.
> Sanguis, ave, lateris Christi de vulnere sparse,
> 410   in cruce pendentis unda salubris, ave».

MODERN EDITIONS OF THE MUSIC: BANKS 1993, II, pp. 54-56 (after Panc.27).

REMARKS: The style of the composition is marked by a number of parallels, clearly intended by the author: fifths (for example between Tenor and Bassus in bb. 16-17, 66-67) and octaves (for example between Cantus and Bassus in bb. 24-25, 42-43).

BIBLIOGRAPHY: BANKS 1993, I, pp. 269-270; CHEVALIER I, no. 3050.

46.
CHRISTI CORPUS AVE,
DE SANCTA VIRGINE NATUM
fol. 29r

[St. Anselm of Aosta?]

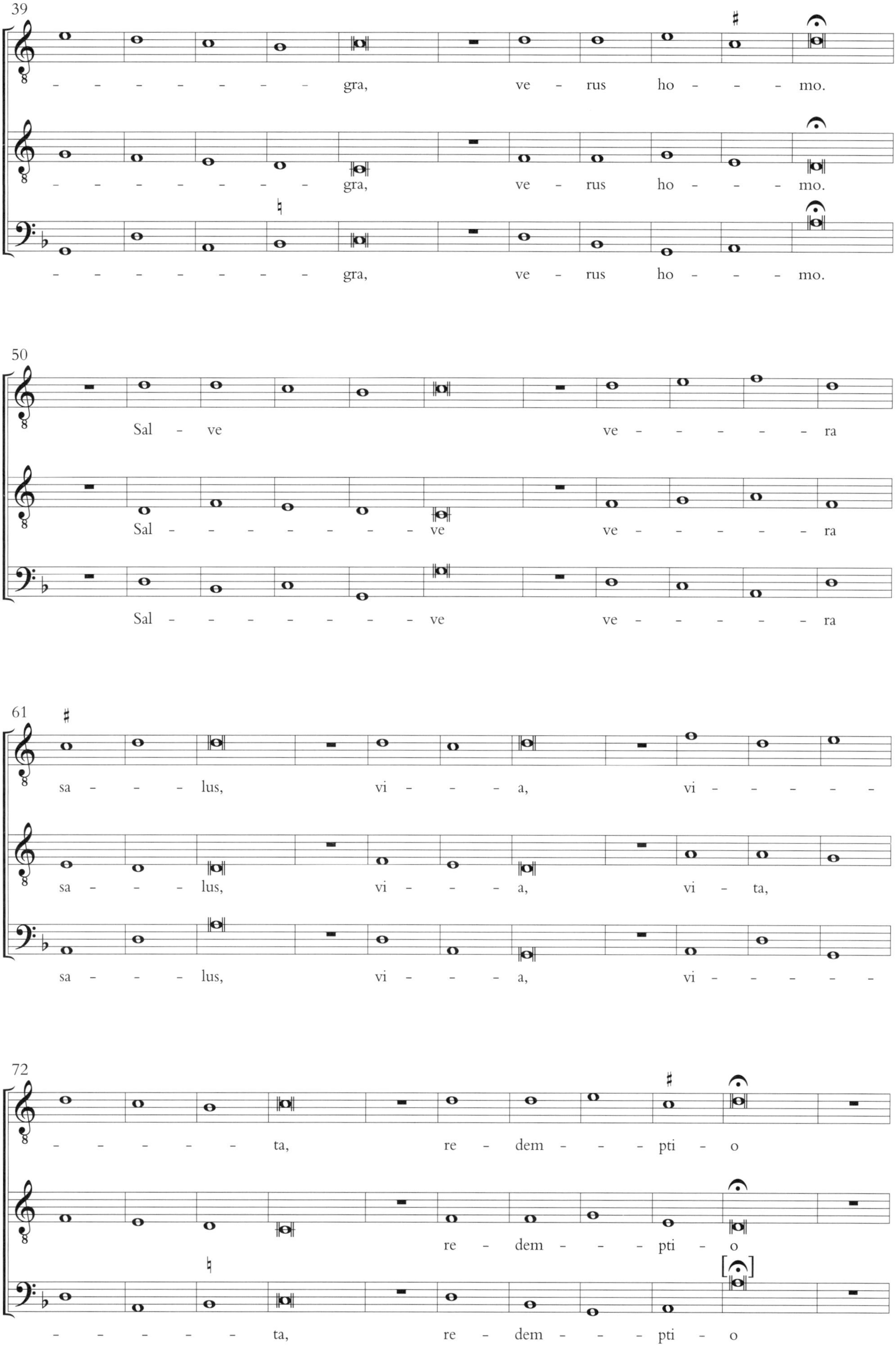
39
gra, ve rus ho mo.
gra, ve rus ho mo.
gra, ve rus ho mo.
50
Sal ve ve ra
Sal ve ve ra
Sal ve ve ra
61
sa lus, vi a, vi
sa lus, vi a, vi ta,
sa lus, vi a, vi
72
ta, re dem pti o
re dem pti o
ta, re dem pti o

mun – – – –

mun – – – –

mun – – – –

– di. Li – be – – – – ret a cun – – –

– di. Li – be – – – ret a cun – – –

– di. Li – be – – – ret a cun – – –

– – – – – ctis nos tu – a

– – – – – ctis nos tu – a

– – – – – ctis nos tu – a

dex – – – – te – ra ma – lis.

dex – – – – te – ra ma – lis.

dex – – – – te – ra ma – lis.

47.

Dolce Regina

fols. 29*v*–30*r* (4 vv.)

[Heading only]

Lauda?[1]

Readings emended in the edition:

Bar	Voice	Original
10/II	A	*a* instead of a rest
27	S,T	*longa* without fermata
32	A	*f'*
58/II	A	*a* instead of *g*
67	T	*a*
70	S	flat before the *f''*
70–71	A	*f'* semibrevis, *e'* semibrevis, and *c'* semibrevis. The whole passage has been corrected on the basis of the concordances

Textual concordances (mss): • *CV. Ch.266* (291*r*), *Dolce regina vergine Maria*

Musical concordances (mss): • CTL G12 (58*v*–60*r*, *olim* 57*v*–58*r*), *Ave dulcis ave pia*

Musical concordances (prints): • PeLaudeII (31*v*–32*r*), *Popule meus quid feci tibi*

Text from *CV. Ch.266*:

    Dolce Regina, Vergine Maria,
    a ˙tte son ritornato,
    tutte di grazia piena e cortesia.
    A chi t'ha invocato,
5   deh, fa che salva sia l'anima mia
    in quel regno beato,
    per carità guidato con tuo scorta.

    Per carità e guidato con tua scorta
    goda nel sonmo bene,
10   gradita chiave e scala, deh,[2] ne 'l porta,
    tormi l'infernal pena,
    e nell'etternal gloria me conforta
    con dolceza serena,
    ché da te vanne e viene ogn'allegreza.

---

[1]. Although there is no musical concordance that would indicate the continuation of the text, Giulio Cattin thinks it probable that it is the lauda *Dolce Regina, Vergine Maria*, present in *CV. Ch.266* (see Cattin 1972a, p. 488, n. 91): three strophes of seven lines (hendecasyllables and settenari) with the scheme AbAbAbC – CdCdCdE – EfEfEfG, with imperfect rhyme in ll. 9 and 11, 18 and 20.

[2]. In the source «del» instead of 'deh'.

15 Ché da 'tte vanne e viene ogn'allegreza,
    per lo divin volere,
    madre degna di Dio sopr'ogn'alteza,
    fanmi nel cor temere
    Iesù tuo figlio, angelica dolceza,
20 soavissimo bene,
    per sempre in lui e godirne, Regina, per amore.

MODERN EDITIONS OF THE MUSIC: CATTIN 1972a, pp. 534-536 (after CTL G12); JEPPESEN 1935, pp. 50-51 (after PeLaudeII).

REMARKS: Although each of the concordances gives a different text, the musical version of Panc.27 is certainly closer to that in CTL G12 than to that of PeLaudeII. Three significant points merit attention: (a) in bar 10/II of the Altus the *a semibrevis* — also in CTL G12 — clashes vertically with the *b′* in the Superius. PeLaudeII gives a *semibrevis* rest instead; (b) the note with fermata in the Bassus of bar 15 is *G brevis* in PeLaudeII and *g longa* in CTL G12. In Panc.27 we find *g longa* but preceded by a *d′ longa* (with fermata) added later and in a smaller size: perhaps the scribe took the initiative to insert the *d′* in order to provide the chord with a fifth, otherwise lacking; (c) in the passage in the Altus in bars 58-59/I — and also in CTL G12 — the *a minima* clashes with the *g′* of the Superius. PeLaudeII has a completely different version at this point: a *semibrevis* rest, dotted *c′ minima*, *d′ semiminima*, *e′ minima* (and *f′ minima*). Many other variants, also melodic, separate the version of Panc.27 from that of Petrucci. The much closer musical version of CTL G12, however, has a concluding «Amen», completely absent in Panc.27 (and also in PeLaudeII).

BIBLIOGRAPHY: BECHERINI 1954, p. 116, n. 1; BOORMAN 2006, p. 935; CATTIN 1972a, pp. 488-489; CATTIN 1973a, p. 198; FRATI 1918, p. 192; JEPPESEN 1969, p. 40, n. 3; LUISI 1983, I, p. 545.

47.
DOLCE REGINA
fols. 29v–30r

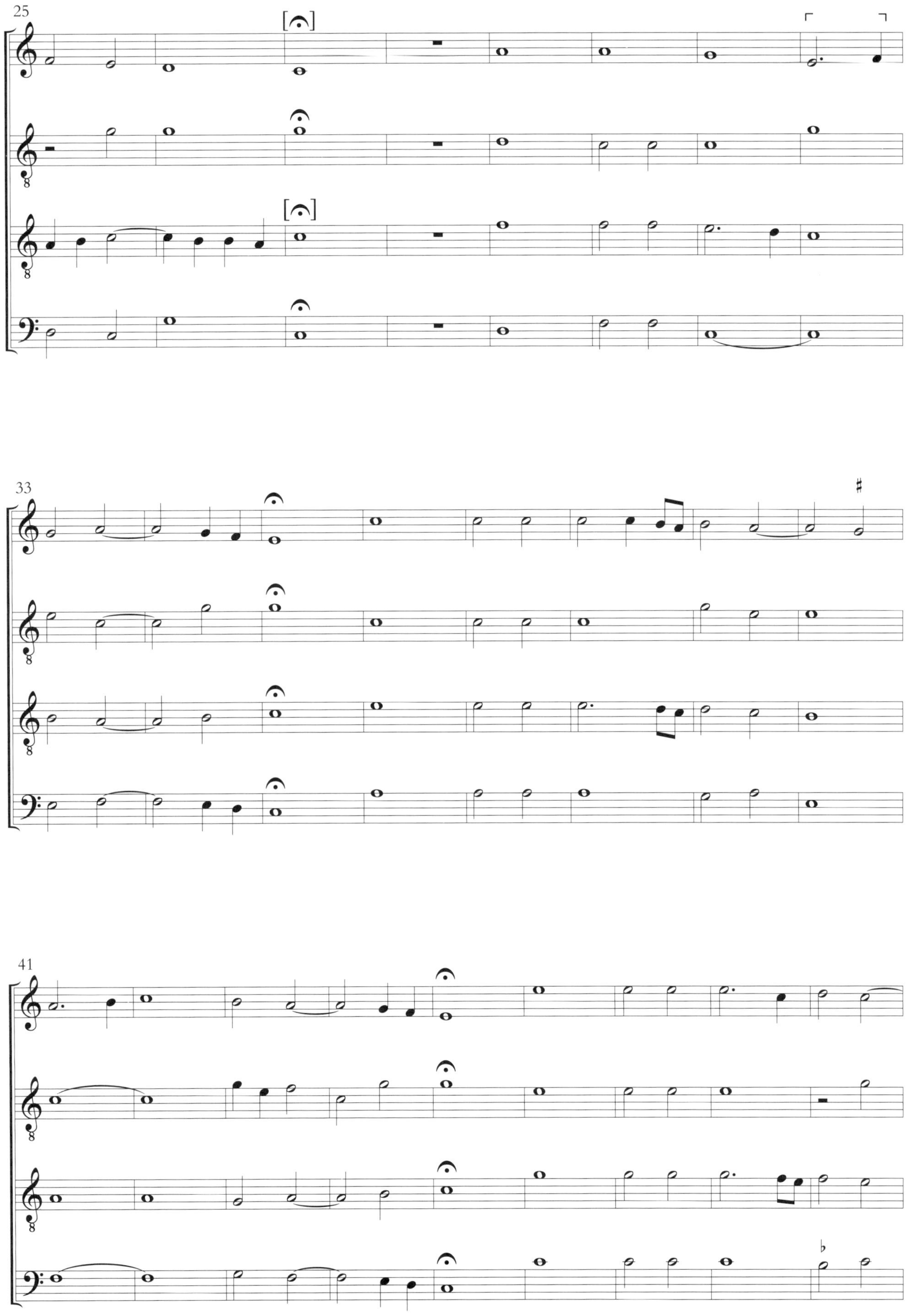
25
33
41

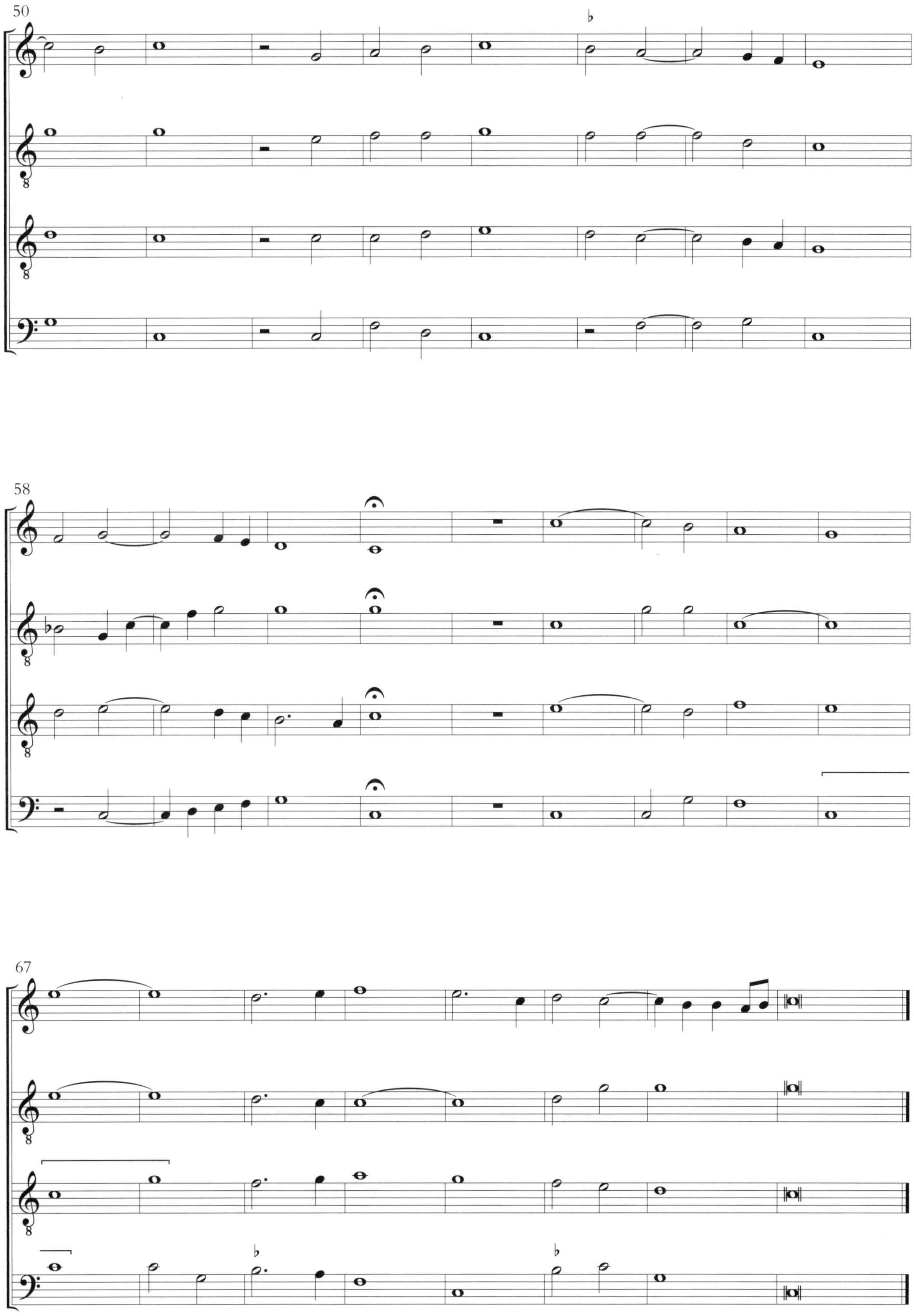
50
58
67

48.

Gaude Virgo, mater Christi

fols. 29*v*-30*r* (4 vv.)

Gaude Virgo, mater Christi,
que per aurem concepisti
Gabriele nuntio.

First strophe of a paraliturgical text for the Feast of the Seven Joys of Mary.

Musical concordances (mss): • BolM 15 (280*r*), *Gaude flore virginali*,[1] 3 vv. (without B) • BolU 2216 (22*r*), *Gaude flore virginali*, 3 vv. (without A, but with a different B) • MilB 49 (84*v*), *Gaude flore virginali*, 2 vv. (S and T only) • TrenF 133 (230-231), 3 vv. (without B) • VenM I145 (127*r*-128*r*), 3 vv. (without A, but with a different B)

Text from *LaudeBonar*, fol. 28*r* (probably, this is the lauda that found its way to Panc.27 and is also present, for example, in *LaudeMisc*, fols. 72*v*-73*r*. It corresponds to the AH 24 version (p. 57), with lines 7-9 and 16-18 lacking. It also corresponds to the two versions published in Mone II: pp. 162-163, where the same two strophes are missing and there are two further strophes, and pp. 163-164, which has five of eight strophes in common):

«Congratulatoria alla Madonna»

Gaude Virgo mater Christi.
Quae per aurem concepisti
Gabriele nuntio,

gaude quia Deo plena,
5   peperisti sine pena,
cum pudoris lilio.

Gaude ut oblatio,
regem, et devotio,
tuo fertur filio.

10   Gaude quia tui nati,
quem dolebas mortem pati
fulget resurrectio.

---

[1]. A parchment codex of the 14th-15th century, which belonged to Giuseppe Mazzatinti, contains 14 texts (anonymous lyric and dramatic laude by the Disciplinati of Gubbio). On fol. 22*r* the following text appears, edited in Mazzatinti 1889, pp. 147-148, which begins the second strophe with *Gaude flore virginali*: «Gaude Virgo mater Christi | quod per flamen concepisti | Gabrielle nuncio. | Gaude flore virginali | onoreque speciali | trascendis splendiferum. | Gaude quod deo plena | peperisti sine pena | cum pudoris lilio. | Gaude magos advenisse | aurum tus mirram tulisse | tuo unigenito. | Gaude quod tui nati | quem dolebas mortem pati | fulget resurrectio. | Gaude Christo resurgente | quod ipso trihumphante | nostra fit redempcio. | Gaude quod post Christum scandis | et est tibi onor grandis | in cellis palacio. | Ubi fructus ventris tui | per te detur nobis frui | in perhenni gaudio. Amen» (Chevalier I, nos. 6808, 6809, 6810).

Gaude Christo asendente,
in coelumque, te vidente,[2]
15   motu fertur proprio.

Gaude quod paraclitus,
missus est divinitus,
in tuo collegio.

Gaude quia post Christum scandis
20   et fit honor tibi grandis,
in celi palatio.

Ubi fructus ventris tui,
per te detur nobis frui,
in eterno gaudio.

MODERN EDITIONS OF THE TEXT: AH 24, p. 57;[3] GALLETTI 1863, p. 145 (after *LaudeMisc*); MONE II, pp. 162-163, 163-164.

MODERN EDITIONS OF THE MUSIC: BANKS 1993, II, p. 80 (after Panc.27); DIEDERICHS 1986, p. 316 (after BolM 15), p. 317 (after VenM I145), p. 318 (after MilB 49), p. 319 (after Panc.27); FEININGER 1975, p. 60 (after TrenF 133).

REMARKS: Written in a residual space on the page, and certainly later than the preceding piece (no. 47), the composition has many parallel octaves between the Tenor and the Bassus (bb. 2/III-3/II, 6/III-8/II, 11/III-12/II). The version of Panc.27 does not appear to be related to any of the known concordances. The musical tradition demonstrates that *Gaude Virgo, mater Christi* typically circulated for three voices without the Bassus in Panc.27: the addition of this voice might be due to the scribe's initiative, but in so doing he has worsened the polyphonic construction of a piece that, as demonstrated by its presence in BolU 2216, was already in circulation since the first decades of the fifteenth century, also with the text beginning *Gaude flore virginali*.

BIBLIOGRAPHY: BANKS 1993, I, pp. 274-275; CHEVALIER I, nos. 7013-7015, 7019; CHEVALIER IV, no. 37592; DIEDERICHS 1986, pp. 110-118; FRATI 1918, p. 198; LUISI 1983, I, p. 546; MAZZATINTI 1889.

---

[2]. The source has «puod [*sic*] in coelumque te vidente». The version emended by GALLETTI 1863, p. 145 (after *LaudeMisc*) is used.

[3]. AH gives several other texts that share the same incipit and various other parts with the version of *LaudeBonar* (AH 15, p. 96: «De Gaudiis BMV» [pium dictamen]; AH 15, p. 97: «De Gaudiis BMV» [pium dictamen]; AH 24, p. 57: «RO [= part of a rhymed office]: De Beata Maria V. Die Martis. Prosa 1»; AH 31, p. 176: «De V Gaudiis BMV» [pium dictamen]; AH 31, pp. 180-181: «De VII Gaudiis BMV» [pium dictamen]; AH 31, pp. 197-198: «De VII Gaudiis BMV terrestribus et totidem caelestibus» [pium dictamen]; AH 42, p. 82: «De [XIV] Gaudiis BMV» [sequentia]; AH 42, p. 83: «De [XII] Gaudiis BMV» [sequentia]; AH 42, pp. 83-84: «Sequentia, quae erit tractus in LXX»; AH 46, pp. 134-135: «De XII Gaudiis BMV» [pium dictamen]).

48.
GAUDE VIRGO, MATER CHRISTI
fols. 29v–30r

Cantus: Gau - de Vir - go, ma - ter Chri - sti, que per au - rem con - ce - pi - sti Ga - bri - e - le nun - ti - o.

Altus: Gau - de Vir - go, ma - ter Chri - sti, que per au - rem con - ce - pi - sti Ga - bri - e - le nun - ti - o.

Tenor: Gau - de

Bassus: Gau - de Vir - go, ma - ter Chri - sti

49.

DEH, FUSSE QUI [CHI MI TO' EL SOMNO! SOMNO]

fol. 30*v* (4 vv.)

[SERAFINO AQUILANO]

[Heading only]

Italian secular piece (echo strambotto toscano?).[1]

TEXTUAL CONCORDANCES (MSS): • *CV. VL. 5159* (93*v*), *De fusse qui chi mi tien sonno: sonno*, (Serafino Aquilano) • *Fer. C. 408* (83*r*), *Deh fusse qui chi mi ti el sonno: sonno*, «Seraphinus» • *Ven. M. I. 66* (300*v*), *Deh fusse qui chi mi to il sonno? sonno*, «Ecco Serap. Aqui.»

TEXTUAL CONCORDANCES (PRINTS):[2] • *Aq1502Bes* (d1*r*), *Deh fusse qui chi mi to el somno! somno*, (Serafino Aquilano), «Ecco» • *Aq1502Bon* (M2*r*), *De fusse qui chi mi to il somno: somno*, (Serafino Aquilano), «ecco» • *Aq1503Baz* (L8*r*), *De fusse qui chi mi to il somno: somno*, (Serafino Aquilano), «Echo» • *Aq1503Bes* (d3*r*), *Deh fusse qui chi mi to el sonno? sonno*, (Serafino Aquilano), «ecco» • *Aq1503Bon* (L1*v*), *De fusse qui chi mi to il somno: sonno*, (Serafino Aquilano), «Ecco» • *Aq1503Man* (m6*r*), (Serafino Aquilano) • *Aq1503Pac* (c4*r*), *Deh fusse qui chi mi to el sonno? somno*, (Serafino Aquilano), «Ecco» • *Aq1503Rug* (M2*r-v*), (Serafino Aquilano) • *Aq1504Bon* (K3*v*), (Serafino Aquilano) • *Aq1504Man* (M3*v*-M4*r*), *De fusse qui chi mi tol somno: somno*, (Serafino Aquilano), «Echo» • *Aq1505Bon(A)* (K3*v*), *Deh fusse qui chi mi to il somno: sonno*, (Serafino Aquilano) • *Aq1505Son* (N4*v*-N5*r*), *Deh fusse qui chi mi to il somno! somno*, (Serafino Aquilano), «Echo» • *Aq1507Son* (N4*v*-N5*r*), (Serafino Aquilano) • *Aq1509Son* (N4*v*-N5*r*), *Dhe* [*sic*] *fusse qui chi mi mi* [*sic*] *to el somno somno*, (Serafino Aquilano) • *Aq1510Tub* (b2*r*), (Serafino Aquilano) • *Aq1511Leg* (g1*v*), (Serafino Aquilano), «Ecco» • *Aq1515Leg* (g1*v*), *De fussi qui chi mi to il somno: somno*, (Serafino Aquilano), «Ecco» • *Aq1516Cas(A)* (g1*v*), *De fussi qui chi mi to il somno: somno*, (Serafino Aquilano), «Ecco» • *Aq1516Cas(B)* (G1*v*), (Serafino Aquilano) • *Aq1516Giu* (139*v*), *Dieh* [*sic*] *fusse qui chi mi mi* [*sic*] *to el sonno, sonno*, (Serafino Aquilano), «Echo» • *Aq1516Son* (N4*v*-N5*r*), *Deh fosse qui chi mi to il sonno, somno*, (Serafino Aquilano) • *Aq1523Vim* (G12*v*), (Serafino Aquilano) • *Aq1530Zop* (R5*r-v*), *De fusse qui chi mi to il sonno, sonno*, (Serafino Aquilano), «Ecco» • *Aq1548Basc* (139*v*), *Deh fusse qui chi mi to il sonno, sonno*, (Serafino Aquilano), «Echo»

---

[1]. Although there is no musical concordance that gives the continuation of the incipit of Panc.27, Giuseppina La Face and Antonio Rossi believe it is the echo strambotto *Deh, fusse qui chi mi to' el somno! Somno* (see LA FACE BIANCONI - ROSSI 1999, p. 110).

[2]. The printed tradition of Serafino's works was almost entirely posthumous; the *editio princeps*, put together by Francesco Flavio to prevent the total loss of the poems, which had already begun, is represented by *Aq1502Bes*, a collection that gave rise to an extremely rich editorial tradition (34 editions in the first 15 years; more than 50 had appeared by 1568), which amplified or varied from time to time the body of texts collected, also inserting some pieces by other authors (see the complete bibliography in ROSSI 2002, pp. 349-399 and ROSSI 2005, pp. 452-494). Most of the editions do not derive directly from the *princeps*, but from *Aq1502Bon*, which appeared barely 25 days later. Other editions on which succeeding editions were based — though scarcely reliable in the question of attribution of the pieces collected, which grew enormously — were the anthologies *Aq1503Baz* and *Aq1516Giu*, in which the text is always implicitly attributed to Serafino, together with many other poems that contemporary sources attribute instead to other authors. More trustworthy are the anthologies *Aq1503Bes* (edited by the humanist Angelo Colocci, who had already been in contact with Serafino in Rome), on which none of the succeeding editions drew, and *Aq1505Son* (edited by Giovan Battista Bonaccursio), which had at least three republications (*Aq1507Son*, *Aq1509Son*, and *Aq1516Son*).

Text from *Aq1502Bes*:

> Deh, fusse qui chi mi to' el somno! Somno.
> Ah, chi responde al mio clamore? Amore.
> Mei prieghi, Amor, stringer te ponno? Ponno.
> Dimi, costei prezza el mio amore? More.
> 5   Dunque li ciel mio ben non vonno? Vonno.
> Chi darrà fine al mio dolore? L'ore.
> E che ho da far lei sia contenta? Tenta.
> Speri poi tu darmela venta? Venta.

Modern editions of the text: Bauer Formiconi 1967, p. 248 (after *Aq1516Giu*); La Face Bianconi – Rossi 1999, pp. 110-111 (after *Aq1502Bes*); Rossi 2002, pp. 167-168 (after *Aq1502Bes*).

Modern editions of the music: La Face Bianconi – Rossi 1999, pp. 192-193 (after Panc.27).

Remarks: Even though it is a musical *unicum*, this piece has been allotted a comfortable layout: by itself, in fact, it occupies the first four staves on the page. The presence of this piece was probably the result of an initial editorial decision to include a group of pieces that all begin with the letter 'D'.

Bibliography: Ferrari Barassi 1993, p. 1493.

49.
DEH, FUSSE QUI [CHI MI TO' EL SOMNO! SOMNO]
fol. 30*v*

[Serafino Aquilano]

50.

DEH, NON PIÙ TANTE PAROLE

fol. 31*r* (4 vv.)

[Heading only]

Italian secular piece (barzelletta?).

REMARKS: See also Remarks to no. 49. Of some interest is the unusual repetition of the passage from bars 11 to 14, which replicate the similar preceding version in *sesquialtera* (bb. 7–10).

50.
Deh, non più tante parole

fol. 31*r*

51.

DA PACEM, DOMINE

fols. 31*v*-32*r* (4 vv.)

Da pacem, Domine,
in diebus nostris,
quia non est alius
qui pugnet pro nobis
5   nisi tu Deus noster.

Antiphon for Peace (AR, p. 146★; LU, pp. 1867-1868); also used as antiphon for the Commemoration of the Holy Maccabees, Martyrs (CAO III, p. 135). See also IGC, p. 106.

READINGS EMENDED IN THE EDITION:

BAR	VOICE	ORIGINAL
13/I	B	the addition of the rest agrees with all the concordances

MUSICAL CONCORDANCES (MSS):[1] • CTL G12 (110*v*-111*r*, *olim* 119*v*-120*r*), 3 vv. (without A) • ParisN F1597 (2*v*-3*r*), 3 vv. (without A)

MUSICAL CONCORDANCES (PRINTS): • PeMotA1502 (45*v*-46*r*), «Si placet» rubric above the A • PeMotA1505 (45*v*-46*r*), «Si placet» rubric above the A

MODERN EDITIONS OF THE MUSIC: CMM 76, pp. 73-74 (after CTL G12); DRAKE 1972, II, pp. 106-108 (after PeMotA1502); SHERR 1991, pp. 91-95 (after PeMotA1502); SHIPP 1960, pp. 244-247 (after ParisN F1597).

REMARKS: The piece is transmitted in three voices (in CTL G12 and in ParisN F1597) and in four voices (in PeMotA1502 and its reprint with a «si placet» Altus), but all three concordances have numerous graphic variants with respect to the version in Panc.27 (ligatures, coloration, rhythmic variants, small ornamentations). Nor can Petrucci's version be the model for Panc.27: the Altus ends with an embellished coda in place of the long final note in the manuscript (bb. 51-54). The chant in AR, p. 146★ and LU, pp. 1867-1868 is quoted at the beginning of each phrase in the Superius.

BIBLIOGRAPHY: BANKS 1993, I, pp. 270-271; BOORMAN 2006, p. 900; BROWN 1990, p. 755, n. 37; CAO III, p. 135; CATTIN 1973a, p. 214; CMM 76, p. xxxii; DRAKE 1972, I, pp. 75-76, 149, 174, 226, 324-325; IGC, p. 106; SHIPP 1960, pp. 159-160.

---

[1]. Stanley Boorman (see BOORMAN 2006, p. 900) lists as well the following manuscript concordances, all anonymous: Amiens, Bibliothèque Municipale, 162, fol. 2*r* (3 vv.), Vatican City, Cappella Sistina, 15, fols. 266*v*-267*r* (4 vv.); Vatican City, San Pietro B 80, 18, fol. 38*v* (3 vv.). In all three cases these are pieces that are not concordant with that in Panc.27.

51.
DA PACEM, DOMINE

fols. 31*v*–32*r*

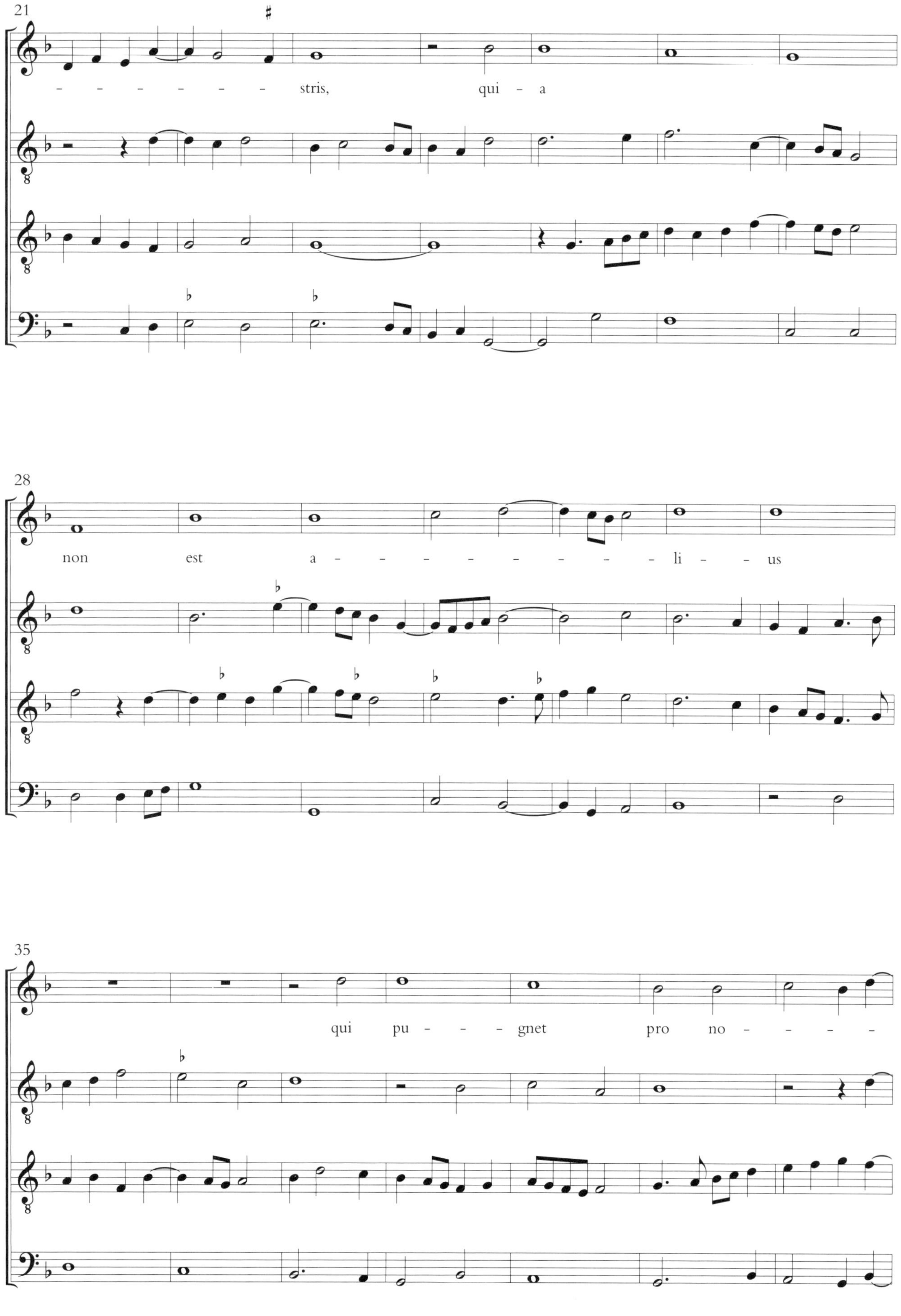
21
- - - - - - - stris, qui - a
28
non est a - - - - - - - - li - - us
35
qui pu - - - gnet pro no - - - -

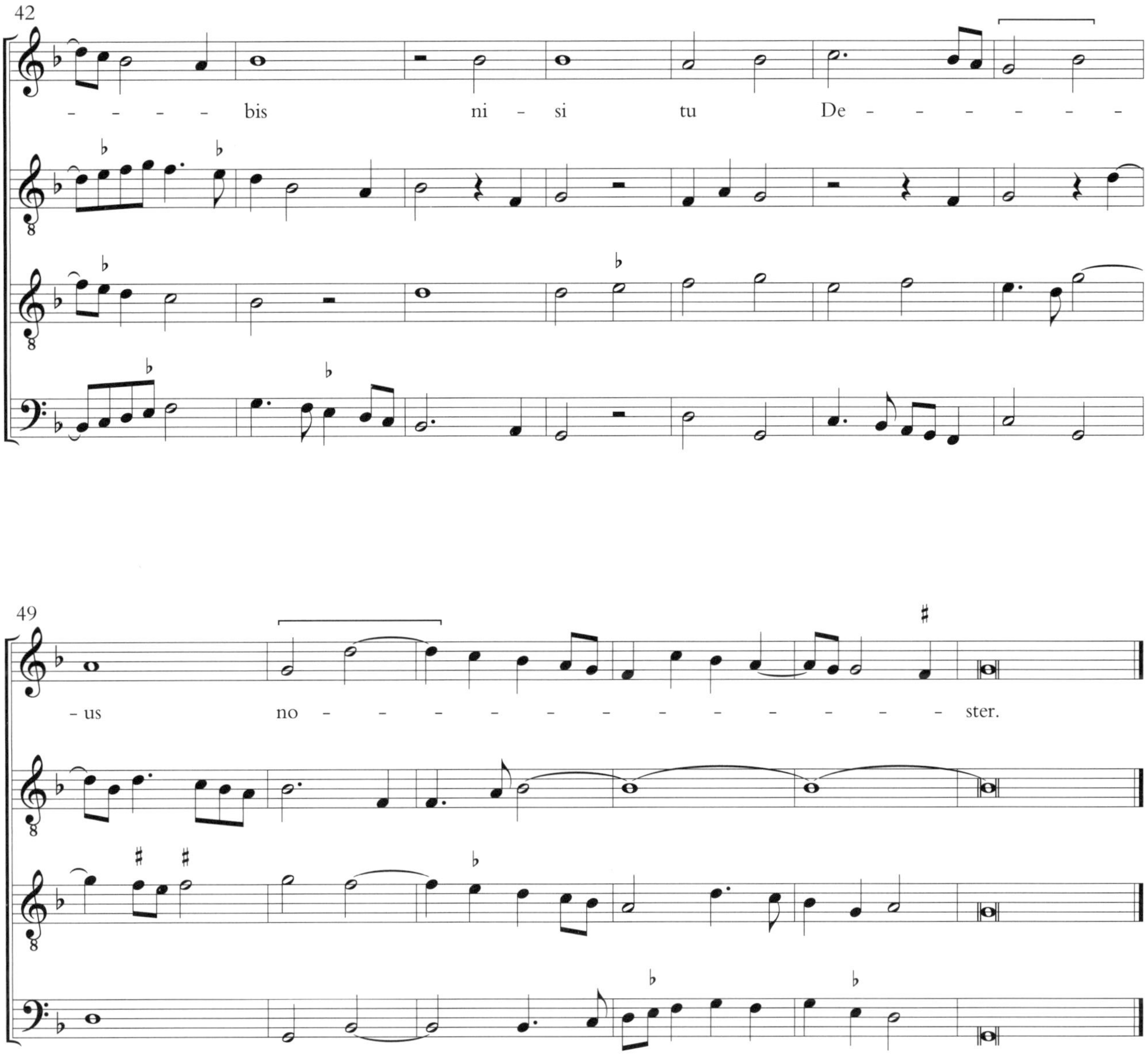
42
- - - - bis ni - si tu De - - - - - - -
49
- us no - - - - - - - - - - - - - ster.

52.

Deh sì, deh no, deh sì

fol. 32*v* (4 vv.)

[Marchetto Cara / Bartolomeo Tromboncino][1]

Deh sì, deh no, deh sì,
deh, 'l to bisogno di'.
      Deh sì, [deh no,] deh sì

Oimè che se 'l dirò,
e ch'ela dica: 'No',
5   so ben che morirò,
meglio è lasar[la] qui.
      Deh sì [...]

Se 'l dico, che serà?
La se scorezarà,
da sé mi scazarà,
10   che serà poi de mi?
      Deh sì [...]

Ecco, vo' dirlo, orsù,
Amor, che farai tu?
Se no mi vorà più,
che serà poi de mi?
      Deh sì [...]

Italian secular piece (ballata antica).

Commentary on the text:

1	over the «o» of «no» there is an abbreviation sign for an «n». I have preferred to ignore it since all the concordances have the more logical reading «no»
2	«tho» instead of 'to'
6	the addition improves the line and is taken from the other sources
7	the *residuum* begins here
9	a caret indicates the correct position of «mi», written after «scazarà». This insertion was probably the result of a later correction, as demonstrated by the lighter ink

Readings emended in the edition:

Bar	Voice	Original
16	C	*longa*

---

[1]. Both attributions appear in Venetian prints by Petrucci, published at slightly more than four years' distance from each other (PeFroI: 28 November 1504; PeBossI1509: 27 March 1509).

| 31 | C, A, T, B | the composition ends with a *custos* and the rubric «ut supra», which refer back to the initial note; it is clear that the piece ends at bar 16 |

MUSICAL CONCORDANCES (MSS): • BolM 18 (14*v*-15*r*) • ParisN Rés27 (25*v*-26*r*)

MUSICAL CONCORDANCES (PRINTS): • PeBossI1509 (28*r*), «B. T.» • PeBossI1515 (28*r*), «B. T.» • PeFroI (14*v*-15*r*), «M. C.»

TEXT FROM BolM 18:

Deh sì, deh no, deh sì,
deh, 'l tuo bisogno di'.
Deh sì […]

Oimè che s'io 'l dirò,
ch'ela dica de no,
5   so ben ch'io morirò,
megl[i]o è 'llasarla qui.

Se 'l dico, che sarà?
La se scarucerà
da 'ssé mi scacerà,
10   che dirà poi di ti?

Eco, io nol dirò,
Amor, che farai tu?
Me non mi vorrà più,
che sarà poi di mi?

15   S'io tacio sempre, oimè,
che mi val la mia fé?
Adonca pur megl[i]o è
non la lassar così.

Che debia far no so,
20   de dirlo ardir non ho,
né ancor tacer si può:
la non può star così.

MODERN EDITIONS OF THE TEXT: CESARI *ET AL.* 1954, p. 7★ (after PeFroI); DISERTORI 1964, p. 363 (after PeBossI1509); FILOCAMO 2000, pp. 113-115 (after Panc.27); GALLICO (1961) 1998, pp. 9-10 (after PeFroI); SCHWARTZ 1935, p. xxix (after PeFroI).

MODERN EDITIONS OF THE MUSIC: CESARI *ET AL.* 1954, pp. 12-13 (after PeFroI); DISERTORI 1964, p. 363 (after PeBossI1509); SCHWARTZ 1935, pp. 11-12 (after PeFroI).

REMARKS: The model for the copying of the piece is certainly PeFroI, a musical version that is completely identical (apart from the scribe's oversight in b. 16 of the Cantus). Even the amount of text is identical in the two sources, but with a few slight differences. Apart from some graphic variants and the different key signature (B flat in all the voices), the version of BolM 18 does not include bars 17-31 of the Tenor. In Panc.27 *Deh sì, deh no, deh sì* concludes the section originally reserved for the letter 'D'.

BIBLIOGRAPHY: BOORMAN 2006, p. 971; FILOCAMO 2004; GALLICO (1961) 1998, pp. 9-11; PRIZER 1980, pp. 77, 94-95, 355; TIBALDI 2005, pp. 499, 509; WEISS 1998, p. 20.

52.
Deh sì, deh no, deh sì
fol. 32*v*

[Marchetto Cara / Bartolomeo Tromboncino]

346

'No',   so   ben che   mo – ri – rò,   me – glio è   la-sar   –   [la]   qui.

Ut supra

53.

La nocte aquieta ogni fiero animale

fol. 33*r* (4 vv.)

[…]¹

> La nocte aquieta ogni fiero animale
> e da fatiche sue resta discio[l]to.
> La notte i vaghi ucel‹li› dan triegua a l'ale
> e la voce, che 'l cantar gli è tolto.
> 5   La nocte, alfin, se possa ogni mortale,
> et io più ne‹lli›i suspiri son involto.
> Né mai ho pace al mio longo martìre,
> ché gran fatiga è de miseria uscire.

Italian secular piece (strambotto toscano).

COMMENTARY ON THE TEXT:

2	the error «discioto» has been corrected on the basis of the other sources
3	the *residuum* begins here
3	the hypermetre can be corrected on the basis of the other literary sources
6	the hypermetre can be corrected on the basis of the other literary sources

TEXTUAL CONCORDANCES (MSS): • *CV. Ca.193* (289*v*) • *CV.VL.5159* (182*r*), (Serafino Aquilano) • *CV. VL.13704* (86*v, olim 96v*) • *Fir.N. 75* (220*v*) • *Ox.B. CI.99* (99*v*) • *Paris.N. I.1543* (225*v*)²

TEXTUAL CONCORDANCES (PRINTS): • *Aq1503Baz* (O2*v*) • *Aq1504Bon* (L2*v*), (Serafino Aquilano) • *Aq1504Man* (O5*r*), (Serafino Aquilano) • *Aq1505Bon(A)* (L2*v*), (Serafino Aquilano) • *Aq1505Bon(B)* (L2*v*), (Serafino Aquilano) • *Aq1505Son* (O5*v*), (Serafino Aquilano) • *Aq1506Bon* (K4*v*), (Serafino Aquilano) • *Aq1507Bon* (K4*v*), (Serafino Aquilano) • *Aq1507Son* (O5*v*), (Serafino Aquilano) • *Aq1508Bon* (K4*v*), (Serafino Aquilano) • *Aq1509Son* (O5*v*), (Serafino Aquilano) • *Aq1510Rus* (K4*v*), (Serafino Aquilano) • *Aq1511Leg* (h3*v*), (Serafino Aquilano) • *Aq1512Bin* (E7*v*), (Serafino Aquilano) • *Aq1513Lov* (110*r-v*), (Serafino Aquilano) • *Aq1513Ses* (K4*v*), (Serafino Aquilano) • *Aq1515Leg* (h3*v*), (Serafino Aquilano) • *Aq1516Bin* (N6*r*), (Serafino Aquilano) • *Aq1516Cas(A)* (h3*v*), (Serafino Aquilano) • *Aq1516Cas(B)* (H3*v*), (Serafino Aquilano) • *Aq1516Giu* (148*r*), (Serafino Aquilano) • *Aq1516Son* (O5*v*), (Serafino Aquilano) • *Aq1518Mon* (O5*r*), (Serafino Aquilano) • *Aq1519Ses* (K4*v*), (Serafino Aquilano) • *Aq1522Rus* (N3*v*), (Serafino Aquilano) • *Aq1523Vim* (I4*v*), (Serafino Aquilano) • *Aq1530Zop* (S5*v*), (Serafino Aquilano) • *Aq1548Basc* (148*r*), (Serafino Aquilano)

MUSICAL CONCORDANCES (PRINTS): • PeFroIV1505 (25*r*) • PeFroIV1507 (25*r*)

MODERN EDITIONS OF THE TEXT: BAUER FORMICONI 1967, p. 297 (after *Aq1516Giu*); FILOCAMO 2000,

---

¹. The attribution to Serafino Aquilano, although accepted by BAUER FORMICONI 1967, is rejected in LA FACE BIANCONI – ROSSI 1999.

². From fol. 223*v* to fol. 227*r* there are several strambotti, mostly by Serafino.

pp. 115-117 (after Panc.27); SCHWARTZ 1935, p. xl (after PeFroIV1505); SPONGANO 1971, p. 73 (after *Ox.B. CI.99*).

MODERN EDITIONS OF THE MUSIC: SCHWARTZ 1935, p. 70 (after PeFroIV1505).

REMARKS: Although PeFroIV1505 (with its reprint) is the only musical concordance and shares the hypermetric poetic readings, there is no question of considering Petrucci's print as the model for the scribe of Panc.27. Three of the four voices (Altus, Tenor, Bassus) are written in other clefs, and have several melodic and graphic variants. The upper voice is musically identical, but the text under the music lacks the adjective «fiero» before «animale».

BIBLIOGRAPHY: BOORMAN 2006, p. 987.

53.
LA NOCTE AQUIETA OGNI FIERO ANIMALE
fol. *33r*

La noc-te a-quie - - ta o - gni fie - ro a-ni-ma -

- - - - - - le e da fa - ti-che su - e

re - sta di - scio[l] - - - - - - - - - to.

54.

La mora

fols. 33*v*-34*r* (3 vv.)

[Henricus Isaac]

La mora[1]

Instrumental piece.

Musical concordances (mss): • BasU 22 (32*v*-34*v*), «Isacius author» • BolM 18 (72*v*-73*r*) • CV G27 (83*v*-84*r*, *olim* 90*v*-91*r*), *Dona gentil*,[2] «Ysach» • FirN BR229 (11*v*-12*r*), textless, «Henricus Yzac» • FirN M107bis (56*v*-57*r*, *olim* 44*v*-45*r*), «Jzac» • FirN M178 (29*v*-30*r*), «Enrigus Yzac» • HeilbS 2 (no. 14), B only, «Isaac» • KøbK 1848 (412) • LeipU 1494 (85*v*-86*r*), textless, «H.Y.» • LeipU 1494 (245*v*-246*r*), *Reple tuorum corda fidelium* • MünS 272 (72*v*-73*r*) • ParisN Rés27 (14*v*-15*r*) • ParisN Rés676 (40*v*-41*r*), C: *Mora: dona gentile*, T: *La Mora: Dona gentile*, Ct: *Muora: dona zentile* • SegC (175*v*), *Elaes*, «Ysaac» • SGS 462 (60*v*-61*r*), *O regina La morra*, 4 vv. (additional A), «Isaac» • SGS 463 (no. 176), 2 vv. (S and A only), «Henricus Isaac», heading: «Dorius» • SGS 530 (93*v*-94*r*), textless, «Heinrich Isaac» • VerCap 757 (39*v*-40*r*), textless, modern hand: «Yzac. La morra» • WML 6 (11), textless, «Ysaac», «Muteta»[3] • ZwR 78/3 (no. 25), textless, «Isaac»

Musical concordances (prints):[4] • EgenLieder (III, no. 34), S only • FormTrium (no. 29), textless, but in the Jena copy only, added by hand: «La mora» • PeOdh1503 (49*v*-50*r*), «Yzac» • PeOdh1504 (49*v*-50*r*), «Yzac» • PeSpinI (26*r*-27*r*), (Francesco Spinacino) • PetreiusNewI (g3*r*-g4*r*), «Jsaac» • PetreiusNewI (p1*v*-p3*r*), «Jsaac» • PhalChansons (8-9), «Benedictus Isaac»[5]

Modern editions of the music: Baker 1978, II, p. 462 (after SegC); Brown 1983, II, pp. 23-25 (after FirN BR229); DTÖ 28, pp. 90-91 (after FirN BR229); 151-152 (after PetreiusNewI, fols. p1*v*-p3*r*), 152-153 (after PetreiusNewI, fols. g3*r*-g4*r*), 154-155 (after BasU 22); EDM 32, p. 113 (after LeipU 1494); EDM 34, pp. 360-361 (after LeipU 1494); Ferrari 1994, pp. 4-6 (after ParisN Rés676); Hewitt 1942, pp. 315-316 (after PeOdh1504); IMM 2, pp. 30-32 (after PeOdh1504); Mönkemeyer 1985, I, p. 50 (after FormTrium); Schmidt 1969, II, pp. 61-63 (after PeSpinI); SM 5, pp. 131-132 (after SGS 462); SM 6, pp. 30-31 (after BasU 22); SM 8, pp. 226-227 (after SGS 530).

---

[1]. There have been many questions about this incipit. The most likely opinions remain those of Helen Hewitt, who considered «Mora» as a homage to Ludovico il Moro, duke of Milan (see Hewitt 1942, p. 76); Federico Ghisi, according to whom the incipit might allude to a popular game, still played in Italy (see Ghisi 1965, p. 5); and Allan Atlas, who hypothesized a relationship between all the texts in the various concordances referring to the incipit «La mora» and an unknown woman or queen Mora (see Atlas 1975-76, I, p. 188). Adhering to one or the other interpretation, scholars have sometimes spelt the word «mora» with a capital 'm'. I prefer to adopt the lower case 'm', since the various editions of the *Odhecaton* always give it thus.

[2]. Is there a slight possibility that this textual incipit refers to the rondeau quatrain *Dona gentile bella come l'oro* set to music by Dufay? See the edition of the text of NHY 91, fols. 43*v*-44*r*, in Perkins - Garey 1979, II, pp. 326-328.

[3]. «Muteta» (= 'motet').

[4]. In PeOdh1501 the pages that should have contained *La mora* (fols. 49*v*-50*r*) are lacking; the piece, however, was the original print, as proved by the table of contents.

[5]. In Staehelin 1977, I, p. 48 it is stated that this piece corresponds to *La mora*. See also Vanhulst 1990, pp. 3 and 5.

Remarks: The only sources distant from the version in Panc.27 are those of KøbK 1848, SegC, SGS 462, SGS 463, VerCap 757, and FormTrium. The other musical sources are instead quite close, and especially FirN M107bis and FirN BR229. The *Odhecaton* version is probably the model used: the differences with Panc.27 are merely graphic (above all *ligaturae cum opposita proprietate* instead of separated notes in the manuscript).

Bibliography: Atlas 1975-76, I, pp. 187-188; Baker 1978; Banks 1999; Boorman 2006, pp. 986-987; Brown 1983, I, pp. 97-98, 211-212; Brown - Polk 2001, pp. 129, 131; Brown - Stein 1999, p. 84; Cattin 1975, pp. 212-213; Christoffersen 1994, II, p. 158; Filocamo 2004; Ghisi 1965, p. 5; Hewitt 1942, pp. 149-150; Kämper 1976, pp. 89, 158; Lama de la Cruz 1994, pp. 275-276; Loach 1969, I, pp. 324, 387; Picker 1991, p. 108; Powers 1994, pp. 459-460; SM 6, p. 123; SM 8, p. 357; Weiss 1998, pp. 31-32.

54.
LA MORA
fols. 33v–34r

[Henricus Isaac]

La mora

354

55.

La stangetta[1]

fols. 34*v*-35*r* (3 vv.)

[Henricus Isaac / Jacob Obrecht / Gaspar van Weerbeke][2]

[Heading only]

Instrumental piece.

Readings emended in the edition:

Bar	Voice	Original
26/I	B	*d minima*
58	T	*brevis* with fermata

Musical concordances (mss): • HeilbS 2 (no. 29), B only • SegC (172*r*), *Ortus de celo flos est*,[3] «Ysaac» • ZwR 78/3 (no. 18), textless, «Obrecht»

Musical concordances (prints): • EgenLieder (III, no. 54), S only • FormTrium (no. 44), textless, but in the Jena copy only, added by hand: «La stangetta» • PeOdh1501 (54*v*-55*r*), «Uuerbech»[4] • PeOdh1503 (54*v*-55*r*) • PeOdh1504 (54*v*-55*r*) • PeSpinII (37*v*-38*v*) • PetreiusNewII (no. VI)

Modern editions of the music: Hewitt 1942, pp. 325-326 (after PeOdh1504); Mönkemeyer 1985, I, pp. 68-69 (after FormTrium); Schmidt 1969, II, pp. 267-269 (after PeSpinII); Wolf O/7, pp. 45-47 (after ZwR 78/3).

---

[1]. As Helen Hewitt was the first to realize, this heading might refer to the noble family Stanga of Cremona (see Hewitt 1942, p. 76). It cannot be proved definitively, but such an interpretation seems plausible, also because it was to a member of the same family, Corradolo Stanga, that Franchino Gaffurio dedicated his *Tractatus practicabilium proportionum* (written between 1481 and 1483). Building on this idea, Allan Atlas hypothesized that *La stangetta* should refer to Corradolo himself (see Atlas 1975-76, I, p. 188, n. 2). Fausto Torrefranca, however, thought that the piece was composed by Marchesino Stange (or Stanga) — faithful secretary of Ludovico il Moro — who belonged to the Cremonese family and died in 1500 (see Torrefranca 1939, p. 208, n. 1), an opinion also shared by Dietrich Kämper (see Kämper 1980, p. 282). Reinhard Strohm too refers to the same family, placing it, however, at Milan (see Strohm 1993, p. 570, n. 614). There was also at least another Stanga in Milan: Antonio, son of Cristoforo, a member of the college of jurists, who was sent to various places in Italy as Milanese ambassador. (I thank Bonnie Blackburn, who referred me to further references to the Stanga family in Cerioni 1970, I, p. 236.) The incipit in PeSpinII, perhaps reflecting the pronunciation 500 years ago, is *La stanghetta*, with the 'h' making the 'g' hard; but perhaps this is merely a graphic variant. In the edition I have preferred to maintain the original spelling, since it is not possible to prove the sounding likeness with the name of the Stanga family. Moreover, I believe that the piece was copied from the *Odhecaton*, in whose various versions the incipit always has a lower case 's' and never an 'h'.

[2]. The attribution to Obrecht is generally judged to be rather improbable, since sources contemporary with him do not give it (see NOE 17, p. lxxxii). Like Dietrich Kämper (Kämper 1980, p. 85), Martin Picker too inclines towards the attribution to Weerbeke (see Picker 1991, p. 95), as do Reinhard Strohm and Emma Kempson in the entry 'Isaac, Heinrich' in NG. As Bonnie Blackburn and Giulio Cattin have remarked (pers. com.), it seems more likely that the piece is by Isaac, since Weerbeke is not known for writing these types of pieces, whereas Isaac is.

[3]. Lama de la Cruz 1994, p. 265, states that this text is unknown.

[4]. Only the copy of the *Odhecaton* in Bologna (PeOdh1501) has the attribution «Uuerbech» (= 'Weerbeke'?) But Jeppesen 1969, p. 291 gives «Uverbeck (= Obrecht?)»; the others do not have any attribution.

REMARKS: The versions in SegC and FormTrium are distant from that in Panc.27, while the MSS HeilbS 2 and ZwR 78/3 are much closer. The *Odhecaton* version was probably the model for the scribe of Panc.27 (it differs only in a few graphic details).[5]

BIBLIOGRAPHY: ATLAS 1981; BAKER 1978, I, p. 453; BANKS 1999; BOORMAN 2006, pp. 987-988; CATTIN 1975, p. 212; FILOCAMO 2004; HEWITT 1942, p. 151; JEPPESEN 1969, p. 63; KÄMPER 1976, pp. 85, 158; KÄMPER 1980; LAMA DE LA CRUZ 1994, p. 265; NOE 17, pp. lxxxi-lxxxii; PICKER 1991, p. 95; REESE 1990, p. 200; TORREFRANCA 1939, p. 208, n. 1.

---

[5]. The copy in Bologna (PeOdh1501) lacks fols. 55r-57v, and the following Contra (fol. 58r) belongs to the piece *Helas le bon temps que j'avoie* by Johannes Tinctoris.

55.
LA STANGETTA
fols. 34v–35r

[Henricus Isaac / Jacob Obrecht / Gaspar van Weerbeke]

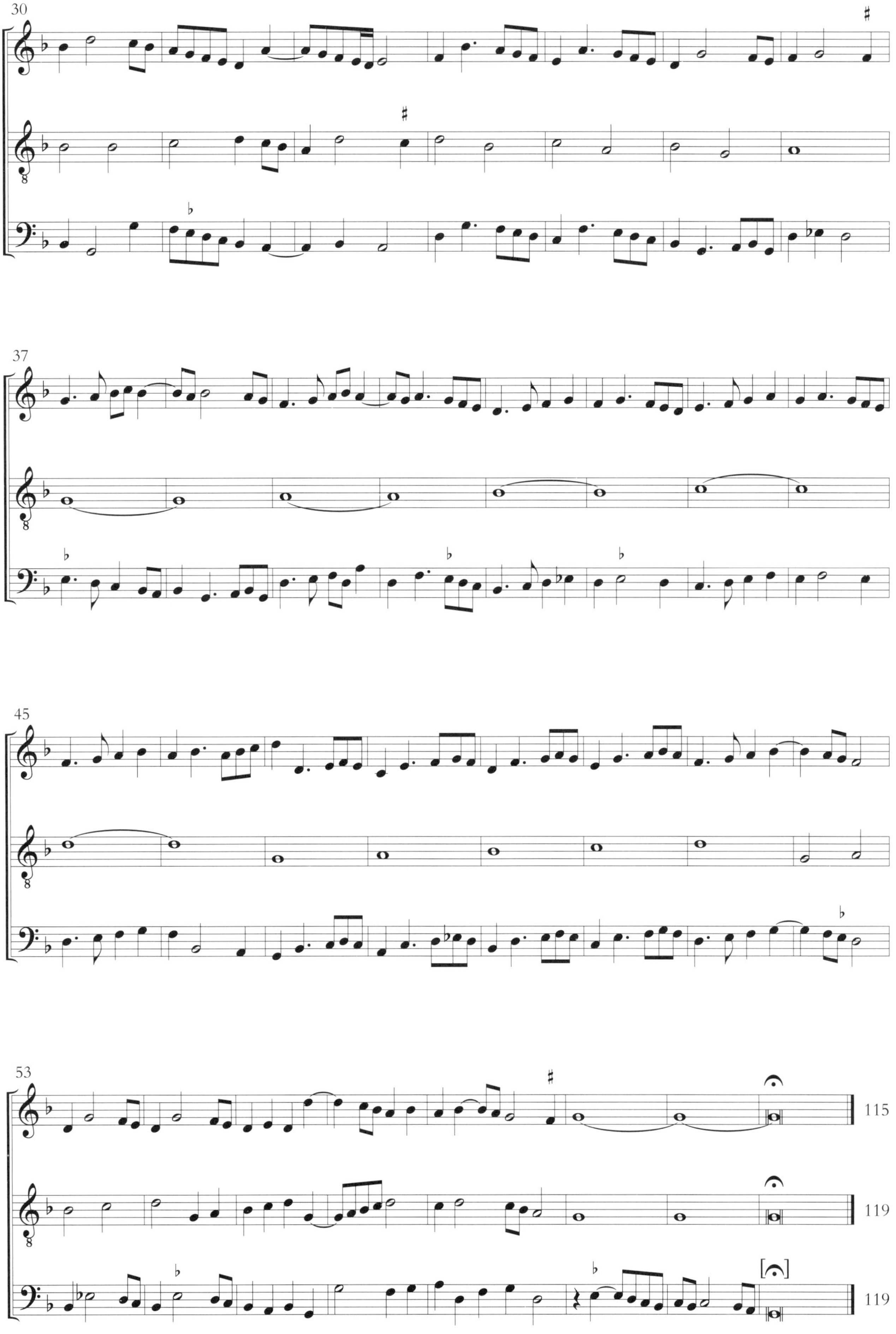
30
37
45
53
115
119
119

56.

HELAS, [QUE POURA DEVENIR]

fols. 35*v*-36*r* (4 vv.)

[FIRMINUS] CARON

Helas

Chanson (rondeau cinquain).

READINGS EMENDED IN THE EDITION:

BAR	VOICE	ORIGINAL
8/II	S	flat before the *f''*
23/II	S	*e' minima* instead of *d'*
39/II	B	*b* erased and substituted with *d*
40/I	A	*b'* instead of *c''*
56/II	A	*e' d'*

TEXTUAL CONCORDANCES (MSS): • *Berl.M. 17* (130*r-v*), *Hellas que pourra devenir*

MUSICAL CONCORDANCES (MSS): • AugsS 25 (4*r*), *Dess mayen lust*, 3 vv. • BolM 16 (128*v*-129*r*), *Elas que pour devenir*, 3 vv. • BolM 18 (35*v*-36*r*), *Helasso* • BratM 33 (no. 1), *Myt treuen herzen hab ich an allen*, 2 vv. (S and T only) • CV G27 (64*v*-65*r*, *olim* 71*v*-72*r*), 3 vv., «Caron» • DijM 517 (78*v*-79*r*, new foliation 81*v*-82*r*), *Helas que*, 3 vv., «Caron» • FirN BR229 (222*v*-223*r*), *Helas que poura devenir*, 3 vv., «Caron» • KrakJ 40098 (no. 8), heading *Der seyden schwantcz*, text under the music *Ave sydus clarissimum*, 3 vv. • ParisN F15123 (33*v*-34*r*), *Hellas que poura devenir*, 3 vv. • ParisN Rés676 (12*v*-13*r*), *Helas que pora advenire*, 3 vv. • PerA 431 (59*v*-60*r*), 3 vv. • RomaCa 2856 (45*v*-46*v*), *Hellas mon cuer*,[1] 3 vv., «Caron» • SegC (114*v*-115*r*), *Elaes*, «Caron» • SevC 43 (39*v*-40*r*), 3 vv. • TrenM 89 (416*v*-417*r*), textless, 3 vv. • UppsU 76a (13*v*-14*r*), *Helas que pourra devenir*, 3 vv. • VerCap 757 (19*v*-20*r*), textless, 3 vv., modern hand: «Caron, Helas que poura devenir (a 4)» • WashC L25 (12*v*-13*r*), 3 vv., later hand: «Caron, Helas m'amour ma tres parfete amye»[2] • WolfA G287 (49*v*-50*r*), *Helas que pourra devenir*, 3 vv.

MUSICAL CONCORDANCES (PRINTS): • Baena (30*r*-31*r*), *Helas qui porra*; index: «Caron. Helas qui pourra. Del otauo [tono]» • PeOdh1501 (15*v*-16*r*), *Helas que poura devenir*, «Caron», «Si placet» rubric above the A • PeOdh1503 (15*v*-16*r*), *Helas que poura devenir*, «Caron», «Si placet» rubric above the A • PeOdh1504 (15*v*-16*r*), *Helas que poura devenir*, «Caron», «Si placet» rubric above the A

TEXT FROM BROWN 1983, I, p. 291 (after DijM 517):

> Helas, que pourra devenir
> mon cueur, s'il ne peut parvenir

---

[1]. Perhaps this is the incipit of the rondeau quatrain *Helas mon cueur helas, mon oeil*, edited in LÖPELMANN 1923, no. 169 (see WOLFF 1970, I, p. 235).

[2]. The music in WashC L25 is provided with another text, the rondeau quatrain *Helas m'amour ma tres parfecte amye* edited in LÖPELMANN 1923, no. 456 and in BROWN 1983, I, p. 291.

a celle haultaine entreprise
où sa voulenté s'est soubmise
5   pour mieulx sur toutes advenir?

C'est chois sans ailleurs revenir:
eslicte pour temps advenir,
avoir plaisance à sa devise.
            Helas, […]

Or est contraint pour l'advenir,
10   car Desir l'a fait convenir
qui l'a mis hors de sa franchise;
et desja la cause est commise
pour en juger à son plaisir.
            Helas, […]

MODERN EDITIONS OF THE TEXT: BROWN 1983, I, p. 291 (after DijM 517); LÖPELMANN 1923, no. 344 (after *Berl.M. 17*).

MODERN EDITIONS OF THE MUSIC: BARRET 1981, p. 488 (after DijM 517); BROWN 1983, II, pp. 478-481 (after FirN BR229); DTÖ 15, pp. 248-249 (after TrenM 89, with the A from PeOdh1504 and Panc.27); EDM 4, pp. 92-93 (after KrakJ 40098); EDM 85, pp. 8-9 (after KrakJ 40098); FERRARI 1994, pp. 10-11 (after ParisN Rés676); GUTIÉRREZ-DENHOFF 1988, p. 72 (after WolfA G287); HEWITT 1942, pp. 246-247 (after PeOdh1504); MOERK 1971, II, pp. 119-120 (after SevC 43); PEASE 1959, II, pp. 100-103 (after ParisN F15123); SELF 1996, pp. 40-43 (after BolM 18); THOMSON 1971-76, II, pp. 175-179; TORREFRANCA 1939, pp. 554-557 (after PeOdh1504); WOLFF 1970, II, pp. 129-131 (after RomaCa 2856).

REMARKS: The piece comes down to us in two traditions: for three and for four voices, with a «si placet» Altus added in only four sources (BolM 18, Panc.27, SegC, PeOdh1501 and its reprints). The version of Panc.27 certainly derives from *Odhecaton*, as demonstrated by two conjunctive errors present in the Altus itself (bb. 40/I and 56/II), which distance these two sources from the only other two for four voices. The piece merited a citation in Tinctoris's *Liber de arte contrapuncti* (Book II, ch. 33), dated 11 October 1477, for the use of a diminished fifth in root position between the Bassus and Tenor in bar 45 (*e - b* flat) — which, moreover, also produces a seventh with the *d′* in the Altus — transmitted in BolM 18 and SegC, but absent both in Panc.27 and *Odhecaton*. From a collation with the other sources it emerges that in three places the Bassus of Panc.27 clearly differs from the manuscript sources: *c′* instead of *a* in bar 30/II (AugsS 25, KrakJ 40098, TrenM 89, WashC L25), a *semibrevis* rest instead of *f* in bar 38 (AugsS 25, DijM 517, FirN BR229, TrenM 89, UppsU 76a, WashC L25), *b* instead of *d* in bar 39/II (AugsS 25, DijM 517, FirN BR229, TrenM 89, UppsU 76a).

BIBLIOGRAPHY: ATLAS 1975-76, I, pp. 146-148, 174-176; BAKER 1978, I, pp. 367-368; BARRET 1981, III, pp. 486-487; BOORMAN 2006, p. 1048; BROWN 1982, pp. 15-21; BROWN 1983, I, pp. 290-291; EDM 86, p. 356; FALLOWS 1999, pp. 181-182; FILOCAMO 2004; HEWITT 1942, pp. 133-134, 171; LAMA DE LA CRUZ 1994, pp. 206-207; MOERK 1971, I, pp. 136-137; PEASE 1959, I, p. 92; THOMSON 1971-76, II, p. iii; WEISS 1998, p. 23; WOLFF 1970, I, pp. 233-238.

56.
HELAS, [QUE POURA DEVENIR]
fols. 35*v*–36*r*

[Firminus] Caron

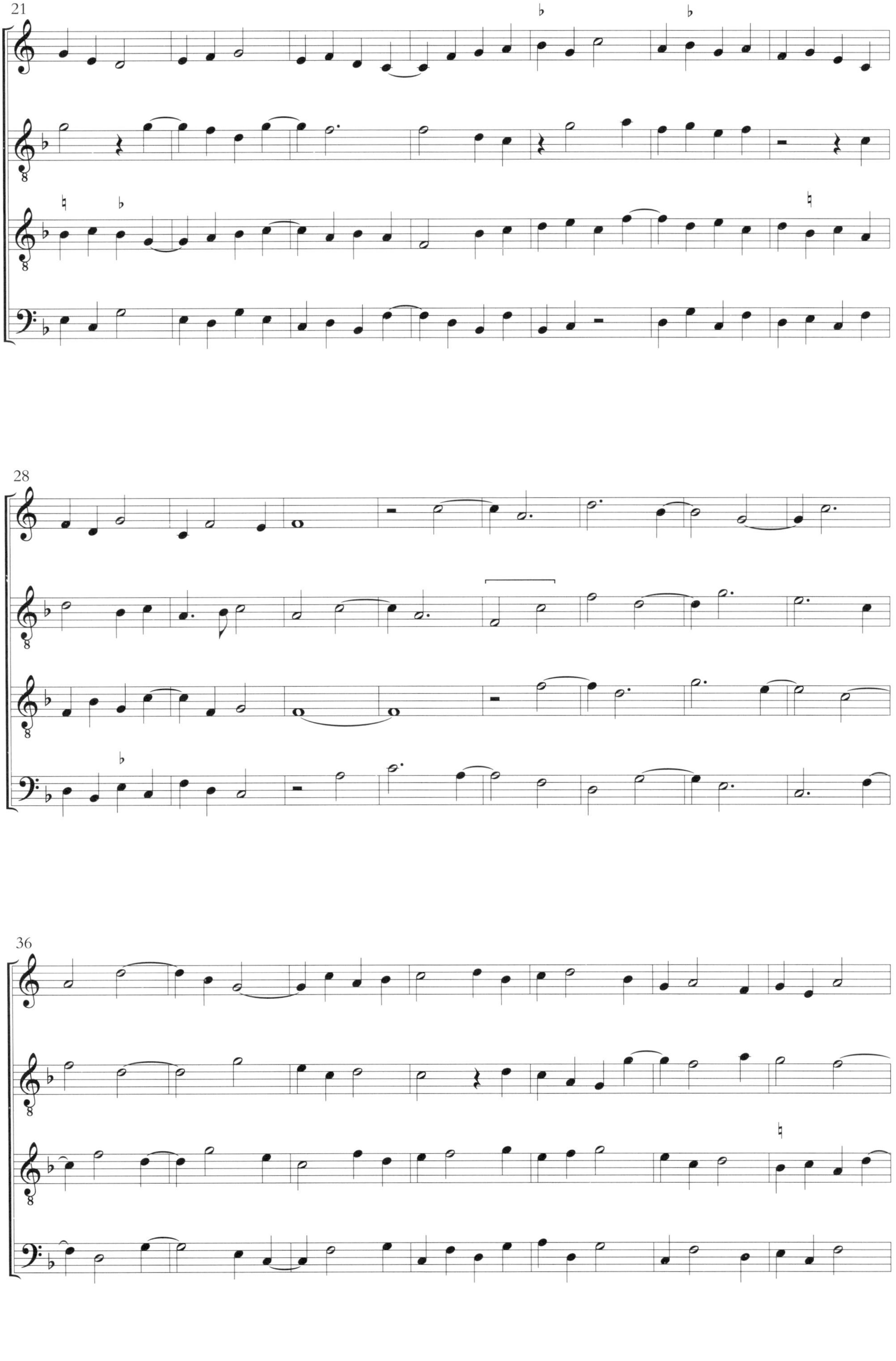
21
28
36

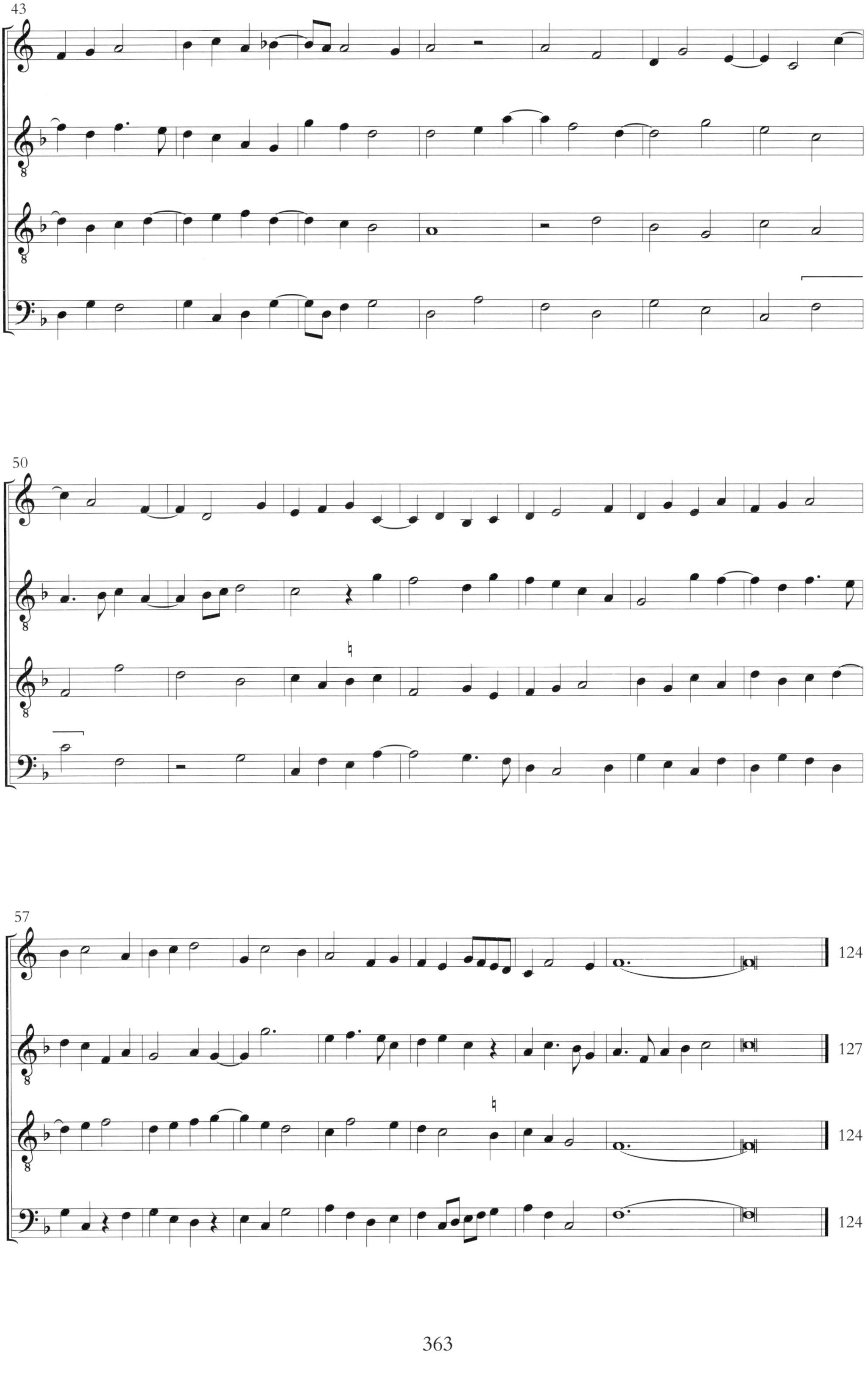
43
50
57
124
127
124
124

57.

Hor oires una canzon

fols. 36*v*-37*r* (5 vv.)

[Johannes de Stokem][1]

[Heading only]

Instrumental piece?

Musical concordances (mss): • IserV 124 (no. 45), textless, 3 vv. incomplete (lacking A and T$_1$), S: «Joannes Stock», B: «Jo. Stocken» • SGS 461 (28-29), *Hor ori un* • VerCap 757 (46*v*-47*r*), textless; a modern hand has written: «Anon. Hor oires une chanzon»

Musical concordances (prints): • PeOdh1501 (5*v*-6*r*) • PeOdh1503 (5*v*-6*r*) • PeOdh1504 (5*v*-6*r*)

Modern editions of the music: Giesbert 1936, I, pp. 28-29 (after SGS 461); Hewitt 1942, pp. 224-225 (after PeOdh1504); Torrefranca 1939, pp. 558-560 (after PeOdh1504).

Remarks: This is the only piece for five voices in the manuscript. *Hor oires una canzon* is probably not an incipit but a type of instruction that indicates the performance of the piece: «Now you will hear a chanson» (= 'a piece of music'). But it is also true that the Tenor II could sing the text *Hor oires una canzon* seven times in all, repeating the motif *g′ g′ f′ d′ e′ e′d′* (with the single variant at b. 12/II, where in place of the second *e′* there is a *g′*, to avoid parallel octaves with the Superius). Despite the fact that the version of *Odhecaton* has the correct rests in bars 39-40 in Tenor II, it is likely that the version in Panc.27 derives directly from the Petrucci print.

Bibliography: Boorman 2006, p. 1048; Hewitt 1942, p. 130.

---

[1]. In the article on 'Stokem, Johannes de' in NG by Pamela F. Starr, as in that in MGG by Philippe Vendrix, no mention is made of the attribution to Stokem of this piece.

57.
HOR OIRES UNA CANZON

fols. 36v-37r

[Johannes de Stokem]

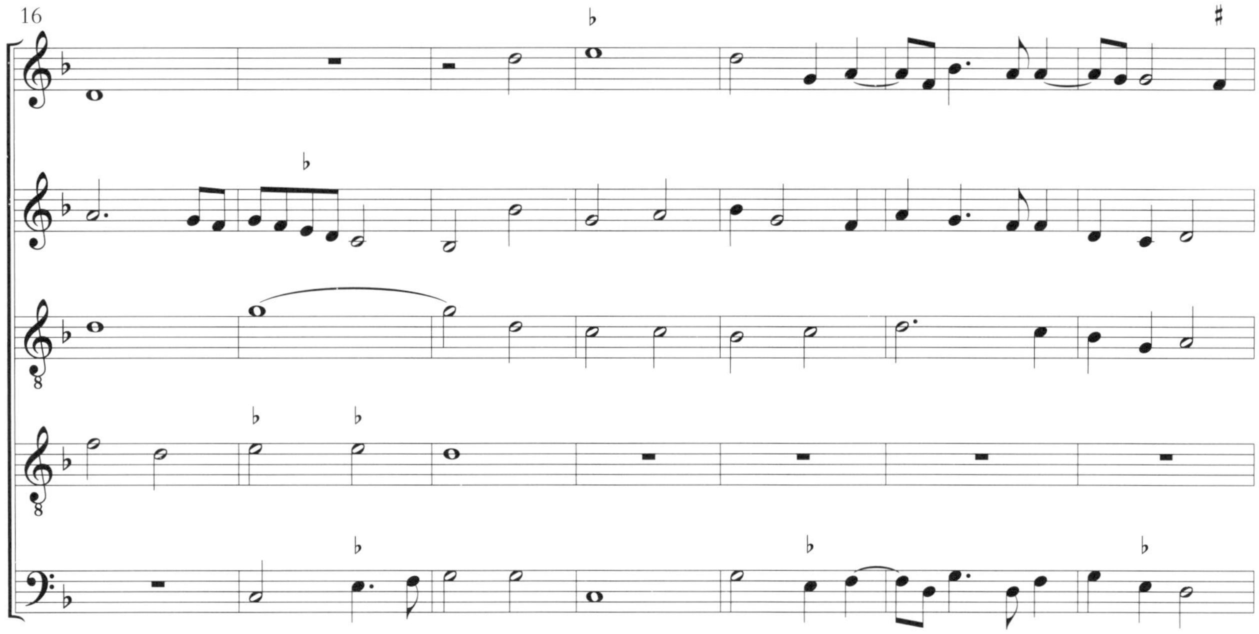
16

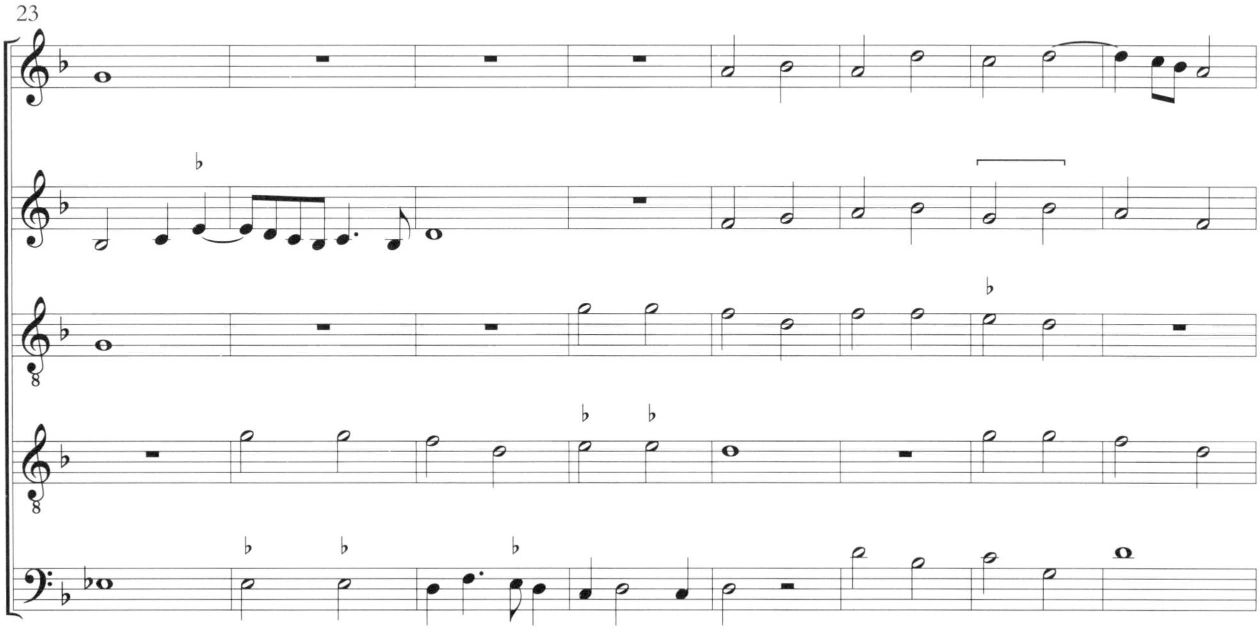
23

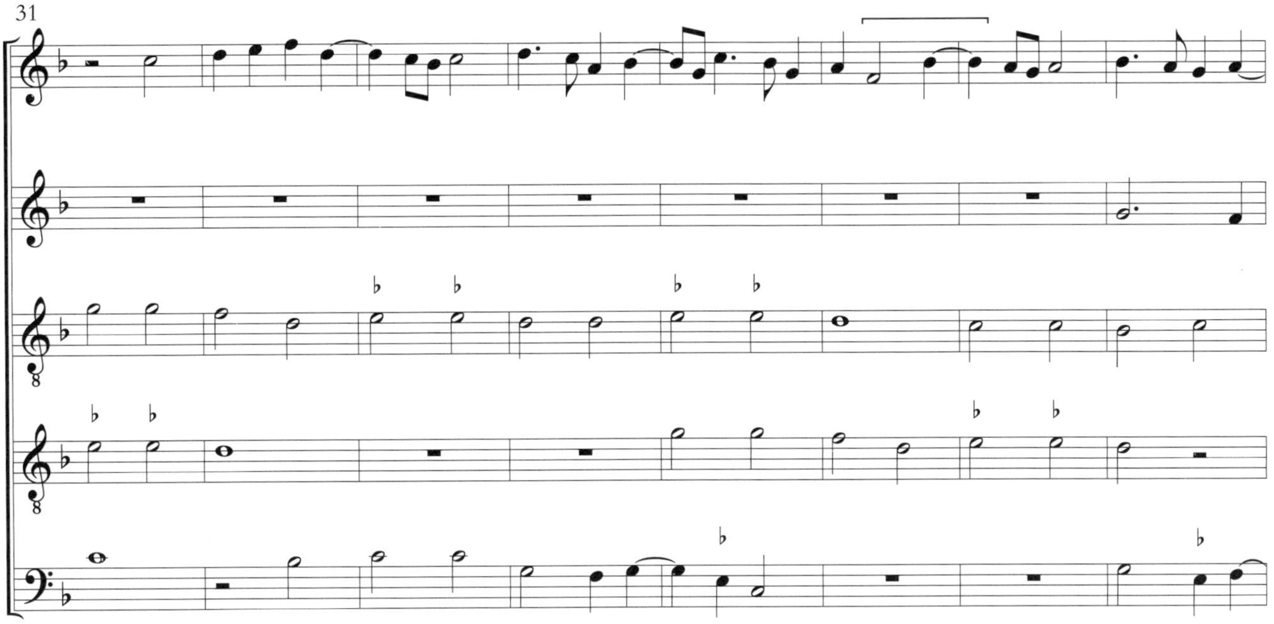
31

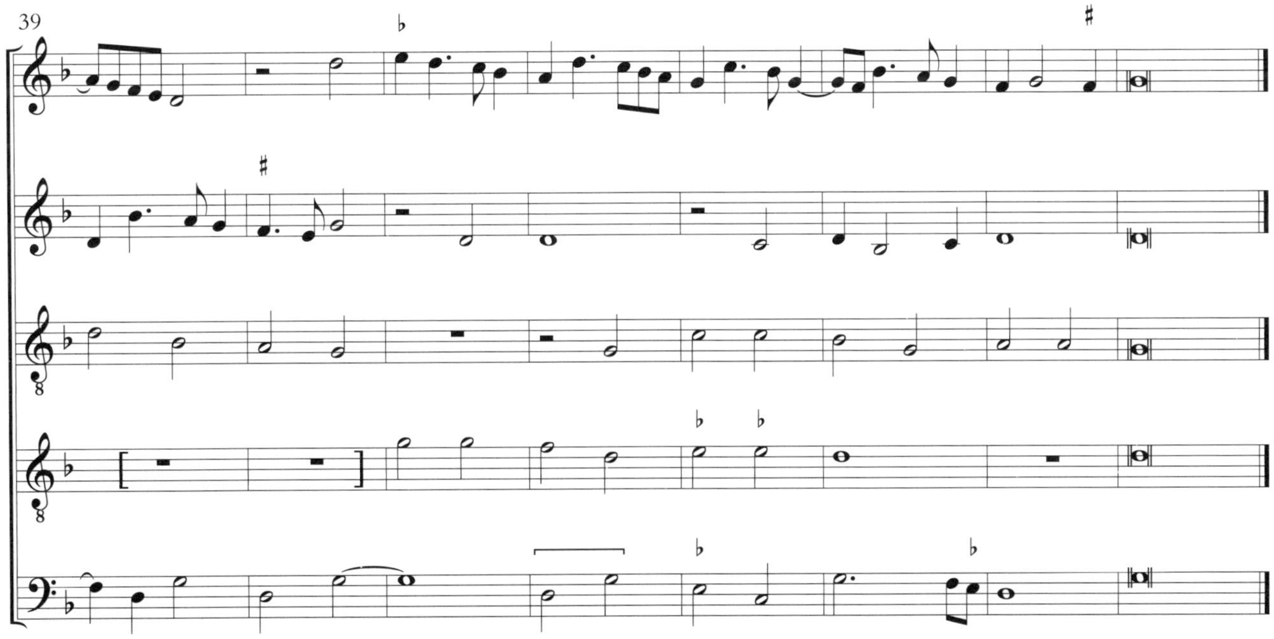
39

58.

[...]

fols. 37*v*-38*r* (3 vv.)

A piece without text, which might imply one of the two texts that circulated in musical concordances: *Illuxit dies* (perhaps identifiable with one of the two texts given below) and *Vidi impium superexaltatum* (from Psalm 36).

MUSICAL CONCORDANCES (MSS): • BerlS 40021 (162*r*), *Illuxit dies* • CTL G12 (115*v*-116*r*, *olim* 124*v*-125*r*), *Vidi impium superexaltatum*

TEXT FROM JUST 1975, II, p. 72 (after MS Munich, Bayerische Staatsbibliothek, Clm 12204, *Missale festivum 1459 aus dem Augustiner-Chorherrenstift Raitenbuch*, fol. 34*v*):[1]

	Illuxit dies quam fecit Dominus
	surrexit hiems fugatur eminus,
	gaudet cara merula,
	modulatur dulciter,
5	vernatur florum arida,
	auster nam flat suaviter,
	ideoque nos formati
	et undique sic instructi
	mirifice depromemus
10	odas nostras hodie
	in caelum vociferantes.
	Alleluia.

TEXT FROM AH 8, 33-34 (*De Paschate*):[2]

1a. Illuxit dies,
     quam fecit Dominus,
     mortem devastans
     et victor suis apparens
     dilectoribus vivus.

1b. Primo Mariae,
     dehinc apostolis,
     docens scripturas,
     cor aperiens, ut clausa
     de ipso reserarent.

2a. Favent igitur
     resurgenti
     Christo cuncta gaudiis,
     flores, segetes

---

[1]. On the nature of the text, Martin Just says: «Carmen, kontrafaziert als Versus Alleluiaticus eines Officium rhythm. Tempore paschali (?)» (see JUST 1975, II, p. 71). The text, in fact, was not used throughout the Easter season but only on Easter Sunday and its Octave (I thank Giulio Cattin for this clarification). The incipit recalls v. 24 of Psalm 117 «haec est dies quam fecit Dominus | exultemur et laetemur in ea» (VULGATA, p. 920).

[2]. Strophe 1a is also found as versicle 16 of the sequence *Laudes salvatori* attributed to Notker Balbulus (AH 53, pp. 65-66, *In Resurrectione Domini*) and discussed in CROCKER 1977, pp. 94-115.

redivivo
fructu vernant
et volucres gelu tristi
terso dulce jubilant.

2b.   Lucet clarius
sol et luna,
morte Christi turbida,
tellus herbida
resurgenti
plaudit Christo,
quae tremula ejus morte
se casuram minitat.

3a.   Ergo die ista
exsultemus,
qua nobis viam vitae
resurgens
patefecit Jesus.

3b.   Astra, solum, mare
jucundentur
et cuncti gratulentur
in coelis
spiritales chori.

TEXT FROM AH 11, p. 224 (*De sancto Quintino*):

1.   Illuxit dies annua
qua victa mundi gloria
Martyr Quintinus rosea
coeli scandit palatia.

2.   Flamma, ferro et carcere
cruciatus mirifice
durisque tensus cocleis
manes insuperabilis.

3.   Vox de coelo te monuit:
O Quintine, constans esto,
pro pena, quam nunc pateris
confestim coronaberis.

4.   Tandem succiso capite
tuo perfusus sanguine
per ascensum purpureum
tribunal scandis amoenum.

5.   Tibi quanta suavitas,
quanta tibi sit gloria,
non sufficit vox promere
nec ulla mens conjicere.

6.   Ergo nostri memor esto,
ut per tua suffragia
vitantes carnis vitia

via curramus ardua.

7.   Honor, virtus, imperium
sit summo regi martyrum,
quos per poenas corporeas
transfert ad sedes placidas.

Text from AH 25, p. 36 (*De sancto Alexio. In 1. Vesperis. Ad Magnificat*):

Illuxit dies celebris,
nullis turbanda tenebris,
qua verae lucis filius
assumptus est Alexius,
verum in tuo lumine
lumen visurus, Domine,
cuius placatus precibus
praesta nobis supplicibus,
ut nos mane et vespere
tibi velis adsistere
teque post cum Alexio
contemplemur in gaudio.

Text from AH 52, pp. 257-258 (*De sancta Martha. Ad Vesperas*):

1.   Illuxit dies Domini;
suo dent laudes nomini
canore gentes carmine
a solis ortus cardine.

2.   Hac die Martha civibus
coniungitur caelestibus;
caterva cum angelica
exsultet aula caelica.

3.   Haec, caelebs dum exsisteret
et vitam sanctam duceret,
erat in te sua quies,
Christe, qui lux es et dies.

4.   Mandatis tuis paruit,
quam ob rem signis claruit
ad salutem fidelium,
Rex Christe, factor omnium.

5.   Dum caros suos aleret,
vinumque iam deficeret,
vertisti lympham in merum,
conditor alme siderum.

6.   Quaete, Christe, quondam pavit,
illam tuis sociavit
dextris sponsam specialem
urbs beata Ierusalem.

7.   Hinc trinitati gloriam
honorem et victoriam

pangamus hymno pistico
ex more docti mystico.

TEXT FROM AH 16, p. 32 (*In Transfiguratione DN. Ad Laudes*):

1.   Illuxit dies inclita,
qua credimus pollicita
condonari poscentibus
Christi sacris operibus.

2.   Qui glorioso lumine
prae solis claritudine
transfiguratur hodie
sub deitatis specie.

3.   Nunc jubilationibus
omnes plaudant cum manibus
in his tantis solemnibus
nobis regum praebentibus.

4.   Ubi jam transiguratum
trinum et unum Dominum
conspiciemus splendidum
ei cantantes canticum.

5.   Gloria tibi, Domine,
splendenti claro lumine,
cum patre et sancto flamine
in sempiterna saecula.

TEXT FROM Psalm 36:35-36 (VULGATA, p. 814):

35.   vidi impium superexaltatum
et elevatum sicut cedros Libani

36.   et transivi et ecce non erat
et quaesivi eum et non est inventus locus eius

MODERN EDITIONS OF THE MUSIC: EDM 77, pp. 234-235 (after BerlS 40021); KÄMPER 1976, pp. vi-ix (after Panc.27).

REMARKS: Many variants separate the musical version of Panc.27 from the concordances. BerlS 40021 cannot have been used as a model; CTL G12 is substantially the same as Panc.27, but the very great number of ligatures and the change of clef in the Bassus, not found in Panc.27, are perplexing. Regarding the text to be sung, it is more likely (but impossible to prove) that Panc.27 sets *Vidi impium superexaltatum*, present in CTL G12, with which it shares a large part of the devotional repertory.

BIBLIOGRAPHY: CATTIN 1973a, pp. 215-216; EDM 78, p. 335; FILOCAMO 2004; JUST 1975, I, pp. 14, 35, 46, 48, 62, 63, 107; JUST II, pp. 71-72; KÄMPER 1976, pp. 92-94; ROTHENBERG 2006, p. 360.

58.

[...]

fols. 37*v*–38*r*

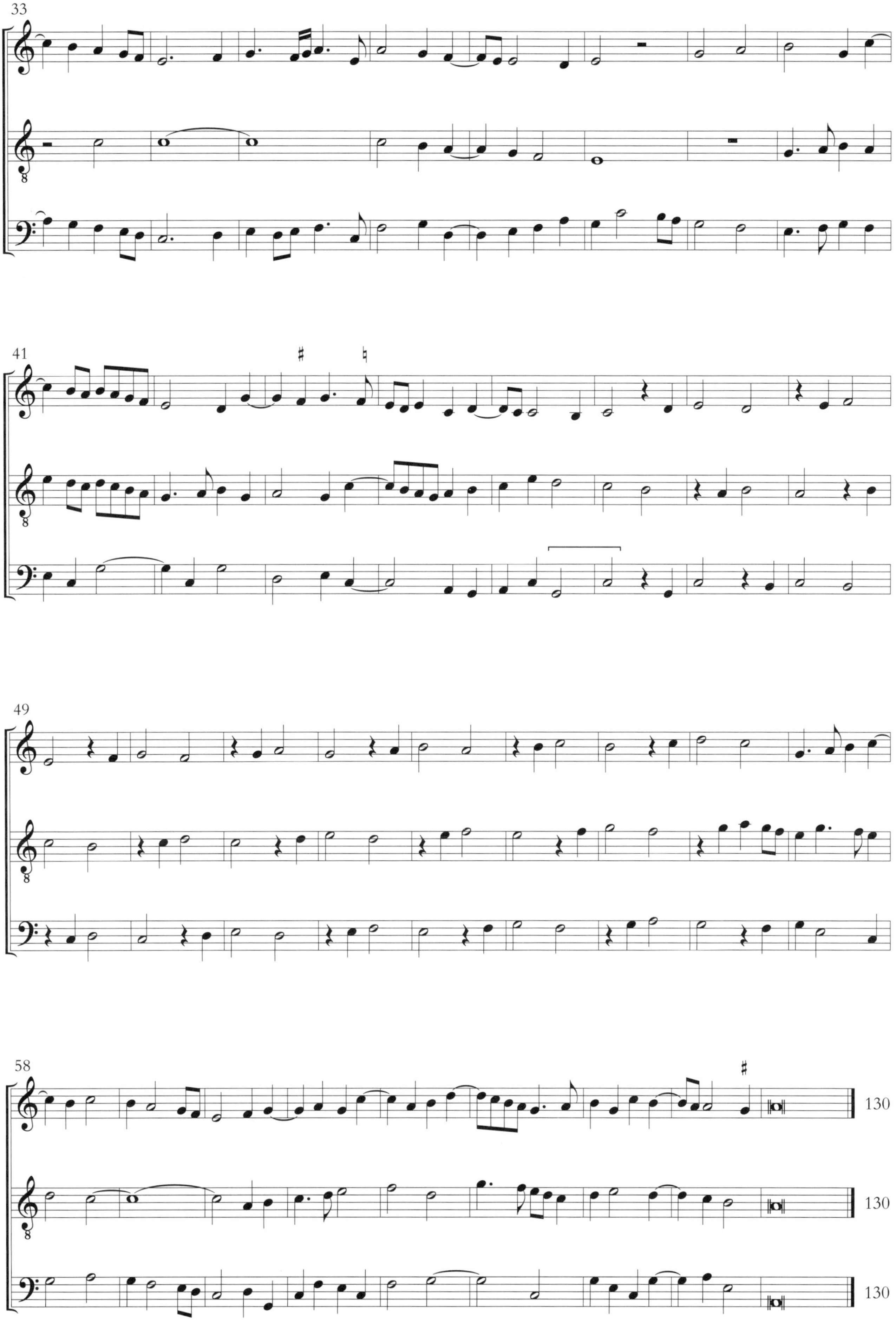
33
41
49
58
130
130
130

59.

Ne doibt [on prendre quant on donne]

fols. 38*v*–39*r* (3 vv.)

[Jean II, duc de Bourbon]   [Loyset] Compere

Ne doibt

Chanson (virelai).

Commentary on the text:

1   Ne] Me S, B

Readings emended in the edition:

Bar	Voice	Original
51/I	B	*c* instead of *d*

Musical concordances (mss): • BolM 18 (87*v*–88*r*), *Me doibt* • DijM 517 (189*v*–191*r*, *olim* 186*v*–188*r*), *Ne doibt on prendre*, «Loyset compere», «Bourbon» • HKK 20 (101), first part of B only, textless, «Compere» • RegB 940-1 (no. 227), *Venit'amant'insieme a pianger forte*, «Foglianus»[1] • ZwR 78/3 (no. 14), textless

Musical concordances (prints): • EgenLieder (III, no. 52), *Me doibt*, S only • GardFesta1543 (12), *Venite amanti insieme a pianger forte*, (Costanzo Festa) • GardFesta1556 (12), *Venite amanti insieme a pianger forte*, (Costanzo Festa) • GardFesta1564 (12), *Venite amanti insieme a pianger forte*, (Costanzo Festa) • MeruloFesta (12), *Venite amanti insieme a pianger forte*, (Costanzo Festa) • PeOdh1501 (51*r*),[2] *Me doibt* • PeOdh1503 (50*v*–51*r*), *Me doibt*, «Compere» • PeOdh1504 (50*v*–51*r*), *Me doibt*, «Compere» • PetreiusNewII (no. 8), *Me dobt*, «Compere» • ScottoFesta1547[3] (12), *Venit'amanti insieme a pianger forte*, (Costanzo Festa) • ScottoFesta1551 (12), *Venite amanti insieme a pianger forte*, (Costanzo Festa) • ScottoFesta1559 (12), *Venite amanti insieme a pianger forte*, (Costanzo Festa)

---

[1]. The attribution to Giacomo Fogliano has a rather complicated history. The musical piece *Ne doibt on prendre quant on donne* is also found in the Venetian print GardFesta of 1543, with the contrafact text of Poliziano's rispetto *Venite amanti insieme a pianger forte* (edited both in Delcorno Branca 1986, no. 58, and in Delcorno Branca 1990, no. 78 with the incipit *Venite insieme amanti [...]*, which inverts the second and third words). This musical source was reprinted several times (see Fenlon - Haar 1988, p. 234), and in the edition of 1547 printed in Venice by Ottaviano Scotto four pieces were added at the end, attributed to Fogliano, a composer honoured by a citation on the title page («una nova gionta di madrigali di Iacomo Fogliano & de altri autori», a new addition of madrigals by Iacomo Fogliano and by other authors). In the editions following that of 1547 the ascription to Fogliano is retained, and the scribe of the musical MS RegB 940-1 extended it erroneously to the 14 pieces he copied from it into his manuscript. Wilfried Brennecke thinks that the copyist of RegB 940-1 used the edition of 1551 (see Brennecke 1953, pp. 76-77), and curiously he chose not to transcribe any piece actually attributable to Fogliano.

[2]. Fol. 50*v*, which should have contained the two upper voices and the attribution to Compère, is lacking.

[3]. In all three of the partbooks [STB] of the exemplar consulted in the Biblioteca Comunale of Trent (shelfmark: BCT 1 / F.b. 28; pezzo 1947/3), page 12 is lacking, which, according to the Tabula of the print, should have contained *Venite amanti insieme a pianger forte*.

Ne doibt on prendre quant on donne
et que son corps on habendonne
a servir, cremir et amer
et pour maistresse réclamer.
5   Espérant que on s'abendonne.

Je suis de telle opinion
que deux cueurs de vray union
doibvent l'ung de l'aultre des cendre.

Et donner clere vision,
10   sans faire nulle avusion,
qu'on veult amer jusques à cuer fendre.

La loy d'amours ainsi l'ordonne.
qui ne le fait se désordonne
et vaultdroit mieulx estre en la mer
15   que trouver party plain d'amer
puis qu'à servir tant on s'adonne.

Ne doibt [...]

MODERN EDITIONS OF THE MUSIC: BARRET 1981, IV, p. 1194 (after DijM 517); CMM 15/V, pp. 35-36 (after PeOdh1504); CMM 25/VII, pp. 24-25; EML 62, no. 3 (after PeOdh1504); HEWITT 1942, pp. 317-318 (after PeOdh1504).

REMARKS: The error in the Bassus in bar 51/I is not shared by any other concordance. It is therefore possible that the scribe of Panc.27 stumbled in copying from a model, perhaps misled by the presence of the *c* two notes further on (already perceived while he would have been copying *d*). Moreover, in bars 14/II-15 of the Tenor (fol. 38*v*, halfway through the fourth stave) the *semibreves b* and *a* were certainly inserted later by the copyist, as indicated by the very narrow space provided for them; this element too encourages the hypothesis that the piece was copied from a model. *Odhecaton* was almost certainly the scribe's model: the Superius and Tenor are identical, while in the Bassus there are three tiny variants (a cautionary B flat is missing, a ligature is divided in Panc.27, and a dot of addition becomes a repeated note in Panc.27). Even the textual incipit is identical, as well as the authorial attribution. Although demonstrably relatively close (with a few graphic differences), the anonymous musical version in BolM 18 gives, in contrast to the versions in Panc.27 and *Odhecaton*, *f* instead of *a* in bar 21/II of the Tenor.

BIBLIOGRAPHY: BARRET 1981, IV, p. 1193; BOORMAN 2006, p. 1060; BRENNECKE 1953, pp. 76-77; CMM 25/VII, p. xvi; FALLOWS 1999, p. 292; FENLON - HAAR 1988, pp. 234-237; HEWITT 1942, pp. 150, 175; WEISS 1998, pp. 36-37.

59.
NE DOIBT [ON PRENDRE QUANT ON DONNE]
fols. 38v–39r

[Jean II, duc de Bourbon]

[Loyset] Compere

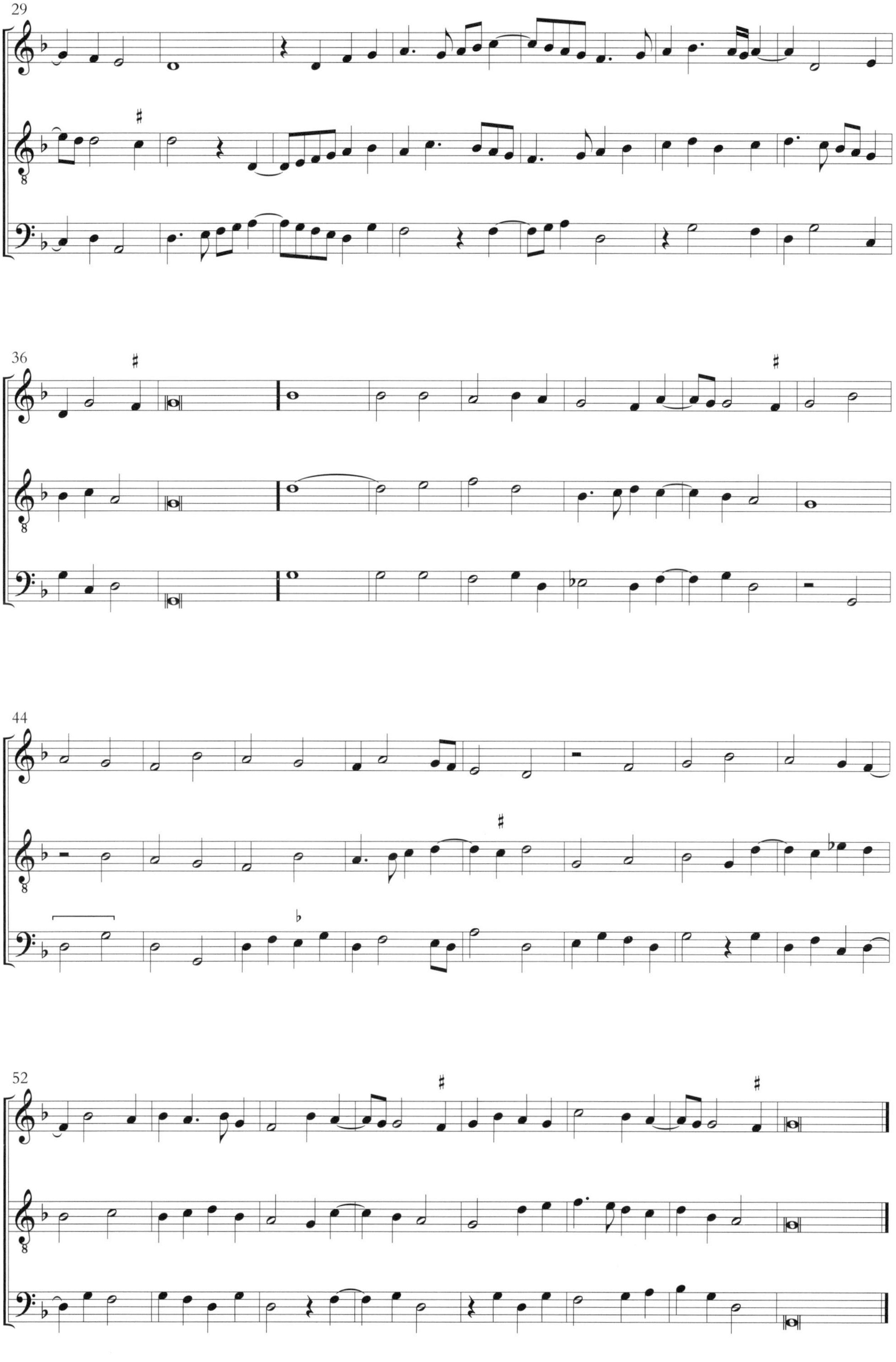
29
36
44
52

60.

Mater digna Dei

fols. 39*v*-40*r* (4 vv.)

[Gaspar van Weerbeke]

Mater digna Dei
venie via luxque diei,
sis tutela rei
duxque comesque mei.
5   Nata Dei,
miserere,
lux alma diei;
digna coli,
regina poli,
10   me relinquere noli.
Me tibi, Virgo pia,
genitrix commendo Maria.
Iesu, fili Dei,
tu miserere mei.

Rhymed prayer in honour of the Blessed Virgin Mary.

COMMENTARY ON THE TEXT:

3   tutela] tutella S
6   the normal version of the text has «miserere mei»

MUSICAL CONCORDANCES (MSS): • CTL G12 (107*v*-108*r*, *olim* 116*v*-117*r*) • MilD 1 (115*v*-116*r*), «Gaspar» • PadCap 17 (156*v*-157*r*) • VerCap 758 (19*v*-20*r*)

MUSICAL CONCORDANCES (PRINTS): • PeMotA1502 (54*v*-55*r*); index: «Gaspar» • PeMotA1505 (54*v*-55*r*); index: «Gaspar»

MODERN EDITIONS OF THE MUSIC: BANKS 1993, II, pp. 115-117 (after Panc.27); DELPORTE 1954; DRAKE 1972, II, pp. 132-134 (after PeMotA1502); TINTORI 1963, pp. 4-7 (after MilD 1).

REMARKS: The version of Panc.27 has surely been copied from PeMotA1502 (or its reprint): it is musically identical, save for the fermata overlooked by the scribe of Panc.27 over the rest of the Tenor in bar 63; moreover, Petrucci's text is more correct (l. 3: «tutela»; l. 6: «miserere mei»; l. 10: «linquere»). *Mater digna Dei*, *Christi mater ave* (no. 99), and *Ave stella matutina* (no. 129) form a compact group of three compositions attributed to Weerbeke, already present in the late fifteenth-century MS MilD 1 (fols. 114*v*-117*r*) and the *Motetti A* print (fols. 50*v*-52*r* and 54*v*-55*r*): together with Panc.27 these two musical sources are the only ones to include all three pieces. But only in MilD 1 are the pieces presented consecutively, in the order *Christi mater ave*, *Mater digna Dei*, *Ave stella matutina*: the complete incipit of the first piece contains the first words of the incipit of the other two («Mater» and «Ave»)![1] The version of CTL G12 contains two substantive variants with respect to Panc.27: the rest in the Altus in bars 29/II–30 is longer, and at bar 42/I in the Bassus there is a *c′ semibrevis* in place of two *minimae a c′*. A number of graphic variants distance the version of Panc.27 from those in MilD 1, PadCap 17, and VerCap 758.

BIBLIOGRAPHY: BANKS 1993, I, p. 280; BOORMAN 2006, p. 921; BROWN 1990, p. 755, n. 38; CATTIN 1973a, p. 213; CHEVALIER II, no. 11335; CROLL 1954, no. 13; DRAKE 1972, I, pp. 78, 140, 141, 164, 165, 285-289; FILOCAMO 2004; RIFKIN 2003, p. 311, n. 155.

---

[1]. As noted in RIFKIN 2003, p. 311, n. 144.

60.
Mater digna Dei
fols. 39*v*-40*r*

[Gaspar van Weerbeke]

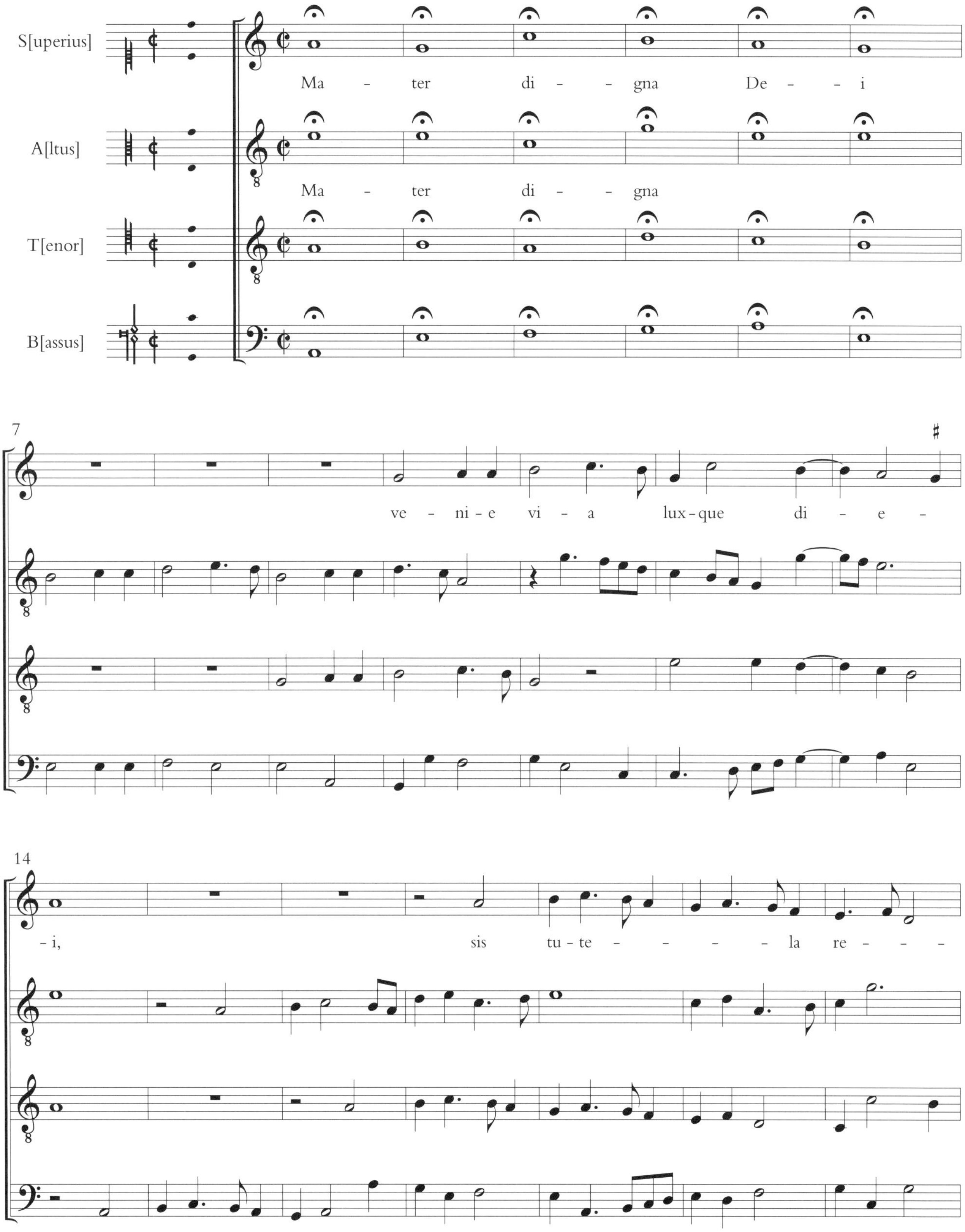

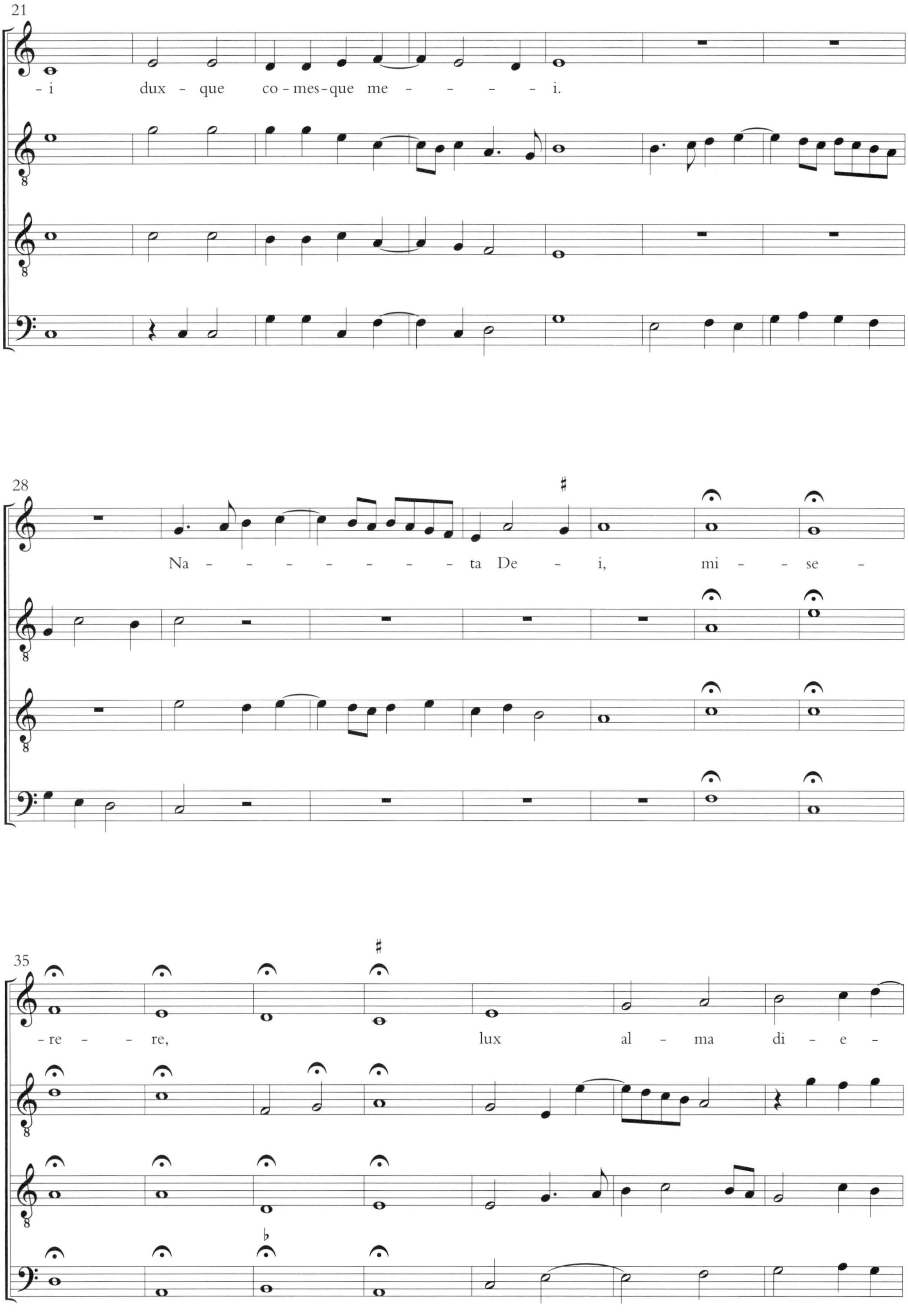
21
-i duxque comesque me - - - - - i.
28
Na - - - - - - - - ta De - i, mi - se -
35
-re - - re, lux al - ma di - e -

42
- - - i; di - gna co - - - - - li, re - gi - na po - li,
49
me re - lin - que - re no - - - - - li. Me ti - bi,
56
Vir - - go pi - a, ge - ni - trix com - men - do Ma - ri - - - - -

-a. Ie - - su, fi - - li De - - i, tu

mi - se - re - re me - - - - - - - i.

61.

Io son de gabbia, non de bosco ocello /
Iste confesor Domini

fol. 40*v* (4 vv.)

[Michele Pesenti]

Io son de gabbia, non de bosco ocello,
che 'l duol, cantando, desacerbo rio.
Lass'i', che fui, che son, ahi meschinello,
povero ocello!

Iste confesor Domini.[1]

Italian secular piece (Sapphic ode).[2] The accessory text is the incipit of *Iste confessor Domini sacratus*, a hymn in sapphic strophes (BR [*Commune Sanctorum*], p. 31; LR, pp. 190-191).[3] Since none of the melodies associated with this hymn (see IGC, pp. 233-234) corresponds to the Tenor or the melodies of the other voices of the polyphonic composition in Panc.27, it is likely that the hymn is

---

[1]. It cannot be the text *Iste confessor Domini colentes* (AM, pp. 655, 656, 664, 668, 669; AR, pp. [49]-[50], [51]-[52], [52]-[53], [53]-[55], [68]-[69], [69]-[70], [71]-[72], [72]-[73]; LU, pp. 1177-1178, 1178-1179, 1179-1180, 1196-1198, 1198-1199, and also Chevalier I, nos. 9131 and 9132; IGC, p. 233), which was introduced thanks to the classicizing reform promoted at the time of Pope Urban VIII. I nevertheless give this text, taken from LU, pp. 1177-1178 (*Commune Confessoris Pontificis. In II. Vesperis*):

1. *Iste confessor Domini, colentes*
    quem pie laudant populi per orbem,
    *hac die laetus meruit beatas (*Si non est dies obitus*: hac die laetus meruit supremos)*
    *scandere sedes. (*Si non est dies obitus*: laudis honores)*
2. *Qui pius, prudens, humilis, pudicus,*
    sobriam duxit sine labe vitam,
    donec humanos animavit aurae
    Spiritus artus.
3. *Cuius ob praestans meritum frequenter,*
    aegra quae passim iacuere membra,
    viribus morbi domitis, saluti
    restituuntur.
4. *Noster hinc illi chorus obsequentem*
    concinit laudem celebresque palmas,
    ut piis eius precibus iuvemur
    omne per aevum.
5. *Sit salus illi, decus, atque virtus,*
    qui super caeli solio coruscans,
    totius mundi seriem gubernat,
    trinus et unus.
    Amen.

[2]. The Latin text underneath the music in the only concordances (*Integer vitae scelerisque purus*) is a Horatian ode reinterpreted in accentual metre (see Lowinsky 1989, pp. 162-165, Schmidt-Beste 1999, p. 371, and Holford-Strevens 1999, p. 408). The complete poetic text can be read in Brancacci 2005, pp. 290-291, taken from *Q. Horatii Flacci Opera*, edited by Stephan Borszák, Leipzig, Teubner (Bibliotheca Scriptorum Graecorum et Romanorum), 1984, p. 23, and with an apparatus that registers the variants in PeFroI.

[3]. The text is discussed in Schmidt-Beste 1999, pp. 368-370 and in Holford-Strevens 1999, p. 402.

a *contrafactum* of the piece itself, substituting for the Latin text *Integer vitae scelerisque purus*[4] found in the other sources.

READINGS EMENDED IN THE EDITION:

BAR	VOICE	ORIGINAL
14/II	C	*f″* as an alternative reading (certainly an error for *g″*) above the *g′*

MUSICAL CONCORDANCES (PRINTS): • PeBossI1509 (36r), *Integer vitae scelerisque purus*, «D. M.»[5] • PeBossI1515 (36r), *Integer vitae scelerisque purus*, «D. M.» • PeFroI (44r), *Integer vitae scelerisque purus*, «Micha»

TEXT FROM BR [*Commune Sanctorum*], p. 31 (*In natali confessoris pontificis*):

1.   Iste confessor Domini sacratus,
        festa plebs cuius celebrat per orbem,
        hodie letus meruit secreta
        scandere celi.

2.   Qui pius, prudens, humilis, pudicus,
        sobrius, castus fuit, et quietus,
        vita dum presens vegetavit eius
        corporis artus.

3.   Ad sacrum cuius tumulum frequenter
        membra languentum modo sanitati,
        quolibet morbo fuerint gravata,
        restituuntur.

4.   Unde nunc noster chorus in honorem
        ipsius hymnum canit hunc libenter,
        ut piis eius meritis iuvemur
        omne per evum.

5.   Sit laus illi, decus, atque virtus,
        qui supra celi residens cacumen,
        totius mundi machinam gubernat
        trinus, et unus.

        Amen.

MODERN EDITIONS OF THE TEXT: FILOCAMO 2003, p. 24 (after Panc.27).

MODERN EDITIONS OF THE MUSIC: BRANCACCI 2005, pp. 305-306 (after PeFroI); CESARI *ET AL.* 1954, p. 35 (after PeFroI);[6] DISERTORI 1964, p. 393 (after PeBossI1509); FILOCAMO 2003, p. 36 (after Panc.27); SCHERING 1931, p. 71 (after PeBossI1509); SCHWARTZ 1935, p. 34 (after PeFroI).

REMARKS: This piece inaugurates a group of three pieces placed on fols. 40v-41r: *Io son de gabbia, non de bosco ocello* (no. 61), *L'ucelo me chiama [che perdo giornata]* (no. 62), and *Io son l'ucello che sopra i rami d'oro* (no. 63). Together with two other compositions (*Io son l'ocel che con le debil ali* of Michele Pesenti, and *Io son l'ocello che non pò volare* of Bartolomeo Tromboncino), William Prizer has singled out a 'cycle'

---

[4]. On the other hand, none of the Petrucci prints that has a musical concordance gives the Italian text.
[5]. Probably «D[ominus] M[ichael]».
[6]. Reprinted in LOWINSKY 1989, p. 164.

of humorous responses between the Ferrarese and Mantuan courts (see PRIZER 1985, p. 28). All the pieces are discussed and edited in FILOCAMO 2003; with respect to this edition, in the present version an alternative interpretation is offered (but not prescribed) of the *musica ficta*: in bars 5-7/I of the Cantus the *f'* moves back to natural, a descending chromatic step (from b. 4 to b. 5), corresponding to the literary image of sorrow («duol»).[7] William Prizer interprets *Iste confessor Domini* as written against Cardinal Ippolito I d'Este,[8] in whose service Pesenti was several times, perhaps from 1504.[9]

BIBLIOGRAPHY: BOORMAN 2006, pp. 913-914; BRANCACCI 2005, pp. 283, 288, 290-291; BROWN – STEIN 1999, p. 90; CAO IV, p. 513; CATTIN 1986, pp. 300-301, n. 96; CESARI *ET AL*. 1954, p. xxix; FILOCAMO 2003, pp. vii-xi; HERCZOG 1997; HOLFORD-STREVENS 1999; IGC, pp. 233-234; KIRKENDALE 1988, pp. 305-306, 309-313, n. 218; LUISI 1977, pp. 331-332; PRIZER 1985, pp. 28-29, n. 104; SCHMIDT-BESTE 1999.

---

[7]. This effective expressive variant I owe to the good taste of Adam Gilbert, who has performed the piece with the Ensemble Ciaramella.

[8]. See PRIZER 1985, p. 28.

[9]. See CATTIN 1986, p. 300.

61.

Io son de gabbia, non de bosco ocello / Iste confesor Domini

fol. 40*v*

[Michele Pesenti]

Cantus: Io son de gab - bia, non de bo - sco o - cel - lo,

Tenor: Iste confesor Domini

che 'l duol, can - tan - do, de - sa - cer - bo ri - o. Las - s'i', che

fui, che son, ahi me - schi - nel - lo, po - ve - ro o - cel - lo!

62.

L'ucelo me chiama [che perdo giornata]

fols. 40*v*-41*r* (3 vv.)

[Francesco Galeota]

L'ucelo me chiama

Italian secular piece (strambotto).[1]

Textual concordances (mss): • *Mod.E. 1168* (116), *L'aucello me chiamo io perdigiornata* • *Nap.N. 1* (34*v*), *L'aucello me chiamo io perdigiornata*

Textual concordances (prints): • *Altissimo 1525* (a4*r*), *L'uccelo mi chiamo perdigornata* [*sic*]

Musical concordances (mss):[2] • ParisN Rés676 (65*v*-66*r*), only S and T in common, *L'ucelo mi chiamo che perdo giornata* • PerA 431 (112*v*-113*r*), 4 vv. (with an additional B), *L'ucello mio chiamo io perdo jornata*

Text from ParisN Rés676:

L'ucelo mi chiamo che perdo giornata,
ch'io bramo e pur aspecto e mai non perde.
Notula son, che sempr'io sto celata
e som batuta, e mai non me difende.
5   Nibio sonto, che mai non fo calata
e sempre giro, e mai non me distende.
Nave son, senza vela abandonata
in mare, senza timone arbor fracasata.

Modern editions of the text: Bronzini 1976, p. 66 (after *Nap.N. 1*); Bronzini 1977, p. 130 (after *Mod.E. 1168*); Filocamo 2003, pp. 10-11 (after ParisN Rés676), 14 (after ModE 9); Hernon 1972, p. 444 (after PerA 431); La Face Bianconi 1990, pp. 205-206 (after ModE 9).

Modern editions of the music: Filocamo 2003, p. 28 (after ParisN Rés676); Hernon 1972, pp. 441-443 (after PerA 431).

Remarks: See also the Remarks to no. 61. Although the composer's name is not given, the composition must have had a wide diffusion from the beginning, at least from the last twenty years of the Quattrocento (the years when the musical manuscript PerA 431 was compiled). The comprehensive tradition of the piece appears to have followed two different paths, which share only the melody of the Superius: one is attested in the version for four voices of ModE 9; the other in all the other

---

[1]. The rhyme scheme of the last distich (AA) prevents a classification as a Sicilian strambotto, even if one might suppose that this unusual scheme resulted from an alteration made in the Sicilian form (see Rossi 1993, pp. 254-256).

[2]. Although not classifiable as a concordance, the following manuscript version for four voices shares only the Superius with Panc.27: ModE 9 (69*v*-70*r*), *L'ocello mi chiamo che perde zornata*. This musical version is edited in La Face Bianconi 1990, pp. 300-302 (commentary at 142-145) and in Filocamo 2003, p. 29.

versions (PerA 431, ParisN Rés676, Panc.27). This second branch of the tradition in turn has several offshoots: one version for four voices (PerA 431) and one for three (ParisN Rés676). As shown in the following synoptic table, the reading for three voices of Panc.27 cannot be linked to the tradition of ParisN Rés676 (the '★' indicates that the voice is labelled «Contra», but in Panc.27 it is a 'Contra [Altus]', whereas in ParisN Rés676 it is a 'Contra [Bassus]'):

	voices	*Superius*	*Altus*	*Tenor*	*Bassus*
ModE 9	4	x	different	different	different
PerA 431	4	x	x	x	x
ParisN Rés676	3	x	–	x	x★
Panc.27	3	x	x★	x	–

The layout in Panc.27 clarifies that the scribe has copied the piece in a residual space on the opening, using the two lowest staves: the Superius occupies the fifth and half the sixth stave of fol. 40*v*; the Tenor begins immediately after in this last line, and continues on the fifth stave of fol. 41*r*; the Contra [Altus] begins at the end of this last line and finishes at the end of the sixth stave. Physically, therefore, there was no more space available on the opening. On the other hand, the awkward counterpoint of the version in Panc.27 (numerous parallel fourths on the strong beat in the two lower voices) suggests the hypothesis that the piece was not originally transmitted in this way, but that the version of Panc.27 derives instead from a model for four voices in which the Bassus was not copied (perhaps for the mere lack of space in Panc.27?).[3]

BIBLIOGRAPHY: CATTIN 1986, p. 285; FILOCAMO 2003, pp. vii-xi; LA FACE BIANCONI 1990, pp. 64, 117–118; PRIZER 1985, p. 28.

---

[3]. I thank Fabrizio Ammetto for his lengthy consideration of the problematic aspects of the piece in Panc.27.

62.
L'UCELO ME CHIAMA [CHE PERDO GIORNATA]

fols. 40*v*–41*r*

[Francesco Galeota]

63.

Io son l'ucello che sopra i rami d'oro

fol. 41*r* (4 vv.)

[Marchetto Cara]

Io son l'ucello che sopra i rami d'oro
d'un arbor verdo in bosco mi lamento

Italian secular piece (strambotto toscano).

Commentary on the text:

1   the hypermetre can be corrected on the basis of the reading of PeFroIV1505 (and its reprint)

Readings emended in the edition:

Bar	Voice	Original
1	A	*a*
7	T	*longa* with fermata
7/I	B	flat, referring to *b* in bar 9
18/II	T	*a*

Textual concordances (mss): • *Bol.FM. 10* (40*v*) • *Fir.N. B.228* (34*v*) • *Fir.N. M.VII.117* (37*v*) • *Fir.N. NA.701* (33*v*) • *Fir.R. 2723* (103*r*) • *Mod.E. 809* (130*r*) • *Pes.O. 54* (121*v*) • *Pes.O. 54* (125*r*) • *Sev.C. 31* (16*v*)[1]

Textual concordances (prints): • *RispSon* (b3*r*)

Musical concordances (mss): • ParisN Rés676 (9*r*), 2 vv. (A and B only); index: «Cara»

Musical concordances (prints):[2] • PeFroIV1505 (2*r*), «Marcus Chara Vero» • PeFroIV1507 (2*r*), «Marcus Chara Vero»

Text from PeFroIV1505:

Io son l'ocel che sopra i rami d'oro
de un arbor verde in bosco me lamento;
io son l'ocel che senza alcun ristoro
dormo la nocte a la tempesta e al vento.
5   Arbor crudel, tu vedi pur ch'io moro,
e ancor non hai pietà del mio tormento;
ma fammi pur, si sai, oltraggio e torto:
servirte son disposto vivo e morto.

---

[1]. On fol. 76*v* the same heading has been struck out, but is still legible.

[2]. Although not classifiable as a concordance, the following printed version shares only the Tenor with Panc.27: *Frottole, libro octavo*, Venice, Ottaviano Petrucci, 21 May 1507 (Munich, Bayerische Staatsbibliothek, Rar. 878/8), fols. 49*v*-50*r*, *Io son l'ocel che con le debil ali*, «D. MI.». This musical version is edited in Boscolo 1999, pp. 231-233 and in Filocamo 2003, pp. 32-34.

MODERN EDITIONS OF THE TEXT: FILOCAMO 2003, pp. 15-17 (after PeFroIV1505); SAVIOTTI 1892, p. 344 (after *Pes. O. 54*); SCHWARTZ 1935, p. xxxviii (after PeFroIV1505).

MODERN EDITIONS OF THE MUSIC: FILOCAMO 2003, pp. 30-31 (after PeFroIV1505); PIRROTTA 1975, pp. 30-31 (after PeFroIV1505, with partial omission of the Altus); SCHWARTZ 1935, p. 45 (after PeFroIV1505).

REMARKS: See also the Remarks to no. 61, and note 1 to entry no. 15. Although certainly having had a model for copying, the piece in Panc.27 does not seem to be connected with any of the known concordances because of the numerous graphic and substantive variants (above all in the Altus of PeFroIV1505 and its reprint).[3]

BIBLIOGRAPHY: BOORMAN 2006, p. 983; BOSCOLO 2003; FILOCAMO 2003, pp. vii–xi; GHISI 1953a, p. 71; JEPPESEN 1968, p. 89; JEPPESEN 1969, p. 123; LOCKWOOD 1987, pp. 138-139; PRIZER 1980, p. 137; PRIZER 1985, pp. 28-29; PRIZER 1986, pp. 24-25, and n. 81; SAVIOTTI 1892, pp. 320-321; VECCHI GALLI 1986a, p. 27.

---

[3]. Lucia Boscolo maintains, incorrectly in my view, that the lauda contrafact *Io son Giesù che sopra i rami d'oro* (set to music in *Razzi*, fols. 133*v*-134*r*) circulated also with the music of *Io son l'ucello che sopra i rami d'oro* (see BOSCOLO 2003, p. 365, n. 31). This conclusion rests on a shaky basis, that the 'cantasi come' indications in the two literary sources (*Laude Vecchie* and *Opera Nova*) have the same status as musical prints (*ibid.*, p. 359). In the absence of a musical source that would confirm this hypothesis, it must be rejected.

63.
Io son l'ucello che sopra i rami d'oro

fol. 41*r*

[Marchetto Cara]

Io son l'u - cel - lo che so - pra i

ra - mi d'o - ro

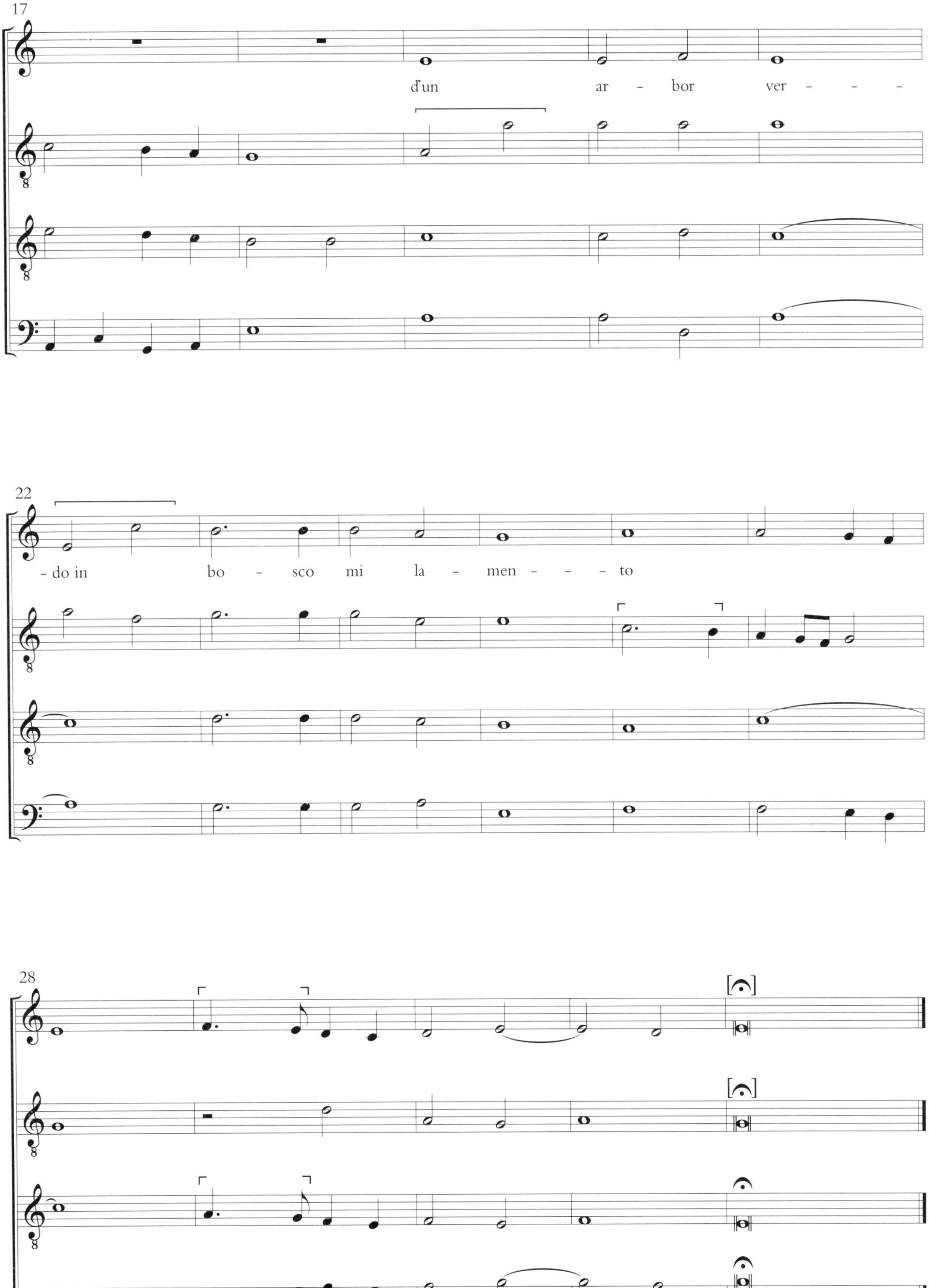
17
d'un ar - bor ver - - -
22
- do in bo - sco mi la - men - - - to
28

64.

CANTI ZOIOSI E DOLCE MELODIA /
JO HAY PRIS AMOR [À MA DEVISE]

fol. 41*v* (3 vv.)

[…]¹

Canti zoiosi e dolce melodia
tuti cantiamo a l'umile Maria.

Lauda (oda). Contrafact on the music of the rondeau quatrain *J'ay pris amours à ma devise*.²

READINGS EMENDED IN THE EDITION:

BAR	VOICE	ORIGINAL
29/II	Ct	*f*
31-32	S	*brevis* with fermata
57	T	*longa* with fermata

TEXTUAL CONCORDANCES (MSS):³ • *Berg.C. 1* (92r-*v*), (Jacopone da Todi) • *Berl.S. H.348* (22r-*v*), (Jacopone da Todi) • *Bol.Car. 34* (60*v*-61*v*) • *Bol.U. 2845* (277-278) • *Borg.P. M.76725* (131r-132r) • *CV. Ch.120* (20*v*-21r, *olim* 170*v*-171r), «De la madona Jacopone» • *CV. Ch.266* (224*v*-225r) • *CV. P.341* (79r-*v*) • *CV. VL.13026* (18r-*v*) • *Fir.L. Ash.1402* (49*v*-50*v*) • *Fir.L. Ash.1402* (171*v*-172*v*) • *Fir.N. 140* (23*v*-24*v*) • *Fir.N. M.27* (118r-119r), (Jacopone da Todi) • *Fir.N. M.1083* (39r-*v*) • *Fir.R. 1502* (9r-*v*)⁴ • *Gub.Maz*⁵ • *Mil.A. 3* (105*v*-106r) • *Mil.A. T.502* (112*v*-113*v*), «Laus B. Jacoponi de assumptione Virginis Marie» • *Mil.B. 27* (4r-5r) • *Mil.T. 92* ([233]r-[234]r) • *Mil.T. 383* (9*v*-10*v*) • *Mil.T. 913* (15r-16r) • *Nap.N. 38* (34r-35r) • *Paris.N. I.559* (104*v*-105r), (Jacopone da Todi) • *Paris.N. I.607* (113*v*-114*v*), (Jacopone da Todi) • *Piac.C. L.15* (24r-25*v*, *olim* 19r-20*v*) • *Piac.C. P.245* (34r-35r) • *Roma.Ang. 2274* (28r-29*v*) • *Roma.Ang. 2275* (111*v*-112r, *olim* 120*v*-121r) • *Roma.Ca. 3828* (160*v*-162r) • *Tessier* (84*v*) • *Ven.C. C.128* (77*v*-78*v*) • *Ven.GR. 120* (83r-84r), (Leonardo Giustinian) • *Ven.M. I.77* (95r-96r) • *Ven.M. I.80* (37r-38*v*) • *Ven.M. I.80* (117r-*v*) • *Ven.M. I.153* (140*v*-141*v*), (Jacopone da Todi, modern hand) • *Ven.M. I.182* (220r-*v*) • *Ven.M. I.230* (30r-31*v*) • *Ven.M. I.313* (24r-25*v*) • *Ver.Civ. 1212* (267-268), (Jacopone da Todi)

---

¹. Disertori suggests an attribution to Caron on stylistic grounds (see DISERTORI 1964, p. 78), as does (independently) MONTAGNA 1987, p. 125.

². See the text, taken from the musical source ParisN Rés57, collated with WashC L25, in TARUSKIN 1982, p. 7.

³. Although the repertory CARBONI 1977, p. 56, lists the lauda in the manuscript Vatican City, Biblioteca Apostolica Vaticana, Patetta 732, this manuscript (19th-century!) has no trace of it. I have carefully checked other codices in the fondo Patetta (734, 736, 739, 744, 746, 781, 980, 1445, 1513), and also Ferraioli 732, but none of these manuscripts contains the text *Canti gioiosi e dolce melodia*.

⁴. The first two lines also on fol. 6r but with the variant «Canti gioiosi e dolce melodia | tucti gridiamo al lume di Maria».

⁵. I have not been able to see this manuscript in person, and have no idea where it is at present. The index of the manuscript in MAZZATINTI 1880 (p. 87) does not mention the lauda, which appears instead in a later article (see MAZZATINTI 1886, p. 40).

TEXTUAL CONCORDANCES (PRINTS): • *Busti1488* (cap. IX) • *Busti1489* (a4r-v) • *Busti1490* (a2r-v) • *Busti1492S* (a2v-a3v), (Bernardino de' Busti) • *Busti1492Z* (a2v-a3r), (Bernardino de' Busti) • *Busti1494* (E1v-E3r), (Bernardino de' Busti) • *Busti1517* (A2v-A3r), (Bernardino de' Busti) • *BustiPon* (cap. IV) • *Compendio1483* (139r-140v) • *Fior1505* (c5v-c6v) • *JacopBen* (p2r-p3r), (Jacopone da Todi) • *JacopMis* (221-222), (Jacopone da Todi) • *JacopSper* (110v-111v), (Jacopone da Todi) • *LaudeBonar* (10v-11r) • *LaudeGiacc* (9r-v) • *LaudeMisc* (70v-71r) • *LaudeVecchie* (h2r-v) • *OperaNova* (58r-v)

MUSICAL CONCORDANCES (MSS): • BolM 16 (138v-139r), *J'a pris amor* • DijM 517 (7r, *olim* 2r), *J'ay pris amours*, 2 vv. (T and Ct only)[6] • EsM 24 (136v), *J'ay prins amours*, T only, in two versions[7] • LinzL 529 (5r), *J'ay pris amours*,[8] opening line of Ct only, with indication of S • LonB A31922 (41v-42r), *J'ay pryse amours* • MünS 352b (159r), textless • MünS L5023 (54v-55v), *O preciosum convivium* with the heading «Discantus de sacramento», 2 vv. (S and T only) • ParisN F15123 (21v-22r), *J'a pris amoris a ma divise* • ParisN NAF4379 (27v-28r), *J'ay prins amours en ma devise* • ParisN Rés57 (71v-72r), *J'ay pris amours a ma devise* • ParisN Ro2973 (23v-24r), *J'ay pris amours a ma devise* • PerA 431 (75v-76r), *J'am pris amore* • PesO 1144 (61-65), *J'a prex amore* • SegC (118v),[9] *J'ay prijs amours*, 2 vv. (S and T only) • TrenC 1947/4 (5v-6r), textless, with different Ct • WashC L25 (31v-32r), *J'ay prins amours a ma devise* • WolfA G287 (37v-38r), *J'ay prins amours a ma devise*

MUSICAL CONCORDANCES (PRINTS): • PeSpinI (23v-25v), *J'ay pris amours*, (Francesco Spinacino) • PeSpinII (13-14), *J'ay pris amours*

TEXT FROM *Bol.U. 2845*:

    Canti zolgiosi e dolze melodia
    tuti cridamo a l'umile Maria.

    L'umile Maria sopra li cieli è zita,
    li anzoli fam festa in quella eterna vita;
5   tuti s'enclina, et ognum d'onor l'anvita
    a la Regina de gran cortexia.

    O Regina dolze, o sancta imperatrice,
    per amor de quello, che lasù te mise,
    fane gustare de quelo che se dice
10   che tu gustasti quando fosti in via.

    Quando te partisti dal tenebroso mundo,
    contra de ti vene quel grande Re iocundo,
    tuti i nemici fugiendo, vano al fondo
    po' che vedeno adimplir la prophetia.

15   O devoti amanti de Maria iocunda,
    presto coreti, avanti che la iunga,
    et annuntiati a quela turba munda
    che s'aparechino a laudar Maria.

---

[6]. One page is missing.

[7]. First version crossed out, second version apparently correct.

[8]. Three staves below the discantus there is an inscription: «Tenor Canon — Conficies altum / sonne diattessaron altus». I thank Herbert Kellman for this information, and Leofranc Holford-Strevens, who has reconstructed a more correct version of the final part as 'sonando diatessaron altius'.

[9]. The following page is lost or not copied: «vacat» is written at the top of the page.

Stano tuti atenti cum aliegre faze,
20 tuti stano pronti et aspetando tace:
como zonzesti cridavam «Pace, pace
a te, beata Virgine Maria».

Anzoli, arcanzoli e le virtute sancte
foron le prime schiere che te som davanti,
25 umilmente inchinavam tuti quanti
dicendo: «Viva l'umile Maria».

Dominatione e podestà beate
cum li principati in uno amor ligate:
chi veduto avesse quant'erano braxate
30 de benedirti zamai non cessaria.

Per li troni sancti passa la Regina,
fra li cherubini va la cherubina,
gratie dolze quela dona divina,
cum quella turba al Creator rendea.

35 *O voi, seraphini ne lo amor somersi,*
per la seraphina mutasti i vostri versi:
de sanctus sanctus, sancta sancta dicesti
po' che 'l piaque a l'alta Signoria.[10]

E le piaze larghe de quel splendiente cielo
40 tuto foccoso corea Gabrielo,
como impazito dicea a questo e quelo:
«A costei feci l'alta ambasaria».

Li propheti sancti faceam sollempne festa,
chi s'inclinava e chi salutava questa;
45 David cantava che questa donna onesta
tracto l'avea fuor di prigionia.

Ma li patriarci tuti ad una schiera
stavam tuti chiusi soto soa bandiera,
e como videno quela gran lumera
50 presto zascuno de soa sema uscia.

Poi da tuto il stuolo tu fosti circundata
cum suave voce prexa e solevata,
presso al tuo fiolo si t'ebero colocata
et onorata, como eterna dea.

55 O Maria dolze, o clemente, o pia,
o rengratiata fia tanta compagnia,
chi non te lauda smarita hano la via
de prevegnire a l'alta psalmodia.

MODERN EDITIONS OF THE TEXT: BRAMBILLA 1903, pp. 49-50 (from a mysterious Neapolitan manuscript, which is not any of those listed so far, and would also contain Enselmino da Montebelluna's *Pianto*); GALLETTI 1863, pp. 142-143 (after *LaudeMisc*); LONGO 1986, pp. 391-393 (after *Borg.P. M.76725*);

---

10. This strophe is lacking in many sources, among which *Bol.U. 2845.*

397

LUISI 1983, I, pp. 293-294 (after *Ven. GR. 120*); MAZZA 1960, pp. 167-168 (after *Berg. C. 15*); PERCOPO 1884, pp. 151-152 (after *Nap. N. 38*).

MODERN EDITIONS OF THE MUSIC: BARRET 1981, II, p. 4 (after DijM 517); DISERTORI 1964, pp. 215-218 (after PeSpinI, and after DijM 517, with S and T after TrenC 1947/4); DTÖ 28, p. 185 (after ParisN NAF4379); EDM 39, p. 400 (after MünS 352b); GUTIÉRREZ-DENHOFF 1988, p. 52 (after WolfA G287); HANEN 1983, pp. 473-476 (after EsM 24, with S and Ct after WashC L25); IVANOFF 1988, p. 93 (after PesO 1144), p. 215 (after DijM 517); KOTTICK 1962, II, p. 62 (after ParisN Ro2973); LUISI 1983, II, p. 24 (after Panc.27); NOE 17, pp. lxiii-lxiv (after WolfA G287); PEASE 1959, II, pp. 62-64 (after ParisN F15123); REESE 1968, p. 79 (after ParisN NAF4379); SCHMIDT 1969, II, p. 194 (after PeSpinII); STEVENS 1962, p. 31 (after LonB A31922); TARUSKIN 1982, pp. 6-7 (after ParisN Rés57), pp. 8-9 (after WashC L25), pp. 10-11 (after LonB A31922), pp. 12-13 (after TrenC 1947/4); THIBAULT - DROZ (1927) 1976, pp. 3-4, (after DijM 517, with S after ParisN F15123 and WolfA G287); THIBAULT - FALLOWS 1991, pp. 34-35 (after ParisN Ro2973); THOMAS 1981, no. 7 (after DijM 517 and MünS 352b); WOLF O/7, pp. 92-94 (after ParisN N4379), pp. 94-96 (after PerA 431).

REMARKS: *J'ay pris amours à ma devise* is one of the most famous chansons of the fifteenth century, which circulated in various musical reworkings (for three voices with a different Contratenor Bassus, with only the Superius in common, with only the Tenor in common, in the form of parodies, etc.). Thoroughly studied by Richard Taruskin, the original musical version might be that transmitted also by Panc.27 (a source not listed in TARUSKIN 1982), despite his belief that the piece circulated also in the form of a Superius-Tenor *bicinium*, as probably happened with many Burgundian chansons (see TARUSKIN 1982, p. 2); no known source, however, transmits the piece for two voices. David Fallows, on the other hand, thinks that the possible original version of the chanson could be a three-voice one with a different Contratenor in the same range as the Tenor; the version of Panc.27 would then be a subsequent reworking (see FALLOWS 1999, p. 195). Despite the extensive diffusion of the musical versions, the testimony of Panc.27 — although differing from the concordances in various graphic and substantive variants — is the only one to transmit the lauda text *Canti gioiosi e dolce melodia*. In the Panciatichi manuscript *Canti zoiosi e dolce melodia / Jo hay pris amor* has an interesting connection with the three preceding pieces (see Remarks to no. 61): the incipit of no. 64 is analogous to that of *Io son l'ocel che con le debil ali*, transmitted uniquely by the printed source *Frottole, libro octavo*, Venice, Ottaviano Petrucci, 21 May 1507 (Munich, Bayerische Staatsbibliothek, Rar. 878/8), fols. 49*v*-50*r*, another piece connected with the 'bird cycle' (see FILOCAMO 2003). The Tenor of this last piece is found in fact in no. 63 of Panc.27 (*Io son l'ucello che sopra i rami d'oro*). If considered from this viewpoint, the placement of no. 64 is logically justified in relation to the compact group of the three preceding pieces.

BIBLIOGRAPHY: BAKER 1978, I, p. 373; BANFI 1956, p. 47; BARRET 1981, II, pp. 1-3; BOORMAN 2006, p. 1049; BROWN 1963, pp. 233-235; CATTIN 1968a, p. 4; CATTIN 1984, p. 424; DISERTORI 1946; DISERTORI 1964, pp. 77-78; FALLOWS 1999, pp. 195-197, 506; FEIST 1889, p. 127; FILOCAMO 2004; FRATI 1917, p. 468; GUIDOBALDI 1995, pp. 50-59; HERNON 1972, pp. 517-518; JEPPESEN 1935, p. xix; KÄMPER 1976, p. 82; LAMA DE LA CRUZ 1994, p. 210; LONGO 1986, p. 220; LUISI 1983, I, p. 544; MECONI 1994; NOE 17, pp. lxii-lxv; PANNELLA 1968, pp. 23, 41; PEASE 1959, I, pp. 88-89; TARUSKIN 1982, pp. 2-5; TENNERONI 1909, p. 74; THIBAULT - DROZ (1927) 1976, p. 115; THIBAULT - FALLOWS 1991, pp. xciii-xcv; WILSON 1998, p. 87.

64.

CANTI ZOIOSI E DOLCE MELODIA / JO HAY PRIS AMOR [À MA DEVISE]

fol. 41*v*

Ma – – ri – – a.   Can – – ti zo –

– io – – si   e   dol – – –

– ce   me – – – – lo – di a   tu – ti   can –

– tia – mo a   l'u – mi – le   Ma – ri – – a.

400

65.

Io mi voglio lamentare

fol. 42*r* (4 vv.)

[Giovanni Brocco]

> Io mi voglio lamentare
> del tuo cor falace e rio:
> tu me lasi per altrui amare.
> Patientia sia cum Dio.

Italian secular piece (oda or barzelletta).[1]

Commentary on the text:

3   hypermetric; can be corrected on the basis of the readings in PeFroIII1505 (and its reprint) and
           MadP 1335

Readings emended in the edition:

Bar	Voice	Original
8/III	B	*semiminima e* in place of *g*, corrected according to ParisN Rés676

Musical concordances (mss): • MadP 1335 (284*v*) • ParisN Rés676 (53*v*-54*r*), 3 vv. (A lacking)

Musical concordances (prints): • PeFroIII1505 (28*r*), «Io. Bro.» • PeFroIII1507 (28*r*), «Io. Bro.»

Text from PeFroIII1505:

> Io mi voglio lamentare
> del tuo cor fallace e rio:
> lassa me per altri amare.
> Patientia sia con Dio.

5   Io te ho amato assai con fede:
     tu 'l sai bene e 'l so ancor io,
     et non hai di me mercede.
     Patientia […]

     Per te sola ho abandonato,
10   donna, sancti, sancte e Dio,
     per te vado atormentato.
     Patientia […]

     Per te, ingrata, ognor si trova
     vivo e morto lo cor mio,
15   per te resto ad ogni prova.
     Patientia […]

---

[1]. The text is transmitted in two metric forms: as an oda in PeFroIII1505 (and its reprint) and MadP 1335, and as a barzelletta in ParisN Rés676.

Non me voglio desperare,
pur ch'io veda il volto pio
se me lassi tormentare.
20   Patientia […]

Patientia io voglio al tuto
supportar per amor tio,
se non voi tu darme adiuto.
Patientia […]

Text from MadP 1335:

Yo me vollo lamentare
del tu' amor falace e rio:
lassa me per altr'amare.
Paçiencia sia cum Dio.

5   Tu mi vedi ad ora ad ora
la mia vita consumare,
y te piache que yo muera
desperato per te amare.

Text from ParisN Rés676:

Io mi voglio lamentare
del to cor ingrato e rio:
laso me per altro amare.
Patientia or sia cum Dio.

5   El mio amor fu dolze e pio,
fu cum fede et cum amore.
Or non stimo el patir mio,
la mia pena e 'l mio dolore.
Io fui già to servitore,
10   sempr' e mai ti volsi amare.
        Io mi voglio […]

Or ch'è perso ogne vigore
de mia forza e de mio ardire,
cum gran fé si fu l'amore
che portai cum gran martìre.
15   Ingrata sei, mi fai languire,
che non posso suportare.
        Io mi voglio […]

Te domando in mercede,
o falsa e traditora,
la mia tanta e pura fede
20   è cagion ch'io stia di fora,
e tu vedi ad ora ad ora
la mia vita consumare.
        Io mi voglio […]

Tanta pena sì m'acuora
quando io penso non amare,
25   et a ti piace ch'io mora.

Meglio ti seria confortare
e il to core donarmi,
che 'l to amante abruxare.
       Io mi voglio [...]

Lasa ormai la dureza!
30   O generosa mia dea
cagnose la toa gentileza.
Conforta l'alma mia rea
e no ti fare cagna zudea:
volere ch'un cor per ti deba crepare.
       Io mi voglio [...]

MODERN EDITIONS OF THE TEXT: BARBIERI 1890, p. 140 (after MadP 1335); CESARI *ET AL.* 1954, pp. 42*-43* (after PeFroIII1505); FILOCAMO 2000, pp. 123-125 (after Panc.27); MME 14/2, p. 481 (after MadP 1335).

MODERN EDITIONS OF THE MUSIC: BARBIERI 1890, p. 446 (after MadP 1335); CESARI *ET AL.* 1954, p. 114 (after PeFroIII1505); MME 10, p. 185 (after MadP 1335).

REMARKS: The version of Panc.27 is not closely related to any of the known concordances, which themselves demonstratively belong to different traditions, as is also confirmed by the differences in the text. With respect to Panc.27, MadP 1335 and ParisN Rés676 transmit the piece with many differences, both graphic and substantive; in PeFroIII1505 (and its reprint), moreover, *Io mi voglio lamentare* is written a tone higher, and entirely lacks the concluding section (bb. 13-15).

BIBLIOGRAPHY: BOORMAN 2006, p. 982; FERRARI BARASSI 1993, pp. 1486-1487, 1494-1498; FERRARI BARASSI 1997, pp. 50, 63.

65.
Io mi voglio lamentare
fol. 42*r*

[Giovanni Brocco]

Io mi vo - glio la - men-ta - re del tuo cor fa-

-la - ce e ri - o: tu me la - si per al-trui a - ma - - re.

Pa - ti-en - tia sia cum Di - o, *pa - ti - en - tia sia cum Di - o.*

66.

In te, domine, speravi

fols. 42*v*-43*r* (4 vv.)

Iosquin D[es Prez]

In te, domine, speravi
per trovar pietà in eterno.
Ma in un t[r]isto e obscuro inferno
fui, e frustra laboravi.
      In te, domine, speravi

5   Roto è al vento ogni speranza:
veggio il ciel voltarmi 'm pianto.
Suspir, lacrime me avanza
del mio tristo sperar tanto.
Fui ferito, se non quanto
10   tribulando ad te clamavi.
      In te, domine […]

Lo cecato voler mio
perfin quin m'ha fato muto,
et or poco al dolor mio
per mio dir vien proveduto.
15   Deh, signor, porgime adiuto,
nam de me iam desperavi.
      In te, domine […]

Barzelletta.[1] The incipit is taken from the opening of Psalms 30 and 70 («In te Domine speravi non/ne confundar in aeternum»), Vulgata, pp. 802-805, 854-857.

Commentary on the text:

5   the *residuum* begins here
12   «quin» means 'qui'

Textual concordances (prints): • *Inamormento* (f4*r*)

Musical concordances (mss): • BasU 17-20 (no. 68; S: 38*v*, A: 37*v*-38*r*, T: 39*v*-40*r*, B: 38*v*) • BasU 22-4 (no. 47; S: 52*r*, B: 50*v*), 2 vv. (S and B only) • BerlS 40196 (262*v*-263*r*) • BolM 18 (12*v*-13*r*), textless • ErlU 473/4 (191*v*-192*r*), *Deo gratias* • FirC B2441 (56*v*-57*r*) • FirN BR337 (84*v*), textless, B only • GreifU 640-1 (no. 1), 2 vv. (S and B only) • HerdF 9822 (no. 14; S: 4*v*, B: 5*v*), *In te Domine speravi non confundar in aeternum*, 2 vv. (S and B only) • KönU 150 (no. 9) • LeipU 51 (no. 45; T: 68*r*, B: 100*r*), *In te Domine speravi non confundar in eternum*, 2 vv. (T and B only) • LonB E3051 (56*v*-57*r*)

---

[1]. Although the piece is sometimes considered a lauda, I agree with the opinion expressed in the NJE, where it appears in a volume of Secular Works.

• MadP 1335 (56r), «Jusquin dascanio» • MünU 326 (13r), *In te Domine speravi non confundar in eternum*, A only • ParisN Rés676 (17v-18r) • RegB 940-1 (no. 42), *In te Domine speravi non confundar in eternum*; index: «Joskin Daskanio» • SGS 463 (no. 25), *In te Domine speravi non confundar in eternum*, S only, «Iosquinus Pratensis», «Ionicus» • SionC 87-4 (4v), *En te Domine speravi non confundar in eternum*, B only • SionC 87-4 (13v), *In te Domine speravi non confundar in eternum*, B only • UlmS 236 (no. 13), as fourth part of another motet *In te Domine speravi non confundar in eternum* • UppsU 478-80 (no. 4), *In te Domine speravi non confundar in eternum*, 3vv. (S lacking) • WrocK 352 (30r-31r)

MUSICAL CONCORDANCES (PRINTS):[2] • GünNew (F3v-F4r) • GutNew (F4r-v) • PeBossI1509 (38v-39r), «Josquin Dascanio» • PeBossI1515 (38v-39r), «Josquin Dascanio» • PeFroI (49v-50r), «Iosquin Dascanio» • RhauSym (no. 1), *In te Domine speravi non confundar in eternum*, «Ioskin Daskanio»

TEXT FROM ParisN Rés676:

> In te, domine, speravi
> per trovare pianto in eterno.
> Ma in un tristo et obscuro inferno
> fui, et frustra laboravi.
>   In te, domine […]

> 5   Rotta al vento ogne speranza
>   del mio tristo sperar tanto.
>   Sospiri, lacrime sol avanza,
>   vego il celo nutrirme in pianto.
>   Sempre affanni, abisso in ogne canto,
> 10   tribulando ad te clamavi.
>   In te, domine […]

> Fin al celo i dolori mei
> son già 'nati,[3] e tu non credi.
> Sol te, sola, che vorei
> star nel stento, e tu il vedi.
> 15   Ma dal dì ch'io ti chiedi
>   ad te oculos levavi.
>   In te, domine […]

> Se nel cello, como si dice,
> del martìr si sente palma,[4]
> presso[5] d'esser felice
> 20   per seguirte, ochi d'alma.
>   E per questa mia degna alma
>   semper lacrimas rigavi.
>   In te, domine […]

The disposition of the Latin–Italian text, which differs among the sources, is summarized in the following chart, in which the arabic numerals indicate the successsion of the stanzas (without considering variants in writing or single words):

---

[2]. Although not classifiable as a concordance, the Cantus of the following printed version shares only the Tenor with Panc.27: *Frottole, libro octavo*, Venice, Ottaviano Petrucci, 21 May 1507 (Munich, Bayerische Staatsbibliothek, Rar. 878/8), fols. 43v-44r, *Poi che in te donna speravi. Resposta*, «N. B.». This musical version is edited in BOSCOLO 1999, pp. 221-222.

[3]. The past participle «'nati» derives from 'annati' (= 'andati').

[4]. «si sente palma» = 'si ricava premio, lode, elogio'.

[5]. From 'appressarsi'? (= 'avvicinarsi').

	PeFroI - PeBossI1509 - PeBoss1515	MadP 1335	ParisN Rés676	FirC B2441 - LonB E3051
Roto è	1	1	1	1
Lo cecato	2	–	–	–
Fin al celo	–	–	2	2
Se nel cello	–	–	3	–

MODERN EDITIONS OF THE TEXT: BARBIERI 1890, pp. 76-77 (after MadP 1335 and PeFroI); BORGHI 1995, pp. 220-221 (after FirC B2441); CESARI ET AL. 1954, p. 19★ (after PeFroI); DISERTORI 1964, p. 405 (after PeBossI1509); FILOCAMO 2000, pp. 125-128 (after Panc.27); MME 14/2, p. 287 (after MadP 1335); NJE 28, II, pp. 255-256 (after FirC B2441); SCHWARTZ 1935, p. xxxvii (after PeFroI).

MODERN EDITIONS OF THE MUSIC: ALBRECHT 1959, pp. 3-4 (after RhauSym); BARBIERI 1890, pp. 311-312 (after MadP 1335 and PeFroI); BORGHI 1995, pp. 403-404 (after FirC B2441); CESARI ET AL. 1954, pp. 38-39 (after PeFroI); DAVISON - APEL (1946) 1977, p. 98 (after PeFroI); DISERTORI 1964, pp. 404-405 (after PeBossI1509); LOACH 1969, II, pp. 46-47 (after SGS 463, with alterations indicated on p. 2); MCCOY 1988, no. 33 (after GünNew); MME 5, p. 110 (after MadP 1335); NJE 28, I, pp. 48-49 (after FirC B2441); SCHWARTZ 1935, pp. 37-38 (after PeFroI); THOMAS 1991, no. 2 (after PeFroI).

REMARKS: This piece is among the most celebrated and widely diffused pieces of the Renaissance, circulating both as a lauda with a bilingual Latin-Italian text, and with Latin text from the beginning of Psalms 30 and 70. The version of Panc.27 certainly derives from PeFroI: the text is the same (with slight graphic variants), and the music is practically identical. The only differences in Panc.27 are the absence of a fermata in the Bassus (b. 12) and the omission of the two *signa congruentiae* in the Altus and Tenor (b. 29/I); moreover, Panc.27 omits (correctly!) the fermata that PeFroI places over the final *f'* of the Superius. David Fallows maintains that, because of these slight differences, the version of Panc.27 might be derived from an exemplar of PeFroI different from those known today at Munich and Vienna (see NJE 28/II, p. 254). It seems to me, however, that the weight of the evidence favours a different interpretation: (a) the omission of bar 12 might be a simple oversight on the part of the copyist; (b) the absence of the *signa congruentiae* in bar 29 (purely intended for performance, and not structural) might be due to the fact that the scribe judged them superfluous, since it was a very famous piece in which the *signa* simply indicate the end of the poetic stanza; (c) the omission of the fermata at the end, finally, is irrelevant, given that in Petrucci it seems to suggest the prolongation *ad libitum* of the final *longa* until the other voices finish.

BIBLIOGRAPHY: ALBRECHT 1959, p. 181; BECHERINI 1954, p. 115, n. 4; BOORMAN 2006, p. 913; BOSCOLO 1999, p. 19; BRENNECKE 1953, p. 31; CATTIN 1984, pp. 434-435; CATTIN 1986, p. 273; DISERTORI 1964, p. 55; FENLON - HAAR 1991, p. 64; FERRARI BARASSI 1993, pp. 1485, 1490; FERRARI BARASSI 1997, pp. 53-54; FILOCAMO 2004; GALLICO 1976, pp. 450-452; LOACH 1969, I, p. 289; LUISI 1995, p. 396; MACEY 1998, pp. 155-156, 237-252; NJE 28, II, pp. 237-264; PRIZER 1996b, pp. 16, 46-47; SHERR 2000b, pp. 425-428; TIBALDI 2005, pp. 560-563; WEISS 1998, p. 20.

66.

IN TE, DOMINE, SPERAVI

fols. 42v–43r

Iosquin D[es Prez]

S[uperius]

In te, do - mi-ne, spe - ra — — — —

A[ltus]

In te, do - mi-ne, spe - ra - vi

T[enor]

In te, do - mi-ne, spe - ra - vi

B[assus]

- vi per   tro - var pie - tà in e - ter — no.

Ma in   un t[r]i - sto e ob-scu - ro in - fer — no fui, e

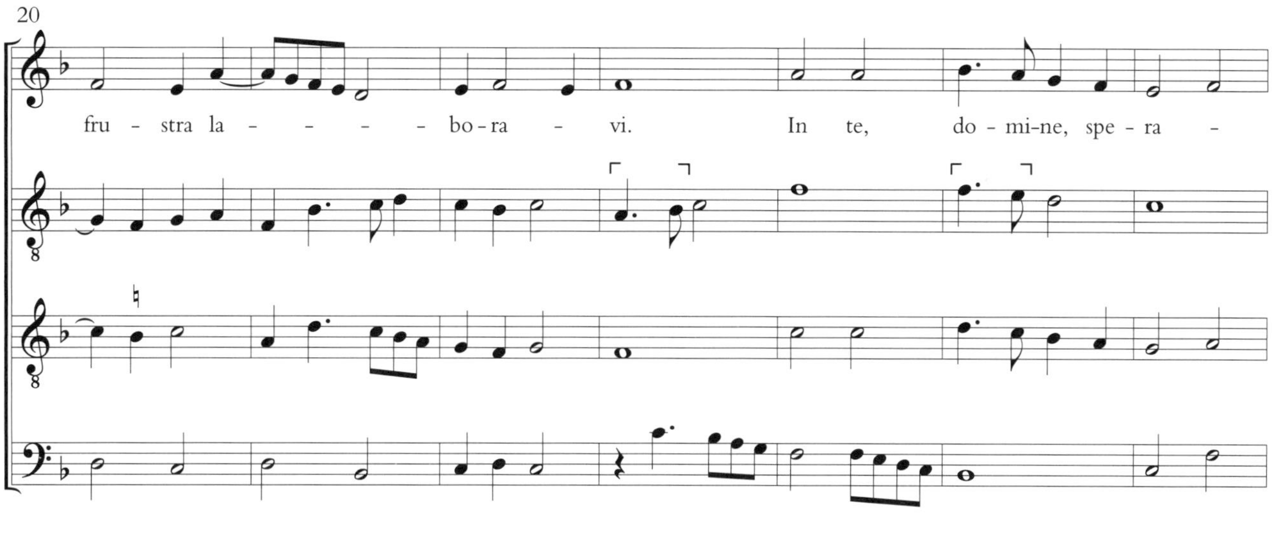

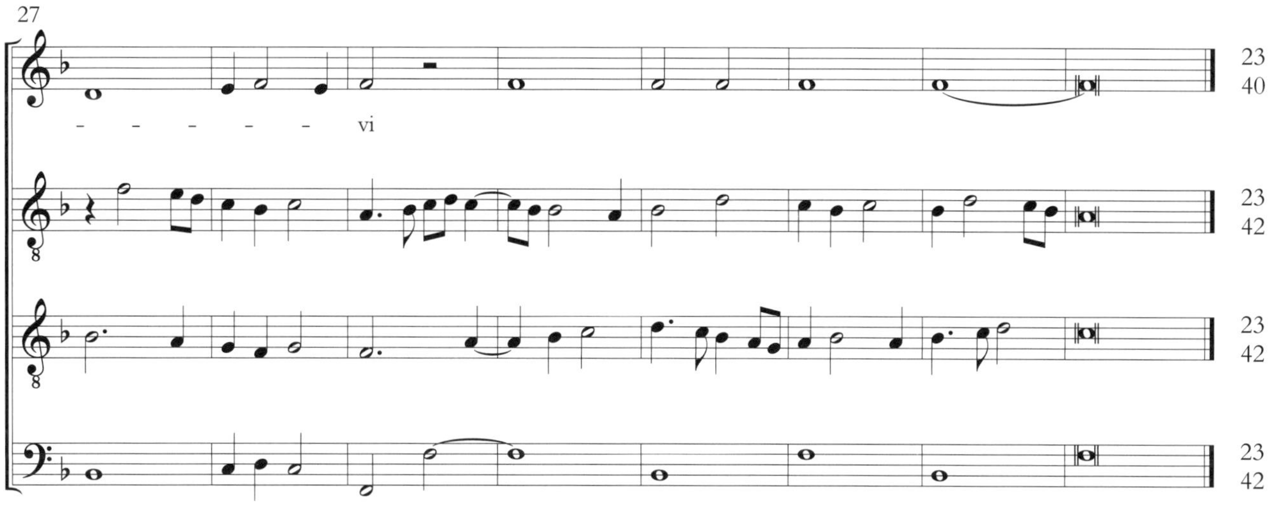

67.

Egli è il tuo bon Iesù

fols. 42v–43r (4 vv.)

[Feo Belcari]   Frater Dionisius Placentinus

> Egli è il tuo bon Iesù
> che ti dà il suo amor.
> Egli è Iesù, sì, è,
> egli è il tuo bon Iesù.

5   El fu per te conficto
> cum gran pena e dolore,
> el fu Iesù, sì, fu,
> el fu per te conficto.

> El t'ha per sua sposa
10   per farte grande onore,
> el t'ha Iesù, sì, ha,
> el t'ha per sua sposa.

> Ama Iesù tuo Dio,
> tuo Dio e bon Signore.
15   Ama Iesù ama,
> ama Iesù tuo Dio.

Lauda (Oda).

COMMENTARY ON THE TEXT:

1–4	placed under the C
5–8	placed under the T
5 and 8	«conflicto» in the MS. A derivation from 'confligo' does not seem very likely
9–12	placed under the A
13–16	placed under the B
15	for the line not to be hypermetric it should be read as *tronco*, with consequent diastole on «ama» (to be read 'amà')

TEXTUAL CONCORDANCES (MSS): • *CV. Ro. 424* (121r), (Feo Belcari) • *Fir. N. M. 690* (51v–52r), (Feo Belcari) • *Rim. C. 38* (131v), «Feo Belchari» • *Roma. Ang. 2274* (53r–54r) • *Roma. Co. 3* (102–103) • *Ven. M. I. 78* (32v–33r), «Di Feo Belcari»

TEXTUAL CONCORDANCES (PRINTS): • *LaudeBonac* (32v–33r), «Di Feo Belbhari [*sic*]» • *LaudeMisc* (12v), «Di Feo Belchari» • *LaudeSper* (17v), «Di Feo Belcari» • *LaudeVecchie* (b3r–v), «Di Feo Belcari» • *LaudiGiunti* (C2r), «Del medesimo» (= Di Feo Belcari) • *LaudiRiccardiana* (g3r), «di Feo Belcari» • *OperaNova* (11v), «Di Feo Belchari»

MODERN EDITIONS OF THE TEXT: GALLETTI 1863, p. 52 (after *LaudeBonac*).

MODERN EDITIONS OF THE MUSIC: JEPPESEN 1935, p. 168 (after Panc.27).

REMARKS: The piece was certainly added later; it is in fact written on a residual portion of the pages and, in addition to having darker ink, the scribal *ductus* is more slovenly with respect to no. 66 on the same opening. Many literary sources cite the 'cantasi come' as *Egli è tutt bon homme*, but it is surprising, in the state of our present knowledge, that the piece is a musical *unicum*.

BIBLIOGRAPHY: CATTIN 1978, p. 36; CATTIN 1984, pp. 418-419; FALLOWS 1999, p. 184; FRATI 1918, p. 194; GHISI 1953a, pp. 66, 69; LUISI 1983, I, pp. 178, 192; TENNERONI 1909, p. 105; WILSON 1998, p. 86.

67.
EGLI È IL TUO BON IESÙ
fols. 42v-43r

[Feo Belcari]

Frater Dionisius Placentinus

- sù,   sì,   è,   e - gli è il   tuo   bon   Ie - sù.
- sù,   sì,   fu,   el   fu   per   te   con - fic-to.
- sù,   sì,   ha,   el   t'ha   per   su   —   —   a   spo-sa.
- sù   a - ma,   a - ma   Ie   -   sù   tuo   Di - o.

- sù,   sì,   è,   e - gli è il   tuo   bon   Ie - sù.
- sù,   sì,   fu,   el   fu   per   te   con - fic-to.
- sù,   sì,   ha,   el   t'ha   per   su   —   —   a   spo-sa.
- sù   a - ma,   a - ma   Ie   -   sù   tuo   Di - o.

- sù,   sì,   è,   e - gli è il   tuo   bon   Ie - sù.
- sù,   sì,   fu,   el   fu   per   te   con - fic-to.
- sù,   sì,   ha,   el   t'ha   per   su   —   —   a   spo-sa.
- sù   a - ma,   a - ma   Ie   -   sù   tuo   Di - o.

- sù,   sì,   è,   e - gli è il   tuo   bon   Ie - sù.
- sù,   sì,   fu,   el   fu   per   te   con - fic-to.
- sù,   sì,   ha,   el   t'ha   per   su   —   —   a   spo-sa.
- sù   a - ma,   a - ma   Ie   -   sù   tuo   Di - o.

68.

A LA CAZA / IAMO A LA CAZA

fols. 43*v*-45*r* (4 vv.)

Iamo a la caza

Italian secular piece.

READINGS EMENDED IN THE EDITION:

BAR	VOICE	ORIGINAL
21/II	S	*g′* instead of *f′*
35	S, T	*longa*
39	A	*semibrevis*
after 46	S, A, T, B	a bar line that would indicate the beginning of the section to be repeated is lacking
53/I	A	*d′* instead of *e′*
54/I	A	*c′* instead of *b*, corrected on the basis of the reading in ParisN Rés676 (see Remarks)
60	A	superfluous black *g′ brevis* between the two *a*'s
72	S, A, T, B	*semibrevis* with fermata

TEXTUAL CONCORDANCES (MSS): • *Fir.N. 42* (82*v*-83*v*), heading: «1485. La chaccia di Roma»

TEXTUAL CONCORDANCES (PRINTS): • *Lamento* (A3*v*-A4*r*) • *Lamento 1524* (A3*v*-A4*r*) • *Lamento 1526* (A3*v*-A4*r*) • *Operetta 1512*[1] (a1*v*), «Canzone de la caccia» • *Operetta 1515* (3*v*-4*r*), «Canzone de la caccia» • *Operetta 1521* (3*v*), «Canzona della caccia»

MUSICAL CONCORDANCES (MSS): • FirN BR337 (80*v*-81*r*), B only • LeipU 1494 (247*v*-248*v*) • ParisN Rés676 (63*v*-65*r*) • SevC 43 (32*v*-34*r*)

TEXT FROM *Fir.N. 42* (substantially the same as in FirN BR337[2] and LeipU 1494):[3]

    Iamo a la caccia,
    iamo a la caccia!
    Su su, ogni om si spaccia!

    Per la porta Pertusa
5   ce n'andiam questa mattina
    sanza più far riposa
    per la Testeverina,
    ché gli è tempo d'andare!

    Comincia a chiamare
10 Iacomello a la brigata,

---

[1]. I thank Antonio Rossi, who alerted me to this concordance in its various versions.

[2]. The text of FirN BR337 gives ll. 1-29, with the following important variants: ll. 9-10 are lacking, which should be placed in bb. 36-39, which, in the single partbook that survives of this manuscript, corresponds to four bars of rests; in place of ll. 24-25 there is the text «a te Agostino a te | a me Spagnuolo a me».

[3]. The text of LeipU 1494 gives only ll. 1-13, with a few graphic variants.

Agostino; fa stare
la gente aparechiata,
quest'è bella giornata!

O messer Marino, Schiavetto,
15 Signor Ieronimo e Tomasino,
Pietro Caranzon e Lorenzetto,
Pietro Matruccio, Alesandro, Macino,
ogni om pigli el suo camino!

O Timoteo,
20 o Iacometto,
vin qua Taddeo,
o Franceschetto,
andate apresso a lo Spagnoletto!

Vigliala vieni, aduna,[4]
25 Rubino sta avanti,
su su su su su su su su,
Cola, vien tu,
ché gli è ora di non restar più!
Uno di voi la via faccia.

30 Orsù alegramente,
tutti di bella brigata:
chiama a 'tte tutta la gente
che stieno aparechiata,
gli è già chiaro el giorno.

35 Suona lo corno, capo caccia:
la lepre sta d'intorno,
gli cani senton la traccia.
Su, spaccia, spaccia, spaccia!

Tien qui, Balzano, tè qui, Lione;
40 tè qui, Fagiano, tè qui, Falcone;
tè qui, Tristano, tè qui, Carbone;
tè qui, Alano, tè qui, Peccione!
Chiama li brachi dal monte, o babbione!
Tè qui, Quatrochi, tè qui, Pazuolo;
45 tè qui, Finochio, tè qui, Spagnolo!
Apri li ochi al capriuolo!

A 'tte, Agostino, a 'tte!
A 'tte, Spagnolo, a 'tte!

Vedila, vedila, vedila, vedila!
50 Cola, pigliala, ché un cam si la straccia,
uno di voi la via faccia!

Iamo a la caccia,
iamo a la caccia!
Su su, ogni om si spaccia!

---

4. The meaning of this line is obscure.

TEXT FROM ParisN Rés676 (substantially the same as in SevC 43):[5]

> A la cazza, a la cazza!
> Su su su, ognon se spazza!
>
> A questa nostra cazza
> venite volontera,
> 5   cum li brachi e levreri.
> Chi vol venire se spazza,
> ché l'è tempo d'andare.
>
> Sona lo corno, capo di cazza!
> Su, spazza, spazza, spazza!
>
> 10   Tè qui, Balzan, tè qui, Lion;
> tè qui, Fasam, tè qui, Falcon;
> tè qui, Tristan, tè qui, Bigolon;
> te qui, Lan, tè qui, Carbon!
> Chiama li brachi dal monte, babion!
> 15   Tè qui, Pezole, tè qui, Spagnolo;
> abi bon ochio al capriolo!
>
> A te, Bigeto, a te Pasaliqua!
> Vìdela, vìdela,
> vìdela, vìdela.
>
> 20   Al colo, al colo pigliala:
> ché li cani non la straza.

TEXT FROM *Operetta 1521* (*Lamento* has the same text, with a few interesting graphic variants):

> Giamo a la caccia, su su a la caccia!
> Su su, ognun si spaccia!
>
> Per la porta Pertusata
> n'andaremo questa matina
> 5   senza fare più posata
> alla Transtyberina,
> ché gli è tempo d'andare!
>
> Comincia a chiamare
> Chaporello e la brigata,
> 10   Augustino; fa stare
> la gente apparechiata,
> questa è la giornata!
>
> O misser Mario, Schiaveto,
> Signor Hieronymo e Thomasino,
> 15   Pietro Charano e Lorenzetto,
> Petro Marcuzzo, Lisandro e Mancino,
> ognun pigli el camino!
> O Timotheo, Iacometto,
> o tu Thadeo, o Franceschetto,
> 20   andate presso al Spagnoletto!

---

5. Apart from graphic differences, the text of SevC 43 has the following important variants: l. 7 («non aspectar el zorno»); l. 17 («a te Augustin a te | a te Spagnolo a te», as attested in the version of *Fir. N. 42*); l. 19 («a quela a quela pilgiala»).

Boniforte, vien a me
e Rubino resta a ‹a› te!
Su su, o Cola, vien tu?[6]
Gli è tempo, non star più!
25   Uno di voi la via faccia.

         Giamo a la caccia […]

Cercaremo la Buraccia,
Castel Nido e Malagrotta,
perché[7] ritti d'ogni faccia
li tre luochi tutti in frotta.
30   Porta del vino e da mangiare,
lo fiasco pieno non ti scordare,
ché possiamo meglio cacciare.

A Campo Salino andiamo,
Campo Merlo non lassiamo,
35   la Magliana e lo pollaio,
Casal Prete e la casetta,
e cercando tuti in fretta
perché ognun lo dover faccia.

         Giamo a la caccia […]

Orsù, su alegramente,
40   tutti di bella brigata:
e chiamate tutta la gente
che stia bene apparechiata,
ché già chiaro è lo giorno.

Sona el corno, tu o capo caccia,
45   ché la lepre è qui d'intorno,
ché li can sentan la traccia.
Su, spaccia, spaccia, spaccia!

Tè qui, Balzan, tè qui, Lion;
tè qui, Fasan, tè qui, Falcon;
50   tè qui, Tristan, tè qui, Pichion;
tè qui, Alan, tè qui, Carbon!
Chiama li cani dal monte, o babion!
Tè qui, Quattrocchi, tè qui, Pezolo;
tè qui, Finocchio, tè qui, Spagnolo!
55   Apri l'occhio al capriolo!

A te, Augustino, a te!
A te, Spagnolo, a te!

Vèdila, vèdila,
vèdila, vèdila!

---

[6]. The question mark is present in the source.
[7]. The source has «porco» instead of 'perché', which, however, is attested in the concordances.

417

60 O Cola, Cola, pigliala,
    ché li cani non la straccia.

     Giamo a la caccia […]

MODERN EDITIONS OF THE TEXT: CARDUCCI (1896) 1973, pp. 86-90 (after *Fir.N. 42* and *Lamento*); PIRROTTA 1975, pp. 66-67 (after ParisN Rés676, but the text is in fact partly different); TORREFRANCA 1939, pp. 279-281 (after ParisN Rés676).

MODERN EDITIONS OF THE MUSIC: EDM 34, pp. 366-368 (after LeipU 1494); JEPPESEN 1970, p. 75 (after SevC 43, bb. 1-5, S only); MOERK 1971, II, pp. 57-61 (after SevC 43); OSTHOFF 1969, II, pp. 45-49 (after Panc.27 and FirN BR337), 50-54 (after SevC 43); PIRROTTA 1975, pp. 67-72 (after ParisN Rés676); TORREFRANCA 1939, pp. 412-417 (after ParisN Rés676).

REMARKS: The version of Panc.27 does not derive from any of the known concordances because of its numerous graphic and substantive variants. Moreover, with the exception of the Bassus of FirN BR337, in all the concordances the piece is divided into two sections: in LeipU 1494, ParisN Rés676, and SevC 43 the second part begins at bar 47, whereas Panc.27 is the only source that divides the piece between bars 50 and 51. Indeed, bars 47-50 themselves are written out in all four concordant versions, and not indicated by a repeat sign, as happens in Panc.27. The problematic passage in the Altus of bar 54/I is interesting: whereas LeipU 1494 and SevC 43 have the same (incorrect) version as Panc.27, only ParisN Rés676 corrects the double dissonance with the Superius (d'') and Bassus (b), but it does not avoid parallel unisons with the Bassus. The textual tradition is very complex, characterized by two substantially different branches: on the one side *Fir.N. 42*, FirN BR337, and LeipU 1494; on the other ParisN Rés676 and SevC 43. The version of Panc.27 (perhaps instrumental?) cannot be securely related to either of the two branches: in fact «A la caza» is the heading of the piece, while «Iamo a la caza» is the textual incipit, placed only in the Altus.

BIBLIOGRAPHY: FALLOWS 1999, p. 528; FILOCAMO 2009a; GALLICO 1996, p. 49; LUISI 1983, I, pp. 197, 235; MOERK 1971, I, p. 125; TORREFRANCA 1939, pp. 143, 280, n. 2, pp. 280-281.

68.
A LA CAZA / IAMO A LA CAZA
fols. 43v–45r

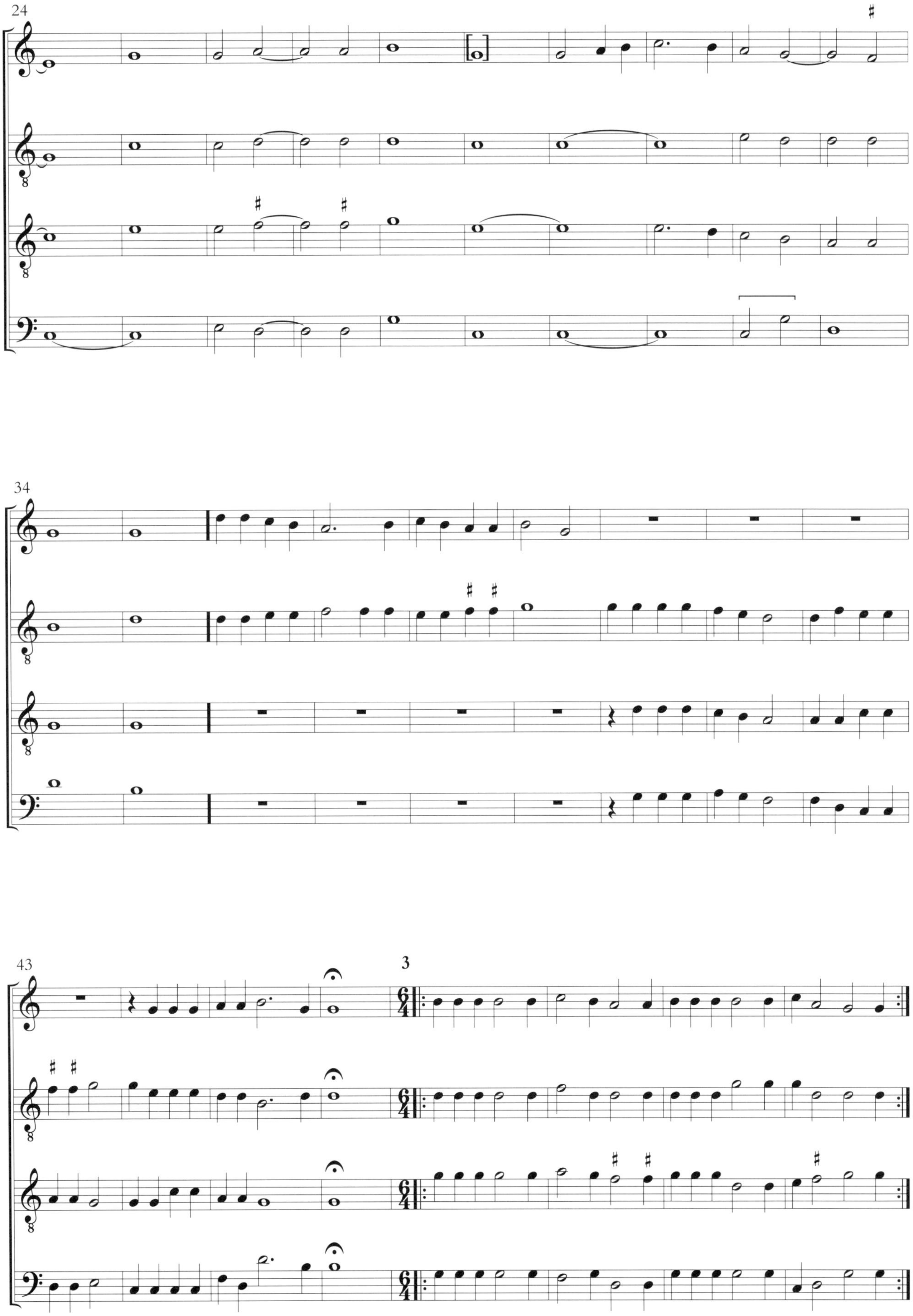
24
34
43
3

Secunda pars

421

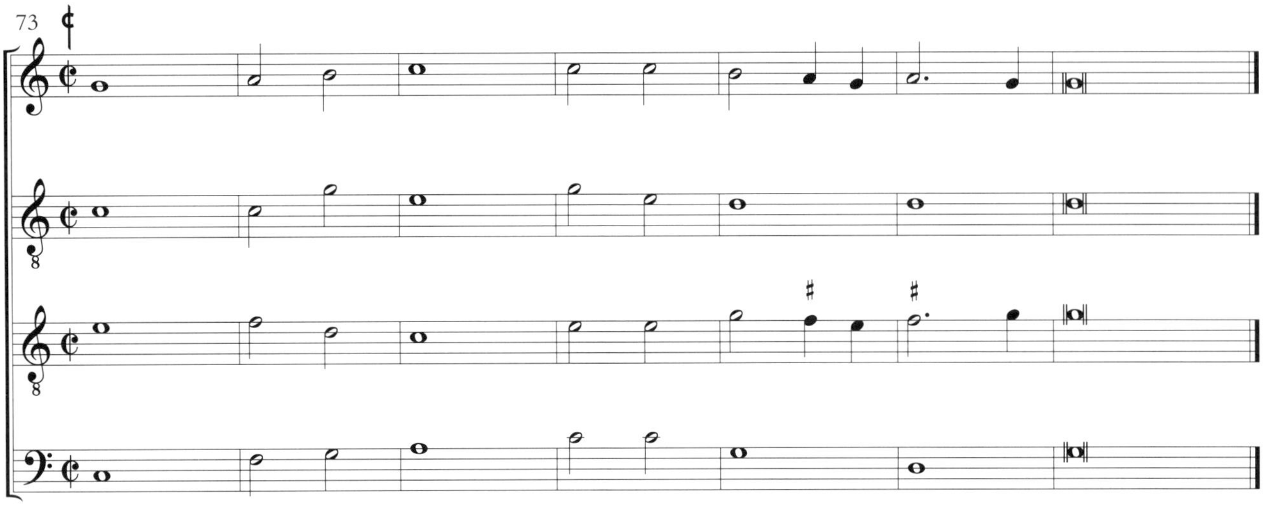
73

69.

Iesù, Iesù, Iesù

fols. 45*v*–46*r* (4 vv.)

[Feo Belcari]

Iesù, Iesù, Iesù,
ognon chiami Iesù.

Chiamati questo nomo
col cor e cum la mente,
5   e sentireti como
egli [è] dolce e clemente.
Chi 'l chiama fidelmente
sente nel cor Iesù.
        Iesù, Iesù […]

El è quel‹lo› nome sancto
10   che dà salute al mondo,
converte il nostro pianto
nel so gaudio iocundo,
e chi vol el cor mundo
ricora al bon Iesù.
        Iesù, Iesù […]

15   Se tu te senti pene
chiama Iesù col core,
e lui per gratia vene
a levarti il dolore.
Sempre fia il to megliore
20   ‹a› chiamar nel cor Iesù.
        Iesù, Iesù […]

Iesù è l'amor mio,
Iesù è 'l mio dilecto,
Iesù benigno e pio,
Iesù senza diffecto,
25   Iesù vero omo e Dio,
che mi fa dir: 'Iesù'.

Lauda (barzelletta). Contrafact on the music of *Visin visin visin*.

Commentary on the text:

6   addition found in concordant sources
9   the *residuum* begins here

| 9 | deletion inferred from the concordant sources |
| 20 | deletion inferred from the concordant sources |

Readings emended in the edition:

Bar	Voice	Original
4-5	B	a *brevis-longa* ligature, with the *brevis* blackened (perhaps optional? see Remarks). In the transcription the length of the final note takes into account the upbeat of the following bar and the initial one
17-18	B	a *brevis-longa* ligature, with the *brevis* blackened (perhaps optional? see Remarks). In the transcription the length of the final note takes into account the initial upbeat: at the end of the strophe, in fact, the ripresa is repeated (to b. 5/I), followed then by the next strophe

Textual concordances (mss): • *Bol.U. 4019* (87r-v), «Belcari» • *CV. BL.3711* (109-110) • CV F84 (42v-43v), text only,[1] «Feo Belchari» • *CV. Ro.424* (186v) • *Fir.M. 262* (26r-v) • *Fir.N. LF.236* (2r-v) • *Fir.N. M.686* (4r-v) • *Fir.N. M.1083* (29r-v) • *Fir.N. P.169* (156v-157v), «Feo Belcari» • *Fir.N. P.173* (164r), «Feo Belcari» • *Fir.R. 1413* (257r) • *Fir.R. 1473* (124r) • *Fir.R. 2895* (27r-v) • *Fir.R. 3112* (222v-223r, olim 219v-220r) • *Rav.C. 63* (208r-v) • *Rim.C. 38* (143r-v), «Di Feo Belchari» • *Roma.Ca. 1432* (28v-31r) • *Siena.C. 14* (62v-63v) • *Siena.C. 15* (29r-30r) • *Siena.C. 17* (115r-116r) • *Siena.C. 41* (44r-v) • *Ven.M. I.78* (61v-62r) • *Ven.M. I.79* (8r-9r)

Textual concordances (prints):[2] • *Colletanio1509* (M1r) • *Colletanio1510* (M1r) • *Colletanio1513* (M1r) • *Colletanio1514Lov* (L3r-v) • *Colletanio1514Rus* (M1r) • *Colletanio1521* (F5r-v), Ognun chiami Iesu | Iesu Iesu Iesu • *Colletanio1524* (F5r-v), Ognun chiami Iesu | Iesu Iesu Iesu • *Colletanio1537* (F5r-v), Ognun chiami Iesu | Iesu Iesu Iesu • *Compendio* (M3r) • *LaudeBonac* (61v-62r), «Di Feo Belchari» • *LaudeBonar* (30r), «Del Beato Giouanni Colombino da Siena Giesuato» • *LaudeFort* (a3r-v), «Di Feo Belcari» • *LaudeMisc* (23v-24r), «Di Feo Belchari» • *LaudeNat* (a3r), «Di Feo Belchari» • *LaudeSper* (31r-v), «Di Feo Belcari» • *LaudeVecchie* (c4v-c5r), «Di Feo Belchari» • *LaudiBad* (a3r), «Di Feo Belcari» • *LaudiGiunti* (C1r-v), «Del medesimo» (= Feo Belcari)[3] • *LaudiRiccardiana* (h3r), «Feo Belcari» • *Opera1515* (M2r-v) • *OperaNova* (20v-21r), «Di Feo Belchari»

Musical concordances (mss): • BerlS 30 (2v), 2 vv. (S and T only) • FirN BR62 (1v), *Visin visin visin*, S only

Musical concordances (prints): • Razzi (60r),[4] 2 vv. (S and T only)[5]

Text from Razzi:

Gesù, Gesù, Gesù,
ognun chiami Gesù.

Chiamate questo nome
col core e con la mente,
5   e sentirete come
egli è dolce e clemente.
Chi 'l chiama fedelmente
sente nel cor Gesù.

---

[1]. Text without music.
[2]. The surviving folios of the only exemplar known of *Colletanio* (imperfect) do not contain the text.
[3]. The previous lauda is headed «Di Feo Belchari».
[4]. On fol. 60v the poetic text is written out, preceded by the rubric «Laude di Feo Belcari».
[5]. With a mensuration sign of *tempus imperfectum diminutum cum prolatione minori*.

Egli è quel nome santo
10   che dà salute al mondo,
converte il nostro pianto
nel suo gaudio giocondo;
se volete il cor mondo
ricorrete a Gesù.

15   Se tu ti senti in pene
chiama Gesù col core,
e lui per grazia viene
a levarti il dolore.
Se fia il tuo migliore,
20   però chiama Gesù.

Gesù sempre chiamiamo
che per noi morì in croce,
Gesù sempre lodiamo
col core e con la voce.
25   Ciaschedun sia veloce
a ringraziar Gesù.

Gesù pien di dolcezza,
Gesù è il mio desio,
Gesù somma bellezza,
30   Gesù ver'uomo e Dio,
Gesù è l'amor mio,
che mi fa dir: 'Gesù'.

MODERN EDITIONS OF THE TEXT: GALLETTI 1863, p. 69 (after *LaudeBonac*); MACEY 1998, p. 47 (after Panc.27); MANCUSO 1984, II, p. 447 (after Razzi); PAPINI 1923, pp. 95-96.

MODERN EDITIONS OF THE MUSIC: GHISI 1937, p. 110; JAENECKE 1979, p. 143 (after BerlS 30); LEVI 1905, p. 296 (after FirN BR62); MACEY 1993, p. 166 (after Panc.27); MACEY 1998, p. 45 (after Panc.27); MANCUSO 1984, II, pp. 449-450 (after Razzi); PRIZER 1993b, p. 177 (after Razzi).

REMARKS: Musically speaking, one cannot say that the version in Panc.27 derives from the concordances noted above: apart from transmitting only two voices, BerlS 30 has a textual *residuum* that is partly different; the fragment of the partbook FirN BR62 gives the text of the well-known carnival song *Visin visin visin | chi vol spazar camin*, the song of the chimney sweeps, dated «from the 1470s» in MACEY 1998, pp. 44-45. Macey's hypothesis concerning the presence of the ligature in the Bassus in bars 4-5 and 17-18 is interesting: it would serve to mimic the upward movement of the broom used by the chimney sweep (see MACEY 1998, p. 46), a clear sexual metaphor. It is possible that in the lauda text of Panc.27 the *G* of the ligature has been blackened (therefore made optional) to mitigate the obscenity of the graphic reference implicit in the famous carnival song.

BIBLIOGRAPHY: BECHERINI 1954, p. 113 and n. 2; CARBONI - ZIINO 1973, p. 280; CATTIN 1978, p. 40; FALLOWS 1999, pp. 566-567; GHISI 1937, pp. 52-53, 100, 109, 192-193; LUISI 1983, I, pp. 190, 196; MACEY 1993, pp. 158-159; MACEY 1998, pp. 44-47; PRIZER 1993b, pp. 176-177; PRIZER 1996a, p. 178; PRIZER 2001, pp. 19-20, 24, 31, 32; ROSTIROLLA (1986) 2001, p. 147; ROSTIROLLA (1990) 2001, pp. 307-310; ROSTIROLLA (1997) 2001, p. 574; TENNERONI 1909, p. 132.

69.
IESÙ, IESÙ, IESÙ
fols. 45v–46r

[Feo Belcari]

Ie - sù, Ie - sù, Ie - sù, o - gnon chia - mi Ie - sù. Chia-

Ie - sù, Ie - sù, Ie - sù

- ma - ti que - sto no - mo col cor e cum la men - te, e sen - ti - re - ti co - mo e-

- gli [è] dol - ce e cle - men - te. Chi 'l chia - ma fi - del - men - te sen - te nel cor Ie - sù.

70.

Alto Iesù, figl[i]olo de Maria

fols. 45v–46r (3 vv.)

Alto Iesù, figl[i]olo de Maria,
il cui nome da lo Eterno fu proveduto
anci che in la madre s[c]endese
ne la umana via.

5   Manifestato già per prophetia,
annuntiato da spiriti lezadri,
poi predicato tra le gente ingrate
in questo mondo pieno de tenèbre,
dèvesse reverentia e gran onore
10   in cielo, in terra et anco nel profondo.

Per cui lu umano geno, da l'errore
originale chiamato, e sue ruine
fu liberato, clarificato e mondo:
Iesù ben se può dire iocondo!
15   Ni lo tuo sancto nome arà memoria
vivendo qua in gratia e poi in gloria.

Amen.

Lauda (a series of lines that strive to be hendecasyllables, mostly in couplets or alternating rhyme).

Commentary on the text:

2	hypermetric
3	hypometric
5	the *residuum* begins here
5	the MS has «manifestata»
12	hypermetric
12	«e» stands for 'ex' (Latinism)
13	hypermetric
14	the MS has «bon»
14	hypometric

Readings emended in the edition:

Bar	Voice	Original
7	Ct	*b*
11/II	T	*d'*
12	T	*brevis* and two *minimae*
12	Ct	*f*
36	Ct	*g*

REMARKS: A poetic and musical *unicum*, the piece presents many problems in reconstruction, of both the text and the music.[1] It is possible that the composer (the scribe himself?) tried out his mediocre contrapuntal talent against a pleasing Cantus melody: all the emendations reported, in fact, involve the lower voices. But it is also legitimate to think that the scribe copied distractedly from his model (the errors corrected here could be explained as simple negligence), completely inventing only the lauda text. The metre and scansion of the lauda verse are in fact disastrous, perhaps the worst of all the texts in Panc.27. The piece was probably added later, as can be deduced from its placement on the empty spaces of the opening.

BIBLIOGRAPHY: FALLOWS 1999, p. 502.

[1]. I thank Bonnie Blackburn and Fabrizio Ammetto, who improved the faulty musical version of the manuscript.

70.
ALTO IESÙ, FIGL[I]OLO DE MARIA
fols. 45*v*-46*r*

ne   la   u - ma   -   na vi   -   -   -   a.

71.

Ave maris stella

fol. 46*v* (3 vv.)

Ave maris stella

Hymn for the Blessed Virgin Mary used, for example, in the first nocturn of the feast of the Purification (AH 2, pp. 39-40), for the Annunciation (AH 51, pp. 140-142), for the Office of the Blessed Virgin Mary on Saturdays (AM, pp. 712-713; AR, pp. [126]-[127], [127]-[128]), and for the Office of various Marian feasts (AM, pp. 704, 704-705; AR, pp. [117]-[118], [118]-[119], [119]-[121]; BR [*Commune Sanctorum*], pp. 75-76; LU, pp. 1259-1260, 1261-1262, 1262-1263; PM, p. 288). See also CAO, IV, p. 509 and IGC, p. 56.

READINGS EMENDED IN THE EDITION:

BAR	VOICE	ORIGINAL
39	Ct	*C*

TEXT FROM BR [*Commune Sanctorum*], pp. 75-76 (*Officium B. Mariae extra Adventum. Hymnus*):

1. Ave maris stella,
    Dei mater alma,
    atque semper virgo,
    felix caeli porta.

2. Sumens illud Ave
    Gabrielis ore,
    funda nos in pace,
    mutans Evae nomen.

3. Solve vincla reis,
    profer lumen caecis,
    mala nostra pelle,
    bona cuncta posce;

4. monstra te esse matrem:
    sumat per te preces,
    qui pro nobis natus,
    tulit esse tuus.

5. Virgo singularis,
    inter omnes mitis,
    nos culpis solutos,
    mites fac, et castos.

6. Vitam praesta puram,
    iter para tutum,
    ut videntes Iesum,
    semper collaetemur.

7.   Sit laus Deo Patri,
      summo Christo decus,
      Spiritui Sancto,
      tribus[1] honor unus.

      Amen.

MODERN EDITIONS OF THE TEXT: AH 2, pp. 39-40; AH 51, pp. 140-142.

MODERN EDITIONS OF THE MUSIC: BANKS 1993, II, pp. 31-32 (after Panc.27).

REMARKS: The beginning of the chant in AM, p. 704; AR, pp. [117]-[118], LU, pp. 1259-1260, PM, p. 288 is cited in the Superius.

BIBLIOGRAPHY: BANKS 1993, I, p. 266; CAO, IV, p. 509; CHEVALIER I, no. 1889; IGC, p. 56; WARD 1980, p. 87.

---

[1]. BR has «trinus».

71.
AVE MARIS STELLA
fol. 46*v*

Ave maris stella

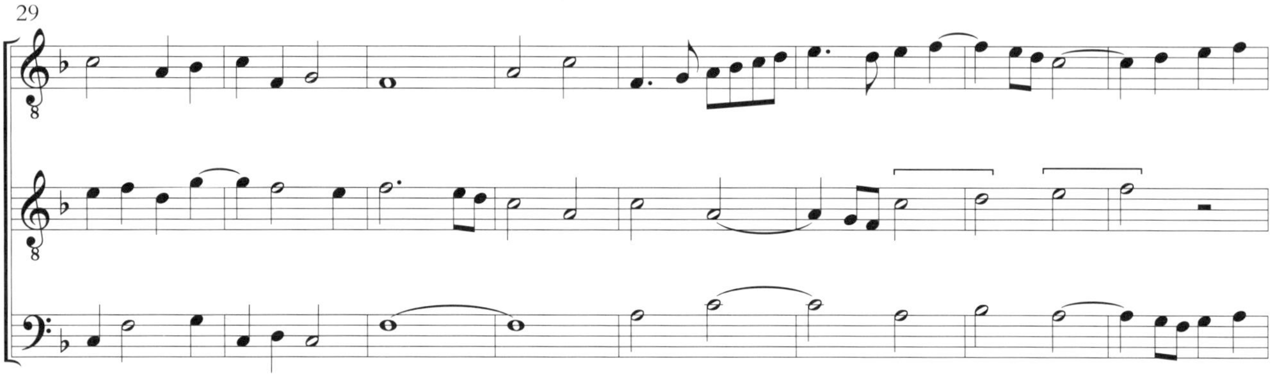
29

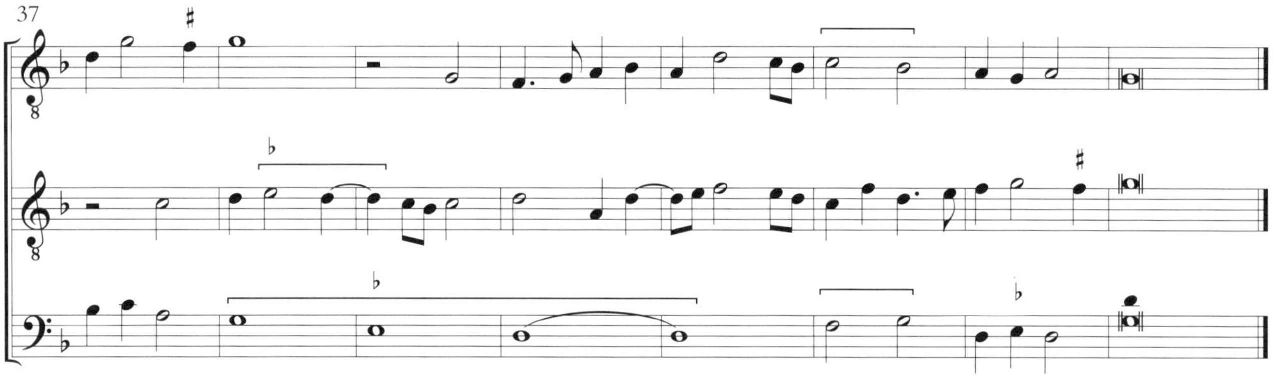
37

72.

AURES AD NOSTRAS [DEITATIS PRECES]

fol. 47r (3 vv.)

[Heading only]

Hymn for Lent in Sapphic stanzas. It is used, for example, at Lauds on Sunday (AH 2, pp. 83-84) or at Vespers (AH 51, pp. 61-63). See also CAO IV, p. 509 and IGC, p. 54.

READINGS EMENDED IN THE EDITION:

BAR	VOICE	ORIGINAL
9-10	Ct	*e′ semibrevis, d′ semiminima, c′ semiminima, b semiminima, a semiminima*
13	Ct	*g a* instead of *b c′*
42/II	Ct	*f*
43	Ct	*c*

TEXT FROM AH 2, pp. 83-84 (*Dominicis diebus in Quadragesima. In matutinis laudibus*) and AH 51, pp. 61-63 (*In Quadragesima. Ad Matutinas Laudes vel Vesperas*):

Aures ad nostras deitatis preces,
Deus, inclina pietate sola
supplicum vota suscipe, precamur,
famuli tui.

5   Respice clemens solio de sancto
vultu sereno, lampadas illustra
lumine tuo, tenebras depelle
pectore nostro.

Crimina laxa pietate multa,
10   ablue sordes, vincula disrumpe,
parce peccatis, releva jacentes
dextera tua.

Te sine tetro mergimur profundo,
labimur alta sceleris sub unda,
15   brachio tuo trahimur ad clara
sidera coeli.

Christe, lux vera, bonitas et vita,
gaudium mundi, pietas immensa,
qui nos a morte roseo salvasti
20   sanguine tuo;

insere tuum, petimus, amorem
mentibus nostris, fidei refunde
lumen aeternum, caritatis auge
dilectionem.

25   Tu nobis dona fontem lacrymarum,
      jejuniorum fortia ministra,
      vitia carnis milia retunde
      framea tua.

      Procul a nobis perfidus absistat
30   Sathan, a tuis viribus confractus,
      Sanctus assistat Spiritus, a tua
      sede dimissus.

      Gloria Deo sit aeterno patri,
      sit tibi semper, genitoris nate,
35   cum quo aequalis spiritus per cuncta
      saecula regnat.

MODERN EDITIONS OF THE TEXT: AH 2, pp. 83-84; AH 51, pp. 61-63.

REMARKS: The chant published in STÄBLEIN 1956, Melody no. 714 (after MS Verona, Biblioteca Capitolare, CIX (102), fols. 115*v*-117*r*) is paraphrased in the Superius.

BIBLIOGRAPHY: CAO IV, p. 509; CHEVALIER I, no. 1612; HOLFORD-STREVENS 1999, p. 402; IGC, p. 54; SCHMIDT-BESTE 1999, pp. 368-370; STÄBLEIN 1956, Melody no. 714; WARD 1980, p. 80.

72.
AURES AD NOSTRAS [DEITATIS PRECES]
fol. 47*r*

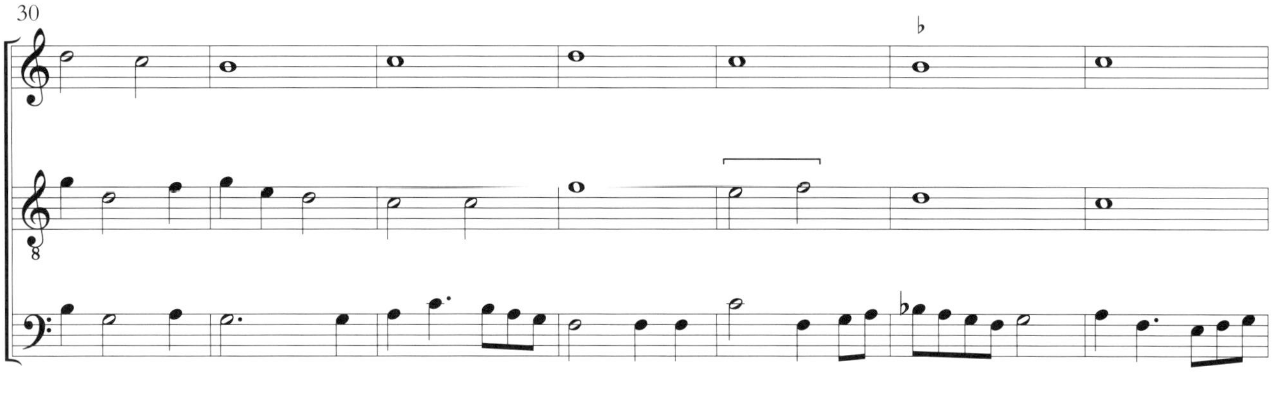
30

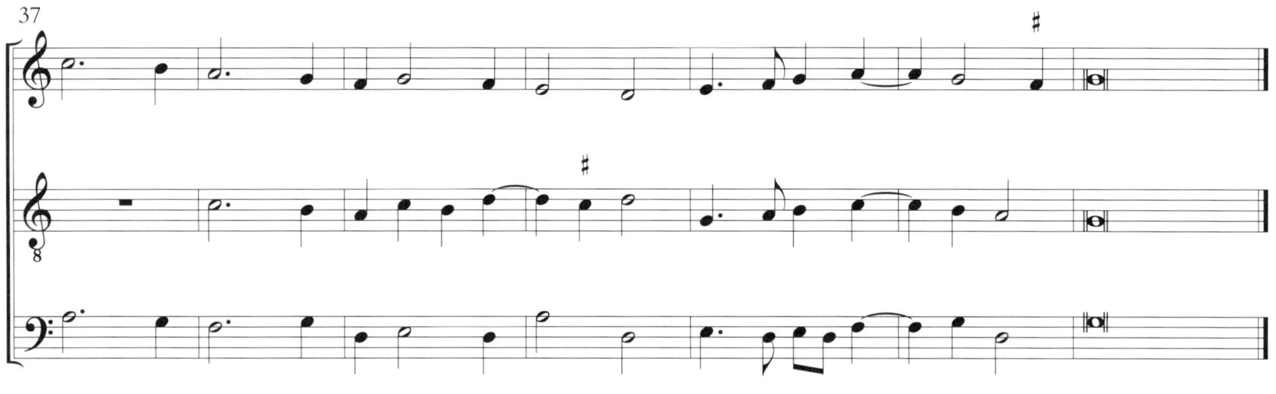
37

73.

Helas, [le bon temps que j'avoie]

fols. 47*v*-48*r* (3 vv.)

[Johannes] Tinctoris / [Loyset Compère][1]

Helas

Chanson (rondeau quatrain).

Readings emended in the edition:

Bar	Voice	Original
35	S	flat before f''
52	S	flat before f''

Musical concordances (mss): • FirN BR229 (214*v*-215*r*) • KrakJ 40098 (no. 269), textless, «K»[2] • SegC (184*r*), *Elaes abraham*,[3] «Loysette Compere» • SevC 43 (44*v*-45*r*), *Helas le bon tempo que i'avoie* • ZwR 78/3 (no. 21), textless

Musical concordances (prints): • PeOdh1501 (58*r*)[4] • PeOdh1503 (57*v*-58*r*), «Tinctoris» • PeOdh1504 (57*v*-58*r*), «Tinctoris»

Text from SevC 43:

> Helas, le bon temps[5] que i'avoie!
> Or m'as[6] tu bien habandonné;
> je suis le plus infortuné
> qui sont [en ce monde sans joye].[7]

Modern editions of the text: Brown 1983, I, p. 289 (after SevC 43).

Modern editions of the music: Brown 1983, II, pp. 460-462 (after FirN BR229); CMM 18, pp. 130-131 (after PeOdh1504); EDM 4, p. 63 (after KrakJ 40098); Gombosi 1925, *Notenanhang*, no. 8 (after PeOdh1504); Hewitt 1942, pp. 331-332 (after PeOdh1504); Moerk 1971, II, pp. 131-132 (after SevC 43).

Remarks: Despite that fact that the versions of Panc.27 and ZwR 78/3 are quite similar, it is almost certain that model for Panc.27 was *Odhecaton*: the collation demonstrates that, except for the unique

---

[1]. The fact that the three known versions of the *Odhecaton* all give Tinctoris as author suggests that the one attribution to Compère is erroneous.

[2]. The alphabet letter 'K' falls within a series running from no. 260, which has the label 'A', up to no. 282, signed with the letter 'X', omitting 'J' and 'U'.

[3]. Lama de la Cruz 1994, p. 288, erroneously gives *Elaes abrayam* and says that the text is unknown.

[4]. Fol. 57*v* is missing, which should have contained the two upper voices and the attribution, given in the index: «Tinctoris».

[5]. «tempo» instead of 'temps'.

[6]. «a» instead of 'as'.

[7]. Howard Mayer Brown supplied the additional words in square brackets (see Brown 1983, I, p. 289).

variant in the Superius in bars 45/II–46/I (in Petrucci the two notes *a′* are joined), the pieces are exactly identical, as is the name of the composer and the textual incipit in each voice.

BIBLIOGRAPHY: ATLAS 1981; BAKER 1978, I, p. 483; BOORMAN 2006, p. 1047; BROWN 1983, I, p. 289; EDM 4, p. 133; FALLOWS 1999, p. 178; HEWITT 1942, p. 152; LAMA DE LA CRUZ 1994, p. 288; MOERK 1971, I, p. 138.

73.
HELAS, [LE BON TEMPS QUE J'AVOIE]

fols. 47*v*–48*r*

[Johannes] Tintoris / [Loyset Compère]

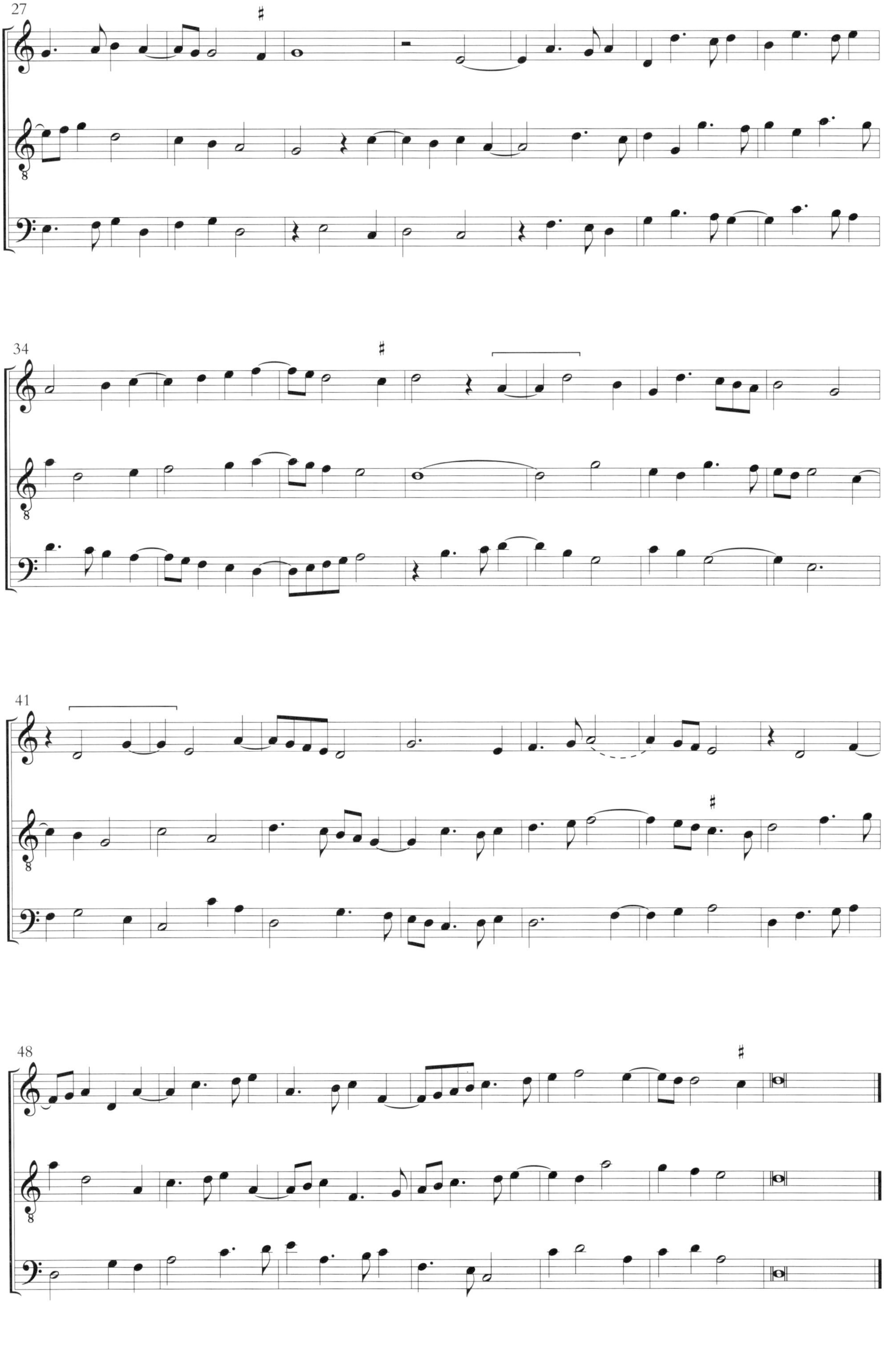
27
34
41
48

74.

Miserere [mei, Deus]

fols. 48*v*-49*r* (4 vv.)

Miserere

Psalm 50:3 (Vulgata, p. 830). Penitential text used, for example, at Lauds in the Office of the Dead (LU, pp. 1800-1801), on Maundy Thursday, Good Friday, and Holy Saturday (AM, pp. 413-414; LU, pp. 646-647, 689-690, 734), and of days without their own antiphon (BR, pp. 40-41); for the burial service (AM, pp. 1161-1162; LU, pp. 1763-1764); generically during Lent (AM, pp. 25-26; AR, pp. 10-11, 156★-159★; LU, pp. 1872, 1873). See also CS, p. 134. Also used as the versicle for the penitential antiphon *Asperges me Domine et mundabor* (LU, pp. 11, 13; MR [*Commune Sanctorum*], fol. 47*r*; PM, p. 9), itself taken from the same Psalm (50:9).

Readings emended in the edition:

Bar	Voice	Original
4	S	*signum congruentiae* instead of a fermata
11/I	B	*D* instead of *C*
13	S	*signum congruentiae* instead of a fermata
18	S	*signum congruentiae* instead of a fermata

Musical concordances (mss): • CTL G12 (36*v*-37*r*, *olim* 35*v*-36*r*), *Miserere mei Deus secundum magnam misericordiam tuam*[1]

Text from Vulgata, pp. 830-832 (*Liber Psalmorum*, L, 3-21):

3. Miserere mei Deus secundum magnam misericordiam tuam
   et secundum multitudinem miserationum tuarum
   dele iniquitatem meam

4. amplius lava me ab iniquitate mea
   et a peccato meo munda me

5. quoniam iniquitatem meam ego cognosco
   et peccatum meum contra me est semper

6. tibi soli peccavi et malum coram te feci
   ut iustificeris in sermonibus tuis
   et vincas cum iudicaris

7. ecce enim in iniquitatibus conceptus sum
   et in peccatis concepit me mater mea

8. ecce enim veritatem dilexisti
   incerta et occulta sapientiae tuae manifestasti mihi

---

[1]. The text is copied over a text that has been erased (see Cattin 1973a, p. 195).

9.   asparges [*sic*] me hysopo et mundabor
    lavabis me et super nivem dealbabor

10.   auditui meo dabis gaudium et laetitiam
    exultabunt ossa humiliata

11.   averte faciem tuam a peccatis meis
    et omnes iniquitates meas dele

12.   cor mundum crea in me Deus
    et spiritum rectum innova in visceribus meis

13.   ne proicias me a facie tua
    et spiritum sanctum tuum ne auferas a me

14.   redde mihi laetitiam salutaris tui
    et spiritu principali confirma me

15.   docebo iniquos vias tuas
    et impii ad te convertentur

16.   libera me de sanguinibus Deus Deus salutis meae
    exultabit lingua mea iustitiam tuam

17.   Domine labia mea aperies
    et os meum adnuntiabit laudem tuam

18.   quoniam si voluisses sacrificium dedissem utique
    holocaustis non delectaberis

19.   sacrificium Deo spiritus contribulatus
    cor contritum et humiliatum Deus non spernet

20.   benigne fac Domine in bona voluntate tua Sion
    et aedificentur muri Hierusalem

21.   tunc acceptabis sacrificium iustitiae oblationes et holocausta
    tunc inponent super altare tuum vitulos

MODERN EDITIONS OF THE MUSIC: CATTIN 1972a, pp. 520-521 (after CTL G12), 522 (after Panc.27).

REMARKS: As Giulio Cattin has observed, it is clear that the versions of Panc.27 and CTL G12 do not derive from the same model (see CATTIN 1972a, p. 485): they are separated by rhythmic variants, ornamentations, and different readings. The missing rest in Panc.27 (Bassus, b. 24) is also lacking in CTL G12, but this coincidence is not sufficient to hypothesize a link between the two versions. It simply confirms that the two manuscripts belonged to an environment in which a common repertory circulated, even though not the same environment (see CATTIN 1972a, p. 486).

BIBLIOGRAPHY: BANKS 1993, I, pp. 280-281; CATTIN 1972a, pp. 485-486; CATTIN 1973a, p. 195; CS, p. 134; IGC, p. 281; JEPPESEN 1969, p. 40, n. 3.

74.
MISERERE [MEI, DEUS]
fols. 48v–49r

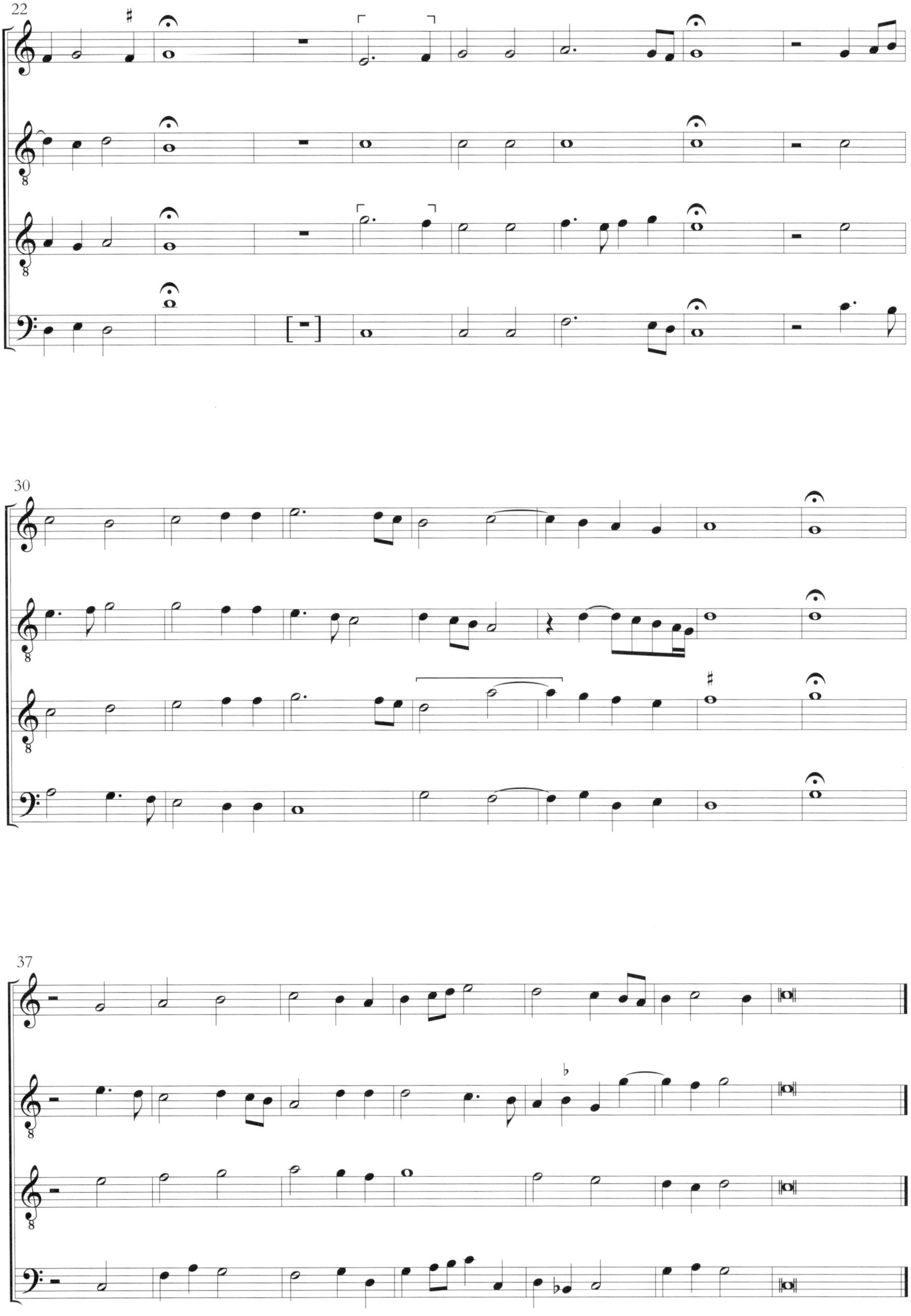
22
30
37

75.

LES BIEN AMORE / OMNIS LABOR HABET FINEM

fols. 49v-50r (3 vv.)

[HENRICUS] IZACH[1]

Les bien amore

Chanson ('cantasi come' *Omnis labor habet finem*).[2]

READINGS EMENDED IN THE EDITION:

BAR	VOICE	ORIGINAL
6/I	B	*f*
18/I	B	*d*
53	B	*longa* with fermata

MUSICAL CONCORDANCES (MSS): • BerlS 40021 (58v), *Ave amator casti consilii* • BolM 16 (8v-9r), *Des biens* • BolM 18 (64v-65r), 4 vv. (with an additional A), *[D]Es bien d'amors* • CTL G12 (119v-120r, olim 136v-137r), *Omnis habet finem labor* • CV G27 (37v-38r, olim 44v-45r), *Des biens*[3] • FirN BR229 (18v-19r), *Les biens*, «Jannes Martini» • FirN M121 (29v-30r), textless • FirN M178 (44v-45r), *La re*, «Josn. Martin» • PerA 431 (86v-87r), *Des biens d'amoris* • RomaCa 2856 (5v-6v), *De biens d'amours*

MUSICAL CONCORDANCES (PRINTS): • FormTrium (no. 77), textless

MODERN EDITIONS OF THE MUSIC: ATLAS 1975-76, II, pp. 25-27 (after CV G27); BROWN 1983, II, pp. 40-41 (after FirN BR229); DTÖ 32, p. 220 (after Panc.27); EDM 76, pp. 175-176, (after BerlS 40021); EVANS 1975, pp. 11-12 (after RomaCa 2856), 13-15 (after BolM 18); MÖNKEMEYER 1985, II, pp. 112-113 (after FormTrium); WOLFF 1970, II, pp. 9-12 (after RomaCa 2856).

REMARKS: The piece has a double tradition: one descends from Martini, the other — probably later — from Isaac. The most important differences in the first version are the passage in bars 17-19, modified contrapuntally in the lower voices, and the section of bars 23-29, extended and changed. Moreover, Isaac adds an initial *d* to the Bassus, realizing thereby a canonic imitation between the three voices. CTL G12 is the only version truly comparable with Panc.27: in addition to sharing the same Latin incipit — with the second and third words reversed and a few more words («Omnis habet finem labor in me regula fallit»)[4] — it clearly has the Panc.27 version of the piece. It cannot

---

[1]. It is likely that this version of the piece is Isaac's revision of a chanson by Johannes Martini (see BROWN 1983, I, p. 213).

[2]. The rondeau cinquain *Des bien d'amours quinconques les depart* of Jean d'Auton (ca. 1466 - 1528) is not old enough to have been set by Martini (see BROWN 1983, I, p. 67, n. 47). Contrary to what Atlas says (ATLAS 1975-76, I, p. 100), the text does not appear in the poetic manuscript *Paris. N. F. 1719*, which was compiled in the Loire Valley in the 1480s. The rondeau, nevertheless, is edited in BROWN 1983, I, pp. 213-214.

[3]. The manuscript attributed the piece to «Ysach» on fol. 37v, but this inscription by Scribe A was then cancelled by Scribe B. Allan Atlas maintains that it is still possible to read it with the aid of an ultraviolet lamp (see ATLAS 1975-76, I, pp. 14 and 101).

[4]. A similar phrase («Omnis labor optat praemium») is quoted in WANDER II, entry 'Habdank', no. 1.

be taken for granted, however, that the two versions are therefore related: even if the Superius is absolutely identical, and in the Tenor only the time signature is lacking, the lower voice has some graphic variants and one substantive variant (b. 18/I: *e* instead of the original *d* of Panc.27).

BIBLIOGRAPHY: ATLAS 1975-76, I, pp. 100-102; ATLAS 1981; BROWN 1982, p. 12, n. 15; BROWN 1983, I, pp. 213-214; CATTIN 1973a, pp. 217-218; EDM 78, p. 327; FALLOWS 1999, pp. 127-128; FILOCAMO 2004; GHISI 1965, p. 4; HERNON 1972, p. 524; JUST 1975, I, pp. 62, 63, 79, 100-101, 105, 107, 125-126; II, pp. 48-50; LITTERICK 1981, p. 120; PICKER 1991, pp. 125-126; POWERS 1994, pp. 512-514; WEISS 1998, pp. 28-29; WOLFF 1970, I, pp. 191-192.

75.
LES BIEN AMORE / OMNIS LABOR HABET FINEM

fols. 49*v*-50*r*

[Henricus] Izach

Les bien amore

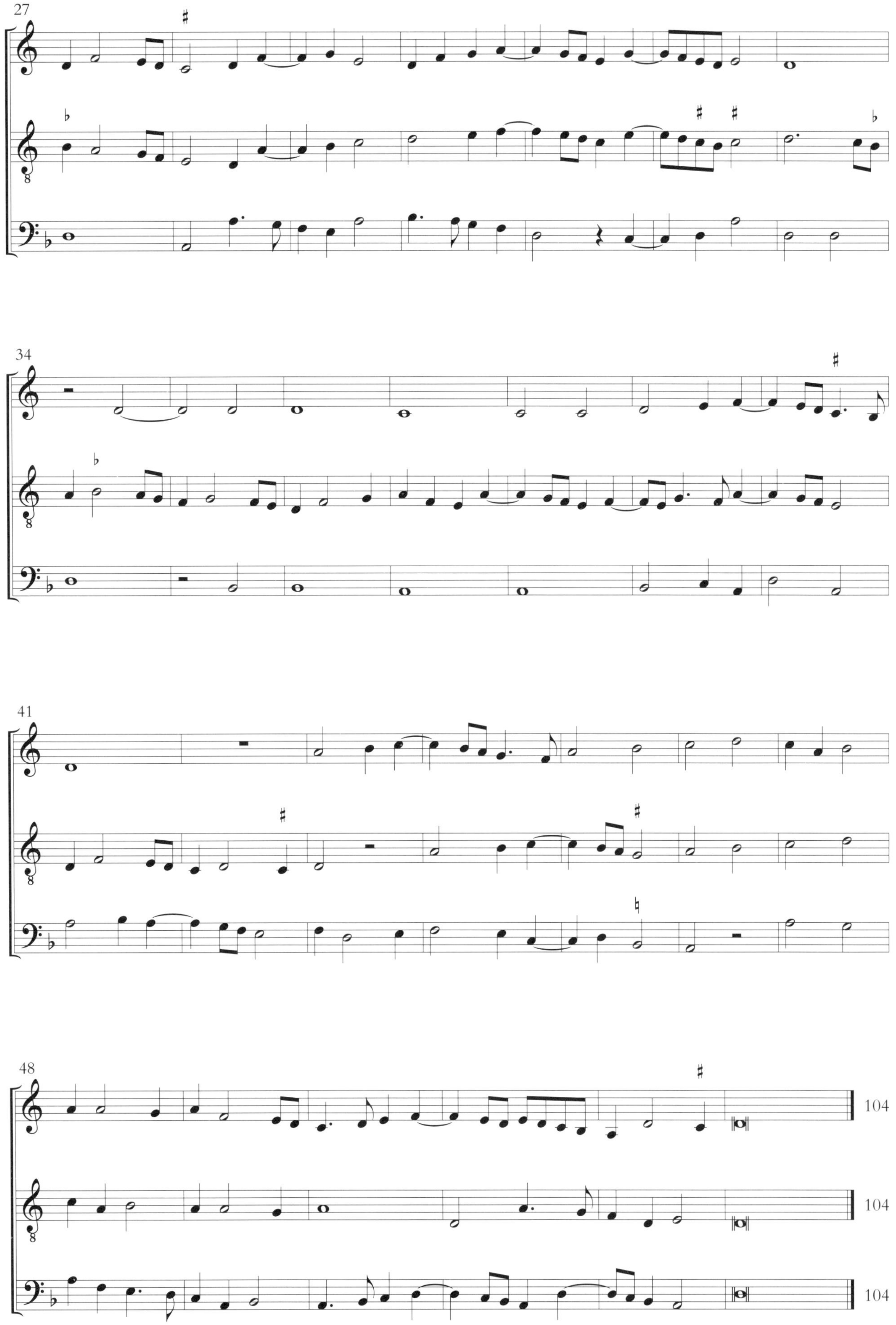
27
34
41
48
104
104
104

76.

O Iesù dolce, o infinito amore

fol. 50*v* (3 vv.)

[Leonardo Giustinian]

> O Iesù dolce, o infinito amore,
> inextimabel dono,
> misero mi, che sono,
> che da ti fugo e tu me segui ogn'ora.

5   Per qual mio merito, o Signor mio benigno,
> o per qual mia bontà
> sì largamenti nel mio cor maligno
> spandi la tua pietà?

Lauda (ballata).

Commentary on the text:

5   hypermetric

Readings emended in the edition:

Bar	Voice	Original
24/II-III	T	*d' c'*

Textual concordances (mss): • *Berg.C. 1* (98*v*) • *Berl.S. H.348* (127r-*v*), (Leonardo Giustinian) • *Bol.U. 1737* (35*v*-36*r*) • *Bol.U. 2672* (54*r*-55*v*) • *Bol.U. 2845* (375) • *Bol.U. 2932* (176*r*-177*v*) • *Bol.U. 4019* (127*v*-128*r*) • *CV. BL.3679* (22*v*-23*v*) • *CV. BL.3711* (42-44)[1] • *CV. Ch.266* (57*r*-*v*) • *CV. OL.251*[2] • *CV. Ro.424* (114*v*-115*v*), «di messer Lionardo Giustiniano» • *CV. VL.5133* (131*v*-132*r*), «Dominus Leonardus Justinianus» • *CV.VL.7714* (97*v*) • *CV.VL.13026* (59*r*-*v*) • *Fer.C. 211* (127*r*-130*r*) • *Fir.L. Ash.480* (146*v*-147*v*) • *Fir.L. Ash.1402* (166*r*-167*r*) • *Fir.M. 262* (2*r*-3*v*) • *Fir.N. 4* (25*r*) • *Fir.N. 35* (184*r*-185*r*) • *Fir.N. 140* (65*r*-66*r*) • *Fir.N. 700* (75*r*-76*v*) • *Fir.N. II.VIII.3* (97*v*-98*v*) • *Fir.N. LF.13* (15*v*-16*r*) • *Fir.N. LF.302* (37*v*-39*v*) • *Fir.N. M.27* (67*r*-69*v*) • *Fir.N. M.30* (8*r*-9*r*) • *Fir.N. M.686* (7*v*-8*r*) • *Fir.N. M.1083* (148*r*) • *Fir.N. P.173* (151*v*-152*r*), «Leonardo Giustiniano» • *Fir.R. 1119* (229*r*-230*r*) • *Fir.R. 1413* (247*v*-249*r*), «Lionardo Giustiniano» • *Fir.R. 1473* (119*v*-121*r*) • *Fir.R. 1502* (57*v*-58*r*) • *Fir.R. 2895* (17*v*-19*r*) • *Fir.R. 2929* (28*v*-29*v*, olim 27*v*-28*v*) • *Fir.R. 3112* (18*r*-19*v*, olim 10*r*-11*r*) • *FrattaPol.Fanan* (141*v*-142*v*), «Nobilissimi Leonardi Justiniani Veneti» • *Mil.A. 35* (101*v*-102*r*), «Leonardo Giustinian» • *Mil.B. 27* (33*v*-35*r*) • *Mil.T. 92* ([208]*v*-[209]*v*) • *Mil.T. 913* (55*r*-56*v*) • *Mün.S. I240* (64*r*) • *Nap.N. 38* (11*v*-16*r*) • *Ox.B.*

---

[1]. Francesco Luisi observes that «the trimming of the page has removed an old annotation, of which there remains only a letter that is perhaps an 'I'; it is likely that it consisted of the initials of 'Leonardo Iustiniano'. Nevertheless, it cannot be excluded that it was an old numeration of the laude» (see Luisi 1983, I, p. 189).

[2]. On fol. 34*r* only the incipit «O Yhesù dolce» is cited, but then the MS does not contain the poem. In Carboni - Ziino 1996, p. 427, it is hypothesized that «the scribe wanted to note down on the page the 'titles' of some secular and sacred musical pieces that he knew well and appreciated. Nevertheless, the reasons why this list was written remain unknown». In the index, on the other hand, Carboni and Ziino assign no. 35 to *O Yhesù dolce*.

CI. 193 (27r-29r) • *Ox.B. CI.263* (66v-67r) • *Paris.N. I.618* (22v-[24v]) • *Piac.C. L.15* (54r-56r, *olim* 49r-51r) • *Prato.R. 186* (no. 2) • *Rim.C. 38* (125v-126r), «Di messer Leonardo Vinitiano» • *Roma.Al. 224* (261r-263v) • *Roma.Ang. 1482* (110v-111r) • *Roma.Ang. 2274* (3v-4v) • *Roma.Ang. 2275* (82v-84r, *olim* 89v-91r) • *Roma.Co. 33* (22v-23v) • *Tessier* (82v) • *Trev.C. 220* (49r-v) • *Ven. GR. 120* (1r-2r), «de misier Lunardo Iustiniam» • *Ven.GR. 121* (48v-50r), (Leonardo Giustinian) • *Ven.M. I.77* (114r-115v) • *Ven.M. I.78* (18v-19v), «di Messer Lionardo Giustiniano» • *Ven.M. I.80* (74v-76r) • *Ven.M. I.182* (144v-145r), «di messer lonardo» • *Ven.M. I.182* (203v, only the last four stanzas of the lauda) • *Ven.M. I.230* (28v-30r) • *Ven.M. I.257* (125r-127r) • *Ven.M. I.313* (84r-86r) • *Ven.M. I.486* (112r-113v) • *Ver.Cap. 737* (52v-53r)

TEXTUAL CONCORDANCES (PRINTS): • *Compendio1483* (128r-129v) • *Fior1505* (i3r-i4r) • *Giust1474* (A1r-A2v), (Leonardo Giustinian) • *Giust1475* (a1r-a2r), (Leonardo Giustinian) • *Giust1483* (a2r-a3r), (Leonardo Giustinian) • *Giust1490* (a1r-a2r), (Leonardo Giustinian) • *Giust1495* (a1r), (Leonardo Giustinian) • *Giust1506* (a1r-a3r), (Leonardo Giustinian) • *Giust1517* (a2r-a3v), (Leonardo Giustinian) • *LaudeBonac* (18v-19v), «Di Messer Lionardo Giustiniano» • *LaudeMisc* (7r-v), «Di Messer Lionardo Giustiniano» • *LaudeVecchie* (a6v-a7r), «Di Messer Lionardo Giustiniano» • *LaudiGiunti* (B1v), «Del medesimo» («Di Messer Lionardo Giustiniano Gentilhuomo Venetiano») • *LaudiRiccardiana* (f2v-f3r), «Leonardo Giustinian» • *OperaNova* (6v-7r), «di Messer Lionardo Giustiniano»

MUSICAL CONCORDANCES (MSS): • CTL G12 (67v-68r, *olim* 66v-67r), 2 vv. (without B) • WashC J6 (110v), T only

MUSICAL CONCORDANCES (PRINTS): • Razzi (61v-62r),[3] 2 vv.[4] (without B, but with different T)

TEXT FROM *Giust1474*:

> O Iesù dolce, o infinito amor,
> inextimabel dono,
> misero me, chi sono,
> che da te fuzo e tu me segui d'ogn'or.

5   Per qual mio merito, o Signor mio benigno,
> o per qual mia bontà
> sì largamente in el mio cor maligno
> spandi la tua pietà?
> L'anima mia che sempre offeso t'ha,
10   sì dolcemente chiami,
> che par ben che tu l'ami
> come bon padre, e non come Signor.

> Zamai non resti a mille dolci modi
> chiamar l'anima a te;
15   or dime, Signor mio, de che te godi,
> ch'ha' tu veduto in me?
> Non pensi qual io sia e qual tu se',
> tu summo ben perfecto
> e io pien de difecto,
20   pien de peccati e pien d'ogni fetor?

---

[3]. On fol. 62v the text is written out, with the indication «Laude di M. Leonardo Giustiniano». Giulio Cattin thinks it arbitrary, however, to attribute the music as well to Giustinian (see CATTIN 1968b, p. 93).

[4]. With a mensuration sign of *tempus imperfectum diminutum cum prolatione minori*.

Co'[5] più te offendo tanto più tu se'
cortese a perdonar,
tanti grevi peccati et error mei
non te pol far turbar,
25 anci, me vieni sì dolce a lusengar
che 'l par che m'abbi offeso,
o amor non inteso,
de che vil cosa sei facto amator!

Non basti che una volta tu portasti
30 sì vil morte per mi,
or non te par che 'l sangue sparto basti
a trar l'anima a ti?
Che mille volte me mandi e ogni dì
tanti doni e sì spessi,
35 che con el minimo d'essi
arder dovresti ogni aghiaciato cor?

S'io non ti cognosesse in altre cosse
sì largo e liberal,
io crederia che tuo doni a mi fosse
40 solo per più mio mal.
Però, che quando tu sei più real
tanto son più obligato,
et essendote ingrato
la tua largheza acresse el mio eror.

45 Ma io so ben, Signor mio, che ciò tu fai
sollo per più mio ben,
l'ardente carità che d'amor mai
celar non se convien.
O cor mio duro, o cor mio, che te tien
50 che non ardi d'amore,
vezendo el tuo factore
arder inamorato per tuo amor?

E tu, anima mia, fata da Dio
tanto bella e zentil,
55 alza da terra un poco el tuo desio,
e non star più sì vil,
che Iesù ha preparato el tuo sedil
ne gli anzelici regni;
e 'l par che non te degni
60 de eser consorte e spoxa al[6] tuo fator.

Iesù, per questo, zà, non te turbare
de porzeme la man,
io sum sumerso e non posso levare
de 'sto fango mondan.
65 Chiamame speso e non me star lutan,
che forsi, qualche volta,

---

  5. *Compendio 1483* has «come». «Co'» probably derives from 'cum' (= 'quanto'): even today in the Veneto «co'» is used
in the same sense. I thank Giulio Cattin for this observation.
  6. «el» in the source.

453

la pecorella stolta
fuzirà lupo e seguirà el pastor.

MODERN EDITIONS OF THE TEXT: GALLETTI 1863, pp. 48-49 (after *LaudeBonac*); LEVI 1905, pp. 191-193; LUISI 1983, I, p. 255 (after *Ven.GR. 120*), II, p. cxiv (after WashC J6, Panc.27, CTL G12, Razzi); MANCUSO 1984, II, pp. 454-455 (after Razzi); MAZZA 1960, p. 181 (after *Berg.C. 15*).

MODERN EDITIONS OF THE MUSIC: BECHERINI 1954, pp. 117 (after Razzi), 118 (after Panc.27); CMM 76, pp. 23 (after CTL G12); LEVI 1905, p. 191 (after Razzi); LUISI 1983, II, p. 88 (after WashC J6), pp. 88-89 (after Panc.27), p. 90 (after CTL G12), pp. 93-94 (after Razzi), p. 228 (after Panc.27, but with the contrafact text *O crudel donna [dispietata] poi che lassato me hay*); MANCUSO 1984, II, pp. 456-460 (after Razzi); WILSON 1992, pp. 271-276 (after CTL G12, Panc.27, Razzi).

REMARKS: With the exception of WashC J6, which transmits only the melody of the Tenor, the two other musical versions (CTL G12 and Razzi) are for two voices: Superius and Tenor. Although the version of Panc.27 is for three voices instead, it nevertheless appears that the contrapuntal structure should be interpreted as a pair of *bicinia* (Superius-Tenor and Superius-Bassus): this is suggested by the frequent instances of parallel fifths and octaves between Tenor and Bassus (bb. 1/III-2/I, 7/I-II, 10/I-II, 11/I-II, 11/III-12/I, 13/II-III, 20/III-21/I, 21/II-III) and between Superius and Bassus (bb. 3/I-II, 15/I-II, 20). Probably, therefore, the scribe of Panc.27 has added the lowest voice at his own initiative, resulting in a rather awkward polyphonic result.[7] The poetic text was widely diffused, and is often accompanied by the rubric 'cantasi come'.

BIBLIOGRAPHY: BECHERINI 1954, pp. 112-113; BECHERINI 1959b, p. 247; CARBONI - ZIINO 1996, pp. 459-461; CATTIN 1968b, pp. 91-96; CATTIN 1973a, pp. 200-201; CATTIN 1978, pp. 29, 33, 34; CMM 76, p. xxiii; FEIST 1889, p. 159; FRATI 1918, p. 322; GHISI 1953a, pp. 66-67, 73; LUISI 1983, I, p. 553; NOSOW 2000, pp. 245, 247; RABBONI 1991, pp. 73, 74, 76, 132-134; TENNERONI 1909, p. 184; WILSON 1992, pp. 171-172.

---

[7]. I owe this conclusion on the contrapuntal structure of the piece to the observations of Bonnie Blackburn and the comments of Fabrizio Ammetto.

76.
O Iesù dolce, o infinito amore
fol. 50*v*

[Leonardo Giustinian]

S[uperius]
T[enor]
Bassus

O Ie - sù dol - ce, o in - fi - ni - to a - mo - re, i - ne-xti-ma -

- bel do-no, mi - se - ro mi, che so-no,

che da ti fu-go e tu me se-gui o-gn'o-ra. Per qual mio me - ri-to, o
sì lar - ga-men-ti nel

Si - gnor mi o - - o be - ni-gno, o per qual mi-a bon - tà
mi - o cor ma-li-gno span-di la tu-a pie-tà?

77.

O MISERO STATO

fol. 51*r* (4 vv.)

[Heading only]

Lauda?

REMARKS: The piece has many parallel progressions, clearly intended by the composer: octaves (Altus–Bassus, b. 16), unisons (Altus–Tenor, bb. 4/II-5), and fifths (Altus–Bassus, b. 4; Cantus–Altus, bb. 8/II-9).

BIBLIOGRAPHY: JEPPESEN 1969, p. 40, n. 3.

77.
O misero stato
fol. 51*r*

78.

Oimè, che moro [per ti, dona crudele]

fol. 51*v* (4 vv.)

Marcetus [Cara]

[Heading only]

Italian secular piece (strambotto toscano).

Readings emended in the edition:

Bar	Voice	Original
6	B	all three *longae* with fermatas are black

Textual concordances (mss): • *Br. Q. 23* (167*v*), *Ahime che mor per te donna crudele*

Musical concordances (mss): • ModE 9 (91*v*-92*r*), *Aime ch'io moro per te donna crudele* • ParisN Rés676 (114*v*-115*r*), *Aime ch'io moro per ti dona crudele*; index: «Cara»

Text from ParisN Rés676:

> Aimè, ch'io moro per ti, dona crudele,
> e non ti curi del mio fidele servire.
> Aimè, ch'io moro, se 'l tuo amaro fielle
> non si converte in dolze al mio martìre.
> 5   Aimè, ch'io moro, Amor, volgie le veglie,[1]
> se non che forza sia il cor finire.
> Aimè, ch'io moro, e tu più dura e forte
> per il mio ben servire mi doni morte.

Modern editions of the text: La Face Bianconi 1990, p. 216 (after ModE 9); Prizer 1980, p. 502 (after ParisN Rés676).

Modern editions of the music: La Face Bianconi 1990, pp. 342-344 (after ModE 9); Prizer 1980, pp. 503-504 (after ParisN Rés676).

Remarks: Both the version in ModE 9 and that in ParisN Rés676 are very distant from Panc.27: apart from graphic differences, there are many substantive variants, sometimes in common. The rubric «Iustus» placed at the bottom of fol. 51*v*, however, gives reason to believe that the piece in Panc.27 was copied from a model not currently known. The odd writing of bar 6 in the Bassus is worth mentioning: contrary to what one might expect, none of the three notes is indicated as the fundamental one; it would have been more logical to find at least the *g* notated as a white *longa*, as happens at the end of the voice.

Bibliography: Prizer 1980, pp. 65, 117-118.

---

[1]. «volgie le veglie» means 'volgi le vele'.

78.
Oimè, che moro [per ti, dona crudele]
fol. 51*v*

Marcetus [Cara]

Iustus

79.

O gloriosa Domina

fol. 52r (3 vv.)

O gloriosa Domina,
excelsa super sidera,
qui te creavit, provide
lactasti sacro ubere.

First strophe of the Marian hymn *O gloriosa Domina*, used, for example, as the hymn at Lauds and the other hours for the Annunciation (AM, p. 864) and on other Marian feasts (AM, p. 709; BR [*Commune Sanctorum*], p. 78). The same stanza is also found in the hymn *Quem terra pontus aethera*, either as the sixth stanza (AH 50, pp. 86-88, *Hymnus Beatae Mariae*) or as the fifth stanza (AH 2, pp. 38-39, *In purificatione S. Mariae ad Vesperas*).

MUSICAL CONCORDANCES (MSS): • CTL G12 (59v-60r, *olim* 58v-59r), 2 vv. (C and T only)[1]

TEXT FROM BR [*Commune Sanctorum*], p. 78 (*Officium S. Mariae. Ad Laudes et per Horas. Hymnus*):

O gloriosa domina
excelsa super sidera,
qui te creavit provide
lactasti sacro ubere.

5   Quod Eva tristis abstulit,
tu reddis almo germine:
intrent ut astra flebiles,
caeli fenestra facta es.

Tu regis alti ianua,
10   et porta lucis fulgida:
vitam datam per virginem
gentes redemptae plaudite.

[G]loria tibi Domine,
qui natus es de virgine,
15   cum Patre et Sancto Spiritu
in sempiterna saecula.

Amen.

MODERN EDITIONS OF THE MUSIC: BANKS 1993, II, p. 142 (after Panc.27); CATTIN 1972a, p. 537 (after CTL G12 and Panc.27).

REMARKS: Although it is the only known concordance, the version of CTL G12 cannot be directly linked with that of Panc.27: in addition to the different mensuration there are many discrepancies in the length of notes, and its important coda is absent in Panc.27. As Cattin points out, we are

---

[1]. The text following the incipit *O gloriosa Domina* has been erased in both voices; it was the text of the following lauda: *Regina ‹de o› del cor mio.*

confronted with the demonstration that the two sources, although often drawing on the same musical reservoir, in reality have taken different paths (see Cattin 1972a, p. 490). As in other pieces in Panc.27, *O gloriosa Domina* has parallel octaves between the Cantus and Contra, clearly intended by the composer (bb. 1 and 10). The first phrase of the chant in AM, pp. 709 and 864 is paraphrased in the Cantus.

Bibliography: Banks 1993, I, p. 283; Cattin 1972a, pp. 489-490; Cattin 1973a, p. 198; Chevalier II, no. 13042; IGC, p. 304; Stäblein 1956, Melody no. 551; Ward 1980, p. 199.

79.
O GLORIOSA DOMINA
fol. 52r

Cantus: O glo – ri – o – sa Do – mi – na, ex –

-cel – sa su – per si – de – ra, qui te cre – a – vit, pro – vi –

-de la – cta – sti sa – cro u – be – re.

80.

GUARDA LE VESTIMENTE

fol. 52*r* (3 vv.)

Guarda le vestimente

Italian secular piece? (strambotto siciliano?)[1]

READINGS EMENDED IN THE EDITION:

BAR	VOICE	ORIGINAL
8/II-9/I	T	*d′ c′ b*

TEXTUAL CONCORDANCES (MSS): • *Mod.E. 1168* (76) • *Nap.N. 1* (12*v*-13*r*)

TEXT FROM *Mod.E. 1168*:

> Guarda li vestimenti negri et tristi,
> guarda com'è tornato il mio colore,
> guarda la fede che me promettisti,
> guarda come è voltato lo to core,
> 5   guarda la pena donde me ponesti,
> guarda che non te fui mai traditore,
> guarda che fin al fine me dicisti
> volerme sostenere con lo tuo amore,
> ché tu probasti et me non cognovisti,
> 10   per essere causa del mio grave dolore.

MODERN EDITIONS OF THE TEXT: BRONZINI 1976, p. 26 (after *Nap.N. 1*); BRONZINI 1977, p. 87 (after *Mod.E. 1168*).

REMARKS: Because it is erroneously displaced by a third, the passage in the Tenor may be the result of careless copying from the model.

BIBLIOGRAPHY: JEPPESEN 1969, p. 125.

---

[1]. Although there is no musical concordance that gives the continuation of the incipit of Panc.27, it is probable that it is the anonymous strambotto *Guarda li vestimenti negri et tristi*. Its unusual form, which adds a 'coda' of two or more lines to the typical Sicilian strambotto, can nevertheless be found in the linguistic region of southern Italy (see ROSSI 1993, p. 256).

80.
GUARDA LE VESTIMENTE
fol. 52*r*

Guarda le vestimente

81.

Omnis laus in fine canitur

fols. 52v-53r (4 vv.)

[Henricus Isaac]

[Heading only][1]

Medieval proverb.

Readings emended in the edition:

Bar	Voice	Original
24/II	B	a blackened *c* appears under the *e*, indicating cancellation

Musical concordances (mss): • CambM 18 (137v-153r: 151v-152r), *Agnus dei I* (after *Missa Chargé de deul*) • CTL G12 (123v-124r, *olim* 140v-141r), «Jsaac» • MilD 2 (151v-159v: 159v), *Agnus dei I* (after *Missa Chargé de deul*), «Isach» • UppsU 76e (1r-11v: 10v-11v), *Agnus dei I* (after *Missa Chargé de deul*), S only, «Henrici Izac»

Musical concordances (prints): • PeIsaac (no. 1), *Agnus dei I* (after *Missa Chargé de deul*), «Henrici Izac»

Modern editions of the text: Binder 1861, no. 2414; Lehmann 1630, p. 173; Walther 1965, p. 644; Wander I, entry 'Ende', no. 47.

Modern editions of the music: Banks 1993, II, pp. 144-145 (after Panc.27); CMM 65/VI, pp. 1-37: 34-36 (after PeIsaac); Fano 1962, pp. 74-113: 108-109 (after MilD 2); Wooldridge 1905, pp. 257-259 (after PeIsaac).

Remarks: In addition to being the only source that transmits the piece with the text *Omnis laus in fine canitur*, CTL G12 has the closest musical reading to Panc.27, despite two missing notes (*e semibrevis* in b. 24/II of the Bassus and *g' semibrevis* in b. 32/II of the Altus), and in five cases two-note ligatures join notes separated in Panc.27. That Panc.27 nevertheless derives from a model may be hypothesized from the mistake in the Bassus in bar 24/II.

Bibliography: Banks 1993, I, p. 284; Boorman 2006, p. 861; Cattin 1973a, pp. 219-220; Fano 1962, p. xxiv; Filocamo 2004; Picker 1991, pp. 23-24; Reese 1990, p. 226; Staehlin 1977, III, pp. 86-94.

---

[1]. The heading comprises the text of the entire proverb.

81.

OMNIS LAUS IN FINE CANITUR

fols. 52v–53r

[Henricus Isaac]

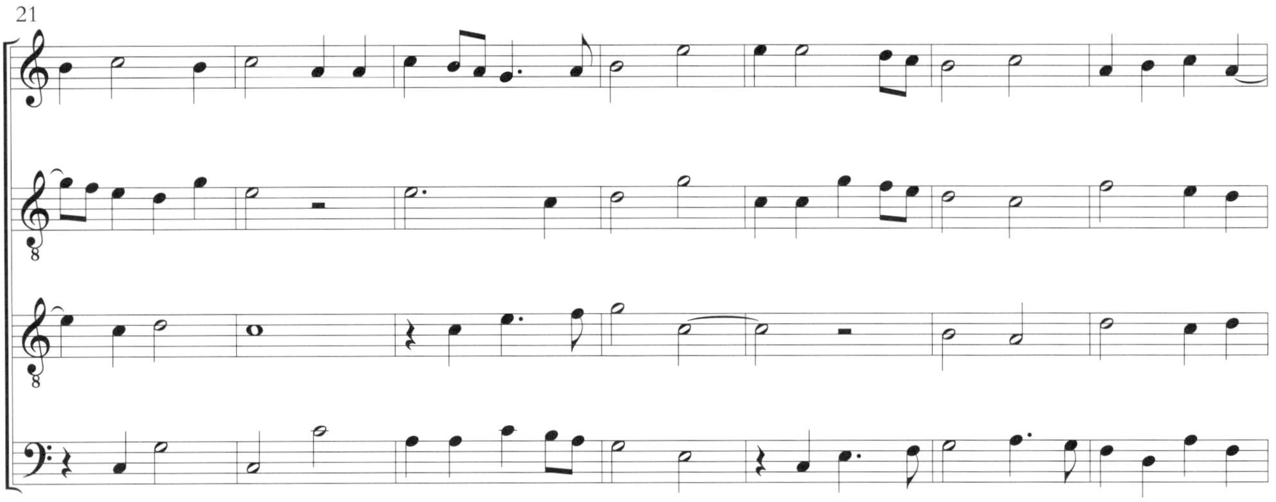
21

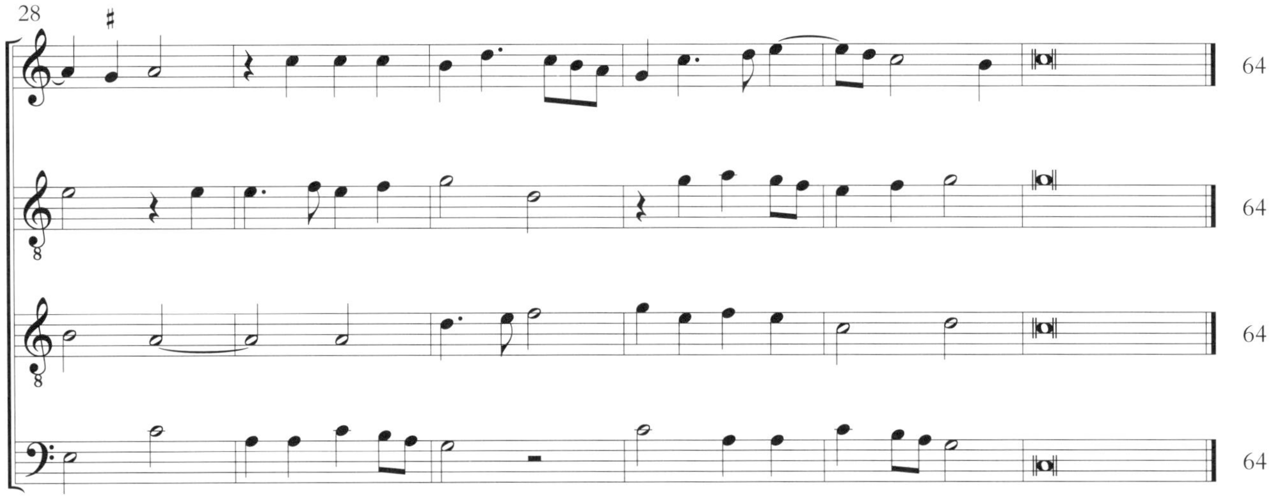
28
64
64
64
64

82.

O madre di Iesù, o dea eterna

fols. 52v–53r (4 vv.)

O madre di Iesù, o dea eterna

Lauda.

REMARKS: Two curved lines in the Superius serve to link single notes to the precise words (b. 2: the second *d'* is linked to «Iesù»; b. 3/I: *f'* is connected with «o»). This seems to be related to a performance of the piece.

82.
O MADRE DI IESÙ, O DEA ETERNA
fols. 52*v*–53*r*

S[uperius]: O ma - dre di Ie - sù, o dea e - ter - na

A[ltus]: O ma - dre di Ie - sù

T[enor]: O ma - dre di Ie - sù

B[assus]: O ma - dre di Ie - sù

83.

O gloriosa Regina mundi

fols. 53*v*-54*r* (3 vv.)

[Johannes Touront]

O gloriosa Regina mundi,
succurre nobis, pia,
ad te clamantibus,
tu que genuisti
5 Salvatorem in gentibus.
Ave Virgo pulcherrima
in gratiis uberrima.
Ave Virgo pulcherrima,
Salvatorem que protulisti.
Amen.

Prayer in honour of the Blessed Virgin Mary.

COMMENTARY ON THE TEXT:

9   protulisti] prodisti B

READINGS EMENDED IN THE EDITION:

Bar	Voice	Original
42	B	*b g*
66/I	S	flat before the *f″*

MUSICAL CONCORDANCES (MSS): • BolM 16 (142*v*-143*r*), *O gloriosa Domina* • CTL G12 (89*v*-90*r*, *olim* 89*v*-90*r*) • FirR 2356 (23*v*-24*r*) • HKK 7 (L2*v*-L3*r*), *O lucis alme sator mundi* • MünS 352b (167*v*), *Ave regina*, «asoirolg» • MünS L5023 (4*v*-6*r*), 2 vv. (without B) • ParisN F15123 (3*v*-4*r*) • ParisN Rés676 (32*v*-33*r*), heading: «Laus virginis Marie», heading over the B: «10 octubris [1502]» • PerA 431 (58*v*-59*r*), «Cecus»[1] • PrahaS 47 (182*v*-183*r*) • RomaCa 2856 (63*v*-65*r*), «Jo. tourant» • SevC 43 (88*v*-89*r*) • TrenM 91 (178*v*) • VerCap 757 (18*v*-19*r*), textless

MODERN EDITIONS OF THE MUSIC: BESSELER 1950, I, pp. 7-8 (after TrenM 91); DAVIS 1978, pp. 176-179 (after ParisN F15123); DTÖ 15, pp. 219-220 (after TrenM 91); EDM 39, pp. 416-417 (after MünS 352b); MOERK 1971, II, pp. 257-260 (after SevC 43); PEASE 1959, II, pp. 5-9 (after ParisN F15123); VINCENT 1857, pp. 675-679 (after ParisN F15123); WOLFF 1970, II, pp. 179-183 (after RomaCa 2856).

---

[1]. Allan Atlas believes that the name 'Cecus' refers to Touront, and therefore does not indicate another composer (see ATLAS 1981, p. 283). Recently Paweł Gancarczyk has found a new document that connects Touront with the Imperial chapel in Vienna in 1460. Here the name is given as 'Tourhout', and he received a benefice in Antwerp Cathedral in the same year. This document would exclude his being blind (see the abstract of the paper *Johannes Touront in Central Europe* read by Gancarczyk at the *Medieval & Renaissance Music Conference 2007*, Vienna, 7-11 August). I thank Bonnie Blackburn for having brought this paper to my attention.

REMARKS: The musical version in Panc.27 is not derived directly from any of the known concordances. Only CTL G12 shows any closeness: it is the only source that shares with Panc.27 a final «Amen» section (bb. 102-106), but only in the Superius and Tenor (it is missing in the Bassus). CTL G12, moreover, has a conjunctive error in bar 42 of the Bassus: the same (erroneous) *semibreves*, but in ligature. Despite this closeness, however, the version of CTL G12 has a number of graphic variants (ligatures in place of separated notes, and some ornaments): thus it seems likely that Panc.27 and CTL G12, although not directly related to each other, derive from a common repertory.

BIBLIOGRAPHY: ATLAS 1981; BANKS 1993, I, p. 284; CATTIN 1973a, pp. 209-210; DAVIS 1978, pp. xxvii-xxviii; FALLOWS 1999, p. 589; FILOCAMO 2004; HERNON 1972, pp. 511-512; LEVERETT 1996, pp. 127-130; PEASE 1959, I, p. 85; WOLFF 1970, I, pp. 261-263.

83.
O GLORIOSA REGINA MUNDI
fols. 53v–54r

[Johannes Touront]

31
cla - man - ti - - - bus, tu que
cla - - man - - ti - -
cla - - - - - man - - ti - - - - - - bus,
39
ge - - - - nu - - - - - - - - - - - - - i - sti
-bus, tu que ge - - - nu - - i - - sti
tu que ge - nu - i - - - - - - - sti Sal -
46
Sal - va - - - - - - - - - to - - - - - rem in
Sal - va - - - to - - - - rem in
- va - to - - - - - - - - - - - rem
53
gen - - - - - ti - bus.
gen - - - ti - - - - bus.
in gen - ti - bus.

60
A - ve Vir - - - - - - - - -
A - - - ve Vir - - - - - go pul -
A - - - ve Vir - - - go pul - - -
67
- - - - - - go pul - cher - ri - ma in gra - ti -
- cher - ri - ma in gra - ti - - - -
- cher - ri - ma in gra - ti - is
75
- is u - - - ber - ri - ma. A - ve Vir - - - -
- is u - - - ber - - - - - - - - ri -
u - ber - - -
82
- - - go pul - cher - - - - - - - - - ri - - - -
- ma. A - ve Vir - - - - - go
- ri - - - - - - - - - - - - ma. A - ve Vir - go

89
-ma, Sal - va - - - - - - to - - - - - - rem que
pul - cher - ri - - - - - - - - - - ma, Sal - va - to - - -
pul - cher - ri - - - - - - - - - - ma, Sal - - - - va - to -
96
pro - - tu - - - - li - sti.
- - - - rem que pro - tu - li - - - - sti.
- rem que pro - - - tu - - - li - - - sti.
102
A - - - - - - - - - - - - - - men.
200
A - - - - - - - - - - - - - - men.
200
A - - - - - - - - - - - - - - men.
200

84.

La speranza me tien vivo

fols. 54v-55r (4 vv.)

La speranza me tien vivo,
ché sperando moro ogn'ora,
ché speranza in gran dimora
ha el sperar de speme privo.
      La speranza me tien vivo,
      ché sperando moro ogn'ora.

5   El sperar che no ven mai,
e l'è doglia tropo forte
a chi vive in pene e guai
no pò aver già pegior sorte.
Ma s'io sum cunducto a morte
10   de speranza no sum privo.

Più no voglio el tuo conforto,
v[i]a da me speme fallace,
perché sum pegio che morto
pur sperando d'aver pace,
15   perché più che morto iace
chi [de] speme [è] in tuto privo.

Italian secular piece (barzelletta).

COMMENTARY ON THE TEXT:

2	ogn'ora] oghora S
5	the *residuum* begins here
16	hypometric; corrected on the basis of the reading of PeFroIII1505 (and its reprint)

MUSICAL CONCORDANCES (MSS): • FirN BR337 (31v), B only

MUSICAL CONCORDANCES (PRINTS): • PeFroIII1505 (47v-48r) • PeFroIII1507 (47v-48r)

MODERN EDITIONS OF THE TEXT: CESARI *ET AL.* 1954, p. 46★ (after PeFroIII1505).

MODERN EDITIONS OF THE MUSIC: CESARI *ET AL.* 1954, pp. 128-129 (after PeFroIII1505).

REMARKS: Between the Bassus of FirN BR337 and that of Panc.27 there are only a few graphic variants, apart from the different mensuration sign (*tempus imperfectum cum prolatione minori*). With regard to Petrucci's print, however, the only difference is that the Tenor is written in the tenor clef. For the rest, apart from the fermata, which in PeFroIII1505 (and its reprint) appears in the form of a *signum congruentiae* (Bassus, b. 31/I), the musical versions are completely identical. The *residuum* is written in a darker ink and with a narrower pen nib than the rest.

BIBLIOGRAPHY: BOORMAN 2006, p. 987; FILOCAMO 2004.

84.
LA SPERANZA ME TIEN VIVO
fols. 54v–55r

19
pri - vo. La spe - ran - za me
25
tien vi - vo, ché spe - ran - do mo - - - - - ro o - gn'o - - -
31
- ra.
72

85.

Se conviene a un cor vilano

fols. 55*v*–56*r* (4 vv.)

[Eneas]

Se conviene a un cor vilano,
che 'l demostra quel che sia,
ch'una rana non potria
viver fuora del pantano.
    Se conviene a un cor vilano,
    che 'l demostra quel che sia.

5   Non alberga un vero amore
    cum el cor ch'è nato vile:
    ben se anida col favore
    in uno altro più virile.
    Dui contrarii, in un sol stile,
10   non pò stare in compagnia,
        ch'una rana non potria
        viver fuora del pantano.

Italian secular piece (barzelletta).

COMMENTARY ON THE TEXT:

9   in un] un in S

MUSICAL CONCORDANCES (PRINTS): • PeFroIII1505 (62*v*-63*r*), «Eneas» • PeFroIII1507 (62*v*-63*r*), «Eneas»

TEXT FROM PeFroIII1505:

Se conviene a un cor villano,
che 'l demostra quel che sia,
ch'una rana non potria
viver fora del pantano.
    Se conviene a un cor villano,
    che 'l demostra quel che sia.

5   Non alberga un vero amore
    con el cor ch'è nato vile:
    ben se anida col favore
    in un altro più virile.
    Doi contrarii, in un sol stile,
10   non può stare in compagnia,
        ch'una rana non potria
        viver fora d'un pantano.

Questo i' so servendo ad una
ch'ha in sé posto ogni beltade.
Questo i' so, che mai alcuna
non serà di tal viltade,
15 e con noi tra questa etade
più de ognuna costei sia,
ch'una rana [...]

Per scoprirmi a questa el pecto
me scopersi a tutto el mondo.
Per sfogar l'ardente effecto
20 più me posi in gran profondo,
et per lei sì grave el pondo,
che qual morto io vo per via,
ch'una rana [...]

Piglia exempio ogn'altro amante
da me lasso e sol meschino.
25 Piglia exempio lo ignorante
del mio crudo e fier destino.
Non se ponga a tal camino
chi del stil non ha la spia,
ch'una rana [...]

MODERN EDITIONS OF THE TEXT: CESARI *ET AL.* 1954, p. 50★ (after PeFroIII1505); FILOCAMO 2000, pp. 132-133 (after Panc.27).

MODERN EDITIONS OF THE MUSIC: CESARI *ET AL.* 1954, p. 141 (after PeFroIII1505).

REMARKS: The unique concordance, PeFroIII1505, is almost certainly the model for the Panc.27 scribe: three of the four voices are completely identical, and the Superius differs only in three repeated notes instead of a dotted note (and always in the same passage: bb. 1, 14, 33/II-34/I). On the textual level, however, the two sources have a few linguistic and graphic variants. Certainly it is not the reprint PeFroIII1507, which in the Superius has the textual variant «Se convine a una [...]» (see BOORMAN 2006, p. 672).

BIBLIOGRAPHY: BOORMAN 2006, p. 1014.

85.

SE CONVIENE A UN COR VILANO

fols. 55*v*–56*r*

[Eneas]

S[uperius]: Se con - vie-ne a un cor vi-la - no, che 'l de-mo - - straquel

A[ltus]: Se con-vie - ne a un cor vi - la - no

T[enor]: Se con-vie - ne a un cor vi - la - no

B[assus]

che si - a, ch'u-na ra - na non po-tri - a vi-ver fuo - ra del pan - ta - no.

Se con - vie-ne a un cor vi-la - no, che 'l de-mo - - stra quel che si - a.

Non al-ber- - -ga un ve-ro a-mo-re cum el cor ch'è na - to vi - le:
ben se a-ni- - -da col fa - vo-re in u-no al-tro più vi-ri - le.

Dui con-tra - rii, in un sol sti - le, non pò sta - re in com - pa-gni-

-a, ch'u-na ra-na non po-tri - a vi-ver fuo - ra del pan-ta - no.

86.

Verbum caro factum est

fol. 56*v* (3 vv.)

Verbum caro factum est
de Virgine Maria.

In hoc anni circulo
[…]
5   nato nobis parvulo
[…]

Paraliturgical text for the Nativity (for the full text, see no. 142). The first line of the text is based on John 1:14: «Et Verbum caro factum est et habitavit in nobis | et vidimus gloriam eius | gloriam quasi unigeniti a Patre plenum gratiae et veritatis» (VULGATA, p. 1658).

READINGS EMENDED IN THE EDITION:

BAR	VOICE	ORIGINAL
10/III	C	*d″*
12/III	Ct	*d* instead of *g*
14-16	C	line 5 is erroneously underlaid here
after 16	C, T, Ct	a *custos* leads back to the initial note. The repetition of bars 1-9 is intended (see Remarks)
after 16	C	inscription «ut supra» after the *custos*

MUSICAL CONCORDANCES (MSS): • Panc.27 (109*v*)

MODERN EDITIONS OF THE TEXT: MONE II, pp. 80-84, with some textual variants.

MODERN EDITIONS OF THE MUSIC: BECHERINI 1954, p. 118 (after Panc.27, only bb. 1-9); LUISI 1983, II, p. 201 (after Panc. 27).[1]

REMARKS: The same text has been set to music four times in Panc.27, for three voices (nos. 86, 136, 142) and two voices (no. 144). In all four cases, lines 5-6 have the same music as lines 1-2, either written out (nos. 136, 142) or indicated by means of a *custos* (nos. 86, 144). Only in no. 86 have lines 4 and 6 of the text been forgotten; the line «nato nobis parvulo» is in fact written in a darker ink and with a slightly smaller body: this suggests the hypothesis that the scribe added it later, disregarding the classical structure of the piece, which he certainly knew, since he uses it exactly in the other three versions (or perhaps he intended an *alternatim* performance of the verses lacking here?). With respect to the concordant no. 142, no. 86 presents an identical Cantus, while in the two lower voices we find a few different notes, which in only two cases modify the polyphonic complex (bb. 5/III-6/II and 14/II). Thus we are perhaps confronted with an instance of reworking by the scribe himself, who, beginning with a traditional Christmas melody, devised

---

[1]. Luisi gives a combined transcription of the two concordant versions in Panc.27.

several musical settings. In general, there are various parallel progressions that seem to be the result of an improvised counterpoint.[2]

BIBLIOGRAPHY: BANKS 1993, I, p. 292; CATTIN (1960) 2003, pp. 62-63; CHEVALIER II, no. 21347; FRATI 1919, p. 88; JAENECKE 1979, p. 134;[3] LUISI 1983, I, p. 552.

---

[2]. I thank Bonnie Blackburn, to whom I owe this observation.

[3]. There reference is made to two compositions of Panc.27, whose Cantus parts are identical with that represented in an intarsia made by the wood carver Giovanni da Verona (Verona, ca. 1457 – Verona, 10 February 1525) kept in the church of Monte Oliveto Maggiore in Siena. The two pieces in reality are the *Verbum caro* no. 86 and the *Verbum caro* no. 142 (fol. 109v), and not the *Verbum caro* no. 144 (fol. 110r) indicated in the caption of pl. 2 (after p. 158) of the English version of REESE 1990.

86.

VERBUM CARO FACTUM EST

fol. 56*v*

Cantus: Ver – bum ca – ro fa – ctum est ... de Vir – gi – ne Ma –

Tenor: Ver – bum ca – ro

Con[tr]a: Ver – bum ca – ro

– ri – – a. In hoc an – ni cir – cu – lo na – to no – bis par – vu – lo

Ut supra

87.

MILLE PROVE [HO GIÀ FACTO PER LEVARMI]

fol. 56*v* (3 vv.)

Mille prove

Italian secular piece (strambotto toscano).

READINGS EMENDED IN THE EDITION:

BAR	VOICE	ORIGINAL
10	C	*longa* with fermata
25/I	C	*b′* instead of *a′*, as in all the musical concordances

TEXTUAL CONCORDANCES (MSS): • *Fir.N. B.228* (24*v*), *Mille prove aggio fatto per levarme* • *Fir.N. NA.701* (41*r*), *Mille prove ho gia fato per levarme* • *Paris.N. I.1020* (147*v*), *Mille prove o gia facto per levarmy* • *Pes.O. 54* (74*v*), *Mille prove angio facto sol per levarmi*

MUSICAL CONCORDANCES (MSS): • FirN BR230 (58*v*-59*r*), *Mille prove io ho gia fatte per levarmi* • ModE 9 (97*v*-98*r*), *Mille prove aggio fatto per levarme*, 4 vv. (with an additional A) • ParisN Rés676 (23*v*-24*r*), *Mille prove ho gia facto per levarmi*

TEXT FROM ParisN Rés676:

> Mille prove ho già facto per levarmi
> da tanta servitù per tua dureza,
> perché hai di diamanto nel pecto l'armi,
> dove ogne sagitta Amor si speza.
> 5   Quando io penso ad altra dona darmi,
> alora parangon facio di to beleza,
> e, sopra ogn'altra se 'l cor mio ti stima,
> io resto più ligato asai che prima.

MODERN EDITIONS OF THE TEXT: CAPPELLI 1868, p. 64 (after ModE 9); CAPPELLI 1975, p. 30 (after ModE 9); LA FACE BIANCONI 1990, p. 218 (after ModE 9); SPONGANO (1966) 1974, p. 237.

MODERN EDITIONS OF THE MUSIC: LA FACE BIANCONI 1990, pp. 358-360 (after ModE 9).

REMARKS: The piece in Panc.27 cannot derive from any of the known models. All three musical concordances are distanced by numerous graphic and some substantive variants. Regarding the reading of bar 25/I in the Cantus, it is possible that the scribe of Panc.27 clearly intended the original *b′*, which — though incorrect vertically (it clashes with both the Tenor and the Contra) — has its own melodic logic in the descending scalar pattern from *d″* in bar 23/II to *g′* in bar 27/II.

87.
MILLE PROVE [HO GIÀ FACTO PER LEVARMI]
fol. 56v

Mil — le pro — ve

88.

MEMENTO MEI

fol. 57*r* (3 vv.)

Memento mei

Lauda?[1]

READINGS EMENDED IN THE EDITION:

BAR	VOICE	ORIGINAL
29	T	G
after 30	Ct	three erased notes (subsequently rewritten a third higher at b. 32): an inadvertent miscopying from a model?

TEXTUAL CONCORDANCES (MSS): • *Ven. GR. 120* (38*v*–40*r*), *Memento mei o sacra Virgo pia*

TEXT FROM *Ven. GR. 120*:

> Memento mei, o sacra Virgo pia,
> memento mei, sì ch'io non sia inganato
> de questo misero mondo sconsolato,
> pieno de acerbe pene.

MODERN EDITIONS OF THE TEXT: LUISI 1983, I, pp. 272-273 (after *Ven. GR. 120*).

MODERN EDITIONS OF THE MUSIC: LUISI 1983, II, pp. 76-77 (after Panc.27).

BIBLIOGRAPHY: BANKS 1993, I, p. 280.

---

[1]. Although there is no musical concordance that would indicate the continuation of the text, Francesco Luisi thinks it probable that it is the lauda *Memento mei o sacra Virgo pia*. Luisi himself acknowledges the hypothetical character of his reconstruction (see LUISI 1983, II, p. cxiii): quatrain of three hendecasyllables and a settenario ABBc.

88.
MEMENTO MEI
fol. 57*r*

89.

Si dedero [somnum oculis meis]

fols. 57*v*-58*r* (3 vv.)

Alex[ander] Agricola[1]

[Heading only]

Psalm 131:4 («si dedero somnum oculis meis | et palpebris meis dormitationem», Vulgata, p. 936). Occasionally used as the verse of the responsory *In pace in idipsum* (after Psalm 4:9, «in pace in id ipsum dormiam et requiescam», Vulgata, p. 772),[2] for Holy Saturday (see CAO IV, p. 232).[3]

Readings emended in the edition:

Bar	Voice	Original
8	B	flat before the *F*

Musical concordances (mss): • BarcC 454 (106*v*-107*r*), 4 vv.[4] • BasU 22 (13*r*-15*v*), «Henricvs Izack componebat» • BolM 16 (135*v*-137*r*), *Si dedero sonnum oculis meis* • BolM 17 (34*v*-35*r*), *Si dedero sompnum oculis meis*, «A. Agricola» • BolM 18 (70*v*-71*r*) • BruxR 11239 (32*v*-33*r*), *Si dedero somnum oculis meis* • ChN 25 (58*r*-59*v*), «canto belisimo mai esta sona a sta foza» • CV G27 (18*v*-19*r*, olim 25*v*-26*r*), *Si dedero sumpnum oculis meis*, «Agricola» • FirN BR229 (69*v*-70*r*), *Si dedero somnum oculis meis*, «Alexander Agricola» • FirN M107bis (31*v*-32*r*/*v*?); index only: *Si dedero*[5] • FirN M178 (31*v*-32*r*), *Si dedero sompnum*, «Alexander» • FirR 2356 (76*v*-77*r*), *Si dedero somnum* • FirR 2794 (14*v*-15*r*), *Si dedero sompnum oculis meis* • GreifU 640-1 (no. 9), *Si dedero somnum*, 2 vv. (S and B only) • KøbK 1848 (100-101) • ParisN F1597 (7*v*-8*r*), *Si dedero somnum oculis meis* • ParisN Rés676 (30*v*-31*r*), *Si dedero somnum*, 4 vv., «Agricola» • RomaCa 2856 (100*v*-102*r*), «Agricola» • SegC (170*v*), «Alexander Agricola» • SGS 462 (35*v*-36*r*), *Si dedero somnum oculis meis* • SGS 463 (no. 16), S only, «Verbonet», «Hypomixolydius» • SGS 530 (17*v*-18*r*), «1. pars Si dedero. Alexander» • VerCap 757 (24*v*-25*r*), textless, modern hand: «Alexander Si dedero»

Musical concordances (prints): • Baena (31*v*-32*r*); index: «Obrec. Si dedero. Del otauo [tono]» • FormTrium (no. 13), textless (in the Jena copy, added by hand: *Si dedero*; in the Berlin copy, added by hand: «Obrecht») • PeOdh1501 (61*v*-62*r*), «Alexander» • PeOdh1503 (61*v*-62*r*), «Alexander» • PeOdh1504 (61*v*-62*r*), «Alexander» • PeSpinII (29*v*-30*v*) • PetreiusNewII (no. 46), «Ja. Obrecht»

Text from Vulgata, pp. 935-936 (*Liber Psalmorum*, CXXXI, 1-5):

1.   Canticum graduum.
    Memento Domine David et omnis mansuetudinis eius

---

[1]. Most of the sources attribute the piece to Agricola. The four sources that give a different attribution — Isaac, Obrecht, [Ghiselin] Verbonnet — are rather late (BasU 22: 1512/13-1532; SGS 463: after 1540; Baena: 1540; PetreiusNewII: 1536).

[2]. See Antiphonale Sarisburiense, pl. 150.

[3]. BR, p. 355, however, has the versicle «Cum invocarem», Psalm 4:2, in that position.

[4]. The added Contratenor Altus differs from the «Altitonans» (= Altus) in ParisN Rés676, even if these are the only two sources that transmit the piece for four voices.

[5]. Considering that the piece is anonymous, it is not entirely clear to which piece it refers in the missing folios.

2.   sicut iuravit Domino votum vovit Deo Iacob

3.   si introiero in tabernaculum domus meae
                 si ascendero in lectum strati mei

4.   si dedero somnum oculis meis
                 et palpebris meis dormitationem

5.   et requiem temporibus meis
                 donec inveniam locum Domino tabernaculum Deo Iacob

TEXT FROM CAO IV, p. 232:

        In pace in idipsum dormiam et requiescam.
      V. Si dedero somnum oculis meis,
        et palpebris meis dormitationem.

MODERN EDITIONS OF THE TEXT: CAO IV, p. 232.

MODERN EDITIONS OF THE MUSIC: BROWN 1983, II, pp. 138-140 (after FirN BR229); CMM 22/IV, pp. 50-51 (after ParisN F1597); DTÖ 28, pp. 163-164 (after BasU 22); FERRARI 1994, pp. 22-24 (after ParisN Rés676); GOMBOSI 1955, pp. 103-106 (after ChN 25); HEWITT 1942, pp. 339-340 (after PeOdh1504); JONES 1971, II, pp. 183-186 (after FirR 2794); VAN MALDEGHEM, *Musique religieuse*, XIX, no. 6 (after BruxR 11239);[6] MÖNKEMEYER 1985, I, pp. 24-25 (after FormTrium); NOE 12, p. xvii (after FirN BR229); NOE 18, pp. 48-49 (after Baena); PICKER 1965, pp. 464-466 (after BruxR 11239); SCHMIDT 1969, II p. 242 (after PeSpinII); SELF 1996, pp. 72-77 (after ParisN Rés676, with Ct after BarcC 454); SHIPP 1960, pp. 266-270 (after ParisN F1597); SM 5, pp. 66-67 (after SGS 462); SM 6, pp. 12-13 (after BasU 22); SM 8, pp. 64 (after SGS 530); TOFT 1992, pp. 148-149 (after ParisN F1597); WOLF O/3, pp. 55-57 (after FormTrium), pp. 58-60 (after PetreiusNewII); WOLFF 1970, II, pp. 268-272 (after RomaCa 2856).

REMARKS: The version of Panc.27 matches that of *Odhecaton* almost exactly: there are few graphic variants, all of minor significance. Thus is it more than likely that Petrucci was the model, considering also that both versions transmit the same amount of text (but spelling the name of the composer differently!). From a collation with the other sources it appears that at bar 58/I in the Bassus some sources — whose readings are often distant from those in Panc.27 (such as BolM 17, CV G27, FirN BR229, FirN M178, FirR 2356, FirR 2794, GreifU 640-1, VerCap 757) — have a *semibrevis* rest instead of *c*.

BIBLIOGRAPHY: ATLAS 1975-76, I, pp. 78-79; ATLAS 1981; BAKER 1978, I, pp. 448-449; BOORMAN 2006, pp. 944-945; BROWN 1983, I, pp. 238-239; CAO IV, p. 232; CHRISTOFFERSEN 1994, II, p. 74; CMM 22/IV, pp. xv-xvii; EDWARDS 2006, p. 409; FALLOWS 1999, pp. 597-599; FILOCAMO 2004; HEWITT 1942, pp. 154-155, 177; JONES 1971, II, pp. 86-88; LAMA DE LA CRUZ 1994, pp. 262-263; LOACH 1969, I, pp. 287, 337; POWERS 1994, pp. 464-469; PRIZER 1995, pp. 184-185; ROS-FÁBREGAS 1992, I, pp. 145-146; SHIPP 1960, pp. 162-163; SM 6, p. 121; SM 8, p. 346; THOMAS 2001; TOFT 1992, pp. 124-130; WEISS 1998, pp. 30-31; WOLFF 1970, I, pp. 302-307.

---

[6]. Ascribed to La Rue, and joined to the preceding piece and the one that follows in the manuscript: *Si dedero* is the second part of the piece labelled «Muteta» (= 'motet').

89.
Si dedero [somnum oculis meis]
fols. 57*v*–58*r*

Alex[ander] Agricola

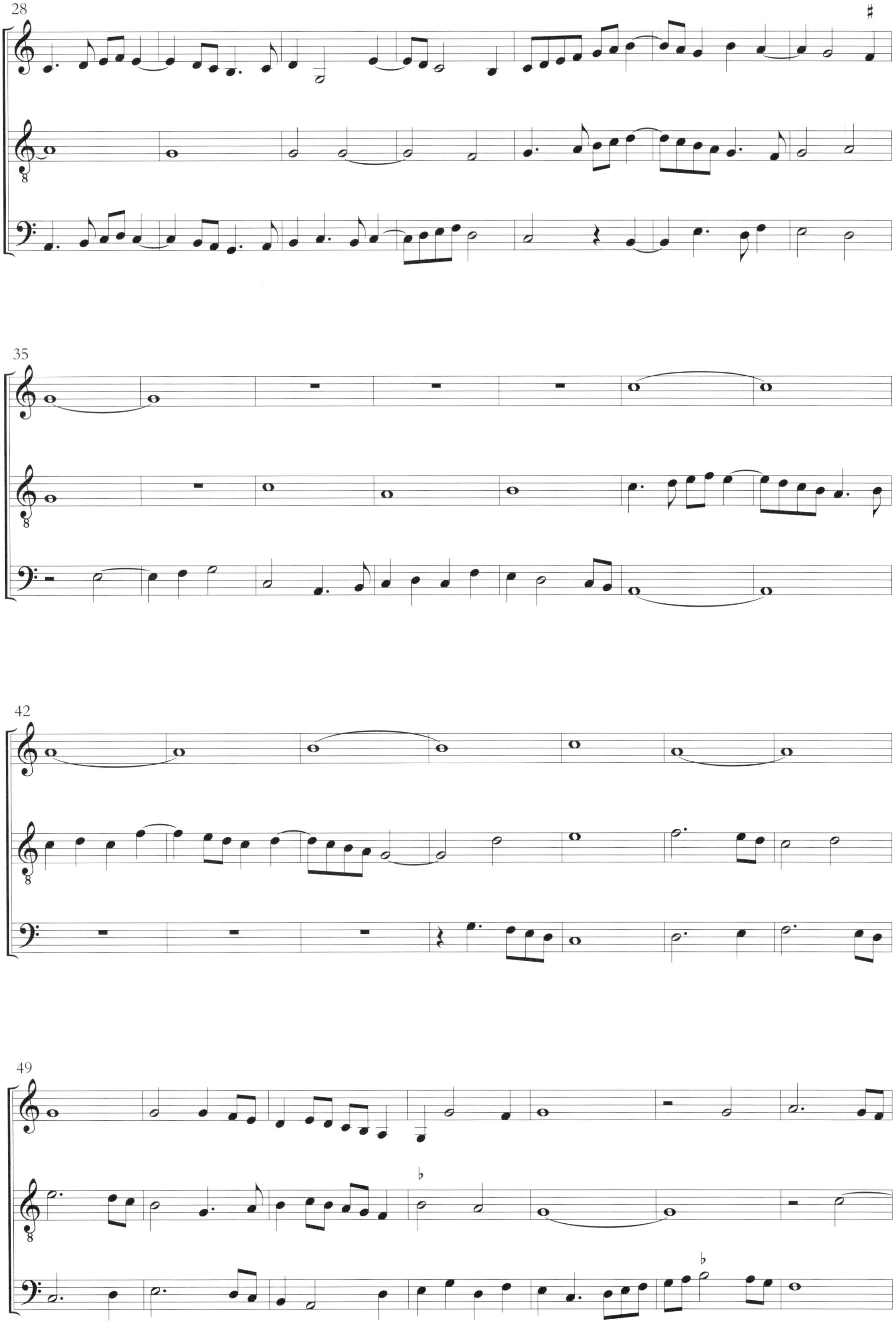
28
35
42
49

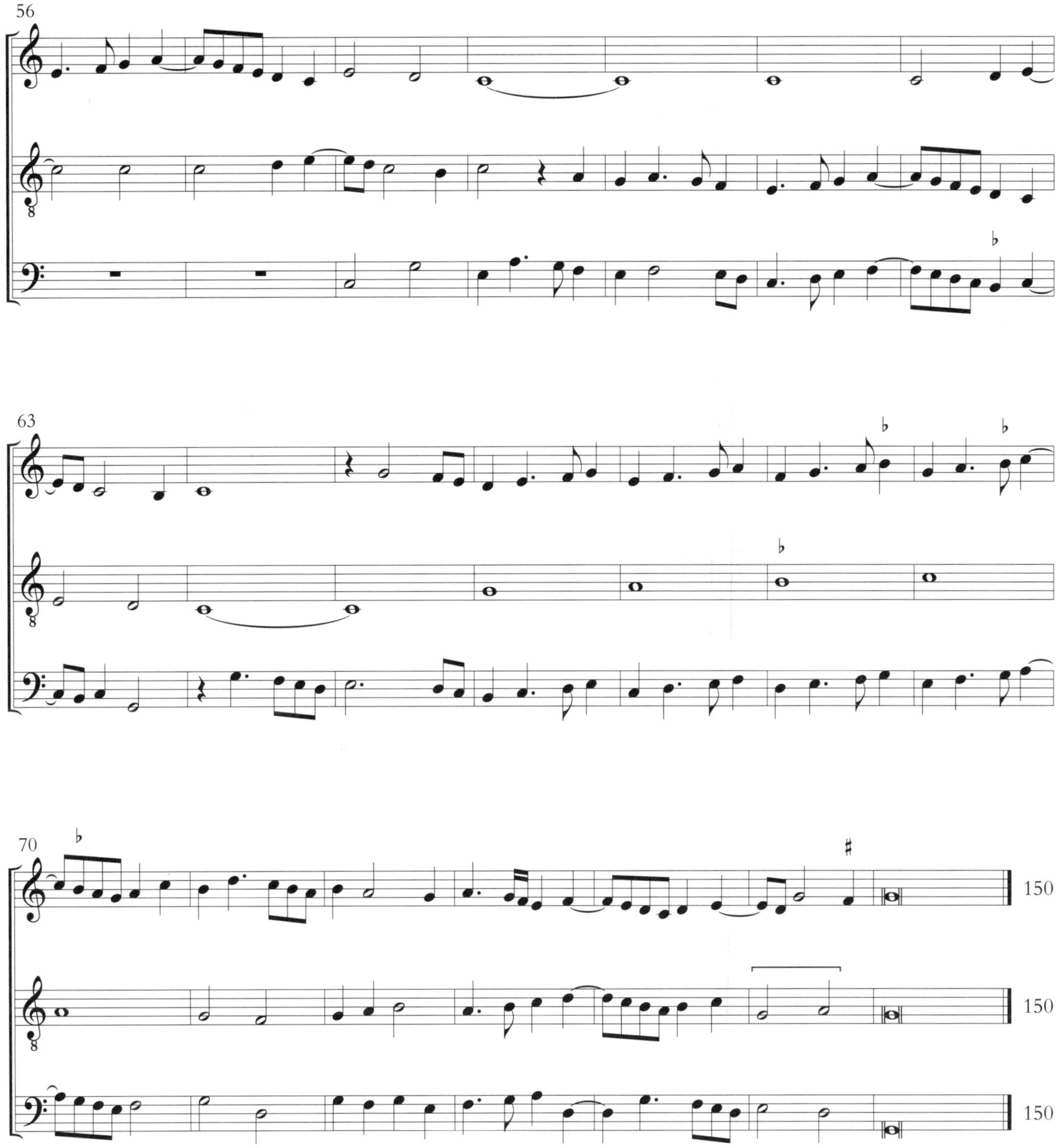
56
63
70
150
150
150

90.

SURGE, PROPERA, AMICA MEA

fols. 58*v*–59*r* (4 vv.)

IO[HANNES] DE PINAROL

Surge, propera, amica mea,
spetiosa mea, et veni,
columba mea,
in foraminibus petre,
5   in caverna macerie.
Ostende mihi fatiem tuam,
sonet vox tua in auribus meis:
vox enim tua dulcis
et faties tua decora.

Marian prayer, based on the Song of Songs 2:10, 13-14 (VULGATA, p. 998). The second section of the text («Ostende mihi […]») was also used independently (see CAO III, p. 391, CS, p. 269, and IGC, p. 318). See also no. 91, where the section «Surge propera […]» continues instead according to the Vulgate text.

READINGS EMENDED IN THE EDITION:

BAR	VOICE	ORIGINAL
3-5	B	*brevis-longa* ligature
4-6	A	*brevis-longa* ligature
7-8	B	*brevis-brevis* ligature
8-10/I	A	*brevis-brevis* ligature with dot
after 65	A	an unusual sign resembling a *semibrevis* rest
79/I	S	*g*′ instead of *a*′
90/I	A	flat before *b*′
97	B	*longa* with fermata

MUSICAL CONCORDANCES (PRINTS):[1] • PeMotA1502 (6*v*-7*r*), «Jo. de Pinarol»

TEXT FROM VULGATA, p. 998 (*Canticum canticorum*, II, 10-14):

10.	et dilectus meus loquitur mihi
	surge propera amica mea formonsa mea et veni
11.	iam enim hiemps transiit imber abiit et recessit
12.	flores apparuerunt in terra tempus putationis advenit
	vox turturis audita est in terra nostra
13.	ficus protulit grossos suos vineae florent dederunt odorem
	surge amica mea speciosa mea et veni
14.	columba mea in foraminibus petrae in caverna maceriae
	ostende mihi faciem tuam sonet vox tua in auribus meis
	vox enim tua dulcis et facies tua decora

---

[1]. The version of PeMotA1505 is lacking, because this recently discovered print, which exists in a unique copy, lacks the entire initial fascicle (see BOORMAN 2006, pp. 576-579).

MODERN EDITIONS OF THE MUSIC: BANKS 1993, II, pp. 186-189 (after Panc.27); DRAKE 1972, II, pp. 15-17 (after PeMotA1502); SHERR 1991, pp. 5-11 (after PeMotA1502).

REMARKS: Although it is the only concordance known, the version of PeMotA1502 does not seem to have been the model for the scribe of Panc.27. The two versions differ graphically on a number of points, and in the print the text is written in a more modern Latin (l. 2 «speciosa», l. 6 «faciem», l. 9 «facies»). However, it is interesting that the attribution to Pinarol is present only in Petrucci prints and in two Renaissance manuscripts thought to depend on them: Panc.27 and the later Munich, Bayerische Staatsbibliothek, Musiksammlung, Mus. 1516 (= MaiM 204).

BIBLIOGRAPHY: BANKS 1993, I, p. 290; BOORMAN 2006, p. 947; BROWN 1990, p. 755, n. 38; CAO III, p. 391; CS, p. 269; DRAKE 1972, I, pp. 174, 276-277; FILOCAMO 2004; IGC, p. 318.

90.
SURGE, PROPERA, AMICA MEA
fols. 58*v*–59*r*

Io[hannes] de Pinarol

499

48
-e. O - sten - de mi - hi fa - ti - em tu - - - - - - -
-e.
-e. O - sten - de mi - hi fa - - - - - - ti - em
-e.
56
- - - - - - - - - am,
so - - - - - - - net vox tu - - - -
tu - - - - - - - - am,
so - - - - - - - net vox tu -
64
-a in au-ri-bus me - - - - - - - - - - - - - - is:
- - - - a in au-ri-bus me - - - - - - - - - - - - is:

72
vox e - nim tu - a dul - - - - - - - - - - - -
vox e - nim tu - a dul - - - - - cis
vox e - nim tu - a dul - cis et fa - - - -
vox e - nim tu - a dul - cis et fa - - - - - - - - - -
81
- cis et fa - ti - es tu - - - - a de - - - -
et fa - - - - - - - - - - ti - es tu - - - a de - - -
- - - - - - - ti - es tu - - - - - - - - - - - a
- - - - - - - ti - es tu - - - - - a de - - - -
89
- - - - - - - - - - - - - - - - - - co - ra. 190
- - - - - - - - - - - - - - - - - - co - ra. 190
de - - - - - - - - - - - - - - - - co - ra. 190
- - - - - - - - - - - - - - - - - - co - ra. 190

91.

O PULCHERRIMA MULIERUM

fols. 59*v*–60*r* (4 vv.)

GASPAR [VAN WEERBEKE]

O pulcherrima mulierum,
surge, propera, amica mea,
columba mea, formosa mea, et veni.
Ostende mihi fatiem tuam,
5 sonet vox tua in auribus meis:
vox enim tua dulcis
et faties tua decora.

Marian prayer based on the Song of Songs 2:10, 14 (VULGATA, p. 998), preceded by the versicle *O pulcherrima mulierum* from the Song of Songs 5:9, 17 (VULGATA, p. 1000). The text is composed of two main parts («Surge, propera […]» and «Ostende mihi […]»), each of which is also used independently (see CAO III, p. 391, CS, pp. 268-269, and IGC, pp. 318, 406).

READINGS EMENDED IN THE EDITION:

BAR	VOICE	ORIGINAL
20/II	T	*e´ minima* instead of a dot, according to PeMotA1502 (and its reprint)

MUSICAL CONCORDANCES (MSS): • CTL G12 (102*r*, *olim* 111*r*), 2 vv. (A and B only)[1]

MUSICAL CONCORDANCES (PRINTS): • PeMotA1502 (40*v*-41*r*), «Gaspar» • PeMotA1505 (40*v*-41*r*), «Gaspar»

TEXT FROM VULGATA, p. 998 (*Canticum canticorum*, II, 10-14): see no. 90.

MODERN EDITIONS OF THE MUSIC: BANKS 1993, II, pp. 145-147 (after Panc.27); DRAKE 1972, II, pp. 95-96 (after PeMotA1502); SHERR 1991, pp. 61-65 (after PeMotA1502).

REMARKS: While it seems risky to me to think that this piece was derived from CTL G12[2] because of the numerous graphic variants in the Altus and the lack of a composer attribution, I think it more plausible that there was some contact between Panc.27 and PeMotA1502 (or its reprint). Very few graphic variants (mostly repeated notes) separate the two versions; moreover, Petrucci gives the complete text in all four voices, even if written in a more modern Latin (l. 4 «faciem»; l. 8 «facies»). The name of the composer, on the other hand, is transmitted identically.

BIBLIOGRAPHY: BANKS 1993, I, p. 284; BOORMAN 2006, p. 931; BROWN 1990, p. 755, n. 38; CAO III, p. 391; CATTIN 1973a, p. 211; CS, pp. 268-269; DRAKE 1972, I, pp. 74, 125-126, 174, 271-272, 276, 291; FILOCAMO 2004; IGC, pp. 318, 406.

---

[1]. The page carrying the Superius and Tenor is lost.
[2]. Despite Giulio Cattin's belief that «the two remaining voices correspond to the version in Panc.27 even in graphic details» (see CATTIN 1973a, p. 211).

91.

O PULCHERRIMA MULIERUM

fols. 59*v*-60*r*

Gaspar [van Weerbeke]

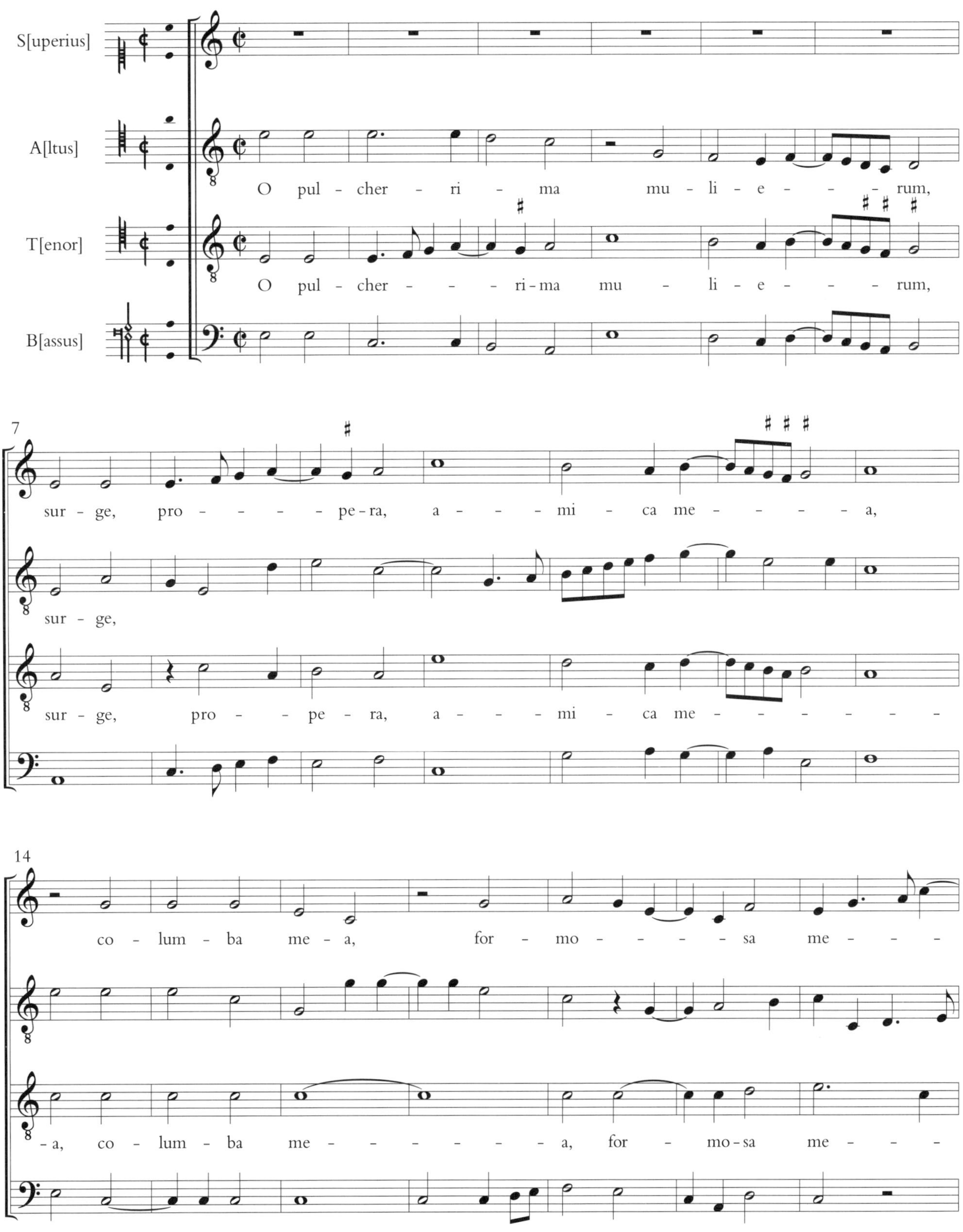

21
- - a, et ve - - - ni. O - sten - de mi - hi
- - a, et ve - - - - - - ni. O - sten - de mi - hi fa - ti -
28
fa - ti - em tu - am, so - net vox tu - a
- em tu - - - - - am, so - net vox tu - a in au -
35
in au - ri - bus me - - - - - - - is:
- ri - bus me - - - - - - - - - is:

vox e- nim tu - a dul - - - -

vox e- nim tu - a dul - - - cis

- cis et fa - ti - es tu - a de - - co - ra.

et fa - ti - es tu - a de - - - - - co - ra.

92.

Si dedero [el mio core al dio d'amore]

fols. 60*v*-61*r* (4 vv.)

[Giacomo Fogliano]

Si dedero

Italian secular piece (strambotto toscano).

Commentary on the text:

1   «dedero» is the future perfect active tense of Latin *do*, *das*, *dedi*, *datum*, *dare* (= 'to give, offer, dedicate'), here 'if I shall have given'

Readings emended in the edition:

Bar	Voice	Original
incipit	A	B flat in the key signature

Musical concordances (mss): • FirN BR230 (18*v*-19*r*), *Si dedero el mio core al dio d'amore*, «Jacobus Foglianus» • FirN M107bis (31*v*-32*r*/*v*?); index only: *Si dedero*[1]

Text from FirN BR230:

> Si dedero el mio core al dio d'amore,
> sarà mie vita dolorosa forte.
> Si dedero el mio core ad un signore,
> i' so che l'ospedale è fin di corte.
5 > Si dedero el mio core cercando ognore
> roba o danarei, egli è sudor di morte.
> Però solo virtù mi sottoscrivo,
> la qual po' morte ancor tien l'omo vivo.

Remarks: The MS FirN BR230, although including a version of the piece that is musically close to that in Panc.27, has almost certainly been copied later. Nevertheless, the variants, mostly graphic, distinguish the two versions only slightly. In the Altus of Panc.27 the presence of B flat in the signature is curious: in fact it would apply to only the first three Bs (bb. 2-4).

Bibliography: Fallows 1999, p. 597; Prizer 2004a, pp. 405, 406.

---

[1]. Considering that the piece is anonymous, it is not entirely clear to which piece it refers in the missing folios.

92.
Sɪ ᴅᴇᴅᴇʀᴏ [ᴇʟ ᴍɪᴏ ᴄᴏʀᴇ ᴀʟ ᴅɪᴏ ᴅ'ᴀᴍᴏʀᴇ]
fols. 60v–61r

[Giacomo Fogliano]

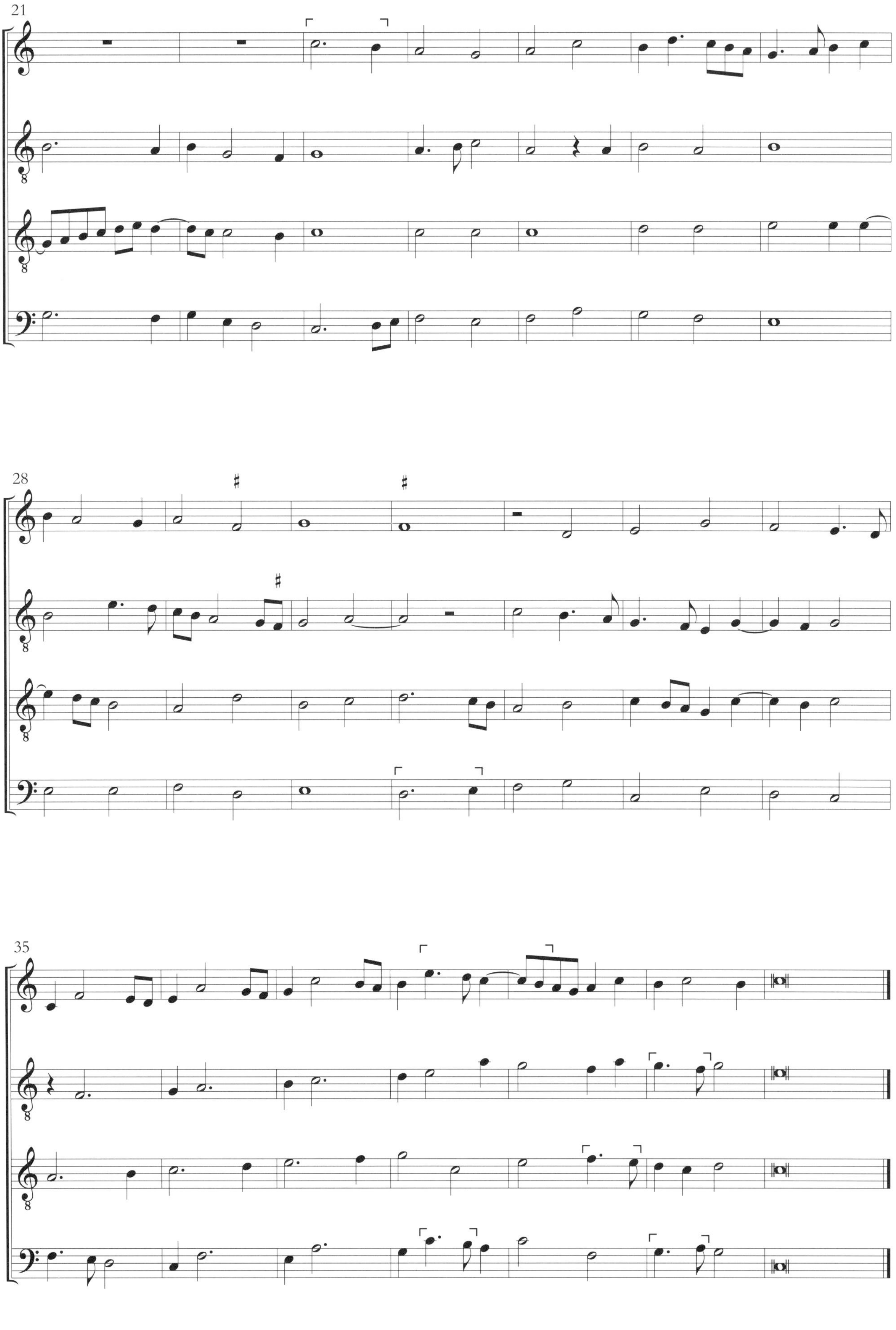
21
28
35

93.

Se ben or [non] scopri el fuoco

fols. 60*v*–61*r* (4 vv.)

[Bartolomeo Tromboncino]

Se ben or [non] scopri el fuoco

Italian secular piece (barzelletta).

COMMENTARY ON THE TEXT:

1	A: «or» lacking
1	the line has been corrected by adding «non» on the basis of the other witnesses

READINGS EMENDED IN THE EDITION:

BAR	VOICE	ORIGINAL
18/II	A	*d' minima* followed by a dot of addition

TEXTUAL CONCORDANCES (MSS): • *Man. C. 4* (132*r*–*v*) • *Mod. E. 809* (188*v*–189*r*)

TEXTUAL CONCORDANCES (PRINTS): • *Inamormento* (f2*v*)

MUSICAL CONCORDANCES (MSS): • BerlS 22048 (1*r*), modern hand: «Tromboncino Bartolomeo» • BolM 18 (3*v*-4*r*) • CTL G12 (75*v*-76*r*, olim 74*v*-75*r*), *L'oration e sempre bona*[1] • FirN BR230 (22*v*-23*r*), «Tronboncino» • LonB E3051 (57*v*-58*r*) • MilT 55 (32*v*-33*r*)

MUSICAL CONCORDANCES (PRINTS): • PeFroI (18*v*-19*r*), «B. T.»

TEXT FROM PeFroI:

> Se ben or non scopro el foco
> ne la amara pena mia,
> questa doglia acœrba e ria
> fia scoperta a tempo e loco.
> > Se ben or non scopro el foco

5
> Verrà tempo che Fortuna
> condurà mie velle in porto.
> Se or patisco pena alcuna,
> già per questo io non son morto,
> e 'l dolor ch'io pato a torto
10
> fia scoperto a tempo e loco.
> > Se ben […]

> Ben serìa nato infelice
> a star sempre in questo stato.
> Se la sorte or me desdice,

---

[1]. The lauda text is to be attributed to Feo Belcari (see CATTIN 1973a, p. 204 and CMM 76, p. 33); for further on *L'orazione è sempre buona* see CARBONI - ZIINO 1973, p. 280.

                   ancor spero esser beato
15   e il martìr mio dispietato
                   fia scoperto a tempo e loco.
                           Se ben […]

                   Doppo l'aspra e ria tempesta
                   sòl tornar el ciel iocondo.
                   Se mia vita iace mesta
20   non starò sempre al profondo
                   e 'l mio mal, che è solo al mondo,
                   fia scoperto a tempo e loco.
                           Se ben […]

                   L'invisibil mio cordoglio,
                   che ad ogn'or mi sparte el core,
25   dir mi fa quel che non soglio:
                   questo advien per troppo amore.
                   Or non più che 'l gran dolore
                   fia scoperto a tempo e loco.
                           Se ben […]

The disposition of the text, which differs considerably among the sources, is summarized in the following chart, in which the arabic numerals indicate the succession of the stanzas (without considering variants in writing or single words):

	PeFroI – *Mod.E. 809*	*Man.C. 4*	BolM 18	MilT 55	LonB E3051	FirN BR230	BerlS 22048
Verrà tempo	1	1	1	1	1	1	2
Ben serìa	2	2	2	2	–	4	1
Doppo l'aspra	3	3	–	–	–	3	3
L'invisibil	4	–	3	–	–	2	4

MODERN EDITIONS OF THE TEXT: CESARI *ET AL.* 1954, p. 8★ (after PeFroI); GIAZOTTO 1959, pp. 63-64 (after MilT 55); JEPPESEN 1970, p. 152 (after MilT 55); SCHWARTZ 1935, p. xxx (after PeFroI); WOLF (1926) 1931, p. 56 (after FirN BR230).

MODERN EDITIONS OF THE MUSIC: BESSELER 1931, p. 220 (after PeFroI); CESARI *ET AL.* 1954, p. 16 (after PeFroI); CMM 76, p. 32 (after CTL G12); GIAZOTTO 1959, pp. 64-65 (after MilT 55); JEPPESEN 1970, pp. 249-250 (after MilT 55); SCHWARTZ 1935, pp. 14-15 (after PeFroI); WOLF (1926) 1931, pp. 55-56 (after FirN BR230).

REMARKS: The version in Panc.27 is certainly derived from a model, as shown by the absence of bar 20 in the Tenor (identical with the preceding one, thus a typical copying error). A collation of the concordances demonstrates that it is not possible to hypothesize any of them as the model for Panc.27: all the musical sources examined present versions that are differentiated by graphic and melodic variants. Moreover, the textual incipit of Panc.27 is defective in both voices that include it (Cantus and Altus): one can deduce from this that the scribe certainly did not understand the sense of what he was copying, and this possibility renders it unlikely that his model was one of the sources that has come down to us.

BIBLIOGRAPHY: BOORMAN 2006, p. 1013; CATTIN 1972a, p. 452; CATTIN 1973a, pp. 204-205; CATTIN 1978, pp. 27, 38; GALLETTI 1863, p. 53; GHISI 1937, p. 97; VECCHI GALLI 1986a, p. 17; WEISS 1998, pp. 18-19.

93.
Se ben or [non] scopri el fuoco

fols. *60v–61r*

[Bartolomeo Tromboncino]

Cantus: Se ben or [non] sco - pri el fuo - co

Altus: Se ben [or non] sco-pri el fuo - co

94.

Regina celi letare

fols. 61*v*-63*r* (4 vv.)

[Antoine] Brumel

Regina celi letare,
alleluia,
quia quem meruisti portare,
alleluia,
5   resurrexit sicut dixit,
alleluia,
ora pro nobis Deum,
alleluia.

Marian antiphon for Paschal Time used as the concluding antiphon at Compline (AM, pp. 176, 179-180; AR, pp. 67-68; BR, p. 110; LR, pp. 48-49; LU, pp. 275 and 278). It is also used, for example, as antiphon to the Benedictus and to the Magnificat in the Office of the Blessed Virgin Mary on Saturdays (AM, pp. 718-719; AR, p. [131]), and in Paschal Time for feasts of the Blessed Virgin Mary (PM, pp. 257-258). See also CAO III, p. 440; IGC, p. 361.

Musical concordances (mss): • CV S42 (123*v*-125*r*), «Brumel» • SGS 530 (87*v*-88*r*), «Brumel» • VerCap 758 (13*v*-15*r*)

Musical concordances (prints): • AttMotetz (no. 6: 7*v*, 8*v*, 9*r*, 8*r*) • PeMotA1502 (19*v*-21*r*), «Brumel» • PeMotA1505 (19*v*-21*r*), «Brumel»

Modern editions of the text: CAO III, p. 440.

Modern editions of the music: Ambros V, pp. 172-179 (after PeMotA1502); CMM 5/V, pp. 95-99; Drake 1972, II, pp. 48-53 (after PeMotA1502); SM 8, pp. 214-216 (after SGS 530).

Remarks: The print AttMotetz is a rather late source (ca. 1528), and the version of CV S42 (a manuscript compiled in the same years as Panc.27) is fairly distant because of the presence of some substantive variants (it differs in the Superius and Tenor in bb. 60-61). The version of PeMotA1502 (and its reprint) is certainly closer to Panc.27, but nevertheless the many differences (graphic and small ornaments) discourage the hypothesis of a direct copy from Petrucci. The chant melody is quoted at the beginning of each phrase: the underlying chant appears to be a version conflating the solemn tone (AM, p. 179, AR, p. 67, LR, p. 48, and LU, p. 275) and the simple tone (AM, p. 180, AR, p. 68, LR, p. 49, and LU, p. 278).[1]

Bibliography: Boorman 2006, p. 940; Brown 1990, p. 752, n. 27, p. 755, n. 38; CAO III, p. 440; Drake 1972, I, pp. 68-69, 123, 163, 164, 198, 235, 241-242; Filocamo 2004; IGC, p. 361; Sherr 1996, p. 170; SM 8, p. 356.

---

[1]. I thank Bonnie Blackburn for this last observation.

94.
REGINA CELI LETARE
fols. 61*v*–63*r*

[Antoine] Brumel

21
- lu - - - ia,
- - - - - - - - ia,
- le - - - lu - - - ia,
28
qui - a quem
qui - a quem
qui - a
qui - a quem me - ru -
35
me - ru - i - - - - - - - - - - - - - sti
me - ru - i - - - - - - - - - - - - - - - -
quem me - ru - i - - - - - - -
- i - - - - - - - - - - - - - - - - - - -

42
por
sti por ta
sti por
sti por ta
49
ta re, al le
re, al le
ta re, al le lu
re, al le lu
57
lu ia,
124
lu ia,
125
ia,
124
ia,
124

[Secunda pars]
64
re - sur - re - - - - xit
re - sur - re - - - - - - - - - - - - xit
re - sur - re - - - - - xit si -
re - sur - re - - - - - - - - - - - xit si - cut
72
si - cut di - xit, al - le - lu - - -
si - cut di - xit, al - le - lu - - - - - - - - - -
- cut di - xit, al - - le - lu - - - - -
di - xit, al - - le - lu - - - ia,
79
- - - - ia, o - ra pro
- - - - ia, o - ra pro no - - - - - - - - - - -
- - - - ia, o - ra pro no - - - -
o - ra pro no - - - - - - - - - - - - - -

86
no - - - - - - - - - bis De - - - - - - - - -
- - - - - bis De - - - - - - - - -
- - - - - - - - - - - - - bis De - - - - - - - - - -
- bis De - - - - - - - - - - - - -
93
- - - um, al - le - lu - ia,
- - - um, al - le - lu - ia, al -
- - - um, al - le - lu - ia, al - - - -
- - um, al - le - lu - ia,
100
al - - - - - le - lu - ia. al - - - - - le - lu -
- - - le - lu - ia.
- le - lu - ia.

108
- ia. al - le - lu - ia.
al - le - lu - ia.
al - le - lu - ia.
al - le - lu - ia.
116
al -
al - - - - - le - lu - ia.
124
132
132
- - - - - - - - - le - - - - - lu - - - ia.
132
132

95.

O QUAM GLORIFICA [LUCE CORUSCAS]

fols. 63*v*-64*r* (3 vv.)

[ALEXANDER] AGRICOLA

O quam glorifica

Hymn in Honour of the Blessed Virgin Mary (AR, pp. 134★-135★; LU, pp. 1864-1865). It has been used, for example, for the Purification (AH 2, p. 40) and for the Assumption (AH 51, pp. 146-147; PM, pp. 180-181). See also CAO IV, p. 516; IGC, p. 306.

READINGS EMENDED IN THE EDITION:

BAR	VOICE	ORIGINAL
66/II	Ct	*A*; *F* has been substituted after ParisN F1597

MUSICAL CONCORDANCES (MSS): • ParisN F1597 (6*v*-7*r*), *O quam glorifica luce coruscas*

MUSICAL CONCORDANCES (PRINTS): • PeMotA1502 (14*v*-15*r*), *O quam glorifica luce coruscas*, «Agricola» • PeMotA1505 (14*v*-15*r*), *O quam glorifica luce coruscas*, «Agricola»

TEXT FROM AR pp. 134★-135★ (*In honorem B. Mariae Virginis*):

1. O quam glorifica luce coruscas,
    stirpis Davidicae regia proles!
    Sublimis residens, Virgo Maria,
    supra caeligenas aetheris omnes.

2. Tu cum virgineo mater honore,
    angelorum Domino pectoris aulam
    sacris visceribus casta parasti;
    natus hinc Deus est corpore Christus.

3. Quem cunctus venerans orbis adorat,
    cui nunc rite genu flectitur omne;
    a quo te, petimus, subveniente,
    abjectis tenebris, gaudia lucis.

4. Hoc largire pater luminis omnis,
    natum per proprium, flamine sacro,
    qui tecum nitida vivit in aethra
    regnans, ac moderans saecula cuncta.

    Amen.

MODERN EDITIONS OF THE TEXT: AH 2, p. 40; AH 51, pp. 146-147.

MODERN EDITIONS OF THE MUSIC: CMM 22/IV, pp. 48-49; DRAKE 1972, II, pp. 36-38 (after PeMotA1502); IGC, p. 306; SHIPP 1960, pp. 261-265 (after ParisN F1597).

REMARKS: Despite being a manuscript of the early sixteenth century (but of French provenance), ParisN F1597 transmits readings quite different from those of Panc.27: there are many ornamental notes and graphic variants (ligatures, repeated notes, coloration, rhythmic differences), and some different notes. On the other hand, very few graphic differences (repeated notes instead of long ones, or vice versa) separate Panc.27 and PeMotA1502 (and its reprint): the closeness of the two versions is also confirmed by the presence in both of the *A* in bar 66/II of the Contra (although correct, it weakens the effect of the entrance of the imitative upbeat). Copying from Petrucci is very plausible, given that there is the same short textual incipit and the same attribution. The chant in AR, pp. 134*-135*, LU, pp. 1864-1865, and PM, pp. 180-181 is paraphrased in the Superius up to bar 66.

BIBLIOGRAPHY: BOORMAN 2006, p. 932; CAO IV, p. 516; CHEVALIER II, no. 13516; DRAKE 1972, I, pp. 66, 149, 174, 225-226; FILOCAMO 2004; IGC, p. 306; SHIPP 1960, pp. 161-162; STÄBLEIN 1956, Melody no. 717.

95.
O QUAM GLORIFICA [LUCE CORUSCAS]

fols. *63v–64r*

[Alexander] Agricola

O quam glorifica

O quam glorifica

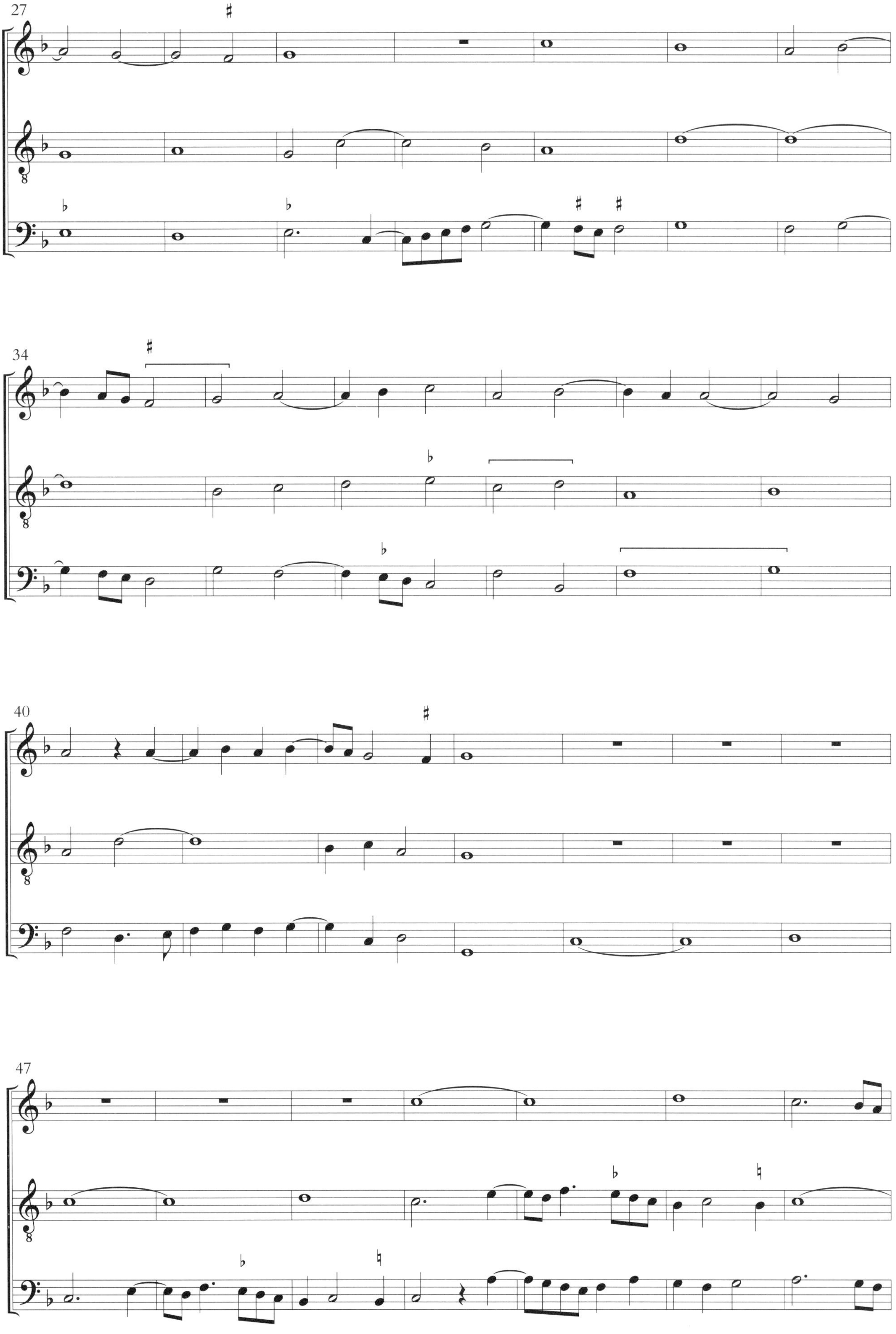
27
34
40
47

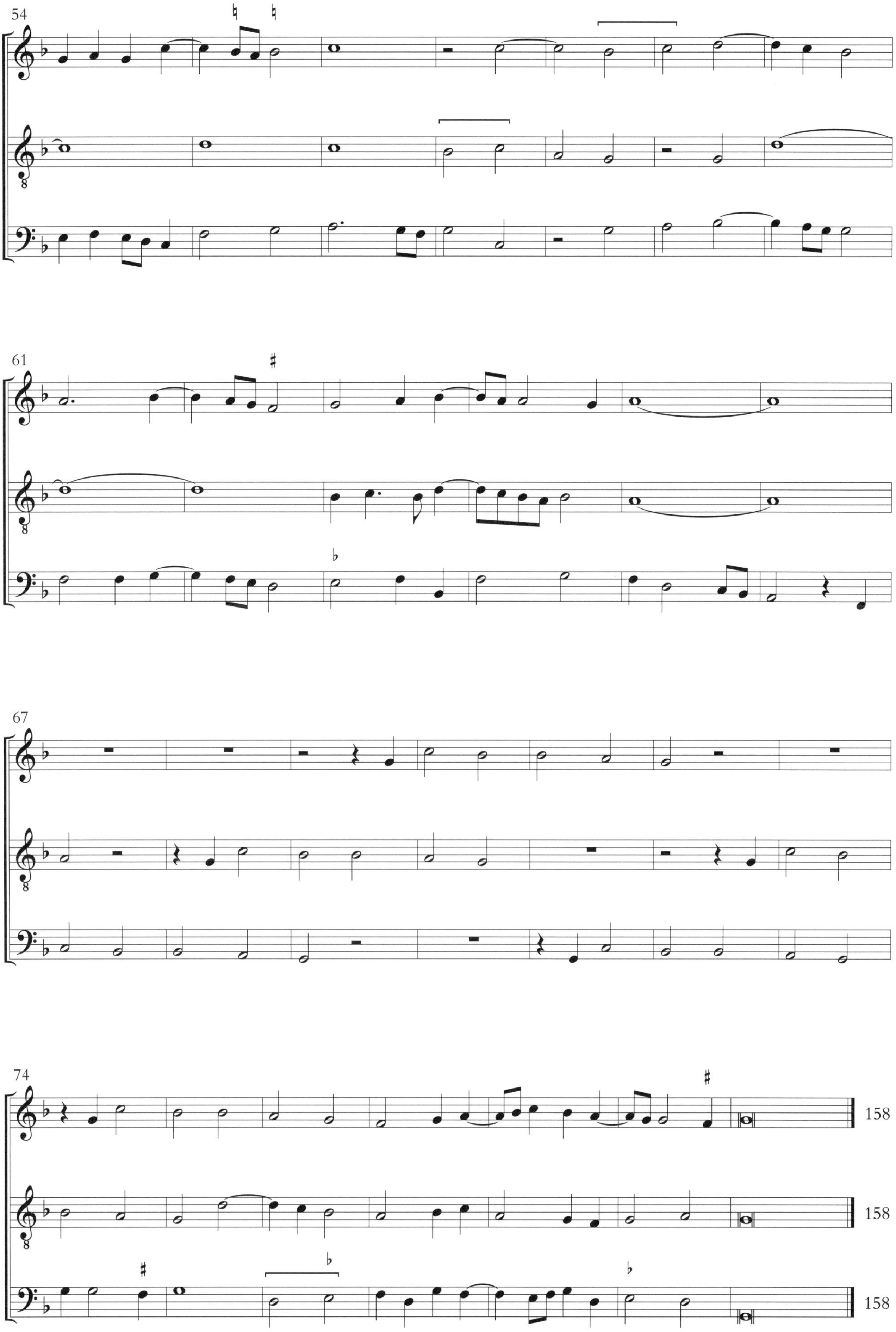
54
61
67
74
158
158
158

96.

Helas, que il est à mon gré

fols. 64*v*–65*r* (4 vv.)

[Johannes] Japart

Helas, que il est à mon gré

Chanson (bergerette).

Readings emended in the edition:

Bar	Voice	Original
incipit	S	flat on the top line of the staff
16	S, T	the change in mensuration occurs in the following bar
23/II-III	B	black *brevis* surmounted with a correction sign « ^ » (see Remarks)

Musical concordances (mss): • CV G27 (47*v*–48*r*, *olim* 54*v*–55*r*), *Elas qu'el este a mon gre* • FirN BR229 (152*v*–153*r*), textless • FirN M107bis (12*r*, *olim* 11*r*), textless, 2 vv. (A and B only);[1] index: *Elas qu'el at a mon gre* • FirN M178 (45*v*–46*r*), *Ch'el et a mon gre* • ParisN F12744 (3*r*), S only[2] • SGS 463 (no. 180), 2 vv. (S and A only), «Japart», «Dorius»

Musical concordances (prints): • PeOdh1501 (33*r*), 2vv. (A and B only)[3] • PeOdh1503 (32*v*–33*r*), «Japart» • PeOdh1504 (32*v*–33*r*), «Japart»

Text from ParisN F12744 (with corrections by Howard Mayer Brown; see Brown 1983, I, p. 267):

Hellas, qu'elle est à mon gré,
celle que je n'ouse nommer!
Hellas, qu'elle est à mon gré,
celle que n'ouse dire!

5   L'autre jour jouer m'alloye,
marchant sur la verdure.

Trouvay la belle en ung pré,
sur l'erbe qui point dure.

D'amours faisoit ung chappellet;
10   vray Dieu, qu'il estoit bien fait!
Par amour luy demanday,
et elle me l'octroye.

Hellas, […]

---

[1]. The page with the Superius and Tenor has been lost.
[2]. The manuscript contains monophonic pieces, and only one for two voices.
[3]. Fol. 32*v*, which would have contained the two other voices and the attribution to Japart, is missing.

MODERN EDITIONS OF THE TEXT: BROWN 1983, I, p. 267 (after ParisN F12744); HELDT 1916, no. 6 (after ParisN F12744); PARIS - GEVAERT 1875, no. 4, (after ParisN F12744).

MODERN EDITIONS OF THE MUSIC: BOER 1938, no. 8 (after PeOdh1504); BROWN 1983, II, pp. 310-313 (after FirN BR229); HEWITT 1942, pp. 284-285 (after PeOdh1504); PARIS - GEVAERT 1875, no. 4 (after ParisN F12744); TORREFRANCA 1939, pp. 554-557 (after PeOdh1504).

REMARKS: The musical version in Panc.27 is distant from the versions in CV G27, FirN BR229, FirN M107bis, FirN M178, which transmit different readings in the Altus (bb. 13-14, 29-33, 38-40). On the other hand, the versions of SGS 463 and *Odhecaton* are close. The most plausible hypothesis is that the piece in Panc.27 derives directly from *Odhecaton*: the Superius and Altus are completely identical. The only graphic differences in the Tenor and Bassus are probably due to the scribe's oversight in copying: in bar 48/I-II of the Tenor the notes *f'* and *g'* are black in Petrucci (the Panc.27 scribe may simply have forgotten to fill the notes in); in bar 23/II-III of the Bassus the scribe realized that he had mistakenly coloured the *brevis e'*, and remedied it by indicating the error with a correction.

BIBLIOGRAPHY: ATLAS 1975-76, I, pp. 121-122; ATLAS 2005, pp. 649, 652; BOORMAN 2006, p. 1048; BROWN 1983, I, pp. 267, 291; HEWITT 1942, pp. 144, 174; LOACH 1969, I, pp. 324, 390; POWERS 1994, pp. 515-516.

96.

HELAS, QUE IL EST À MON GRÉ

fols. 64*v*-65*r*

[Johannes] Japart

Helas, que il est

Helas, que il est à mon gré

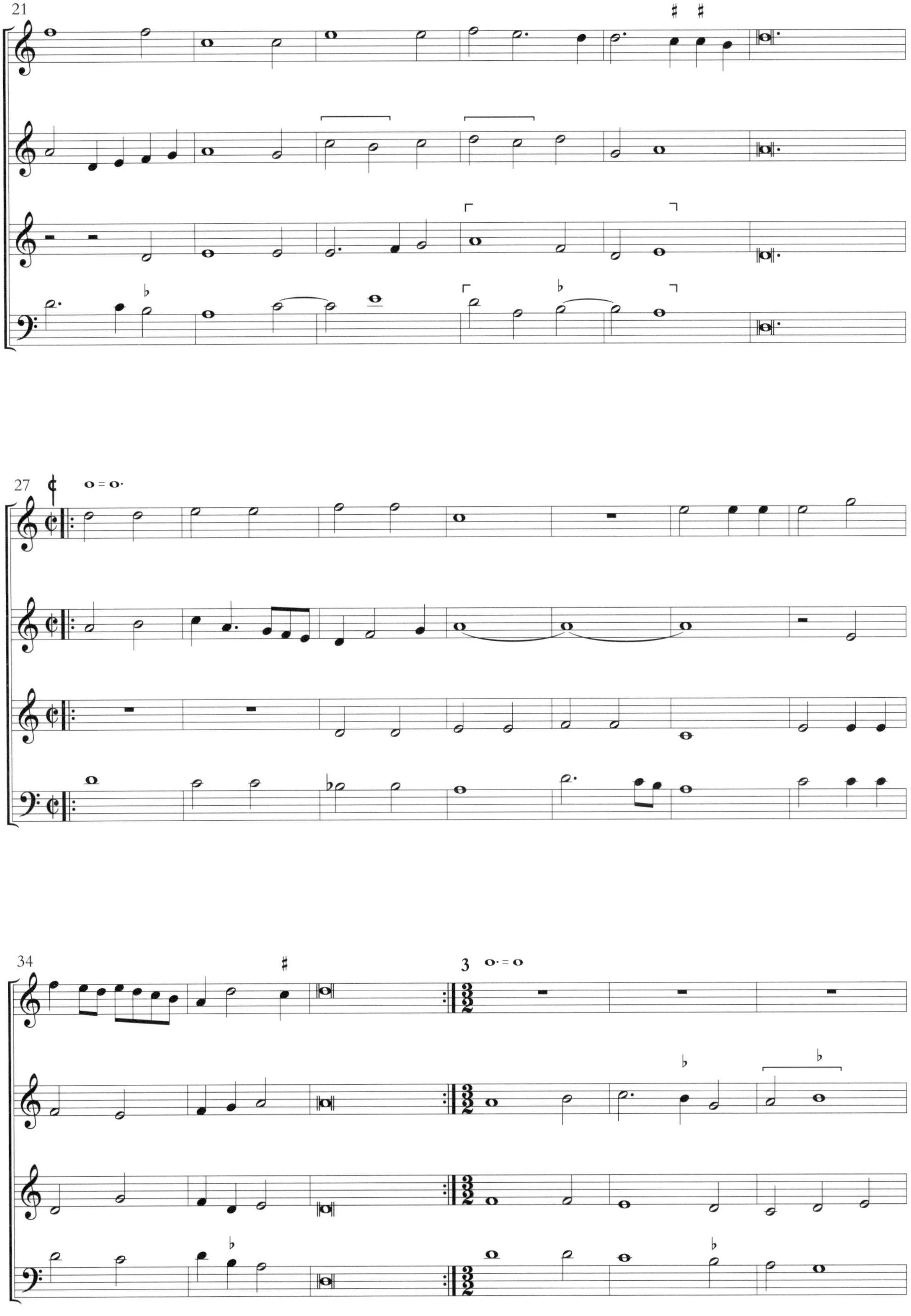
21
27
34
3

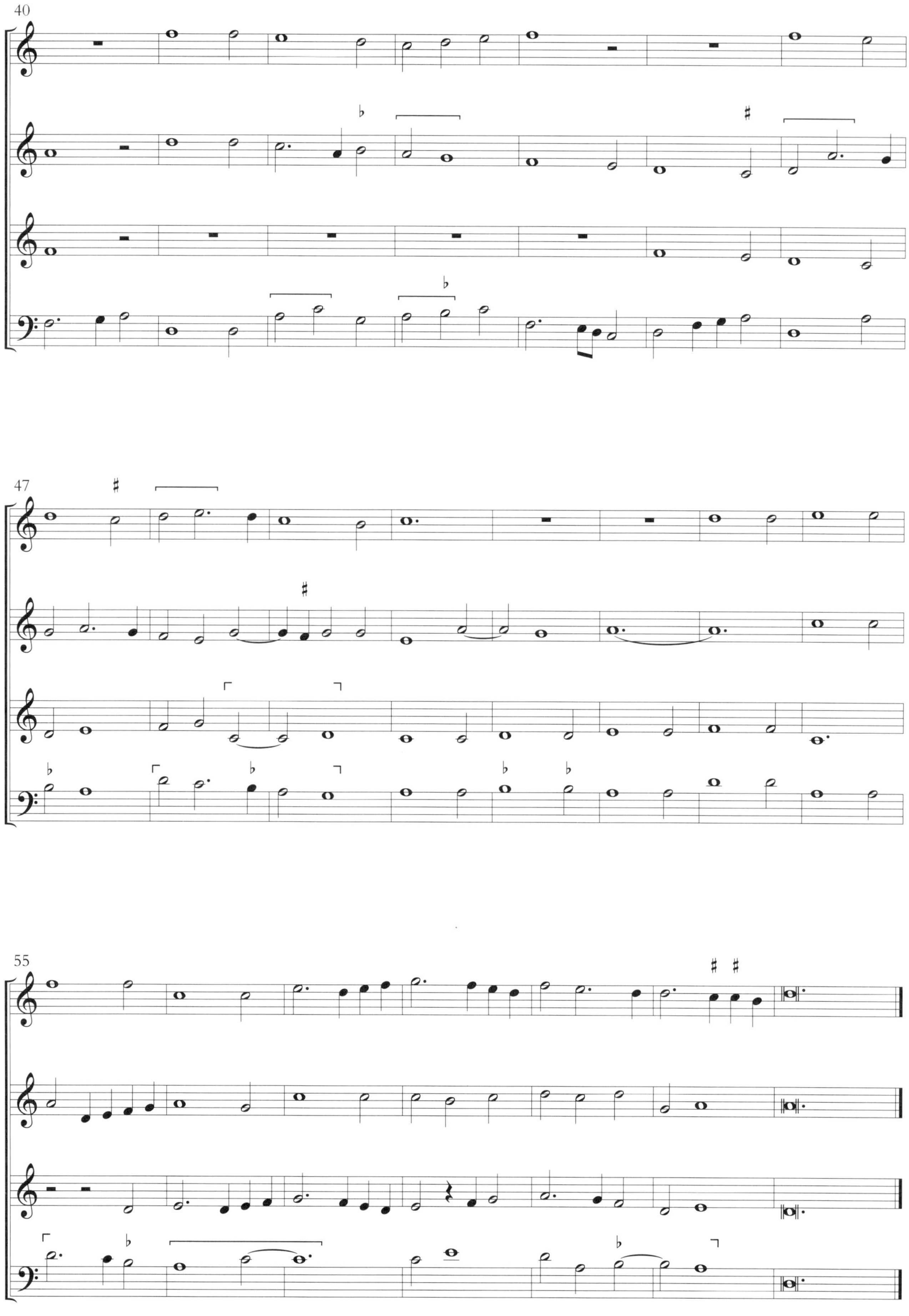
40
47
55

97.

Helas, [ce n'est pas sans rayson]

fols. 65v–66r (4 vv.)

[Johannes de] Sthokem

Helas

Chanson.

Readings emended in the edition:

Bar	Voice	Original
after 19	S	repeat sign that indicates the repetition of bars 1–19 (written out in the transcription)
after 50	S	*g′ brevis* and *f′ semibrevis* erroneously duplicated

Musical concordances (mss): • SGS 461 (64), *Helas ce n'est pas*, «Stoken»

Musical concordances (prints): • PeOdh1501 (21v-22r), *Helas ce n'est pas sans rayson*, «Sthokem» • PeOdh1503 (21v-22r), *Helas ce n'est pas sans rayson*, «Sthokem» • PeOdh1504 (21v-22r), *Helas ce n'est pas sans rayson*, «Sthokem»

Text from PeOdh1504:

> Helas ce n'est pas sans rayson
> se y ai melancolie.

Modern editions of the music: Giesbert 1936, II, pp. 74-75 (after SGS 461); Hewitt 1942, pp. 261-262 (after PeOdh1504); Torrefranca 1939, pp. 550-553 (after PeOdh1504).

Remarks: Significantly, the erroneous doubling of the *brevis g′* and *semibrevis f′* after bar 50 is also found in *Odhecaton*. There is no difference between the two versions, not even graphic, which clearly suggests that the version in Panc. 27 (practically without text) derives from Petrucci. Even the odd spelling of the name is the same in both.

Bibliography: Boorman 2006, p. 1047; Hewitt 1942, pp. 137, 172.

97.
HELAS, [CE N'EST PAS SANS RAYSON]

fols. 65*v*–66*r*

[Johannes de] Sthokem

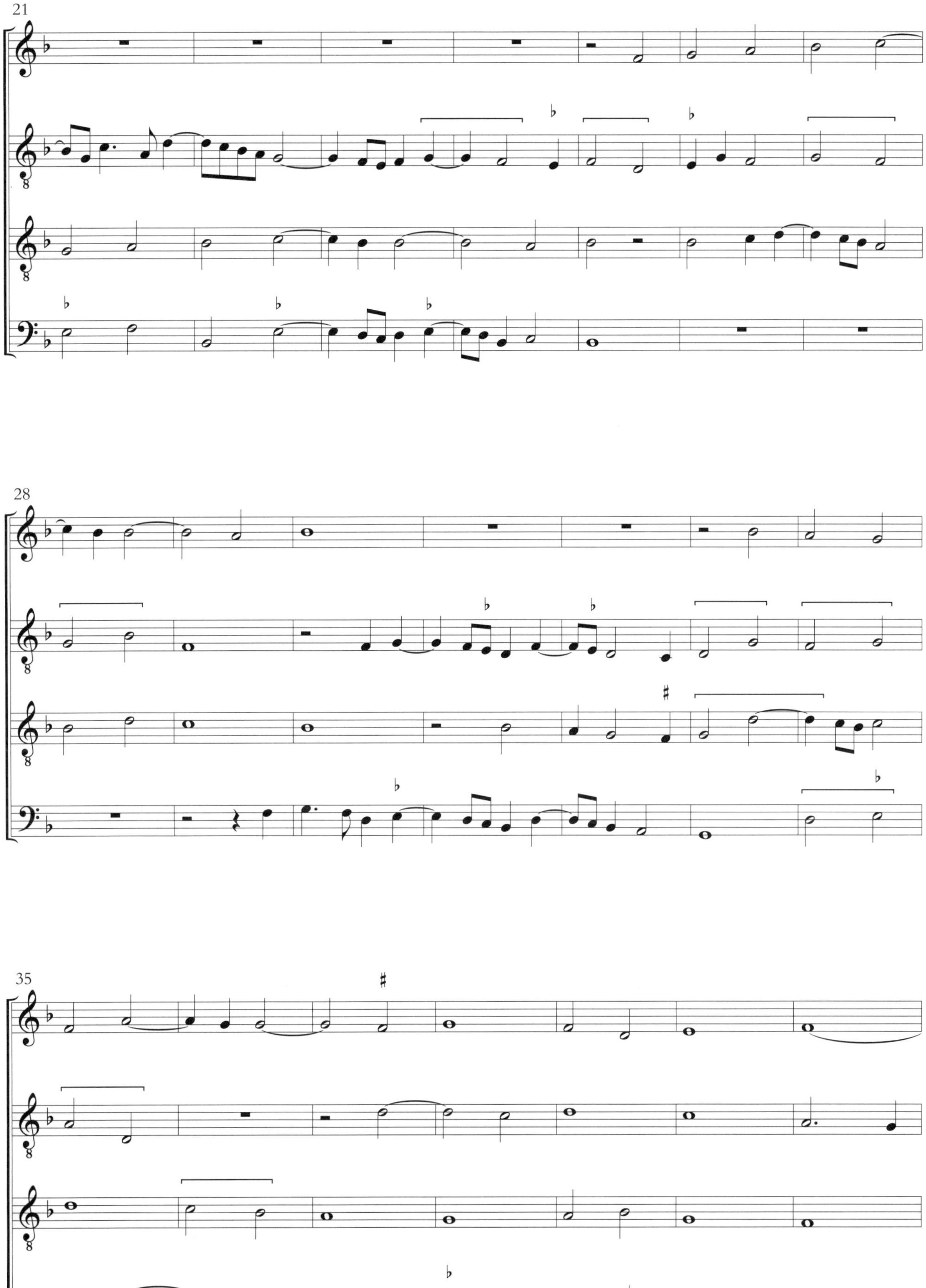
21
28
35

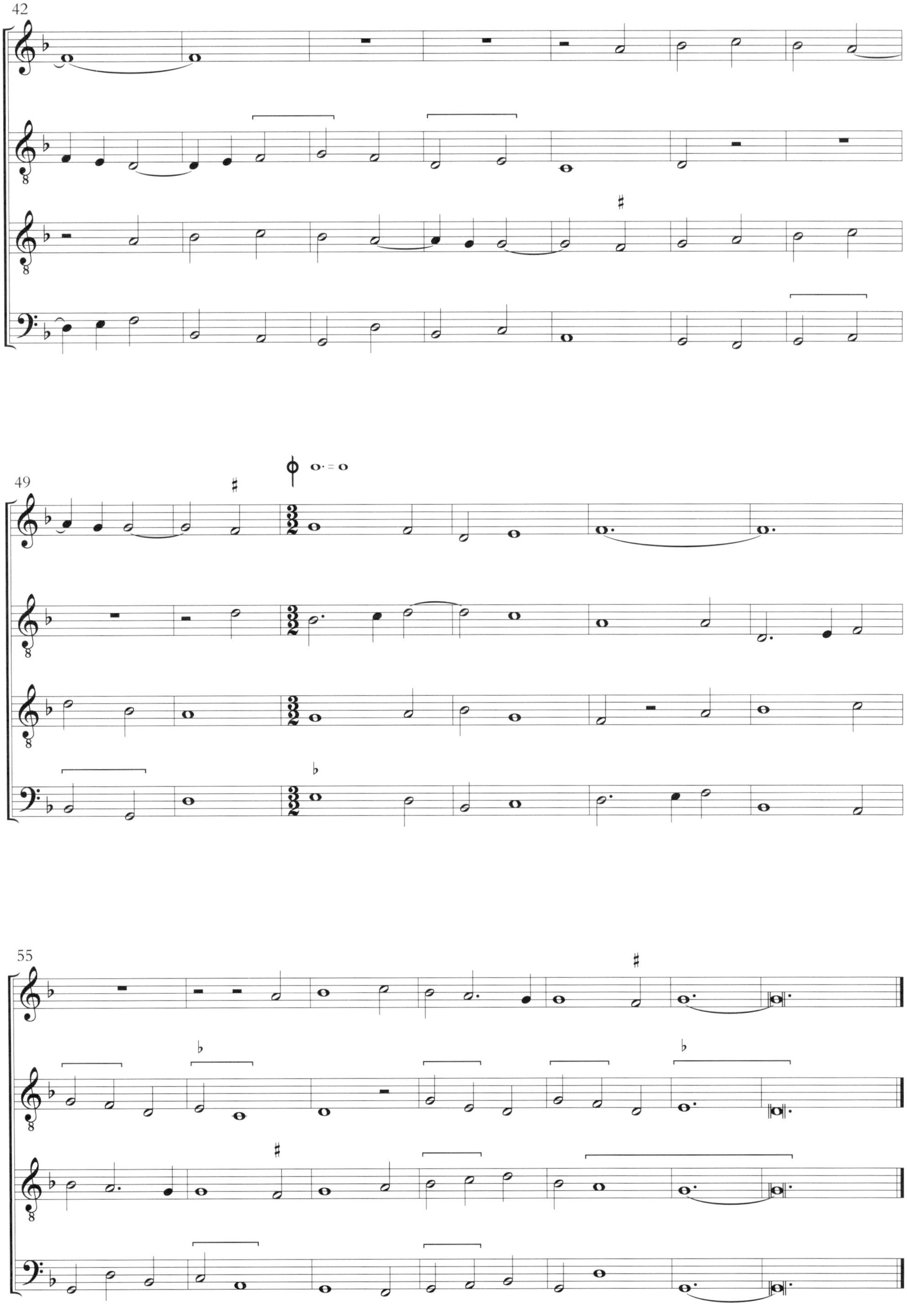
42
49
55

98.

Virgo Maria, non est tibi similis nata

fols. 66v-67r (4 vv.)

Gaspar [van Weerbeke]

Virgo Maria, non est tibi similis nata
in mundo inter omnes mulieres,
florens ut rosa, fragrans sicut lilium,
intercede pro nobis ad Dominum Iesum Christum.

Processional antiphon for the Nativity of the Blessed Virgin Mary (PM, pp. 186-187) and other Marian feasts (see CAO III, p. 543).

Musical concordances (mss): • SGS 530 (89v), «Gaspar» • SienaC 2 (120v-121r)

Musical concordances (prints): • PeMotA1502 (21v-22r), «Gaspar» • PeMotA1505 (21v-22r), «Gaspar»

Text from CAO III, p. 543 (*Assumptio S. Mariae*):

Virgo Maria, non est tibi similis nata
in mundo in mulieres,
flores ut rosa, odor sicut lilium,
ora pro nobis ad tuum Filium.

Modern editions of the text: CAO III, p. 543.

Modern editions of the music: Ambros V, pp. 183-185 (after PeMotA1502); Banks 1993, II, pp. 210-211 (after Panc.27); Delporte 1953; Drake 1972, II, pp. 54-55 (after PeMotA1502); Lenaerts 1962, pp. 54-55 (after PeMotA1502); Sherr 1991, pp. 33-36 (after PeMotA1502); SM 8, p. 218 (after SGS 530).

Remarks: Although the version of SienaC 2 is certainly older and very close to Panc.27, the piece in Panc.27 clearly derives from PeMotA1502 (or its reprint): the Cantus and Bassus are absolutely identical; the single graphic difference in the Altus, a long note in Petrucci, is subdivided in Panc.27 into two repeated notes, and the Tenor has the reverse case. Moreover, Panc.27 has the same amount of text and the same attribution. The performance orientation of Panc.27 is demonstrated by the presence of a line that joins the syllable «no-» (of «nobis») to the c' of bar 39/I in the Altus (fol. 67r, third system). Some words in the Altus («pro nobis», «ad Dominum») and Tenor («in mundo», «mulieres», «ad Dominum») are underlined with dots, but in this case they probably do not mean cancellation for the purpose of repositioning the syllables.

Bibliography: Banks 1993, I, pp. 293-294; Boorman 2006, p. 953; Brown 1990, p. 755, n. 38; CAO III, p. 543; Dickey 2005, p. 17; Drake 1972, I, pp. 69, 175, 272-273, 275, 284; Filocamo 2004; IGC, p. 443; SM 8, p. 356.

98.

VIRGO MARIA, NON EST TIBI SIMILIS NATA

fols. 66v-67r

Gaspar [van Weerbeke]

19
- ter o - mnes mu - li - e - - - - - - - - -
- ter o - mnes
in - ter o - mnes mu - li - e - - - - -
- - - mnes mu - - - - - li - e - res,
25
- res, fra -
fra - grans si - cut
- res, flo - rens ut ro - - - - - - - - sa,
flo - rens ut ro - - - - - - - - - - - - - sa,
32
- grans si - cut li - li - - - - um, in - ter - ce - - - de pro
li - - - - - li - - - - um, in - ter - ce - de pro
in - ter - ce - - - de pro
si - cut li - li - - - um, in - ter - ce - - - de pro

no – – bis ad Do – – – mi – num Ie – – sum Chri –

no – – bis ad Do – – mi – num Ie – –

no – – bis ad Do – – mi – num Ie – – sum Chri –

no – – bis ad Do – – mi – num Ie – – – –

96

104

96

104

– – – – – – stum.

– – – – – – sum Chri – – – – stum.

– – – – – – stum.

– – – – – – sum Chri – – – – stum.

99.

CHRISTI MATER, AVE

fols. 67*v*–68*r* (4 vv.)

GASPAR [VAN WEERBEKE]

Christi mater, ave,
sanctissima Virgo Maria,
Virgo post partum,
sicut et ante, manens.
5   Virgo que Christum peperisti,
lacte educasti,
me rege, me serva, me tueare potens,
me tibi commendo,
me, Virgo, linquere noli;
10   ne peream, Christo
funde, Maria, preces.

Devotional prayer to the Blessed Virgin Mary, present also in the *Vita scolastica* (ca. 1290–1300) of
Bonvesin de la Riva.

COMMENTARY ON THE TEXT:

7	serva] salva S
9–10	B: «linquere noli ne peream Christo» has been written in a small size above the original, but slightly earlier. Moreover, where the copyist originally wrote «relinquere», the addition has «linquere»

READINGS EMENDED IN THE EDITION:

BAR	VOICE	ORIGINAL
35/I	A	*g*, corrected according to MilD 1

MUSICAL CONCORDANCES (MSS): • MilD 1 (114*v*–115*r*), «Gaspar»

MUSICAL CONCORDANCES (PRINTS): • PeMotA1502 (50*v*–51*r*), «Gaspar» • PeMotA1505 (50*v*–51*r*), «Gaspar»

TEXT FROM BONVESIN DE LA RIVA, p. 63 (ll. 339–344):[1]

Mater ave Cristi, sanctissima Virgo Maria,
partu post partum, sicut et ante, manens.
Virgo, que Cristum peperisti, lacte educasti,
me rege, me serva, me tueare potens.
5   Me tibi commendo, me, Virgo, relinquere noli.
Ne peream, Cristo funde, Maria, preces.

---

[1]. With slight differences from the text in Panc.27.

MODERN EDITIONS OF THE MUSIC: BANKS 1993, II, pp. 56-58 (after Panc.27); DRAKE 1972, II, pp. 121-122 (after PeMotA1502); TINTORI 1963, pp. 1-3 (after MilD 1).

REMARKS: (See also the Remarks to no. 60.) Although it is certainly earlier, the version of MilD 1 cannot be the model for the scribe of Panc.27: too many graphic variants separate the two sources, and MilD 1's correct version of bar 35/I in the Altus (c') further demonstrates its distance from Panc.27. It is interesting to compare the version in PeMotA 1502 and its reprint, which are substantially identical with that of Panc.27; there is a single important variant in the placement of the Altus clef (tenor in PeMotA1502 and its reprint, alto in Panc.27). The same amount of text is found in both sources, and it is highly probable that the scribe of Panc.27 copied from the print (and not vice versa), since the manuscript was certainly written after the date of the publication of *Motetti A* (9 May 1502). The conjunctive error of the Altus in bar 35/I creates a clear link between the two sources: the copyist transposed the entire Altus part (because he used a different clef), faithfully transcribing Petrucci's error.

BIBLIOGRAPHY: BANKS 1993, I, p. 270; BOORMAN 2006, p. 897; BROWN 1990, p. 755; DRAKE 1972, I, pp. 77, 140, 285-289; FILOCAMO 2004; GASSER 1999, pp. 216, 218; RIFKIN 2003, p. 311, n. 155.

99.
Christi mater, ave
fols. 67*v*–68*r*

Gaspar [van Weerbeke]

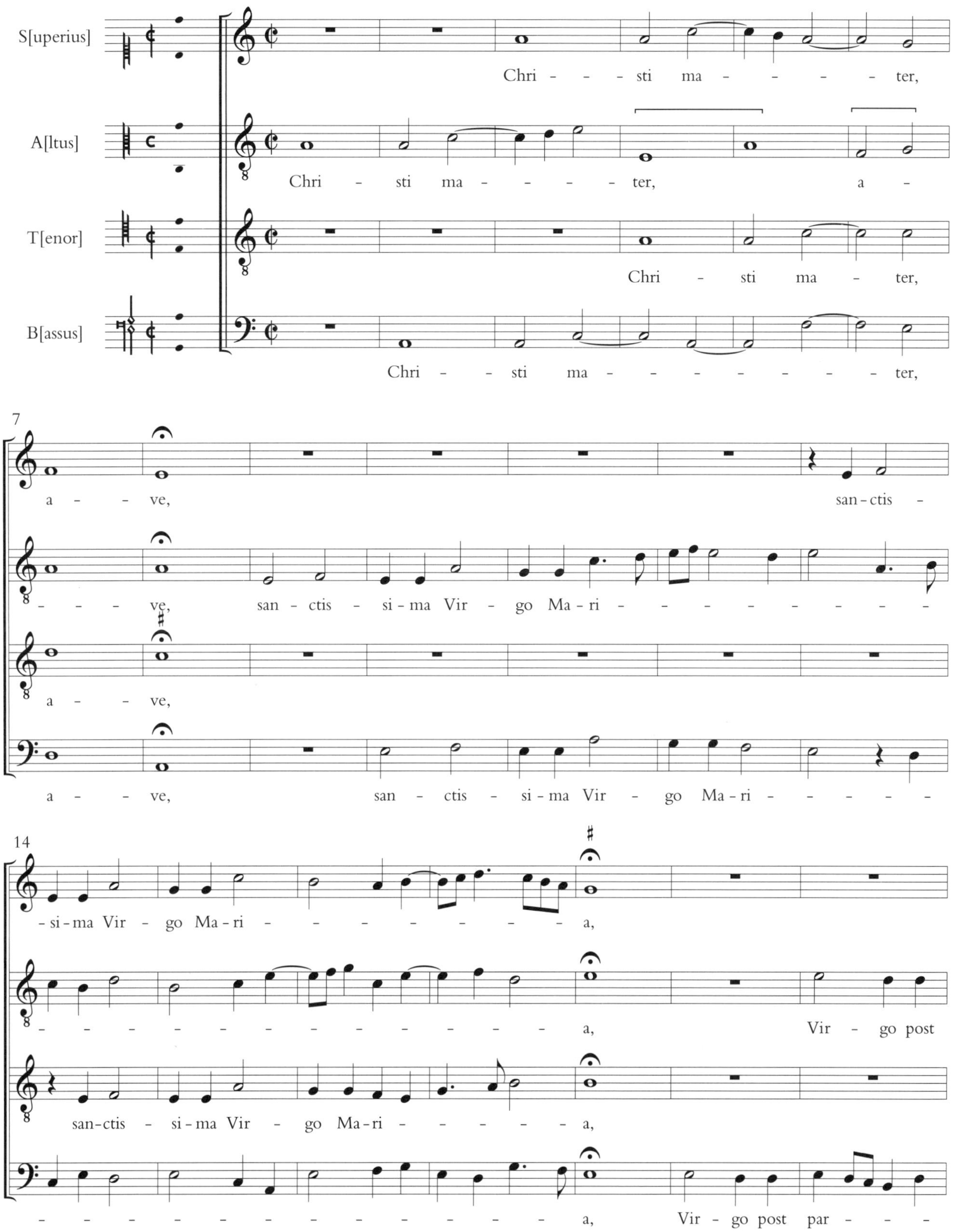

21
Vir -
par - - - - tum, si - cut et an - te, ma - nens.
Vir - go que Chri -
- - tum, si - cut et an - te, ma - - - - - nens.
28
- go que Chri - stum pe - pe - ri - sti, la - cte e - du - ca - sti, me
la - cte e - du - ca - sti, me re - - - - ge, me ser - -
- stum pe - pe - ri - sti, la - cte e - du - ca - sti, me re - ge, me
la - cte e - du - ca - sti, me re - ge, me ser - va, me
35
re - ge, me ser - va, me tu - e - a - re po - tens, me ti - bi com - men - do,
- va, me tu - e - a - re po - - - tens, me ti - bi com - men - do,
ser - va, me tu - e - a - re po - - - tens, me ti - bi com - men - do,
tu - e - a - re po - - - - - - - - - tens, me ti - bi com - men - do,

me, Vir-go, lin - - que - re no - - li; ne pe - re-am, Chri - sto

me, Vir-go, lin - - que - re no - - li; ne pe - re-am, Chri-sto

me, Vir-go, lin - - que - re no - - li; ne pe - re-am, Chri - sto

me, Vir-go, lin - - que - re no - - li; ne pe - re-am, Chri - sto

fun - de, Ma - ri - a, pre - - - - - - ces.

fun - de, Ma - ri - a, pre - - - - - - ces.

fun - de, Ma - ri - - a, pre - - - - - ces.

fun - de, Ma - ri - a, pre - - - - - ces.

14
18
68

100.

TRISTA È LA SORTE DI CHI SERVE AL VENTO

fols. 68*v*–69*r* (4 vv.)

Trista è la sorte di chi serve al vento
e chi se pasce de speranza incerta.

Italian secular piece (strambotto toscano).

TEXT FROM MilT 55:[1]

Trista è la sorte de chi serve al vento
e chi se passe de speranza incerti.
Chi prova el sa che de fatica et stento
se porta ingratitudine per merti.
5   Non iova esser fidel, eser atento,
et nostri dolzi zorni andar deserti,
che senza colpa, et sol per fantaxia,
in un momento al ben servir se oblia.

---

[1]. At fols. 52*v*–53*r* the musical MS MilT 55 contains a strambotto that is not concordant with the version in Panc.27. The text, however, quite possibly is the same in both manuscripts. The text of MilT 55 has been edited in GIAZOTTO 1959, p. 89 and in JEPPESEN 1970, p. 157.

100.
TRISTA È LA SORTE DI CHI SERVE AL VENTO
fols. 68v–69r

25
e chi se pa - - - - - - sce de spe -
chi se pa - - - - - - sce de
chi se pa - - - - - - sce de spe - ran -
chi se pa - - - - sce de spe - ran - -
33
- ran - - - - - - - za in - cer - - - - - - - ta.
spe - ran - - - - za in - cer - - - - - - - ta.
- - - - - - - - za in - cer - - - - - - - ta.
- - - - - - - - za in - cer - - - - - - - ta.

101.

Piange Pisa

fols. 68v–69r (4 vv.)

Piange Pisa

Italian secular piece.

READINGS EMENDED IN THE EDITION:

BAR	VOICE	ORIGINAL
9	S	the sharp sign appears under the first *c'*, in a hand different from that of scribe A. The sharp is then followed by another indication (perhaps «AT»?)
12	S	the sharp sign appears under the first *c'* in the same hand that added it at bar 9

MODERN EDITIONS OF THE MUSIC: JEPPESEN 1969, pp. 323-324 (after Panc.27).

REMARKS: This competent composition is written in the space left over on the opening (the last two staves of each page). Even if written with the same type of ink used for the piece just above (no. 100), the greater elegance of the script demonstrates that *Piange Pisa* was added later. The reference to the city of Pisa in the incipit of this piece and in the name given to the musician is one of the motives that has led in the past to the mistaken assumption that Panc.27 was a source compiled in Tuscany.

BIBLIOGRAPHY: JEPPESEN 1969, pp. 37-39.

101.
PIANGE PISA

fols. 68v–69r

Bar[tholomeus?] Pisanus

Piange Pisa

102.

Stella celi extirpavit

fols. 69*v*–70*r* (4 vv.)

Stella celi extirpavit,
que lactavit Dominum,
pestem quam plantavit
primus parens hominum.

5   Ipsa stella nunc dignetur
sidera compescere,
quorum bella plebem scindunt
dire mortis ulcere.

Rhymed votive antiphon in honour of the Blessed Virgin Mary, sung in time of plague (AH 31, pp. 210-211).

Commentary on the text:

3   the word 'mortis' is lacking before «pestem»

Readings emended in the edition:

Bar	Voice	Original
21	B	a flat before *F* appears to have been added later

Musical concordances (prints): • PeMotA1502 (41*v*–42*r*) • PeMotA1505 (41*v*–42*r*)

Text from AH 31, pp. 210-211 (*Ad BMV, tempore pestilentiae*):

Stella caeli exstirpavit,
quae lactavit Dominum,
mortis pestem, quam plantavit
primus parens hominum.

5   Ipsa stella nunc dignetur
sidera compescere,
quorum bella plebem caedunt
diro mortis ulcere.

Virga Iesse germinavit
10   florem veri luminis,
quem benigne ros rigavit
septiformis spiritus.

Ipsa virgo nunc compescat
daemonum insidias,
15   ut in nobis nunc virescat
laus et omnis bonitas.

Mater Dei amicta sole,
luna tui pedibus
subest, nunc a cladis mole
20   serva nos in aedibus.

Ipsa mater deprecetur
filium piissimum,
ut viventes hunc laudemus,
patrem et paraclitum.

MODERN EDITIONS OF THE MUSIC: BANKS 1993, II, pp. 181–183 (after Panc.27); DRAKE 1972, II, pp. 97–99 (after PeMotA1502); SHERR 1991, pp. 67-73 (after PeMotA1502).

REMARKS: The collation with PeMotA1502 (and its reprint) is extremely interesting for two contrasting reasons. On the one hand, the notable graphic differences in the Tenor discourage the hypothesis of a direct copying from PeMotA1502 (or its reprint): in the print it is written in the tenor clef, it has eight ligatures absent in Panc.27, and a *longa* in place of two *breves*. On the other hand, there is only a single variant in the Superius: in bar 18/I-II the version of Panc.27 correctly gives an *e′ semibrevis*, whereas Petrucci mistakenly has *d′*. I think, however, that the scribe of Panc.27 first copied *d′*: next to the *e′* one can in fact see an erasure corresponding to the *d′*. It is possible, therefore, that after copying from the model the scribe realized and then corrected the error. In addition to the numbers placed at the end of each voice, under the last stave of fol. 70*v*, to the right, appear in column format the numbers '144' and '3': they apply respectively to the number of *semibreves* of the Superius, Tenor, and Bassus, excluding the final *longa*, and to the difference in *semibreves* between the comprehensive number in the Altus and that in the other voices. Is it perhaps an indication of compositional planning on the part of Scribe A, who may have had in mind to reuse the music?

BIBLIOGRAPHY: BANKS 1993, I, p. 290; BOORMAN 2006, p. 947; BROWN 1990, pp. 752, 755, n. 38; CHEVALIER II, no. 19438; DRAKE 1972, I, pp. 74, 128, 174, 175, 217–221; FILOCAMO 2004.

102.
STELLA CELI EXTIRPAVIT
fols. *69v–70r*

pe - stem quam plan - ta - vit

pri - mus pa - rens ho - - - mi -

- num. I - psa stel - - - la nunc di - - - gne -

41
- tur si - de - ra com - pe -
48
- - - sce - re, quo - rum bel - - - - - la
55
ple - - - - bem scin - - - dunt di -

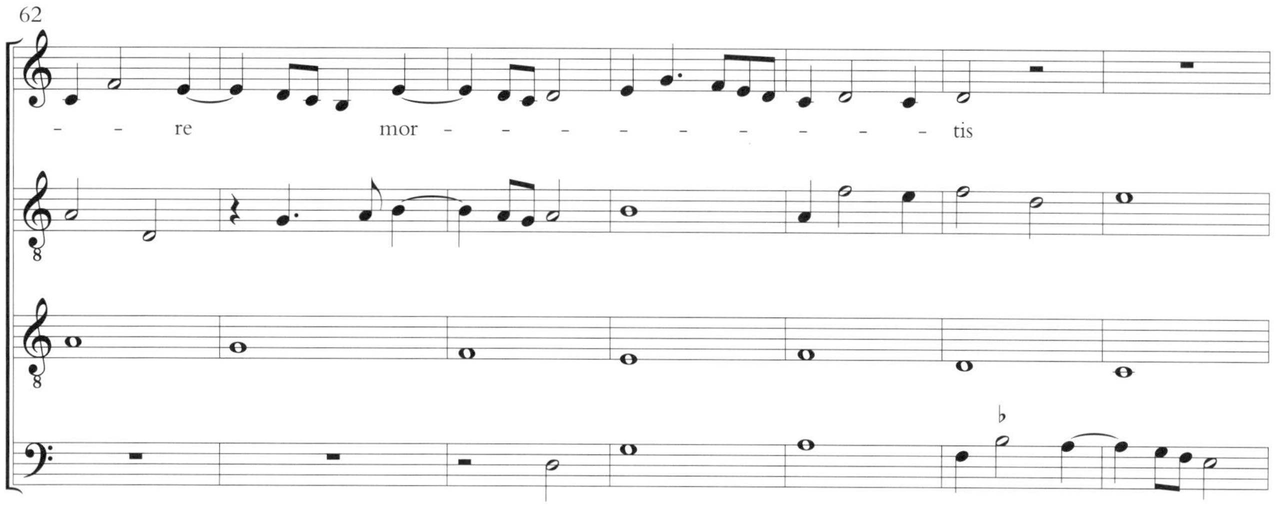
62
– – re mor – – – – – – – – – – tis

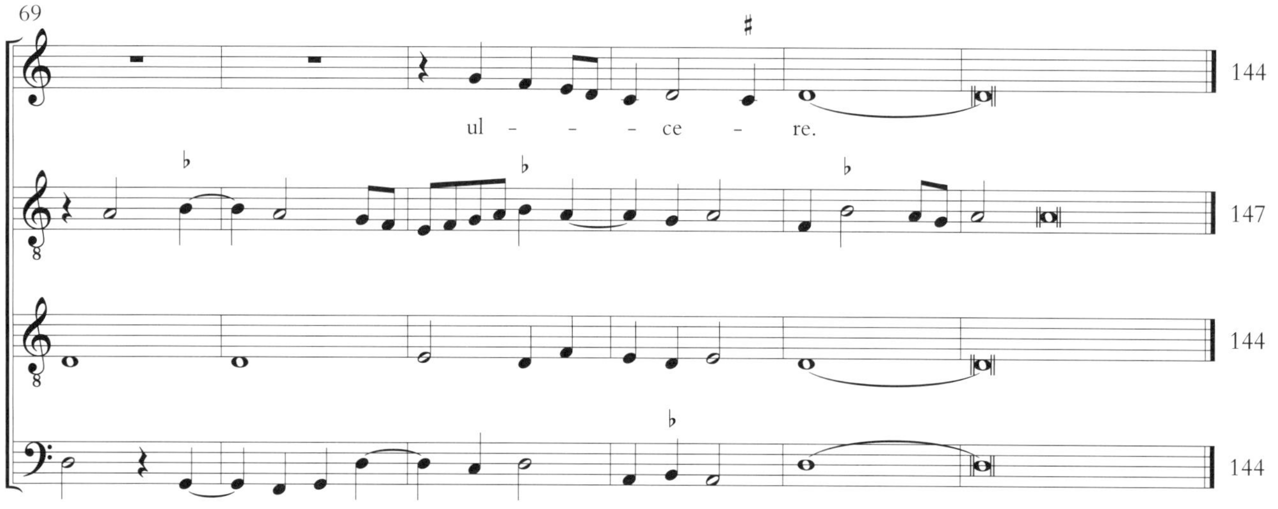
69
ul – – – ce – re.
144
147
144
144

103.

ADONAI, [SANCTISSIME DOMINE]

fols. 70*v*-71*r* (4 vv.)

GASPAR [VAN WEERBEKE]

Adonai

Non-liturgical penitential prayer based in part on Judith 16:16 («Adonai Domine magnus es tu et praeclarus in virtute et quem superare nemo potest», VULGATA, p. 710), on Esther 13:17 («exaudi deprecationem meam et propitius esto sorti et funiculo tuo | et converte luctum nostrum in gaudium | ut viventes laudemus nomen tuum Domine | et non claudas ora te canentium», VULGATA, p. 726), on the Magnificat antiphon at Vespers and Matins responsory *Adonai Domine*, Saturday before the fourth Sunday in September (AM, pp. 586-587, AR, p. 549, GR, pp. 74-75, LR, p. 424, and LU, p. 993: «Adonai Domine Deus»), Matins responsory on the fourth Sunday in September (LR, p. 424), and on the antiphon *Iuxta/Inter vestibulum* for the blessing of the ashes on Ash Wednesday (MR, p. 66: «Iuxta vestibulum et altare plorabunt sacerdotes ministri domini, et dicent: parce domine, parce populo tuo: et ne dissipes ora canentium domine»;[1] LU, pp. 523-524: «et ne dissipes ora clamantium ad te, Domine»).[2] See also AMS, p. 253.

MUSICAL CONCORDANCES (MSS): • SGS 463 (no. 104), *Adonaÿ sanctissime Domine*, 2 vv. (S and A only), «Gaspar», «Hÿpodorius, idest secundus tonus» • SGS 530 (82*v*-84*r*), *Adonay sanctissime*, «Gaspar»,

MUSICAL CONCORDANCES (PRINTS): • PeMotA1502 (15*v*-16*r*), *Adonay sanctissime Domine*, «Gaspar» • PeMotA1505 (15*v*-16*r*), *Adonay sanctissime Domine*, «Gaspar»

TEXT FROM PeMotA1502:

> Adonai, sanctissime Domine,
> Deus omnipotens,
> exaudi preces servorum tuorum
> et da nobis locum penitentiae
> 5   et ne claudas ora canentium te Domine.

MODERN EDITIONS OF THE TEXT: DRAKE 1972, I, p. 275 (after PeMotA1502).

MODERN EDITIONS OF THE MUSIC: BANKS 1993, II, pp. 3-5 (after Panc.27); DRAKE 1972, II, pp. 38-41 (after PeMotA1502); LOACH 1969, II, pp. 156-159 (after SGS 463, with T and B after PeMotA1502); SHERR 1991, pp. 21-26 (after PeMotA1502); SM 8, pp. 204-205 (after SGS 530).

REMARKS: PeMotA1502 (with its reprint) is the only one of the three concordant sources that is

---

[1]. In the *Missale Romanum ex decreto sacrosancti Concilii Tridentini restitutum [...]*, Venice, Nicola Pezzana, 1690, p. 45: «Inter vestibulum et altare plorabunt sacerdotes ministri domini, et dicent: parce domine, parce populo tuo: et ne claudas ora canentium te domine».

[2]. Clearly Weerbeke's text is not any of these liturgical sources. Such a compilation of various biblical sources sounds very much like the Milanese *motetti missales* texts, yet this piece does not appear there. Perhaps it was Weerbeke who started the tradition? I thank Bonnie Blackburn for having suggested this hypothesis.

closely related to the version in Panc.27 (SGS 463 is a later source in partbooks, many of whose compositions have been taken from Petrucci prints, while SGS 530 is a keyboard intabulation). Collation with *Motetti A* shows that Panc.27 is substantially identical with the print; the only differences are the following: a change of clef in *Motetti A* Superius (from b. 56/II to the end); a tenor clef for the Altus (alto clef in Panc.27); and the lack of a precautionary B flat at bar 9/II in the Bassus (which may have been added later in Panc.27). That Panc.27 was copied from *Motetti A* is shown not only by the presence of the complete text in the print, but also from the publication date of PeMotA1502 and its 1505 reprint, probably earlier than that of the copying of the manuscript.

BIBLIOGRAPHY: AMS, p. 253; BANKS 1993, I, p. 262; BOORMAN 2006, p. 886; BROWN 1990, p. 755, n. 36 and n. 39; DRAKE 1972, I, pp. 67, 175, 193, 275-276; FILOCAMO 2004; LOACH 1969, I, p. 306; SM 8, p. 355.

103.
ADONAI, [SANCTISSIME DOMINE]

fols. *70v–71r*

Gaspar [van Weerbeke]

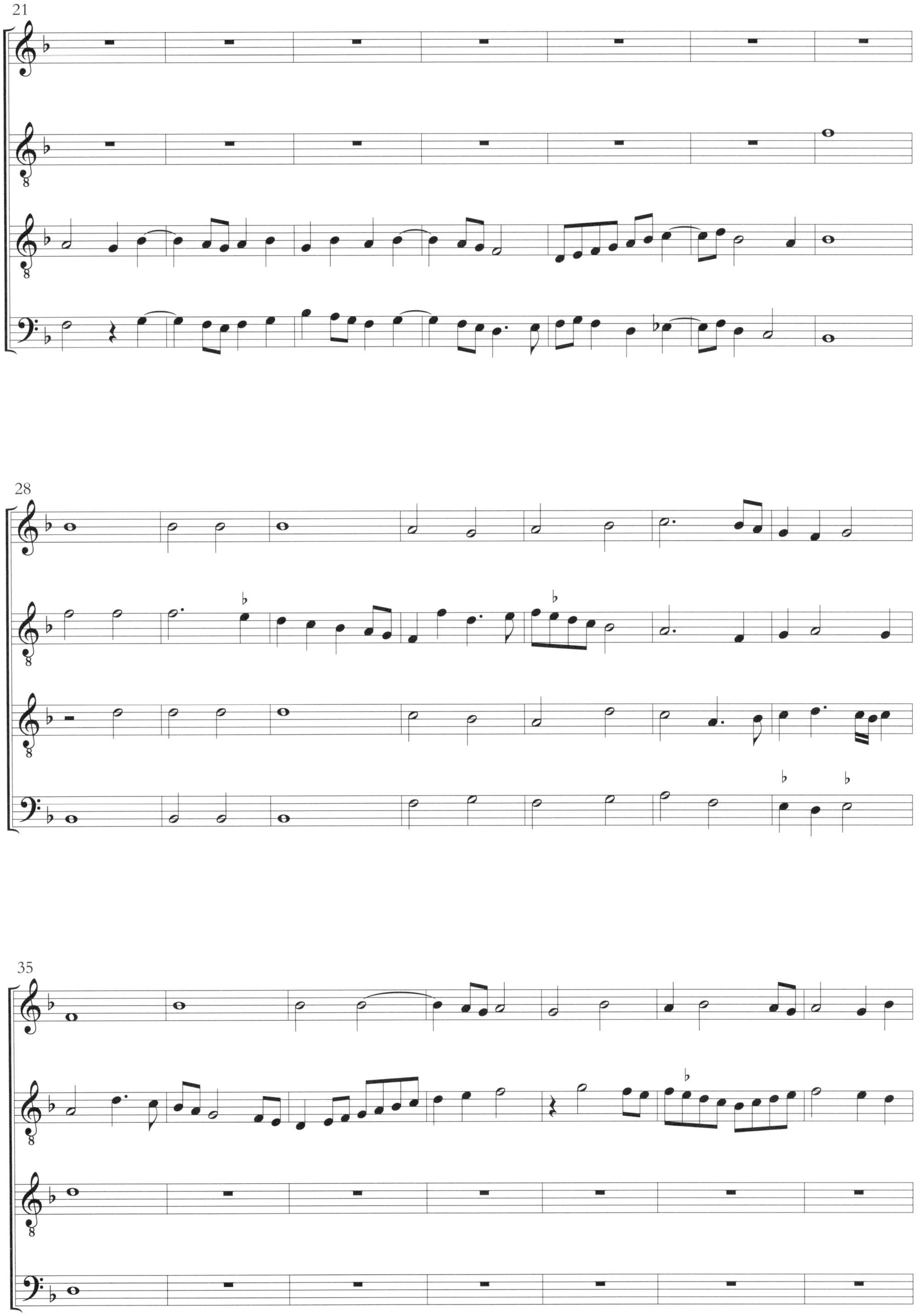
21
28
35

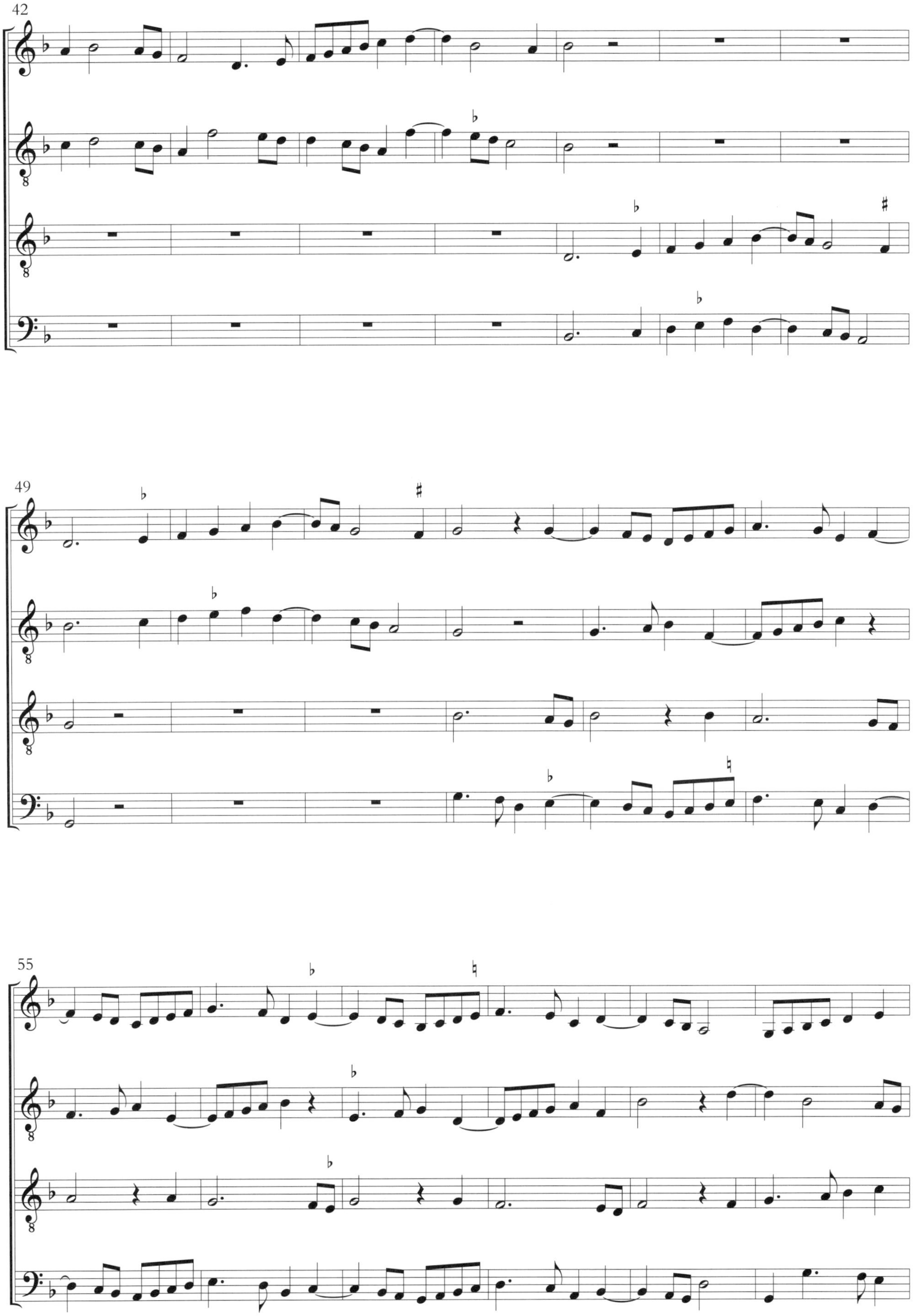
42
49
55

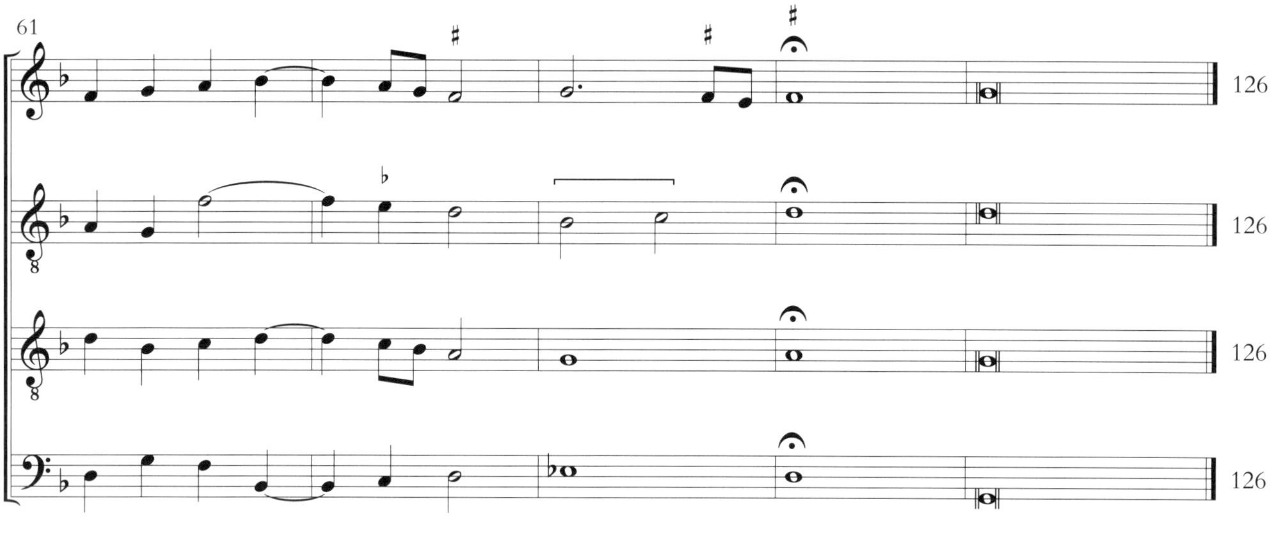
61
126
126
126
126

104.

Tristitia vestra convertetur in gaudium

fols. 71*v*-72*r* (4 vv.)

Renaldo

Tristitia vestra convertetur in gaudium, alleluia.
Mundus autem gaudebit, vos vero contristabimini,
sed tristitia vestra convertetur in gaudium, alleluia, alleluia.

Based on John 16:20 («amen amen dico vobis | quia plorabitis et flebitis vos | mundus autem gaudebit | vos autem contristabimini | sed tristitia vestra vertetur in gaudium», Vulgata, p. 1688). Used, for example, as eighth responsory for the third Sunday after Easter (BR, p. 392), and as the second responsory of first Nocturns for the feast of Apostles and Martyrs in Paschaltide (BR [*Commune Sanctorum*], p. 18; LR, pp. 165-166). See also CAO IV, p. 437 and IGC, p. 419.

Modern edition of the text: CAO IV, p. 437.

Modern editions of the music: Banks 1993, II, pp. 192-194 (after Panc.27).

Remarks: The necessary added notes in bar 33 of the Bassus suggest that the scribe mistakenly copied from his model, omitting at this point the repetition of the previous motif (b. 32) a step higher.[1]

Bibliography: Banks 1993, I, p. 291; CAO IV, p. 437; CS, p. 480; Filocamo 2004; IGC, p. 419.

---

[1]. I thank Bonnie Blackburn for having suggested this emendation.

104.

TRISTITIA VESTRA CONVERTETUR IN GAUDIUM

fols. 71*v*-72*r*

Renaldo

22
-tur in gau - di - um, al - le - lu - - ia. Mun - dus au - tem
-tur in gau - di - um, al - le - lu - - ia, al - le - lu - ia. Mun - dus au - tem
-tur in gau - di - um, al - le - - - lu - ia. Mun - dus au - tem
-tur in gau - di - um, al - le - lu - ia, al - le - lu - ia. Mun - dus au - tem
30
gau - de - bit, vos ve - ro con - tri - sta-bi-mi - ni,
gau - de - bit, vos ve - ro con - tri - sta - - - bi-mi - ni,
gau - de - bit, vos ve - ro con - tri-sta - bi - mi - ni,
gau - de - bit, vos ve - ro con - tri-sta - bi - mi - ni,
38
sed tri - sti - ti - a
con - tri-sta - bi - mi - ni, sed tri - sti - ti - a ve - stra
sed tri - sti - ti - a ve - stra
con - tri-sta - - - - bi - mi - ni, sed tri - sti - ti - a

45
ve - - - - - - stra
con-ver-te-tur in gau -
con - ver - te-tur in gau-di - - - - - -
con-ver - te-tur in gau - di - - - - - -
ve - - - - - - - stra
51
- di - um,
al-le - lu-
- - um,
al-le-lu -
- - um,
con - ver - te-tur in gau - di - um,
al - le-lu - - -
con - ver - te - tur in gau - di - um,
al - le - lu - ia,
58
- ia, al - le-lu - ia, al - le - lu-ia, al - le - lu - ia.
- ia, al-le - - - lu - ia, al-le-lu - ia, al-le-lu - - - - ia.
- ia, al-le - - - lu - ia, al - le-lu - ia, al-le - lu - - - ia.
al - le - lu - ia, al - le - lu - ia, al - le - lu - - - ia.
75
52

105.

Meskim [es u cutkin ru?]

fol. 72*v* (3 vv.)

[Jacob Obrecht]

Meskim

Flemish song.

Readings emended in the edition:

Bar	Voice	Original
30	C	*longa* with fermata

Musical concordances (mss): • FirN BR229 (179*v*-180*r*), 4 vv., textless, «Jacobus Obrech» • FirN M178 (76*v*-77*r*), *Adiu adiu*, 4 vv., «Jacobi Obret» • SegC (134*v*), S Ct B: *Meiskin es u cutkin ru*, T: *Wat heb dier mo te doene*,[1] 4 vv., «Jacobus Hobrecht» • SGS 463; index only: *Meskim* • SGS 530 (84*r*), *Messkin es hu*

Musical concordances (prints):[2] • PeOdh1503 (103*v*), *Meskin es hu*, 4 vv. • PeOdh1504 (103*v*), *Meskin es hu*, 4 vv.

Text from NOE 17, p. 36:

    Meiskin es u cutkin ru?
    Wat heb dier me te doene?
    Laetet mi tasten dat bid ic u.
    O bid' tot morghen tnoene.
5   Jeso ruaer,
    jeso daschaer
    ist afternaer.
    O bid' tot morghen tnoene.

Modern editions of the text: Blackburn 1981b, p. 143 (after FirN M121); Brown 1983, I, p. 278 (after FirN M121); NOE 17, p. 36 (after SegC and FirN M121).

Modern editions of the music: Ambros V, pp. 34-35 (after FirN BR229); Brown 1983, II, pp. 383-384 (after FirN BR229); Hewitt 1942, p. 421 (after PeOdh1504); NOE 17, pp. 35-36 (a conflation of all the vocal sources); NOE 18, pp. 68-69 (after SGS 530); SM 8, pp. 206-207 (after SGS 530); Wolf O/7, pp. 1-2 (after PeOdh1504), 78-79 (after SGS 530).

Remarks: Panc.27 is the only source that transmits the piece with three voices: the Tenor of Panc.27 combines the melodic phrases that alternate between the Altus and Tenor in the version for four voices. The version of FirN M178, both text and music, is quite different from the others.

---

[1]. This is the second line of this Flemish song.
[2]. In PeOdh1501 the folio that would have contained the piece is lacking.

BIBLIOGRAPHY: BAKER 1978, I, p. 393; BLACKBURN 1981b, pp. 141-148; BONDA 1996, p. xxxix, pp. 42, 190; BOORMAN 2006, p. 1072; BROWN 1983, I, pp. 278-279; FALLOWS 1999, p. 292; FILOCAMO 2004; HEWITT 1942, p. 167; JICKELI 1994, p. 173; LAMA DE LA CRUZ 1994, p. 223; NOE 17, pp. xxxviii-xxxix; POWERS 1994, pp. 597-598; REESE 1990, pp. 199-200; SM 8, p. 355; WEGMAN 1994, p. 157.

105.
MESKIM [ES U CUTKIN RU?]
fol. 72v

[Jacob Obrecht]

106.

Q‍UEMADMODUM DESIDERAT CERVUS

fol. 73*r* (3 vv.)

Quemadmodum desiderat cervus ad fontes aquarum,
ita desiderat anima mea ad te, Deus.

Psalm 41:2 (V‍ULGATA, p. 492). The whole psalm is used, for example, on Tuesday at Sext (AR, pp. 116-117; BR, p. 45), at Matins of the Office of the Dead (AR, p. [170]) and at the second Nocturn of Matins of Corpus Christi (LU, pp. 930-931).[1] See also IGC, p. 344.

T‍EXT FROM V‍ULGATA, pp. 492-493 (*Liber Psalmorum*, XLI, 2-13):

I‍N FINEM IN INTELLECTUM FILIIS CORE

2.   Quemadmodum desiderat cervus ad fontes aquarum
     ita desiderat anima mea ad te Deus

3.   sitivit anima mea ad Deum fortem vivum
     quando veniam et parebo ante faciem Dei

4.   fuerunt mihi lacrimae meae panis die ac nocte
     dum dicitur mihi cotidie ubi est Deus tuus

5.   haec recordatus sum et effudi in me animam meam
     quoniam transibo in loco tabernaculi admirabilis usque ad domum Dei
     in voce exsultationis et confessionis sonus epulantis

6.   quare tristis es anima mea et quare conturbas me
     spera in Deo quoniam confitebor illi
     salutare vultus mei

7.   Deus meus
     ad me ipsum anima mea conturbata est
     propterea memor ero tui
     de terra Iordanis et Hermoniim a monte modico

8.   Abyssus ad abyssum invocat
     in voce cataractarum tuarum
     omnia excelsa tua et fluctus tui super me transierunt

9.   in die mandavit Dominus misericordiam suam
     et nocte canticum eius
     apud me oratio Deo vitae meae

10. dicam Deo susceptor meus es quare oblitus es mei
     quare contristatus incedo
     dum adfligit me inimicus

---

[1]. The text in the version *Sicut cervus desiderat ad fontes aquarum* could have been used, according to the Sarum tradition (preceding the Council of Trent), as an alternative Tract for the Requiem Mass.

11.   dum confringuntur ossa mea exprobraverunt mihi qui tribulant me
         dum dicunt mihi per singulos dies ubi est Deus tuus

12.   quare tristis es anima mea et quare conturbas me
         spera in Deum quoniam adhuc confitebor illi
         salutare vultus mei et Deus meus

MODERN EDITIONS OF THE MUSIC: BANKS 1993, II, pp. 157-158 (after Panc.27).

REMARKS: The craftsmanship of the piece, rich in imitation, indicates that we are probably in the presence of a master musician. The text contrasts with the musical style: might this be a contrafact of an instrumental piece or a section of a mass?[2]

BIBLIOGRAPHY: BANKS 1993, I, p. 286; CS, p. 118; FILOCAMO 2004; FILOCAMO 2009c; IGC, p. 344.

---

[2]. My thanks to Bonnie Blackburn for this suggestion.

106.
Quemadmodum desiderat cervus
fol. 73*r*

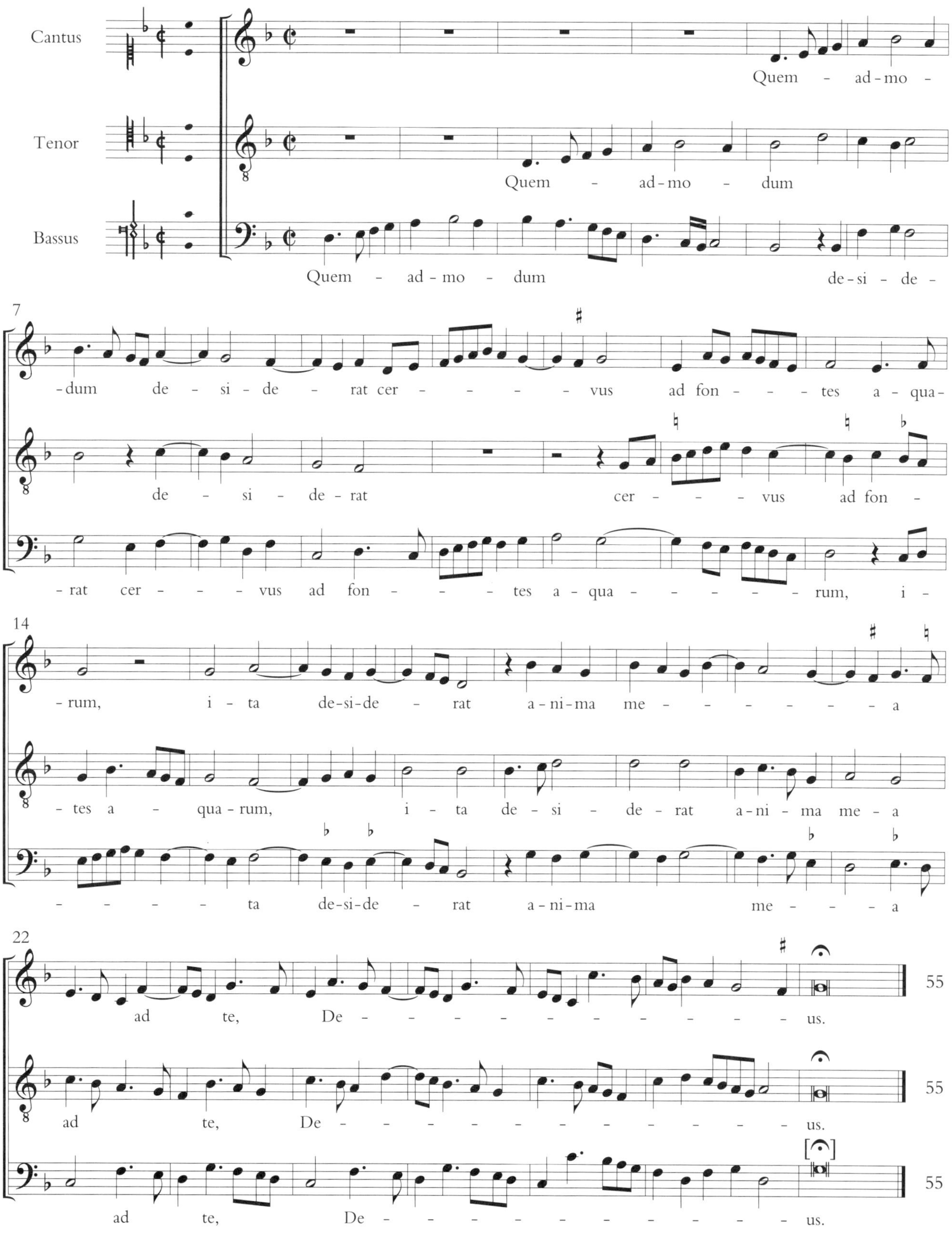

107.

Veni Creator Spiri[tus]

fols. *73v-74r* (3 vv.)

Veni Creator Spiri[tus]

Hymn invoking the Holy Spirit (AM, p. 1254; AR, pp. 73★-74★; GR, pp. 135★-136★). It is used principally on Vespers of Pentecost (AM, pp. 518-519; AR, pp. 500-502; BR, p. 436; LU, pp. 885-886; PM, p. 89). See also CAO IV, p. 520 and IGC, p. 430.

Readings emended in the edition:

Bar	Voice	Original
49	T	the higher alternative note is f'

Text from BR, p. 436 (*In festo Pentecostes. Ad Vesperas. Hymnus*):

Veni Creator Spiritus,
mentes tuorum visita,
imple superna gratia,
quae tu creasti pectora.

5   Qui paraclitus diceris,
donum Dei altissimi,
fons vivus, ignis, charitas,
et spiritalis unctio.

Tu septiformis munere,
10   dextrae Dei tu digitus,
tu rite promissum Patris,
sermone ditans guttura.

Accende lumen sensibus,
infunde amorem cordibus,
15   infirma nostri corporis
virtute firmans perpeti:[1]

Hostem repellas longius,
pacemque dones protinus:
ductore sic te praevio
20   vitemus omne noxium.

Per te sciamus da Patrem,
noscamus, atque Filium,
te utriusque Spiritum
credamus omni tempore.

---

[1]. BR has «perpetim».

25   Gloria Patri Domino,
      natoque, qui a mortuis
      surrexit, ac paraclito,
      in saeculorum saecula.

      Amen.

MODERN EDITIONS OF THE TEXT: AH 2, pp. 93-94; AH 50, pp. 193-194; MONE, I, pp. 241-242.

MODERN EDITIONS OF THE MUSIC: BANKS 1993, II, pp. 196-197 (after Panc.27).

REMARKS: The alternative readings in the final chord of the Tenor are rather unlikely: they exceed the normal ambitus of the voice, and the black notes are reached melodically by an unusual leap. Certainly this passage can be counted among the various less felicitous experiments of Scribe A in Panc.27. The beginning of the chant in AM, p. 1254, AR, pp. 73★-74★, GR, pp. 135★-136★, LU, pp. 885-886, and PM, p. 89 is paraphrased in the Superius and Tenor.

BIBLIOGRAPHY: BANKS 1993, I, pp. 291-292; CAO IV, p. 520; CHEVALIER II, no. 21204; IGC, p. 430; STÄBLEIN 1956, Melody no. 17; WARD 1980, p. 274.

107.
VENI CREATOR SPIRI[TUS]
fols. *73v–74r*

Veni Creator Spiri[tus]

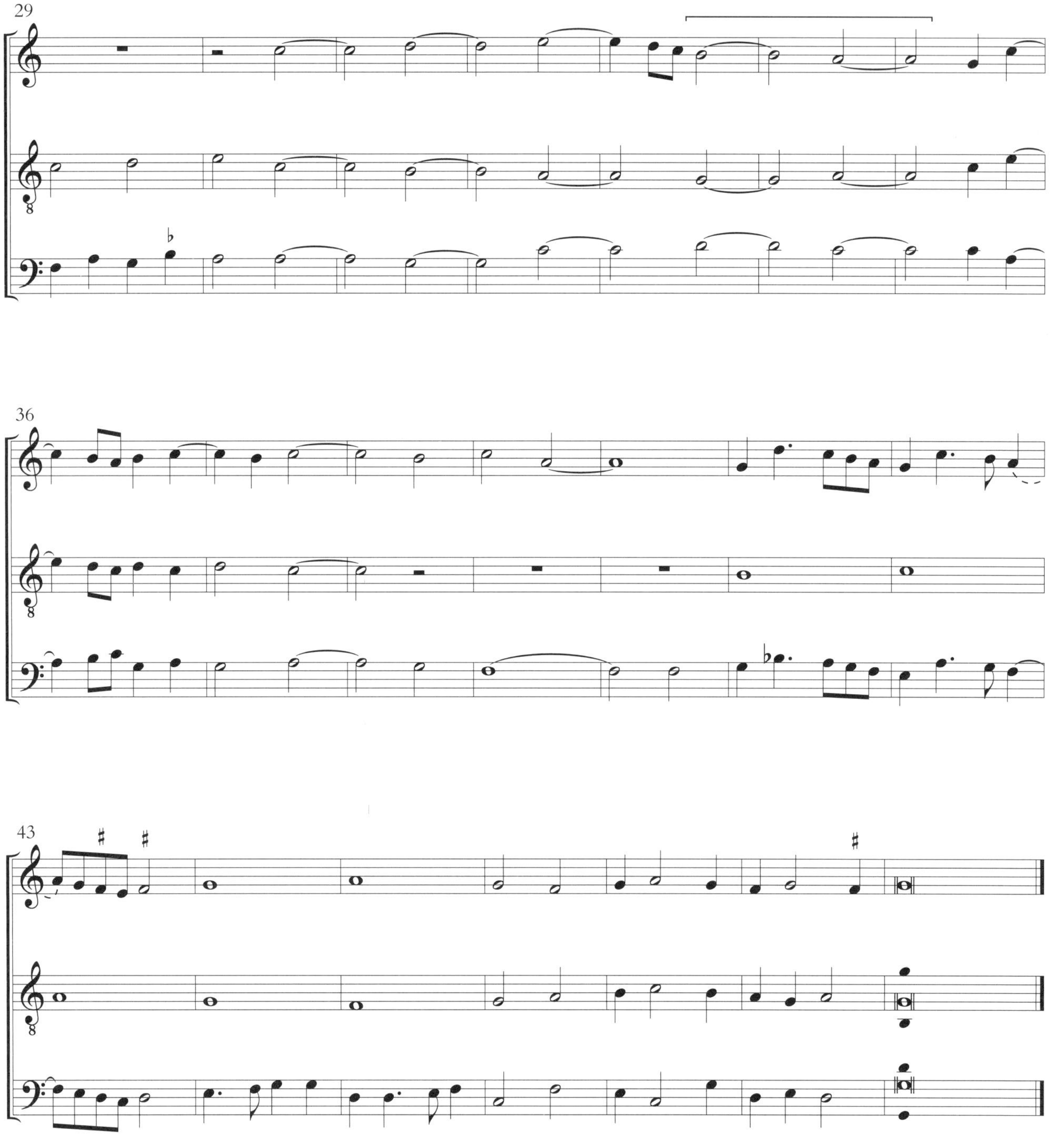
29
36
43

108.

Kyrie eleison

fols. 74v-75r (3 vv.)

Kyrie eleison,
Christe eleison,
Kyrie eleison.

Kyrie of the Ordinary of the Mass. The text is also used as an act of penitence at the beginning of litanies.

Commentary on the text:

1	Kyrie]	Chyrie C; «Chirie» cancelled T; Chirie Ct
1	eleison]	eleyson C
2	eleison]	eleyson C
3	Kyrie]	Chirie C, Ct
3	eleison]	eleyson C

Readings emended in the edition:

Bar	Voice	Original
9/II	C	*g'*
17	T	*longa* with fermata
30/I	T	*a*
35–36	C	*longa* with fermata
36	T	*longa* with fermata
between 36 and 37	C	bar line missing

REMARKS: This Kyrie is completely isolated; positioned between two hymns, it does not even share a liturgical function with them.

BIBLIOGRAPHY: IGC, pp. 249-256.

108.
KYRIE ELEISON
fols. 74v-75r

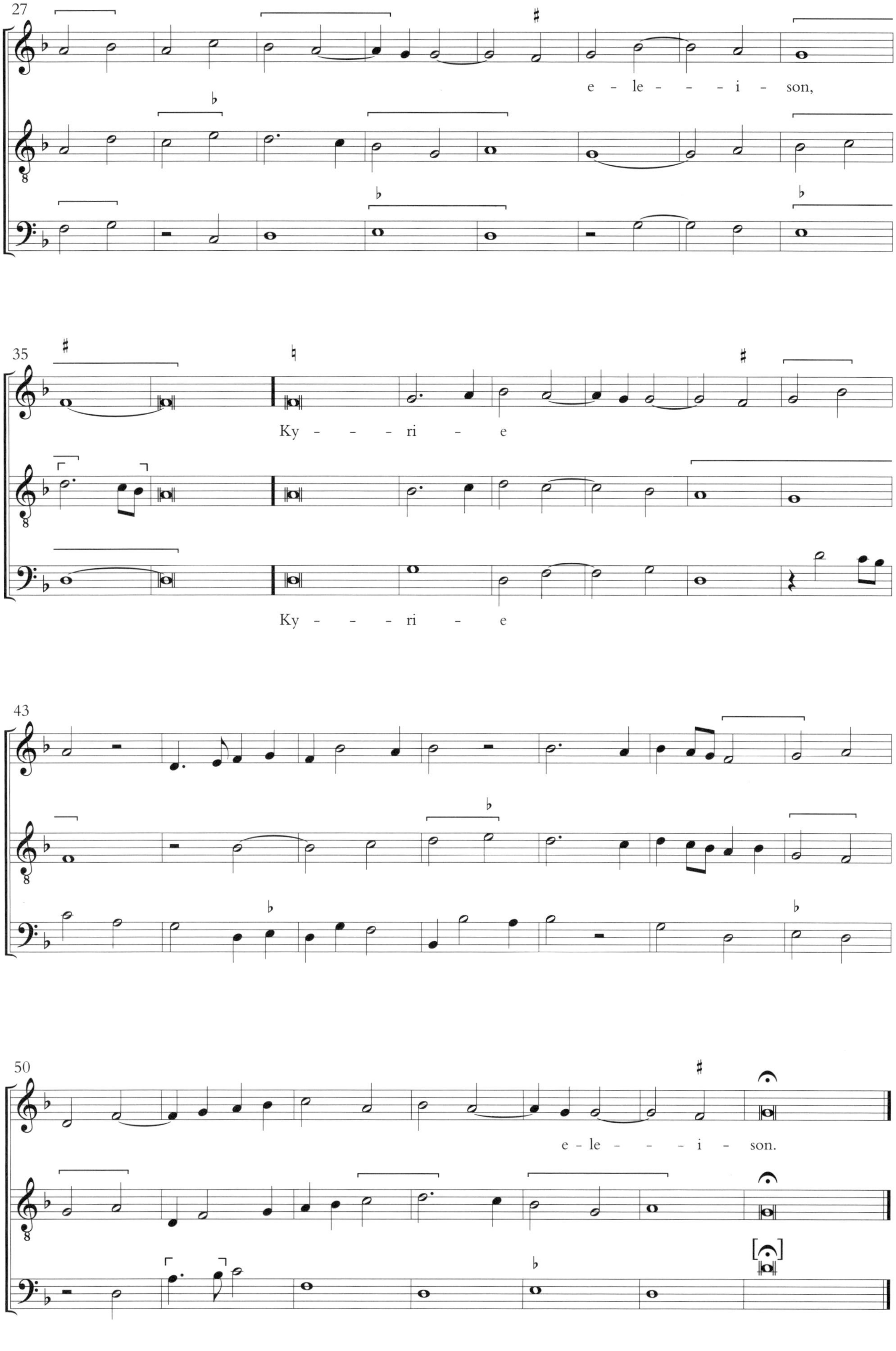
27
e - le - - - i - son,
35
Ky - - - ri - - e
Ky - - - ri - - e
43
50
e - le - - - i - son.

109.

LUCIS CREATOR OPTIME

fols. *75v–76r* (3 vv.)

Lucis Creator optime

For the text see no. 165.[1]

READINGS EMENDED IN THE EDITION:

BAR	VOICE	ORIGINAL
39/II	Ct	*c*
48	S	*longa* with fermata

MODERN EDITIONS OF THE TEXT: See no. 165.

MODERN EDITIONS OF THE MUSIC: BANKS 1993, II, pp. 112-113 (after Panc.27).

REMARKS: Possibly a contrafact of a chanson?[2]

BIBLIOGRAPHY: BANKS 1993, I, p. 279; CHEVALIER II, no. 10691; FILOCAMO 2004; WARD 1980, p. 192.

---

[1]. In AH 37, p. 211, is found the text of the hymn in tercets for St. Lucy, which begins «Lucis creator optime, | Luciae nobilissimae | Splendor mentem illuminans». But since the musical incipit of no. 109 is similar to that of no. 165, which has the standard text for Sunday at Vespers, it is likely that also no. 109 is a setting of the same lines.

[2]. This hypothesis was suggested by Bonnie Blackburn.

109.
LUCIS CREATOR OPTIME
fols. 75v–76r

S[uperius]

Lucis Creator optime

T[enor]

Con[tr]a

Lucis Creator

578

110.

[…]

fol. 76*v* (4 vv.)

Instrumental piece?

Readings emended in the edition:

Bar	Voice	Original
13/I	B	*a* instead of *g*
16/I	B	*a* instead of *g*

Remarks: In the manuscript the repetition sign appears only at the end of bar 17, and it is not clear which section should be repeated: bars 1-17, 18-24, or 12-17? The lack of a text impedes a clear understanding of the musical form, but the solution chosen in the present edition (that is, beginning the repeat at b. 12) creates a balance between the four sections (A: bb. 1-4; B: bb. 5-11; C: bb. 12-17; B: bb. 18-24). The repetition of section C reinforces the contrast with section B, heard before and after.

110.

[...]

fol. 76*v*

111.

Regina celi [letare]

fol. 77r (3 vv.)

[Loyset] Compere

Regina celi

For the text see no. 94.

Readings emended in the edition:

Bar	Voice	Original
12	S	*minim c″*
12/II-13/I	S	insertion according to both concordances

Musical concordances (mss): • BolM 17 (5*v*-6*r*), S and T: *Royne du ciel*, Ct: *Regina celi*, with a slightly different musical incipit, «Prioris»

Musical concordances (prints): • PeOdh1501 (91*r*), S: *Royne du ciel*, Ct: *Regina celi*, «Compere», • PeOdh1503 (91*r*), S: *Royne du ciel*, Ct: *Regina celi*, «Compere» • PeOdh1504 (91*r*), S: *Royne du ciel*, Ct: *Regina celi*, «Compere»

Modern editions of the music: CMM 15/V, p. 7 (after PeOdh1504); CMM 90/III, pp. 124-125 (after BolM 17); Hewitt 1942, pp. 395-396 (after PeOdh1504).

Remarks: The version of the late fifteenth-century manuscript BolM 17 differs from that of Panc.27 in the musical incipit (bb. 1-5 of Panc.27 correspond, extended and slightly modified, to bb. 1-7 of BolM 17), in the attribution (to Prioris), and in the text *Royne du ciel* in the upper voices. Similarly, the passage at bars 40-43/I is significantly different from Panc.27: the Tenor differs rhythmically in bars 40-41/I, and at bar 42/II it has *d* instead of *c′*; the Superius has *g′* instead of *b′* at bar 43/I. The version of *Odhecaton* is related to that in BolM 17 only in the analogous passage in the Tenor of bars 40-43/I and in the presence of the supplementary text *Royne du ciel* (but only in the Superius). The Contra and the Superius — although written in different clef — are substantially identical with Panc.27; the errors in the Superius in bars 12-13/I are attributable to the faulty copying of the scribe, who certainly had a different version of the piece as model. The first phrase of the chant in AM, pp. 179-180, AR, pp. 67-68, LR, pp. 48-49, and LU, pp. 275 and 278 is treated as a rising ostinato in the Contra.

Bibliography: Atlas 1981; Boorman 2006, p. 1066; CAO III, p. 440; CMM 90/III, p. xxi; Fallows 1999, p. 352; Filocamo 2004; Finscher 1964, pp. 211-213; Hewitt 1942, pp. 165, 180; IGC, p. 361; Rothenberg 2006, p. 381.

111.
REGINA CELI [LETARE]
fol. 77r

[Loyset] Compere

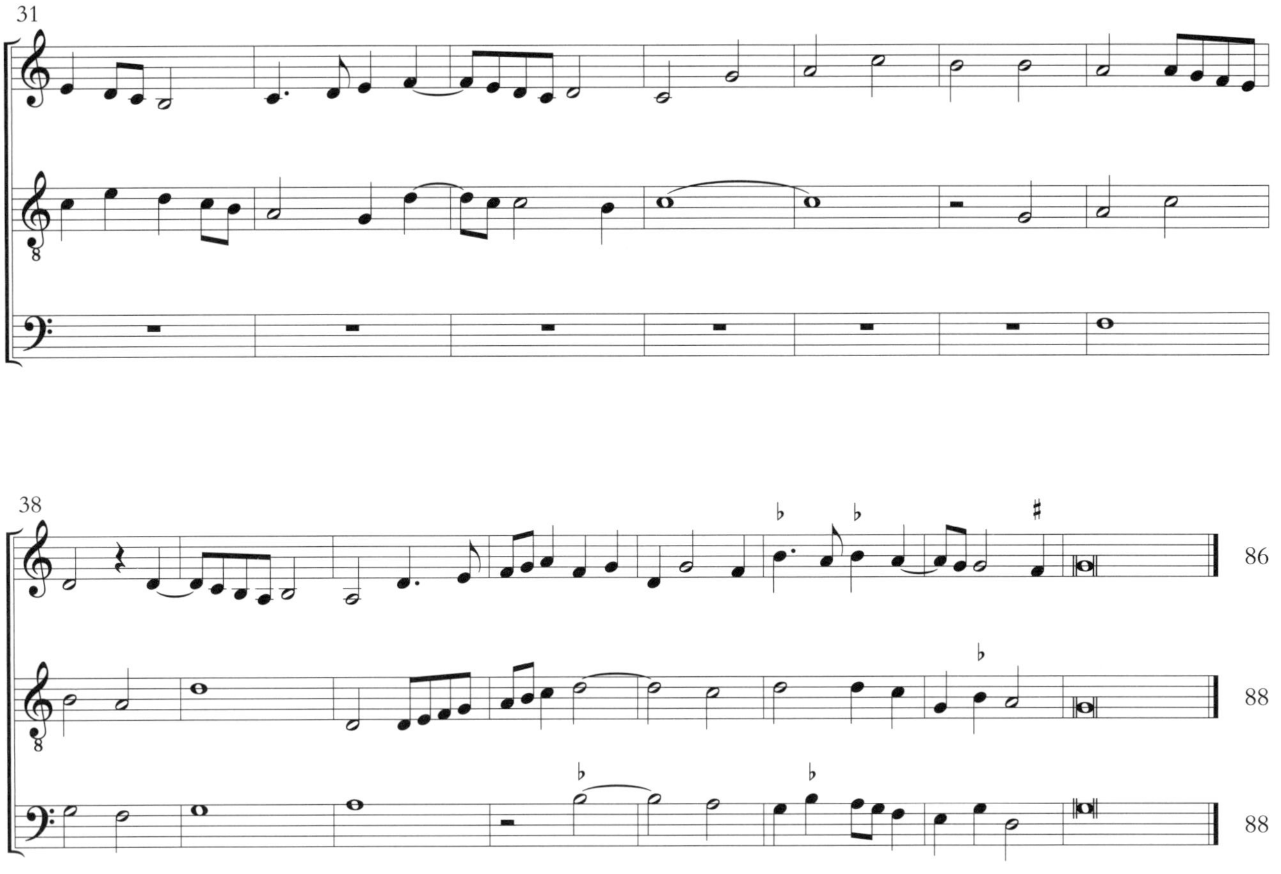
31
38
86
88
88

112.

Miserere al mio perire

fols. *77v–78r* (4 vv.)

Miserere al mio perire,
o Maria, in ciel regina,
prega la bontà divina
che mi facia al ciel venire.

5   Deh, risguarda il peccatore,
tuto alflicto nel peccato:
questo mundo pien de errore
cum tristitia m'ha inganato.
Or ch'io l'ho abandunato
10   vo' emendare el mio errore.
         Miserere al mio perire,
         o Maria, in ciel regina.

A mal passo io sum venuto,
sente nel cor gran tormento,
per mal far io son caduto:
sempre a viver malcontento.
15   Per usir de questo stento
son disposto a Dio servire.

Mai riposo non si trova,
né dilecto in questo mundo.
Ben cognosce chi lo prova,
20   non si pò trovar iocundo,
ma più tosto nel profundo
sta sommerso da martìre.

Sol i[n] Dio, ch'è summo bene,
trovarà leticia vera.
25   Chi vorà finir le pene
in lui solo creda e spera,
abi carità sincera,
se sua voglia vol seguire.

A Maria, cum bon desio,
30   tutti andiam divotamente,
pregarà el so figliol pio:
che conservi nostra mente
dal leone rugiente,
diffenda ne[l] morire.

Amen.

Lauda (barzelletta).

COMMENTARY ON THE TEXT:

4	facia] faci T
6	alflicto] aflito T
10	vo'] voglio S
11	the *residuum* begins here
34	the MS has «moriree»

READINGS EMENDED IN THE EDITION:

BAR	VOICE	ORIGINAL
10	B	*A*
14/I	A	*minimae f′* and *g′*
18/I	A	dotted *semibrevis g′*
25/I	A	*b*
28	A	*semibrevis*
29/I	A	*brevis*
37/I	A	*minimae f′* and *g′*
41/I	A	dotted *semibrevis g′*
after 47	A	an erroneous repetition of bars 25-33 with two variants: coloration (corresponding to 29/I) and a *longa* for the last note
57	A	*brevis* with fermata
57	B	*A*

TEXTUAL CONCORDANCES (PRINTS): • *Fior1505* (p2v-p4v)

REMARKS: This form, a barzelletta, has three musical phrases: A (bb. 1-10) for lines 1-2; B (bb. 11-24) for lines 3-4; C (bb. 25-33, repeated) for lines 5-6 and 7-8. The musical material of the piece ends at this point, since lines 9-10 repeat phrase B (bb. 34-47), and the abbreviated refrain reuses phrase A (bb. 48-57). Although an *unicum*, the piece in Panc.27 has certainly been copied from a model with an Altus that was already problematic, which perhaps ended at bar 33, after the complete exposition of the musical material. The scribe of Panc.27 has probably expanded the original structure, adapting it more closely to the lauda text: the errors present in the manuscript are repeated faithfully from each musical phrase in its repetition (b. 10 → 57; b. 14/I → 37/I; b. 18/I → 41/I), as also happens with the two omissions (b. 5/II → 52/II; b. 22/II → 45/II).[1] It seems likely that the copyist himself devised the lauda contrafact on the basis of a secular model, which can be identified as *Fior1505*: after the concluding «Amen», the text of the *residuum* continues erroneously with the line *Son su passo de la morte*, which is in fact the *incipit* of the following text in *Fior1505*; he then subsequently suspended copying without crossing out the extraneous line, here listed under the following number (see also the Remarks to no. 112bis).[2] This way of working gives credence to the hypothesis that Scribe A was an 'experimenter' who extracted the texts to be set to music from literary sources, as is shown in many entries in this edition.

---

[1]. I thank Fabrizio Ammetto, who discovered the musical errors and corrected them.

[2]. I thank Antonio Rossi for notifying me that *Son su passo de la morte* is the incipit of a different poem, rather than the continuation of the lines of the text of no. 112, as the graphic disposition in Panc.27 would suggest.

112.
MISERERE AL MIO PERIRE
fols. 77v–78r

20
ciel ve-ni - - - - - - - - re. Deh, ri - sguar-da il
que - - - sto mun - do
ciel ve-ni - - - - - - - - re. Deh, ri - sguar-da il
que - - - sto mun - do
27
pec - ca - to - re, tu - to al - flic - to nel pec-ca - to:
pien de er - ro - re cum tri - sti - tia m'ha in - ga-na - to.
pec - ca - to - re, tu - to al - flic - to nel pec-ca - to:
pien de er - ro - re cum tri - sti - tia m'ha in - ga-na - to.
34
Or ch'io l'ho a - ban - du - - - na - - - - - to
Or ch'io l'ho a - ban - du - - - na - - - - - to

40
vo' e - men - da - - re el mio er - ro - - - - - - - - -
vo' e - - - men - da - re el mio er - ro - - - - - - -
47
- re. Mi - se - re - re al mio pe - ri - - - re, o Ma -
- re. Mi - se - re - re al mio pe - ri - - - re, o Ma -
53
- ri - a, in ciel re - gi - - - - na.
- ri - a, in ciel re - gi - - - na.

112bis.

SON SU PASSO DE LA MORTE

fol. 78*r* (text only)

Son su passo de la morte

Lauda (barzelletta).

TEXTUAL CONCORDANCES (PRINTS): • *Fior1505* (p3*r-v*)

TEXT FROM *Fior1505*:

      Son su passo de la morte
      pien de viti e pene amare,
      e mi vego al fin andare
      cum amara e dura sorte.

5   Ben cognosco el falir mio
      e 'l tormento ch'io aspeto
      per le offese fate a Dio.
      Andarò nel so conspeto
      manifesto el mio diffeto
10   fra la celeste corte.

      Quando io risguardo e miro
      el dì extremo, ch'è vicino,
      cum sudor tremo e suspiro,
      del iuditio in me divino,
15   ripensando a quel camino
      al qual convien corer forte.

      Li mie giorni van mancando
      come al sole fa la neve,
      oimè quando vo pensan[d]o
20   quanto è stato el piacer breve,
      parmi più che penna lieve
      chi si fa al mundo consorte.[1]

      Vego che 'l tempo più vola
      che non fa la folia al vento,
25   già la morte m'è a la gola
      che me dà crudel spavento;
      sol mi fano mal contento
      le mie vie che son torte.

      Signor mio, nel morire,
30   al qual so ch'io son vicino,
      dami gratia de pentire

---

[1]. In the source «consorre» instead of 'consorte'.

e drizar el mio camino.
A te, summo ben divino
e del ciel, me apri le porte!

REMARKS: There is no music for this incipit; the copyist has supplied only the first line at the end of the *residuum* of *Miserere al mio perire* (no. 112), probably taken from *Fior1505* (see Remarks to no. 112). In the repertories of *poesia per musica* consulted, the *incipit Son su passo della morte* refers only to GNACCARINI 1909, which lists the printed secular verse that Giosuè Carducci knew. This census, in turn, goes back to the *Rime antiche di su antiche stampe e manoscritti (per nozze Menghini-Zannoni)*, edited by Severino Ferrari (Bologna, Zanichelli, 1893); the publication contains, among other things, the modern edition of the 'tre canzonette' that follow strambotti by Serafino and Giustinian in a printed book preserved at the Biblioteca Universitaria of Bologna (*Strambotti in proposito di ciascuno amatore. Li quali scrisse di sua propria mano il Nobile Missier Leonardo Giustiniano*, Treviso, Girolamo Righettini, 1637, shelfmark: Tab.III.M.II.16). The three canzonette in question, all anonymous, are grouped under the title *Sventurato pellegrino*, and the second of them (fol. A2r) begins «Son sul ponto [*recte*: 'passo'] de la morte»:[2]

Son sul passo[3] de la morte
e d'amarti son contento;
vedo ben, che indarno stento;
così vuol mia dura sorte.
    Son sul passo de la morte
    e d'amarti son contento.

5   Cuor non ho altro che pensi
se no[n] a te, che m'hai disfatto;
aggio perso tutti i sensi,
poi non so come sia fatto;
tanto son di doglia stratto[4]
10   che le membra mi son torte.
    Son sul passo de la morte
    e d'amarti son contento.

Io son gionto a tal partito,
con inganno, e tradimento;
peggio m'è ch'io son schernito,
né mai fece fallimento;
15   or te mostrarò ch'io sento
le mie guance afflitte e smorte.
    Son sul passo de la morte
    e d'amarti son contento.

Ben m'avveggio e sì m'accorgo
che non son quel ch'io soleva;
non ti vedo, non ti scorgo
20   più di fuor come faceva;
questo trato non credeva
mai aver da te sì forte.

---

[2]. After the Remarks, see the complete text taken from the Bolognese print; the poem is present in at least another print, pointed out to me by Antonio Rossi, preserved at the New York Public Library, Spencer Coll. Ital. 151-Giustiniani (*Barzelette del sventurato pellegrino*, no typ. info.).

[3]. «ponto» instead of 'passo'.

[4]. Severino Ferrari corrects «stretto», which is in the source, to 'attratto'. The New York print has «stracio».

Son sul passo de la morte
e d'amarti son contento.

'Sto dolor patir non posso
di morir sì giovinetto:
25   questa morte m'ha constretto
con lo corpo ne lo fosso:
e son sì da dolor mosso
e da iniqua crudel sorte.
        Son sul passo de la morte
        e d'amarti son contento.

Sia con Dio, riman' in pace,[5]
30   ché 'l mi è forza lagrimare:
io mi butto in le tue brazze[6]
ch'io mi sento il cuor mancare:
io non posso più parlare
poiché m'hai chiuse le porte.
        Son sul passo de la morte
        e d'amarti son contento.

Apart from the incipit, the continuation of the text is completely different from that in *Fior1505*, which, in my opinion, was the model from which the copyist of Panc.27 took the line *Son su passo de la morte*, believing it at first to be the continuation of the text of no. 112. In effect the graphic disposition of the texts could easily mislead: there is no sign whatsoever that separates one text from the other. This is why I lean towards the idea that the text erroneously copied by the Scribe A of Panc.27 is that of *Fior1505*, which is not found in any repertory of *poesia per musica*.

---

[5]. Severino Ferrari corrects «pace» to 'paze'. The New York print has «pace».
[6]. Severino Ferrari corrects «brazze» to 'braze'. The New York print has «brace».

112bis.
SON SU PASSO DE LA MORTE
fol. 78*r*

No music

113.

SCONSOLATA PHYLOMENA

fol. 78*v* (4 vv.)

Sconsolata phylomena

Italian secular piece (barzelletta).

COMMENTARY ON THE TEXT:

1	«phylomena» is the poetic image of the nightingale

READINGS EMENDED IN THE EDITION:

BAR	VOICE	ORIGINAL
4	T	*longa* with fermata
17	A, T	*brevis* with fermata
21	S, T, B	*longa* with fermata

MUSICAL CONCORDANCES (MSS): • ParisN Rés676 (104*v*-105*r*), heading: «Propter odium contra fratrem»[1]

TEXT FROM ParisN Rés676:

> Sconsolata philomena
> sol ch'io piango il perso nido,
> io scio ben che bramo et crido
> in deserto la mia pena.
>> Sconsolata filo[mena]

5	Parmi asai ch'è facta sorda
	la iustitia et la ragione,
	più di me non si ricorda
	piatà nì compassione.
	Non mi giova più oratione,
10	né mei versi in cantilena.
	Sconsolata […]

REMARKS: Although it is the only concordance, the version in ParisN Rés676 has various graphic variants with respect to that of Panc.27 (for example, omission of some fermatas, *breves* in place of *longae* or in place of two repeated *semibreves*, different coloration patterns). It cannot be proved that the two pieces are directly related, even if it is possible that they make reference to a shared repertory.

---

[1]. Bonnie Blackburn has decoded the inscription, which seems to have been written over an erasure; it means 'because of hatred against a brother', or possibly 'friar'.

113.
SCONSOLATA PHYLOMENA
fol. 78*v*

Scon - so - la - ta phy-lo-me - na

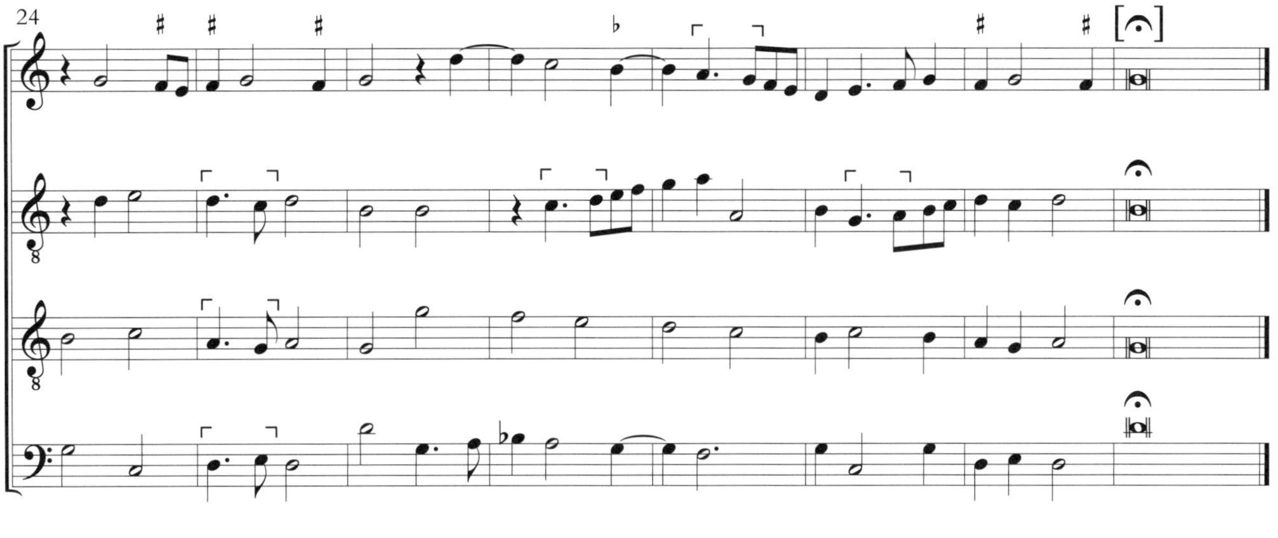
24

114.

Cum desiderio vo cercando

fol. 79*r* (3 vv.)

[Bianco da Siena]

Cum desiderio vo cercando
de trovare quel amoroso
Iesù Cristo dilectoso
per cui amore io vo suspirando.

5   Suspirando per amore
vado cercando el mio dilecto;
posa non trova il mio core,
tanto è per amor constreto.
Cum desiderio pur aspeto
10   de trova[r] da lui mercede;
datoli ho il cor e la fede,
sempre a lui me ricommando.

Ricommandoli el cor mio,
poiché d'amor l'ho infiamato,
15   prego lui che 'l mio desio
no li sia dismentigato.
Quanto l'ho desiderato
no lo dico in questo canto,
ma più volte, cum gran pianto,
20   per amor el vo chiamando.

Lauda (barzelletta). See also no. 29.

Commentary on the text:

1	hypermetric
2	hypermetric
4	hypermetric
5	the *residuum* begins here
6	hypermetric
9	hypermetric

Readings emended in the edition:

Bar	Voice	Original
19/II	S	*e´ minima* with the tail erased, transforming it into a *semibrevis*
34	T	*longa* with fermata

Textual concordances (mss): See no. 29.

TEXTUAL CONCORDANCES (PRINTS): See no. 29.

MUSICAL CONCORDANCES (MSS):[1] • CTL G12 (*68v-69r, olim 67v-68r*)

MODERN EDITIONS OF THE TEXT: See no. 29.

MODERN EDITIONS OF THE MUSIC: CMM 76, p. 24 (after CTL G12); DIEDERICHS 1986, pp. 302-303 (after Panc.27); GHISI 1953a, p. 55 (after Panc.27, partial transcription); LUISI 1983, II, pp. 32-33 (after Panc.27).

REMARKS: Despite the substantial closeness between the musical versions of Panc.27 and CTL G12, several graphic variants discourage the hypothesis of a direct relation between the two sources (in all three voices of CTL G12 the mensuration sign is lacking and the final note has a fermata). The rhythm of the last two descending notes in bar 3/I of the Superius of CTL G12 is slower (*minima* followed by two *semiminimae*); the missing rest in Panc.27 in bar 17/I of the Superius is present in CTL G12, and the ambiguous note in bar 19/II is given in the correct form. The poetic text is present in the same quantity in both manuscripts, but with numerous graphic differences.

BIBLIOGRAPHY: CATTIN 1973a, p. 201; CMM 76, p. xxiii; D'ANCONA (1878) 1906, p. 479; FALLOWS 1999, pp. 504-505; FRATI 1917, pp. 476, 478; GHISI 1953a, pp. 52-56, 69; JEPPESEN 1969, pp. 40-41; LONGO 1986, p. 221; LUISI 1983, I, p. 544; NOSOW 2000, pp. 243, 245; WILSON 1992, p. 172.

---

[1]. The piece *Ben lo sa Dio se sum vergine e pura* of the fiftheenth-century source ParisN Ro2973 (fols. *1v-2r*) – edited in THIBAULT - FALLOWS 1991, pp. 4-5 – shares the Superius and Tenor of Panc.27, slightly modified (see THIBAULT - FALLOWS 1991, p. lxxv).

114.
CUM DESIDERIO VO CERCANDO
fol. 79*r*

[Bianco da Siena]

115.

Tᴜ sᴏʟᴜs ǫᴜɪ ꜰᴀᴄɪs ᴍɪʀᴀʙɪʟɪᴀ

fols. 79*v*–80*r* (4 vv.)

Iᴏsǫᴜɪɴ [ᴅᴇs Pʀᴇᴢ]

Tu solus qui facis mirabilia,
tu solus creator qui creasti nos,
tu solus redemptor qui redemisti nos
sanguine tuo preciosissimo.

5   […]
In te solum confidimus,
nec alium adoramus,
Iesu Christe.

Ad te preces effundimus,
10   exaudi quod supplicamus,
et concede quod petimus,
rex benigne.

Freely composed prayer to Christ, whose opening line recalls Psalm 135:4 («qui facit mirabilia magna solus | quoniam in aeternum misericordia eius», Vᴜʟɢᴀᴛᴀ, p. 938).

Cᴏᴍᴍᴇɴᴛᴀʀʏ ᴏɴ ᴛʜᴇ ᴛᴇxᴛ:

5   the text of line 5 («ad te solum confugimus») should have been placed only under the music of the T and B (bb. 38-41)

Mᴜsɪᴄᴀʟ ᴄᴏɴᴄᴏʀᴅᴀɴᴄᴇs (ᴍss): • CV S41 (155*v*-156*r*), *Missa D'ung aultre amer, loco Benedictus et Osanna II*; index: «Iosquini» • ModD IV (14*v*-15*r*), *Missa D'ung aultre amer, loco Benedictus et Osanna II*, modern hand: «Josquin», T cut off from bar 52 to end • RMN (45*v*-46*r*), bars 1-37 only[1] • SGS 463 (no. 95), 2 vv. (S and A only), «Iosquinus Pratensis», «Dorius i. Primus» • WashC M6 (80*r*-81*r*), *O mater Dei et hominis*, bars 1-37 are missing in the S and T[2]

Mᴜsɪᴄᴀʟ ᴄᴏɴᴄᴏʀᴅᴀɴᴄᴇs (ᴘʀɪɴᴛs): • GiuJosqII (20*r-v*), *Missa D'ung aultre amer, loco Benedictus et Osanna II*, (Josquin) • PeJosqII1505 (no. 6), *Missa D'ung aultre amer, loco Benedictus et Osanna II*, (Josquin) • PeJosqII1515Gothic (no. 6), *Missa D'ung aultre amer, loco Benedictus et Osanna II*, «Josquin» • PeJosqII1515Roman (no. 6), *Missa D'ung aultre amer, loco Benedictus et Osanna II*, «Josquin» • PeLaudeII (25*v*-26*r*), *O mater Dei et hominis* • PeMotB (57*v*-59*r*: 57*v*-58*r*), «Josquin»

Mᴏᴅᴇʀɴ ᴇᴅɪᴛɪᴏɴs ᴏꜰ ᴛʜᴇ ᴛᴇxᴛ: Dʀᴀᴋᴇ 2002, p. 56 (after PeMotB); NJE 22, II, pp. 43-44.

Mᴏᴅᴇʀɴ ᴇᴅɪᴛɪᴏɴs ᴏꜰ ᴛʜᴇ ᴍᴜsɪᴄ: Bᴇᴄʜᴇʀɪɴɪ 1954, p. 120 (after Panc.27, bb. 1-21); Dʀᴀᴋᴇ 1972, II, pp.

---

[1]. Fol. 47 is lacking in the manuscript.
[2]. The first page of the piece has been lost.

262-265: 262-263; D<small>RAKE</small> 2002, pp. 254-258: 254-256 (after PeMotB); D<small>RAKE</small> 2005, pp. 453-454 (after PeMotB); J<small>EPPESEN</small> 1935, pp. 40-41 (after PeLaudeII); NJE 7, I, pp. 1-20: 15-17 (after CV S41); NJE 22, I, pp. 38-42: 38-41 (after PeMotB); S<small>MIJERS</small> J/4, pp. 56-58 (after PeMotB); S<small>MIJERS</small> J/23, pp. 131–133 (after PeJosqII1505).

R<small>EMARKS</small>: The tradition of this piece has been thoroughly studied by Bonnie Blackburn (NJE 22, II, pp. 39-51): the three types of transmission (as an indendent composition, as an alternative to the *Benedictus* and *Osanna II* of the *Missa D'ung aultre amer*, and as the lauda *O mater Dei et hominis*) do not correspond to three different stemmatic filiations. The musical version of Panc.27 is not directly linked to any of the known concordances,[3] since it has various unique readings. The distance from the Petrucci sources edited by Petrus Castellanus is demonstrated also by the different mensuration sign ('3' in Panc.27 instead of 'O' over '3' in Petrucci) in bar 53 (see NJE 22, II, p. 40, and B<small>LACKBURN</small> 2005, p. 422, n. 24). That Panc.27 nevertheless derives from another source is shown by the transmission of the text, which is placed correctly only in the Cantus and Altus. In the Tenor the text is missing after the middle of the third line; the Bassus has the correct text from beginning to end, but the copyist of Panc.27 forgot to copy line 5, putting in its place line 6 (bb. 38-41), confusing lines 5 and 6 perhaps because of their assonance. It therefore follows that the lack of line 5 is purely a scribal oversight and not a true textual omission.[4]

B<small>IBLIOGRAPHY</small>: B<small>LACKBURN</small> 2001a, p. 36; B<small>OORMAN</small> 2006, p. 949; B<small>ROWN</small> 1990, pp. 748, 752, 755, n. 39; C<small>UMMINGS</small> 1981, p. 52; D<small>RAKE</small> 1972, I, pp. 91, 105, 131, 145, 165, 175, 179, 180, 193, 331, 339, 341-342; D<small>RAKE</small> 2002, pp. 8-9, 56-57; D<small>RAKE</small> 2005; F<small>INSCHER</small> 2000, pp. 257-258; L<small>OACH</small> 1969, I, pp. 304, 356; NJE 22, II, pp. 30-46; N<small>OBLE</small> 1985, p. 12; R<small>IFKIN</small> 2003, p. 242, n. 11, p. 260, n. 51; R<small>OTHENBERG</small> 2006, p. 380; S<small>HERR</small> 1996, p. 154.

---

[3]. Even though Warren Drake maintains that it was copied from PeMotB (see D<small>RAKE</small> 2002, p. 56).
[4]. I thank Fabrizio Ammetto for this observation.

115.

Tu solus qui facis mirabilia

fols. 79*v*-80*r*

Iosquin [des Prez]

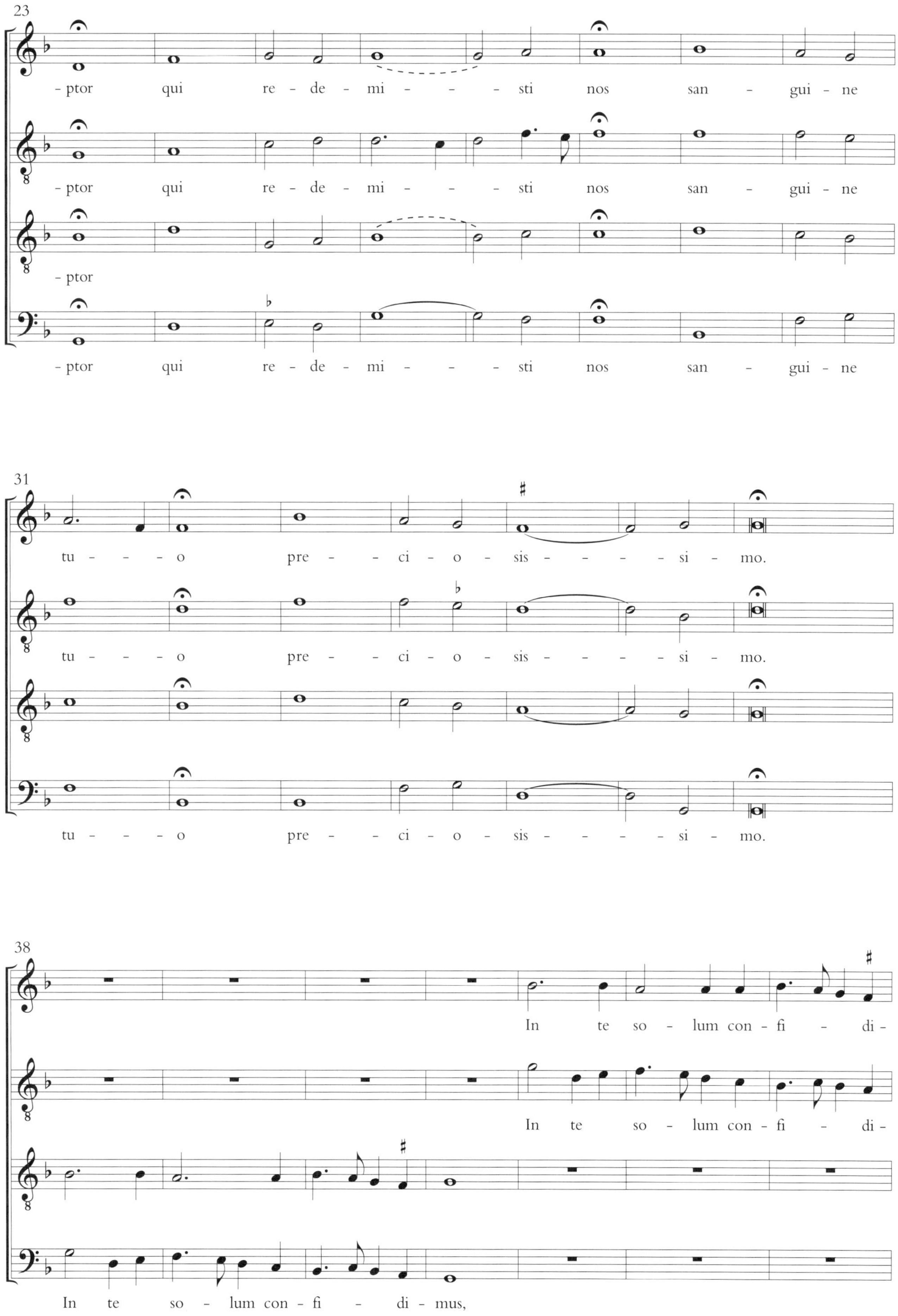
23
-ptor qui re - de - mi - - - - sti nos san - gui - ne
-ptor qui re - de - mi - - - - sti nos san - gui - ne
-ptor
-ptor qui re - de - mi - - - - sti nos san - gui - ne
31
tu - - - o pre - - ci - o - sis - - - - - si - mo.
tu - - - o pre - - ci - o - sis - - - - - si - mo.
tu - - - o pre - - ci - o - sis - - - - - si - mo.
38
In te so - lum con - fi - di -
In te so - lum con - fi - di -
In te so - lum con - fi - di - mus,

45
-mus, nec a-li-um a-do-ra-mus, Ie-su Chri-ste.
-mus, nec a-li-um a-do-ra-mus, Ie-su Chri-ste.
nec a-li-um a-do-ra-mus, Ie-su Chri-ste.
53
3
ex-au-di quod sup-pli-ca-mus, et
ex-au-di quod sup-pli-ca-mus, et
Ad te pre-ces ef-fun-di-mus, et
61
con-ce-de quod pe-ti-mus, rex be-ni-gne.
con-ce-de quod pe-ti-mus, rex be-ni-gne.
con-ce-de quod pe-ti-mus, rex be-ni-gne.

116.

'Patientia' [ognun me dice]

fols. 80*v*–81*r* (4 vv.)

'Patientia' […]

Sempre il sano […]

Altra cosa […]

El gi è tropo […]

    'Patientia' […]

Italian secular piece (barzelletta).

Readings emended in the edition:

Bar	Voice	Original
after 12	A	superfluous *semibrevis e*
25	A	*semibrevis*
after 53	A	superfluous *semibrevis a*
68	A	*e*

Textual concordances (mss): • *CV. Ca. 193* (97*r*–*v*), *Patientia ogniun me dice* • *Fir. N. NA. 701* (100*r*–*v*), *Patientia ognun me dice* • *Fir. R. 1258* (127*v*)

Textual concordances (prints): • *Historia* (1*v*) • *Patientia* (1*v*) • *Rado* (3*v*)

Musical concordances (mss): • CTL G12 (80*v*–82*r*, olim 79*v*–81*r*), *Patientia ognum me dice* • ParisN Rés27 (39*r*), *Patientia ogniun mi dice* • ParisN Rés676 (18*v*–19*r*), *Pacientia ognom mi dice*

Musical concordances (prints): • PeDalza (54*v*–55*r*), *Patientia ognun me dice*

Text from *CV. Ca. 193*:
> 'Patientia' ognun me dice,
> facto sta poterla avere,
> ch'aver male e poi tacere
> non satisfa uno infelice.

5   Io pur vivo e sempre stento,
> a patientia ognun me exorta.
> Fin non vedo al mio tormento,
> ma pur dice ognun: 'Supporta'.
> È sì[1] tal chi mi conforta

---

[1]. The manuscript has «ci».

10   che se fusse in el mio stato
        ogni afflicto e tribulato
        più di me diria felice.
                'Pacientia' ognun me dice.

        Sempre el sano a chi è dolente
        bon conforto porger sòle.
15   Ma colui che mal se sente
        non se passe de parole.
        Altra cossa l'uomo vole
        che pacientia per soccorso,
        che gli è tropo amaro morso
20   a mangiar simel radice.
                'Pacientia' ognun me dice.

        Io non trovo calendaro
        che patientia per sancta abia.
        La si mangia col cugiaro
        de la maledeta rabia.
25   Chi non ha sul corpo scabia
        si non fa come si gratti;
        le parole non son fatti,
        a dir tutto non me lice.
                'Pacientia' ognun me dice.

        Quando arò dato licentia
30   al gran mal che mi tormenta,
        voglio alor aver pacientia,
        ché la mente sia contenta.
        Ma per dir che sempre stenta
        e ognora esser passuto,
35   di pacientia senza aiuto
        non la vo' per adiutrice.
                'Pacientia' ognun me dice.

MODERN EDITIONS OF THE TEXT: BIZZARRI 1941, pp. 864-865 (after CTL G12); VITALETTI 1920-21, pp. 310-311 (after *Historia*).

MODERN EDITIONS OF THE MUSIC: CMM 76, pp. 70-72 (after CTL G12).

REMARKS: While the shorter version in ParisN Rés676 (which ends at b. 38) is musically distant from Panc.27, the version in CTL G12 is closely related: all the errors in the Altus in Panc.27 are present in CTL G12 as well, including the missing parts (added in the present edition). It would not be prudent to say that one version derives from the other, because of the notable textual differences. The deficient poem present in Panc.27 (which completely ignores the first strophe of CTL G12, corresponding to ll. 5-12) gives as initial strophe «sempre il sano [a chi è dolente]» (appearing as *residuum* instead in CTL G12). Moreover, the incipit «altra cosa» in Panc.27 becomes «ch'altra cosa» in CTL G12, while the incipit «el gi è tropo» becomes «perché è troppo». It is possible, however, to hypothesize with a high degree of probability that the two versions of the piece derive from a common model. In the present edition the simultaneous rests have been added in all the voices at four specific places (bb. 17/I, 26/I, 39/I, 51/I):[2] such additions replicate the initial upbeat rhythm,

---

[2]. I thank Adam Gilbert for this useful suggestion.

maintaining in each section the typical propelling movement of the dance, to which this piece is related.[3]

BIBLIOGRAPHY: BOORMAN 2006, p. 1003; CATTIN 1972a, pp. 453, n. 14, 491, n. 98; CATTIN 1973a, p. 206; CMM 76, p. xi; DISERTORI 1964, p. 85; FILOCAMO 2004; GALLO 1979; GHISI 1953a, p. 64, n. 17; HEARTZ 1978, p. 374; SPARTI 1993, pp. 138-140; TORREFRANCA 1939, p. 272.

---

[3]. The bassedance *Patientia* with choreography by Guglielmo Ebreo is attested in the following manuscripts: Florence, Biblioteca Medicea Laurenziana, Antinori 13 (1510), fols. 23*v*-29*r*; Florence, Biblioteca Nazionale Centrale, Magliabechiano XIX.88 (15th c.), fol. 23*r*; New York, Public Library, Dance Collection, 'Giorgio' Manuscript, *MGZMB-Res. 72-254 (15th c.), fol. 10*r*; Paris, Bibliothèque Nationale de France, Fonds It. 476 (1474), fol. 40*v*; Paris, Bibliothèque Nationale de France, Fonds It. 973 (1463), fol. 31*r*; Siena, Biblioteca Comunale degli Intronati, L.V.29 (written ca. 1474), fol. 56*r* (see GALLO 1979).

116.
'PATIENTIA' [OGNUN ME DICE]
fols. 80v–81r

Sempre il sano

Sempre

Sempre il sano

Sempre

Altra cosa

El gi è tropo

'Patientia'

'Patientia'

'Patientia'

117.

VERBUM CARO, PANEM VERUM

fols. *81v–82r* (4 vv.)

Verbum caro, panem verum
Verbo carnem efficit:
fitque sanguis Christi merum,
et si sensus deficit,
5   ad firmandum cor sincerum
sola fides sufficit.

Fourth stanza of the hymn *Pange lingua gloriosi corporis mysterium* (AH 50, pp. 586-587; AR, pp. 103★, 104★), used on the feast of Corpus Christi for the procession of the Holy Sacrament at the end of Mass (GR, pp. 137★, 138★; LU, pp. 950-952) and for Vespers (AM, pp. 547-548; AR, pp. 527-529; BR, p. 454; LU, pp. 957-959).

COMMENTARY ON THE TEXT:

2	Verbo] verbum C	
4	deficit] defficit C, B	

READINGS EMENDED IN THE EDITION:

BAR	VOICE	ORIGINAL
25/I	B	the insertion is justified by analogy with the imitative entries in the preceding voices
50-52	T	*longa* with fermata

TEXT FROM BR, p. 454 (*In festo Corporis Christi. Ad Vesperas. Hymnus*):

1.   Pange lingua gloriosi
corporis mysterium,
sanguinisque pretiosi,
quem in mundi pretium
fructus ventris generosi
rex effudit gentium.

2.   Nobis datus, nobis natus
ex intacta Virgine,
et in mundo conversatus,
sparso verbi semine,
sui moras incolatus
miro clausit ordine.

3.   In supremae nocte cenae
recumbens cum fratribus,
observata lege plene
cibis in legalibus,
cibum turbae duodenae
se dat suis manibus.

4. Verbum caro panem verum
    verbo carnem efficit,
    fitque sanguis Christi merum,
    et si sensus deficit,
    ad firmandum cor sincerum
    sola fides sufficit.

5. Tantum ergo Sacramentum
    veneremur cernui:
    et antiquum documentum
    novo cedat ritui:
    praestet fides supplementum
    sensuum defectui.

6. Genitori, genitoque
    laus, et iubilatio,
    salus, honor, virtus quoque
    sit, et benedictio:
    procedenti ab utroque
    compar sit laudatio.

    Amen.

MODERN EDITIONS OF THE TEXT: AH 50, pp. 586-587.

MODERN EDITIONS OF THE MUSIC: BANKS 1993, II, pp. 200-202 (after Panc.27).

REMARKS: The Cantus paraphrases the melodic incipit of each stanza of the Gregorian hymn in AR, pp. 527-529 and 103★, GR, pp. 137★, LU, pp. 957-959.

BIBLIOGRAPHY: BANKS 1993, I, p. 293; CHEVALIER II, nos. 14467 and 21349; IGC, p. 319; WARD 1980, p. 223.

117.
Verbum caro, panem verum
fols. 81v–82r

22
-que san - - - - - guis Chri - - - - sti me -
san - - - - - guis Chri - sti me - - - - - - -
fit - que san - - - guis Chri - - - - - sti me - - - - - -
fit - que san - - - - guis Chri - - - - sti
29
- - rum, et si sen - sus de - fi - cit,
- - rum, et si sen - sus de - - - fi - cit, ad
- - rum, et si sen-sus de - - - fi - cit,
me - rum, et si sen - sus de - fi - - - - - - - -
37
ad fir - - - man - - - dum cor sin - ce-rum
fir - - - - - man - - - - dum cor sin - - - - ce - - - - - - rum
ad fir - - - - - man - - - - - - dum cor sin - ce - rum
- cit, ad fir - - - - - man - dum cor sin -

so – – la fi – – – – – des suf-fi – cit.

so – la fi – – des suf-fi – – – – – cit.

so – la fi – des suf-fi – – – cit.

– ce - rum so - la fi – – – – – des suf-fi – – – cit.

118.

Incipit oratio Ieremie prophete

fols. 82v–84r (3 vv.)

	Incipit oratio Ieremie prophete.
	Recordare, Domine, quid acciderit nobis:
	intuere, et respice oprobrium nostrum.
	Hereditas nostra versa est ad alienos:
5	domus nostre ad extraneos.
	Pupilli facti sumus absque patre,
	matres nostre quasi vidue.
	Aquam nostram pecunia bibimus:
	ligna nostra pretio comparavimus.
10	Cervicibus minabamur,
	et lassis non dabatur requies.
	Egipto dedimus manum,
	et Assiriis, ut saturaremur pane.
	Patres nostri peccaverunt, et non sunt:
15	et nos iniquitates eorum portavimus.
	Servi dominati sunt nostri:
	et non fuit qui redimeret nos de manibus eorum.
	Ierusalem, Ierusalem, convertere ad Dominum Deum tuum.

Lamentations of Jeremiah, 5:1–8 (Vulgata, p. 1254), with the addition of the final invocation «Ierusalem, Ierusalem, convertere ad Dominum Deum tuum» (likewise in no. 178). Used for the third lesson at the first Nocturn in Matins of Holy Saturday (BR, p. 356).

COMMENTARY ON THE TEXT:

11	Vulgata: «et» lacking
17	Vulgata: «non fuit qui redimeret de manu eorum»

READINGS EMENDED IN THE EDITION:

Bar	Voice	Original
39	B	*d semibrevis* with fermata, corrected in analogy with bar 52
84	T	*semibrevis* with fermata
101/I	B	*d* instead of *e*
143/I	B	*a semibrevis*

TEXT FROM Vulgata, pp. 1254–1255 (*Threni idest Lamentationes Ieremiae prophetae*, V, 1–22):

	Oratio Ieremiae prophetae
1.	recordare Domine quid acciderit nobis
	intuere et respice obprobrium nostrum
2.	hereditas nostra versa est ad alienos
	domus nostrae ad extraneos

3. pupilli facti sumus absque patre
   matres nostrae quasi viduae
4. aquam nostram pecunia bibimus
   ligna nostra pretio conparavimus
5. cervicibus minabamur
   lassis non dabatur requies
6. Aegypto dedimus manum
   et Assyriis ut saturaremur pane
7. patres nostri peccaverunt et non sunt
   et nos iniquitates eorum portavimus
8. servi dominati sunt nostri
   non fuit qui redimeret de manu eorum
9. in animabus nostris adferebamus panem nobis
   a facie gladii in deserto
10. pellis nostra quasi clibanus exusta est
    a facie tempestatum famis
11. mulieres in Sion humiliaverunt
    virgines in civitatibus Iuda
12. principes manu suspensi sunt
    facies senum non erubuerunt
13. adulescentibus inpudice abusi sunt
    et pueri in ligno corruerunt
14. senes de portis defecerunt
    iuvenes de choro psallentium
15. defecit gaudium cordis nostri
    versus est in luctu chorus noster
16. cecidit corona capitis nostri
    vae nobis quia peccavimus
17. propterea maestum factum est cor nostrum
    ideo contenebrati sunt oculi nostri
18. propter montem Sion quia disperiit
    vulpes ambulaverunt in eo
19. tu autem Domine in aeternum permanebis
    solium tuum in generatione et generatione
20. quare in perpetuum ob900livisceris nostri
    derelinques nos in longitudine dierum
21. converte nos Domine ad te et convertemur
    innova dies nostros sicut a principio
22. sed proiciens reppulisti nos
    iratus es contra nos vehementer

MODERN EDITIONS OF THE MUSIC: BANKS 1993, II, pp. 95-98 (after Panc.27); BECHERINI 1954, p. 121 (after Panc.27, bb. 1-16).

REMARKS: A *signum congruentiae* appears over each of the two fermatas in the Cantus (bb. 7 and 10), which probably refer to the performance of the piece.

BIBLIOGRAPHY: BANKS 1993, I, p. 277; CS, pp. 346-347.

118.
Incipit oratio Ieremie prophete
fols. 82v–84r

Cantus: In – ci – pit o – ra – ti – o Ie – re – mi – e pro – phe – – – – – – – – te. Re – cor – da – re, Do – mi – ne, quid ac – ci – de – rit no – bis: in – tu – e – re, et re – spi – ce o – pro – bri – um no – – – strum.

[Tenor]: In – ci – pit o – ra – ti – o Ie – re – mi – e pro – phe – – – – – – – – te. Re – cor – da – re, Do – mi – ne, quid ac – ci – de – rit no – bis: in – tu – e – re, et re – spi – ce o – pro – bri – um no – – – strum.

[Bassus]: In – ci – pit o – ra – ti – o Ie – re – mi – e pro – phe – – – – – – – – te. Re – cor – da – re, Do – mi – ne, quid ac – ci – de – rit no – bis: in – tu – e – re, et re – spi – ce o – pro – bri – um no – – – strum.

33
He - re - di - tas no - stra ver - sa est ad a - li - e - nos:
40
do - mus no - stre ad ex - tra - ne - os.
47
Pu - pil - li fa - cti su - mus ab - sque pa - tre, ma - tres
54
no - stre qua - si vi - du -

61
- - - - e. A - quam no - stram pe - cu - - - ni -
- - - - e. A - quam no - stram pe - cu - - - ni -
- - - - e. A - quam no - stram pe - - - - cu - ni -
68
- a bi - bi - - mus: li - gna no - - stra pre - ti - - - o
- a bi - bi - - mus: li - gna no - - stra pre - ti - - - o
- a bi - bi - - mus: li - gna no - - stra pre - - - ti - - -
75
com-pa-ra - - - - - - vi - mus. Cer - vi - ci - bus mi - na -
com-pa-ra - - - - - - vi - mus. Cer - vi - ci - bus mi - na -
- - o com-pa - ra - - - vi - mus. Cer - vi - ci - bus mi - na -
82
- ba - - - - - mur, et las - - sis non da - ba -
- ba - - - - - - mur, et las - - - sis non da - ba -
- ba - - - - - - - mur, et las - - - sis non da - ba -

89
- - tur re - - - - qui - es. E - gi - pto de - di - mus ma - num,
- - tur re - - - qui - es. E - gi - pto de - di - mus ma - num,
- - tur re - - - qui - es. E - gi - pto de - di - mus ma - num,
96
et As - si - ri - is, ut sa - tu - ra - re - mur pa - - - -
et As - si - ri - is, ut sa - tu - ra - re - mur pa - - - -
et As - si - ri - is, ut sa - - tu - ra - re - mur pa - - - -
103
- ne. Pa - tres no - stri pec - ca - ve - runt, et non sunt:
- ne. Pa - tres no - stri pec - ca - ve - runt, et non sunt:
- ne. Pa - tres no - stri pec - ca - ve - runt, et non sunt:
110
et nos i - ni - qui - ta - tes e - o - rum por - ta - - - - vi -
et nos i - ni - qui - ta - tes e - o - rum por - ta - - - - vi -
et nos i - ni - qui - ta - tes e - o - rum por - ta - vi - - - - -

116 Ser - vi do - mi - na - ti sunt no - stri: et non fu -

123 - it qui re - di - me - ret nos de ma - ni - bus e -

130 - o - rum. Ie - ru - sa - lem, Ie - ru - sa -

137 - lem, con - ver - te - re ad Do - mi - num De - um tu - um.

119.

(Credo) Patrem omnipotentem

fols. 84*v*–86*r* (2 vv.)

Patrem omnipotentem, factorem celi et terre, visibilium omnium, et invisibilium.
Et in unum Dominum Iesum Christum, filium Dei unigenitum.
Et ex Patre natum ante omnia secula.
Deum de Deo, lumen de lumine, Deum verum de Deo vero.
5   Genitum, non factum, consubstantialem Patri: per quem omnia facta sunt.
Qui propter nos homines, et propter nostram salutem descendit de celis.
Et incarnatus est de Spiritu Sancto ex Maria Virgine: et homo factus est.
Crucifixus etiam pro nobis: sub Pontio Pilato passus, et sepultus est.
Et resurrexit tertia die, secundum scripturas.
10   Et ascendit in celum: sedet ad dexteram Patris.
Et iterum venturus est cum gloria, iudicare vivos et mortuos: cuius regni non erit finis.
[…]

Amen.

Credo of the Ordinary of the Mass. The text was also recited silently at the beginning of all the Hours and at the end of Compline (BR, pp. 1, 110).

COMMENTARY ON THE TEXT:

5   consubstantialem] cūsubstantiale T_1, T_2

READINGS EMENDED IN THE EDITION:

Bar	Voice	Original
54/I	T_1	*brevis*
106/II–107/I	T_2	*semibrevis*
after 116	T_2	bar line missing, but the page turn follows
139	T_1	*longa*
140	T_2	*b* instead of *c′*
156	T_2	*b* instead of *c′*
173–174/I	T_1	*brevis-brevis-brevis* ligature
174/II–178	T_1	*brevis-brevis-brevis-brevis-brevis-brevis-brevis-longa* ligature
179	T_1	*brevis-brevis* ligature
179/II	T_2	*brevis*

REMARKS: The piece was probably copied from a model, as indicated by missing notes in bars 126/II (Tenor I) and 165/III (Tenor II) and the erasure at the end of Tenor I (fol. 85*v*, fourth stave) of the music of the «Amen», written at the same melodic height, but graphically a third lower and in a different clef. The scribe stopped transcribing the text of the Credo (omitting the sections after «Et in Spiritum Sanctum Dominum») at the point where he turned from fol. 84*v* to fol. 85*v* (Tenor I): perhaps he also forgot to copy the remainder of the text from his model? The piece is littered with parallel fifths and octaves, probably intended by the composer himself. The chant of Credo IV (GR, pp. 67★–69★; LU, pp. 71–73) appears nearly literally in the Superius.

BIBLIOGRAPHY: IGC, p. 98.

119.
(CREDO) PATREM OMNIPOTENTEM
fols. 84v–86r

39
De-um ve - rum de De-o ve - - - ro. Ge-ni-tum, non fa - ctum,
De-um ve - rum
47
con-sub-stan-ti - a - lem Pa - tri: per quem o - mni-a fa - cta sunt.
54
Qui pro - pter nos ho-mi-nes, et pro-pter no-stram sa - lu - tem de-scen-dit de
62
ce - - - lis. Et in-car-na-tus est de Spi - ri-tu San - cto ex Ma-ri -
70
- a Vir-gi - ne: et ho-mo fa-ctus est. Cru - ci - fi - - - xus
78
e - ti-am pro no - - - bis: sub Pon-ti - o Pi-la - to pas-sus, et se -

-pul - tus est. Et re-sur-re - xit ter-ti - a di – – e,

se - cun - dum scri - ptu – – ras. Et a – scen - dit in ce - lum:

se - det ad dex-te - ram Pa – tris. Et i - te-rum ven - tu - rus est cum

glo - ri - a, iu - di - ca - re vi - vos et mor-tu – os: cu - ius re-gni

non e - rit fi - nis.

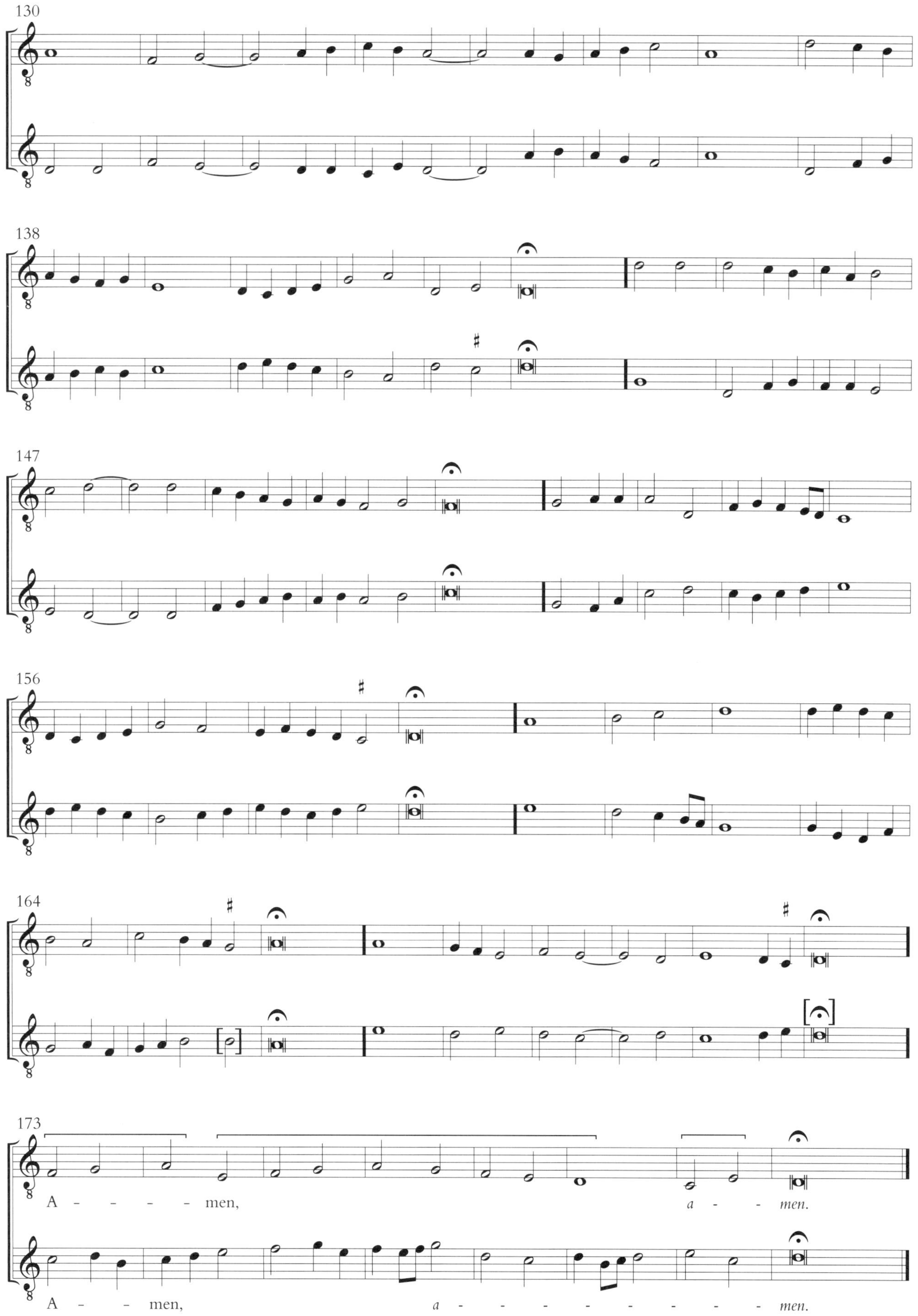
130
138
147
156
164
173
A - - - - men, a - - men.
A - - men, a - - - - - - - - - - - men.

120.

O Domine Iesu Christe

fols. 86v-87r (4 vv.)

[Antoine Brumel]

O Domine Iesu Christe,
te supplices exoramus
ut N. servum tuum languescentem
et molesta febre pressum,
5   ab omni egretudinis
gravamine incolumen per merita
tue passionis sanitatisque munere
letum reddere digneris.

Prayer to Christ connected with the *Officium de Passione* known as the 'Prayers of St. Gregory': seven prayers, all with the same beginning, *O Domine Iesu Christe*; this is a variant of the fourth prayer. See also no. 121.

Commentary on the text:

3   «N.» stands for *nomen*; it is to be replaced by the name of the person for whom the text is being sung[1]

Readings emended in the edition:

Bar	Voice	Original
16	A	dot missing after the *c'*
22/II	T	after the *d* follow four superfluous notes: *g semibrevis, f semiminima, e semiminima, d minima*
23/I	A	*c' semibrevis*
31	A	*f longa* with fermata
54/II	S	*c'*
54/II	B	*F*

Musical concordances (mss): • BolM 19 (93v-94r), with text *O domine Iesu Christe pastor bone iustos conserva peccatores iustifica*, «A. Brumel»

Text from BolM 19:

O Domine Iesu Christe,
pastor bone, iustos conserva,
peccatores iustifica.
Et omnibus fidelibus defunctis miserere,
et propicius esto michi peccatori.
Amen.

---

[1]. My thanks to Bonnie Blackburn for resolving the abbreviation.

MODERN EDITIONS OF THE TEXT: BLACKBURN 1997, p. 606, n. 20.

MODERN EDITIONS OF THE MUSIC: BANKS 1993, II, pp. 139-140 (after Panc.27); CMM 5/V, pp. 86-88 (after BolM 19).

REMARKS: Although there is a musical concordance, the text — which prays for the healing from illness of a person whose name is to be substituted («N.») — is not otherwise known. The repetition of the passage in the Tenor (b. 22/II) is surely due to an oversight in copying from the model, which was certainly not a source similar to BolM 19,[2] and all the more if we take into account the musical reading itself, which shows graphic variants and some different notes. See also the Remarks to no. 121.

BIBLIOGRAPHY: BANKS 1993, I, p. 283; BLACKBURN 1997, pp. 599-603.

---

[2]. Panc.27 is clearly earlier than BolM 19: one of its pieces is dated 1518, and the manuscript is probably north Italian, even if its provenance has not been proved (see BLACKBURN 2001c, p. 148, n. 71).

120.
O Domine Iesu Christe
fols. 86*v*–87*r*

[Antoine Brumel]

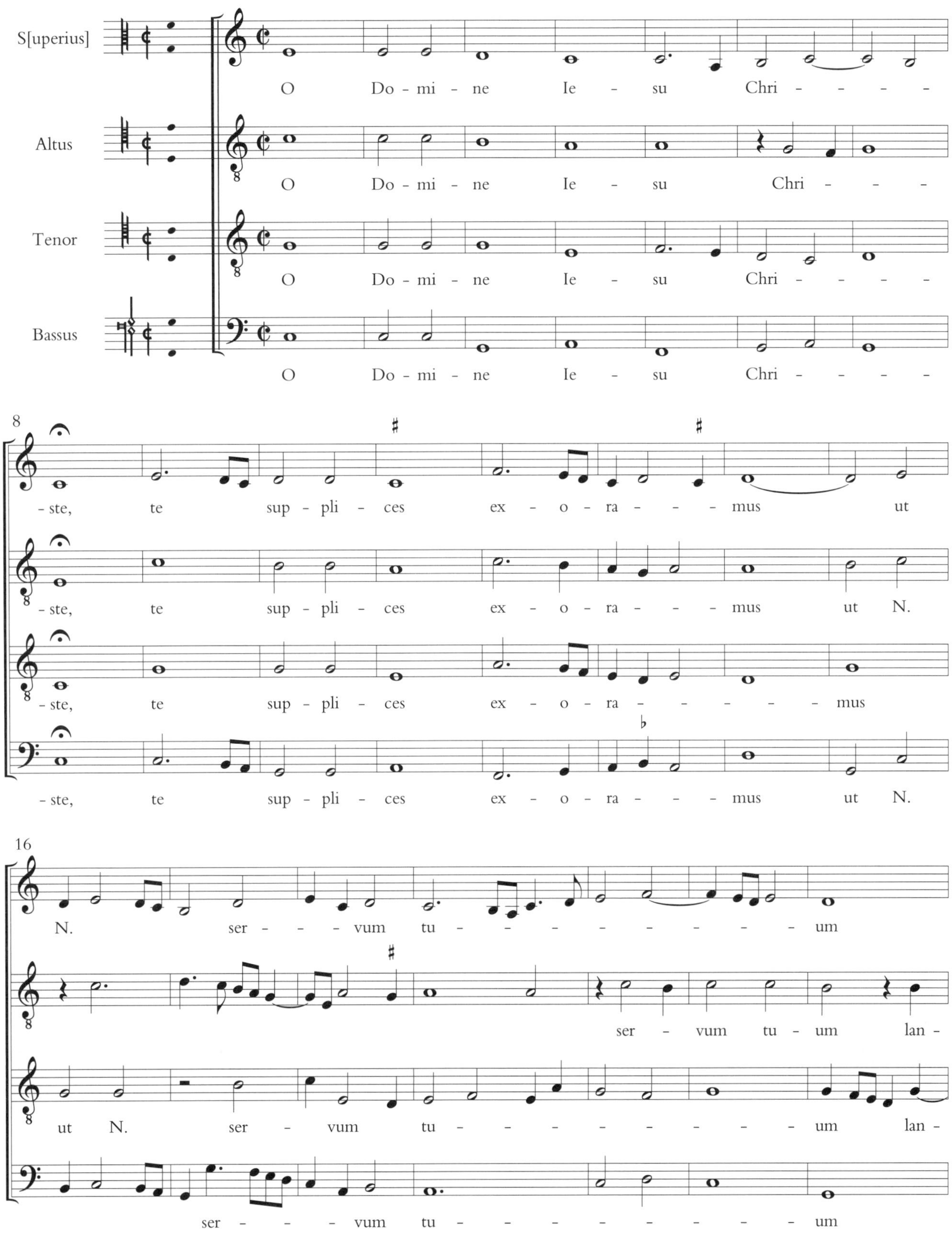

23
lan - - - gue - scen - - - - - - - - - tem et mo - le - sta fe -
- - - gue - scen - - - - tem et mo - le - sta fe - bre
- - - gue - scen - - - - tem et mo - le - sta fe - bre
lan - - - gue - scen - - - - tem et mo - le - sta fe - - - - - bre
30
- bre pres - sum, ab o - - mni e - gre - tu -
pres - - - - sum, ab o - - mni e - gre - tu -
pres - - - - sum, ab o - - - - - mni e - - gre - - - tu -
pres - - - - sum, ab o - - - - - mni e - - - - - gre - tu -
37
- di - - - - - - nis gra - - - va - mi - ne in - co - lu - - - -
- di - nis gra - va - - - - mi - - - ne in - co - lu - -
- di - - - - - nis gra - va - - - mi - - ne in - co - lu - -
- di - - - - - - nis gra - va - mi - - - - - ne in - co - lu - -

45
-men per me-ri-ta tu-e pas - si - - - - - - - o - nis sa - ni - ta -
-men per me-ri-ta tu-e pas - si - - - - - - o - nis sa-ni-ta-tis -
-men per me-ri-ta tu-e pas - - si - - o - - - nis
-men per me-ri-ta tu-e pas - si - - - - - - o - - - - nis sa-ni-ta-tis -
53
- tis - que mu-ne - - - - - - - re le - - - - - - - tum
- - - que mu-ne - - - re le - - - -
sa - ni - ta - tis - - - que mu-ne - - - - - - - re
- - - que mu-ne - - - - - - - - re le - - - - - - - - -
61
red - de - - - - re di - gne - - - - - - ris.
-tum red - - - de - re di - - gne - ris.
le - - - tum red-de - re di - gne - - ris.
-tum red - - - - - de - re di - gne - - ris.

121.

O Domine Iesu Christe

fols. 87*v*–88*r* (4 vv.)

[POPE GREGORY I 'THE GREAT'?]   [ANTOINE BRUMEL?][1]

> O Domine Iesu Christe,
> propter illam amaritudinem
> quam pro me
> sustinuisti in cruce, maxime in illa hora
> 5   quando sanctissima anima tua egressa est de corpore tuo:
> miserere anime mee in egressu suo.
> Amen.

Prayer to Christ connected with the *Officium de Passione* known as the 'Prayers of St. Gregory', where it is the fifth prayer. See also no. 120.

COMMENTARY ON THE TEXT:

2	amaritudinem] amaratudinem A
6	mee] me B
6	egressu] egressuo A

READINGS EMENDED IN THE EDITION:

BAR	VOICE	ORIGINAL
between 38/I and 38/II	T	superfluous *a minima*
39/II–40/I	T	superfluous dot following the *a semibrevis*
55	T	*longa* with fermata

MODERN EDITIONS OF THE TEXT: BLACKBURN 1997, p. 600 (after Bernardino de' Busti, *Thesaurus spiritualis cum quamplurimis alijs additis noviter impressus*, Lyon, Nicolaus Wolff, 23 March 1500);[2] DRAKE 2002, pp. 35-36 (after PeMotB).

REMARKS: Bonnie Blackburn's hypothesis that pieces nos. 120 and 121 are stylistically similar (and also assignable to the same composer) is supported also by the graphical aspect of fol. 86*v*: on the fifth stave of this page the Cantus of no. 121 has been copied up to the end of bar 28. This line was then struck through and rewritten at the beginning of fol. 87*v*. Perhaps the scribe too thought of the two pieces as a linked pair, and written by the same composer. The Panc.27 Latin text does not exactly correspond with the one edited in BLACKBURN 1997, nor the one in PeMotB.

BIBLIOGRAPHY: BLACKBURN 1997, pp. 599-603; BROWN 1990, p. 751; DRAKE 2002, pp. 11-13; FILOCAMO 2004.

---

[1]. Bonnie Blackburn considers no. 121 «stylistically [...] a pair with Brumel's [no. 120]» (see BLACKBURN 1997, p. 603). In n. 20 of the same article she speaks of *O Domine Iesu Christe, propter illam* as the 'secunda pars' of *O Domine Iesu Christe, te supplices* [no. 120] and suggests that Brumel may be the composer of this piece as well.

[2]. There are copies in New York, New York Public Library; Paris, Bibliothèque Nationale de France (imperfect); Washington, DC, Library of Congress.

121.
O Domine Iesu Christe

fols. 87*v*–88*r*

[Pope Gregory I 'the Great'?]

[Antoine Brumel?]

633

il - la ho - - - - - - - - - - ra

ma - - xi - - - me in il - la ho - -

ma - xi - me in il - - la ho -

quan - - - - - do san - ctis - si - ma a - ni - ma

- ra quan - do san - ctis - si - ma a - - ni - -

- ra quan - - - do san - ctis - si - ma a - ni - ma tu -

quan - do san - ctis - si - ma

tu - - - - - a e - - - - gres - - - sa est de

- ma tu - - a e - gres - sa est de cor-po - re

- a e - gres - - - sa est de cor-

a - ni - ma tu - a e - gres - - - sa est de

42
cor - po - re tu - - - o: mi - se - re - - - - re
tu - - - o: mi - se - - - re - re a - ni - me me -
- po - re tu - - - - - o: mi - se - re - - - re a -
cor - po - re tu - o: mi - - - se - re - re a - ni - me
49
a - ni - me me - - - - e in e - gres - su su - - - o.
- e in e - gres - - - - su su - - - - - - - o.
- ni - me me - e in e - gres - - su su - - - - - - o.
me - e in e - gres - su su - - - - - - - o.
56
A - - - - - - - - - - - - - - - - - men.
108
13
A - - - - - - - - - - - - - - - - - men.
108
13
A - - - - - - - - - - - - - - men.
A - - - - - - - - - - - - - - - - - men.
108
13

122.

3i toni. Nunc dimittis servum tuum

fol. 88*v* (3 vv.)

Nunc dimittis servum tuum, Domine,
secundum verbum tuum in pace.
[…]¹
Quod parasti ante fatiem omnium populorum.
5   […]
Gloria Patri et Filio et Spiritui Sancto
[…]

Canticle of Simeon (Luke 2:29-32, Vulgata, p. 1609), followed by the first part of the Lesser Doxology («Gloria Patri et Filio et Spiritui Sancto»). Used every day at Compline (AM, pp. 437, 452, 1109; AR, p. 64; BR, pp. 108-109; LU, pp. 271, 764, 784, 1735). The text is also used in the feast of the Purification of the Virgin as a Tract (GR, pp. 412-413; LU, pp. 1363-1364), and, divided into versicles, it is sung interspersed with the antiphon *Lumen ad revelationem gentium* for the benediction of the candles (GR, p. 406; LU, pp. 1357-1358); see also CAO III, p. 360 and CAO IV, pp. 310, 496).

Commentary on the text:

| 2 | verbum tuum in] verbum in T |
| 4 | Vulgata: «faciem» instead of 'fatiem' |

Readings emended in the edition:

Bar	Voice	Original
30	Ct	*longa* with fermata
47	Ct	superfluous *a fusa* before the *e*

Text from Vulgata, p. 1609 (*Evangelium secundum Lucam*, II, 29-32):

29.	nunc dimittis servum tuum Domine
	secundum verbum tuum in pace
30.	quia viderunt oculi mei salutare tuum
31.	quod parasti ante faciem omnium populorum
32.	lumen ad revelationem gentium
	et gloriam plebis tuae Israhel

Modern editions of the music: Banks 1993, II, pp. 132-134 (after Panc.27).

Remarks: This the only case in the whole manuscript for which the copyist specifies the mode of the piece: the rubric «3i toni» occurs as a heading. It is possible that the missing rest in the Contra (b. 20) is due to copying from a model, so far unknown. The chant in GR, p. 406, LU, pp. 271, 764, 784, 1357, 1735 is paraphrased in the Cantus.

Bibliography: Banks 1993, I, p. 282; CAO III, p. 360; CAO IV, pp. 310, 496; CS; pp. 438-440; Hoyer 1992, pp. 21, 44, 128, 171; IGC, p. 299.

---

¹. The absence of alternating verses such as this indicates *alternatim* performance, with the missing verses in plainchant.

122.

3i toni. Nunc dimittis servum tuum

fol. 88*v*

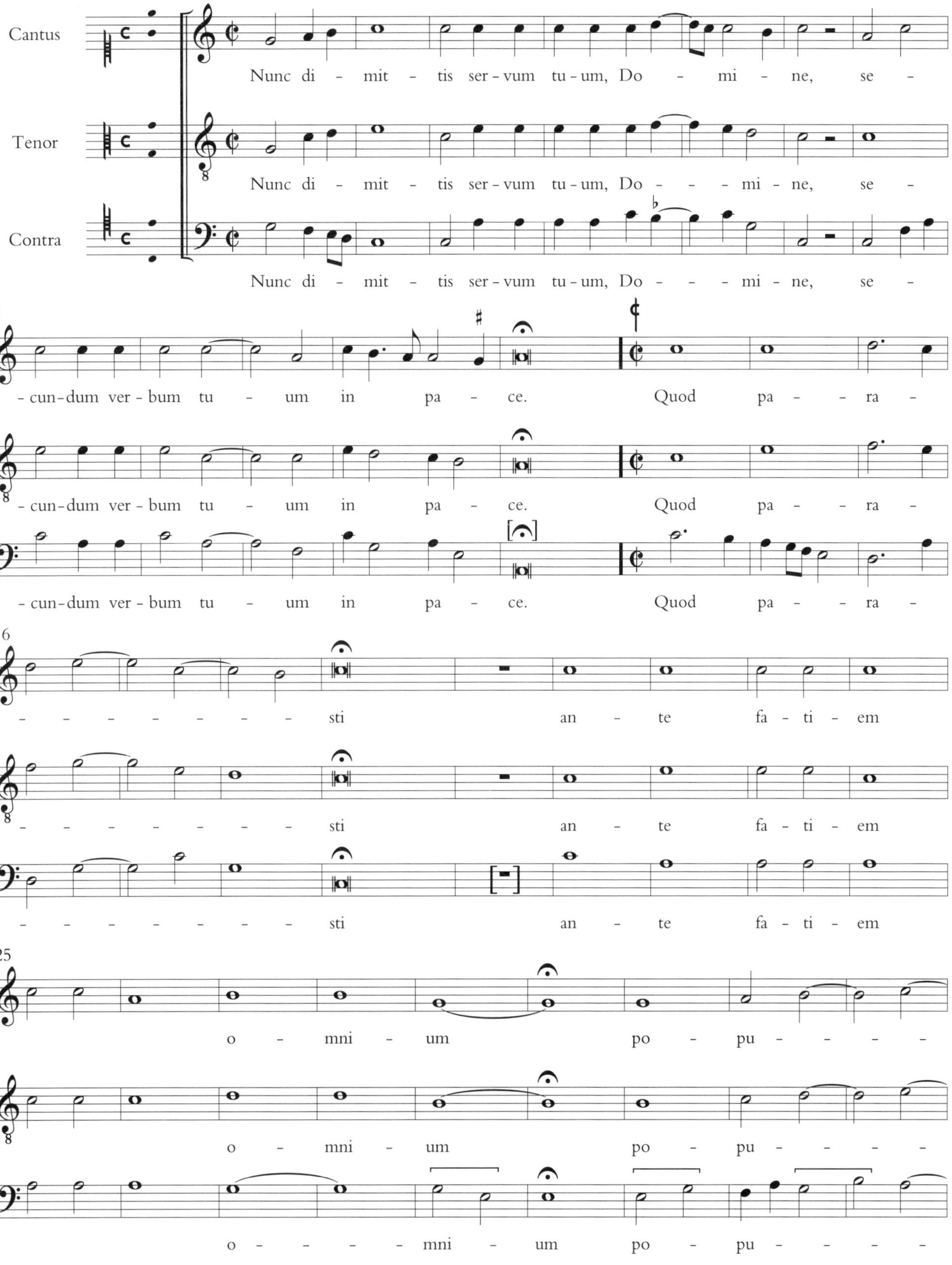

34
C
- - lo - - - rum. Glo - ri - a Pa - tri et Fi - li - - - - - - -
- - lo - - - rum. Glo - ri - a Pa - tri et Fi - li - - - - - - -
- - lo - - - rum. Glo - ri - a Pa - tri et Fi - li - - - - -
42
- o et Spi - ri - tu - - - - i San - - - - - - - cto
- o et Spi - ri - tu - - - - i San - - - - - - - cto
- o et Spi - ri - tu - - - - i San - - - - - - - - - cto

123.

Magnificat anima mea Dominum

fols. 89*v*-91*r* (4/3 vv.)

[…][1]

Magnificat anima mea Dominum
[…][2]
Quia respexit humilitatem ancille sue,
ecce enim ex hoc beatam me dicent omnes generationes.
5   […]
   […]
Et misericordia eius a progenie in progenies timentibus eum
   […]
   […]
10   Deposuit potentes de sede, et exaltavit humiles
   […]
Suscepit Israel puerum suum, recordatus misericordie sue
   […]
   […]

Gloria Patri et Filio et Spiritui Sancto
   […]

Canticle of the Blessed Virgin Mary (*Magnificat*) based on Luke 1:46-55 (Vulgata, p. 1607), followed by the first part of the Lesser Doxology («Gloria Patri et Filio et Spiritui Sancto») as for Vespers (AM, pp. 129, 727; AR, pp. 52, 102; BR, p. 87; LU, pp. 207-218 (18 melodies), 260). See also CS, pp. 430-433; IGC, p. 270.

Commentary on the text:

7	Vulgata: «in progenies et progenies» instead of 'a progenie in progenies'	
12	Vulgata: «memorari misericordiae» instead of 'recordatus misericordie sue'	

Readings emended in the edition:

Bar	Voice	Original
incipit	S	the intonation «Magnificat» is in black notation
13/I	S	two *semibreves* instead of two *minimae*
25	B	*c′ longa* above the *d*

---

[1]. In RISM B IV/5, p. 148, an attribution to Johannes Prioris is suggested, referring to Wexler 1974. But Richard Wexler refers in fact to a different Magnificat (VIII toni) for 2/3/4 voices in MS Florence, Archivio del Duomo, II.27 (fols. 85*v*-90*r*), with an inscription «del Priore» in the index, which is listed under the Dubious Works (Wexler 1974, pp. 205-208 and 377). Also CMM 90/II, which lists all the Requiem and Magnificat settings attributed to Prioris, does not include the music of this Magnificat.

[2]. The absence of alternating verses such as this indicates *alternatim* performance, with the missing verses in plainchant.

52/I	S	*g′ semiminima* above *e′*
53	B	*semibrevis* with fermata

TEXT FROM VULGATA, p. 1607 (*Evangelium secundum Lucam*, I, 46-55):

46. et ait Maria
    Magnificat anima mea Dominum
47. et exultavit spiritus meus in Deo salutari meo
48. quia respexit humilitatem ancillae suae
    ecce enim ex hoc beatam me dicent omnes generationes
49. quia fecit mihi magna qui potens est
    et sanctum nomen eius
50. et misericordia eius in progenies et progenies timentibus eum
51. fecit potentiam in brachio suo
    dispersit superbos mente cordis sui
52. deposuit potentes de sede et exaltavit humiles
53. esurientes implevit bonis et divites dimisit inanes
54. suscepit Israhel puerum suum memorari misericordiae
55. sicut locutus est ad patres nostros
    Abraham et semini eius in saecula

REMARKS: This is the only piece in Panc.27 in which the archaic labels «Contratenor Altus» (= Altus) and «Contratenor Bassus» (= Bassus) are used. The mensuration sign 'Ø' that introduces the *Quia respexit* section (b. 8) had likewise largely fallen out of use by the early sixteenth century: the sign, though unique in the manuscript, does not appear in the table of symbols drawn up by the copyist on fol. 216*v*. These signs probably indicate that the piece was copied from an earlier source. The chant in LU, pp. 207 and 213 (*Tonus 1.*) is paraphrased in the Superius and the Tenor.

BIBLIOGRAPHY: CAO III, pp. 323-324; CS, pp. 430-433; IGC, p. 270; KIRSCH 1966, p. 144.

123.
Magnificat anima mea Dominum
fols. 89*v*–91*r*

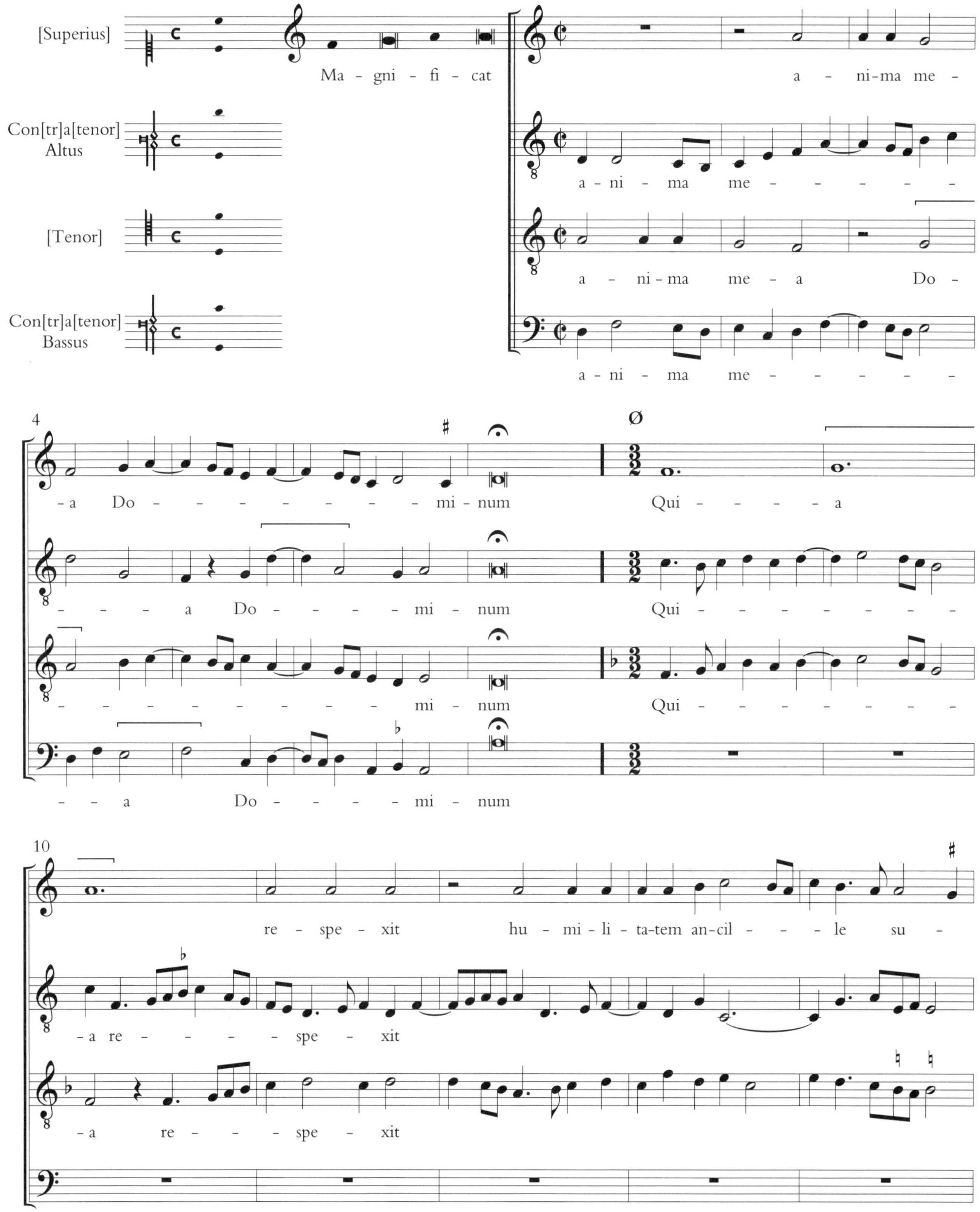

15
-e, ec - - ce e-nim ex hoc be-a - tam me di - - - cent
me di - - - cent

20
o - mnes ge-ne-ra - - ti - - - o - nes.
o - mnes ge-ne-ra - - ti - - - - o - nes.

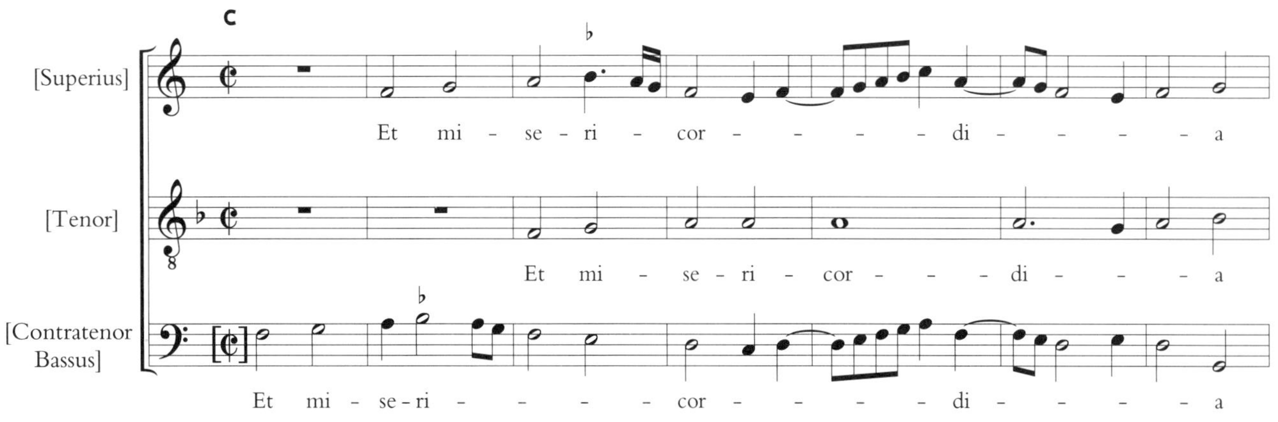
C
[Superius]
Et mi - se - ri - cor - - - - di - - - - a
[Tenor]
Et mi - se - ri - cor - - - - di - - - - a
[Contratenor Bassus]
Et mi - se-ri - - - - - cor - - - - - di - - - - a

643

Su - sce - pit I - sra - el pu - e - rum su - um,
Su - sce - pit
Su - sce - pit
54
re - cor - da - - - - tus mi -
61
- se - ri - cor - di - - - - - - - - e su - - - - - - e
68
Glo - - - - - ri - - - a Pa - tri et Fi - - - li - - -
Glo - - - - - ri - - - a
Glo - - - - - ri - - - a

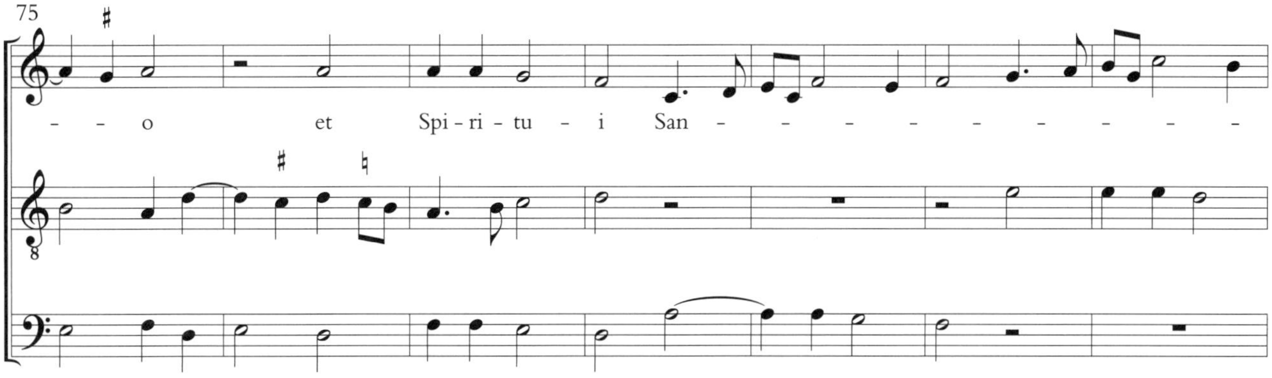
75
- - o et Spi - ri - tu - i San - - - - - - - - - - -

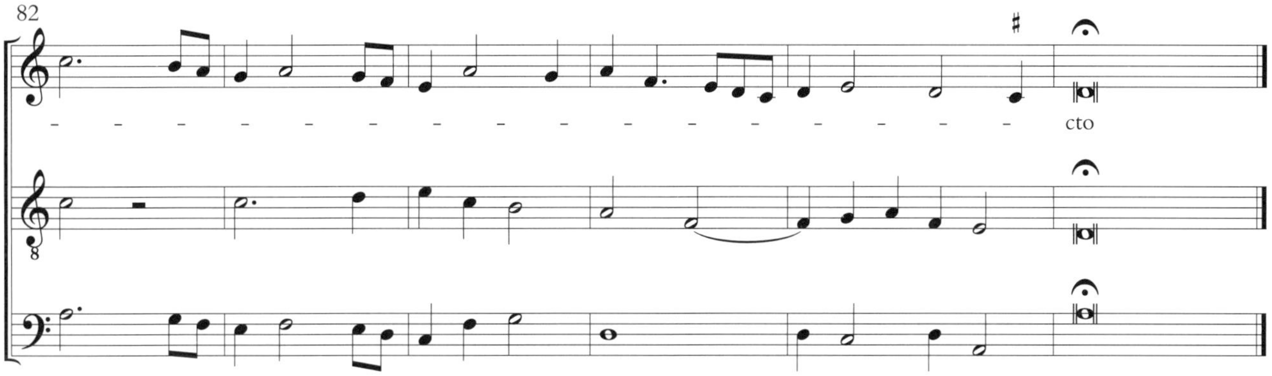
82
- - - - - - - - - - - - - - - - - cto

124.

La Spagna

fols. 91*v*–94*r* (4 vv.)

Io[HANNES] GHISELIN

La Spagna

Instrumental fantasy on a basse danse melody.[1]

READINGS EMENDED IN THE EDITION:

BAR	VOICE	ORIGINAL
19/II	B	*g semibrevis* corrected to *minima*
78/III	B	flat before *B*

MUSICAL CONCORDANCES (MSS):[2] • ParisN Rés27 (19*v*-20*v*), *Spagna*

MUSICAL CONCORDANCES (PRINTS):[3] • HanZanger (O2*v*-P1*r*), textless, «Ioannis Gyselini» • PeMotA1502 (31*v*-34*r*), «Jo. Ghiselin» • PeMotA1505 (31*v*-34*r*), «Jo. Ghiselin»

MODERN EDITIONS OF THE MUSIC: CMM 23/IV, pp. 32-36 (after PeMotA1502); DRAKE 1972, II, pp. 74-79 (after PeMotA1502).

REMARKS: Leaving out of consideration the manuscript intabulation and the print HanZanger (very late and with various graphic and substantive differences), the tradition of the piece in Panc.27 can be related only to PeMotA1502 (and its reprint). Although certainly earlier, it is rather improbable that Petrucci's print could have been the model copied by the scribe of Panc.27: the whole Superius of *Motetti A* is written in the mezzosoprano clef; it has an ornamental figure instead of the *g′ semibrevis* in bar 60/III; the two errors in the Bassus of Panc.27 do not appear there, and it lacks the B flat before the *B* in bar 10/III. Moreover, the layout of this very long piece is different graphically, even if in both sources the piece occupies six pages altogether. The copyist of Panc.27 has subdivided the piece into three homogenous sections of 30 bars each (the last section has 31 because of the cadential close) without any musical justification, while in the layout of *Motetti A* the three sections (bb. 1-28, 29-56, 57-91, not indicated by any rubric) always coincide with a cadence. Probably the copyist of Panc.27 was calculating the length of each section purely mechanically, confirmed also

---

[1]. The basse danse *La Spagna*, with choreography, is attested in the following manuscripts: Florence, Biblioteca Medicea Laurenziana, Antinori 13 (copied in 1510), fols. 28*v*-29*r*: anonymous choreography *La bassa di Castiglia*; New York, Public Library, Dance Collection, 'Giorgio' Manuscript, ★MGZMB-Res. 72-254 (written ca. 1480), fol. 36*r*: anonymous choreography; Siena, Biblioteca Comunale degli Intronati, L.V.29 (written ca. 1474), fol. 36*v*: anonymous choreography (see GALLO 1979, pp. 70 and 76).

[2]. Although not classifiable as concordances, the following manuscript versions are nevertheless more or less directly linked with the piece, because they share the same Tenor, sometimes transposed: BolM 16 (73*v*-74*r*); BolM 18 (48*v*-49*r*); BolM 18 (49*v*-50*r*); LeipU 1494 (63*v*-64*r*); MadP 1335 (223*r*); ParisN Rés27 (15*r*-16*v*); PerA 431 (95*v*-96*r*); PerA 431 (103*v*-104*r*); Perugia, Biblioteca Comunale Augusta, 1013 (*olim* M.36) (100*v*-102*r* and 112*v*-113*r*).

[3]. Although not classifiable as concordances, the following printed versions are nevertheless more or less directly linked with the piece, because they share the same Tenor: PeCantiC (147*v*-149*r*); PeSpinII (31*r*-33*r*).

by the little numbers added at the end of the *Prima* and *Tertia pars* and referring to the number of *semibreves*, excluding the final *longa* (see FILOCAMO 2004).

BIBLIOGRAPHY: ATLAS 1985, pp. 153-154; ATLAS 1998b, pp. 230-233; BOORMAN 1995, p. 48; BOORMAN 1995, p. 1078; BRAINARD 1985, pp. 80-81, n. 7; BROWN - POLK 2001, pp. 118, 129; BUKOFZER 1950, pp. 195-210; CATTIN 1975, p. 199; DISERTORI 1964, p. 72; DRAKE 1972, I, pp. 71-72; EDWARDS 1981, pp. 87-88; FALLOWS 1999, p. 529; FILOCAMO 2004; GALLO 1979; GUIDOBALDI 1995, pp. 66, 71, n. 68, 71-72; HEARTZ 1966; KÄMPER 1976, pp. 57, 89-91, 102-103; KINKELDEY 1959, pp. 6, 22, 26-27; LITTERICK 1981, pp. 124-125; PESCERELLI 1974, pp. 50, 52; REESE 1990, pp. 187, 226, 281, 545, 651, 699; SPARTI 1993.

124.
LA SPAGNA
fols. 91*v*-94*r*

Io[hannes] Ghiselin

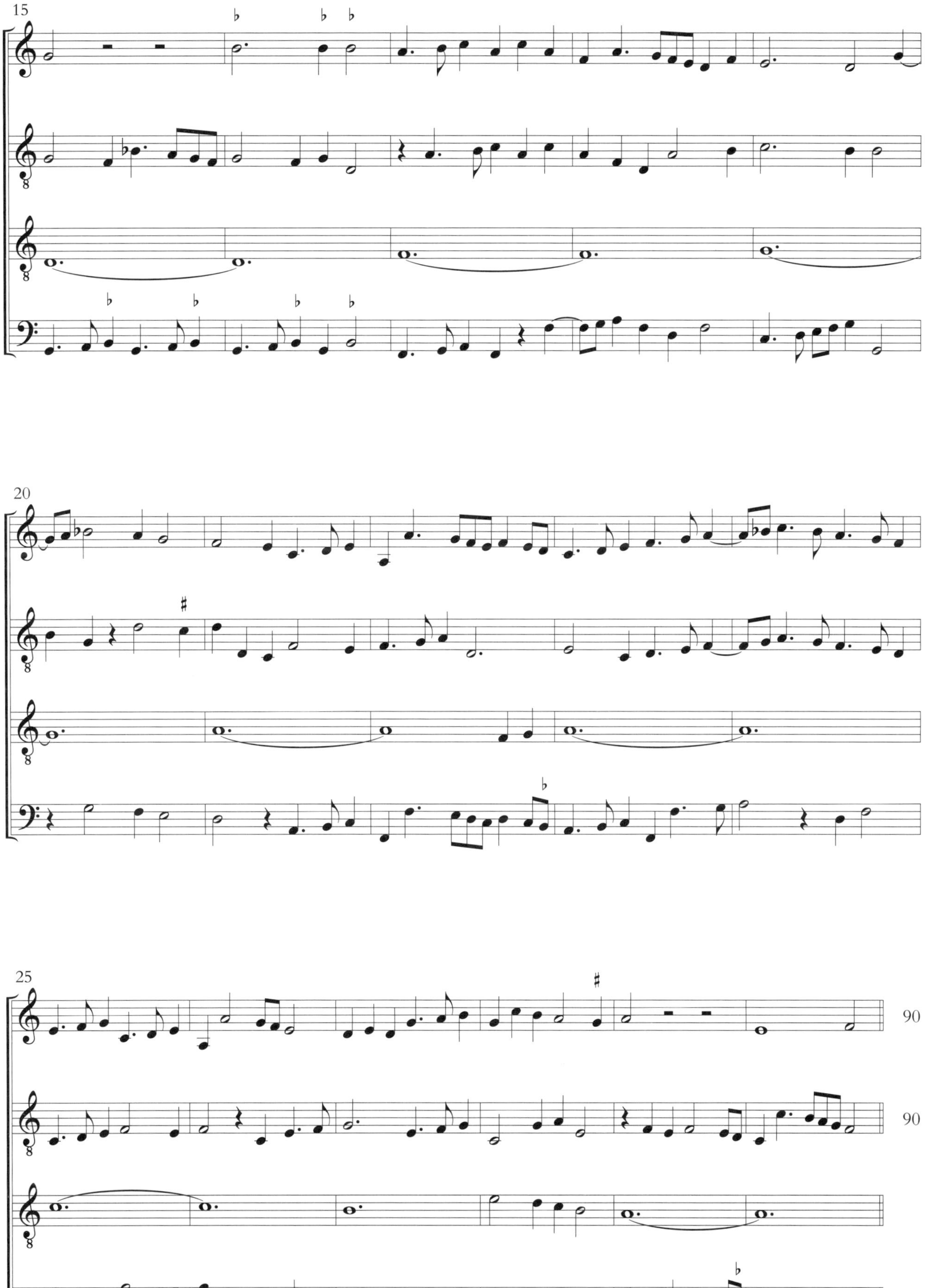
15
20
25
90
90

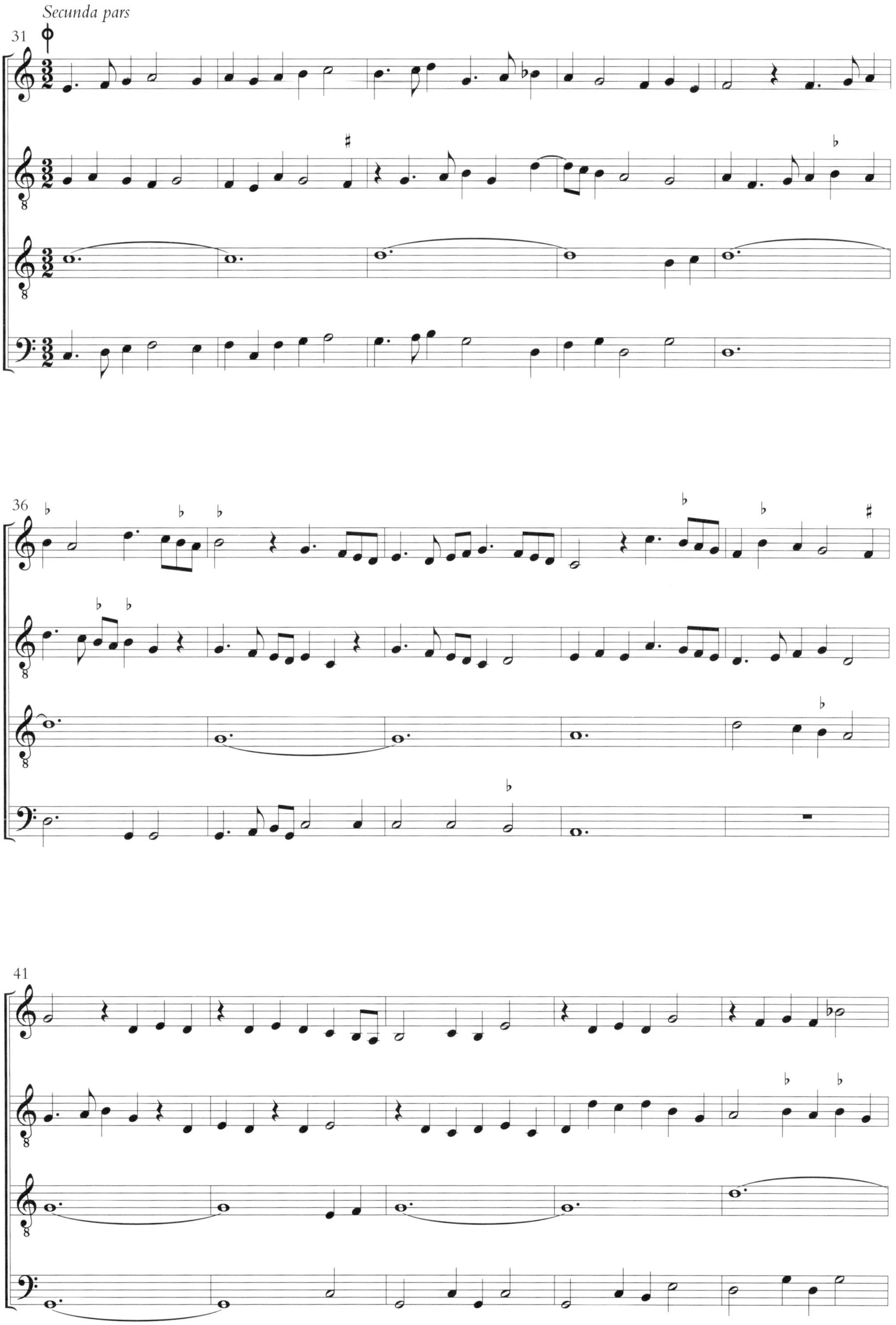
Secunda pars
31
36
41

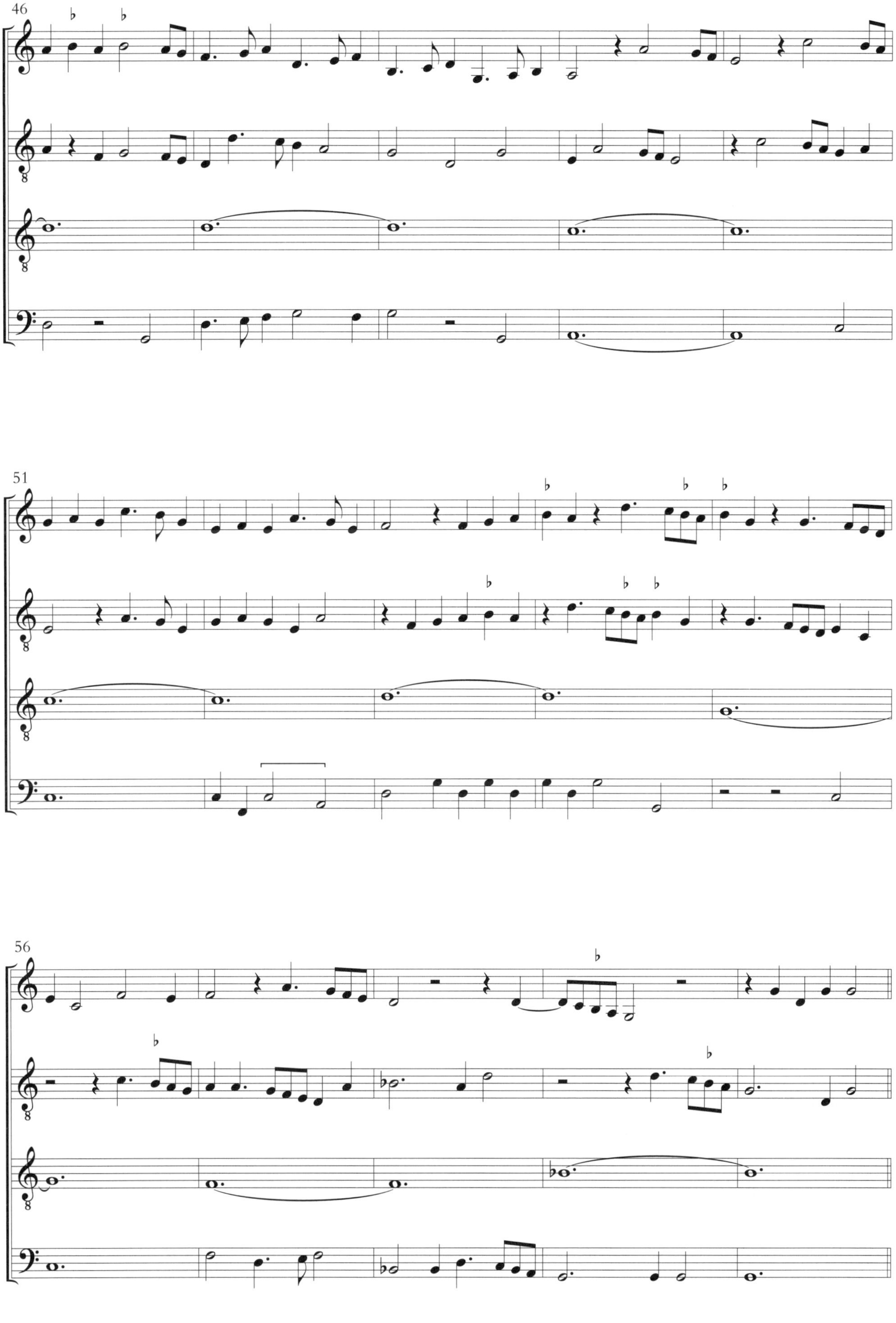
46
51
56

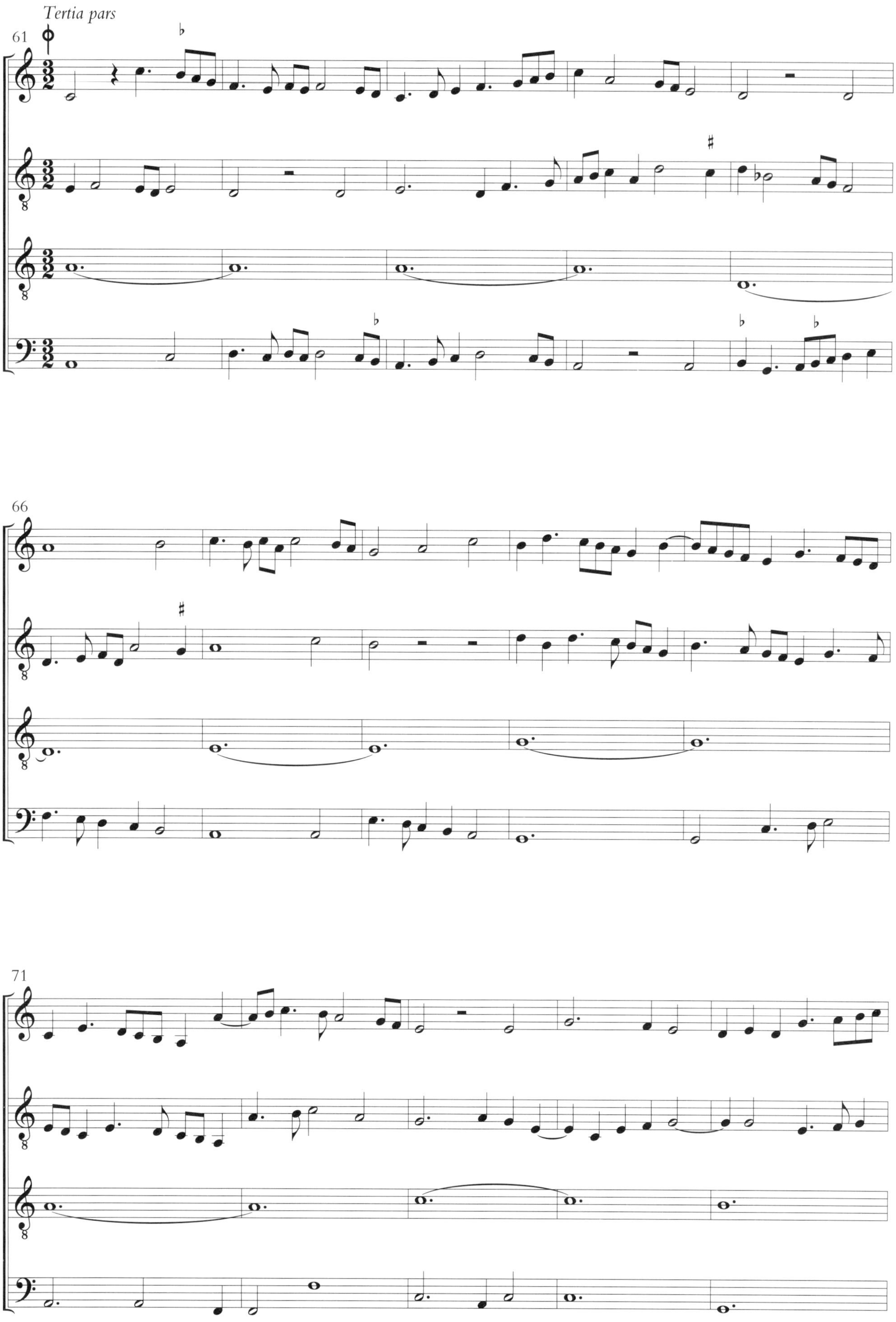
Tertia pars
61
66
71

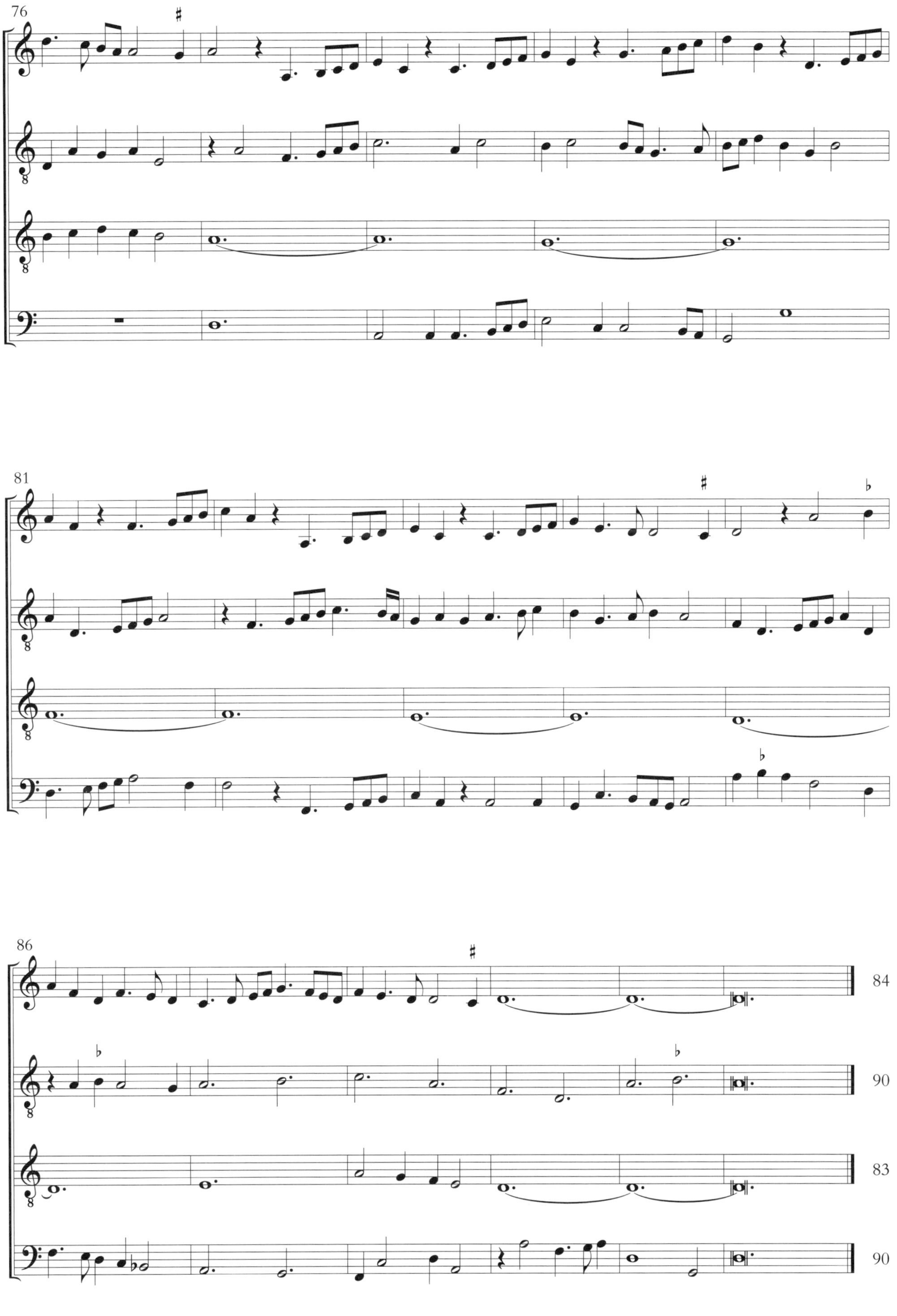
76
81
86
84
90
83
90

125.

Regina celi [letare]

fols. 94*v*-95*r* (3 vv.)

Antonius Perag[ulfus] Luc[ensis]

Regina celi

For the text see no. 94.

Readings emended in the edition:

Bar	Voice	Original
73/I	S	*g′ brevis*, corrected to a *semibrevis* with a rising stem on the left[1]
125-128	T	under each of the four white *breves* appears the figure «3»

Modern editions of the music: Banks 1993, II, pp. 160-163 (after Panc.27).

Remarks: At the end of fol. 94*v* (sixth stave, corresponding to b. 108 of the Tenor) there is a little hand with the index finger pointing to the next page, with a sign « + »: this is the only instance in the manuscript of a clear reference of this type to the following page. The use of a little hand as a pointer occurs quite often in older manuscripts, and it is surprising that in Panc.27 it is used so infrequently. In this *Regina celi* the hand is superfluous (the *custos* would be sufficient, which is also present), but it would have been very useful, on the other hand, in other situations where voices from different pieces are crowded together on the same opening (a prominent example is on fols. 210*v*-211*r*). The chant in AM, pp. 179-180, AR, pp. 67-68, LR, pp. 48-49, and LU, pp. 275 and 278 is paraphrased in all voices, but most closely in the Tenor.

Bibliography: Banks 1993, I, p. 287; CAO III, p. 440; Filocamo 2004; IGC, p. 361.

---

[1]. An analogous case is mentioned by Giovanni Spataro in a letter to Pietro Aaron dated 6 November 1523 (see Blackburn *et al.* 1991, p. 282). I thank Bonnie Blackburn for having brought this document to my attention.

125.
REGINA CELI [LETARE]
fols. 94v–95r

Antonius Perag[ulfus] Luc[ensis]

S[uperius] — Regina celi

T[enor] — Regina celi

Contra — Regina

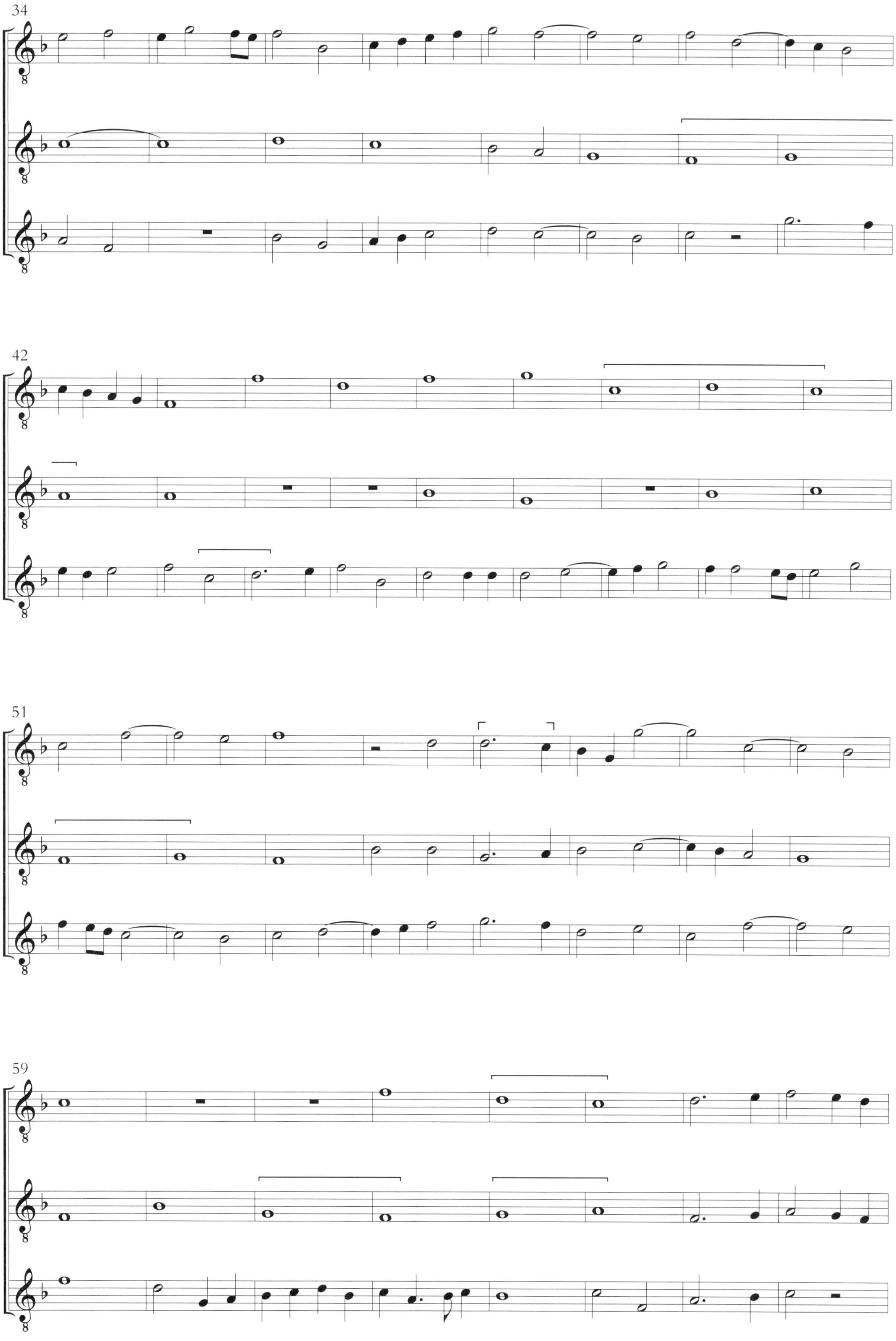
34
42
51
59

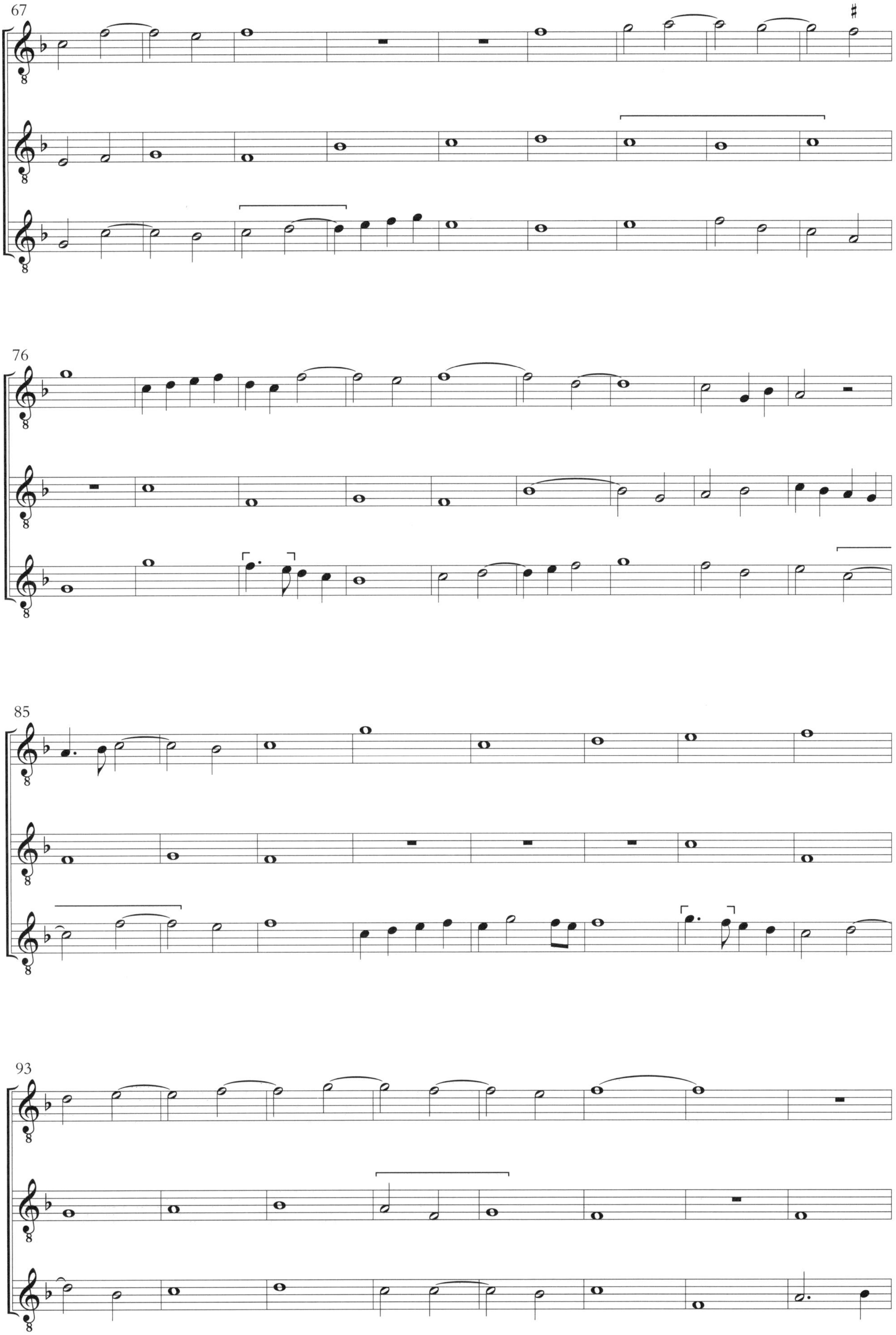
67
76
85
93

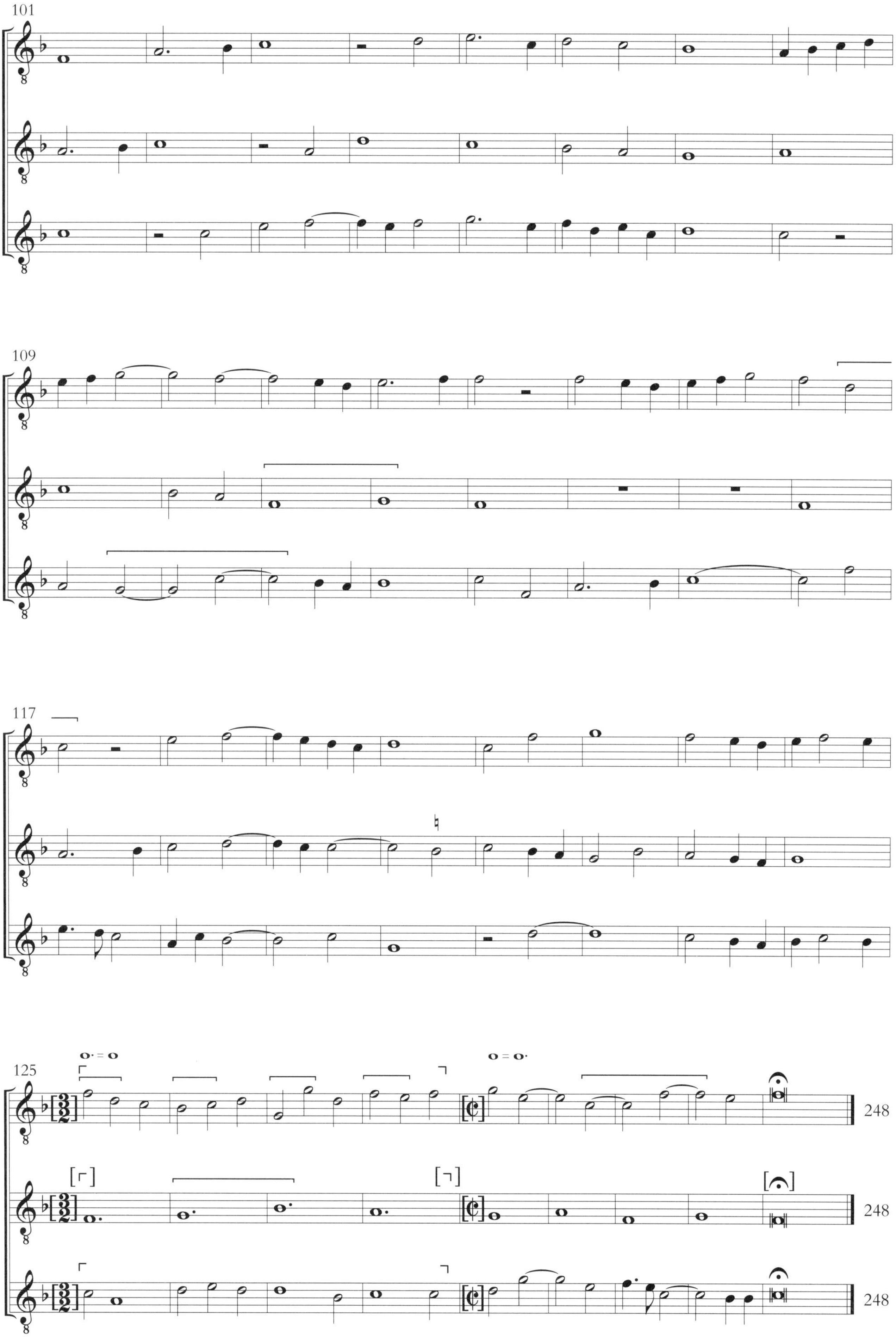
101
109
117
125
248
248
248

126.

PROPTER GRAVAMEN [ET TORMENTUM]

fols. 95*v*-97*r* (4 vv.)

[LOYSET] COMPERE

Propter gravamen […]

Memento nostri […]

Intercessory prayer to the Blessed Virgin Mary.

READINGS EMENDED IN THE EDITION:

BAR	VOICE	ORIGINAL
101	B	the *Secunda pars* opens with a mensuration sign of *tempus perfectum diminutum cum prolatione minori*
128	A	*longa* with fermata

MUSICAL CONCORDANCES (MSS): • BarcC 454 (133*v*-135*r*), *Propter gravamen et tormentum* • CambM 125-8 (S: 71*v*-72*r*, A: 71*v*-72*r*, T: 71*v*-72*r*, B: 71*v*-72*r*), *Propter gravamen et tormentum* • CV S15 (193*v*-196*r*), *Propter gravamen et tormentum* • SGS 530 (78*v*-79*r*), *Propter gravame* [*sic*], *Prima pars* only, «Compere» • WrocU 428 (196*v*-198*r*), *Propter gravamen et tormentum*, «Compere»

MUSICAL CONCORDANCES (PRINTS): • PeMotA1502 (10*v*-13*r*), *Propter gravamen et tormentum*, «Compere» • PeMotA1505 (10*v*-13*r*), *Propter gravamen et tormentum*, «Compere»

TEXT FROM PeMotA1502:

> Propter gravamen et tormentum,
> quod torquebatur spiritum tuum et cor tuum, Virgo Maria,
> quando filium tuum per doloribus voce magna clamantem,
> et te matrem d[u]lcissimam Ioanni commendantem,
> 5   et in manu Patris commendato Spiritum deficientem attendebas:
> Succurre nobis peccatoribus,
> quando lingue nostre non potuerunt amplius nominare,
> oculi obscurabuntur, aures surdescent,
> omnesque vires et sensus anime deficient.
>
> 10   Memento nostri, piissima mater misericordie,
> quae nunc perfugimus ad aures tue pietatis,
> et subveni in hora ultima et extreme necessitatis,
> per quem a cunctis terroribus servamus,
> et ad celestis patrie requiem,
> 15   in pro teque duce pervenire mereamur.
>
> Amen.

MODERN EDITIONS OF THE MUSIC: CMM 15/IV, pp. 45-48 (after PeMotA1502); DRAKE 1972, II, pp. 26-32 (after PeMotA1502); SM 8, pp. 193-194 (after SGS 530).

REMARKS: The version of Panc.27 is clearly distant from that of all the manuscripts because of several substantive variants, two of which — in the Altus — are shared by more than one other manuscript: bar 63, *a* instead of *f* (BarcC 454, CambM 125-8); bar 176/II, *d′* instead of *e′* (BarcC 454, CambM 125-8, CV S15). The scribe of Panc.27 certainly used Petrucci's print as a model: throughout this very long piece there are very few graphic variants, not significant for the transmission (a dot of addition instead of a repeated note in the Superius, some ligatures instead of separated notes or vice versa), while the Tenor is completely identical. The text is complete in PeMotA1502 (and its reprint), whereas Panc.27 has only the incipit.

BIBLIOGRAPHY: BOORMAN 2006, p. 936; BROWN 1990, p. 755, n. 38; DRAKE 1972, I, pp. 65-66, 144, 185, 186, 198, 312-313; FILOCAMO 2004; ROS-FÁBREGAS 1992, I, pp. 152-153; SHERR 1996, p. 120; SM 8, p. 354.

126.
PROPTER GRAVAMEN [ET TORMENTUM]

fols. 95*v*–97*r*

[Loyset] Compere

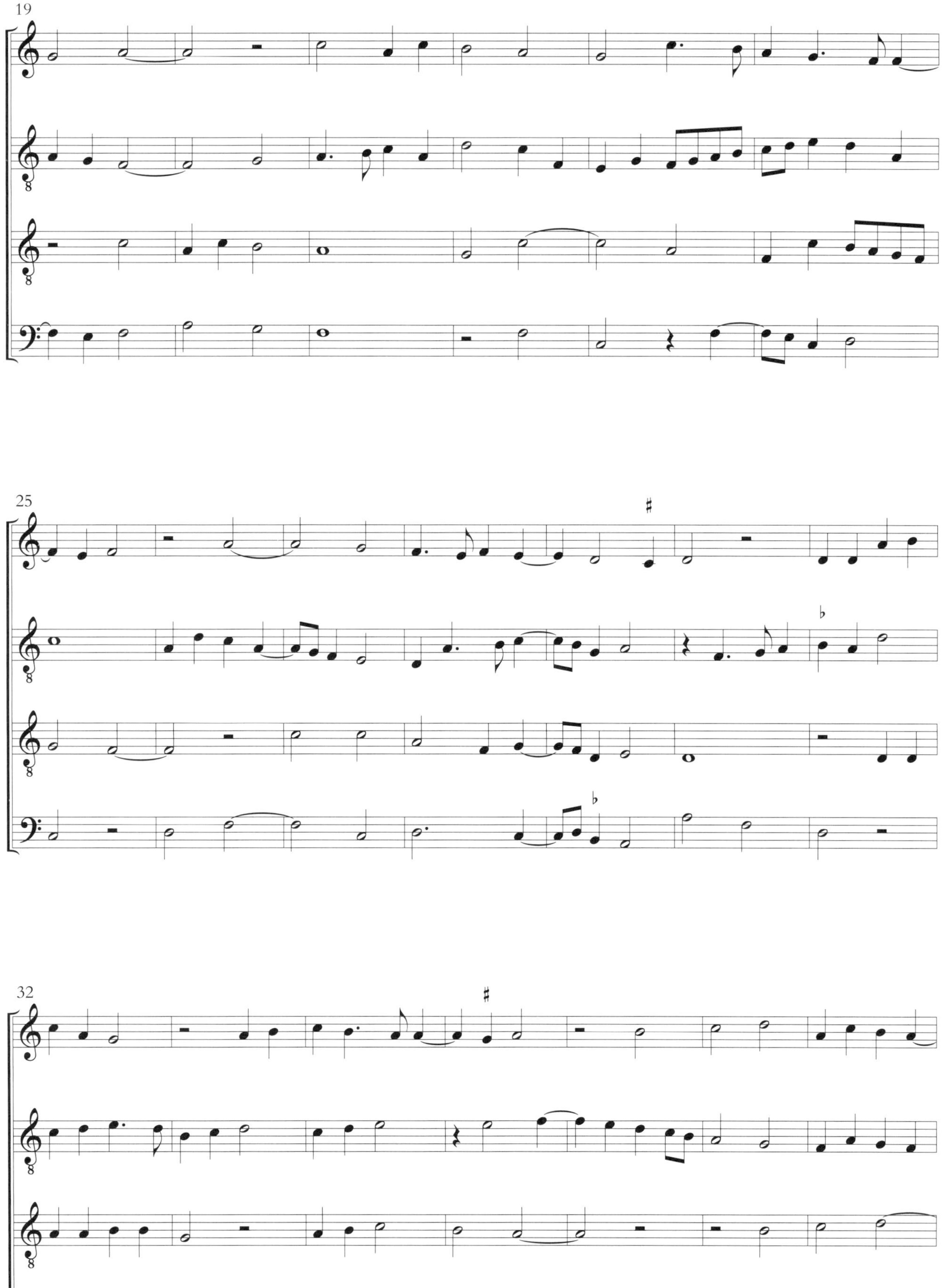
19
25
32

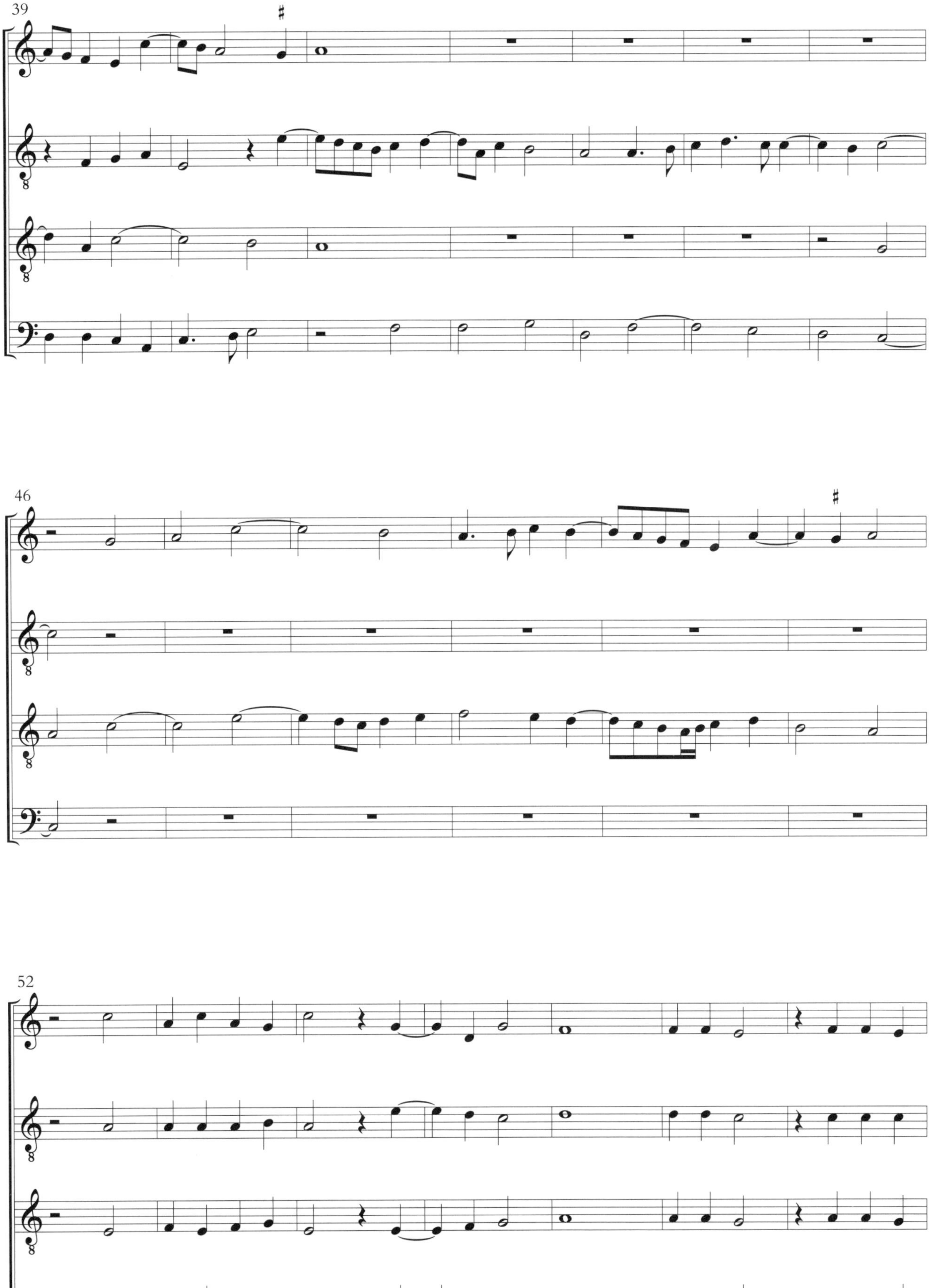
39
46
52

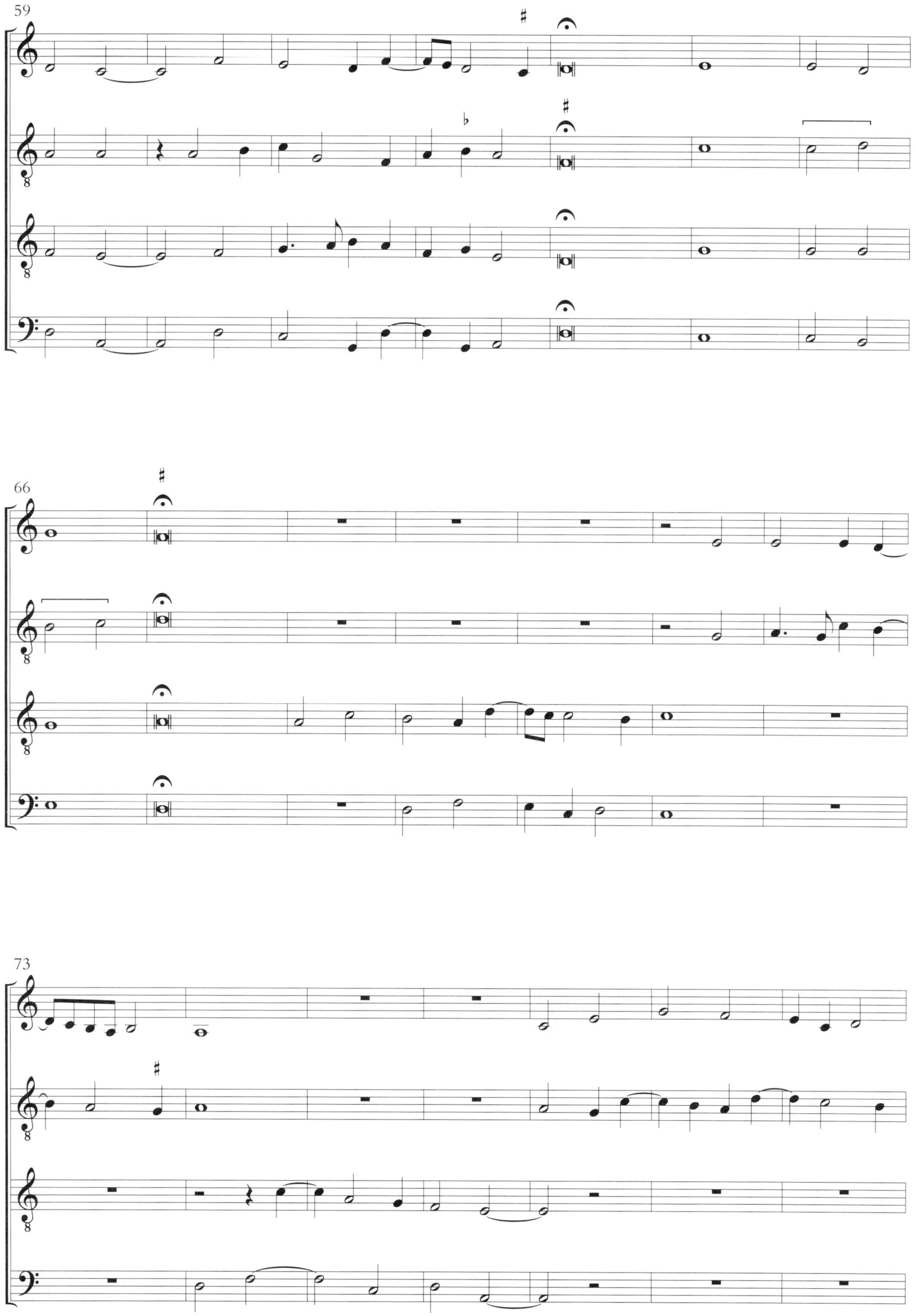
59
66
73

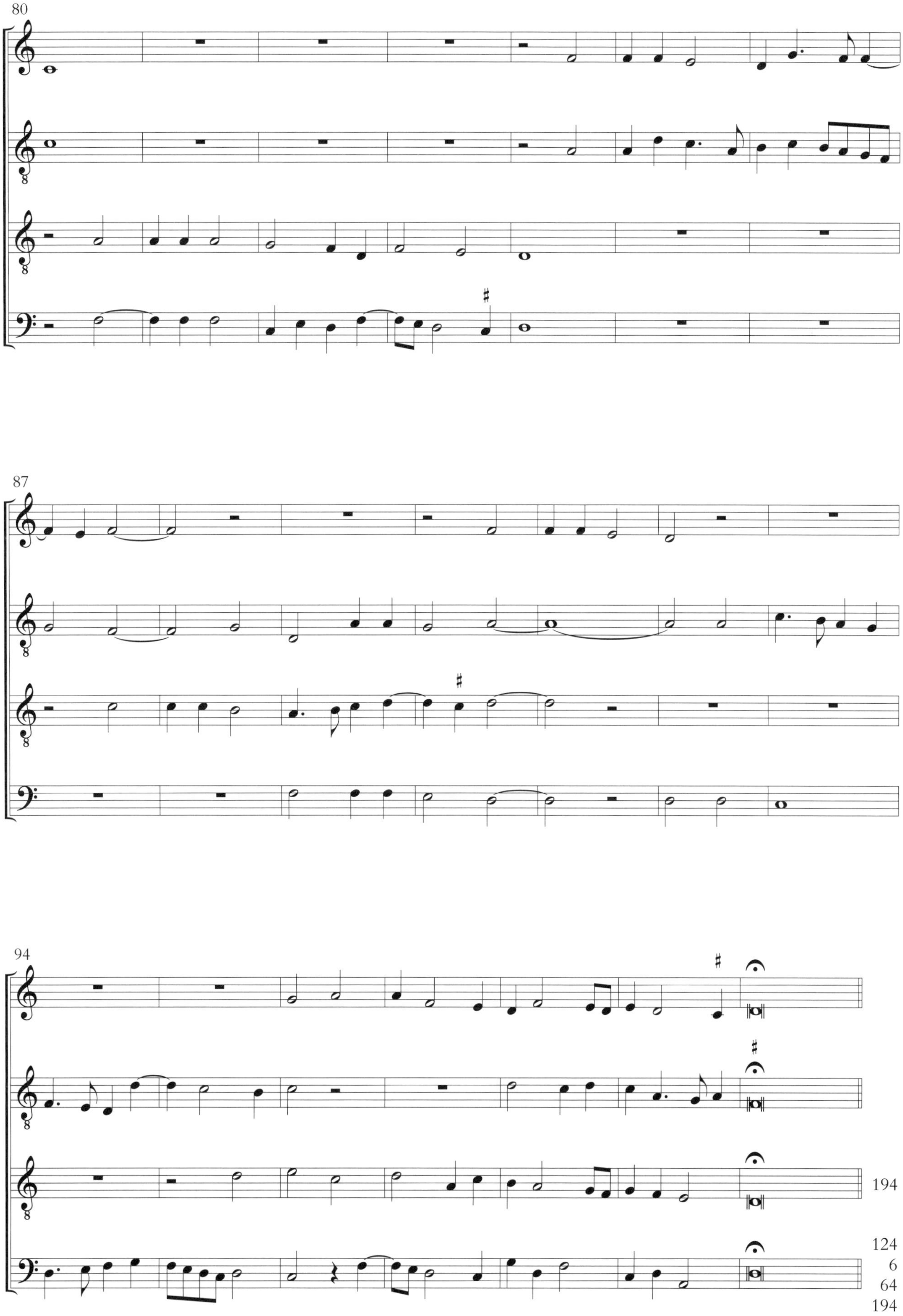
80
87
94
194
124
6
64
194

Secunda pars

Memento nostri

Memento nostri

Memento nostri

Memento

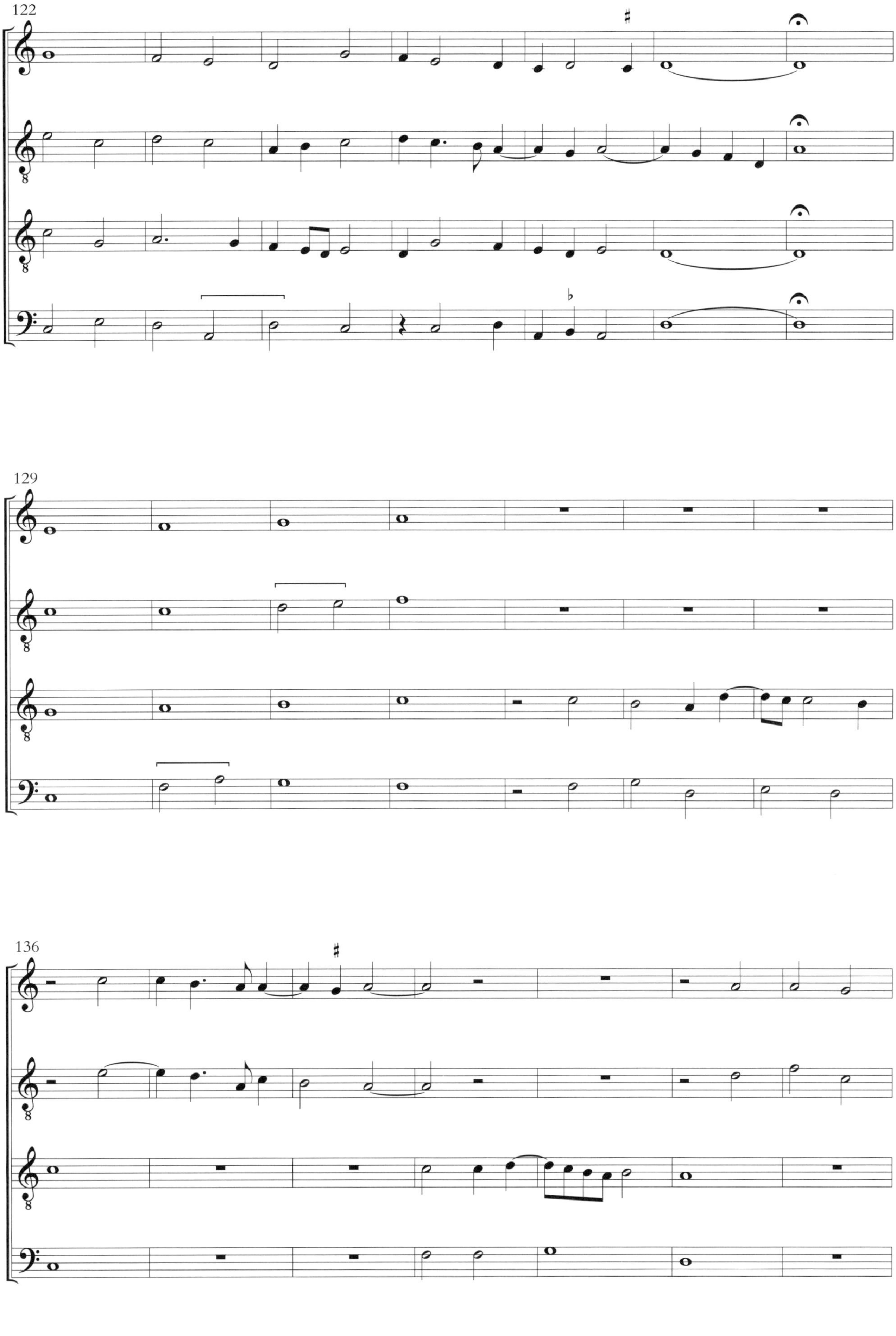
122
129
136

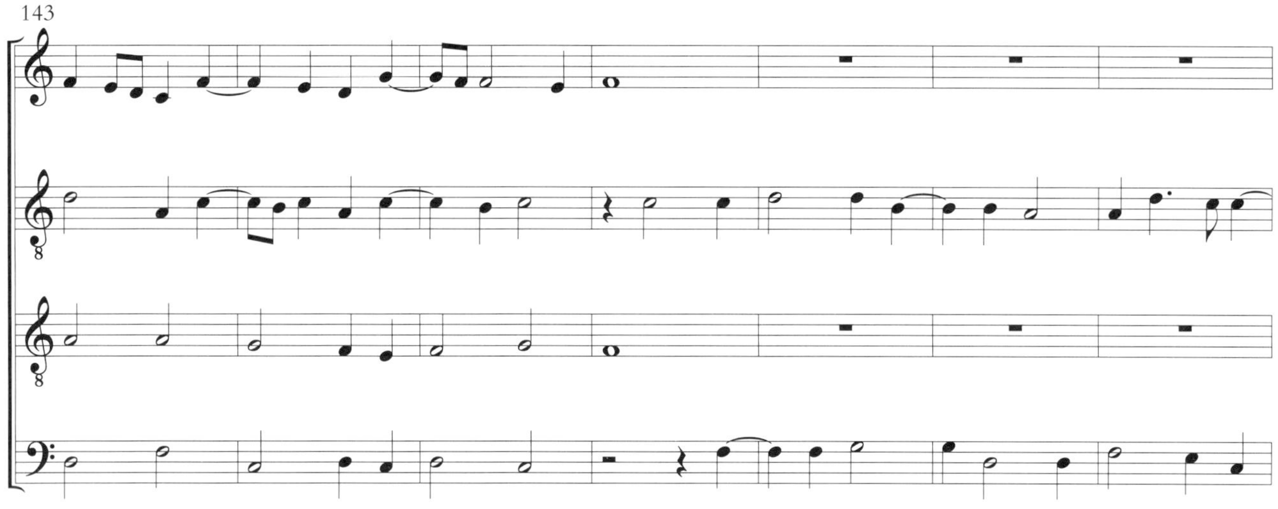
143

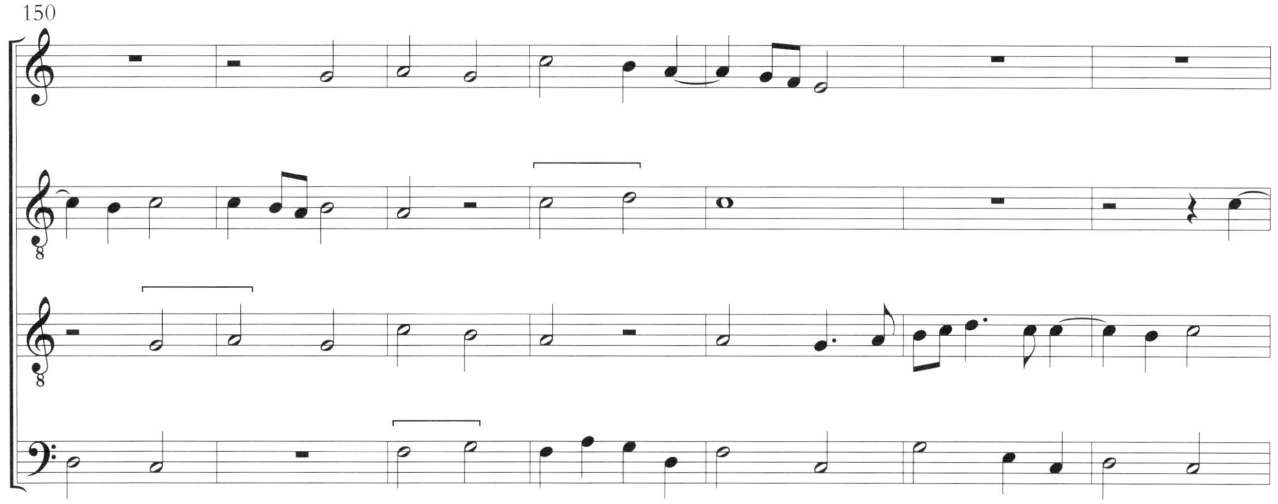
150

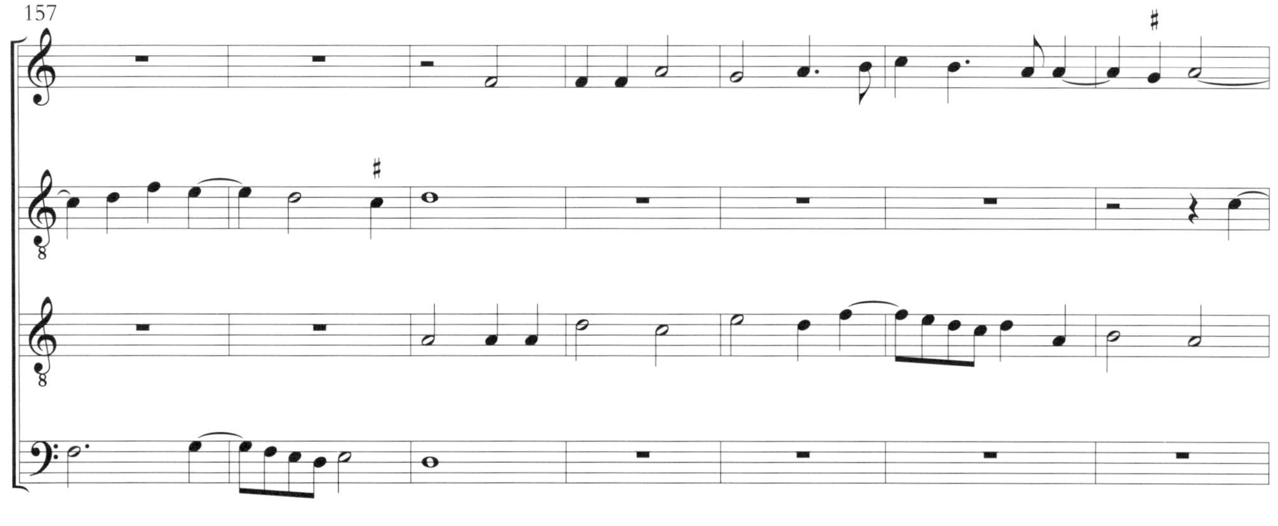
157

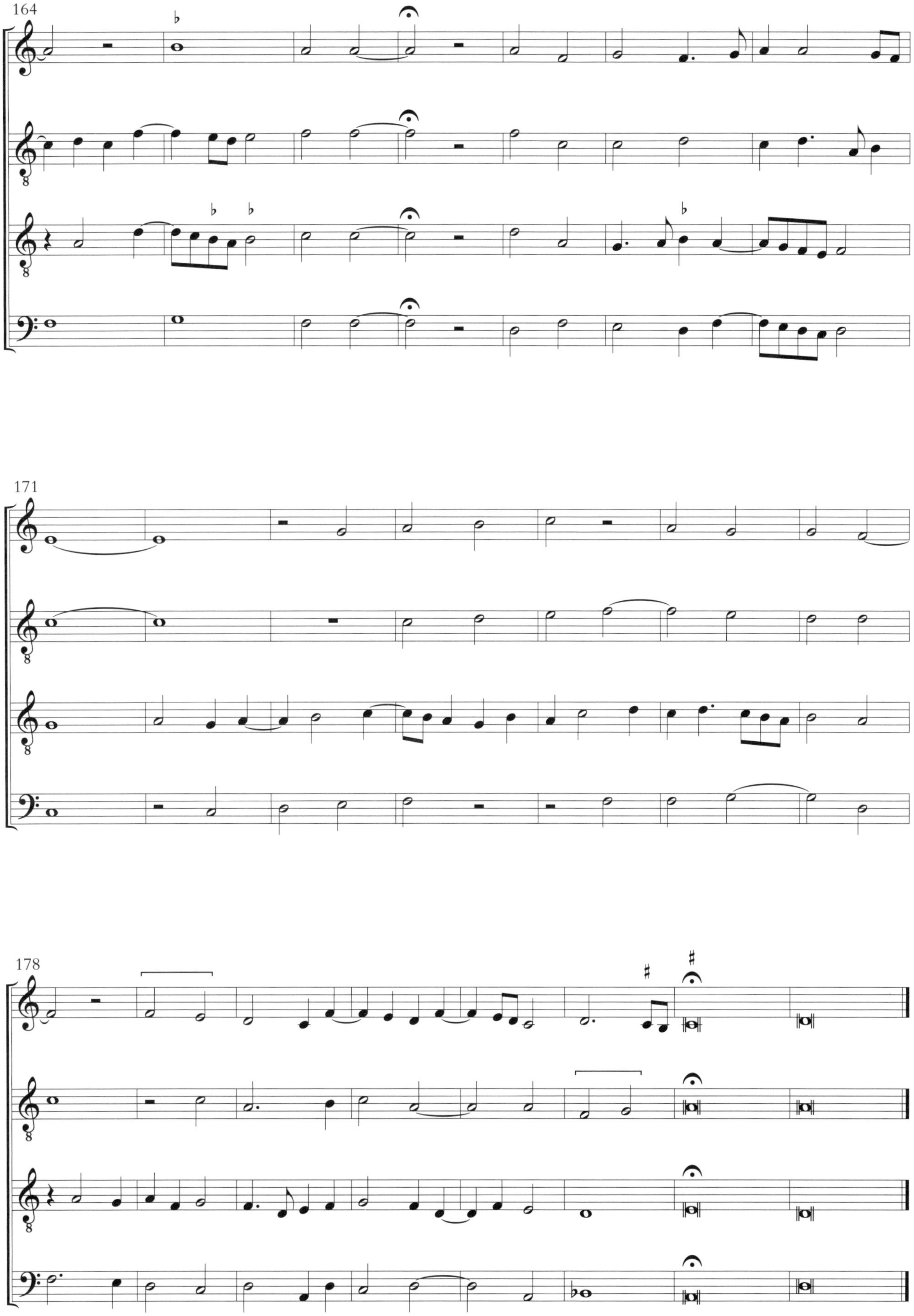
164
171
178

127.

ALES REGRES, [VUIDEZ DE MA PRESENCE]

fols. 97*v*–98*r* (3 vv.)

[JEAN II, DUC DE BOURBON]   HAYNE [VAN GHIZEGHEM]

Ales regres

Chanson (rondeau cinquain).

READINGS EMENDED IN THE EDITION:

BAR	VOICE	ORIGINAL
48/II	Ct	*f* instead of *g*

TEXTUAL CONCORDANCES (MSS): • *Paris.N. F.1719* (30*v*), *Alles regretz vuiduez de ma presence* • *Paris.N. F.1719* (144*v*), only ll. 1–3, *Allez regretz vuidez de ma presence*

MUSICAL CONCORDANCES (MSS): • BerlS 40026 (21*r*–22*v*), *Ales regres in fa* • BolM 17 (30*v*–31*r*), «Hayne» • BruxR 90 / TournaiV 94 (S: 1*v*–2*v*(?),[1] T: 1*v*–3*r*), 2 vv. (S and T only) • BruxR 11239 (2*v*–4*r*) • ChN 25 (37*v*–38*v*) • CV G27 (20*v*–21*r*, *olim* 27*v*–28*r*), «Hayne» • FirN BR229 (242*v*–243*r*) • FirN M107bis (43*v*–44*r*, *olim* 32*v*–33*r*), S: *Ales rigret ales aglor Squoris votra autas* • FirN M117 (32*v*–33*r*, *olim* 38*v*–39*r*), *Alles regretz vuidez de ma plaisance* • FirN M178 (42*v*–43*r*), «Hayne» • FirR 2356 (91*v*–92*r*) • FirR 2794 (58*v*–59*r*), *Allez regret vuidez de ma plaisance*, «Heyne» • KøbK 1848 (414) • LeipU 49-50 (S: 211*r*–*v*, Ct: 210*v*–211*r*), *secunda pars* of the motet *Nuptiae factae sunt* of Martin Agricola («M. Agr») with the text *Dulcis conjugi bonum sit omen*, 2 vv. (S and Ct only) • LonB A31922 (5*v*–6*r*), *Alles regretz vuidez* • LonB RXVI (20*v*–21*r*), *Alez regret vuydes de ma presence* • ParisN F1597 (11*v*–12*r*), *Allez regretz vuidez* • ParisN F2245 (17*v*–18*r*), «Hayne», «bourbon» • RomaCa 2856 (96*v*–98*r*), «Haine» • SegC (163*v*), «Scoen (Groen?) Heyne» • TorN 27 (12*v*), *Alles regret vuydes de ma presance* • UppsU 76a (1*r*), *Allez regretz vuidez de ma presence*, 2 vv. (T and Ct only), later hand: «[Hayne van Ghizeghem]», • VerCap 757 (28*v*–29*r*), textless, modern hand: «Hayne Ales regres» • WashC L25 (140*v*–142*r*) • ZwR 78/3 (no. 11), textless

MUSICAL CONCORDANCES (PRINTS): • EgenLieder (III, no. 26), S only • FormGerle (43*v*–44*v*) • FormTrium (no. 7), textless, but in the Jena copy only, added by hand: «Hayne. Ales regres» • PeOdh1501 (62*v*–63*r*), «Hayne» • PeOdh1503 (62*v*–63*r*), «Hayne» • PeOdh1504 (62*v*–63*r*), «Hayne»

TEXT FROM FirR 2794 (but according to the version emended in BROWN 1983, I, p. 297):

    Allez Regret, vuidez de ma presence;
    allez ailleurs querir vostre acointance;
    assés avés tourmenté mon las cueur
    rempli de dueil pour estre serviteur
5   d'une sans per que j'ay amée d'enfance.

    Fait luy avés longuement ceste offence.
    Où est celuy qui onc fut né en France

---

[1]. Incomplete; fol. 3 is lacking in BruxR 90.

qui endurast tel mortel deshonneur?
    Allez Regret, […]

N'y tournés plus, car, par ma conscience,
10   se plus vous voy prochain de ma plaisance,
devant chascun vous feray tel honneur
que l'en dira que la main d'ung seigneur
vous a bien mis en la malle meschance.
    Allez Regret, […]

MODERN EDITIONS OF THE TEXT: AMAURY 1894, p. 117 (after TournaiV 94); BROWN 1983, I, p. 297 (after FirR 2794); CHRISTOFFERSEN 1994, I, p. 121 (after FirR 2794); CMM 22/V, p. xxii (after *Paris.N. F.1719*, 30*v*); FRANÇON 1934, p. 184 (after BruxR 11239 and after *Paris.N. F.1719*, 30*v*); GACHET 1849, p. 61 (after BruxR 11239); GREENBERG - MAYNARD 1975, p. 163 (after LonB A31922); LITTERICK 1995, p. 160 (after the musical version of CMM 74; the final line of the refrain is taken from LonB RXVI); PICKER 1965, p. 418; SHIPP 1960, II, p. 287 (with the *residuum* from WALLIS 1929); WALLIS 1929, no. 237 (after LonB RXVI).

MODERN EDITIONS OF THE MUSIC: BECHERINI 1942-43, pp. 344-347 (after FirR 2794); BROWN 1983, II, pp. 527-529 (after FirN BR229); CHRISTOFFERSEN 1994, I, pp. 122-124 (after KøbK 1848); CMM 74, pp. 3-5; DROZ - THIBAULT 1924 (1976), pp. 49-54 (after ParisN F2245); EDM 91, pp. 32-34, (after BerlS 40026); GERLE 1976, p. 17 (after FormGerle); GOMBOSI 1925, *Notenanhang*, no. 3 (after PeOdh1504); GOMBOSI 1955, pp. 62-64 (after ChN 25); GREENBERG - MAYNARD 1975, pp. 164-166 (after LonB A31922); HEWITT 1942, pp. 341-342 (after PeOdh1504); IMM 4, pp. 16-19 (after ParisN F2245); JONES 1971, II, pp. 277-279 (after FirR 2794); LITTERICK 1976, pp. 250-251 (after LonB RXVI); LITTERICK 1995, pp. 161-162 (after CMM 74); van MALDEGHEM, *Musique profane*, XIII, no. 34 (after BruxR 11239) (headed *"Recommandation" Recueillez-vous*, and considered a work of Compère); MARIX 1937, pp. 118-120 (after ParisN F2245); MÖNKEMEYER 1985, I, p. 16 (after FormTrium); PIERCE 1973, II, p. 367 (after FormGerle); PICKER 1965, pp. 416-418, (after BruxR 11239); SHIPP 1960, II, pp. 285-288 (after ParisN F1597); SMIJERS J/43, pp. 83-84 (after PeOdh1504); STEVENS 1962, p. 3 (after LonB A31922); VILLANIS 1905, *Supplemento*, no. 1, pp. 2-5 (after TorN 27); WOLFF 1970, II, pp. 262-264, (after RomaCa 2856).

REMARKS: The version in Panc.27 can be directly linked only with *Odhecaton* and ZwR 78/3 (a version that Martin Picker believes is derived from Petrucci).[2] Panc.27 has few differences with respect to *Odhecaton*: it adds a fermata at the end of the Superius and Tenor, has a change of clef in the Contra on a new stave (whereas Petrucci needed to add an upper ledger line covering bb. 48/II-52), and substitutes a repeated *c′* for the dot of addition in Contra, bar 25/II (but in this case too a change of stave is involved, after the first *c′*). Considering the presence of the same attribution, the same amount of text in *Odhecaton* and Panc.27, and the conjunctive error in bar 48/II of the Contra, it is reasonable to hypothesize that the scribe had Petrucci as a model.

BIBLIOGRAPHY: ATLAS 1975-76, I, pp. 81-82; BAKER 1978, I, pp. 431-432; BOORMAN 2006, pp. 1032-1033; BROWN 1963, pp. 186-187; BROWN 1983, I, pp. 296-297; CHOLIJ 1992; CHRISTOFFERSEN 1994, I, pp. 120-128, 160-161; CMM 74, pp. xxxiv-xxxv; DROZ - THIBAULT 1924 (1976), p. 83; EDM 92, p. 151; FALLOWS 1999, pp. 81-83; FERY-HUE 1991, pp. 40, 119; FILOCAMO 2004; GEERING 1933, p. 235; GREENBERG - MAYNARD 1975, pp. 162-163; HEWITT 1942, pp. 155-156, 177; JONES 1971, II, pp. 133-136; LAMA DE LA CRUZ 1994, pp. 247-248; LITTERICK 1976, pp. 197-199; LITTERICK 1995; MARIX 1939, p. 236; MECONI 1994; POWERS 1994, pp. 504-509; SCHWOB 1905, p. 27; SHIPP 1960, pp. 164-166; WOLFF 1970, I, pp. 296-302.

---

[2]. See PICKER 1965, p. 150.

127.
ALES REGRES, [VUIDEZ DE MA PRESENCE]
fols. 97*v*–98*r*

[Jean II, duc de Bourbon]   Hayne [van Ghizeghem]

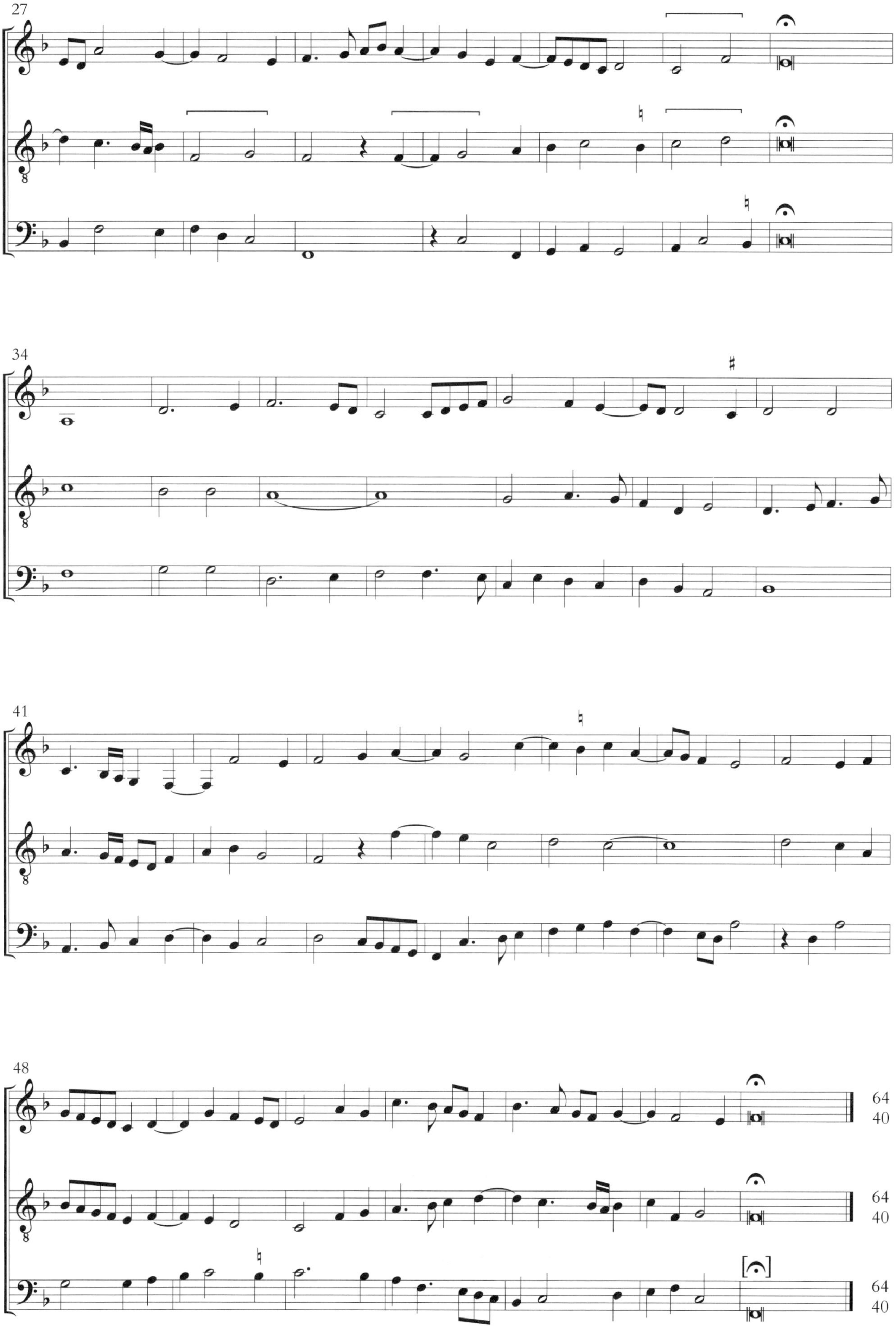
27
34
41
48
64
40

128.

LA ALFONSINA[1]

fols. 98*v*-99*r* (3 vv.)

IO[HANNES] GHISELIN

[Heading only]

Instrumental piece.

MUSICAL CONCORDANCES (MSS): • SGS 461 (80-81), «Io. Gisilin»

MUSICAL CONCORDANCES (PRINTS): • EgenLieder (III, no. 53), S only • FormTrium (no. 49), textless, but in the Jena copy only, added by hand: «Joh. Ghiselin. La alfonsina» • HanZanger (E3*v*-F1*r*), textless, «Io. Ghiselin» • PeOdh1501 (87*v*-88*r*), «Jo. Ghiselin» • PeOdh1503 (87*v*-88*r*), «Jo. Ghiselin» • PeOdh1504 (87*v*-88*r*), «Jo. Ghiselin» • PetreiusNewII (no. XV), «Jo. Ghiselin»

MODERN EDITIONS OF THE MUSIC: AMBROS V, pp. 190-192 (after PeOdh1501); ATLAS 1998a, pp. 265-266 (after PeOdh1504); CESARI *ET AL.* 1954, pp. xliv-xlv (after PeOdh1504); CMM 23/IV, pp. 36-38 (after PeOdh1504); GIESBERT 1936, II, pp. 92-93 (after SGS 461); HEWITT 1942, pp. 387-388 (after PeOdh1504); MÖNKEMEYER 1985, I, pp. 74-75 (after FormTrium).

REMARKS: The version of Panc.27 is identical with that of SGS 461, if one excepts the lack of the precautionary B flat before the *b* (Contra, b. 25/II) and the different spelling of the attribution. Although the sources are probably contemporary, a direct contact between the two manuscripts is unlikely, since SGS 461 comes from a German-speaking area. The various printed sources that transmit the piece are all rather late (from the 1530s to after the mid-1550s), with the single exception of *Odhecaton*. The version of Panc.27 was certainly copied from this print, but on this point an observation may be made: certainly the model for the copyist of Panc.27 was not the exemplar in the Biblioteca Capitolare of Treviso (PeOdh1504) because certain graphic elements distance it from the exemplars of the Museo Internazionale e Biblioteca della Musica in Bologna (PeOdh1501) and the Library of Congress in Washington, DC (PeOdh1504, which therefore cannot be considered a copy of the same printing as the copy in Treviso). The discrepancies in the copy in Treviso are the following: at bar 21/II of the Tenor the note head of the *b* is missing; at bar 38 of the Tenor the *c′* was not printed; at bar 60/II of the Contra the *semibrevis c* is black rather than white.

BIBLIOGRAPHY: BOORMAN 2006, p. 985; BROWN - POLK 2001, p. 131; BROWN - STEIN 1999, p. 84; CESARI *ET AL.* 1954, p. ix; EDWARDS 1981, pp. 89-90; FILOCAMO 2004; HEWITT 1942, p. 163; KÄMPER 1976, pp. 74, 87-88, 131; REESE 1990, pp. 281-282; TORREFRANCA 1939, p. 208.

---

[1]. Many scholars prefer to capitalize the initial 'a' in 'alfonsina', since they believe that the piece may refer to Alfonso, the son of Ercole I d'Este, who was to inherit the title of Duke of Ferrara in 1505 (see, for example, STROHM 1993, p. 570, n. 612). The hypothesis is suggestive and not implausible, since Ghiselin had known professional contacts with Ferrara. Helen Hewitt enlarges the range of possibilities, suggesting that it might allude to Alfonsina de' Medici, wife of Piero, son of Lorenzo il Magnifico (see HEWITT 1942, p. 76, n. 73). But I prefer to adopt a lower-case 'a' because, apart from there being no proof of a dedication to well-known real people, I believe that the piece was copied from Petrucci's *Odhecaton*, in which the various editions always use a lower-case 'a'.

128.
LA ALFONSINA
fols. 98*v*-99*r*

Io[hannes] Ghiselin

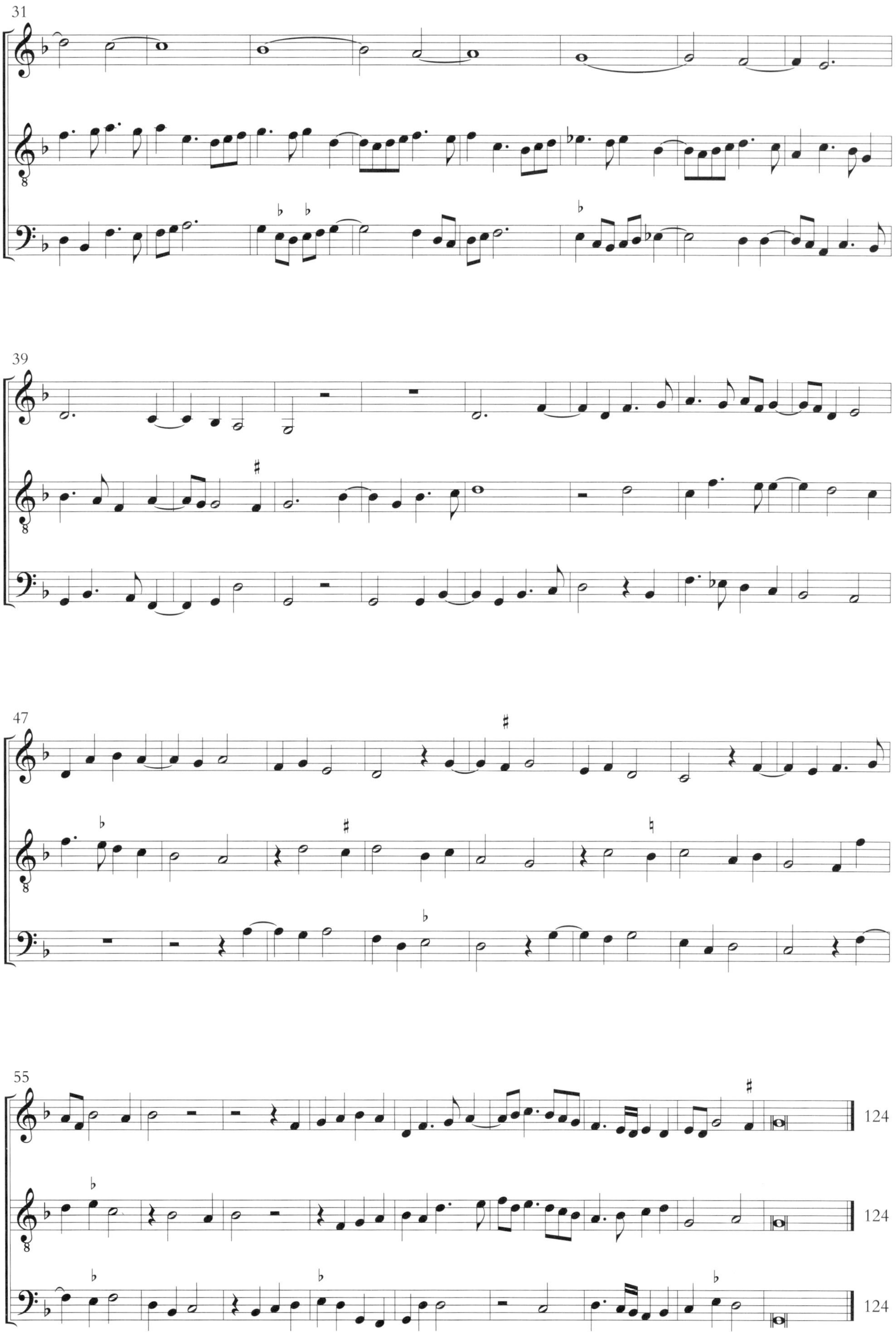
31
39
47
55
124
124
124

129.

AVE STELLA MATUTINA

fols. 99*v*-100*r* (4 vv.)

GASPAR [VAN WEERBEKE]

Ave stella matutina
vita nostra lux divina
lucens omne seculum.

[…]
5   que […]

Rhymed prayer to the Blessed Virgin Mary.

READINGS EMENDED IN THE EDITION:

BAR	VOICE	ORIGINAL
incipit	A	the MS has «Ave» underneath the initial rests
74/II-III	B	*d*, corrected according to MilD 1

MUSICAL CONCORDANCES (MSS): • MilD 1 (116*v*-117*r*), «Gaspar»

MUSICAL CONCORDANCES (PRINTS): • PeMotA1502 (51*v*-52*r*), «Gaspar» • PeMotA1505 (51*v*-52*r*), «Gaspar»

TEXT FROM PeMotA1502:

Ave, stella matutina,
vita nostra lux divina,
lucens omne seculum.

Nos defende a ruina,
5   que es nostra medicina
peccatorum omnium.

Aures tuas nunc inclina,
cum pietatis sis Regina,
audi nostra cantica,

10   quibus tibi nostras voces,
supplicamus ite duces,
omni cum familia,

ut te duce semper tui
sint et possit per te duci
15   tecum ad celestia.

O gloriosa, o benedicta, celi Regina,
audi, exaudi nos, Virgo Maria.

MODERN EDITIONS OF THE TEXT: DRAKE 1972, I, p. 287 (after PeMotA1502).

MODERN EDITIONS OF THE MUSIC: BANKS 1993, II, pp. 40-42 (after Panc.27); DRAKE 1972, II, pp. 123-126 (after PeMotA1502); TINTORI 1963, pp. 8-12 (after MilD 1).

REMARKS: (See also the Remarks to no. 60.) Although it is certainly earlier, the version of MilD 1 cannot be the model for the scribe of Panc.27: few graphic variants separate the two sources, and MilD 1's correct version of bar 74/II-III in the Bassus (*e*) further demonstrates its distance from Panc.27. As in the case of no. 99 (*Christi mater, ave*), it is interesting to compare the version in PeMotA1502 (and its reprint), which is substantially identical with that of Panc.27; the conjunctive error of the Bassus in bar 74/II-III clearly connects the two sources. That the scribe of Panc.27 copied from the print (and not vice versa) is proved not only by the earlier date of *Motetti A*, but also the fact that there is more text in Petrucci's print.

BIBLIOGRAPHY: BANKS 1993, I, p. 267; BOORMAN 2006, p. 893; BROWN 1990, p. 755, n. 38; DRAKE 1972, I, pp. 77, 130, 131, 140, 277, 285-289; FILOCAMO 2004; RIFKIN 2003, p. 311, n. 155.

129.
AVE STELLA MATUTINA
fols. 99*v*–100*r*

Gaspar [van Weerbeke]

Ave stella matutina
vita nostra lux divina lucens omne seculum.
que

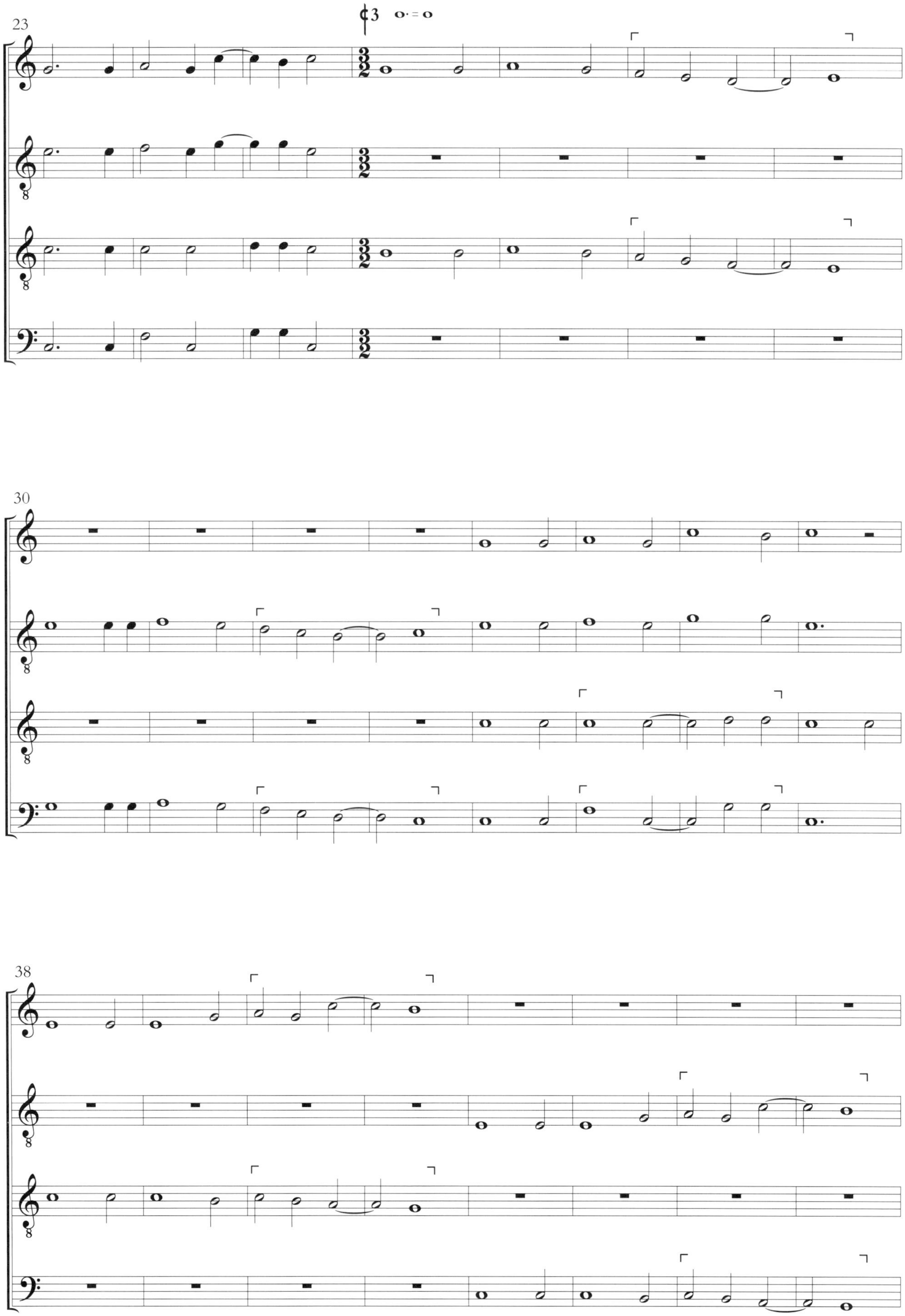
23
30
38

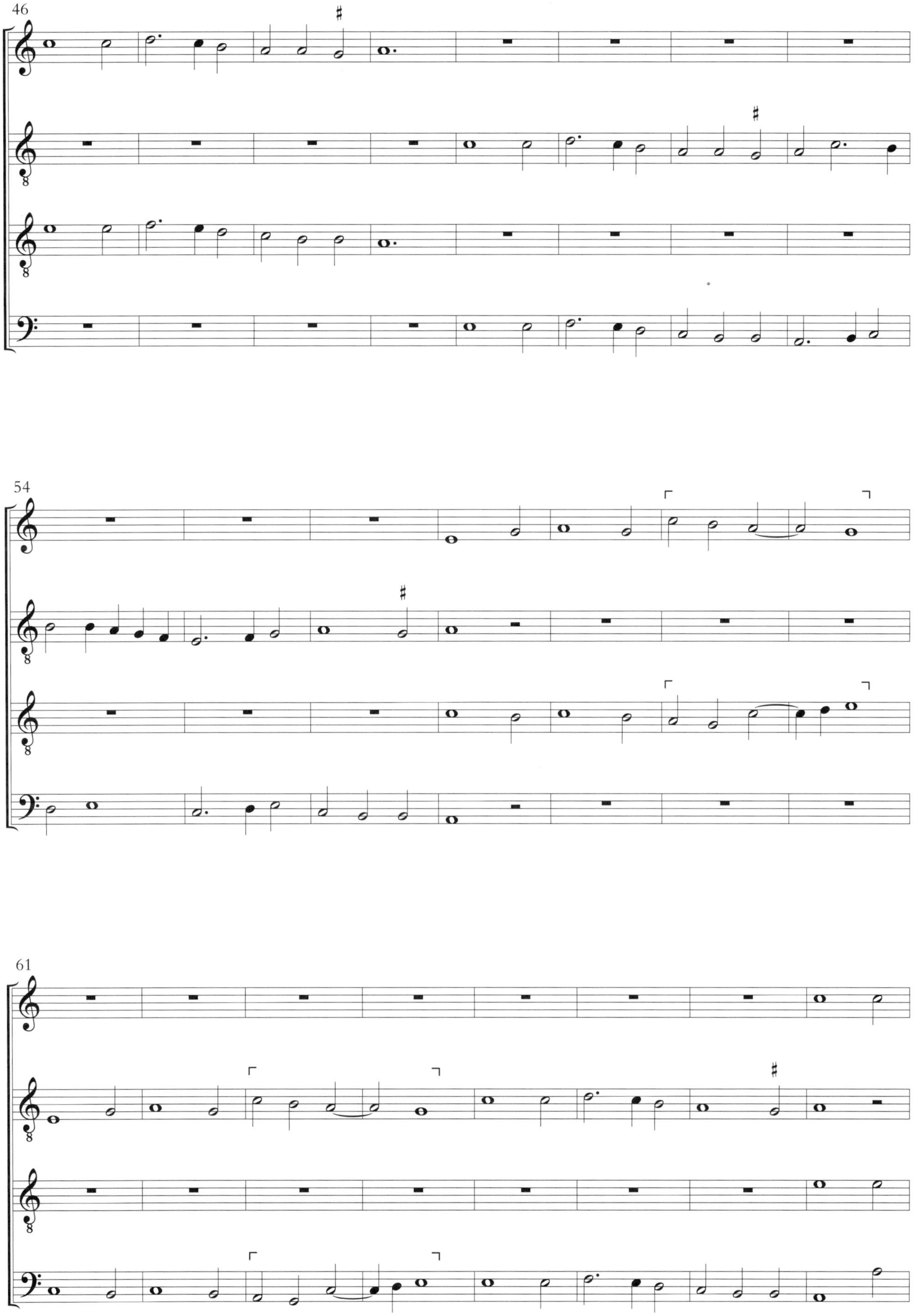
46
54
61

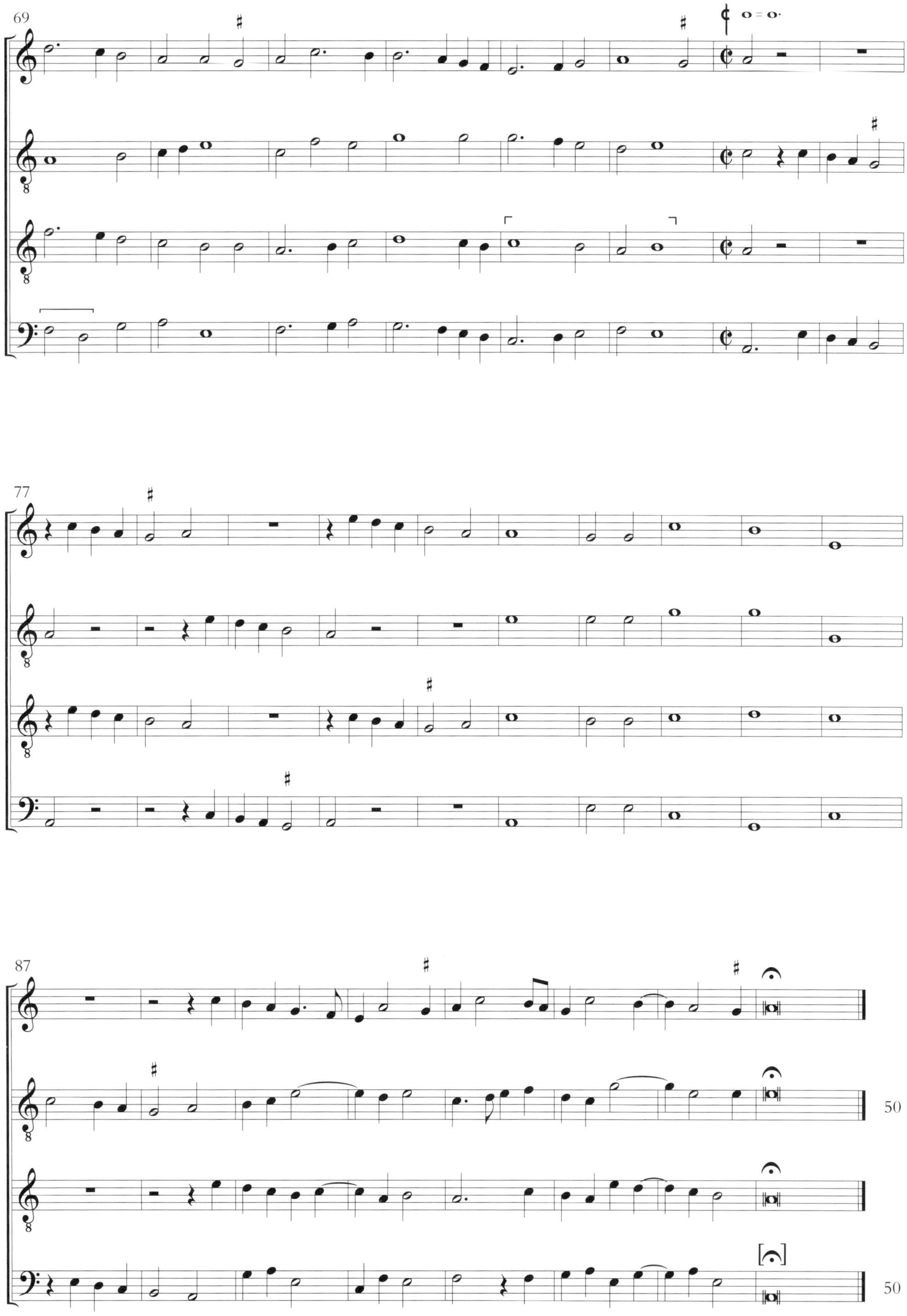
69
77
87
50
50

130.

IBO MIHI AD MONTEM MIRRHE

fols. 100*v*–101*r* (4 vv.)

[GASPAR VAN WEERBEKE]

Ibo mihi ad montem mirrhe
et ad colles Libani.
Tota spetiosa, amica mea,
et macula non est in te.
5   Veni de Libano, sponsa mea,
veniens transibis ad montem
Hermon, a cubilibus leonum,
et a montibus leopardorum.

Based on Song of Songs 4:6-8 (VULGATA, p. 999). See CAO III, p. 264, a version of the twelfth century (but with versicle and respond) that seems to be the earliest so far attested.[1] In the Sarum rite a similar text is a processional Marian antiphon and also an antiphon to the Benedictus at Lauds, Octave of the Nativity of the Blessed Virgin Mary.[2] It is also found in the Worcester Antiphoner (MS F.160 of the library of Worcester Cathedral).[3] The text «Vadam ad montem myrrhae, et ad collem thuris» is otherwise used as a Marian antiphon in the Roman rite, for example in the Office of the Seven Sorrows of the Virgin (AR, p. 674; LU, pp. 1422-1423), and it is also the antiphon for Lauds in the Office of the Passion (see CS, p. 271).

COMMENTARY ON THE TEXT:

1   VULGATA: «Vadam ad montem» instead of 'Ibo mihi ad montem'[4]
5   sponsa] spetiosa T

READINGS EMENDED IN THE EDITION:

BAR	VOICE	ORIGINAL
35	A	*longa* with fermata

MUSICAL CONCORDANCES (PRINTS): • PeMotA1502 (37*v*-38*r*), «Gaspar» • PeMotA1505 (37*v*-38*r*), «Gaspar»

TEXT FROM CAO III, p. 264 (*In Letania*):

Ibo mihi ad montem myrrhae et ad collem Libani, et loquar sponsae meae: «Tota speciosa es, proxima mea, et macula non est in te. Veni a Libano, veni, et transibis ad montem Seir et Hermon, a cubilibus leonum, a montibus leopardorum, alleluia».
℣. Pulchrae genae tuae et turturis, collum tuum sicut monilia. Veni.

---

[1]. My thanks to Cesarino Ruini for pointing this out.
[2]. See ANTIPHONALE SARISBURIENSE, pl. 528.
[3]. See PALÉOGRAPHIE MUSICALE XII, p. 361.
[4]. The ANTIPHONALE SARISBURIENSE has «Ibo michi ad montem», which is closer to Weerbeke's text, but it is not exactly the same thereafter. My thanks to Bonnie Blackburn for pointing this out.

> Ibo michi ad montem mirre
> et ad colles Libani et loquar sponse mee:
> «Tota speciosa es, amica mea,
> et macula non est in te.
> 5   Veni ad Libanum, sponsa,
> venies et transibis a monte Sanyr
> et Hermon, a cubilibus leonum,
> a montibus leopardorum».

TEXT FROM VULGATA, pp. 998-999 (*Canticum Canticorum Salomonis*, IV, 1-15):

1. quam pulchra es amica mea quam pulchra es
   oculi tui columbarum absque eo quod intrinsecus latet
   capilli tui sicut greges caprarum
   quae ascenderunt de monte Galaad
2. dentes tui sicut greges tonsarum
   quae ascenderunt de lavacro
   omnes gemellis fetibus et sterilis non est inter eas
3. sicut vitta coccinea labia tua et eloquium tuum dulce
   sicut fragmen mali punici ita genae tuae
   absque eo quod intrinsecus latet
4. sicut turris David collum tuum
   quae aedificata est cum propugnaculis
   mille clypei pendent ex ea omnis armatura fortium
5. duo ubera tua sicut duo hinuli capreae gemelli
   qui pascuntur in liliis
6. donec adspiret dies et inclinentur umbrae
   vadam ad montem murrae et ad collem turis
7. tota pulchra es amica mea et macula non est in te
8. veni de Libano sponsa
   veni de Libano veni coronaberis
   de capite Amana de vertice Sanir et Hermon
   de cubilibus leonum de montibus pardorum
9. vulnerasti cor meum soror mea sponsa
   vulnerasti cor meum in uno oculorum tuorum
   et in uno crine colli tui
10. quam pulchrae sunt mammae tuae soror mea sponsa
    pulchriora ubera tua vino
    et odor unguentorum tuorum super omnia aromata
11. favus distillans labia tua sponsa
    mel et lac sub lingua tua
    et odor vestimentorum tuorum sicut odor turis
12. hortus conclusus soror mea sponsa
    hortus conclusus fons signatus
13. emissiones tuae paradisus malorum punicorum
    cum pomorum fructibus cypri cum nardo
14. nardus et crocus fistula et cinnamomum
    cum universis lignis Libani
    murra et aloe cum omnibus primis unguentis
15. fons hortorum puteus aquarum viventium
    quae fluunt impetu de Libano

MODERN EDITIONS OF THE MUSIC: BANKS 1993, II, pp. 90-91 (after Panc.27); DRAKE 1972, II, pp. 89-91 (after PeMotA1502); SHERR 1991, pp. 45-49 (after PeMotA1502).

REMARKS: The version of *Motetti A* is probably the model for the scribe of Panc.27: there are very few graphic variants, and the only notable difference is the change of clef at bar 24/II in the Tenor of Panc.27 (corresponding to line break), not present in the print. The textual error in the Tenor in line 5, a typical copying error, increases the probability of copying from a model. However, all voices of PeMotA1502 and its reprint have «speciosa» in line 3.

BIBLIOGRAPHY: BANKS 1993, I, p. 276; BOORMAN 2006, p. 911; BROWN 1990, p. 755, n. 38; CAO III, p. 264; DRAKE 1972, I, pp. 73, 132-133, 174, 177, 270-272, 273; FILOCAMO 2004; IGC, p. 209.

130.
Ibo mihi ad montem mirrhe
fols. 100v–101r

[Gaspar van Weerbeke]

12
spe - ti - o - sa, a - mi - ca me - a, et ma - cu - la non
a - mi - ca me - a, et ma - cu - la non est
a - mi - ca me - a, et ma - cu - la non est in
a - mi - ca me - a, et ma - cu - la non
16
est in te. ve - ni de Li - - ba -
in te. ve - ni de Li - - - ba - no, spon -
te. ve - ni de Li - - ba - no, spon - -
est in te. spon -
20
- no, spon - - - - - sa me - a, ve - ni de Li - - ba -
- sa me - - - - - a, ve - - - - - - ni de Li - - - ba - no,
- sa me - - - - - - - - a, ve - ni de Li - - ba -
- sa me - - - - - a, ve - ni de Li - - ba -

-no, veniens transi - - bis ad mon-tem Her - - mon,

veniens transi - bis ad mon - - - - tem Her - - mon,

-no, veniens tran-si-bis ad mon-tem Her - - mon,

-no, veniens tran-si - - bis ad mon-tem Her - - mon,

a cu-bi-li - - - bus le-o - - num, et a mon -

a cu-bi-li - - bus le - o - num, et a mon -

a cu-bi-li-bus le-o-num, et a mon -

a cu-bi-li - - - bus le-o - num, et a mon -

- - ti-bus le - o-par - - - do - - rum.

- - ti-bus le-o-par - - do - - rum.

-ti - bus le - o-par - - - do - - rum.

-ti - bus le - o - par - - - - do - - - rum.

131.

Mater patris [et filia]

fols. 101*v*-102*r* (3 vv.)

[Antoine] Brumel

Mater patris

Rhymed substitute antiphon from an *Officium Beatae Virginis Mariae in Sabbato* found in a breviary (MS 368) in the Municipal Library of Porto, datable after 1317. There the antiphons proper to the season as used at Second Vespers are specified: *Alma redemptoris*, or *Speciosa*, or *Mater patris et filia*. That this was a text principally found in the Iberian peninsula may be confirmed from its setting in the form of a conductus in MS Madrid, Biblioteca Nacional, 20486 (formerly Hh 167, and before that Toledo, Catedral, Biblioteca Capitular, 930/33.23),[1] fols. 117*v*-118*v*, and in MS BurHu, fols. 147*r*-150*r*.

Readings emended in the edition:

Bar	Voice	Original
37/I	S	*brevis g'* and *brevis g'* erroneously rewritten and then struck out
58	S	*brevis* with fermata
73	Ct	*longa* with fermata

Musical concordances (mss): • BarcC 454 (136*v*-137*r*), *Mater patris et filia* • BolM 18 (75*v*-76*r*), only the Ct agrees; the S and T, after the first notes, are completely different • MünU 322-5 (no. 18), *Mater patris et filia* • SegC (157*v*-158*r*), *Mater patris et filia*, «Anthonius brumel» • SevC 20 (19*v*-20*r*)

Musical concordances (prints): • Baena (28*r*-29*v*), *Mater patris et filia*; index: «Luyset [Compère]. Mater patris. Del primero [tono]» • FormTrium (no. 55), textless (in the Jena copy, added by hand: «Ant. Brumel Mater patris»; in the Berlin copy, added by hand: «Henricus Brumel Pater matris [*sic*]») • PeOdh1501 (67*v*-68*r*), «Brunel» [*sic*] • PeOdh1503 (67*v*-68*r*), «Brunel» [*sic*] • PeOdh1504 (67*v*-68*r*), «Brumel» • PeSpinII (33*v*-34*v*), *Mater patris et filia* • PetreiusNewII (no.V), «A. Brumel», «Trium»

Text from MünU 322-5:

> Mater patris et filia,
> mulierum laetitia,
> stella maris eximia,
> audi nostra suspiria.

5   Regina poli curiae,
> mater misericordiae,
> in hac valle miseriae,
> [...][2]

---

[1]. From Spain, middle or 3rd quarter of the 13th century (see the entry 'Sources', NG XXIII, p. 873, and RISM B IV/1, pp. 245-256).

[2]. In the version set by Brumel, the line «sis reis porta veniae», present in all the versions in AH, is lacking.

10 Maria, propter filium,
confer nobis remedium.
Bone Jesu, fili Dei,
nostras preces exaudi
et precibus nostris
dona nobis remedium.
Amen.

Text from AH 46, p. 202 (*Ad Beatam Mariam V.*):		Text from AH 49, p. 331 (*In Assumptione Beatae M. V.*):		Text from AH 45a, p. 26 (*Ad Magnificat*):	
1.	Mater patris et filia, supernorum laetitia, stella maris eximia, audi nostra suspiria.	1a. 1b.	Mater patris et filia, mulierum laetitia, stella maris eximia, audi nostra suspiria.	1.	Mater patris et filia, mulierum laetitia, stella maris eximia, audi nostra suspiria.
2.	Regina poli curiae, mater misericordiae, in hac valle miseriae sis reis porta veniae.	2a. 2b.	Regina poli curiae, mater misericordiae, in hac valle miseriae sis reis porta veniae.	2.	Regina poli curiae, mater misericordiae. In hac valle miseriae sis reis dona veniae.
3.	Maria, propter filium confer nobis praesidium; bone fili, prece matris dona tuis regnum patris.	3a. 3b. 4a. 4b.	Per tuum, virgo, filium confer nobis remedium. Bone fili, prece matris perduc nos ad regna patris.	3.	Maria, propter filium confer reis remedium; bone fili, preces matris dona tuis regna patris.

Modern editions of the text (the text used by Brumel does not correspond exactly to any of the versions published in AH: it includes variants from each one, and sometimes differs from all; see CMM 5/V, p. xxxiv): AH 45a, p. 26; AH 46, p. 202; AH 49, p. 331; Lama de la Cruz 1994, p. 232 (after SegC).

Modern editions of the music: CMM 5/V, pp. 63-65 (after PeOdh1504); Disertori 1940, pp. 107-109 (after PeOdh1504); Disertori 1964, pp. 232-237 (after PeSpinII); Greenberg – Maynard 1975, pp. 95-98 (after PeOdh1504); Hewitt 1942, pp. 351-352 (after PeOdh1504); Mönkemeyer 1985, II, pp. 81-82 (after FormTrium); Schmidt 1969, II, pp. 254-258 (after PeSpinII); Smijers V/5, pp. 138-139 (after PeOdh1501, with the text taken from MünU 322-5).

Remarks: The musical version of Panc.27 plausibly derives from *Odhecaton*: even if the imitative entry of the Superius in bars 3-4/I and 61/I-II differs rhythmically (a long note instead of two repeated notes), there are very few graphic variants, of minor significance. The change of clef in the Superius (b. 59) in Panc.27 has all the appearance of a later correction, perhaps due to copying at a different pitch from the model: the new clef is in fact written in a small space and in a smaller size. Panc.27 and *Odhecaton* also share the same amount of text and the same attribution. The tradition of the other concordant sources, however, is distant. The most substantial shared variants occur in bars 22-23 of the Superius (BarC 454, MünU 322-5, SegC, SevC 20) and the Tenor (MünU 322-3, SegC, SevC 20).

Bibliography: Baker 1978, I, p. 429; Boorman 2006, p. 921; Chevalier II, no. 11349; Chevalier IV, no. 38899; CMM 5/V, pp. xxxiii-xxxiv; Filocamo 2004; Greenberg – Maynard 1975, p. 94; Hewitt 1942, pp. 157-158, 178; Lama de la Cruz 1994, p. 232; Ros-Fábregas 1992, I, pp. 153-154; Weiss 1998, p. 33.

131.
MATER PATRIS [ET FILIA]
fols. 101v–102r

[Antoine] Brumel

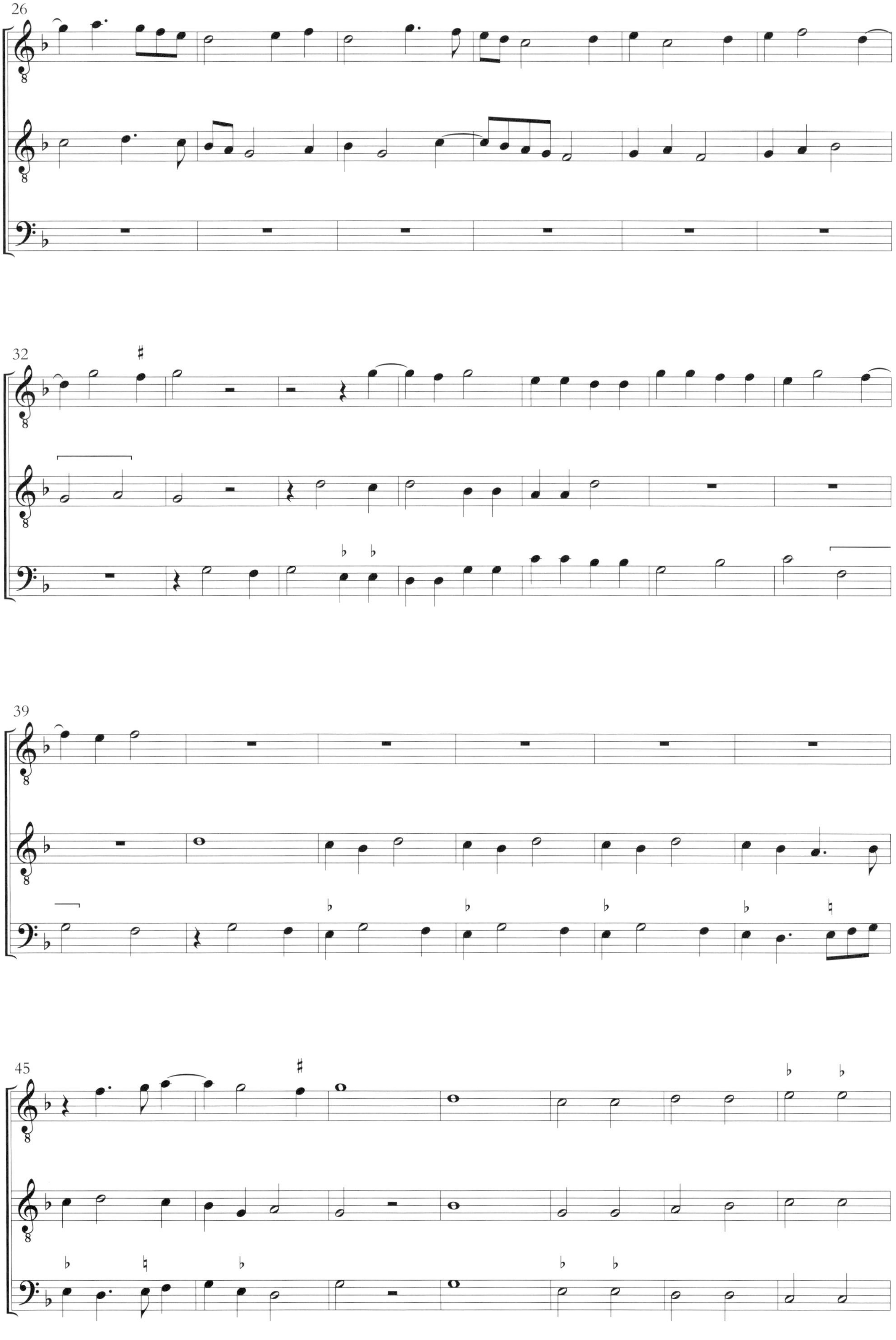
26
32
39
45

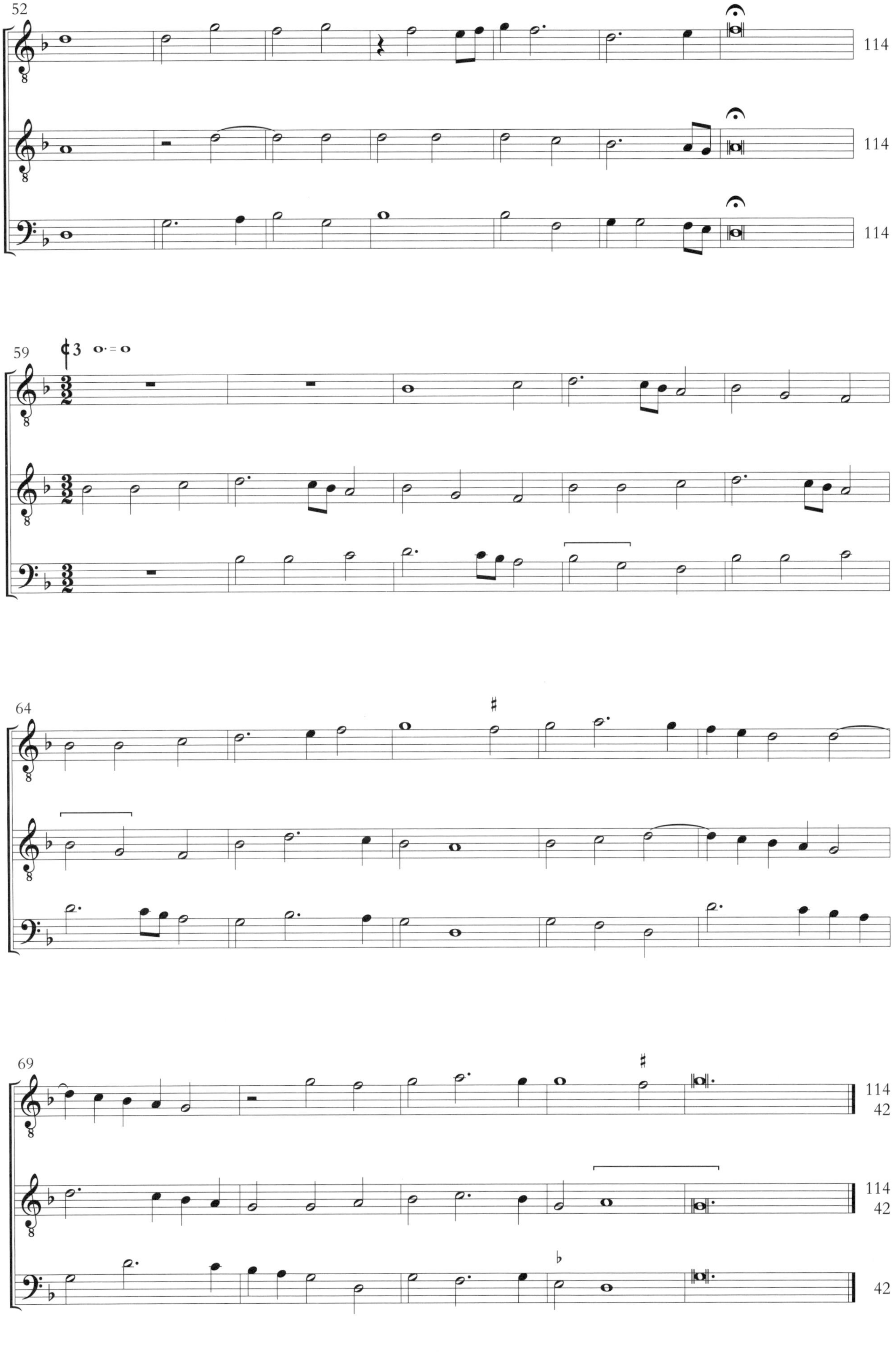

132.

Ave Maria, gratia plena

fols. 102*v*–103*r* (4 vv.)

Ave Maria, gratia plena, Dominus tecum;
benedicta tu in mulieribus,
et benedictus fructus ventris tui, Iesus.
Sancta Maria, mater Dei,
5   ora pro nobis peccatoribus,
nunc et in hora mortis nostre.
Amen.

For the text see no. 2.

Readings emended in the edition:

Bar	Voice	Original
43	S	*longa* with fermata

Musical concordances (mss): • Panc.27 (4*v*–5*r*)

Remarks: The same *Ave Maria* appears in the first fascicle of Panc.27 (no. 6), with small musical and graphic variants (for example, the presence or absence of fermatas and ligatures) and a rhythmic variant (*semibrevis*, two *minimae*, and *brevis* in place of a *longa*, Altus, bb. 15–16).

Bibliography: See no. 6.

132.
Ave Maria, gratia plena
fols. 102*v*-103*r*

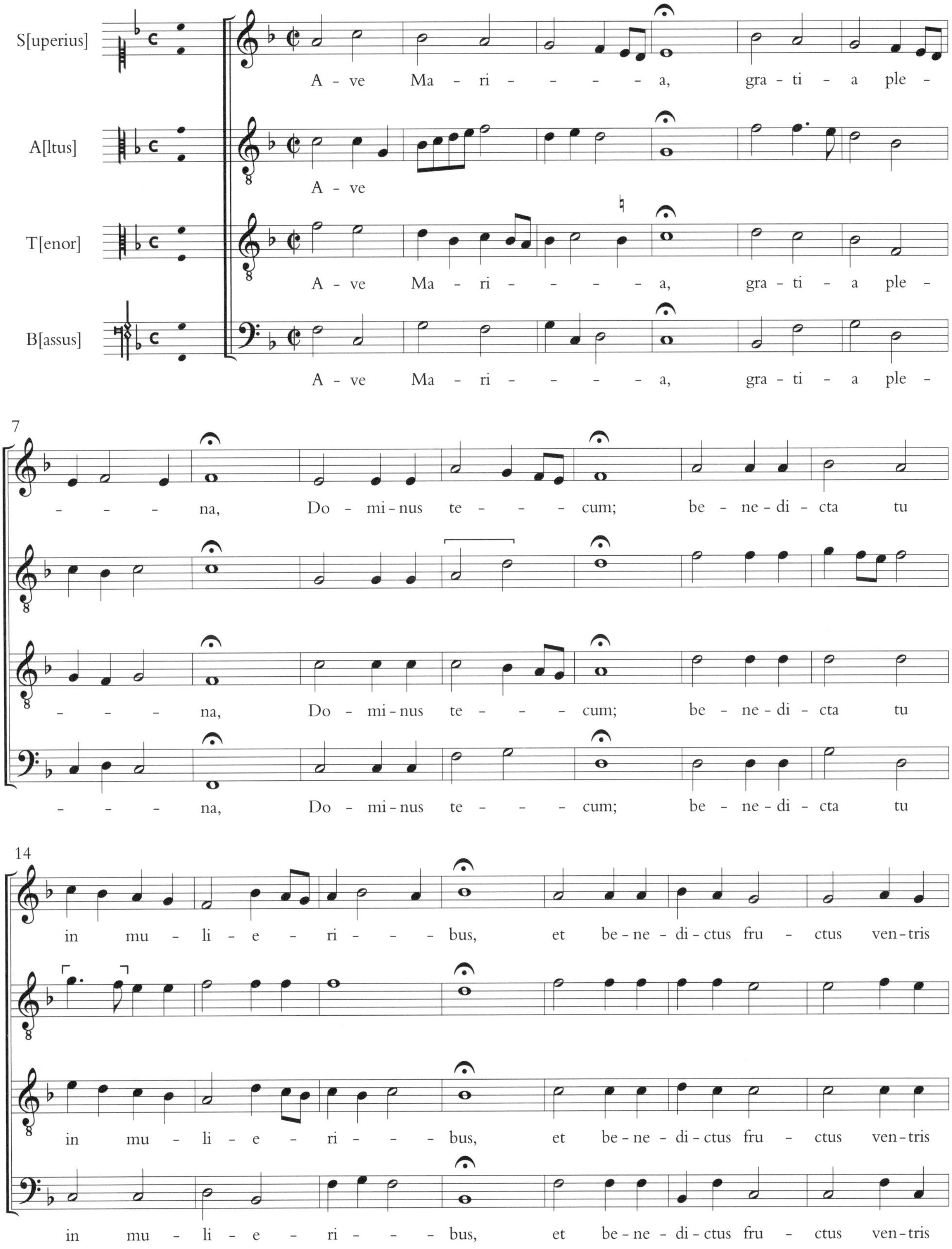

21
tu - - - i, Ie - sus. San - cta Ma - ri - a, ma - - - - - ter
Ie - - sus
tu - - - i, Ie - sus. San - cta Ma - ri - a, ma - - - - - ter
tu - - - i, Ie - sus. San - cta Ma - ri - a, ma - - - - - ter
29
De - i, o - ra pro no - bis pec - ca - to - ri - - - - - - - bus,
De - i, o - ra pro no - bis pec - ca - to - ri - - - - - - - bus,
De - i, o - ra pro no - bis pec - ca - to - ri - - - - - - - bus,
36
nunc et in ho - ra mor - tis no - stre. A - men.
nunc et in ho - ra mor - tis no - stre. A - men.
nunc et in ho - ra mor - tis no - stre. A - men.

133.

Letanie. SANCTA MARIA, ORA PRO NOBIS

fol. 102*v* (4 vv.)

Sancta Maria,
ora pro nobis ad Deum Iesum Christum.

«Sancta Maria» is the first in a long series of prayer invocations (after the initial act of penitence) in the Litanies of the Blessed Virgin Mary (Litany of Loreto, LU, pp. 1857-1858, 1860), but also in the Litanies of the Saints (BR [*Commune Sanctorum*], pp. 87-89, 91-92; GR, pp. 213-215; LU, pp. 756-758; MR, 228-229), and in the Litanies to St. Joseph (LU, p. 1877); the response «Ora pro nobis ad Deum Iesum Christum» is more extended than that in the liturgical books («Ora pro nobis»).[1]

COMMENTARY ON THE TEXT: The complete text appears only in the Bassus. On fol. 102*v* the scribe has written the rubric «Letanie», in the plural; the designation clearly applies to the following piece as well (no. 134).

READINGS EMENDED IN THE EDITION:

BAR	VOICE	ORIGINAL
8/II-9/I	A	*d′* and *c′ minima* and *semibrevis* in place of *semibrevis* and *minima*

MODERN EDITIONS OF THE MUSIC: BANKS 1993, II, p. 174 (after Panc.27).

BIBLIOGRAPHY: BANKS 1993, I, pp. 288-289.

---

[1]. The text of the Litany of Loreto was increasing diffused in the first half of the sixteenth century, and was codified in 1587 by a decree of Pope Sixtus V, a native of Grottammare, near the Sanctuary of Loreto.

133.

Letanie. SANCTA MARIA, ORA PRO NOBIS

fol. 102*v*

134.

Sancta Maria, ora pro nobis

fol. 103*r* (3 vv.)

Sancta Maria,
ora pro nobis ad Deum Iesum Christum.

For the text see no. 133.

Commentary on the text: On fol. 102*v*, at the beginning of the previous piece (no. 133), the scribe
has written the rubric «Letanie», in the plural; the designation clearly applies to this piece as well.

Readings emended in the edition:

Bar	Voice	Original
7	B	*A*

Modern editions of the music: Banks 1993, II, p. 174 (after Panc.27).

Bibliography: Banks 1993, I, p. 289.

134.
SANCTA MARIA, ORA PRO NOBIS
fol. 103*r*

Cantus: San — cta Ma — ri — a, o — ra pro no — bis

Tenor: San — cta Ma — ri — a, o — ra pro no — bis

Bassus: San — cta Ma — ri — a, o — ra pro no — bis

ad De — — — um Ie — sum Chri — stum.

ad De — — — um Ie — sum Chri — stum.

ad De — — — um Ie — sum Chri — stum.

135.

(LIBERA ME, DOMINE)
Duo. DIES ILLA, DIES IRE
TREMENS FACTUS SUM EGO
REQUIEM ETERNAM

fol. 103*v* (2 vv.)

Dies illa, dies ire,
calamitatis et miserie,
dies magna et amara valde.

Tremens factus sum ego, et timeo,
5   dum discusio venerit, atque ventura ira.

Requiem eternam dona eis, Domine,
et lux perpetua luceat eis.

The three versicles of the Responsory *Libera me, Domine*, used in the Office of the Dead (AR, pp. [174]-
[175]; BR [*Commune Sanctorum*], p. 86; PM, pp. 321-322), and at the end of the Requiem Mass, for the
Absolution of the Dead (GR, pp. 103★-104★; LU, pp. 1767-1768). Here the three sections do not follow
the canonical order: the *Tremens* follows the *Dies illa* instead of preceding it.

COMMENTARY ON THE TEXT:

4-5   normally the section *Tremens factum sum* precedes the section *Dies irae, dies illa* instead of following
            it

READINGS EMENDED IN THE EDITION:

BAR	VOICE	ORIGINAL
16	B$_2$	black *brevis*
17	B$_2$	black *brevis* with fermata
25	B$_2$	*longa* with fermata
36	B$_2$	*brevis* without fermata
58/II	B$_1$	*brevis* with fermata

MUSICAL CONCORDANCES (MSS): • Panc.27 (210*v*-211*r*), *Tremens factus sum ego / Dies illa, dies ire / Requiem
   eternam*, with the voices exchanged

TEXT FROM BR [*Commune Sanctorum*], p. 86 (*Officium defunctorum. Lectio IX. Responsorium*):
   Libera me Domine de morte aeterna, in die illa tremenda,
   quando caeli movendi sunt, et terra,
   dum veneris iudicare saeculum per ignem.

   V. Tremens factus sum ego, et timeo
   dum discussio venerit, atque ventura ira.
   Quando [...].

℣. Dies illa, dies irae, calamitatis, et miseriae,
dies magna, et amara valde.
Dum ven[…].

℣. Requiem aeternam […].

Libera me, […].

MODERN EDITIONS OF THE MUSIC: BANKS 1993, II, pp. 70-72 (after Panc.27).

REMARKS: Apart from the exchange of the two voices, nos. 135 and 184 share identical musical material: slight differences — such as different clefs, cadential ornamentation, the presence or absence of simultaneous rests after the notes with fermatas — do not affect the substantial mirroring of one piece in the other. (Moreover, it is interesting to note that the incipit of the *Dies illa, dies ire* section corresponds exactly to the incipit of the *Requiem* section, at least up to the second note with fermata.) The only substantive musical difference (intended, or purely accidental?) is a different note in the *Requiem*: in no. 135 *f* appears in bar 59/II (Bassus I), whereas at the corresponding point in no. 184 (b. 47/II, Bassus II) there is an *e*. A sure indication of performance found in no. 135 is the line drawn by the scribe connecting the syllable «-em» of the word *Requiem* with the *brevis* with fermata in bar 52 (Bassus II).

BIBLIOGRAPHY: BANKS 1993, I, p. 272; FILOCAMO 2009c.

135.
(Libera me, Domine)
Duo. Dies illa, dies ire
Tremens factus sum ego
Requiem eternam
fol. 103*v*

et ti-me-o, dum di-scu-si-o ve - ne - rit,

et ti-me-o, dum di-scu-si-o ve - ne - rit,

at - que ven-tu - ra i - - - - - - - - - ra.

at - que ven-tu - ra i - - - - - - - - - ra.

Re - - qui - em e - - ter - - nam

Re - - qui - em e - - ter - - nam

do - - na e - - is, Do - - mi - ne,

do - - na e - - is, Do - - mi - ne,

et lux per - pe-tu - a lu-ce - at e - - is.

et lux per - pe-tu-a lu - ce - at e - - is.

136.

Verbum caro factum est

fol. 104*v* (3 vv.)

Verbum caro factum est
de Virgine Maria.

In hoc anni circulo
vita datur seculo
5   nato nobis parvulo
de Virgine Maria.

For the text see no. 86. It is impossible to establish if the (hypothetical) missing text continues as in no. 142, no. 144, or in still another way.

Readings emended in the edition:

Bar	Voice	Original
28/I	T, Ct	*brevis*

Modern editions of the text: See no. 86.

Modern editions of the music: Luisi 1983, II, p. 200 (after Panc. 27).[1]

Remarks: See the Remarks to no. 86. Whereas in the versions of nos. 86, 142, and 144 the *cantus firmus* is in the highest voice, in no. 136 the pre-existing melody is placed in the Tenor. Of the four, this is the only *Verbum caro* in duple metre, written in a version perhaps ornamented by the scribe himself. The omission of the rests in bars 28/II-29/I of the Tenor, together with the erroneous transcription of the note values in bar 28/I, are not necessarily errors in copying from a model: since bars 24-34 repeat bars 1-11, the copyist might in fact have mistranscribed them by recopying from the initial section already in place.

Bibliography: See no. 86.

---

[1]. Luisi transcribes the piece in triple metre, believing that the original indication of *tempus imperfectum* is erroneous.

136.
VERBUM CARO FACTUM EST
fol. 104*v*

137.

Alleluia

fol. 105*r* (3 vv.)

Dominicus

Alleluia.

Acclamation, used, for example, in the Office as an invitatory or antiphon, and in the Mass as part of the Proper (except in Lent). See also CAO III, pp. 3-4, 37-43; CAO IV, pp. 17-19, 508; and IGC, pp. 15-39.

Readings emended in the edition:

Bar	Voice	Original
35	S	*longa* with fermata

Modern editions of the music: Banks 1993, II, pp. 5-6 (after Panc.27).

Remarks: Despite the parallel fifths (b. 9/II between Tenor and Bassus), this is the piece of a competent composer: the movement in parallel tenths between the Superius and the Bassus (bb. 14-16/I, 18/II-20, 25/II-28/I) recalls the words of Gaffurius in the third book of the *Practica musice* (1496).[1]

Bibliography: Banks 1993, I, p. 262; CAO III, pp. 3-4, 37-43; CAO IV, pp. 17-19, 508; Filocamo 2004; IGC, pp. 15-39.

---

[1]. «[…] Est & celeberrimus quidam in contrapuncto processus notularum videlicet Baritonantis ad cantus notulas institutus consimilibus notulis per decimam inuicem procedentibus: tenore ad singulos concorditer commeante. quem Tinctoris: Gulielmus guarnerij: Iusquin despret: Gaspar: Alexander agricola: Loyset: Obrech: Brumel: Isaac ac reliqui Iucundissimi compositores in suis cantilenis saepius observarunt. quod & praesentis concentus consideratione percipitur» (see Gaffurio 1496, *Liber Tertius, De Consimilibus perfectis concordantijs in contrapuncto consequenter tolerandis, Caput duodecimum*).

137.

ALLELUIA

fol. 105*r*

Dominicus

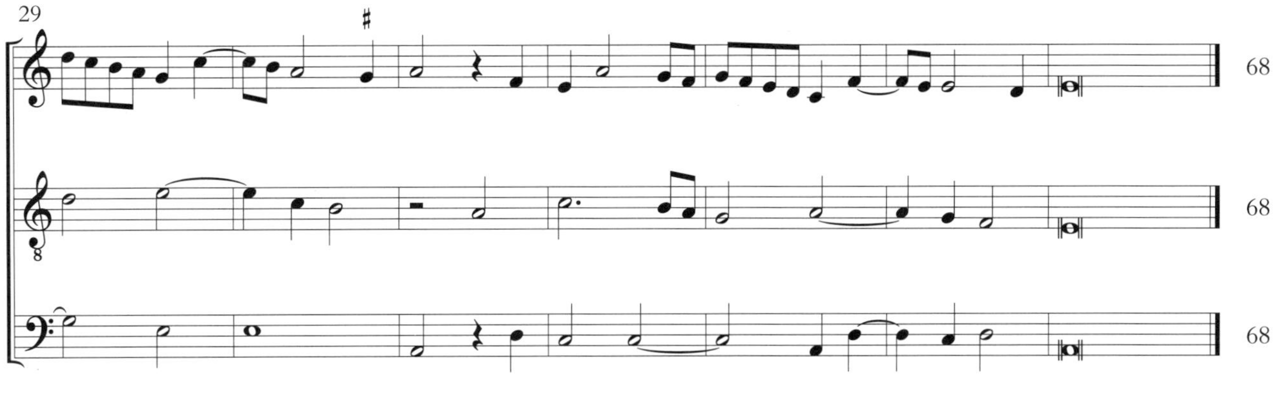
29
68
68
68

138.

Alleluia

fols. 105*v*–106*r* (4 vv.)

[Henricus Isaac]

Alleluia.

For the text see no. 137. Contrafact on the music of *Salve Regina*.

Readings emended in the edition:

Bar	Voice	Original
28	A	*d′ e′* instead of *c′ d′*

Musical concordances (mss): • BerlS 40021 (69*r*-72*r*: 69*v*-70*r*), *Ad te clamamus* (after *Salve Regina*), «Heyn. Ysack»; index: «Salve regina. h. Isaac etc.» • BolM 18 (79*v*-80*r*), ATB: *Thysis*, S: *Thisis* • DresL 505 (436*r*-445*r*: 437*r*-438*v*), *Ad te clamamus* (after *Salve Regina*), «H. Isack» • FirN BR229 (272*v*-273*r*), textless, «Henricus Yzac» • ParisN Rés676 (50*v*-51*r*), B: *Gratis accepistis et gratis date*,[1] SAT: *Gratis accepistis* • SegC (67*v*-71*r*: 68*v*-69*r*), *Ad te clamamus* (after *Salve Regina*), «Isaac» • StuttL 39 (149*v*-184*r*: 157*v*-162*r*), *Ad te clamamus* (after *Salve rex misericordiae*) • WarU 5892 (73*v*-77*r*: 73*v*), *Ad te clamamus* (after *Salve Regina*)

Modern editions of the music: Banks 1993, II, pp. 6-7 (after Panc.27); Brown 1983, II, pp. 593-595 (after FirN BR229); Davison - Apel (1946) 1977, pp. 91-92 (after DTÖ 28); DTÖ 28, p. 119 (after FirN BR229); EDM 76, pp. 202-216: 205-206 (after BerlS 40021).

Remarks: The version of Panc.27 is the only one with the text «Alleluia»: the piece in fact follows the only other Alleluia in the manuscript, no. 137. The text is a contrafact, since the composition forms part of Isaac's *Salve Regina* and paraphrases the chant (*Dominica ad Completorium*, LU, p. 276) very loosely at the beginning of the Superius, Altus, and Tenor. The note added in bar 23/I of the Superius is present in all the concordances, whereas the erroneous notes in bar 28 of the Altus are not found in any other version of the piece (this passage differs only in SegC). It is likely, therefore, that the musical version of Panc.27 was copied from a model that has not come down to us, also considering all the graphic variants that separate its readings from the concordant sources.

Bibliography: Banks 1993, I, pp. 262-263; Baker 1978, I, p. 312; Brown 1983, I, p. 303; EDM 78, p. 328; Filocamo 2004; IGC, pp. 15-39; Just 1975, II, pp. 119-120; Lama de la Cruz 1994, pp. 179-180; Picker 1991, p. 92; Prizer 1995, p. 184; Weiss 1998, pp. 34-35.

---

[1]. «Freely have you received, freely give» (Matt. 10:8): this may have been extracted from a sermon of Savonarola, perhaps for Advent 1485 (see Prizer 1995, p. 184 and Cattin 1973b, p. 90).

138.
ALLELUIA
fols. 105*v*–106*r*

[Henricus Isaac]

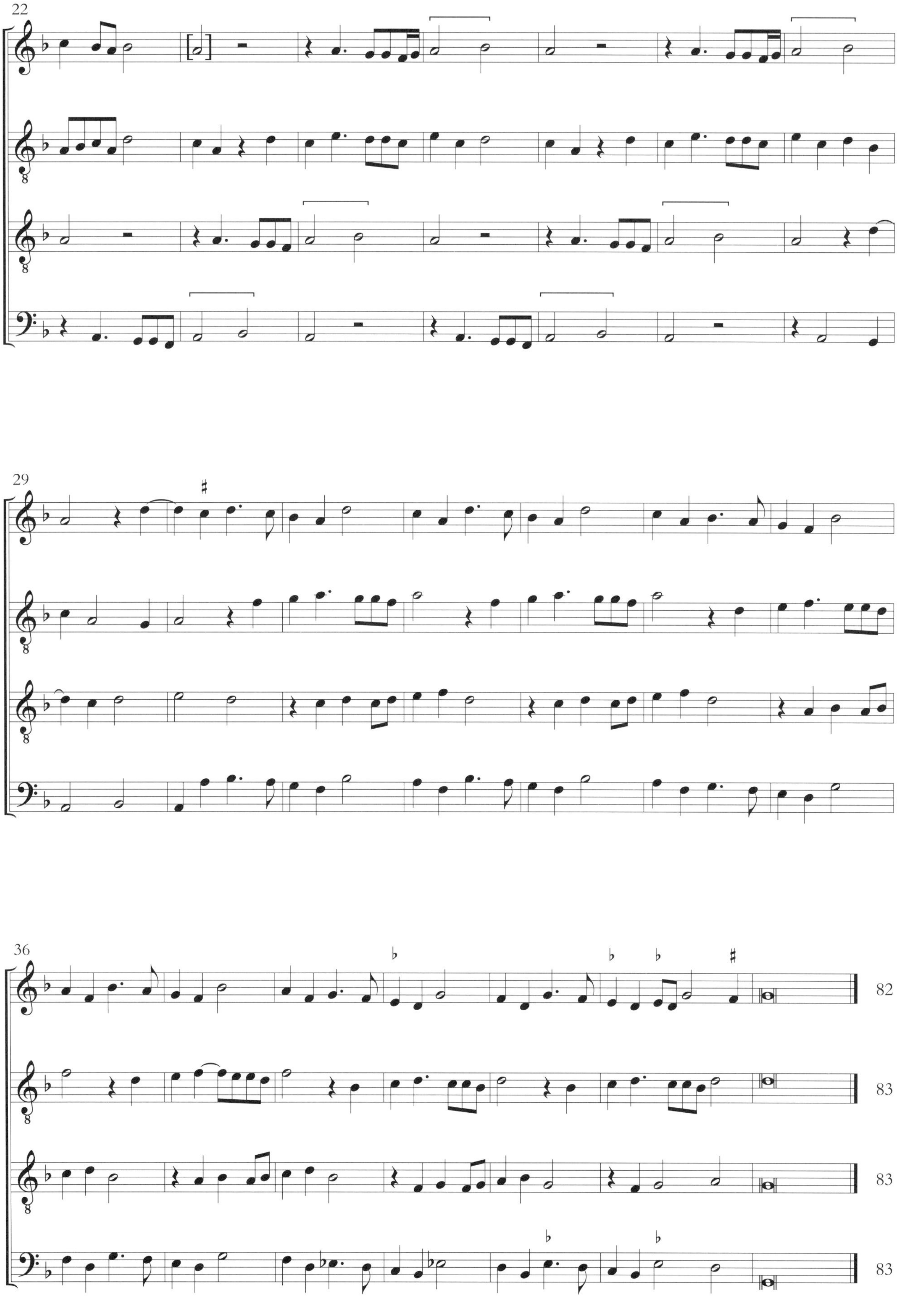
22
29
36
82
83
83
83

139.

Fortuna d'um gran tempo

fols. 106v-107r (3 vv.)

[Josquin des Prez]

[Heading only]

Instrumental piece, based on a folksong.[1]

Readings emended in the edition:

Bar	Voice	Original
14	T	two *semibreves g*, with a small «b» (= *brevis*) underneath; see Remarks

Musical concordances (mss):[2] • BasU 22 (18r-19v), «Iosquin» • BasU 26c (7v-8v), textless • BerlS 40026 (20r-21r)

Musical concordances (prints):[3] • EgenLieder (III, no. 10), S only • PeOdh1501 (80v-81r), «Josquin» • PeOdh1503 (80v-81r) • PeOdh1504 (80v-81r) • PeSpinI (8r-v), (Francesco Spinacino)

Modern editions of the music: van Benthem 1980, pp. 47-48 (after PeOdh1501 and PeSpinI); Disertori 1964, pp. 176-179 (after PeOdh1504 and PeSpinI); EDM 91, pp. 30-31, (after BerlS 40026); Hewitt 1942, pp. 375-376 (after PeOdh1504); Lowinsky 1943, pp. 51-53 (after PeOdh1504); NJE 27, I, pp. 18-19 (after PeOdh1504); Schmidt 1969, II, pp. 17-19 (after PeSpinI); SM 6, pp. 16-17 (after BasU 22), pp. 95-96 (after BasU 26c); Smijers J/55, pp. 62-64, 64-65 (after PeOdh1504); Torrefranca 1939, pp. 458-460 (after PeOdh1504); Warburton 1980, pp. 95-96 (after BerlS 40026).

Remarks: This celebrated piece by Josquin has occupied scholars for more than sixty years. Edward Lowinsky was the first to confront its modal complexities, proposing stimulating connections with

---

[1]. The musical MS FirN BR229 has the following text on fols. 156v-158r:

> Fortuna d'un gran tempo mi se' stata
> tanto leggiadra, gratiosa et bella.
> Solo una gratia t'aggio adimandata,
> et a quella mi se' stata ribella.
> Et chi lo vuol sapere, sì, lo sappia:
> in questa terra volea bene ad una.
> Un degli sua amanti mi minaccia,
> credendo ch'io la lasci per paura.

This text has been edited in Torrefranca 1939, p. 205 (in l. 1 he gives «ch'un» instead of 'd'un', deriving the variant from the *Stanze dello Sparpaglia* of Anton Francesco Doni; see Torrefranca 1939, p. 205, n. 2, and p. 207, n. 1); Lowinsky 1943, p. 64; Brown 1983, I, p. 269. Nevertheless, it is not possible to prove that this is the text intended by the Panc.27 copyist.

[2]. Although not classifiable as concordances, the following manuscript versions are nevertheless more or less directly linked with the piece: Florence, Biblioteca Nazionale Centrale, Magliabechiano XIX.164-167 (49r-v), quodlibet; FirN BR229 (154v-156r), quodlibet; FirN BR229 (156v-158r).

[3]. Although not classifiable as concordances, the following printed versions are nevertheless more or less directly linked with the piece: *Frottole, libro septimo*, Venice, Ottaviano Petrucci, 6 June 1507 (12v-13r); *Frottole, libro nono*, Venice, Ottaviano Petrucci, 22 January 1508 (1509 modern style) (38v-39r), quodlibet; *Canti B. Numero Cinquanta*, Venice, Ottaviano Petrucci, 5 February 1501 (1502 modern style) (35v-36r); PeCantiC (52v-53r).

the cultural and artistic context (see LOWINSKY 1943); moreover, he hypothesized a date of 1499, «under the immediate impression of the fall of the house of Sforza» (see LOWINSKY 1976, pp. 71-72). The problematic nub of the piece is the interpretation of the *musica ficta*; according to Lowinsky *Fortuna d'un gran tempo* is one of the first compositions to use the whole chromatic scale, making a systematic use of modulation (see LOWINSKY 1943, p. 58). A more recent article by Jaap van Benthem reconsiders Lowinsky's authoritative view: there is no need to interpret the *musica ficta* as the outcome of modulation around the circle of fifths, and thus the three different key signatures in the three voices can return to their normal function in the modal system (see VAN BENTHEM 1980, p. 35). With regard to *musica ficta*, the most problematic spot is the conclusion (bb. 44/II-46), which has false relations between the Superius and Contra caused by the alternation of *e'* (natural) and *e* (flat); Francesco Spinacino's lute tablature (published by March 1507), from which one might expect a definitive clarification, avoids the problem by eliminating all the *e*s from the lower voice in the final passage. On the basis of numerological studies by Willem Elders — who had attributed the number '99' to 'Josquin' and the number '88' to 'des Prez' (see ELDERS 1969, p. 179) — van Benthem counts 88 notes in the melody segments and the contrapuntal lines against them, and 187 (88 + 99) in the remaining notes (VAN BENTHEM 1980, p. 38). The Panc.27 scribe's mistranscription in bar 14 of the Tenor falls right in the first half of the piece: to write two repeated notes instead of a long one would certainly damage the imitative design with the Superius (b. 12) and the Contra (b. 16), but it would also spoil the suggestive numerological plan proposed by van Benthem (see VAN BENTHEM 1980, p. 45, n. 87). The copyist himself, however, seems to have realized his error: under the two *g* *semibreves* he has written a small «b» (= *brevis*), a reading that was certainly in his model, which was surely *Odhecaton* (from which Panc.27 differs in this sole variant); the absence of the attribution excludes the exemplar now in Bologna (PeOdh1501) as the model.

BIBLIOGRAPHY: VAN BENTHEM 1980; BOORMAN 2006, p. 978; EDM 92, p. 151; ELDERS 1969, pp. 183-185; FILOCAMO 2004; GALLICO 1996, pp. 87, 148-149, 170; HEWITT 1942, pp. 161, 179; KÄMPER 1976, pp. 77-78, 131; LOWINSKY 1943; LOWINSKY 1945, p. 254; LOWINSKY 1976, pp. 71-72; NJE 27, II, pp. 79-90; REESE 1990, pp. 167, 226, 243; SM 6, pp. 121, 129; TORREFRANCA 1939, pp. 205-208.

139.
Fortuna d'um gran tempo
fols. 106*v*–107*r*

[Josquin des Prez]

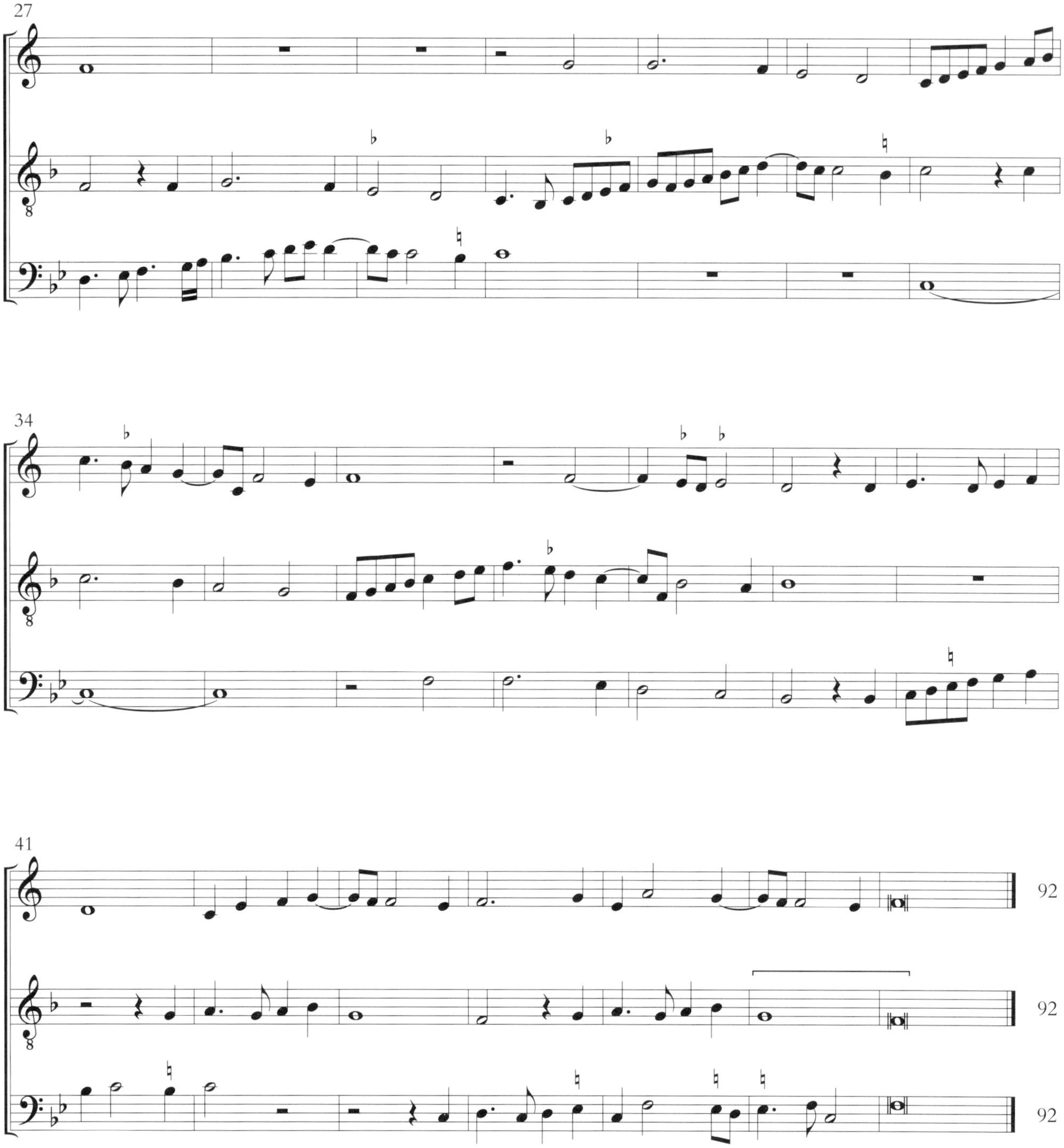
27
34
41
92
92
92

140.

Tenebre facte sunt

fols. 107v-108r (4 vv.)

Tenebre facte sunt,
dum crucifixissent Iesum Iudei,
et circa horam nonam
exclamavit voce magna: «Deus meus,
5   ut quid dereliquisti me?».
Et inclinato capite,
emisit spiritum.

Based on Matthew 27:45-50 (Vulgata, pp. 1572-1573), Mark 15:33-37 (Vulgata, pp. 1603-1604), and John 19:30 (Vulgata, p. 1694). The text is used, for example, as the fifth responsory in the second Nocturn of Matins on Good Friday (BR, p. 353; LU, pp. 680-681). See also CAO IV, p. 432 and IGC, p. 413.

Commentary on the text:

4   BR gives «Iesus» after «exclamavit»
5   BR gives «ut quid me dereliquisti?»

Text from BR, p. 353 (*Feria VI in Parasceve. Lectio V. Responsorium*):

Tenebrae factae sunt
dum crucifixissent Iesum Iudaei:
et circa horam nonam
exclamavit Iesus voce magna: «Deus meus
5   ut quid me dereliquisti?».
Et inclinato capite
emisit spiritum.

V. Exclamans Iesus voce magna ait:
«Pater in manus tuas
10   commendo spiritum meum».

Et inclinato […].

Modern editions of the text: CAO IV, p. 432.

Modern editions of the music: Banks 1993, II, pp. 189-191 (after Panc.27).

Bibliography: Banks 1993, I, p. 291; CAO IV, p. 432; CS, pp. 412, 483; IGC, p. 413.

140.
Tenebre facte sunt
fols. 107v–108r

21
ho - - - - - ram no - - - - - nam ex - cla - ma - - - vit
- ca ho - - ram no - nam ex - cla - ma - - - vit vo - ce
ho - - - - ram no - nam ex - cla - ma - - -
ho - - - - ram no - nam ex - cla-ma - - - - -
28
vo - ce ma - - - - - gna: «De - us, De -
ma - - - - - - - - - gna: «De - us, De -
- vit vo - - - - ce ma - - - gna: «De - us, De -
- vit vo - - - - ce ma - - - gna: «De - us, De -
35
- us me - us, ut quid de - re -
- us me - us, ut quid de - re - li -
- us me - us, ut quid de - re - li - qui - sti
- us me - us, ut quid de - re - li - qui - sti

-li - qui - sti me?». Et in-cli - na - to ca-pi - te, e - mi - sit spi - ri -

-qui - sti me?». Et in-cli - na - to ca-pi - te, e - mi - sit spi - ri -

me?». Et in-cli - na - to ca-pi - te, e - mi - sit spi - ri -

me?». Et in-cli - na - to ca-pi - te, e - mi - sit spi - ri -

- tum, et in-cli - na - to ca-pi - te, e - mi - sit spi - ri - tum.

- tum, et in-cli - na - to ca-pi - te, e - mi - sit spi - ri - tum.

- tum, et in-cli - na - to ca-pi - te, e - mi - sit spi - ri - tum.

- tum, et in-cli - na - to ca-pi - te, e - mi - sit spi - ri - tum.

141.

Ave sanctissima Maria

fols. 108*v*-109*r* (4 vv.)

[Pope Sixtus IV?]

> Ave sanctissima Maria,
> mater Dei, regina celi,
> porta paradisi, domina mundi,
> pura singularis, tu es virgo;
> 5 tu concepisti Iesum sine peccato,
> tu peperisti Creatorem et Salvatorem mundi,
> in quo non dubito.
> Libera me ab omni malo,
> et ora pro peccatis.
> Amen.

Fifteenth-century prayer to the Blessed Virgin Mary (Immaculate Conception), perhaps with the purpose of obtaining indulgences.

Readings emended in the edition:

Bar	Voice	Original
18	A	*g*
69	C, A, T, B	*longa* with fermata

Modern editions of the text: Blackburn 1999, pp. 168-170.

Modern editions of the music: Banks 1993, II, pp. 34-36 (after Panc.27).

Bibliography: Banks 1993, I, p. 267; Blackburn 1999; Blackburn 2003, pp. 171-173.

141.
Ave sanctissima Maria
fols. 108*v*-109*r*

[Pope Sixtus IV?]

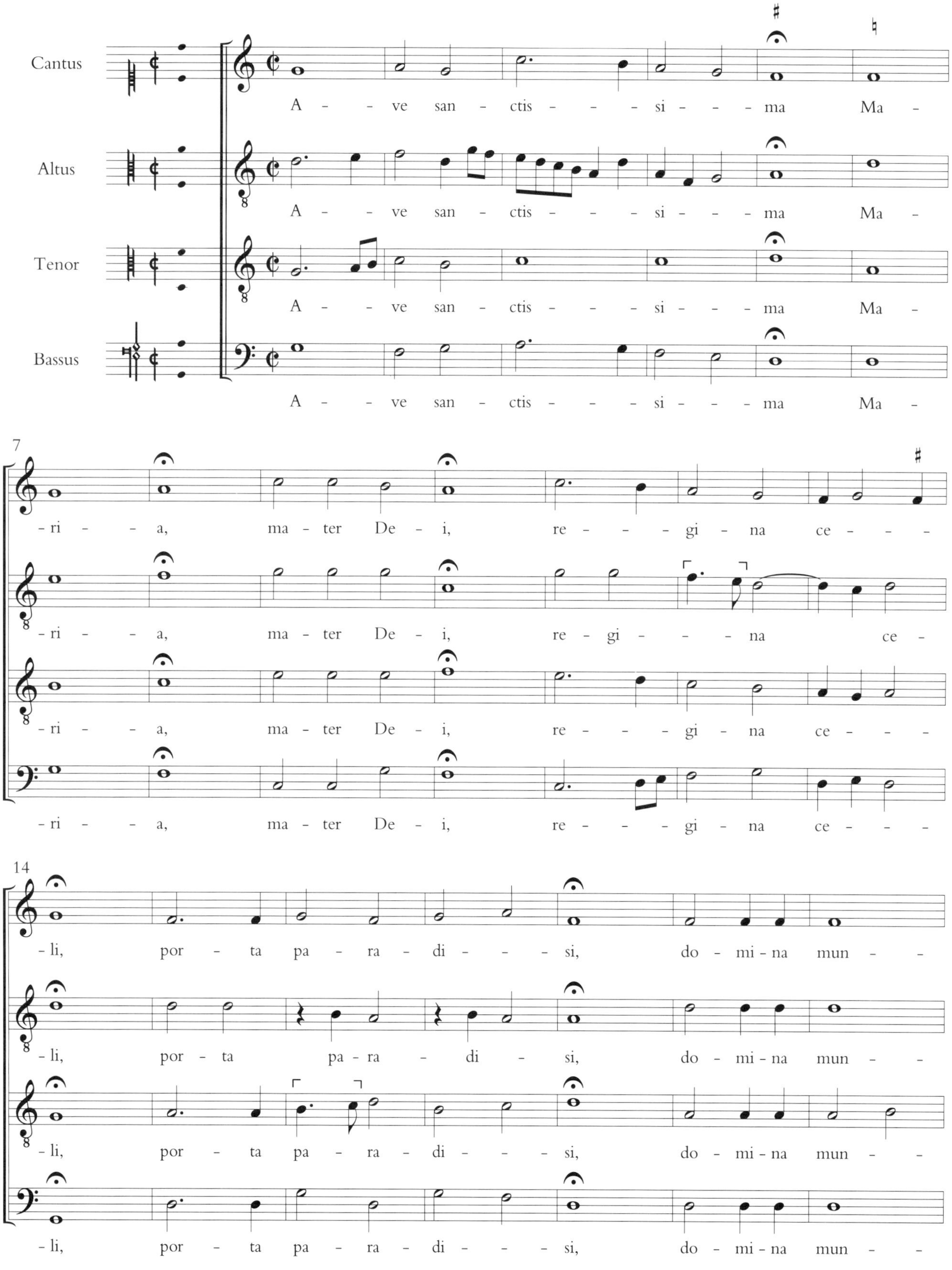

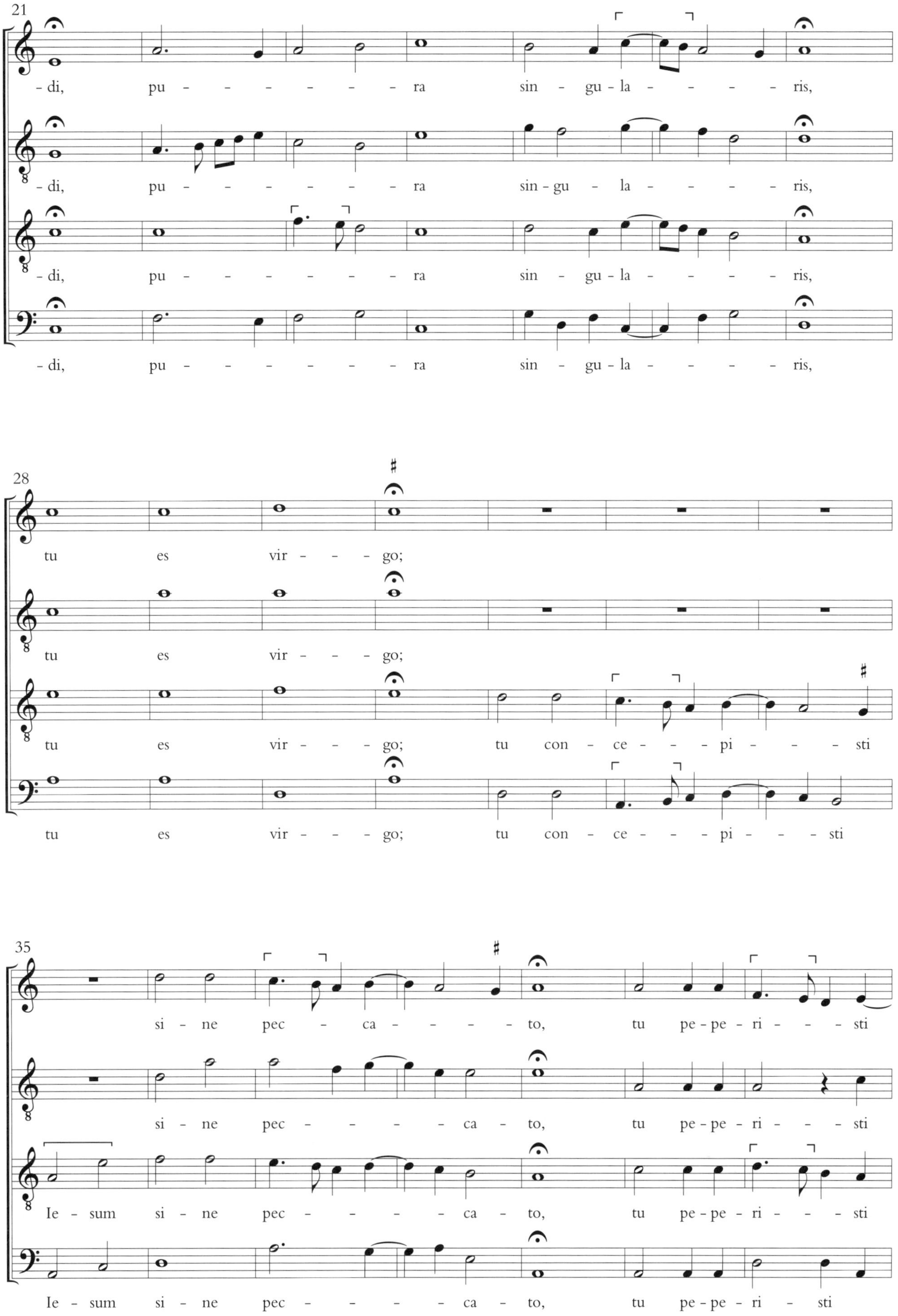
21
- di, pu - - - - - - - ra sin - gu - la - - - - - ris,
- di, pu - - - - - - - ra sin - gu - la - - - - - ris,
- di, pu - - - - - - - ra sin - gu - la - - - - - ris,
- di, pu - - - - - - - ra sin - gu - la - - - - - ris,
28
tu es vir - - - go;
tu es vir - - - go;
tu es vir - - - go; tu con - ce - - - pi - - - sti
tu es vir - - - go; tu con - ce - - - pi - - - sti
35
si - ne pec - ca - - - - - to, tu pe - pe - ri - - - sti
si - ne pec - - - - - ca - to, tu pe - pe - ri - - - sti
Ie - sum si - ne pec - - - - - ca - to, tu pe - pe - ri - - - sti
Ie - sum si - ne pec - - - - - ca - to, tu pe - pe - ri - sti

42
Cre - a - to - rem et Sal - va - to - - rem mun - di,
Cre - a - to - - - rem et Sal - va - to - rem mun - di,
Cre-a-to - rem et Sal - va - to - rem mun - di,
Cre - a - - - to - rem et Sal - va - to - rem mun - di,
50
in quo non du - bi - to. Li - be - ra me ab o - mni
in quo non du - bi - to. Li - be - ra me ab o - mni
in quo non du - bi - to. Li - be - ra me ab
in quo non du - bi - to. Li - be - ra me ab o - mni
57
ma - - - - - - - lo, et o - ra pro pec - - -
ma - - - - - - - lo, et o - ra pro pec -
o - mni ma - lo, et o - ra pro pec -
ma - - - - - - - lo, et o - ra pro pec - - -

-ca – – – – tis

-ca – – – – tis

-ca – – – – tis

-ca – – – – tis, pro pec - - ca - – – – – tis.

A – – men.

A – – men.

A – – men.

A – – men.

725

142.

Verbum caro factum est

fol. 109v (3 vv.)

Verbum caro factum est
de Virgine Maria.

In hoc anni circulo
vita datur seculo
5   nato nobis parvulo
de Virgine Maria.

Fons de suo rivulo
nascitur pro populo,
fracto mortis vinculo,
10   in Virgine Maria.

Quos vetustas suffocat
nos ad vitam revocat,
nam se Deus collocat
in Virgine Maria.

15   Stella solem protulit,
sol salutem contulit,
nihil tamen abstulit
a Virgine Maria.

Sine viri copula
20   florem dedit virgula,
qui manet in secula
cum Virgine Maria.

Ex Virgine regia,
summi regis filia
25   plena datur gratia
pro Virgine Maria.

O stupor in mentibus
tam altum videntibus
ligati in vilibus
30   a Virgine Maria.

O pastores currite,
gregem nostrum sinite,
Deum verum colite
cum Virgine Maria.

35   Mundi factor inditus,
      patris unigenitus
      nobis datur celitus
      de Virgine Maria.

      O beata femina,
40   cuius ventris sarcina
      mundi lavit crimina
      de Virgine Maria.

      In presepe ponitur
      et a brutis noscitur,
45   vello mortis tegitur
      a Virgine Maria.

      Puer circumciditur,
      sanguis eius funditur,
      puer Iesus patitur
50   cum Virgine Maria.

      Nomen sacrum ponitur
      Iesus Christus dicitur
      et purusque nascitur
      de Virgine Maria.

55   Tres reges de gentibus
      Iesum cum muneribus
      orant flexis genibus
      cum Virgine Maria.

      In Bethelem qui natus est,
60   Ierusalem delatus est,
      et in templo oblatus est
      a Virgine Maria.

For the text see no. 86.

COMMENTARY ON THE TEXT:

7	the *residuum* begins here
55	over this stanza is written «In epiphania», which probably indicates that it should be sung only on Epiphany[2]

MUSICAL CONCORDANCES (MSS): • Panc.27 (56*v*)

MODERN EDITIONS OF THE TEXT: MONE II, pp. 80-84,[1] with some textual variants.

MODERN EDITIONS OF THE MUSIC: See no. 86.

---

[1]. The common strophes appear in a different order; in MONE II ll. 27-30 and 51-54 are lacking.
[2]. I thank Bonnie Blackburn for deciphering this inscription.

Remarks: See the Remarks to no. 86. With respect to the concordant piece on fol. 56*v*, the few changes made — perhaps by the scribe himself — in the Tenor and in the Contra correct some of the parallel progressions, though creating others (bb. 5/III–6/II between Cantus and Contra; bb. 10/III–11/II between Cantus and Tenor; b. 14/I–II between Cantus and Contra; b. 14/II–III between Tenor and Contra). The piece occupies the entire page, with an erased heading *Aures ad nostras*. With respect to the text, nos. 142 and 144 probably contain some traces of oral corruption, both in the strophes found in MONE and in the supplementary ones.

Bibliography: See no. 86.

142.

VERBUM CARO FACTUM EST

fol. 109*v*

Cantus: Ver - bum ca - ro fa - ctum est de Vir - gi - ne Ma -

Tenor

Contra: Ver - bum ca - ro fa - ctum est de Vir - gi - ne Ma -

- ri - a. In hoc an - ni cir - cu - lo vi - ta da - tur se - cu - lo

- ri - a.

na - to no - bis par - vu - lo de Vir - gi - ne Ma - ri - a.

143.

Se per te mia fin serà

fol. 110r (4 vv.)

[Heading only]

Italian secular piece (barzelletta?).[1]

READINGS EMENDED IN THE EDITION:

BAR	VOICE	ORIGINAL
8/I	A	*b* instead of *c′*
9	B	two *minimae* in place of two *semibreves*

REMARKS: Although this is a musical *unicum*, it is possible that the piece derives from a model: the error in bar 9 is quite typical of the copying process; moreover, at the bottom of the piece appears the rubric «Iustus», which might refer to a pre-existing model. Furthermore, the presence of a flat in the signature of the Bassus is curious: there seems to be no reason for it, since the voice does not have even one B.

---

[1]. The musical structure of the piece suggests this form.

143.
SE PER TE MIA FIN SERÀ
fol. 110*r*

Iustus

144.

Verbum caro factum est

fol. 110*r* (2 vv.)

Verbum caro factum est
de Virgine Maria.

In hoc anni circulo
vita datur seculo
5   nato nobis parvulo
de Virgi[ne Maria].

Cum in templo presentatur
Simeon hunc amplexatur
et de Iesu prophetatur
10   cum Virgine Maria.

Sidus quodque comparatur
Anna sibi gratulatur
sicque festum terminatur
cum Virgine Maria.

15   Die hac sanctissima
omnibus gratissima
nobis datur gratia
cum Virgine Maria.

Illi laus et gloria,
20   decus et victoria,
qui manet in secula
cum Virgine Maria.

Amen.

For the text see no. 86.

Commentary on the text:

7   the *residuum* begins here[1]

Readings emended in the edition:

Bar	Voice	Original
after 17	C, T	a *custos* in place of a repetition sign

---

[1]. I thank Bonnie Blackburn, who helped me decipher the text.

MODERN EDITIONS OF THE TEXT: MONE II, pp. 80-84 (ll. 1-6 only, with some textual variants).

MODERN EDITIONS OF THE MUSIC: LUISI 1983, II, p. 202 (after Panc.27).

REMARKS: See the Remarks to no. 86. No. 144 is the simplest of the four settings of *Verbum caro* in the manuscript: it is the only one for two voices and has a very uniform modal structure. Written in a lighter ink in an unused space (the last two staves of fol. 110*r*) and certainly copied later with respect to the preceding no. 143, the piece seems to have originated as a *bicinium*, perhaps the result of a compositional experiment by the copyist himself. The different texts of the *Verbum caro* settings no. 144 and no. 142 (see the relative entries) are destined for successive feasts of the Nativity (Nativity of Jesus, Circumcision, Epiphany, Presentation in the Temple).[2]

BIBLIOGRAPHY: See no. 86.

---

[2]. I thank Giulio Cattin for this observation.

144.
VERBUM CARO FACTUM EST
fol. 110*r*

145.

Se non dormi, donna, ascolta

fols. 110*v*–111*r* (4 vv.)

[? C.]¹

Se non dormi, donna, ascolta
la passion che me tormenta,
perché [l'alma] è quasi spenta
che ne[l] cor era ricolta.

5   Se tu dormi, vegio e canto,
non però che n‹a›'abia voglia,
se te narro col mio pianto
el piacer e la mia voglia,
questa dura mia gran doglia
10   che nel pecto m'è ricolta.
        Se non dormi, donna, ascolta
        la pas[sion che me tormenta]

Italian secular piece (barzelletta).

COMMENTARY ON THE TEXT:

1	non] no S (first enunciation of the line)
3	hypometric; corrected on the basis of the reading in *Fir.L. Ant.158*, *Fir.N. T.227*, FirC B2441, ParisN Rés676
6	the letter ‹a› is not present in FirC B2441, ParisN Rés676, PeFroIII1505 (and its reprint)

READINGS EMENDED IN THE EDITION:

BAR	VOICE	ORIGINAL
12	B	*longa* with fermata
22/I	A	*c semibrevis*, corrected in analogy with the passage in bar 10/I

TEXTUAL CONCORDANCES (MSS):² • *Fir.L. Ant.158* (41*v*–42*v*), «Cantilena placida ad canendum» • *Fir.N. T.227* (16*v*)

---

¹. Although the facsimile of ParisN Rés676 does not show it correctly (see LESURE 1979, p. 126), on the original MS an abbreviation composed of two letters can be observed at the head of the composition: the second is a «C», while the first is a quivering stroke written in a lighter ink ('I'?, 'L'?, part of an 'M'?). Considering the letters as the abbreviation of the name of the composer, Nanie Bridgman assumed that the first letter was an 'L', and therefore attributed the piece to Loyset Compère (see BRIDGMAN 1953-56, p. 226). Prizer maintains instead that it may be an 'M', hypothesizing Marchetto Cara as author (see PRIZER 1996b, p. 13, n. 7). The modern edition of the piece appears in vol. 15/V of the CMM edition dedicated to Compère, as an *opus dubium*: Ludwig Finscher, however, prefers to leave the question of attribution open (see CMM 15/V, p. II). The musical style of the piece, nevertheless, suggests that an attribution to Cara is more plausible; similarly, the few sources transmitting the piece would also point in Cara's direction. In Petrucci's publications, Cara himself is often indicated simply with his initials «M. C.».

². The bassadanza *Se no dormi dona alsciolta* with choreography is found in the MS Florence, Biblioteca Medicea Laurenziana, Antinori 13 (copied in 1510), fols. 56*v*-57*r*: the choreography is anonymous (see GALLO 1979).

Musical concordances (mss): • FirC B2441 (34*v*–35*r*) • LonB E3051 (40*v*–41*r*) • ParisN Rés676 (67*v*–68*r*), «[…+…] C.»

Musical concordances (prints): • PeFroIII1505 (53*v*–54*r*) • PeFroIII1507 (53*v*–54*r*)

Text from PeFroIII1505:

Se non dormi, donna, ascolta
la passion che me tormenta,
perché [l'alma] è quasi spenta
che nel cor era ricolta.
         Si non dormi, donna, ascolta
         la passion che me tormenta.

5   Se tu dormi, veghio e canto,
non però che n'abia voglia,
sol ti narro col mio pianto
el piacere e la mia voglia,
questa dura mia gran doglia
10   che nel petto m'è recolta.
         Se non dormi, donna, ascolta
         la passion che me tormenta.

Io sto intorno a le tue mura,
non dormendo, e non veghiando,
ma cognosco ben sei dura!
Questo viver intanto sprando,
15   andarà ad ognor menando
la mia vita paza e stolta.
         Se non dormi […]

Damme almen qualche resposta,
quando a tuo servo el pò dare.
Verità non fia nascosta
20   in quel tanto tuo sapere.
Non me far or pene avere
fa mia vita in gaudio volta.
         Se non dormi […]

Se non hai di me pietade,
damme almen un bel combiato,[3]
25   che non stia in calamitade
se non da te morto io cado.
Ben servir in cotal stato,
me nutrisco in pena molta.
         Se non dormi […]

Text from FirC B2441 (ripresa, first, second, third stanza, followed by an additional stanza):

Gionto son dona al laccio,
io non posso più fugire.
Fa di me qualche più stratio.
Son disposto a te servire
con ingegno, forza e ardire,

---

[3]. The term «combiato» is a dialectal form of 'commiato' (= 'leave-taking') (see Battaglia III, p. 371).

finché vita a me sia tolta.
      Se non dormi […]

TEXT FROM *Fir.L.Ant.158* (ripresa, first, fifth, second stanza, and two additional stanzas):

Non ti posso dinegare
chi non venga al mie fallire.
Chi ti venga a risvegliare
nel più bel del tuo dormire?
Quel che ora non posso dire
scoprirollo un'altra volta.
      Se non dormi […]

E m'incresce di svegliarti,
ma mi sforza el troppo amore
che m'induce a palesarti
el segreto del mio core.
Perché sempre vive e more
questa vita doglia molta.
      Se non dormi […]

TEXT FROM LonB E3051 (it begins with the first stanza, without the text of the initial ripresa, followed by an additional stanza):

Se tu credi el mio cantare
e 'l sia sol per darmi spasso,
egli è sol per dimonstrare
el crudo affanno pel cor lasso.
Sol per te, donna, mi spasso,
poiché l'alma tu m'ha' tolta.

The disposition of the text, which differs considerably among the sources, is summarized in the following chart, in which the arabic numerals indicate the successsion of the stanzas (without considering variants in writing or single words):

	PeFroIII1505 - PeFroIII1507	FirC B2441	ParisN Rés676	*Fir.L.Ant.158*	*Fir.N.T.227*	LonB E3051
Se tu dormi	1	1	1	1	1	1
Io sto intorno	2	2	2	3	–	–
Damme almen	3	3	–	–	–	–
Se non hai	4	–	–	–	–	–
Gionto son	–	4	–	2	2	–
Se tu credi	–	–	–	–	–	2
Non ti posso	–	–	–	4	–	–
E m'incresce	–	–	–	5	–	–

MODERN EDITIONS OF THE TEXT: BORGHI 1995, pp. 191-193 (after FirC B2441); CESARI *ET AL.* 1954, pp. 47*-48* (after PeFroIII1505); FILOCAMO 2000, pp. 145-148 (after Panc.27).

MODERN EDITIONS OF THE MUSIC: BORGHI 1995, pp. 365-366 (after FirC B2441); CESARI *ET AL.* 1954, pp. 133-134 (after PeFroIII1505); CMM 15/V, pp. 68-69 (after PeFroIII1505).

REMARKS: The version in Panc.27 is not related to any of the known concordances; all arrange the musical sections in a different manner (FirC B2441 and ParisN Rés676 end at b. 24; LonB E3051 at b. 18; PeFroIII1505 and its reprint repeat bb. 1-6 after b. 12). Moreover, ParisN Rés676 has a completely different Altus, and the piece is transposed a fourth higher. FirC B2441 and LonB E3051 have numerous graphic and rhythmic variants, and in LonB E3051 the first strophe of the text is lacking. On the whole, therefore, the version closest to Panc.27 is Petrucci's: the lack of «l'alma» in line 3 is an important conjunctive element, but the numerous rhythmic and graphic variants discourage the hypothesis of direct copying. More plausible is the idea that both versions derive from a common model that has not come down to us, even if the rhythmic variant in bar 7/I (a *semibrevis* rest isolates LonB E3051, *minimae d′* and *e′* unite FirC B2441 with Panc.27, and *minima* rest, *semiminimae d′* and *e′* unite Paris Rés676 with PeFroIII1505 and its reprint) opens up other hypotheses as to transmission.

BIBLIOGRAPHY: BOORMAN 2006, p. 1017; BRIDGMAN 1953-56, p. 226; GALLO 1979; PESCERELLI 1974, pp. 50-51, 54-55; PRIZER 1986, p. 22; PRIZER 1996b, pp. 13, n. 7, 43; PRIZER 2004a, pp. 402, 404; SPARTI 1996, pp. 146, 149-150.

145.
SE NON DORMI, DONNA, ASCOLTA

fols. 110*v*-111*r*

[? C.]

Se non dor - mi, don - na, a - scol - ta la pas - sion che me tor-

Se non dor - mi, don - na, a - scol - ta

-men - ta, per - ché [l'al - ma] è qua - si spen - ta che ne[l] cor e - ra ri - col - ta.

Se tu dor - mi, ve - gio e can - to, non pe - rò che n'a - bia vo - glia,
se te nar - ro col mio pian - to el pia - cer e la mia vo - glia,

que – sta du – ra mia gran do – glia che nel pec – to m'è ri – col – ta.

Se non dor – mi, don – na, a – scol – ta la pas – [sion che me tor – men – ta.]

146.

SIAMO, DONE, TREI ROMERI

fols. 110*v*–111*r* (3 vv.)

Siamo, done, trei romeri
che elemosina ‹noi› cerchiamo,
perché d'altro non viviamo.
Però, done, socorete
5   ‹a› noi tre poveri romeri!

Per gram forsa siamo usciti
de la nostra abitatio',
se alcun ben voi ne fareti,
no saremo ingrati noi.

10   Deh, madona, se posseti
un bocon de quel ch'è tale
noi chiamemo a segurtate
‹de› quel che sta soto el scosale.

Italian secular piece (carnival song).

COMMENTARY ON THE TEXT:

1	«trei»: dialectal form derived from the Latin 'tres'[1]
1	«romeri»: the 'romeo' was the pilgrim going to Rome[2]
2	hypermetric; the hypothesis of deletion is justified by the scansion of the verse and because it is impossible to insert an extra syllable under the music
3	«vivemo» instead of 'viviamo'
5	hypermetric; the extra syllable could also be accommodated under the notes, but would result in a faulty accentual correspondence between the text and the music. One could also delete, if one wished, «trei» instead of 'a', but I prefer to eliminate «a» because in modern Italian the verb 'soccorrere' is transitive, and thus the following «a» would sound incorrect
6	the *residuum* begins here
12	«chiamemo»: with the sense of 'invoke', 'solicit'[3]
12	«segurtate»: from the Latin 'secur(um)' with its derivative 'securitas' = 'security'[4]
13	hypermetric. «Scosale»: the 'cosciale' was a garment or a part of it used to cover the thighs in order to protect them[5]

---

[1]. SEE CORTELAZZO – ZOLLI V, pp. 1368–1369.
[2]. See CORTELAZZO – ZOLLI IV, p. 1104.
[3]. See CORTELAZZO – ZOLLI I, p. 229.
[4]. See CORTELAZZO – ZOLLI V, p. 1200.
[5]. See CORTELAZZO – ZOLLI I, p. 290.

READINGS EMENDED IN THE EDITION:

BAR	VOICE	ORIGINAL
incipit	C, T, Ct	transcribed presuming the use of *tempus imperfectum diminutum cum prolatione minori*, considering the fact the writing is primarily in *semibreves* and *miminae*
6/I	Ct	*e* instead of *f*
after 11	Ct	the repeat sign is lacking
12	C, Ct	under the new mensural sign of *tempus imperfectum diminutum cum prolatione minori* the arabic number '3' is missing. The transcription follows the indication in the Tenor (*tactus* sign above the number '3')
20/II	C	*d′* instead of *c′*

MODERN EDITIONS OF THE TEXT: GALLUCCI 1966, I, pp. 324–325 (after Panc.27); GHISI 1937, p. 55 (after Panc.27, only the first stanza).

MODERN EDITIONS OF THE MUSIC: GALLUCCI 1966, II, pp. 234–235 (after Panc.27).

REMARKS: This carnival song has the typical homorhythmic structure for three voices and the characteristic alternation between duple and triple metre. The piece was probably added later: it is in fact written in the remaining portion of the opening, with the *residuum* crowded into a tiny corner of fol. 110*v*.

BIBLIOGRAPHY: GHISI 1937, pp. 55, 119, 195; PRIZER 1996b, p. 24; PRIZER 2005, pp. 240-241.

146.
Siamo, done, trei romeri

fols. 110*v*–111*r*

Cantus: Sia - mo, do - ne, trei ro - me - ri che e - le - mo - si - na cer - chia - mo, per - ché d'al - tro non vi - via - mo.

Tenor: Sia - mo, do - ne, trei ro - me - ri

Co[n]tra: Sia - mo, do - ne, trei ro - me - ri

Pe - rò, do - ne, so - co - re - te noi trei po - ve - ri ro - me - ri!

147.

Alzando li oghii vidi Maria bella

fol. 110*v* (text only)

Alzando li oghii vidi Maria bella,
cum lo libro in mano e l'anzelo li favella.

Davanti a lei stava inzenogiato
l'anzelo Gabriele tanto relucente

Lauda (barzelletta).

Textual concordances (mss): • *Berl.S. H.348* (161*v*) • *Bol.U. 2845* (275-276) • *CV. BL.4047* (121*r*) • *CV. Ch.266* (37*v*-38*r*) • *CV.VL.13026* (26*r-v*) • *Fer.C. 211* (96*v*-97*v*) • *Fir.L. Ash.480* (105*v*-106*r*) • *Fir.L. Ash.852* (77*v*-78*v*) • *Fir.L. Ash.1402* (169*v*-170*r*) • *Fir.M. 262* (77*v*-78*r*) • *Fir.N. 58* (80*v*-81*r*) • *Fir.N. 140* (4*v*-5*r*) • *Fir.N. LF.249* (45*r-v*) • *Fir.N. M.27* (177*r*) • *Fir.N. M.30* (39*r*-40*r*) • *Fir.N. M.285* (87*r*-88*r*) • *Fir.N. M.686* (1*r-v*) • *Fir.R. 1473* (92*r*-93*r*) • *Fir.R. 1502* (14*r-v*) • *Fir.R. 1666* (12*r-v*) • *Fir.R. 2895* (59*r*-60*r*) • *Fir.R. 2929* (64*r*-65*r, olim 63*r*-64*r*) • *Mil.A. 3* (84*r-v*) • *Parma.P. Pal.37* (109*r-v*) • *Piac.C. L.15* (8*v*-9*v, olim 3*v*-4*v*) • *Roma.N. V.24* (142*r-v*) • *Siena.C. 13* (18*v*-19*r*) • *Siena.C. 14* (69*r*-70*v*) • *Siena.C. 15* (20*v*-21*v*) • *Siena.C. 17* (75*v*-77*r*) • *Siena.C. 41* (34*v*-35*v*) • *Ven.M. I.77* (86*r*-87*r*) • *Ven.M. I.182* (258*v*-259*r*) • *Ven.M. I.230* (26*r*-27*r*) • *Ven.M. I.313* (109*v*-110*v*), *Volgendo gli ochi vidi Maria bella* • *Ven.M. I.324* (123*v*-124*r*)

Textual concordances (prints): • *Fior1505* (b4*v*-b5*r*) • *LaudeBonar* (1*v*) • *LaudeMisc* (57*v*-58*r*) • *LaudeVecchie* (g1*v*-g2*r*) • *OperaNova* (49*v*-50*r*)

Text from *Bol.U. 2845*:

Alzando li ochi vidi Maria bella,
col libro in man e l'anzol li favella.

Denanzi a lei inzenochiom li stava
quel anzolo Gabriel tanto lucente,
5   umilmente che lui li parlava:
«Vergine pura, non temer niente:
messazo son de Cristo[1] onipotente,
che lui t'ha ellecta e vol te per spoxella».

Standose solleta in la soa cella,
10 vergognosamente respondea,
però che la donzella ad omo non favella
e grande meravelgia de questo se facea.
E l'anzolo li disse: «Ave Maria,
tu sei piena de gratia, o chiara stella.

---

[1]. It would be more correct if instead of «Cristo» there were 'Dio', as edited in Galletti 1863, p. 121.

15   Sapi, Madona, che in cielo è ordinato
      che tu sia madre del fiol de Dio;
      li anzoli e tuti i sancti l'ham pregato,
      che per amor s'adempia 'o lor desio.
      Dio fece l'omo bom e puo' fo rio,
20   e però la benedictiom a voi s'apella».

Queste parole de tanta adorneza
e circundate de virtù d'amore,
bem parve che dal ciel fosse mandata,
tanta alegreza n'ebe il [p]urro cuore:
25   «Daspoi che 'l piace al mio dolze Signore,
      ecco ch'io son la sua umile ancella».

Alor in lei desexe il Spirito Sancto,
cum uno razo de sole ha circundata.
Dentro da lei intrò quel fructo sancto
30   in quela sacristia tanto sacrata;
      poi parturisti, o Virgo inviolata,
      e remanesti virgine polzella.

O fini amanti, mirati a costei
che de virtute è tanto adorna.
35   Il cielo e la terra s'amirano per lei,
      luce del cielo e del mondo columna;[2]
      chi vol vedere la polzella adorna
      vada a veder la nuntiata bella.

MODERN EDITIONS OF THE TEXT: GALLETTI 1863, pp. 121-122 (after *LaudeMisc*).

REMARKS: The text *Alzando li oghii vidi Maria bella* is found at the bottom of fol. 110*v*, under the Tenor of the carnival song *Siamo, donne, trei romeri* (no. 146).[3] It cannot be a question of a contrafact of the carnival song, given that the differing metres of the two texts inhibits an adaption to a devotional text. The same goes for the music that follows, composed to the text *Signora, anci, mea dea* (no. 148, fol. 111*v*). The only hypothesis that seems to me likely to explain the presence of this unique text without music in Panc.27 is that the scribe wrote down the text in the margin with the idea of joining it to music later. Perhaps he changed his mind or forgot it! As demonstrated by the long list of poetic concordances given above, the text was widely diffused (there are also numerous 'cantasi come' and other contrafacts): the scribe could easily have taken it from some literary source; this might also be confirmed by the presence of a semicolon after «relucente» (l. 4).

BIBLIOGRAPHY: DAMILANO 1963, p. 63; FRATI 1917, p. 454; GHISI 1937, pp. 55, 119, 195; GHISI 1953a, p. 68; LUISI 1983, I, pp. 132, 144, 200, 208; PRIZER 1996b, p. 24; TENNERONI 1909, p. 53.

---

[2]. The MS has «columpna».

[3]. The lauda was not mentioned in the inventory of Panc.27 drawn up by Morpurgo at the end of the nineteenth century (see MORPURGO *ET AL.* 1887-1962, pp. 54-58), but it is present in the catalogue by Bianca Becherini (see BECHERINI 1959a, pp. 118-122). RISM B IV/5 (pp. 141-150), on the other hand, does not mention the presence of the lauda at all.

147.

ALZANDO LI OGHII VIDI MARIA BELLA

fol. 110*v*

No music

148.

Signora, anci, mea dea

fol. 111*v* (4 vv.)

Barth[olomeo] T[romboncino][1]

Signora, anci, mea dea,
so ben che avesti a sdegno
che senza moto o segno
me partisse,

5   e che a te non venisse,
umil, cum reverentia,
a chiederti licentia
qual bon servo,

sì che forsi protervo,
10   vilano, iniquo e ingrato
serò da te chiamato,
benché a torto.

Però che vivo e morto
trovomi ov'io mi voglia,
15   no vo' che mai si soglia
da te el core.

E se di nostro errore
sapesti la cagione,
son certo che ragione
20   mi daresti.

Italian secular piece (oda).

Commentary on the text:

1   «mia» in no. 150
5   the *residuum* begins here
15   «soglia»: with the meaning of 'sciolga'

Musical concordances (mss): • Panc.27 (112*r*), common Cantus

Musical concordances (prints): • PeFroIII1505 (63*v*), «B.T.», only the Cantus agrees • PeFroIII1507 (63*v*), «B.T.», only the Cantus agrees

---

[1]. This attribution probably refers only to the upper voice of the piece. See Remarks to no. 150.

TEXT FROM PeFroIII1505:

Signora, anzi, mia dea,
so ben che avesti a sdegno
che senza motto o segno
mi partisse.

5   E che a te non venisse,
umil, con reverentia,
a chiederti licentia
qual bon servo.

Sì che forsi protervo,
10   villano, iniquo e ingrato
serò da te chiamato,
benché a torto.

Però che vivo e morto
trovemi ov'io mi voglia,
15   non vo' che mai si soglia
da te el core.

E se di nostro errore
sapesti la cagione,
son certo che ragione
20   mi daresti.

E se 'l te fur molesti
nel mio partir tal modi,
se mai la causa tu odi,
lauderàmi.

25   Non men per questo averàmi²
disposto al tuo servitio,
ch'ogni tuo benefitio
scripto ho in petto.

E se pur per diffetto
30   di cieli o de mia sorte
non poss'io avanti morte
farti certa,

quest'ultima mia offerta
de ch'èn³ contenti i dei,
35   perché tu simil sei,
fiati grata.

E a te sia dedicata
mia alma e ogni mio senso,
ché ad altro mai non penso
40   che obedirti.

---

². «averàmi» stands for 'avrammi'.
³. «èn» stands for 'enno' (= 'sono').

Se a toi sublimi spirti
tal dono picol parti,
io non so più che darti
che me stesso.

Modern editions of the text: Cesari *et al.* 1954, p. 50★ (after PeFroIII1505).

Remarks: See no. 150.

Bibliography: Boorman 2006, p. 1021; Einstein 1949, I, p. 92; Jeppesen 1969, pp. 37-38.

148.
SIGNORA, ANCI, MEA DEA
fol. 111*v*

Barth[olomeo] T[romboncino]

Cantus: Si - gno - ra, an-ci, mea de - a, so ben che a-ve-sti a sde-gno

Altus: Si - gno - ra

Cantus: che sen - za mo-to o se-gno me par-tis - se

149.

La virtù se vol seguire

fols. 111*v*-112*r* (3 vv.)

La virtù se vol‹e› seguire,
non fortuna: in quelle è vana,
da virtù no se lontana
chi felice vol morire.

5   Per virtù se aquista regno
e in su quel se mantene.
La virtù fa l'omo degno
‹e› sie la fin del summo bene.
Quello mai non vene in pene,
10   chi virtù vol pur seguire.

Chi se fonda in la fortuna
alfin se trova in basso.

Italian secular piece (barzelletta).

COMMENTARY ON THE TEXT:

1	hypermetric; «vole» has been corrected on the basis of the readings in ParisN Rés676 and *Pes. O. 54*
8	hypermetric; the hypothesis of deletion is justified by the scansion of the verse and because it is impossible to insert an extra syllable under the music
9	the *residuum* begins here
12	hypometric

READINGS EMENDED IN THE EDITION:

BAR	VOICE	ORIGINAL
17	S	*longa* with fermata
after 17	S, T	mensuration sign of *tempus imperfectum diminutum cum prolatione minori*

TEXTUAL CONCORDANCES (MSS): • *CV. Ca. 193* (88*r-v*) • *Fir. L. Ant. 158* (14*r-v*) • *Fir. N. M. 735* (12*r-v*) • *Pes. O. 54* (125*v*)

MUSICAL CONCORDANCES (MSS): • FirN M121 (17*v*-18*r*), 4 vv. (with an additional A) • ParisN Rés676 (71*v*-72*r*), 4 vv. (with an additional A)

---

¹. In his doctoral dissertation of 1974, William Prizer attributed the piece to Marchetto Cara, on the basis of its musical relation with *In eterno io voglio amarte* in PeFroI (fols. 10*v*-11*r*), which bears the attribution «M. C.». But this piece, besides having an extra Altus, is not concordant with the version of Panc.27 (it has only the first notes in common). In the recent entry dedicated to Cara ('Cara, Marchetto', in NG), however, Prizer does not list the piece among those attributable to Marchetto.

Text from ParisN Rés676:

La virtù se vol seguire,
non fortuna iniqua e vana,
da virtù non s'alontana
chi felice vol morire.

5   Per virtù s'aquista regno
e cum quella se mantiene.
La virtù fa l'omo degno
a la fin del summo bene.
Qual è, donca, più bel pegno
10   che volere virtù finire?[4]

Chi s'affonda in la fortuna
a la fin s'atrova al basso.
Or è chiara et or è bruna,
e d'un sei fa spesse un asso.
15   Sarà, adonca, il nero spesso,
la virtù per non perire.
              La virtù se vol seguire.

Viva, viva, viva, viva,
viva, adonca, la virtute.
La virtù sie nostra guida,
20   che donare ci pò salute.
Da virtude non se priva,
chi nel cello si vol salire.
              La virtù se vol seguire.

Modern editions of the text: Filocamo 2000, pp. 151-153 (after Panc.27); Prizer 1980, p. 505 (after ParisN Rés676); Saviotti 1892, pp. 327-328 (after *Pes. O. 54*).

Modern editions of the music: Mancuso 1984, II, pp. 299-303 (after Razzi); Prizer 1980, pp. 507-508 (after ParisN Rés676).

Remarks: The version of Panc.27 — the only one transmitted in three voices — is distant from the other known concordances, both from the musical and the literary point of view: very many graphic and substantive variants from all the other witnesses separate it from the tradition. In the manuscript the piece has surely been added later: it occupies in fact a residual portion of space, and is inserted in a group of pieces dedicated to the letter 'S'.

Bibliography: Blackburn 1981b, pp. 125-126, 151-152; Cesari *et al.* 1954, pp. lxxxv, 5★-6★, 9; Prizer 1980, p. 161; Prizer 2004a, pp. 403-405; Prizer 2009; Schwartz 1935, pp. xxviii, 7-8.

---

[2]. On fol. 9*r* the poetic text is written out, preceded by the rubric «Laude di authore incerto».
[3]. The modern edition of this text can be found in Mancuso 1984, II, p. 297.
[4]. «finire» perhaps has the sense of 'realize completely'.

149.
LA VIRTÙ SE VOL SEGUIRE
fols. 111*v*-112*r*

S[uperius]

T[enor]

Con[tr]a

La vir-tù se vol se-gui-re, non for-tu-na: in

La vir-tù

La vir-tù

quel-le è va - - na, da vir-tù no se lon-

-ta - na chi fe-li-ce vol mo-ri-re. Per vir-tù se a-qui-
La vir-tù fa l'o-

-sta re - gno e in su quel se man-te-ne.
-mo de - gno sie la fin del sum-mo be-ne.

150.

SIGNORA, ANCI, MIA DEA

fol. 112*r* (4 vv.)

[BARTOLOMEO TROMBONCINO]

Signora, anci, mia dea,
[so ben che avesti a sdegno
che senza moto o segno
me partisse.]¹

For the text see no. 148.

COMMENTARY ON THE TEXT:

1	the line is placed under the Bassus
1	«mea» in no. 148

READINGS EMENDED IN THE EDITION:

BAR	VOICE	ORIGINAL
1-16	C	in the margin of the corresponding stave (blank) appears the note *Cantus ut supra* instead of the complete voice. The same higher voice of no. 148 has therefore been transcribed
incipit	T	mensuration sign of *tempus imperfectum diminutum cum prolatione minori*
4/I	A	*e′ minima*
8	C	the barline, absent in no. 148, is inferred from the other voices

MUSICAL CONCORDANCES (MSS): • Panc.27 (111*v*), common Cantus

MUSICAL CONCORDANCES (PRINTS): • PeFroIII1505 (63*v*), «B. T.» • PeFroIII1507 (63*v*), «B. T.»

MODERN EDITIONS OF THE TEXT: CESARI *ET AL.* 1954, p. 50★ (after PeFroIII1505).

MODERN EDITIONS OF THE MUSIC: CESARI *ET AL.* 1954, p. 142 (after PeFroIII1505); EINSTEIN 1949, III, pp. 7-8.

REMARKS: Nos. 148 and 150 merit a joint commentary. Whereas the version of no. 150 is probably taken from the Petrucci print (Panc.27 differs only in a ligature instead of two separated notes in the Tenor and the Bassus, the use of two different clefs in the Altus and Bassus, and slight graphic linguistic variants), no. 148 is perhaps the result of an independent reworking (by the scribe of Panc.27?) based on the version transcribed on the same opening. The Cantus of no. 148 is that of Petrucci, with a single insignificant melodic variant (b. 10/III) and the last two notes are separated instead of in ligature. A comparison of the two versions of Panc.27 serves to clarify the type of 'revision' undertaken by the anonymous composer: whereas the Bassus differs substantially only in bars 3/I, 9/I, and 10/I, the Tenor varies bars 1-3/I and 9/I, and the Altus is completely different. It

---

¹. While the first line is written under the music of the Bassus, ll. 2-4 are taken from the Cantus of no. 148.

is possible that the copyist inserted the two versions of *Signora, anci mia dea* at the same time: no. 149 (fols. 111*v*-112*r*), in fact, was clearly copied at a later time, as one can see from its placement on the last three remaining staves of the two pages, and the darker ink.

BIBLIOGRAPHY: BOORMAN 2006, p. 1021; EINSTEIN 1949, I, p. 92; JEPPESEN 1969, pp. 37-38.

150.
SIGNORA, ANCI, MIA DEA
fol. 112*r*

[Bartolomeo Tromboncino]

Cantus
ut supra
[no. 148]

Altus

Tenor

Bassus

[Si-gno - ra, an - ci, mea de - a,   so ben che a - ve - sti a sde-gno

Si - gno-ra, an - ci, mia de - a

che sen - za mo - to o se - gno   me par - tis - se]

151.

Poca pace e molta guerra

fols. 112*v*-113*r* (4 vv.)

[Bartolomeo Tromboncino]

[Heading only]

Italian secular piece (barzelletta).

Readings emended in the edition:

Bar	Voice	Original
5/II	S	*d'*, corrected on the basis of the version in PeFroV
19/II	S	*d'*, corrected on the basis of the version in PeFroV

Musical concordances (mss): • FirN BR337 (24*v*), B only • ParisN Rés27 (41*r*-*v*)[1] • ParisN Rés676 (101*v*-102*r*), «Trombetino»

Musical concordances (prints): • PeFroV (31*v*-32*r*); index: «T»

Text from PeFroV:

> Poca pace e molta guerra
> mi sta sempr'intorno al core;
> se sto un dì senza dolore,
> l'altro bramo esser sotto terra.
>   Poca pace […]

5   Or in gaudio et ora in pace
> l'alma mia sta lieta e trista,
> quando parla, quando tace,
> qualche male si mi contrista.
> Poco perde e poco aquista
10   quel che al mio voler s'afferra.
>   Poca pace […]

> Sempre hai teco l'amo e l'esca,
> la piatà, l'ira e lo sdegno;
> quando par di me t'incresca,
> quando par che m'abi a sdegno.
15   Son fra vènti un debil legno
> chi me spinge in mare e in terra.
>   Poca pace […]

---

[1]. Although there is no attribution on the relative pages, both Thibault and Lesure provide an index of the contents of the tablature, and in both cases they write «Trombetino» — an ascription that appears in none of the concordances known — next to the piece *Poca pace e molta guerra* (see Thibault 1958, p. 54 and Lesure 1981, *Index*).

Remarks: With respect to the lowest voice in Panc.27, the Bassus of FirN BR337 has rhythmic variants (repeated notes instead of long ones or vice versa, and the last four notes are not in ligature) and the mensuration sign of *tempus imperfectum cum prolatione minori*. The version in ParisN Rés676 too contains some rhythmic and graphic variants, and the highest voice is written in a different clef (a third higher, as in PeFroV). Only the Petrucci print permits us to correct the repeated error in Panc.27 (S, bb. 5/II and 19/II), where ParisN Rés676 shares the incorrect *d'*. It is therefore not possible to hypothesize Panc.27's direct derivation from either of the known concordances.

Bibliography: Boorman 2006, p. 1006; Filocamo 2004.

151.

POCA PACE E MOLTA GUERRA

fols. 112*v*–113*r*

[Bartolomeo Tromboncino]

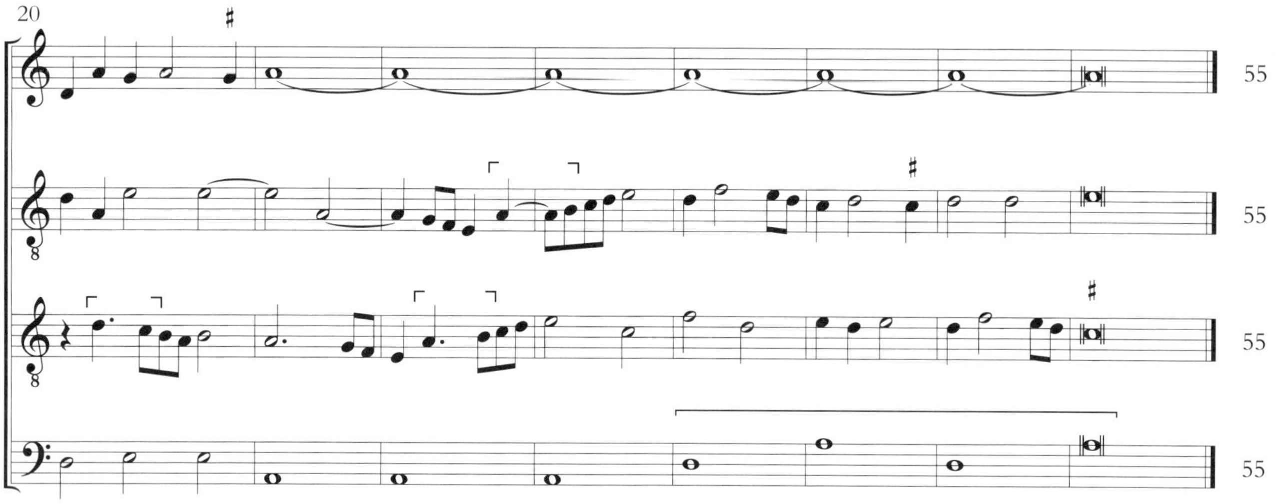
20
55
55
55
55

152.

Se l'ortolana vene a la città

fols. 112*v*-113*r* (4 vv.)

Se l'ortolana vene a la città,
el so marito la segue pian piam.
Va in là vilan. Tiene [...+...] fontana

Questa ortolana va per le contrade,
5   un compagno la prende per la man.
           Va in là vilan.

E io lei voglio comprare [...+...]
[...+...] ristoro ch'in piaza fan.
           Va in là [...]

Lua[...+...]
[...+...]
           Va in là [...]

10   In persto che voi, caro fratello
      poi laseme andare se no me vateram.
           Va in là vi[...]

Tornato [...+...]
[...+...]
           Va in là [...]

V[...+...]
15   [...+...]
           Va in là [...]

Voglio dar [...+...]
[...+...]
           Va in là [...]

Se [...+...]
[...+...]
           Va in là [...]

20   A [...+...]
      [...+...]
           Va in là [...]

Italian secular piece.

COMMENTARY ON THE TEXT:

3	the text breaks off after «Tiene»
after 9	from here on, the placement of the lines is problematic: the lines following labelled 10-16 are only in the Bassus, whereas the others are above the Altus. It is not clear which is the correct sequence, because it is possible that those above the Altus were written there for lack of further space under the Bassus
10	«In persto» perhaps stands for 'in presto'
11	«vateram» perhaps has the sense of 'batteranno' (= 'beat')

READINGS EMENDED IN THE EDITION:

BAR	VOICE	ORIGINAL
5/I	A	c'

MODERN EDITION OF THE TEXT: GALLICO 1996, p. 149 (only the first three lines).

REMARKS: It is highly probable that the text of this composition was rather indecent: the scribe (or someone for him) has considered it opportune to cover a large part of the text, rendering it impossible to read today, except in part (and only with the help of a Wood lamp). Certainly this piece was inserted in the manuscript at a later stage: the space used, in fact, exploits the blank space left on the opening (the last two staves on each page). The mensuration sign indicated in each of the four voices is *tempus imperfectum diminutum cum prolatione minori*, but I have preferred to use triple metre, which matches the prosody of the text more closely.[1]

BIBLIOGRAPHY: FILOCAMO 2004; GALLICO 1996, p. 124.

---

[1]. I thank Fabrizio Ammetto, who suggested this more cogent rhythmic interpretation.

152.
Se l'ortolana vene a la città
fols. 112v–113r

S[uperius]

Se l'or-to-la - na ve-ne a la ci - tà, el so ma-
Que-sta or-to-la - na va per le con - tra - de, un com-pa-

A[ltus]

T[enor]

Se l'or-to-la - na ve-ne a la ci - tà, el so ma-

B[assus]

...+...

-ri-to la se-gue pian piam. Va in là vi-lan. Tie-ne ...+... fon - ta-na
-gno la pren-de per la man. Va in là vi-lan.

-ri-to la se-gue pian piam. Va in là vi-lan. ...+...

153.

[...]

fols. 113*v*–114*r* (4 vv.)

Vocal piece, without text, probably Italian (canto carnascialesco?).

Readings emended in the edition:

Bar	Voice	Original
3	B	*g*
5	B	*g semibrevis* with fermata
6–8	B	*d e f g a a b b*
10	A, B	*longa* with fermata
15	A, T	*longa* with fermata
16	B	dotted *minima* and *semiminima*
27/II	A	*brevis* rest instead of *semibrevis* rest
29	T	dot of addition lacking
30	S	*brevis* with fermata
50	S	superfluous black *semibrevis a′* between *a′* and *b′*
51/II–III	A	*b*
52/I–II	B	*brevis* mistakenly white
52/III	B	*f*
55	B	white *longa* with fermata

Remarks: Although this piece has no text, it has the typical structure of a canto carnascialesco, alternating duple- and triple-meter sections.[1] The piece was certainly copied from a model, as demonstrated by the omission of several notes (Bassus, bb. 27/I and 40/III; Altus, b. 29), the mistake in bars 6–8 of the Bassus — correct if they were to be read in the bass clef —, and the probable oversight in omitting B flat in the signature of the Superius, Altus, and Bassus. The constant presence of *signa congruentiae* over nearly all the fermatas refers to performance, but given the errors in the version of Panc.27, it is unlikely that the piece was actually performed from this manuscript. It is more plausible that the scribe simply copied the *signa congruentiae* from his model.

---

[1]. I thank Bonnie Blackburn for this suggestion.

153.

[...]

fols. 113v–114r

765

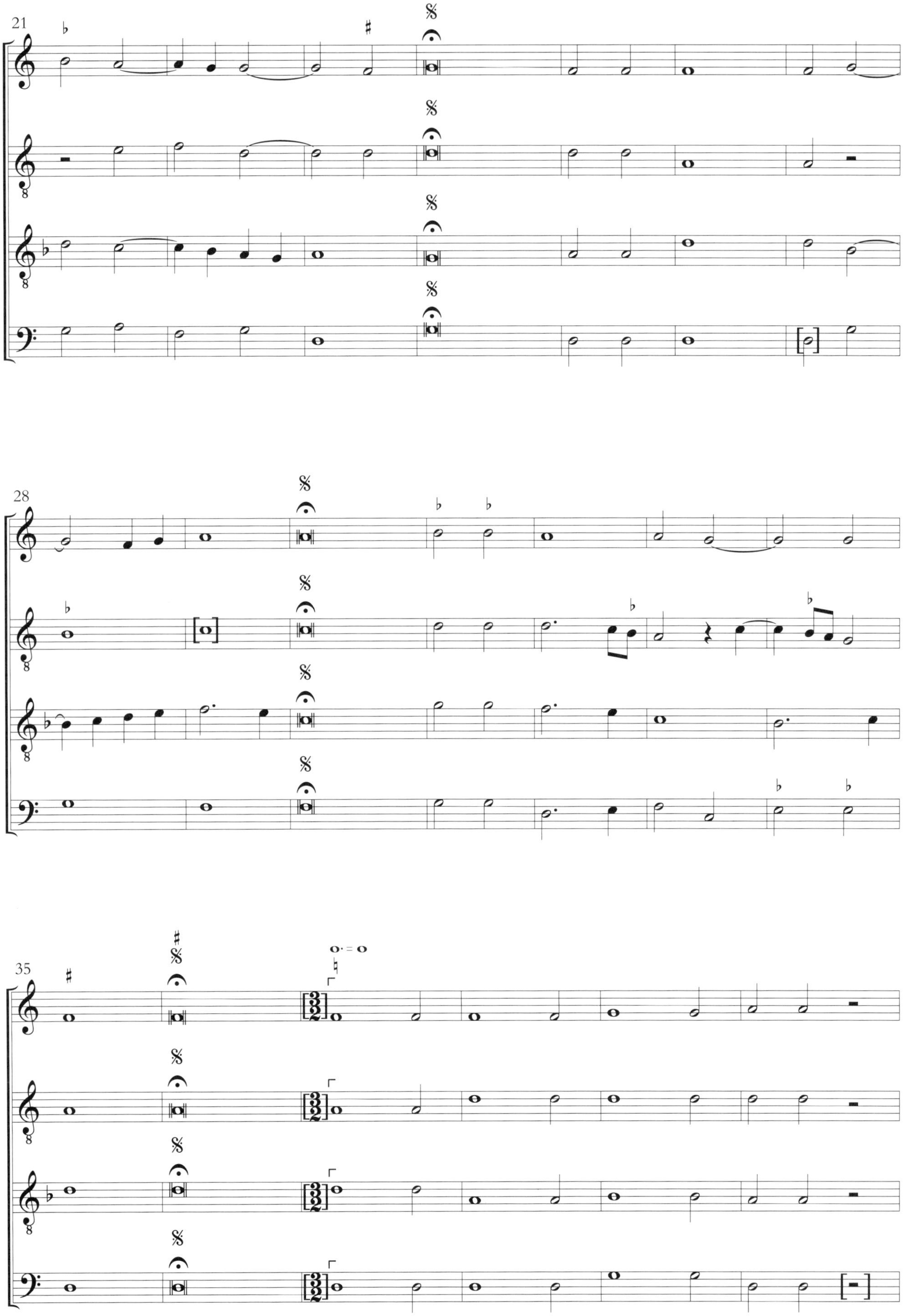
21
28
35

767

154.

[F]AMMI CIÒ CHE VÒI, CRUDEL SIGNORA

fols. 113*v*–114*r* (4 vv.)

[F]ammi[1] ciò che vòi, crudel signora,
che tanto più te sum partiale.
Tormentimi e amazemi, traditora,
cum tuto questo no ti voglio male.
5   Se mi vòi morto non far più dimora,
ecoti el cor, asicurati e dalli,
bem scriver farò a la sepultura:
'questo meschino l'ocisse la tale'.

Italian secular piece (strambotto siciliano).

COMMENTARY ON THE TEXT:

2	hypometric
5	the *residuum* begins here
6	imperfect rhyme. One would expect an ending with the rhyme '-ale'
7	Sicilian rhyme: «–ura» instead of '-ora'

READINGS EMENDED IN THE EDITION:

BAR	VOICE	ORIGINAL
3	B	*longa*
9	T	*semibrevis*
10	T	*longa*
12/II	A	*e-f semibrevis-semibrevis* ligature omitted
20/II	B	*g*

REMARKS: This piece initiates a sequence of four homogeneous strambotti (nos. 154–157), all musical *unica*: metrically eccentric and contrapuntally awkward, they are perhaps poetic-musical experiments by the same inexpert creator (only no. 155 has a literary concordance). They share a common poetic theme — unrequited love — and in three of the four texts the speaker is a man (only in no. 155 does a woman lament): perhaps the intention was to create a contradictory amorous composite in which each of the protagonists would have the right to speak? No. 154 is particularly problematic from a contrapuntal point of view: the corrections made in the edition do not solve the entire gamut of compositional imperfections, consisting of many parallel progressions and vertical clashes, above all in the Altus part (probably added later).[2]

---

[1]. The first letter of the word is lacking. Morpurgo's catalogue opted for an 'F' (see MORPURGO ET AL. 1887-1962, p. 56), but Bianca Becherini adds 'D' (see BECHERINI 1959a, p. 122), as does RISM (B IV/5, p. 149). The older interpretation seems more sensible to me. As Antonio Rossi observes, the incipit is nevertheless quite common in the strambotto repertory of the end of the fifteenth and beginning of the sixteenth century.

[2]. I thank Bonnie Blackburn, who suggested this hypothesis.

154.
[F]AMMI CIÒ CHE VÒI, CRUDEL SIGNORA
fols. 113v–114r

Cantus / Altus / Tenor / Bassus

[F]am - mi ciò che vò - i, cru - del si - gno -
Tor - men - ti - mi e a - ma - ze - mi, tra - di - to -

- - ra,   che
- - ra,   cum

tan - to più te sum par - - ti a - - - - le.
tu - to que - sto no ti vo - glio ma - - - - le.

155.

In foco ardente moro como fenice

fols. 114*v*–115*r* (4 vv.)

In foco ardente moro como fenice,
da ti lontano vivendo in parte strana,
ricordate di me, tua servitrice.
Signore mio caro, benché sia lontana,
5   'Amore vole fede sempre' mai se dice,
fa adunca la promesa non sia vana.
Ricordate di me, caro signore,
che sempre t'ho scolpito nel mezo del core.

Italian secular piece (strambotto toscano).

Commentary on the text:

1	hypermetric
2	hypermetric; the original version «strane» has been corrected to 'strana' to respect the rhyme with lines 4 and 6. The version of *Ox.B. CI.99* also gives «strana»
4	hypermetric; the original version «lontano» has been corrected to 'lontana' to respect the rhyme with lines 2 and 6
5	hypermetric; the *residuum* begins here
8	hypermetric

Textual concordances (mss): • *Ox.B. CI.99* (80*r*)

Modern editions of the text: Filocamo 2000, pp. 156-157 (after Panc.27); Spongano 1971, pp. 28-29 (after *Ox.B. CI.99*).

Remarks: See the Remarks to no. 154.

155.

IN FOCO ARDENTE MORO COMO FENICE

fols. 114*v*–115*r*

vi – ven – do in par – – te stra – – na,
-ro, ben – ché sia lon – – ta – – – – – na

156.

Seràno li [...] mei tanto cocenti

fols. 114*v*–115*r* (3 vv.)

Seràno li [...] mei tanto cocenti,[1]
che movirano li sassi aver mercede,
e volarano al ciel li mei lamenti
per dimonstrare al mundo che amai con fede.
5   E poi che fiano intesi i mei tormenti
da quella che el mio male curato crede,
adopri, poi, Fortuna ogni sua possa,
ch'a lei ho dato l'alma, el cor‹o› e l'ossa.

Italian secular piece (strambotto toscano).

COMMENTARY ON THE TEXT:

1	hypometric; the scansion suggests that a monosyllabic word should be added (perhaps 'dì'?)[2] between «li» and «mei», or between «mei» and «tanto»
2	hypermetric
4	hypermetric
5	«interso» instead of 'intesi', corrected to improve logic
5	«li» instead of 'i'. The hypermeter has been emended on the basis of the scansion of the line in the music
6	hypermetric; «incurato» instead of 'curato', corrected to improve logic

READINGS EMENDED IN THE EDITION:

BAR	VOICE	ORIGINAL
2	Ct	white *f brevis*, instead of black *brevis* in coloration
17	T	white *a brevis*, instead of black *brevis* in coloration

REMARKS: See the Remarks to no. 154. Lines 1-4 are written under the Superius, lines 5-8 under the Tenor.

---

[1]. In the catalogue of the Panciatichi MSS MORPURGO *ET AL.* 1887-1962, p. 56, this line is arranged differently: *Seràno li mei [...] tanto cocenti.* The Italianists I have consulted believe that it is preferable to place the lacuna after the second word.

[2]. I thank Bonnie Blackburn for this hypothesis.

156.
Seràno li [...] mei tanto cocenti
fols. 114*v*–115*r*

S[uperius]

Se – rà – – no li [...] mei tan – to co –
e vo – – la – ra – no al ciel li mei la –
E poi che fia – no in – te – si i mei tor –
a – do – pri, poi, For – tu – na o – gni sua

Tenor

Se – rà – – no li [...] mei tan – to co –
e vo – – la – ra – no al ciel li mei la –
E poi che fia – no in – te – si i mei tor –
a – do – pri, poi, For – tu – na o – gni sua

Contra

Se – rà – – no li [...] mei

– – – – cen – ti,
– – – – men – ti
– – – – men – ti
pos – – sa,

– – – – – cen – ti,
– – – – – men – ti
– – – – – men – ti
pos – – sa,

che mo – vi – ra – no li sas – si
per di – mon – stra – re al mun – do
da quel – la che el mio ma – le
ch'a le – i ho da – to l'al – ma,

che mo – vi – ra – no li sas – si
per di – mon – stra – re al mun – do
da quel – la che el mio ma – le
ch'a le – i ho da – to l'al – ma,

a - - - ver mer - - - - - - ce - - - de,
che a - mai con fe - - - de.
cu - - ra - - to cre - - - de,
el cor e l'os - - - sa.

a - - - ver mer - - - - - - ce - - - de,
che a - mai con fe - - - de.
cu - - ra - - to cre - - - de,
el cor e l'os - - - sa.

157.

Non naque al mondo mai el più scontento

fols. 114*v*–115*r* (3 vv.)

> Non naque al mondo mai el più scontento,
> né più infelice e più desventurato,
> né che sentisse mai tanto tormento
> quale sento ora misero infelice.
> 5   Cerco la morte per mio contento,
> ma lei me fuge per ciascum lato.
> Cusì sono nemico a celo e terra
> per quella che me tene in tanta guerra.

Italian secular piece (strambotto toscano).

COMMENTARY ON THE TEXT:

4   the line ends in an irregular manner: the metric form would require an ending in '-ato'
5   the *residuum* begins here

READINGS EMENDED IN THE EDITION:

BAR	VOICE	ORIGINAL
14–15	S	*brevis*
26/I	Ct	*g*

REMARKS: This poetic and musical *unicum* is the fruit of a very modest literary and compositorial competence, perhaps the work of the scribe himself. Vertical clashes between the Superius and Tenor (bb. 12/II and 28/II) and parallel unisons between Tenor and Contra (b. 9) seem to have been intended by the composer.

157.
Non naque al mondo mai el più scontento

fols. 114v–115r

S[uperius] / Tenor / Con[tr]a

Non na - que al mon - do mai
né che sen - tis - se mai
Non
Non na - que

el più scon - ten - - - - - - - - - - - - to,
tan - to tor - men - - - - - - - - - to

né più in - fe - - li - - ce e più de - -
qua - le sen - - to o - ra mi - se - - - -

- - - - - - - sven - - tu - ra - - to,
- - - - - - - ro in - - fe - li - - ce.

158.

Poiché vivo sopra la terra

fols. 115*v*–116*r* (3 vv.)

> Poiché vivo sopra la terra
> […]
> […]
> […]
>
> 5   La mia pura iuventute
> […]
> mercé, pace, né salute
> […]

Italian secular piece (barzelletta?).[1]

Readings emended in the edition:

Bar	Voice	Original
25/II	Ct	*d semibrevis* (the correction *f-e* in the transcription is taken from the version in ParisN F15123)
27/I	Ct	the added rest is taken from the version in ParisN F15123

Musical concordances (mss): • MontA 871; index only (no. 88): *Poy che bivo super* • ParisN F15123 (98*v*–99*r*)

Text from ParisN F15123:

> Poiché vivo sopra la terra
> con tam mala triste sorte,
> Dio volesse che la morte
> sola me facesse guerra.
>
> 5   La mia prima ioventute
> se consuma ad poco ad poco:
> merçé, pace né salute
> non trovo, posa né loco.

Modern editions of the text: Liuzzi 1946, p. 58 (after ParisN F15123).

Modern editions of the music: Pease 1959, II, pp. 283-286 (after ParisN F15123).

Remarks: The only known concordance for the piece is found in an illuminated manuscript of the end of the fifteenth century, of Florentine provenance. The version in ParisN F15123 cannot, however, be considered as related to that of Panc.27: they are differentiated, in fact, by a large number of graphic variants, rhythmic and melodic. In the version of Panc.27 the three voices of the piece

---

[1]. The text does not allow a definite classification of its form.

move quite awkwardly, with vertical clashes (b. 49/II) and parallel motion: fifths (Superius-Contra, b. 39) and octaves (Superius-Tenor, b. 51).

BIBLIOGRAPHY: FALLOWS 1999, pp. 14, 556; FILOCAMO 2004; PEASE 1959, I, p. 103.

158.
Poiché vivo sopra la terra

fols. 115*v*–116*r*

La mia pu-
mer - cé, pa-
La mia
La mia pu-

- ra iu - ven - tu - te
- ce, né sa - lu - te
- ra

159.

Giù per la mala via

fol. 116r (4 vv.)

[Feo Belcari][1]

> Giù per la mala via

Archaic type of lauda (*laisse* of double seven-syllable monorhymed lines).[2]

Readings emended in the edition:

Bar	Voice	Original
18	C, A, T, B	*semibrevis* with fermata

Textual concordances (mss): • *CV. Ro. 424* (181r-v), (Feo Belcari) • *CV. VL. 13026* (75r-v) • *Fir. L. Ash. 480* (154r-155r) • *Fir. M. 262* (152r-v) • *Fir. N. 35* (194r-195r) • *Fir. N. M. 367* (97r) • *Fir. N. M. 690* (23r-24r), (Pheo Belcari) • *Fir. N. M. 1083* (129v-130r), «Feo Belchari» • *Fir. R. 1413* (249v-250v), «Feo Belcari» • *Fir. R. 3112* (index only)[3] • MilA 5 (51r-v)[4] • *Mil. A. 25* (165r) • *Rim. C. 38* (128r-v), «Feo Belchari» • *Roma. Ang. 2274* (20r-21v) • *Roma. Co. 3* (45-47) • *Siena. C. 16* (37r-38r) • *Ven. M. I. 78* (24v)[5]

Textual concordances (prints): • *Fior1505* (f1v-f2v) • *LaudeBonac* (24v-25r), «Di Feo Belchari» • *LaudeBonar* (27r), «di Francesco dal Bizo» • *LaudeGiacc* (30r-v) • *LaudeMisc* (9v), «Di Feo Belchari» • *LaudeSper* (13v), «Di Feo Belcari» • *LaudeVecchie* (a8v), «Di Feo Belchari» • *LaudiGiunti* (C1v), «Del medesimo» (= Feo Belcari) • *LaudiRiccardiana* (f8r-v), «Feo Belcari» • *OperaNova* (8v), «Di Feo Belchari»

---

[1]. The true paternity of this text has been attributed to Belcari or to Savonarola. In his critical edition of the poetry of Savonarola, Mario Martelli rejected the text as a work of the Ferrarese preacher, assigning it to Belcari (see Martelli 1968, pp. 96-99); Carlo Castiglioni maintained that the attribution to either author was impossible since the lauda was included in the manuscript *Mil. A. 25*, which according to him was written around the middle of the fifteenth century (see Castiglioni 1932, pp. 245-247). The manuscript is in fact dated 1443 (on fol. 1r), but considering that Feo Belcari was born in 1410, he could have been the author of the text. On the other hand, Giulio Cattin writes that in the Milanese manuscript the lauda seems to be «a later addition, written on blank pages»; see Cattin (1971a) 2003, p. 143, n. 27.

[2]. Although there is no musical concordance that would indicate the continuation of the text, many scholars think it probable that it is the lauda *Giù per la mala via - l'anima mia ne va*. Poetry in double seven-syllable lines (translating French alexandrines) is a very old metric form, especially in northern Italy. For example, one of the archetypal north Italian laude of the type, *Rayna possentissima, - sovr'el cel si' asaltaa*, is a monorhymed *laisse* of double seven-syllable lines. I thank Paolo Trovato for this explanation.

[3]. The index indicates that the text should be found on fol. 125 (old numeration). In fact, the old fol. 125 is lacking, and the old foliation jumps from fol. 124 to fol. 126. The more recent foliation, however, does not take the missing folio into consideration, which suggests that fol. 125 was lost before the manuscript was renumbered.

[4]. The 'Codice Borromeo' (MilA 5) contains poems and a single musical lauda (*Hora mai sono in età*).

[5]. At the end of fol. 24v there is an annotation in another hand: «mancasci una carta» (a folio is lacking). The manuscript continues on fol. 26r with another poem that had begun on the missing folio, which is a «cantasi come O Iesù dolce di Feo Belchri [sic]».

TEXT FROM *LaudeBonar.*

> Giù per la mala via – l'anima mia ne va;
> se la non ha soccorso – presto morta sarà.
> Il demonio l'ha inganà – con la sua falsità
> e 'l senso li promette – ch'ogni piacer darà,
5. e 'l mondo ancor la invita – a far la iniquità:
> l'anima mia tentata – or chi l'aiutarà?
> Aiùtati, meschina, – col don che Dio ti dà:
> tu hai libero arbitrio, – che meritar ti fa;
> ricorri a Giesù Cristo, – che ‹con›fitto in croce sta;
10. se tu 'l preghi umilmente, – la gratia ti darà.
> Abbi fede e speranza, – che forte ti farà:
> tu non puoi esser vinta – senza tua volontà;
> più potente è la gratia – che ogni adversità.
> Pensa ben della morte, – che presto ne verrà;
15. contempla poi l'inferno, – pien di penalità;
> risguarda il paradiso – con sua giocondità;
> accèndite in fervore, – pien d'ogni carità;
> e poi ogni fatica – più lieve ti parrà.
> Giesù, tuo dolce sposo, – allor t'abbracciarà;
20. daratti il braccio suo, – pien di soavità;
> l'arra di vita eterna – la mente gustarà;
> giubilo, canto e festa – il tuo cor sentirà,
> cantando: 'Amor, amore, – amor, summa bontà'.
> Va', dunque, per la strada, – che Dio mostrata t'ha,
25. laudando il summo Dio – in santa Trinità.
> Amen.

MODERN EDITIONS OF THE TEXT: CASTIGLIONI 1932, p. 247 (after *Mil.A. 25*); GALLETTI 1863, pp. 50-51 (after *LaudeBonac*); LEVI 1905, pp. 121-122; MARTELLI 1968, pp. 96-99 (after *Fir.N. 35*).

MODERN EDITIONS OF THE MUSIC: BECHERINI 1954, p. 119 (after Panc.27).

REMARKS: The piece is curiously characterized by a very restricted range in all four voices: a fourth (Altus, Tenor, and Bassus) and a fifth (Cantus). Considering in addition the extremely wide diffusion of the text, confirmed by the very large number of concordances in literary sources, it can reasonably be suggested that it was perhaps the scribe who attempted a musical setting for a group of inexperienced singers. The fact that the piece occupies the remainder of the space on fol. 116*r* (the last four staves, precisely filled!) might confirm the hypothesis of a compositional experiment, perhaps extempore, on the part of the copyist.

BIBLIOGRAPHY: BECHERINI 1954, pp. 113-114; CASTIGLIONI 1932, pp. 245-247; CATTIN (1971a) 2003, pp. 142-143; CATTIN 1978, p. 34; FRATI 1918, pp. 201-202; GHISI 1953a, pp. 67, 71; LUISI 1983, I, pp. 177, 195, 235; MARTELLI 1968, pp. 96-99; ROSTIROLLA (1986) 2001, pp. 41, 143; ROSTIROLLA (1995) 2001, p. 508; TENNERONI 1909, p. 118; WILSON 1998, p. 99.

159.
Giù per la mala via
fol. 116*r*

[Feo Belcari]

Giù per la mala via

160.

CAMINATA

fols. 116*v*-117*r* (4 vv.)

Caminata[1]

Instrumental dance.

READINGS EMENDED IN THE EDITION:

BAR	VOICE	ORIGINAL
incipit	A	the B flat signature in the clef is present till bar 20, at the only stave break. The absence thereafter is probably an oversight on the part of the copyist and the signature has been reinstated.

MUSICAL CONCORDANCES (MSS): • AugsS 142a (20*v*-21*r*), 3 vv.,[2] without A, heading: « x ‹ y », textless[3]

MODERN EDITIONS OF THE MUSIC: JONAS 1983, I, pp. 66-67 (after AugsS 142a); WOLF (1926) 1931, pp. 66-67 (after Panc.27).

REMARKS: The tripartite structure of the piece (ABA': bb. 1-16, 17-20, 21-33) is certainly a function of its accompaniment of dance. The unique concordance, a version for three voices in AugsS 142a, is in fact much more extended: it contains 'polyphonic variations' that have not been noticed heretofore because they occur in separate, non-contiguous phrases, placed haphazardly. But, in contrast to Panc.27, the A section does not comprise 16 bars because at the end of bar 8 a repeat sign occurs in all voices; section B, on the other hand, writes out 4 bars of the repeat only in the higher voice; the Tenor and Bassus resolve the sign so that they cover 8 bars. In Panc.27, therefore, the piece cannot end at bar 33: the variant A' with repeated notes does not repeat section A exactly, but stops at bar 33 since the conclusion corresponding to bars 13-16 is missing; perhaps the purpose of writing out section A' was merely to suggest an alternative performance (incomplete) of the analogous section A. It is more likely that the two sections A and B were repeated *ad libitum* until the end of the dance, concluding with section A, or, even more likely, with section B.[4] The numerous rhythmic and melodic variants in AugsS 142a discourage the hypothesis of a direct contact between the two musical versions of the piece, even if it is possible to hypothesize that an instrumentalist sent the piece from Mantua to Augsburg (where MS AugsS 142a was compiled), varying it polyphonically. With respect to the previous piece in Panc.27, the ink of *Caminata* is much darker; the scribal *ductus* becomes more regular and ordered.

BIBLIOGRAPHY: FILOCAMO 2009b; GOMBOSI 1936, pp. 119-120, 127, n. 2; JONAS 1983, II, p. 37; KÄMPER 1976, pp. 58-60, 196; MOE 1956, I, pp. 235-236; POLK 1996, p. 332.

---

[1]. The term 'caminata' might refer to the great hall with fireplace present in aristocratic palaces. For Tommaseo 'camminata' / 'caminata' denotes a long part of the building, such as a passageway, a loggia, a corridor (see BATTAGLIA II, p. 585).

[2]. The fourth voice present on fol. 21*r* is in fact an alternative bass (bb. 1-16 only), probably intended for an instrument in the tenor range to be used in place of the bass instrument.

[3]. At the bottom of the page there is a rubric that I have tried unsuccessfully to decipher.

[4]. I thank Bonnie Blackburn and Fabrizio Ammetto for having helped me greatly in reflecting on the formal structure of this piece.

160.
Caminata
fols. 116*v*–117*r*

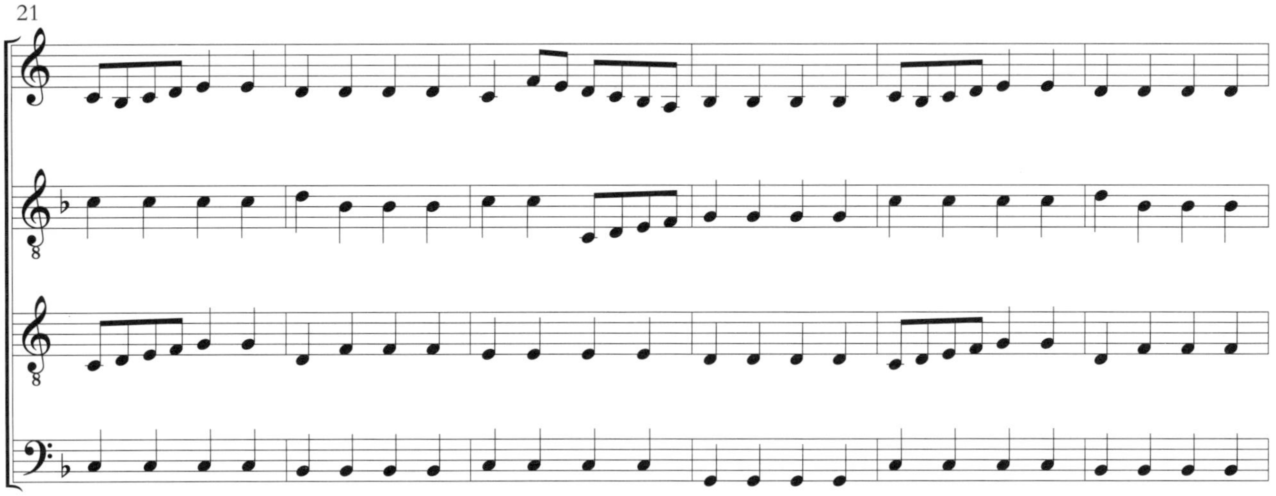
21

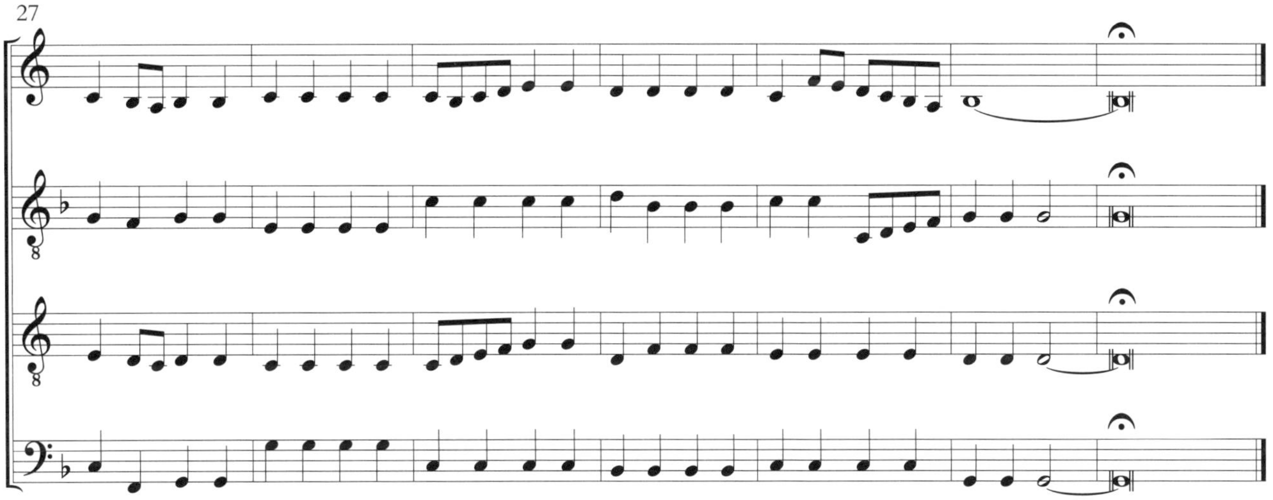
27

161.

(Magnificat) Et exultavit

fols. 117*v*-118*r* (4 vv.)

[…]¹
Et exultavit spiritus meus in Deo salutari meo
[…]
[…]
5   Quia fecit mihi magna qui potens est,
et sanctum nomen eius
[…]
Fecit potentiam in brachio suo,
dispersit superbos mente cordis sui
10   […]
Esurientes […]
[…]
Sicut locutus est […]
[…]

[…]
Sicut erat in principio et nunc […].

For the text see no. 123. The text concludes with the second part of the Lesser Doxology («Sicut erat in principio et nunc […]»), as also at Vespers.

Readings emended in the edition:

Bar	Voice	Original
2/II	B	*e* instead of *f*
10/III–12/II	T	three *brevis-brevis* ligatures instead of three *semibrevis-semibrevis* ligatures
14/II	T	*f′* instead of *d′*
19	C, A, T	*semibrevis* with fermata
22/II	A	*c′* instead of *d′*
27/II-III	C	*b′ a′ g′* instead of *c″ b′ a′*
30	B	*longa* with fermata
33/III	B	*f* instead of *d*

Remarks: The three musical sections of this *Magnificat* (bb. 1-13, 14-23, 24-36) are separated by single or double bars. But the text underlay, reproduced exactly in the edition, makes it clear that none of these bars can be interpreted as indicating a repetition, either of the previous or the new section; otherwise the standard disposition of the text would be disrupted. Therefore, the music was intended to be sung twice, from beginning to end. The chant in GR, pp. 218-219 and LU, pp. 212, 218 (*Tonus 8.*) is paraphrased in the Cantus.

Bibliography: CAO III, pp. 323-324; CS, pp. 430-433; IGC, p. 270; Kirsch 1966, p. 423.

---

¹. The absence of alternating verses such as this indicates *alternatim* performance, with the missing verses in plainchant.

161.
(MAGNIFICAT) ET EXULTAVIT
fols. 117v-118r

Cantus: Et ex - ul - ta - - - - - vit
E - su - ri - en - - - - tes

spi - ri - tus me - - - - us in De - o sa - lu - ta - ri me - -

- - - o Qui - a fe - cit mi - - hi ma - gna qui po - -
Si - cut lo - cu - tus est

A[ltus]: E[t]

tens est, et san-ctum no — — — men e — — — ius

Fe — cit po — ten — ti — am in bra-chi — o su — — — — o,
Si — cut e — — — rat in prin-ci-pi — o et nunc

di — sper-sit su — per — bos men — te cor — dis su — — — i

162.

Kyrie [eleison]

fols. 118*v*–119*r* (4 vv.)

Kyrie
Christe
Kyrie

For the text see no. 108.

COMMENTARY ON THE TEXT:

1   Kyrie] yrie S

REMARKS: This Kyrie is completely isolated; positioned between two Magnificats, it does not even share a liturgical function with them. Nevertheless, the Tenor cites the first phrase of the Kyrie IX *Cum jubilo* (GR, p. 32★ and LU, p. 40), used on feasts of the Blessed Virgin Mary.

BIBLIOGRAPHY: IGC, pp. 249-256.

162.
KYRIE [ELEISON]
fols. 118*v*-119*r*

18
Christe
Christe
Christe
Christe
25
32
Kyrie
Kyrie
Kyrie
Kyrie

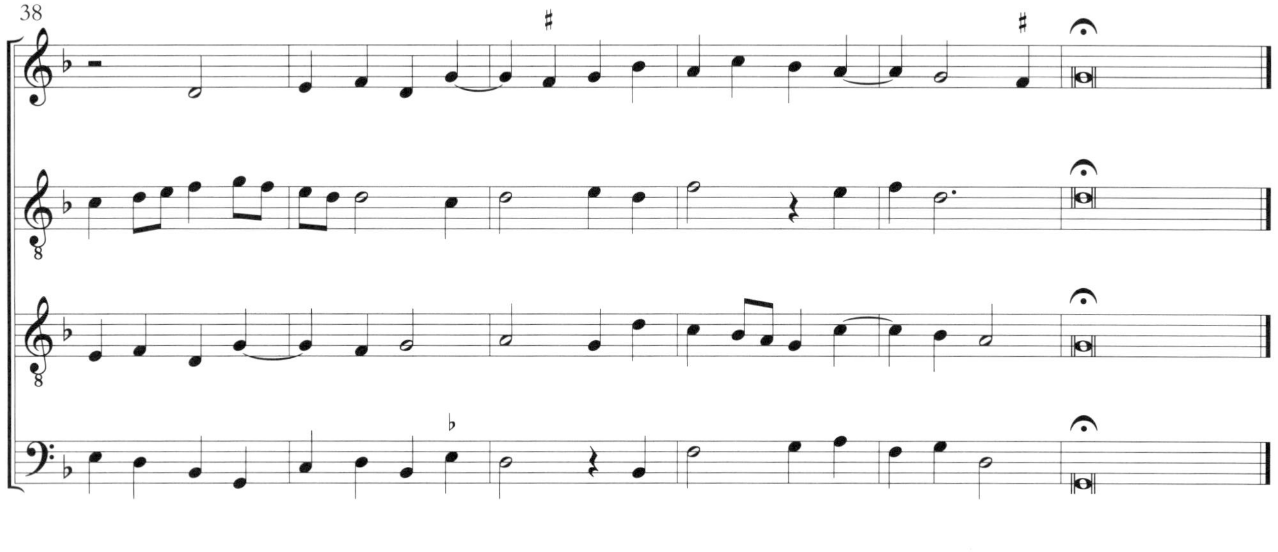
38

163.

(Magnificat) Et exultavit

fols. 119v-120r (4 vv.)

```
        [...]¹
        Et exultavit spiritus
        [...]
        [...]
5       Quia fecit mihi
        [...]
        [...]
        Fecit potentiam
        [...]
10      [...]
        [...]
        [...]
        [...]
        [...]
```

For the text see no. 123, without the concluding Lesser Doxology.

Readings emended in the edition:

Bar	Voice	Original
51	B	*A semibrevis*, *B minima*, *c minima*, corrected by analogy with bars 28 and 75
52	B	*f*
between 75/I and 75/II	B	*A brevis* deleted

Remarks: The chant in LU, pp. 207 and 213 (*Tonus 1.*) is paraphrased in the Superius.

Bibliography: CAO III, pp. 323-324; CS, pp. 430-433; IGC, p. 270; Kirsch 1966, p. 161.

---

¹. The absence of alternating verses such as this indicates *alternatim* performance, with the missing verses in plainchant.

163.
(Magnificat) Et exultavit
fols. 119v-120r

Quia fecit mihi

Quia fecit mihi

Quia fecit

Quia fecit

Fecit potentiam

Fecit potentiam

Fecit potentiam

Fecit potentiam

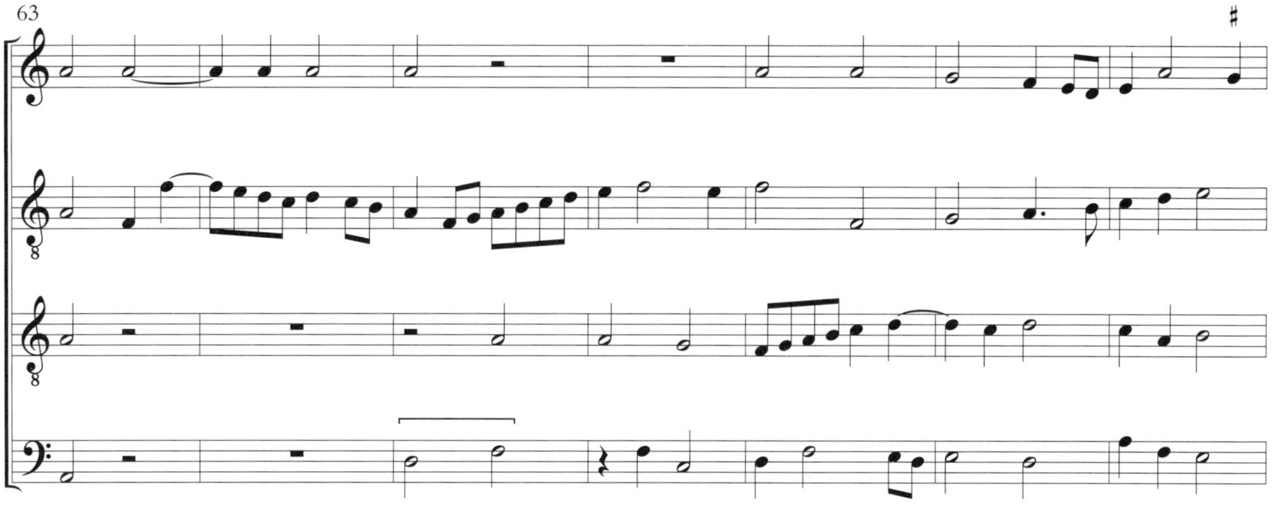
63

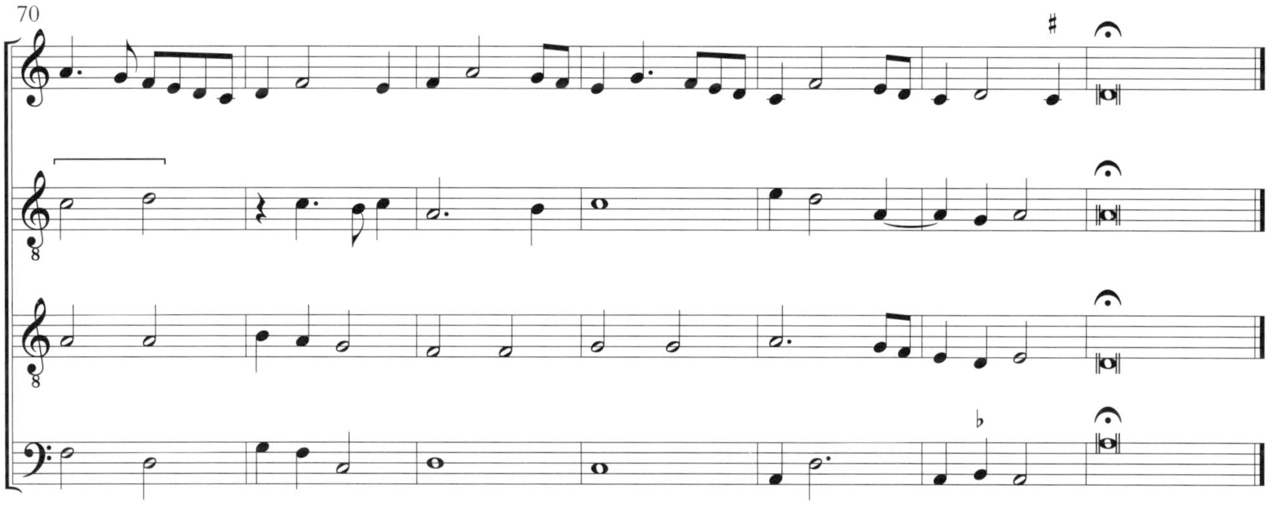
70

164.

Felix namque

fols. 130*v*–132*r* (4 vv.)

Felix namque

This may be the Marian antiphon *Felix namque es, sacra Virgo Maria* (AR, pp. 127*-128*).[1] It has been used, for example, as the Offertory at the Saturday Mass for the Blessed Virgin Mary from Christmas to the Purification (GR, pp. [95]-[96]; MR [*Commune Sanctorum*], fol. 27*r*), and ninth responsory, third Nocturn of Matins on feasts of the Blessed Virgin Mary (BR, p. 847; LR, pp. 255-256). See also CAO III, p. 226, CAO IV, p. 183, and IGC, p. 184.

Readings emended in the edition:

Bar	Voice	Original
77/II	T	two *minimae*
78	S	four *minimae*
78	T	dotted *semibrevis* and *minima*

Text from MR [*Commune Sanctorum*], fol. 27*r* (*Missa votiva de Sancta Maria. A nativitate usque ad purificationem. Offertorium*):

Felix namque,[2]
sacra Virgo Maria,
et omni laude dignissima:
quia ex te ortus est sol iustitie,
5   Christus Deus noster.

Modern editions of the music: Banks 1993, II, pp. 76-79 (after Panc.27).

Remarks: The Bassus has a first alternative version corresponding to bars 16-26/I, introduced by the rubric «Loco istarum pausarum» (= 'instead of these rests'), and a further variant for the entire *Secunda pars* (bb. 51-88) accompanied by the rubric «alio mo(do) notat(um)» (= 'written in a different manner'). While the new version in the *Prima pars* is a true alternative to the sequences of rests in this section, in the *Secunda pars* the copyist has rewritten the entire Bassus, even duplicating two whole sections of the original Bassus (bb. 59-65 and 76-88). In his evident *horror vacui* caused by a row of rests in the lowest voice, the scribe tested himself by filling in these empty musical spaces, but in so doing he fell into contrapuntal difficulties: for example, the alternative Bassus at bar 16 (*a*) begins with a disagreeable clash with the Altus, and at bars 57-58 creates twelfth/fifth parallels first with the Superius (*B-f′*, *c-g′*), then with the Altus (*c-g*, *d-a*), etc.

Bibliography: Banks 1993, I, p. 274; CAO III, p. 226; CAO IV, p. 183; Filocamo 2004; IGC, p. 184.

---

[1]. For other possible texts with the same incipit, see CAO III, p. 226, CAO IV, p. 183, and IGC, p. 184.

[2]. MR does not have «es» after «namque».

164.
Felix namque
fols. 130*v*–132*r*

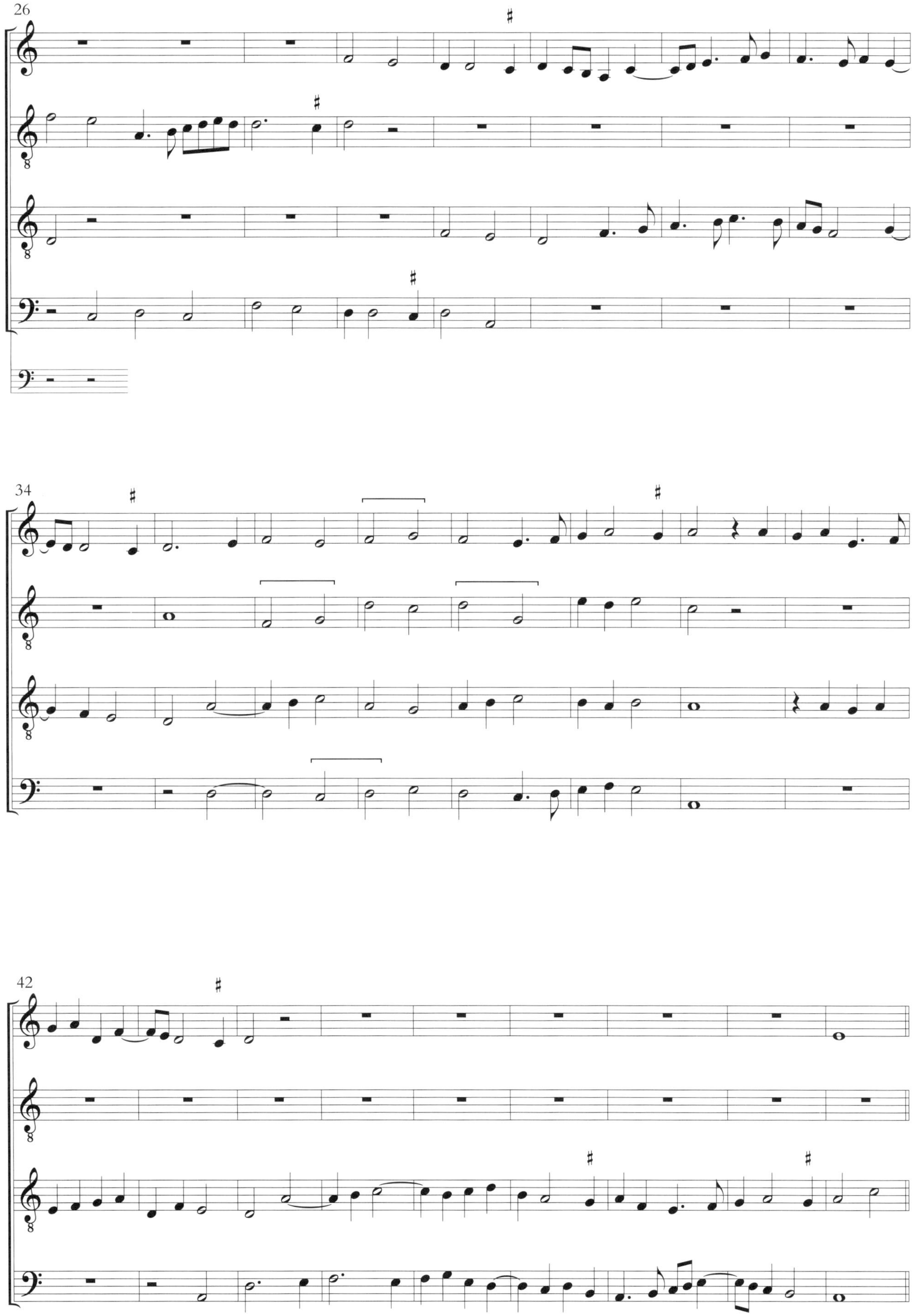
26
34
42

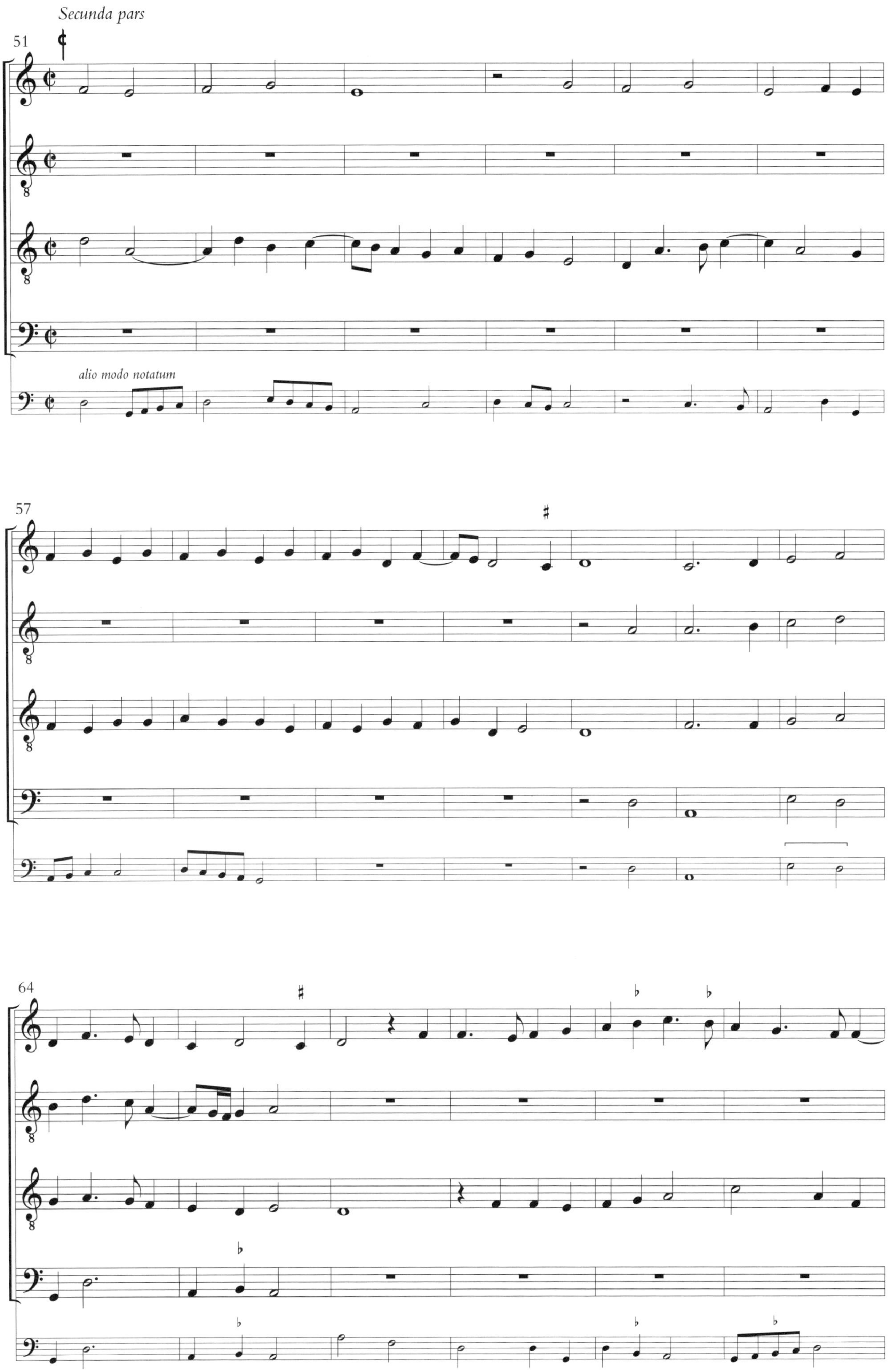
Secunda pars
51
alio modo notatum
57
64

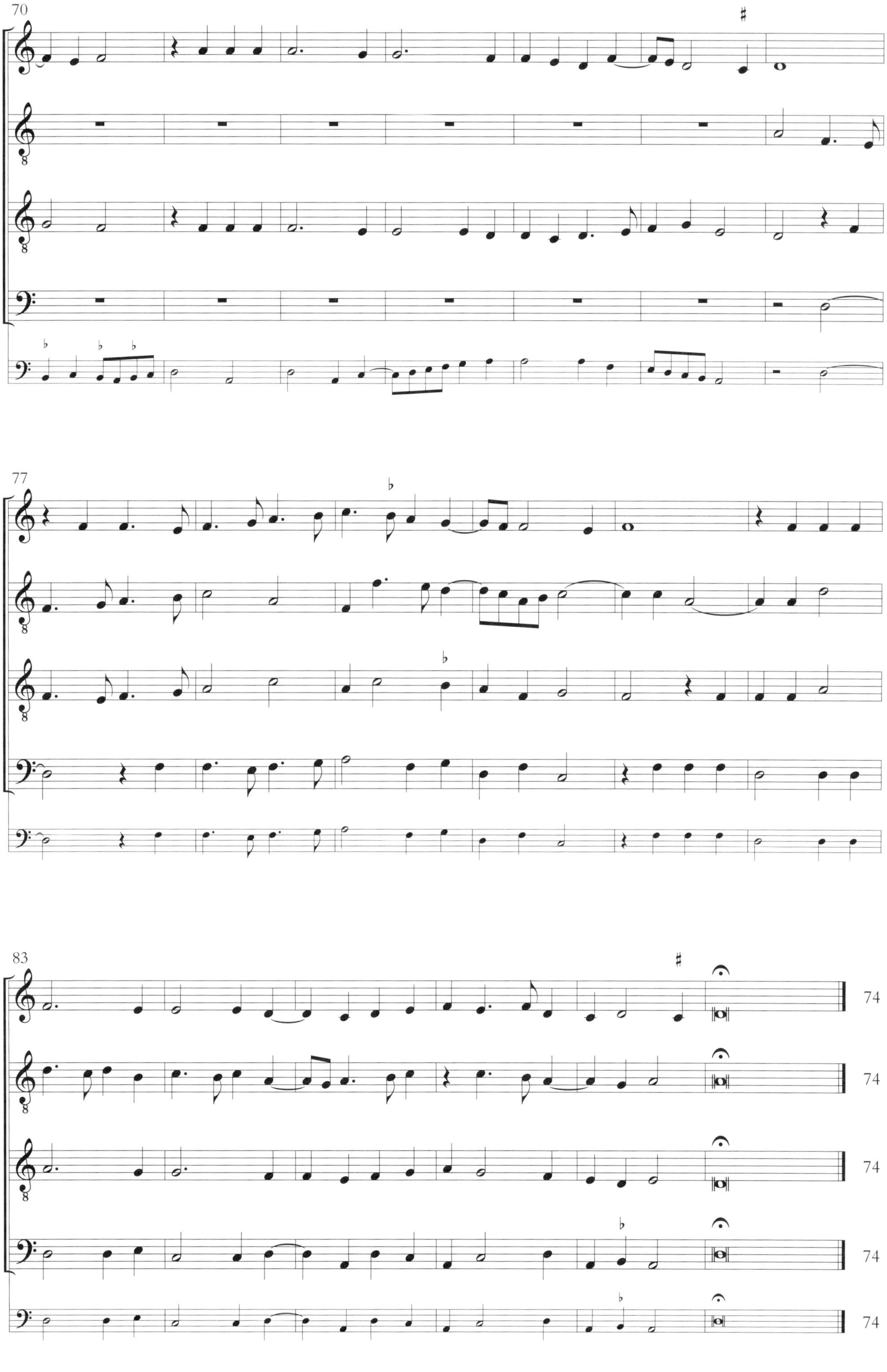
70
77
83
74
74
74
74
74

165.

Lucis Creator optime

fols. 132*v*-133*r* (3 vv.)

Lucis Creator optime,
lucem dierum proferens,
primordiis lucis nove
mundi parans originem.

First strophe of a hymn. Used at Vespers on Sundays throughout the year (AM, pp. 128-129, two melodies; AR, pp. 48-49, 49-50, 51-52; BR, pp. 93-94; LU, pp. 256-257; 257-258; 258-259). See also CAO IV, p. 514 and IGC, p. 267.

Commentary on the text:

4	primordiis] primodiis S	

Readings emended in the edition:

Bar	Voice	Original
9/I-II	B	*a f*
26/III	B	*f*

Text from BR, pp. 93-94 (*Dominica ad vesperas. Hymnus*):

1. Lucis Creator optime,
   lucem dierum proferens,
   primordiis lucis novae
   mundi parans originem,

2. qui mane iunctum vesperi
   diem vocari praecipis,
   tetrum chaos illabitur,
   audi preces cum fletibus:

3. ne mens gravata crimine,
   vitae sit exul munere,
   dum nil perenne cogitat,
   seseque culpis illigat.

4. Caelorum pulset intimum.
   Vitale tollat praemium:
   vitemus omne noxium,
   purgemus omne pessimum.

5. Praesta, Pater […].

Modern editions of the text: AH 51, pp. 34-35; Mone, I, pp. 82-83.

Modern editions of the music: Banks 1993, II, pp. 114-115 (after Panc.27).

REMARKS: The chant in AR, pp. 49-50 and LU, pp. 257-258 appears in Tenor, partly paraphrased and partly quoted. Although it is so far an *unicum*, the piece has certainly been written by a competent composer.

BIBLIOGRAPHY: BANKS 1993, I, p. 279; CAO IV, p. 514; CHEVALIER II, no. 10691; FILOCAMO 2004; IGC, p. 267; STÄBLEIN 1956, Melody no. 186; WARD 1980, p. 188.

165.
LUCIS CREATOR OPTIME
fols. *132v–133r*

15
-is lu - - - cis no - - - - - ve mun - - - - - - - - -
- - - - mor - - - - - di - - - - - is lu - - -
-cis no - ve
20
-di pa - rans o - ri - gi - - - - - - - -
-cis no - - - - ve mun - - -
mun - - - - - - di pa - - - - - rans o - - - - - ri - gi -
26
- - - - - - - - - - - - - - - - - - - nem.
-di pa - - - - - rans o - - ri - gi - - - nem.
- - - - - - - - - - - - - - - - - - - nem.
84

166.

MAGNI[FIC]AT ANIMA MEA DOMINUM

fols. 133v-135r (3 vv.)

Magni[fic]at anima mea Dominum
[…][1]
Quia respexit humilitatem ancille sue,
ecce enim ex hoc beatam me dicent omnes generationes.
5   […]
     […]
     Et misericordia eius a progenie in progenies timentibus eum
     […]
     […]
10   Deposuit potentes de sede, et exaltavit humiles
     […]
     Suscepit Israel puerum suum, recordatus misericordie sue
     […]
     […]

     Gloria Patri et Filio et Spiritui Sancto
     […]

For the text see no. 123.

READINGS EMENDED IN THE EDITION:

BAR	VOICE	ORIGINAL
incipit	S	the intonation «Magnificat» is in black notation
62	B	rubric: «Deposuit tacet»
93/II	B	*a semiminima*, corrected on the basis of TorN 27

MUSICAL CONCORDANCES (MSS): • TorN 27 (87r-88r)

REMARKS: The text underlay is problematic (in many places the writing seems almost instrumental). Two types of ink are used: dark for the notes (and the single intonation «Magni.ᵃᵗ») and light for the text, a clear sign that the text was copied later. In the highest stave on fol. 134r the musical incipit of the Tenor (bb. 1-6, without text) has been entered and then erased; the complete part is placed on the last three staves of fol. 133v. I believe that this error derives from a mistake in copying from the model: traditionally the space at the top of the recto is reserved for the Altus, which frequently shares the same ambitus and clef as the Tenor. The scribe may absentmindedly have copied the incipit of the Tenor a second time, thinking he was transcribing the beginning of the Altus (not present in this piece). The model, however, is certainly not TorN 27: although it is a north Italian source of the early sixteenth century, many graphic variants and at least two

---

[1]. The absence of alternating verses such as this indicates *alternatim* performance, with the missing verses in plainchant.

substantial variants separate it from this *Magnificat*. Although the piece is written in the sixth mode, all the voices paraphrase the chant in LU, p. 207 (*Tonus 1.*).

BIBLIOGRAPHY: CAO III, pp. 323-324; CS, pp. 430-433; FILOCAMO 2004; IGC, p. 270; KIRSCH 1966, p. 296.

166.
Magni[fic]at anima mea Dominum
fols. 133*v*–135*r*

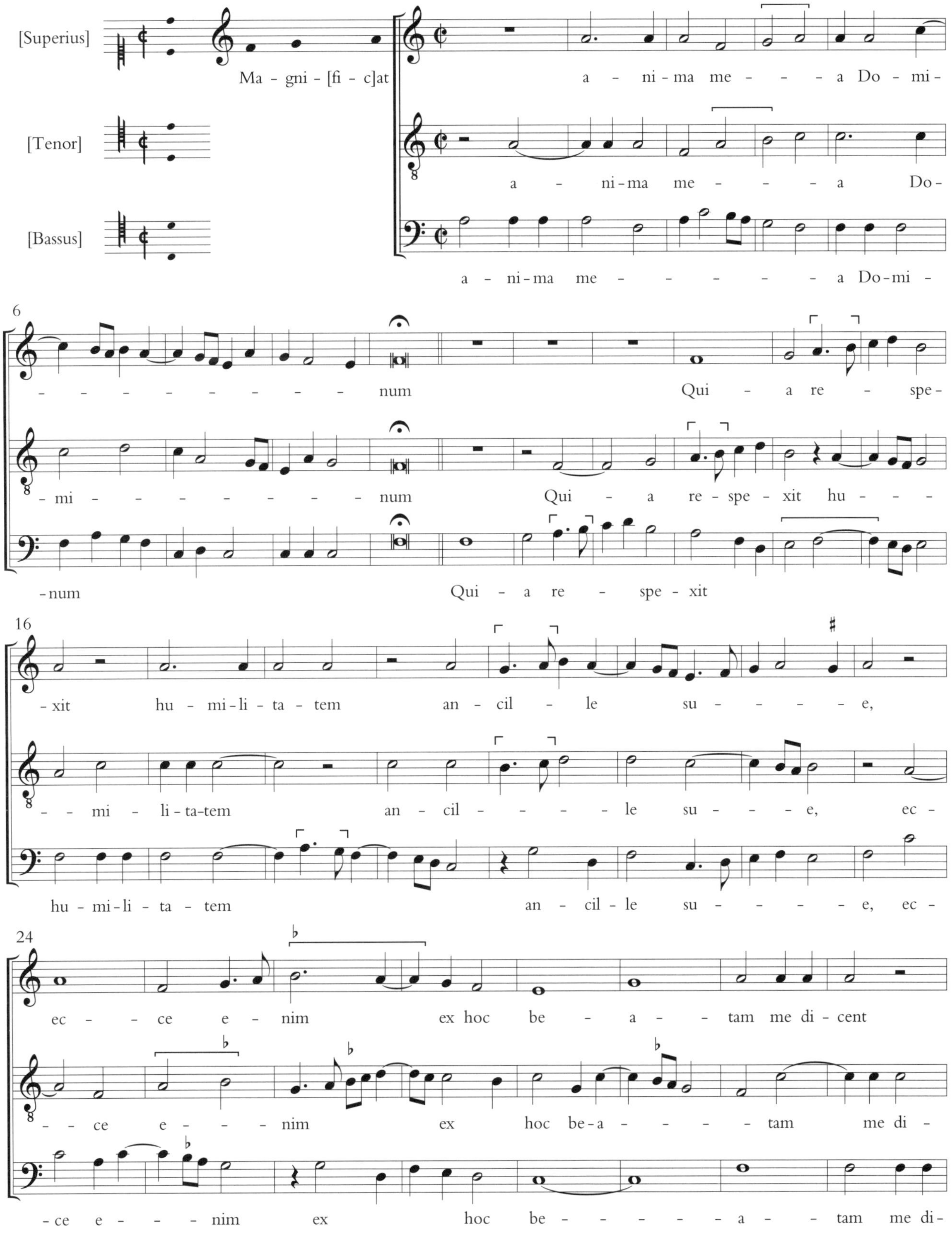

32
o - mnes ge - ne - - - - - - - - ra - ti - o - nes.
- cent o - - - - - mnes ge - ne - ra - ti - o - nes.
- cent o - mnes ge - ne - - - - - - - - ra - ti - o - nes.
40
Et mi - se - ri - cor - di - a
Et mi - se - ri - cor - di - - - a
Et mi - se - ri - cor - di - a
47
e - ius a pro - ge - ni - e in pro - ge - ni - es
e - ius a pro - ge - ni - e in pro - ge -
e - ius a pro - ge - ni - e in pro - ge - ni - - - es
55
ti - men - ti - bus e - - - um
- ni - - - - - - - - - es ti - men - ti - bus e - um
ti - men - ti - bus e - - - - - - - um
16
58
43

Duo
S[uperius]
T[enor]
De - - - po-su-it po-ten - - - - - - -
De - - - po-su-it
68
- - tes de se - - - de, et ex-al -
po-ten - tes de se - - - - - de, et ex-al - - - - - - - - -
75
-ta - - - - - - vit humi - - - - - - - - - - les
-ta - - - - - - vit hu-mi - - - - - - - - - les
S[uperius]
T[enor]
[Bassus]
Su - - - - - sce - pit I - sra - el
Su-sce-pit I - - - sra - el
Su-sce-pit I - sra - el
88
pu - e-rum su - - - - - - - - - - um,
pu - e - rum su - - - - um,
pu - e - rum su - - - - - - - - um,

re – cor-da-tus mi-se-ri-cor-di – – e su – – – e

re – cor-da-tus mi-se-ri-cor – di – e su – e

re – cor-da-tus mi-se – ri – cor-di – e su – – – – e

Glo – – ri – a Pa – – – tri

Glo – – ri – a Pa – – – – – tri

Glo – ri – – – – – – a Pa – tri

et Fi – li – o et

et Fi – li – o

et Fi – li – o et Spi-ri – tu – i

Spi-ri – tu – i San – – – – – – cto

et Spi – ri – tu – i San – – cto

San – – – – – cto

814

167.

(Magnificat) Anima mea Dominum

fols. 135v-138r (4 vv.)

Anima mea Dominum

[...]¹

Quia respexit humilitatem ancille sue,

ecce enim ex hoc beatam me dicent omnes generationes.

5   [...]

[...]

Et misericordia eius a progenie in progenies timentibus eum

[...]

[...]

10   Deposuit potentes de sede, et exaltavit humiles

[...]

Suscepit Israel puerum suum, recordatus misericordie sue

[...]

[...]

Gloria Patri et Filio et Spiritui Sancto

[...]

For the text see no. 123.

Readings emended in the edition:

Bar	Voice	Original
after 15	T	rubric: «Quia respexit tacet»
after 109	A	rubric: «Deposuit tacet»
after 127	T	rubric: «Tenor tacet Suscepit»
142	A	*signum congruentiae*
after 186	A	rubric: «Gloria tacet»

Remarks: The piece is written in very light ink, perhaps copied at the same time that the scribe added the text to the *Magnificat* immediately preceding (no. 166). The *signum congruentiae* at bar 142 in the Altus might suggest that the composition was performed: even if the sign appears at the end of a clausula, it cannot be interpreted as a fermata; more likely it indicates to the singer of the Altus part that this is the entrance point of the Bassus (to whom, perhaps, he makes a sign during the performance), which had not sung the beginning of the *Suscepit*. The chant in GR, pp. 218-219, and LU, pp. 212, 218 (*Tonus 8.*) is very loosely paraphrased in the upper three voices.

Bibliography: CAO III, pp. 323-324; CS, pp. 430-433; Filocamo 2004; IGC, p. 270; Kirsch 1966, p. 398.

---

¹. The absence of alternating verses such as this indicates *alternatim* performance, with the missing verses in plainchant.

167.
(MAGNIFICAT) ANIMA MEA DOMINUM

fols. 135*v*–138*r*

S[uperius]
A[ltus]
B[assus]
Qui - - - - - a re-spe - xit
Qui - a re - spe - xit
25
hu-mi-li - ta-tem an - cil - - - -
hu - mi-li - ta - tem
34
- le su - - - - e,
an - cil - le su - e,
Qui - a re - spe - - - - - - - - - - - -
42
ec - - - - - - ce e -
ec - ce e - nim
- - - - - - xit hu - mi - li - ta - - - - - - tem

50
- - - nim ex hoc
ex hoc be - a - - tam
an - cil - le su - -
59
be - a - - - - - - - - tam
me di - - - - - - - cent
- - - - - - - - e, ec - ce e - - - - - - nim
67
me di - cent o - mnes ge -
o - mnes ge - ne - - - - - - -
ex hoc be - a - tam me di - cent
76
- - ne - ra - - - - - ti - - - - - - - o - - - nes.
- - - - ra - - - - ti - - - - - - - - - - o - nes.
o - mnes ge - - - ne - ra - - - - ti - - - - o - nes.
42
132

S[uperius]
A[ltus]
T[enor]
[Bassus]
Et mi-se-ri - cor - - - - di - a e-ius
Et mi-se-ri - cor-di - a e - - - - ius a pro-ge-ni-e
Et mi-se-ri - - - cor - - - - - di - a e-ius a
Et mi - se-ri - cor-di - a e-ius a pro-ge - ni-
92
a pro-ge-ni - - - - - e in pro - - - ge - ni - es
in pro - ge - ni - es ti - men - ti - - - bus
pro-ge-ni - - - e in pro-ge - - - - - - - ni-es
-e in pro-ge - ni - es
101
ti-men-ti - - - - - bus e - - - - - - um
e - - - - - - - um
52
ti-men - ti - - - - - bus e - - - - - - - - - - um
ti - men - ti - bus e - - - - - um

S[uperius]
T[enor]
[Bassus]
De - - - po - - su - - - - - - it po - ten - tes de se-de,
De - - - po - su-it po - ten - - - - - - tes de
De - po - su - it po - ten - tes de se - - - - -
115
se - de, et
- de,
119
et ex-al - ta - vit hu-mi - - - - - - -
ex-al - ta - vit hu - mi - - - - - - - - - - - - -
et ex-al - ta - - - - - vit
124
- - - - - - - - - - - - - - - - - les
- - - - - - - - - - - - - - - - - les
hu - - - - - mi - - les
52
51

S[uperius]
A[ltus]
B[assus]
Su - sce - - - pit I - - - sra - el
Su - sce - - - - - - pit I - - - sra - el pu - e -
136
pu - - e - rum su - - - um,
- rum su - - - - - - - - - - - - - um, re -
Re -
143
re - - - - cor -
- - - cor - da - - - - - - - - - - - - - - - - - -
- - - cor - da - - - - - - - - - - - tus
151
- da - - - - - - - - tus
- tus
mi - - - - - - se - ri - cor - - - - - di - e

158
mi - - - se - ri - cor - - - - di - e
mi - - - se - - - ri - cor - - - - - - - - - - - - - -
165
- - - - - - - - di - e
172
su - - - - - - - - - - - - - - - - -
180
- - - - - - - - - - - - - - - - - - - e
su - - - - - - - - - - - - - - - - e
116
su - - - - - - - - - - - - - - - e.
116

S[uperius]
Glo - - - ri - a Pa - - - - - - - - - tri
T[enor]
Glo - - - ri - - - a Pa - - - - - - - - - -
B[assus]
Glo - - - - - ri - a Pa - - - - - - - - - - - - -
198
et Fi - - li - - -
- - tri et Fi - li - - - -
- tri et Fi - - - li - - - - - o
208
- - - - - - - - - - - - - - o
- - - o et
et Spi - - - - - - - - - - ri - tu - i
219
et Spi - ri - tu - i San - - - cto
116
85
Spi - - - ri - tu - - - - i San - - - - - - cto
85
San - - - - - - - - - - - - - - - - - - cto
85

168.

Helas, [que devera mon cueur]

fols. 138v–139r (3 vv.)

[Henricus] Isach

Helas

Chanson (rondeau cinquain).[1]

Readings emended in the edition:

Bar	Voice	Original
11	Ct	*d′* instead of *c′*

Musical concordances (mss): • BolM 34 (6v–8r), textless, score format,[2] «Josquini» • CV G27 (76v–77r, olim 83v–84r), «Ysach» • FirN BR229 (5v–6r), *Helas que devera mon cuer*, «Henricus Yzac» • HeilbS 2 (no. 31), Ct only, «Henri. Isaac» • HKK 20 (101), textless, Ct only, «H. I.» • ModE 8 (71v), Ct only • SegC (177r), *Elaes*, «Ysaac» • SGS 530 (28v–29r), «Heinrich Isaac» • VerCap 757 (20v–21r), textless, modern hand: «Ysaac Helas (que devera mon cueur)» • ZwR 78/3 (no. 23), textless, «Isaac»

Musical concordances (prints):[3] • EgenLieder (III, no. 55), C only • FormTrium (no. 3), textless, but in the Jena copy only, added by hand: «H. Isac, Helas je suis mary» • PeOdh1503 (55v–56r), «Yzac» • PeOdh1504 (55v–56r), «Yzac»

Modern editions of the music: Brown 1983, II, pp. 11–13 (after FirN BR229); DTÖ 28, p. 75 (after FirN BR229); DTÖ 32, p. 234 (after SGS 530); Hewitt 1942, pp. 327–328 (after PeOdh1504); Mönkemeyer 1985, II, p. 12 (after FormTrium); SM 8, pp. 86–87 (after SGS 530).

Remarks: The musical version of Panc.27 is not directly related to any of the concordant sources. Even if the reading of *Odhecaton* seems the closest, many graphic variants (tiny embellishments, divided notes, a rest in place of a note) and the error in bar 11 (absent in Petrucci) discourage the notion of direct contact. The Contra in Panc.27 begins in the alto clef (but changes to tenor at the beginning of the next stave), in contrast to what happens in the other sources, where the part is written throughout in the tenor clef. The error in bar 11 is not found in the other concordances. Thus it is difficult to posit a certain 'kinship' with the piece in Panc.27; it is perhaps more likely that this piece, widely diffused, was transmitted in other sources that have not survived and which the scribe of Panc.27 could have drawn on. From this piece to no. 172 there is a change in the graphic aspect of the writing, which becomes much more vigorous with respect to the previous piece.

---

[1] According to Howard Mayer Brown (see Brown 1983, I, p. 209), Isaac is probably referring to the text *Helas, que pourra devenir* (see no. 56).

[2] This is a manuscript copied in Rome at the beginning of the seventeenth century (1613). The chronological limits of the sources cited in this edition are thereby exceeded, but inclusion of the manuscript is justified by the fact that it bears a (unique) attribution of this piece to Josquin.

[3]. In PeOdh1501 the folios that would have contained the piece are lacking.

BIBLIOGRAPHY: ATLAS 1975-76, I, pp. 174-177; BAKER 1978, I, p. 483; BOORMAN 2006, pp. 1047-1048; BROWN 1983, I, p. 209; FILOCAMO 2004; HEWITT 1942, p. 151; KÄMPER 1976, p. 78; LAMA DE LA CRUZ 1994, p. 278; LOWINSKY 1943, p. 57; NJE 27, II, pp. 105-107; PICKER 1991, p. 102; SM 8, p. 347.

168.
HELAS, [QUE DEVERA MON CUEUR]

fols. 138*v*-139*r*

[Henricus] Isach

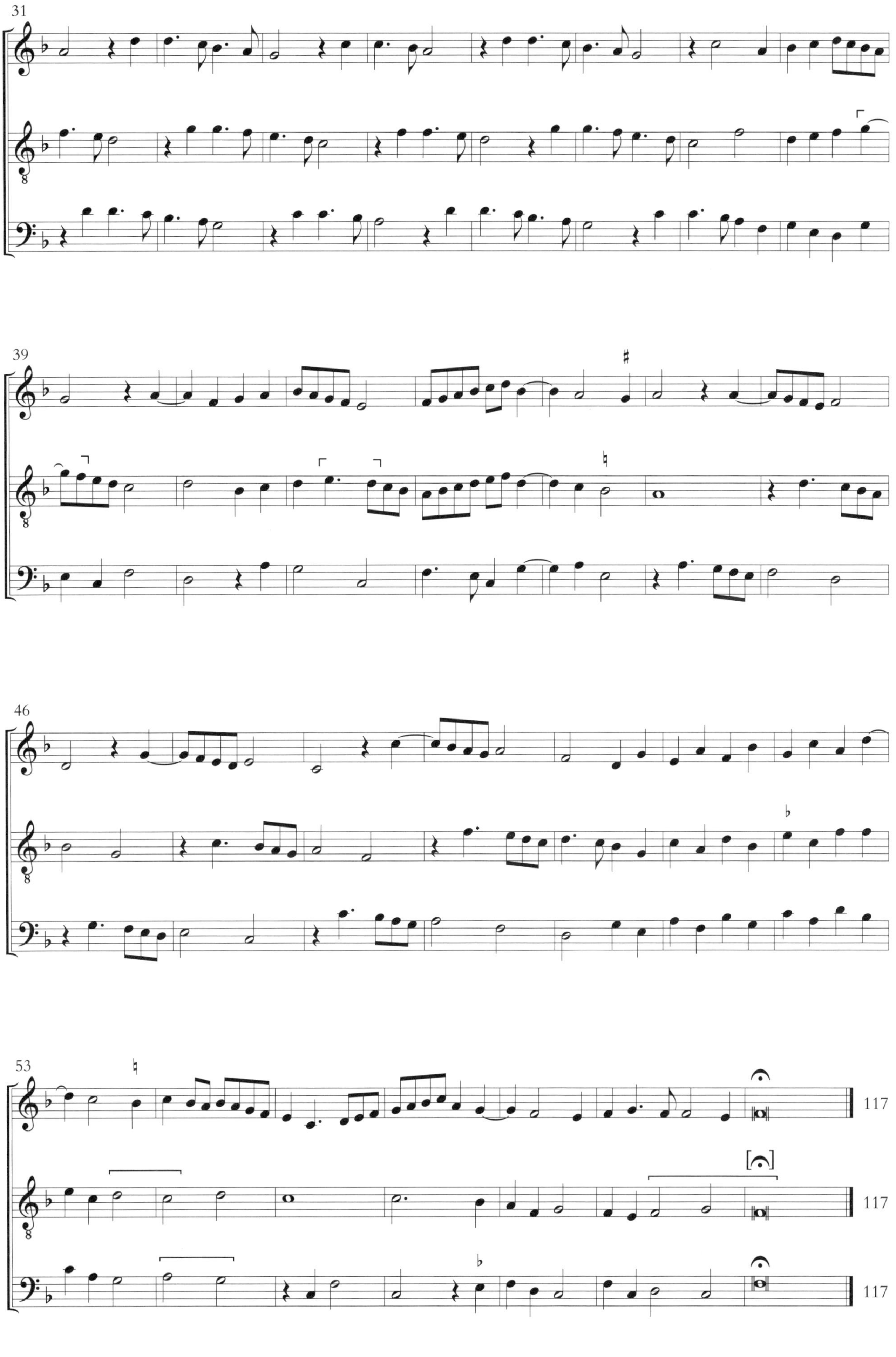
31
39
46
53
117
117
117

169.

Non desina

fols. 139*v*–140*r* (4 vv.)

Non desina

Instrumental piece?

COMMENTARY ON THE TEXT:

1 «desina»: perhaps from the verb *desino, is, desii, desitum, ere* = 'to stop, leave out, abandon'

READINGS EMENDED IN THE EDITION:

BAR	VOICE	ORIGINAL
6/II	A	*minima*
20	C	the missing notes have been conjectured from the motion in parallel tenths with the Bassus (bb. 18–21/I)
49	B	*g*
55/II	C	*d'*
between 56 and 57	B	superfluous *semiminima c'*, omitted to make the melodic passage conform to that appearing in various voices (e.g. C, bb. 51–52; A, b. 57/II–59; T, bb. 59–60; B, bb. 60/II–62/I, etc.)

MODERN EDITIONS OF THE MUSIC: BANKS 1993, II, pp. 130–132 (after Panc.27).

REMARKS: The composition is well crafted, and certainly the work of an important composer, probably a northerner. In the eighteenth fascicle of Panc.27 *Non desina* follows a composition by Isaac (*Helas, [que devera mon cuer]*, no. 168) and precedes another piece (*Turis*, no. 170), also anonymous, and likewise of first-rate musical quality, for which no concordances have been discovered so far. It is improbable that the scribe of the manuscript, a mediocre composer, is the author. *Non desina* is written with the same very dark ink and with the same scribal *ductus* as nos. 168 and 170; possibly the copyist of Panc.27 had in mind to put together a collection of pieces written by Isaac? (Asked about the stylistic characteristics of *Non desina*, Bonnie Blackburn suggested the paternity of Isaac or Agricola.)

BIBLIOGRAPHY: BANKS 1993, I, pp. 281–282.

169.
NON DESINA
fols. 139v–140r

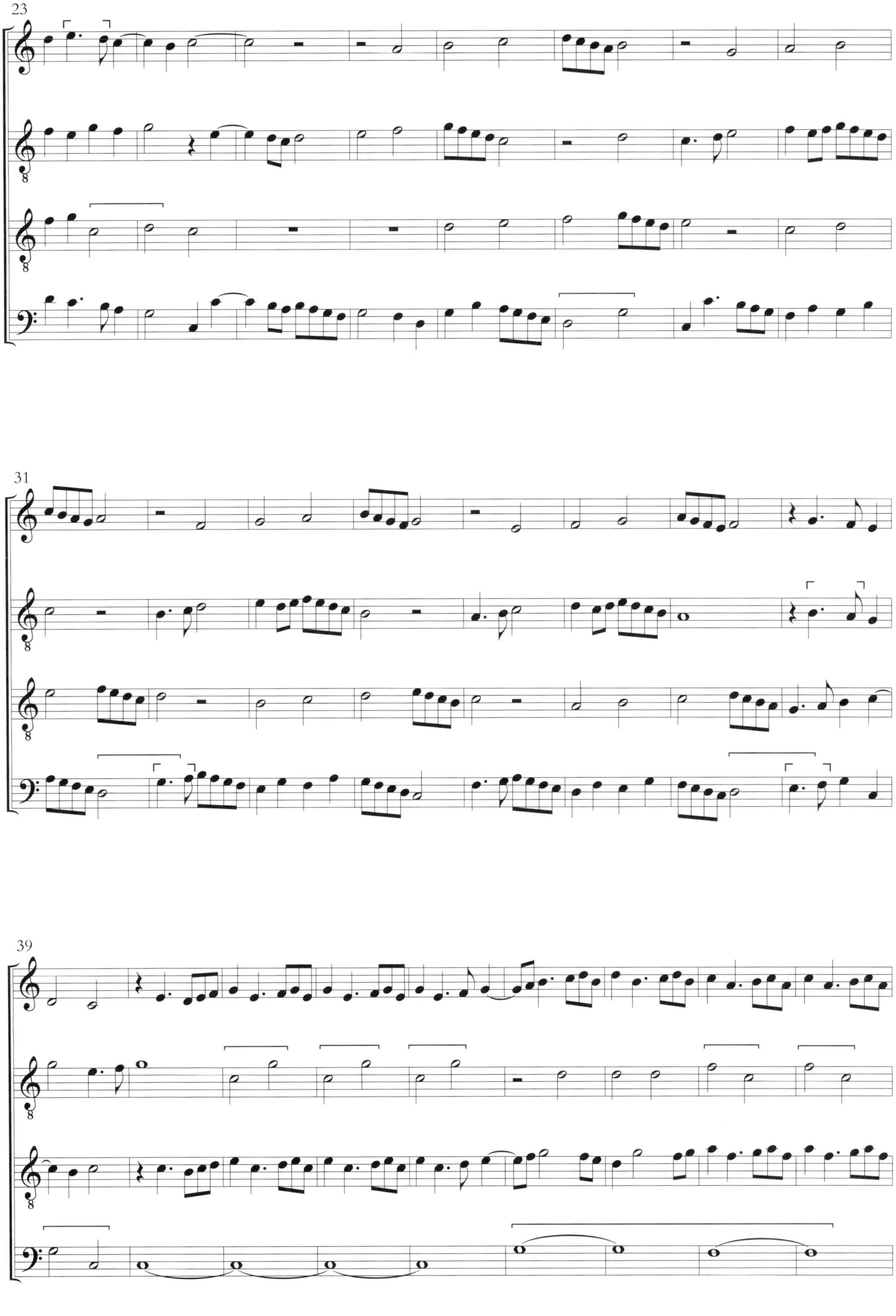
23
31
39

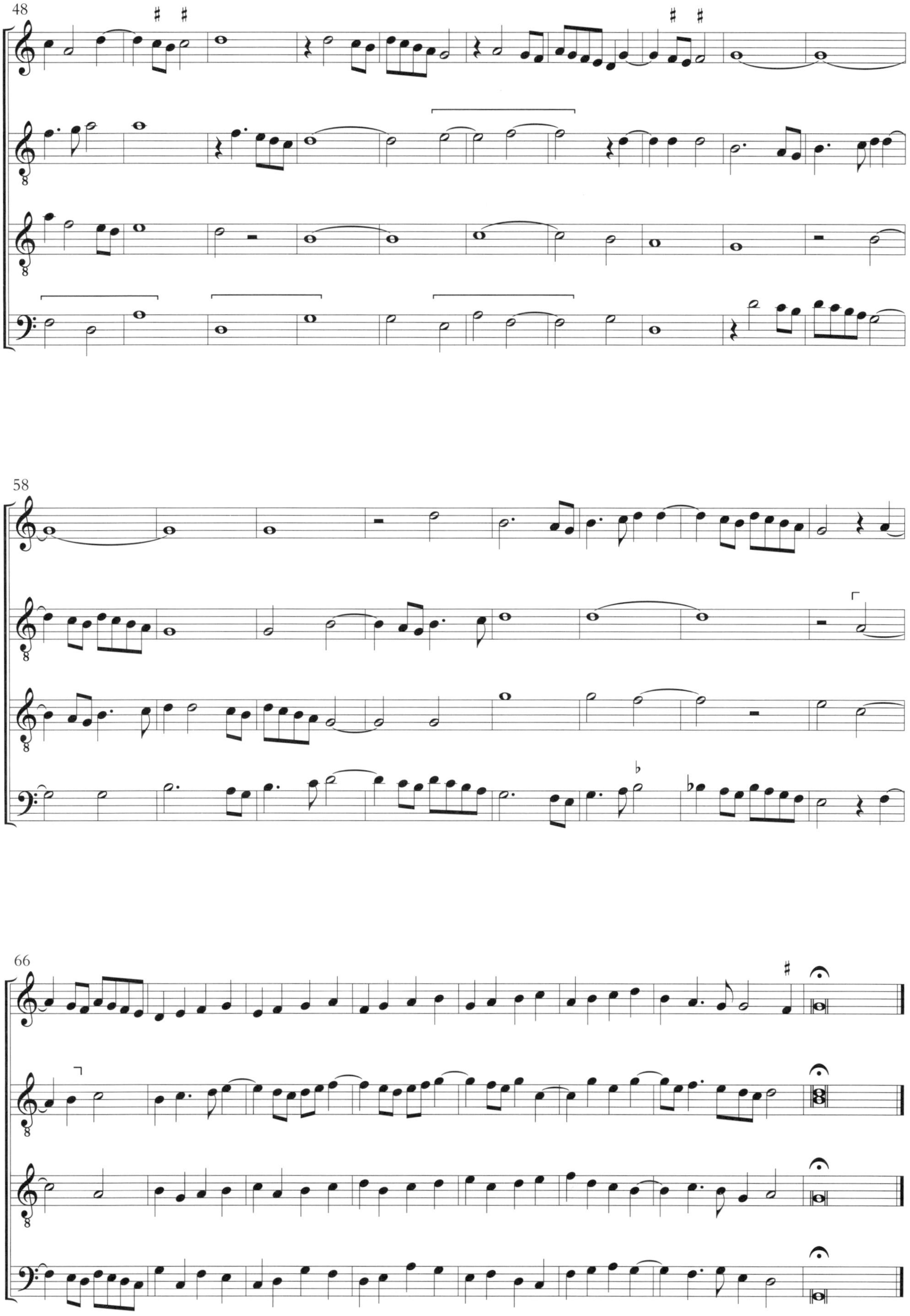
48
58
66

170.

Turis

fols. 140*v*–141*r* (3 vv.)

[Heading only]

Instrumental piece?

Commentary on the text: Traditionally «Turis» is considered to be the name of the composer of the piece. If instead «Turis» is a textual incipit, it might be the genitive of the Latin *tus* (*thus*), incense, as in the case of the motet by Gaspard Le Roux *Thuris odor volet ad auras* for the Elevation and Adoration of the Holy Sacrament. Another possibility is that it might be *turris* (= 'tower, castle, palace / dovecote, pigeon house'), a typical epithet of the Virgin (turris eburnea, turris David) and the beginning of texts such as *Turris David ascenditur* (AH 5, p. 137), or *Turris his davidica* (AH 48, p. 203), or *Turris fortissima nomen Domini*, set to music by Nicolaus Rost.

Readings emended in the edition:

Bar	Voice	Original
45-46	T	*brevis* with fermata

Modern editions of the music: Kämper 1976, p. 73 (after Panc.27, incipit only).

Remarks: Notwithstanding the fact that the Tenor and Bassus have a B flat key signature, it is likely that in the second section of the piece (bb. 17-46) all the Bs in these two voices should be natural: the change from transposed Dorian (with B flat) to Mixolydian (with B natural) may seem unusual, but it helps to attenuate the tritones and false relations with the Cantus in the long ascending sequence (bb. 25-40). The general impression is that we are dealing with an instrumental composition; moreover, there is no text under the music. The artistic quality of the piece is noteworthy (see also the Remarks to no. 169).

Bibliography: Kämper 1976, pp. 73-74.

170.
TURIS
fols. 140*v*–141*r*

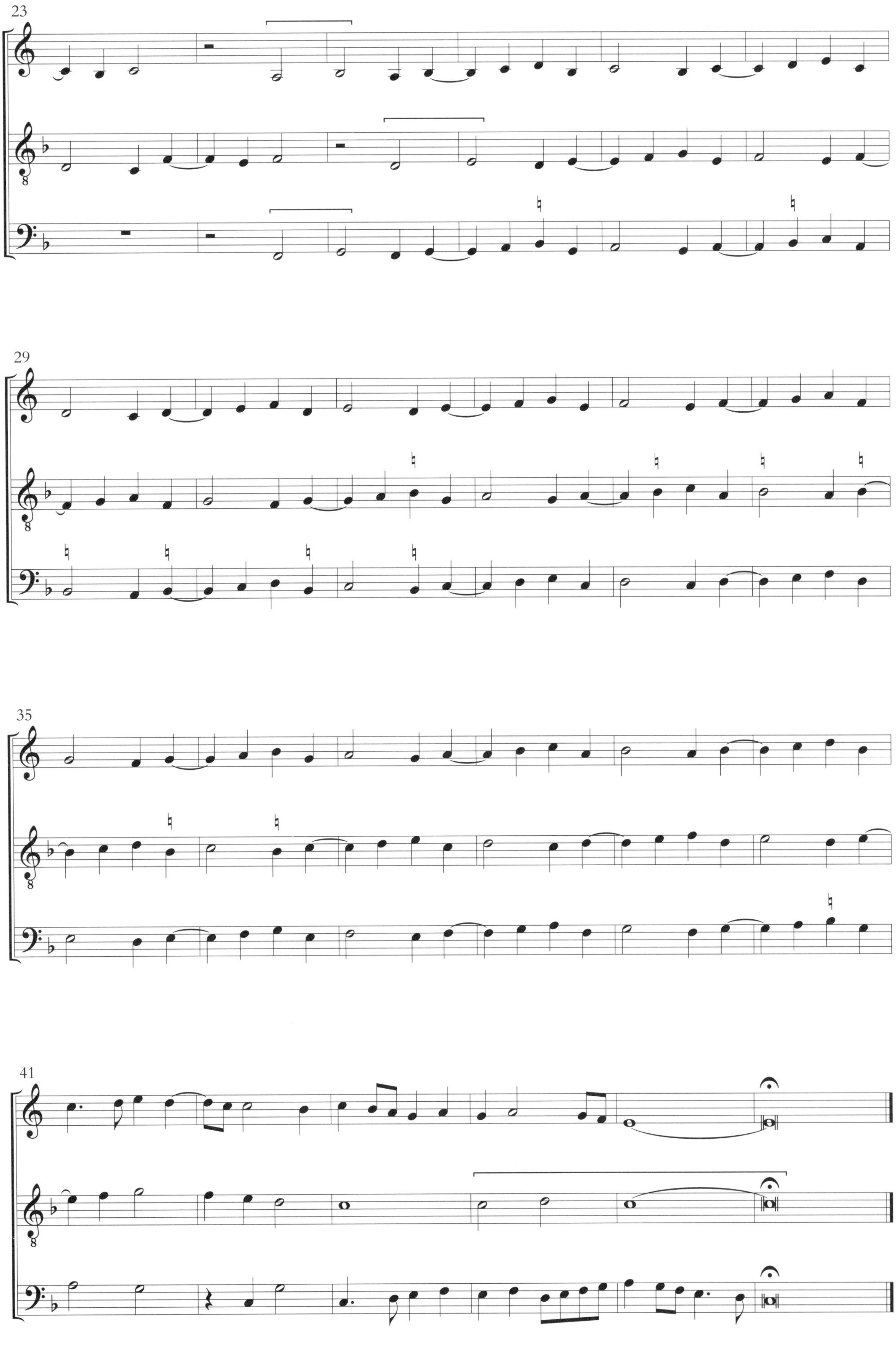
23
29
35
41

171.

Bianca più che neve sei chiamata

fols. 141*v*-142*r* (3 vv.)

Bianca più che neve sei chiamata

Italian secular piece?

READINGS EMENDED IN THE EDITION:

BAR	VOICE	ORIGINAL
42/II	S	dotted *d″ minima*, transcribed as *minima* (b. 42/II) and *semiminima* (b. 44/II); between the two repeated notes a supplement has been inserted (see Remarks)

REMARKS: Although no musical concordances are known, the piece was certainly copied from a model: this is demonstrated by the missing passage, restored here, of a rising sequential progression in bars 42/II-44/II.[1]

---

[1]. I thank Fabrizio Ammetto for having suggested this solution.

171.
BIANCA PIÙ CHE NEVE SEI CHIAMATA
fols. 141*v*-142*r*

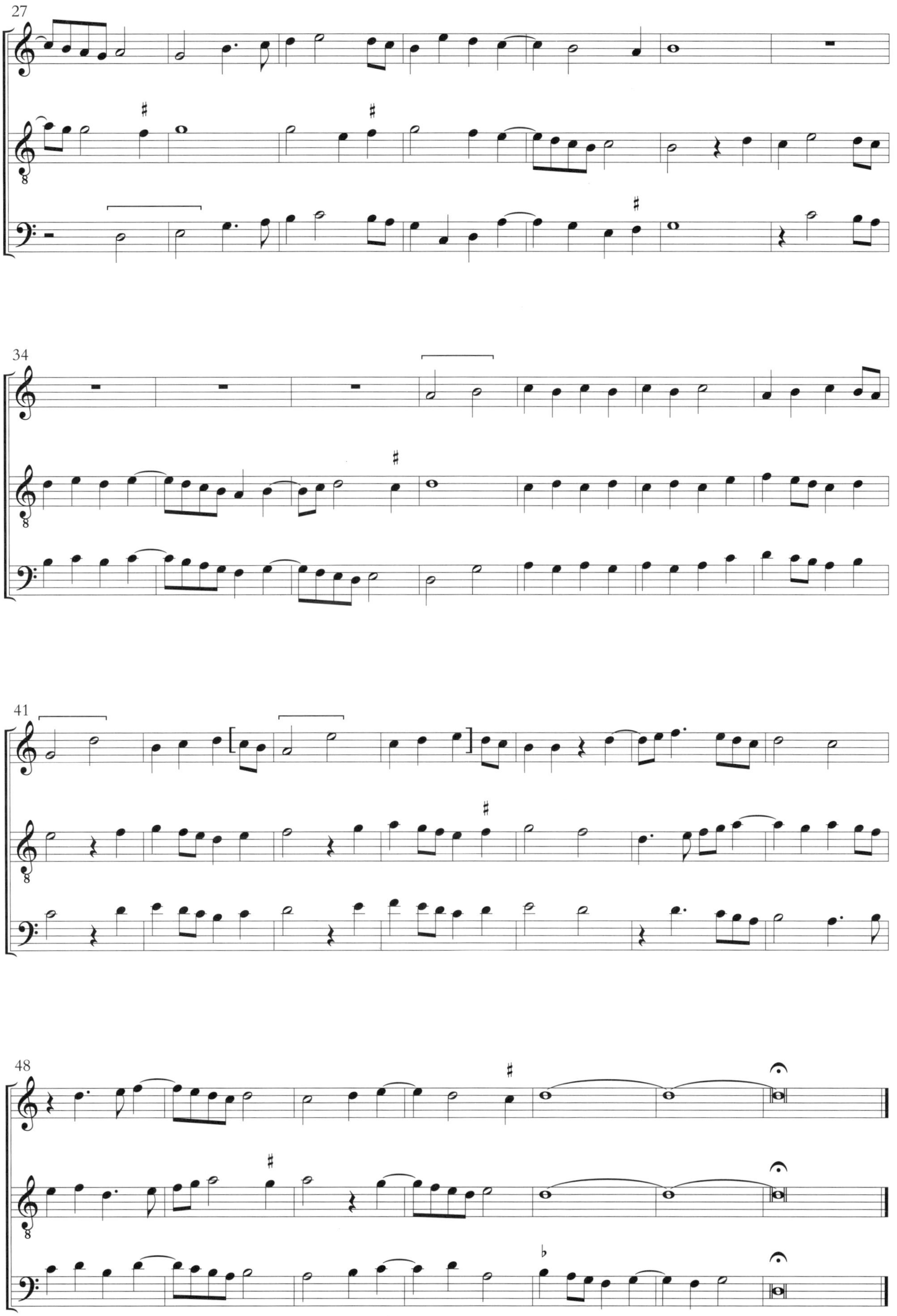
27
34
41
48

172.

Sine fraude

fols. 142v–143r (3 vv.)

Sine fraude

Instrumental piece?

COMMENTARY ON THE TEXT:

1 «fraude» derives of course from the Latin *fraus, fraudis* (= 'fraud, cheating, deception, treachery, deceit / sin, wickedness / detriment, harm, error, danger, illusion')

READINGS EMENDED IN THE EDITION:

BAR	VOICE	ORIGINAL
47/II–49/I	B	the missing part has been reconstructed on the basis of the repetition of the T (bb. 45/II–47/I), which moves in parallel thirds with the B
50	C	*d″* and *c″*
51	T	*c′ minima*

MODERN EDITIONS OF THE MUSIC: BANKS 1993, II, pp. 175-176 (after Panc.27).

REMARKS: The piece has probably been copied from another source, and the copyist overlooked the section of the Bassus that has been restored in the present edition. The little numbers appended at the end of each voice surely served in this case to assure the comprehensive counting of the *semibreves*: 112 in all, since the rest in bar 7 was missing as well as bars 47/II to 49/I.

BIBLIOGRAPHY: BANKS 1993, I, p. 289.

172.
SINE FRAUDE
fols. *142v–143r*

Cantus: Sine fraude

Tenor: Sine fraude

Bassus

Sine fraude

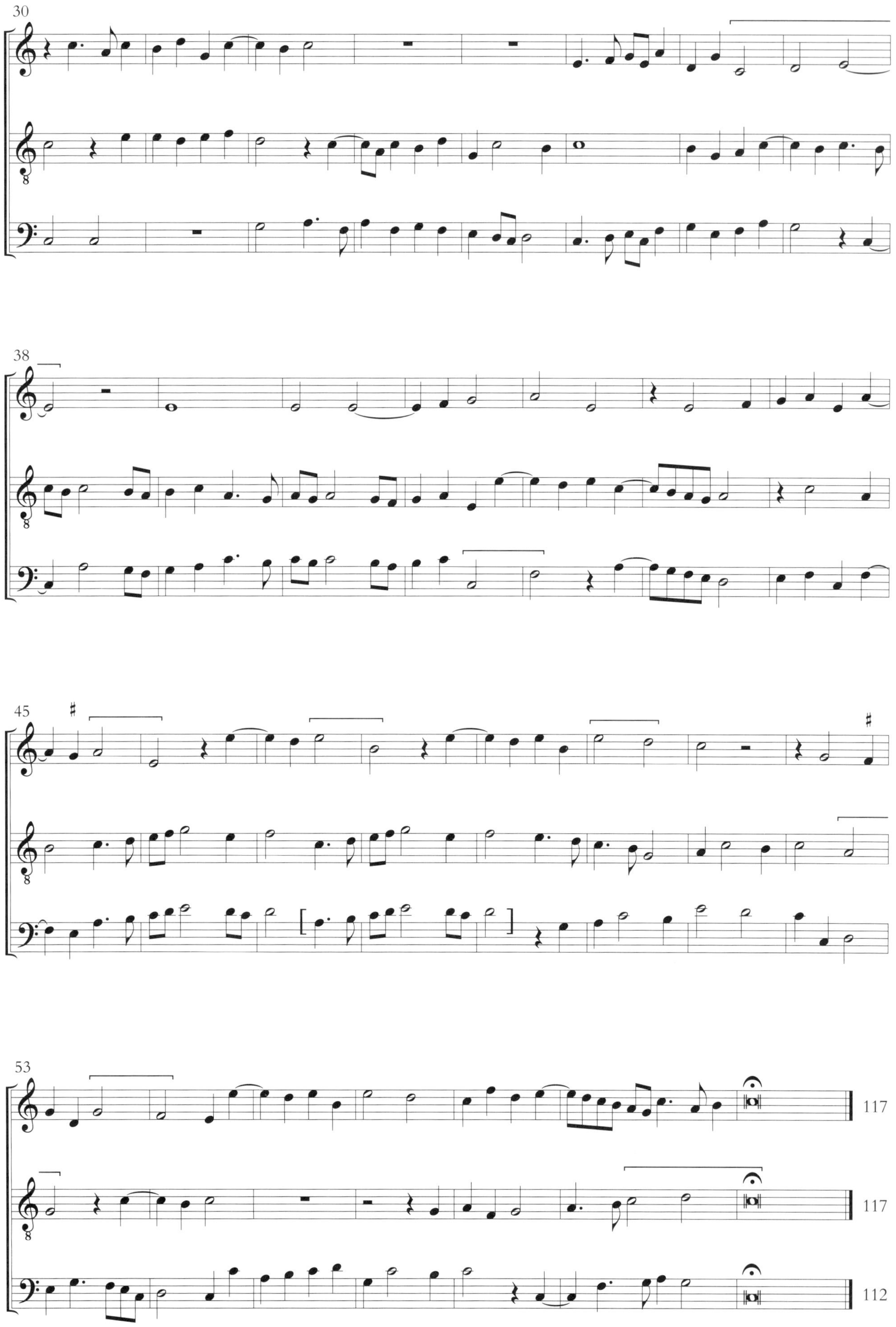
30
38
45
53
117
117
112

173.

Ave Maria, gratia plena

fols. 143*v*–144*r* (4 vv.)

Ave Maria, gratia plena, Dominus tecum;
benedicta tu in mulieribus,
et benedictus fructus ventris tui, Iesus.
Sancta Maria, mater Dei,
5   ora pro nobis peccatoribus,
nunc et in hora mortis nostre.
Amen.

For the text see no. 2.

MODERN EDITIONS OF THE MUSIC: BANKS 1993, II, pp. 14-15 (after Panc.27).

REMARKS: The many repeated notes make the text underlay problematic to the extent of contradicting prosodic rhythm (for example, bb. 5, 7, 9, 10, 12). It is therefore possible that the piece is a contrafact of an instrumental piece; moreover, the missing repeated note in the Bassus (b. 20/II) suggests copying from a model.

BIBLIOGRAPHY: BANKS 1993, I, p. 263; CAO III, pp. 5, 64; CAO IV, pp. 40, 42, 476; CS, pp. 424-425, 428-429; FREEMAN 1991, p. 202; IGC, p. 55.

173.
AVE MARIA, GRATIA PLENA
fols. 143v–144r

21
De - i, o - ra pro no - - - bis pec - ca - to - ri - bus,
De - i, o - ra pro no - - - bis pec - ca - to - ri - bus,
De - i, o - ra pro no - - - bis pec - ca - to - ri - bus,
De - i, o - ra pro no - - - bis pec - ca - to - ri - bus,
28
nunc et in ho - ra mor - tis no - - - - - - - - stre.
nunc et in ho - ra mor - tis no - - - - - - - - stre.
nunc et in ho - ra mor - tis no - - - - - - - - stre.
nunc et in ho - ra mor - tis no - - - - - - - - stre.
35
A - - - men.
A - - - men.
A - - - men.
A - - - men.

174.

Incipit lamentatio Ieremie prophete

fols. 144*v*-145*r* (4 vv.)

[Erasmus (Lapicida?)[1]]

Incipit lamentatio Ieremie prophete.

Aleph.
Quomodo sedet sola civitas plena populo!
Facta est quasi vidua domina gentium,
princeps provinciarum facta est sub tributo.

Lamentations of Jeremiah, 1:1 (Vulgata, p. 1248). The sections from *Aleph* to *Vau* are used for the first lesson at the first Nocturn in Matins on Maundy Thursday (BR, p. 346); the sections from *Zain* to *Caph* are used for the second lesson at the same Nocturn (BR, pp. 346-347).

Commentary on the text:

2 Vulgata: «sedit» instead of 'sedet'

Musical concordances (prints):[2] • PeLamII (F3*v*-G2*r*: F3*v*-F4*r*), «Erasmus»

Text from Vulgata, pp. 1248-1250 (*Threni idest Lamentationes Ieremiae prophetae*, I, 1-22):

1. Aleph
Quomodo sedit sola civitas plena populo
facta est quasi vidua domina gentium
princeps provinciarum facta est sub tributo

2. Beth
plorans ploravit in nocte et lacrimae eius in maxillis eius
non est qui consoletur eam ex omnibus caris eius
omnes amici eius spreverunt eam et facti sunt ei inimici

3. Gimel
migravit Iuda propter adflictionem et multitudinem servitutis
habitavit inter gentes nec invenit requiem
omnes persecutores eius apprehenderunt eam inter angustias

4. Deleth
viae Sion lugent eo quod non sint qui veniant ad sollemnitatem
omnes portae eius destructae sacerdotes eius gementes
virgines eius squalidae et ipsa oppressa amaritudine

---

[1]. Even though it is not specified either in Panc.27 or PeLamII, it is very likely that this 'Erasmus' is the better-known 'Lapicida'. Stanley Boorman, for his part, interprets 'Erasmus' as 'Desiderius Erasmus' in the index of Boorman 2006 (p. 1265), although elsewhere he consistently does not attribute the same paternity.

[2]. I thank Peter Scott for kindly having given me some information from his doctoral dissertation on the two books of Lamentations printed by Petrucci (Scott 2004).

5.   He
facti sunt hostes eius in capite inimici illius locupletati sunt
quia Dominus locutus est super eam propter multitudinem iniquitatum eius
parvuli eius ducti sunt captivi ante faciem tribulantis

6.   Vav
et egressus est a filia Sion omnis decor eius
facti sunt principes eius velut arietes non invenientes pascuam
et abierunt absque fortitudine ante faciem subsequentis

7.   Zai
recordata est Hierusalem dierum adflictionis suae et praevaricationis
omnium desiderabilium suorum quae habuerat a diebus antiquis
cum caderet populus eius in manu hostili et non esset auxiliator
viderunt eam hostes et deriserunt sabbata eius

8.   Heth
peccatum peccavit Hierusalem propterea instabilis facta est
omnes qui glorificabant eam spreverunt illam quia viderunt ignominiam eius
ipsa autem gemens et conversa retrorsum

9.   Teth
sordes eius in pedibus eius nec recordata est finis sui
deposita est vehementer non habens consolatorem
vide Domine adflictionem meam quoniam erectus est inimicus

10.   Ioth
manum suam misit hostis ad omnia desiderabilia eius
quia vidit gentes ingressas sanctuarium suum
de quibus praeceperas ne intrarent in ecclesiam tuam

11.   Caph
omnis populus eius gemens et quaerens panem
dederunt pretiosa quaeque pro cibo ad refocilandam animam
vide Domine considera quoniam facta sum vilis

12.   Lamed
o vos omnes qui transitis per viam adtendite et videte
si est dolor sicut dolor meus quoniam vindemiavit me
ut locutus est Dominus in die irae furoris sui

13.   Mem
de excelso misit ignem in ossibus meis et erudivit me
expandit rete pedibus meis convertit me retrorsum
posuit me desolatam tota die maerore confectam

14.   Nun
vigilavit iugum iniquitatum mearum in manu eius convolutae sunt
et inpositae collo meo infirmata est virtus mea
dedit me Dominus in manu de qua non potero surgere

15.   Samech
abstulit omnes magnificos meos Dominus de medio mei
vocavit adversum me tempus ut conteret electos meos
torcular calcavit Dominus virgini filiae Iuda

16. AIN

idcirco ego plorans et oculus meus deducens aquam
quia longe factus est a me consolator convertens animam meam
facti sunt filii mei perditi quoniam invaluit inimicus

17. FE

expandit Sion manus suas non est qui consoletur eam
mandavit Dominus adversum Iacob in circuitu eius hostes eius
facta est Hierusalem quasi polluta menstruis inter eos

18. SADE

iustus est Dominus quia os eius ad iracundiam provocavi
audite obsecro universi populi et videte dolorem meum
virgines meae et iuvenes mei abierunt in captivitatem

19. COPH

vocavi amicos meos et ipsi deceperunt me
sacerdotes mei et senes mei in urbe consumpti sunt
quia quaesierunt cibum sibi ut refocillarent animam suam

20. RES

vide Domine quoniam tribulor venter meus conturbatus est
subversum est cor meum in memet ipsa quoniam amaritudine plena sum
foris interfecit gladius et domi mors similis est

21. SEN

audierunt quia ingemesco ego et non est qui consoletur me
omnes inimici mei audierunt malum meum laetati sunt quoniam tu fecisti
adduxisti diem consolationis et fient similes mei

22. THAV

ingrediatur omne malum eorum coram te
et devindemia eos sicut vindemiasti me propter omnes iniquitates meas
multi enim gemitus mei et cor meum maerens

MODERN EDITIONS OF THE MUSIC: MASSENKEIL 1965, pp. 51-59: 51-52 (after PeLamII).

REMARKS: There are no substantive variants between the version of Panc.27 and that of PeLamII: the two sources differ only graphically (repeated notes). The closeness of the two sources seems to indicate direct contact. But the piece in Panc.27 is only the initial part of Petrucci's version: if one was copied from the other, it can only be so in the case of the scribe of Panc.27, who might have had before him Petrucci's second book of Lamentations, published on 29 May 1506. No conjunctive error joins them definitively, but if the remarkable similarity of the two sources were enough to prove contact, Scribe A's work on the manuscript would extend to after Petrucci's publication. The very dark ink perhaps indicates that this piece was not copied at the same time as the previous piece. Two pages follow (fols. 145v-146r) that have staves but no music.

BIBLIOGRAPHY: BOORMAN 2006, p. 916; CS, pp. 339-342; MASSENKEIL 1965, pp. 7*-9*; SCOTT 2004, pp. 59-82.

174.
INCIPIT LAMENTATIO IEREMIE PROPHETE
fols. 144*v*–145*r*

[Erasmus (Lapicida?)]

22
Quo - - mo - do se - det so - - la ci - vi - - tas
Quo - - mo - do se - det so - la ci - vi - - tas
Quo - - mo - do se - det so - - la ci - vi - tas ple -
Quo - - mo - do se - det so - - la ci - vi - - tas
30
ple - na po - pu - - - - lo! Fa - cta est
ple - na po - - - pu - - - lo! Fa - - - - - - - - - -
- - na po - pu - lo! Fa - cta
ple - na po - - - pu - - - lo! Fa - - -
37
qua - - - si vi - du - a do - - - - - - -
- cta est qua - - - - - si vi - du - a do - - - - -
est qua - - si vi - du - a do - - - mi - - - -
- - - - cta est qua - si vi - du - a do - - - - - - -

44
- mi - - - na gen - - - - ti - - - - - um,
- - mi - na gen - - ti - - - - - um, prin - - - - - -
- - - na gen - - - - - - - - ti - um, prin - - - - - -
- mi - na gen - - - - ti - - - - - - - um, prin - - - - - -
51
prin - - - - - ceps pro - vin - ci - a - - -
- - - - ceps pro - - - - vin - - - - - - ci - - - a - - -
- - - - ceps pro - - - - - vin - - - - - - - ci - - - a -
- ceps pro - - - - - vin - - - - ci - a - - - - - - rum
58
- rum fa - - - - - - - - - cta est sub tri - bu - to.
- rum fa - - - cta est sub tri - bu - to.
- rum fa - - - - - - - - - cta est sub tri - bu - to.
fa - - - - - - - cta est sub tri - bu - to.

175.

AVE MARIA, GRATIA PLENA

fols. 146*v*-147*r* (4 vv.)

[BARTOLOMEO TROMBONCINO]

Ave Maria, gratia plena, Dominus tecum;
benedicta tu in mulieribus,
et benedictus fructus ventris tui, Iesus.
Sancta Maria, mater Dei,
5   ora pro nobis peccatoribus,
nunc et in hora mortis nostre.
Amen.

For the text see no. 2.

READINGS EMENDED IN THE EDITION:

BAR	VOICE	ORIGINAL
4	T, B	*brevis* with fermata, analogous to the identical passage in bar 53
53	T, B	*longa* with fermata
after 53	T	bar line

MUSICAL CONCORDANCES (PRINTS): • Motetti1520 (S: 10*v*-11*r*; A: 11*v*-12*r*; T: 12*r*; B: 10*r-v*); in the index of each voice part: «B.T.» • PeLaudeII (33*v*-34*r*)

MODERN EDITIONS OF THE MUSIC: BANKS 1993, II, pp. 29-30 (after Panc.27); JEPPESEN 1935, pp. 54-55 (after PeLaudeII).

REMARKS: The version of Panc.27 is not related to that of PeLaudeII — substantial variants separate them — nor with the version of Motetti1520, which has a large number of graphic variants. The piece is certainly not a contrafact (that is, it has not been changed from a secular to a devotional text), as is demonstrated by the presence of the litany chant at *Sancta Maria, ora pro nobis* (LU, p. 757), corresponding to the section *Sancta Maria* in the Superius, bars 40-43 (see also PRIZER 1993b, p. 182).

BIBLIOGRAPHY: BANKS 1993, I, p. 266; BOORMAN 2006, p. 889; CAO III, pp. 5, 64; CAO IV, pp. 40, 42, 476; CS, pp. 424-425, 428-429; IGC, p. 55; PRIZER 1993b, pp. 181-182.

175.
AVE MARIA, GRATIA PLENA
fols. 146*v*-147*r*

[Bartolomeo Tromboncino]

A – ve Ma – ri – a, gra – ti – a

A – ve Ma – ri – a, gra – ti – a

A – ve Ma – ri – a, gra – ti – a

A – ve Ma – ri – a, gra – ti – a

ple – na, Do – mi-nus te – cum; be – ne-di – cta

ple – na

ple – na, Do – mi-nus te – cum

ple – na

tu in mu – li – e – ri – bus, et be –

19
- ne - di - ctus fru - ctus ven - tris tu - - - - i, Ie - - -
25
- sus. San - cta Ma -
32
- ri - a, ma - ter De - i,

San - cta Ma - ri - a, o - ra pro no - bis pec -

- ca - to - ri - bus, nunc et in ho - - - - - ra mor -

- tis no - - - stre. A - - - men.

A - - - - men.

A - - - - - men.

A - - - - - - men.

176.

Incipit oratio Ieremie prophete

fols. 147*v*-149*r* (4 vv.)

Incipit oratio Ieremie prophete.
Recordare, Domine, quid acciderit nobis:
intuere, et respice obbrobrium nostrum.
Hereditas nostra versa est ad alienos:
5   domus nostre ad extraneos.
Pupilli facti sumus absque patre,
matres nostre quasi vidue.
Aquam nostram pecunia bibimus:
ligna nostra pretio comparavimus.

Lamentations of Jeremiah, 5:1-4 (Vulgata, p. 1254). For the text see no. 118.

Readings emended in the edition:

Bar	Voice	Original
13/I	B	*semibrevis* rest instead of *d semibrevis*
17	C	*brevis* with fermata
29/I	A	*f* instead of *g*
48/II-49/I	B	*e minima*
53/II	B	*a minima*

Modern editions of the music: Banks 1993, II, pp. 99-102 (after Panc.27).

Remarks: The piece has certainly been copied from a model, as proved by the frequent erasures (for example, the fermata above the *longa* in bars 84-85 in the third stave of fol. 148*v*, and the section comprising bars 99-102/I in the fifth stave of fol. 149*r*, completely erased and rewritten with other notes), and above all the irregular disposition of the beginning of the Bassus on fol. 148*r* (bb. 1-65): at the start of the fourth stave, instead of the beginning of the voice, we find bars 42-62/II, finishing on the fifth stave (bb. 62/II-65). But at this point the scribe must have realized that he had forgotten to copy the beginning of the voice (bb. 1-41); he then wrote this part and, having arrived at bar 41, indicated the problem with a *custos*, the rubric «Ibi supra hereditas», and a *signe de renvoi*, duplicated at the beginning of the fourth stave. Probably performance-related is the copyist's cancellation of the word «bibimus» in the Cantus, bar 92 (fol. 148*v*, first stave): «bibimus» was rewritten a little later, perhaps to indicate that the melisma on «-bi» should be extended up to the cadence of bars 95-96.

Bibliography: Banks 1993, I, pp. 277-278; CS, pp. 346-347.

176.
Incipit oratio Ieremie prophete
fols. 147*v*–149*r*

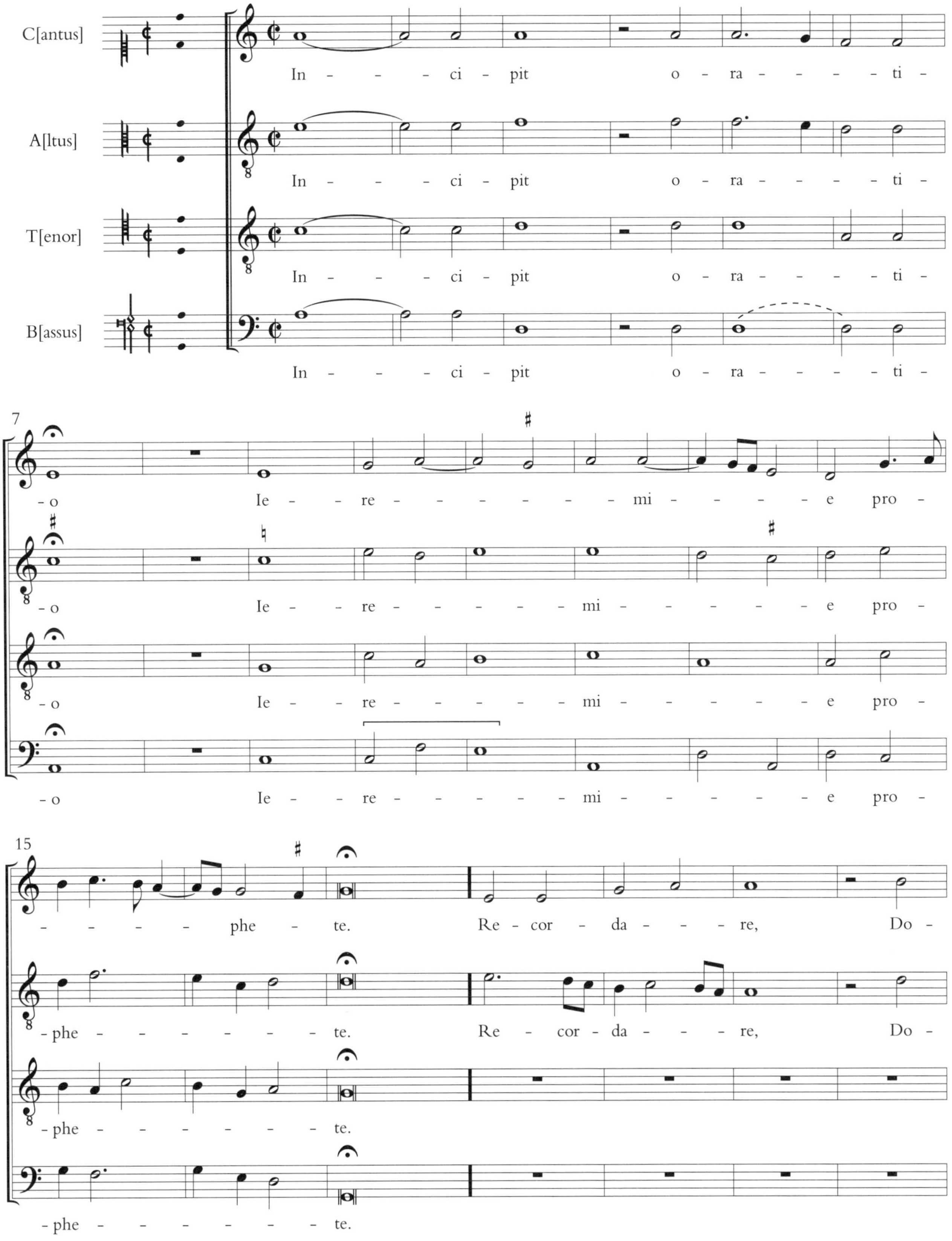

22
-mi - - - - - - ne, quid ac - ci - de - rit no - -
-mi - - - - - - ne, quid ac - ci - - - - - de - rit no - -
30
-bis: in - tu - e - re, et re - spi - ce ob - bro - - - - bri -
-bis: in - tu - e - re, et re - - - spi - ce ob - bro -
in - - - tu - e - re, et re - spi - ce ob - bro - bri - - - -
in - - - tu - e - re, et re - spi - ce ob - bro - - - - bri -
38
-um no - - - - - strum, no - - - - - - strum.
-bri - - - - um no - - - - - - - - strum. He - re - di - - -
-um no - - - - - - - - - - - strum. He - re - di - - -
- - - - um no - - - - - - - - strum. He - re - di - - -

857

66
Pu - pil - li fa - - - - cti su - mus ab - - - - - sque pa - -
Pu - - pil - - - - li fa - - - - cti su - - - - - - - mus ab - -
73
ma - - - - - tres no -
- - - - - - - - - - - - tre, ma - - - - - tres no - stre
- - - - - - - sque pa - - - tre, ma - - - - tres no -
ma - - - - - tres no -
80
-stre qua - si vi - - - du - - e. A - quam no -
qua - - - si vi - - - - du - - - e. A - quam no - stram pe -
-stre qua - si vi - - - - du - - - - e.
-stre qua - si vi - - - du - - - - e. A - quam no - - - - -

859

177.

Rex autem David

fols. 149*v*-150*r* (4 vv.)

[Adrian Willaert?[1]]

Rex autem David
operuit caput suum
et clamabat voce magna, dicens:
«Absalon fili mi, fili mi Absalon!
5   Quis mihi tribuat ut ego moriar pro te,
fili mi, fili mi Absalon, Absalon fili mi, fili mi?».

Based on 2 Samuel (2 Kings) 19:4 («porro rex operuit caput suum et clamabat voce magna | fili mi Absalom Absalom fili mi fili mi», Vulgata, p. 444) and 18:33 («contristatus itaque rex ascendit cenaculum portae | et flevit et sic loquebatur vadens | fili mi Absalom fili mi Absalom | quis mihi tribuat ut ego moriar pro te | Absalom fili mi fili mi», Vulgata, p. 444).

Readings emended in the edition:

Bar	Voice	Original
7	B	*longa* with fermata
24-25	A	*brevis* with fermata
25	B	*longa* with fermata
34	C	*longa* with fermata
42	B	*longa* with fermata
after 46/I	A	there is a part erased and then rewritten the same
54	C	*brevis* with fermata

Musical concordances (mss): • BasU 5-9 (no. 29) • CoimU 48 (123*v*), score format • GreifU 640-1 (no. 43), 2 vv. (C and B only) • MünU 326 (18*v*), A only • RegB 220-2 (no. 52) • RegB 940-1 (no. 29) • SionC 87-4 (31*r*), B only • SGS 463 (no. 108), 2 vv. (C and A only), «Adrianus Villaert», rubric «Phrÿgius id est tertius» • VerCap 760 (49*v*-50*r*)

Musical concordances (prints): • RhauSym (no. 43)

---

[1]. The attribution to Willaert is highly suspect; appearing only in SGS 463, copied towards the middle of the sixteenth century, it poses serious chronological problems. Willaert was born ca. 1490, and even if his first presence in Italy is documented at Rome in the year 1515 (a payment of 8 July 1515 places him in the service of Cardinal Ippolito I d'Este; published in Lockwood 1985, doc. 1; see also pp. 87-88, where it is suggested that he may have been the unnamed singer hired in October 1514), music did not necessarily travel with the composer. If the composition should be by Willaert, the redaction of Panc.27 would need to be advanced by at least several years from the *terminus post quem* of 29 May 1506 (though still within the first decade of the sixteenth century), and one would be forced to hypothesize an extremely precocious Italian circulation of Willaert's music, as he would be less than 20 years old. Even Lockwood expresses doubts on the paternity of *Rex autem David*; the piece is included among the 'Doubtful and Misattributed Works' in the article on Willaert in NG.

TEXT FROM after CAO III, p. 445:

> Rex autem David,
> cooperto capite incedens,
> lugebat filium, dicens:
> «Absalon fili mi, fili mi Absalon,
> 5   quis mihi det ut ego moriar pro te,
> fili mi Absalon?».

MODERN EDITIONS OF THE TEXT: CAO III, p. 445.

MODERN EDITIONS OF THE MUSIC: ALBRECHT 1959, pp. 151-153 (after RhauSym); BANKS 1993, II, pp. 169-171 (after Panc.27); LOACH 1969, II, pp. 170-172 (after SGS 463, with T and B after RegB 940-1).

REMARKS: The musical version of Panc.27 is not related to any of the concordant sources. A great number of substantial variants are found at specific points: b instead of c' in bar 18/II of the Tenor (RegB 220-2, SGS 463, RhauSym), b instead of a in bar 28/II of the Altus (MünU 326, RegB 220-2, RhauSym), c' instead of e' in bar 51/I of the Cantus (RegB 220-2, SGS 463, RhauSym). Another factor distancing the version of Panc.27 from RegB 220-2, SGS 463, and RhauSym is their substitution of the words «cooperto capite» in line 2 for «operuit caput» (in the Vulgata). It is possible that the text was added later by the copyist, since the ink is paler with respect to that of the music.

BIBLIOGRAPHY: ALBRECHT 1959, p. 189; BANKS 1993, I, p. 288; CAO III, p. 445; IGC, p. 466; LOACH 1969, I, p. 307.

177.
REX AUTEM DAVID

fols. 149*v*-150*r*

[Adrian Willaert?]

gna, di - - - - - cens: «Ab - sa - lon

fi - li mi, fi - li mi Ab - sa - lon!

Quis mi - hi tri - bu - at ut e - go mo - ri - ar pro

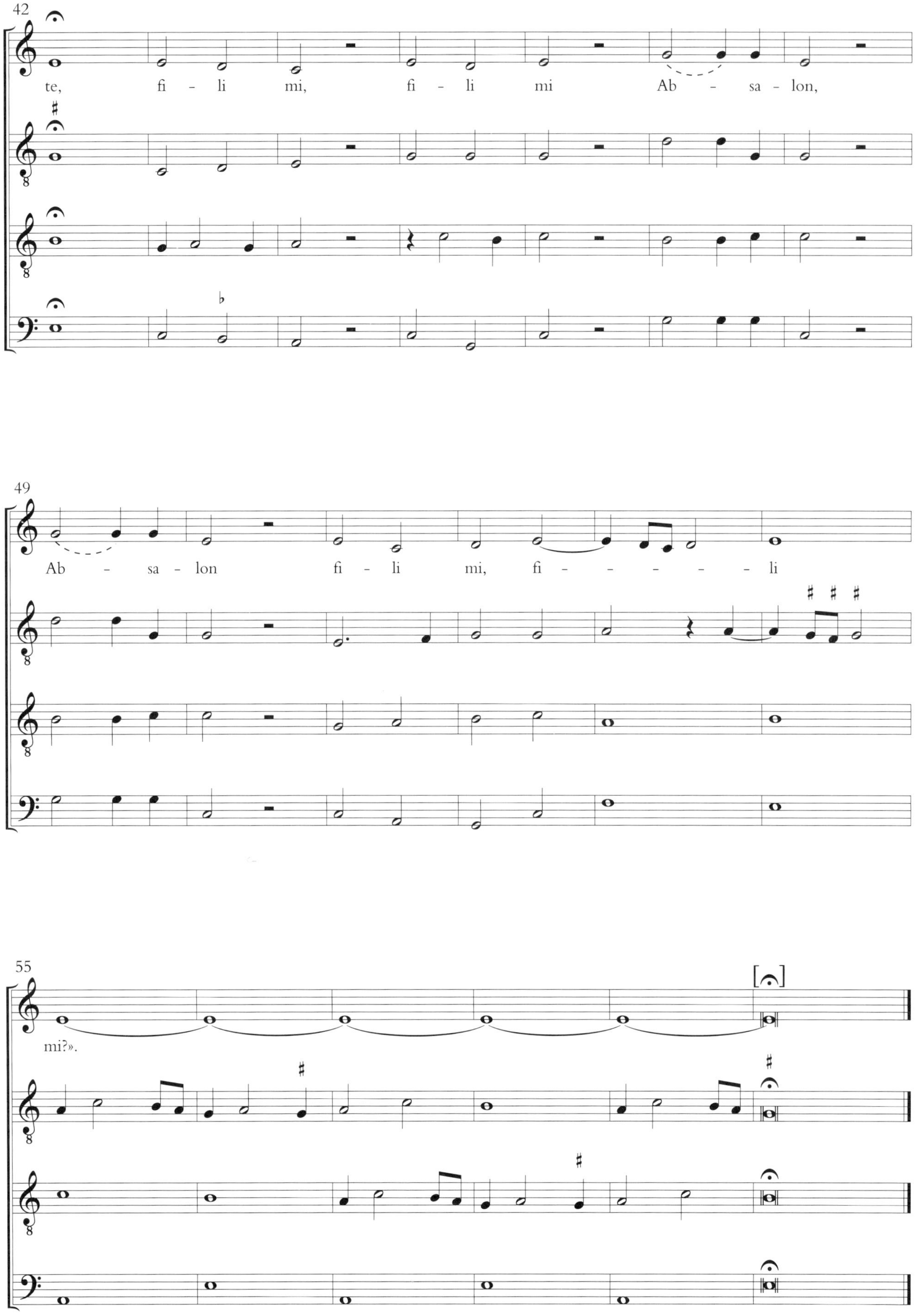
42
te, fi - li mi, fi - li mi Ab - sa - lon,
49
Ab - sa - lon fi - li mi, fi - - - - li
55
mi?».

178.

INCIPIT LAMENTATIO IEREMIE PROPHETE

fols. 150*v*-156*r* (4 vv.)

Incipit lamentatio Ieremie prophete.

ALEPH.
> Quomodo sedet sola civitas plena populo!
Facta est quasi vidua domina gentium,
princeps provinciarum facta est sub tributo.

5 BETH.
> Plorans ploravit in nocte, et lacrime eius in maxillis eius,
non est qui consoletur eam ex omnibus caris eius:
omnes amici eius spreverunt eam, et facti sunt ei inimici.

Ierusalem, Ierusalem, convertere ad Dominum Deum tuum.

GIMEL.
> Migravit Iudas propter afflictionem, et multitudinem servitutis,
10 habitavit inter gentes, nec invenit requiem:
omnes persecutores eius apprehenderunt eam inter angustias.

DALETH.
> Vie Sion lugent, eo quod non sint qui veniant ad solemnitatem:
omnes porte eius destructe, sacerdotes eius gementes,
virgines eius squalide, et ipsa oppressa est amaritudine.

15 Ierusalem, Ierusalem, convertere ad Dominum Deum tuum.

HE.
> Facti sunt hostes eius in capite, inimici illius locuplectati sunt,
quare Dominus locutus est super eam propter multitudinem iniquitatum eius,
parvuli eius ducti sunt in captivitatem ante faciem tribulantis.

VAU.
> Egressus est a filia Sion omnis decor eius:
20 facti sunt principes velut arietes non invenientes pascua
et abierunt absque fortitudine ante faciem subsequentis.

ZAY.
> Recordata est Ierusalem dierum afflictionis sue, et prevaricationis,
omnium desiderabilium suorum, que habuerat a diebus antiquis,
cum caderet populus eius in manu hostili, et non esset auxiliator.

25 Ierusalem, Ierusalem, convertere ad Dominum Deum tuum.

Lamentations of Jeremiah, 1:1-7 (Vulgata, p. 1248) with the last verse incomplete (see the complete text in no. 174), with the added invocation «Ierusalem, Ierusalem, convertere ad Dominum Deum tuum» (also in no. 118).

Commentary on the text:

9	Vulgata gives «Iuda» instead of 'Iudas'
14	Vulgata: «est» lacking
16	Vulgata gives «locupletati» instead of 'locuplectati'
17	Vulgata gives «quia» instead of 'quare'
18	Vulgata gives «captivi» instead of 'in captivitatem'
19	Vulgata gives «et egressus» instead of 'Egressus'
20	Vulgata gives «principes eius» instead of 'principes'
20	Vulgata gives «pascuam» instead of 'pasqua'

Readings emended in the edition:

Bar	Voice	Original
15	B	*longa* without fermata
19	B	*longa* with fermata
34	A	*longa* with fermata
88	S	dot missing after the *g'*
90	A	*longa* with fermata
108	B	*brevis* with fermata
128	T	*f*
128	B	*longa* without fermata
141	S	*brevis* with fermata
145	S	*longa* with fermata
160	S	*brevis* with fermata
after 165	A	the *custos* mistakenly indicates *f'* rather than *d'*
181	A	*brevis* with fermata
188	S, T	*longa* without fermata
194	A, T, B	*brevis* with fermata
213	S	*longa* without fermata
227/II-228/I	B	*e*
247	T	*brevis* with fermata
253	T	*b* flat
270	T	*longa* with fermata
295	B	*longa* with fermata
330	T, B	*longa* with fermata
332	T	superfluous *c' semibrevis* between *c'* and *b*

Modern editions of the music: Massenkeil 1965, pp. 142-148 (after Panc.27).

Remarks: RISM[1] classified this set of Lamentations as three different compositions: I, fols. 150*v*-152*r* (= bb. 1-104); II, fols. 152*v*-154*r* (= bb. 105-229); III, fols. 154*v*-156*r* (= bb. 230-337); instead it comprises one set of Lamentations, from fol. 150*v* to fol. 156*r*. The sections are unified by a number of elements: they are in the same mode (mode 6), the music of the refrain «Ierusalem, Ierusalem, convertere» is the same in all three sections (bb. 91-99/I; 182-190/I; 324-332/I); the music of the five Hebrew letters Aleph, Ghimel, He, Vau, Zain is very similar, as is that for Beth and Daleth.[2]

---

[1]. See RISM B IV/5, p. 150.

[2]. My thanks to Herbert Kellman, whose help has been indispensable in resolving this complicated case.

This set of Lamentations has certainly been copied from a model that is not known, as suggested by the omission of a note (b. 221, Altus), the frequent exchange of *breves* and *longae* with fermatas in cadences, a mistaken *custos* in the Altus (after b. 165), and the erroneous repeated note in the Tenor (b. 332). These Lamentations preserve performance-related indications: frequent lines drawn between syllables and notes (for example, in the Superius at fol. 151*v*, second stave, and fol. 152*v*, second and third staves; in the Altus, fol. 153*r*, second stave, and fol. 156*r*, first stave). After this lengthy composition begins a long section of the manuscript with ruled staves but without music (fols. 156*v*-207*r*).

BIBLIOGRAPHY: CS, pp. 339-342; MASSENKEIL 1965, pp. 7★-9★.

178.
INCIPIT LAMENTATIO IEREMIE PROPHETE

fols. 150*v*-156*r*

[Superius] In – ci – pit la – men – ta – ti – o

[Altus] In – ci – pit la – men – ta – ti – o

[Tenor] In – ci – pit la – men – ta – ti – o

[Bassus] In – ci – pit la – men – ta – ti – o

Ie – re – mi – e pro – phe – te.

Ie – re – mi – e pro – phe – te.

Ie – re – mi – e pro – phe – te.

Ie – re – mi – e pro – phe – te.

A – leph. Quo –

A – leph. Quo – mo –

A – leph. Quo –

A – leph. Quo –

-mo - do se - det so - la ci - vi - tas ple - na po - pu - lo!

- do se - det so - la ci - vi - tas ple - na po - pu - lo!

-mo - do se - det so - la ci - vi - tas ple - na po - pu - lo!

-mo - do se - det so - la ci - vi - tas ple - na po - pu - lo!

Fa - cta est qua - si vi - du - a do - mi - na gen - ti - um,

Fa - cta est qua - si vi - du - a do - mi - na gen - ti - um,

Fa - cta est qua - si vi - du - a do - mi - na gen - ti - um,

Fa - cta est qua - si vi - du - a do - mi - na gen - ti - um,

prin - ceps pro - vin - ci - a - - - - rum fa - cta est

prin - ceps pro - vin - ci - a - - - - rum fa - cta est

prin - ceps pro - vin - ci - a - - - - rum fa - cta est

prin - ceps pro - vin - ci - a - - - - rum fa - cta est

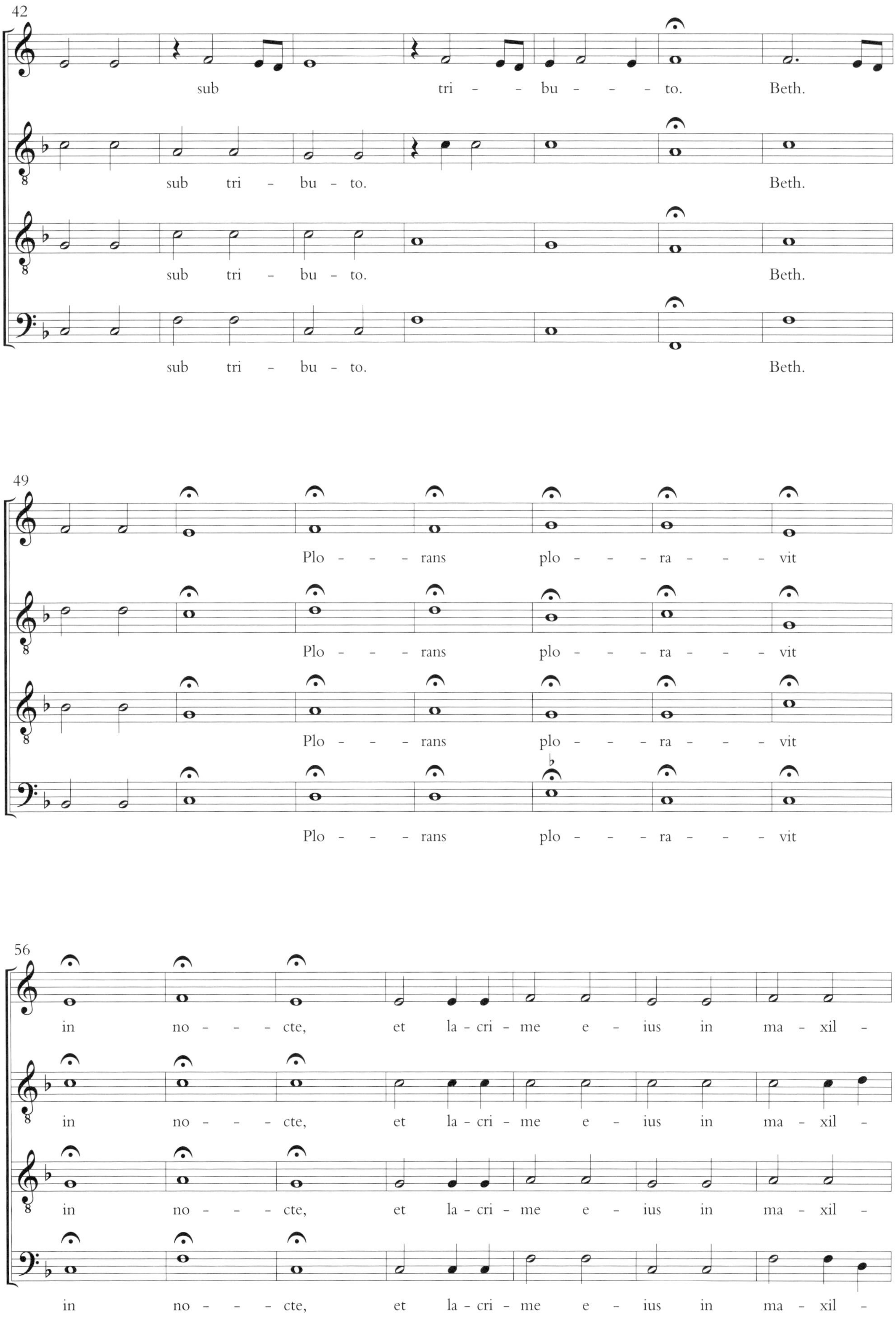
42
sub tri - - bu - - - to. Beth.
sub tri - bu - to. Beth.
sub tri - bu - to. Beth.
sub tri - bu - to. Beth.
49
Plo - - - rans plo - - - ra - - - vit
Plo - - - rans plo - - - ra - - - vit
Plo - - - rans plo - - - ra - - - vit
Plo - - - rans plo - - - ra - - - vit
56
in no - - - cte, et la - cri - me e - ius in ma - xil -
in no - - - cte, et la - cri - me e - ius in ma - xil -
in no - - - cte, et la - cri - me e - ius in ma - xil -
in no - - - cte, et la - cri - me e - ius in ma - xil -

63
-lis e - ius, non est qui con-so - le - tur e - - - - am
-lis e - ius, non est qui con-so - le - tur e - - - - am
-lis e - ius, non est qui con-so - le - tur e - - - - am
-lis e - ius, non est qui con-so - le - tur e - - - - am
70
ex o - mni - bus ca - ris e - ius: o - mnes a - mi - ci
ex o - mni - bus ca - ris e - ius: o - mnes a - mi - ci
ex o - mni - bus ca - ris e - ius: o - mnes a - mi - ci
ex o - mni - bus ca - ris e - ius: o - mnes a - mi - ci
77
e - ius spre - ve - runt e - - - am, et fa - cti sunt e -
e - ius spre - ve - runt e - - - am, et fa - cti sunt e -
e - ius spre - ve - runt e - - - am, et fa - cti sunt e -
e - ius spre - ve - runt e - - - am, et fa - cti sunt e -

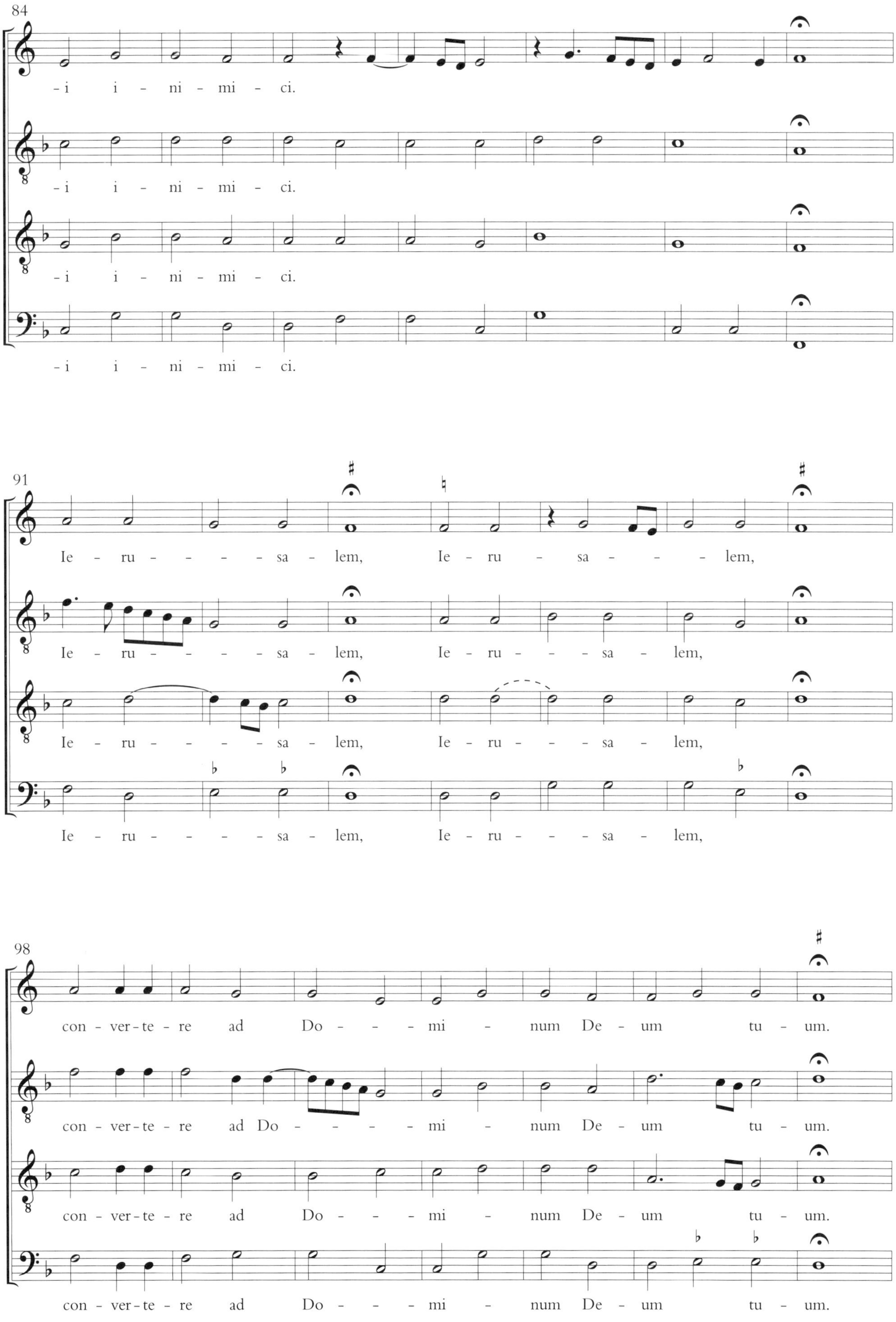
84
-i i - ni - mi - ci.
-i i - ni - mi - ci.
-i i - ni - mi - ci.
-i i - ni - mi - ci.
91
Ie - ru - - - - sa - lem, Ie - ru - sa - - - lem,
Ie - ru - - - - sa - lem, Ie - ru - - - sa - lem,
Ie - ru - - - - sa - lem, Ie - ru - - - sa - lem,
Ie - ru - - - - sa - lem, Ie - ru - - - sa - lem,
98
con - ver - te - re ad Do - - mi - num De - um tu - um.
con - ver - te - re ad Do - - - mi - num De - um tu - um.
con - ver - te - re ad Do - - mi - num De - um tu - um.
con - ver - te - re ad Do - - mi - num De - um tu - um.

105
Gi - - - mel. Mi - gra - vit Iu - das
Gi - - - mel. Mi - gra - vit Iu - das
Gi - - - mel. Mi - gra - vit Iu - das
Gi - - - mel. Mi - gra - vit Iu - das
111
pro - pter af - fli - cti - o - - - nem, et mul - ti - tu - di - nem ser - vi - tu -
pro - pter af - fli - cti - o - - - nem, et mul - ti - tu - di - nem ser - vi - tu -
pro - pter af - fli - cti - o - - - nem, et mul - ti - tu - di - nem ser - vi - tu -
pro - pter af - fli - cti - o - - - nem, et mul - ti - tu - di - nem ser - vi - tu -
118
- tis: ha - bi - ta - vit in - ter gen - - - tes, nec in - - - ve -
- tis: ha - bi - ta - vit in - ter gen - - - tes, nec in - ve - nit
- tis: ha - bi - ta - vit in - ter gen - - - tes, nec in - ve - nit
- tis: ha - bi - ta - vit in - ter gen - - - tes, nec in - ve - nit

125
- - nit re - - - - qui - em: o - mnes per - se - cu - to - res
re - qui - em: o - mnes per - se - cu - to - res
re - qui - em: o - mnes per - se - cu - to - res
re - qui - em: o - mnes per - se - cu - to - res
132
e - ius ap - pre - - hen - de - runt e - am in - ter
e - ius ap - pre - - hen - de - runt e - am in - ter
e - ius ap - pre - - hen - de - runt e - am in - ter an - - -
e - ius ap - pre - - hen - de - runt e - am in - ter an - - -
139
an - - gu - sti - as. Da - - leth.
an - gu - sti - - - as. Da - - - leth.
- - gu - - - sti - - - as. Da - - leth.
- - gu - - - sti - - - as. Da - - leth.

146
Vi - e Si - on lu - - - - - gent, e - o quod non sint
153
qui ve - ni - ant ad so - le - - - - - mni - - - - - ta - - -
160
- tem: o - mnes por - te e - ius de - stru - cte, sa - cer - do -

167
-tes e - ius ge - men - tes, vir - gi - nes e - ius squa - li - de,
-tes e - ius ge - men - tes, vir - gi - nes e - ius squa - li - de,
-tes e - ius ge - men - tes, vir - gi - nes e - ius squa - li - de,
-tes e - - - ius ge-men - tes, vir - gi - nes e - ius squa - li - de,
174
et ip - sa op - pres - - sa est a - ma - ri - tu - - - - diet ip - sa op - pres - - sa est a - ma - ri - tu - - - di - - -
et ip - sa op - pres - - sa est a - ma - ri - tu - - - di - - -
et ip - sa op - pres - - sa est a - ma - ri - tu - - - di - - -
181
-ne. Ie - ru - - - sa - lem, Ie - ru - sa-lem,
-ne. Ie - ru - - - sa - lem, Ie - ru - sa - lem,
-ne. Ie - ru - - - sa - lem, Ie - ru - sa - lem,
-ne. Ie - ru - - - sa - lem, Ie - ru - sa - lem,

188
con - ver - te - re ad Do - - - mi - num De - um tu - um.
con - ver - te - re ad Do - - - mi - num De - um tu - um.
con - ver - te - re ad Do - - - mi - num De - um tu - um.
con - ver - te - re ad Do - - - mi - num De - um tu - um.
195
He. Fa - - - cti sunt ho - stes
He. Fa - - - cti sunt ho - stes e -
He. Fa - - - cti sunt ho - stes
He. Fa - - - cti sunt ho - stes
202
e - - - ius in ca - pi - te, i - ni - mi - ci il - li -
- - - ius in ca - pi - te, i - ni - mi - ci il - li -
e - - - ius in ca - pi - te, i - ni - mi - ci il - li -
e - - - ius in ca - pi - te, i - ni - mi - ci il - li -

209
-us lo - cu - ple - - - cta - ti sunt, qua - re Do - mi - nus
-us lo - cu - ple - - - cta - - - ti sunt, qua - re Do - mi - nus
-us lo - cu - ple - - - cta - - - ti sunt, qua - re Do - mi - nus
-us lo - cu - ple - - - cta - - - ti sunt, qua - re Do - mi - nus
216
lo - cu - tus est su - per e - - - - am
lo - cu - tus est su - - - per e - - - am
lo - cu - tus est su - per e - - - - am
lo - cu - tus est su - per e - - - - am
223
pro - pter mul - ti - tu - di - nem i - ni - qui - ta - tum e - - - - - - ius,
pro - pter mul - ti - tu - di - nem i - ni - qui - ta - tum e - - - - - ius,
pro - pter mul - ti - tu - di - nem i - ni - qui - ta - tum e - - - - - - ius,
pro - pter mul - ti - tu - di - nem i - ni - qui - ta - tum e - - - - - - ius,

230
par - vu - li e - ius du - cti sunt in ca - pti - vi - - - ta -
par - vu - li e - ius du - cti sunt in ca - pti - - - vi - ta -
par - vu - li e - ius du - cti sunt in ca - pti - - - vi - ta -
par - vu - li e - ius du - cti sunt in ca - pti - vi - - - ta -
237
- - tem an - te fa - ci - em tri - bu - lan - - - - - - - - - -
- - tem an - te fa - ci - em tri - bu - lan - - - tis.
- - tem an - te fa - ci - em tri - bu - lan - - - - - - - - - -
- - tem an - te fa - ci - em tri - bu - lan - - - tis.
244
- tis. Vau. E - gres-sus est
Vau. E - gres-sus est
- tis. Vau. E - gres-sus est
Vau. E - gres-sus est

251
a fi - li - a Si - on o - mnis de - - - cor e - ius:
a fi - li - a Si - on o - mnis de - cor e - ius:
a fi - li - a Si - on o - mnis de - - - cor e - ius:
a fi - li - a Si - on o - mnis de - - - cor e - ius:
259
fa - cti sunt prin - ci - - pes ve - lut a - ri - e - tes
fa - cti sunt prin - ci - - pes ve - - lut a - ri - e - tes
fa - cti sunt prin - - - ci - pes ve - - lut a - ri - e - tes
fa - cti sunt prin - ci - - pes ve - - lut a - ri - e - tes
267
non in - ve - ni - en - tes pa - scu - a: et a - bi - e - runt ab - sque
non in - ve - ni - en - tes pa - scu - a: et a - bi - e - runt ab - sque
non in - ve - ni - en - tes pa - scu - a: et a - bi - e - runt ab - sque
non in - ve - ni - en - tes pa - scu - a: et a - bi - e - runt ab - sque

274
for - ti - tu - di - ne an - te fa - ci - em sub - se - - - quen - - - - -
for - ti - tu - di - ne an - te fa - ci - em sub - se - quen - - - tis.
for - ti - tu - di - ne an - te fa - ci - em sub - se - quen - - - - - -
for - ti - tu - di - ne an - te fa - ci - em sub - se - - - quen - tis.
281
- - - - - tis. Zay. Re - cor - da - ta est Ie -
Zay. Re - cor - da - ta est Ie -
- - - - - tis. Zay. Re - cor - da - ta est Ie -
Zay. Re - cor - da - ta est Ie -
289
- ru - sa - lem di - e - rum af - fli - cti - o - nis su - - - - e, et pre -
- ru - sa - lem di - e - rum af - fli - cti - o - nis su - - - - e, et pre -
- ru - sa - lem di - e - rum af - fli - cti - o - nis su - - - - e, et pre -
- ru - sa - lem di - e - rum af - fli - cti - o - nis su - - - - e, et pre -

297
-va-ri-ca-ti-o-nis, o-mni-um de-si-de-ra-bi-li-um su-
-va-ri-ca-ti-o-nis, o-mni-um de-si-de-ra-bi-li-um su-
-va-ri-ca-ti-o-nis, o-mni-um de-si-de-ra-bi-li-um su-
-va-ri-ca-ti-o-nis, o-mni-um de-si-de-ra-bi-li-um su-
304
-o-rum, que ha-bu-e-rat a di-e-bus an-ti-quis, cum ca-de-
-o-rum, que ha-bu-e-rat a di-e-bus an-ti-quis, cum ca-de-
-o-rum, que ha-bu-e-rat a di-e-bus an-ti-quis, cum ca-de-
-o-rum, que ha-bu-e-rat a di-e-bus an-ti-quis, cum ca-de-
311
-ret po-pu-lus e-ius in ma-nu ho-sti-li, et non
-ret po-pu-lus e-ius in ma-nu ho-sti-li, et non
-ret po-pu-lus e-ius in ma-nu ho-sti-li, et non
-ret po-pu-lus e-ius in ma-nu ho-sti-li, et non

es – set au – xi – li – – a – – – – – – tor.   Ie – ru –

es – set au – xi – li – a – tor.   Ie – ru –

es – set au – xi – li – – a – – – – – tor.   Ie – ru –

es – set au – xi – li – a – tor.   Ie – ru –

– – sa – lem,   Ie – ru – sa – lem,   con – ver – te –

– – sa – lem,   Ie – ru – sa – lem,   con – ver – te –

– – sa – lem,   Ie – ru – sa – lem,   con – ver – te –

– – sa – lem,   Ie – ru – sa – lem,   con – ver – te –

– re ad Do – – mi – num De – um tu – – – um.

– re ad Do – – mi – num De – um tu – – um.

– re ad Do – – mi – num De – um tu – – um.

– re ad Do – – mi – num De – um tu – – um.

179.

Tuto el mundo è fantasia

fols. 207*v*–208*r* (4 vv.)

[Jo(hannes?) Hesdimois]

Tuto el mundo è fantasia,
e ciascun‹o› segue suo lege;
ogi questa impera et rege,
de seguirlla ognun desia.

5   L'uno cerca ‹d'›esser‹e› lodatto,
e [più] d'altro non si cura;
l'altro va tuto adombratto,
e 'l pensier d'altri misura.

Italian secular piece (barzelletta).

Commentary on the text:

2	hypermetric; corrected according to the two concordant sources
4	corrected according to the two concordant sources
5	hypermetric; corrected according to AntCanzoni
6	hypometric; corrected according to the two concordant sources

Readings emended in the edition:

Bar	Voice	Original
20/II	A	flat before *a'*, perhaps an oversight of the copyist, who intended it to apply to the following *b'*
32	A	*longa*
38	S, A, T	*longa*
43/II	T	*f'* changed to *d'* to avoid parallel octaves with the B
46/II–54	B	at *a* begins a section that was struck out, then recopied with a few graphic variants
48/III	B	the second *d* is erroneously blackened
51/II	A	*c' minima*

Textual concordances (mss): • *Man.C. 4* (141*v*–142*r*)[1]

Musical concordances (prints): • AntCanzoni (2*v*–3*r*), «Io. Hesdimois»

---

[1]. In the first and third stanzas the second line is in fact in the place of the third.

TEXT FROM AntCanzoni:

> Tucto il mundo è fantasia,
> et ciascun segue sua legge;
> ogi questa impera et regge,
> de seguirla ognun desia.

5   L'uno cerca esser lodato,
     et più d'altro non se cura;
     l'altro va tutto adombrato,
     e 'l pensier d'altri mesura.
     Tal è, poi che non ha cura
10   né de altrui, né de sua via.
          Tucto il mundo è fantasia.

     Questo il gioco molto apreza,
     quello i dati,[2] questo carte,
     l'altro i scacchi, e il resto spreza,
     questo Baccho, l'altro Marte.
15   Cusì ognun dal ver si parte
     sequitando sua pazia.
          Tucto […]

     Chi di bianco et chi di nero,
     chi de azuro al fin si veste,
     chi dilecta il segno intero,
20   chi del quadro fa gran feste.
     Però son le voglie preste
     de seguir la lor follia.
          Tucto […]

MODERN EDITIONS OF THE TEXT: FILOCAMO 2000, pp. 161-162 (after Panc.27).

REMARKS: This piece and the following one are the only ones copied by Scribe B, who was certainly less skilled in music and rather careless in its presentation. It is interesting that he chose the last leaves of the penultimate fascicle (XXVI) of the manuscript, which was preceded by five quaternions (XXI-XXV) on which staves had been drawn but no music entered, as well as the second half of XX and the first three quarters of XXVI. After this Scribe A returns, leaving only the second half of fascicle XXVII empty. That Scribe B is less expert than his colleague can also be shown by the very Italian designation of the vocal parts (in *Tuto el mundo è fantasia* he gives «Soprano», «Alto», «Tinor[e]»; in *Di pensier in pensier, di monte in monte* he gives «Soprano», «Alto», «Tinore», «Basso»). The text, written in an ugly cursive mercantile script, is difficult to read in both pieces. The version of the music of *Tuto el mundo è fantasia* in AntCanzoni is very close to that of Panc.27: the two versions differ in minor variants, some of which are errors of the Panc.27 scribe. It is highly likely that the scribe copied this piece directly from Antico's publication, dated 9 October 1510 (the conjunctive error of b. 43/II also supports this hypothesis); the reverse is less likely since Panc.27 has less text.

BIBLIOGRAPHY: EINSTEIN 1951.

---

2. «dati» stands for 'dadi'.

179.
TUTO EL MUNDO È FANTASIA

fols. *207v-208r*

[Jo(hannes?) Hesdimois]

Tu-to el mun - do è fan - ta - si - a, e cia - scun se -

- gue suo le - ge. O - gi que - sta im - pe - ra et re - ge, de se - guir -

- lla o - gnun de - si - a, *de se - guir - lla* o - gnun de - si -

L'u-no cer - - - ca es-ser lo-dat - - - to, e [più] d'al - - -
l'al-tro va tu-to a - dom-brat - - - to, e 'l pen - sier

-tro non si - cu - ra;
d'al - tri mi - su - ra.

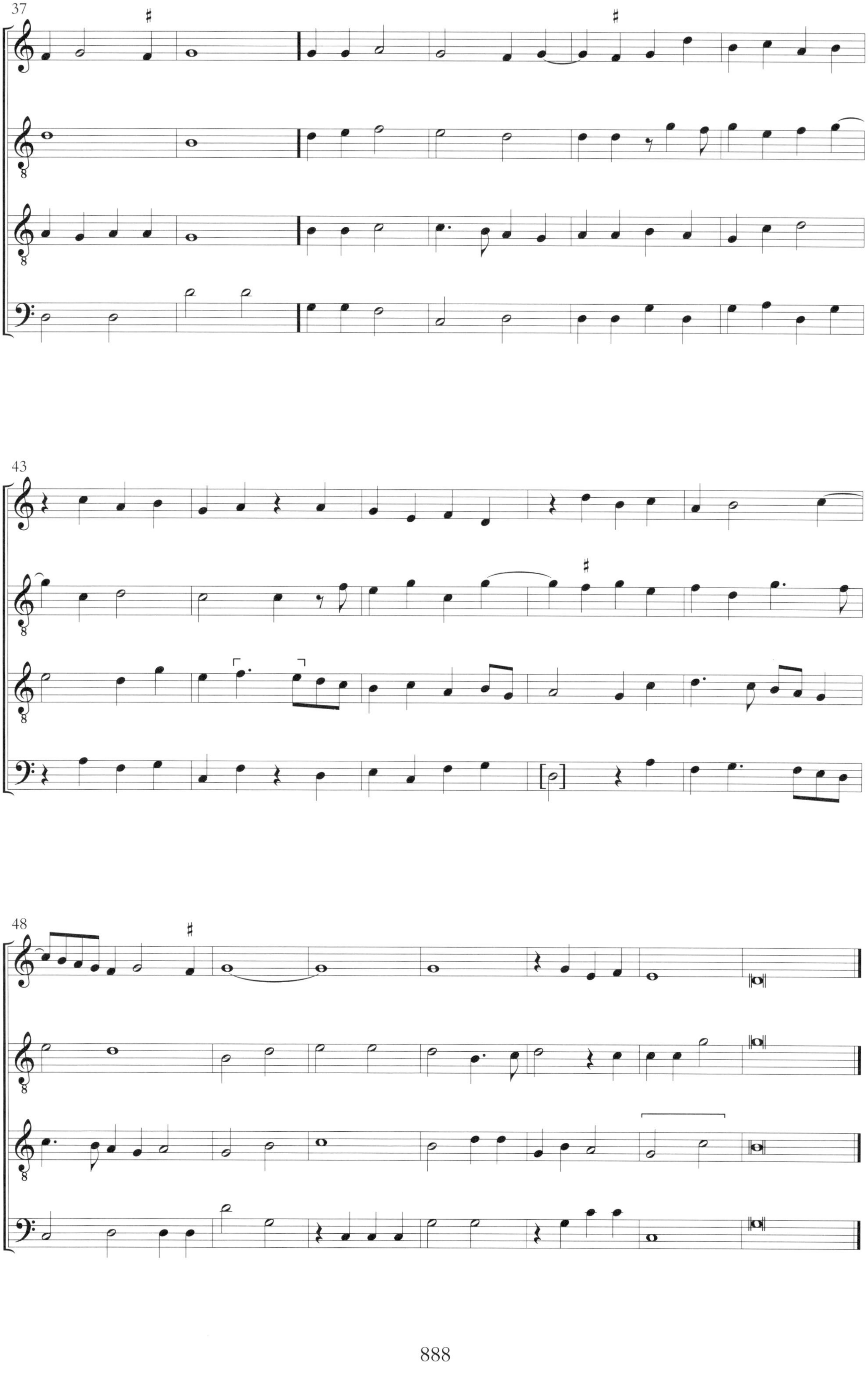
37
43
48

180.

Di pensier in pensier, di monte in monte

fols. 208*v*-209*r* (4 vv.)

[Francesco Petrarca]

Di pensier in pensier, di monte in monte,
mi guida Amore, ch'ogni segnato calle
provo contrario alla tranquilla vita.
Se 'n solitaria piagia, rivo o fonte,
5   se 'n fra duo pogi siede ombrosa valle,
ivi s'aquetta l'alma sbigotitta;
e come Amor l'envitta,
or ride, or piange, or teme, or s'asecura;
e 'l volto che 'llei segue ov'ella el mena
10 se turba e raserena,
e im un eser‹e› piciol tempo dura;
onde alla vista om di tal vita 'sperto
dirìa: «Questo arde e di suo stato è incerto».

First stanza of a canzone of five stanzas, no. 129 of Petrarch's *Rerum vulgarium fragmenta* (*Canzoniere*).[1]

Commentary on the text:

| 2 | hypermetric |
| 11 | hypermetric; corrected according to AntCanzoni |

Readings emended in the edition:

Bar	Voice	Original
28/II	B	*minima*
29/II	B	*a semibrevis*
55	T	*f' semibrevis* instead of dotted *minima*

Textual concordances (mss):[2] • *CV. Ch.176* (66r-v), (Francesco Petrarca) • *CV. VL.3195* (29r-v), (Francesco Petrarca)

---

[1]. The canzone was written at Selvapiana in 1341-42 or, more likely, in 1344-45 (see Bigi 1983). It already formed part of a primitive redaction of the *Canzoniere* (lost), destined among others for Azzo da Correggio, datable to 1356-58.

[2]. The manuscript tradition of Petrarch's *Canzoniere* begins with the MS *CV. Ch.176*: a preliminary redaction in Boccaccio's hand (ca. 1363), it was limited to only 204 poems; among other manuscripts showing intermediate recensions and authorial variants, *CV. VL.3195* is considered instead as the basis for the definitive version (*Francisci Petrarche laureati poete Rerum vulgarium fragmenta*), largely copied by Petrarch's personal scribe, Giovanni Malpaghini (1366-67), and added to in several stages by the poet himself, up to the year of his death. The successive manuscript diffusion — in the form of complete or partial copies, or even of single pieces — was enormous, and even today not under complete control (see the series *Censimento dei codici petrarcheschi*, Padua, Antenore, 1964-, in progress).

Textual concordances (prints):[3] • *Petr1470* (56*v*-57*v*), (Francesco Petrarca)

Musical concordances (prints): • AntCanzoni (34*v*-35*r*)

Text from *CV.VL.3195*:

Di pensier in pensier, di monte in monte
mi guida Amor, ch'ogni segnato calle
provo contrario a la tranquilla vita.
Se 'n solitaria piaggia, rivo o fonte,
5   se 'n fra duo poggi siede ombrosa valle,
ivi s'acqueta l'alma sbigottita;
et come Amor l'envita,
or ride, or piange, or teme, or s'assecura;
e 'l volto che lei segue ov'ella il mena
10   si turba et rasserena,
et in un esser picciol tempo dura;
onde a la vista uom di tal vita experto
dirìa: «Questo arde, et di suo stato è incerto».

Per alti monti et per selve aspre trovo
15   qualche riposo: ogni abitato loco
è nemico mortal degli occhi miei.
A ciascun passo nasce un penser novo
de la mia donna, che sovente in gioco
gira 'l tormento ch'i' porto per lei;
20   et a pena vorrei
cangiar questo mio viver dolce amaro
ch'i' dico: «Forse ancor ti serva Amore
ad un tempo migliore;
forse, a te stesso vile, altrui se' caro».
25   Et in questa trapasso sospirando:
«Or porrebbe esser vero? or come? or quando?».

Ove porge ombra un pino alto od un colle
talor m'arresto, et pur nel primo sasso
disegno co' la mente il suo bel viso.
30   Poi ch'a me torno, trovo il petto molle
de la pietate, et alor dico: «Ahi lasso,
dove se' giunto! et onde se' diviso!».
Ma mentre tener fiso
posso al primo pensier la mente vaga,
35   et mirar lei, et obliar me stesso,
sento Amor sì da presso
che del suo proprio error l'alma s'appaga:
in tante parte et sì bella la veggio
che, se l'error durasse, altro non cheggio.

40   I' l'ho più volte (or chi fia che mi 'l creda?)
ne l'acqua chiara et sopra l'erba verde
veduto viva, et nel troncon d'un faggio

---

3. The printed tradition of Petrarch's *Canzoniere* (often joined with the *Trionfi*) begins very early, starting with *Petr1470* (which nevertheless has a different order of pieces from the definitive one) and continuing on the average of almost one print per year up to the middle of the sixteenth century, with no fewer than twenty-nine incunables (for a detailed list, see Ley et al. 2002).

e 'n bianca nube, sì fatta che Leda
avria ben detto che sua figlia perde,
45   come stella che 'l sol copre col raggio;
et quanto in più selvaggio
loco mi trovo e 'n più deserto lido,
tanto più bella il mio pensier l'adombra.
Poi quando il vero sgombra
50   quel dolce error, pur lì medesmo assido
me freddo, pietra morta in pietra viva,
in guisa d'uom che pensi et pianga et scriva.

Ove d'altra montagna ombra non tocchi,
verso 'l maggiore e 'l più expedito giogo
55   tirar mi suol un desiderio intenso;
indi i miei danni a misurar con gli occhi
comincio (e 'ntanto lagrimando sfogo
di dolorosa nebbia il cor condenso)
alor ch'i' miro et penso
60   quanta aria dal bel viso mi diparte,
che sempre m'è sì presso et sì lontano.
Poscia fra me pian piano:
«Che sai tu, lasso? forse in quella parte
or di tua lontanança si sospira;
65   et in questo penser l'alma respira».

Canzone, oltra quell'alpe,
là dove il ciel è più sereno et lieto,
mi rivedrai sovr'un ruscel corrente,
ove l'aura si sente
70   d'un fresco et odorifero laureto.
Ivi è 'l mio cor, et quella che 'l m'invola;
qui veder pôi l'imagine mia sola.

MODERN EDITIONS OF THE TEXT: BETTARINI 2005, pp. 623-633; CONTINI 1949, pp. 129-132; CONTINI 1964,[4] pp. 179-181; CONTINI 2004, pp. 129-132; FILOCAMO 2000, pp. 162-163 (after Panc.27); LEVI 1905, pp. 69-71; SANTAGATA 1996, pp. 625-634; SANTAGATA 2004, pp. 631-640.

MODERN EDITIONS OF THE MUSIC: DISERTORI 1964, pp. 133-136 (after AntCanzoni).

REMARKS: In this case too the version of Panc.27 is extremely close to that of the only known musical concordance: between the two there are only slight graphic differences, but some aspects connect them unequivocally. The passsages added to the modern edition have been taken from the version of AntCanzoni. Such necessary adjustments reveal Scribe B's habits in copying from the printed source (see also the Remarks to no. 179). Proof is based principally on the fact that in Antico's print the section between bars 17 and 32 (which repeats bb. 1-16) is written out in full in the Soprano, Alto, and Basso, whereas in the «Tinore» (sic) the repeat is indicated only with a ritornello sign; the scribe of Panc.27 copies pedantically from his model, AntCanzoni, but forgets to place the ritornello sign at the end of bar 16 of the «Tinore». Moreover, in Antico's print there is more poetic text, which is a further confirmation of the direction in the process of copying.[5]

---

[4]. With numerous misprints, corrected sporadically in successive reprintings after that of 1973.

[5]. I thank Marco Beghelli, who helped me to sort out the textual tradition of the poem and its bibliography.

BIBLIOGRAPHY: AGOSTI 1993, pp. 62-67; ANTONETTI 1964; BERTONE 1999, pp. 103-107; BIGI 1983; DIONISOTTI 1974, p. 84; DISERTORI 1964, pp. 38; EINSTEIN 1951; FUBINI (1962) 1975, pp. 247-254; GANTERT 2000; LANYI 1979; PRIZER 1985, pp. 17, 20-22; PRIZER 1986, p. 30; PRIZER 1991, pp. 13-15; STIERLE 1989.

180.

Di pensier in pensier, di monte in monte

fols. 208v-209r

[Francesco Petrarca]

Di pen - sier in pen - sier, di mon-te in mon -

- te, mi gui-da A - mo - re, ch'o-gni se-gna - to cal - le pro-vo con-tra-rio al -

- la tran-quil - la vi - ta. Se 'n so - li - ta - ria pia - gia, ri-vo o fon -

22
-te, se 'n fra duo po - - - gi sie - de om - bro - sa val - le, i - vi s'a - quet - ta
30
l'al - ma sbi - go - tit - ta; e co - me A - mor l'en - vit - ta, or ri - de, or pian - ge, or te - me, or
37
s'a - - - - se - cu - ra; e 'l vol - to che •llei se - gue o - v'el - la el me - na se tur - ba e

ra - se - re - na,   e im un e - ser pi - ciol tem - po du - ra;   on -

- - de al - la vi - - sta om di tal vi - ta 'sper - to di - rìa: «Que -

- sto ar-de e di suo sta-to è in - - cer - - - - to».

181.

Requiem eternam dona eis, Domine

fols. 209*v*–210*r* (4 vv.)

Requiem eternam dona eis, Domine,
et lux perpetua luceat eis.
Te decet [h]imnus, Deus, in Sion.
Et tibi reddetur votum in Ierusalem.
5   Exaudi orationem meam,
ad te omnis caro veniet.

Introit for the Requiem Mass (GR, p. 95★; LU, p. 1807; MR [*Commune Sanctorum*], fols. 41*r*, 42*r*, 43*r*, 43*v*).

Readings emended in the edition:

Bar	Voice	Original
12	C	*d′*
62	T	*longa* with fermata
84/II	C	*e′*

Modern editions of the music: Banks 1993, II, pp. 167-169 (after Panc.27).

Remarks: The final section of the manuscript begins here, marked by the return of Scribe A, who reappears after an interruption of more than fifty folios. This section is written with a much darker ink compared with that used by Scribe B. In this Requiem the many ligatures are not interpretable as such, but rather as a grouping of notes of equal value to which single syllables are underlaid. The chant in GR, p. 95★ and LU, p. 1807 is used in the Tenor. See also no. 182.

Bibliography: Banks 1993, I, pp. 287-288; Filocamo 2009c; IGC, p. 364.

181.
REQUIEM ETERNAM DONA EIS, DOMINE
fols. *209v-210r*

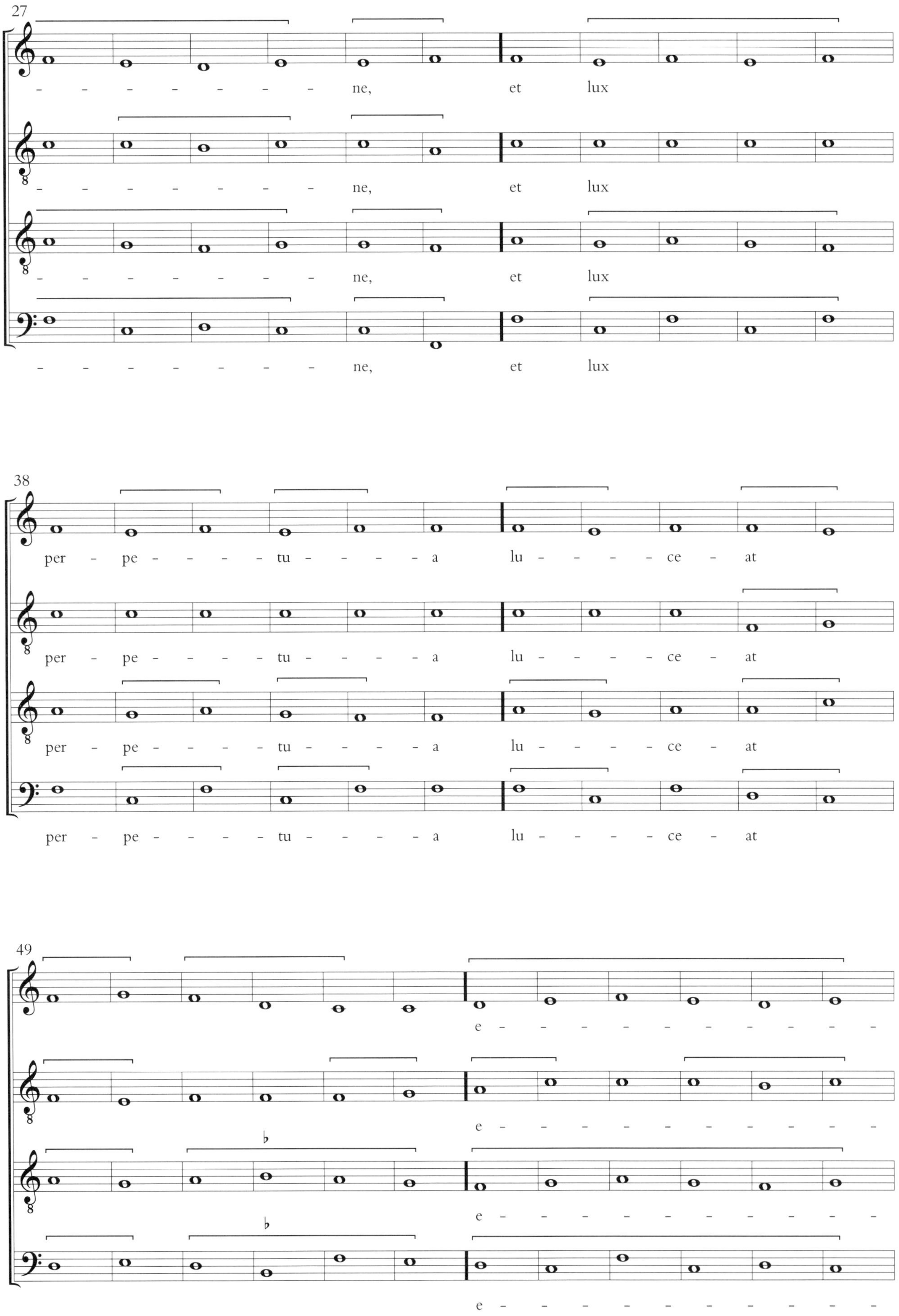
27
- - - - - - - ne, et lux
- - - - - - - ne, et lux
- - - - - - - ne, et lux
- - - - - - - ne, et lux
38
per - pe - - - - tu - - - - a lu - - - - ce - at
per - pe - - - - tu - - - - a lu - - - - ce - at
per - pe - - - - tu - - - - a lu - - - - ce - at
per - pe - - - - tu - - - - a lu - - - - ce - at
49
e - - - - - - - - - - -
e - - - - - - - - - - -
e - - - - - - - - - - -
e - - - - - - - - - - -

61
- is.
- is.
- is. Te de - - - cet [h]i - mnus, De - us, in Si - on.
- is.
73
Et ti - bi red - de - tur vo - tum in Ie - ru - sa - lem. E - xau -
Et ti - bi red - de - tur vo - tum in Ie - ru - sa - lem. E - xau -
Et ti - bi red - de - tur vo - tum in Ie - ru - sa - lem. E - xau -
Et ti - bi red - de - tur vo - tum in Ie - ru - sa - lem. E - xau -
80
- - di o - ra - tio-nem me - am, ad te o - mnis ca - ro ve - ni - et.
- - di o - ra - tio-nem me - am, ad te o - mnis ca - ro ve - ni - et.
- - di o - ra - tio-nem me - am, ad te o - mnis ca - ro ve - ni - et.
- - di o - ra - tio-nem me - am, ad te o - mnis ca - ro ve - ni - et.

182.

Kyrie eleison

fols. 210*v*-211*r* (4 vv.)

Kyrie eleison,
Christe eleison,
Kyrie [e]leison.

Kyrie of the Requiem Mass (see Remarks).

COMMENTARY ON THE TEXT:

1   eleison] leyson A, B
2   eleison] leyson A, B

REMARKS: That this *Kyrie* is clearly connected with the Requiem no. 181 is proved by the melody of the Tenor, which is the chant of the Kyrie of the Mass for the Dead (GR, p. 95★, LU, p. 1807). Over the very long ligature at the end of the Tenor the scribe has placed a series of 2s almost over every note: I think it is an indication with a view towards performance, to allow the singers to calculate exactly the value of every note.

BIBLIOGRAPHY: FILOCAMO 2009c; IGC, p. 254.

182.
Kyrie eleison
fols. 210*v*-211*r*

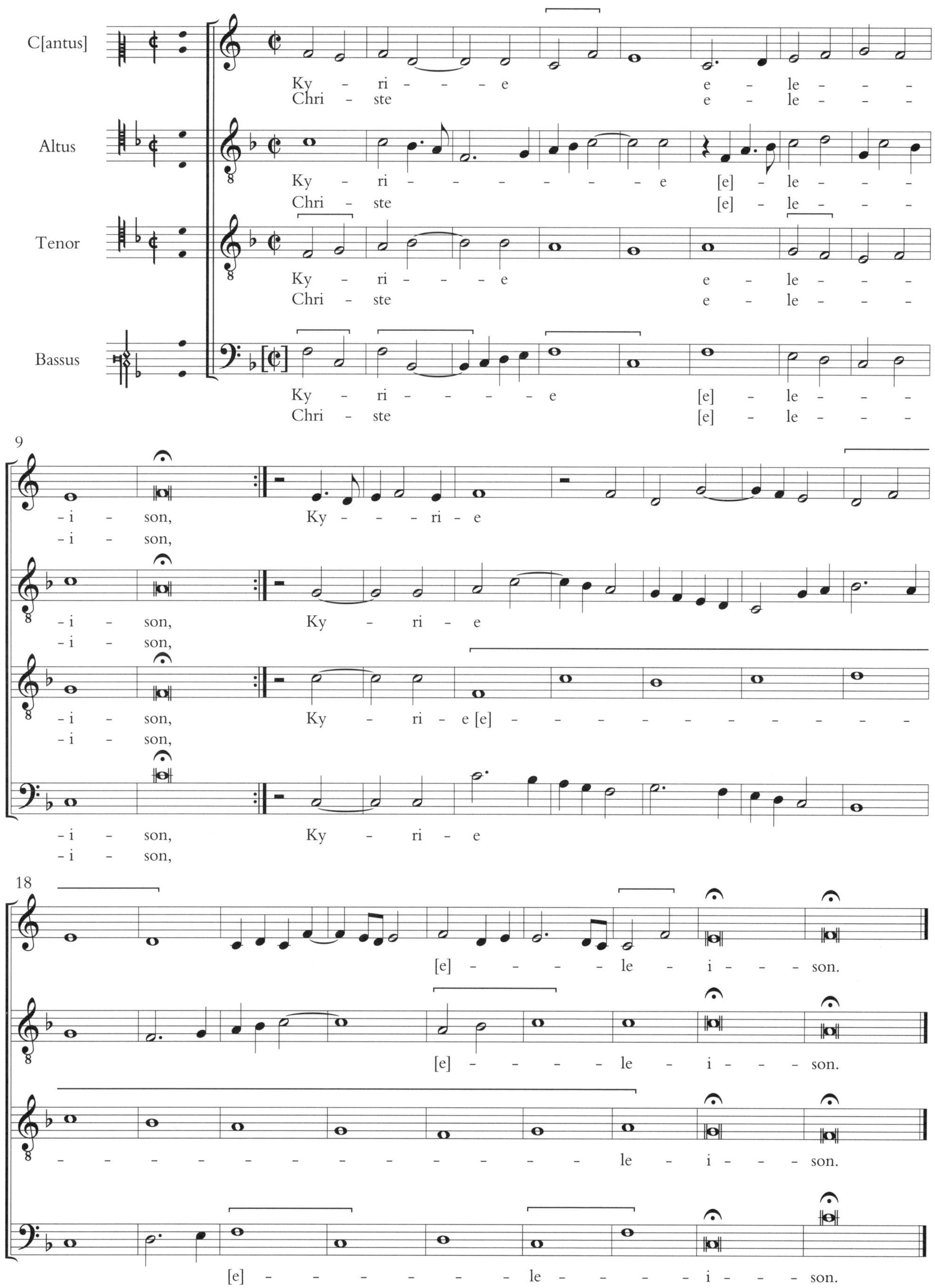

183.

Amen

fols. 210*v*-211*r* (2 vv.?)

Amen.

Amen of the Sequence of the Requiem Mass (see Remarks).

Readings emended in the edition:

Bar	Voice	Original
6	[?]	*B*
6	B	*f*

Remarks: Folios 210*v*-211*r* contain also a *Kyrie* 'pro defunctis' for four voices (no. 182), the three sections of *Libera me, Domine* for two voices (no. 184), and the beginning of the sequence *Dies ire* for two voices (no. 185). The Tenor of the *Amen* (no. 183) uses the chant of the «Amen» that concludes the monodic sequence *Dies irae* (GR, pp. 97★-100★: 100★ and LU, pp. 1810-1813: 1813).[1] It is not out of the question that the four voices of this *Amen* are to be read as four-voice polyphony: given the chant in the Tenor, one might hypothesize that the scribe-composer wished to experiment with various polyphonic combinations applicable at the end of no. 185. In fact, while the combination of the four voices is rather clumsy (also since all voices are in a low register), it is more manageable to place each voice individually with the Tenor, thus producing three *bicinia*. If so, the question would remain open about the placement of this *Amen* on fols. 210*v*-211*r*, instead of at the end of the sequence no. 185 (fols. 211*v*-212*r*).

Bibliography: Filocamo 2009c.

---

[1]. I thank Bonnie Blackburn, who identified the *Amen*.

183.
AMEN
fols. 210*v*–211*r*

184.

(Libera me, Domine)
Tremens factus sum ego
Dies illa, dies ire
Requiem eternam

fols. 210*v*–211*r* (2 vv.)

Tremens factus sum ego, et timeo
dum discusio venerit, atque ventura ira.

Dies illa, dies ire,
calamitatis et miserie,
5   dies magna et amara valde.

Requiem eternam dona eis, Domine,
et lux perpetua luceat eis.

For the text see no. 135. Here, the three sections follow the standard order.

Musical concordances (mss): • Panc.27 (103*v*), *Dies illa, dies ire / Tremens factus sum ego / Requiem eternam*, with the voices exchanged

Modern editions of the music: Banks 1993, II, pp. 72-74 (after Panc.27).

Remarks: See the Remarks to no. 135. With respect to the writing of the music, the ink used for the text is mostly lighter.

Bibliography: Banks 1993, I, pp. 272-273; Filocamo 2009c.

184.
(Libera me, Domine)
Tremens factus sum ego
Dies illa, dies ire
Requiem eternam
fols. 210*v*–211*r*

33
et a - ma - - - - - - - - - - - - ra val - - - de.
et a - ma - ra, et a-ma - ra val - - - - de.
Re - - - - qui - em e - - - ter - - - nam do - - -
Re - - - - qui - em e - - - ter - - - nam do - - -
46
- na e - - - is, Do - - - mi - - - - - - - ne,
- - na e - - - is, Do - - - mi - - - - - - - ne,
53
et lux per - pe-tu-a lu - ce - at e - - - is.
et lux per - pe - tu - a lu-ce - at e - - - is.

185.

Dies ire, dies illa

fols. 210v-212r (2 vv.)

Dies ire, dies illa,
solvet seclum in favilla
teste David cum Sibilla.

For the text see no. 39.

Readings emended in the edition:

Bar	Voice	Original
after 41	B$_2$	bar line missing
between 54 and 55	B$_2$	superfluous *f brevis*
55/II	B$_1$	*brevis*
68/II	B$_2$	*f*

Modern editions of the text: AH 54, pp. 269-270.

Modern editions of the music: Banks 1993, II, p. 75 (after Panc.27, bb. 1-18 only).

Remarks: Heretofore it has always been thought that bars 19 ff. were a separate piece. Instead, that section is a continuation of the sequence *Dies ire, dies illa* (GR, pp. 97★-100★ and LU, pp. 1810-1813): in fact, bars 1-18 of the Bassus II carry the chant of the first two strophes («Dies irae» and «Quantus tremor»), bars 19-41 of the Bassus I have the chant of the third and fourth strophes («Tuba mirum» and «Mors stupebit»), bars 42-64 of the Bassus II have the chant of the fifth and sixth strophes («Liber scriptus» and «Judex ergo»), and bars 65-79 of the Bassus I have the chant of the eighteenth strophe («Lacrimosa»). Furthermore, from a graphical point of view, the copyist began to write the Bassus I of the *Tuba mirum* section at the end of fol. 210v (following the last bar of the *Dies ire* section). He then struck out this beginning and rewrote it on fol. 211v, placing the clef and notes a third lower (though keeping the same pitch).

Bibliography: Banks 1993, I, p. 273; Chevalier I, no. 4626; Filocamo 2009c.

185.
DIES IRE, DIES ILLA
fols. 210v–212r

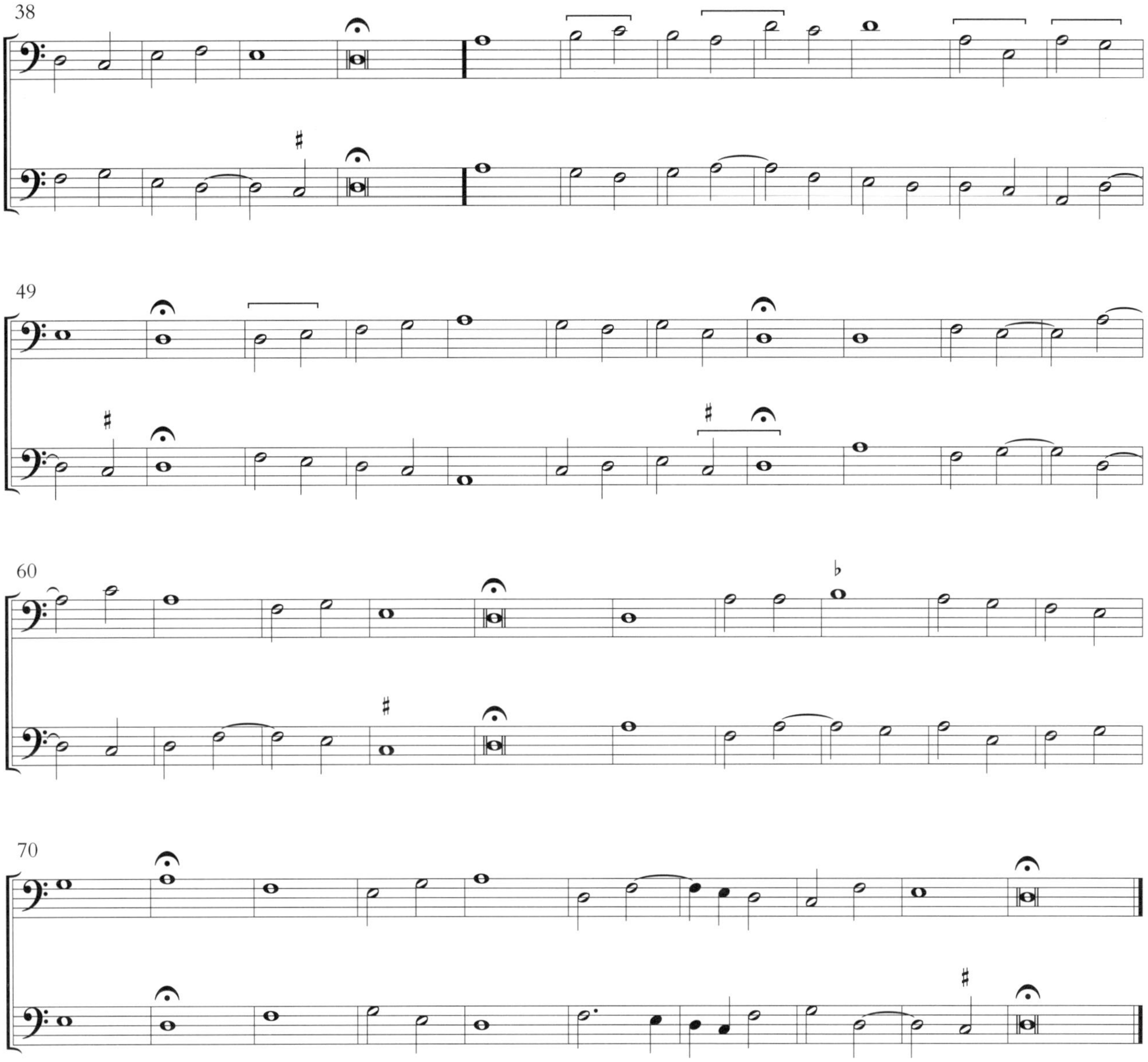
38
49
60
70

186.

DIES IRE, DIES ILLA

fols. 212v-213r (4 vv.)

Dies ire, dies illa,
solvet seclum in favilla
teste David cum Sibilla.

Quid sum miser

Qui Mariam

For the text see no. 39.

COMMENTARY ON THE TEXT:

3   Sibilla] Sibbilla B

READINGS EMENDED IN THE EDITION:

BAR	VOICE	ORIGINAL
5-6/I	T	*a minima, g semibrevis, f semibrevis* in place of *f e d*; the passage has been corrected on the basis of bars 12-13

MODERN EDITIONS OF THE TEXT: AH 54, pp. 269-270.

MODERN EDITIONS OF THE MUSIC: BANKS 1993, II, pp. 75-76 (after Panc.27).

REMARKS: The beginning of the chant in GR 97★-100★ and LU, pp. 1810-1813 is lightly paraphrased in the Tenor. This *Dies ire* is the last piece in the manuscript. The copyist's hand returns only on fol. 216v (the last page of the last fascicle; see FIG. 15, p. 912), to illustrate for performers the various note shapes (with their corresponding rests) and to clarify how to perform the note values under the different mensuration signs, both simple and proportional.

BIBLIOGRAPHY: BANKS 1993, I, pp. 273-274; CHEVALIER I, no. 4626; FILOCAMO 2009c.

186.
Dies ire, dies illa
fols. 212v–213r

C[antus]

A[ltus]

Di - es i - re, di - es il - la,
Quid sum mi - ser
Qui Ma - ri - am

T[enor]

Di - es i - re, di - es il - la,
Quid sum mi - ser
Qui Ma - ri - am

B[assus]

Di - es i - re, di - es il - la,

sol - vet se - clum in fa - vil - la te -

sol - vet se - clum in fa - vil - la

sol - vet se - clum in fa - vil - la te -

Da - vid cum Si - bil - la.

- ste Da - vid cum Si - bil - la.

te - ste Da - vid cum Si - bil - la.

- ste Da - vid cum Si - bil - la.

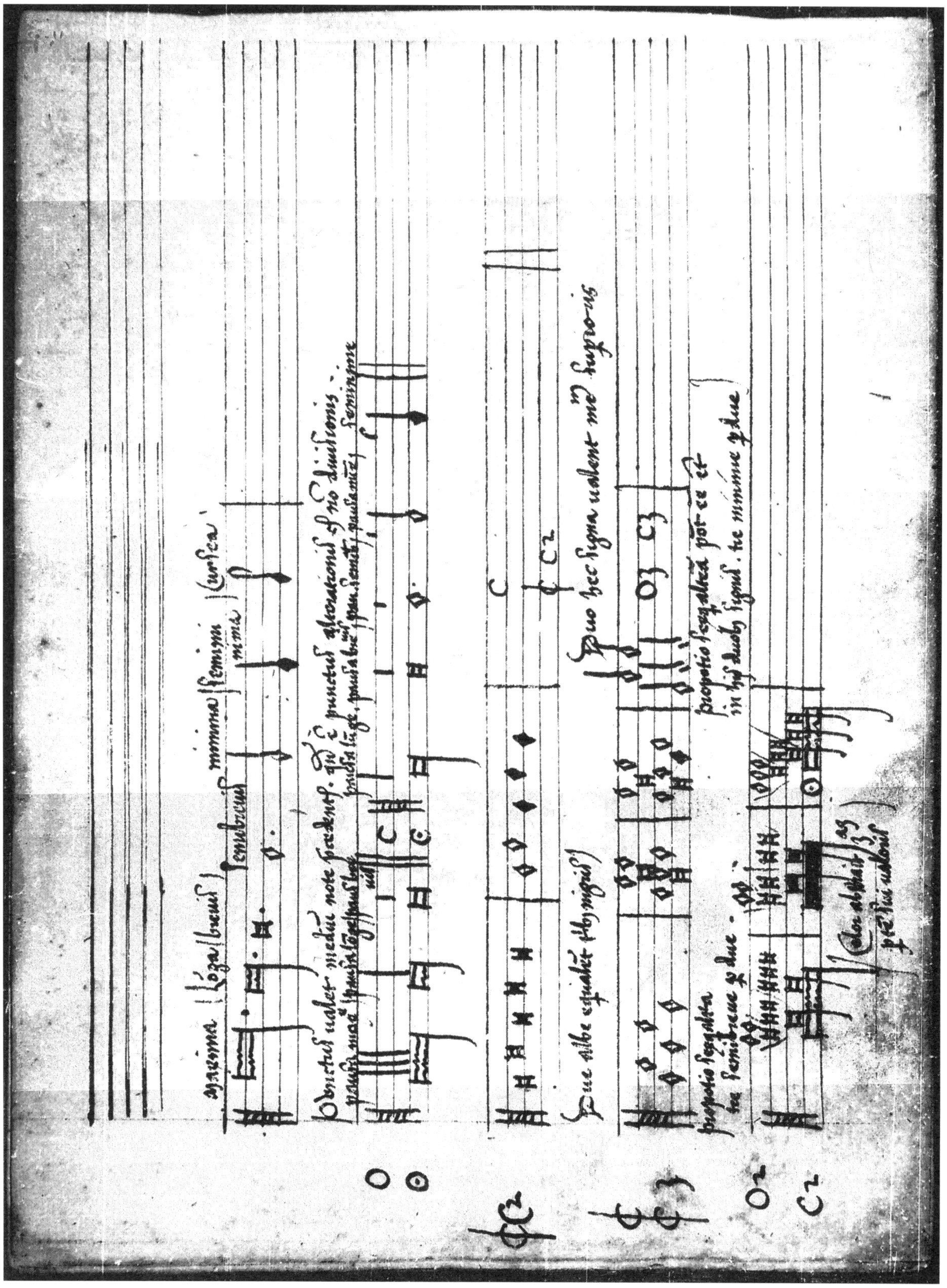

FIG. 15: Rules of mensural notation, fól. 216ʋ. Photo Mario Setter – GAP.

Index of Compositions and Alternative Texts
(with 'cantasi come', *contrafacta*, and references to more complete compositions)

Note: • The titles in roman are those edited in Panc.27; • the titles in italic are taken from concordances ('cantasi come' and *contrafacta*) and appear as they are written in the sources; • the italic titles within parentheses refer to the complete compositions from which parts are excerpted in Panc.27; • the arrow → indicates the relevant piece in Panc.27; • the names of the poets are all taken from concordances; they appear within curly brackets and have been normalized; • the names of the composers have been normalized (when known) and appear within square brackets if taken from concordances; • the numbers in boldface refer to the order in which the pieces appear in the manuscript.

Amice, ad quid venisti? attende tibi, ALEXANDER AGRICOLA, **no. 16**
    Dictes le moy
    Dictes moy toutes

Anima mea Dominum → (Magnificat) Anima mea Dominum [*Octavi toni*], **no. 167**

Arda el ciel e 'l mundo tuto, **no. 43**
    Crida el ciello e 'l mondo tuto

Aures ad nostras [deitatis preces], **no. 72**

Ave amator casti consilii → Les bien amore, **no. 75**

Ave di celli imperatrice santa → Contento in foco sto como fenice, **no. 33**

Ave dulcis ave pia → Dolce Regina, **no. 47**

Ave Maria, gratia plena, **no. 6** (= **no. 132**)

Ave Maria, gratia [plena], **no. 28**

Ave Maria, gratia plena, **no. 132** (= **no. 6**)

Ave Maria, gratia plena, **no. 173**

Ave Maria, gratia plena, LORENZO BERGOMOZZI, **no. 2**

Ave Maria, gratia plena, MARCHETTO CARA / [BARTOLOMEO TROMBONCINO], **no. 4**

Ave Maria, gratia plena, GIACOMO FOGLIANO, **no. 3**

Ave Maria, [gratia plena], MUSIPULA, **no. 8**

Ave Maria, gratia plena, BARTOLOMEO TROMBONCINO, **no. 9**

Ave Maria, gratia plena, [BARTOLOMEO TROMBONCINO], **no. 175**

Ave maris stella, **no. 71**

Ave regina → O gloriosa Regina mundi, **no. 83**

Ave Regina, Virgo gloriosa / Sofrire son disposto [ogni tormento], {ENSELMINO DA MONTEBELLUNA}, **no. 13**
    Pianto della Vergine

Ave sanctissima civitas - O virgo felix nondum edita → A la bataglia, **no. 11**

Ave sanctissima Maria, {POPE SIXTUS IV?}, **no. 141**

Ave stella fulgida → Poi che t'ebi nel core / Fortuna desperata, **no. 36**

Ave stella matutina, GASPAR VAN WEERBEKE, **no. 129**

Ave sydus clarissimum → Helas, [que poura devenir], **no. 56**

Ave victorioso, **no. 14**
    Ave victorioso e sancto legno

Ave victorioso e sancto legno → Ave victorioso, **no. 14**

Benedicamus Domino, **no. 22**

Benedicamus Domino, **no. 23**

Benedicamus Domino, **no. 24**

Benedicamus Domino, **no. 25**

Benedicamus Domino, **no. 26**

Benedictus → La mora, **no. 54**

Benedictus - Osanna II (Missa D'ung aultre amer) → Tu solus qui facis mirabilia, **no. 115**

Benedictus (*Missa Quant j'ay au cueur*), HENRICUS ISAAC, **no. 21**
    Plytzgan / Plitzgen

Dolce Regina, **no. 47**

    Ave dulcis ave pia

    Dolce regina vergine Maria

    Popule meus quid feci tibi

Dolce regina vergine Maria → Dolce Regina, **no. 47**

Dona gentile → La mora, **no. 54**

Dulcis conjugi bonum sit omen (Nuptiae factae sunt) → Ales regres, [vuidez de ma presence], **no. 127**

Egli è il tuo buon Iesù, {Feo Belcari}, Frater Dionisius Placentinus, **no. 67**

Elaes → La mora, **no. 54**

Elaes abraham → Helas, [le bon temps que j'avoie], **no. 73**

Elas qu'el at a mon gre → Helas, que il est à mon gré, **no. 96**

Et exultavit → (Magnificat) Et exultavit [*Octavi toni*], **no. 161**

Et exultavit → (Magnificat) Et exultavit [*Primi toni*], **no. 163**

[F]ammi ciò che vòi, crudel signora, **no. 154**

Felix namque, **no. 164**

Fortuna, che te giova de straciarme, **no. 35**

Fortuna desperata → Poi che t'ebi nel core / Fortuna desperata, **no. 36**

Fortuna desperata | iniqua e maladecta → Poi che t'ebi nel core / Fortuna desperata, **no. 36**

Fortuna desperata quae te dementia cepit → Poi che t'ebi nel core / Fortuna desperata, **no. 36**

Fortuna desperata quae te dementia vertit → Poi che t'ebi nel core / Fortuna desperata, **no. 36**

Fortuna d'um gran tempo, [Josquin des Prez], **no. 139**

Fortune esperee → Poi che t'ebi nel core / Fortuna desperata, **no. 36**

Gaude flore virginali → Gaude Virgo, mater Christi, **no. 48**

Gaude Virgo, mater Christi, **no. 48**

    Gaude flore virginali

Giù per la mala via, {Feo Belcari}, **no. 159**

Gratis accepistis et gratis date → Alleluia, **no. 138**

Guarda le vestimente, **no. 80**

    Guarda li vestimenti negri et tristi

Guarda li vestimenti negri et tristi → Guarda le vestimente, **no. 80**

Helas, [ce n'est pas sans rayson], Johannes de Stokem, **no. 97**

Helas je suis mary → Helas, [que devera mon cueur], **no. 168**

Helas, [le bon temps que j'avoie], Johannes Tinctoris / [Loyset Compère], **no. 73**

    Elaes abraham

Helas m'amour ma tres parfete amye → Helas, [que poura devenir], **no. 56**

Helas, [que devera mon cueur], Henricus Isaac, **no. 168**

    Helas je suis mary

Helas, que il est à mon gré, Johannes Japart, **no. 96**

    Ch'el et a mon gre

    Elas qu'el at a mon gre

Helas, [que poura devenir], Firminus Caron, **no. 56**

Ave sydus clarissimum
Der seyden schwantcz
Dess mayen lust
Helas m'amour ma tres parfete amye
Hellas mon cuer
Myt treuen herzen hab ich an allen

Hellas mon cuer → Helas, [que poura devenir], **no. 56**

Hor oires una canzon, [Johannes de Stokem], **no. 57**

Iamo a la caza → A la caza / Iamo a la caza, **no. 68**

Ibo mihi ad montem mirrhe, [Gaspar van Weerbeke], **no. 130**

Iesù, Iesù, Iesù, {Feo Belcari}, **no. 69**
   Ognun chiami Iesù | Iesù Iesù Iesù
   Visin visin visin

Illuxit dies → […], **no. 58**

Incipit lamentatio Ieremie prophete (Lamentations of Jeremiah), **no. 178**

Incipit lamentatio Ieremie prophete (Lamentations of Jeremiah), [Erasmus (Lapicida?)], **no. 174**

Incipit oratio Ieremie prophete (Lamentations of Jeremiah), **no. 118**

Incipit oratio Ieremie prophete (Lamentations of Jeremiah), **no. 176**

In foco ardente moro como fenice, **no. 155**

In te Domine speravi non confundar in aeternum → In te, domine, speravi | per trovar pietà in eterno, **no. 66**

In te, domine, speravi | per trovar pietà in eterno, Josquin des Prez, **no. 66**
   In te Domine speravi non confundar in aeternum

Integer vitae scelerisque purus → Io son de gabbia, non de bosco ocello / Iste confesor Domini, **no. 61**

Io mi voglio lamentare, [Giovanni Brocco], **no. 65**

Io son de gabbia, non de bosco ocello / Iste confesor Domini, [Michele Pesenti], **no. 61**
   Integer vitae scelerisque purus

Io son l'ucello che sopra i rami d'oro, [Marchetto Cara], **no. 63**

Iste confesor Domini → Io son de gabbia, non de bosco ocello, **no. 61**

Jo hay pris amor [à ma devise] → Canti zoiosi e dolce melodia, **no. 64**

Kyrie eleison, **no. 108**

Kyrie [eleison], **no. 162**

Kyrie eleison, **no. 182**

La alfonsina, Johannes Ghiselin, **no. 128**

(Lamentations of Jeremiah) → Incipit lamentatio Ieremie prophete, **no. 174**

(Lamentations of Jeremiah) → Incipit lamentatio Ieremie prophete, **no. 178**

(Lamentations of Jeremiah) → Incipit oratio Ieremie prophete, **no. 118**

(Lamentations of Jeremiah) → Incipit oratio Ieremie prophete, **no. 176**

La mora, [Henricus Isaac], **no. 54**
   Benedictus
   Dona gentile
   Elaes
   O regina La morra
   Reple tuorum corda fidelium

Nunc dimittis servum tuum (*3i toni*), **no. 122**

Nuptiae factae sunt → Ales regres, [vuidez de ma presence], **no. 127**

O admirabile comertium!, **no. 10**

O Domine Iesu Christe, [Antoine Brumel], **no. 120**

O Domine Iesu Christe, {Pope Gregory I 'the Great'?}, [Antoine Brumel?], **no. 121**

O dulcedo virginalis → A la bataglia, **no. 11**

Ogi è 'l tempo, peccatore, **no. 42**

O gloriosa Domina, **no. 79**
> Quem terra pontus aethera

O gloriosa Domina → O gloriosa Regina mundi, **no. 83**

O gloriosa Regina mundi, [Johannes Touront], **no. 83**
> *Ave regina*
> *O gloriosa Domina*
> *O lucis alme sator mundi*

Ognun chiami Iesù | Iesù Iesù Iesù → Iesù, Iesù, Iesù, **no. 69**

O Iesù dolce, o infinito amore, {Leonardo Giustinian}, **no. 76**

Oimè, che moro [per ti, dona crudele], Marchetto Cara, **no. 78**
> *Aime ch'io moro per ti dona crudele*

Oime il core oime la testa → Aimè el cor, aimè la testa, **no. 12**

Oime lo capo oime la testa → Aimè el cor, aimè la testa, **no. 12**

O lucis alme sator mundi → O gloriosa Regina mundi, **no. 83**

O madre di Iesù, o dea eterna, **no. 82**

O mater Dei et hominis → Tu solus qui facis mirabilia, **no. 115**

O mia infelice sorte, **no. 38**

O misero stato, **no. 77**

Omnis habet labor finem → Les bien amore, **no. 75**

Omnis labor habet finem → Les bien amore, **no. 75**

Omnis laus in fine canitur, [Henricus Isaac], **no. 81**
> *Agnus Dei I (Missa Chargé de deul)*

O panis vite venerande → Poi che t'ebi nel core / Fortuna desperata, **no. 36**

O praeclarissima atque graciosa → A la bataglia, **no. 11**

O preciosum convivium → Canti zoiosi e dolce melodia / Jo hay pris amor [à ma devise], **no. 64**

O pulcherrima mulierum, Gaspar van Weerbeke, **no. 91**

O quam glorifica [luce coruscas], Alexander Agricola, **no. 95**

Oratio Ieremie prophete → Incipit oratio Ieremie prophete, **no. 118**

Oratio Ieremie prophete → Incipit oratio Ieremie prophete, **no. 176**

O regina La morra → La mora, **no. 54**

Ortus de celo flos est → La stangetta, **no. 55**

Pange lingua gloriosi corporis mysterium → Verbum caro, panem verum, **no. 117**

'Patientia' [ognun me dice], **no. 116**

Patrem omnipotentem → (Credo) Patrem omnipotentem, **no. 119**

Piange Pisa, Bar[tholomeus?] Pisanus, **no. 101**

Pianto della Vergine → Ave Regina, Virgo gloriosa, **no. 13**

Planctus Mariae → Cum autem venissem ad locum, **no. 45**

Plytzgan / Plitzgen → Benedictus, **no. 21**

Poca pace e molta guerra, [Bartolomeo Tromboncino], **no. 151**

Poi che sei dal mondo tolta, {Leonardo Giustinian}, Ben, **no. 27**

Poi che t'ebi nel core / Fortuna desperata, {Francesco degli Albizzi}, **no. 36**
> *Ave stella fulgida*
> *Fortuna desperata | iniqua e maladecta*
> *Fortuna desperata quae te dementia cepit*
> *Fortuna desperata quae te dementia vertit*
> *Fortune esperee*
> *O panis vite venerande*
> *Virginis alme parens*

Poiché vivo sopra la terra, **no. 158**

Popule meus quid feci tibi → Dolce Regina, **no. 47**

Propter gravamen [et tormentum], Loyset Compère, **no. 126**

Quemadmodum desiderat cervus, **no. 106**

Quem terra pontus aethera → O gloriosa Domina, **no. 79**

Qui nos fecit ex nihilo, **no. 20**

Qui seminant in lacrimis, **no. 5**

Rappresentazione di Abramo e Isacco → Chi serve a Dio cum purità di cor[e], **no. 30**

Regina celi letare, Antoine Brumel, **no. 94**

Regina celi [letare], Loyset Compère, **no. 111**
> *Royne du ciel*

Regina celi [letare], Antonio Peragulfo, **no. 125**

Reple tuorum corda fidelium → La mora, **no. 54**

Requiem eternam → (Requiem Mass: *Libera me, Domine*), **no. 135**

Requiem eternam → (Requiem Mass: *Libera me, Domine*), **no. 184**

Requiem eternam dona eis, Domine, **no. 181**

(Requiem Mass: *Libera me, Domine*) → Dies illa, dies ire - Tremens factus sum ego - Requiem eternam, **no. 135**

(Requiem Mass: *Libera me, Domine*) → Tremens factus sum ego - Dies illa, dies ire - Requiem eternam, **no. 184**

(Requiem Mass, sequence) → Amen, **no. 183**

(Requiem Mass, sequence) → Dies ire, dies illa, **no. 39**

(Requiem Mass, sequence) → Dies ire, dies illa, **no. 185**

(Requiem Mass, sequence) → Dies ire, dies illa, **no. 186**

Rex autem David, [Adrian Willaert?], **no. 177**

Royne du ciel → Regina celi [letare], **no. 111**

Salve Regina → Alleluia, **no. 138**

Sancta Maria, ora pro nobis, **no. 133**

Sancta Maria, ora pro nobis, **no. 134**

Sconsolata phylomena, **no. 113**

Se a Maria fonte d'amore → A Maria, fonte d'amore / Vive lieto [e non temere], **no. 15**

Se ben or [non] scopri el fuoco, [BARTOLOMEO TROMBONCINO], **no. 93**
    L'oration e sempre bona

Se conviene a un cor vilano, [ENEAS], **no. 85**

Se l'ortolana vene a la cità, **no. 152**

Se non dormi, donna, ascolta, [? C.], **no. 145**

Se per te mia fin serà, **no. 143**

Seràno li […] mei tanto cocenti, **no. 156**

Siamo, done, trei romeri, **no. 146**

Si dedero [el mio core al dio d'amore], [GIACOMO FOGLIANO], **no. 92**

Si dedero [somnum oculis meis], ALEXANDER AGRICOLA, **no. 89**

Signora, anci, mea dea, BARTOLOMEO TROMBONCINO, **no. 148**

Signora, anci, mia dea, [BARTOLOMEO TROMBONCINO], **no. 150**

Sine fraude, **no. 172**

Sofrire son disposto [ogni tormento] → Ave Regina, Virgo gloriosa, **no. 13**

Son su passo de la morte (text only), **no. 112bis**

Stella celi extirpavit, **no. 102**

Surge, propera, amica mea, JOHANNES DE PINAROL, **no. 90**

Tenebre facte sunt, **no. 140**

Thysis / Thisis → Alleluia, **no. 138**

Tremens factus sum ego → (Requiem Mass: *Libera me, Domine*), **no. 135**

Tremens factus sum ego → (Requiem Mass: *Libera me, Domine*), **no. 184**

Trista è la sorte di chi serve al vento, **no. 100**

Tristitia vestra convertetur in gaudium, RENALDO, **no. 104**

Turis, **no. 170**

Tu solus qui facis mirabilia, JOSQUIN DES PREZ, **no. 115**
    Benedictus - Osanna II (Missa D'ung aultre amer)
    O mater Dei et hominis

Tuto el mundo è fantasia, [JO(HANNES?) HESDIMOIS], **no. 179**

Utile consilium, **no. 44**

Veni Creator Spiri[tus], **no. 107**

Venite amanti insieme a pianger forte → Ne doibt [on prendre quant on donne], **no. 59**

Verbum caro factum est, **no. 86 (= no. 142)**

Verbum caro factum est, **no. 136**

Verbum caro factum est, **no. 142 (= no. 86)**

Verbum caro factum est, **no. 144**

Verbum caro, panem verum, **no. 117**
    Pange lingua gloriosi corporis mysterium

Libraries and their Holdings

The list includes all the libraries (listed alphabetically by country and city) that possess sources concordant with the music or texts in Panc.27. After the name of each library the sources are listed in the following order:

T-ms = Textual manuscripts
T-pr = Textual prints
M-ms = Musical manuscripts
M-pr = Musical prints

AUSTRIA

Güssing, Franziskaner-Kloster, Bibliothek (• **M-pr**: PeIsaac, PeJosqII1515Gothic)

Linz, Oberösterreichische Landesbibliothek (*ex* Bundesstaatliche Studienbibliothek) (• **M-ms**: LinzL 529)

Wien, Österreichische Nationalbibliothek (• **T-pr**: *Aq1516Bin, Aq1516Giu, Petr1470* • **M-ms**: WienN 11883, WienN 18688 • **M-pr**: GardFesta1556, GiuJosqII, MüllerHeckel, PeBossI1509, PeCantiC, PeDalza, PeFroI, PeFroIII1507, PeFroIV1507, PeFroV, PeIsaac, PeJosqII1515Gothic, PeJosqII1515Roman)

BELGIUM

Brussel/Bruxelles, Koninklijke Bibliotheek van België / Bibliothèque Royale de Belgique (• **T-pr**: *Petr1470* • **M-ms**: BruxR 90, BruxR 11239 • **M-pr**: MüllerHeckel, PeDalza, PeJosqII1515Roman, PetreiusNewII, Razzi)

Leuven, Katholieke Universiteit, Universiteitsbibliotheek (• **T-pr**: *Petr1470*)

Liège, Bibliothèque de l'Université de Liège (• **T-pr**: *Busti1492S*)

Tournai, Bibliothèque de la Ville (• **M-ms**: TournaiV 94)

CZECH REPUBLIC

Hradec Králové, Krajské Muzeum, Literární Archiv (• **M-ms**: HKK 7, HKK 20)

Praha, Strahovský Klášter - Knihovna (• **M-ms**: PrahaS 47)

DENMARK

København, Kongelige Bibliotek (• **T-pr**: *TebOp1498* • **M-ms**: KøbK 291, KøbK 1848 • **M-pr**: PetreiusNewI)

FRANCE

Besançon, Bibliothèque Municipale (• **M-pr**: PhalChansons)

Cambrai, Médiathèque Municipale (• **M-ms**: CambM 18, CambM 125-8)

CHANTILLY, Bibliothèque du Musée Condé (• **T-PR**: *Aq1520Pen, Lamento1524, Non1524, Petr1470, Rado*)

DIJON, Bibliothèque Municipale (• **M-MS**: DijM 517)

MONTPELLIER, Bibliothèque Municipale (• **T-PR**: *Aq1516Giu*)

PARIS, Bibliothèque de l'Institut National d'Histoire de l'Art (• **T-PR**: *Chasse*)

—, Bibliothèque Mazarine (• **T-PR**: *Aq1516Giu, Aq1530Zop, Busti1492S, Giust1490, LaudeMisc*)

—, Bibliothèque Nationale de France (• **T-MS**: *Paris.N. F.1719, Paris.N. I.559, Paris.N. I.560, Paris.N. I.607, Paris.N. I.618, Paris.N. I.1020, Paris.N. I.1543* • **T-PR**: *Aq1502Bon, Aq1548Basc, AqMis, Giust1475* [2 copies], *Petr1470, Pianto1483, Pianto1537, SetteDolori, TebOp1498, TebSon1499* • **M-MS**: ParisN F1597, ParisN F2245, ParisN F12744, ParisN F15123, ParisN NAF4379, ParisN NAL401, ParisN Rés27, ParisN Rés57, ParisN Rés676, ParisN Ro2973 • **M-PR**: AttMotetz, EgenLieder, GiuJosqII, HanZanger, MüllerHeckel, PeBossI1509, PeCantiC, PeLamI, PeLamII, PeMotB, PeOdh1504, ScottoFesta1559)

—, Bibliothèque Sainte-Geneviève (• **M-PR**: HanZanger, PeFroV)

—, Musée Jacquemart-André (Bibliothèque de l'Institut) (• **T-MS**: *Paris.JA. 2075*)

STRASBOURG, Bibliothèque Nationale et Universitaire (• **M-PR**: Razzi)

—, Bibliothèque du Séminaire Protestant (• **M-PR**: PetreiusNewI)

VERSAILLES, Bibliothèque Municipale (• **M-PR**: AttMotetz)

GERMANY

AUGSBURG, Staats- und Stadtbibliothek (• **M-MS**: AugsS 25, AugsS 142a • **M-PR**: HanZanger)

BERLIN, Freie Universität Berlin, Universitätsbibliothek (• **M-PR**: FormTrium)

—, Staatliche Museen der Stiftung Preußischer Kulturbesitz, Kupferstichkabinett (• **T-MS**: *Berl.M. 17*)

—, Staatsbibliothek, Preußischer Kulturbesitz (• **T-MS**: *Berl.S. H.348* • **T-PR**: *Aq1548Basc, LaudeBonac* • **M-MS**: BerlS 30, BerlS 22048, BerlS 40021, BerlS 40026, BerlS 40196, BerlS 40632 • **M-PR**: FormGerle, HanZanger, MüllerHeckel, PeIsaac, PeJosqII1515Gothic, PetreiusNewI, PetreiusNewII)

BERLIN-CHARLOTTENBURG, Bibliothek der Hochschule für Musik und Darstellende Kunst (• **M-PR**: FormTrium)

DARMSTADT, Universitäts- und Landesbibliothek (*ex* Hessische Landes- und Hochschulbibliothek) (• **M-PR**: HanZanger)

DRESDEN, Sächsische Landesbibliothek – Staats- und Universitätsbibliothek (• **M-MS**: DresL 505 • **M-PR**: MüllerHeckel, RhauSym)

EICHSTÄTT, Universitätsbibliothek Eichstätt-Ingolstadt (*ex* Staatliche Bibliothek Eichstätt) (• **M-PR**: AttMotetz)

ERLANGEN, Universitätsbibliothek (• **M-MS**: ErlU 473/4)

FRANKFURT AM MAIN, Universitätsbibliothek Johann Christian Senckenberg (• **T-PR**: *Aq1503Rug* • **M-MS**: FMU 20)

GOTHA, Forschungs- und Landesbibliothek (• **M-PR**: HanZanger)

GÖTTINGEN, Niedersächsische Staats- und Universitätsbibliothek (• **M-PR**: HanZanger)

GREIFSWALD, Universitätsbibliothek (• **M-MS**: GreifU 640-1)

HALLE AN DER SAALE, Martin-Luther-Universität, Universitäts- und Landesbibliothek Sachsen-Anhalt (• **M-PR**: PetreiusNewI, PetreiusNewII)

HAMBURG, Staats- und Universitätsbibliothek Carl von Ossietzky, Musikabteilung (• **M-PR**: WyssHeckel [lost])

HEILBRONN, Stadtarchiv (• **M-MS**: HeilbS 2 • **M-PR**: HanZanger, RhauSym)

HERDRINGEN, Schloss Fürstenberg, Bibliothek (• **M-MS**: HerdF 9822)

ISERLOHN, Evangelische Kirkengemeinde, Varnhagen Bibliothek (• **M-MS**: IserV 124)

JENA, Thüringer Universitäts- und Landesbibliothek (• **M-MS**: JenaU 31 • **M-PR**: FormTrium, HanZanger, RhauSym)

KARLSRUHE, Badische Landesbibliothek (• **M-PR**: GünNew)

KASSEL, Landesbibliothek und Murhardsche Bibliothek der Stadt Kassel (• **M-MS**: KasL 53/2)

LEIPZIG, Städtische Bibliotheken, Muzikbibliothek (• **M-PR**: PetreiusNewI [2 copies])

—, Universitätsbibliothek, Bibliotheca Albertina (• **M-MS**: LeipU 49-50, LeipU 51, LeipU 1494)

MÜNCHEN, Bayerische Staatsbibliothek (• **T-MS**: *Mün.S. I240, Mün.S. I265* • **T-PR**: *Aq1502Bes, Aq1516Son, AqStramb(B), Busti1494, Operetta1515, Operetta1521, SetteDolori, TebEp1506* • **M-MS**: MünS 272, MünS 352b, MünS L5023 • **M-PR**: AttTrezeMotetz [lost, but a photocopy is preserved], GardFesta1556, HanZanger, MüllerHeckel, PeFroI, PeFroIII1505, PeFroIV1505, PeFroV, PetreiusNewI, RhauSym)

—, Universitätsbibliothek der Ludwig-Maximilians-Universität (• **M-MS**: MünU 322-5, MünU 326, MünU 718)

NÜRNBERG, Bibliothek des Germanische Nationalmuseum (• **M-PR**: GutNew, PetreiusNewII)

REGENSBURG, Bischöfliche Zentralbibliothek (• **M-MS**: RegB 220-2, RegB 940-1 • **M-PR**: GiuJosqII, PeFroIII1507)

—, Fürst Thurn und Taxis Hofbibliothek und Zentralarchiv (• **M-PR**: GardFesta1564)

ROSTOCK, Universitätsbibliothek (• **M-PR**: RhauSym)

STUTTGART, Württembergische Landesbibliothek (• **T-PR**: *Aq1509Son* • **M-MS**: StuttL 39 • **M-PR**: HanZanger)

TRIER, Stadtbibliothek (• **M-PR**: MüllerHeckel)

ULM, Von Schermar'sche Familienstiftung, Bibliothek (• **M-MS**: UlmS 236, UlmS 237)

WOLFENBÜTTEL, Herzog August Bibliothek (• **T-PR**: *Aq1548Basc, Non1568* • **M-MS**: WolfA 78, WolfA G287 • **M-PR**: HanZanger [2 copies], PeJosqII1505, PetreiusNewI, PetreiusNewII)

ZWICKAU, Ratsschulbibliothek (• **T-PR**: *AqStramb(B), Non1500a, Non1500b* • **M-MS**: ZwR 78/2, ZwR 78/3, ZwR 86/2 • **M-PR**: RhauSym)

HUNGARY

BUDAPEST, Országos Széchényi Könyvtár (• **M-PR**: PeMotA1505, PeMotB)

SZOMBATHELY, Püspöki Könyvtár (• **M-PR**: PeJosqII1515Roman)

IRELAND

DUBLIN, Trinity College Library (• **T-PR**: *Petr1470*)

Amelia, Biblioteca del Seminario Vescovile (• **M-pr**: LiberSac1537)

Ancona, Biblioteca Comunale Luciano Benincasa (• **T-pr**: *Giust1483*)

Aosta, Biblioteca del Seminario Maggiore (• **T-pr**: *Aq1511Leg*)

L'Aquila, Biblioteca Provinciale Salvatore Tommasi (• **T-pr**: *Aq1530Zop*)

Arezzo, Istituzione Biblioteca Città di Arezzo (• **T-pr**: *Aq1505Son*)

Assisi, Biblioteca del Centro di Documentazione Francescana del Sacro Convento di S. Francesco (• **T-pr**: *JacopSper*)

—, Biblioteca Comunale (• **M-pr**: PeJosqII1515Gothic)

—, Biblioteca della Porziuncola (Basilica di S. Maria degli Angeli) (• **M-pr**: Razzi)

Bergamo, Civica Biblioteca - Archivi Storici Angelo Mai (• **T-ms**: *Berg.C. 1* • **T-pr**: *Aq1515Leg*, *Giust1474*, *JacopBen* • **M-pr**: LiberSac1537, PeJosqII1515Roman)

Bologna, Archivio Storico della Provincia di Cristo Re dei Frati Minori dell'Emilia Romagna (• **T-ms**: *Bol.FM. 10*)

—, Biblioteca Arcivescovile (• **T-ms**: *Bol.Arciv. 4880*)

—, Biblioteca di Casa Carducci (• **T-ms**: *Bol.Car. 34* • **T-pr**: *Aq1502Bon*, *Aq1548Basc*, *LaudeSper*, *TebOp1498*)

—, Biblioteca Comunale dell'Archiginnasio (• **T-pr**: *Aq1516Giu* • **M-ms**: BolA 179 • **M-pr**: GiuCant1536)

—, Biblioteca Provinciale dei Frati minori dell'Emilia. Sezione Biblioteca dell'Osservanza (• **M-pr**: LiberSac1537)

—, Biblioteca Universitaria (• **T-ms**: *Bol.U. 12*, *Bol.U. 157*, *Bol.U. 1242*, *Bol.U. 1737*, *Bol.U. 2618*, *Bol.U. 2672*, *Bol.U. 2690*, *Bol.U. 2845*, *Bol.U. 2932*, *Bol.U. 3795*, *Bol.U. 4019* • **T-pr**: *Aq1502Bon*, *Aq1503Baz*, *Busti1494*, *LaudeBonar*, *Opera1515*, *Pianto1481L* • **M-ms**: BolU 2216)

—, Museo Internazionale e Biblioteca della Musica (*ex* Civico Museo Bibliografico Musicale) (• **M-ms**: BolM 13, BolM 15, BolM 16, BolM 17, BolM 18, BolM 19, BolM 34 • **M-pr**: GardFesta1556, GiuCant1523, GiuCant1536, LiberSac1523, PeIsaac, PeJosqII1505, PeJosqII1515Gothic, PeLamI, PeLamII, PeMotA1502, PeMotB, PeOdh1501, Razzi, ScottoFesta1551)

Borgomanero, Biblioteca Pubblica e Casa della Cultura - Fondazione Achille Marazza (• **T-ms**: *Borg.P. M.76725*)

Brescia, Biblioteca Civica Queriniana (• **T-ms**: *Br.Q. 16*, *Br.Q. 23* • **T-pr**: *Giust1495*, *JacopMis*, *Petr1470*)

Bressanone, Biblioteca del Seminario Vescovile Vinzentinum (• **M-pr**: MeruloFesta)

Broni, Biblioteca della Collegiata di S. Pietro Apostolo (• **M-pr**: LiberSac1523)

Cassino, Biblioteca Statale del Monumento Nazionale di Montecassino (• **T-pr**: *TebOp1498* • **M-ms**: MontA 871)

Cava de' Tirreni, Biblioteca Comunale Canonico Aniello Avallone (• **M-pr**: LiberSac1537)

Cesena, Biblioteca dell'Abbazia di S. Maria del Monte (• **M-pr**: GiuCant1536)

Chiavari, Biblioteca della Società Economica (• **T-pr**: *Aq1548Basc*, *LaudeSper*)

Como, Archivio Storico della Diocesi, Fondo Curia Vescovile (• **T-ms**: *Como.C.*)

—, Biblioteca dei Musei Civici (• **T-pr**: *Petr1470*)

CREMONA, Biblioteca Statale (*ex* Governativa) (• **M-PR**: GiuCant1536)

FANO, Biblioteca Comunale Federiciana (• **T-PR**: *Aq1505Son, Aq1509Son, Aq1516Bin, Aq1516Son*)

FERMO, Biblioteca Comunale (• **T-PR**: *TebOp1498*)

FERRARA, Biblioteca Comunale Ariostea (• **T-MS**: *Fer.C. 211, Fer.C. 408* • **T-PR**: *TebOp1498*)

FIESOLE, Biblioteca Bandiniana (• **T-PR**: *JacopSper, LaudeSper*)

FIRENZE, Accademia della Crusca (• **T-PR**: *LaudeMisc, LaudeVecchie*)

—, Biblioteca della Cassa di Risparmio, Fondo Roberto Ridolfi (• **T-PR**: *Giust1490, LaudeBonac, LaudeVecchie*)

—, Biblioteca del Conservatorio Luigi Cherubini (• **M-MS**: FirC B2441 • **M-PR**: Razzi [2 copies])

—, Biblioteca Marucelliana (• **T-MS**: *Fir.M. 262* • **T-PR**: *Aq1507Son, JacopBen* • **M-PR**: PeJosqII1505)

—, Biblioteca Medicea Laurenziana (• **T-MS**: *Fir.L. Ant.158, Fir.L. Ash.480, Fir.L. Ash.539, Fir.L. Ash.567, Fir.L. Ash.598, Fir.L. Ash.852, Fir.L. Ash.1177, Fir.L. Ash.1402, Fir.L. R.121, Fir.L. S.17* • **T-PR**: *Petr1470*)

—, Biblioteca Nazionale Centrale (• **T-MS**: *Fir.N. 4, Fir.N. 12, Fir.N. 35, Fir.N. 42, Fir.N. 54, Fir.N. 58, Fir.N. 75, Fir.N. 140, Fir.N. 291, Fir.N. 700, Fir.N. II.IV.3, Fir.N. II.VIII.3, Fir.N. B.228, Fir.N. CS.488, Fir.N. LF.13, Fir.N. LF.236, Fir.N. LF.249, Fir.N. LF.302, Fir.N. M.27, Fir.N. M.30, Fir.N. M.85, Fir.N. M.285, Fir.N. M.367, Fir.N. M.376, Fir.N. M.686, Fir.N. M.690, Fir.N. M.735, Fir.N. M.738, Fir.N. M.744, Fir.N. M.1083, Fir.N. M.1114, Fir.N. M.1163, Fir.N. M.VII.117, Fir.N. NA.701, Fir.N. P.13, Fir.N. P.169, Fir.N. P.172, Fir.N. P.173, Fir.N. P.219, Fir.N. P.445, Fir.N. T.227* • **T-PR**: *Altissimo1525, Aq1502Bon, Aq1503Baz, Aq1503Pac, Aq1509Son, Aq1515Leg, Aq1516Giu, Aq1518Mon, BelcLBart, BelcLBen, BelcR1485, Colletanio1524, Giust1475* [2 copies], *JacopBen, JacopSper, Lamento, LaudeBonac, LaudeBonar, LaudeFort, LaudeMisc* [2 copies], *LaudeNat, LaudeSper, LaudeVecchie, LaudiGiunti, NonF, OperaNova, Petr1470, Ricco1511, RispSon, TebSon1499* • **M-MS**: FirN BR62, FirN BR229, FirN BR230, FirN BR337, FirN M107bis, FirN M117, FirN M121, FirN M178 • **M-PR**: LiberSac1523, Razzi)

—, Biblioteca Riccardiana (• **T-MS**: *Fir.R. 1094, Fir.R. 1106, Fir.R. 1119, Fir.R. 1258, Fir.R. 1294/2760, Fir.R. 1413, Fir.R. 1473, Fir.R. 1501, Fir.R. 1502, Fir.R. 1661, Fir.R. 1666, Fir.R. 1720, Fir.R. 1721, Fir.R. 1763, Fir.R. 2723, Fir.R. 2816, Fir.R. 2893, Fir.R. 2894, Fir.R. 2895, Fir.R. 2896, Fir.R. 2929, Fir.R. 2971, Fir.R. 3112* • **T-PR**: *Aq1503Bes, Historia, LaudeBonac, LaudeVecchie, LaudiRiccardiana* • **M-MS**: FirR 2356, FirR 2794)

—, Duomo, Archivio Musicale dell'Opera di S. Maria del Fiore (• **M-MS**: FirD 21)

—, Private Collection (• **T-PR**: *Aq1504Man*)

FOLIGNO, Biblioteca Ludovico Jacobilli (• **T-PR**: *LaudeBonac*)

FRATTA POLESINE, Private Collection of Giorgio Fanan (• **T-MS**: *FrattaPol.Fanan* • **M-PR**: Razzi)

GENOVA, Biblioteca della Badia dei Benedettini di S. Andrea della Castagna (• **M-PR**: GiuCant1536)

—, Biblioteca Durazzo (• **T-PR**: *Petr1470*)

—, Biblioteca Universitaria (• **T-PR**: *Aq1513Lov, JacopBen, LaudeSper*)

GROTTAFERRATA, Biblioteca Statale del Monumento Nazionale (Biblioteca della Badia Greca) (• **T-PR**: *JacopBen*)

LIVORNO, Biblioteca Comunale Labronica Francesco Domenico Guerrazzi (• **T-PR**: *JacopBen*)

LUCCA, Biblioteca Statale (*ex* Governativa) (• **T-MS**: *Luc.S. 1302* • **T-PR**: *JacopBen, LaudeMisc, NonF, OperaFregoso, TebOp1498* • **M-PR**: LiberSac1523, Razzi)

Lugo di Romagna, Biblioteca Comunale Fabrizio Trisi (• **T-pr**: *JacopBen*)

Mantova, Biblioteca Comunale (• **T-ms**: *Man.C. 4*)

Messina, Biblioteca Provinciale dei Frati Minori Cappuccini Madonna di Pompei (• **M-pr**: LiberSac1523, LiberSac1537)

—, Biblioteca Regionale Universitaria (• **T-pr**: *JacopSper, LaudeSper* • **M-pr**: LiberSac1537)

Milano, Archivio della Veneranda Fabbrica del Duomo, Sezione Musicale (• **M-ms**: MilD 1, MilD 2)

—, Biblioteca Ambrosiana (• **T-ms**: *Mil.A. 3, Mil.A. 25, Mil.A. 35, Mil.A. 80, Mil.A. 94, Mil.A.T.502* • **T-pr**: *Aq1516Giu, Aq1523Vim, Busti1489, Busti1492S, Busti1492Z, Giust1474, Giust1475* • **M-ms**: MilA 5 • **M-pr**: LiberSac1537)

—, Biblioteca e Archivio del Capitolo Metropolitano (• **T-pr**: *LaudeBonac* • **M-pr**: LiberSac1523, LiberSac1537)

—, Biblioteca dell'Archivio Storico Civico e Biblioteca Trivulziana (• **T-ms**: *Mil.T. 92, Mil.T. 383, Mil.T. 545, Mil.T. 913* • **T-pr**: *Aq1516Cas(B), Aq1523Vim, Busti1492S, Collectanio1514Rus, Colletanio1509, Colletanio1521, Colletanio1524, Compendio1483, Fior1505, Fior1518, Fior1522, Giust1474, Giust1475, Giust1495, Giust1506, JacopMis, JacopSper, LaudeBonac, LaudeMisc, LaudeNat, LaudeSper, LaudeVecchie, LaudiGiunti, NonM, NonVav1, OperaNova, Petr1470, Pianto1481L, TebEp1545, TebSon1499, VitaSB* • **M-ms**: MilT 55 • **M-pr**: Razzi)

—, Biblioteca del Conservatorio Giuseppe Verdi (• **M-pr**: PeIsaac, PeJosqII1505)

—, Biblioteca del Museo Poldi Pezzoli (• **T-pr**: *OperaNova*)

—, Biblioteca Nazionale Braidense (• **T-ms**: *Mil.B. 27, Mil.B. 28* • **T-pr**: *Aq1516Giu, Busti1490, Giust1495, JacopBen, JacopMis, LaudeBonac, LaudeMisc, Petr1470, Pianto1493, TebEp1509, TebSon1499* • **M-ms**: MilB 49 • **M-pr**: LiberSac1523, LiberSac1537)

Modena, Biblioteca Estense Universitaria (• **T-ms**: *Mod.E. 81, Mod.E. 381, Mod.E. 809, Mod.E. 1168, Mod.E. 1277* • **T-pr**: *Aq1508Bon, Aq1516Giu, Aq1548Basc, Collectanio1514Lov, Colletanio1521, Fior1510, Inamormento, JacopSper, Pianto1477, TebOp1498, TebOp1500* • **M-ms**: ModE 8, ModE 9 • **M-pr**: LiberSac1537)

—, Duomo, Biblioteca e Archivio Capitolare (• **M-ms**: ModD IV • **M-pr**: LiberSac1537)

Monreale, Biblioteca Popolare Pax – S. Martino delle Scale (• **M-pr**: GiuCant1536)

Napoli, Biblioteca dell'Accademia Pontaniana (• **T-pr**: *Aq1548Basc*)

—, Biblioteca Nazionale Vittorio Emanuele III (• **T-ms**: *Nap.N. 1, Nap.N. 14, Nap.N. 31, Nap.N. 38* • **T-pr**: *Aq1512Bin, Aq1522Rus, Aq1548Basc, Colletanio1510, Fior1521, Giust1474* [2 copies], *Giust1506, LaudeBonac, Petr1470, TebOp1498*)

—, Biblioteca Oratoriana del Monumento Nazionale dei Girolamini (• **T-pr**: *Aq1502Bon, Aq1548Basc, TebSon1499*)

—, Biblioteca Universitaria (• **T-pr**: *Aq1548Basc, LaudeBonac*)

Novara, Biblioteca Comunale Carlo Negroni (• **M-pr**: LiberSac1523)

Padova, Biblioteca Antoniana (• **T-pr**: *Giust1490* • **M-pr**: PeLamI)

—, Biblioteca Capitolare (• **M-ms**: PadCap 17)

—, Biblioteca Civica (• **T-ms**: *Pad.Civ. 4*)

—, Biblioteca del Convento dei Frati Cappuccini (• **T-pr**: *JacopSper*)

—, Biblioteca del Monumento Nazionale di S. Giustina (• **M-pr**: LiberSac1537)

—, Biblioteca del Seminario Vescovile (• **T-ᴘʀ**: *JacopSper, LaudeSper*)

—, Biblioteca Universitaria (• **T-ᴍs**: *Pad.U. 1151, Pad.U. 1357* • **T-ᴘʀ**: *Aq1515Leg* • **M-ᴘʀ**: GardFesta1564, GiuCant1536)

Pᴀʟᴇʀᴍᴏ, Biblioteca Centrale della Regione Siciliana Alberto Bombace (• **M-ᴘʀ**: GiuCant1536)

—, Biblioteca Comunale (• **T-ᴍs**: *Pal.C. 8*)

Pᴀʀᴍᴀ, Biblioteca Palatina (• **T-ᴍs**: *Parma.P. Pal.37, Parma.P. Par.201, Parma.P. Par.3072* • **T-ᴘʀ**: *Aq1502Bon, Giust1475, Giust1490, Giust1517, JacopBen* [lost], *LaudeBonac, LaudeVecchie, Pianto1505, TebSon1499* • **M-ᴍs**: ParmaP Par3597 • **M-ᴘʀ**: LiberSac1523)

Pᴀᴠɪᴀ, Biblioteca Universitaria (• **T-ᴍs**: *Pav.U.A.355, Pav.U.A.378, Pav.U.A.474* • **M-ᴍs**: PavU A361, PavU A362)

Pᴇʀᴜɢɪᴀ, Biblioteca Comunale Augusta (• **M-ᴍs**: PerA 431)

—, Biblioteca S. Basilio del Seminario Arcivescovile (• **M-ᴘʀ**: LiberSac1537)

Pᴇsᴀʀᴏ, Biblioteca Oliveriana (• **T-ᴍs**: *Pes.O. 54* • **T-ᴘʀ**: *PiantoOratione* • **M-ᴍs**: PesO 1144)

Pᴇsᴄᴀʀᴀ, Biblioteca Comunale Vittoria Colonna (• **T-ᴘʀ**: *Aq1548Basc*)

Pɪᴀᴄᴇɴᴢᴀ, Biblioteca Comunale Passerini-Landi (• **T-ᴍs**: *Piac.C. L.15* [stolen, but a microfilm is preserved], *Piac.C. P.245*)

—, Biblioteca del Seminario Vescovile (• **M-ᴘʀ**: LiberSac1537)

Pɪsᴀ, Biblioteca Universitaria (• **T-ᴘʀ**: *JacopBen, JacopSper, LaudeSper*)

Pʀᴀᴛᴏ, Biblioteca Roncioniana (• **T-ᴍs**: *Prato.R. 186* [lost])

Rᴀᴠᴇɴɴᴀ, Istituzione Biblioteca Classense (• **T-ᴍs**: *Rav.C. 63, Rav.C. 177, Rav.C. 464* • **T-ᴘʀ**: *Aq1516Gɪᴜ, Colletanio1524, Giust1474* • **M-ᴘʀ**: GiuCant1523, GiuCant1536)

Rᴇɢɢᴇʟʟᴏ, Biblioteca dell'Abbazia di Vallombrosa (• **M-ᴘʀ**: GiuCant1536)

Rᴇɢɢɪᴏ ɴᴇʟʟ'Eᴍɪʟɪᴀ, Biblioteca Municipale Antonio Panizzi (• **T-ᴘʀ**: *Aq1505Son*)

Rɪᴇᴛɪ, Biblioteca Comunale Paroniana (• **T-ᴘʀ**: *LaudeBonac*)

Rɪᴍɪɴɪ, Biblioteca Civica Alessandro Gambalunga (• **T-ᴍs**: *Rim.C. 38* • **T-ᴘʀ**: *Colletanio*)

Rᴏᴄᴄᴀ ᴅɪ Mᴇᴢᴢᴏ, Chiesa di S. Maria della Neve, Museo d'Arte Sacra Cardinale Agnifili (• **M-ᴍs**: RMN)

Rᴏᴍᴀ, Biblioteca dell'Accademia Nazionale dei Lincei e Corsiniana (• **T-ᴍs**: *Roma.Co. 3, Roma.Co. 27, Roma.Co. 33* • **T-ᴘʀ**: *Fior1518, Giust1474, JacopSper, LaudeBonac, LaudeSper, LaudiGiunti, OperaNova, Petr1470, Pianto1481H* • **M-ᴘʀ**: Razzi)

—, Biblioteca Angelica (• **T-ᴍs**: *Roma.Ang. 1482, Roma.Ang. 2274, Roma.Ang. 2275* • **T-ᴘʀ**: *Aq1505Son, Fior1509* • **M-ᴘʀ**: LiberSac1523)

—, Biblioteca Paolo Baffi della Banca d'Italia (• **T-ᴘʀ**: *NonVav2*)

—, Biblioteca della Basilica di S. Paolo (• **M-ᴘʀ**: GiuCant1536)

—, Biblioteca Casanatense (• **T-ᴍs**: *Roma.Ca. 817, Roma.Ca. 1432, Roma.Ca. 3828* • **T-ᴘʀ**: *Aq1504Man, Aq1505Bon(B), Aq1516Gɪᴜ, Compendio, Giust1483, JacopBen, LaudeVecchie, SepteDolori, TebEp1500Bes, TebEp1500Sil* • **M-ᴍs**: RomaCa 2856 • **M-ᴘʀ**: LiberSac1523, LiberSac1537)

—, Biblioteca Musicale Governativa del Conservatorio S. Cecilia (• **M-ᴘʀ**: Razzi [2 copies])

—, Biblioteca Nazionale Centrale Vittorio Emanuele II (• **T-ᴍs**: *Roma.N. S.413, Roma.N. V.24, Roma.N. VE.483* • **T-ᴘʀ**: *Aq1502Bes, Aq1505Bon(A), Aq1509Son, Aq1516Gɪᴜ, Aq1530Zop, JacopBen, JacopSper, LaudeBonar, Petr1470* • **M-ᴘʀ**: GiuCant1536)

—, Biblioteca del Pontificio Ateneo Antonianum (• **T-pr**: *JacopSper*, *LaudeSper*)

—, Biblioteca del Senato della Repubblica (• **T-ms**: *Roma.S. 2*)

—, Biblioteca Universitaria Alessandrina (• **T-ms**: *Roma.Al. 224*, *Roma.Al. 301* • **T-pr**: *Aq1510Rus*)

Rovereto, Biblioteca Civica Girolamo Tartarotti (• **T-pr**: *Aq1507Bon*)

Siena, Biblioteca Comunale degli Intronati (• **T-ms**: *Siena.C. 13*, *Siena.C. 14*, *Siena.C. 15*, *Siena.C. 16*, *Siena.C. 17*, *Siena.C. 41*, *Siena.C. II.37*, *Siena.C. VIII.37* • **T-pr**: *LaudeBonar*, *LaudeGiacc* • **M-ms**: SienaC 2 • **M-pr**: GiuCant1536)

Spoleto, Biblioteca Comunale Giosuè Carducci (• **T-pr**: *JacopBen* [lost])

Teolo, Biblioteca del Monumento Nazionale di Praglia (• **M-pr**: GiuCant1536)

Torino, Biblioteca Nazionale Universitaria (• **T-pr**: *Aq1516Bin*, *Aq1516Giu* • **M-ms**: TorN 27)

Trento, Museo Castello del Buonconsiglio, Monumenti e Collezioni Provinciali (*ex* Museo Provinciale d'Arte) (• **M-ms**: TrenM 89, TrenM 91)

—, Biblioteca Comunale (• **M-ms**: TrenC 1947/4 • **M-pr**: ScottoFesta1547)

—, Biblioteca Musicale Laurence Feininger (• **M-ms**: TrenF 133 • **M-pr**: LiberSac1523)

—, Biblioteca Provinciale dei Padri Cappuccini (• **M-pr**: LiberSac1537)

—, Fondazione Biblioteca S. Bernardino (• **M-pr**: LiberSac1523)

Treviso, Biblioteca Capitolare della Cattedrale (• **M-pr**: PeCantiC, PeOdh1504)

—, Biblioteca Comunale (• **T-ms**: *Trev.C. 22*, *Trev.C. 188*, *Trev.C. 220* • **T-pr**: *Aq1504Bon*, *Aq1506Bon*, *Aq1519Ses*, *Colletanio1510* • **M-pr**: LiberSac1523)

Trieste, Biblioteca Civica Attilio Hortis (• **T-pr**: *Petr1470*)

Udine, Biblioteca Civica Vincenzo Joppi (• **T-pr**: *Aq1530Zop*)

Venezia, Biblioteca d'Arte del Museo Civico Correr (• **T-ms**: *Ven.C. C.128* • **T-pr**: *Aq1516Son*, *Fior1505*, *Giust1474*, *JacopSper*, *Pianto1493*)

—, Biblioteca della Fondazione Querini Stampalia (• **T-pr**: *Giust1506*, *JacopBen*)

—, Biblioteca Giustinian-Recanati (• **T-ms**: *Ven.GR. 120*, *Ven.GR. 121*)

—, Biblioteche della Fondazione Giorgio Cini (• **T-pr**: *Aq1502Bon*, *Colletanio1513*, *Fior1522*, *Giust1474*, *JacopBen*, *LaudeVecchie*)

—, Biblioteca Nazionale Marciana (• **T-ms**: *Ven.M. I.3*, *Ven.M. I.9*, *Ven.M. I.28*, *Ven.M. I.30*, *Ven.M. I.38*, *Ven.M. I.61*, *Ven.M. I.66*, *Ven.M. I.75*, *Ven.M. I.77*, *Ven.M. I.78*, *Ven.M. I.79*, *Ven.M. I.80*, *Ven.M. I.153*, *Ven.M. I.182*, *Ven.M. I.230*, *Ven.M. I.257*, *Ven.M. I.269*, *Ven.M. I.313*, *Ven.M. I.324*, *Ven.M. I.486*, *Ven.M. IZ.60* • **T-pr**: *Aq1502Bon*, *Aq1505Bon(B)*, *Aq1519Ses*, *Aq1530Zop*, *Aq1548Basc*, *Colletanio1510*, *Fior1510*, *Giust1483*, *LaudeBonac* [2 copies], *LaudeMisc*, *LaudeVecchie*, *LaudiGiunti*, *OperaNova*, *Patientia*, *Petr1470* [2 copies], *SolaVirtus* • **M-ms**: VenM I145 • **M-pr**: LiberSac1523, Razzi)

Ventimiglia, Biblioteca Civica Aprosiana (• **T-pr**: *Aq1502Bes*, *Aq1548Basc*)

Vercelli, Biblioteca Civica (• **T-pr**: *Aq1548Basc*)

Verona, Biblioteca dell'Accademia Filarmonica (• **M-pr**: GardFesta1556)

—, Biblioteca Capitolare (• **T-ms**: *Ver.Cap. 737*, *Ver.Cap. 811* • **T-pr**: *TebOp1498* • **M-ms**: VerCap 690, VerCap 757, VerCap 758, VerCap 760)

—, Biblioteca Civica (• **T-ms**: *Ver.Civ. 1212* • **T-pr**: *Pianto1490*)

Vicenza, Archivio di Stato (• **T-ms**: *Vic.A. 32bis*)

—, Biblioteca Civica Bertoliana (• **T-ms**: *Vic.C. 65, Vic.C. 111* • **T-pr**: *Aq1516Son, Giust1475, Pianto1481L*)

THE NETHERLANDS

Den Haag, Koninklijke Bibliotheek (• **T-pr**: *JacopMis*)

Maastricht, Rijksarchief van Limburg (• **M-ms**: MaaR)

POLAND

Kraków, Biblioteka Jagiellońska (• **M-ms**: KrakJ 40098 • **M-pr**: GardFesta1543, MeruloFesta, MüllerHeckel, PeSpinI, PeSpinII, Razzi, WyssHeckel)

Poznań, Miejska Biblioteka Publiczna im. Edwarda Raczyńskiego, Dział Zbiorów Specjalnych (• **M-ms**: PozR 1361)

Warszawa, Biblioteka Narodowa (• **M-ms**: WarN P364 [destroyed, but a microfilm is preserved])

—, Biblioteka Uniwersytecka, Oddział Zbiorów Muzycznych (• **M-ms**: WarU 5892)

Wrocław (Breslau), Biblioteka Kapitulna (• **M-ms**: WrocK 352)

—, Biblioteka Uniwersytecka (• **M-ms**: WrocU 428)

PORTUGAL

Coimbra, Biblioteca Geral da Universidade (• **M-ms**: CoimU 48)

RUSSIA

Kaliningrad (Königsberg), former Staats- und Universitätsbibliothek (• **M-ms**: KönU 150 [lost])

St. Peterburg, Rossijskaja Nacional'naja Biblioteka (• **T-pr**: *Giust1483* • **M-pr**: Razzi)

SLOVAKIA

Bratislava, Miestne Pracovisko Matice Slovenskej (• **M-ms**: BratM 33 [lost, but partially known through a photocopy])

SOUTH AFRICA

Cape Town, National Library of South Africa (*ex* South African Public Library) (• **M-ms**: CTL G12)

SPAIN

Ávila, Biblioteca Pública (• **T-pr**: *LaudeBonac*)

Barcelona, Biblioteca de Catalunya (*ex* Biblioteca Central) (• **M-ms**: BarcC 454 • **M-pr**: GiuJosqII, PeJosqII1515Gothic)

—, Biblioteca de la Institució Milà i Fontanals, Consejo Superior de Investigaciones Científicas (*ex* Biblioteca del Instituto Español de Musicologia) (• **M-pr**: ScottoFesta1547)

—, Biblioteca de la Universitat (• **T-PR**: *Aq1516Giu*)

Burgos, Monasterio de las Huelgas (• **M-MS**: BurHu)

El Escorial, Real Monasterio de San Lorenzo, Biblioteca y Archivo de Música (• **M-MS**: EsM 24)

Madrid, Biblioteca Nacional de España (• **T-PR**: *Aq1502Bes, Aq1513Ses, Aq1516Giu*)

—, Biblioteca del Palacio Real (• **M-MS**: MadP 1335 • **M-PR**: Baena)

—, Private Collections (• **M-PR**: PeFroI, PeFroIII1505, PeOdh1504 [*olim* Madrid, Biblioteca de la Casa Ducal de Medinaceli])

Segovia, Archivo Capitular de la Catedral (• **M-MS**: SegC)

Sevilla, Biblioteca Capitular y Colombina (• **T-MS**: *Sev.C. 31, Sev.C. 52* • **T-PR**: *Aq1510Tub, Busti1517, BustiPon, Colletanio1509, ContrFi, Giust1483, Infantia1515, OperaNova, Operetta1512, SetteDolori, TebEp1509* • **M-MS**: SevC 20, SevC 43 • **M-PR**: PeBossI1509, PeLaudeII, PeOdh1503)

València, Universitat de València, Biblioteca General e Històrica (• **T-PR**: *Aq1507Bon, Aq1516Giu*)

SWEDEN

Örebro, Karolinska Läroverkets Bibliotek (• **M-PR**: HanZanger)

Stockholm, Kungliga Biblioteket (• **T-MS**: *Stock.K. 5* • **T-PR**: *Petr1470*)

Uppsala, Universitetsbiblioteket (• **M-MS**: UppsU 76a, UppsU 76e, UppsU 478-80)

SWITZERLAND

Basel, Öffentliche Bibliothek der Universität (• **M-MS**: BasU 5-9, BasU 10, BasU 17-20, BasU 22, BasU 22-4, BasU 26c • **M-PR**: AntCanzoni, MüllerHeckel)

Bern, Stadt- und Universitätsbibliothek (• **M-PR**: PetreiusNewI)

Cologny, Fondation Martin Bodmer, Bibliotheca Bodmeriana (• **T-PR**: *Petr1470*)

Genève, Fondation Barbier-Müller (Université, Faculté des Lettres) (• **T-PR**: *Aq1510Rus*)

Lugano, Biblioteca Cantonale (• **T-PR**: *Giust1490*)

St. Gallen, Stiftsbibliothek (• **M-MS**: SGS 461, SGS 462, SGS 463, SGS 530)

Sion (Sitten), Archives du Chapitre de la Cathédrale (• **M-MS**: SionC 87-4)

Zofingen, Stadtbibliothek (• **M-PR**: PetreiusNewI)

UNITED KINGDOM

Cambridge, King's College Library (• **T-PR**: *Petr1470* [2 copies])

—, University Library (• **T-PR**: *Aq1530Zop, Giust1517, LaudeMisc* [one page only])

Edinburgh, National Library of Scotland (• **T-PR**: *Aq1548Basc*)

Liverpool, Public Libraries, Central Library (• **T-PR**: *Petr1470*)

London, British Library (• **T-MS**: *Lon.B.A.16439, Lon.B.A.27549* • **T-PR**: *Aq1502Bon, Aq1505Bon(B), Aq1505Son, Aq1508Bon, Aq1515Leg, Aq1516Bin, Aq1516Cas(B), Aq1516Giu, AqStramb(A), AqVav,*

Busti1517, Chasse, Fior1505, Giust1474, Giust1483, Giust1490, JacopMis, Lamento1526, LaudeBonac, LaudeMisc, Non1520, Non1528, Non1540M, Petr1470 [2 copies], *Pianto1481L, Ricco1511, Ricco1520, TebSon1499* • **M‑MS**: LonB A31922, LonB A35087, LonB E3051, LonB RXVI • **M‑PR**: FormGerle [2 copies], GiuJosqII, MüllerHeckel, PeIsaac, PeJosqII1515Gothic, PeJosqII1515Roman, PeLamI, PeLamII, PeMotB, Razzi [2 copies])

—, Private Collection of Nessa Glen (*olim* WERTHEIM AM MAIN, Fürstlich Löwenstein'sche Bibliothek) (• **M‑MS**: WML 6)

—, Royal College of Music (• **M‑PR**: MüllerHeckel)

—, Society of Antiquaries (• **T‑PR**: *Giust1475*)

MANCHESTER, John Rylands Library (• **T‑PR**: *Giust1475, Petr1470*)

OXFORD, Bodleian Library (• **T‑MS**: *Ox.B. CI.99, Ox.B. CI.180, Ox.B. CI.193, Ox.B. CI.208, Ox.B. CI.240, Ox.B. CI.263, Ox.B. CI.301, Ox.B. CL.317, Ox.B. CL.363* • **T‑PR**: *Aq1502Bon, Aq1505Son, Aq1548Basc, Giust1474, LaudeBonac, Petr1470, TebEp1557* • **M‑PR**: Razzi)

—, Private Collection of David Rogers (• **T‑PR**: *Pianto1495*)

UNITED STATES OF AMERICA

ATLANTA (GA), Emory University Library (• **T‑PR**: *LaudeBonac*)

BALTIMORE, Walters Art Gallery (• **T‑PR**: *TebSon1499*)

BOSTON, Public Library, Music Department (• **M‑PR**: GiuCant1523, GiuCant1536)

BRYN MAWR (PA), Bryn Mawr College, Marjorie Walter Goodhart Medieval Library (• **T‑PR**: *BelcLBart, LaudeMisc*)

CAMBRIDGE (MA), Harvard University, Houghton Library (• **T‑PR**: *Aq1502Bon, Aq1516Son, Aq1522Rus, LaudeBonac, Petr1470*)

CHICAGO, Newberry Library (• **T‑PR**: *Petr1470* • **M‑MS**: ChN 25 • **M‑PR**: GiuCant1536, PeBossI1515, PeDalza)

CLAREMONT (CA), Honnold Library (Bodman Collection), Associated Colleges (• **T‑PR**: *LaudeBonac*)

CORVALLIS (OR), Oregon State University Library (• **T‑PR**: *LaudeMisc*)

DURHAM (NC), Duke University, Perkins Library (• **T‑PR**: *Aq1503Man*)

ITHACA (NY), Cornell University Library, Kroch Library Rare & Manuscripts (• **T‑PR**: *Petr1470* • **M‑PR**: HanZanger)

LOS ANGELES, University of California Library (• **T‑PR**: *Aq1516Son, Giust1483*)

MINNEAPOLIS (MN), Minneapolis Public Library (• **M‑PR**: GiuCant1536)

NEW HAVEN, Yale University, Beinecke Rare Book and Manuscript Library (• **M‑MS**: NHY 91 • **T‑PR**: *Aq1502Bes, Aq1509Son, JacopMis*)

NEW YORK, Columbia University (• **T‑MS**: *N.Y.C. 195*)

—, Jewish Theological Seminary of America Library (• **T‑PR**: *Aq1505Son*)

—, Pierpont Morgan Library (• **T‑PR**: *Giust1475, Petr1470* • **M‑PR**: Motetti1520, PeOdh1504)

—, New York Public Library, Humanities‑Rare Books Division (• **T‑PR**: *Aq1502Bon*)

—, New York Public Library, Spencer Collection (• **T‑PR**: *Aq1529Mor, Non1540R*)

PHILADELPHIA, Rosenbach Museum and Library (• **T-PR**: *Petr1470*)

—, University of Pennsylvania Library, J. Robert van Pelt Library (• **T-PR**: *Aq1516Cas(A)*, *Aq1516Cas(B)*, *Aq1519Ses*)

PRINCETON, University Library (• **T-PR**: *Aq1516Giu*)

PROVIDENCE (RI), Annmary Brown Memorial Library, Brown University (• **T-PR**: *Pianto1478*)

ROCHESTER (NY), Sibley Music Library, Eastman School of Music, University of Rochester (• **M-PR**: GiuCant1536, PeJosqII1505, PeJosqII1515Gothic)

ST. MEINRAD (IN), Archabbey Library of St. Meinrad (• **M-PR**: GiuCant1536)

SAN MARINO (CA), Henry E. Huntington Library (• **T-PR**: *JacopMis*)

UNIVERSITY PARK (PA), Pennsylvania State University Libraries (• **T-PR**: *Aq1503Bes*)

WASHINGTON, DC, Folger Shakespeare Library (• **T-PR**: *Aq1503Bon, Fior1510*)

—, Library of Congress (• **T-PR**: *Aq1548Basc, Giust1490, Petr1470* • **M-MS**: WashC J6, WashC L25, WashC M6 • **M-PR**: HanZanger, PeOdh1504, PetreiusNewI)

VATICAN CITY

CITTÀ DEL VATICANO, Biblioteca Apostolica Vaticana (• **T-MS**: *CV. BL.3679, CV. BL.3695, CV. BL.3711, CV. BL.4047, CV. Ca.193, CV. Ch.120, CV. Ch.176, CV. Ch.266, CV. OL.251, CV. OL.3322, CV. P.113, CV. P.341, CV. P.1513, CV. ReL.478, CV. Ro.229, CV. Ro.424, CV. Ro.651, CV. Ro.1002, CV.VL.3195, CV.VL.3213, CV.VL.5133, CV.VL.5159, CV.VL.5170, CV.VL.7714, CV. VL.8191, CV.VL.13026, CV.VL.13704* • **T-PR**: *Aq1503Baz, Aq1503Bon, Aq1505Son, Aq1515Leg, Aq1516Cas(A), Aq1516Giu, Aq1530Zop, Busti1492S, Colletanio1537, Fior1505, Giust1495, JacopBen, JacopMis, JacopSper, LaudeBonac* [3 copies], *OperaFregoso, Petr1470* [2 copies], *Pianto1481L* • **M-MS**: CV F84, CV G27, CV S15, CV S35, CV S41, CV S42 • **M-PR**: GiuCant1523, LiberSac1523, LiberSac1537, PeJosqII1515Roman)

CURRENT LOCATION UNKNOWN

• **T-MS**: *Brambilla, Gub.Maz, Spithöver, Tessier* • **T-PR**: *Busti1488, Infantia1513, Infantia1541* • **M-PR**: PeBossI1509 (private possession), PeFroI (private possession), PeFroIII1505 (private possession), PeFroIV1505 (private possession), PeOdh1503 (private possession)

BIBLIOGRAPHICAL REFERENCES

ABERT 1927

ABERT, Hermann Joseph. *Illustriertes Musik-Lexikon*, Stuttgart, Engelhorns, 1927.

AGNELLI 1902

AGNELLI, Giovanni. 'Il Libro dei battuti di San Defendente di Lodi. Saggio di dialetto lodigiano del secolo decimo quarto', in: *Archivio storico per la città e comuni del circondario di Lodi*, XXI (1902), pp. iii-xv, 1-106.

AGOSTI 1993

AGOSTI, Stefano. *Gli occhi, le chiome. Per una lettura psicoanalitica del Canzoniere di Petrarca*, Milan, Feltrinelli, 1993.

AH

Analecta hymnica medii aevi, edited by Guido Maria Dreves, Clemens Blume, and Henry Marriott Bannister, 55 vols, Leipzig, Fues Verlag (R. Reisland), 1886-1922.

ALBRECHT 1959

Symphoniae Jucundae atque adeo breves 4 vocum, ab optimis quibusque musicis compositae 1538, edited by Hans Albrecht, Kassel, Bärenreiter - Saint Louis (MO), Concordia Edition, 1959.

ALLOCCO-CASTELLINO 1926

BELCARI, Feo. *Sacre rappresentazioni e laude*, introduction and notes by Onorato Allocco-Castellino, Turin, UTET, 1926 (I classici italiani, 16).

ALM *ET AL*. 1996

Musica Franca: Essays in Honor of Frank A. D'Accone, edited by Irene Alm, Alyson McLamore, and Colleen Reardon, Stuyvesant (NY), Pendragon Press, 1996 (Festschrift Series, 18).

AM

Antiphonale monasticum pro diurnis horis, Paris-Tournai-Rome, Desclée et Socii, 1934.

AMAURY 1894

AMAURY, Louys, Baron de La Grange. 'L'album de musique du XVe siècle du musée de Tournai', in: *Annales de la Société d'archéologie de Bruxelles. Mémoires, rapports et documents*, VIII (1894), pp. 114-119.

AMBROS I-V

AMBROS, August Wilhelm. *Geschichte der Musik* (3rd edn.), 5 vols, Leipzig, Leuckart, 1887-1911 (vol. V: *Auserwählte Tonwerke der berühmsten Meister des 15. und 16. Jahrhunderts. Eine Beispielsammlung zu dem dritten Bande der Musikgeschichte von A. W. Ambros nach dessen unvollendet hinterlassenem Notenmaterial mit zahlreiche Vermehrungen*, edited by Otto Kade, 2nd rev. edn., Leipzig, Leuckart, 1889).

AMORTH 1998

AMORTH, Luigi. *Modena capitale. Storia di Modena e dei suoi duchi dal 1598 al 1860*, no pl., Banca Popolare dell'Emilia Romagna, 1998.

AMS

Antiphonale Missarum Sextuplex, d'apres le graduel de Monza et les antiphonaires de Rheinau, du Mont-Blandin, de Compiègne, de Corbie et de Senlis, edited by René-Jean Hesbert, Brussels, Vromant & C., 1935; rpt. Rome, Herder, 1985.

ANDREOSE 2001

ANDREOSE, Alvise. 'Censimento dei manoscritti del *Pianto della Vergine* (*Lamentatio beatae Virginis*) di Enselmino da Montebelluna conservati alla Biblioteca Nazionale Marciana', in: *Quaderni veneti*, XVII/33 (2001), pp. 7-28.

ANGLÉS 1931

    El còdex musical de las Huelgas (Música a veus dels segles XIII-XIV), introduction, facsimile, and transcription by Higinio Anglés, 3 vols, Barcelona, Institut d'Estudis Catalanis - Biblioteca de Catalunya, 1931.

ANTIPHONALE SARISBURIENSE

    Antiphonale Sarisburiense: A Reproduction in Facsimile of a Manuscript of the 13th Century, edited by Walter Howard Frere, 6 vols, London, Plainsong and Mediaeval Music Society, 1901-1924; rpt. Farnborough, Gregg Press, 1966.

ANTONETTI 1964

    ANTONETTI, Pierre. 'Poésie et littérature dans la canzone: *Di pensier in pensier…* (Pétrarque, "Canzoniere", CXXIX)', in: *Annales de la Faculté des Lettres d'Aix*, XXXVIII (1964), pp. 195-204.

AR

    Antiphonale Sacrosanctae Romanae Ecclesiae pro diurnis horis, Paris-Tournai-Rome, Desclée et Socii, 1924.

ARS NOVA V

    L'Ars nova italiana del Trecento, V, edited by Agostino Ziino, Palermo, Enchiridion, 1985.

ATLAS 1975-76

    ATLAS, Allan W. *The Cappella Giulia Chansonnier (Rome, Biblioteca Apostolica Vaticana, C.G. XIII.27)*, 2 vols, Brooklyn, Institute of Mediaeval Music, 1975-1976 (Wissenschaftliche Abhandlungen - Musicological Studies, XXVII, 1).

ATLAS 1981

    ATLAS, Allan W. 'Conflicting Attributions in Italian Sources of the Franco-Netherlandish Chanson, *c.*1465 - *c.*1505: A Progress Report on a New Hypothesis', in: FENLON 1981, pp. 249-293.

ATLAS 1985

    ATLAS, Allan W. *Music at the Aragonese Court of Naples*, Cambridge, Cambridge University Press, 1985.

ATLAS 1993

    ATLAS, Allan W. 'Aragonese Naples and Medicean Florence: Musical Interrelationships and Influence in the Late Fifteenth Century', in: GARGIULO 1993, pp. 15-45.

ATLAS 1998a

    Anthology of Renaissance Music, edited by Allan W. Atlas, New York - London, Norton, 1998.

ATLAS 1998b

    ATLAS, Allan W. *Renaissance Music. Music in Western Europe, 1400-1600*, New York - London, Norton, 1998.

ATLAS 2005

    ATLAS, Allan W. 'Petrucci's Songbooks and Japart's Biography', in: CATTIN - DALLA VECCHIA 2005, pp. 645-660.

AUGSBURGER LIEDERBUCH 1997

    Das Augsburger Liederbuch … Sign. CIM 43 (2° Cod. 142a) der Staats- und Stadtbibliothek Augsburg, Stuttgart, Cornetto, 1997 (Faksimile-Edition Augsburg, 3).

BAKER 1978

    BAKER, Norma Klein. *An Unnumbered Manuscript of Polyphony in the Archives of the Cathedral of Segovia: Its Provenance and History*, 2 vols, Ph.D. diss., College Park (MD), University of Maryland, 1978.

BANFI 1956

    BANFI, Luigi. 'Lo zibaldone quattrocentesco di Giovanni de' Dazi', in: *Acme*, IX (1956), pp. 25-51.

BANFI (1963) 1974

    Sacre rappresentazioni del Quattrocento, edited by Luigi Banfi, Turin, UTET, 1963; rev. edn. 1974.

BANKS 1993

    BANKS, Jon. *The Motet as a Formal Type in Northern Italy ca. 1500*, 2 vols, New York, Garland, 1993.

BANKS 1999

    BANKS, Jon. 'Performing the Instrumental Music in the Segovia Codex', in: *Early Music*, XXVII (1999), pp. 295-309.

BARBIERI 1890

Cancionero musical de los siglos XV y XVI transcrito y comentado por Francisco Asenjo Barbieri, Madrid, Real Academia de Bellas Artes de San Fernando, 1890; rpt. edited by Emilio Casares Rodicio, [Malaga], Departamento de Publicaciones del Centro Cultural de la "Generación del 27", [1987].

BARRET 1981

BARRET, Charles Edward. *A Critical Edition of the Dijon Chansonnier: Dijon, Bibliothèque de la ville, Ms. 517 (ancien 295)*, 4 vols, Ph.D. diss., Nashville (TN), George Peabody College - Vanderbilt University, 1981.

BASILE 1983

BASILE, Tania. *Per il testo critico delle rime del Tebaldeo*, Messina, Centro di Studi umanistici, 1983 (Itinerari eruditi, 1).

BASILE - MARCHAND 1989-92

TEBALDEO, Antonio. *Rime*, edited by Tania Basile and Jean-Jacques Marchand, 3 vols, Modena, Panini, 1989-1992.

BATTAGLIA

BATTAGLIA, Salvatore. *Grande dizionario della lingua italiana*, 21 vols, Turin, UTET, 1961-2002.

BAUER FORMICONI 1967

BAUER FORMICONI, Barbara. *Die Strambotti des Serafino dall'Aquila*, Munich, Fink, 1967 (Freiburger Schriften zur romanischen Philologie, 10).

BECHERINI 1942-43

BECHERINI, Bianca. 'Alcuni canti dell'*Odhecaton* e del codice fiorentino 2794', in: *Bulletin de l'Institut historique belge de Rome*, XXII (1942-43), pp. 327-348.

BECHERINI 1953

BECHERINI, Bianca. 'La canzone *Alla battaglia* di Henricus Isac', in: *Revue belge de Musicologie*, VII (1953), pp. 5-25.

BECHERINI 1954

BECHERINI, Bianca. 'Musica italiana a Firenze nel XV secolo', in: *Revue belge de Musicologie*, VIII (1954), pp. 109-121.

BECHERINI 1959a

BECHERINI, Bianca. *Catalogo dei manoscritti musicali della Biblioteca Nazionale di Firenze*, Kassel, Bärenreiter, 1959.

BECHERINI 1959b

BECHERINI, Bianca. 'Poesia e musica in Italia ai primi del XV secolo', in: *L'Ars nova. Recueil d'études sur la musique du XIVe siècle. Les colloques de Wégimont, II-1955*, Paris, Les belles lettres, 1959, pp. 239-250.

BENDISCIOLI 1960

BENDISCIOLI, Mario. 'Finalità tradizionali e motivi nuovi in una confraternita a Mantova del terzo decennio del Cinquecento', in: *Problemi di vita religiosa in Italia nel Cinquecento. Atti del Convegno di Storia della Chiesa in Italia, Bologna, 2-6 settembre 1958*, Padua, Antenore, 1960 (Italia Sacra: Studi e documenti di Storia ecclesiastica, 2), pp. 91-101.

BENT 1969

BENT, Margaret. *The Old Hall Manuscript: A Paleographical Study*, Ph.D. diss., Cambridge, University of Cambridge, 1969.

BENT 1984

BENT, Margaret. 'Text Setting in Sacred Music of the Early 15th Century: Evidence and Implications', in: GÜNTHER - FINSCHER 1984, pp. 291-326; rpt. EADEM. *Counterpoint, Composition and Musica Ficta*, New York - London, Routledge, 2002, pp. 273-300.

BENTE 1968

BENTE, Martin. *Neue Wege der Quellenkritik und die Biographie Ludwig Senfls*, Wiesbaden, Breitkopf & Härtel, 1968.

VAN BENTHEM 1980

BENTHEM, Jaap van. '*Fortuna* in Focus: Concerning "Conflicting" Progressions in Josquin's *Fortuna dun gran tempo*', in: *Tijdschrift van de Koninklijke Vereniging voor Nederlandse Muziekgeschiedenis*, XXX (1980), pp. 1-50.

BERNOULLI 1910

BERNOULLI, Eduard. *Aus Liederbüchern der Humanistenzeit: Eine bibliographische und notentypographische Studie*, Leipzig, Breitkopf & Härtel, 1910.

BERTOLOTTI 1890

BERTOLOTTI, Antonio. *I Musici alla corte dei Gonzaga in Mantova dal secolo XV al XVIII*, Milan, Ricordi, 1890; rpt. Bologna, Forni, 1969.

BERTONE 1999

BERTONE, Giorgio. *Lo sguardo escluso. L'idea di paesaggio nella letteratura occidentale*, Novara, Interlinea, 1999.

BESSELER 1931

BESSELER, Heinrich. *Die Musik des Mittelalters und der Renaissance*, Potsdam, Athenaion, 1931 (Handbuch der Musikwissenschaft, 2).

BESSELER 1950

Capella: Meisterwerke mittelalterlicher Musik, I, edited by Heinrich Besseler, Kassel, Bärenreiter, 1950; rpt. 1959.

BETTARINI 2005

PETRARCA, Francesco. *Canzoniere. Rerum vulgarium fragmenta*, edited by Rosanna Bettarini, 2 vols, Turin, Einaudi, 2005.

BEVILACQUA 1994

BEVILACQUA, Claudio. *Fra Enselmino da Montebelluna frate laudario O.E.S.A. (ca 1285 - ca 1355) ed "El planto de la Verzene Maria"*, Trieste, Kuhar, 1994.

BIADEGO 1892

BIADEGO, Giuseppe. *Catalogo descrittivo dei manoscritti della Biblioteca Comunale di Verona*, Verona, Civelli, 1892.

BIADENE 1885

BIADENE, Leandro. 'La Passione e Risurrezione. Poemetto veronese del sec. XIII', in: *Studi di Filologia romanza*, I (1885), pp. 215-275, 449-452.

BIADENE 1887   .

BIADENE, Leandro. 'Un manoscritto di rime spirituali (cod. Hamilton 348)', in: *Giornale storico della letteratura italiana*, IX (1887), pp. 186-214.

BIGI 1983

BIGI, Emilio. 'La canzone CXXIX, in: *Lectura Petrarce*, III (1983), pp. 79-97; then in: IDEM. *Poesia latina e volgare nel Rinascimento italiano*, Naples, Morano, 1989, pp. 9-30.

BINDER 1861

Novus thesaurus adagiorum latinorum. Lateinischer Sprichwörterschatz…, edited by Wilhelm Binder, Stuttgart, Fischhaber, 1861; rpt. Niederwalluf bei Wiesbaden, M. Sandig, 1971.

BINI 1851

Laudi spirituali del Bianco da Siena, povero Gesuato del sec. XIV, edited by Telesforo Bini, Lucca, Giusti, 1851 (partial rpt. as *Laude mistiche del Bianco da Siena*, edited by Gennaro Maria Monti, Lanciano, G. Carabba, 1925).

BINI 1852

Rime e prose del buon secolo della lingua, edited by Telesforo Bini, Lucca, Giusti, 1852.

BIZZARRI 1941

BIZZARRI, Edoardo. 'Inediti italiani della *Grey Collection*', in: *La Rinascita*, IV (1941), pp. 860-870.

BLACK 1989

BLACK, Christopher F. *Italian Confraternities in the Sixteenth Century*, Cambridge, Cambridge University Press, 1989.

BLACKBURN 1981b

BLACKBURN, Bonnie J. 'Two "Carnival Songs" Unmasked: A Commentary on MS Florence Magl. XIX.121', in: *Musica Disciplina*, XXXV (1981), pp. 121-178.

BLACKBURN 1996

BLACKBURN, Bonnie J. 'Lorenzo de' Medici, a Lost Isaac Manuscript, and the Venetian Ambassador', in: ALM *ET AL.* 1996, pp. 19-44; rpt. BLACKBURN 2000, no. V.

BLACKBURN 1997

    BLACKBURN, Bonnie J. 'For Whom Do the Singers Sing?', in: *Early Music*, XXV (1997), pp. 593-609.

BLACKBURN 1999

    BLACKBURN, Bonnie J. 'The Virgin in the Sun: Music and Image for a Prayer Attributed to Sixtus IV', in: *Journal of the Royal Music Association*, CXXIV (1999), pp. 157-195.

BLACKBURN 2000

    BLACKBURN, Bonnie J. *Composition, Printing and Performance*, Aldershot, Ashgate, 2000.

BLACKBURN 2001a

    BLACKBURN, Bonnie J. 'The Dispute about Harmony *c.*1500, and the Creation of a New Style', in: *Théorie et analyse musicales 1450-1650. Actes du colloque international Louvain-la-Neuve, 23-25 septembre 1999*, edited by Anne-Emmanuelle Ceulemans and Bonnie J. Blackburn, Louvain-la-Neuve, Département d'histoire de l'art et d'archéologie - Collège Érasme, 2001 (Publications d'histoire de l'art et d'archéologie de l'Université Catholique de Louvain - C; Musicologica Neolovaniensia, Studia 9), pp. 1-37.

BLACKBURN 2001b

    BLACKBURN, Bonnie J. 'Canonic Conundrums: The Singer's Petrucci', in: *Basler Jahrbuch für historische Musikpraxis*, XXV (2001), pp. 53-69.

BLACKBURN 2003

    BLACKBURN, Bonnie J. 'Messages in Miniature: Pictorial Programme and Theological Implications in the Alamire Choirbooks', in: *The Burgundian-Habsburg Court Complex of Music Manuscripts (1500-1535) and the Workshop of Petrus Alamire. Colloquium Proceedings Leuven 25-28 November 1999*, general editors Bruno Bouckaert and Eugeen Schreurs, Leuven-Neerpelt, Alamire Foundation, 2003 (Yearbook of the Alamire Foundation, 5), pp. 161-184.

BLACKBURN 2005

    BLACKBURN, Bonnie J. 'The Sign of Petrucci's Editor', in: CATTIN - DALLA VECCHIA 2005, pp. 415-429.

BLACKBURN *ET AL.* 1991

    A Correspondence of Renaissance Musicians, edited by Bonnie J. Blackburn, Edward E. Lowinsky, and Clement A. Miller, Oxford, Clarendon Press, 1991.

BLOXAM *ET AL.* 2009

    "Uno gentile et subtile ingenio": Studies in Renaissance Music in Honour of Bonnie Blackburn, edited by M. Jennifer Bloxam, Gioia Filocamo, and Leofranc Holford-Strevens, Turnhout, Brepols, 2009 (Épitome musical).

BOER 1938

    BOER, Coenraad L. W. *Chansonvormen op het einde van de XVde eeuw: Een studie naar aanleiding van Petrucci's "Harmonice musices Odhecaton"*, Amsterdam, H. J. Paris, 1938.

BONDA 1996

    BONDA, Jan Willem. *De meerstemmige Nederlandse liederen van de vijftiende en zestiende eeuw*, Ph.D. diss., Utrecht, Universiteit Utrecht, 1996; Hilversum, Verloren, 1996.

BONFANTINI 1942

    Le sacre rappresentazioni italiane. Raccolta di testi dal sec. XIII al secolo XVI, edited by Mario Bonfantini, Milan, Bompiani, [1942].

BONVESIN DE LA RIVA

    BONVESIN DE LA RIVA, 'Vita scolastica', in: *Quinque claves sapientiae. Incerti auctoris "Rudium doctrina". Bonvicini de Ripa "Vita scolastica"*, edited by Anežka Vidmanová-Schmidtová, Leipzig, Teubner, 1969 (Bibliotheca scriptorum Graecorum et Romanorum Teubneriana).

BOORMAN 1981a

    BOORMAN, Stanley. 'Limitations and Extensions of Filiation Technique', in: FENLON 1981, pp. 319-346.

BOORMAN 1995

    BOORMAN, Stanley. 'Composition-Copying: Performance-Re-Creation: The Matrix of Stemmatic Problems for Early Music', in: BORGHI - ZAPPALÀ 1995, pp. 45-55.

BOORMAN 2006

    BOORMAN, Stanley. *Ottaviano Petrucci: A Catalogue Raisonné*, New York, Oxford University Press, 2006.

BOORMAN – BEEBE 2001

    Ottaviano Petrucci. Harmonice Musices Odhecaton A, facsimile, edited by Stanley Boorman and Ellen S. Beebe, New York, Broude Trust, 2001 (Critical Facsimiles, 7).

BORGHI 1995

    BORGHI, Renato. *Il manoscritto Basevi 2441 della Biblioteca del Conservatorio "L. Cherubini" di Firenze. Edizione critica*, tesi di dottorato in Filologia musicale, Cremona, Università di Pavia, a.a. 1994-95.

BORGHI – ZAPPALà 1995

    L'edizione critica tra testo musicale e testo letterario, edited by Renato Borghi and Pietro Zappalà, Lucca, LIM, 1995 (Studi e testi musicali, n.s., 3).

BOSCOLO 1999

    Frottole, Libro Octavo. Ottaviano Petrucci, Venezia 1507, edited by Lucia Boscolo, Padua, CLUEP, 1999 (Octaviani Petrutii Forosemproniensis Froctolae, II).

BOSCOLO 2003

    BOSCOLO, Lucia. '*Son passaro solitario tornato…*: post scriptum al *ciclo dell'uccello*', in: *Musica e Storia*, XI (2003), pp. 347-368.

BOUQUET 1968

    BOUQUET, Marie-Thérèse. 'La Cappella musicale dei Duchi di Savoia dal 1450 al 1500', in: *Rivista italiana di Musicologia*, III (1968), pp. 233-285.

BR

    Breviarium Romanum ex Decreto Sacrosancti Concilii Tridentini restitutum, Pii V. Pont. Max. iussu editum, Rome, Paolo Manuzio, 1568; rpt. *Breviarium Romanum, Editio Princeps (1568)*; rpt., introduction and appendix edited by Manlio Sodi and Achille Maria Triacca, with the collaboration of Maria Gabriella Foti, Vatican City, Libreria Editrice Vaticana, 1999.

BRAINARD 1985

    BRAINARD, Ingrid. 'L'arte del danzare in transizione: un documento tedesco sconosciuto sulla danza di corte', in: *La Danza italiana*, III (1985), pp. 77-89.

BRAMBILLA 1903

    BRAMBILLA, Ettore. *Rime ascetiche trascritte da un codice napoletano e da un comense del secolo XV*, Cuneo, Tipografia Isoardi, 1903.

BRANCACCI 2005

    BRANCACCI, Fiorella. 'Dal canto umanistico su versi latini alla frottola. La tradizione dell'ode saffica', in: *Studi musicali*, XXXIV (2005), pp. 267-318.

BRENNECKE 1953

    BRENNECKE, Wilfried. *Die Handschrift A.R. 940/41 der Proske-Bibliothek zu Regensburg*, Kassel-Basel, Bärenreiter, 1953.

BRIDGMAN 1953-56

    BRIDGMAN, Nanie. 'Un manuscrit italien du début du XVIe siècle à la Bibliothèque nationale (Département de la musique, Rés.Vm.⁷ 676)', in: *Annales musicologiques: Moyen-Age et Renaissance*, I (1953), pp. 177-267; IV (1956), pp. 259-260.

BRIQUET

    BRIQUET, Charles-Moïse. *Les filigranes: Dictionnaire historique des marques du papier dès leur apparition vers 1282 jusqu'en 1600*, 4 vols, Paris, A. Picard & fils - Geneva, A. Jullien, 1907; rpt. edited by Allan Stevenson, Amsterdam, Paper Publications Society, 1968.

BRONZINI 1976

    Testi e temi di letteratura popolare, II, edited by Giovanni Battista Bronzini, Bari, Adriatica, 1976.

BRONZINI 1977

    Testi e temi di letteratura popolare, III, edited by Giovanni Battista Bronzini, Bari, Adriatica, 1977.

BROOKS 1951

  BROOKS, Catherine V. *Antoine Busnois as a Composer of Chansons*, 3 vols, Ph.D. diss., New York, New York University, 1951.

BROWN 1963

  BROWN, Howard Mayer. *Music in the French Secular Theater, 1400-1550*, Cambridge (MA), Harvard University Press, 1963.

BROWN 1982

  BROWN, Howard Mayer. 'Emulation, Competition, and Homage: Imitation and Theories of Imitation in the Renaissance', in: *Journal of the American Musicological Society*, XXXV (1982), pp. 1-48.

BROWN 1983

  A Florentine Chansonnier from the Time of Lorenzo the Magnificent. Florence, Biblioteca Nazionale Centrale MS Banco Rari 229, edited by Howard M. Brown, 2 vols, Chicago-London, University of Chicago Press, 1983 (Monuments of Renaissance Music, 7).

BROWN 1990

  BROWN, Howard Mayer. 'The Mirror of Man's Salvation: Music in Devotional Life about 1500', in: *Renaissance Quarterly*, XLIII (1990), pp. 744-773.

BROWN – POLK 2001

  BROWN, Howard Mayer – POLK, Keith. 'Instrumental Music, *c.*1300 – *c.*1520', in: *Music as Concept and Practice in the Late Middle Ages*, edited by Reinhard Strohm and Bonnie J. Blackburn, Oxford, Oxford University Press, 2001 (The New Oxford History of Music, III/1), pp. 97-161.

BROWN – STEIN 1999

  BROWN, Howard Mayer – STEIN, Louise K. *Music in the Renaissance*, Upper Saddle River (NJ), Prentice Hall, 1999.

BRUNELLI 1986

  BRUNELLI, Roberto. *Diocesi di Mantova*, Brescia, Editrice La Scuola, 1986 (Storia religiosa della Lombardia, 8).

BRZEZIŃSKA 1986

  BRZEZIŃSKA, Barbara. *Repertuar polskich tabulatur organowych z pierwszej połowy XVI wieku* [Repertoire of the Polish organ tablatures from the first half of the 16th c.], Kraków, Polskie Wydawn. Muzyczne, 1987.

BUKOFZER 1950

  BUKOFZER, Manfred Fritz. *A Polyphonic Basse Dance of the Renaissance*, in: IDEM. *Studies in Medieval and Renaissance Music*, New York, Norton, 1950, pp. 190-216.

BUSSE BERGER 1993

  BUSSE BERGER, Anna Maria. *Mensuration and Proportion Signs: Origins and Evolution*, Oxford, Clarendon Press, 1993.

CALZAVARA 1950

  FRA ENSELMINO, *El pianto de la Verzene Maria*, edited by Ernesto Calzavara, Milan, All'insegna del pesce d'oro, 1950.

CANAL (1879) 1881

  CANAL, Pietro. *Della musica in Mantova: notizie tratte principalmente dall'Archivio Gonzaga ed esposte dal M.E. Ab. Pietro Canal*, [Venice, Tipografia Antonelli], 1881; rpt. Bologna, Forni, 1977.

CAO

  Corpus Antiphonalium Officii, edited by René-Jean Hesbert, 6 vols, Rome, Herder, 1963-1979 (Rerum Ecclesiasticarum Documenta Cura Pontifici Athenaei Sancti Anselmi de Urbe Edita, Series maior. Fontes, 7-12).

CAPPELLI 1868

  Poesie musicali dei secoli XIV, XV e XVI tratte da vari codici, edited by Antonio Cappelli, Bologna, Romagnoli, 1868.

CAPPELLI 1975

  CAPPELLI, Antonio. *Ballate, rispetti d'amore e poesie varie tratte da codici musicali dei secoli XIV, XV e XVI*, Modena, Cappelli, 1866 (per le nozze Cappelli - Saltini); new edn. Bologna, Forni, 1975.

CAPPONI 1747

  Catalogo della libreria Capponi, o sia de' libri italiani del fu Marchese Alessandro Gregorio Capponi, Rome, Bernabò e Lazzarini, 1747.

CARBONI 1977

    CARBONI, Fabio. *Incipitario della lirica italiana dei secoli XIII e XIV. I: Biblioteca Apostolica Vaticana, fondi Archivio S. Pietro - Urbinate latino*, Vatican City, Biblioteca Apostolica Vaticana, 1977 (Studi e Testi, 277).

CARBONI – ZIINO 1973

    CARBONI, Fabio - ZIINO, Agostino. 'Laudi musicali del XVI secolo: il manoscritto Ferrajoli 84 della Biblioteca Apostolica Vaticana', in: *Cultura neolatina*, XXXIII (1973), pp. 273-329.

CARBONI – ZIINO 1996

    CARBONI, Fabio - ZIINO, Agostino. 'Un elenco di composizioni musicali della seconda metà del Quattrocento', in: ALM *ET AL.* 1996, pp. 425-487.

CARDUCCI 1863

    Le Stanze, l'Orfeo e le Rime di messer Angelo Ambrogini Poliziano, edited by Giosuè Carducci, Florence, Barbèra, 1863.

CARDUCCI (1896) 1973

    CARDUCCI, Giosuè. *Cacce in rima dei secoli XIV e XV*, Bologna, Zanichelli, 1896; Bologna, A.M.I.S., 1973.

CASIMIRI 1941

    CASIMIRI, Raffaele. 'Musica e musicisti nella Cattedrale di Padova nei sec. XIV, XV, XVI. Contributo per una storia', in: *Note d'archivio per la storia musicale*, XVIII (1941), pp. 1-31, 101-180, 181-214. (The study continues in vol. XIX (1942), pp. 49-92.)

CASNATI – RE 1965

    CASNATI, Francesco - RE, Maria Luisa. 'Il Pianto di fra' Enselmino nel laudario dei Battuti comaschi', in: *Ausonia* XX/1 (1965), pp. 15-18.

CASTIGLIONI 1932

    CASTIGLIONI, Carlo. 'Di una lauda attribuita al Savonarola e al Belcari e di un codice dell'Ambrosiana', in: *Convivium*, IV (1932), pp. 245-247.

CATALOGUE PARIS

    Catalogue de la musique imprimée avant 1800 conservée dans les bibliothèques publiques de Paris, published under the direction of François Lesure, Paris, Bibliothèque Nationale de France, 1981.

CATTIN 1968a

    CATTIN, Giulio. 'Le composizioni musicali del ms. Pavia Aldini 361', in: *L'Ars nova italiana del Trecento*, II, edited by F. Alberto Gallo, Certaldo, Centro di Studi sull'Ars nova italiana del Trecento, 1968, pp. 1-21; rpt. CATTIN 2003, pp. 115-133.

CATTIN 1968b

    CATTIN, Giulio. 'Polifonia quattrocentesca italiana nel codice Washington, Library of Congress, ML 171 J 6', in: *Quadrivium*, IX (1968), pp. 87-102; rpt. CATTIN 2003, pp. 97-113.

CATTIN 1969

    CATTIN, Giulio, in: *Quadrivium*, X/2 (1969), pp. 5-47 (an untitled essay comprising: 1. *Il presbyter Johannes de Quadris*, pp. 5-12; 2. *Le opere*, pp. 12-17; 3. *Iste confessor*, pp. 17-20; 4. *Lamentationes Jeremiae Prophetae*, pp. 20-35; 5. *Processio in die Veneris Sancti*, pp. 35-42; 6. *Opere profane attribuite*, pp. 43-45).

CATTIN 1970

    CATTIN, Giulio. 'Tradizione e tendenze innovatrici nella normativa e nella pratica liturgico-musicale della Congregazione di S. Giustina', in: *Benedictina*, XVII (1970), pp. 254-299.

CATTIN (1971a) 2003

    CATTIN, Giulio. 'Le poesie del Savonarola nelle fonti musicali', in: *Quadrivium*, XII/1 (1971), pp. 259-281; rpt. CATTIN 2003, pp. 135-151.

CATTIN 1971b

    CATTIN, Giulio. *Johannes de Quadris: musico del sec. XV*, Bologna, Forni, 1971 (Biblioteca di *Quadrivium*. Serie musicologica, 12).

CATTIN 1972a

    CATTIN, Giulio. 'Canti polifonici del repertorio benedettino in uno sconosciuto *Liber quadragesimalis* e in altre fonti italiane dei sec. XV e XVI inc.', in: *Benedictina*, XIX (1972), pp. 445-537.

CATTIN 1972b

    Johannis de Quadris Opera, edited by Giulio Cattin, Bologna, AMIS, 1972 (Antiquae Musicae Italicae Monumenta, Monumenta Veneta Sacra, II).

CATTIN 1973a

    CATTIN, Giulio. 'Nuova fonte italiana della polifonia intorno al 1500 (Ms. Cape Town, Grey 3.b.12)', in: *Acta musicologica*, XLV (1973), pp. 165-221; rpt. CATTIN 2003, pp. 153-226.

CATTIN 1973b

    CATTIN, Giulio. *Il primo Savonarola: poesie e prediche autografe dal Codice Borromeo*, Florence, Olschki, 1973 (Biblioteca di *Lettere italiane*, 12); the section *Le poesie*, pp. 191-234, is reprinted in CATTIN 2003, pp. 227-267.

CATTIN 1975

    CATTIN, Giulio. 'Canti, canzoni a ballo e danze nelle Maccheronee di Teofilo Folengo', in: *Rivista italiana di Musicologia*, X (1975), pp. 180-215.

CATTIN 1977

    CATTIN, Giulio. 'Testi melici e organizzazione rituale nella Processione fiorentina di "Depositio" secondo il manoscritto 21 dell'Opera di S. Maria del Fiore', in: *Dimensioni drammatiche della liturgia medioevale. Atti del I Convegno di studio, Viterbo, 31 maggio, 1-2 giugno 1976*, Milan, Bulzoni - Viterbo, Agnesotti, 1977, pp. 243-265.

CATTIN 1978

    CATTIN, Giulio. 'I *cantasi come* in una stampa di laude della Biblioteca Riccardiana (Ed. r. 196)', in: *Quadrivium*, XIX/2 (1978), pp. 5-52; rpt. CATTIN 2003, pp. 313-354.

CATTIN 1983a

    CATTIN, Giulio. 'Il repertorio polifonico sacro nelle fonti napoletane del Quattrocento', in: BIANCONI - BOSSA 1983, pp. 29-45.

CATTIN 1983b

    CATTIN, Giulio. 'Le rime del Poliziano nelle fonti musicali', in: MISCELLANEA BRANCA III, pp. 379-396.

CATTIN 1984

    CATTIN, Giulio. '*Contrafacta* internazionali: musiche europee per laude italiane', in: GÜNTHER - FINSCHER 1984, pp. 411-442; rpt. CATTIN 2003, pp. 401-424.

CATTIN 1985

    CATTIN, Giulio. 'Persistenza e variazioni in un tropo polifonico al *Benedicamus*' in: ARS NOVA V, pp. 46-56.

CATTIN 1986

    CATTIN, Giulio. 'Il Quattrocento', in: *Letteratura italiana*, edited by Alberto Asor Rosa, VI: *Teatro, musica, tradizione dei classici*, Turin, Einaudi, 1986, pp. 265-318.

CATTIN 1990

    CATTIN, Giulio. 'Nomi di rimatori per la polifonia profana italiana del secondo Quattrocento', in: *Rivista italiana di Musicologia*, XXV (1990), pp. 209-311.

CATTIN 2003

    CATTIN, Giulio. *Studi sulla lauda offerti all'autore da F. A. Gallo e F. Luisi*, edited by Patrizia Dalla Vecchia, Rome, Torre d'Orfeo, 2003.

CATTIN - DALLA VECCHIA 2005

    Venezia 1501. Petrucci e la stampa musicale. Atti del convegno internazionale, Venezia - Palazzo Giustinian Lolin 10-13 ottobre 2001, edited by Giulio Cattin and Patrizia Dalla Vecchia, Venice, Fondazione Levi, 2005.

CC

    Census-Catalogue of Manuscript Sources of Polyphonic Music 1400-1550, edited by Herbert Kellman (I-V) and Charles Hamm (I only), 5 vols, Neuhausen-Stuttgart, American Institute of Musicology - Hänssler, 1979-1988 (Renaissance Manuscript Studies, 1).

CERIONI 1970

    CERIONI, Lydia. *La diplomazia sforzesca nella seconda metà del Quattrocento e i suoi cifrari segreti*, 2 vols, Rome, Il Centro di Ricerca, 1970 (Fonti e Studi del Corpus membranarum italicarum, 7).

CERUTI BURGIO 1972

    CERUTI BURGIO, Anna. *Una miscellanea di poesie cortigiane: il codice Parmense 201*, Parma, Università degli studi di Parma - Istituto di Filologia moderna, 1972.

CESARI *ET AL.* 1954

    CESARI, Gaetano - MONTEROSSO, Raffaello - DISERTORI, Benvenuto. *Le frottole nell'edizione principe di Ottaviano Petrucci. Testi e musiche pubblicati in trascrizione integrale*, I, Cremona, Athenaeum Cremonese, 1954 (Instituta et Monumenta, I, 1).

CHAPMAN 1964

    CHAPMAN, Catherine Weeks. *Andrea Antico*, Ph.D. diss., Cambridge (MA), Harvard University, 1964.

CHAPMAN 1968

    CHAPMAN, Catherine Weeks. 'Printed Collections of Polyphonic Music Owned by Ferdinand Columbus', in: *Journal of the American Musicological Society*, XXI (1968), pp. 34-84.

CHEVALIER

    CHEVALIER, Ulysse. *Repertorium hymnologicum: Catalogue des chantes, hymnes, proses, séquences, tropes en usage dans l'Eglise Latin e depuis les origines jusqu'à nos jours*, 4 vols, Louvain, Lefever - Polleunis & Ceuterick, 1892-1912.

CHOLIJ 1992

    CHOLIJ, Irena. 'Borrowed Music. *Allez regrets* and the Use of Pre-Existent Material', in: *Companion to Medieval and Renaissance Music*, edited by Tess Knighton and David Fallows, London, Dent, 1992; Oxford, Oxford University Press, 1997, pp. 165-176.

CHRISTOFFERSEN 1994

    CHRISTOFFERSEN, Peter Woetmann. *French Music in the Early Sixteenth Century: Studies in the Music Collection of a Copyist of Lyons, the Manuscript Ny kgl. Samling 1848 2° in the Royal Library, Copenhagen*, 3 vols, Copenhagen, Museum Tusculanum Press - University of Copenhagen, 1994.

CIBOTTO 1960

    ENSELMINO DA MONTEBELLUNA, 'El planto de la verzene Maria', in: *Teatro veneto*, edited by Gian Antonio Cibotto, Parma, Guanda, 1960 (La Fenice del Teatro, 6), pp. 69-113.

CIONI 1961

    CIONI, Alfredo. *Bibliografia delle sacre rappresentazioni*, Florence, Sansoni, 1961 (Biblioteca Bibliografica Italica, 22).

CMM 5/V

    Antoine Brumel: Opera omnia, V: *Motets*, edited by Barton Hudson, no pl., American Institute of Musicology, 1972 (Corpus Mensurabilis Musicae, 5).

CMM 15/IV

    Loyset Compère: Opera omnia, IV: *Motets*, edited by Ludwig Finscher, no pl., American Institute of Musicology, 1961 (Corpus Mensurabilis Musicae, 15).

CMM 15/V

    Loyset Compère: Opera omnia, V [Secular works], edited by Ludwig Finscher, no pl., American Institute of Musicology, 1972 (Corpus Mensurabilis Musicae, 15).

CMM 18

    Johannes Tinctoris: Opera omnia, edited by William Melin, no pl., American Institute of Musicology, 1976 (Corpus Mensurabilis Musicae, 18).

CMM 22/IV

    Alexander Agricola: Opera omnia, IV: *Motetta, Contrafacta*, edited by Edward R. Lerner, no pl., American Institute of Musicology, 1966 (Corpus Mensurabilis Musicae, 22).

CMM 22/V

Alexander Agricola: Opera omnia, V: *Cantiones, Musica instrumentalis, Opera dubia*, edited by Edward R. Lerner, no pl., American Institute of Musicology, 1970 (Corpus Mensurabilis Musicae, 22).

CMM 23/IV

Johannes Ghiselin-Verbonnet: Opera omnia, IV: *Chansons*, edited by Clytus Gottwald, no pl., American Institute of Musicology, 1968 (Corpus Mensurabilis Musicae, 23).

CMM 25/VII

Costanzo Festa: Opera omnia, VII: *Madrigals*, edited by Albert Seay, Neuhausen-Stuttgart, American Institute of Musicology, 1977 (Corpus Mensurabilis Musicae, 25).

CMM 32/I

Bernardo Pisano: Collected Works, edited by Frank A. D'Accone, no pl., American Institute of Musicology, 1966 (Corpus Mensurabilis Musicae, 32/I).

CMM 65/VI

Heinrich Isaac: Opera omnia, VI [Four-voice Masses I], edited by Edward R. Lerner, Neuhausen-Stuttgart, American Institute of Musicology - Hänssler, 1984 (Corpus Mensurabilis Musicae, 65).

CMM 65/VII

Heinrich Isaac: Opera omnia, VII [Four-voice Masses I], edited by Edward R. Lerner, Neuhausen-Stuttgart, American Institute of Musicology - Hänssler, 1984 (Corpus Mensurabilis Musicae, 65).

CMM 74

Hayne van Ghizeghem: Opera omnia, edited by Barton Hudson, Neuhausen-Stuttgart, American Institute of Musicology - Hänssler, 1977 (Corpus Mensurabilis Musicae, 74).

CMM 76

Italian Laude and Latin Unica in MS Capetown, Grey 3.b.12, edited by Giulio Cattin, Neuhausen-Stuttgart, American Institute of Musicology - Hänssler, 1977 (Corpus Mensurabilis Musicae, 76).

CMM 79

The Las Huelgas Manuscript: Burgos, Monasterio de Las Huelgas, edited by Gordon A. Anderson, 2 vols., Neuhausen-Stuttgart, American Institute of Musicology - Hänssler, 1982 (Corpus Mensurabilis Musicae, 79).

CMM 90/II

Johannes Prioris: Collected Works, II: [Requiem, 5 Magnificats], edited by T. Herman Keahey, Neuhausen-Stuttgart, American Institute of Musicology - Hänssler, 1982 (Corpus Mensurabilis Musicae, 90).

CMM 90/III

Johannes Prioris: Collected Works, III: *Motets and Chansons*, edited by Conrad Douglas, Neuhausen-Stuttgart, American Institute of Musicology - Hänssler, 1985 (Corpus Mensurabilis Musicae, 90).

COLLECTANEA

Collectanea historiae musicae, 4 vols, Florence, Olschki, 1953-1966 (Biblioteca degli *Historiae Musicae Cultores*, 22).

COLOMB DE BATINES 1852

COLOMB DE BATINES, Paul. *Bibliografia delle antiche rappresentazioni italiane sacre e profane stampate nei secoli XV e XVI*, Florence, Società Tipografica, 1852; rpt. Milan, Görlich, 1958.

CONTINI 1949

PETRARCA, Francesco. *Rerum vulgarium fragmenta*, edited by Gianfranco Contini, Paris, Tallone, 1949.

CONTINI 1964

PETRARCA, Francesco. *Canzoniere*, critical text and introduction by Gianfranco Contini, annotations by Daniele Ponchiroli, Turin, Einaudi, 1964; rev. edn. 1992.

CONTINI 2004

PETRARCA, Francesco. *Canzoniere (Rerum vulgarium fragmenta)*, edited by Gianfranco Contini, [Alpignano], Tallone, 2004.

CORBIN 1960

CORBIN, Solange. *La déposition liturgique du Christ au Vendredi saint. Sa place dans l'histoire des rites et du théâtre religieux (Analyse de documents portugais)*, Paris, Les belles lettres - Lisbon, Livraria Bertrand, 1960.

CORTELAZZO - ZOLLI

CORTELAZZO, Manlio - ZOLLI, Paolo. *Dizionario etimologico della lingua italiana*, 5 vols, Bologna, Zanichelli, 1979-1988.

CREMA 2002

CREMA, Elisabetta. 'L'indizio di una prolungata fortuna: il *Pianto della Vergine* di Enselmino da Montebelluna nella *Passione di Revello*', in: *Aevum. Rassegna di scienze storiche, linguistiche e filologiche*, LXXVI (2002), pp. 609-618.

CREMA 2005

CREMA, Elisabetta. 'Iconografia della Passione nel *Pianto della Vergine* di Enselmino da Montebelluna', in: *Il teatro delle statue. Gruppi lignei di Deposizione e Annunciazione tra XII e XIII secolo*, edited by Francesca Flores d'Arcais, Milan, Vita e Pensiero, 2005 (Storia dell'arte / Ricerche), pp. 33-59.

CROCKER 1977

CROCKER, Richard. *The Early Medieval Sequence*, Berkeley - Los Angeles - London, University of California Press, 1977.

CROLL 1954

CROLL, Gerhard. *Das Motettenwerk Gaspars van Weerbeke*, Ph.D. diss., Göttingen, Universität Göttingen, 1954.

CS

Carmina Scripturarum, scilicet Antiphonas et Responsoria ex Sacro Scripturae Fonte in Libros Liturgicos Sanctae Ecclesiae Romanae derivata, collected and edited by Carl Marbach, Strasburg, LeRoux, 1907; rpt. Hildesheim, G. Olms, 1994.

CUMMINGS 1981

CUMMINGS, Anthony M. 'Toward an Interpretation of the Sixteenth-Century Motet', in: *Journal of the American Musicological Society*, XXXIV (1981), pp. 43-59.

CYRUS 2000

De tous biens plaine. Twenty-Eight Settings of Hayne van Ghizeghem's Chansons, edited by Cynthia J. Cyrus, Madison (WI), A-R Editions, 2000 (Recent Researches in the Music of the Middle Ages and Early Renaissance, 36).

D'ACCONE 1961

D'ACCONE, Frank A. 'The Singers of San Giovanni in Florence during the 15th Century', in: *Journal of the American Musicological Society*, XIV (1961), pp. 307-358.

D'ACCONE 1963

D'ACCONE, Frank A. 'Heinrich Isaac in Florence: New and Unpublished Documents', in: *The Musical Quarterly*, IL (1963), pp. 464-483.

D'ACCONE 1997

D'ACCONE, Frank A. *The Civic Muse. Music and Musicians in Siena during the Middle Ages and the Renaissance*, Chicago-London, University of Chicago Press, 1997.

DAHLHAUS (1968) 1988

DAHLHAUS, Carl. *Untersuchungen über die Entstehung der harmonischen Tonalität*, Kassel, Bärenreiter, (1968) 1988.

D'ALESSI 1925

D'ALESSI, Giovanni. *Il tipografo fiammingo Gerardo de Lisa, cantore e maestro di cappella nella cattedrale di Treviso (1463-1496)*, Vedelago (Treviso), Tipografia A.E.R., 1925.

D'ALESSI 1938

D'ALESSI, Giovanni. 'Maestri e Cantori fiamminghi nella Cappella Musicale del Duomo di Treviso (Italia) (1411-1561)', in: *Tijdschrift van de Koninklijke Vereniging voor Nederlandse Muziekgeschiedenis*, XV (1938), pp. 147-165.

D'AMICO 1955

Teatro italiano, I: *Le origini e il Rinascimento*, edited by Silvio D'Amico, Milan, Nuova Accademia, 1955.

DAMILANO 1963
DAMILANO, Piero. 'Fonti musicali della lauda polifonica intorno alla metà del sec. XV', in: COLLECTANEA III, pp. 59-90.

D'ANCONA 1872
D'ANCONA, Alessandro. *Sacre rappresentazioni dei secoli XIV, XV e XVI*, 3 vols, Florence, Le Monnier, 1872.

D'ANCONA (1878) 1906
D'ANCONA, Alessandro. *La poesia popolare italiana*, Livorno, Vigo, 1878; 2nd enlarged edn. 1906; rpt. Bologna, Forni, 1974.

DAVIS 1978
Johannes Vincenet: The Collected Works, edited by Bertran E. Davis, Madison (WI), A-R Editions, 1978 (Recent Researches in the Music of the Middle Ages and Early Renaissance, 9-10).

DAVISON - APEL (1946) 1977
Historical Anthology of Music, edited by Archibald T. Davison and Willi Apel, I: *Oriental, Medieval, and Renaissance Music*, Cambridge (MA), Harvard University Press, (1946); rev. edn. 1977.

DBI
Dizionario biografico degli italiani, Rome, Istituto della Enciclopedia italiana, 1960-.

DE ANGELIS 1818
DE ANGELIS, Luigi. *Capitoli dei disciplinati della venerabile Compagnia della Madonna sotto le volte dell'I. e R. Spedale di S. Maria della Scala di Siena*, Siena, Porri, 1818.

DE BARTHOLOMAEIS 1943
Laude drammatiche e rappresentazioni sacre, edited by Vincenzo De Bartholomaeis, 3 vols, Florence, Le Monnier, 1943.

DE FEO 1981
DE FEO, Francesco. *Carte di Cesare Guasti: Inventario*, Florence, Olschki, 1981 (Carteggi di Cesare Guasti, 7).

DELCORNO BRANCA 1971
DELCORNO BRANCA, Daniela. 'Per un catalogo delle *Rime* del Poliziano', in: *Lettere italiane*, XXIII (1971), pp. 225-252.

DELCORNO BRANCA 1979
DELCORNO BRANCA, Daniela. *Sulla tradizione delle Rime del Poliziano*, Florence, Olschki, 1979 (Biblioteca di *Lettere italiane*, 23).

DELCORNO BRANCA 1983
DELCORNO BRANCA, Daniela. 'Da Poliziano a Serafino', in: MISCELLANEA BRANCA III, pp. 423-450.

DELCORNO BRANCA 1986
POLIZIANO, Angelo. *Rime*, edited by Daniela Delcorno Branca, Florence, Accademia della Crusca, 1986.

DELCORNO BRANCA 1987
DELCORNO BRANCA, Daniela. 'Il laboratorio del Poliziano. Per una lettura delle *Rime*', in: *Lettere italiane*, XXXIX (1987), pp. 153-206.

DELCORNO BRANCA 1990
POLIZIANO, Angelo. *Rime*, edited by Daniela Delcorno Branca, Venice, Marsilio, 1990.

DELPORTE 1953
WEERBEKE, Gaspar van. *Virgo Maria*, edited by Jules Delporte, Paris, Editions musicales de la Schola cantorum et de la Procure générale de musique, 1953.

DELPORTE 1954
WEERBEKE, Gaspar van. *Mater digna Dei*, edited by Jules Delporte, Paris, Editions musicales de la Schola cantorum et de la Procure générale de musique, 1954.

DE ROBERTIS 1966
DE ROBERTIS, Domenico. 'L'esperienza poetica del Quattrocento', in: *Storia della letteratura italiana*, III, Milan, Garzanti, 1966, pp. 357-566.

DEUMM

Dizionario enciclopedico universale della musica e dei musicisti, *Le Biografie*, 8 vols, Turin, UTET, 1985-1988.

DICKEY 2005

DICKEY, Timothy J. 'Rethinking the Siena Choirbook: A New Date and Implications for its Musical Contents', in: *Early Music History*, XXV (2005), pp. 1-52.

DI CROLLALANZA III

DI CROLLALANZA, Giovanni Battista. *Dizionario storico-blasonico delle famiglie nobili e notabili italiane estinte e fiorenti*, III, Pisa, presso la direzione del Giornale Araldico, 1890; rpt. Bologna, Forni, 1965.

DIEDERICHS 1986

DIEDERICHS, Elisabeth. *Die Anfänge der mehrstimmigen Lauda vom Ende des 14. bis zur Mitte des 15. Jahrhunderts*, Tutzing, Schneider, 1986 (Münchner Veröffentlichungen zur Musikgeschichte, 41).

DI GIOVANNI 1874

DI GIOVANNI, Vincenzo. 'Una laude a Maria Vergine', in: *Il Propugnatore*, VII (1874), pp. 431-437.

DIONISOTTI 1950

Maria Savorgnan - Pietro Bembo: carteggio d'amore (1500-1501), edited by Carlo Dionisotti, Florence, Le Monnier, 1950.

DIONISOTTI 1974

DIONISOTTI, Carlo. 'Fortuna del Petrarca nel Quattrocento', in: *Italia medioevale e umanistica*, XVII (1974), pp. 61-113.

DISERTORI 1940

DISERTORI, Benvenuto. 'Campane in un mottetto del Quattrocento', in: *Rivista musicale italiana*, XLIV (1940), pp. 106-111.

DISERTORI 1946

DISERTORI, Benvenuto. 'Il manoscritto 1947-4 di Trento e la canzone *I'ay prins amours*', in: *Rivista musicale italiana*, XLVIII (1946), pp. 1-29.

DISERTORI 1964

DISERTORI, Benvenuto. *Le Frottole per canto e liuto intabulate da Franciscus Bossinensis*, Milan, Ricordi, 1964 (Istituzioni e monumenti dell'arte musicale italiana, n.s., III).

DONESMONDI 1612

DONESMONDI, Ippolito. *Dell'historia ecclesiastica di Mantova*, 2 vols, Mantua, Aurelio & Lodovico Osanna, 1612; rpt. Bologna, Forni, 1977.

DRAKE 1972

DRAKE, Warren. *The First Printed Books of Motets. Petrucci's Motetti A Numero Trentatre (Venice 1502) and Motetti de Passione, de Cruce, de Sacramento, de Beata Virgine et huiusmodi B, (Venice 1503)*, 2 vols, Ph.D. diss., Urbana-Champaign (IL), University of Illinois at Urbana-Champaign, 1972.

DRAKE 2002

Ottaviano Petrucci, Motetti de Passione, de Cruce, de Sacramento, de Beata Virgine et huiusmodi B, Venice, 1503, edited by Warren Drake, Chicago-London, University of Chicago Press, 2002 (Monuments of Renaissance Music, XI).

DRAKE 2005

DRAKE, Warren. 'Motetti B and its Relation to the Lauda Repertory circa 1500', in: CATTIN - DALLA VECCHIA 2005, pp. 441-454.

DROZ - THIBAULT (1924) 1976

Poètes et musiciens du XVᵉ siècle, edited by Eugénie Droz and Geneviève Thibault, Paris, Jeanbin, 1924 (Documents artistiques du XVᵉ siècle, 1); rpt. Geneva, Slatkine Reprints, 1976.

DTÖ 14-15

Sechs Trienter Codices: geistliche und weltliche Kompositionen des XV. Jahrhunderts, edited by Guido Adler and Oswald Koller, Vienna, Artaria, 1900; rpt. Graz, Akademische Druck- u. Verlagsanstalt, 1959 (Denkmäler der Tonkunst in Österreich, 14-15, Jahrg. VII).

DTÖ 28

    Heinrich Isaac: Weltliche Werke, I, edited by Johannes Wolf, Vienna, Artaria - Leipzig, Breitkopf & Härtel, 1907; rpt. Graz, Akademische Druck- u. Verlagsanstalt, 1959 (Denkmäler der Tonkunst in Österreich, 28, Jahrg. XIV/1).

DTÖ 32

    Heinrich Isaac: Choralis Constantinus, II, edited by Anton von Webern, *mit einem Nachtrag zu den weltlichen Werken von Heinrich Isaac (vgl. Jahrgang XIV, Band I)*, edited by Johannes Wolf, Vienna, Artaria - Leipzig, Breitkopf & Härtel, 1909; rpt. Graz, Akademische Druck- u. Verlagsanstalt, 1959 (Denkmäler der Tonkunst in Österreich, 32, Jahrg. XVI/1).

EARP 1983

    EARP, Lawrence M. *Scribal Practice, Manuscript Production and the Transmission of Music in Late Medieval France: The Manuscripts of Guillaume de Machaut*, Ph.D. diss., Princeton, Princeton University, 1983.

EARP 1991

    EARP, Lawrence M. 'Texting in 15th-Century French Chansons: A Look Ahead from the 14th Century', in: *Early Music*, XIX (1991), pp. 195-210.

EDIT 16

    Le edizioni italiane del 16. secolo: censimento nazionale, 6 vols, Rome, ICCU, 1986-2007.

EDM 4

    Das Glogauer Liederbuch: Erster Teil: Deutsche Lieder und Spielstücke, edited by Heribert Ringmann and Joseph Klapper, Kassel, Bärenreiter, 1936 (Das Erbe deutscher Musik, 4: Abteilung Mittelalter, 1); rpt. 1954.

EDM 8

    Das Glogauer Liederbuch: Zweiter Teil: Ausgewählte lateinische Sätze, edited by Heribert Ringmann and Joseph Klapper, Kassel, Bärenreiter, 1937 (Das Erbe deutscher Musik, 8: Abteilung Mittelalter, 3); rpt. 1954.

EDM 32-34

    Der Mensuralkodex des Nikolaus Apel (Ms. 1494 der Universitätsbibliothek Leipzig), edited by Rudolf Gerber (I-II), Ludwig Finscher, and Wolfgang Dömlig (III), 3 vols, Kassel, Bärenreiter, 1956, 1960, 1975 (Das Erbe deutscher Musik, 32-34: Abteilung Mittelalter, 4-6).

EDM 37-39

    Das Buxheimer Orgelbuch, edited by Bertha Antonia Wallner, 3 vols, Kassel, Bärenreiter, 1958-1959 (Das Erbe deutscher Musik, 37-39: Abteilung Mittelalter, 7-9).

EDM 76-78

    Der Kodex Berlin 40021. Staatsbibliothek Preußischer Kulturbesitz Berlin Mus. ms. 40021, edited by Martin Just, 3 vols, Kassel, Bärenreiter, 1990-1991 (Das Erbe deutscher Musik, 76-78: Abteilung Mittelalter, 14-16).

EDM 85-86

    Das Glogauer Liederbuch: Dritter (Vierter) Teil, edited by Christian Väterlein, 2 vols, Kassel, Bärenreiter, 1981 (Das Erbe deutscher Musik, 85-86: Abteilung Mittelalter, 22-23).

EDM 91-92

    Die Orgeltabulatur des Leonhard Kleber, edited by Karin Berg-Kotterba with Martin Staehlin, 2 vols, Frankfurt, Henry Litolff, 1987 (Das Erbe deutscher Musik, 91-92: Abteilung Orgel/Klavier/Laute, 7-8).

EDWARDS 1974

    EDWARDS, Warwick. 'The Walsingham Consort Books', in: *Music & Letters*, LV (1974), pp. 209-214.

EDWARDS 1981

    EDWARDS, Warwick. 'Songs without Words by Josquin and his Contemporaries', in: FENLON 1981, pp. 79-92.

EDWARDS 2006

    EDWARDS, Warwick. 'Alexander Agricola and Intuitive Syllable Deployment', in: *Early Music*, XXXIV (2006), pp. 409-425.

EINSTEIN 1949
    EINSTEIN, Alfred. *The Italian Madrigal*, 3 vols, Princeton, Princeton University Press, 1949.

EINSTEIN 1951
    EINSTEIN, Alfred. 'Andrea Antico's *Canzoni nove* of 1510', in: *The Musical Quarterly*, XXXVII (1951), pp. 330-339.

EITNER
    EITNER, Robert. *Biographisch-bibliographisches Quellen-Lexikon der Musiker und Musikgelehrten*, 11 vols, Leipzig, Breitkopf & Härtel, 1900-1904, rpt. Graz, Akademische Druck- u. Verlagsanstalt, 1959-1960.

ELDERS 1969
    ELDERS, Willem. 'Das Symbol in der Musik von Josquin des Prez', in: *Acta musicologica*, XLI (1969), pp. 164-185.

EML 62
    Loyset Compère: 3 Chansons for 3 Voices or Instruments, edited by Bernard Thomas, [Brighton], London Pro Musica Edition, 1989 (Early Music Library, 62).

EML 97
    Hayne van Ghizeghem: 2 Famous Rondeaux for 3 Voices or Instruments, edited by Bernard Thomas, [Brighton], London Pro Musica Edition, 1991 (Early Music Library, 97).

ENCICLOPEDIA DEI PAPI
    Enciclopedia dei papi, 3 vols, Rome, Istituto della Enciclopedia italiana fondata da Giovanni Treccani, 2000.

ESSLING
    PRINCE D'ESSLING, *Études sur l'art de la gravure sur bois à Venise. Les livres à figures vénitiens de la fin du XVe siècle et du commencement du XVIe*, 5 vols, Florence, Olschki – Paris, Leclerc, 1909-1914.

EVANS 1975
    Johannes Martini: Secular Pieces, edited by Edward G. Evans, Jr., Madison (WI), A-R Editions, 1975 (Recent Researches in the Music of the Middle Ages and Early Renaissance, 1).

FABRIS 2001
    FABRIS, Dinko. 'The Origin of Italian Lute Tablature: Venice circa 1500 or Naples before Petrucci?', in: *Basler Jahrbuch für historische Musikpraxis*, XXV (2001), pp. 143-158.

FABRIS 2005
    FABRIS, Dinko. 'Le prime intavolature italiane per liuto', in: CATTIN – DALLA VECCHIA 2005, pp. 473-490.

FACCIOLI 1975
    Il teatro italiano I. Dalle origini al Quattrocento, edited by Emilio Faccioli, Turin, Einaudi, 1975 (Gli Struzzi, 75*).

FALLOWS 1995
    Oxford, Bodleian Library, MS. Canon. Misc. 213, with an introduction and inventory by David Fallows, Chicago-London, University of Chicago Press, 1995 (Late Medieval and Early Renaissance Music in Facsimile, 1).

FALLOWS 1999
    FALLOWS, David. *A Catalogue of Polyphonic Songs, 1415-1480*, Oxford, Oxford University Press, 1999.

FALLOWS 2005
    FALLOWS, David. 'I volumi dei canti di Petrucci: finalità e repertorio', in: CATTIN – DALLA VECCHIA 2005, pp. 661-676. (Italian trans. of the article 'Petrucci's Canti Volumes: Scope and Repertory', previously published in: *Basler Jahrbuch für historische Musikpraxis*, XXV (2001), pp. 39-51.)

FALLOWS 2007
    FALLOWS, David. Review of BOORMAN, Stanley. *Ottaviano Petrucci: A Catalogue Raisonné*, New York, Oxford University Press, 2006, in: *Journal of the American Musicological Society*, LX (2007), pp. 415-421.

FALLOWS 2009
    FALLOWS, David. *Josquin*, Turnhout, Brepols, 2009 (Épitome musical).

Fano 1962

 Heinrich Isaac: Messe, edited by Fabio Fano, Milan, Veneranda Fabbrica del Duomo di Milano, 1962 (Archivium Musices Metropolitanum Mediolanense, 10).

Feininger 1975

 Feininger, Laurence. 'Eine neue Quelle zur Polyphonie des 15 Jahrhunderts', in: *Festschrift Walter Senn zum 70. Geburtstag*, edited by Ewald Fassler, Munich-Salzburg, Katzbichler, 1975, pp. 53-63.

Feist 1889

 Feist, Alfred. 'Mitteilungen aus älteren Sammlungen italienischer geistlicher Lieder', in: *Zeitschrift für romanische Philologie*, XIII (1889), pp. 115-185.

Fenlon 1981

 Music in Medieval and Early Modern Europe: Patronage, Sources and Texts, edited by Iain Fenlon, Cambridge, Cambridge University Press, 1981.

Fenlon - Haar 1988

 Fenlon, Iain - Haar, James. *The Italian Madrigal in the Early Sixteenth Century. Sources and Interpretation*, Cambridge-London, Cambridge University Press, 1988.

Fenlon - Haar 1991

 Fenlon, Iain - Haar, James. *Il madrigale italiano nel primo Cinquecento. Le fonti e la loro storia*, Turin, Einaudi, 1991. (Italian translation of only the first part of *The Italian Madrigal in the Early Sixteenth Century. Sources and Interpretation*, Cambridge-London, Cambridge University Press, 1988 = Fenlon - Haar 1988.)

Ferrari 1994

 10 Fantasie a 3 e 4 voci dal ms. Rés. Vm.⁷ 676 di Parigi (1502), edited by Marco Ferrari, Bologna, Ut Orpheus Edizioni, 1994 (Ricercare Capriccio Fantasia, 3).

Ferrari Barassi 1993

 Ferrari Barassi, Elena. 'Frottole en el *Cancionero Musical de Palacio*', in: *Actas del XV Congreso de la Sociedad Internacional de Musicología, Culturas musicales del Mediterraneo y sus ramificaciones (Madrid, 3-10.IV.1992), Revista de Musicología*, XVI (1993), pp. 1482-1498.

Ferrari Barassi 1997

 Ferrari Barassi, Elena. 'Alcune frottole "petrucciane" fra Italia, Spagna e Germania', in: *Nuova Rivista musicale italiana*, XXXI (1997), pp. 47-70.

Fery-Hue 1991

 Au grey d'amours ... (Pièces inédites du manuscrit Paris, Bibl. nat., fr. 1719): étude et édition, edited by Françoise Fery-Hue, Montreal, Ceres, 1991 (Le moyen français, 27-28).

Fétis

 Biographie universelle des musiciens et Bibliographie générale de la musique, 2nd rev. and augmented edn. by F[rançois]-J[oseph] Fétis, 8 vols, Paris, Librairie de Firmin Didot frères, fils et Cⁱᵉ, 1860-1865; rpt. Brussels, Culture et civilisation, 1963.

Filocamo 2000

 Filocamo, Gioia. *Il repertorio profano con testo italiano del codice Panciatichi 27*, tesi di dottorato in Filologia musicale, Cremona, Università di Pavia, a.a. 1999-2000.

Filocamo 2003

 Poesia e musica alle corti di Mantova e Ferrara. 1. Il 'ciclo dell'uccello', edited by Gioia Filocamo, Bologna, Ut Orpheus Edizioni, 2003 (Odhecaton, 16).

Filocamo 2004

 Filocamo, Gioia. 'Numeri "servi" o "padroni"? Un'ipotesi sulla funzione del codice Panciatichi 27', in: *La scrittura come rappresentazione del pensiero musicale*, edited by Gianmario Borio, Pisa, Edizioni ETS, 2004, pp. 125-155.

Filocamo 2009a

 Filocamo, Gioia. '*Suona lo corno, capo caccia!*: un'antica caccia romana in musica edita da Carducci', in: *Qual musica attorno a Giosue. Nel centenario della morte di Carducci. Atti del convegno Bologna, Accademia Filarmonica (28-29 settembre 2007)*, edited by Piero Mioli, Bologna, Pàtron, 2009, pp. 67-76.

FILOCAMO 2009b

FILOCAMO, Gioia. 'Sulle orme di Ulrich Schubinger "il giovane": repertorio "vivo" dal codice musicale AugsS 142a', in: BLOXAM *ET AL.* 2009, pp. 233-248.

FILOCAMO 2009c

FILOCAMO, Gioia. 'Democratizing the Requiem: Mercantile Mentality and the Fear of Death in Italy', in: *Journal of the Alamire Foundation*, I (2009), pp. 27–48.

FINSCHER 1964

FINSCHER, Ludwig. *Loyset Compère (c.1450-1518), Life and Works*, no pl., American Institute of Musicology, 1964 (Musicological Studies and Documents, 12).

FINSCHER 2000

FINSCHER, Ludwig. 'Four-Voice Motets', in: SHERR 2000a, pp. 249-279.

FINZI 1893

FINZI, Vittorio. 'Il pianto della B. Vergine attribuito a frate Enselmino da Treviso, una laude di Leonardo Giustiniani, alcune orazioni di S. Gregorio Magno, ed altri componimenti tratti dal codice lucchese, 1302', in: *Il Propugnatore*, n.s., VI/2, 1893, pp. 168-194.

FINZI 1894

FINZI, Vittorio. 'Il *Pianto della B. Vergine* giusta la lezione di due codici lucchesi', in: *Zeitschrift für romanische Philologie*, XVIII (1894), pp. 319–380.

FRANCESCHINI 1977

FRANCESCHINI, Adriano. 'Inventari inediti di biblioteche ferraresi del sec. XV. Parte A: La biblioteca di Francesco de Lignamine Vescovo di Ferrara (1446-1460)', in: *Atti e Memorie della Deputazione Provinciale Ferrarese di Storia Patria*, s. III, vol. 24, 1977, pp. 51-86.

FRANCESCHINI 1982

FRANCESCHINI, Adriano. 'Inventari inediti di biblioteche ferraresi del sec. XV. Parte B: La biblioteca del capitolo dei Canonici della Cattedrale', in: *Atti e Memorie della Deputazione Provinciale Ferrarese di Storia Patria*, s. IV, vol. 2, 1982, pp. 5-174.

FRANÇON 1934

Albums poétiques de Marguerite d'Autriche, edited by Marcel Françon, Cambridge (MA), Harvard University Press - Paris, Droz, 1934.

FRATI 1909

FRATI, Carlo. 'La Biblioteca Marciana nel triennio 1906-08. Parte II', in: *L'ateneo veneto*, XXXII/2 (1909), pp. 43-71.

FRATI 1917-18

FRATI, Lodovico. 'Giunte agli *Inizii di antiche poesie italiane religiose e morali* a cura di Annibale Tenneroni', in: *Archivum romanicum*, I (1917), pp. 441-480; II (1918), pp. 185-207, 325-343. (The study continues in vol. III (1919), pp. 62-94.)

FREEMAN 1991

FREEMAN, Daniel. 'On the Origins of the *Pater noster - Ave Maria* of Josquin des Prez', in: *Musica Disciplina*, XLV (1991), pp. 169-219.

FUBINI (1962) 1975

FUBINI, Mario. *Metrica e poesia. Lezioni sulle forme metriche italiane*, I: *Dal Duecento al Petrarca*, Milan, Feltrinelli, 1962; 3rd edn. 1975.

FULLER 1969

FULLER, Sarah. 'Additional Notes on the 15th-Century Chansonnier Bologna Q 16', in: *Musica Disciplina*, XXIII (1969), pp. 81-103.

GACHET 1849

Albums et œuvres poétiques de Marguerite d'Autriche, Gouvernante des Pays-Bas, edited by Émile Gachet, Brussels, Librairie Scientifique et Litteraire, 1849 (Societé des Bibliophiles belges, XVII).

GAFFURIO 1496

Practica musice Franchini Gafori laudensis, Milan, Giovan Pietro Lomazzo for Guillaume Le Signerre, 1496; rpt. edited by Giuseppe Vecchi, Bologna, Forni, 1972.

GALLETTI 1833

GALLETTI, Gustavo Camillo. *Le rappresentazioni di Feo Belcari ed altre di lui poesie edite ed inedite citate come testo di lingua nel Vocabolario degli Accademici della Crusca*, Florence, Moutier, 1833.

GALLETTI 1863

GALLETTI, Gustavo Camillo. *Laude spirituali di Feo Belcari, di Lorenzo d'Albizzo, di Castellano Castellani e di altri comprese nelle quattro più antiche raccolte*, 4 vols, Florence, Molini e Cecchi, 1863.

GALLI 1947

GALLI, Giuseppe. 'Due ignote edizioni quattrocentine della *Corona della Beatissima Vergine Maria* di Fra' Bernardino de' Busti', in: *Miscellanea bibliografica in memoria di Don Tommasi Accurti*, edited by Lamberto Donati, Rome, Edizioni di "Storia e Letteratura", 1947 (Storia e Letteratura, 15), pp. 103-124.

GALLICO 1961

GALLICO, Claudio. *Un libro di poesia per musica dell'epoca d'Isabella d'Este*, Mantua, no pr., 1961 ("Quaderni" del *Bollettino Storico Mantovano*, 4).

GALLICO 1976

GALLICO, Claudio. 'Josquin's Compositions on Italian Texts and the Frottola', in: LOWINSKY – BLACKBURN 1976, pp. 446-454; rpt. GALLICO 2001, pp. 227-235.

GALLICO 1996

GALLICO, Claudio. *Rimeria musicale popolare italiana nel Rinascimento*, Lucca, LIM, 1996.

GALLICO (1961) 1998

GALLICO, Claudio. *"Forse che sì forse che no" fra poesia e musica*, Mantua, Istituto Carlo d'Arco, 1961; rpt. with a new postface by the author, Mantua, Edizioni Tre Lune, 1998.

GALLO 1966

GALLO, F. Alberto. '*Cantus planus binatim*: polifonia primitiva in fonti tardive', in: *Quadrivium*, VII (1966), pp. 79-89.

GALLO 1979

GALLO, F. Alberto. 'Il "ballare lombardo" (circa 1435-1475). I balli e le basse danze di Domenico da Piacenza e di Guglielmo da Pesaro', in: *Studi musicali*, VIII (1979), pp. 61-84.

GALLO 1985

GALLO, F. Alberto. 'The Practice of *cantus planus binatim* in Italy from the Beginning of the 14th to the Beginning of the 16th Century', in: ARS NOVA V, pp. 13-30.

GALLUCCI 1966

GALLUCCI, Joseph J., Jr. *Festival Music in Florence, ca. 1480 - ca. 1520: Canti Carnascialeschi, Trionfi and Related Forms*, 2 vols, Ph.D. diss., Cambridge (MA), Harvard University, 1966.

GANTERT 2000

GANTERT, Ruth. '*Canzoniere* CXXIX: *Di pensier in pensier, di monte in monte*', in: *Petrarca e i suoi lettori*, edited by Vittorio Ceratozzolo and Georges Güntert, Ravenna, Longo, 2000, pp. 55-77.

GARGAN 1978

GARGAN, Luciano. *Cultura e arte nel Veneto al tempo del Petrarca*, Padua, Antenore, 1978 (Studi sul Petrarca, 5).

GARGIULO 1993

La musica a Firenze al tempo di Lorenzo il Magnifico. Atti del Congresso internazionale di studi (Firenze, 15-17 giugno 1992), edited by Piero Gargiulo, Florence, Olschki, 1993 (Quaderni della Rivista italiana di Musicologia, 30).

GASPARI

Catalogo della Biblioteca del Liceo Musicale di Bologna compilato da Gaetano Gaspari compiuto e pubblicato da Luigi Torchi per cura del Municipio, 4 vols, Bologna, Libreria Romagnoli Dall'Acqua, 1890-1905; rpt. with corrections edited by Napoleone Fanti, Oscar Mischiati, and Luigi Ferdinando Tagliavini: GASPARI, Gaetano. *Catalogo della Biblioteca musicale "G.B. Martini" di Bologna*, Bologna, Forni, 1961.

GASSER 1999

GASSER, Nolan. '*Beata et venerabilis virgo*: Music and Devotion in Renaissance Milan', in: *Crossing Boundaries: Issues of Cultural and Individual Identity in the Middle Ages and the Renaissance*, edited by Sally McKee, Turnhout, Brepols, 1999 (Arizona Studies in the Middle Ages and the Renaissance, 3), pp. 203-238.

GDE

Grande Dizionario Enciclopedico, founded by Pietro Fedele, 4th edn., Turin, UTET, 1984-2005.

GEERING 1933

GEERING, Arnold. *Die Vokalmusik in der Schweiz zur Zeit der Reformation*, Aarau, H. R. Sauerländer, 1933 (Schweizerisches Jahrbuch für Musikwissenschaft, 6).

GERBER (1812) 1966

GERBER, Ernst L. *Neues Historisch-biographisches Lexikon der Tonkünstler*, edited by Othmar Wessely, 2 vols, Graz, Akademische Druck- u. Verlagsanstalt, (1812) 1966.

GERLE 1976

Tabulature pour les luths: Nuremberg, Formschneider, 1533 / Hans Gerle, edited by Groupe E.R.A.T.T.O. du C.N.R.S., Hélène Chamassé and Raymond Meylan, 5 vols, Paris, Heugel, 1975-1978 (Publications de la Société française de musicologie; 5 sér., vol. 1), III: *Chansons françaises et trios*, 1976.

GHISI 1937

GHISI, Federico. *I canti carnascialeschi nelle fonti musicali del XV e XVI secolo*, Florence, Olschki, 1937; rpt. Bologna, A.M.I.S., 1970.

GHISI 1939

GHISI, Federico. 'Poesie musicali italiane', in: *Note d'archivio per la storia musicale*, XVI (1939), pp. 40-73.

GHISI 1953a

GHISI, Federico. 'Strambotti e laude nel travestimento spirituale della poesia musicale del Quattrocento', in: COLLECTANEA I, pp. 45-78.

GHISI 1953b

GHISI, Federico. 'Un processionale inedito per la Settimana Santa nell'Opera del Duomo di Firenze', in: *Rivista musicale italiana*, LV (1953), pp. 362-369.

GHISI 1965

GHISI, Federico. 'Alcune note in margine alle fonti italiane profane intonate da Arrigo il Tedesco (Isaac)', in: *Analecta musicologica*, II (1965), pp. 1-5.

GIALDRONI - ZIINO 1995

GIALDRONI, Giuliana - ZIINO, Agostino. 'Due nuovi frammenti di musica profana del primo Quattrocento nell'Archivio di stato di Frosinone', in: *Studi musicali*, XXIV (1995), pp. 185-208.

GIAZOTTO 1959

GIAZOTTO, Remo. 'Onde musicali nella corrente poetica di Serafino dell'Aquila', in: IDEM. *Musurgia nova*, Milan, Ricordi, 1959, pp. 3-119.

GIESBERT 1936

GIESBERT, Franz Julius. *Ein altes Spielbuch aus der Zeit um 1500: Pergament-Handschrift (Liber Fridolini Sichery) der Stiftsbibliothek zu St. Gallen*, 2 vols, Mainz, Schott, 1936.

GLIXON 1990

GLIXON, Jonathan. 'The Polyphonic Laude of Innocentius Dammonis', in: *The Journal of Musicology*, VIII (1990), pp. 19-53.

Gnaccarini 1909

Indice delle rime volgari a stampa che fanno parte della Biblioteca Carducci, edited by Giulio Gnaccarini, 2 vols, Bologna, Romagnoli - Dall'Acqua, 1909.

Goff (1964) 1973

Incunabula in American Libraries. A Third Census of Fifteenth-Century Books Recorded in North American Collections, edited by Frederick R. Goff, 3rd edn., New York, Bibliographical Society of America, 1964; rpt. of the copy annotated by the editor, Millwood (NY), Kraus Reprint, 1973.

Goldthwaite (1995) 1999

Goldthwaite, Richard A. *Wealth and the Demand for Art in Italy 1300-1600*, Baltimore-London, Johns Hopkins University Press, 1993; Italian trans. as *Ricchezza e domanda nel mercato dell'arte in Italia dal Trecento al Seicento. La cultura materiale e le origini del consumismo*, Milan, Unicopli, (1995) 1999.

Gombosi 1925

Gombosi, Otto. *Jacob Obrecht. Eine stilkritische Studie*, Leipzig, Breitkopf & Härtel, 1925 (Sammlung musikwissenschaftlicher Einzeldarstellungen, 4).

Gombosi 1936

Gombosi, Otto. 'Zur Frühgeschichte der Folia', in: *Acta musicologica*, VIII (1936), pp. 119-129.

Gombosi 1955

Compositione di Meser Vincenzo Capirola: Lute-book (circa 1517), edited by Otto Gombosi, Neuilly-sur-Seine, Société de musique d'autrefois, 1955 (Publications de la Société de musique d'autrefois. Textes musicaux, 1).

GR

Graduale Sacrosanctae Romanae Ecclesiae de tempore et de sanctis…, Paris-Tournai-Rome, Desclée et Socii, 1924.

Graf 1884

Graf, Arturo. 'Di un codice riccardiano di leggende volgari', in: *Giornale storico della letteratura italiana*, III (1884), pp. 401-414.

Grandi 1989

Grandi, Oler. 'Gli statuti quattrocenteschi dei Disciplini di Canneto sull'Oglio', in: *I Disciplini. Ricerche sulle confraternite del Mantovano*, edited by Claudio Ghisini and Giuseppe Rubini, Mantua, Gianluigi Arcari Editore - Cassa Rurale ed Artigiana di Castel Goffredo, 1989, pp. 87-136.

Grand Robert des noms propres

Grand Robert des noms propres: Dictionnaire universel alphabétique et analogique des noms propres, under the direction of Paul Robert, Paris, Le Robert, 1984.

Greenberg - Maynard 1975

An Anthology of Early Renaissance Music, edited by Noah Greenberg and Paul Maynard, New York, Norton, 1975.

Guerrini 1926

Guerrini, Paolo. 'Di alcuni organisti della Cattedrale di Brescia nel Cinquecento', in: *Note d'archivio per la storia musicale*, III (1926), pp. 246-256.

Guerrini 1939

Guerrini, Paolo. 'Gli organi e gli organisti della Cattedrale di Brescia in alcuni documenti del Comune, della Fabbrica e del Capitolo', in: *Note d'archivio per la storia musicale*, XVI (1939), pp. 205-225.

Guerrini 1942

Guerrini, Paolo. 'L'organaro bresciano G. B. Fachetti e l'organo di Merlin Cocaio', in: *Note d'archivio per la storia musicale*, XIX (1942), pp. 136-144.

Guidobaldi 1995

Guidobaldi, Nicoletta. *La musica di Federico. Immagini e suoni alla corte di Urbino*, Florence, Olschki, 1995 (Studi e testi per la storia della musica, 11).

Günther - Finscher 1984

Musik und Text in der Mehrstimmigkeit des 14. und 15. Jahrhunderts, edited by Ursula Günther and Ludwig Finscher, Kassel, Bärenreiter, 1984 (Göttinger Musikwissenschaftliche Arbeiten, 10).

GUTIÉRREZ-DENHOFF 1985

GUTIÉRREZ-DENHOFF, Martella. *Der Wolfenbütteler Chansonnier, Wolfenbüttel, Herzog August Bibliothek Codex Guelf. 287 Extrav. Untersuchungen zu Repertoire und Überlieferung*, Wiesbaden, Harrassowitz, 1985 (Wolfenbütteler Forschungen, 29).

GUTIÉRREZ-DENHOFF 1988

Der Wolfenbütteler Chansonnier: Herzog August Bibliothek, Wolfenbüttel Codex Guelf. 287 Extrav., edited by Martella Gutiérrez-Denhoff, Mainz-London, Schott, 1988 (Musikalische Denkmäler, 10).

HABERL 1888

HABERL, Franz Xaver. *Die römische "schola cantorum" und die päpstlichen Kapellsänger bis zur Mitte des 16. Jahrhunderts: Sonderabdruck aus der Vierteljahrsschrift für Musikwissenschaft*, III, Leipzig, Breitkopf & Härtel, 1888; rpt. Hildesheim - New York, G. Olms, 1971.

HAGGH 1999

HAGGH, Barbara. 'Busnoys and "Caron" in Documents from Brussels', in: HIGGINS 1999, pp. 295-315.

HANEN 1983

HANEN, Martha K. *The Chansonnier El Escorial IV.a.24*, 3 vols, Henryville (PA), Institute of Mediaeval Music, 1983 (Wissenschaftliche Abhandlungen / Musicological Studies, 36).

HEARTZ 1966

HEARTZ, Daniel. 'Hoftanz and Basse Dance', in: *Journal of the American Musicological Society*, XIX (1966), pp. 13-36.

HEARTZ 1978

HEARTZ, Daniel. *A 15th-Century Ballo: Rôti Bouilli Joyeux*, in: LARUE 1978, pp. 359-375.

HELDT 1916

Französische Virelais aus dem 15. Jahrhundert, edited by Elisabeth Heldt, Halle (Saale), Niemeyer, 1916.

HERCZOG 1997

HERCZOG, Johann. '*Exordium in varietate*. La musica in Germania tra Umanesimo e borghesia', in: *Nuova Rivista musicale italiana*, XXXI (1997), pp. 71-99.

HERCZOG 2005

HERCZOG, Johann. *Marte armonioso. Trionfo della Battaglia musicale nel Rinascimento*, Galatina, Mario Congedo Editore, 2005 (Università degli studi di Lecce, Dipartimento dei Beni, delle Arti e della Storia, 22).

HERNON 1972

HERNON, Michael A. *Perugia, Ms. 431 (G 20): A Study of the Secular Italian Pieces*, Ph.D. diss., Nashville (TN), George Peabody College for Teachers - Vanderbilt University, 1972.

HERVIEUX 1884

Phedre et ses anciens imitateurs directs et indirects, edited by Leopold Hervieux, 2 vols, Paris, Firmin Didot, 1884 (Les fabulistes latins: depuis le siècle d'Auguste jusqu'à la fin du Moyen Âge, 1-2).

HEWITT 1942

Harmonice Musices Odhecaton A, edited by Helen Hewitt; edition of the literary texts by Isabel Pope, Cambridge (MA), Medieval Academy of America, 1942; rpt. New York, Da Capo Press, 1978.

HIGGINS 1999

Antoine Busnoys: Method, Meaning, and Context in Late Medieval Music, edited by Paula Higgins, Oxford, Clarendon Press, 1999.

HOLFORD-STREVENS 1999

HOLFORD-STREVENS, Leofranc. 'Metrics for Musicians: Response to Thomas Schmidt-Beste', in: *Studi musicali*, XXVIII (1999), pp. 397-409.

HOUDOY 1880

HOUDOY, Jules. *Histoire artistique de la cathédrale de Cambrai, ancienne église métropolitaine Notre-Dame: Comptes, inventaires et documents inédits, avec une vue et un plan de l'ancienne cathédrale*, Lille, impr. de Danel, 1880; rpt. Geneva, Minkoff, 1972.

HOYER 1992

HOYER, Johannes. *Die mehrstimmigen Nunc dimittis-Vertonungen vom 15. bis zum frühen 17. Jahrhundert-Überlieferung, Stil und Funktion*, Augsburg, Verlegt bei Dr. Bernd Wißner, 1992 (Collectanea musicologica herausgegeben von Franz Krautwurst, 2).

IGC

An Index of Gregorian Chant, I: *Alphabetical Index*, compiled by John R. Bryden and David G. Hughes, Cambridge (MA), Harvard University Press, 1969.

IMBRIANI 1883

La rappresentazione ossia Festa di Abraam e Isaac scritta da Feo di Feo di Coppo Belcari fiorentino, edited by Vittorio Imbriani, Naples, no pr., 1883.

IMM

Invitation to Medieval Music, edited by Thurston Dart and Brian Trowell, 4 vols, London, Stainer & Bell, 1967, 1969, 1976, 1978 (Music of the Mid-Fifteenth Century).

INNOCENTI 1984

INNOCENTI, Piero. *Il bosco e gli alberi. Storie di libri, storie di biblioteche, storie di idee*, I, Florence, Giunta regionale toscana - La Nuova Italia, 1984 (Archivi e biblioteche, 10).

INSKO 1992

Krakowska Tabulatura Organowa: The Cracow Tablature (ca. 1548), edited by Wyatt Insko, Łódź, Ludowy Instytut Muzyczny, 1992 (Dawna Muzyka Organowa).

IVANOFF 1988

Eine zentrale Quelle der frühen italienischen Lautenpraxis. Edition der Handschrift Pesaro, Biblioteca Oliveriana, MS. 1144, edited by Vladimir Ivanoff, Tutzing, Schneider, 1988 (Münchner Editionen zur Musikgeschichte, 7).

JAENECKE 1979

JAENECKE, Joachim. 'Eine unbekannte Laudensammlung des 15. Jahrhunderts', in: *Renaissance-Studien: Helmuth Osthoff zum 80. Geburtstag*, edited by Ludwig Finscher, Tutzing, Schneider, 1979 (Frankfurter Beiträge zur Musikwissenschaft, 11), pp. 127-144.

JEPPESEN 1927

Der Kopenhagener Chansonnier: Das Manuskript Thott 291⁸ der Königlichen Bibliothek Kopenhagen, edited by Knud Jeppesen, Copenhagen, Levin & Munksgaard - Leipzig, Breitkopf & Härtel, 1927; rev. edn. Viggo Brondal, New York, Broude, 1965.

JEPPESEN 1935

Die mehrstimmige italienische Laude um 1500, edited by Knud Jeppesen, Copenhagen, Levin & Munksgaard - Leipzig, Breitkopf & Härtel, 1935; rpt. Bologna, A.M.I.S., 1971.

JEPPESEN 1968

JEPPESEN, Knud. *La Frottola. Bemerkungen zur Bibliographie der ältesten weltlichen Notendrucke in Italien*, Aarhus-Copenhagen, Munksgaard, 1968 (Acta Jutlandica, XL, 2).

JEPPESEN 1969

JEPPESEN, Knud. *La Frottola*, II: *Zur Bibliographie der handschriftlichen musikalischen Überlieferung des weltlichen italienischen Lieds um 1500*, Aarhus-Copenhagen, Hansen, 1969 (Acta Jutlandica, XLI, 1).

JEPPESEN 1970

JEPPESEN, Knud. *La Frottola*, III: *Frottola und Volkslied: Zur musikalischen Überlieferung des folkloristischen Guts in der Frottola. Beilage: Vollständige, kritische Neuausgabe vom älteren Teil des Ms. 55 der Biblioteca Trivulziana, Milano*, Aarhus-Copenhagen, Hansen, 1970 (Acta Jutlandica, XLII, 1).

JICKELI 1994

JICKELI, Carl F. *Textlose Kompositionen um 1500*, Frankfurt am Main, Lang, 1994.

JONAS 1983

 JONAS, Luise. *Das Augsburger Liederbuch: die Musikhandschrift 2° Codex 142a der Staats- und Stadtbibliothek Augsburg: Edition und Kommentar*, 2 vols, Munich-Salzburg, Katzbichler, 1983 (Berliner musikwissenschaftliche Arbeiten, 21).

JONES 1971

 JONES, George Morton. *The 'First' Chansonnier of the Biblioteca Riccardiana, Codex 2794: A Study in the Method of Editing 15th-Century Music*, 2 vols, Ph.D. diss., New York, New York University, 1971.

JUST 1975

 JUST, Martin. *Der Mensuralkodex Mus. Ms. 40021 der Staatsbibliothek Preußischer Kulturbesitz Berlin: Untersuchungen zum Repertoire einer deutschen Quelle des 15. Jahrhunderts*, 2 vols, Tutzing, Hans Schneider, 1975 (Würzburger musikhistorische Beiträge, 1).

KÄMPER 1976

 KÄMPER, Dietrich. 'Studien zur Instrumentalen Ensemblemusik des 16. Jahrhunderts in Italien', in: *Analecta musicologica*, X (1970); Italian trans. as *La musica strumentale nel Rinascimento*, Turin, ERI, 1976.

KÄMPER 1980

 KÄMPER, Dietrich. 'La stangetta: eine Instrumentalkomposition Gaspars van Weerbeke?', in: *Ars musica, musica scientia: Festschrift Heinrich Hüschen zum fünfundsechzigsten Geburtstag am 2. März 1980*, edited by Detlef Altenburg, Cologne, Gitarre und Laute Verlagsgesellschaft, 1980, pp. 277-288.

KENT 2004

 KENT, F. William. 'Heinrich Isaac's Music in Laurentian Florence: New Documents', in: *Die Lektüre der Welt. Zur Theorie, Geschichte und Soziologie kultureller Praxis. Festschrift für Walter Veit*, edited by Helmut Heinze and Christiane Weller, Frankfurt am Main, Lang, 2004 (Forschungen zur Literatur- und Kulturgeschichte, 74), pp. 367-371.

KING 1999

 KING, Jonathan. 'Texting Practices in Manuscript Sources of Early Fifteenth-Century Polyphony', in: *Journal of the Royal Musical Association*, CXXIV (1999), pp. 1-25.

KINKELDEY 1910

 KINKELDEY, Otto. *Orgel und Klavier in der Musik des 16. Jahrhunderts; ein Beitrag zur Geschichte der Instrumentalmusik*, Leipzig, Breitkopf & Härtel, 1910; rpt. Hildesheim, G. Olms, 1968.

KINKELDEY 1959

 KINKELDEY, Otto. 'Dance Tunes of the Fifteenth Century', in: *Instrumental Music. A Conference at Isham Memorial Library, Harvard University, May 4, 1957*, edited by David G. Hughes, Cambridge (MA), Harvard University Press, 1959, pp. 3-30.

KIRKENDALE 1988

 KIRKENDALE, Warren. 'Franceschina, Girometta and their Companions in a Madrigal "a diversi linguaggi" by Luca Marenzio and Orazio Vecchi', in: *Acta musicologica*, XLIV (1972), pp. 181-213; Italian trans. as 'La Franceschina, la Girometta e soci in un madrigale "a diversi linguaggi" di Luca Marenzio e Orazio Vecchi', in: *Il Madrigale fra Cinque e Seicento*, edited by Paolo Fabbri, Bologna, Il Mulino, 1988, pp. 249-331.

KIRSCH 1966

 KIRSCH, Winfried. *Die Quellen der mehrstimmigen Magnificat- und Te Deum-Vertonungen bis zur Mitte des 16. Jahrhunderts*, Tutzing, Schneider, 1966.

KLÖCKNER 2004

 Heinrich Isaac, Battaglia zu vier Stimmen, edited by Dieter Klöckner, Stuttgart, Cornetto, 2004.

KOTTICK 1962

 KOTTICK, Edward L. *The Music of the Chansonnier Cordiforme, Paris, Bibliothèque Nationale, Rothschild 2973*, 2 vols, Ph.D. diss., Chapel Hill (NC), University of North Carolina at Chapel Hill, 1962.

KRISTELLER 1897

Early Florentine Woodcuts with an Annotated List of Florentine Illustrated Books, edited by Paul Kristeller, London, Kegan Paul, 1897.

LA FACE BIANCONI 1990

LA FACE BIANCONI, Giuseppina. *Gli strambotti del codice estense α.F.9.9*, Florence, Olschki, 1990 (Studi e testi per la storia della musica, 8).

LA FACE BIANCONI - ROSSI 1990

LA FACE BIANCONI, Giuseppina - ROSSI, Antonio. '*Soffrir "non" son disposto ogni tormento*. Serafino Aquilano: figura letteraria, fantasma musicologico', in: POMPILIO ET AL. 1990, II, pp. 240-254.

LA FACE BIANCONI - ROSSI 1999

LA FACE BIANCONI, Giuseppina - ROSSI, Antonio. *Le Rime di Serafino Aquilano in musica*, Florence, Olschki, 1999 (Studi e testi per la storia della musica, 13).

LAMA DE LA CRUZ 1994

LAMA DE LA CRUZ, Victor de. *Cancionero musical de la Catedral de Segovia*, Salamanca, Junta de Castilla y León, Consejería de Cultura y Turismo, 1994.

LANYI 1979

LANYI, Gabriel. 'The 129th Poem in Petrarch's *Canzoniere*: An Analysis', in: *Forum Italicum*, XIII (1979), pp. 201-212.

LARGHI 1998

LARGHI, Gerardo. 'Recuperi da un laudario comasco', in: *Archivio storico della Diocesi di Como*, IX (1998), pp. 57-101.

LECCISOTTI 1939

Congregationis S. Iustinae de Padua O. S. B. Ordinationes Capitulorum Generalium - Parte I (1424-1474), edited by Don Tommaso Leccisotti, 2 vols, Isola del Liri, A. Macioce & Pisani, 1939 (Miscellanea Cassinese, 16-17).

LEHMANN 1630

Florilegium Politicum. Politischer Blumengarten durch Christophorum Lehmann, no pl., Getruckt impensis autoris, 1630; rpt. of the 1639 edn. edited by Wolfgang Mieder, Bern - Frankfurt am Main - New York, Lang, 1986.

LENAERTS 1962

Die Kunst der Niederländer, edited by René Bernard Lenaerts, Cologne, Arno Volk Verlag, 1962 (Das Musikwerk, 22).

LESURE 1979

Manuscrit italien de frottole, 1502. Facsimilé du MS de la Bibliothèque Nationale, Paris, Rés. Vm.7 676, edited by François Lesure, Geneva, Minkoff, 1979.

LESURE 1981

Tablature de luth italienne. Cent dix pièces pour luth seul et accompagnements pour luth d'œuvres vocales. Fac-similé du ms. de la Bibliotheque nationale, Paris. Rés. Vmd. ms. 27. ca. 1505, edited by François Lesure, Geneva, Minkoff, 1981.

LEVERETT 1996

LEVERETT, Adelyn Peck. 'Works by Vincenet in Trent 91', in: *I codici musicali trentini: nuove scoperte e nuovi orientamenti della ricerca*, edited by Peter Wright, Trent, Servizi beni librari e archivistici, 1996, pp. 121-147.

LEVI 1905

LEVI, Eugenia. *Lirica italiana antica. Novissima scelta di rime dei secoli XIII, XIV, XV*, Florence, Olschki, 1905.

LEY ET AL. 2002

LEY, Klaus, with the collaboration of Christine MUNDT-ESPÍN and Charlotte KRAUSS. *Die Drucke von Petrarcas "Rime", 1470-2000. Synoptische Bibliographie der Editionen und Kommentare, Bibliotheksnachweise*, Hildesheim, G. Olms, 2002.

LINDER 1898

Plainte de la Vierge en vieux vénitien: texte critique précédé d'une introduction linguistique et littéraire, edited by Alfred Linder, Uppsala, E. Berling, 1898.

LITTERICK 1976

LITTERICK, Louise. *The Manuscript Royal 20.A.XVI of the British Library*, Ph.D. diss., New York, New York University, 1976.

LITTERICK 1980

LITTERICK, Louise. 'Performing Franco-Netherlandish Secular Music of the Late 15th Century: Texted and Untexted Parts in the Sources', in: *Early Music*, VIII (1980), pp. 474-485.

LITTERICK 1981

LITTERICK, Louise. 'On Italian Instrumental Ensemble Music in the Late Fifteenth Century', in: FENLON 1981, pp. 117-130.

LITTERICK 1995

LITTERICK, Louise. 'Vocal or Instrumental? A Methodology for Ambiguous Cases', in: VACCARO 1995, pp. 157-178.

LIUZZI 1946

LIUZZI, Fernando. *I musicisti italiani in Francia*, I: *Dalle origini al secolo XVII*, Rome, Danesi, 1946 (L'opera del genio italiano all'estero).

LIZ

Letteratura italiana Zanichelli in CD-Rom, edited by Pasquale Stoppelli and Eugenio Picchi, 6 CD-Roms, Bologna, Zanichelli, 1998.

LOACH 1969

LOACH, Donald G. *Aegidius Tschudi's Songbook (St. Gall MS 463): A Humanistic Document from the Circle of Heinrich Glarean*, 2 vols, Ph.D. diss., Berkeley, University of California at Berkeley, 1969.

LOCKWOOD 1979

LOCKWOOD, Lewis. 'Jean Mouton and Jean Michel: Evidence on French Music and Musicians in Italy, 1505-1520', in: *Journal of the American Musicological Society*, XXXII (1979), pp. 191-246.

LOCKWOOD 1985

LOCKWOOD, Lewis. 'Adrian Willaert and Cardinal Ippolito d'Este: New Light on Willaert's Early Career in Italy', in: *Early Music History*, V (1985), pp. 85-112.

LOCKWOOD 1987

LOCKWOOD, Lewis. *Music in Renaissance Ferrara, 1400-1505: The Creation of a Musical Centre in the Fifteenth Century*, Cambridge (MA), Harvard University Press - Oxford, Oxford University Press, 1984 (Studies in the History of Music, 2); Italian trans. as *La musica a Ferrara nel Rinascimento. La creazione di un centro musicale nel XV secolo*, Bologna, Il Mulino, 1987.

LONGO 1986

LONGO, Pier Giorgio. *Letteratura e pietà a Novara tra XV e XVI secolo*, Novara-Borgomanero, Associazione di storia della Chiesa novarese - Fondazione Achille Marazza, 1986.

LÖPELMANN 1923

Die Liederhandschrift des Cardinals de Rohan, 15. Jahrh., nach der berliner Hs. Hamilton 674, edited by Martin Löpelmann, Göttingen, Niemeyer, 1923 (Gesellschaft für romanische Literatur, 44).

LOWINSKY 1943

LOWINSKY, Edward E. 'The Goddess Fortuna in Music', in: *The Musical Quarterly*, XXIX (1943), pp. 45-77; rpt. LOWINSKY 1989, I, no. 9.

LOWINSKY 1945

LOWINSKY, Edward E. 'The Function of Conflicting Signatures in Early Polyphonic Music', in: *The Musical Quarterly*, XXXI (1945), pp. 227-260; rpt. LOWINSKY 1989, II, no. 27.

LOWINSKY 1948

LOWINSKY, Edward E. 'On the Use of Scores by Sixteenth-Century Musicians', in: *Journal of the American Musicological Society*, I (1948), pp. 17-23; rpt. with small changes in LOWINSKY 1989, II, no. 34.

LOWINSKY 1962

LOWINSKY, Edward E. *Tonality and Atonality in Sixteenth-Century Music*, Berkeley - Los Angeles, University of California Press, 1962.

LOWINSKY 1976

LOWINSKY, Edward E. 'Ascanio Sforza's Life: A Key to Josquin's Biography and an Aid to the Chronology of his Works', in: LOWINSKY - BLACKBURN 1976, pp. 31-75.

LOWINSKY 1989

LOWINSKY, Edward E. *Music in the Culture of the Renaissance and Other Essays*, edited by Bonnie J. Blackburn, 2 vols, Chicago-London, University of Chicago Press, 1989.

LR

Liber responsorialis pro festis I. classis et communi sanctorum juxta ritum monasticum, Solesmes, Abbaye St-Pierre, 1895.

LU

Liber Usualis Missae et Officii pro dominicis et festis. Cum cantu gregoriano ex editione vaticana adamussim excerpto…, Paris-Tournai-Rome, Desclée et Socii, 1935.

LUISI 1977

LUISI, Francesco. *Del cantar a libro […] o sulla viola. La musica vocale nel Rinascimento. Studi sulla musica vocale profana in Italia nei secoli XV e XVI*, Turin, ERI, 1977.

LUISI 1983

Laudario giustinianeo, edited by Francesco Luisi, 2 vols, Venice, Fondazione Levi, 1983.

LUISI 1995

LUISI, Francesco. 'Questioni di ecdotica in rapporto alla prassi compositiva del repertorio profano italiano della fine del Quattrocento', in: BORGHI - ZAPPALÀ 1995, pp. 389-403.

LUISI 2005

LUISI, Francesco. 'Scrittura e riscrittura del repertorio profano italiano nelle edizioni petrucciane', in: CATTIN - DALLA VECCHIA 2005, pp. 177-214.

McCOY 1988

Hans Newsidler: Das erst Buch (1544), edited and transcribed into French tablature by Stewart McCoy, London, Lute Society Music Editions, 1988.

MACEY 1993

MACEY, Patrick. 'Some New Contrafacta for Canti Carnascialeschi and Laude in Late Quattrocento Florence', in: GARGIULO 1993, pp. 143-166.

MACEY 1998

MACEY, Patrick. *Bonfire Songs. Savonarola's Musical Legacy*, Oxford, Clarendon Press, 1998.

McGEE 1983a

McGEE, Timothy J. '*Alla battaglia*: Music and Ceremony in Fifteenth-Century Florence', in: *Journal of the American Musicological Society*, XXXVI (1983), pp. 287-302.

McGEE 1983b

McGEE, Timothy J. 'Vocal Music for a Renaissance Military Ceremony', in: *American Choral Review*, XXV/3 (1983), pp. 3-11.

McMURTRY 1967

McMURTRY, William. *The British Museum Manuscript Additional 35087: A Transcription of the French, Italian and Latin Compositions with Concordance and Commentary*, Ph.D. diss., Denton (TX), North Texas State University, 1967.

VAN MALDEGHEM

Trésor musical: collection authentique de musique sacrée et profane des anciens maîtres belges, edited by Robert Julien van Maldeghem, 6 vols, Brussels, Muquardt, 1865-1893; rpt. Vaduz, Liechtenstein, Kraus Reprint, 1965.

MANCUSO 1984

MANCUSO, Margaret Ann. *Serafino Razzi's "Libro Primo delle Laudi Spirituali" (Venice: Rampazetto for Giunti, 1563): A Critical Edition and Commentary*, 2 vols, M.A. thesis, Long Beach (CA), California State University, 1984.

MARIX 1937

Les Musiciens de la cour de Bourgogne au XVᵉ siècle (1420-1467): Gilles de Binche (Binchois), Pierre Fontaine, Jacques Vide, Nicole Grenon, Gilles Joye, Hayne de Ghizeghem, Robert Morton: messes, motets, chansons, edited by Jeanne Marix, Paris, L'Oiseau-Lyre, 1937.

MARIX 1939

   Histoire de la musique et des musiciens de la cour de Bourgogne sous le règne de Philippe le Bon (1420-1467), edited by Jeanne Marix, Strasbourg, Heitz, 1939; rpt. Geneva, Minkoff, 1972.

MARTELLI 1968

   GIROLAMO SAVONAROLA, *Poesie*, edited by Mario Martelli, Rome, Angelo Belardetti Editore, 1968 (Edizione nazionale delle opere di Girolamo Savonarola, [8]).

MASSENKEIL 1965

   Mehrstimmige Lamentationen aus der ersten Hälfe des 16. Jahrhunderts, edited by Günther Massenkeil, Mainz, B. Schott's Söhne, 1965 (Musikalische Denkmäler, VI).

MAZZA 1960

   MAZZA, Giuseppe. *Il laudario jacoponico Delta VII 15 della biblioteca civica "Angelo Maj" di Bergamo*, Bergamo, Editrice San Marco, 1960.

MAZZATINTI 1880

   MAZZATINTI, Giuseppe. 'I Disciplinati di Gubbio e i loro uffizi drammatici', in: *Giornale di Filologia romanza*, VI (1880), pp. 85-102.

MAZZATINTI 1886

   MAZZATINTI, Giuseppe. 'Alcuni codici delle rime di Iacopone da Todi', in: *Miscellanea francescana di storia, di lettere, di arti*, I (1886), pp. 33-40.

MAZZATINTI 1889

   MAZZATINTI, Giuseppe. 'Laudi dei disciplinati di Gubbio', in: *Il Propugnatore*, n.s., II/1 (1889), pp. 145-196.

MECONI 1994

   MECONI, Honey. 'Art-Song Reworking: An Overview', in: *Journal of the Royal Musical Association*, CXIX (1994), pp. 1-42.

MECONI 1999

   MECONI, Honey. 'Poliziano, *Primavera*, and Perugia 431: New Light on *Fortuna desperata*', in: HIGGINS 1999, pp. 465-503.

MECONI 2001a

   Fortuna desperata: Thirty-Six Settings of an Italian Song, edited by Honey Meconi, Middleton (WI), A-R Editions, 2001 (Recent Researches in the Music of the Middle Ages and Early Renaissance, 37).

MEERSSEMAN 1977

   MEERSSEMAN, Gilles Gérard. 'Les confréries de Saint-Pierre Martyr', in: *Archivum fratrum praedicatorum*, XXI (1951), pp. 51-196, Italian trans. as *Le confraternite di San Pietro Martire*, in: IDEM. *Ordo fraternitatis. Confraternite e pietà dei laici nel Medioevo*, with the collaboration of Gian Piero Pacini, 3 vols, Rome, Herder, 1977, II, pp. 754-920.

MENSI 1899

   MENSI, Luigi. *Dizionario biografico piacentino*, Piacenza, A. Del Maino, 1899; rpt. Bologna, Forni, 1979.

MESSEDAGLIA 1944

   MESSEDAGLIA, Luigi. *Arbizzano e Novare. Storia di una terra della Valpolicella*, Verona, La Tipografica Veronese, 1944.

MGG

   Die Musik in Geschichte und Gegenwart: … zweite, neubearbeitete Ausgabe, Personenteil, edited by Ludwig Finscher, 17 vols, Kassel, Bärenreiter – Stuttgart, Metzler, 1994-2007.

MIGLIORINI 1954

   MIGLIORINI, Bruno. 'Latino e volgare nel Quattrocento', in: *Lettere italiane*, VI (1954), pp. 321-335.

MISCELLANEA BRANCA

   Miscellanea di studi in onore di Vittore Branca, 7 vols (I: *Dal Medioevo al Petrarca*; III: *Umanesimo e Rinascimento a Firenze e Venezia*), Florence, Olschki, 1983.

MISCHIATI 2001

    MISCHIATI, Oscar. 'Per una bibliografia delle fonti a stampa della lauda post-tridentina (1563-1952)', revised with additions by Giancarlo Rostirolla, in: ROSTIROLLA *ET AL.* 2001, pp. 741-784.

MME 5

    La Música en la Corte de los Reyes Católicos, II: *Polifonía profana: Cancionero Musical de Palacio (Siglos XV-XVI)*, I, edited by Higinio Anglés, Barcelona, Consejo Superior de Investigaciones Científicas - Instituto Español de Musicología, 1947 (Monumentos de la Música Española, 5).

MME 10

    La Musica en la Corte de los Reyes Católicos, III: *Polifonía profana: Cancionero Musical de Palacio (Siglos XV-XVI)*, II, edited by Higinio Anglés, Barcelona, Consejo Superior de Investigaciones Científicas - Instituto Español de Musicología, 1951 (Monumentos de la Música Española, 10).

MME 14/2

    La Música en la Corte de los Reyes Católicos, IV-2: *Cancionero Musical de Palacio (Siglos XV-XVI)*, III-B, edited by José Romeu Figueras, Barcelona, Consejo Superior de Investigaciones Científicas - Instituto Español de Musicología, 1965 (Monumentos de la Música Española, 14/2).

MOE 1956

    MOE, Lawrence Henry. *Dance Music in Printed Italian Lute Tablatures from 1507 to 1611*, 2 vols, Ph.D. diss., Cambridge (MA), Harvard University, 1956.

MOERK 1971

    MOERK, Alice A. *The Seville Chansonnier: An Edition of Sevilla 5-I-43 and Paris N.A. Fr. 4379 (Pt. 1)*, 2 vols, Ph.D. diss., Morgantown (WV), West Virginia University, 1971.

MOLMENTI 1895

    MOLMENTI, Pompeo. 'L'organo della Cattedrale di Salò', in: *Gazzetta musicale di Milano*, L (24 February 1895), pp. 130-131.

MONE

    Hymni Latini Medii Aevi, edited by Franz Joseph Mone, 3 vols, Freiburg im Breisgau, Herder, 1853-1855; rpt. Bologna, Forni, 1969.

MÖNKEMEYER 1985

    FORMSCHNEYDER, Hieronymus. *Trium vocum carmina*, edited by Helmut Mönkemeyer, 2 vols, Celle, Moeck, 1985 (Monumenta musicae ad usum praticum: eine Denkmalreihe für Freunde alter Musik, 1-2).

MONTAGNA 1987

    MONTAGNA, Gerald. 'Caron, Hayne, Compère: A Transmission Reassessment', in: *Early Music History*, VII (1987), pp. 107-157.

MORAWSKI 1972

    Średniowiecze. The Middle Ages, edited by Jerzy Morawski, 2 vols, Kraków, Polskie Wydawnictwo Muzyczne, 1972 (Musica Antiqua Polonica, I).

MORPURGO 1883

    MORPURGO, Salvatore. 'Un codice scritto da un prigioniero triestino', in: *Archivio storico per Trieste, l'Istria e il Trentino*, II, 1883, pp. 391-395.

MORPURGO *ET AL.* 1887-1962

    Catalogo dei manoscritti panciatichiani della Biblioteca Nazionale Centrale di Firenze, I, edited by Salomone Morpurgo, Pasquale Papa, and Berta Maracchi Biagiarelli, Florence, Bencini, 1887 - Rome, Istituto Poligrafico dello Stato, 1962 (Indici e cataloghi, 7).

MORSOLIN 1890

    MORSOLIN, Bernardo. 'Frammento del *Lamentum Virginis*, poema del secolo decimoquarto', in: *Atti del Reale Istituto Veneto di Scienze, Lettere ed Arti*, XXXVIII, s. VII, vol. I, 1890, pp. 933-965.

MORSOLIN 1891

    MORSOLIN, Bernardo. 'I presunti autori del *Lamentum Virginis*, poema del secolo decimoquarto', in: *Atti del Reale Istituto Veneto di Scienze, Lettere ed Arti*, XXXVIII, s. VII, vol. II, 1891, pp. 535-555.

Moscardi 1899

Moscardi, Vincenzo. 'Serafino Ciminello nel IV centenario della sua morte', in: *Bollettino della Società di Storia Patria Anton Ludovico Antinori negli Abruzzi*, XI, 1899, pp. 259-285.

Moser 1930

Frühmeister der deutschen Orgelkunst, edited by Hans Joachim Moser, Wiesbaden, Breitkopf & Härtel, 1930 (Veröffentlichungen der Staatlichen Akademie für Kirchen- und Schulmusik Berlin, 1).

MR

Missale Romanum ex decreto Sacrosancti Concilii Tridentini restitutum, Pij V. Pont. Max. iussu editum, Venice, Giovanni Varisco ed eredi di Bartolomeo Faletti, e soci, 1570; rpt. *Missale Romanum. Editio Princeps (1570)*, edited by Manlio Sodi and Achille Maria Triacca, Vatican City, Libreria Editrice Vaticana, 1998.

Murphy 1999

Murphy, Paul V. 'Politics, Piety, and Reform. Lay Religiosity in Sixteenth-Century Mantua', in: *Confraternities and Catholic Reform in Italy, France, and Spain*, edited by John Patrick Donnelly and Michael W. Maher, Dexter (MI), Thomas University Press at Truman State University, 1999 (Sixteenth Century Essays and Studies, 44), pp. 45-54.

Musiques anciennes

*Musiques anciennes. Instruments et partitions, XVI-XVIII*ᵉ *siècles. Catalogue de l'exposition (Paris, Bibliothèque Nationale, 7 novembre - 7 décembre 1980)*, Paris, Bibliothèque Nationale de France, 1980.

Muzyka staropolska 1966

Muzyka staropolska; wyb'or nie publikowanych utwor'ow z XII-XVIII wieku / Old Polish Music; A Selection of Hitherto Unpublished Works from the XIIth-XVIIIth Centuries, edited by Hieronim Feicht, [Kraków], Polskie Wydawnictwo Muzyczne, 1966.

Nerici 1880

Nerici, Luigi. *Storia della musica in Lucca*, Lucca, Tipografia Giusti, 1880 (Memorie e documenti per servire alla storia di Lucca, XII).

Newbigin 1981

Newbigin, Nerida. 'Il testo e il contesto dell'*Abramo e Isac* di Feo Belcari', in: *Studi e problemi di critica testuale*, XXIII (1981), pp. 13-27.

Newbigin 1983

Nuovo Corpus di Sacre Rappresentazioni fiorentine del Quattrocento edite e inedite tratte da manoscritti coevi o ricontrollate su di essi, edited by Nerida Newbigin, Bologna, Commissione per i testi di lingua, 1983 (Collezione di opere inedite o rare, 139).

NG

The New Grove Dictionary of Music and Musicians, edited by Stanley Sadie, executive editor John Tyrrell, 29 vols, London, Macmillan, 2001.

Nicastro 1924

Inventario dei Manoscritti della Raccolta Guasti di Prato, edited by Sebastiano Nicastro, Florence, Olschki, 1924.

NJE 7

New Josquin Edition, 7: Masses Based on Secular Polyphonic Songs, edited by Thomas Noblitt, 2 vols, Utrecht, Koninklijke Vereniging voor Nederlandse Muziekgeschiedenis, 1997.

NJE 22

New Josquin Edition, 22: Motets on Non-Biblical Texts "De domino Jesu Christo" 2, edited by Bonnie J. Blackburn, 2 vols, Utrecht, Koninklijke Vereniging voor Nederlandse Muziekgeschiedenis, 2003.

NJE 27

New Josquin Edition, 27: Secular Works for Three Voices, edited by Jaap van Benthem and Howard Mayer Brown, 2 vols, Utrecht, Koninklijke Vereniging voor Nederlandse Muziekgeschiedenis, 1987 and 1991.

NJE 28

New Josquin Edition, 28: Secular Works for Four Voices, edited by David Fallows, 2 vols, Utrecht, Koninklijke Vereniging voor Nederlandse Muziekgeschiedenis, 2005.

NOBLE 1978

 NOBLE, Jeremy. 'Ottaviano Petrucci: His Josquin Editions and Some Others', in: *Essays Presented to Myron P. Gilmore*, edited by Sergio Bertelli and Gloria Ramakus, II, Florence, La Nuova Italia, 1978, pp. 433-445.

NOBLE 1985

 NOBLE, Jeremy. 'The Function of Josquin's Motets', in: *Tijdschrift van de Koninklijke Vereniging voor Nederlandse Muziekgeschiedenis*, XXXV (1985), pp. 9-31.

NOE 4

 New Obrecht Edition, 4: *Missa De tous biens playne, Missa Fors seulement, Missa Fortuna desperata*, edited by Barton Hudson, Utrecht, Koninklijke Vereniging voor Nederlandse Muziekgeschiedenis, 1986.

NOE 12

 New Obrecht Edition, 12: *Missa Si dedero, Missa Sub tuum presidium, Missa Veci la danse Barbari*, edited by Thomas Noblitt, Utrecht, Koninklijke Vereniging voor Nederlandse Muziekgeschiedenis, 1992.

NOE 17

 New Obrecht Edition, 17: *Secular Works and Textless Compositions*, edited by Leon Kessels and Eric Jas, Utrecht, Koninklijke Vereniging voor Nederlandse Muziekgeschiedenis, 1997.

NOE 18

 New Obrecht Edition, 18: *Supplement*, edited by Eric Jas, Utrecht, Koninklijke Vereniging voor Nederlandse Muziekgeschiedenis, 1999.

NOSOW 2000

 NOSOW, Robert. 'Binchois's Songs in the Feo Belcari Manuscripts', in: *Binchois Studies*, edited by Andrew Kirkman and Dennis Slavin, New York - Oxford, Oxford University Press, 2000, pp. 221-248.

NOVATI 1907

 NOVATI, Francesco. 'Contributi alla storia della lirica musicale neo-latina', in: *Studi medioevali*, II (1907), pp. 318-322.

OSTHOFF 1969

 OSTHOFF, Wolfgang. *Theatergesang und darstellende Musik in der italienischen Renaissance (15. und 16. Jahrhundert)*, 2 vols, Tutzing, Schneider, 1969 (Münchner Veröffentlichungen zur Musikgeschichte, 14).

OWENS 1997

 OWENS, Jessie A. *Composers at Work. The Craft of Musical Composition 1450-1600*, New York - Oxford, Oxford University Press, 1997.

PAGANI 1968

 PAGANI, Walter. *Repertorio tematico della scuola poetica siciliana*, Bari, Adriatica, 1968.

PAGANUZZI 1976

 PAGANUZZI, Enrico. 'Medioevo e Rinascimento', in: *La musica a Verona*, Verona, Banca Mutua Popolare, 1976, pp. 3-216.

PALÉOGRAPHIE MUSICALE XII

 Antiphonaire monastique, XIII siècle: Codex F. 160 de la Bibliothèque de la Cathédrale de Worcester, published under the direction of André Mocquereau, Tournai, Desclée - Paris, A. Picard & fils, 1922 (Paléographie musicale, XII); rpt. Bern, Lang, 1971.

PANNELLA 1968

 PANNELLA, Liliana. 'Le composizioni profane di una raccolta fiorentina del Cinquecento', in: *Rivista italiana di Musicologia*, III (1968), pp. 3-47.

PAPINI 1923

 Antologia della poesia religiosa italiana, edited by Giovanni Papini, Milan, Vita e Pensiero, 1923 (Il pensiero cristiano, 6).

PARIS - GEVAERT 1875

 Chansons du XV siècle publiées d'après le manuscrit de la Bibliothèque Nationale de Paris, edited by Gaston Bruno, Paulin Paris, and François Auguste Gevaert, Paris, Firmin Didot, 1875 (Société des anciens textes français).

PEASE 1959

 PEASE, Edward J. *An Edition of the Pixérécourt Manuscript: Paris, Bibliothèque Nationale, ms. Fonds français 15123*, 3 vols, Ph.D. diss., Bloomington (IN), University of Indiana, 1959.

PELICELLI 1916

 PELICELLI, Nestore. *La cappella corale della Steccata nel secolo XVI*, Parma, Fresching & C., 1916.

PELICELLI 1931

 PELICELLI, Nestore. 'Musicisti in Parma nei secoli XV-XVI', in: *Note d'archivio per la storia musicale*, VIII (1931), pp. 132-142, 196-215, 278-299.

PERCOPO 1884-86

 PERCOPO, Erasmo. 'Le laudi di fra Jacopone da Todi nei mss. della Biblioteca Nazionale di Napoli. Contributo alla edizione critica', in: *Il Propugnatore*, XVII/2 (1884), pp. 127-173, 376-410; XVIII/1 (1885), pp. 106-135, 370-400; XVIII/2 (1885), pp. 136-188; XIX/1 (1886), pp. 239-258, 365-404.

PERINI 1938

 PERINI, P. Davide Aurelio. *Bibliographia Augustiniana cum notis biographicis: Scriptores Itali*, IV, Florence, Libreria Fiorentina, 1938.

PERKINS – GAREY 1979

 The Mellon Chansonnier, edited by Leeman L. Perkins and Howard Garey, 2 vols, New Haven, Yale University Press, 1979.

PERZ – KOWALEWICZ 1976

 Sources of Polyphony up to c.1500. Transcriptions, edited by Mirosław Perz and Henryk Kowalewicz, Graz, Akademische Druck- und Verlagsanstal – Warsaw, PWN, 1976 (Antiquitates Musicae in Polonia, 14).

PESCERELLI 1974

 PESCERELLI, Beatrice. 'Una sconosciuta redazione del trattato di danza di Guglielmo Ebreo', in: *Rivista italiana di Musicologia*, IX (1974), pp. 48-55.

PETRUCCI 1992

 PETRUCCI, Armando. *Medioevo da leggere. Guida allo studio delle testimonianze scritte del Medioevo italiano*, Turin, Einaudi, 1992.

PEVERADA 1991

 PEVERADA, Enrico. *Vita musicale nella chiesa ferrarese del Quattrocento*, Ferrara, Capitolo Cattedrale, 1991.

PICKER 1965

 PICKER, Martin. *The Chanson Albums of Marguerite of Austria: MSS 228 and 11239 of the Bibliothèque Royale de Belgique, Brussels*, Berkeley – Los Angeles, University of California Press, 1965.

PICKER 1977

 PICKER, Martin. 'The Motet Anthologies of Andrea Antico', in: *A Musical Offering: Essays in Honor of Martin Bernstein*, edited by Edward H. Clinkscale and Claire Brook, New York, Pendragon Press, 1977, pp. 211-237.

PICKER 1991

 PICKER, Martin. *Henricus Isaac: A Guide to Research*, New York, Garland, 1991.

PIERCE 1973

 PIERCE, Jane I. *Hans Gerle: Sixteenth-Century Lutenist and Pedagogue*, 2 vols, Ph.D. diss., Chapel Hill (NC), University of North Carolina at Chapel Hill, 1973.

PIRROTTA 1975

 PIRROTTA, Nino. *Li due Orfei: da Poliziano a Monteverdi*, 2nd rev. edn., Turin, Einaudi, 1975.

PIRROTTA 1984

 PIRROTTA, Nino. 'Tradizione orale e tradizione scritta della musica', in: *L'Ars nova italiana del Trecento*, III, edited by F. Alberto Gallo, Certaldo, Centro di Studi sull'Ars nova italiana del Trecento, 1970; also in: IDEM. *Musica tra Medioevo e Rinascimento*, Turin, Einaudi, 1984, pp. 177-184.

PIRROTTA 1994

    PIRROTTA, Nino. 'Before the Madrigal', in: *The Journal of Musicology*, XII (1994), pp. 237-252.

PLAMENAC 1928

    PLAMENAC, Dragan. 'Autour d'Ockeghem', in: *La Revue musicale*, IX (1928), pp. 26-47.

PM

    Processionale monasticum ad usum Congregationis Gallicae Ordinis Sancti Benedicti, Solesmes, Abbaye St-Pierre, 1893.

POLK 1994

    POLK, Keith. 'Innovation in Instrumental Music 1450-1520: The Role of German Performers within European Music', in: *Music in the German Renaissance: Sources, Styles, and Contexts*, edited by John Kmetz, Cambridge, Cambridge University Press, 1994, pp. 202-214.

POLK 1996

    POLK, Keith. 'Foreign and Domestic in Italian Instrumental Music of the Fifteenth Century', in: ALM *ET AL.* 1996, pp. 323-332.

POMPILIO *ET AL.* 1990

    Atti del XIV congresso della Società Internazionale di Musicologia (Bologna, 27 agosto - 1° settembre 1987; Ferrara-Parma 30 agosto 1987), edited by Angelo Pompilio *et al.*, 3 vols, Turin, EDT/Musica, 1990.

PONTE 1969

    PONTE, Giovanni. *Attorno al Savonarola. Castellano Castellani e la sacra rappresentazione in Firenze tra '400 e '500*, Genoa, [Pagano], 1969.

PONTE 1974

    Sacre rappresentazioni fiorentine del Quattrocento, edited by Giovanni Ponte, Milan, Marzorati, 1974.

POPE – KANAZAWA 1978

    The Musical Manuscript Montecassino 871. A Neapolitan Repertory of Sacred and Secular Music of the Late Fifteenth Century, edited by Isabel Pope and Masakata Kanazawa, Oxford, Oxford University Press, 1978.

POWERS 1994

    POWERS, Wendy Jane. *The Music Manuscript Fondo Magliabechi XIX.178 of the Biblioteca Nazionale Centrale, Florence: A Study in the Changing Role of the Chanson in Late Fifteenth-Century Florence*, Ph.D. diss., New York, Columbia University, 1994.

PRIZER 1980a

    PRIZER, William F. *Courtly Pastimes. The Frottole of Marchetto Cara*, Ann Arbor (MI), UMI Research Press, 1980 (Studies in Musicology, 33).

PRIZER 1985

    PRIZER, William F. 'Isabella d'Este and Lucrezia Borgia as Patrons of Music. The Frottola at Mantua and Ferrara', in: *Journal of the American Musicological Society*, XXXVIII (1985), pp. 1-33.

PRIZER 1986

    PRIZER, William F. 'The Frottola and the Unwritten Tradition', in: *Studi musicali*, XV (1986), pp. 3-37.

PRIZER 1990

    PRIZER, William F. 'Paris, Bibliothèque Nationale, Rés. Vm.[7] 676 and Music at Mantua', in: POMPILIO *ET AL.* 1990, II, pp. 235-239.

PRIZER 1991

    PRIZER, William F. 'Games of Venus: Secular Vocal Music in the Late Quattrocento and Early Cinquecento', in: *The Journal of Musicology*, XI (1991), pp. 3-56.

PRIZER 1993b

    PRIZER, William F. 'Laude di popolo, laude di corte: Some Thoughts on the Style and Function of the Renaissance Lauda', in: GARGIULO 1993, pp. 167-194.

PRIZER 1995

    PRIZER, William F. 'Instrumental Music / Instrumentally Performed Music ca. 1500: The Genres of Paris, Bibliothèque Nationale, Ms. Res. Vm.⁷ 676', in: VACCARO 1995, pp. 179-198.

PRIZER 1996a

    PRIZER, William F. '*Facciamo pure noi carnevale*: Non-Florentine Carnival Songs of the Late Fifteenth and Early Sixteenth Centuries', in: ALM *ET AL.* 1996 pp. 173-211.

PRIZER 1996b

    PRIZER, William F. 'Secular Music at Milan during the Early Cinquecento: Florence, Biblioteca del Conservatorio, MS Basevi 2441', in: *Musica Disciplina*, L (1996), pp. 9-57.

PRIZER 2001

    PRIZER, William F. 'The Music Savonarola Burned: The Florentine Carnival Song in the Late 15th Century', in: *Musica e Storia*, IX (2001), pp. 5-33.

PRIZER 2004a

    PRIZER, William F. 'Wives and Courtesans: The Frottola in Florence', in: *Music Observed: Studies in Memory of William C. Holmes*, edited by Colleen Reardon and Susan Parisi, Warren (MI), Harmonie Park Press, 2004, pp. 401-415.

PRIZER 2004b

    PRIZER, William F. 'Reading Carnival: The Creation of a Florentine Carnival Song', in: *Early Music History*, XXIII (2004), pp. 185-252.

PRIZER 2005

    PRIZER, William F. 'Petrucci and the Carnival Song: On the Origins and Dissemination of a Genre', in: CATTIN - DALLA VECCHIA 2005, pp. 215-251.

PRIZER 2009

    PRIZER, William F. 'The "Virtue" of Lorenzo Lotto: A Musical Intarsia in the Basilica of Santa Maria Maggiore in Bergamo', in: BLOXAM *ET AL.* 2009, pp. 617-626.

RABBONI 1991

    RABBONI, Renzo. *Laudari e canzonieri nella Firenze del '400. Scrittura privata e modelli nel "Vat. Barb. lat. 3679"*, Bologna, CLUEB, 1991.

REESE 1968

    REESE, Gustave. 'Musical Compositions in Renaissance Intarsia', in: *Medieval and Renaissance Studies. Proceedings of the Southeastern Institute of Medieval and Renaissance Studies*, II (Summer 1968), edited by John L. Lievsay, Durham (NC), Duke University Press, 1968, pp. 74-97.

REESE 1990

    REESE, Gustave. *La musica nel Rinascimento*, Florence, Le Lettere, 1990 (Italian trans. of *Music in the Renaissance*, New York - London, Norton & C., 1954; rev. edn. London, Dent - New York, Norton, 1959).

RESTORI 1894

    RESTORI, Antonio. 'Un codice musicale pavese', in: *Zeitschrift für romanische Philologie*, XVIII (1894), pp. 381-401.

REYNOLDS 1995

    REYNOLDS, Christopher A. *Papal Patronage and the Music of St. Peter's, 1380-1513*, Berkeley - Los Angeles - London, University of California Press, 1995.

RIFKIN 1999

    RIFKIN, Joshua. 'Busnoys and Italy: The Evidence of Two Songs', in: HIGGINS 1999, pp. 505-571.

RIFKIN 2003

    RIFKIN, Joshua. 'Munich, Milan, and a Marian Motet: Dating Josquin's *Ave Maria … virgo serena*', in: *Journal of the American Musicological Society*, LVI (2003), pp. 239-350.

RISM B I

    Répertoire International des Sources Musicales, B I: *Recueils imprimés, XVIᵉ-XVIIᵉ siècles*, edited by François Lesure, Munich-Duisburg, Henle, 1960.

RISM B IV/1

Répertoire International des Sources Musicales, B IV/1: *Manuscripts of Polyphonic Music, 11th - Early 14th Century*, edited by Gilbert Reaney, Munich-Duisburg, Henle, 1966.

RISM B IV/5

Répertoire International des Sources Musicales, B IV/5: *Manuscrits de musique polyphonique, XVe et XVIe siècles. Italie*, edited by Nanie Bridgman, Munich, Henle, 1991.

RMF 13

Modena, Biblioteca Estense e Universitaria, MS alpha.F.9.9, introduction by Frank A. D'Accone, New York - London, Garland, 1987 (Renaissance Music in Facsimile, 13).

RMF 23

Vatican City, Biblioteca Apostolica Vaticana, San Pietro B 80, introduction by Christopher A. Reynolds, New York - London, Garland, 1987 (Renaissance Music in Facsimile, 23).

ROBERTSON 1988

ROBERTSON, Anne Walters. '*Benedicamus Domino*: The Unwritten Tradition', in: *Journal of the American Musicological Society*, XLI (1988), pp. 1-62.

ROGERS 1993

ROGERS, David. 'An Unrecorded Milanese Incunable', in: *The Italian Book (1465-1800). Studies Presented to Daniel E. Rhodes on his 70th Birthday*, edited by Denis V. Reidy, London, British Library, 1993, pp. 7-10.

ROKSETH 1930

Treize motets et un prélude pour orgue, parus chez Pierre Attaingnant en 1531, edited by Yvonne Rokseth, Paris, Droz, 1930 (Publications de la Société Française de Musicologie, ser. 1, vol. 5); rpt. Paris, Heugel, 1968.

ROS-FÁBREGAS 1992

ROS-FÁBREGAS, Emilio. *The Manuscript Barcelona, Biblioteca de Catalunya, M. 454: Study and Edition in the Context of the Iberian and Continental Manuscript Traditions*, 2 vols, Ph.D. diss., New York, City University of New York, 1992.

ROSSI 1882

"Il cantico del sole" in quattro diverse lezioni cavate dai codici manoscritti di Assisi, di Perugia, di Norcia e dal Libro delle conformità, edited by Adamo Rossi, published on the occasion of the seventh centenary of St. Francis, Foligno, Sgariglia, 1882.

ROSSI 1993

ROSSI, Antonio. 'Prima ch'i' die principio a' mie strambotti', in: *Di selva in selva. Studi e testi offerti a Pio Fontana…*, edited by Paolo Di Stefano and Giovanni Fontana, Bellinzona, Casagrande, 1993, pp. 251-264.

ROSSI 2002

SERAFINO AQUILANO. *Strambotti*, edited by Antonio Rossi, Parma-Milan, Fondazione Pietro Bembo - Ugo Guanda, 2002.

ROSSI 2005

SERAFINO AQUILANO. *Sonetti e altre rime*, edited by Antonio Rossi, Rome, Bulzoni, 2005 (Europa delle Corti, 119).

ROSTIROLLA (1986) 2001

ROSTIROLLA, Giancarlo. 'La musica a Roma al tempo del cardinal Baronio. L'oratorio e la produzione laudistica in ambiente romano', in: *Baronio e l'arte. Atti del Convegno internazionale di studio (Sora, 10-13 ottobre 1984)*, edited by Agostino Borromeo *et al.*, Sora, Centro di Studi Soriani V. Patriarca, 1986, pp. 573-771; rpt. ROSTIROLLA *ET AL.* 2001, pp. 1-210.

ROSTIROLLA (1990) 2001

ROSTIROLLA, Giancarlo. 'Laudi e canti religiosi per l'esercizio spirituale della Dottrina cristiana al tempo di Roberto Bellarmino', in: *Bellarmino e la Controriforma. Atti del Convegno internazionale di studi (Sora, 15-18 ottobre 1986)*, edited by Agostino Borromeo *et al.*, Sora, Centro di Studi Soriani V. Patriarca, 1990, pp. 663-847; rpt. ROSTIROLLA *ET AL.* 2001, pp. 275-472.

ROSTIROLLA (1995) 2001

ANIMUCCIA, Giovanni - SOTO, Francesco *ET AL.* *Il Terzo Libro delle Laudi Spirituali (Roma, Blado, 1577)*, facsimile with five musical transcriptions edited by Giancarlo Rostirolla, Rome, Fondazione italiana per la Musica antica della Società italiana del flauto dolce - Recercare - Hortus Musicus, 1995; rpt. ROSTIROLLA *ET AL.* 2001, pp. 473-514.

ROSTIROLLA (1997) 2001

ROSTIROLLA, Giancarlo. 'Laudi e canti spirituali nelle edizioni della prima "controriforma" milanese', in: *Carlo Borromeo e l'opera della "grande riforma". Cultura, religione e arti del governo nella Milano del primo Cinquecento*, edited by Franco Buzzi and Danilo Zardin, introduction by Gianfranco Ravasi, [Milan], Credito Artigiano, 1997, pp. 159-176; rpt. ROSTIROLLA *ET AL.* 2001, pp. 563-594.

ROSTIROLLA *ET AL.* 2001

ROSTIROLLA, Giancarlo - ZARDIN, Danilo - MISCHIATI, Oscar. *La lauda spirituale tra Cinque e Seicento. Poesia e canti devozionali nell'Italia della Controriforma. Volume offerto a Giancarlo Rostirolla nel suo sessantesimo compleanno*, edited by Giuseppe Filippi *et al.*, Rome, IBiMus, 2001.

ROTH 1991

ROTH, Adalbert. *Studien zum frühen Repertoire der päpstlichen Kapelle unter dem Pontifikat Sixtus' IV. (1471-1484). Die Chorbücher 14 und 51 des Fondo Cappella Sistina der Biblioteca Apostolica Vaticana*, Vatican City, Biblioteca Apostolica Vaticana, 1991 (Capellae apostolicae sixtinaeque collectanea acta monumenta, 1).

ROTHENBERG 2006

ROTHENBERG, David J. 'The Marian Symbolism of Spring, ca. 1200 - ca. 1500: Two Case Studies', in: *Journal of the American Musicological Society*, LIX (2006), pp. 319-398.

SACCHETTI-SASSETTI 1940

SACCHETTI-SASSETTI, Angelo. 'La Cappella musicale del Duomo di Rieti', in: *Note d'archivio per la storia musicale*, XVII (1940), pp. 89-104, 121-170.

SANTAGATA 1996

PETRARCA, Francesco. *Canzoniere*, edited by Marco Santagata, Milan, Mondadori, 1996 (I Meridiani).

SANTAGATA 2004

PETRARCA, Francesco. *Canzoniere*, edited by Marco Santagata, new updated edn., Milan, Mondadori, 2004 (I Meridiani).

SARTORI 1956

SARTORI, Claudio. 'Josquin des Prés cantore del Duomo di Milano (1459-1472)', in: *Annales musicologiques*, IV (1956), pp. 55-83.

SAVIOTTI 1892

SAVIOTTI, Alfredo. 'Rime inedite del secolo XV (dal codice Oliveriano 54)', in: *Il Propugnatore*, n.s., V/2 (1892), pp. 303-345.

SAVONA 1973

SAVONA, Eugenio. *Repertorio tematico dello Stil Novo*, Bari, Adriatica, 1973.

SCARDIN 1939

SCARDIN, Gian Piero. 'Le laude non-Jacoponiche dei manoscritti marciani', in: *La bibliofilia*, XLI (1939), pp. 81-102.

SCHAVRAN 1978

SCHAVRAN, Henrietta. *The Manuscript Pavia, Biblioteca Universitaria, Codice Aldini 362: A Study of Song Traditions in Italy circa 1440-1480*, 2 vols, Ph.D. diss., New York, New York University, 1978.

SCHERING 1931

SCHERING, Arnold. *Geschichte der Musik in Beispielen*, Leipzig, Breitkopf & Härtel, 1931.

SCHMIDT 1969

SCHMIDT, Henry Louis. *The First Printed Lute Books: Francesco Spinacino's "Intabolatura de Lauto, Libro Primo" and "Libro Secondo" (Venice: Petrucci, 1507)*, 2 vols, Ph.D. diss., Chapel Hill (NC), University of North Carolina at Chapel Hill, 1969.

SCHMIDT-BESTE 1999

SCHMIDT-BESTE, Thomas. 'Verse Metre, Word Accent and Rhythm in the Polyphonic Hymn of the Fifteenth Century', in: *Studi musicali*, XXVIII (1999), pp. 363-396.

SCHUTTE 1980

SCHUTTE, Anne Jacobson, 'Printing, Piety and the People in Italy: The First Thirty Years', in: *Archiv für Reformationsgeschichte*, LXXI (1980), pp. 5-20.

SCHWARTZ 1920

SCHWARTZ, Rudolf. 'Zur Partitur im 16. Jahrhundert', in: *Archiv für Musikwissenschaft*, II (1920), pp. 73-78.

SCHWARTZ 1935

Ottaviano Petrucci, Frottole, Buch I und IV nach dem Erstlingsdrucken von 1504 und 1505, edited by Rudolf Schwartz, [Leipzig, Breitkopf & Härtel], 1935; rpt. Hildesheim, G. Olms, 1967 (Publikationen älterer Musik veröffentlicht ... bei der Deutschen Gesellschaft für Musikwissenschaft unter der Leitung von Theodor Kroyer, VIII).

SCHWOB 1905

Le Parnasse satyrique du quinzième siècle: anthologie de pièces libres, edited by Marcel Schwob, Paris, H. Welter, 1905; rpt. Geneva, Slatkine Reprints, 1969.

SCOTT 2004

SCOTT, Peter James David. *Ottaviano Petrucci's Lamentationum liber primus and liber secundus (1506/1 and 1506/2): A Bibliographical, Contextual and Analytical Study*, Ph.D. diss., Durham, University of Durham, 2004.

SEAY 1955

SEAY, Albert. 'The Dialogus Johannis Ottobi Anglici in arte musica', in: *Journal of the American Musicological Society*, VIII (1955), pp. 86-100.

SEAY 1975

Johannis Tinctoris, Opera Theoretica, edited by Albert Seay, II, no pl., American Institute of Musicology, 1975 (Corpus Scriptorum de Musica, 22).

SEAY 1978

Johannis Tinctoris, Opera Theoretica, edited by Albert Seay, IIa, no pl., American Institute of Musicology - Hänssler, 1978 (Corpus Scriptorum de Musica, 22).

SELF 1996

The "si placet" Repertoire of 1480-1530, edited by Stephen Self, Madison (WI), A-R Editions, 1996 (Recent Researches in the Music of the Renaissance, 106).

SERENA 1891

SERENA, Augusto. *Fra Enselmino da Montebelluna e la "Lamentatio Virginis"*, Treviso, Tipografia Istituto Mander, 1891.

SERENA 1893

SERENA, Augusto. 'L'autore del *Pietoso lamento*', in: *Il Propugnatore*, n.s., VI/2 (1893), pp. 5-38; rpt. then as '*El pianto de la Verzene Maria* (alla ricerca dell'autore)', in: IDEM. *Pagine letterarie*, Rome, Forzani, 1900, pp. 21-51.

SERENA 1909

El pianto de la Verzene Maria: luoghi scelti, edited by Augusto Serena, Treviso, Tipografia Istituto Turazza, 1909.

SHERR 1990

SHERR, Richard. 'The Relationship between a Vatican Copy of the Gloria of Josquin's Missa de Beata Virgine and Petrucci's Print', in: POMPILIO *ET AL.* 1990, II, pp. 266-271.

SHERR 1991

Selections from "Motetti A numero trentatre" (Venice, 1502), edited by Richard Sherr, New York - London, Garland, 1991 (Motets from Anthologies, 1502-1555 - Sixteenth-Century Motet, 1).

SHERR 1996

SHERR, Richard. *Papal Music Manuscripts in the Late Fifteenth and Early Sixteenth Centuries*, Neuhausen-Stuttgart, Hänssler, 1996 (Renaissance Manuscript Studies, 5).

SHERR 1997

SHERR, Richard. 'Conflicting Levels of Meaning and Understanding in Josquin's *O admirabile commercium* Motet Cycle', in: PESCE 1997, pp. 193-212.

SHERR 2000a

The Josquin Companion, edited by Richard Sherr, New York, Oxford University Press, 2000.

SHERR 2000b

SHERR, Richard. 'Three Settings of Italian Texts and Two Secular Motets', in: SHERR 2000a, pp. 423-430.

SHIPP 1960

SHIPP, Clifford M. A Chansonnier of the Dukes of Lorraine: The Paris Manuscript fonds français 1597, Ph.D. diss., Denton (TX), North Texas State University, 1960.

SLIM 1988

SLIM, H. Colin. 'An Iconographical Echo of the Unwritten Tradition in a Verdelot Madrigal', in: Studi musicali, XVII (1988), pp. 33-54.

SM 5

Das Liederbuch des Johannes Heer von Glarus. Ein Musikheft aus der Zeit des Humanismus (Codex 462 der Stiftsbibliothek St. Gallen), edited by Arnold Geering and Hans Trümpy, Basel, Bärenreiter, 1967 (Schweizerische Musikdenkmäler, 5).

SM 6

Die Tabulaturen aus dem Besitz des Basler Humanisten Bonifacium Amerbach, edited by Hans Joachim Marx, Basel, Bärenreiter, 1967 (Schweizerische Musikdenkmäler, 6).

SM 8

St. Galler Orgelbuch. Die Orgeltabulatur des Fridolin Sicher (St. Gallen, Codex 530), edited by Hans Joachim Marx and Thomas Warburton, Winterthur, Amadeus, 1992 (Schweizerische Musikdenkmäler, 8).

SMIJERS J/4

Werken van Josquin des Prés, uitgegeven door Prof. Dr. A[lbert] Smijers, 4: Motetten, II, Amsterdam, Alsbach-Leipzig, Siegel, 1923 (Vereniging voor Nederlandse Muziekgeschiedenis).

SMIJERS J/13

Werken van Josquin des Prés, uitgegeven door Prof. Dr. A[lbert] Smijers, 13: Missen, IV: Missa Fortuna desperata, Leipzig, Kistner & Siegel, 1929 (Vereniging voor Nederlandse Muziekgeschiedenis).

SMIJERS J/23

Werken van Josquin des Prés, uitgegeven door Prof. Dr. A[lbert] Smijers, 23: Missen, XI: Missa D'ung aultre amer, Amsterdam, Alsbach, 1950 (Vereniging voor Nederlandse Muziekgeschiedenis).

SMIJERS J/43

Werken van Josquin des Prés, uitgegeven door Prof. Dr. A[lbert] Smijers, edited by Albert Smijers and Johanneke van Dorp, 43: Missen, XX: Missa Allez regretz, Amsterdam, Alsbach, 1956 (Vereniging voor Nederlandse Muziekgeschiedenis).

SMIJERS J/53

Werken van Josquin des Prés, uitgegeven door Prof. Dr. A[lbert] Smijers, 53: Wereldlijke Werken, IV, edited by Mirosław Antonowycz and Willem Elders, Amsterdam, no pr., 1965 (Vereniging voor Nederlandse Muziekgeschiedenis).

SMIJERS J/55

Werken van Josquin des Prés, uitgegeven door Prof. Dr. A[lbert] Smijers, 55: Supplement, edited by Mirosław Antonowycz and Willem Elders, Amsterdam, no pr., 1969 (Vereniging voor Nederlandse Muziekgeschiedenis).

SMIJERS V/5

Van Ockeghem tot Sweelinck: Nederlandse muziegeschiedenis in voorbeelden, uitgegeven door Prof. Dr. A[lbert] Smijers, V, Amsterdam, no pr., 1949 (Vereniging voor Nederlandse Muziekgeschiedenis).

SMITH 1991

SMITH, A. William. 'References to Dance in Fifteenth-Century Italian Sacre Rappresentazioni', in: Dance Research Journal, XXIII (1991), pp. 17-24.

SPAGNOLO 1996

I Manoscritti della Biblioteca Capitolare di Verona. Catalogo descrittivo redatto da don Antonio Spagnolo, edited by Silvia Marchi, Verona, Mazziana, 1996.

SPARTI 1993

GUGLIELMO EBREO OF PESARO. *De pratica seu arte tripudii: On the Practice or Art of Dancing*, edited by Barbara Sparti, Oxford, Clarendon Press, 1993.

SPARTI 1996

SPARTI, Barbara. 'Would You Like to Dance This Frottola? Choreographic Concordances in Two Early Sixteenth-Century Tuscan Sources', in: *Musica Disciplina*, L (1996), pp. 135-165.

SPONGANO (1966) 1974

SPONGANO, Raffaele. *Nozioni ed esempi di metrica italiana*, Bologna, Pàtron, (1966) 1974.

SPONGANO 1971

Rispetti e strambotti del Quattrocento. I "Rispetti di più persone" nel Ms. Can. It. 99 della Bodleian Library di Oxford, edited by Raffaele Spongano, Bologna, Tamari, 1971.

STÄBLEIN 1956

Hymnen (I). Die mittelalterlichen Hymnenmelodien des Abendlandes, edited by Bruno Stäblein, Kassel-Basel, Bärenreiter, 1956 (Monumenta Monodica Medii Aevi, 1).

STAEHELIN 1977

Die Messen Heinrich Isaacs, edited by Martin Staehelin, 3 vols, Bern-Stuttgart, P. Haupt, 1977 (Publications de la Société suisse de musicologie, 2ᵉ série, 28, I-III).

STATUTI SENATO

Biblioteca del Senato della Repubblica. Catalogo della raccolta di Statuti, consuetudini, leggi, decreti, ordini e privilegi dei Comuni, delle associazioni e degli enti locali italiani, dal Medioevo alla fine del secolo XVIII, II, Rome, Senato della Repubblica, 1950.

STEVENS 1962

Music at the Court of Henry VIII, edited by John Stevens, London, Stainer & Bell, 1962 (Musica Britannica, 18).

STICCA 1984

STICCA, Sandro. *Il Planctus Mariae nella tradizione drammatica del Medio Evo*, Sulmona, Teatro Club, 1984.

STIERLE 1989

STIERLE, Karlheinz. '*Di pensier in pensier, di monte in monte*. Landschaftserfahrung und Selbsterfahrung in Petrarcas *Canzoniere*', in: *Italienisch*, XXII (1989), pp. 21-34.

STROHM 1968

STROHM, Reinhard. 'Ein unbekanntes Chorbuch des 15. Jahrhunderts', in: *Die Musikforschung*, XXI (1968), pp. 40-42.

STROHM 1981

STROHM, Reinhard. 'European Politics and the Distribution of Music in the Early Fifteenth Century', in: *Early Music History*, I (1981), pp. 305-323.

STROHM 1985

STROHM, Reinhard. 'Polifonie più o meno primitive. Annotazioni alla relazione di base e nuove fonti', in: ARS NOVA V, pp. 83-97.

STROHM 1993

STROHM, Reinhard. *The Rise of European Music, 1380-1500*, Cambridge, Cambridge University Press, 1993.

STROHM 2008

The Lucca Choirbook: Lucca, Archivio di Stato, MS 238; Lucca, Archivio Arcivescovile, MS 97; Pisa, Archivio Arcivescovile, Biblioteca Maffi, Cartella 11/III, edited and with an introduction and inventory by Reinhard Strohm, Chicago-London, University of Chicago Press, 2008.

TARGIONI TOZZETTI 1904

TARGIONI TOZZETTI, Ottaviano. *Antologia della poesia italiana*, edited by Francesco Carlo Pellegrini, first rpt. of the 8th edn. Livorno, Giusti, 1901.

TARUSKIN 1982

TARUSKIN, Richard. *J'ay pris amours: Twenty-Eight Settings in Two, Three, and Four Parts*, Miami (FL), Ogni Sorte Editions, 1982.

TENNERONI 1909

TENNERONI, Annibale. *Inizii di antiche poesie italiane religiose e morali*, Florence, Olschki, 1909.

TESTAVERDE – EVANGELISTA 1988

Sacre rappresentazioni manoscritte e a stampa conservate nella Biblioteca Nazionale Centrale di Firenze, edited by Anna Maria Testaverde and Anna Maria Evangelista, Florence, Giunta Regionale Toscana – Milan, Editrice Bibliografica, 1988 (Inventari e Cataloghi toscani, 25).

THIBAULT 1958

THIBAULT, Geneviève. 'Un manuscrit italien pour luth des premières années du XVIᵉ siècle', in: *Le luth et sa musique*, edited by Jean Jacquot, Paris, Centre National de la Recherche Scientifique, 1958, pp. 43-76.

THIBAULT – DROZ (1927) 1976

Trois chansonniers français du XVᵉ siècle, edited by Geneviève Thibault and Eugénie Droz, I, Paris, Droz, 1927 (Documents artistiques du XVᵉ siècle, 4); rpt. Geneva, Slatkine Reprints, 1976; rpt. New York, Da Capo Press, 1978.

THIBAULT – FALLOWS 1991

Chansonnier de Jean de Montchenu (Bibliothèque nationale, Rothschild 2973) [I.5.13], edition by Geneviève Thibault, commentary by David Fallows, Paris, Société française de musicologie, 1991 (Publications de la Société française de musicologie, première série, 23).

THOMAS 1981

Ten French Songs of the Fifteenth Century. Companion Edition to: Music from the Buxheim Organ Book, I, edited by Bernard Thomas, [Brighton], London Pro Musica Edition, 1981 (The Keyboard Repertoire, 4a).

THOMAS 1985

Heinrich Isaac: "A la bataglia", edited by Bernard Thomas, [Brighton], London Pro Musica Edition, 1985 (Art of the Netherlanders, 1).

THOMAS 1991

Josquin des Prés: 2 Italian Songs for 4 Voices or Instruments, edited by Bernard Thomas, [Brighton], London Pro Musica Edition, 1991 (Early Music Library, 99).

THOMAS 2001

THOMAS, Jennifer. 'The Core Motet Repertory of 16th-Century Europe: A View of Renaissance Musical Culture', in: *Essays on Music and Culture in Honor of Herbert Kellman*, edited by Barbara Haggh, Paris, Minerve – Tours, Centre d'Étude Supérieures de la Renaissance, 2001 (Épitome musical, 8), pp. 335-376.

THOMSON 1959

THOMSON, James. *The Works of Caron. A Study in Fifteenth-Century Style*, 2 vols, Ph.D. diss., New York, New York University, 1959.

THOMSON 1971-76

Les Œuvres complètes de Philippe(?) Caron, edited by James Thomson, 2 vols, Brooklyn, Institute of Mediaeval Music, 1971 and 1976 (Gesamtausgaben/Collected Works, 6).

TIBALDI 2005

TIBALDI, Rodobaldo. 'Repertorio tràdito e coevo nelle intavolature per canto e liuto', in: CATTIN – DALLA VECCHIA 2005, pp. 491-590.

TINTORI 1963

Gaspar van Weerbeke: Messe e mottetti, edited by Giampiero Tintori, [Milan], Veneranda Fabbrica del Duomo, c.1963 (Archivium Musices Metropolitanum Mediolanense, 11).

TIRABOSCHI 1787-94

TIRABOSCHI, Girolamo. *Storia della letteratura italiana*, 2nd Modenese edn., revised, corrected, and enlarged by the author, 9 vols, Modena, Società Tipografica, 1787-1794.

TOBLER 1878

    TOBLER, Adolf. 'Vita del beato fra Jacopone da Todi', in: *Zeitschrift für romanische Philologie*, II (1878), pp. 25-39.

TOFT 1992

    TOFT, Robert. *Aural Images of Lost Traditions*, Toronto, University of Toronto Press, 1992.

TORREFRANCA 1939

    TORREFRANCA, Fausto. *Il segreto del Quattrocento. Musiche ariose e poesia popolaresca*, Milan, Hoepli, 1939; rpt. Bologna, Forni, 1972.

TOSCANI 1993

    TOSCANI, Bernard. *I canti carnascialeschi e le laude di Lorenzo: elementi di cronologia*, in: GARGIULO 1993, pp. 131-142.

TROVATO 2005

    TROVATO, Paolo. 'In margine alle edizioni critiche del corpus petrucciano. Appunti linguistici, stilistici e metrici', in: CATTIN - DALLA VECCHIA 2005, pp. 253-276.

TURA 2001

    TURA, Adolfo. *Edizioni fiorentine del Quattrocento e primo Cinquecento in Trivulziana*, Milan, Comune di Milano, 2001.

VACCARO 1995

    Le Concert des voix et des instruments à la Renaissance: Actes du XXXIVe Colloque international d'études humanistes Tours, Centre d'Études Supérieures de la Renaissance, 1-11 juillet 1991, edited by Jean-Michel Vaccaro, Paris, CNRS, 1995.

VANDER STRAETEN

    VANDER STRAETEN, Edmond. *La musique aux Pays-Bas avant le XIXe siècle*, 8 vols, Brussels, C. Muquardt, Librairie Européenne (I), G.-A. van Trigt, Editeur-Libraire (II-VII), Schott Frères, Editeurs de Musique (VIII), 1867-1888; rpt. New York, Dover, 1969.

VANHULST 1990

    VANHULST, Henri. *Catalogue des Éditions de musique publiées à Louvain par Pierre Phalèse et ses fils 1545-1578*, Brussels, Palais des Académies, 1990.

VANZOLINI 1894

    VANZOLINI, Giuliano. 'Guglielmo o Enselmino da Treviso', in: *Rassegna bibliografica della letteratura italiana*, II (1894), pp. 18-19.

VECCHI GALLI 1986a

    VECCHI GALLI, Paola. 'Accessioni polizianee in una miscellanea di poesie cortigiane. (Il nuovo testimone delle *Stanze*)', in: *Studi e problemi di critica testuale*, XXXII (1986), pp. 13-29.

VELA 1984

    VELA, Claudio. 'Un capitolo extravagante della metrica italiana: l'"oda" per musica', in: IDEM. *Tre studi sulla poesia per musica*, Pavia, Aurora, 1984, pp. 67-81.

VERNARECCI 1882

    VERNARECCI, Augusto. *Ottaviano de' Petrucci da Fossombrone*, Bologna, Romagnoli, 1882; rpt. 1884; rpt. Bologna, Forni, 1971.

VILLANIS 1905

    VILLANIS, Luigi Alberto. 'Alcuni codici manoscritti di musica del secolo XVI posseduti dalla Biblioteca Nazionale di Torino', in: *Atti del congresso internazionale di scienze storiche, Roma, 1-9 aprile 1903*, VIII: *Storia dell'arte musicale e drammatica*, Rome, no pr., 1905, pp. 319-360 + pp. 16 appendix with reproductions and transcriptions.

VINCENT 1857

    VINCENT, Alexandre-Joseph-Hidulphe. 'Note sur la modalité du chant ecclésiastique', in: *Revue archéologique*, XIV (1857), pp. 620-632, 662-684.

VITALETTI 1920-21

    VITALETTI, Guido. 'Le stampe popolari della Miscellanea Malfatti nella Riccardiana di Firenze', in: *La bibliofilia*, XXII (1920-21), pp. 299-315.

VULGATA

Biblia Sacra iuxta vulgatam versionem, edited by Robert Weber *et al.*, 4th edn. edited by Roger Gryson *et al.*, Stuttgart, Deutsche Bibelgesellschaft, 1994.

WALLIS 1929

Anonymous French Verse. An Anthology of Fifteenth Century Poems Collected from Manuscripts in the British Museum, edited by Norbert Hardy Wallis, London, University of London Press, 1929.

WALTHER 1965

WALTHER, Hans. *Proverbia sententiaeque Latinitatis Medii Aevi*, III, Göttingen, Vandenhoeck & Ruprecht, 1965 (Carmina Medii Aevi Posterioris Latina, II/3).

WALTHER 1967

WALTHER, Hans. *Proverbia sententiaeque Latinitatis Medii Aevi*, V, Göttingen, Vandenhoeck & Ruprecht, 1967 (Carmina Medii Aevi Posterioris Latina, II/5).

WANDER

WANDER, Karl Friedrich Wilhelm. *Deutsches Sprichwörter-Lexikon. Ein Hausschatz für das deutsche Volk*, 5 vols, Leipzig, F. A. Brockhaus, 1867-1880; rpt. Aalen, Scientia Verlag, 1963; rpt. Darmstadt, Wissenschaftliche Buschgesellschaft, 1964; rpt. Stuttgart, Athenaion, 1987.

WARBURTON 1980

Keyboard Intabulations of Music by Josquin des Prez, edited by Thomas Warburton, Madison (WI), A-R Editions, 1980 (Recent Researches in the Music of the Renaissance, 34).

WARD 1980

WARD, Tom R. *The Polyphonic Office Hymn 1400-1520: A Descriptive Catalogue*, Neuhausen-Stuttgart, American Institute of Musicology – Hänssler, 1980 (Renaissance Manuscript Studies, 3).

WEGMAN 1994

WEGMAN, Rob C. *Born for the Muses: The Life and Masses of Jacob Obrecht*, Oxford, Oxford University Press, 1994.

WEISS 1998

Bologna Q. 18 [facsimile edn.], introduction by Susan Forscher Weiss, Peer, Alamire, 1998.

WEISSMAN 1991

WEISSMAN, Ronald F. E. 'Cults and Contexts: In Search of the Renaissance Confraternity', in: *Crossing the Boundaries: Christian Piety and the Arts in Italian Medieval and Renaissance Confraternities*, edited by Konrad Eisenbicher, Kalamazoo (MI), Medieval Institute Publications, 1991 (Early Drama, Art, and Music Monograph Series, 15), pp. 201-220.

WEXLER 1974

WEXLER, Richard M. *The Complete Works of Johannes Prioris*, Ph.D. diss., New York, New York University, 1974.

WILSON 1992

WILSON, Blake. *Music and Merchants: The Laudesi Companies of Republican Florence*, Oxford – New York, Oxford University Press – Clarendon Press, 1992.

WILSON 1998

WILSON, Blake. 'Song Collections in Renaissance Florence: The *cantasi come* Tradition and its Manuscript Sources', in: *Recercare*, X (1998), pp. 69-102.

WILSON 2006

WILSON, Blake. 'Heinrich Isaac among the Florentines', in: *The Journal of Musicology*, XXIII (2006), pp. 97-152.

WOLF (1926) 1931

Sing- und Spielmusik aus älterer Zeit, edited by Johannes Wolf, Leipzig, Quelle & Meyer, 1926; 2nd edn. 1931.

WOLF O/1

Werken van Jacob Obrecht, edited by Johannes Wolf, I: *Missen*, Amsterdam, Alsbach – Leipzig, Breitkopf & Härtel, no d. (Vereeniging voor Noord-Nederlands Muziekgeschiedenis).

WOLF O/3

Werken van Jacob Obrecht, edited by Johannes Wolf, III: *Missen*, Amsterdam, Alsbach - Leipzig, Breitkopf & Härtel, no d. (Vereeniging voor Noord-Nederlands Muziekgeschiedenis).

WOLF O/7

Werken van Jacob Obrecht, edited by Johannes Wolf, VII: *Wereldlijke Werken*, Amsterdam, Alsbach - Leipzig, Breitkopf & Härtel, no d. (Vereeniging voor Noord-Nederlands Muziekgeschiedenis).

WOLFF 1970

WOLFF, Arthur S. *The Chansonnier Biblioteca Casanatense 2865: Its History, Purpose, and Music*, 2 vols, Ph.D. diss., Denton (TX), North Texas State University, 1970.

WOOLDRIDGE 1905

WOOLDRIDGE, Harry Ellis. 'The Polyphonic Period', II: *Method of Musical Art, 1300-1600*, in: *The Oxford History of Music*, II, Oxford, Clarendon Press, 1905.

YOUNG 1933

YOUNG, Karl. *The Drama of the Medieval Church*, 2 vols, Oxford, Clarendon Press, 1933.

ZAMBON 1983

ZAMBON, Francesco. 'Sulla fenice del Petrarca', in: MISCELLANEA BRANCA I, pp. 411-425.

ZAMBRINI 1878

ZAMBRINI, Francesco. *Opere volgari a stampa dei secoli XIII e XIV*, Bologna, Zanichelli, 4th edn. with an appendix, 1878.

ZENO 1752

ZENO, Apostolo. *Lettere*, edited by Marco Forcellini, 3 vols, Venice, Valvasense, 1752.

INDEX OF NAMES

BENT, Margaret xvii, 53n, 128n
BENTE, Martin 121n
BENTHEM, Jaap van 713, 714
BENVENUTO, Giovanni di Francesco Cartolaio 47
BERGAMI, Lorenzo 103
BERGOMOZZI, Cesare 103
BERGOMOZZI, Lorenzo (BERGOMOTIUS, Laurentius) 73, 77, 80n, 81, 103, 147, 148, 914
BERNARD, St. 194n, 195, 196
BERNARDINO, St. 48
BERNARDINO DA CASTELLO 36
BERNARDO PISANO (PAGOLI, Bernardo) 102
BERNOULLI, Eduard 279
BERTOCCO, Dionisio 41
BERTOLOTTI, Antonio 105, 106n, 107n
BERTONE, Giorgio 892
BESICKEN, Giovanni 34, 47
BESSELER, Heinrich 471, 510
BETTARINI, Rosanna 891
BEVILACQUA, Claudio 194n, 202, 203
BIADEGO, Giuseppe 33
BIADENE, Leandro 194n, 202, 203
BIANCHI, Vincenzo 110
BIANCO DA SIENA 73, 75, 252, 255, 596, 598, 915
BIGI, Emilio 118, 889n, 892
BINDER, Wilhelm 466
BINDONI, Alessandro 36, 41
BINDONI, Francesco 42, 44
BINI, Telesforo 194n, 195n, 202, 254
BISCIONI, Antonmaria 51n
BIZZARRI, Edoardo 605
BLACK, Christopher F. 125n, 126n, 127n
BLACKBURN, Bonnie J. xvii, xix, 19n, 43n, 54n, 93n, 103n, 107n, 111n, 119, 119n, 125n, 126n, 174n, 229n, 262n, 284n, 355n, 428n, 454n, 471n, 485n, 512n, 553n, 559n, 563, 564, 567n, 576n, 593n, 600, 627n, 628, 628n, 632, 632n, 654n, 683n, 721, 727n, 732n, 752, 764n, 768n, 773n, 785n, 828, 902n
BLAISE D'AURIOL 39
BOCCACCIO, Giovanni 196, 889n
BOER, Coenraad L. W. 525
BOESCH GAJANO, Sofia 118
BOIARDO, Matteo Maria 273
BONACCORSI, Francesco 42
BONACCURSIO, Giovan Battista 335n
BONARDO, Pellegrino 43
BONDA, Jan Willem 564
BONELLI, Manfredo 34, 35, 270n
BONFANTINI, Mario 259
BONVESIN DE LA RIVA 323, 537
BOORMAN, Stanley 17, 17n, 103, 103n, 106n, 108, 108n, 109, 109n, 112n, 122n, 131, 153, 170, 192, 203, 206n, 219, 229n, 230, 280, 285, 288, 313, 321, 328, 340, 340n, 345, 349, 352, 356, 360, 364, 375, 379, 386, 392, 398, 403, 407, 440, 466, 477, 481, 492, 496n, 497, 502, 510, 512, 520, 525, 529, 533, 538, 548, 554, 564, 581, 600, 606, 647, 660, 671, 674, 678, 685, 690, 714, 738, 749, 755, 758, 825, 844n, 846, 850
BORGHETTI, Vincenzo 108, 109, 117
BORGHI, Renato 192, 285, 313, 407, 737
BORGO, Giovanni Antonio 44, 46

BORROMEO, Giberto, count 8
BORSZÁK, Stephan 384n
BOSCOLO, Lucia 391n, 392, 392n, 406n, 407
BOSSINENSIS, Francesco 17, 108
BOTTRIGARI, Ercole 106, 109
BOUQUET, Marie-Thérèse 115
BRAINARD, Ingrid 647
BRAMBILLA, Ettore 22, 202, 203, 397
BRAMBILLA AGENO, Franca 117
BRANCACCI, Fiorella 384n, 385, 386
BRENNECKE, Wilfried 374n, 375, 407
BRIDGMAN, Nanie 203, 735n, 738
BRIQUET, Charles-Moïse 52, 52n
BRITANNICO, Angelo 42
BRITANNICO, Giacomo 40
BROCCO, Giovanni 73, 74, 82, 103, 103n, 104, 104n, 218, 220, 401, 404, 913, 917
BRONZINI, Giovanni Battista 388, 388n, 464
BROOKS, Catherine V. 279
BROWN, Howard Mayer 119n, 121n, 125n, 127n, 214, 214n, 215, 230, 295n, 296, 297, 340, 351, 352, 359, 359n, 360, 379, 386, 398, 439, 439n, 440, 447, 447n, 448, 492, 497, 502, 512, 524, 525, 533, 538, 548, 554, 563, 564, 600, 632, 647, 660, 670, 671, 674, 678, 685, 710, 713n, 824, 824n, 825
BRUMEL, Antoine xv, 74, 75, 82, 82n, 104, 512, 513, 627, 629, 632, 632n, 633, 689, 689n, 690, 691, 707n, 918, 919, 920
BRUNELLI, Roberto 128, 128n, 129n
BRZEZIŃSKA, Barbara 12n
BUCHNER, Hans 278
BUKOFZER, Manfred Fritz 647
BURGOMOZO, Laurentio see BERGOMOZZI, Lorenzo
BUSNOIS, Antoine 279
BUSSE BERGER, Anna Maria 321
BUSTI, Bernardino de' 38, 39, 194n, 196n, 197, 197n, 396, 632
BUSTI, Ubertino da 40

C

CALELLA, Michele 102, 108
CALZAVARA, Ernesto 202
CANAL, Pietro 105, 105n, 106, 106n
CAPIROLA, Vincenzo 6
CAPPELLI, Antonio 487
CAPPONI, Alessandro Gregorio 41, 197n
CARA, Marchetto xv, 73, 74, 75, 82, 104, 120n, 122n, 153, 154, 191, 193, 206n, 284, 286, 344, 346, 391, 393, 458, 459, 735n, 751n, 913, 914, 915, 917, 919
CARBONI, Fabio 260, 395n, 425, 451n, 454, 509n
CARDUCCI, Giosuè 271, 418, 590
CARMINATE, Giovanni Battista 45
CARON, Firminus 74, 104, 105, 210, 359, 361, 395n, 916
CARON, Jean 105
CARON, Philippe 105
CASIMIRI, Raffaele 112
CASNATI, Francesco 195n, 202, 203
CASTELLANI, Castellano 43n
CASTELLANUS, Petrus 109, 600
CASTELLI, Bartolomeo di Matteo 34
CASTIGLIONI, Carlo 782n, 783

ERASMUS (LAPICIDA?) 18, 76, 82, 108, 844, 844n, 847, 917
ESSLING, Victor Masséna, prince of 41, 197n
ESTE, family 106n
ESTE, Alfonso I d', duke of Ferrara 120n, 674n
ESTE, Beatrice d', duchess of Milan 120n
ESTE, Ercole I d', duke of Ferrara 112n, 120, 674n
ESTE, Ferrante d' 120n
ESTE, Ippolito I d', cardinal 120n, 386, 860n
ESTE, Isabella d', marquess of Mantua 120, 120n, 129n
ESTE, Sigismondo d' 120n
EVANGELISTA, Anna Maria 258n
EVANS, Edward G. Evans, Jr. 447

F

FABRIS, Dinko 132
FACCIOLI, Emilio 259
FALLOWS, David xix, 17n, 19n, 104, 105, 106n, 109, 112n, 114, 114n, 115, 116, 116n, 117, 117n, 118, 210, 215, 254, 267, 280, 296, 297, 360, 375, 398, 407, 411, 418, 425, 428, 440, 448, 472, 492, 506, 564, 581, 597, 597n, 647, 671, 779
FANAN, Giorgio 20, 27, 927
FANO, Fabio 230, 466
FEININGER, Laurence 333
FEIST, Alfred 210, 254, 398, 454
FENLON, Iain 118, 374n, 375, 407
FERDINAND I (FERRANTE), king of Naples and Sicily 115
FERRARI, Marco 230, 351, 492
FERRARI, Severino 590, 590n, 591n
FERRARI BARASSI, Elena 336, 403, 407
FERRO, G. B. 106
FERY-HUE, Françoise 671
FESTA, Costanzo 14, 15, 16, 20, 374, 374n
FÉTIS, François-Joseph 107, 107n, 111, 111n
FÉVIN, Antoine de 113, 113n
FILARETE, Francesco 178n
FILIPPO DA LAVAGNA 46
FILIPPO DI LORENZO BENCI 135
FILOCAMO, Gioia 54n, 85n, 120n, 121n, 122n, 125n, 145, 147, 150, 153, 156, 162, 165, 174, 181, 215, 297, 345, 348, 352, 356, 360, 371, 379, 385, 386, 388, 388n, 389, 391n, 392, 398, 403, 407, 418, 448, 466, 472, 477, 481, 492, 497, 502, 512, 520, 533, 534, 537, 538, 548, 554, 559, 564, 567, 576, 581, 606, 632, 647, 654, 660, 671, 674, 678, 685, 690, 702, 707, 710, 714, 737, 752, 758, 762, 770, 779, 785, 800, 806, 810, 815, 825, 885, 891, 896, 900, 902, 904, 907, 910
FINSCHER, Ludwig 105, 109, 110, 581, 600, 735n
FINZI, Vittorio 202, 203
FITCH, Fabrice 102
FLAVIO, Francesco 34, 35, 335n
FOGLIANO, Giacomo 20, 73, 74, 82, 108, 150, 151, 374, 506, 507, 914, 921
FOGLIANO, Lodovico 270n
FOLENGO, Teofilo 122n
FORMSCHNEIDER, Hieronymus 14
FORTUNATI, Pier Antonio 43
FRANCESCHINI, Adriano 102, 102n, 107, 107n
FRANCIGENA, Raynaldus see RENALDO
FRANCISCUS F. 106

FRANÇON, Marcel 671
FRATI, Carlo 32n
FRATI, Lodovico 116, 116n, 203, 254, 260, 328, 333, 398, 411, 454, 485, 597, 745, 783
FREEMAN, Daniel 153, 159, 165, 250, 841
FREGOSO, Antonio Phileremo 45
FROMSON, Michele 115
FUBINI, Mario 892
FUGGER, family 17
FULLER, Sarah 132

G

GACHET, Émile 671
GAFFURIO, Franchino 355n, 707, 707n
GALEOTA, Francesco 74, 117, 388, 390, 918
GALETTI, Paola 117
GALHARDE, Germão 14
GALLAGHER, Sean 104
GALLETTI, Gustavo Camillo 210, 210n, 254, 259, 279, 333, 333n, 397, 411, 425, 454, 510, 744n, 745, 783
GALLI, Giuseppe 38, 196n
GALLICO, Claudio 209n, 221, 280, 345, 407, 418, 714, 762
GALLO, F. Alberto 122n, 227, 606, 606n, 646n, 647, 735n, 738
GALLUCCI, Joseph J., Jr. 742
GANCARCZYK, Paweł 471n
GANTERT, Ruth 892
GARDANO, Antonio 14, 15
GAREY, Howard 295n, 296, 297, 351n
GARGAN, Luciano 117n
GASPARI, Gaetano 106, 109, 113, 113n
GASSER, Nolan 538
GEERING, Arnold 671
GENTILE ARETINO (BECCHI, Gentile?), bishop of Arezzo 73, 117, 178, 178n, 179, 182, 913
GERBER, Ernst L. 107
GERLE, Hans 671
GESSI, Antonio xix
GEVAERT, François Auguste 525
GHISELIN (VERBONNET), Johannes 75, 82, 108, 490, 490n, 646, 648, 674, 674n, 675, 917, 918
GHISI, Federico 181, 203, 254, 260, 321, 351n, 352, 392, 411, 425, 448, 454, 510, 597, 606, 742, 745, 783
GIACCARELLI, Anselmo 43
GIACOMO, mastro 106, 106n
GIALDRONI, Giuliana 93n
GIANSTEFANO DI CARLO 43
GIAZOTTO, Remo 27, 270n, 271, 510, 542n
GIESBERT, Franz Julius 364, 529, 674
GILBERT, Adam xix, 178n, 386n, 605n
GIOVANNI, gesuato 258
GIOVANNI ANTONIO DA GANDINO 37
GIOVANNI COLOMBINO DA SIENA, Blessed 424
GIOVANNI DA CASCIA xvii
GIOVANNI DA VERONA 485n
GIOVANNI DI PINEROLO see PINAROL, Johannes de
GIOVANNI DOMENICO DA BERGAMO, fra 33
GIOVANNI DOMENICO DA NOLA 107n
GIOVANNI DOMINICO 107
GIOVANNI GIACOMO DA LEGNANO 34, 36, 37, 48